Lecture Notes in Computer Science 15825

The series Lecture Notes in Computer Science (LNCS), including its subseries Lecture Notes in Artificial Intelligence (LNAI) and Lecture Notes in Bioinformatics (LNBI), has established itself as a medium for the publication of new developments in computer science and information technology research, teaching, and education.

LNCS enjoys close cooperation with the computer science R & D community, the series counts many renowned academics among its volume editors and paper authors, and collaborates with prestigious societies. Its mission is to serve this international community by providing an invaluable service, mainly focused on the publication of conference and workshop proceedings and postproceedings. LNCS commenced publication in 1973.

Marc Fischlin · Veelasha Moonsamy
Editors

Applied Cryptography and Network Security

23rd International Conference, ACNS 2025
Munich, Germany, June 23–26, 2025
Proceedings, Part I

Springer

Editors
Marc Fischlin
TU Darmstadt
Darmstadt, Germany

Veelasha Moonsamy
Ruhr-Universität Bochum
Bochum, Germany

ISSN 0302-9743 ISSN 1611-3349 (electronic)
Lecture Notes in Computer Science
ISBN 978-3-031-95760-4 ISBN 978-3-031-95761-1 (eBook)
https://doi.org/10.1007/978-3-031-95761-1

This Springer imprint is published by the registered company Springer Nature Switzerland AG
The registered company address is: Gewerbestrasse 11, 6330 Cham, Switzerland

Preface

ACNS 2025, the 23rd International Conference on Applied Cryptography and Network Security, was held in Munich, Germany, on June 23–26, 2025. The conference covered all technical aspects of applied cryptography, network and computer security and privacy, representing both academic research work as well as developments in industrial and technical frontiers. Authors were explicitly asked to detail ethical considerations for vulnerability disclosure, if applicable. This year, ACNS also solicited the submission of Systematization of Knowledge (SoK) papers to put complex questions into a broader context.

The conference had two submission cycles, one in September 2024 and one in January 2025. Authors submitted a total of 241 submissions over the two cycles to ACNS, 116 in the first cycle and 125 in the second cycle. The Program Committee eventually selected 55 papers for publication in the proceedings of the conference, resulting in an acceptance rate of 22.8%. The three volumes of the conference proceedings contain the revised versions of these 55 papers. In addition to the presentations of the contributed papers, ACNS 2025 was also fortunate to have Shweta Shinde and Bart Preneel as invited speakers. Shweta's talk was on "Confidential Computing in Three Acts" and Bart's talk was on "Crypto Wars Revisited" (abstract included in the proceedings).

The program committee of ACNS 2025 consisted of 69 leading experts in the area of applied cryptography and security, supported by 71 external reviewers. The selection process followed a double-blinded approach. Each submission was assigned to at least three reviewers, taking into consideration potential conflicts of interest. The reviewers, after providing an evaluation of the submissions in a "silent" phase, discussed their viewpoints and deliberated on the final decision. The program chairs were not allowed to submit papers and did not handle any submissions they were in conflict with.

Traditionally, ACNS gives a best student paper award to encourage promising students to publish their best results at the conference. This year the award was given to Karen Azari and Andreas Ellison for their work on "Tighter provable security for TreeKEM", and to Mahdi Rahimi for the work "PARSAN-Mix: Packet-Aware Routing and Shuffling with Additional Noise for Latency Optimization in Mix Networks". The award recipients shared a monetary prize of 2,000 EUR generously sponsored by Springer (1,500 EUR for the best student papers and 500 EUR for the workshop).

Running a conference is a team effort. It starts with the steering committee of ACNS, Moti Yung and Jianying Zhou, and their trust in the designated Program Chairs to successfully carry out the next edition of ACNS. We would also like to thank the General Chairs Johannes Kinder and Stefan Katzenbeisser for a smooth organization, as well as Mark Manulis as Workshop Program Chair, Daniel Slamanig as Poster Chair, and Elif Bilge Kavun as Sponsorship Chair. We would also like to thank our contacts at Springer, for an effortless publication process on our side. Needless to say that the conference would be impossible without all the authors submitting their creative works and the program committee and the reviewers evaluating these works. The Program Chairs are indebted to all these colleagues for their honorary engagement.

June 2025

Marc Fischlin
Veelasha Moonsamy

Organization

General Chairs

Johannes Kinder	Ludwig-Maximilians-Universität München, Germany
Stefan Katzenbeisser	University of Passau, Germany

Program Committee Chairs

Marc Fischlin	Technische Universität Darmstadt, Germany
Veelasha Moonsamy	Ruhr University Bochum, Germany

Steering Committee

Moti Yung	Google, USA
Jianying Zhou	Singapore University of Technology and Design, Singapore

Program Committee

Elena Andreeva	TU Wien, Austria
Daniel Arp	TU Berlin, Germany
Andrea Basso	IBM Research Europe, Switzerland
Sebastian Berndt	Technische Hochschule Lübeck, Germany
Sarani Bhattacharya	Indian Institute of Technology Kharagpur, India
Marcus Botacin	Texas A&M University, USA
Jacqueline Brendel	Technische Universität Darmstadt, Germany
Xavier Bultel	INSA Centre Val de Loire, France
Anirban Chakraborty	Max Planck Institute for Security and Privacy, Germany
Guangke Chen	Pengcheng Laboratory, China
Shan Chen	Southern University of Science and Technology, China
Lukasz Chmielewski	Masaryk University, Czech Republic
Daniel Collins	Purdue University, USA

Bernardo David	IT University of Copenhagen, Denmark
Steven Duong	University of Wollongong, Australia
Alessandro Erba	Karlsruhe Institute of Technology, Germany
Reo Eriguchi	National Institute of Advanced Industrial Science and Technology, Japan
Anna Lisa Ferrara	University of Molise, Italy
Danilo Francati	George Mason University, USA
Ankit Gangwal	IIIT Hyderabad, India
Fatemeh Ganji	Worcester Polytechnic Institute, USA
Matteo Große-Kampmann	Rhine-Waal University of Applied Sciences, Germany & AWARE7 GmbH, Germany
Yanqi Gu	Meta, USA
Berk Gulmezoglu	Iowa State University, USA
Shuai Han	Shanghai Jiao Tong University, China
Julius Hermelink	Max Planck Institute for Security and Privacy, Germany
Murtuza Jadliwala	University of Texas at San Antonio, USA
Nesrine Kaaniche	Institut Polytechnique de Paris, France
Hamidreza Khoshakhlagh	Aarhus University, Denmark
Alexander Koch	CNRS, IRIF, Université Paris Cité, France
Christoph Krauß	Darmstadt University of Applied Sciences, Germany
Duc Le	Visa Research, USA
Antonin Leroux	Université de Rennes, France
Eleonora Losiouk	University of Padua, Italy
Stefan Lucks	Bauhaus-Universität Weimar, Germany
Monosij Maitra	Indian Institute of Technology Kharagpur, India
Suryadipta Majumdar	Concordia University, Canada
Barbara Masucci	University of Salerno, Italy
Jeremias Mechler	Karlsruhe Institute of Technology, Germany
Elena Pagnin	Chalmers University of Technology, Sweden
Lorenz Panny	Technische Universität München, Germany
Sikhar Patranabis	IBM Research, India
Thomas Peters	UC Louvain, Belgium
Prabhu Karthikeyan Rajasekaran	Google, USA
Shahram Rasoolzadeh	Ruhr University Bochum, Germany
Leonardo Regano	Università degli Studi di Cagliari, Italy
Doreen Riepel	UC San Diego, USA
Arnab Roy	University of Innsbruck, Austria
Sushmita Ruj	University of New South Wales, Australia
Vadim Safronov	University of Oxford, UK
Yusuke Sakai	AIST, Japan

Antonio Sanso	Ethereum Foundation, Switzerland
Theodore Schnitzler	Maastricht University, The Netherlands
Dave Singelee	KU Leuven, Belgium
Mridula Singh	CISPA Helmholtz Center for Information Security, Germany
Juraj Somorovsky	Paderborn University, Germany
Yongsoo Song	Seoul National University, South Korea
Claudio Soriente	NEC Laboratories Europe, Germany
Angelo Spognardi	Sapienza University of Rome, Italy
Riccardo Spolaor	Shandong University, China
Paul Staat	Max Planck Institute for Security and Privacy, Germany
Igors Stepanovs	Amazon, Spain
Christine Utz	Radboud University, The Netherlands
Daniele Venturi	Sapienza University of Rome, Italy
Alexios Voulimeneas	TU Delft, The Netherlands
Benedikt Wagner	Ethereum Foundation, Switzerland
Avishai Wool	Tel Aviv University, Israel
Chen Yan	Zhejiang University, China
Zeyu Yang	Singapore University of Technology and Design, Singapore

Additional Reviewers

Renas Bacho
Robin Berger
Aymen Boudguiga
Dung Bui
Jean-Paul Bultel
Daniele Canavese
Panagiotis Chatzigiannis
Bohang Chen
Clément Dell'Aiera
Jesko Dujmovic
Sayon Duttagupta
Prastudy Fauzi
Christian Forler
Daniele Friolo
Clemente Galdi
Rachit Garg
Satrajit Ghosh
Soumyadyuti Ghosh
David Gérault
Jincheol Ha
Keisuke Hara
Aditya Hegde
Keitaro Hiwatashi
Jonas Janneck
Mingming Jiang
Aaron Kaiser
Vukašin Karadžić
Alireza Kavousi
Akshaya Kumar
Baiyu Li
Eik List
Xiangyu Liu
You Lyu
Simon Masson
Jeremias Mechler
Bart Mennink

Miran Miran
Nimish Mishra
Arup Mondal
Montassar Naghmouchi
Aysan Nishaburi
Charles Olivier-Anclin
Edoardo Di Paolo
Jeongeun Park
Peter Pessl
Richard Petri
Sihang Pu
Rishabh Ranjan
Angela Robinson
Rajat Sadhukhan
Ashish Sai
Olga Sanina
Christian Scano
Marek Sefranek
István András Seres
Harshal Bhadreshkumar Shah
Laura Shea
Lu Shi
Xuanyu Shi
Animesh Singh
Sayani Sinha
Erkan Tairi
Kaoru Takemure
Tianxin Tang
Toi Tomita
Kien Tuong Truong
Anshu Yadav
Hongyu Yi
Zhenfei Zhang
Yu Zhou
Yunxiao Zhou

Crypto Wars Revisited (Abstract of Invited Talk)

Bart Preneel

ESAT/COSIC KU Leuven, Kasteelpark Arenberg 10, Bus 2452, 3001 Leuven, Belgium
bart.preneel@esat.kuleuven.be

Abstract. The Crypto Wars reflect the ongoing conflict between governments seeking access to encrypted data for national security and crime prevention and the protection of individual and collective privacy. The Crypto Wars go back five decades, starting with the suppression of research on cryptography, access to secure communications (the Clipper Chip), access to stored data (Apple versus the FBI) and spyware (NSO Group). In recent years, the focus has shifted to dealing with end-to-end encryption communications through client-side scanning: all information transmitted would be filtered at large scale on devices prior to encryption or directly after decryption. While officially aimed at detecting Child Sexual Abuse Material (CSAM), this technology is also positioned for use against terrorism and organized crime. However, universal client-side scanning technology violates the essence of end-to-end encryption, would be easy to bypass and—like all other third-party access methods—is prone to misuse and abuse. Moreover, its effectiveness remains highly questionable. Serious flaws have been identified in perceptual hash functions that are essential to detect known CSAM without revealing the content itself. These hash functions map visually similar content to similar short hash values. Our recent work shows that a broad class of designs (including all widely used schemes) result in very high false positive and false negative rates. Regulatory proposals have also put forward the use of AI for the detection of new and in particular AI-generated CSAM; these raise further concerns about technical feasibility and reliability. In April 2025, the EU has published the ProtectEU Communication (https://eur-lex.europa.eu/legal-content/EN/TXT/PDF/?uri=CELEX:52025PC0148). This new internal security strategy calls for a technology roadmap for solutions that give law enforcement access to encrypted data and for expanding access to metadata, thus opening a new battle in the Crypto Wars. Over the past decade, law enforcement agencies have gained vast amounts of metadata, biometric data, surveillance data from cameras, data stored in social media and in public clouds, supported by increasingly powerful analytical tools. These capabilities may well offset the challenges posed by encryption. The priority should be strengthening cybersecurity and privacy while ensuring transparency around interception technologies. A broader societal debate is essential to balance the right to security with other fundamental rights.

Keywords: cryptographic policy · key escrow · CSAM detection · data retention

Contents – Part I

Multi-party Computation

Network Security

Cryptographic Primitives and Protocols

Contents – Part II

Side Channels

Information Security

Privacy and Anonymity

Contents – Part III

Machine Learning

Encryption and Secret Sharing

Registered Matchmaking Encryption

Danilo Francati[1(✉)], Valeria Huang[2], and Daniele Venturi[2]

[1] Royal Holloway, University of London, Egham, UK
danilo.francati@rhul.ac.uk
[2] Sapienza University of Rome, Rome, Italy

Abstract. Matchmaking encryption (ME) is a generalization of attribute-based encryption (ABE) in which both the sender and the receiver (each with their own attributes) can specify access policies the other party must satisfy in order for the message to be revealed. Security guarantees that during decryption nothing is leaked beyond the fact whether a match occurred or not. Similarly to ABE, ME requires a trusted key generation center (KGC) that can potentially decrypt all ciphertexts.

We cast ME in the framework of registered encryption, in which the KGC is replaced by an untrusted key curator that registers public keys, attributes and policies of the users, but is not allowed to decrypt ciphertexts. Our main contribution is a black-box construction of registered ME (RME) using registered ABE (RABE) and lockable obfuscation. As we show, our construction can be instantiated under standard assumptions in the plain model yielding RME for expressive classes of policies.

Keywords: matchmaking encryption · registered encryption · public-key cryptography · lockable obfuscation

1 Introduction

Attribute-Based Encryption. Attribute-based encryption (ABE) [21,25] enhances the standard concept of public-key encryption (PKE) by providing more flexibility in describing who can access the plaintext. While in PKE a ciphertext created using a specific public key pk can be accessed only by who knows the corresponding secret key sk, in ABE, ciphertexts are associated to policies $\mathbb{R}$ specified by the sender, and secret keys to attributes ρ for the receiver, in such a way that the plaintext can be decrypted whenever the attributes satisfy the policy (i.e., $\mathbb{R}(\rho) = 1$). This yields so-called cipertext-policy ABE (CP-ABE); in key-policy ABE (KP-ABE) the role of policies and attributes are swapped, i.e. ciphertexts are associated to attributes σ for the sender, and secret keys to policies $\mathbb{S}$ specified by the receiver. In turn, KP-ABE and CP-ABE are a generalization of identity-based encryption (IBE) [26], which basically corresponds to ABE for the equality predicate (i.e., $\sigma = \rho$).

V. Huang—This work is based on the author's Master's thesis.

M. Fischlin and V. Moonsamy (Eds.): ACNS 2025, LNCS 15825, pp. 3–32, 2025.
https://doi.org/10.1007/978-3-031-95761-1_1

An intrinsic limitation of IBE and ABE systems is that a receiver cannot generate secret keys on its own. For this reason, a trusted-third party known as key generation center (KGC) is introduced; the KGC has its own master public key mpk and master secret key msk, and the latter is used to generate the actual secret keys for the users. This approach yields the so-called *key escrow* problem, as the KGC can decrypt all the ciphertexts.

Registered Encryption (RE). Recently, a new approach to tackle the key escrow problem has been proposed. The idea is to replace the KGC with an untrusted *key curator* whose job is to aggregate users' public keys. This yields the concept of registered IBE (RIBE) [8,9,16–18,22] and registered ABE (RABE) [3,14,15,23,30]. For instance, in CP-RABE, exactly as in PKE, each user independently generates their own public/secret key pair $(\mathsf{pk}, \mathsf{sk})$. Then, they register[1] their public key pk with the key curator along with their attributes ρ. The key curator takes each public keys $\mathsf{pk}_1, \ldots, \mathsf{pk}_L$ and the attributes $\sigma_1, \ldots, \sigma_L$ from different users, and aggregates them together into a single short master public key mpk.[2] Importantly, the size of the aggregated mpk needs to be minimized and we would like to be polylogarithmic in the number of users L. Finally, a ciphertext encrypted with respect to a policy $\mathbb{R}$ can be decrypted by any registered user whose attributes ρ satisfy the policy.

Since the master public key in RE is periodically updated, registered users must receive helper decryption keys hsk from the key curator; these keys will be used during decryption. Once again, the number of updates should be polylogarithmic in the number of users L. In fact, as shown in [24], $\Omega(\log L/\log\log L)$ updates are required (under mild assumptions).

Matchmaking Encryption. A natural generalization of CP-ABE and KP-ABE was recently proposed by Ateniese *et al.* [1,2] under the name of matchmaking encryption (ME). In ME, the sender specifies both a policy $\mathbb{R}$ (to be satisfied by the receiver) and its own attributes σ, whereas the receiver has decryption keys associated to its own attributes ρ and policies $\mathbb{S}$ (to be satisfied by the sender).[3] Correctness requires that the plaintext can be opened in the case of a match (i.e., when $\mathbb{R}(\rho) = \mathbb{S}(\sigma) = 1$). Security requires that in the case of a mismatch (i.e., when either $\mathbb{R}(\rho) = 0$ or $\mathbb{S}(\sigma) = 0$) nothing else is leaked (this is the so-called CPA-1-sided security); additionally, we can also require that in the case of a match nothing beyond the plaintext (and the fact that a match happened) is revealed (this is the so-called CPA-2-sided security). Finally, the original paper introducing ME put forward an additional *authenticity* requirement basically saying that an attacker not possessing attributes σ should not be able to create a valid ciphertext w.r.t. any access policy that is satisfied by σ (this captures security in the presence of malicious senders). Following [11,12],

[1] The key curator is responsible for validating the attributes the users claim.

[2] This aggregation is performed incrementally, i.e., on receiving pk_i, the key curator aggregates pk_i with olds registered public keys and outputs mpk_i.

[3] For flexibility, there are two separate decryption keys (one associated to attributes and one associated to a policy).

we do not consider this property in the paper as it is orthogonal to CPA-1-sided and CPA-2-sided security.

Ateniese *et al.* [1,2] construct ME for arbitrary policies under rather strong assumptions related to obfuscation, and ME for equality policies (a.k.a. identity-based ME) using pairings (in the random oracle model). Subsequent work improved the assumptions for identity-based ME [4–7,13]; more recently, Francati *et al.* [11,12] gave a construction of ME for arbitrary policies (in the plain model) from LWE.

Similarly to IBE and ABE, ME suffers from the key escrow problem. Hence, the question:

How to define and construct registered ME (RME)?

1.1 Our Contributions

In this work, as our first contribution, we put forward a formal treatment of RME. Our treatment is the natural extension of the already existing definitions for CP-RABE and KP-RABE. In particular, in RME, each user generates two pairs of public and secret keys $(\mathsf{pk}_{\mathsf{attr}}, \mathsf{sk}_{\mathsf{attr}})$ and $(\mathsf{pk}_{\mathsf{pol}}, \mathsf{sk}_{\mathsf{pol}})$ which can be registered to attributes or policies, respectively. To register its attributes, the user submits an *attribute-key-registration* request (composed of $\mathsf{pk}_{\mathsf{attr}}$ and attributes ρ) to key curator which will aggregate $\mathsf{pk}_{\mathsf{attr}}$ and olds attribute public keys into a compact *attribute* master public key $\mathsf{mpk}_{\mathsf{attr}}$. This process is completely verifiable and transparent since it is deterministic and does not involve any secret. The act of registering a policy is identical: the user submits a *policy-key-registration* request $(\mathsf{pk}_{\mathsf{pol}}, \mathbb{R})$ which will result in the aggregation and the creation of a compact *policy* master public key $\mathsf{mpk}_{\mathsf{pol}}$.[4]

Next, a user with attributes σ can encrypt a message with respect to a policy $\mathbb{R}$ using the master public keys $(\mathsf{mpk}_{\mathsf{attr}}, \mathsf{mpk}_{\mathsf{pol}})$ of the key curator. Decryption of the ciphertext is possible if and only if there is a match. Of course, RME must obey the same efficiency requirements as in RABE. Similarly to ABE and ME, the security definition can be formulated in the two variants of CPA-1-sided and CPA-2-sided security. We refer the reader to Sect. 3 for the details.

As our second contribution, we provide a construction of RME for arbitrary policies in the plain model. Our construction combines CP-RABE and KP-RABE with a so-called lockable obfuscator (LO) [19,27] (which can be instantiated from LWE). In particular, in Sect. 4, we show:

Theorem 1 (Informal). *There is a construction of CPA-1-sided (resp. CPA-2-sided) RME from CPA secure (resp. CPA-2-sided) CP-RABE, CPA secure (resp. CPA-2-sided) KP-ABE, and LO.*

Combining Theorem 1 with known constructions of RABE and RIBE (in particular, [10,18,30]) and LO [19,27], we obtain several instantiations of RME with different levels of expressiveness and efficiency. For instance, we get:

[4] Similarly to ME, for flexibility, the users can register their attributes and policies separately. This results in two separate master public keys instead of one (and two separate registration and update procedures).

- CPA-2-sided secure RME for arbitrary circuits assuming iO and LWE;
- CPA-2-sided secure RME for zero inner product predicates assuming LWE and the bilinear generic group model;
- CPA-1-sided secure RME for span program predicates assuming MDDH and LWE;
- CPA-1-sided secure RME for equality predicates (a.k.a. identity-based RME) assuming DBDH in prime order groups and LWE.

1.2 Overview of Our Construction

In order to explain the main intuition behind our construction, let us start with a failed attempt to construct RME from CP-RABE and KP-RABE: We first encrypt the message using the CP-ABE scheme, and then encrypt the ciphertext using the KP-ABE scheme. Unfortunately, this construction fails to achieve CPA-1-sided security as the attacker can check which layer of the ciphertext fails to decrypt in case of a mismatch (in particular, it suffices that either $\mathbb{S}(\sigma) = 0$ or $\mathbb{R}(\rho) = 0$ but not both).

We fix this attempt using LO. Recall that LO allows to obfuscate a circuit $\mathbb{C}$ under a lock y together with a message m, in such a way that evaluating the obfuscated circuit, on input x, returns m whenever $\mathbb{C}(x) = y$. As for security, an obfuscated circuit can be simulated in a virtual black-box (VBB) fashion as long as the lock is random and unknown to the adversary. In our construction, we sample a random lock y and encrypt it using CP-RABE obtaining a ciphertext c'. Then, we encrypt c' using KP-RABE obtaining a ciphertext c''. Finally, we let the ciphertext be a LO with respect to lock y, message m, and circuit $\mathbb{C}_{\mathsf{c}''}$ that upon input the secret keys of the underlying KP-ABE and CP-ABE schemes first decrypts c'' and then decrypts c'. Intuitively, in the proof of CPA-1-sided security, VBB security of LO hides everything beyond the fact that a mismatch happened (assuming the ABE schemes are also CPA secure). The proof of CPA-2-sided security is similar, but of course requires the underlying ABE schemes to also satisfy CPA-2-sided security.

Our scheme can be thought of as a generalization of the construction of ME in [11,12]. However, our construction is simpler (and the proof more streamlined) as we remove the abstraction of two-key predicate encryption.

1.3 Related Work

The key curator in RIBE and RABE schemes is fully deterministic and maintains no long-term secrets. This guarantees that, even if the key curator is corrupted, the adversary cannot decrypt any past ciphertext; on the other hand, such an adversary would be able to register a key that decrypts all future ciphertexts. An RE in which such a behavior is publicly detectable by auditing the state of the key curator is called *verifiable* [20].

The concept of registration-based cryptography has also been applied to attribute-based signatures [28], and to functional encryption (FE) [10,29] (yielding RFE). On the one hand, we note that it is not known whether FE implies

ME in a black-box manner (and thus if RFE directly implies RME). On the other hand, RFE implies both CP-RABE and KP-RABE for arbitrary policies.

2 Preliminaries

2.1 Notation

We write $[n] = \{1, 2, \ldots, n\}$. Capital bold-face letters (such as $\mathbf{X}$) are used to denote random variables, small letters (such as x) to denote concrete values, calligraphic letters (such as $\mathcal{X}$) to denote sets, serif letters (such as A) to denote algorithms. All of our algorithms are modeled as (possibly interactive) Turing machines. For a string $x \in \{0,1\}^*$, we let $|x|$ be its length; if $\mathcal{X}$ is a set or a list, $|\mathcal{X}|$ represents the cardinality of $\mathcal{X}$. When x is chosen uniformly in $\mathcal{X}$, we write $x \leftarrow \mathcal{X}$. If A is an algorithm, we write $y \leftarrow \mathsf{A}(x)$ to denote a run of A on input x and output y; if A is randomized, y is a random variable and $\mathsf{A}(x; r)$ denotes a run of A on input x and (uniform) randomness r. An algorithm A is *probabilistic polynomial-time* (PPT) if A is randomized and for any input $x, r \in \{0,1\}^*$ the computation of $\mathsf{A}(x; r)$ terminates in a polynomial number of steps (in the input size). We write $y \leftarrow \mathbb{C}(x)$ to denote the evaluation of the circuit $\mathbb{C}$ on input x and output y. Similarly, for a policy $\mathbb{R}$ (e.g., predicate, boolean formula), we write $\mathbb{R}(x) \in \{0,1\}$ to denote the outcome of evaluating the policy $\mathbb{R}$ on input x.

Negligible Functions. We denote by $\lambda \in \mathbb{N}$ the security parameter and we implicitly assume that every algorithm takes as input the security parameter (written in unary). A function $\nu : \mathbb{N} \to [0,1]$ is called *negligible* in the security parameter λ if it vanishes faster than the inverse of any polynomial in λ, i.e. $\nu(\lambda) \in O(1/p(\lambda))$ for all positive polynomials $p(\lambda)$. We write $\mathsf{negl}(\lambda)$ (resp., $\mathsf{poly}(\lambda)$) to denote an unspecified negligible function (resp., polynomial function) in the security parameter.

2.2 Ciphertext-Policy and Key-Policy Registered Attribute-Based Encryption

Ciphertext-Policy Registered Attribute-Based Encryption. A ciphertext-policy registered attribute-based encryption scheme (CP-RABE) with attribute space $\mathcal{X}$, policy space $\mathcal{P}$ and message space $\mathcal{M}$ consists of a tuple of efficient algorithms $\Pi_{\mathsf{CP\text{-}RABE}} = (\mathsf{Setup}, \mathsf{KGen}, \mathsf{RegPK}, \mathsf{Enc}, \mathsf{Update}, \mathsf{Dec})$ defined as follows:

- $\mathsf{Setup}(1^\lambda) \to \mathsf{crs}$: On input the security parameter 1^λ, the setup algorithm outputs a common reference string crs.
- $\mathsf{KGen}(\mathsf{crs}, \mathsf{aux}) \to (\mathsf{pk}, \mathsf{sk})$: On input the common reference string crs, a (possibly empty) state aux, the key-generation algorithm outputs a public key pk and a secret key sk.

- $\mathsf{RegPK}(\mathsf{crs}, \mathsf{aux}, \mathsf{pk}, \rho) \rightarrow (\mathsf{mpk}, \mathsf{aux}')$: On input the common reference string crs, a (possible empty) state aux, a public key pk, and some attributes $\rho \in \mathcal{X}$, the registration algorithm *deterministically* outputs the master public key mpk and an updated state aux'.
- $\mathsf{Enc}(\mathsf{mpk}, \mathbb{S}, m) \rightarrow \mathsf{c}$: On input the master public key mpk, an access policy $\mathbb{S} \in \mathcal{P}$, and a message $m \in \mathcal{M}$, the encryption algorithm outputs a ciphertext c.
- $\mathsf{Update}(\mathsf{crs}, \mathsf{aux}, \mathsf{pk}) \rightarrow \mathsf{hsk}$: On input the common reference string crs, a state aux, and a public key pk, the algorithm *deterministically* outputs a helper decryption key hsk.
- $\mathsf{Dec}(\mathsf{sk}, \mathsf{hsk}, \mathsf{c}) \rightarrow m$: On input a secret key sk, a helper decryption key hsk, and a ciphertext c, the decryption algorithm either outputs a message $m \in \mathcal{M}$, a special symbol $\perp$ to indicate a decryption failure, or a special flag $\mathsf{GetUpdatepdate}$ that indicates an updated helper decryption key is needed to decrypt.

Correctness, Compactness, and Efficiency of CP-RABE. We require a CP-RABE scheme to be correct, i.e., a honestly computed ciphertext decrypts correctly whenever the receiver's attributes ρ satisfies the sender's policy $\mathbb{S}$ (satisfaction is denoted as $\mathbb{S}(\rho) = 1$). This must hold even in the presence of maliciously chosen registered public keys. To capture this, correctness is defined as a game between a challenger and an adversary.

In addition, we are interested in measuring the efficiency of CP-RABE according to the following aspects: (*i*) size of crs, (*ii*) KGen's runtime, (*iii*) RegPK's runtime, (*iv*) size of mpk, (*v*) size of hsk, and (*vi*) maximum number of updates that each user needs to receive during the lifetime of the system.[5] Following [10], we measure the runtimes of algorithms in the RAM model of computation. In such a model, the runtime of an algorithm can be sublinear in the size of its inputs.

The formal definitions follows.

Definition 1 (Correctness of CP-RABE). *Let* $\Pi_{\mathsf{CP\text{-}RABE}} = (\mathsf{Setup}, \mathsf{KGen}, \mathsf{RegPK}, \mathsf{Enc}, \mathsf{Update}, \mathsf{Dec})$ *be a CP-RABE scheme with attribute space* $\mathcal{X}$, *policy space* $\mathcal{P}$, *and a message space* $\mathcal{M}$. *For any adversary* A, *define the following security game* $\mathbf{G}^{\mathsf{CP\text{-}correctness}}_{\Pi_{\mathsf{CP\text{-}RABE}}, \mathsf{A}}$ *between* A *and the challenger:*

- ***Setup phase:*** *the challenger starts by sampling the common reference string* $\mathsf{crs} \leftarrow \mathsf{Setup}(1^\lambda)$. *It then initializes the auxiliary input* $\mathsf{aux} \leftarrow \perp$ *and the initial master public key* $\mathsf{mpk}_0 \leftarrow \perp$. *It also initializes a counter* $\mathsf{ctr}[\mathsf{reg}] \leftarrow 0$ *to keep track of the number of registration queries and another counter* $\mathsf{ctr}[\mathsf{enc}] \leftarrow 0$ *to keep track of the number of encryption queries. It initializes* $\mathsf{ctr}[\mathsf{reg}^*] \leftarrow \infty$ *as the index for the target key (which will also be updated during the game). Finally, it gives* crs *to* A.

[5] Optimally, we would like those complexity to be poly-logarithmic in the number of users.

- ***Query phase:*** *during the query phase, the adversary* A *is able to make the following queries.*
  - ***Register non-target key query:*** *In a non-target-key registration query, the adversary* A *specifies a public key* pk *and a some attributes* $\rho \in \mathcal{X}$. *The challenger first increments the counter* $\mathsf{ctr[reg]} \leftarrow \mathsf{ctr[reg]} + 1$ *and then register the key by computing* $(\mathsf{mpk}_{\mathsf{crt[reg]}}, \mathsf{aux}') \leftarrow \mathsf{RegPK}(\mathsf{crs}, \mathsf{aux}, \mathsf{pk}, \rho)$. *The challenger updates its auxiliary data by setting* $\mathsf{aux} \leftarrow \mathsf{aux}'$ *and replies to* A *with* $(\mathsf{ctr[reg]}, \mathsf{mpk}_{\mathsf{ctr[reg]}}, \mathsf{aux})$.
  - ***Register target key query:*** *In a target-key registration query, the adversary specifies some attributes* $\rho^* \in \mathcal{X}$. *If the adversary has previously made a target-key registration query, then the challenger replies with* $\perp$. *Otherwise, the challenger increments the counter* $\mathsf{ctr[reg]} \leftarrow \mathsf{ctr[reg]} + 1$, *computes* $(\mathsf{pk}^*, \mathsf{sk}^*) \leftarrow \mathsf{KGen}(\mathsf{crs}, \mathsf{aux})$, *and registers* pk^* *by computing* $(\mathsf{mpk}_{\mathsf{ctr[reg]}}, \mathsf{aux}') \leftarrow \mathsf{RegPK}(\mathsf{crs}, \mathsf{aux}, \mathsf{pk}^*, \rho^*)$. *Then, it computes the helper decryption key* $\mathsf{hsk}^* \leftarrow \mathsf{Update}(\mathsf{crs}, \mathsf{aux}, \mathsf{pk}^*)$. *The challenger updates its auxiliary data by setting* $\mathsf{aux} \leftarrow \mathsf{aux}'$, *stores the index of the target identity* $\mathsf{ctr[reg^*]} \leftarrow \mathsf{ctr[reg]}$, *and replies to* A *with* $(\mathsf{ctr[reg]}, \mathsf{mpk}_{\mathsf{ctr[reg]}}, \mathsf{aux}, \mathsf{pk}^*, \mathsf{hsk}^*, \mathsf{sk}^*)$.
  - ***Encryption query:*** *In an encryption query, the adversary submits the index* $\mathsf{ctr[reg^*]} \leq i \leq \mathsf{ctr[reg]}$ *of a public key, a message* $m_{\mathsf{ctr[enc]}} \in \mathcal{M}$, *and a policy* $\mathbb{S}_{\mathsf{ctr[enc]}} \in \mathcal{P}$. *If the adversary has not yet registered a target key, or if the target set of attributes* ρ^* *does not satisfy the policy* $\mathbb{S}_{\mathsf{ctr[enc]}}$, *the challenger replies with* $\perp$. *Otherwise, the challenger increments the counter* $\mathsf{ctr[enc]} \leftarrow \mathsf{ctr[enc]} + 1$ *and computes* $\mathsf{c}_{\mathsf{ctr[enc]}} \leftarrow \mathsf{Enc}(\mathsf{mpk}_i, \mathbb{S}_{\mathsf{ctr[enc]}}, m_{\mathit{ctr[enc]}})$. *The challenger returns* $(\mathsf{ctr[enc]}, \mathsf{c}_{\mathsf{ctr[enc]}})$ *to* A.
  - ***Decryption query:*** *In a decryption query, the adversary submits a ciphertext index* $1 \leq j \leq \mathsf{ctr[enc]}$. *The challenger computes* $m'_j \leftarrow \mathsf{Dec}(\mathsf{sk}^*, \mathsf{hsk}^*, \mathsf{c_j})$. *If* $m'_j = \mathsf{getupdate}$, *then the challenger computes an updated helper decryption key* $\mathsf{hsk}^* \leftarrow \mathsf{Update}(\mathsf{crs}, \mathsf{aux}, \mathsf{pk}^*)$ *and recomputes* $m'_j \leftarrow \mathsf{Dec}(\mathsf{sk}^*, \mathsf{hsk}^*, \mathsf{c_j})$. *If* $m'_j \neq m_j$, *the experiment halts with output* $b = 1$.
- *If the adversary has finished making queries and the experiment has not halted (as a result of a decryption query), then the experiment outputs* $b = 0$.

We say that $\Pi_{\mathit{CP\text{-}RABE}}$ *is correct if for all (possible unbounded) adversary* A *making at most a polynomial number of queries, we have:*

$$\mathbb{P}\left[\mathbf{G}^{\mathit{CP\text{-}correctness}}_{\Pi_{\mathit{CP\text{-}RABE}},\mathsf{A}}(\lambda) = 1\right] \leq \mathsf{negl}(\lambda).$$

Definition 2 (Compactness and efficiency of CP-RABE). *We say an CP-ABE scheme* $\Pi_{\mathit{CP\text{-}RABE}} = (\mathsf{Setup}, \mathsf{KGen}, \mathsf{RegPK}, \mathsf{Enc}, \mathsf{Update}, \mathsf{Dec})$ *with attribute space* $\mathcal{X}$, *policy space* $\mathcal{P}$, *and a message space* $\mathcal{M}$ *is* $(t_{\mathsf{crs}}, t_{\mathsf{mpk}}, t_{\mathsf{hsk}})$*-compact and* $(t_{\mathsf{KGen}}, t_{\mathsf{RegPK}}, t_{\mathsf{num}}, t_{\mathsf{Update}})$*-efficient if for every unbounded adversary* A *making at most a polynomial number of queries, the following conditions hold in each step of the execution of experiment* $\mathbf{G}^{\mathit{CP\text{-}correctness}}_{\Pi_{\mathit{CP\text{-}RABE}}}$:

$(t_{\mathsf{crs}}, t_{\mathsf{mpk}}, t_{\mathsf{hsk}})$**-compactness.**

- t_{crs}**-compact** crs: *The size of the common reference string is bounded by* t_{crs}.
- t_{mpk}**-compact** mpk: *The size of the each master public key is bounded by* t_{mpk}.
- t_{hsk}**-compact** hsk: *The size of the each helper decryption key is bounded by* t_{hsk}.

$(t_{\mathsf{KGen}}, t_{\mathsf{RegPK}}, t_{\mathsf{num}}, t_{\mathsf{Update}})$**-efficiency.**

- t_{KGen}**-efficient** KGen: *The key-generation (worst-case) runtime is bounded by* t_{KGen}.
- t_{RegPK}**-efficient** RegPK: *The registration (worst-case) runtime is bounded by* t_{RegPK}.
- $(t_{\mathsf{num}}, t_{\mathsf{Update}})$**-efficient** Update: *The challenger executes* Update *at most (worst-case)* t_{num} *times and each invocation runs in time (worst-case)* t_{Update}.

The runtimes of the above algorithms are in the RAM model of computation.

Security of CP-RABE. As for security, a CP-RABE scheme must satisfy CPA-2-sided security, i.e., it is computationally infeasible for an adversary to distinguish between $\mathsf{Enc}(\mathsf{mpk}, \mathbb{S}_0, m_0)$ and $\mathsf{Enc}(\mathsf{mpk}, \mathbb{S}_1, m_1)$ whenever $\mathbb{S}_0(\rho) = \mathbb{S}_1(\rho)$ for every of the attributes ρ (associated to a registered public key pk) whose corresponding secret key sk is held by the adversary.[6] Sometimes, we make use of a weaker definition of security, named CPA security, which guarantees computational indistinguishability of $\mathsf{Enc}(\mathsf{mpk}, \mathbb{S}, m_0)$ and $\mathsf{Enc}(\mathsf{mpk}, \mathbb{S}, m_1)$ only when $\mathbb{S}(\rho) = 0$ (i.e., policy is not hidden). The formal definition follows.

Definition 3 (Security of CP-RABE). *Let* $\Pi_{\mathsf{CP\text{-}RABE}}$ = *(Setup, KGen, RegPK, Enc, Update, Dec) be a CP-RABE scheme with attribute space* $\mathcal{X}$*, policy space* $\mathcal{P}$*, and a message space* $\mathcal{M}$*. For any adversary* A*, define the following security game* $\mathbf{G}^{\mathsf{CP\text{-}security}}_{\Pi_{\mathsf{CP\text{-}RABE}},\mathsf{A}}$ *between* A *and the challenger:*

- ***Setup phase:*** *The challenger samples the common reference string* $\mathsf{crs} \leftarrow \mathsf{Setup}(1^\lambda)$*. It then initializes the auxiliary input* $\mathsf{aux} \leftarrow \perp$ *and the initial master public key* $\mathsf{mpk} \leftarrow \perp$*, a counter* $\mathsf{ctr} \leftarrow 0$ *for the number of honest-key-registration queries the adversary has made, an empty set of keys* $\mathcal{C} \leftarrow \emptyset$ *to keep track of corrupted public keys, and an empty dictionary mapping public keys to registered attribute sets* $\mathsf{D} \leftarrow \emptyset$*. For notational convenience, if* $\mathsf{pk} \notin \mathsf{D}$*, then we define* $\mathsf{D}[\mathsf{pk}] := \emptyset$ *to be the empty set. The challenger gives the* crs *to* A.
- ***Query phase:*** *Adversary* A *can now issue the following queries:*
  - ***Register corrupted key query:*** *In a corrupted-key-registration query, the adversary* A *submits a public key* pk *and some attributes* $\rho \in \mathcal{X}$ *to the oracle. The challenger registers the key by computing* $(\mathsf{mpk}', \mathsf{aux}') \leftarrow \mathsf{RegPK}(\mathsf{crs}, \mathsf{aux}, \mathsf{pk}, \rho)$*. The challenger updates its copy of the public key* $\mathsf{mpk} \leftarrow \mathsf{mpk}'$*, its auxiliary data* $\mathsf{aux} \leftarrow \mathsf{aux}'$*, adds* pk *to* $\mathcal{C}$*, and updates* $\mathsf{D}[\mathsf{pk}] \leftarrow \mathsf{D}[\mathsf{pk}] \cup \rho$*. It replies to* A *with* $(\mathsf{mpk}', \mathsf{aux}')$.

[6] To rule out trivial attacks, we require $m_0 = m_1$ if $\mathbb{S}_0(\rho) = \mathbb{S}_1(\rho) = 1$ for some corrupted attribute ρ.

- ***Register honest key query:*** *In an honest-key-registration query, the adversary specifies a attributes* $\rho \in \mathcal{X}$. *The challenger increments the counter* $\mathsf{ctr} \leftarrow \mathsf{ctr} + 1$ *and samples* $(\mathsf{pk}_{\mathsf{ctr}}, \mathsf{sk}_{\mathsf{ctr}}) \leftarrow \mathsf{KGen}(\mathsf{crs}, \mathsf{aux})$, *and registers* $\mathsf{pk}_{\mathsf{ctr}}$ *by executing* $(\mathsf{mpk}', \mathsf{aux}') \leftarrow \mathsf{RegPK}(\mathsf{crs}, \mathsf{aux}, \mathsf{pk}_{\mathsf{ctr}}, \rho)$. *The challenger updates its master public key* $\mathsf{mpk} \leftarrow \mathsf{mpk}'$, *its auxiliary data* $\mathsf{aux} \leftarrow \mathsf{aux}'$ *and* $\mathsf{D}[\mathsf{pk}_{\mathsf{ctr}}] \leftarrow \mathsf{D}[\mathsf{pk}_{\mathsf{ctr}}] \cup \rho$. *It replies to* A *with* $(\mathsf{ctr}, \mathsf{mpk}', \mathsf{aux}', \mathsf{pk}_{\mathsf{ctr}})$.
- ***Corrupt honest key query:*** *In a corrupt-honest-key query, the adversary specifies an index* $1 \le i \le \mathsf{ctr}$. *Let* $(\mathsf{pk_i}, \mathsf{sk_i})$ *be the* i^{th} *public/secret key the challenger samples when responding to the* i^{th} *honest-key-registration query. The challenger adds* pk_i *to* $\mathcal{C}$ *and replies to* A *with* sk_i.

- ***Challenge phase:*** *The adversary* A *chooses two messages* $m_0^*, m_1^* \in \mathcal{M}$ *and an two access policies* $\mathbb{S}_0^*, \mathbb{S}_1^* \in \mathcal{P}$. *The challenger samples a random* $b \in \{0,1\}$ *and replies with the challenge ciphertext* $\mathsf{c}^* \leftarrow \mathsf{Enc}(\mathsf{mpk}, \mathbb{S}_b^*, m_b^*)$.
- ***Output phase:*** *At the end of the game, the adversary* A *outputs a bit* $b' \in \{0,1\}$. *If* $b' = b$, *then the challenger sets to* 1 *the output of the experiment. Otherwise, it sets the output to* 0.

We say that $\Pi_{\mathsf{CP\text{-}RABE}}$ *is CPA-2-sided secure (reps. CPA secure) if for all valid PPT adversary* A, *we have:*

$$\mathbb{P}\left[\mathbf{G}^{\mathsf{CP\text{-}security}}_{\Pi_{\mathsf{CP\text{-}RABE}},\mathsf{A}}(\lambda) = 1\right] \le \mathsf{negl}(\lambda).$$

Let $\mathcal{S} = \{\rho \in \mathsf{D}[\mathsf{pk}] : \mathsf{pk} \in \mathcal{C}\}$ *the corrupted attributes. An adversary* A *is called valid if:*

- *(CPA security) For every corrupted attribute* $\rho \in \mathcal{S}$, *we have*[7]

$$\mathbb{S}_0^*(\rho) = \mathbb{S}_1^*(\rho) = 0 \wedge \mathbb{S}_0^* = \mathbb{S}_1^*.$$

- *(CPA-2-sided security) For every corrupted attribute* $\rho \in \mathcal{S}$, *we have*

$$\textit{either } \mathbb{S}_0^*(\rho) = \mathbb{S}_1^*(\rho) = 0 \textit{ or } \mathbb{S}_1^*(\rho) = \mathbb{S}_0^*(\rho) \wedge m_0^* = m_1^*.$$

Remark 1 (Post-challenge queries). As mentioned in previous works [10,23], security without post-challenge queries implies security with post-challenge queries. See [10, Remark 1].

Key-Policy Registered Attribute-Based Encryption. In a nutshell, a Key-Policy Registered Attribute-Based Encryption (KP-RABE) scheme is the dual version of CP-ABE. Specifically, the attributes are attached to ciphertext whereas policies are attached to secret keys. The KP-ABE's syntax, correctness, compactness, efficiency, and security definitions are simply adaptations of those of CP-RABE. To meet space constrains, we omit the formal definitions.

[7] The constraint $\mathbb{S}_0^* = \mathbb{S}_1^*$ is required to capture an adversary submitting a single challenge sender's policy as required by CPA security.

2.3 Lockable Obfuscation

Given as input a circuit $\mathbb{C}$, a lock y, and a message m, a lockable obfuscator Obf outputs an obfuscated circuit $\tilde{\mathbb{C}}$ such that, on input x, $\tilde{\mathbb{C}}(x)$ returns m only if the original circuit $\mathbb{C}(x)$ returns the lock y. Otherwise, if $\mathbb{C}(x) \neq y$, then $\tilde{\mathbb{C}}(x) = \perp$.

Let $n(\cdot), s(\cdot), d(\cdot)$ be polynomials, and $\mathcal{C}_{n,s,d}(\lambda)$ be the family of circuits of depth $d(\lambda)$ with input size $n(\lambda)$ and output size $s(\lambda)$. A lockable obfuscator for the circuit family $\mathcal{C}_{n,s,d}(\lambda)$ and message space $\mathcal{M}$ is composed of the following efficient algorithms:

- $\mathsf{Obf}(1^\lambda, \mathbb{C}, y, m) \rightarrow \tilde{\mathbb{C}}$: On input the security parameter 1^λ, a circuit $\mathbb{C} \in \mathcal{C}_{n,s,d}(\lambda)$, a lock $y \in \{0,1\}^{s(\lambda)}$ and a message $m \in \mathcal{M}$, the randomized lockable obfuscator algorithm outputs a circuit $\tilde{\mathbb{C}}$.
- $\mathsf{Eval}(\tilde{\mathbb{C}}, x) \rightarrow m$: On input an obfuscated circuit $\tilde{\mathbb{C}}$ and an input $x \in \{0,1\}^{n(\lambda)}$, the deterministic evaluation algorithm outputs a message $m \in \mathcal{M} \cup \{\perp\}$.

Definition 4 (Semi-statistical correctness of lockable obfuscation). *A lockable obfuscator $\Pi = (\mathsf{Obf}, \mathsf{Eval})$ for the circuit family $\mathcal{C}_{n,s,d}(\lambda)$ and message space $\mathcal{M}$ satisfies semi-statistical correctness if:*

1. $\forall \lambda \in \mathbb{N}, \forall x \in \{0,1\}^{n(\lambda)}, m \in \mathcal{M}, \forall \mathbb{C} \in \mathcal{C}_{n,s,d}(\lambda)$ *such that* $\mathbb{C}(x) = y$, *we have*
$$\mathbb{P}\left[\mathsf{Eval}(\mathsf{Obf}(1^\lambda, \mathbb{C}, y, m), x) = m\right] = 1$$
2. $\forall \lambda \in \mathbb{N}, \forall x \in \{0,1\}^{n(\lambda)}, m \in \mathcal{M}, \forall \mathbb{C} \in \mathcal{C}_{n,s,d}(\lambda)$ *such that* $\mathbb{C}(x) \neq y$, *we have*
$$\mathbb{P}\left[\mathsf{Eval}(\mathsf{Obf}(1^\lambda, \mathbb{C}, y, m), x) = m\right] \leq \mathsf{negl}(\lambda)$$

As of security, a lockable obfuscator guarantees that nothing is leaked when the lock is randomly sampled. This is defined by saying that there exits a PPT simulator ables to simulates an obfuscated circuit $\tilde{\mathbb{C}}$ without having access to $\mathbb{C}$, y, and m.

Definition 5 (Security of lockable obfuscation). *A lockable obfuscator $\Pi = (\mathsf{Obf}, \mathsf{Eval})$ for the circuit family $\mathcal{C}_{n,s,d}(\lambda)$ and message space $\mathcal{M}$ is secure if there exists a PPT simulator S such that for every PPT adversary A we have:*
$$\left|\mathbb{P}\left[\mathbf{G}^{\textsf{lock-sim}}_{\Pi,\mathsf{A},\mathsf{S}}(\lambda) = 1\right] - \frac{1}{2}\right| \leq \mathsf{negl}(\lambda)$$
where $\mathbf{G}^{\textsf{lock-sim}}_{\Pi,\mathsf{A},\mathsf{S}}(\lambda)$ is defined as follows:

- *A sends $(\mathbb{C}, m)$ to the challenger.*
- *The challenger samples a random lock $y \leftarrow s(\lambda)$, a random bit $b \leftarrow \{0,1\}$, and computes $\tilde{\mathbb{C}}_0 \leftarrow \mathsf{Obf}(1^\lambda, \mathbb{C}, y, m)$ and $\tilde{\mathbb{C}}_1 \leftarrow \mathsf{S}(1^\lambda, 1^{|\mathbb{C}|}, 1^{|m|})$.*
- *The challenger sends $\tilde{\mathbb{C}}_b$ to A.*
- *Finally, the adversary outputs $b' \in \{0,1\}$.*

3 Registered Matchmaking Encryption

Following the core functionality of ME, Registered Matchmaking Encryption (RME) allows both the sender and the receiver to choose their access policies that together describe the access rights both parties must satisfy in order to decrypt a particular ciphertext.

As in other registered encryption scheme, also in RME, the trusted authority (required to generate decryption keys in ME) is replaced with a *key curator*. Such key curator accepts registration queries from the receiver in order to register both its attributes ρ and policy $\mathbb{R}$ to some public keys, allowing the receiver to later decrypt (using the corresponding secret keys) a ciphertext according to ρ and $\mathbb{R}$.

Formally, a RME scheme with sender's policy and attributes space $\mathcal{P}_1$ and $\mathcal{X}_1$, receiver's policy and attributes space $\mathcal{P}_2$ and $\mathcal{X}_2$, and message space $\mathcal{M}$, consists of a tuple of efficient algorithms $\Pi_{\mathsf{RME}} = (\mathsf{Setup}, \mathsf{AttrKGen}, \mathsf{PolKGen}, \mathsf{AttrRegPK}, \mathsf{PolRegPK}, \mathsf{Enc}, \mathsf{AttrUpdate}, \mathsf{PolUpdate}, \mathsf{Dec})$ defined as follows:

- $\mathsf{Setup}(1^\lambda) \to \mathsf{crs}$: On input the security parameter 1^λ, the setup algorithm outputs a common reference string crs.
- $\mathsf{AttrKGen}(\mathsf{crs}, \mathsf{aux}) \to (\mathsf{pk_{attr}}, \mathsf{sk_{attr}})$: On input the common reference string crs, a (possibly empty) state aux, the key-generation algorithm outputs a public key $\mathsf{pk_{attr}}$ and a secret key $\mathsf{sk_{attr}}$ associated with receiver's attributes.
- $\mathsf{PolKGen}(\mathsf{crs}, \mathsf{aux}) \to (\mathsf{pk_{pol}}, \mathsf{sk_{pol}})$: On input the common reference string crs, a (possibly empty) state aux, the key-generation algorithm outputs a public key $\mathsf{pk_{pol}}$ and a secret key $\mathsf{sk_{pol}}$ associated with receiver's policies.
- $\mathsf{AttrRegPK}(\mathsf{crs}, \mathsf{aux}, \mathsf{pk_{attr}}, \rho) \to (\mathsf{mpk_{attr}}, \mathsf{aux}')$: On input the common reference string crs, a (possible empty) state aux, a public key $\mathsf{pk_{attr}}$ and attributes $\rho \in \mathcal{X}_2$, the registration algorithm *deterministically* outputs the attribute master public key $\mathsf{mpk_{attr}}$ and an updated state aux.
- $\mathsf{PolRegPK}(\mathsf{crs}, \mathsf{aux}, \mathsf{pk_{pol}}, \mathbb{R}) \to (\mathsf{mpk_{pol}}, \mathsf{aux}')$: On input the common reference string crs, a (possible empty) state aux, a public key $\mathsf{pk_{pol}}$ and an access policies $\mathbb{R} \in \mathcal{P}$, the registration algorithm *deterministically* outputs the policy master public key $\mathsf{mpk_{pol}}$ and an updated state aux'.
- $\mathsf{Enc}(\mathsf{mpk_{attr}}, \mathsf{mpk_{pol}}, \sigma, \mathbb{S}, m) \to \mathsf{c}$: On input two master public keys $\mathsf{mpk_{attr}}$ and $\mathsf{mpk_{pol}}$, attributes $\sigma \in \mathcal{X}_1$, an access policy $\mathbb{S} \in \mathcal{P}_1$, and a message $m \in \mathcal{M}$, the encryption algorithm outputs a ciphertext c.
- $\mathsf{AttrUpdate}(\mathsf{crs}, \mathsf{aux}, \mathsf{pk_{attr}}) \to \mathsf{hsk_{attr}}$: On input the common reference string crs, a state aux, and a public key $\mathsf{pk_{attr}}$, the algorithm *deterministically* outputs a helper decryption key $\mathsf{hsk_{attr}}$.
- $\mathsf{PolUpdate}(\mathsf{crs}, \mathsf{aux}, \mathsf{pk_{pol}}) \to \mathsf{hsk_{pol}}$: On input the common reference string crs, a state aux, and a public key $\mathsf{pk_{pol}}$, the algorithm *deterministically* outputs a helper decryption key $\mathsf{hsk_{pol}}$.
- $\mathsf{Dec}(\mathsf{sk_{attr}}, \mathsf{sk_{pol}}, \mathsf{hsk_{attr}}, \mathsf{hsk_{pol}}, \mathsf{c}) \to m$: On input the master public key mpk, secret keys $\mathsf{sk_{attr}}, \mathsf{sk_{pol}}$, helper decryption keys $\mathsf{hsk_{attr}}, \mathsf{hsk_{pol}}$, and a ciphertext c, the decryption algorithm either outputs a message $m \in \mathcal{M}$, a special symbol $\perp$ to indicate a decryption failure, or a special flag $\mathsf{getupdate}$ that indicates an updated helper decryption key is needed to decrypt.

Correctness, Compactness, and Efficiency of RME. Intuitively, RME must be correct, i.e., a honestly computed ciphertext decrypts correctly whenever $\mathbb{S}(\rho) = \mathbb{R}(\sigma) = 1$ where (σ, ρ) and $(\mathbb{S}, \mathbb{R})$ are sender's and receiver's attributes and policies, respectively. Similarly to CP-RABE and KP-RABE, correctness must hold even in the presence of adversarial registered public keys. The formal definition follows.

Definition 6 (Correctness of RME). *Let* $\Pi_{\mathsf{RME}} = (\mathsf{Setup}, \mathsf{AttrKGen}, \mathsf{PolKGen}, \mathsf{AttrRegPK}, \mathsf{PolRegPK}, \mathsf{Enc}, \mathsf{AttrUpdate}, \mathsf{PolUpdate}, \mathsf{Dec})$ *be a RME scheme with sender's policy and attributes space* $\mathcal{P}_1$ *and* $\mathcal{X}_1$*, receiver's policy and attributes space* $\mathcal{P}_2$ *and* $\mathcal{X}_2$*, and message space* $\mathcal{M}$*. For any adversary* A*, define the following security game* $\mathbf{G}^{\mathsf{RME\text{-}correctness}}_{\Pi_{\mathsf{RME}},\mathsf{A}}$ *between* A *and the challenger:*

- ***Setup phase:*** *The challenger starts by sampling the common reference string* $\mathsf{crs} \leftarrow \mathsf{Setup}(1^\lambda)$*. It then initializes the auxiliary input* $\mathsf{aux} \leftarrow \perp$ *and the initial master public keys* $(\mathsf{mpk}^0_{\mathsf{attr}}, \mathsf{mpk}^0_{\mathsf{pol}}) \leftarrow (\perp, \perp)$*. It also initializes two counters* $\mathsf{ctr}[\mathsf{regAttr}] \leftarrow 0$ *and* $\mathsf{ctr}[\mathsf{regPol}] \leftarrow 0$ *to keep track of the number of attribute and policy registration queries, and another counter* $\mathsf{ctr}[\mathsf{enc}] \leftarrow 0$ *to keep track of the number of encryption queries. It then initializes* $\mathsf{ctr}[\mathsf{regAttr}^*] \leftarrow \infty$ *and* $\mathsf{ctr}[\mathsf{regPol}^*] \leftarrow \infty$ *as the indices for the target attribute/policy keys (which will also be updated during the game). Finally, it gives* crs *to* A*.*
- ***Query phase:*** *During the query phase, the adversary* A *is able to make the following queries.*
  - ***Register non-target attribute-key query:*** *In a non-target-attribute-key registration query, the adversary* A *specifies a public key* $\mathsf{pk}_{\mathsf{attr}}$ *and attributes* $\rho \in \mathcal{X}_2$*. The challenger first increments the counter* $\mathsf{ctr}[\mathsf{regAttr}] \leftarrow \mathsf{ctr}[\mathsf{regAttr}] + 1$ *and registers the key by computing* $(\mathsf{mpk}^{\mathsf{ctr}[\mathsf{regAttr}]}_{\mathsf{attr}}, \mathsf{aux}') \leftarrow \mathsf{AttrRegPK}(\mathsf{crs}, \mathsf{aux}, \mathsf{pk}_{\mathsf{attr}}, \rho)$*. The challenger updates its auxiliary data by setting* $\mathsf{aux} \leftarrow \mathsf{aux}'$ *and returns* $(\mathsf{ctr}[\mathsf{regAttr}], \mathsf{mpk}^{\mathsf{ctr}[\mathsf{regAttr}]}_{\mathsf{attr}}, \mathsf{aux})$ *to* A*.*
  - ***Register non-target policy-key query:*** *In a non-target-policy-key registration query, the adversary* A *specifies a public key* $\mathsf{pk}_{\mathsf{pol}}$ *and a policy* $\mathbb{R} \in \mathcal{P}_2$*. The challenger first increments the counter* $\mathsf{ctr}[\mathsf{regPol}] \leftarrow \mathsf{ctr}[\mathsf{regPol}] + 1$ *and registers the key by computing* $(\mathsf{mpk}^{\mathsf{ctr}[\mathsf{regPol}]}_{\mathsf{pol}}, \mathsf{aux}') \leftarrow \mathsf{PolRegPK}(\mathsf{crs}, \mathsf{aux}, \mathsf{pk}_{\mathsf{pol}}, \mathbb{R})$*. The challenger updates its auxiliary data by setting* $\mathsf{aux} \leftarrow \mathsf{aux}'$ *and replies to* A *with* $(\mathsf{ctr}[\mathsf{regPol}], \mathsf{mpk}^{\mathsf{ctr}[\mathsf{regPol}]}_{\mathsf{pol}}, \mathsf{aux})$*.*
  - ***Register target attribute-key query:*** *In a target-attribute-key registration query, the adversary specifies some attributes* $\rho^* \in \mathcal{X}$*. If the adversary has previously made a target-attribute-key registration query, then the challenger replies with* $\perp$*. Otherwise, it increments the counter* $\mathsf{ctr}[\mathsf{regAttr}] \leftarrow \mathsf{ctr}[\mathsf{regAttr}] + 1$*, samples* $(\mathsf{pk}^*_{\mathsf{attr}}, \mathsf{sk}^*_{\mathsf{attr}}) \leftarrow \mathsf{AttrKGen}(\mathsf{crs}, \mathsf{aux})$*, and registers* $\mathsf{pk}^*_{\mathsf{attr}}$ *by executing* $(\mathsf{mpk}^{\mathsf{ctr}[\mathsf{regAttr}]}_{\mathsf{attr}}, \mathsf{aux}') \leftarrow \mathsf{AttrRegPK}(\mathsf{crs}, \mathsf{aux}, \mathsf{pk}^*_{\mathsf{attr}}, \rho^*)$*. Then, the challenger computes the helper decryption key* $\mathsf{hsk}^*_{\mathsf{attr}} \leftarrow \mathsf{AttrUpdate}(\mathsf{crs}, \mathsf{aux}, \mathsf{pk}^*_{\mathsf{attr}})$*, stores the index of the target attribute* $\mathsf{ctr}[\mathsf{regAttr}^*] \leftarrow \mathsf{ctr}[\mathsf{regAttr}]$*, updates its auxiliary*

data by setting $\mathsf{aux} \leftarrow \mathsf{aux}'$, *and returns* $(\mathsf{ctr}[\mathsf{regAttr}], \mathsf{mpk}_{\mathsf{attr}}^{\mathsf{ctr}[\mathsf{regAttr}]}, \mathsf{aux}, \mathsf{pk}^*_{\mathsf{attr}}, \mathsf{hsk}^*_{\mathsf{attr}}, \mathsf{sk}^*_{\mathsf{attr}})$ *to* A.

- ***Register target policy-key query:*** *In a target-policy-key registration query, the adversary specifies a policy* $\mathbb{R}^* \in \mathcal{P}_2$. *If the adversary has previously made a target-policy-key registration query, then the challenger replies with* $\perp$. *Otherwise, the challenger increments the counter* $\mathsf{ctr}[\mathsf{regPol}] \leftarrow \mathsf{ctr}[\mathsf{regPol}] + 1$, *runs* $(\mathsf{pk}^*_{\mathsf{pol}}, \mathsf{sk}^*_{\mathsf{pol}}) \leftarrow \mathsf{PolKGen}(\mathsf{crs}, \mathsf{aux})$ *and registers* $(\mathsf{mpk}_{\mathsf{pol}}^{\mathsf{ctr}[\mathsf{regPol}]}, \mathsf{aux}') \leftarrow \mathsf{PolRegPK}(\mathsf{crs}, \mathsf{aux}, \mathsf{pk}^*_{\mathsf{pol}}, \mathbb{R}^*)$. *It computes the helper decryption key* $\mathsf{hsk}^*_{\mathsf{pol}} \leftarrow \mathsf{PolUpdate}(\mathsf{crs}, \mathsf{aux}, \mathsf{pk}^*_{\mathsf{pol}})$. *The challenger updates its auxiliary data by setting* $\mathsf{aux} \leftarrow \mathsf{aux}'$, *stores the index of the target identity* $\mathsf{ctr}[\mathsf{regPol}^*] \leftarrow \mathsf{ctr}[\mathsf{regPol}]$, *and replies to* A *with* $(\mathsf{ctr}[\mathsf{regPol}], \mathsf{mpk}_{\mathsf{pol}}^{\mathsf{ctr}[\mathsf{reg}]}, \mathsf{aux}, \mathsf{pk}^*_{\mathsf{pol}}, \mathsf{hsk}^*_{\mathsf{pol}}, \mathsf{sk}^*_{\mathsf{pol}})$.
- ***Encryption query:*** *In an encryption query, the adversary submits the two indexes* $\mathsf{ctr}[\mathsf{regAttr}^*] \leq i_{\mathsf{attr}} \leq \mathsf{ctr}[\mathsf{regAttr}]$ *and* $\mathsf{ctr}[\mathsf{regPol}^*] \leq i_{\mathsf{pol}} \leq \mathsf{ctr}[\mathsf{regPol}]$ *of two master public keys, a message* $m_{\mathsf{ctr}[\mathsf{enc}]} \in \mathcal{M}$, *some attributes* $\sigma_{\mathsf{ctr}[\mathsf{enc}]} \in \mathcal{X}_1$ *and a policy* $\mathbb{S}_{\mathsf{ctr}[\mathsf{enc}]} \in \mathcal{P}_1$. *If the adversary has not yet registered both the target attribute-key and policy-key, or if the target attributes* ρ^* *does not satisfy the policy* $\mathbb{S}_{\mathsf{ctr}[\mathsf{enc}]}$, *or if the target policy* $\mathbb{R}^*$ *is not satisfied by the attributes* $\sigma_{\mathsf{ctr}[\mathsf{enc}]}$, *the challenger replies with* $\perp$. *Otherwise, the challenger increments the counter* $\mathsf{ctr}[\mathsf{enc}] \leftarrow \mathsf{ctr}[\mathsf{enc}] + 1$ *and executes* $\mathsf{c}_{\mathsf{ctr}[\mathsf{enc}]} \leftarrow \mathsf{Enc}(\mathsf{mpk}_{\mathsf{attr}}^{i_{\mathsf{attr}}}, \mathsf{mpk}_{\mathsf{pol}}^{i_{\mathsf{pol}}}, \sigma_{\mathsf{ctr}[\mathsf{enc}]}, \mathbb{S}_{\mathsf{ctr}[\mathsf{enc}]}, m_{\mathsf{ctr}[\mathsf{enc}]})$. *The challenger replies to* A *with* $(\mathsf{ctr}[\mathsf{enc}], \mathsf{c}_{\mathsf{ctr}[\mathsf{enc}]})$.
- ***Decryption query:*** *In a decryption query, the adversary submits a ciphertext index* $1 \leq j \leq \mathsf{ctr}[\mathsf{enc}]$. *The challenger computes* $m'_j \leftarrow \mathsf{Dec}(\mathsf{sk}^*_{\mathsf{attr}}, \mathsf{sk}^*_{\mathsf{pol}}, \mathsf{hsk}^*_{\mathsf{attr}}, \mathsf{hsk}^*_{\mathsf{pol}}, \mathsf{c}_j)$. *If* $m'_j = \mathsf{getupdate}$, *the challenger computes updated helper decryption keys* $\mathsf{hsk}^*_{\mathsf{attr}} \leftarrow \mathsf{AttrUpdate}(\mathsf{crs}, \mathsf{aux}, \mathsf{pk}^*_{\mathsf{attr}})$ *and* $\mathsf{hsk}^*_{\mathsf{pol}} \leftarrow \mathsf{PolUpdate}(\mathsf{crs}, \mathsf{aux}, \mathsf{pk}^*_{\mathsf{pol}})$, *and recomputes* $m'_j \leftarrow \mathsf{Dec}(\mathsf{sk}^*_{\mathsf{attr}}, \mathsf{sk}^*_{\mathsf{pol}}, \mathsf{hsk}^*_{\mathsf{attr}}, \mathsf{hsk}^*_{\mathsf{pol}}, \mathsf{c}_j)$. *If* $m'_j \neq m_j$, *the experiment halts with output* $b = 1$.

– *If the adversary has finished making queries and the experiment has not halted (as a result of a decryption query), then the experiment outputs* $b = 0$.

We say that Π_{RME} *is correct if for all (possible unbounded) adversary* A *making at most a polynomial number of queries, we have:*

$$\mathbb{P}\left[\mathbf{G}^{\textit{RME-correctness}}_{\Pi_{RME},\mathsf{A}}(\lambda) = 1\right] \leq \mathsf{negl}(\lambda).$$

In addition to correctness, we are interested in measuring (asymptotically) the following efficiency aspects of RME: (*i*) size of crs, (*ii*) runtime of key-generation algorithms (i.e., $\mathsf{AttrKGen}$ and $\mathsf{PolKGen}$), (*iii*) runtime of registration algorithms (i.e., $\mathsf{AttrRegPK}$ and $\mathsf{PolRegPK}$), (*iv*) size of master public keys (i.e., $|\mathsf{mpk}_{\mathsf{attr}}| + |\mathsf{mpk}_{\mathsf{pol}}|$), (*v*) size of helper decryption keys (i.e., $|\mathsf{hsk}_{\mathsf{attr}}| + |\mathsf{hsk}_{\mathsf{pol}}|$, and (*vi*) maximum number of updates (i.e., invocations of both $\mathsf{AttrUpdate}$ and

PolUpdate) that each user needs to receive during the lifetime of the system.[8] As usual, we measure the runtimes of algorithms in the RAM model of computation.

Definition 7 (Compactness and efficiency of RME). *We say a RME scheme* Π_{RME} = Setup, AttrKGen, PolKGen, AttrRegPK, PolRegPK, Enc, AttrUpdate, PolUpdate, Dec) *with sender's policy and attributes space* $\mathcal{P}_1$ *and* $\mathcal{X}_1$*, receiver's policy and attributes space* $\mathcal{P}_2$ *and* $\mathcal{X}_2$*, and message space* $\mathcal{M}$*, is* $(t_{\mathsf{crs}}, t_{\mathsf{mpk}_\star}, t_{\mathsf{hsk}_\star})$*-compact and* $(t_{\star\mathsf{KGen}}, t_{\star\mathsf{RegPK}}, t_{\mathsf{num}}, t_{\star\mathsf{Update}})$*-efficient if for every unbounded adversary* A *making at most a polynomial number of queries, the following conditions hold in each step of the execution of experiment* $\mathbf{G}^{\mathsf{RME\text{-}correctness}}_{\Pi_{\mathsf{RME}}}$:

$(t_{\mathsf{crs}}, t_{\mathsf{mpk}_\star}, t_{\mathsf{hsk}_\star})$**-compactness.**

- t_{crs}**-compact** crs**:** *The size of the common reference string is bounded by* t_{crs}.
- $t_{\mathsf{mpk}_\star}$**-compact master public keys:** *The size of the each master public key (output by either* AttrRegPK *or* PolKGen*) is bounded by* $t_{\mathsf{mpk}_\star}$.
- $t_{\mathsf{hsk}_\star}$**-compact helper decryption keys:** *The size of the each helper decryption key (output by either* AttrUpdate *or* PolUpdate*) is bounded by* $t_{\mathsf{hsk}_\star}$.

$(t_{\star\mathsf{KGen}}, t_{\star\mathsf{RegPK}}, t_{\mathsf{num}}, t_{\star\mathsf{Update}})$**-efficiency.**

- $t_{\star\mathsf{KGen}}$**-efficient key generation:** *The (worst-case) runtime of* AttrKGen *and the (worst-case) runtime of* PolKGen *are bounded by* $t_{\star\mathsf{KGen}}$.
- $t_{\star\mathsf{RegPK}}$**-efficient key registration:** *The (worst-case) runtime of* AttrRegPK *and the (worst-case) runtime of* PolRegPK *are bounded by* $t_{\star\mathsf{RegPK}}$.
- $(t_{\mathsf{num}}, t_{\star\mathsf{Update}})$**-efficient updates:** *The challenger executes* AttrUpdate *and* PolUpdate *at most (worst-case)* t_{num} *times (i.e., the cumulative number of* AttrUpdate *and* PolUpdate *executions is at most* t_{num}*). Moreover, the (worst-case) runtime of* AttrUpdate *and the (worst-case) runtime of* PolUpdate *are bounded by* $t_{\star\mathsf{Update}}$.

The runtimes of the above algorithms are in the RAM model of computation.[9]

Security of RME. We define security of RME according to both CPA-1-sided and CPA-2-sided security settings (see [12, Section 6.1]).[10] Specifically, CPA-1-sided security of RME guarantees that the output distributions of Enc($\mathsf{mpk}_{\mathsf{attr}}$, $\mathsf{mpk}_{\mathsf{pol}}$,

---

[8] Optimally, we would like those complexity to be poly-logarithmic in the number of users.

[9] Definition 7 merges compactness and efficiency requirements of attribute- and policy-related algorithms together. This is because, in this work, we are interested in measuring the (worst-case) asympotic efficiency of the scheme. To measure concrete efficiency, a more fine-grained definition can be used by setting an individual constraint for each key and algorithm of RME.

[10] We highlight that CPA-1-sided (reps. CPA-2-sided) security corresponds to only the "mismatch condition" (resp. both "mismatch and match condition") introduced by the seminal paper of Ateniese et al. [1,2].

$\sigma_0, \mathbb{S}_0, m_0)$ and $\mathsf{Enc}(\mathsf{mpk}_{\mathsf{attr}}, \mathsf{mpk}_{\mathsf{pol}}, \sigma_1, \mathbb{S}_1, m_1)$ looks computationally indistinguishable in the presence of an adversary holding secret keys (necessary for decryption) whose registered attributes $\{\rho\}$ and policies $\{\mathbb{R}\}$ do not permit to have a match with sender's attributes and policies (i.e., decryption failure).

In addition to the above, CPA-2-sided guarantees indistinguishability of the same distributions even in the presence of adversaries able to decrypt the ciphertext. When decryption is possible (i.e., CPA-2-sided case), it is necessary to constraint $m_0 = m_1$ and $\mathbb{S}_0(\rho) = \mathbb{S}_1(\rho)$, and $\mathbb{R}(\sigma_0) = \mathbb{R}(\sigma_1)$ to rule out trivial attacks ([1,2] for more details).

Definition 8 (Security of RME). *Let* $\Pi_{\mathsf{RME}} = (\mathsf{Setup}, \mathsf{AttrKGen}, \mathsf{PolKGen}, \mathsf{AttrRegPK}, \mathsf{PolRegPK}, \mathsf{Enc}, \mathsf{AttrUpdate}, \mathsf{PolUpdate}, \mathsf{Dec})$ *be a RME scheme with sender's policy and attributes space* $\mathcal{P}_1$ *and* $\mathcal{X}_1$*, receiver's policy and attributes space* $\mathcal{P}_2$ *and* $\mathcal{X}_2$*, and message space* $\mathcal{M}$*. For any adversary* A*, define the following security game* $\mathbf{G}^{\mathit{RME\text{-}security}}_{\Pi_{\mathit{RME}},\mathsf{A}}$ *between* A *and the challenger:*

- ***Setup phase:*** *The challenger starts by sampling the common reference string* $\mathsf{crs} \leftarrow \mathsf{Setup}(1^\lambda)$*. It then initializes the auxiliary input* $\mathsf{aux} \leftarrow \perp$ *and the initial master public keys* $(\mathsf{mpk}^0_{\mathsf{attr}}, \mathsf{mpk}^0_{\mathsf{pol}}) \leftarrow (\perp, \perp)$*. It then initializes the auxiliary inputs* $\mathsf{aux} \leftarrow \perp$ *and the initial master public key* $\mathsf{mpk} \leftarrow (\perp, \perp)$*, a counter* $\mathsf{ctr}[\mathsf{regAttr}] \leftarrow 0$ *for the number of honest-attribute-key-registration queries and a counter* $\mathsf{ctr}[\mathsf{regPol}] \leftarrow 0$ *for the number of honest-policy-key-registration queries the adversary has made, empty sets of keys* $\mathcal{C}_{\mathsf{attr}} \leftarrow \emptyset$ *to keep track of corrupted public attribute-keys and* $\mathcal{C}_{\mathsf{pol}} \leftarrow \emptyset$ *to keep track of corrupted public policy-keys, and empty dictionaries mapping public keys to registered attribute/policy sets* $\mathsf{D}_{\mathsf{attr}} \leftarrow \emptyset, \mathsf{D}_{\mathsf{pol}} \leftarrow \emptyset$*. For notational convenience, if* $\mathsf{pk} \notin \mathsf{D}$*, then we define* $\mathsf{D}[\mathsf{pk}] := \emptyset$*. The challenger sends the* crs *to* A*.*
- ***Query phase:*** *Adversary* A *can now issue the following queries.*

  - ***Register corrupted attribute-key query:*** *On submitting a corrupted-attribute-key-registration query, the adversary* A *specifies a public key* $\mathsf{pk}_{\mathsf{attr}}$ *and attributes* $\rho \in \mathcal{X}_2$*. The challenger registers the key by computing* $(\mathsf{mpk}'_{\mathsf{attr}}, \mathsf{aux}') \leftarrow \mathsf{AttrRegPK}(\mathsf{crs}, \mathsf{aux}, \mathsf{pk}_{\mathsf{attr}}, \rho)$*. The challenger updates its copy of the master public key* $\mathsf{mpk}_{\mathsf{attr}} \leftarrow \mathsf{mpk}'_{\mathsf{attr}}$*, its auxiliary data* $\mathsf{aux} \leftarrow \mathsf{aux}'$*, adds* $\mathsf{pk}_{\mathsf{attr}}$ *to* $\mathcal{C}_{\mathsf{attr}}$*, and sets* $\mathsf{D}_{\mathsf{attr}}[\mathsf{pk}_{\mathsf{attr}}] \leftarrow \mathsf{D}_{\mathsf{attr}}[\mathsf{pk}_{\mathsf{attr}}] \cup \rho$*. It replies to* A *with* $(\mathsf{mpk}'_{\mathsf{attr}}, \mathsf{aux}')$*.*
  - ***Register corrupted policy-key query:*** *On submitting a corrupted-policy-key-registration query, the adversary* A *specifies a public key* $\mathsf{pk}_{\mathsf{pol}}$ *and a policy* $\mathbb{R} \in \mathcal{P}_1$*. the challenger registers the key by computing* $(\mathsf{mpk}'_{\mathsf{pol}}, \mathsf{aux}') \leftarrow \mathsf{PolRegPK}(\mathsf{crs}, \mathsf{aux}, \mathsf{pk}_{\mathsf{pol}}, \mathbb{R})$*. The challenger updates its copy of the master public key* $\mathsf{mpk}_{\mathsf{pol}} \leftarrow \mathsf{mpk}'_{\mathsf{pol}}$*, its auxiliary data* $\mathsf{aux} \leftarrow \mathsf{aux}'$*, adds* $\mathsf{pk}_{\mathsf{pol}}$ *to* $\mathcal{C}_{\mathsf{pol}}$*, and updates* $\mathsf{D}_{\mathsf{pol}}[\mathsf{pk}_{\mathsf{pol}}] \leftarrow \mathsf{D}_{\mathsf{pol}}[\mathsf{pk}_{\mathsf{pol}}] \cup \mathbb{R}$*. It replies to* A *with* $(\mathsf{mpk}'_{\mathsf{pol}}, \mathsf{aux}')$*.*
  - ***Register honest attribute-key query:*** *On submitting an honest-attribute-key-registration query, the adversary specifies attributes* $\rho \in \mathcal{X}_2$*. The challenger increments the counter* $\mathsf{ctr}[\mathsf{regAttr}] \leftarrow \mathsf{ctr}[\mathsf{regAttr}] + 1$ *and samples* $(\mathsf{pk}^{\mathsf{ctr}[\mathsf{regAttr}]}_{\mathsf{attr}}, \mathsf{sk}^{\mathsf{ctr}[\mathsf{regAttr}]}_{\mathsf{attr}}) \leftarrow \mathsf{AttrKGen}(\mathsf{crs}, \mathsf{aux})$*, and registers the key*

$\mathsf{pk}_{\mathsf{attr}}^{\mathsf{ctr}[\mathsf{regAttr}]}$ *by computing* $(\mathsf{mpk}'_{\mathsf{attr}}, \mathsf{aux}') \leftarrow \mathsf{AttrRegPK}(\mathsf{crs}, \mathsf{aux}, \mathsf{pk}_{\mathsf{attr}}^{\mathsf{ctr}[\mathsf{regAttr}]}, \rho)$. *Then, it updates its public key* $\mathsf{mpk}_{\mathsf{attr}} \leftarrow \mathsf{mpk}'_{\mathsf{attr}}$, *its auxiliary data* $\mathsf{aux} \leftarrow \mathsf{aux}'$ *and* $\mathsf{D}_{\mathsf{attr}}[\mathsf{pk}_{\mathsf{attr}}^{\mathsf{ctr}[\mathsf{regAttr}]}] \leftarrow \mathsf{D}_{\mathsf{attr}}[\mathsf{pk}_{\mathsf{attr}}^{\mathsf{ctr}[\mathsf{regAttr}]}] \cup \rho$. *Finally, the challenger returns* $(\mathsf{ctr}[\mathsf{regAttr}], \mathsf{mpk}'_{\mathsf{attr}}, \mathsf{aux}', \mathsf{pk}_{\mathsf{attr}}^{\mathsf{ctr}[\mathsf{regAttr}]})$ *to* A.

- ***Register honest policy-key query:*** *On submitting an honest-policy-key-registration query, the adversary specifies a policy* $\mathbb{R} \in \mathcal{P}_2$. *The challenger increments the counter* $\mathsf{ctr}[\mathsf{regPol}] \leftarrow \mathsf{ctr}[\mathsf{regPol}] + 1$ *and computes* $(\mathsf{pk}_{\mathsf{pol}}^{\mathsf{ctr}[\mathsf{regPol}]}, \mathsf{sk}_{\mathsf{pol}}^{\mathsf{ctr}[\mathsf{regPol}]}) \leftarrow \mathsf{PolKGen}(\mathsf{crs}, \mathsf{aux})$, *and registers the key* $\mathsf{pk}_{\mathsf{pol}}^{\mathsf{ctr}[\mathsf{regPol}]}$ *by computing* $(\mathsf{mpk}'_{\mathsf{pol}}, \mathsf{aux}') \leftarrow \mathsf{PolRegPK}(\mathsf{crs}, \mathsf{aux}, \mathsf{pk}_{\mathsf{pol}}^{\mathsf{ctr}[\mathsf{regPol}]}, \mathbb{R})$. *The challenger updates its public key* $\mathsf{mpk}_{\mathsf{pol}} \leftarrow \mathsf{mpk}'_{\mathsf{pol}}$, *its auxiliary data* $\mathsf{aux} \leftarrow \mathsf{aux}'$ *and* $\mathsf{D}_{\mathsf{pol}}[\mathsf{pk}_{\mathsf{pol}}^{\mathsf{ctr}[\mathsf{regPol}]}] \leftarrow \mathsf{D}_{\mathsf{pol}}[\mathsf{pk}_{\mathsf{pol}}^{\mathsf{ctr}[\mathsf{regPol}]}] \cup \mathbb{R}$. *Finally, the challenger returns* $(\mathsf{ctr}[\mathsf{regPol}], \mathsf{mpk}'_{\mathsf{pol}}, \mathsf{aux}', \mathsf{pk}_{\mathsf{pol}}^{\mathsf{ctr}[\mathsf{regPol}]})$ *to* A.
- ***Corrupt honest attribute-key query:*** *In a corrupt-honest-attribute-key query, the adversary specifies an index* $1 \leq i \leq \mathsf{ctr}[\mathsf{regAttr}]$. *Let* $(\mathsf{pk}_{\mathsf{attr}}^i, \mathsf{sk}_{\mathsf{attr}}^i)$ *be the* i^{th} *attribute public/secret key the challenger samples when responding to the* i^{th} *honest-attribute-key-registration query. The challenger adds* $\mathsf{pk}_{\mathsf{attr}}^i$ *to* $\mathcal{C}_{\mathsf{attr}}$ *and replies to* A *with* $\mathsf{sk}_{\mathsf{attr}}^i$.
- ***Corrupt honest policy-key query:*** *On submitting a corrupt-honest-policy-key query, the adversary specifies an index* $1 \leq i \leq \mathsf{ctr}[\mathsf{regPol}]$. *Let* $(\mathsf{pk}_{\mathsf{pol}}^i, \mathsf{sk}_{\mathsf{pol}}^i)$ *be the* i^{th} *policy public/secret key the challenger samples when responding to the* i^{th} *honest-policy-key-registration query. The challenger adds* $\mathsf{pk}_{\mathsf{pol}}^i$ *to* $\mathcal{C}_{\mathsf{pol}}$ *and replies to* A *with* $\mathsf{sk}_{\mathsf{pol}}^i$.

- ***Challenge phase:*** *The adversary* A *chooses two messages* $m_0^*, m_1^* \in \mathcal{M}$, *two attributes* $\sigma_0^*, \sigma_1^* \in \mathcal{X}_1$, *and two policies* $\mathbb{S}_0^*, \mathbb{S}_1^* \in \mathcal{P}_1$. *The challenger replies with the challenge ciphertext* $\mathsf{c}^* \leftarrow \mathsf{Enc}(\mathsf{mpk}_{\mathsf{attr}}, \mathsf{mpk}_{\mathsf{pol}}, \sigma^*, \mathbb{S}_b^*, m_b^*)$.
- ***Output phase:*** *At the end of the game, the adversary* A *outputs a bit* $b' \in \{0, 1\}$.

For $t \in [2]$, *we say that* Π_{RME} *is CPA-t-sided secure if for all valid PPT adversary* A, *we have:*

$$\mathbb{P}\left[\mathbf{G}_{\Pi_{\mathsf{RME}},\mathsf{A}}^{\mathsf{RME\text{-}security}}(\lambda) = 1\right] \leq \mathsf{negl}(\lambda).$$

Let $\mathcal{S}_{\mathsf{attr}} = \{\rho \in \mathsf{D}_{\mathsf{attr}}[\mathsf{pk}] : \mathsf{pk} \in \mathcal{C}_{\mathsf{attr}}\}$ *be the set of corrupted attributes and* $\mathcal{S}_{\mathsf{pol}} = \{\mathbb{R} \in \mathsf{D}_{\mathsf{pol}}[\mathsf{pk}] : \mathsf{pk} \in \mathcal{C}_{\mathsf{pol}}\}$ *be the set of corrupted policies. An adversary* A *is called valid if:*

- *(CPA-1-sided security) For every corrupted attributes* $\rho \in \mathcal{S}_{\mathsf{attr}}$ *and for every corrupted policy* $\mathbb{R} \in \mathcal{S}_{\mathsf{pol}}$, *we have*

$$\mathbb{S}_0^*(\rho) = \mathbb{S}_1^*(\rho) = 0 \vee \mathbb{R}(\sigma_0^*) = \mathbb{R}(\sigma_1^*) = 0 \vee$$
$$\mathbb{S}_0^*(\rho) = \mathbb{R}(\sigma_1^*) = 0 \vee \mathbb{S}_1^*(\rho) = \mathbb{R}(\sigma_0^*) = 0.$$

- *(CPA-2-sided security) For every corrupted attributes* $\rho \in \mathcal{S}_{\mathsf{attr}}$ *and for every corrupted policy* $\mathbb{R} \in \mathcal{S}_{\mathsf{pol}}$*, we have*

$$\begin{aligned} &\textit{either } \mathbb{S}_0^*(\rho) = \mathbb{S}_1^*(\rho) = 0 \vee \mathbb{R}(\sigma_0^*) = \mathbb{R}(\sigma_1^*) = 0 \vee \\ &\qquad \mathbb{S}_0^*(\rho) = \mathbb{R}(\sigma_1^*) = 0 \vee \mathbb{S}_1^*(\rho) = \mathbb{R}(\sigma_0^*) = 0 \\ &\textit{or } \mathbb{S}_0^*(\rho) = \mathbb{S}_1^*(\rho) \wedge \mathbb{R}(\sigma_0^*) = \mathbb{R}(\sigma_1^*) \wedge m_0^* = m_1^*. \end{aligned}$$

$\mathbb{C}_{\mathsf{c}}(\mathsf{sk}_{\mathsf{attr}}, \mathsf{sk}_{\mathsf{pol}}, \mathsf{hsk}_{\mathsf{attr}}, \mathsf{hsk}_{\mathsf{pol}})$
return $\mathsf{Dec}_1(\mathsf{sk}_{\mathsf{attr}}, \mathsf{hsk}_{\mathsf{attr}}, \mathsf{Dec}_2(\mathsf{sk}_{\mathsf{pol}}, \mathsf{hsk}_{\mathsf{pol}}, \mathsf{c}))$

Fig. 1. Definition of the circuit $\mathbb{C}_c$ of Construction 1.

4 Construction

In this section, we present our RME construction based on KP-RABE, CP-ABE, and lockable obfuscation. The sender's and receiver's attributes and policies supported by RME corresponds to that of the underlying RABE schemes.

Construction 1. *Consider the following ingredients:*

1. *Let* $\Pi_1 = (\mathsf{Setup}_1, \mathsf{KGen}_1, \mathsf{RegPK}_1, \mathsf{Enc}_1, \mathsf{Update}_1, \mathsf{Dec}_1)$ *be a CP-RABE scheme with message spaces* $\mathcal{M}_1 = \{0,1\}^{s(\lambda)}$*, attribute space* $\mathcal{X}_2$*, policy space* $\mathcal{P}_1$*, and ciphertext space* $\mathcal{Y}_1$*.*
2. *Let* $\Pi_2 = (\mathsf{Setup}_2, \mathsf{KGen}_2, \mathsf{RegPK}_{\mathsf{pol}}, \mathsf{Enc}_2, \mathsf{Update}_2, \mathsf{Dec}_2)$ *be a KP-RABE scheme with message space* $\mathcal{M}_2 = \mathcal{Y}_1$*, attribute space* $\mathcal{X}_1$*, policy space* $\mathcal{P}_2$*.*
3. *Let* $\Pi_3 = (\mathsf{Obf}, \mathsf{Eval})$ *be a lockable obfuscation scheme with message space* $\mathcal{M}$ *for the circuits family* $\mathcal{C}_{n,s,d}(\lambda) = \{\mathbb{C}_{\mathsf{c}}\}$ *as defined in Fig. 1 where* $n(\lambda), s(\lambda), d(\lambda)$ *depends on the schemes* Π_1 *and* Π_2 *used.*

We build a RME scheme Π_{RME} *with sender's policy and attributes space* $\mathcal{P}_1$ *and* $\mathcal{X}_1$*, receiver's policy and attributes space* $\mathcal{P}_2$ *and* $\mathcal{X}_2$*, and message space* $\mathcal{M}$ *in the following way:*

- $\mathsf{Setup}(1^\lambda) \to \mathsf{crs}$*: On input the security parameter* 1^λ*, the setup algorithm outputs* $\mathsf{crs} = (\mathsf{crs}_1, \mathsf{crs}_2)$*, where* $\mathsf{crs}_1 \leftarrow \mathsf{Setup}_1(1^\lambda)$ *and* $\mathsf{crs}_2 \leftarrow \mathsf{Setup}_2(1^\lambda)$*.*
- $\mathsf{AttrKGen}(\mathsf{crs}, \mathsf{aux}) \to (\mathsf{pk}_{\mathsf{attr}}, \mathsf{sk}_{\mathsf{attr}})$*: On input the common reference string* $\mathsf{crs} = (\mathsf{crs}_1, \mathsf{crs}_2)$*, a (possibly empty) state* $\mathsf{aux} = (\mathsf{aux}_1, \mathsf{aux}_2)$*, the attribute-key-generation algorithm outputs* $(\mathsf{pk}_{\mathsf{attr}}, \mathsf{sk}_{\mathsf{attr}}) \leftarrow \mathsf{KGen}_1(\mathsf{crs}_1, \mathsf{aux}_1)$*.*
- $\mathsf{PolKGen}(\mathsf{crs}, \mathsf{aux}) \to (\mathsf{pk}_{\mathsf{pol}}, \mathsf{sk}_{\mathsf{pol}})$*: On input the common reference string* $\mathsf{crs} = (\mathsf{crs}_1, \mathsf{crs}_2)$*, a (possibly empty) state* $\mathsf{aux} = (\mathsf{aux}_1, \mathsf{aux}_2)$*, the policy-key-generation algorithm outputs* $(\mathsf{pk}_{\mathsf{pol}}, \mathsf{sk}_{\mathsf{pol}}) \leftarrow \mathsf{KGen}_2(\mathsf{crs}_2, \mathsf{aux}_2)$*.*

- $\mathsf{AttrRegPK}(\mathsf{crs}, \mathsf{aux}, \mathsf{pk}_{\mathsf{attr}}, \rho) \to (\mathsf{mpk}_{\mathsf{attr}}, \mathsf{aux}')$: *On input the common reference string* $\mathsf{crs} = (\mathsf{crs}_1, \mathsf{crs}_2)$, *a (possible empty) state* $\mathsf{aux} = (\mathsf{aux}_1, \mathsf{aux}_2)$, *a public key* $\mathsf{pk}_{\mathsf{attr}}$ *and attributes* $\rho \in \mathcal{X}_2$, *the attribute-registration algorithm outputs* $(\mathsf{mpk}_{\mathsf{attr}}, \mathsf{aux}') = (\mathsf{mpk}_{\mathsf{attr}}, (\mathsf{aux}_1', \mathsf{aux}_2))$ *where* $(\mathsf{mpk}_{\mathsf{attr}}, \mathsf{aux}_1') \leftarrow \mathsf{RegPK}_1(\mathsf{crs}_1, \mathsf{aux}_1, \mathsf{pk}_{\mathsf{attr}}, \rho)$.
- $\mathsf{PolRegPK}(\mathsf{crs}, \mathsf{aux}, \mathsf{pk}_{\mathsf{pol}}, \mathbb{R}) \to (\mathsf{mpk}_{\mathsf{pol}}, \mathsf{aux}')$: *On input the common reference string* $\mathsf{crs} = (\mathsf{crs}_1, \mathsf{crs}_2)$, *a (possible empty) state* $\mathsf{aux} = (\mathsf{aux}_1, \mathsf{aux}_2)$, *a public key* $\mathsf{pk}_{\mathsf{pol}}$ *and a policy* $\mathbb{R} \in \mathcal{P}_2$, *the policy-registration algorithm outputs* $(\mathsf{mpk}_{\mathsf{pol}}, \mathsf{aux}') = (\mathsf{mpk}_{\mathsf{pol}}, (\mathsf{aux}_1, \mathsf{aux}_2'))$ *where* $(\mathsf{mpk}_{\mathsf{pol}}, \mathsf{aux}_2') \leftarrow \mathsf{RegPK}_{\mathsf{pol}}(\mathsf{crs}_2, \mathsf{aux}_2, \mathsf{pk}_{\mathsf{pol}}, \mathbb{R})$.
- $\mathsf{Enc}(\mathsf{mpk}_{\mathsf{attr}}, \mathsf{mpk}_{\mathsf{pol}}, \sigma, \mathbb{S}, m) \to \mathsf{c}$: *On input the master public keys* $\mathsf{mpk}_{\mathsf{attr}}$ *and* mpk_{pol}, *attributes* $\sigma \in \mathcal{X}_1$, *a policy* $\mathbb{S} \in \mathcal{P}_1$, *and a message* $m \in \mathcal{M}$, *the encryption algorithm outputs a ciphertext* c, *computed as follows:*
  1. *Sample a random lock* $y \leftarrow \{0,1\}^{s(\lambda)}$.
  2. *Compute* $\mathsf{c}' \leftarrow \mathsf{Enc}_1(\mathsf{mpk}_{\mathsf{attr}}, \mathbb{S}, y)$ *and* $\mathsf{c}'' \leftarrow \mathsf{Enc}_2(\mathsf{mpk}_{\mathsf{pol}}, \sigma, c')$.
  3. *Set* $\mathsf{c} = \tilde{\mathbb{C}} \leftarrow \mathsf{Obf}(1^\lambda, \mathbb{C}_{\mathsf{c}''}, y, m)$.
- $\mathsf{AttrUpdate}(\mathsf{crs}, \mathsf{aux}, \mathsf{pk}_{\mathsf{attr}}) \to \mathsf{hsk}_{\mathsf{attr}}$: *On input the common reference string* $\mathsf{crs} = (\mathsf{crs}_1, \mathsf{crs}_2)$, *a state* $\mathsf{aux} = (\mathsf{aux}_1, \mathsf{aux}_2)$, *and a public key* $\mathsf{pk}_{\mathsf{attr}}$, *the attribute-update algorithm outputs* $\mathsf{hsk}_{\mathsf{attr}} \leftarrow \mathsf{Update}_1(\mathsf{crs}_1, \mathsf{aux}_1, \mathsf{pk}_{\mathsf{attr}})$.
- $\mathsf{PolUpdate}(\mathsf{crs}, \mathsf{aux}, \mathsf{pk}_{\mathsf{pol}}) \to \mathsf{hsk}_{\mathsf{pol}}$: *On input the common reference string* $\mathsf{crs} = (\mathsf{crs}_1, \mathsf{crs}_2)$, *a state* $\mathsf{aux} = (\mathsf{aux}_1, \mathsf{aux}_2)$, *and a public key* $\mathsf{pk}_{\mathsf{pol}}$, *the policy-update algorithm outputs* $\mathsf{hsk}_{\mathsf{pol}} \leftarrow \mathsf{Update}_2(\mathsf{crs}_2, \mathsf{aux}_2, \mathsf{pk}_{\mathsf{pol}})$.
- $\mathsf{Dec}(\mathsf{sk}_{\mathsf{attr}}, \mathsf{sk}_{\mathsf{pol}}, \mathsf{hsk}_{\mathsf{attr}}, \mathsf{hsk}_{\mathsf{pol}}, \mathsf{c}) \to m$: *On input the master public key* mpk, *the secret keys* $\mathsf{sk}_{\mathsf{attr}}, \mathsf{sk}_{\mathsf{pol}}$, *the helper decryption keys* $\mathsf{hsk}_{\mathsf{attr}}, \mathsf{hsk}_{\mathsf{pol}}$, *and a ciphertext* $\mathsf{c} = \tilde{\mathbb{C}}$, *the decryption algorithm computes* $m = \mathsf{Eval}(\tilde{\mathbb{C}}, (\mathsf{sk}_{\mathsf{attr}}, \mathsf{sk}_{\mathsf{pol}}, \mathsf{hsk}_{\mathsf{attr}}, \mathsf{hsk}_{\mathsf{pol}}))$. *If* $m = \perp$, *it returns* getupdate; *otherwise, it returns* m.

As for correctness, efficiency/compactness, and security, we establish the following results.

Theorem 2 (Correctness of Π_{RME}). *Let* Π_1, Π_2, *and* Π_3 *as defined in Construction 1. If* Π_1 *and* Π_1 *are correct (Definition 1), and* Π_3 *satisfies semi-statistical correctness (Definition 4), then* Π_{RME} *from Construction 1 is correct (Definition 6).*

Proof. Assume the RME scheme Π_{RME} is not correct (Definition 6): There exists an adversary A winning the correctness game $\mathbf{G}^{\mathsf{RME\text{-}correctness}}_{\Pi_{\mathsf{RME}},\mathsf{A}}$ with non negligible probability ϵ_{RME}, i.e.,

$$\mathbb{P}\left[\mathbf{G}^{\mathsf{RME\text{-}correctness}}_{\Pi_{\mathsf{RME}},\mathsf{A}}(\lambda) = 1\right] = \epsilon_{\mathsf{RME}}$$

We show that we can use A to build an adversary able to break the correctness of the underlying CP-RABE scheme Π_1 or KP-RABE scheme Π_2.

We observe that $\mathbb{P}\left[\mathbf{G}^{\mathsf{RME\text{-}correctness}}_{\Pi_{\mathsf{RME}},\mathsf{A}}(\lambda) = 1\right] = \epsilon_{\mathsf{RME}}$ means that, with non negligible probability, there exists $1 \le j \le \mathsf{ctr}[\mathsf{enc}]$ such that $m_j' \neq m_j$. Let j^* be the index of the first decryption query that fails (i.e., for which the correctness experiment halts with output $b = 1$). This implies that $\mathsf{Dec}(\mathsf{sk}^*_{\mathsf{attr}}, \mathsf{sk}^*_{\mathsf{pol}}, \mathsf{hsk}^*_{\mathsf{attr}}, \mathsf{hsk}^*_{\mathsf{pol}}, \mathsf{c}_{\mathsf{j}^*}) \neq m_{j^*}$, which happens when $\mathsf{Eval}(\tilde{\mathbb{C}}_{\mathsf{j}^*}, (\mathsf{sk}^*_{\mathsf{attr}}, \mathsf{sk}^*_{\mathsf{pol}}, \mathsf{hsk}^*_{\mathsf{attr}}, \mathsf{hsk}^*_{\mathsf{pol}})) \neq m_{j^*}$ (for $\mathsf{c}_{j^*} = \tilde{\mathbb{C}}$) where $\tilde{\mathbb{C}}_{j^*}$ is computed honestly during the $(j^*)^{\text{th}}$ encryption query.

By leveraging the definition of the circuit $\mathbb{C}_{\mathsf{c}}$ (see Fig. 1) and the fact that Π_3 scheme satisfies semi-statistical correctness, $\mathsf{Eval}(\tilde{\mathbb{C}}_{\mathsf{j}^*}, (\mathsf{sk}^*_{\mathsf{attr}}, \mathsf{sk}^*_{\mathsf{pol}}, \mathsf{hsk}^*_{\mathsf{attr}}, \mathsf{hsk}^*_{\mathsf{pol}})) \neq m_{j^*}$ only if either Dec_1 (of Π_1) or Dec_2 (of Π_2) fail during decryption, i.e.,

1. $\mathsf{c}'_{j^*} = \mathsf{Dec}_2(\mathsf{sk}^*_{\mathsf{pol}}, \mathsf{hsk}^*_{\mathsf{pol}}, \mathsf{c}''_{j^*})$ but $\mathsf{Dec}_1(\mathsf{sk}^*_{\mathsf{attr}}, \mathsf{hsk}^*_{\mathsf{attr}}, \mathsf{c}'_{j^*}) \neq y_{j^*}$, which leads us to break CP-RABE correctness with non negligible probability; or
2. $\mathsf{c}'_{j^*} \neq \mathsf{Dec}_2(\mathsf{sk}^*_{\mathsf{pol}}, \mathsf{hsk}^*_{\mathsf{pol}}, \mathsf{c}''_{j^*})$, which allows us to break KP-RABE correctness with non negligible probability.

We prove the above two cases individually.

Case 1. Assuming Case 1 holds (Item 1), we build the adversary A' against the correctness of the CP-RABE scheme Π_1:

- **Setup phase:** A' receives crs_1 from the challenger and sets $\mathsf{crs} = (\mathsf{crs}_1, \mathsf{crs}_2)$ where $\mathsf{crs}_2 \leftarrow \mathsf{Setup}_2(1^\lambda)$. It initializes the auxiliary input $\mathsf{aux} = (\mathsf{aux}_1, \mathsf{aux}_2) \leftarrow (\perp, \perp)$ and the initial master public keys $\mathsf{mpk}^0_{\mathsf{pol}} \leftarrow \perp$ and $\mathsf{mpk}^0_{\mathsf{attr}} \leftarrow \perp$. It also initializes a counter $\mathsf{ctr}[\mathsf{regPol}] \leftarrow 0$ and $\mathsf{ctr}[\mathsf{enc}] \leftarrow 0$ to keep track of the number of policy registration queries and encryption queries, respectively. It then initializes $\mathsf{ctr}[\mathsf{regPol}^*] \leftarrow \infty$ as the index for the target policy key. Finally, it gives crs to A.
- **Query phase:** A' answers to the incoming oracle queries from A as follows:
  - **Register non-target attribute-key query:** On input a public key $\mathsf{pk}_{\mathsf{attr}}$ and attributes $\rho \in \mathcal{X}_2$, A' forwards the query to the challenger and the latter replies with $(\mathsf{ctr}[\mathsf{regAttr}], \mathsf{mpk}^{\mathsf{ctr}[\mathsf{regAttr}]}_{\mathsf{attr}}, \mathsf{aux}'_1)$. Finally, A' updates $\mathsf{aux}_1 \leftarrow \mathsf{aux}'_1$ and returns $(\mathsf{ctr}[\mathsf{regAttr}], \mathsf{mpk}^{\mathsf{ctr}[\mathsf{regAttr}]}_{\mathsf{attr}}, \mathsf{aux})$ to A.
  - **Register non-target policy-key query:** On input a public key $\mathsf{pk}_{\mathsf{pol}}$ and a policy $\mathbb{R} \in \mathcal{P}_2$, the adversary A' increments the counter $\mathsf{ctr}[\mathsf{regPol}] \leftarrow \mathsf{ctr}[\mathsf{regPol}] + 1$, registers the key by computing $(\mathsf{mpk}^{\mathsf{crtPol}[\mathsf{reg}]}_{\mathsf{pol}}, \mathsf{aux}'_2) \leftarrow \mathsf{RegPK}_{\mathsf{pol}}(\mathsf{crs}_2, \mathsf{aux}_2, \mathsf{pk}_{\mathsf{pol}}, \mathbb{R})$, updates its auxiliary data by setting $\mathsf{aux}_2 \leftarrow \mathsf{aux}'_2$, and replies to A with $(\mathsf{ctr}[\mathsf{regPol}], \mathsf{mpk}^{\mathsf{ctr}[\mathsf{regPol}]}_{\mathsf{pol}}, \mathsf{aux})$.
  - **Register target attribute-key query:** On input attributes $\rho^* \in \mathcal{X}_2$, A' forwards it to the challenger. If the challenger returns $\perp$, A' returns $\perp$ to A. Otherwise, if the challenger returns $(\mathsf{ctr}[\mathsf{regAttr}^*], \mathsf{mpk}^{\mathsf{ctr}[\mathsf{regAttr}^*]}_{\mathsf{attr}}, \mathsf{aux}_1, \mathsf{pk}^*_{\mathsf{attr}}, \mathsf{hsk}^*_{\mathsf{attr}}, \mathsf{sk}^*_{\mathsf{attr}})$ then A updates $\mathsf{aux}_1 \leftarrow \mathsf{aux}'_1$. Finally, it returns $(\mathsf{ctr}[\mathsf{regAttr}^*], \mathsf{mpk}^{\mathsf{ctr}[\mathsf{regAttr}^*]}_{\mathsf{attr}}, \mathsf{aux}, \mathsf{pk}^*_{\mathsf{attr}}, \mathsf{hsk}^*_{\mathsf{attr}}, \mathsf{sk}^*_{\mathsf{attr}})$ to A
  - **Register target policy-key query:** On input a policy $\mathbb{R}^* \in \mathcal{P}_2$, if A has previously made a target-policy-key registration query, then A' replies with $\perp$. Otherwise, A' increments $\mathsf{ctr}[\mathsf{regPol}] \leftarrow \mathsf{ctr}[\mathsf{regPol}] + 1$, samples $(\mathsf{pk}^*_{\mathsf{pol}}, \mathsf{sk}^*_{\mathsf{pol}}) \leftarrow \mathsf{KGen}_2(\mathsf{crs}_2, \mathsf{aux}_2)$, registers $(\mathsf{mpk}^{\mathsf{ctr}[\mathsf{regPol}]}_{\mathsf{pol}}, \mathsf{aux}'_2) \leftarrow$

$\mathsf{RegPK}_2(\mathsf{crs}_2, \mathsf{aux}_2, \mathsf{pk}_2^*, \mathbb{R}^*)$, computes the helper decryption key $\mathsf{hsk}_{\mathsf{pol}}^* \leftarrow \mathsf{Update}_2(\mathsf{crs}_2, \mathsf{aux}_2, \mathsf{pk}_{\mathsf{pol}}^*)$, updates its auxiliary data by setting $\mathsf{aux}_2 \leftarrow \mathsf{aux}_2'$, stores the index of the target identity $\mathsf{ctr}[\mathsf{regPol}^*] \leftarrow \mathsf{ctr}[\mathsf{regPol}]$, and replies to A with $(\mathsf{ctr}[\mathsf{regPol}], \mathsf{mpk}_{\mathsf{pol}}^{\mathsf{ctr}[\mathsf{regPol}]}, \mathsf{aux}, \mathsf{pk}_{\mathsf{pol}}^*, \mathsf{hsk}_{\mathsf{pol}}^*, \mathsf{sk}_{\mathsf{pol}}^*)$.

- **Encryption query:** On input $\mathsf{ctr}[\mathsf{regAttr}^*] \leq i_{\mathsf{attr}} \leq \mathsf{ctr}[\mathsf{regAttr}]$ and $\mathsf{ctr}[\mathsf{regPol}^*] \leq i_{\mathsf{pol}} \leq \mathsf{ctr}[\mathsf{regPol}]$ of two master public keys, a message $m_{\mathsf{ctr}[\mathsf{enc}]} \in \mathcal{M}$, an attribute $\sigma_{\mathsf{ctr}[\mathsf{enc}]} \in \mathcal{X}_1$, and a policy $\mathbb{S}_{\mathsf{ctr}[\mathsf{enc}]} \in \mathcal{P}_1$ from A, A' proceeds as follows:
  * If A has not yet registered the target policy-key, or has not yet registered the target attribute-key ρ^*, or if the target set of attributes ρ^* does not satisfy the policy $\mathbb{S}_{\mathsf{ctr}[\mathsf{enc}]}$, or if the target policy set $\mathbb{R}^*$ is not satisfied by the attribute $\sigma_{\mathsf{ctr}[\mathsf{enc}]}$, A' replies with $\perp$ as the answer of the encryption query.
  * Otherwise, A' increments the counter $\mathsf{ctr}[\mathsf{enc}] \leftarrow \mathsf{ctr}[\mathsf{enc}] + 1$, samples $y_{\mathsf{ctr}[\mathsf{enc}]} \leftarrow \{0,1\}^{s(\lambda)}$ and forwards $(i_{\mathsf{attr}}, y_{\mathsf{ctr}[\mathsf{enc}]}, \mathbb{S}_{\mathsf{ctr}[\mathsf{enc}]})$ to the challenger.
  * A' receives $(\mathsf{ctr}[\mathsf{enc}], \mathsf{c}'_{\mathsf{ctr}[\mathsf{enc}]})$ and computes $\mathsf{c}''_{\mathsf{ctr}[\mathsf{enc}]} \leftarrow \mathsf{Enc}_2(\mathsf{mpk}_{\mathsf{pol}}^{i_{\mathsf{pol}}}, \sigma_{\mathsf{ctr}[\mathsf{enc}]}, \mathsf{c}'_{\mathsf{ctr}[\mathsf{enc}]})$, $\tilde{\mathbb{C}} \leftarrow \mathsf{Obf}(1^\lambda, \mathbb{C}_{\mathsf{c}''_{\mathsf{ctr}[\mathsf{enc}]}}, y_{\mathsf{ctr}[\mathsf{enc}]}, m_{\mathsf{ctr}[\mathsf{enc}]})$.
  * Finally, it replies to A with $(\mathsf{ctr}[\mathsf{enc}], \mathsf{c}_{\mathsf{ctr}[\mathsf{enc}]})$ where $\mathsf{c}_{\mathsf{ctr}[\mathsf{enc}]} \leftarrow \tilde{\mathbb{C}}$.
- **Decryption query:** On input a ciphertext index $1 \leq j^* \leq \mathsf{ctr}[\mathsf{enc}]$, A' forwards j^* to the challenger. If the challenger returns 1, A' halts. Otherwise, A' continues with the experiment.

Since Π_3 satisfies semi-statical correctness, A' can safely skip the execution of $\tilde{\mathbb{C}}$ without compromising the simulation of the final decryption query phase. Moreover, conditioned to Case 1 (Item 1), we know that Dec_2 decrypts correctly returning c'_{j^*}, i.e., the ciphertext computed during $(j^*)^{\text{th}}$ encryption query. This allows A' to safely send j^* to the challenger as the final target ciphertext. Finally, again conditioned to Case 1, we know that $\mathsf{Dec}_1(\mathsf{sk}_{\mathsf{attr}}^*, \mathsf{hsk}_{\mathsf{attr}}^*, \mathsf{c}'_{j^*}) \neq y_{j^*}$ with non-negligible probability ϵ_{RME}. This concludes the proof.

Case 2. The proof of this second case (Item 2) follows by using an analogous (and symmetric) approach to that of Case 1 (Item 1).

Theorem 3 (Compactness and efficiency of Π_{RME}). *Let Π_1, Π_2, and Π_3 as defined in Construction 1. If Π_1 is $(t_{\mathsf{crs}}^1, t_{\mathsf{mpk}}^1, t_{\mathsf{hsk}}^1)$-compact and $(t_{\mathsf{KGen}}^1, t_{\mathsf{RegPK}}^1, t_{\mathsf{num}}^1, t_{\mathsf{Update}}^1)$-efficient, and Π_2 is $(t_{\mathsf{crs}}^2, t_{\mathsf{mpk}}^2, t_{\mathsf{hsk}}^2)$-compact and $(t_{\mathsf{KGen}}^2, t_{\mathsf{RegPK}}^2, t_{\mathsf{num}}^2, t_{\mathsf{Update}}^2)$-efficient (Definition 2), then Π_{RME} from Construction 1 is $(t_{\mathsf{crs}}, t_{\mathsf{mpk}_\star}, t_{\mathsf{hsk}_\star})$-compact and $(t_{\star\mathsf{KGen}}, t_{\star\mathsf{RegPK}}, t_{\mathsf{num}}, t_{\star\mathsf{Update}})$-efficient (Definition 7) where*

$$(t_{\mathsf{crs}}, t_{\mathsf{mpk}_\star}, t_{\mathsf{hsk}_\star}) = (t_{\mathsf{crs}}^1 + t_{\mathsf{crs}}^2, \max\{t_{\mathsf{mpk}}^1, t_{\mathsf{mpk}}^2\}, \max\{t_{\mathsf{hsk}}^1, t_{\mathsf{hsk}}^2\}) \quad \text{and}$$

$$(t_{\star\mathsf{KGen}}, t_{\star\mathsf{RegPK}}, t_{\mathsf{num}}, t_{\star\mathsf{Update}}) =$$
$$(\max\{t_{\mathsf{KGen}}^1, t_{\mathsf{KGen}}^2\}, \max\{t_{\mathsf{RegPK}}^1, t_{\mathsf{RegPK}}^2\}, t_{\mathsf{num}}^1 + t_{\mathsf{num}}^2, \max\{t_{\mathsf{Update}}^1, t_{\mathsf{Update}}^2\})$$

Proof We prove each property of Π_{RME} from Construction 1 individually.

- $(t^1_{\mathsf{crs}} + t^2_{\mathsf{crs}})$**-compact** crs**:** The common reference string is composed by the concatenation of KP-RABE's and CP-RABE's ones. Thus, Π_{RME} is $(t^1_{\mathsf{crs}}+t^2_{\mathsf{crs}})$-compact.
- $(\mathsf{max}\{t^1_{\mathsf{mpk}}, t^2_{\mathsf{mpk}}\})$**-compact master public keys:** Each master public key corresponds to that of the underlying schemes. Thus, each master public key is at most of size $\mathsf{max}\{t^1_{\mathsf{mpk}}, t^2_{\mathsf{mpk}}\}$.
- $(\mathsf{max}\{t^1_{\mathsf{hsk}}, t^2_{\mathsf{hsk}}\})$**-compact helper decryption keys:** Each helper decryption key corresponds to that of the underlying schemes. Thus, each helper decryption key is at most of size $\mathsf{max}\{t^1_{\mathsf{hsk}}, t^2_{\mathsf{hsk}}\}$.
- $(\mathsf{max}\{t^1_{\mathsf{KGen}}, t^2_{\mathsf{KGen}}\})$**-efficient key generation:** AttrKGen and PolKGen correspond to the key generation algorithms of CP-RABE and KP-RABE, respectively. Thus, the running time of the former algorithms are both bounded by $\mathsf{max}\{t^1_{\mathsf{KGen}}, t^2_{\mathsf{KGen}}$.
- $(\mathsf{max}\{t^1_{\mathsf{RegPK}}, t^2_{\mathsf{RegPK}}\})$**-efficient key registration:** AttrRegPK and PolRegPK correspond to the registration algorithms of CP-RABE and KP-RABE, respectively. Thus, the running time of the former algorithms are both bounded by $\mathsf{max}\{t^1_{\mathsf{RegPK}}, t^2_{\mathsf{RegPK}}$.
- $(t^1_{\mathsf{num}} + t^2_{\mathsf{num}}, \mathsf{max}\{t^1_{\mathsf{Update}}, t^2_{\mathsf{Update}}\})$**-efficient updates:** AttrUpdate and PolUpdate correspond to the updation algorithms of CP-RABE and KP-RABE, respectively. Thus, the running time of the former algorithms are both bounded by $\mathsf{max}\{t^1_{\mathsf{Update}}, t^2_{\mathsf{Update}}\}$. Moreover, the cumulative number of AttrUpdate and PolUpdate corresponds to the summation of the number of updates t^1_{num} of CP-RABE and the number of updates t^2_{num} of KP-RABE.

Theorem 4 (Security of Π_{RME}). *Let Π_1, Π_2, and Π_3 as defined in Construction 1.*

- *If Π_1 and Π_2 are CPA secure (Definition 3) and Π_3 is secure (Definition 5) then Π_{RME} from Construction 1 is CPA-1-sided secure (Definition 8).*
- *If Π_1 and Π_2 are CPA-2-sided secure (Definition 3) and Π_3 is secure (Definition 5) then Π_{RME} from Construction 1 is CPA-2-sided secure (Definition 8).*

Proof. **CPA-1-sided security.** Recall the definition of a valid adversary of CPA-1-sided security: For every corrupted attributes $\rho \in \mathcal{S}_{\mathsf{attr}}$ and for every corrupted policy $\mathbb{R} \in \mathcal{S}_{\mathsf{pol}}$, we have

$$\mathbb{S}^*_0(\rho) = \mathbb{S}^*_1(\rho) = 0 \vee \mathbb{R}(\sigma^*_0) = \mathbb{R}(\sigma^*_1) = 0 \vee$$
$$\mathbb{S}^*_0(\rho) = \mathbb{R}(\sigma^*_1) = 0 \vee \mathbb{S}^*_1(\rho) = \mathbb{R}(\sigma^*_0) = 0,$$

where $\mathcal{S}_{\mathsf{attr}} = \{\rho \in \mathsf{D}_{\mathsf{attr}}[\mathsf{pk}] : \mathsf{pk} \in \mathcal{C}_{\mathsf{attr}}\}$ is the set of corrupted attributes, and $\mathcal{S}_{\mathsf{pol}} = \{\mathbb{R} \in \mathsf{D}_{\mathsf{pol}}[\mathsf{pk}] : \mathsf{pk} \in \mathcal{C}_{\mathsf{pol}}\}$ is the set of corrupted policies.

The satisfaction of the above validity condition can be rewritten as:

$$\exists i, j \in [2],\ \mathbf{Validity}_{i,j} \text{ holds},$$

where

- **Validity**$_{1,1}$: $\mathbb{S}_0^*(\rho) = \mathbb{S}_1^*(\rho) = 0,\ \forall \rho \in \mathcal{S}_{\mathsf{attr}}$;
- **Validity**$_{2,2}$: $\mathbb{R}(\sigma_0^*) = \mathbb{R}(\sigma_1^*) = 0,\ \forall \mathbb{R} \in \mathcal{S}_{\mathsf{pol}}$;
- **Validity**$_{1,2}$: $\mathbb{S}_0^*(\rho) = \mathbb{R}(\sigma_1^*) = 0,\ \forall \rho \in \mathcal{S}_{\mathsf{attr}}, \forall \mathbb{R} \in \mathcal{S}_{\mathsf{pol}}$;
- **Validity**$_{2,1}$: $\mathbb{S}_1^*(\rho) = \mathbb{R}(\sigma_0^*) = 0,\ \forall \rho \in \mathcal{S}_{\mathsf{attr}}, \forall \mathbb{R} \in \mathcal{S}_{\mathsf{pol}}$.

We want to show that, for a valid adversary A, the probability of winning the security game, conditioned to **Validity**$_{i,j}$, is at most negligibly greater than $\frac{1}{2}$. We will prove this for each of the above 4 cases.

Lemma 1. *If Π_1 is CPA secure (Definition 3) and Π_3 is secure (Definition 5), then*

$$\mathbb{P}\left[\mathbf{G}_{\Pi_{RME},\mathsf{A}}^{\mathit{RME\text{-}security}}(\lambda) = 1 : \mathbf{Validity}_{1,1}\right] \leq \mathsf{negl}(\lambda).$$

Proof. Consider the following hybrid experiments:

- $\mathbf{H}_0^b(\lambda)$: This is exactly the CPA-1-sided game conditioned to **Validity**$_{1,1}$, where the challenge bit is b.
- $\mathbf{H}_1^b(\lambda)$: Same as $\mathbf{H}_0^b(\lambda)$, except that the challenger runs $\mathsf{c}' \leftarrow \mathsf{Enc}_1(\mathsf{mpk}_{\mathsf{attr}}, \mathbb{S}_b^*, 0^{s(\lambda)})$ during the challenge phase.
- $\mathbf{H}_2^b(\lambda)$: Same as $\mathbf{H}_1^b(\lambda)$, except that the challenger computes $\tilde{\mathbb{C}}$ (during the challenge phase) using the simulator of the lockable obfuscation scheme Π_3, i.e. $\tilde{\mathbb{C}} \leftarrow \mathsf{S}(1^\lambda, 1^{|\mathbb{C}_{c''}|}, 1^{|m_b^*|})$.

Claim 1. $\mathbf{H}_0^b(\lambda) \approx_c \mathbf{H}_1^b(\lambda)$.

Proof. Suppose there exists a PPT distinguisher D that distinguishes between $\mathbf{H}_0^b(\lambda)$ and $\mathbf{H}_1^b(\lambda)$ with non-negligible probability. Then we can build an adversary A that breaks the CPA security of Π_1. The adversary A is defined as follows:

1. Receive crs_1 from the challenger.
2. Initialize $\mathsf{aux} = (\mathsf{aux}_1, \mathsf{aux}_2) \leftarrow (\bot, \bot)$, $(\mathsf{mpk}_{\mathsf{attr}}\mathsf{mpk}_{\mathsf{pol}}) \leftarrow (\bot, \bot)$, $\mathsf{ctr}[\mathsf{regAttr}] \leftarrow 0$, and $\mathsf{ctr}[\mathsf{regPol}] \leftarrow 0$.
3. Send $\mathsf{crs} = (\mathsf{crs}_1, \mathsf{crs}_2)$ to D, where $\mathsf{crs}_2 \leftarrow \mathsf{Setup}_2(1^\lambda)$.
4. A answers the incoming oracle queries as follows:
   - **Register corrupted attribute-key query:** On input a public key $\mathsf{pk}_{\mathsf{attr}}$ and attributes $\rho \in \mathcal{X}_2$, A forwards the query as a corrupted-key-registration query to the challenger, receives the answer $(\mathsf{mpk}'_{\mathsf{attr}}, \mathsf{aux}'_1)$ from the challenger, sets $\mathsf{aux}_1 \leftarrow \mathsf{aux}'_1$ and $\mathsf{mpk}_{\mathsf{attr}} \leftarrow \mathsf{mpk}'_{\mathsf{attr}}$, and forwards $(\mathsf{mpk}_{\mathsf{attr}}, \mathsf{aux})$ to D.
   - **Register corrupted policy-key query:** On input a public key $\mathsf{pk}_{\mathsf{pol}}$ and a policy $\mathbb{R} \in \mathcal{P}_2$, A computes $(\mathsf{mpk}'_{\mathsf{pol}}, \mathsf{aux}'_2) \leftarrow \mathsf{RegPK}_2(\mathsf{crs}_2, \mathsf{aux}_2, \mathsf{pk}_{\mathsf{pol}}, \mathbb{R})$, updates $\mathsf{mpk}_{\mathsf{pol}} \leftarrow \mathsf{mpk}'_{\mathsf{pol}}$ and $\mathsf{aux}_2 \leftarrow \mathsf{aux}'_2$, adds $\mathsf{pk}_{\mathsf{pol}}$ to $\mathcal{C}_{\mathsf{pol}}$, and updates $\mathsf{D}_{\mathsf{pol}}[\mathsf{pk}_{\mathsf{pol}}] \leftarrow \mathsf{D}_{\mathsf{pol}}[\mathsf{pk}_{\mathsf{pol}}] \cup \mathbb{R}$. It replies to D with $(\mathsf{mpk}_{\mathsf{pol}}, \mathsf{aux})$.
   - **Register honest attribute-key query:** On input attributes $\rho \in \mathcal{X}_2$, A forwards the query as an honest-key-registration query to the challenger and receives the answer $(\mathsf{ctr}'[\mathsf{regAttr}], \mathsf{mpk}'_{\mathsf{attr}}, \mathsf{aux}'_1, \mathsf{pk}_{\mathsf{attr}}^{\mathsf{ctr}'[\mathsf{regAttr}]})$. The adversarial A updates $\mathsf{ctr}[\mathsf{regAttr}] \leftarrow \mathsf{ctr}'[\mathsf{regAttr}]$, $\mathsf{mpk}_{\mathsf{attr}} \leftarrow \mathsf{mpk}_{\mathsf{attr}}$, and $\mathsf{aux}_1 \leftarrow \mathsf{aux}'_1$. Finally, A returns $(\mathsf{ctr}[\mathsf{regAttr}], \mathsf{mpk}_{\mathsf{attr}}, \mathsf{aux}, \mathsf{pk}_{\mathsf{attr}}^{\mathsf{ctr}[\mathsf{regAttr}]})$ to D.

- **Register honest policy-key query:** On input a policy $\mathbb{R} \in \mathcal{P}_2$, A increments the counter $\mathsf{ctr}[\mathsf{regPol}] \leftarrow \mathsf{ctr}[\mathsf{regPol}] + 1$, samples $(\mathsf{pk}_{\mathsf{pol}}^{\mathsf{ctr}[\mathsf{regPol}]}, \mathsf{sk}_{\mathsf{pol}}^{\mathsf{ctr}[\mathsf{regPol}]}) \leftarrow \mathsf{KGen}_2(\mathsf{crs}_2, \mathsf{aux}_2)$, and registers $(\mathsf{mpk}_{\mathsf{pol}}, \mathsf{aux}_2) \leftarrow \mathsf{RegPK}_2(\mathsf{crs}_2, \mathsf{aux}_2, \mathsf{pk}_{\mathsf{pol}}^{\mathsf{ctr}[\mathsf{regPol}]}, \mathbb{R})$. It updates $\mathsf{mpk}_{\mathsf{pol}} \leftarrow \mathsf{mpk}'_{\mathsf{pol}}$ and $\mathsf{aux}_2 \leftarrow \mathsf{aux}'_2$, sets $\mathsf{D}_{\mathsf{pol}}[\mathsf{pk}_{\mathsf{pol}}^{\mathsf{ctr}[\mathsf{regPol}]}] \leftarrow \mathsf{D}_{\mathsf{pol}}[\mathsf{pk}_{\mathsf{pol}}^{\mathsf{ctr}[\mathsf{regPol}]}] \cup \mathbb{R}$. Finally, A replies to D with $(\mathsf{ctr}[\mathsf{regPol}], \mathsf{mpk}_{\mathsf{pol}}, \mathsf{aux}, \mathsf{pk}_{\mathsf{pol}}^{\mathsf{ctr}[\mathsf{regPol}]})$.
- **Corrupt honest attribute-key query:** On input an index $1 \leq k \leq \mathsf{ctr}[\mathsf{regAttr}]$, it forwards the query as an honest-key-corruption query to the challenger. Then, A receives $\mathsf{sk}_{\mathsf{attr}}^k$ which is returned to D.
- **Corrupt honest policy-key query:** On input an index $1 \leq k \leq \mathsf{ctr}[\mathsf{regPol}]$, let $(\mathsf{pk}_{\mathsf{pol}}^k, \mathsf{sk}_{\mathsf{pol}}^k)$ be the kth policy public/secret key sampled by the adversary A when asked to responding to the kth honest-policy-key-registration query. A replies to D with $\mathsf{sk}_{\mathsf{pol}}^k$.

5. **Challenge phase:** A receives the challenge $(m_0^*, m_1^*, \sigma_0^*, \sigma_1^*, \mathbb{S}_0^*, \mathbb{S}_1^*)$ from D and proceeds as follows:
   - Send the challenge $(y, 0^{s(\lambda)}, \mathbb{S}_b^*, \mathbb{S}_b^*)$ to the challenger where y is a random lock sampled from $\{0,1\}^{s(\lambda)}$.
   - Receive the challenge ciphertext c^* and compute $\mathsf{c}'' \leftarrow \mathsf{Enc}_2(\mathsf{mpk}_{\mathsf{pol}}, \sigma_b^*, \mathsf{c}^*)$.

   Finally, A returns $\mathsf{c} \leftarrow \tilde{\mathbb{C}}$ to D where $\tilde{\mathbb{C}} \leftarrow \mathsf{Obf}(1^\lambda, \mathbb{C}_{\mathsf{c}''}, y, m_b^*)$
6. **Output phase:** Return the same output of D.

Let d be the challenge bit sampled by the challenger. The adversary A perfectly simulates the view of D. In particular, if $d = 0$, A simulates $\mathbf{H}_0^b(\lambda)$. On the other hand, if $d = 1$, A simulates $\mathbf{H}_1^b(\lambda)$.

Moreover, we can observe that A is valid since D satisfies condition $\mathbf{Validity}_{1,1}$. Indeed, the latter condition implies that $\mathbb{S}_0^*(\rho) = \mathbb{S}_1^*(\rho) = 0$, for every corrupted attribute $\rho \in \mathcal{S}_{\mathsf{attr}}$ (recall that $\mathbb{S}_0^* = \mathbb{S}_1^* = \mathbb{S}_b^*$ since A sends two identical challenge policies). This concludes the proof.

Claim 2. $\mathbf{H}_1^b(\lambda) \approx_c \mathbf{H}_2^b(\lambda)$.

Proof. Suppose there exists a PPT distinguisher D that distinguishes between $\mathbf{H}_1^b(\lambda)$ and $\mathbf{H}_2^b(\lambda)$ with non-negligible probability. Then, we build an adversary A able to break the security of lockable obfuscation Π_3. A is defined as follows:

1. A computes $(\mathsf{crs}_1, \mathsf{crs}_2) = \mathsf{crs} \leftarrow \mathsf{Setup}(1^\lambda)$. It then initializes the auxiliary input $\mathsf{aux} = (\mathsf{aux}_1, \mathsf{aux}_2) \leftarrow (\perp, \perp)$ and the initial master public keys $(\mathsf{mpk}_{\mathsf{attr}}, \mathsf{mpk}_{\mathsf{pol}}) \leftarrow (\perp, \perp)$, two counters $\mathsf{ctr}[\mathsf{regAttr}] \leftarrow 0$ and $\mathsf{ctr}[\mathsf{regPol}] \leftarrow 0$.
2. A answers all the incoming queries (until the challenge phase) as defined in $\mathbf{H}^b(\lambda)_1$. To accomplish this, A uses the values computed during the initialization (see Item 1).
3. **Challenge phase:** A receives the challenge $(m_0^*, m_1^*, \sigma_0^*, \sigma_1^*, \mathbb{S}_0^*, \mathbb{S}_1^*)$ from D. Then, it proceeds as follows:
   - Compute $\mathsf{c}'' \leftarrow \mathsf{Enc}_2(\mathsf{mpk}_{\mathsf{pol}}, \sigma_b^*, \mathsf{Enc}_1(\mathsf{mpk}_{\mathsf{attr}}, \mathbb{S}_b^*, 0^{s(\lambda)}))$.

- Send $(\mathbb{C}_{\mathsf{c}''}, m_b^*)$ to the challenger and receive the challenge obfuscation $\tilde{\mathbb{C}}$.

Finally, A returns $\mathsf{c} = \tilde{\mathbb{C}}$ to D.

4. **Output phase:** Return the same output of D.

Let d be the challenge bit sampled by the challenger. When $d = 0$, A simulates $\mathbf{H}_1^b(\lambda)$. On the other hand, if $d = 1$, A simulates $\mathbf{H}_2^b(\lambda)$. Thus, A retains the same non-negligible advantage of D. This concludes the proof.

Claim 3. $\mathbf{H}_2^b(\lambda) \equiv \mathbf{H}_2^{1-b}(\lambda)$.

Proof. The claim follows by observing that these experiments do not depend on the challenge bit b.

Lemma 1 follows by combining Claims 1 and 3.

Lemma 2. *If Π_2 is CPA secure and Π_3 is secure (Definition 5), then*

$$\mathbb{P}\left[\mathbf{G}_{\Pi_{\mathsf{RME}},\mathsf{A}}^{\mathsf{RME\text{-}security}}(\lambda) = 1 : \mathbf{Validity}_{2,2}\right] \leq \mathsf{negl}(\lambda).$$

Proof. Consider the following hybrid experiments:

- $\mathbf{H}_0^b(\lambda)$: This is exactly the CPA-1-sided game conditioned to $\mathbf{Validity}_{2,2}$, where the challenge bit is b.
- $\mathbf{H}_1^b(\lambda)$: Same as $\mathbf{H}_0^b(\lambda)$, except that the challenger runs $\mathsf{c}'' \leftarrow \mathsf{Enc}_2(\mathsf{mpk}_{\mathsf{pol}}, \sigma_b^*, w)$ during the challenge phase, where w is randomly sampled from the ciphertext space of $\mathcal{Y}_1$ of Π_1.
- $\mathbf{H}_2^b(\lambda)$: Same as $\mathbf{H}_1^b(\lambda)$, except that the challenger computes $\tilde{\mathbb{C}}$ (during the challenge phase) using the simulator of the lockable obfuscation scheme Π_3, i.e. $\tilde{\mathbb{C}} \leftarrow \mathsf{S}(1^\lambda, 1^{|\mathbb{C}_{\mathsf{c}''}|}, 1^{|m_b^*|})$.

Claim 4. $\mathbf{H}_0^b(\lambda) \approx_c \mathbf{H}_1^b(\lambda)$.

Proof. The claim follows by using a similar strategy to that of Claim 1 and making a reduction to the security of KP-RABE.

Claim 5. $\mathbf{H}_1^b(\lambda) \approx_c \mathbf{H}_2^b(\lambda)$.

Proof. The claim follows by using an identical argument to that of Claim 2.

Claim 6. $\mathbf{H}_2^b(\lambda) \equiv \mathbf{H}_2^{1-b}(\lambda)$.

Proof. The claim follows by observing that these experiments do not depend on the challenge bit b.

Lemma 2 follows by combining Claims 4 and 6.

Lemma 3. *If Π_1 and Π_2 are CPA secure (Definition 3), and Π_3 is secure (Definition 5), then*

$$\mathbb{P}\left[\mathbf{G}_{\Pi_{\mathsf{RME}},\mathsf{A}}^{\mathsf{RME\text{-}security}}(\lambda) = 1 : \mathbf{Validity}_{1,2}\right] \leq \mathsf{negl}(\lambda).$$

Proof. Consider the following hybrid experiments:

- $\mathbf{H}_0^b(\lambda)$: This is exactly the CPA-1-sided game conditioned to $\mathbf{Validity}_{1,2}$, where the challenge bit is b.
- $\mathbf{H}_1^b(\lambda)$: Same as $\mathbf{H}_0^b(\lambda)$, except that:
  (If $b = 0$**)** The challenger computes $\mathsf{c}' \leftarrow \mathsf{Enc}_1(\mathsf{mpk}_{\mathsf{attr}}, \mathbb{S}_0^*, 0^{s(\lambda)})$ during the challenge phase.
  (If $b = 1$**)** The challenger computes $\mathsf{c}'' \leftarrow \mathsf{Enc}_2(\mathsf{mpk}_{\mathsf{pol}}, \sigma_1^*, w)$ during the challenge phase, w is randomly sampled from the ciphertext space of $\mathcal{Y}_1$ of Π_1.
- $\mathbf{H}_2^b(\lambda)$: Same as $\mathbf{H}_1^b(\lambda)$, except that the challenger computes $\tilde{\mathbb{C}}$, during the challenge phase, using the simulator of the lockable obfuscation scheme Π_3, i.e. $\tilde{\mathbb{C}} \leftarrow \mathsf{S}(1^\lambda, 1^{|\mathbb{C}_{c''}|}, 1^{|m_b^*|})$.

Claim 7. $\mathbf{H}_0^b(\lambda) \approx_c \mathbf{H}_1^b(\lambda)$.

Proof. If $b = 0$, the proof is identical to that of Claim 1. On the other hand, if $b = 1$, the proof is identical to that of Claim 4.

Claim 8. $\mathbf{H}_1^b(\lambda) \approx_c \mathbf{H}_2^b(\lambda)$.

Proof. If $b = 0$, the proof is identical to that of Claim 2. On the other hand, if $b = 1$, the proof is identical to that of Claim 5.

Claim 9. $\mathbf{H}_2^b(\lambda) \equiv \mathbf{H}_2^{1-b}(\lambda)$.

Proof. The claim follows by observing that these experiments do not depend on the challenge bit b.

Lemma 3 follows by combining Claims 7 and 9.

Lemma 4. *If Π_1 and Π_2 are CPA secure (Definition 3), and Π_3 is secure (Definition 5), then*

$$\mathbb{P}\left[\mathbf{G}_{\Pi_{RME},\mathsf{A}}^{RME\text{-}security}(\lambda) = 1 : \mathbf{Validity}_{2,1}\right] \le \mathsf{negl}(\lambda).$$

Proof. The lemma follows by using a symmetrical argument to that of Lemma 3.

By combining Lemmas 1 to 4, we obtain that, if Π_1 and Π_2 are CPA secure (Definition 3) and Π_3 is secure (Definition 5), then Π_{RME} from Construction 1 is CPA-1-sided secure. This concludes the proof.

CPA-2-Sided Security. Recall the definition of a valid adversary of CPA-2-sided security: For every corrupted attributes $\rho \in \mathcal{S}_{\mathsf{attr}}$ and for every corrupted policy $\mathbb{R} \in \mathcal{S}_{\mathsf{pol}}$, we have

$$\begin{aligned}\text{either } &\mathbb{S}_0^*(\rho) = \mathbb{S}_1^*(\rho) = 0 \vee \mathbb{R}(\sigma_0^*) = \mathbb{R}(\sigma_1^*) = 0 \vee \\ &\mathbb{S}_0^*(\rho) = \mathbb{R}(\sigma_1^*) = 0 \vee \mathbb{S}_1^*(\rho) = \mathbb{R}(\sigma_0^*) = 0 \\ \text{or } &\mathbb{S}_0^*(\rho) = \mathbb{S}_1^*(\rho) \wedge \mathbb{R}(\sigma_0^*) = \mathbb{R}(\sigma_1^*) \wedge m_0^* = m_1^*,\end{aligned}$$

where $\mathcal{S}_{\mathsf{attr}} = \{\rho \in \mathsf{D}_{\mathsf{attr}}[\mathsf{pk}] : \mathsf{pk} \in \mathcal{C}_{\mathsf{attr}}\}$ is the set of corrupted attributes and $\mathcal{S}_{\mathsf{pol}} = \{\mathbb{R} \in \mathsf{D}_{\mathsf{pol}}[\mathsf{pk}] : \mathsf{pk} \in \mathcal{C}_{\mathsf{pol}}\}$ is the set of corrupted policies.

Consider the following events:

- **Validity**$_{1,1}$: $\mathbb{S}_0^*(\rho) = \mathbb{S}_1^*(\rho) = 0, \ \forall \rho \in \mathcal{S}_{\mathsf{attr}}$;
- **Validity**$_{2,2}$: $\mathbb{R}(\sigma_0^*) = \mathbb{R}(\sigma_1^*) = 0, \ \forall \mathbb{R} \in \mathcal{S}_{\mathsf{pol}}$;
- **Validity**$_{1,2}$: $\mathbb{S}_0^*(\rho) = \mathbb{R}(\sigma_1^*) = 0, \ \forall \rho \in \mathcal{S}_{\mathsf{attr}}, \forall \mathbb{R} \in \mathcal{S}_{\mathsf{pol}}$;
- **Validity**$_{2,1}$: $\mathbb{S}_1^*(\rho) = \mathbb{R}(\sigma_0^*) = 0, \ \forall \rho \in \mathcal{S}_{\mathsf{attr}}, \forall \mathbb{R} \in \mathcal{S}_{\mathsf{pol}}$;
- **Validity**$_\star$: $\mathbb{S}_0^*(\rho) = \mathbb{S}_1^*(\rho) \wedge \mathbb{R}(\sigma_0^*) = \mathbb{R}(\sigma_1^*) \wedge (m_0^* = m_1^*), \ \forall \rho \in \mathcal{S}_{\mathsf{attr}}, \ \forall \mathbb{R} \in \mathcal{S}_{\mathsf{pol}}$.

Then, the satisfaction of the validity condition can be rewritten as follows:

$$\begin{aligned} &\text{either } \left(\exists i, j \in [2], \ \mathbf{Validity}_{i,j} \text{ holds } \right) \\ &\text{or } \left(\mathbf{Validity}_\star \text{ holds}\right). \end{aligned}$$

We want to show that, for a valid adversary A, the probability of winning the security game, conditioned to any of the above five validity conditions, is at most negligibly greater than $\frac{1}{2}$. We will prove this for each of the above 5 cases.

Lemma 5. *If Π_1 and Π_2 are CPA-2-sided secure (Definition 3),*[11] *and Π_3 is secure (Definition 5), then*

$$\forall i, j \in [2], \ \mathbb{P}\left[\mathbf{G}_{\Pi_{\mathsf{RME}}, \mathsf{A}}^{\mathsf{RME\text{-}security}}(\lambda) = 1 : \mathbf{Validity}_{i,j}\right] \leq \mathsf{negl}(\lambda).$$

Proof. The lemma follows by using an identical approach to that of CPA-1-sided security (see proofs of Lemmas 1 to 4).

Lemma 6. *If Π_1 and Π_2 are CPA-2-sided secure (Definition 3), then*

$$\mathbb{P}\left[\mathbf{G}_{\Pi_{\mathsf{RME}}, \mathsf{A}}^{\mathsf{RME\text{-}security}}(\lambda) = 1 : \mathbf{Validity}_\star\right] \leq \mathsf{negl}(\lambda).$$

Proof. Consider the following hybrid experiments:

- $\mathbf{H}_0^b(\lambda)$: This is exactly the CPA-2-sided security experiment **Validity**$_\star$ where the challenge bit is b.
- $\mathbf{H}_1^b(\lambda)$: Same as $\mathbf{H}_0^b(\lambda)$, except that the challenger runs $\mathsf{c}' \leftarrow \mathsf{Enc}_1(\mathsf{mpk}_{\mathsf{attr}}, \mathbb{S}_{1-b}, y)$ where y is a random lock sampled from $\{0,1\}^{s(\lambda)}$.
- $\mathbf{H}_2^b(\lambda)$: Same as $\mathbf{H}_1^b(\lambda)$, except that the challenger runs $\mathsf{c}'' \leftarrow \mathsf{Enc}_2(\mathsf{mpk}_{\mathsf{pol}}, \sigma_{1-b}, \mathsf{c}')$.

Claim 10. $\mathbf{H}_0^b(\lambda) \approx_c \mathbf{H}_1^b(\lambda)$.

Proof. Suppose there exists a PPT distinguisher D that distinguishes between $\mathbf{H}_0^b(\lambda)$ and $\mathbf{H}_1^b(\lambda)$ with non-negligible probability. Then we can build an adversary A that breaks the CPA-2-sided of Π_1. The adversary A is defined as follows:

1. Receive crs_1 from the challenger.
2. Initialize $\mathsf{aux} = (\mathsf{aux}_1, \mathsf{aux}_2) \leftarrow (\perp, \perp)$, $(\mathsf{mpk}_{\mathsf{attr}} \mathsf{mpk}_{\mathsf{pol}}) \leftarrow (\perp, \perp)$, $\mathsf{ctr}[\mathsf{regAttr}] \leftarrow 0$, and $\mathsf{ctr}[\mathsf{regPol}] \leftarrow 0$.
3. Send $\mathsf{crs} = (\mathsf{crs}_1, \mathsf{crs}_2)$ to D, where $\mathsf{crs}_2 \leftarrow \mathsf{Setup}_2(1^\lambda)$.

[11] For completeness, we stress that the lemma follows even if Π_1 and Π_2 are only CPA secure (as in Lemmas 1 to 4).

4. A answers the incoming oracle queries as follows:
   - **Register corrupted attribute-key query:** On input a public key $\mathsf{pk}_{\mathsf{attr}}$ and attributes $\rho \in \mathcal{X}_2$, A forwards the query as a corrupted-key-registration query to the challenger, receives the answer $(\mathsf{mpk}'_{\mathsf{attr}}, \mathsf{aux}'_1)$ from the challenger, sets $\mathsf{aux}_1 \leftarrow \mathsf{aux}'_1$ and $\mathsf{mpk}_{\mathsf{attr}} \leftarrow \mathsf{mpk}'_{\mathsf{attr}}$, and forwards $(\mathsf{mpk}_{\mathsf{attr}}, \mathsf{aux})$ to D.
   - **Register corrupted policy-key query:** On input a public key $\mathsf{pk}_{\mathsf{pol}}$ and a policy $\mathbb{R} \in \mathcal{P}_2$, A computes $(\mathsf{mpk}'_{\mathsf{pol}}, \mathsf{aux}'_2) \leftarrow \mathsf{RegPK}_2(\mathsf{crs}_2, \mathsf{aux}_2, \mathsf{pk}_{\mathsf{pol}}, \mathbb{R})$, updates $\mathsf{mpk}_{\mathsf{pol}} \leftarrow \mathsf{mpk}'_{\mathsf{pol}}$ and $\mathsf{aux}_2 \leftarrow \mathsf{aux}'_2$, adds $\mathsf{pk}_{\mathsf{pol}}$ to $\mathcal{C}_{\mathsf{pol}}$, and updates $\mathsf{D}_{\mathsf{pol}}[\mathsf{pk}_{\mathsf{pol}}] \leftarrow \mathsf{D}_{\mathsf{pol}}[\mathsf{pk}_{\mathsf{pol}}] \cup \mathbb{R}$. It replies to D with $(\mathsf{mpk}_{\mathsf{pol}}, \mathsf{aux})$.
   - **Register honest attribute-key query:** On input attributes $\rho \in \mathcal{X}_2$, A forwards the query as an honest-key-registration query to the challenger and receives the answer $(\mathsf{ctr}'[\mathsf{regAttr}], \mathsf{mpk}'_{\mathsf{attr}}, \mathsf{aux}'_1, \mathsf{pk}_{\mathsf{attr}}^{\mathsf{ctr}'[\mathsf{regAttr}]})$. The adversarial A updates $\mathsf{ctr}[\mathsf{regAttr}] \leftarrow \mathsf{ctr}'[\mathsf{regAttr}]$, $\mathsf{mpk}_{\mathsf{attr}} \leftarrow \mathsf{mpk}_{\mathsf{attr}}$, and $\mathsf{aux}_1 \leftarrow \mathsf{aux}'_1$. Finally, A returns $(\mathsf{ctr}[\mathsf{regAttr}], \mathsf{mpk}_{\mathsf{attr}}, \mathsf{aux}, \mathsf{pk}_{\mathsf{attr}}^{\mathsf{ctr}[\mathsf{regAttr}]})$ to D.
   - **Register honest policy-key query:** On input a policy $\mathbb{R} \in \mathcal{P}_2$, A increments the counter $\mathsf{ctr}[\mathsf{regPol}] \leftarrow \mathsf{ctr}[\mathsf{regPol}] + 1$, samples $(\mathsf{pk}_{\mathsf{pol}}^{\mathsf{ctr}[\mathsf{regPol}]}, \mathsf{sk}_{\mathsf{pol}}^{\mathsf{ctr}[\mathsf{regPol}]}) \leftarrow \mathsf{KGen}_2(\mathsf{crs}_2, \mathsf{aux}_2)$, and registers $(\mathsf{mpk}_{\mathsf{pol}}, \mathsf{aux}_2) \leftarrow \mathsf{RegPK}_2(\mathsf{crs}_2, \mathsf{aux}_2, \mathsf{pk}_{\mathsf{pol}}^{\mathsf{ctr}[\mathsf{regPol}]}, \mathbb{R})$. It updates $\mathsf{mpk}_{\mathsf{pol}} \leftarrow \mathsf{mpk}'_{\mathsf{pol}}$ and $\mathsf{aux}_2 \leftarrow \mathsf{aux}'_2$, sets $\mathsf{D}_{\mathsf{pol}}[\mathsf{pk}_{\mathsf{pol}}^{\mathsf{ctr}[\mathsf{regPol}]}] \leftarrow \mathsf{D}_{\mathsf{pol}}[\mathsf{pk}_{\mathsf{pol}}^{\mathsf{ctr}[\mathsf{regPol}]}] \cup \mathbb{R}$. Finally, A replies to D with $(\mathsf{ctr}[\mathsf{regPol}], \mathsf{mpk}_{\mathsf{pol}}, \mathsf{aux}, \mathsf{pk}_{\mathsf{pol}}^{\mathsf{ctr}[\mathsf{regPol}]})$.
   - **Corrupt honest attribute-key query:** On input an index $1 \leq k \leq \mathsf{ctr}[\mathsf{regAttr}]$, it forwards the query as an honest-key-corruption query to the challenger. Then, A receives $\mathsf{sk}_{\mathsf{attr}}^k$ which is returned to D.
   - **Corrupt honest policy-key query:** On input an index $1 \leq k \leq \mathsf{ctr}[\mathsf{regPol}]$, let $(\mathsf{pk}_{\mathsf{pol}}^k, \mathsf{sk}_{\mathsf{pol}}^k)$ be the kth policy public/secret key sampled by the adversary A when asked to responding to the kth honest-policy-key-registration query. A replies to D with $\mathsf{sk}_{\mathsf{pol}}^k$.
5. **Challenge phase:** A receives the challenge $(m_0^*, m_1^*, \sigma_0^*, \sigma_1^*, \mathbb{S}_0^*, \mathbb{S}_1^*)$ from D and proceeds as follows:
   - Send the challenge $(y, y, \mathbb{S}_b^*, \mathbb{S}_{1-b}^*)$ to the challenger where y is a random lock sampled from $\{0,1\}^{s(\lambda)}$.
   - Receive the challenge ciphertext c^* and compute $\mathsf{c}'' \leftarrow \mathsf{Enc}_2(\mathsf{mpk}_{\mathsf{pol}}, \sigma_b^*, \mathsf{c}^*)$.

   Finally, A returns $\mathsf{c} \leftarrow \tilde{\mathbb{C}}$ to D where $\tilde{\mathbb{C}} \leftarrow \mathsf{Obf}(1^\lambda, \mathbb{C}_{\mathsf{c}''}, y, m_b^*)$
6. **Output phase:** Return the same output of D.

Let d be the challenge bit sampled by the challenger. The adversary A perfectly simulates the view of D. In particular, if $d = 0$, A simulates $\mathbf{H}_0^b(\lambda)$. On the other hand, if $d = 1$, A simulates $\mathbf{H}_1^b(\lambda)$.

Moreover, we can observe that A is valid since D satisfies condition $\mathbf{Validity}_\star$. Indeed, the latter condition implies that $\mathbb{S}_0^*(\rho) = \mathbb{S}_1^*(\rho)$, for every corrupted attribute $\rho \in \mathcal{S}_{\mathsf{attr}}$. This concludes the proof.

Claim 11. $\mathbf{H}_1^b(\lambda) \approx_c \mathbf{H}_2^b(\lambda)$.

Proof. The claim follows by using a similar argument to that of Claim 10 and making a reduction to the security of KP-RABE.

Claim 12. $\mathbf{H}_2^b(\lambda) \equiv \mathbf{H}_0^{1-b}(\lambda)$.

Proof. The only difference between $\mathbf{H}_2^b(\lambda)$ and $\mathbf{H}_0^{1-b}(\lambda)$ is about the encrypted message. In particular, the challenge ciphertext of $\mathbf{H}_2^b(\lambda)$ is computed by encrypting m_b^*. On the other hand, the challenge ciphertext of $\mathbf{H}_0^{1-b}(\lambda)$ is computed by encrypting m_{1-b}^*. However, conditioned to $\textbf{Validity}_\star$, we have that $m_b^* = m_{1-b}^*$. This concludes the proof.

Lemma 6 follows by combining Claims 10 to 12.

By combining Lemmas 5 and 6, we obtain that, if Π_1 and Π_2 are CPA-2-sided secure (Definition 3) and Π_3 is secure (Definition 5), then Π_{RME} from Construction 1 is CPA-2-sided secure. This concludes the proof.

Acknowledgements. Daniele Venturi is member of the Gruppo Nazionale Calcolo Scientifico Istituto Nazionale di Alta Matematica (GNCS-INdAM). His research was supported by project SERICS (PE00000014) and by project PARTHENON (B53D23013000006), under the MUR National Recovery and Resilience Plan funded by the European Union-NextGenerationEU.

References

1. Ateniese, G., Francati, D., Nuñez, D., Venturi, D.: Match me if you can: matchmaking encryption and its applications. In: Boldyreva, A., Micciancio, D. (eds.) CRYPTO 2019, Part II. LNCS, vol. 11693, pp. 701–731. Springer, Cham (2019). https://doi.org/10.1007/978-3-030-26951-7_24
2. Ateniese, G., Francati, D., Nuñez, D., Venturi, D.: Match me if you can: matchmaking encryption and its applications. J. Cryptol. **34**(3), 1–50 (2021). https://doi.org/10.1007/s00145-021-09381-4
3. Attrapadung, N., Tomida, J.: A modular approach to registered ABE for unbounded predicates. In: Reyzin, L., Stebila, D. (eds.) CRYPTO 2024, Part III. LNCS, vol. 14922, pp. 280–316. Springer, Cham (2024). https://doi.org/10.1007/978-3-031-68382-4_9
4. Boyen, X., Li, Q.: Identity-based matchmaking encryption with enhanced privacy - a generic construction with practical instantiations. In: Tsudik, G., Conti, M., Liang, K., Smaragdakis, G. (eds.) ESORICS 2023, Part II. LNCS, vol. 14345, pp. 425–445. Springer, Cham (2023). https://doi.org/10.1007/978-3-031-51476-0_21
5. Chen, J., Li, Y., Wen, J., Weng, J.: Identity-based matchmaking encryption from standard assumptions. In: Agrawal, S., Lin, D. (eds.) ASIACRYPT 2022, Part III. LNCS, vol. 13793, pp. 394–422. Springer, Cham (2022). https://doi.org/10.1007/978-3-031-22969-5_14
6. Chiku, S., Hara, K., Shikata, J.: Identity-based matchmaking encryption secure against key generation center. In: Zhang, M., Au, M.H., Zhang, Y. (eds.) ProvSec 2023. LNCS, vol. 14217, pp. 251–273. Springer, Cham (2023). https://doi.org/10.1007/978-3-031-45513-1_14

7. Cimorelli Belfiore, R., De Cosmo, A., Ferrara, A.L.: Identity-based matchmaking encryption from standard lattice assumptions. In: International Conference on Applied Cryptography and Network Security, pp. 163–188. Springer (2024). https://doi.org/10.1007/978-3-031-54773-7_7
8. Cong, K., Eldefrawy, K., Smart, N.P.: Optimizing registration based encryption. In: Paterson, M.B. (ed.) 18th IMA International Conference on Cryptography and Coding. LNCS, vol. 13129, pp. 129–157. Springer, Cham (2021). https://doi.org/10.1007/978-3-030-92641-0_7
9. Fiore, D., Kolonelos, D., de Perthuis, P.: Cuckoo commitments: registration-based encryption and key-value map commitments for large spaces. In: Guo, J., Steinfeld, R. (eds.) ASIACRYPT 2023, Part V. LNCS, vol. 14442, pp. 166–200. Springer, Singapore (2023). https://doi.org/10.1007/978-981-99-8733-7_6
10. Francati, D., Friolo, D., Maitra, M., Malavolta, G., Rahimi, A., Venturi, D.: Registered (inner-product) functional encryption. In: Guo, J., Steinfeld, R. (eds.) ASIACRYPT 2023, Part V. LNCS, vol. 14442, pp. 98–133. Springer, Singapore (2023). https://doi.org/10.1007/978-981-99-8733-7_4
11. Francati, D., Friolo, D., Malavolta, G., Venturi, D.: Multi-key and multi-input predicate encryption from learning with errors. In: Hazay, C., Stam, M. (eds.) EUROCRYPT 2023, Part III. LNCS, vol. 14006, pp. 573–604. Springer, Cham (2023). https://doi.org/10.1007/978-3-031-30620-4_19
12. Francati, D., Friolo, D., Malavolta, G., Venturi, D.: Multi-key and multi-input predicate encryption (for conjunctions) from learning with errors. J. Cryptol. **37**(24), 100 (2024). https://doi.org/10.1007/s00145-024-09504-7
13. Francati, D., Guidi, A., Russo, L., Venturi, D.: Identity-based matchmaking encryption without random oracles. In: Adhikari, A., Küsters, R., Preneel, B. (eds.) INDOCRYPT 2021. LNCS, vol. 13143, pp. 415–435. Springer, Cham (2021). https://doi.org/10.1007/978-3-030-92518-5_19
14. Freitag, C., Waters, B., Wu, D.J.: How to use (plain) witness encryption: Registered ABE, flexible broadcast, and more. In: Handschuh, H., Lysyanskaya, A. (eds.) CRYPTO 2023, Part IV. LNCS, vol. 14084, pp. 498–531. Springer, Cham (2023). https://doi.org/10.1007/978-3-031-38551-3_16
15. Garg, R., Lu, G., Waters, B., Wu, D.J.: Reducing the CRS size in registered ABE systems. In: Reyzin, L., Stebila, D. (eds.) CRYPTO 2024, Part III. LNCS, vol. 14922, pp. 143–177. Springer, Cham (2024). https://doi.org/10.1007/978-3-031-68382-4_5
16. Garg, S., Hajiabadi, M., Mahmoody, M., Rahimi, A.: Registration-based encryption: Removing private-key generator from IBE. In: Beimel, A., Dziembowski, S. (eds.) TCC 2018, Part I. LNCS, vol. 11239, pp. 689–718. Springer, Cham (2018). https://doi.org/10.1007/978-3-030-03807-6_25
17. Garg, S., Hajiabadi, M., Mahmoody, M., Rahimi, A., Sekar, S.: Registration-based encryption from standard assumptions. In: Lin, D., Sako, K. (eds.) PKC 2019, Part II. LNCS, vol. 11443, pp. 63–93. Springer, Cham (2019). https://doi.org/10.1007/978-3-030-17259-6_3
18. Glaeser, N., Kolonelos, D., Malavolta, G., Rahimi, A.: Efficient registration-based encryption. In: Meng, W., Jensen, C.D., Cremers, C., Kirda, E. (eds.) ACM CCS 2023, pp. 1065–1079. ACM Press (2023). https://doi.org/10.1145/3576915.3616596
19. Goyal, R., Koppula, V., Waters, B.: Lockable obfuscation. In: Umans, C. (ed.) 58th FOCS, pp. 612–621. IEEE Computer Society Press (2017). https://doi.org/10.1109/FOCS.2017.62

20. Goyal, R., Vusirikala, S.: Verifiable registration-based encryption. In: Micciancio, D., Ristenpart, T. (eds.) CRYPTO 2020, Part I. LNCS, vol. 12170, pp. 621–651. Springer, Cham (2020). https://doi.org/10.1007/978-3-030-56784-2_21
21. Goyal, V., Pandey, O., Sahai, A., Waters, B.: Attribute-based encryption for fine-grained access control of encrypted data. In: Juels, A., Wright, R.N., De Capitani di Vimercati, S. (eds.) ACM CCS 2006, pp. 89–98. ACM Press (2006). https://doi.org/10.1145/1180405.1180418. Available as Cryptology ePrint Archive Report 2006/309
22. Hajiabadi, M., Mahmoody, M., Qi, W., Sarfaraz, S.: Lower bounds on assumptions behind registration-based encryption. In: Rothblum, G.N., Wee, H. (eds.) TCC 2023, Part II. LNCS, vol. 14370, pp. 306–334. Springer, Cham (2023). https://doi.org/10.1007/978-3-031-48618-0_11
23. Hohenberger, S., Lu, G., Waters, B., Wu, D.J.: Registered attribute-based encryption. In: Hazay, C., Stam, M. (eds.) EUROCRYPT 2023, Part III. LNCS, vol. 14006, pp. 511–542. Springer, Cham (2023). https://doi.org/10.1007/978-3-031-30620-4_17
24. Mahmoody, M., Qi, W., Rahimi, A.: Lower bounds for the number of decryption updates in registration-based encryption. In: Kiltz, E., Vaikuntanathan, V. (eds.) TCC 2022, Part I. LNCS, vol. 13747, pp. 559–587. Springer, Cham (2022). https://doi.org/10.1007/978-3-031-22318-1_20
25. Sahai, A., Waters, B.R.: Fuzzy identity-based encryption. In: Cramer, R. (ed.) EUROCRYPT 2005. LNCS, vol. 3494, pp. 457–473. Springer, Berlin, Heidelberg (2005). https://doi.org/10.1007/11426639_27
26. Shamir, A.: Identity-based cryptosystems and signature schemes. In: Blakley, G.R., Chaum, D. (eds.) CRYPTO 1984. LNCS, vol. 196, pp. 47–53. Springer, Heidelberg (1984). https://doi.org/10.1007/3-540-39568-7_5
27. Wichs, D., Zirdelis, G.: Obfuscating compute-and-compare programs under LWE. In: Umans, C. (ed.) 58th FOCS, pp. 600–611. IEEE Computer Society Press (2017). https://doi.org/10.1109/FOCS.2017.61
28. Zhang, Y., Zhao, J., Zhu, Z., Gong, J., Chen, J.: Registered attribute-based signature. In: Tang, Q., Teague, V. (eds.) PKC 2024, Part I. LNCS, vol. 14601, pp. 133–162. Springer, Cham (2024). https://doi.org/10.1007/978-3-031-57718-5_5
29. Zhu, Z., Li, J., Zhang, K., Gong, J., Qian, H.: Registered functional encryptions from pairings. In: Joye, M., Leander, G. (eds.) EUROCRYPT 2024, Part II. LNCS, vol. 14652, pp. 373–402. Springer, Cham (2024). https://doi.org/10.1007/978-3-031-58723-8_13
30. Zhu, Z., Zhang, K., Gong, J., Qian, H.: Registered ABE via predicate encodings. In: Guo, J., Steinfeld, R. (eds.) ASIACRYPT 2023, Part V. LNCS, vol. 14442, pp. 66–97. Springer, Singapore (2023). https://doi.org/10.1007/978-981-99-8733-7_3

Sum-Preserving Encryption: Improved Bounds and Constructions for Long Vectors

Sarah Miracle and Scott Yilek(✉)

University of St. Thomas, St. Paul, USA
{sarah.miracle,syilek}@stthomas.edu

Abstract. Sum-preserving encryption, introduced by Tajik, Gunasekaran, Dutta, Ellia, Bobba, Rosulek, Wright, and Feng (NDSS 2019), allows the encryption of a vector of integers into another vector with the same sum. Tajik et al. proposed a construction resembling a shuffling algorithm and used it to build a type of image encryption called thumbnail-preserving encryption. Later work by Miracle and Yilek (Asiacrypt 2022) introduced additional applications, provided mixing time bounds on the Tajik et al. scheme, and proposed rankings that could be used in the rank-encipher-unrank technique from format-preserving encryption. We build on previous work and improve on their results specifically for the encryption of long vectors with thousands of elements or more. First, we provide an improved analysis of the Tajik et al. construction that relies on a more complex coupling argument than the analysis of Miracle and Yilek. In one of our target applications, this new analysis reduces the number of rounds from about 160,000 to just under 2,600. Our second result is the first analysis of a generalization of the Tajik et al. construction that we call a grouping-based scheme. This solves an open problem given by Miracle and Yilek and provides schemes with improved performance that should scale better as vector size increases.

Keywords: Sum-preserving encryption · Format-preserving encryption

1 Introduction

A sum-preserving encryption scheme is a type of format-preserving encryption [2,3] in which both plaintexts and ciphertexts are vectors of n integers and the sum of the ciphertext vector equals the sum of the plaintext vector. Typically, each integer in the vectors is at most a component bound d. Tajik, Gunasekaran, Dutta, Ellis, Bobba, Rosulek, Wright, and Feng [14] first used sum-preserving encryption as a tool to build thumbnail-preserving encryption [9,16], which allows one to encrypt an image but ensure the thumbnail of the ciphertext image is identical to the thumbnail of the plaintext image. Tajik et al. described

M. Fischlin and V. Moonsamy (Eds.): ACNS 2025, LNCS 15825, pp. 33–61, 2025.
https://doi.org/10.1007/978-3-031-95761-1_2

one construction of a sum-preserving encryption scheme and analyzed its security and efficiency. A later paper by Miracle and Yilek [10] provided a formal security analysis of the Tajik et al. scheme, introduced new constructions, and proposed additional applications.

To see why sum-preserving encryption is useful and understand some of the challenges, let us consider two of the applications proposed in previous work: thumbnail-preserving encryption and dataset encryption. In thumbnail-preserving encryption, we can take n-by-n blocks of pixel values (each 0–255) from an image and apply sum-preserving encryption to the resulting vector of length n^2. The ciphertext will be another vector of n^2 pixel values with the same sum as the original vector. Since the sum and length are preserved, the mean is also preserved. Thus, if a thumbnail of the image is generated by replacing each n-by-n block of pixels with its mean pixel value, then the thumbnail of the ciphertext will be the same as the thumbnail of the original image, giving us thumbnail-preserving encryption. Tajik et al. implemented this idea and deployed a browser extension that works with a modern photo sharing service.

Miracle and Yilek proposed additional dataset encryption applications for sum-preserving encryption. For example, a company with user reviews might want to encrypt a large dataset of thousands of user ratings (each integers 0–4) in a format-preserving way. If sum-preserving encryption is used, then the ciphertext vector will appear to be a vector with thousands of random ratings, but with the same sum and mean, as the original rating data. Miracle and Yilek proposed additional examples in which it may be useful to encrypt data with sum-preserving encryption so that a statistical measure like mean can be computed on the encrypted data.

Looking forward, we will see that previous constructions of sum-preserving encryption suffer from performance issues in both of the applications mentioned above as the vector length n increases.

1.1 Previous Approaches

There are currently two known approaches to building sum-preserving encryption schemes. We follow [10] in referring to them as ranking-based and matching-based constructions.

RANKING-BASED. Ranking-based constructions are based on the rank-encipher-unrank algorithm [2] widely used in Format-Preserving Encryption [3,4,6]. In rank-encipher-unrank, plaintexts in a set $\mathcal{X}$ are first mapped to integers using a rank algorithm, then the resulting integer in $\{0, \ldots, |\mathcal{X}| - 1\}$ is encrypted into another integer in the same range, before finally an unrank algorithm maps this second integer back into the original set $\mathcal{X}$. Thus, this construction relies on the existence of efficient rank and unrank algorithms for a given domain $\mathcal{X}$.

To see how this can be applied to sum-preserving encryption, let us first define an (n, d, S)-vector to be a vector of n integers $(x_1, \ldots, x_n)$ such that each $0 \leq x_i \leq d$ and the sum of the x_i's is S. If we wish to encrypt an (n, d, S)-vector with rank-encipher-unrank, we would first need to find an efficient rank algorithm to map our vector to $\{0, \ldots, N-1\}$, where N is the number of possible vectors with the same vector length n, component bound d, and sum S as our vector. Then, we would encrypt the resulting integer to get another integer in $\{0, \ldots, N-1\}$. Finally, we would apply an efficient unrank algorithm to get another (n, d, S)-vector.

The main challenge here is finding efficient rank and unrank algorithms. Previous work [8] on format-preserving encryption has shown that it is possible to rank and unrank languages based on regular expressions and DFAs. While it is possible to describe (n, d, S)-vectors with regular expressions and then apply these techniques, Tajik et al. argue this approach would be completely impractical. As a result, custom ranking algorithms are instead needed.

Towards this, Tajik et al. described how some simple equations give a way to rank (n, d, S)-vectors if $n = 2$. Miracle and Yilek then found two ways to rank longer vectors, which they refer to as lexicographic ranking and recursive-block ranking. These algorithms rely on precomputing large tables using either dynamic programming or generating functions. All of these ranking approaches are described in more detail in Sect. 2.

Matching-based. Tajik et al. gave a construction for sum-preserving encryption of (n, d, S)-vectors that more closely resembles card shuffling algorithms from the Markov chain community. Their algorithm, which we refer to as a matching-based algorithm, proceeds in rounds. In each round, the n elements of the vector are randomly rearranged using a shuffling algorithm, and then adjacent points are matched. Each pair of adjacent points is then encrypted, in a sum-preserving way, to form a new pair of points (each point still between 0 and d) with the same sum as the original pair. This pair encryption is done using rank-encipher-unrank combined with the equations we mentioned above that can be used to rank and unrank $(2, d, S)$-vectors. After each pair of points in the vector has been encrypted into a new pair, this entire process repeats again for many rounds. It is easy to see that if pairs of vector elements always become new pairs with the same sum, then the overall algorithm will be sum-preserving.

For any choice of n, d, and S, careful analysis is needed to prove how many rounds are necessary to ensure the resulting vector is indistinguishable from a random (n, d, S)-vector. Tajik et al. gave a heuristic analysis and argued about 1000 rounds should be sufficient for their target application (thumbnail-preserving encryption). Miracle and Yilek then proved explicit mixing time bounds using Markov chain techniques.

Drawbacks. Miracle and Yilek gave a detailed performance analysis of the above algorithms when used in four different applications. In short, they found the matching-based algorithm is the best choice for applications with small vector length n and large component bound d, while the ranking-based algorithms perform better as n grows and d isn't too large. However, as the vector size n gets into the thousands, all of the algorithms start to become impractical. For the matching-based algorithm, this is due to each pair of points in the vector needing to be encrypted in every one of the thousands of rounds. In the case of the two ranking-based algorithms, the time and space needed for the precomputed tables becomes impractical.

Unfortunately, the two applications we mentioned above (image block encryption with blocks 32×32 pixels or larger and rating dataset encryption) are both examples with large vector length n. Thus, satisfactory solutions do not yet exist for these applications. Looking forward, our results will finally provide a path to more practical solutions.

One additional unanswered question from previous work is just how many rounds of the matching-based scheme are needed to provide security. There is currently a significant gap between the number of rounds suggested by Tajik et al. and the number of rounds given by the proofs of Miracle-Yilek. For example, in the 32×32 block image encryption application, Tajik et al. proposed 1000 rounds might be sufficient, and Miracle-Yilek's performance tests actually used those numbers. However, Miracle and Yilek's mixing time proof shows that over 36,000 rounds are actually sufficient to argue security. The gap is even larger for the rating dataset application, with the proof showing that over 160,000 rounds are needed!

1.2 Our Results

We build on the previous work of Tajik et al. and Miracle-Yilek and have two main contributions. First, we provide an improved analysis of the matching-based scheme of Tajik et al., narrowing the gap between theory and practice. The improvement is particularly evident in the rating dataset application. For this application, with 5000 movie ratings between 0 and 4, the original bound in [10] requires 164,647 rounds while our new bound only requires 2,594 rounds.

Miracle and Yilek prove their original bound using a path coupling technique. The general idea is to first define a distance metric on pairs on configurations and then show that the expected distance between the pairs decreases with each round. Path coupling allows them to only consider two configurations that differ on two points. They show that if the two points where the configurations differ are matched together, which happens with probability $1/n$, the distance decreases to 0 and if they are not then the distance remains unchanged. We improve on their result by giving a significantly more complicated coupling for which we are able to show a decrease in distance for half of the matchings. The coupling and proof are given in Sect. 3.

Our second result is an analysis of what we call grouping-based schemes for sum-preserving encryption. The idea is to generalize the matching-based scheme so that in each round, after the points are shuffled, they are no longer matched into pairs, but instead bundled into groups of 3 or larger. These groups are then encrypted with rank-encipher-unrank to form new groups with the same group sum, and the process again repeats for many rounds. Miracle and Yilek briefly mentioned this idea at the end of their paper as a way to deal with larger vector lengths, but they left its analysis as an open problem.

We solve this open problem by formally analyzing such grouping-based schemes. For groups of size 3, we formally define a Markov chain $\mathcal{M}_T$ and show that the mixing time satisfies $\tau_{\mathcal{M}_T}(\epsilon) \leq \binom{n}{2} \ln(\min(dn, 2S)\epsilon^{-1})$. For larger groups of size $k > 3$, we formally define the chain $\mathcal{M}_k$, however the proof becomes much more complicated and we are unable to give a general bound on the mixing time. The complicated part is showing that there exists a way to couple sets of size k which does not increase the distance. This is especially challenging because in order to define the coupling we need to respect the transition probabilities of the Markov chain. For a group of size k with sum S, the chain will pick uniformly from all valid configurations with the same sum while not violating the component bound d. The challenge is that different sums can have different numbers of valid configurations and thus these are chosen with different probabilities.

While we do not give a general proof, we give a coupling that we conjecture does not increase the distance between the configurations. Additionally, we provide an algorithm that allows one to computationally prove that the coupling works for a particular d and k. We verify this holds for all of the values given in Fig. 2. Assuming it has been computationally verified that the coupling meets the constraints for a particular d and k, then we show that the mixing time satisfies $\tau_{\mathcal{M}_k}(\epsilon) \leq \left(\frac{n}{k-1}\right) \ln(\min(dn, 2S)\epsilon^{-1})$.

Grouping-based schemes give us more efficient options for applications with large vectors. For example, in the 32×32 pixel block application, the mixing-time proof from Miracle-Yilek says that over 36,000 rounds of the matching-based scheme would be needed. If we extrapolate from their performance results, we can see that such an encryption could take about 280 s. With a grouping-based scheme, we can select a group size of 256 (meaning the vector is divided into 4 groups). We have computationally verified our coupling works for this choice of parameters, and then our bound shows that about 143 rounds are needed. This sounds like a massive improvement, but we need to keep in mind that the ranking done on each group now needs to be the more complex (and slower) ranking from Miracle-Yilek instead of the equation-based ranking that could be done on pairs of points. We can again extrapolate from the performance results of Miracle-Yilek, since they did ranking performance tests on vectors of size 256 pixels. Using their data, we estimate it would take about 7.4 s to encrypt the 32×32 pixel block.

Similar improvement should be possible for rating dataset encryption. In that application, we have computationally verified our coupling works for a group size of $k = 1250$, meaning in each round the vector of 5000 ratings can be split into four groups. Our bound shows that we would need 132 rounds in this scenario, as opposed to the 2,600 rounds for the matching-based scheme our first result says are needed. Even though each of the 132 rounds will require four applications of the slower Miracle-Yilek ranking algorithms, instead of 2500 applications of the equation-based ranking in the matching-based scheme, the overall performance should still be superior and should scale better as n increases. Further investigation is needed to determine the ideal choice of group size k for this and other applications.

2 Definitions and Prior Sum-Preserving Constructions

2.1 Definition of Sum-Preserving Encryption

We now formally define a sum-preserving encryption scheme, closely following the previous definitions in [14] and [10]. Let $\mathcal{X}_{n,d}$ be the set of all vectors $(x_1, \ldots, x_n)$ of length n and with each x_i an integer such that $0 \leq x_i \leq d$. A sum-preserving encryption scheme for $\mathcal{X}_{n,d}$ consists of encryption algorithm E and decryption algorithm D. The deterministic encryption algorithm $\mathsf{E} : \mathcal{K} \times \mathcal{X}_{n,d} \to \mathcal{X}_{n,d}$ takes a key K from a keyspace $\mathcal{K}$ and a plaintext vector $(x_1, \ldots, x_n) \in \mathcal{X}_{n,d}$, and outputs a ciphertext vector $(y_1, \ldots, y_n)$ that is also in $\mathcal{X}_{n,d}$. Importantly, the sum of the plaintext vector must equal the sum of the ciphertext vector. Specifically, for every $K \in \mathcal{K}$ and every vector $(x_1, \ldots, x_n) \in \mathcal{X}_{n,d}$, it is true that $\sum(x_1, \ldots, x_n) = \sum \mathsf{E}(K, (x_1, \ldots, x_n))$.

The decryption algorithm $\mathsf{D} : \mathcal{K} \times \mathcal{X}_{n,d} \times \mathcal{X}_{n,d}$ should then be such that for all $K \in \mathcal{K}$ and every message vector $(x_1, \ldots, x_n)$ in $\mathcal{X}_{n,d}$, $\mathsf{D}(K, \mathsf{E}(K, (x_1, \ldots, x_n))) = (x_1, \ldots, x_n)$, meaning that decryption always undoes encryption. Note that decryption will then also be sum-preserving.

Previous work [10,14] formally defined and discussed formal security notions for sum-preserving encryption. In short, a good sum-preserving encryption scheme should be indistinguishable from a random sum-preserving function. The key difficulty in proving security then shifts to analyzing the mixing time of the underlying Markov chains, which is our focus in this paper.

2.2 Previous Ranking-Based Constructions

Tajik et al. [14] gave a straightforward algorithm to rank vectors of length two ($n = 2$) with sum S and component bound d. Consider a general such vector (x, y) with $S = x + y$. If $S \leq d$ then there are $S + 1$ valid vectors: $(0, S), (1, S - 1), \ldots, (S, 0)$. In this case, let $\texttt{rank}((x, y)) = x$. Conversely if $S > d$ then there are $2d - S + 1$ valid vectors: $(S - d, d), \ldots, (d, S - d)$. In this case, let $\texttt{rank}((x, y)) = d - x$. To unrank the vectors, let $\texttt{unrank}(t) = (t, S - t)$ if $S \leq d$ and $\texttt{unrank}(t) = (d - t, S - d + t)$ if $S > d$.

In [10] Miracle and Yilek give two practical algorithms to rank and unrank vectors that are larger than 2. Their first rank and unrank algorithms use a lexicographical ranking and are based on an algorithm by Stein [13] for ranking restricted n-compositions.[1] More formally, given two vectors x and y, let j be the first point such that $x(j) \neq y(j)$. If $x(j) < y(j)$ then $x < y$ and otherwise $x > y$. To rank a general vector x according to this ordering, we need to determine how many vectors are less than x according to the lexicographical ranking. Miracle and Yilek [10] do this with the help of a precomputed table C_d where $C_d(n, S)$ stores the number of vectors of length n with sum S and component bound d.

[1] Vectors of length n with sum S are also called n-part compositions of S. There has been work studying bounded or restricted compositions where a component bound is also included. Much of the previous work in this area has involved counting or enumerating such compositions (see e.g., [1,11,15]).

The size of the table grows with n and S and again becomes impractical for large values. They give two algorithms for filling this table. One is based on a dynamic programming algorithm and the other uses generating functions to compute $C_d(n, S)$ directly. Given this precomputed information, they give a recursive definition for $\texttt{rank}(x)$. As a base case, for vectors of length 1, $\texttt{rank}(x) = 0$. Otherwise, we have the following recurrence:

$$\texttt{rank}_{n,S}(x_1, \ldots, x_n) = \sum_{0 \leq i < x_1} C_d(n-1, S-i) + \texttt{rank}_{n,S}(x_2, \ldots, x_n).$$

It's straightforward to see how to turn this definition into an algorithm to find $\texttt{rank}(x)$. Miracle and Yilek also give an unrank algorithm again based on the same recurrence.

Miracle and Yilek give a second more efficient ranking algorithm based on what they refer to as "recursive block order." In this ranking, a vector x is split in half to become x_L and x_R. To determine how two vectors x and y related to each other, you first consider (recursively) x_L and y_L. If $x_L < y_L$ then $x < y$ and similarly if $x_L > y_L$ then $x > y$. Finally if $x_L = x_R$ then we consider x_R and y_R. If $x_R < y_R$ then $x < y$, if $x_R > y_R$ then $x > y$ and finally if $x_R = y_R$ then $x = y$. Based on this order they again come up with recursive rank (and unrank) algorithms. The key improvement here is that since the size of the vectors is cut in half at each step they get a significant reduction in the size of the precomputed table C_d. Roughly they only need to store $C_d(n, S)$ for values of n that are powers of 2.

2.3 Previous Grouping-Based Constructions

In [14] Tajik et al. give an algorithm for sum-preserving encryption based on a shuffling approach which proceeds in rounds. As described in the introduction, the general idea is in each round to randomly shuffle all of the n points. Adjacent points are then "paired" together. For each of these pairs they apply a rank-encipher-unrank approach using the rank and unrank algorithms for vectors of length 2 described in Sect. 2.2. This ensures that each pair is replaced uniformly from all available pairs with the same sum and the overall sum remains unchanged. Miracle and Yilek [10] reframe this algorithm as a Markov chain and formally analyze the mixing time. Here we give the formal definition of the equivalent Markov chain.

The Sum-Preserving Shuffle Markov chain $\mathcal{M}_S$

`Starting at any valid configuration` $x_0 \in \Omega$`, iterate the following:`

- At time t, choose a random shuffling R on all points uniformly at random (u.a.r.).
- Pair adjacent points in R to create a perfect matching M.
- Independently, for each matched pair of points $(p_i, p_j) \in M$ select values for $x_{t+1}(p_i)$ and $x_{t+1}(p_j)$ u.a.r. from all valid choices that preserve the sum. Namely, all choices that satisfy $x_t(p_i)+x_t(p_j) = x_{t+1}(p_i)+x_{t+1}(p_j)$, $x_{t+1}(i) \leq d$, and $x_{t+1}(j) \leq d$.

Miracle and Yilek [10] show that this Markov chain is irreducible and converges to the uniform distribution. They bound the number of rounds needed by showing that the mixing time $\tau_{\mathcal{M}_S}(\epsilon)$ of the Sum-Preserving Shuffle Markov chain satisfies $\tau_{\mathcal{M}_S}(\epsilon) \leq n \ln(\min(dn, 2S)\epsilon^{-1})$, where d is the component bound, S is the sum, and n is the vector length. Informally, the mixing time $\tau_{\mathcal{M}}$ of a Markov chain $\mathcal{M}$ is the number of rounds needed to converge to the stationary distribution μ for the chain $\mathcal{M}$. Formally, let $\mathcal{P}^t(x, y)$ be the t-step transition probability, Ω be the state space of the Markov chain, and $||\mathcal{P}^t - \mu|| = \max_{x\in\Omega}(1/2)\sum_{y\in\Omega}|\mathcal{P}^t(x, y) - \mu(y)|$ be the total variation distance at time t (i.e. after t rounds). Given these definitions then the *mixing time* of the Markov chain $\mathcal{M}$ is formally defined as

$$\tau_{\mathcal{M}}(\epsilon) = \min\{t : ||\mathcal{P}^{t'} - \mu|| \leq \epsilon, \forall t' \geq t\}.$$

In Sect. 3, we give an improved bound on the mixing time of $\mathcal{M}_S$. In the remaining sections, we will generalize the algorithm $\mathcal{M}_S$ so instead of grouping the shuffled points into groups of 2, we group them into groups of size 3 and larger. We formally define and analyze our new algorithms in Sects. 4 and 5.

3 Improved Mixing Time Bound for the Sum-Preserving Markov Chain $\mathcal{M}_S$

In this section, we give an improved bound on the mixing time of the sum-preserving Markov chain $\mathcal{M}_S$ introduced by Tajik et al. [14] and formally defined in Sect. 2.3.

3.1 Background on Path Coupling and $\mathcal{M}_S$

Our proof bounding the mixing time of $\mathcal{M}_S$ will use the path coupling technique (see e.g., [5]). This is the same general technique used by Miracle and Yilek [10] thus we will begin by briefly describing the technique and their original proof. A coupling is a pair of random variables $(X_t, Y_t)_{t=0}^{\infty}$ defined on $\Omega \times \Omega$ such that viewed in isolation both X_t and Y_t simulate the Markov chain and once they collide they will always agree (i.e., if $X_t = Y_t$, then X_{t+1}, Y_{t+1}). The coupling time is the minimum time until both processes (X and Y) agree and can be used to bound the mixing time of a Markov chain as follows.

Theorem 1. *(see e.g. [7]) Define the coupling time T as*

$$T = \max_{x,y\in\Omega} \mathbf{E}\left[\min\{t : X_t = Y_t | X_0 = x, Y_0 = y\}\right].$$

Given this definition of T, the mixing time $\tau(\epsilon)$ satisfies

$$\tau(\epsilon) \leq \lceil Te \ln \epsilon^{-1} \rceil.$$

A standard argument is to define a distance metric on pairs on configurations $x, y \in \Omega$, then carefully define a coupling for which the distance between all pairs of configurations decreases with each step of the Markov chain, and finally bound the coupling time and subsequently the mixing time. Path coupling (see e.g. [7]) simplifies this technique by only requiring one to show that the distance is decreasing for certain pairs of configuration instead of all pairs. As in [10], we will use the following path coupling theorem due to Dyer and Greenhill [7].

Theorem 2. *Let ϕ be an integer valued metric defined on $\Omega \times \Omega$ which takes values in $\{0, ..., B\}$. Let U be a subset of $\Omega \times \Omega$ such that for all $(x_t, y_t) \in \Omega \times \Omega$ there exists a path $x_t = z_0, z_1, ..., z_r = y_t$ between x_t and y_t such that $(z_i, z_{i+1}) \in U$ for $0 \leq i < r$ and $\sum_{i=0}^{r-1} \phi(z_i, z_{i+1}) = \phi(x_t, y_t)$. Let $\mathcal{M}$ be a Markov chain on Ω with transition matrix P. Consider any random function $f : \Omega \to \Omega$ such that $\Pr[f(x) = y] = P(x, y)$ for all $x, y \in \Omega$, and define a coupling of the Markov chain by $(x_t, y_t) \to (x_{t+1}, y_{t+1}) = (f(x_t), f(y_t))$. If there exists $\beta < 1$ such that $E[\phi(x_{t+1}, y_{t+1})] \leq \beta\phi(x_t, y_t)$, for all $(x_t, y_t) \in U$, then the mixing time of $\mathcal{M}$ satisfies*

$$\tau(\epsilon) \leq \frac{\ln(B\epsilon^{-1})}{1 - \beta}.$$

We begin by giving a brief summary of the path coupling argument used in [10]. Miracle and Yilek use the Manhattan distance

$$\phi(x, y) = \sum_{i=1}^{n} |x(i) - y(i)| \tag{1}$$

and define U to be the set of pairs of configurations that differ by exactly two points. They show that for all pairs $(x, y) \in \Omega$ there exists a path between x and y that only changes two points in each step as required by Theorem 2. Their coupling selects the same matching (i.e. the same shuffling) in both processes. If the two points that differ are matched together (which happens with probability $1/n$) the distance between the two processes x and y is decreased to zero in a single step. They then show that for all other matchings the distance remains the same. For pairs in the matching that have the same values in both x and y using the same choices in both processes will insure they continue to have the same values. However pairs that contain one of the two points the differ will have different sums and thus it is not obvious that a coupling exists that ensures that the distance does not increase. This is especially complicated because the Markov chain chooses uniformly between all valid choices for the pairs. However with different sums there can be a different number of choices and thus each choice is chosen with a different probability in each of the chains. For example, consider a pair of points that has sum 7 in x and 4 in y with component bound $d = 4$. The choices for x are $(3, 4)$ and $(4, 3)$ each with probability $1/2$. For y the choices are $(0, 4), (1, 3), (2, 2), (3, 1), (4, 0)$ each with probability $1/4$. To complete their proof Miracle and Yilek prove the following lemma showing there exists a coupling between all possible pairs of points so that coupled pairs are not at a greater distance than the original pair and thus the overall distance between the configurations does not increase.

Lemma 1. *[10] Given two arbitrary points i and j with $x_t(i) = y_t(i)$ and $x_t(j) \neq y_t(j)$, there exists a coupling such that*

$$|x_t(j) - y_t(j)| \geq |x_{t+1}(i) - y_{t+1}(i)| + |x_{t+1}(j) - y_{t+1}(j)|.$$

3.2 Proof Bounding the Mixing Time of $\mathcal{M}_S$

Our proof will also use the Manhattan distance (defined in Eq. 1) but a more complex coupling that will allow us to decrease the distance for every matching regardless of whether the points that differ are matched together thus showing that the distance decreases at a greater rate (β is smaller). We prove the following theorem bounding the mixing time of $\mathcal{M}_S$.

Theorem 3. *Let n be the vector length, S the sum, and d the component bound and $p^* = (d^2 + d)^{-1}$. Given these definitions, the mixing time $\tau_{\mathcal{M}_S}(\epsilon)$ of the sum-preserving Markov chain $\mathcal{M}_S$ satisfies*

$$\tau_{\mathcal{M}_S}(\epsilon) \leq \left(\frac{4n}{np^* + 4 - p^*}\right) \ln(\min(dn, 2S)\epsilon^{-1}).$$

Proof. As in [10] we will only consider pairs of configurations that differ by exactly two points. Consider the example $x_t(a) = 40, x_t(b) = 3, x_t(c) = 4$, and $x_t(d) = 1$. For ease of notation, we will write $x = \{40, 3, 4, 1\}$ and $y = \{40, 6, 1, 1\}$. More generally, we assume x and y differ only on points b and c and in the matching M, b is matched to a point $a \neq c$ and c is matched to point d. If we use the same matching M in x_t and y_t it is not possible to decrease the distance. However, if we use the original matching M in x_t and in y_t we use a different matching M' which is identical to M except that b is matched to d (instead of a) and c to a (instead of d) then the configurations $(37, 6, 4, 1)$ and $(40, 3, 1, 4)$ are possible configurations for both x_{t+1} and y_{t+1}. If these are coupled together then the distance would decrease to zero. The general idea is to use the positions a and d to add or remove value in order to decrease the distance to zero even when b and c (the points that differ between x and y) are not matched together.

While this approach seems promising there are several complications. First, it is possible that position a (or d) does have a high enough (or low enough value) to reduce the distance to 0 (e.g. $x_t(a) < y_t(b) - x_t(b)$). For example in the previous example if $x_t(a) = y_t(a) = 0$ then we would not be able to increase position $x_t(b)$ or $y_t(c)$. In order to show that we can decrease the distance in at least half of the matchings we will pair matchings together. We will pair the matching M with the matching M' as defined above (here a is matched to c and b is matched to d). Without loss of generality assume that $x_t(b) > y_t(b)$ and $x_t(c) < y_t(c)$. If position a has value less than $d/2$ then if we use matching M in x and matching M' in y there exists a valid configuration that decreases the distance by $d' = 2 * \min(d/2, 2 * (x_t(b) - y_t(b)))$: $x_{t+1} = (x_t(a) + d'/2, x_t(b) - d'/2, x_t(c), x_t(d))$ and $y_{t+1} = (x_t(a) + d'/2, y_t(b), y_t(c) - d'/2, x_t(d))$. Similarly if position a has value greater than $d/2$ then if we use matching M' in x and matching M in y there exists a valid configuration that decreases the distance by $d' = 2 * \min(d/2, 2 * (x_t(b) - y_t(b)))$. Thus regardless of the value of $x_t(a) = y_t(a)$ there will always be at least one valid configuration using M or M' in x and respectively M' or M in y that deceases the distance by at least a factor of 2 (since the maximum distance is $2d$).

Although using matching M in x and M' in y (or vice versa) will sometimes decrease the distance, we cannot couple these together for all configurations because there will be other pairs that significantly increase the distance. Consider the example $x = (0, 1, 0, 500), y = (0, 0, 1, 500)$, and $d = 500$. If we match M and M' there are two good configurations valid in both x and y: $(1, 0, 0, 500)$ and $(0, 1, 1, 499)$. However in x (with matching M) position b is equally like to be 1 and 0 while in y this position can take on values 0 through 500. Thus there is no way to couple these in order to maintain the original distance of 2. In order to get around this problem we will only use different matchings in x and y for the cases where the distance decreases and for all other cases we will use the same matching for both x and y and rely on the coupling of pairs of points defined previously in [10]. At a high-level we will show that pulling out these "special" configurations with a small enough probability and coupling them differently does not change the original coupling given in [10] too much and we can repair it to ensure the distance does not increase.

More formally for some minimum probability $p^* = (d^2 + d)^{-1}$ we will couple a single matching M' in x with M in y and M in x with M' in y. We will choose the configurations so that in one pairing the distances decreases by at least a half as shown above. In the other pairing we will choose the original configurations which we know are valid choices and do not change the distance. The proof that we can modify the coupling given in [10] as desired is in Appendix A. Thus with probability $\left(\frac{n-1}{n}\right)(p^*/2)$ we reduce the distance by $1/2$. To summarize if the matching pairs the points that differ together the distance decreases to 0 while in all other cases with probability $p^*/2$ the distance is decreased by half and with the remaining probability it remains the same. Thus we can bound the change in distance as follows.

$$E[\phi(x_{t+1}, y_{t+1})] \leq \left(\frac{1}{n}\right) 0 + \left(\frac{n-1}{n}\right) \left(\left(\frac{p^*}{2}\right) \frac{\phi(x_t, y_t)}{2} + \left(1 - \frac{p^*}{2}\right) \phi(x_t, y_t) \right).$$

Simplifying shows that we can let $\beta = \frac{n-1}{n}(1 - p^*/4)$. Using this choice of β, $B \leq \min(dn, 2S)$, and applying Theorem 2 gives

$$\tau(\epsilon) \leq \left(\frac{4n}{np^* + 4 - p^*} \right) \ln(\min(dn, 2S)\epsilon^{-1}).$$

where $p^* = (d \cdot (d-1))^{-1}$. Note that if d is a constant relative to n then we have

$$\tau(\epsilon) = O(\ln(\min(n, 2S)\epsilon^{-1})).$$

4 Groups of Three Argument

In this section, we generalize the shuffling-based approached introduced by Tajik et al. [14] by grouping the n points in larger groups of 3 instead of 2. In each round the points are shuffled and then adjacent points are grouped into sets of 3. Each set of three is then encrypted to form a new set of three using a rank-encipher-unrank approach. Here we can apply either of the rank and unrank algorithms introduced by Miracle and Yilek and described in Sect. 2.2. These algorithms will encrypt each set of three with a new set of three with the same sum thus preserving the overall vector sum.

4.1 The Sum-Preserving Shuffle Markov Chain on Groups of Three

We begin by formally describing our new shuffling-based algorithm as a Markov chain $\mathcal{M}_T$, and then proving that it connects the state space Ω (all vectors with n points, component bound d, and sum S) and converges to the uniform distribution. Finally, we will give a path coupling argument to bound the mixing time of $\mathcal{M}_T$.

The Sum-Preserving Shuffle Markov chain on Groups of Three $\mathcal{M}_T$
`Starting at any valid configuration` $x_0 \in \Omega$, `iterate the following:`

- At time t, choose a random shuffling R on all points uniformly at random (u.a.r.).
- Divide the points into adjacent sets of three according to R.
- Independently, for each set of points $(p_i, p_j, p_k) \in R$ select values for $x_{t+1}(p_i)$, $x_{t+1}(p_j)$, and $x_{t+1}(p_k)$ u.a.r. from all valid choices that preserve the sum. Namely, all choices that satisfy $x_t(p_i)+x_t(p_j)+x_t(p_k) = x_{t+1}(p_i)+x_{t+1}(p_j)+x_{t+1}(p_k)$, $x_{t+1}(p_i) \leq d$, $x_{t+1}(p_j) \leq d$, and $x_{t+1}(p_k) \leq d$.

Next we show that this Markov chain is irreducible (i.e. the state space Ω is connected) and thus has a unique stationary distribution (see e.g., [7]) and that the stationary distribution is uniform. In [10] they argue that the original sum-preserving chain is irreducible because given any two configurations $x, y \in \Omega$ with $\phi(x, y) \neq 0$ (ϕ is defined as the Manhattan distance as in Eq. 1) there exists a pair of points p^+, p^- where $x_{p+} > y_{p+}$ and $x_{p-} < y_{p-}$. Given a matching that pairs these points together it's possible to choose new values for p^+ and p^- in x that decreases the distance from y. Thus applying this repeatedly will give a path from x to y. For our new chain we will modify this argument as follows. We will choose a shuffling that has p^* and p^- in the same set of three. Now we can leave the third point in the set of three (not p^+ or p^-) unchanged and modify p^+ and p^- in x so as to decrease the distance thus showing the chain connects the state space and is therefore irreducible.

We are now ready to prove the following theorem bounding the mixing time of $\mathcal{M}_T$.

Theorem 4. *Let n be the vector length, S the sum, and d the component bound. Given these definitions, the mixing time* $\tau_{\mathcal{M}_T}(\epsilon)$ *satisfies*

$$\tau_{\mathcal{M}_T}(\epsilon) \leq \binom{n}{2} \ln(\min(dn, 2S)\epsilon^{-1}).$$

Proof. As in Sect. 3, we will use the path coupling theorem (Theorem 2) due to Dyer and Greenhill [5]. In order to apply the theorem, we will define a distance metric ϕ and set $U \subset \Omega \times \Omega$, and then show that the expected distance between any pair of configurations $(x, y) \in U$ decreases after a single step of the Markov chain $\mathcal{M}_T$. Again define the distance $\phi(x, y)$ as the Manhattan distance (formally defined in Eq. 1) and U to be the set of configurations x and y at distance exactly two. We begin by showing that for our choice of U and ϕ, there exists a path $x_t = z_0, z_1, ..., z_r = y_t$ between x_t and y_t such that $(z_i, z_{i+1}) \in U$ for $0 \leq i < r$ and $\sum_{i=0}^{r-1} \phi(z_i, z_{i+1}) = \phi(x_t, y_t)$. It is straightforward to modify the path given above in the proof of connectivity to meet these requirements. Recall that in this path at each step two points p^+ and p^- are selected with $x_{p+} > y_{p+}$ and $x_{p-} < y_{p-}$. An ordering is selected where these 2 points are in the same group of three. Next only these two points are modified so as to decrease the distance to y. Given our definition of U we will decrease x_{p+} by one and increase x_{p-} by one thus decreasing the distance by exactly two. Repeatedly applying this procedure gives a path between every pair of configurations x and y that satisfies the conditions of the theorem.

As in [10] it is straightforward to show that $B \leq \min(dn, 2S)$. Recall that S is the sum over all points $S = \sum_{i=1}^{n} x(i)$. Since each point can contribute at most d to ϕ and there are n points, B satisfies $B \leq \min(dn, 2S)$.

In our coupling we will use the same shuffling in both x and y. If the two points that differ are included in the same triplet then the distance between x and y decreases to 0. We will show that this happens with probability $\frac{2}{n-1} > \frac{2}{n}$. Consider the group containing one of the points where they differ. The probability that the other two points in the group do not contain the other point where the chains differ is $\binom{n-2}{2}/\binom{n-1}{2}$ since these points are chosen uniformly at random from the remaining points. Thus the probability both points that differ are in the same triplet is

$$1 - \frac{\binom{n-2}{2}}{\binom{n-1}{2}} = \frac{2}{n-1}.$$

Otherwise, if the points that differ are not in the same set, we will show there exists a coupling so that the distance remains the same. Thus we have:

$$E[\phi(x_{t+1}, y_{t+1}] \leq \left(\frac{2}{n}\right) \cdot 0 + \left(\frac{n-2}{n}\right) \cdot \phi(x_t, y_t) = \left(\frac{n-2}{n}\right) \cdot \phi(x_t, y_t).$$

Letting $\beta = \left(\frac{n-2}{n}\right)$ and applying Theorem 2 we have

$$\tau_{\mathcal{M}_T}(\epsilon) \leq \binom{n}{2} \ln(\min(dn, 2S)\epsilon^{-1}).$$

4.2 The Coupling on Groups of Three Points

It remains to show that if we consider two triplets with different sums (that differ by one) there exists a coupling so that the expected change in distance is at most zero. Formally, we will prove the following lemma.

Lemma 2. *Given three arbitrary points i, j, and k with $x_t(i) = y_t(i)$, $x_t(j) = y_t(j)$, and $x_t(k) = y_t(k) + 1$, there exists a coupling such that*

$$|x_{t+1}(i) - y_{t+1}(i)| + |x_{t+1}(j) - y_{t+1}(j)| + |x_{t+1}(k) - y_{t+1}(k)| \leq 1$$

Proof. Without loss of generality, we will assume $S_x = S_y + 1$. Notice that we only have to consider sums that differ by one because of our definition of U above (from Theorem 2). We give a coupling of the two points $x(k), y(k)$ such that $y_{t+1}(k) + 1 \geq x_{t+1}(k) \geq y_{t+1}(k)$. In other words $x_{t+1}(k) = y_{t+1}(k)$ or $x_{t+1}(k) = y_{t+1}(k) + 1$. Given this coupling of point k we can rely on the coupling given by [10] to coupling the remaining two points i and j in x and y. In [10] they prove the following lemma.

Lemma 3. *[10] Given two arbitrary points i and j with $x_t(i) = y_t(i)$ and $x_t(j) \neq y_t(j)$, there exists a coupling such that*

$$|x_t(j) - y_t(j)| \geq |x_{t+1}(i) - y_{t+1}(i)| + |x_{t+1}(j) - y_{t+1}(j)|.$$

Given the coupling of point k, we have $x_{t+1}(k) - y_{t+1}(k) = \gamma \leq 1$ and the remaining two points have sums which differ by $1 - \gamma$ (γ can be either 1 or 0). Applying Lemma 3 we gives a coupling of points i and j such that $|x_{t+1}(i) - y_{t+1}(i)| + |x_{t+1}(j) - y_{t+1}(j)| \leq 1 - \gamma$ and therefore the total distance between the points at time $t + 1$ is at most $\gamma + 1 - \gamma = 1$ as desired.

It remains to give a coupling for point k. This is challenging because in defining the coupling we need to respect the transition probabilities of the $\mathcal{M}_T$ Markov chain and thus each possible point value is not selected uniformly from 0 to d but instead is selected with probability proportional to the number of valid configurations with that point value. For example, if $S_x = 2$, $S_y = 1$, and $d = 4$ where S_x is the sum of the three points in x at time t and S_y is the sum of the three points in y at time t then the options for x at time $t + 1$ are $(0, 0, 2), (0, 1, 1), (0, 2, 0), (1, 0, 1), (1, 1, 0), (2, 0, 0)$ and the options for y are $(0, 0, 1), (0, 1, 0), (1, 0, 0)$. Thus in x, the first point is 0 with probability 1/2 (3 of the 6 configurations start with 0) while in y it is 0 with probability 2/3. More generally, the probability that $x_{t+1}(k) = a$ is $C_d(d, S_x - a)/n_x$ where the $C_d(2, S)$ is the number of unique valid configurations of two points with sum S as defined in Eq. 3 and n_x is the total number of valid configurations for x. We will couple $x(k)$ and $y(k)$ according to the standard lexicographical order (i.e., increasing order). The coupling for our example is given in Fig. 1. The remaining proof that this coupling has desired property $y_{t+1}(k) + 1 \geq x_{t+1}(k) \geq y_{t+1}(k)$ is given in Appendix B. The proof relies on a complex case analysis depending on how the sums S_x and S_y relate to the component bound d.

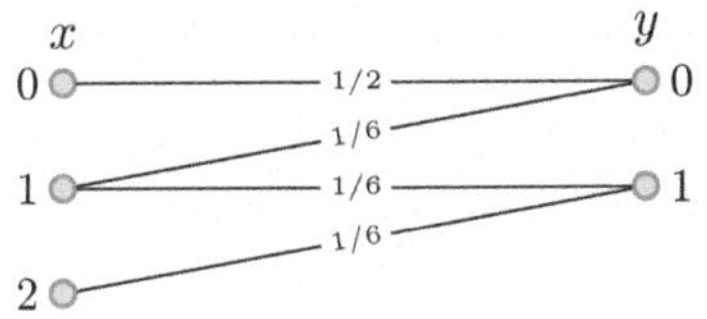

Fig. 1. The bipartite graph visualizing the coupling between the first points for $S_x = 2$, $S_y = 1$, and $d = 4$.

5 Grouping by Sets Larger Than Three

Next we generalize the shuffling-based algorithm $\mathcal{M}_T$ from Sect. 4 to groups of size k where $k > 3$. Again, in each round we begin by shuffling the n points. However, in this more general algorithm we next group the points into adjacent sets of size k instead of 3. Each set of size k is again encrypted to form a new set of size k with the same sum using a rank-encipher-unrank approach. To rank and unrank, we can again use either of the algorithms introduced by Miracle and Yilek and described in Sect. 2.2.

5.1 The Sum-Preserving Shuffle Markov Chain on Groups of Size k

We begin by formally describing this new algorithm as a Markov chain $\mathcal{M}_k$ and proving that it converges to the uniform distribution.

The Sum-Preserving Shuffle Markov chain on Groups of size k $\mathcal{M}_k$
`Starting at any valid configuration` $x_0 \in \Omega$, `iterate the following:`

- At time t, choose a random shuffling R on all points uniformly at random (u.a.r.).
- Divide the points into adjacent sets of size k according to R.
- Independently, for each set of points $(p_i, p_{i+1}, \ldots, p_{i+k-1}) \in R$ select values for $x_{t+1}(p_i), x_{t+1}(p_{i+1}), \ldots, x_{t+1}(p_{i+k-1})$ u.a.r. from all valid choices that preserve the sum. Namely, all choices that satisfy $x_t(p_i) + x_t(p_{i+1}) + \ldots + x_t(p_{i+k-1}) = x_{t+1}(p_i) + x_{t+1}(p_{i+1}) + \ldots + x_{t+1}(p_{i+k-1})$ and $x_{t+1}(p_{i+j}) \leq d$, for all $0 \leq j \leq k-1$.

Next we show that this Markov chain is irreducible (i.e. the state space Ω is connected) and thus has a unique stationary distribution (see e.g., [7]) and that the stationary distribution is uniform. In Sect. 4.1 we prove that the chain $\mathcal{M}_T$ is irreducible by showing there is a path between each pair of configurations that at each step modifies only two points. Since these transitions only modify two points at each step they are also valid transitions for the chain $\mathcal{M}_k$. More formally if the two points are p_1 and p_2 select a permutation where these points are grouped in the same set of k. It is clear from the definition of the transitions of $\mathcal{M}_k$ that changing only the values of p_1 and p_2 while leaving all other points unchanged and maintaining the sum is a valid transition of $\mathcal{M}_k$.

5.2 Bounding the Mixing Time of $\mathcal{M}_k$

In order to bound the mixing time of $\mathcal{M}_k$, we will follow the same technique as for Theorem 4 and use path coupling (Theorem 2). We will again define the distance metric ϕ as the Manhattan distance and set $U \subset \Omega \times \Omega$, to be the set of configurations that are at distance two. In other words, all points except two are identical and for each of these two points the two chains differ by exactly one. In our coupling we will use the same shuffling in both x and y. As in the proof of Theorem 4 if the two points that differ are in the same set of size k then the distance decreases to zero. If the two points that differ are in different sets we would like to prove that there exists a coupling such that the distance does not increase. We conjectures that this is true for all choices of d and k.

Conjecture 1. *Given k arbitrary points $p_1, \dots p_k$ which satisfy $x_t(p_1) = y_t(p_1)$, $x_t(p_2) = y_t(p_2), \dots, x_t(p_{k-1}) = y_t(p_{k-1})$ and $x_t(p_k) = y_t(p_k) - 1$, there exists a coupling such that*

$$\sum_{i=1}^{k} |x_{t+1}(p_i) - y_{t+1}(p_i)| \leq 1.$$

While Conjecture 1 remains open, we have proven the existence of such a coupling for sets of size greater than three with the specific parameters (i.e., fixed values of k and d) listed in Fig. 2. Our proof in Sect. 5.3 gives a coupling and we programmatically verify the coupling meets the necessary conditions for the specific values of k and d in Fig. 2 and all possible sums S_x, S_y. We further conjecture that this coupling will satisfy the constraints of Conjecture 1 for all parameters but have been unable to prove this generally. However, we describe the coupling below and give the algorithm used for verification in Sect. 5.3. It would be

Component Bound d	Set size k	Upper bound on the mixing time $\tau_{\mathcal{M}_k}(\epsilon)$ of $\mathcal{M}_k$.
4	4	$(n/3)\ln(\min(4n, 2S)\epsilon^{-1})$
4	5	$(n/4)\ln(\min(4n, 2S)\epsilon^{-1})$
4	6	$(n/5)\ln(\min(4n, 2S)\epsilon^{-1})$
100	4	$(n/3)\ln(\min(100n, 2S)\epsilon^{-1})$
100	5	$(n/4)\ln(\min(100n, 2S)\epsilon^{-1})$
100	6	$(n/5)\ln(\min(100n, 2S)\epsilon^{-1})$
255	4	$(n/3)\ln(\min(255n, 2S)\epsilon^{-1})$
255	5	$(n/4)\ln(\min(255n, 2S)\epsilon^{-1})$
255	6	$(n/5)\ln(\min(255n, 2S)\epsilon^{-1})$
100000	4	$(n/3)\ln(\min(100000n, 2S)\epsilon^{-1})$
100000	5	$(n/4)\ln(\min(100000n, 2S)\epsilon^{-1})$
100000	6	$(n/5)\ln(\min(100000n, 2S)\epsilon^{-1})$
255	256	$(n/255)\ln(\min(255n, 2S)\epsilon^{-1})$
4	1250	$(n/1249)\ln(\min(4n, 2S)\epsilon^{-1})$

Fig. 2. Computationally proven bounds for particular values of d and k.

straightforward to verify that the conjecture holds for additional parameters and thus prove bounds on the mixing time for those parameters as given in Eq. 2.

Next, we prove a bound on the mixing time of $\mathcal{M}_k$ for the cases where Conjecture 1 holds.

Theorem 5. *Let n be the vector length and S be the sum. If Conjecture 1 holds for group size k and component bound d then the mixing time $\tau_{\mathcal{M}_k}(\epsilon)$ of the chain $\mathcal{M}_k$ satisfies*

$$\tau_{\mathcal{M}_k}(\epsilon) \leq \left(\frac{n}{k-1}\right) \ln(\min(dn, 2S)\epsilon^{-1}).$$

Proof. In order to satisfy the requirements of the path coupling theorem (Theorem 2), we begin by showing that for our choice of U and ϕ, there exists a path $x_t = z_0, z_1, ..., z_r = y_t$ between x_t and y_t such that $(z_i, z_{i+1}) \in U$ for $0 \leq i < r$ and $\sum_{i=0}^{r-1} \phi(z_i, z_{i+1}) = \phi(x_t, y_t)$. Again the path given in Sect. 4.1 between any two pairs of states that modifies only two points at a time (increasing a point by one and decreasing another point by one) satisfies this requirement. The transitions in this path are a subset of the transitions in both $\mathcal{M}_T$ and $\mathcal{M}_k$. Again as in Sect. 4.1 we will use the following upper bound on the maximum distance between configurations

$$B \leq \min(dn, 2S).$$

In our coupling we will use the same shuffling in both x and y. If the two points that differ are included in the same set of size k then the distance decreases to zero. This happens with probability $k/n-1 > k/n$. To see why, consider the group containing one of the points where they differ. The probability that the other $k-1$ points do not contain the other point where the chains differ is $\binom{n-2}{k-1}/\binom{n-1}{k-1}$. Thus the probability they are both in the same group of size k is

$$1 - \frac{\binom{n-2}{k-1}}{\binom{n-1}{k-1}} = \frac{k-1}{n-1}.$$

If the points where the chains differ are not in the same group of k, since Conjecture 1 holds this proves that there exists a coupling for which the distance remains the same. Thus we have

$$E[\phi(x_{t+1}, y_{t+1}] \leq \left(\frac{k-1}{n}\right) \cdot 0 + \left(\frac{n-k+1}{n}\right) \cdot \phi(x_t, y_t) = \left(\frac{n-k+1}{n}\right) \cdot \phi(x_t, y_t).$$

Letting $\beta = \left(\frac{n-k+1}{n}\right)$ and applying Theorem 2 gives

$$\tau_{\mathcal{M}_k}(\epsilon) \leq \left(\frac{n}{k-1}\right) \ln(\min(dn, 2S)\epsilon^{-1}). \tag{2}$$

5.3 Computational Proof of Conjecture 1 for Particular *d* and *k*

It remains to define the coupling and show for the particular values in Fig. 2 that if we consider two sets with different sums then there exists a coupling so that the expected change in distance is at most zero. Lemma 2 gives this result for sets of size three and Miracle and Yilek [10] prove it for sets of size two. For general sets of size greater than three this remains open.

Lemma 4. *Conjecture 1 holds for the values of k and d given in Fig. 2.*

Proof. In order to complete this proof all that remains is to show that Conjecture 1 holds for the values of k and d given in Fig. 2. In the proof of Lemma 2 (which proves Conjecture 1 holds for $k = 3$) above we gave a coupling of the first two points and then relied on the result of [10] for a method of coupling the remaining two points. This technique can easily be extended to four points by giving a coupling of the first points again that satisfies the same conditions and then relying on the Lemma 2 for a coupling of the remaining three points. Applying this technique inductively would give the result. However, it becomes increasingly more complicated to give a coupling of the first two points. Again this is especially challenging because we need to respect the transition probabilities of the Markov chain and thus each possible value is selected with different probabilities depending on how many configurations start with that value which changes depending on the number of remaining points and remaining sum. Again, let $C_d(n, S)$ to be the number of configurations with vector length n, component bound d and sum S. Letting n be the vector length and S the sum, then the probability of the first point having value i is $C_d(n-1, S-i)/C_d(n, S)$, the number of configurations that start with i divided by the total number of configurations. In [10] Miracle and Yilek show that

$$C_d(n, S) = \sum_{k=0}^{n} (-1)^k \binom{n}{k} \binom{n + S - (d+1)k - 1}{n - 1}.$$

For reference, in Fig. 7 we show the function $C_d(2, S)$. As n increases the number of pieces of the C function increases and thus also the complexity of proving the coupling meets the constraints.

As shown in Fig. 1, a valid coupling of the first points can be visualized as a weighted bipartite graph where the vertices in one partition represents the valid values for the first point in x and the other partition represents the valid values for the first point in y. A coupling is a set of edges with weights corresponding to the probability with which those values are paired together. In this more general setting, in order to respect the transition probabilities of $\mathcal{M}_k$, the sum of the weight of the edges adjacent to each vertex in x (the vertices in the "x partition") with value i must be the probability with which that value is selected, namely $C_d(n_x - 1, S_x - i)/C_d(n_x, S_x)$. Similarly the sum of the edge weights adjacent to each vertex in y with value i must have weight $C_d(n_y - 1, S_y - i)/C_d(n_y, S_y)$. Fig. 3 gives an example. Note that the numbers in parentheses are the probability that the number is the first point in the configuration. For example, there are

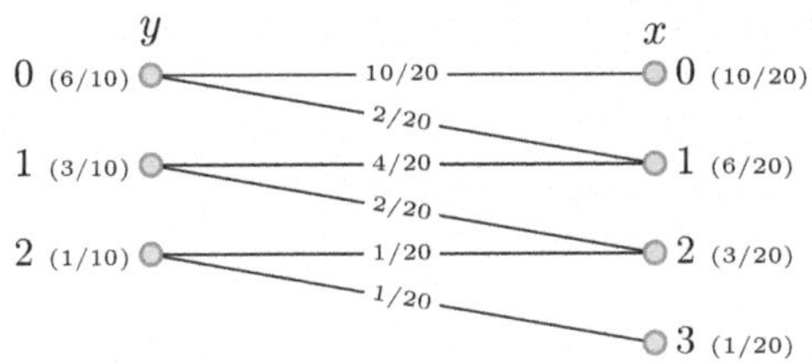

Fig. 3. The bipartite graph visualizing the coupling between the first points for $S_y = 2$, $S_x = 3$, $d = 3$, and $k = 4$.

6 configurations for x which start with 0 and 10 valid configurations total so the probability 0 is the first point is 6/10. For the coupling we will again use the lexicographic coupling introduced in Sect. 4.2. Algorithmically the coupling is created by looping through each vertex in x. For each vertex, repeatedly add an edge to the lowest vertices(s) in y with available probability until the correct weight for x is reached. This procedure will always result in a coupling since the weights on the vertices are probabilities and all sum of all the vertices in x is equal to the sum of all the vertices in y which is 1.

For the parameters given in Fig. 2 we prove programmatically that the standard lexicographical coupling on the first points holds by simulating the coupling for all possible sums and verifying that it meets the desired constraints. We assume without loss of generality that $S_y < S_x = S_y + 1$. Since we have defined U (from the path coupling theorem) as the set of configurations that are at distance two, we only need to consider sums that differ by one. For a fixed choice of d and k we loop through all possible values of S_x and S_y and simulate the coupling. Specifically S_y can take on values from 0 to $k \cdot d - 1$. For each of these choices of S_y and $S_x = S_y + 1$ we run the `verifyCoupling` algorithm given in Fig. 4. Note that our proof relies on induction on the first point. Thus if you were interested in verifying Conjecture 1 for $k = 6$ you would need to first verify for $k = 4$ then $k = 5$ (each for all possible choices of S_x and S_y). More generally, to verify the conjecture for a particular k and component bound d you would need to verify for $4, 5, \ldots k$ each using the same component bound d and all possible sums S_x and $S_y = S_x - 1$.

For a particular choice of S_x, S_y, d and k we verify the coupling by looping through each edge (`coord1_x`, `coord1_y`) in the coupling where `coord1_x` is the value of the first point in x and `coord1_y` is the value of the first point in y. For each edge (`coord1_x`, `coord1_y`) we verify that `coord1_x` = `coord1_y` or `coord1_x` = `coord1_y`+1. If this is satisfied then the distance between the final coupled configurations is the distance between the first points plus the distance between the remaining points. By induction we have that the distance between the remaining points is at most the difference in the sums of the remaining points (either 0 or 1). If `coord1_x` = `coord1_y` then the final distance is the distance

```
procedure verifyCoupling (S_x, S_y, k, d)
    if S_x ≠ S_y − 1 then
        return ERROR
    total_x ← countConfigs (S_x, k, d)
    total_y ← countConfigs (S_y, k, d)
    coord1_x ← 0
    coord1_y← 0
    num_x ← countConfigs (S_x − coord1_x, k − 1, d)
    num_y ← countConfigs (S_y − coord1_y, k − 1, d)
    while num_x < total_x or num_y < total_y do
        if coord1_x > coord1_y or coord1_x < coord1_y - 1 then
            return FAIL
        if num_x / total_x < num_y / total_y then
            coord1_x ← coord1_x + 1
            num_x ← num_x + countConfigs (S_x − coord1_x, k − 1, d)
        else if num_X / total_X > num_Y / total_Y then
            coord1_y ← coord1_y + 1
            num_y ← num_y + countConfigs (S_y − coord1_y, k − 1, d)
        else
            coord1_x ← coord1_x + 1
            coord1_y ← coord1_y + 1
            num_x ← num_x + countConfigs (S_x − coord1_x, k − 1, d)
            num_y ← num_y + countConfigs (S_y − coord1_y, k − 1, d)
    if coord1_x > coord1_y or coord1_x < coord1_y - 1 then
        return FAIL
    return SUCCESS
```

Fig. 4. Algorithm for Verifying the Lexicographical Coupling.

between the first points which is 0 plus the difference in the remaining sums

$$\begin{aligned}|(S_x - \texttt{coord1\_x}) - (S_y - \texttt{coord1\_y})| &= |(S_x - \texttt{coord1\_y}) - (S_y - \texttt{coord1\_y})| \\ &= |S_x - S_y| = 1.\end{aligned}$$

Similarly, if $\texttt{coord1\_x} = \texttt{coord1\_y}{+}1$ then the remaining sums are equal and so the final distance is 1. To determine the edges in the coupling we use that fact that each value `coord1_x` for the first point in x is selected with probability $C_d(n-1, S_x - \texttt{coord1\_x})/C_d(n, S_x)$ and similarly each value `coord1_y` is selected with probability $C_d(n-1, S_y - \texttt{coord1\_y})/C_d(n, S_y)$. The C function is called `countConfigs` in Fig. 4 and again counts the number of valid configurations given n, S, and d and can be easily implemented using formulas derived using generating functions (see e.g. [1,12]) or with dynamic programming [10].

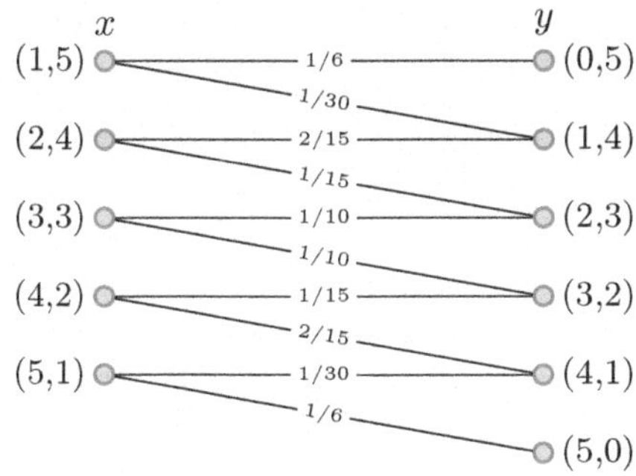

Fig. 5. The bipartite graph visualizing the coupling for $S_x = 6$, $S_y = 5$, and $d = 5$.

A Complete Proof from Sect. 3.2

This section completes the proof of Theorem 3 from Sect. 3.2 which gives an improved bound on the mixing time of the sum-preserving Markov chain $\mathcal{M}_S$.

It remains to show that we can modify the coupling on pairs of points given in [10] by as described at the end of Sect. 3.2. We begin by giving a brief summary of the lexicographical coupling on pairs of points given in [10]. Without loss of generality assume we have two pairs of points $(x(i), x(j))$ and $(y(i), y(j))$ with sums $S_x = x(i) + x(j)$ and $S_y = y(i) + y(j)$ respectively. Configurations are ordered by increasing first coordinate and then coupled according to this ordering while maintaining the appropriate probabilities. For example if we have two pairs of points with $S_x = 6$, $S_y = 5$, and $d = 5$ then the valid choices for x are $(1,5), (2,4), (3,3), (4,2), (5,1)$ and each is selected with probability $1/5$ since there are 5 valid options. For y the choices are $(0,5), (1,4), (2,3), (3,2), (4,1), (5,0)$ and each is selected with probability $1/6$. The coupling can be visualized as a weighted bipartite graph where the options for x form one partition and the options for y form another partition. The edge weights correspond to the probability with which the pair of options is coupled together. In order to respect the probabilities of the Markov chain the total weight of the edges adjacent to each configuration in x must add to $1/n_x$ where n_x is the number of valid options for x and similarly the edges adjacent to each configuration in y must add to $1/n_y$. For our example, the coupling for $S_x = 6$, $S_y = 5$, and $d = 5$ is given in Fig. 5. To determine the coupling (or weighted edges in the graph), iterate through each option for x according to the ordering (top to bottom in the example). While there is still weight (or probability) remaining, add an edge to the next available configuration in y (again according to the ordering, top to bottom) without violating the constraint that the total edge weight adjacent to each option in y is at most $1/n_y$. Because the total vertex weights on each side sum to 1 it is clear this will result in a valid coupling. In [10] they prove that for any valid sums S_x and S_y when using this coupling, each of the pairs that are coupled together are at distance at most $|S_x - S_y|$.

In order to complete our proof, we will need the following lemma which gives a lower bound on the minimum weight edge in the coupling.

Lemma 5. *Each edge of the coupling given in [10] has weight at least*

$$p^* = (d^2 + d)^{-1}.$$

Proof. Given the constructive definition of the coupling from above, a straightforward inductive proof shows that each edge has weight $z/(n_x \cdot n_y)$ for some integer $1 < z < \min(n_x, n_y)$. As a base case the first edge added has weight $\min(n_x, n_y)/(n_x \cdot n_y)$. We can inductively assume that all edges i previously added have weight $z_i/(n_x \cdot n_y)$ for some integer $1 < z_i < \max(n_x, n_y)$ and then it is straightforward to see that the next edge added will meet the constraints. This implies that the minimum weight edge has weight at least $(n_x, n_y)^{-1}$. We know that $n_x, n_y < d + 1$. Additionally if $n_x = n_y$ then all edges have weight $(n_x)^{-1} > (n_x, n_y)^{-1}$. Thus, the minimum weight is at least $(d \cdot (d + 1))^{-1}$ as desired. □

We are now ready to prove the following lemma which shows we can modify the coupling defined in [10] as desired.

Lemma 6. *Define $p^* = (d^2 + d)^{-1}$. Given the coupling defined in [10] between two points i and j with $x_t(i) = y_t(i)$ and $x_t(j) \neq y_t(j)$ it is possible to remove any configuration from x and any from y each with probability p^* and repair the coupling while maintaining the property that*

$$|x_t(j) - y_t(j)| \geq |x_{t+1}(i) - y_{t+1}(i)| + |x_{t+1}(j) - y_{t+1}(j)|.$$

Proof. We need to show that we can remove probability p^* from a point on each side and it is possible to repair the coupling without violating the property that each coupled pair is at distance at most $|S_x - S_y|$. By removing two points one from x and one from y we leave two points $p_x = (i, S_x - i)$ and $p_y = (j, S_y - j)$ open in our coupling each with probability p^* we will call these holes. Note that the points removed may have had edges to multiple points each with weight at least p^* by Lemma 5. We will choose the points that are closest together (i.e. at minimum distance) to be our holes (i.e. p_x and p_y). If these two holes are at distance at most $\delta = |S_x - S_y|$ then we can couple them together with probability p^* (i.e., add an edge between them with weight p^*) and this will repair the coupling. The remainder of the proof will handle the case where the distance between these points p_x and p_y is more than δ. Without loss of generality assume that $n_x < n_y$ (which implies that $1/n_x > 1/n_y$). We will handle the case where $n_x = n_y$ separately. We know from [10] that each x configuration has at least one y configuration that is at distance δ (see [10] Lemma 3). Thus there exists a x configuration either above or below p_x that is at distance at most δ from p_y. We will show it is possible to restructure the coupling so that the hole is moved up to $p_{x-1} = (i - 1, S_x - i + 1)$ or down to $p_{x+1} = (i + 1, S_x - i - 1)$. Thus we can apply this procedure iteratively to move the hole up or down until it is at distance at most δ from p_y. Once the two holes are at distance δ we can add an edge between them with weight p^* and our coupling is repaired.

Consider the point $p_{x-1} = (i-1, S_x - i + 1)$. Since $1/n_x > 1/n_y$ we know this point must have edges to at least two points in y each with probability at least p^* from Lemma 5. More specifically there exists two points $p_{y1} = (k-1, S_y - k + 1)$ and $p_{y2} = (k, S_y - k)$. both at distance at most δ from p_{x-1}. Thus $|(i-1)-(k-1)| + |(S_x - i + 1) - (S_y - k)| \leq \delta$. Simplifying shows that $|i-k| + |S_x - i - S_y + k| \leq \delta$ which implies that p_{y2} is at distance at most δ from p_x. We can then add an edge between p_x and p_{y2} with probability p^* and decrease the edge from p_{x-1} and p_{y2} by p^*. Now the hole has moved from p_x to p_{x-1}. A similar argument shows that it is possible to shift the hole down to p_{x+1}. Thus by repeating this procedure (either the shift up or down) we can move the hole until it is at distance at most δ from p_y.

Finally, we need to handle the case where $n_x = n_y$. Let $C_d(2, S)$ be the number of unique valid configurations of two points with sum S and component bound d. Using standard generating function techniques as shown in [10] we have the following result.

$$C_d(2,S) = \begin{cases} 0 & \text{if } S > 2d+1 \\ 2d+1-S & \text{if } 2d+1 \geq S > d \\ S+1 & \text{if } S \leq d \end{cases} \quad (3)$$

By assumption $S_x \neq S_y$ thus if $n_x = n_y$, we can assume without loss of generality that $S_x \leq d$ and $d < S_y \leq 2d$. Additionally there are $S_x + 1 = 2d - S_y + 1$ possible configurations in both x and y. Specifically the configurations are $(0, S_x), (1, S_x - 1), \ldots (S_x, 0)$ in x and $(S_y - d, d), (S_y - d + 1, d - 1) \ldots (d, S_y - d)$ in y. Further since $S_x \neq S_y$ and $n_x = n_y$, this implies that $S_x \neq d$. The coupling when $n_x = n_y$ is a matching with a single edge with weight $1/n_x = 1/n_y$ between $(i, S_x - i)$ in x and $(S_y - d + i, d - i)$ in y (see the example give in Fig. 6).

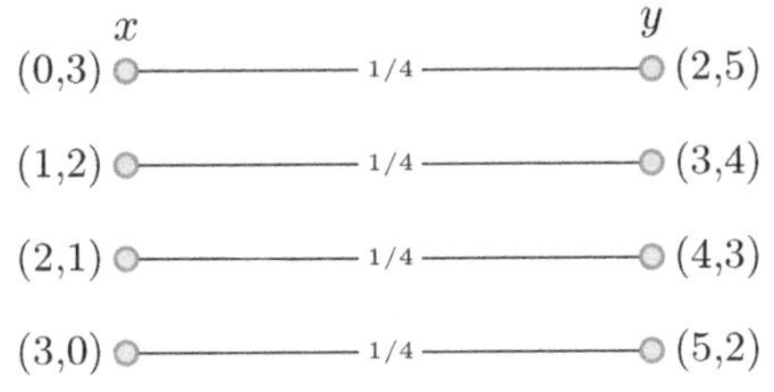

Fig. 6. The bipartite graph visualizing the coupling for $S_x = 3$, $S_y = 7$, and $d = 5$.

Notice that it suffices to show that each configuration $(i, S_x - i)$ in x is at distance at most δ from the point above and below $(S_y - d + i, d - i)$. This would imply that we can move the hole up or down as show in the case where $n_x \neq n_y$.

Basic algebra gives the result as follows:

$$\begin{aligned}\phi((i, S_x - i), (S_y - d + i + 1, d - i - 1)) &= |d - S_y - 1| + |S_x - d + 1| \\ &= (S_y - \max +1) + (d - S_x - 1) \\ &= S_y - S_x - \delta.\end{aligned}$$

A similar argument shows that $(i - 1, S_x - i + 1)$ and $(S_y - d + i - 1, d - i + 1)$ are at distance δ thus completing the proof. □

B Complete Proof from Sect. 4.2

In this section, we complete the proof of Lemma 2 by showing that coupling $x(k)$ and $y(k)$ according to the standard lexicographical order (i.e., increasing order) has the desired property that $y_{t+1}(k)+1 \geq x_{t+1}(k) \geq y_{t+1}(k)$. Recall that Fig. 1 gives an example of the coupling for the running example described in Sect. 4.2.

We begin by defining some useful notation. For our proof it will again help to understand the $C_d(2, S)$ function where $C_d(2, S)$ is the number partitions of S into 2 parts with component bound d; see Fig. 7. This graph comes from Eq. 3 given in Sect. A. For simplicity we will abuse notation and let $C_x(a)$ be the number configurations with three points, first point a, and sum S_x. Given this definition, $C_x(a) = C_d(2, S_x - t)$ and similarly $C_y(a) = C_d(2, S_y - t)$. For a particular sum $C_x(s)$ (or $C_y(s)$) for valid values of s is represented by a portion of the C curve of width d (see Fig. 7). As s (the first point) increases the sum decreases so the value $C_x(s)$ is moving to the left along the C curve. Define $w_x(a)$ to be the cumulative weight of the valid x configurations where the first point satisfies $x_{t+1}(k) \leq a$,

$$w_x(a) = \frac{1}{n_x}\sum_{s=0}^{a} C_d(2, S_x - s) = \frac{1}{n_x}\sum_{s=0}^{a} C_x(s).$$

Similarly, define

$$w_y(a) = \frac{1}{n_y}\sum_{s=0}^{a} C_y(s).$$

To show that our coupling satisfies $y_{t+1}(k) + 1 \geq x_{t+1}(k) \geq y_{t+1}(k)$, we need to prove the following two statements.

1. For all $0 \leq a < d$, $w_x(a) \leq w_y(a)$.
2. For all $1 \leq a < d$, $w_x(a) \geq w_y(a - 1)$.

The first statement ensures that $x_{t+1}(k) \geq y_{t+1}(k)$ and the second ensures $x_{t+1}(k) \leq y_{t+1}(k) + 1$. Note that since these are probability distributions $w_x(d) = w_y(d) = 1$. Define $w'_x(a)$ to be the weight of the x configurations where the first point $x_{t+1}(k) \geq a$. More formally, let

$$w'_x(a) = \frac{1}{n_x}\sum_{s=a}^{d} C_x(s) = 1 - w_x(a - 1),$$

and let

$$w'_y(a) = \frac{1}{n_y}\sum_{s=a}^{d} C_y(s) = 1 - w_y(a-1).$$

Given these definitions, the two statements above are equivalent to the following.

1. For all $0 < a \leq d$, $w'_x(a) \geq w'_y(a)$.
2. For all $1 < a \leq d$, $w'_x(a) \leq w'_y(a-1)$.

We begin by proving the following lemma and then we show that we can use the lemma to handle every possible choice of S_x and $S_y = S_x - 1$.

Lemma 7. *Under each of the conditions listed below we have that for all* $0 \leq a < d$, $w_x(a) \leq w_y(a)$.

1. $n_y \geq n_x$ *and there exists a* $a_0 < d$ *such that for all a satisfying* $0 \leq a \leq a_0, C_x(a) = 0$ *and for* $a_0 < a \leq d$, $C_y(a+1) - C_y(a) \leq C_x(a+1) - C_x(a)$.
2. $n_y \leq n_x$ *and there exists a* $a_0 > 0$ *such that for all a satisfying* $a_0 \leq a \leq d, C_y(a) = 0$ *and for* $0 \leq a < a_0$, $C_y(a+1) - C_y(a) \leq C_x(a+1) - C_x(a)$.

Proof. We will now prove each of the cases in the lemma separately.

Case 1. By way of contradiction, let a be the smallest a such that $0 \leq a < d$ and $w_x(a) > w_y(a)$. Since for $a \leq a_0$ we have that $C_x(a) = 0$ we know that $a > a_0$. Since this is the smallest a for which this is true we must have that $\frac{1}{n_x}C_x(a) > \frac{1}{n_y}C_y(a)$. Next we will show this implies $\frac{1}{n_x}C_x(a+1) > \frac{1}{n_y}C_y(a+1)$. By assumption we have $C_y(a+1) - C_y(t) \leq C_x(a+1) - C_x(a)$ and $1/n_y \leq 1/n_x$ (since $n_y > n_x$). Combining these shows that

$$\begin{aligned}
\frac{1}{n_x}C_x(a+1) &= \frac{1}{n_x}C_x(a) + \frac{1}{n_x}(C_x(a+1) - C_x(a)) \\
&> \frac{1}{n_y}C_y(a) + \frac{1}{n_y}(C_y(a+1) - C_y(a)) \\
&= \frac{1}{n_y}C_y(a+1).
\end{aligned}$$

Applying this argument inductively we have that $\frac{1}{n_x}C_x(a') > \frac{1}{n_y}C_y(a')$ for all $a' > a$. This implies that for all $a' > a$ we have $w_x(a') > w_y(a')$ and specifically $w_x(d) > w_y(d)$. However this contradicts the fact that these are probability distributions and $w_x(d) = w_y(d) = 1$. Thus there can be no s such that $w_x(a) > w_y(a)$ under the assumptions given.

Case 2. This case is essentially the reverse of the previous case. Here we will prove that $w'_x(a) \geq w'_y(a)$ for all $0 \leq a \leq d$ which, as explained previously, is equivalent to showing that $w_x(a) \leq w_y(a)$ for $0 \leq a \leq d$. Again, by way of contradiction, let a be the largest a such that $0 \leq a \leq d$ and $w'_x(a) < w'_y(a)$. We know that if $a \geq a_0$ then $C_y(a) = 0$ which implies that $w'_y(a) = 0$. Thus we must have that $a < a_0$.

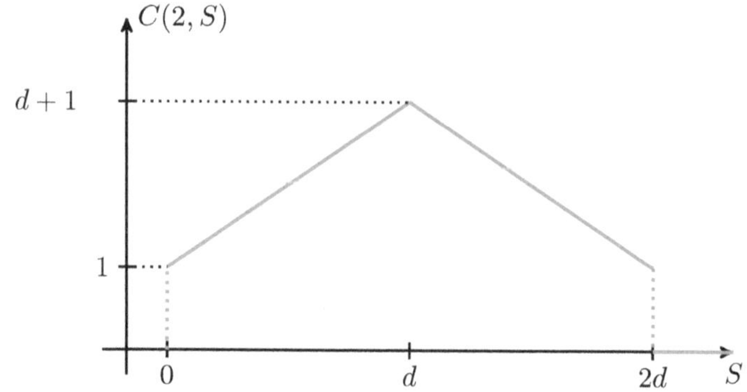

Fig. 7. The function $C(2, S)$.

Since by assumption this is the largest a for which $w'_x(a) < w'_y(a)$ we must have that $\frac{1}{n_x}C_x(a) < \frac{1}{n_y}C_y(a)$. Next we will show this implies $\frac{1}{n_x}C_x(a-1) < \frac{1}{n_y}C_y(a-1)$. By assumption we have $C_y(a+1) - C_y(a) \leq C_x(a+1) - C_x(a)$ for $0 \leq a < a_0$ which implies that $C_x(a-1) - C_x(a) \leq C_y(a-1) - C_y(a)$ for $0 < a \leq a_0$. Similarly by assumption we have that $1/n_x \leq 1/n_y$ (since $n_y \leq n_x$). Combining these shows that

$$\begin{aligned}\frac{1}{n_x}C_x(a-1) &= \frac{1}{n_x}C_x(t) + \frac{1}{n_x}(C_x(a-1) - C_x(t)) \\ &< \frac{1}{n_y}C_y(a) + \frac{1}{n_y}(C_y(a-1) - C_y(a)) \\ &= \frac{1}{n_y}C_y(a-1).\end{aligned}$$

Applying this argument inductively we have that $\frac{1}{n_x}C_x(t') < \frac{1}{n_y}C_y(t')$ for all $a' < a$ This implies that for all $a' < a$ we have $w'_x(a') < w'_y(a')$ and specifically $w'_x(0) < w'_y(0)$. However this contradicts the fact that these are probability distributions and $w'_x(0) = w'_y(0) = 1$. Thus there can be no a such that $w'_x(a) < w'_y(a)$ under the assumptions given. □

Next we will show that all possible values of S_x and S_y satisfy one of the conditions of Lemma 7. We will consider 6 different cases (shown in Fig. 8) depending on the values of S_x and S_y. Since we have three points and each can have a maximum value of d, we have three choices for S.

1. $S >= 2d + 1$
2. $d < S \leq 2d$
3. $S <= d$

Since we have assumed without loss of generality that $S_x = S_y + 1$ we have six choices listed in Fig. 8. It is straightforward to see from Fig. 7 that each of the six cases satisfies the conditions of Lemma 7 for the case given in the last column (Lemma 7 Case).

Conditions	Lemma 7 Case
$S_x > S_y >= 2d + 1$	Case 1
$S_x >= 2d + 1 > S_y > d$	Case 1
$2d + 1 > S_x > S_y > d, n_y \leq n_x$	Case 2
$2d + 1 > S_x > S_y > d, n_y > n_x$	Case 1
$S_x = d + 1, S_y = d$	Case 2
$d >= S_x > S_y$	Case 2

Fig. 8. The six cases for S_x and S_y.

It remains to prove that the second condition that for all $1 \leq a \leq d, w_x(a) \geq w_y(a-1)$. Our proof will consider two cases based on how n_y relates to n_x.

Case $n_y \geq n_x$. We want to show that $w_x(a) \geq w_y(a-1)$. Since $n_y \geq n_x$, we know that $\frac{1}{n_x} > \frac{1}{n_y}$. By definition we have that $C_x(s) = C_y(s-1)$,

$$\begin{aligned} C_x(s) &= C_d(2, S_x - s) \\ &= C_d(2, S_y + 1 - s) \\ &= C_d(2, S_y - (s-1)) = C_y(s-1). \end{aligned}$$

Combining these gives the following result,

$$\begin{aligned} w_x(a) = \frac{1}{n_x} \sum_{s=0}^{a} C_x(s) \geq & \frac{1}{n_y} \sum_{s=0}^{a} C_x(s) \\ \geq & \frac{1}{n_y} \sum_{s=1}^{a} C_x(s) \\ = & \frac{1}{n_y} \sum_{s=1}^{a} C_y(s-1) \\ = & \frac{1}{n_y} \sum_{s=0}^{a-1} C_y(s) = w_y(a-1). \end{aligned}$$

Case $n_y \geq n_x$. Here we will prove the equivalent fact that $w'_x(a) \leq w'_y(a-1)$ for $0 < a \leq d$ as shown above. In this case we have $\frac{1}{n_x} < \frac{1}{n_y}$ and again we will use the fact that $C_x(s) = C_y(s-1)$.

$$
\begin{aligned}
w'_y(a-1) =& \frac{1}{n_y} \sum_{s=a-1}^{d} C_y(s) \\
\geq& \frac{1}{n_y} \sum_{s=a-1}^{d-1} C_y(s) \\
=& \frac{1}{n_y} \sum_{s=a-1}^{d-1} C_x(s+1) \\
=& \frac{1}{n_y} \sum_{s=a}^{d} C_x(s) \\
\geq& \frac{1}{n_x} \sum_{s=a}^{d} C_x(s) = w'_x(a)
\end{aligned}
$$

References

1. Abramson, M.: Restricted combinations and compositions. Fibonacci Q. **14** (1976)
2. Bellare, M., Ristenpart, T., Rogaway, P., Stegers, T.: Format-preserving encryption. In: Jacobson, M.J., Rijmen, V., Safavi-Naini, R. (eds.) SAC 2009. LNCS, vol. 5867, pp. 295–312. Springer, Heidelberg (2009). https://doi.org/10.1007/978-3-642-05445-7_19
3. Brightwell, M., Smith, H.: Using datatype-preserving encryption to enhance data warehouse security. In: National Information Systems Security Conference (NISSC) (1997)
4. Dworkin, M.: Recommendation for block cipher modes of operation: Methods for format preserving-encryption. NIST Special Publication 800-38G (2016). http://dx.doi.org/10.6028/NIST.SP.800-38G
5. Dyer, M., Greenhill, C.: A more rapidly mixing Markov chain for graph colorings. Random Struct. Algor. **13**, 285–317 (1998)
6. Financial services - symmetric key cryptography for the financial services industry - format-preserving encryption. ANSI X9.124 Standard (2020). https://webstore.ansi.org/standards/ascx9/ansix91242020
7. Levin, D.A., Peres, Y., Wilmer, E.L.: Markov chains and mixing times. American Mathematical Society (2006)
8. Luchaup, D., Dyer, K.P., Jha, S., Ristenpart, T., Shrimpton, T.: Libfte: a toolkit for constructing practical, format-abiding encryption schemes. In: Proceedings of the 23rd USENIX Security Symposium, pp. 877–891 (2014)
9. Marohn, B., Wright, C.V., Feng, W., Rosulek, M., Bobba, R.B.: Approximate thumbnail preserving encryption. In: Multimedia Privacy and Security – MPS@CCS 2017, pp. 33–43. ACM (2017)
10. Miracle, S., Yilek, S.: New algorithms and analyses for sum-preserving encryption. In: Agrawal, S., Lin, D. (eds.) ASIACRYPT 2022, Part III. LNCS, vol. 13793, pp. 3–31. Springer, Heidelberg (2022). https://doi.org/10.1007/978-3-031-22969-5_1

11. Opdyke, J.: A unified approach to algorithms generating unrestricted and restricted integer compositions and integer partitions. J. Math. Model. Algor. **9**, 53–97 (2010). https://doi.org/10.1007/s10852-009-9116-2
12. Riordan, J.: An Introduction to Combinatorial Analysis. Dover Publications, Inc. (1980). https://doi.org/10.1515/9781400854332
13. Stein, T.: Uniform random samples for second-order restricted k-compositions (2020). http://essay.utwente.nl/80718/
14. Tajik, K., et al.: Balancing image privacy and usability with thumbnail-preserving encryption. In: NDSS 2019. The Internet Society (2019)
15. Walsh, T.: Loop-free sequencing of bounded integer compositions. JCMCC. J. Comb. Math. Comb. Comput. **33** (2000)
16. Wright, C.V., Feng, W., Liu, F.: Thumbnail-preserving encryption for JPEG. In: ACM Workshop on Information Hiding and Multimedia Security – IH&MMSec 2015, pp. 141–146. ACM (2015)

Fully Secure Searchable Encryption from PRFs, Pairings, and Lattices

Hirotomo Shinoki(✉), Hisayoshi Sato, and Masayuki Yoshino

Hitachi, Ltd., Tokyo, Japan
hirotomo.shinoki.sw@hitachi.com

Abstract. Searchable encryption is a cryptographic primitive that allows us to perform searches on encrypted data. Searchable encryption schemes require that ciphertexts do not leak information about keywords. However, most of the existing schemes do not achieve the security notion that trapdoors do not leak information about the searched keyword. Shen et al. (TCC 2009) proposed a security notion called full security, which includes both ciphertext privacy and trapdoor privacy, but there are few fully secure constructions. Full security is defined for the secret key setting since it is known that public key schemes cannot achieve the trapdoor privacy in principle.

In this paper, we construct a query-bounded fully secure scheme from pseudorandom functions. In addition, we propose three types of efficient (unbounded) fully secure schemes. One of them is based on bilinear groups, and the others are based on lattices. We then analyze the existing constructions. First, we simplify the Cheng et al. scheme (Information Sciences 2023) and prove its security. This scheme had not been proved to be secure. Second, we show that the Li-Boyen pairing-based scheme (IACR CiC 2024) does not achieve the trapdoor privacy, not as claimed.

Keywords: Searchable Encryption · Predicate Encryption · Trapdoor Privacy · Full Security

1 Introduction

Searchable encryption is a cryptosystem that allows keyword search on encrypted data. There are two types of searchable encryption: Searchable Symmetric Encryption (SSE) [40] and Public key Encryption with Keyword Search (PEKS) [10]. The secret key is used for encryption in SSE, while the public key is used for encryption in PEKS. To search for a keyword w, one generates a trapdoor T_w using the secret key. Then, by running the test algorithm, anyone can check whether the given ciphertext is associated with w.

Searchable encryption requires that ciphertexts leak no information on the keywords. However, most of the existing schemes do not satisfy the security notion that trapdoors leak no information about the associated keyword. With respect to the public key setting, it is known that PEKS cannot achieve trapdoor

M. Fischlin and V. Moonsamy (Eds.): ACNS 2025, LNCS 15825, pp. 62–88, 2025.
https://doi.org/10.1007/978-3-031-95761-1_3

privacy in principle. In fact, Byun et al. [13] showed that PEKS is vulnerable to the Keyword Guessing Attack (KGA) and the associated keyword is leaked from the trapdoor when the keyword space is small. In KGA, the attacker tries to find which keyword corresponds to the given trapdoor. The attacker can choose a keyword, encrypt it, and check whether the chosen keyword corresponds to the trapdoor by running the test algorithm. If the number of candidate keywords is small, the attacker can easily find the correct keyword. SSE can achieve the trapdoor privacy, but many SSE schemes use deterministic trapdoor generation algorithms. In these cases, anyone can know whether the given two trapdoors are associated with the same keyword.

In 2009, Shen et al. [39] proposed the security notion of predicate privacy for Predicate-Only Encryption (POE), which is a variant of Predicate Encryption (PE), in the secret key setting. They proposed an POE for inner product with selective predicate privacy using the composite-order bilinear groups. They also formulated the notion of full security, which implies both ciphertext privacy and trapdoor privacy. The basic functionality of predicate-private POE for equality is equivalent to trapdoor-private SSE, although there are some differences in the style of definitions. In this paper, we use the former style to apply these security notions and call it Per-keyword SSE (PSSE).

Predicate privacy can be generalized to Functional Encryption (FE), and there has been a lot of research on function-private FE such as Inner Product Functional Encryption (IPFE) [2,3,9,16,25,27,28,41] and FE/PE for circuits [5,12]. However, IPFE schemes do not directly imply PSSE. FE/PE for circuits supports richer functionalities, but the constructions are somewhat complicated. To the best of our knowledge, until recently, there has been no research on the construction of simplified schemes by restricting the functionality to the equality predicate.

In 2024, Li and Boyen [26] proposed two efficient trapdoor-private PSSE schemes. These schemes are based on pairings and lattices respectively. They also proposed a generic construction of Public key Authenticated Encryption with Keyword Search (PAEKS) from trapdoor-private PSSE and Non-Interactive Key Exchange (NIKE). PAEKS is a variant primitive of PEKS, which was introduced by Huang and Li [24] in 2017 to prevent KGA. As mentioned above, PEKS is vulnerable to KGA in principle. In PAEKS, the data sender has its own secret key to authenticate the ciphertext. Since the test algorithm works correctly only if the ciphertext is authenticated, PAEKS has the potential to prevent KGA. Many PAEKS schemes have been proposed [14,15,19,29,35–37], but most PAEKS schemes achieve only limited trapdoor privacy. Besides the Li-Boyen constructions, there are two PAEKS with (unlimited) trapdoor privacy [14,15]. These schemes imply trapdoor-private PSSE.

1.1 Our Contributions

In this paper, we propose four types of fully secure PSSE.

The first construction uses a pseudorandom function. This construction achieves the bounded version of full security. In the bounded full security setting, the upper bound of the number of queries must be determined before the key generation phase. Although this setting is a weaker variant, the security can be proved without any additional assumption. The other schemes that we propose achieve (unbounded) full security by introducing additional assumptions.

The second construction uses a pseudorandom function and prime-order bilinear groups. This construction is based on the Uniform Matrix Decisional Diffie-Hellman assumption, which we write as U_k-MDDH. This assumption is parameterized by an integer $k \geq 1$. Increasing k makes the assumption weaker, but makes the scheme less efficient. Note that the U_k-MDDH assumption is weaker than the k-Lin assumption.

The third construction uses a pseudorandom function and lattices. This construction is based on the (Ring) Learning with Errors assumption. In addition, it is quite simple compared to the existing schemes. In fact, it does not involve complicated lattice algorithms such as the preimage sampling.

The forth construction is also based on a pseudorandom function and lattices. By introducing the NTRU assumption, this scheme is more efficient than the third construction.

Comparison with Prior Works. The comparison of PSSE schemes with trapdoor privacy is summarized in Table 1. In combination with the Li-Boyen generic construction of PAEKS, which inherits the ciphertext size and the trapdoor size from PSSE, this table can also be seen as the efficiency comparison of PAEKS schemes.

CM22 and CQFM23 are PAEKS with trapdoor privacy. It has been claimed that the security of CQFM23 follows from the Computational Oracle Diffie-Hellman (CODH) assumption in [15], but Li and Boyen [26] pointed out that there is an error in the security analysis. It was also shown that CODH is insufficient and that at least the Decisional Bilinear Diffie-Hellman (DBDH) assumption is required. Thus, no security proof has been given for CQFM23. Note that it seems difficult to prove the security directly from the DBDH assumption. This is because the bilinear map only appears in the test algorithm and does not appear in the security analysis. In this paper, we simplify CQFM23 and show that its security is based on the Decisional Linear (DLin) assumption. This scheme can be seen as a variant of our U_2-MDDH-based construction and can be extended to k-Lin-based construction. We also show that CQFM23 can be generalized to the asymmetric bilinear group setting. In this case, the full security is based on the bilateral k-Lin (bil-k-Lin) assumption.

We also analyze the existing constructions by Li and Boyen [26]. In particular, their security proof for the pairing-based scheme (LB24-P) is incorrect, and the trapdoor privacy can be broken. The Li-Boyen lattice-based construction framework can be used to construct LWE-based scheme, RLWE-based scheme, and NTRU-based scheme. We write them as LB24-L, LB24-R, and LB24-N respectively.

PSSE1 is an efficient PSSE from symmetric primitives that achieves bounded trapdoor privacy. PSSE2 is more efficient or based on weaker assumptions than the existing pairing-based constructions, depending on k. For lattice-based constructions, PSSE3-L is much more efficient than CM22 and LB24-L. Similarly, PSSE3-R and PSSE4 are more efficient than LB24-R and LB24-N respectively. The existing lattice-based constructions use the lattice trapdoor generation algorithm [6,18,32] or the preimage sampling algorithm [22]. On the other hand, our lattice-based constructions do not use such complicated algorithms and consist only of simple computations. CPSSE denotes the generalized version of CQFM23.

Table 1. Comparison of PSSE with Trapdoor Privacy

	Ciphertext	Trapdoor	Assumptions	Remarks
CM22 [14]	$\Omega(\kappa_{ct} n \log^2 q)$	$\Omega(\kappa_{td} n \log^2 q)$	LWE	
CQFM23 [15]	$4\|G\|$	$4\|G\|$	**PRF, DLin**	Modified
LB24-P [26]	$2\|G_1\| + \|G_T\|$	$2\|G_2\|$	(PRF, DBDH)	**Broken**
LB24-L [26]	$\Omega(\kappa_{ct} n \log^2 q)$	$\Omega(\kappa_{td} n \log^2 q)$	PRF, LWE	
LB24-R [26]	$\Omega(N \log^2 q)$	$\Omega(N \log^2 q)$	PRF, RLWE	
LB24-N [26]	$\approx \frac{3}{2} N \log q$	$\approx \frac{3}{2} N \log q$	PRF, RLWE, NTRU	
PSSE1	$Q_{ct} + Q_{td} \cdot \|\mathbb{F}\|$	$Q_{td} + Q_{ct} \cdot \|\mathbb{F}\|$	PRF	Q-bounded
PSSE2	$2k\|G_1\|$	$2k\|G_2\|$	PRF, U_k-MDDH	
PSSE3-L	$\kappa_{ct} \cdot 3n \log q$	$\kappa_{td} \cdot 3n \log q$	PRF, LWE	
PSSE3-R	$3N \log q$	$3N \log q$	PRF, RLWE	
PSSE4	$N \log q$	$N \log q$	PRF, NTRU	
CPSSE	$2k\|G_1\|$	$2k\|G_2\|$	PRF, bil-k-Lin	

The description of "PRF" is not necessary except for PSSE1, but it is specified to show that PRF is actually used.
For a finite set S, $|S|$ denotes the bit size of a random element in S. CQFM23 uses a symmetric bilinear map from $G \times G$. LB24-P, PSSE2, and CPSSE use a bilinear map from $G_1 \times G_2$ to G_T. Q_{ct} and Q_{td} denote upper bounds of the number of ciphertext queries and trapdoor queries respectively. For simplicity, it is assumed that Q_{ct} and Q_{td} are large enough in PSSE1.

As below, there are some other prior constructions related to PSSE, which we omitted from Table 1 for simplicity of description.

- Bounded fully secure FE from PRFs (or equivalently from OWFs) can also be constructed by applying the generic transformation [12] to OWF-based bounded-collusion FE [7,23]. The functionality and security of PSSE1 is limited compared to them (the ciphertext queries are bounded). However, assuming $Q_{td} = Q_{ct}$ and $|\mathbb{F}| = \Theta(\lambda)$ where λ is the security parameter, PSSE1 has quite shorter ciphertext than these schemes. For example, the ciphertext of the FE scheme [7] consists of at least $\Theta(Q_{td} \cdot \lambda^6)$ ciphertext of another scheme (called 1fe). Constructing equality-specialized efficient PSSE with stronger security (e.g. Q_{ct}-unbounded, dynamically bounded [4,21], unbounded) from PRFs is an interesting direction for future work.

- Expressive PAEKS by Meng et al. [31] achieves both ciphertext privacy and trapdoor privacy, but is based on the generic group model. Its ciphertext and trapdoor consists of at least three group elements, which is more than U_1-MDDH-based PSSE2. Broadcast Authenticated Encryption with Keyword Search (BAEKS) by Mukherjee [33] also achieves both ciphertext privacy and trapdoor privacy. In the single-receiver setting, it implies PSSE, but the ciphertext size and the trapdoor size are $2(k+1)|G_1|+|G_T|$ and $2(k+1)|G_2|$ respectively.
- While PSSE is the POE for equality, we can consider the PE version of PSSE. This can be called secret-key anonymous IBE with predicate privacy, and De Caro et al. [17] proposed a construction based on composite-order bilinear groups. By modifying our PSSE schemes, we can construct such schemes from PRFs, prime-order bilinear groups, and lattices. See the full version for the details.

Finally, we note that ciphertext privacy and trapdoor privacy have been considered in the previous research, but full security has not. Full security implies "ciphertext privacy and trapdoor privacy," but not vice versa. Intuitively, full security guarantees that the keyword cannot be leaked even if the adversary has both the ciphertext and the trapdoor, which is not covered by "ciphertext privacy and trapdoor privacy". In this paper, we prove that our constructions achieve full security instead of proving ciphertext privacy and trapdoor privacy.

1.2 Paper Organization

In Sect. 2, we summarize the basic definitions used in this paper. In Sect. 3, 4, and 5, we propose the PRF-based bounded construction (PSSE1), the pairing-based construction (PSSE2), and the lattice-based construction (PSSE3-L, PSSE3-R, and PSSE4) respectively. In Sect. 6, we analyze the existing schemes. We simplify Cheng et al. scheme (CQFM23) and show that its security can be reduced to the bil-DLin assumption. In addition, we give an attack for the pairing-based Li-Boyen scheme (LB24-P).

2 Preliminaries

The basic notations used in this paper are summarized here. "Probabilistic Polynomial-Time" is abbreviated to "PPT". For a finite set S, $x \xleftarrow{\$} S$ means sampling x uniformly at random from S, and $\mathsf{Unif}(S)$ denotes the uniform distribution over S. We say that a function $f : \mathbb{N} \to \mathbb{R}$ is negligible and write $f(n) = \mathsf{negl}(n)$ if for any positive integer k there exists an integer n_k such that $|f(n)| < n^{-k}$ for any $n > n_k$. We say that a probability $p(n)$ is overwhelming if $1 - p(n)$ is negligible. Let $\mathbb{Z}_q$ denote the quotient ring $\mathbb{Z}/q\mathbb{Z}$. Let $\log x$ denote $\log_2 x$. We use the following notations for matrix concatenation:

$$[A|B] = \begin{pmatrix} A & B \end{pmatrix}, \quad [A;C] = \begin{pmatrix} A \\ C \end{pmatrix}.$$

2.1 Pseudorandom Function (PRF)

Let $\{\mathcal{K}_\lambda\}_{\lambda\in\mathbb{N}}$, $\{\mathcal{X}_\lambda\}_{\lambda\in\mathbb{N}}$, and $\{\mathcal{Y}_\lambda\}_{\lambda\in\mathbb{N}}$ be families of finite sets. A family of functions $F = \{F_\lambda : \mathcal{K}_\lambda \times \mathcal{X}_\lambda \to \mathcal{Y}_\lambda\}_{\lambda\in\mathbb{N}}$ is said to be pseudorandom if for any PPT adversary $\mathcal{A}$,

$$\mathsf{Adv}^{\mathsf{PRF}}_{\mathcal{A},F}(\lambda) := \frac{1}{2}\left|\Pr[\mathsf{K} \xleftarrow{\$} \mathcal{K}_\lambda : 1 \leftarrow \mathcal{A}^{F_\lambda(\mathsf{K},\cdot)}(1^\lambda)] - \Pr[f \xleftarrow{\$} \mathsf{Func}[\mathcal{X}_\lambda, \mathcal{Y}_\lambda] : 1 \leftarrow \mathcal{A}^{f(\cdot)}(1^\lambda)]\right|$$

is negligible in λ. Here, $\mathsf{Func}[A, B]$ denotes the set of all functions from A to B. In this paper, we often omit the description of λ and write $F_\lambda(\mathsf{K}, x)$ as $F(\mathsf{K}, x)$ or $F_\mathsf{K}(x)$.

2.2 Bilinear Groups

The bilinear group generator $\mathcal{G}$ is a PPT algorithm that outputs the parameter $\mathbb{G} := (p, G_1, G_2, G_T, g_1, g_2, e) \leftarrow \mathcal{G}(1^\lambda)$. Here, p is a prime of $\Theta(\lambda)$ bits, G_1, G_2, G_T are cyclic groups of order p, g_1 is a generator of G_1, g_2 is a generator of G_2, and $e : G_1 \times G_2 \to G_T$ is a non-degenerate bilinear map. For a matrix $A = (a_{i,j}) \in \mathbb{Z}_p^{m\times n}$, we write $[A]_1 := (g_1^{a_{i,j}}) \in G_1^{m\times n}$, $[A]_2 = (g_2^{a_{i,j}}) \in G_2^{m\times n}$, and $[A]_T = (e(g_1, g_2)^{a_{i,j}}) \in G_T^{m\times n}$. Also, for matrices A and B, we write $e([A]_1, [B]_2) := [AB]_T$. Note that $[AB]_T$ is efficiently computable from $([A]_1, [B]_2)$.

Definition 1 (Matrix Diffie-Hellman Assumption). *Let $\ell > k$ and $\mathcal{D}_{\ell,k}$ be a distribution on $\mathbb{Z}_p^{\ell\times k}$. We say that the $\mathcal{D}_{\ell,k}$-Matrix Decisional Diffie-Hellman ($\mathcal{D}_{\ell,k}$-MDDH) assumption on G_i ($i = 1, 2$) holds if $(\mathbb{G}, [A]_i, [Ar]_i)$ is computationally indistinguishable from $(\mathbb{G}, [A]_i, [u]_i)$ where $A \leftarrow \mathcal{D}_{\ell,k}$, $r \xleftarrow{\$} \mathbb{Z}_p^k$, and $u \xleftarrow{\$} \mathbb{Z}_p^\ell$. We just say that the $\mathcal{D}_{\ell,k}$-MDDH assumption holds if it holds for both G_1 and G_2.*

We say that the bilateral $\mathcal{D}_{\ell,k}$-Matrix Decisional Diffie-Hellman (bil-$\mathcal{D}_{\ell,k}$-MDDH) assumption holds if $(\mathbb{G}, [A]_1, [Ar]_1, [A]_2, [Ar]_2)$ is computationally indistinguishable from $(\mathbb{G}, [A]_1, [u]_1, [A]_2, [u]_2)$.

In this paper, we mainly consider the case that $\ell = k+1$ and $\mathcal{D}_{\ell,k}$ is uniform. We call this case the U_k-MDDH assumption. It is known that U_k-MDDH is weaker than any $\mathcal{D}_{k+1,k}$-MDDH. In particular, the k-Lin assumption implies the U_k-MDDH assumption. We use U_k-MDDH in the following form.

Lemma 1. *For $i = 1, 2$ and $r \in \mathbb{Z}_p^k$, let $\mathcal{O}^r_{G_i}$ be an oracle that samples $a \xleftarrow{\$} \mathbb{Z}_p^k$ and outputs $([a]_i, [a^\top r]_i)$. Let $\mathcal{O}_{G_i}$ be an oracle that samples $a \xleftarrow{\$} \mathbb{Z}_p^k$, $u \xleftarrow{\$} \mathbb{Z}_p$ and outputs $([a]_i, [u]_i)$. If the U_k-MDDH assumption on G_i holds, for any PPT algorithm $\mathcal{A}$,*

$$\mathsf{Adv}^{U_k\text{-}\mathsf{MDDH}}_{i,\mathcal{A}}(\lambda) := \frac{1}{2}\left|\Pr[1 \leftarrow \mathcal{A}^{\mathcal{O}^r_{G_i}}(1^\lambda)] - \Pr[1 \leftarrow \mathcal{A}^{\mathcal{O}_{G_i}}(1^\lambda)]\right|$$

is negligible for a randomly chosen secret $r \xleftarrow{\$} \mathbb{Z}_p^k$.

Proof. Using a U_k-MDDH instance $([A]_i, [s]_i)$, the oracles in this lemma can be simulated in the following way: one samples $t \xleftarrow{\$} \mathbb{Z}_p^{k+1}$ and outputs $([t^\top A]_i, [t^\top s]_i)$. Since the bit length of p is $\Theta(\lambda)$, $A \in \mathbb{Z}_p^{(k+1)\times k}$ is rank k with an overwhelming probability. Thus, it simulates $\mathcal{O}_{G_i}^r$ when $s = Ar$. Similarly, when s is random, $[A|s] \in \mathbb{Z}_p^{(k+1)\times(k+1)}$ is full-rank with an overwhelming probability. Thus, it simulates $\mathcal{O}_{G_i}$ in this case. □

For $m \geq 2$, m-instance version of U_k-MDDH is defined by replacing $r \xleftarrow{\$} \mathbb{Z}_p^k$ with $r \xleftarrow{\$} \mathbb{Z}_p^{k\times m}$ and $u \xleftarrow{\$} \mathbb{Z}_p$ with $u \xleftarrow{\$} \mathbb{Z}_p^m$ in the setting of Lemma 1. In this case, we write the advantage as $\mathsf{Adv}_{i,\mathcal{A}}^{U_k\text{-}\mathsf{MDDH}_m}(\lambda)$. Then, the following tight reduction holds.

Lemma 2 ([20]). *For any PPT algorithm $\mathcal{A}$, there exists a PPT algorithm $\mathcal{B}$ such that*

$$\mathsf{Adv}_{i,\mathcal{A}}^{U_k\text{-}\mathsf{MDDH}_m}(\lambda) \leq \mathsf{Adv}_{i,\mathcal{B}}^{U_k\text{-}\mathsf{MDDH}}(\lambda) + \frac{1}{2(p-1)}.$$

2.3 Lattices

We introduce the assumptions on lattices used in this paper.

Definition 2 (LWE Assumption). *For each positive integer λ, let $n(\lambda)$ be a positive integer, $q(\lambda) \geq 3$ be an integer, and $\chi(\lambda)$ be an error distribution on $\mathbb{Z}_q$.*

(Normal) LWE [38]. *For $s \in \mathbb{Z}_q^n$, let $\mathcal{O}_s$ be the oracle that samples $a \xleftarrow{\$} \mathbb{Z}_q^n$, $x \leftarrow \chi$ and outputs $(a, a^\top s + x)$. Let $\mathcal{O}_\$$ be the oracle that outputs $(a, b) \xleftarrow{\$} \mathbb{Z}_q^n \times \mathbb{Z}_q$. We say that the (n, q, χ)-LWE assumption holds if for any PPT algorithm $\mathcal{A}$,*

$$\mathsf{Adv}_{\mathcal{A}}^{\mathsf{LWE}_{(n,q,\chi)}}(\lambda) := \frac{1}{2}\left|\Pr[1 \leftarrow \mathcal{A}^{\mathcal{O}_s}(1^\lambda)] - \Pr[1 \leftarrow \mathcal{A}^{\mathcal{O}_\$}(1^\lambda)]\right|$$

is negligible for a randomly chosen secret $s \xleftarrow{\$} \mathbb{Z}_q^n$. If $\mathcal{A}$ makes at most m queries, we write the advantage as $\mathsf{Adv}_{\mathcal{A}}^{\mathsf{LWE}_{n,m,q,\chi}}(\lambda)$. We use similar notations for the LWE-variant assumptions and the NTRU assumption defined below.

Non-uniform LWE [11]. *Let η be a distribution on $\mathbb{Z}_q^n$. For $s \in \mathbb{Z}_q^n$, let $\mathcal{O}_s^\eta$ be the oracle that samples $a \leftarrow \eta$, $x \leftarrow \chi$ and outputs $(a, a^\top s + x)$. Let $\mathcal{O}_\$^\eta$ be the oracle that outputs $(a, b) \leftarrow \eta \times \mathrm{Unif}(\mathbb{Z}_q)$. We say that the (n, q, χ, η)-NLWE assumption holds if for any PPT algorithm $\mathcal{A}$,*

$$\mathsf{Adv}_{\mathcal{A}}^{\mathsf{NLWE}_{(n,q,\chi,\eta)}}(\lambda) := \frac{1}{2}\left|\Pr[1 \leftarrow \mathcal{A}^{\mathcal{O}_s^\eta}(1^\lambda)] - \Pr[1 \leftarrow \mathcal{A}^{\mathcal{O}_\$^\eta}(1^\lambda)]\right|$$

is negligible for a randomly chosen secret $s \xleftarrow{\$} \mathbb{Z}_q^n$.

Boneh et al. [11] proved that the (k, q, χ, η)-NLWE problem is as hard as the (n, q, χ)-LWE problem if η satisfies the property called coset sampleability.

Definition 3 (Coset Sampleability [11]). *A distribution η on $\mathbb{Z}_q^k$ is called n-coset sampleable if there exist two PPT algorithms* $\mathsf{MatrixGen}$ *and* $\mathsf{SamplePre}$ *such that:*

- $\mathsf{MatrixGen}(1^\lambda)$ *outputs $M \in \mathbb{Z}_q^{n\times k}$ and auxiliary data T.*
- $\mathsf{SamplePre}(z \in \mathbb{Z}_q^n, M, T)$ *outputs $y \in \mathbb{Z}_q^k$ such that $My = z$. In addition, if z is sampled uniformly at random, the distribution of y is η.*

Lemma 3 ([11]). *If η is n-coset sampleable, the (k, q, χ, η)-NLWE problem is at least as hard as the (n, q, χ)-LWE problem. Namely, for any PPT algorithm $\mathcal{A}$, there exists a PPT algorithm $\mathcal{B}$ such that*

$$\mathsf{Adv}_{\mathcal{A}}^{\mathsf{NLWE}_{k,m,q,\chi,\eta}}(\lambda) \leq \mathsf{Adv}_{\mathcal{B}}^{\mathsf{LWE}_{n,m,q,\chi}}(\lambda).$$

Next, we review the notion of Ring-LWE (RLWE) assumption.

Definition 4 (RLWE Assumption). *Let $N(\lambda)$ be a power of 2, $q(\lambda)$ be a positive integer, and $\mathcal{R}_q := \mathbb{Z}_q[X]/(X^N + 1)$. Let $\chi(\lambda)$ be an error distribution on $\mathcal{R}_q$. For $s \in \mathcal{R}_q$, let $\mathcal{O}_s$ be the oracle that samples $a \xleftarrow{\$} \mathcal{R}_q$, $x \leftarrow \chi$ and outputs $(a, as + x)$. Let $\mathcal{O}_\$$ be the oracle that outputs $(a, b) \xleftarrow{\$} \mathcal{R}_q^2$. We say that the (N, q, χ)-RLWE assumption holds if for any PPT algorithm $\mathcal{A}$,*

$$\mathsf{Adv}_{\mathcal{A}}^{\mathsf{RLWE}_{(N,q,\chi)}}(\lambda) := \frac{1}{2}\left|\Pr[1 \leftarrow \mathcal{A}^{\mathcal{O}_s}(1^\lambda)] - \Pr[1 \leftarrow \mathcal{A}^{\mathcal{O}_\$}(1^\lambda)]\right|$$

is negligible for a randomly chosen secret $s \xleftarrow{\$} \mathcal{R}_q$.

Finally, we introduce the NTRU assumption.

Definition 5 (NTRU assumption). *Let $N(\lambda)$ and $q(\lambda)$ be positive integers, and $\mathcal{R}_q := \mathbb{Z}_q[X]/(X^N + 1)$. Let $\chi(\lambda)$ be a distribution on $\mathcal{R}_q$ and $\chi^\times$ be the conditional distribution of χ on $\mathcal{R}_q^\times$, where $\mathcal{R}_q^\times$ is the multiplicative group of $\mathcal{R}_q$. For $f \in \mathcal{R}_q^\times$, let $\mathcal{O}_f$ be the oracle that samples $g \leftarrow \chi$ and outputs $f^{-1}g$. Let $\mathcal{O}_\$$ be the oracle that outputs $h \xleftarrow{\$} \mathcal{R}_q$. We say that the (N, q, χ)-NTRU assumption holds if for any PPT algorithm $\mathcal{A}$,*

$$\mathsf{Adv}_{\mathcal{A}}^{\mathsf{NTRU}_{(N,q,\chi)}}(\lambda) := \frac{1}{2}\left|\Pr[1 \leftarrow \mathcal{A}^{\mathcal{O}_f}(1^\lambda)] - \Pr[1 \leftarrow \mathcal{A}^{\mathcal{O}_\$}(1^\lambda)]\right|$$

is negligible for $f \leftarrow \chi^\times$.

2.4 Searchable Symmetric Encryption

The following definition of Per-keyword Searchable Symmetric Encryption (PSSE) is a special case of the symmetric predicate-only encryption proposed by Shen et al. [39]. It is called Symmetric-Key Equality-Predicate Encryption (EPE) in [26].

- $\mathsf{KeyGen}(1^\lambda)$: Given a security parameter λ, it outputs a public parameter pp and a secret key K.
- $\mathsf{Enc}(\mathsf{pp}, \mathsf{K}, w)$: Given a public parameter pp, a secret key K, and a keyword w, it outputs a ciphertext C.
- $\mathsf{Trapdoor}(\mathsf{pp}, \mathsf{K}, w)$: Given a public parameter pp, a secret key K, and a keyword w, it outputs a trapdoor T.
- $\mathsf{Test}(\mathsf{pp}, T, C)$: Given a public parameter pp, a trapdoor T, and a ciphertext C, it outputs a bit $b \in \{0, 1\}$.

For simplicity, we often omit the description of pp from the input of algorithms.

We say that the PSSE scheme is correct if $\mathsf{Test}(T, C)$ almost always outputs 1 when T and C have been generated from the same keyword. We say that the PSSE scheme is consistent if $\mathsf{Test}(T, C)$ almost always outputs 0 when T and C have been generated from different keywords. Our formulations below are based on the definitions of correctness and computational consistency for PEKS [1]. Computational consistency is weaker than statistical consistency, but is often used since it does not limit the keyword space and allows flexible construction.

Definition 6 (Correctness). *We say that an PSSE scheme is correct if the minimum value of*

$$\Pr[(\mathsf{pp}, \mathsf{K}) \leftarrow \mathsf{KeyGen}(1^\lambda); C \leftarrow \mathsf{Enc}(\mathsf{K}, w); T \leftarrow \mathsf{Trapdoor}(\mathsf{K}, w) : \mathsf{Test}(T, C) = 1]$$

with respect to w is overwhelming in λ.

Definition 7 (Consistency). *We say that an PSSE scheme is (computationally) consistent if for any PPT algorithm $\mathcal{A}$,*

$$\Pr[(\mathsf{pp}, \mathsf{K}) \leftarrow \mathsf{KeyGen}(1^\lambda); (w, w') \leftarrow \mathcal{A}(1^\lambda, \mathsf{pp}); C \leftarrow \mathsf{Enc}(\mathsf{K}, w); \\ T \leftarrow \mathsf{Trapdoor}(\mathsf{K}, w') : \mathsf{Test}(T, C) = 0 \vee w = w']$$

is overwhelming in λ.

We introduce the notion of full security for PSSE. As weaker properties, the definitions of ciphertext privacy and trapdoor privacy are given in Appendix A.

Definition 8 (Full security [39]). *We say that an PSSE scheme Σ is fully secure if for any PPT algorithm $\mathcal{A}$, the advantage*

$$\mathsf{Adv}^{\mathsf{Full}}_{\mathcal{A},\Sigma}(\lambda) := \Big| \Pr[(\mathsf{pp}, \mathsf{K}) \leftarrow \mathsf{KeyGen}(1^\lambda); b \xleftarrow{\$} \{0, 1\}; \\ b' \leftarrow \mathcal{A}^{\mathcal{O}^b_{\mathsf{ct}}(\mathsf{K},\cdot,\cdot), \mathcal{O}^b_{\mathsf{td}}(\mathsf{K},\cdot,\cdot)}(1^\lambda, \mathsf{pp}) : b = b'] - \frac{1}{2} \Big|$$

is negligible in λ. *Here,* $\mathcal{O}^b_{\mathsf{ct}}(\mathsf{K},\cdot,\cdot)$ *outputs* $C \leftarrow \mathsf{Enc}(\mathsf{K}, w_b)$ *given* (w_0, w_1) *as input.* $\mathcal{O}^b_{\mathsf{td}}(\mathsf{K},\cdot,\cdot)$ *outputs* $T \leftarrow \mathsf{Trapdoor}(\mathsf{K}, w_b)$ *given* (w_0, w_1) *as input. The restriction is that for any input* (x_0, x_1) *to* $\mathcal{O}^b_{\mathsf{ct}}$ *and any input* (y_0, y_1) *to* $\mathcal{O}^b_{\mathsf{td}}$, $(x_0, x_1) = (y_0, y_1)$ *or "*$x_0 \neq y_0 \wedge x_1 \neq y_1$*" holds.*

Let $Q_{\mathsf{ct}}(\lambda)$ (resp. $Q_{\mathsf{td}}(\lambda)$) be an upper bound polynomial of the number of ciphertext (resp. trapdoor) queries. In the "bounded version" of full security, Q_{td} and Q_{ct} are determined before KeyGen phase. We write $\mathsf{KeyGen}(1^\lambda, Q_{\mathsf{td}}, Q_{\mathsf{ct}})$ instead of $\mathsf{KeyGen}(1^\lambda)$ when considering bounded full security. We write the advantage of the bounded full security game as $\mathsf{Adv}^{\mathsf{BFull}}_{\mathcal{A},\Sigma}(\lambda)$.

3 Bounded Fully Secure PSSE from PRF

In this section, we propose an PSSE construction from PRF, which we write as PSSE1. In addition, we show that PSSE1 satisfies correctness, consistency, and bounded full security.

3.1 Construction

Let $\mathbb{F}$ be a finite field of order $q(\lambda) = 2^{\omega(\log \lambda)}$. Let $\mathcal{W}$ denote the keyword space. The construction of PSSE1 is as follows:

- $\mathsf{KeyGen}(1^\lambda, Q_{\mathsf{td}}, Q_{\mathsf{ct}})$:
  1. Sets $d_1 \geq Q_{\mathsf{td}}$ and $d_2 \geq Q_{\mathsf{ct}}$.
  2. Chooses a pseudorandom function $F : \mathcal{K} \times \mathcal{W} \to \mathbb{F}^{d_1 \times d_2}$.
  3. Chooses a distribution η_i on $\mathbb{F}^{d_i}$ for $i = 1, 2$. For each η_i, it is required that d_i independent samples from η_i become linearly independent with an overwhelming probability.
  4. Samples $\mathsf{K} \xleftarrow{\$} \mathcal{K}$.
  5. Outputs the public parameter F, η_1, η_2 and the secret key K.
- $\mathsf{Enc}(\mathsf{K}, w)$: Samples $x \leftarrow \eta_2$ and outputs $(c_1, c_2) := (x, F_{\mathsf{K}}(w)x)$.
- $\mathsf{Trapdoor}(\mathsf{K}, w)$: Samples $y \leftarrow \eta_1$ and outputs $(t_1, t_2) := (y, F_{\mathsf{K}}(w)^\top y)$.
- $\mathsf{Test}((t_1, t_2), (c_1, c_2))$: Outputs 1 if $c_1^\top t_2 = c_2^\top t_1$, otherwise outputs 0.

$\eta_i = \mathrm{Unif}(\mathbb{F}^{d_i})$ satisfies the above condition since $q = 2^{\omega(\log \lambda)}$. Instead, different distributions may be used for more efficient constructions. For example, when q is prime and $\eta_i = \mathrm{Unif}(\{0,1\}^{d_i})$, the probability that d_i samples are linearly independent is $1 - O(1/p) - 2^{-\Omega(d_i)}$ [30,34]. By setting $d_i = \omega(\log \lambda)$, this example satisfies the condition.

3.2 Properties

We show that PSSE1 satisfies correctness, consistency, and bounded full security.

Correctness easily follows from the definition. Consistency follows from the pseudorandomness of F.

Theorem 1. PSSE1 *is consistent provided that* F *is pseudorandom.*

Proof. Suppose that the consistency adversary outputs (w, w') where $w \neq w'$. For $(c_1, c_2) \leftarrow \mathsf{Enc}(\mathsf{K}, w)$ and $(t_1, t_2) \leftarrow \mathsf{Trapdoor}(\mathsf{K}, w')$,

$$c_1^\top t_2 - c_2^\top t_1 = x^\top (F_\mathsf{K}(w') - F_\mathsf{K}(w))^\top y$$

holds. By the pseudorandomness of F, it is sufficient to show that

$$\Pr\left[x \leftarrow \eta_2, y \leftarrow \eta_1; M \xleftarrow{\$} \mathbb{F}^{d_1 \times d_2} : x^\top M^\top y = 0\right]$$

is negligible. Since $x, y \neq 0$ with an overwhelming probability, the probability that $x^\top M^\top y = 0$ is negligible. □

Bounded full security also follows from the pseudorandomness of F. We prove the following theorem in the next subsection.

Theorem 2. PSSE1 *is bounded fully secure provided that* F *is pseudorandom. Namely, for any PPT adversary* $\mathcal{A}$ *that makes a bounded number of queries, there exists a PPT algorithm* $\mathcal{B}$ *such that*

$$\mathsf{Adv}^{\mathsf{BFull}}_{\mathcal{A},\mathsf{PSSE1}}(\lambda) \leq 2\mathsf{Adv}^{\mathsf{PRF}}_{\mathcal{B},F}(\lambda) + \mathsf{negl}(\lambda).$$

3.3 Proof of Theorem 2

Let $\mathcal{O}^b_\mathsf{K}$ denote the pair of the oracles $(\mathcal{O}^b_\mathsf{ct}(\mathsf{K}, \cdot, \cdot), \mathcal{O}^b_\mathsf{td}(\mathsf{K}, \cdot, \cdot))$. Consider the following pair of stateful oracles $\mathcal{O}^\mathsf{M} = (\mathcal{O}^\mathsf{M}_\mathsf{ct}(\cdot, \cdot), \mathcal{O}^\mathsf{M}_\mathsf{td}(\cdot, \cdot))$.

1. $\mathsf{List} = \emptyset$ at the beginning.
2. $\mathcal{O}^\mathsf{M}_\mathsf{ct}(w_0, w_1)$ samples $x \leftarrow \eta_2$. If $((w_0, w_1), M) \in \mathsf{List}$ for some $M \in \mathbb{F}^{d_1 \times d_2}$, it returns (x, Mx). Otherwise, it samples $M \xleftarrow{\$} \mathbb{F}^{d_1 \times d_2}$ and returns (x, Mx). Then, $((w_0, w_1), M)$ is appended to List.
3. $\mathcal{O}^\mathsf{M}_\mathsf{td}(w_0, w_1)$ samples $y \leftarrow \eta_1$. If $((w_0, w_1), M) \in \mathsf{List}$ for some $M \in \mathbb{F}^{d_1 \times d_2}$, it returns $(y, M^\top y)$. Otherwise, it samples $M \xleftarrow{\$} \mathbb{F}^{d_1 \times d_2}$ and returns $(y, M^\top y)$. Then, $((w_0, w_1), M)$ is appended to List.

We prove that any PPT adversary cannot distinguish $\mathcal{O}^0_\mathsf{K}$ (or equivalently $\mathcal{O}^1_\mathsf{K}$) with $\mathcal{O}^\mathsf{M}$ with a non-negligible advantage provided that F is pseudorandom.

Now, we define $\mathcal{O}^0$ by replacing the pseudorandom function in $\mathcal{O}^0_\mathsf{K}$ with the randomly chosen function. Let $\mathsf{FList} = \emptyset$ at the beginning. When the oracles compute $F_\mathsf{K}(w)$ for the first time, it chooses $M \xleftarrow{\$} \mathbb{F}^{d_1 \times d_2}$ and appends (w, M) to FList. After that, the oracles use M instead of $F_\mathsf{K}(w)$. Then, for any PPT adversary $\mathcal{A}$, there exists a PPT algorithm $\mathcal{B}$ such that

$$\left|\Pr[1 \leftarrow \mathcal{A}^{\mathcal{O}^0_\mathsf{K}}(1^\lambda)] - \Pr[1 \leftarrow \mathcal{A}^{\mathcal{O}^0}(1^\lambda)]\right| \leq 2\mathsf{Adv}^{\mathsf{PRF}}_{\mathcal{B},F}(\lambda).$$

Here, the description of pp is omitted from the input.

Next, we define the intermediate oracles between $\mathcal{O}^0$ and $\mathcal{O}^\mathsf{M}$. $\mathcal{O}^{0,i}$ $(i = 0, 1, \ldots, Q)$ sets $\mathsf{List} = \emptyset$ and $\mathsf{FList} = \emptyset$ at the beginning. Then, $\mathcal{O}^{0,i}_\mathsf{ct}(\cdot, \cdot)$ behaves as follows:

1. It samples $x \leftarrow \eta_2$.
2. If $((w_0, w_1), M) \in \mathsf{List}$ for some $M \in \mathbb{F}^{d_1 \times d_2}$, it returns (x, Mx).
3. If $|\mathsf{List}| < i$, it samples $M \xleftarrow{\$} \mathbb{F}^{d_1 \times d_2}$ and returns (x, Mx). Then, $((w_0, w_1), M)$ is appended to List.
4. If $(w_0, M) \in \mathsf{FList}$ for some $M \in \mathbb{F}^{d_1 \times d_2}$, it returns (x, Mx).
5. Otherwise, it samples $M \xleftarrow{\$} \mathbb{F}^{d_1 \times d_2}$ and returns (x, Mx). Then, (w_0, M) is appended to FList.

$\mathcal{O}^{0,i}_{\mathsf{td}}(\cdot, \cdot)$ are defined in the same way. They sample $y \leftarrow \eta_1$ and return $(y, M^\top y)$. We have $\mathcal{O}^0 = \mathcal{O}^{0,0}$ and $\mathcal{O}^{\mathsf{M}} = \mathcal{O}^{0,Q}$.

We prove that $\mathcal{O}^{0,i}$ and $\mathcal{O}^{0,i+1}$ are computationally indistinguishable. Regarding $\mathcal{O}^{0,i}$, let Q_{i+1} denote the query in which the first element is appended to FList. In the case of $\mathcal{O}^{0,i+1}$, this corresponds to the query in which the $(i+1)$-th element is appended to List. The difference between these oracles is the behaviour when receiving Q_{i+1}. Let $(w_{0,i+1}, w_{1,i+1})$ be the pair of keywords corresponding to Q_{i+1}.

Let E denote the event that $(w_{0,i+1}, w_{1,i+1})$ has not been queried both to the ciphertext oracle and the trapdoor oracle throughout the game. In the case of $\neg E$, queries of the form $(w_{0,i+1}, \cdot)$ except $(w_{0,i+1}, w_{1,i+1})$ are not allowed. Thus, seen from the outside, $\mathcal{O}^{0,i}$ and $\mathcal{O}^{0,i+1}$ behave in the same way. It follows that for any PPT adversary $\mathcal{A}$,

$$\Pr[1 \leftarrow \mathcal{A}^{\mathcal{O}^{0,i}}(1^\lambda) \wedge \neg E] = \Pr[1 \leftarrow \mathcal{A}^{\mathcal{O}^{0,i+1}}(1^\lambda) \wedge \neg E].$$

E can be divided into two cases: E_1 and E_2. E_1 denotes the case that $(w_{0,i+1}, w_{1,i+1})$ has been queried only to the ciphertext oracle. E_2 denotes the case that $(w_{0,i+1}, w_{1,i+1})$ has been queried only to the trapdoor oracle.

By symmetry, we consider the case of E_1. Then, trapdoor queries of the form $(w_{0,i+1}, \cdot)$ are not allowed. Let $\mathcal{O}^{0,i+1/3}$ denote the oracle constructed by modifying $\mathcal{O}^{0,i}$ in the following way:

For Q_{i+1} or ciphertext queries of the form $\mathsf{input} = (w_{0,i+1}, \cdot)$ after Q_{i+1},
1. If $(\mathsf{input}, M) \in \mathsf{List}$ for some $M \in \mathbb{F}^{d_1 \times d_2}$, it returns (x, Mx) where $x \leftarrow \eta_2$.
2. Otherwise, it returns $(x, u) \leftarrow \eta_2 \times \mathrm{Unif}(\mathbb{F}^{d_1})$.

In addition, let $\mathcal{O}^{0,2/3}$ be the oracle defined by applying the above modification only to Q_{i+1}.

When considering $\mathcal{O}^i$, the responses to the ciphertext queries on $(w_{0,i+1}, \cdot)$ that are not in List are summarized in Table 2. Q^+_{i+1} denotes the next such ciphertext query of Q_{i+1} that satisfies $\mathsf{input} \neq (w_{0,i+1}, w_{1,i+1})$. $\mathsf{List}(\cdot)$ denotes M such that $(\cdot, M) \in \mathsf{List}$, and $\mathsf{FList}(\cdot)$ denotes M such that $(\cdot, M) \in \mathsf{FList}$. "Random" means that the oracle returns a sample from $\eta_2 \times \mathrm{Unif}(\mathbb{F}^{d_1})$.

In the case of $\mathcal{O}^i$, let $x_1, x_2, \ldots, x_k$ ($k \le Q_{\mathsf{ct}}$) be the set of x sampled in such queries. Since $x_1, x_2, \ldots, x_k$ are linearly independent with an overwhelming probability,

$$([x_1|x_2|\cdots|x_k], \mathsf{FList}(w_{0,i+1}) \cdot [x_1|x_2|\cdots|x_k])$$

Table 2. Responses to ciphertext queries on $(w_{0,i+1}, \cdot)$ that are not in List

	Q_{i+1}	Q_{i+1}^{+}	Others	
$\mathcal{O}^{i}$	○ uses $\mathsf{FList}(w_{0,i+1})$	uses $\mathsf{FList}(w_{0,i+1})$	uses $\mathsf{FList}(w_{0,i+1})$	
$\mathcal{O}^{i+1/3}$	random	random	random	
$\mathcal{O}^{i+2/3}$	random	○ uses $\mathsf{FList}(w_{0,i+1})$	random	(1)
			uses $\mathsf{FList}(w_{0,i+1})$	(2)
$\mathcal{O}^{i+1}$	○ uses $\mathsf{List}(\mathsf{input})$	○ uses $\mathsf{FList}(w_{0,i+1})$	uses $\mathsf{List}(\mathsf{input})$	(1)
			uses $\mathsf{FList}(w_{0,i+1})$	(2)

(1) Cases that $\mathsf{input} = (w_{0,i+1}, w_{1,i+1})$ (2) Otherwise
○ The oracle samples M and appends it to List or FList.

is statistically close to the distribution $\eta_2^k \times \mathrm{Unif}(\mathbb{F}^{d_1 \times k})$. Since $\mathsf{FList}(w_{0,i+1})$ is independent of the other view of $\mathcal{A}$, we have

$$|\Pr[1 \leftarrow \mathcal{A}^{\mathcal{O}^{0,i}}(1^\lambda) \wedge E_1] - \Pr[1 \leftarrow \mathcal{A}^{\mathcal{O}^{0,i+1/3}}(1^\lambda) \wedge E_1]| = \mathsf{negl}(\lambda).$$

In the same way, we have

$$|\Pr[1 \leftarrow \mathcal{A}^{\mathcal{O}^{0,i+(t-1)/3}}(1^\lambda) \wedge E_1] - \Pr[1 \leftarrow \mathcal{A}^{\mathcal{O}^{0,i+t/3}}(1^\lambda) \wedge E_1]| = \mathsf{negl}(\lambda)$$

for each $t = 2, 3$. Since this property holds also for E_2, we have

$$|\Pr[1 \leftarrow \mathcal{A}^{\mathcal{O}^{0,i}}(1^\lambda)] - \Pr[1 \leftarrow \mathcal{A}^{\mathcal{O}^{0,i+1}}(1^\lambda)]| = \mathsf{negl}(\lambda).$$

Therefore,

$$\left|\Pr[1 \leftarrow \mathcal{A}^{\mathcal{O}_{\mathsf{K}}^{0}}(1^\lambda)] - \Pr[1 \leftarrow \mathcal{A}^{\mathcal{O}^{\mathsf{M}}}(1^\lambda)]\right| \leq 2\mathsf{Adv}_{\mathcal{B},F}^{\mathsf{PRF}}(\lambda) + \mathsf{negl}(\lambda)$$

and this completes the proof.

4 Pairing-Based PSSE with Full Security

In this section, we propose an PSSE construction based on pairings, which we write as $\mathsf{PSSE2}$. Full security is reduced to the uniform MDDH assumption.

4.1 Construction

Let $\mathcal{G}$ be a bilinear group generation algorithm and k be a positive integer. For simplicity of description, we assume that the group order p can be regarded as a deterministic function of the security parameter λ. Let $\mathcal{W}$ denote the keyword space and $F : \mathcal{K} \times \mathcal{W} \to \mathbb{Z}_p^{k \times k}$ be a pseudorandom function. The construction of $\mathsf{PSSE2}$ is as follows:

- $\mathsf{KeyGen}(1^\lambda)$:
  1. Runs $\mathbb{G} := (p, G_1, G_2, G_T, g_1, g_2, e) \leftarrow \mathcal{G}(1^\lambda)$.

2. Samples $\mathsf{K} \xleftarrow{\$} \mathcal{K}$.
3. Outputs the public parameter $\mathbb{G}$ and the secret key K.

- $\mathsf{Enc}(\mathsf{K}, w)$: Samples $x \xleftarrow{\$} \mathbb{Z}_p^k$ and outputs $(c_1, c_2) := ([x]_1, [F_{\mathsf{K}}(w)x]_1)$.
- $\mathsf{Trapdoor}(\mathsf{K}, w)$: Samples $y \xleftarrow{\$} \mathbb{Z}_p^k$ and outputs $(t_1, t_2) := ([y]_2, [F_{\mathsf{K}}(w)^\top y]_2)$.
- $\mathsf{Test}((t_1, t_2), (c_1, c_2))$: Outputs 1 if $e(c_1^\top, t_2) = e(c_2^\top, t_1)$, otherwise outputs 0.

k determines the underlying assumption of $\mathsf{PSSE2}$.

4.2 Properties

It is easy to see that $\mathsf{PSSE2}$ satisfies correctness. In fact, if a ciphertext (c_1, c_2) and a trapdoor (t_1, t_2) are associated with the same keyword w,

$$e(c_1^\top, t_2) = \left[x^\top F_{\mathsf{K}}(w)^\top y\right]_T = e(c_2^\top, t_1).$$

Consistency follows from the pseudorandomness of F.

Theorem 3. $\mathsf{PSSE2}$ *is consistent provided that F is pseudorandom.*

Proof. Suppose that the consistency adversary outputs (w, w') where $w \neq w'$. For $(c_1, c_2) \leftarrow \mathsf{Enc}(\mathsf{K}, w)$ and $(t_1, t_2) \leftarrow \mathsf{Trapdoor}(\mathsf{K}, w')$,

$$e(c_1^\top, t_2)/e(c_2^\top, t_1) = \left[x^\top (F_{\mathsf{K}}(w') - F_{\mathsf{K}}(w))^\top y\right]_T$$

holds. By the pseudorandomness of F, it is sufficient to show that

$$\Pr\left[x, y \xleftarrow{\$} \mathbb{Z}_p^k; M \xleftarrow{\$} \mathbb{Z}_p^{k \times k} : x^\top M y = 0\right]$$

is negligible. Since $x, y \neq 0$ with an overwhelming probability, the probability that $x^\top M y = 0$ is negligible. $\square$

Full security follows from the pseudorandomness of F and the U_k-MDDH assumption.

Theorem 4. $\mathsf{PSSE2}$ *is fully secure provided that F is pseudorandom and the U_k-MDDH assumption holds. Namely, for any PPT adversary $\mathcal{A}$ that makes at most Q queries, there exist PPT algorithms $\mathcal{B}_1, \mathcal{B}_2, \mathcal{B}_3$ such that*

$$\mathsf{Adv}^{\mathsf{Full}}_{\mathcal{A},\mathsf{PSSE2}}(\lambda) \leq 2\mathsf{Adv}^{\mathsf{PRF}}_{\mathcal{B}_1,F}(\lambda) + 6Q\left(\mathsf{Adv}^{U_k\text{-}\mathsf{MDDH}}_{1,\mathcal{B}_2}(\lambda) + \mathsf{Adv}^{U_k\text{-}\mathsf{MDDH}}_{2,\mathcal{B}_3}(\lambda)\right) + \mathsf{negl}(\lambda).$$

The proof is given in Appendix B.1.

5 Lattice-Based PSSE with Full Security

In this section, we propose PSSE constructions with full security based on lattices. First, we describe an LWE-based construction, which we write as $\mathsf{PSSE3}\text{-}\mathsf{L}$. Then, we show that the RLWE-based scheme $\mathsf{PSSE3}\text{-}\mathsf{R}$ can be constructed in the same way. Finally, we propose an NTRU-based construction $\mathsf{PSSE4}$, which is more efficient than the (R)LWE-based schemes.

5.1 Revisiting Coset Sampleability

For constructing PSSE, we use an n-coset sampleable distribution η on $\mathbb{Z}_q^k$ that outputs short vectors. Boneh et al. [11] proposed two examples of such distributions.

In the first example, η is the uniform distribution on $\{0,1\}^k$ where $k = n\lceil \log q \rceil$. q is restricted to a power of 2 if q is polynomially bounded. In the second example, η is a discrete Gaussian distribution with the deviation σ where $k = \Omega(n \log q)$ and $\sigma = \Omega(\sqrt{n \log q})$.

In both of these cases, $k \geq n \log q$ holds. We propose a generalized construction of the first example. For an integer $d(\lambda) \geq 2$, we define n-coset sampleable distributions η_d with the dimension $k = dn$ as follows. Let $q_0 = \lceil q^{1/d} \rceil$.

- $\mathsf{MatrixGen}(1^\lambda)$: It outputs

$$M = \left[q_0^{d-1} I_n | q_0^{d-2} I_n | \cdots | I_n\right] \in \mathbb{Z}_q^{n \times k}$$

  and auxiliary data $T = \emptyset$.
- $\mathsf{SamplePre}(z \in \mathbb{Z}_q^n, M, T)$: It treats z as $z \in (-q/2, q/2]^n$ and sets $y_{d-1} = \lfloor z/q_0^{d-1} \rceil$, $z_{d-1} = z - q_0^{d-1} y_{d-1}$. Then, it inductively sets $y_i = \lfloor z_{i+1}/q_0^i \rceil$ and $z_i = z_{i+1} - q_0^i y_i$ for $i = d-2, \ldots, 0$. Finally, it outputs $[y_{d-1}; \cdots; y_0] \in [-q_0/2, q_0/2]^k$.

5.2 LWE-Based Construction

Let $m(\lambda), q(\lambda), \kappa_{\mathsf{td}}(\lambda), \kappa_{\mathsf{ct}}(\lambda)$ be positive integers such that $\kappa_{\mathsf{td}} \kappa_{\mathsf{ct}} = \omega(\log \lambda)$. Let $\chi(\lambda)$ be an error distribution on $\mathbb{Z}_q$ and $\eta(\lambda)$ be a distribution that outputs short vectors. Let $\mathcal{W}$ denote the keyword space and $F : \mathcal{K} \times \mathcal{W} \rightarrow \mathbb{Z}_q^{m \times m}$ be a pseudorandom function. The construction of $\mathsf{PSSE3\text{-}L}$ is as follows:

- $\mathsf{KeyGen}(1^\lambda)$:
  1. Samples $\mathsf{K} \xleftarrow{\$} \mathcal{K}$.
  2. Outputs the secret key K.
- $\mathsf{Enc}(\mathsf{K}, w)$:
  1. Samples $c_j \leftarrow \eta$ and $x_j \leftarrow \chi^m$ for $j = 1, \ldots, \kappa_{\mathsf{ct}}$.
  2. Computes $d_j = F_{\mathsf{K}}(w) c_j + x_j$ for each j.
  3. Outputs $\{c_j, d_j\}_{j=1}^{\kappa_{\mathsf{ct}}}$.
- $\mathsf{Trapdoor}(\mathsf{K}, w)$:
  1. Samples $t_i \leftarrow \eta$ and $y_i \leftarrow \chi^m$ for $i = 1, \ldots, \kappa_{\mathsf{td}}$.
  2. Computes $u_i = F_{\mathsf{K}}(w)^\top t_i + y_i$ for each i.
  3. Outputs $\{t_i, u_i\}_{i=1}^{\kappa_{\mathsf{td}}}$.
- $\mathsf{Test}(\{t_i, u_i\}_{i=1}^{\kappa_{\mathsf{td}}}, \{c_j, d_j\}_{j=1}^{\kappa_{\mathsf{ct}}})$:
  1. Computes $\alpha_{i,j} = c_j^\top u_i - d_j^\top t_i \in \mathbb{Z}_q$ for each $(i,j) \in [1, \kappa_{\mathsf{td}}] \times [1, \kappa_{\mathsf{ct}}]$.
  2. Treats $\alpha_{i,j}$ as an integer in $(-q/2, q/2]$. Outputs 1 if $-\lfloor q/4 \rfloor < \alpha_{i,j} < \lfloor q/4 \rfloor$ for every (i,j), otherwise outputs 0.

5.3 Properties

First, we consider correctness of PSSE3-L. Suppose that $\{t_i, u_i\}_{i=1}^{\kappa_{\mathsf{td}}}$ and $\{c_j, d_j\}_{j=1}^{\kappa_{\mathsf{ct}}}$ are generated from the same keyword. Then, for any (i,j), $|\alpha_{i,j}| = |c_j^\top y_i - x_j^\top t_i|$ holds. This value is relatively small, so this scheme can achieve correctness in appropriate parameter settings.

For example, consider the case that $\eta = \eta_2$ and $m = 2n$. In order that the worst-case to average-case reduction works, let χ be the discrete Gaussian with the deviation $\sigma = \Theta(\sqrt{n})$. Correctness holds if

$$q = \sqrt{2n} q_0 \sigma \cdot \omega(\sqrt{\log n}).$$

Thus, when $q = \omega(n^2 \log n)$, our scheme is correct. As another example, when $\eta = \eta_{\lceil \log q \rceil}$, smaller $q = \omega(n \log n)$ can be used. However, since m is large in this example, η_2 seems to be more attractive in terms of efficiency.

Consistency and full security follow from the pseudorandomness of F and the NLWE assumption. By Lemma 3, if η is n-coset sampleable, this NLWE assumption follows from the LWE assumption with the dimension n.

Theorem 5. PSSE3-L *is consistent provided that F is pseudorandom and the (m, q, χ, η)-NLWE assumption holds.*

Proof. By the pseudorandomness of F and the (m, q, χ, η)-NLWE assumption, it is sufficient to show that

$$\begin{aligned} \Pr[c_j \leftarrow \eta, d_j \xleftarrow{\$} \mathbb{Z}_q^m \text{ for } j = 1, \ldots, \kappa_{\mathsf{ct}};\\ t_i \leftarrow \eta, u_i \xleftarrow{\$} \mathbb{Z}_q^m \text{ for } i = 1, \ldots, \kappa_{\mathsf{td}} :\\ 1 \leftarrow \mathsf{Test}(\{t_i, u_i\}_{i=1}^{\kappa_{\mathsf{td}}}, \{c_j, d_j\}_{j=1}^{\kappa_{\mathsf{ct}}})] \end{aligned}$$

is negligible. Let $z_{i,j} \leftarrow \chi$ for each $(i,j) \in [1, \kappa_{\mathsf{td}}] \times [1, \kappa_{\mathsf{ct}}]$. Then, by the (m, q, χ, η)-NLWE assumption and the hybrid argument, $\{c_j^\top u_i + z_{i,j}\}_{i,j}$ is computationally indistinguishable from random. Moreover, since d_j, u_i are independent of $c_j, u_i, z_{i,j}$, $\{c_j^\top u_i - d_j^\top t_i + z_{i,j}\}_{i,j}$ is also computationally indistinguishable from random. Suppose that the output of χ is in $[-E, E]$ with an overwhelming probability. If Test outputs 1, $|c_j^\top u_i - d_j^\top t_i + z_{i,j}| < q/4 + E$ holds for any (i,j). Thus, this probability is bounded above by $(1/2 + 2E/q)^{\kappa_{\mathsf{td}}\kappa_{\mathsf{ct}}} + \mathsf{negl}(\lambda)$. When κ_{td} and κ_{ct} are large enough that $\kappa_{\mathsf{td}}\kappa_{\mathsf{ct}} = \omega(\log \lambda)$, PSSE3-L is consistent. □

Theorem 6. PSSE3-L *is fully secure provided that F is pseudorandom and the (m, q, χ, η)-NLWE assumption holds. Namely, for any PPT adversary $\mathcal{A}$ that makes at most Q queries, there exist PPT algorithms $\mathcal{B}_1, \mathcal{B}_2$ such that*

$$\mathsf{Adv}^{\mathsf{Full}}_{\mathcal{A},\mathsf{PSSE3\text{-}L}}(\lambda) \leq 2\mathsf{Adv}^{\mathsf{PRF}}_{\mathcal{B}_1,F}(\lambda) + 12mQ \cdot \mathsf{Adv}^{\mathsf{NLWE}_{m,\kappa Q,q,\chi,\eta}}_{\mathcal{B}_2}(\lambda)$$

where $\kappa := \max\{\kappa_{\mathsf{td}}, \kappa_{\mathsf{ct}}\}$.

The proof is given in Appendix B.2.

5.4 RLWE-Based Construction

We can construct the RLWE-based variant PSSE3-R of PSSE3-L in the same way. Let $k(\lambda)$ be a positive integer. Let $\chi(\lambda)$ be an error distribution on $\mathcal{R}_q$ and $\eta(\lambda)$ be a distribution on $\mathcal{R}_q^k$ that outputs short vectors. Let $\mathcal{W}$ denote the keyword space and $F : \mathcal{K} \times \mathcal{W} \rightarrow \mathcal{R}_q^{k\times k}$ be a pseudorandom function. The construction of PSSE3-R is as follows:

- $\mathsf{KeyGen}(1^\lambda)$:
  1. Samples $\mathsf{K} \xleftarrow{\$} \mathcal{K}$.
  2. Outputs the secret key K.
- $\mathsf{Enc}(\mathsf{K}, w)$:
  1. Samples $c \leftarrow \eta$ and $x \leftarrow \chi^k$.
  2. Computes $d = F_{\mathsf{K}}(w)c + x$.
  3. Outputs (c, d).
- $\mathsf{Trapdoor}(\mathsf{K}, w)$:
  1. Samples $t \leftarrow \eta$ and $y \leftarrow \chi^k$.
  2. Computes $u = F_{\mathsf{K}}(w)^\top t + y$.
  3. Outputs (t, u).
- $\mathsf{Test}((t, u), (c, d))$:
  1. Computes $\alpha = c^\top u - d^\top t \in \mathcal{R}_q$.
  2. Treats the coefficients of α as integers in $(-q/2, q/2]$. Outputs 1 if they are in $(-\lfloor q/4 \rfloor, \lfloor q/4 \rfloor)$ for $\Theta(\lambda)$ coefficients in a fixed position, otherwise outputs 0. Note that $N > \lambda$ holds for practical RLWE parameters.

Lemma 3 holds also for the RLWE setting. Thus, for appropriate k (e.g. $k = 2$) and η, full security of this scheme is reduced to the RLWE assumption. See the full version for the details.

5.5 NTRU-Based Construction

We construct the NTRU-based scheme PSSE4. Let $\chi(\lambda)$ be a distribution on $\mathcal{R}_q$ that outputs polnomials with small coefficients. Let $\mathcal{W}$ denote the keyword space and $F : \mathcal{K} \times \mathcal{W} \rightarrow \mathcal{R}_q^\times$ be a pseudorandom function. The construction of PSSE4 is as follows:

- $\mathsf{KeyGen}(1^\lambda)$:
  1. Samples $\mathsf{K} \xleftarrow{\$} \mathcal{K}$.
  2. Outputs the secret key K.
- $\mathsf{Enc}(\mathsf{K}, w)$:
  1. Samples $a \leftarrow \chi$.
  2. Outputs $c = a \cdot F_{\mathsf{K}}(w)$.
- $\mathsf{Trapdoor}(\mathsf{K}, w)$:
  1. Samples $b \leftarrow \chi$.
  2. Outputs $t = b \cdot F_{\mathsf{K}}(w)^{-1}$.
- $\mathsf{Test}(t, c)$:
  1. Computes $\alpha = c \cdot t \in \mathcal{R}_q$.

2. Treats the coefficients of α as integers in $(-q/2, q/2]$. Outputs 1 if they are in $(-\lfloor q/4 \rfloor, \lfloor q/4 \rfloor)$ for $\Theta(\lambda)$ coefficients in a fixed position, otherwise outputs 0.

If c and t are generated from the same keyword, $ct = ab$ has relatively small coefficients since $a, b \leftarrow \chi$. For example, when χ is distributed on $[-p(\lambda), p(\lambda)]$, the negative false does not occur if we set $q > 4Np(\lambda)^2$. Note that the function p should be $\omega(1)$ to prevent a recent attack [8].

If c and t are generated from different keywords, $(c, t) \in \mathcal{R}_q \times \mathcal{R}_q$ is indistinguishable from uniform by the NTRU assumption. The RLWE assumption ensures that ct is relatively close to uniform, as in the case of PSSE3-R.

Full security follows from the pseudorandomness of F and the (N, q, χ)-NTRU assumption. For any PPT adversary $\mathcal{A}$ of PSSE4 that makes at most Q queries, there exist PPT algorithms $\mathcal{B}_1, \mathcal{B}_2$ such that

$$\mathsf{Adv}^{\mathsf{Full}}_{\mathcal{A},\mathsf{PSSE4}}(\lambda) \leq 2\mathsf{Adv}^{\mathsf{PRF}}_{\mathcal{B}_1,F}(\lambda) + 12Q \cdot \mathsf{Adv}^{\mathsf{NTRU}_{N,Q,q,\chi}}_{\mathcal{B}_2}(\lambda).$$

The proof is the same as that of the other constructions, but note that NTRU instances can be converted to "the ciphertext/trapdoor form" in the proof. Let h be an NTRU instance and $h' = hr$ where $r \xleftarrow{\$} \mathcal{R}_q^\times$. If $h = f^{-1}g$, $h' = (f^{-1}r)g$ where $f^{-1}r$ is uniformly random in $\mathcal{R}_q^\times$. If h is uniformly random, h' is also uniformly random.

6 Analysis of Existing Schemes

First, we analyze the Cheng et al. PAEKS scheme [15]. This scheme is essentially the combination of NIKE and PSSE, so we focus on the PSSE part. It has been unknown whether the PSSE part is secure since Li and Boyen [26] pointed out that the original proof is not correct. We simplify and generalize this scheme. Then, we show that full security is reduced to the bilateral DLin assumption.

Second, we show that the Li-Boyen pairing-based PSSE [26] is not trapdoor-private, not as claimed.

6.1 Simplifying Cheng et al. PSSE Scheme

We propose a simplified version of the Cheng et al. scheme, which we write as CPSSE. For the details of the simplification, see the full version of this paper.

Let $F : \mathcal{K} \times \mathcal{W} \to \mathbb{Z}_p$ be a pseudorandom function. In the original scheme, the symmetric bilinear map is used. In this paper, we generalize it to the bilinear map $e : G_1 \times G_2 \to G_T$ where $G_1 = G_2$ does not necessarily hold.

- $\mathsf{KeyGen}(1^\lambda)$:
  1. Runs the bilinear group generation algorithm $\mathbb{G} = (p, G_1, G_2, G_T, g_1, g_2, e) \leftarrow \mathcal{G}(1^\lambda)$.
  2. Samples $x, y \xleftarrow{\$} \mathbb{Z}_p$.

3. Samples $\mathsf{K} \xleftarrow{\$} \mathcal{K}$.
4. Outputs the public parameter $\mathbb{G}$ and the secret key $\mathsf{K}' = (\mathsf{K}, x, y)$.

- $\mathsf{Enc}(\mathsf{K}', w)$: Samples $r_1, r_2 \xleftarrow{\$} \mathbb{Z}_p$ and outputs a ciphertext (C_1, C_2, C_3, C_4) where

$$C_1 = g_1^{F_{\mathsf{K}}(w)r_1 + yr_2},\ C_2 = g_1^{xr_1},\ C_3 = g_1^{r_2},\ C_4 = g_1^{r_1}.$$

- $\mathsf{Trapdoor}(\mathsf{K}', w)$: Samples $s_1, s_2 \xleftarrow{\$} \mathbb{Z}_p$ and outputs a trapdoor (T_1, T_2, T_3, T_4) where

$$T_1 = g_2^{F_{\mathsf{K}}(w)s_1 + xs_2},\ T_2 = g_2^{ys_1},\ T_3 = g_2^{s_2},\ T_4 = g_2^{s_1}.$$

- $\mathsf{Test}((T_1, T_2, T_3, T_4), (C_1, C_2, C_3, C_4))$: Outputs 1 if $e(C_1, T_4) \cdot e(C_2, T_3) = e(C_4, T_1) \cdot e(C_3, T_2)$, otherwise outputs 0.

Note that instead of setting (x, y) as a part of the secret key, we can set $(g_1^x, g_1^y, g_2^x, g_2^y)$ as a part of the public parameter.

Let $G_{\mathsf{K}'} : \mathcal{W} \to \mathbb{Z}_p^{2\times 2}$ denote the function defined by

$$G_{\mathsf{K}'}(w) := \begin{pmatrix} F_{\mathsf{K}}(w) & y \\ x & 0 \end{pmatrix}.$$

Using $G_{\mathsf{K}'}$, ciphertexts and the trapdoors can be written in the similar form to $\mathsf{PSSE2}$ based on the $\mathcal{U}_2$-MDDH assumption.

- Ciphertext: $([r]_1, [G_{\mathsf{K}'}(w)r]_1)$ where $r \xleftarrow{\$} \mathbb{Z}_p^2$.
- Trapdoor: $([s]_2, [G_{\mathsf{K}'}(w)^\top s]_2)$ where $s \xleftarrow{\$} \mathbb{Z}_p^2$.

Compared to $\mathcal{U}_2$-MDDH-based $\mathsf{PSSE2}$, the ciphertext size and the trapdoor size is the same. The advantage is the improved computational cost due to the smaller range of F. The disadvantage is that the security is reduced to a stronger assumption.

Correctness and consistency can be easily proved in the same way as $\mathsf{PSSE2}$. We analyze the security of CPSSE. In the (bil-)$\mathcal{U}_2$-MDDH assumption, the matrix distribution is $\mathrm{Unif}(\mathbb{Z}_p^{3\times 2})$. In the (bil-)DLin assumption, the matrix distribution is

$$A = \begin{pmatrix} a_1 & 0 \\ 0 & a_2 \\ 1 & 1 \end{pmatrix} \text{ where } a_1, a_2 \xleftarrow{\$} \mathbb{Z}_p\,.$$

Full security of CPSSE is reduced to the bil-MDDH assumption such that the matrix distribution is

$$\begin{pmatrix} b_1 & b_2 \\ b_3 & b_4 \\ 0 & 1 \end{pmatrix} \text{ where } b_1, b_2, b_3, b_4 \xleftarrow{\$} \mathbb{Z}_p,$$

which we write as $\mathcal{V}_2$ in this paper. We show that the (bil-)DLin assumption implies the (bil-)$\mathcal{V}_2$-MDDH assumption using the MDDH reduction method [20].

Let L, R be the matrices defined as

$$L = \begin{pmatrix} 1 & 0 & l_1 \\ 0 & 1 & l_2 \\ 0 & 0 & 1 \end{pmatrix} \quad \text{where } l_1, l_2 \xleftarrow{\$} \mathbb{Z}_p, \quad R = \begin{pmatrix} 1 & 0 \\ -1 & 1 \end{pmatrix}.$$

For a bil-DLin instance $([A]_1, [z]_1, [A]_2, [z]_2)$, the distribution of LAR is V_2 since

$$LAR = \begin{pmatrix} a_1 & l_1 \\ -a_2 & a_2 + l_2 \\ 0 & 1 \end{pmatrix}.$$

By the invertibility of R, $([LAR]_1, [LAz]_1, [LAR]_2, [LAz]_2)$ is a bil-V_2-MDDH instance. Thus, the (bil-)DLin assumption implies the (bil-)V_2-MDDH assumption.

Theorem 7. *The modified Cheng et al. PSSE scheme* CPSSE *is fully secure provided that F is pseudorandom and the bil-V_2-MDDH assumption holds.*

The proof is given in Appendix B.3.

This scheme can be generalized to the constructions based on the bilateral k-Lin assumption by setting $F : \mathcal{K} \times \mathcal{W} \to \mathbb{Z}_p^{(k-1)\times(k-1)}$, $x, y \xleftarrow{\$} \mathbb{Z}_p^k$, and

$$G_{\mathsf{K}'}(w) := \begin{pmatrix} F_{\mathsf{K}}(w) & y \\ x^\top & 0 \end{pmatrix}.$$

6.2 Attack on Li-Boyen Pairing-Based Scheme

First, we describe the algorithms of the Li-Boyen pairing-based scheme [26]. Let $F : \mathcal{K} \times \mathcal{W} \to \mathbb{Z}_p$ be a pseudorandom function.

- $\mathsf{KeyGen}(1^\lambda)$:
  1. Runs $\mathbb{G} := (p, G_1, G_2, G_T, g_1, g_2, e) \leftarrow \mathcal{G}(1^\lambda)$.
  2. Samples $z \xleftarrow{\$} \mathbb{Z}_p$ and sets $u_1 = g_1^z$, $u_2 = g_2^z$.
  3. Samples $h_2 \xleftarrow{\$} G_2$.
  4. Samples $\mathsf{K} \xleftarrow{\$} \mathcal{K}$.
  5. Outputs the public parameter $(\mathbb{G}, u_1, u_2, h_2)$ and the secret key K.
- $\mathsf{Enc}(\mathsf{K}, w)$: Samples $s \xleftarrow{\$} \mathbb{Z}_p$ and outputs $(c_1, c_2, c_3) := (e(g_1, h_2)^{F_{\mathsf{K}}(w)\cdot s}, u_1^s, g_1^s)$.
- $\mathsf{Trapdoor}(\mathsf{K}, w)$: Samples $r \xleftarrow{\$} \mathbb{Z}_p$ and outputs $(t_1, t_2) := \left(h_2^{F_{\mathsf{K}}(w)} u_2^r, g_2^r\right)$.
- $\mathsf{Test}((t_1, t_2), (c_1, c_2, c_3))$: Outputs 1 if $e(c_3, t_1) = c_1 \cdot e(c_2, t_2)$, otherwise outputs 0.

They claimed that its ciphertext privacy can be reduced to the DBDH assumption, and its trapdoor privacy can be reduced to the DDH assumption on G_2 (See Appendix A for the definitions of ciphertext/trapdoor privacy). However, incorrect DDH definition is used in the proof, and trapdoor privacy can be broken in the following way.

Theorem 8. *The Li-Boyen pairing-based PSSE does not satisfy trapdoor privacy.*

Proof. The adversary chooses arbitrary challenge keywords w_0^*, w_1^* $(w_0^* \neq w_1^*)$ and receives a challenge trapdoor $(t_1^*, t_2^*) = \left(h_2^{F_\mathsf{K}(w_b^*)} u_2^{r^*}, g_2^{r^*}\right)$ where $b \xleftarrow{\$} \{0,1\}$. In addition, the adversary receives a trapdoor $(t_1, t_2) = \left(h_2^{F_\mathsf{K}(w_0^*)} u_2^r, g_2^r\right)$ of w_0^* and a ciphertext $(c_1, c_2, c_3) = \left(e(g_1, h_2)^{F_\mathsf{K}(w) \cdot s}, u_1^s, g_1^s\right)$ of an arbitrary keyword w $(w \notin \{w_0^*, w_1^*\})$. Then, we have $e(c_3, t_1^*)/e(c_2, t_2^*) = e(g_1, h_2)^{F_\mathsf{K}(w_b^*) \cdot s}$ and $e(c_3, t_1)/e(c_2, t_2) = e(g_1, h_2)^{F_\mathsf{K}(w_0^*) \cdot s}$. By checking whether they are equal, the adversary can guess whether $b = 0$ with an overwhelming probability. □

In this attack, (u_1, g_1) can be used instead of (c_2, c_3). However, we used (c_2, c_3) to indicate that keeping (u_1, g_1) as secret in this scheme does not affect the proof.

A Supplementary Definitions

We describe the definitions of ciphertext privacy and trapdoor privacy. Note that full security implies both of them.

Let $\mathcal{O}_{\mathsf{ct}}(\mathsf{K}, \cdot)$ be the oracle that outputs $C \leftarrow \mathsf{Enc}(\mathsf{K}, w)$ given a keyword w as input. Let $\mathcal{O}_{\mathsf{td}}(\mathsf{K}, \cdot)$ be the oracle that outputs $T \leftarrow \mathsf{Trapdoor}(\mathsf{K}, w)$ given a keyword w as input.

Definition 9 (Ciphertext Privacy). *We say that an PSSE scheme is ciphertext-private if for any PPT algorithm $\mathcal{A}$, the advantage*

$$\Big| \Pr[(\mathsf{pp}, \mathsf{K}) \leftarrow \mathsf{KeyGen}(1^\lambda); (w_0^*, w_1^*, \mathsf{st}) \leftarrow \mathcal{A}^{\mathcal{O}_{\mathsf{ct}}(\mathsf{K},\cdot), \mathcal{O}_{\mathsf{td}}(\mathsf{K},\cdot)}(\mathsf{find}, \mathsf{pp});$$

$$b \xleftarrow{\$} \{0,1\}; C^* \leftarrow \mathsf{Enc}(\mathsf{K}, w_b^*); b' \leftarrow \mathcal{A}^{\mathcal{O}_{\mathsf{ct}}(\mathsf{K},\cdot), \mathcal{O}_{\mathsf{td}}(\mathsf{K},\cdot)}(\mathsf{guess}, \mathsf{st}, C^*) : b = b'] - \frac{1}{2} \Big|$$

is negligible in λ. The challenge keyword w_0^*, w_1^* cannot be input to $\mathcal{O}_{\mathsf{td}}(\mathsf{K}, \cdot)$.

Definition 10 (Trapdoor Privacy). *We say that an PSSE scheme is trapdoor-private if for any PPT algorithm $\mathcal{A}$, the advantage*

$$\Big| \Pr[(\mathsf{pp}, \mathsf{K}) \leftarrow \mathsf{KeyGen}(1^\lambda); (w_0^*, w_1^*, \mathsf{st}) \leftarrow \mathcal{A}^{\mathcal{O}_{\mathsf{ct}}(\mathsf{K},\cdot), \mathcal{O}_{\mathsf{td}}(\mathsf{K},\cdot)}(\mathsf{find}, \mathsf{pp});$$

$$b \xleftarrow{\$} \{0,1\}; T^* \leftarrow \mathsf{Trapdoor}(\mathsf{K}, w_b^*); b' \leftarrow \mathcal{A}^{\mathcal{O}_{\mathsf{ct}}(\mathsf{K},\cdot), \mathcal{O}_{\mathsf{td}}(\mathsf{K},\cdot)}(\mathsf{guess}, \mathsf{st}, T^*) : b = b'] - \frac{1}{2} \Big|$$

is negligible in λ. The challenge keyword w_0^*, w_1^* cannot be input to $\mathcal{O}_{\mathsf{ct}}(\mathsf{K}, \cdot)$.

B Supplementary Proofs

B.1 Proof of Theorem 4

Let Q be an upper bound of the number of queries. We define the oracles $\mathcal{O}^0_{\mathsf{K}}$, $\mathcal{O}^{0,t/3}(t = 0, 1, \ldots, 3Q)$ and the events E, E_1, E_2 in the same way as the proof of Theorem 2.

First, there exists a PPT algorithm $\mathcal{B}_1$ such that

$$\left|\Pr[1 \leftarrow \mathcal{A}^{\mathcal{O}^0_{\mathsf{K}}}(1^\lambda)] - \Pr[1 \leftarrow \mathcal{A}^{\mathcal{O}^0}(1^\lambda)]\right| \leq 2\mathsf{Adv}^{\mathsf{PRF}}_{\mathcal{B}_1,F}(\lambda).$$

Then, we evaluate the computational difference between $\mathcal{O}^{0,i}$ and $\mathcal{O}^{0,i+1}$ for $i = 0, 1, \ldots, Q-1$. We have

$$\Pr[1 \leftarrow \mathcal{A}^{\mathcal{O}^{0,i}}(1^\lambda) \wedge \neg E] = \Pr[1 \leftarrow \mathcal{A}^{\mathcal{O}^{0,i+1}}(1^\lambda) \wedge \neg E],$$

so we consider the case of E_1 by symmetry. By treating $\mathsf{FList}(w_{0,i+1})$ as the k-instance MDDH secret, it follows that there exists a PPT algorithm $\mathcal{B}_{2,1}$ such that

$$\left|\Pr[1 \leftarrow \mathcal{A}^{\mathcal{O}^{0,i}}(1^\lambda) \wedge E_1] - \Pr[1 \leftarrow \mathcal{A}^{\mathcal{O}^{0,i+1/3}}(1^\lambda) \wedge E_1]\right| \leq 2\mathsf{Adv}^{\mathcal{U}_k\text{-}\mathsf{MDDH}_k}_{1,\mathcal{B}_{2,1}}(\lambda).$$

Similarly, there exist PPT algorithms $\mathcal{B}_{2,t}$ $(t = 2, 3)$ such that

$$\left|\Pr[1 \leftarrow \mathcal{A}^{\mathcal{O}^{0,i+(t-1)/3}}(1^\lambda) \wedge E_1] - \Pr[1 \leftarrow \mathcal{A}^{\mathcal{O}^{0,i+t/3}}(1^\lambda) \wedge E_1]\right| \leq 2\mathsf{Adv}^{\mathcal{U}_k\text{-}\mathsf{MDDH}_k}_{1,\mathcal{B}_{2,t}}(\lambda).$$

Thus, for some PPT algorithm $\mathcal{B}_2$,

$$\left|\Pr[1 \leftarrow \mathcal{A}^{\mathcal{O}^{0,i}}(1^\lambda) \wedge E_1] - \Pr[1 \leftarrow \mathcal{A}^{\mathcal{O}^{0,i+1}}(1^\lambda) \wedge E_1]\right| \leq 6\mathsf{Adv}^{\mathcal{U}_k\text{-}\mathsf{MDDH}_k}_{1,\mathcal{B}_2}(\lambda)$$

holds. By symmetry, there exists a PPT algorithm $\mathcal{B}_3$ such that

$$\left|\Pr[1 \leftarrow \mathcal{A}^{\mathcal{O}^{0,i}}(1^\lambda) \wedge E_2] - \Pr[1 \leftarrow \mathcal{A}^{\mathcal{O}^{0,i+1}}(1^\lambda) \wedge E_2]\right| \leq 6\mathsf{Adv}^{\mathcal{U}_k\text{-}\mathsf{MDDH}_k}_{2,\mathcal{B}_3}(\lambda).$$

By Lemma 2, the inequality in Theorem 4 holds.

B.2 Proof of Theorem 6

Let Q be an upper bound of the number of queries. We define the oracles $\mathcal{O}^0_{\mathsf{K}}$, $\mathcal{O}^{0,t/3}(t = 0, 1, \ldots, 3Q)$ and the events E, E_1, E_2 in the same way as the proof of Theorem 2.

First, there exists a PPT algorithm $\mathcal{B}_1$ such that

$$\left|\Pr[1 \leftarrow \mathcal{A}^{\mathcal{O}^0_{\mathsf{K}}}(1^\lambda)] - \Pr[1 \leftarrow \mathcal{A}^{\mathcal{O}^0}(1^\lambda)]\right| \leq 2\mathsf{Adv}^{\mathsf{PRF}}_{\mathcal{B}_1,F}(\lambda).$$

Then, we evaluate the computational difference between $\mathcal{O}^{0,i}$ and $\mathcal{O}^{0,i+1}$ for $i = 0, 1, \ldots, Q-1$. We have

$$\Pr[1 \leftarrow \mathcal{A}^{\mathcal{O}^{0,i}}(1^\lambda) \wedge \neg E] = \Pr[1 \leftarrow \mathcal{A}^{\mathcal{O}^{0,i+1}}(1^\lambda) \wedge \neg E],$$

so we consider the case of E_1 by symmetry. By treating $\mathsf{FList}(w_{0,i+1})$ as the m-instance NLWE secret and using the hybrid argument, it follows that there exists a PPT algorithm $\mathcal{B}_{2,1}$ such that

$$\left|\Pr[1 \leftarrow \mathcal{A}^{\mathcal{O}^{0,i}}(1^\lambda) \wedge E_1] - \Pr[1 \leftarrow \mathcal{A}^{\mathcal{O}^{0,i+1/3}}(1^\lambda) \wedge E_1]\right| \leq 2m\mathsf{Adv}_{\mathcal{B}_{2,1}}^{\mathsf{NLWE}_{m,\kappa_{\mathsf{ct}}Q,q,\chi,\eta}}(\lambda).$$

Similarly, there exist PPT algorithms $\mathcal{B}_{2,t}$ $(t = 2, 3)$ such that

$$\left|\Pr[1 \leftarrow \mathcal{A}^{\mathcal{O}^{0,i+(t-1)/3}}(1^\lambda) \wedge E_1] - \Pr[1 \leftarrow \mathcal{A}^{\mathcal{O}^{0,i+t/3}}(1^\lambda) \wedge E_1]\right| \leq 2m\mathsf{Adv}_{\mathcal{B}_{2,t}}^{\mathsf{NLWE}_{m,\kappa_{\mathsf{ct}}Q,q,\chi,\eta}}(\lambda).$$

Thus, for some PPT algorithm $\mathcal{B}_2$,

$$\left|\Pr[1 \leftarrow \mathcal{A}^{\mathcal{O}^{0,i}}(1^\lambda) \wedge E_1] - \Pr[1 \leftarrow \mathcal{A}^{\mathcal{O}^{0,i+1}}(1^\lambda) \wedge E_1]\right| \leq 6m\mathsf{Adv}_{\mathcal{B}_2}^{\mathsf{NLWE}_{m,\kappa_{\mathsf{ct}}Q,q,\chi,\eta}}(\lambda)$$

holds. By symmetry, there exists a PPT algorithm $\mathcal{B}_2'$ such that

$$\left|\Pr[1 \leftarrow \mathcal{A}^{\mathcal{O}^{0,i}}(1^\lambda) \wedge E_2] - \Pr[1 \leftarrow \mathcal{A}^{\mathcal{O}^{0,i+1}}(1^\lambda) \wedge E_2]\right| \leq 6m\mathsf{Adv}_{\mathcal{B}_2'}^{\mathsf{NLWE}_{m,\kappa_{\mathsf{td}}Q,q,\chi,\eta}}(\lambda).$$

Therefore, the inequality in Theorem 6 holds.

B.3 Proof of Theorem 7

Similarly to U_k-MDDH, the following lemma holds. The proof is almost the same as that of Lemma 1.

Lemma 4. *For $r \in \mathbb{Z}_p^2$, let $\mathcal{O}^r$ be an oracle that samples $a \stackrel{\$}{\leftarrow} \mathbb{Z}_p^2$ and outputs $([a]_1, [a^\top r]_1, [a]_2, [a^\top r]_2)$. Let $\mathcal{O}$ be an oracle that samples $a \stackrel{\$}{\leftarrow} \mathbb{Z}_p^2$, $u \stackrel{\$}{\leftarrow} \mathbb{Z}_p$ and outputs $([a]_1, [u]_1, [a]_2, [u]_2)$. If the bil-$V_2$-MDDH assumption holds, for any PPT algorithm $\mathcal{A}$,*

$$\mathsf{Adv}_{\mathcal{A}}^{\mathsf{bil}\text{-}V_2\text{-}\mathsf{MDDH}}(\lambda) := \frac{1}{2}\left|\Pr[1 \leftarrow \mathcal{A}^{\mathcal{O}^r}(1^\lambda, [y]_1, [y]_2)] - \Pr[1 \leftarrow \mathcal{A}^{\mathcal{O}}(1^\lambda, [y]_1, [y]_2)]\right|$$

is negligible for a randomly chosen secret $r = (x, y)^\top \stackrel{\$}{\leftarrow} \mathbb{Z}_p^2$.

Proof. Using the bil-V_2-MDDH instance $([A]_1, [s]_1, [A]_2, [s]_2)$, the view of $\mathcal{A}$ in this lemma can be simulated. $[y]_1$ and $[y]_2$ are set as the third components of $[s]_1$ and $[s]_2$ respectively. The oracle simulator samples $t \stackrel{\$}{\leftarrow} \mathbb{Z}_p^3$ and outputs $([t^\top A]_1, [t^\top s]_1, [t^\top A]_2, [t^\top s]_2)$. Since the bit length of p is $\Theta(\lambda)$ and two rows of A are uniformly random, $A \in \mathbb{Z}_p^{3\times 2}$ is rank 2 with an overwhelming probability. Thus, it simulates $\mathcal{O}^r$ when $s = Ar$. When s is random, $[A|s] \in \mathbb{Z}_p^{3\times 3}$ is full-rank with an overwhelming probability since two rows of $[A|s]$ are uniformly random. Thus, it simulates $\mathcal{O}$ in this case. $\square$

Let Q be an upper bound of the number of queries. We define the oracles $\mathcal{O}^0_{\mathsf{K}'}$, $\mathcal{O}^{0,t/3}_{x,y}(t = 0, 1, \ldots, 3Q)$ and the events E, E_1, E_2 in the same way as the proof of Theorem 2. Note that the secret key K' contains x, y in CPSSE, so the oracles depend on x, y.

First, there exists a PPT algorithm $\mathcal{B}_1$ such that

$$\left|\Pr[1 \leftarrow \mathcal{A}^{\mathcal{O}^0_{\mathsf{K}'}}(1^\lambda)] - \Pr[1 \leftarrow \mathcal{A}^{\mathcal{O}^0_{x,y}}(1^\lambda)]\right| \leq 2\mathsf{Adv}^{\mathsf{PRF}}_{\mathcal{B}_1,F}(\lambda).$$

In addition, we have

$$\Pr[1 \leftarrow \mathcal{A}^{\mathcal{O}^{0,i}_{x,y}}(1^\lambda) \wedge \neg E] = \Pr[1 \leftarrow \mathcal{A}^{\mathcal{O}^{0,i+1}_{x,y}}(1^\lambda) \wedge \neg E].$$

In the case of E_1, consider treating $(\mathsf{FList}(w_{0,i+1}), y)$ as the secret and constructing a bil-V_2-MDDH solver using the oracle distinguisher of $\mathcal{O}^{0,i}_{x,y}$ and $\mathcal{O}^{0,i+1/3}_{x,y}$. The solver samples $x \overset{\$}{\leftarrow} \mathbb{Z}_p$. Since the solver knows $(x, [y]_1, [y]_2)$, it can correctly respond to queries from the distinguisher. Note that in this case, "random" in Table 2 means that the oracle returns $([(r_1, r_2)^\top]_1, [(r_3, r_1 x)^\top]_1)$ where $r_1, r_2, r_3 \overset{\$}{\leftarrow} \mathbb{Z}_p$. Thus, it follows that there exists a PPT algorithm $\mathcal{B}_{2,1}$ such that

$$\left|\Pr[1 \leftarrow \mathcal{A}^{\mathcal{O}^{0,i}_{x,y}}(1^\lambda) \wedge E_1] - \Pr[1 \leftarrow \mathcal{A}^{\mathcal{O}^{0,i+1/3}_{x,y}}(1^\lambda) \wedge E_1]\right| \leq 2\mathsf{Adv}^{\mathsf{bil}\text{-}V_2\text{-}\mathsf{MDDH}}_{\mathcal{B}_{2,1}}(\lambda).$$

Similarly, there exist PPT algorithms $\mathcal{B}_{2,t}$ $(t = 2, 3)$ such that

$$\left|\Pr[1 \leftarrow \mathcal{A}^{\mathcal{O}^{0,i+(t-1)/3}_{x,y}}(1^\lambda) \wedge E_1] - \Pr[1 \leftarrow \mathcal{A}^{\mathcal{O}^{0,i+t/3}_{x,y}}(1^\lambda) \wedge E_1]\right| \leq 2\mathsf{Adv}^{\mathsf{bil}\text{-}V_2\text{-}\mathsf{MDDH}}_{\mathcal{B}_{2,t}}(\lambda).$$

Thus, for some PPT algorithm $\mathcal{B}_2$,

$$\left|\Pr[1 \leftarrow \mathcal{A}^{\mathcal{O}^{0,i}_{x,y}}(1^\lambda) \wedge E] - \Pr[1 \leftarrow \mathcal{A}^{\mathcal{O}^{0,i+1}_{x,y}}(1^\lambda) \wedge E]\right| \leq 12\mathsf{Adv}^{\mathsf{bil}\text{-}V_2\text{-}\mathsf{MDDH}}_{\mathcal{B}_2}(\lambda).$$

holds. Therefore,

$$\mathsf{Adv}^{\mathsf{Full}}_{\mathcal{A},\mathsf{CPSSE}}(\lambda) \leq 2\mathsf{Adv}^{\mathsf{PRF}}_{\mathcal{B}_1,F}(\lambda) + 12Q\mathsf{Adv}^{\mathsf{bil}\text{-}V_2\text{-}\mathsf{MDDH}}_{\mathcal{B}_2}(\lambda)$$

holds and this completes the proof.

References

1. Abdalla, M., et al.: Searchable encryption revisited: consistency properties, relation to anonymous IBE, and extensions. In: Shoup, V. (ed.) CRYPTO 2005. LNCS, vol. 3621, pp. 205–222. Springer, Heidelberg (2005)
2. Abdalla, M., Catalano, D., Fiore, D., Gay, R., Ursu, B.: Multi-input functional encryption for inner products: function-hiding realizations and constructions without pairings. In: Shacham, H., Boldyreva, A. (eds.) CRYPTO 2018. LNCS, vol. 10991, pp. 597–627. Springer, Cham (2018). https://doi.org/10.1007/978-3-319-96884-1_20

3. Agrawal, S., Agrawal, S., Badrinarayanan, S., Kumarasubramanian, A., Prabhakaran, M., Sahai, A.: On the practical security of inner product functional encryption. In: Katz, J. (ed.) PKC 2015. LNCS, vol. 9020, pp. 777–798. Springer, Heidelberg (2015). https://doi.org/10.1007/978-3-662-46447-2_35
4. Agrawal, S., Maitra, M., Vempati, N.S., Yamada, S.: Functional encryption for Turing machines with dynamic bounded collusion from LWE. In: Malkin, T., Peikert, C. (eds.) CRYPTO 2021. LNCS, vol. 12828, pp. 239–269. Springer, Cham (2021). https://doi.org/10.1007/978-3-030-84259-8_9
5. Agrawal, S., Yamada, S.: CP-ABE for circuits (and more) in the symmetric key setting. In: Pass, R., Pietrzak, K. (eds.) TCC 2020. LNCS, vol. 12550, pp. 117–148. Springer, Cham (2020). https://doi.org/10.1007/978-3-030-64375-1_5
6. Alwen, J., Peikert, C.: Generating shorter bases for hard random lattices. In: Theory of Computing Systems, vol. 48, pp. 535–553 (2011)
7. Ananth, P., Vaikuntanathan, V.: Optimal bounded-collusion secure functional encryption. In: Hofheinz, D., Rosen, A. (eds.) TCC 2019. LNCS, vol. 11891, pp. 174–198. Springer, Cham (2019). https://doi.org/10.1007/978-3-030-36030-6_8
8. Bai, S., Jangir, H., Ngo, T., Youmans, W.: An algebraic algorithm for breaking NTRU with multiple keys. Des. Codes Cryptogr. **92**, 3895–3918 (2024)
9. Bishop, A., Jain, A., Kowalczyk, L.: Function-hiding inner product encryption. In: Iwata, T., Cheon, J. (eds) ASIACRYPT 2015. LNCS, vol. 9452, pp. 470–491. Springer, Heidelberg (2015)
10. Boneh, D., Di Crescenzo, G., Ostrovsky, R., Persiano, G.: Public key encryption with keyword search. In: Cachin, C., Camenisch, J.L. (eds.) EUROCRYPT 2004. LNCS, vol. 3027, pp. 506–522. Springer, Heidelberg (2004). https://doi.org/10.1007/978-3-540-24676-3_30
11. Boneh, D., Lewi, K., Montgomery, H., Raghunathan, A.: Key homomorphic PRFs and their applications. In: Canetti, R., Garay, J.A. (eds.) CRYPTO 2013. LNCS, vol. 8042, pp. 410–428. Springer, Heidelberg (2013). https://doi.org/10.1007/978-3-642-40041-4_23
12. Brakerski, Z., Segev, G.: Function-private functional encryption in the private-key setting. J. Cryptol. **31**, 202–225 (2018)
13. Byun, J.W., Rhee, H.S., Park, H.-A., Lee, D.H.: Off-line keyword guessing attacks on recent keyword search schemes over encrypted data. In: Jonker, W., Petković, M. (eds.) SDM 2006. LNCS, vol. 4165, pp. 75–83. Springer, Heidelberg (2006). https://doi.org/10.1007/11844662_6
14. Cheng, L., Meng, F.: Public key authenticated encryption with keyword search from LWE. In: Atluri, V., Di Pietro, R., Jensen, C.D., Meng, W. (eds.) ESORICS 2022. LNCS, vol. 13554, pp. 303–324. Springer, Cham (2022)
15. Cheng, L., Qin, J., Feng, F., Meng, F.: Security-enhanced public-key authenticated searchable encryption. Inf. Sci. **647**, 119454 (2023)
16. Datta, P., Dutta, R., Mukhopadhyay, S.: Functional encryption for inner product with full function privacy. In: Cheng, C.M., Chung, K.M., Persiano, G., Yang, B.Y. (eds.) PKC 2016. LNCS, vol. 9614, pp. 164-195. Springer, Heidelberg (2016)
17. De Caro, A., Iovino, V., Persiano, G.: Fully secure anonymous HIBE and secret-key anonymous IBE with short ciphertexts. In: Joye, M., Miyaji, A., Otsuka, A. (eds.) Pairing 2010. LNCS, vol. 6487, pp. 347–366. Springer, Heidelberg (2010)
18. Ducas, L., Lyubashevsky, V., Prest, T.: Efficient identity-based encryption over NTRU lattices. In: Sarkar, P., Iwata, T. (eds.) ASIACRYPT 2014. LNCS, vol. 8874, pp. 22–41. Springer, Heidelberg (2014). https://doi.org/10.1007/978-3-662-45608-8_2

19. Emura, K.: Generic construction of public-key authenticated encryption with keyword search revisited: stronger security and efficient construction. In: ACM APKC 2022, pp. 39–49 (2022)
20. Escala, A., Herold, G., Kiltz, E., Ràfols, C., Villar, J.: An algebraic framework for Diffie–Hellman assumptions. J. Cryptol. **30**, 242–288 (2017)
21. Garg, R., Goyal, R., Lu, G., Waters, B.: Dynamic collusion bounded functional encryption from identity-based encryption. In: Dunkelman, O., Dziembowski, S. (eds.) EUROCRYPT 2022. LNCS, vol. 13276, pp. 736–763. Springer, Cham (2022)
22. Gentry, C., Peikert, C., Vaikuntanathan, V.: Trapdoors for hard lattices and new cryptographic constructions. In: ACM STOC 2008, pp. 197–206 (2008)
23. Gorbunov, S., Vaikuntanathan, V., Wee, H.: Functional encryption with bounded collusions via multi-party computation. In: Safavi-Naini, R., Canetti, R. (eds.) CRYPTO 2012. LNCS, vol. 7417, pp. 162–179. Springer, Heidelberg (2012). https://doi.org/10.1007/978-3-642-32009-5_11
24. Huang, Q., Li, H.: An efficient public-key searchable encryption scheme secure against inside keyword guessing attacks. Inf. Sci. **403**, 1–14 (2017)
25. Kim, S., Lewi, K., Mandal, A., Montgomery, H., Roy, A., Wu, D.J.: Function-hiding inner product encryption is practical. In: Catalano, D., De Prisco, R. (eds.) SCN 2018. LNCS, vol. 11035, pp. 544–562. Springer, Cham (2018). https://doi.org/10.1007/978-3-319-98113-0_29
26. Li, Q., Boyen, X.: Public-key authenticated encryption with keyword search made easy. In: IACR Communications in Cryptology, vol. 1, no. 2 (2024)
27. Lin, H.: Indistinguishability obfuscation from SXDH on 5-linear maps and locality-5 PRGs. In: Katz, J., Shacham, H. (eds.) CRYPTO 2017. LNCS, vol. 10401, pp. 599–629. Springer, Cham (2017). https://doi.org/10.1007/978-3-319-63688-7_20
28. Lin, H., Vaikuntanathan, V.: Indistinguishability obfuscation from DDH-like assumptions on constant-degree graded encodings. In: IEEE FOCS 2016, pp. 11–20 (2016)
29. Liu, ZY., Tseng, YF., Tso, R., Mambo, M., Chen, YC.: Public-key authenticated encryption with keyword search: cryptanalysis, enhanced security, and quantum-resistant instantiation. In: ACM ASIACCS, pp. 423–436 (2022)
30. Maples, K.: Singularity of random matrices over finite fields. arXiv preprint arXiv:1012.2372 (2010)
31. Meng, L., Chen, L., Tian, Y., Manulis, M., Liu, S.: FEASE: fast and expressive asymmetric searchable encryption. In: USENIX Security 2024, pp. 2545–2562 (2024)
32. Micciancio, D., Peikert, C.: Trapdoors for lattices: simpler, tighter, faster, smaller. In: Pointcheval, D., Johansson, T. (eds.) EUROCRYPT 2012. LNCS, vol. 7237, pp. 700–718. Springer, Heidelberg (2012). https://doi.org/10.1007/978-3-642-29011-4_41
33. Mukherjee, S.: Statistically consistent broadcast authenticated encryption with keyword search. In: Simpson, L., Rezazadeh Baee, M.A. (eds.) ACISP 2023. LNCS, vol. 13915, pp. 523–552. Springer, Cham (2023)
34. Nguyen, H.H., Paquette, E.: Surjectivity of near-square random matrices. Comb. Probab. Comput. **29**(2), 267–292 (2020)
35. Noroozi, M., Eslami, Z.: Public key authenticated encryption with keyword search: revisited. IET Inf. Secur. **13**(4), 336–342 (2019)
36. Qin, B., Chen, Y., Huang, Q., Liu, X., Zheng, D.: Public-key authenticated encryption with keyword search revisited: security model and constructions. Inf. Sci. **516**, 515–528 (2020)

37. Qin, B., Cui, H., Zheng, X., Zheng, D.: Improved security model for public-key authenticated encryption with keyword search. In: Huang, Q., Yu, Y. (eds.) ProvSec 2021. LNCS, vol. 13059, pp. 19–38. Springer, Cham (2021)
38. Regev, O.: On lattices, learning with errors, random linear codes, and cryptography. J. ACM **56**(6), 1–40 (2009)
39. Shen, E., Shi, E., Waters, B.: Predicate privacy in encryption systems. In: Reingold, O. (ed.) TCC 2009. LNCS, vol. 5444, pp. 457–473. Springer, Heidelberg (2009). https://doi.org/10.1007/978-3-642-00457-5_27
40. Song, D.X., Wagner, D., Perrig, A.: Practical techniques for searches on encrypted data. In: IEEE S&P 2000, pp. 44–55 (2000)
41. Tomida, J., Abe, M., Okamoto, T.: Efficient functional encryption for inner-product values with full-hiding security. In: Bishop, M., Nascimento, A. (eds.) ISC 2016. LNCS, vol. 9866, pp. 408–425. Springer, Cham (2016). https://doi.org/10.1007/978-3-319-45871-7_24

Pre-constructed Publicly Verifiable Secret Sharing and Applications

Karim Baghery(✉), Noah Knapen, Georgio Nicolas, and Mahdi Rahimi

COSIC, KU Leuven, Leuven, Belgium
{karim.baghery,mahdi.rahimi}@kuleuven.be,
georgio.nicolas@esat.kuleuven.be

Abstract. Conventional Publicly Verifiable Secret Sharing (PVSS) protocols allow a dealer to share a secret among n parties without interaction, ensuring that any $t+1$ parties (where $t+1 \leq n$) can recover the secret, while anyone can publicly verify the validity of both the individual shares and the reconstructed secret. PVSS schemes are shown to be a key tool in a wide range of practical applications. In this paper, we introduce Pre-constructed PVSS (PPVSS), an extension of standard PVSS schemes, highlighting its enhanced utility and efficiency in various protocols. Unlike standard PVSS, PPVSS requires the dealer to publish a commitment or encryption of the main secret and incorporates a novel secret reconstruction method. We show that these refinements make PPVSS more practical and versatile than conventional PVSS schemes. To build a PPVSS scheme, we first point out that the well-known PVSS scheme by Schoenmakers (CRYPTO'99) and its pairing-based variant presented by Heidarvand and Villar (SAC'08) can be seen as special cases of PPVSS, where the dealer also publishes a commitment to the main secret. However, these protocols are not practical for many applications due to efficiency limitations and are less flexible compared to a standard PPVSS scheme. To address this, we propose a general strategy for transforming a Shamir-based PVSS scheme into a PPVSS scheme. Using this strategy, we construct two practical PPVSS schemes in both the Random Oracle (RO) and plain models, grounded in state-of-the-art PVSS designs. Leveraging the new RO-based PPVSS scheme, we revisit some applications and present more efficient variants. Notably, we propose a new universally verifiable e-voting protocol that improves on the alternative scheme by Schoenmakers (CRYPTO'99), reducing the verification complexity with m voters from $O(n^2m)$ to $O(nm)$ exponentiations–a previously unattainable goal with standard PVSS schemes. Our implementation results demonstrate that both our proposed PPVSS schemes and the new universally verifiable e-voting protocol significantly outperform existing alternatives in terms of efficiency.

Keywords: Publicly Verifiable Secret Sharing · PVSS · Pre-Constructed Publicly Verifiable Secret Sharing · Universally Verifiable E-Voting

M. Fischlin and V. Moonsamy (Eds.): ACNS 2025, LNCS 15825, pp. 89–119, 2025.
https://doi.org/10.1007/978-3-031-95761-1_4

1 Introduction

Secret sharing schemes allow a dealer to divide a secret into shares and distribute them among n participants, such that any subset of $t+1$ participants can collaborate to reconstruct the secret, while any subset of t or fewer participants learn nothing about it. This $(t+1, n)$-threshold structure ensures resilience and confidentiality in settings where trust is distributed among multiple parties. Secret sharing protocols have found applications in secure multi-party computation, threshold cryptography, and decentralized systems such as blockchain.

Verifiable Secret Sharing. In the well-known secret sharing protocol proposed by Shamir [24], a dealer shares a secret f_0 among n parties using a secret degree-t polynomial $f(X)$. To do this, the dealer sets $f(0) := f_0$, and each party P_i privately receives $f(i)$ as their individual share of the main secret $f_0 = f(0)$. However, basic secret sharing schemes, while providing security guarantees, assume that both the dealer and participants are honest. This assumption is problematic in adversarial environments, where malicious actors could compromise the protocol by distributing incorrect shares or refusing to participate honestly. To address this issue, *Verifiable Secret Sharing* (VSS) schemes were developed, allowing parties to verify the correctness of their shares [1,2,5,13,16,22]. Feldman's VSS scheme [16] is a pioneering work in this area, utilizing homomorphic commitments to enable verification of the shares in Shamir's scheme, ensuring that they are consistent with a unique secret polynomial. Feldman's approach guarantees that the shares are correct, but it does not hide the secret polynomial's coefficients, limiting its privacy guarantees and making it suitable only for sharing high-entropy secrets. Pedersen's VSS [22] extended this idea by using his homomorphic commitment and incorporating additional randomness, providing both verifiability and secrecy of the shared values. A recent work by Atapoor, Baghery, Cozzo, and Pedersen [1] presented a highly efficient VSS scheme based on Shamir's protocol, using hash-based (i.e., non-homomorphic) commitments.

Publicly Verifiable Secret Sharing. In VSS schemes, the share verification phase might require interaction between the dealer and the parties, and verification can only be done by the shareholders. As cryptographic protocols evolved, the need arose for schemes that allow external parties to verify the correctness of the process. *Publicly VSS* (PVSS) was proposed to meet this demand, allowing also external auditors to verify the shares and the reconstructed secret [3,8,9,18,19,23]. In PVSS schemes, a dealer publishes shares encrypted under the public keys of parties along with a Non-Interactive Zero-Knowledge (NIZK) proof, enabling anyone to verify the correctness of the shares. Schoenmakers' PVSS scheme [23] is a well-known example of such a scheme, built on Feldman's VSS in the Random Oracle (RO) model. His protocol has been particularly useful for applications requiring transparency, such as universally verifiable e-voting, robust public-key infrastructure, threshold software key escrow, and many more [23]. However, while Schoenmakers' PVSS scheme guarantees public verifiability, it suffers from inefficiencies, particularly in the verification phase, where $O(n^2)$ exponentiations are required. This computational overhead makes Schoenmakers' scheme unsuitable for applications requiring scalability, such as large-scale elections or randomness beacons in decentralized protocols.

Despite its foundational role, the complexity of Schoenmakers' PVSS scheme has driven the development of more efficient alternatives. Several works have sought to reduce the computational and communication costs associated with PVSS. Heidarvand and Villar [20] proposed a pairing-based variant of Schoenmakers' PVSS scheme in the plain model, but it still requires $O(nt)$ exponentiations and $O(n)$ pairing operations in the verification phase, which are computationally expensive. In ACNS'17, Cascudo and David [8] improved upon Schoenmakers' work [23] and its pairing-based variant [20] by designing two PVSS schemes that reduce the complexity of share verification to $O(n)$ exponentiations, making the schemes more suitable for large-scale applications. This improvement in verification was achieved through a coding-theory technique, employing a random codeword from the dual code of the Reed-Solomon code used for secret sharing. The authors [8] also used their proposed PVSS schemes to construct the SCRAIP protocol, a publicly verifiable randomness beacon protocol in the honest-majority setting. Several follow-up works [3,9,11] have proposed new PVSS schemes that are concretely more efficient than those in [8]. For a detailed comparison, we refer to the full version of paper [4]. We highlight that PVSS schemes are mainly categorized into two classes, each suited to different applications: the schemes where the secret is g^{f_0}, and those where it is f_0, with g as the generator of a cyclic group of prime order. The PVSS schemes proposed in [3,8,9,11,23] belong to the first category, where each party obtains a share g^{f_i} and, in the reconstruction phase, the parties collectively reconstruct g^{f_0}. Conversely, the schemes in [10,19] belong to the second category.

Our Contributions. Our contributions can be summarized as follows:

Pre-constructed Publicly Verifiable Secret Sharing. As the first contribution of this paper, we define Pre-Constructed PVSS (PPVSS) as an extension of standard PVSS schemes. PPVSS offers all the capabilities of standard PVSS but also requires the dealer to pre-construct and publish a commitment/encryption of the main secret. This subtle modification allows us to have a novel secret reconstruction approach specific to PPVSS schemes. Beyond a novel reconstruction approach, by enabling the dealer to publish a commitment to the main secret and prove its well-formedness alongside other shares in the same round, a PPVSS scheme provides enhanced functionality compared to PVSS schemes. Using this new reconstruction approach, which we call *optimistic reconstruction*, the dealer can open a single commitment to the (pre-constructed) secret during the reconstruction phase, rather than involving at least $t+1$ shareholders to reconstruct the same secret or opening the entire secret polynomial, as done in some current PVSS-based protocols [9]. Opening the entire polynomial by the dealer incurs a communication cost of at least $O(t\lambda)$ bits and a computation cost of $O(t)$ for each verifier, where λ and t are the security and threshold parameters, respectively. In some applications of PVSS schemes, each player usually acts as the dealer once. Since we assume the majority of parties are honest, most dealers can use the proposed optimistic reconstruction approach. If reconstruction of a malicious dealer's secret is needed and the dealer does not open the commitment, any $t+1$ honest parties can use their shares along with the classic reconstruction approach–here referred to as the *pessimistic reconstruction*–to reconstruct the secret. Our analysis show that a PPVSS scheme can be more versatile and broadly applicable than standard PVSS schemes.

Schoenmakers' PVSS is a Special PPVSS. We show that Schoenmakers' PVSS and its pairing-based variant [20,23], which are built on Feldman VSS [16], can be seen as a special type of PPVSS. In addition to encrypting the shares, the dealer also publishes a commitment to the main secret. However, his scheme requires $O(n^2)$ exponentiations during verification and is not as flexible as our defined and proposed PPVSS schemes. The reason for this reduced flexibility is that, following Feldman VSS [15], in Schoenmakers' (P)PVSS scheme [23], the commitment to the main secret has to be based on the same group generator used in other commitments and cannot be based on the public key of a specific party. Due to this limitation, while constructing threshold binding ElGamal based on his proposed (P)PVSS scheme [23, Section 6.1], Schoenmakers had to separately encrypt $g^{f(0)}$ under the public key pk_0 of the target party and use a Chaum-Pedersen protocol [12] to prove that the commitment $C_0 = g^{f(0)}$ commits to the same value encrypted under the target public key pk_0. This approach incurs additional computational and communication costs. As we demonstrate later, in our proposed PPVSS schemes, this can be achieved for free, by simply replacing the commitment key with the target public key pk_0.

In [8], Cascudo and David presented two PVSS protocols that improve Schoenmakers' scheme and its paring-based variant [20,23], by reducing the number of exponentiations required for verification from $O(n^2)$ to $O(n)$. All the follow-up works, like [3,8,9,11,23], also present a better efficiency compared to Schoenmakers' PVSS and its paring-based variant [20,23]. However, all the follow-up PVSS schemes with $O(n)$ verification complexity lack the pre-constructability feature of Schoenmakers' original design. Since the goal of PVSS is typically to allow public verifiability of the shares and the dealer only needs to encrypt the shares under each participant's public key. The main secret is not shared with any individual, and thus the pre-constructability found in Schoenmakers' scheme was inherited from Feldman VSS and not carried forward into the follow-up and more efficient PVSS designs. Our analysis show that this property is crucial for some applications like universally verifiable e-voting and robust public-key infrastructure [23].

General Strategy for Building PPVSS. As the next contribution of this paper, we introduce a general strategy to convert a Shamir-based PVSS scheme into an efficient PPVSS scheme with minimal computational and communication overhead. Our approach is inspired by the design of the Shamir secret sharing scheme. We note that in Shamir's scheme, the individual shares $f(i)$ and the main secret $f(0)$ are all distinct points on the same secret polynomial $f(X)$. In a standard Shamir-based PVSS scheme, given the parties' public keys $\{\mathsf{pk}_i\}_{i=1}^n$ and a secret degree-t polynomial $f(X)$, a dealer generates a Non-Interactive Zero-Knowledge (NIZK) proof for $C_i = \mathsf{Enc}(f(i), \mathsf{pk}_i)$ for $i = 1, \ldots, n$, where $n \geq 2t + 1$ and Enc is a public key encryption algorithm. We show that, with minimal modifications, the dealer can extend the NIZK proof scheme to the case $i = 0, 1, \ldots, n$, where $f(0)$ denotes the main secret and pk_0 is a commitment key or the public key of a designated party. Notably, in terms of efficiency, the computational and communication overhead in the resulting PPVSS scheme is negligible compared to the original PVSS scheme, increasing by only a factor of $1/n$ for both the dealer and the verifier.

Practical PPVSS Schemes. Using the proposed strategy, we build two practical PPVSS schemes based on the PVSS schemes proposed in [3,8,9]. Our focus is on these practical PVSS schemes, where the secret is g^{f_0}, however, we believe that our strategy is general enough to be used with other Shamir-based PVSS schemes as well, including the ones that the secret is f_0 [10]. Our initial PPVSS scheme can be seen as a more efficient alternative to Schoenmakers' PPVSS scheme [23], as both are constructed in the RO model. While the second proposed PPVSS scheme is constructed in the plain model and can be seen as a more efficient alternative to the paring-based variant of Schoenmakers' PPVSS scheme [23], proposed by Heidarvand and Villar [20]. In terms of efficiency, the new PPVSS schemes are more efficient than the (special) PPVSS schemes proposed in [20,23], and notably reducing the verification complexity from $O(n^2)$ to $O(n)$. Compared to the original PVSS schemes [3,8,9], the resulting PPVSS schemes have very close efficiency, while presenting new functionalities, and enabling a more efficient reconstruction approach. Table 1 provides a summary of performance metrics for the proposed PPVSS schemes.

More Efficient Universally Verifiable E-Voting Protocol. Schoenmakers demonstrated how his (P)PVSS scheme could be applied to various use cases, including a universally verifiable e-voting protocol [23]. In Schoenmakers' voting protocol, the computational cost for the verification step is approximately $m(nt+4.5n)$ exponentiations, where m and n are the number of voters and talliers, respectively, and $t = \lfloor \frac{n-1}{2} \rfloor$ is the threshold. In some cases, such as boardroom elections, each participant may act as both a voter and a tallier, meaning $m = n$. In such cases, the verification phase requires $O(n^3)$ exponentiations.

Table 1. A comparison of new PPVSS schemes with those of Schoenmakers [23] and its paring-based variant [20]. BC: Dealer's Broadcast size, Dow.: Download size by a verifier, Opt. Reconst.: Optimistic Reconstruction, Pes. Reconst.: Pessimistic Reconstruction, PDL: Polynomial Discrete Logarithm, DDH: Decisional Diffie-Hellman, DBS: Decisional Bilinear Square, RO: Random Oracle, Plain: Plain Model, n: Number of parties, t: threshold parameter ($t \approx n/2$), $P_{\mathbb{G}}$: Pairing Operation, $E_{\mathbb{G}}$: Exponentiation in group $\mathbb{G}$, $M_{\mathbb{G}}$: Multiplication in group $\mathbb{G}$, $\mathcal{PE}$: degree-t Polynomial Evaluation, $|\mathbb{G}|$: $\mathbb{G}$ element size, $|\mathbb{Z}_q|$: $\mathbb{Z}_q$ element size.

PPVSS & Security	Share	Broadcast & Dow	Verification	Opt. Reconst.	Pes. Reconst.
Schoenmakers [23] (DDH, RO)	$4.5n\ E_{\mathbb{G}}$ $1n\ \mathcal{PE}$	BC: $1.5n\lvert\mathbb{G}\rvert + n\lvert\mathbb{Z}_q\rvert$ Dow: $2.5n\lvert\mathbb{G}\rvert + n\lvert\mathbb{Z}_q\rvert$	$nt + 4n\ E_{\mathbb{G}} +$ $nt + 2n\ M_{\mathbb{G}}$	$1\ E_{\mathbb{G}}$	$5t\ E_{\mathbb{G}}$ $+ t\ M_{\mathbb{G}}$
Sec. 4.2 (PDL, DDH, RO)	$2n\ E_{\mathbb{G}}$ $2n\ \mathcal{PE}$	BC: $n\lvert\mathbb{G}\rvert + 0.5n\lvert\mathbb{Z}_q\rvert$ Dow: $2n\lvert\mathbb{G}\rvert + 0.5n\lvert\mathbb{Z}_q\rvert$	$2n\ E_{\mathbb{G}} +$ $n\ \mathcal{PE} + n\ M_{\mathbb{G}}$	$1\ E_{\mathbb{G}}$	$5t\ E_{\mathbb{G}} +$ $t\ M_{\mathbb{G}}$
Hei-Vil [20] (DBS, Plain)	$1.5n\ E_{\mathbb{G}}$ $1n\ \mathcal{PE}$	BC: $1.5n\lvert\mathbb{G}\rvert$ Dow: $2.5n\lvert\mathbb{G}\rvert$	$nt\ E_{\mathbb{G}} + 2n\ P_{\mathbb{G}}$ $+ nt\ M_{\mathbb{G}}$	$1\ E_{\mathbb{G}}$	$2t\ P_{\mathbb{G}} + t\ E_{\mathbb{G}}$ $+ t\ M_{\mathbb{G}}$
Sec. 4.3 (DBS, Plain)	$2n\ E_{\mathbb{G}}$ $1n\ \mathcal{PE}$	BC: $2n\lvert\mathbb{G}\rvert$ Dow: $3n\lvert\mathbb{G}\rvert$	$n\ E_{\mathbb{G}} + 2n\ P_{\mathbb{G}}$ $+ n\ M_{\mathbb{G}}$	$1\ E_{\mathbb{G}}$	$2t\ P_{\mathbb{G}} + t\ E_{\mathbb{G}}$ $+ t\ M_{\mathbb{G}}$

As an additional contribution of this paper, leveraging our proposed RO-based PPVSS scheme, we revisit the universally verifiable e-voting protocol presented by Schoenmakers [23] and introduce an improved version. The new e-voting protocol outperforms Schoenmakers' construction in several ways, notably reducing the verification phase to $O(mn)$ exponentiations rather than $O(mn^2)$. This improvement makes the new e-voting protocol viable for elections with a large value of n. To assess the performance of the new e-voting protocol, we present a prototype Rust implementation of both the original and our revisited protocols. Detailed performance evaluations and comparisons are provided in Sect. 5.3. For $(n, t) = (512, 255)$, we demonstrate that the new e-voting scheme requires $90\times$ less time for a single ballot verification. Additionally, for the same parameter sizes, the improved e-voting protocol requires 40% less time for ballot casting and 40% less (broadcast) communication by each voter.

Outline. In Sect. 2, we present some preliminaries. In Sect. 3, we discuss the definitions for PPVSS and introduce a general strategy to build a PPVSS scheme. In Sect. 4, we present two practical PPVSS schemes along with some implementation results. In Sect. 5, we use the new RO-based PPVSS scheme and revisit Shoenmakers' e-voting protocol and evaluate its performance with a prototype implementation. Finally, in Sect. 6, we conclude the paper.

2 Preliminaries

Notation. We denote by λ the security parameter. Throughout this paper, p and q represent two large primes such that q divides $p - 1$. We define $\mathbb{G}$ as the unique subgroup of $\mathbb{Z}_p^\star$ with order q, and let g be a generator of the cyclic group $\mathbb{G}$ of prime order q. The group $\mathbb{G}$ is chosen such that computing DL within $\mathbb{G}$, i.e., finding $\log_g h$ for some $h \in \mathbb{G}$, is computationally hard.

2.1 Sigma Protocols

Next, we recall the definition of sigma protocols (Σ-protocols). Here the algorithms are Probabilistic Polynomial-Time (PPT), unless mentioned. Let $X = X(\lambda)$ and $W = W(\lambda)$ be sets. Let R be a relation on $X \times W$ that defines a language $L = \{x \in X : \exists w \in W, R(x, w) = 1\}$. Given $x \in L$, an element $w \in W$ such that $R(x, w) = 1$ is called a witness. Let relation generator $\mathcal{R}$ be a PPT algorithm such that $\mathcal{R}(1^\lambda)$ outputs pairs (x, w) such that $R(x, w) = 1$.

A sigma-protocol (Σ-protocol) for the relation R is a 3-round interactive protocol between two PPT algorithms: a prover P and a verifier V. P holds a witness w for $x \in L$ and V is given x. In first round, P sends a commitment value a to V, and then in second round, V answers with a randomly sample challenge value d. A Σ-protocol is called public-coin if the challenge value d is a public and random string rather than something derived in a complex or private way. Finally, P answers with a response z, and V verifies the proof and outputs `true` or `false`. The triple $\mathsf{trans} := (a, d, z)$ is called a transcript of the Σ-protocol. A Σ-protocol is supposed to satisfy *Completeness*, *Honest Verifier Zero-Knowledge* (HVZK), and *Special Soundness* defined below.

Definition 1 (Completeness). *A Σ-protocol with parties (P, V) is* complete *for $\mathcal{R}$, if for all $(x, w) \in R$, the honest V will always accept the honest P.*

Definition 2 (HVZK). *A Σ-protocol with parties (P, V) satisfies* HVZK *for $\mathcal{R}$, if there exists a PPT algorithm $\mathcal{S}$ that given $x \in X$, can simulate the* trans *of the scheme, s.t. for all $x \in L$, $(x, w) \in R$,*

$$\mathsf{trans}(P(x, w) \leftrightarrow V(x)) \approx \mathsf{trans}(\mathcal{S}(x))$$

where $\mathsf{trans}(P(\cdot) \leftrightarrow V(\cdot))$ indicates the transcript of the Σ-protocol with (P, V), and $\approx$ denotes the indistinguishability of transcripts.

Definition 3 (Special Soundness). *A Σ-protocol with parties (P, V) is* special sound *for $\mathcal{R}$, if there exists a PPT extractor $\mathcal{E}$, such that for any $x \in L$, given two valid transcripts (a, d, z) and (a, d', z') for the same message a but $d \neq d'$, then $\mathcal{E}(a, d, z, d', z')$ outputs a witness w for the relation R.*

In the Random Oracle (RO) model, using Fiat-Shamir transform [17], a public-coin, complete, HVZK, and special soundness Σ-protocol can be turned into a Non-Interactive Zero-Knowledge (NIZK) proof or argument of knowledge.

Chaum-Pedersen Protocol for DL Equality. Let $\mathbb{G}$ be a group with hard DL, and g, h be two group elements, where g is the group generator. Let a prover aim to convince a verifier that for the public statement g, h, a, b, he knows a witness x which holds in the following relation,

$$R_{DLEQ} = \{(g, h, a, b), x \mid a = g^x \wedge b = h^x\}. \tag{1}$$

This relation is known as DL EQuality (DLEQ). In [12], Chaum and Pedersen introduced an efficient NIZK proof of knowledge for DLEQ, as summarized in Fig. 1. This protocol is widely employed in various cryptographic protocols, including threshold decryption, e-voting systems, PVSS schemes, etc.

Prover: Given the statement $(g, h, a, b) \in \mathbb{G}$ and the witness value $x \in \mathbb{Z}_q$, proceed as follows and output a proof π.

1. Sample $r \leftarrow\$ \mathbb{Z}_q$ uniformly at random; and set $c_1 = g^r$ and $c_2 = h^r$.
2. Set $d \leftarrow \mathcal{H}(a, b, c_1, c_2)$, where $\mathcal{H}$ is a random oracle.
3. Set $z = r + d \cdot x \mod q$; and Return $\pi := (d, z)$

Verifier: Given the statement $(g, h, a, b) \in \mathbb{G}$ and the proof $\pi = (d, z)$, checks if $d = \mathcal{H}(a, b, \frac{g^z}{a^d}, \frac{h^z}{b^d})$ and outputs `true` or `false`.

Fig. 1. Chaum-Pedersen NIZK proof of knowledge for DLEQ [12].

NIZK Proof of Binary Vote. In the ballot casting phase of the e-voting protocol proposed by Schoenmakers [23], a voter V casts a binary vote $v \in \{0, 1\}$ by running the sharing phase for the (P)PVSS scheme, using a random secret $s \in \mathbb{Z}_q$, and computing the value $U = G^{s+v}$. In addition, the voter generates a proof π_U to show that $v \in \{0, 1\}$ without revealing any information on v. The proof π_U refers to the commitment $C_0 = g^s$, which is published as part of the (P)PVSS transcript, and proves that:

$$\log_G U = \log_g C_0 \ \vee \ \log_G U = 1 + \log_g C_0.$$

The proof π_U is constructed using the technique of [14], and its protocol can be summarized as follows:

1. The prover sets $a_v = g^w$ and $b_v = G^w$ for random $w \in_R \mathbb{Z}_q$. The prover also sets $a_{1-v} = g^{r_{1-v}} C_0^{d_{1-v}}$ and $b_{1-v} = G^{r_{1-v}} (U/G^{1-v})^{d_{1-v}}$, for random $r_{1-v}, d_{1-v} \in_R \mathbb{Z}_q$. The prover sends a_0, b_0, a_1, b_1 in this order to the verifier.
2. The verifier sends a random challenge $c \in_R \mathbb{Z}_q$ to the prover.
3. The prover sets $d_v = c - d_{1-v} \pmod q$ and $r_v = w - sd_v \pmod q$, and sends d_0, r_0, d_1, r_1 in this order to the verifier.
4. The verifier checks that $c = d_0 + d_1 \pmod q$ and that

$$a_0 = g^{r_0} C_0^{d_0}, \quad b_0 = G^{r_0} U^{d_0}, \quad a_1 = g^{r_1} C_0^{d_1}, \quad \text{and} \quad b_1 = G^{r_1} \left(\tfrac{U}{G}\right)^{d_1}.$$

The protocol is proven to satisfy completeness, special soundness and honest verifier zero-knowledge; hence, its non-interactive version achieves ZK and releases no information on v in the random oracle model. This protocol is also used in our revised e-voting protocol.

2.2 Bilinear Groups and Computational Assumptions

We present one of our proposed PPVSS schemes over a symmetric bilinear group, which are defined as below.

Definition 4 (Bilinear Groupc). *A bilinear group is a tuple* $(q, \mathbb{G}, \mathbb{G}_T, e)$, *where* $\mathbb{G}$ *and* $\mathbb{G}_T$ *are groups of prime order* q, *and* $e : \mathbb{G} \times \mathbb{G} \to \mathbb{G}_T$ *is a bilinear map with the following properties:*

- ***Bilinearity:*** $e(g^\alpha, g^\beta) = e(g, g)^{\alpha\beta}$ *for every* $g \in \mathbb{G}$ *and* $\alpha, \beta \in \mathbb{Z}_q$.
- ***Non-degeneration:*** $e(g, g) \neq 1$ *unless* $g = 1$.
- ***Efficiency:*** *There are efficient algorithms for computing group operations in* $\mathbb{G}$, $\mathbb{G}_T$, *and evaluating* $e(x, y)$ *for* $x, y \in \mathbb{G}$.

The security of Cascudo and David's paring-based PVSS scheme [8] is proven under the Decisional Bilinear Square (DBS) assumption [20], which was shown to be related to the Decisional Bilinear Diffie-Hellman assumption.

Definition 5 (Decisional Bilinear Square (DBS) Assumption [20]). *Let* $(q, \mathbb{G}, \mathbb{G}_T, e)$ *be a bilinear group. For a generator* $g \in \mathbb{G}$, *random values* $\mu, \nu, s \leftarrow \mathbb{Z}_q$, *and given* $u = g^\mu$ *and* $v = g^\nu$, *the following probability distributions are computationally indistinguishable:*

$$D_0 = (g, u, v, T_0 = e(u, u)^\nu) \approx D_1 = (g, u, v, T_1 = e(u, u)^s)$$

Polynomial Discrete Problem. In [3], Baghery generalize Discrete Logarithm (DL) relation over polynomials and introduce the Polynomial Discrete Logarithm (PDL) relation denoted as R_{PDL}, which is defined as follows,

$$R_{PDL} = \{(g, x_i, F_i), f(X) \mid F_i = g^{f(x_i)} \text{ for } i = 1, 2, \ldots, n\}.$$

Here, $f(X) \in \mathbb{Z}_q[X]_t$ is a (at most) degree $t \leq n - 1$ witness polynomial with coefficients from $\mathbb{Z}_q$, and $\{x_i\}_{i=1}^n$ are n *distinct* elements from $\mathbb{Z}_q$. The R_{PDL} relation is based on the PDL problem, defined as follows, which is shown to be reducible to the DL problem [3].

Definition 6 (Polynomial Discrete Logarithm Problem [3]). *Let* $\mathbb{G}$ *be a finite cyclic group of order* q *generated by* g. *Given* $F_1, \ldots, F_n$ *from* $\mathbb{G}$ *and distinct elements* $x_1, \ldots, x_n$ *from* $\mathbb{Z}_q$, *find a polynomial* $f(X) \in \mathbb{Z}_q[X]_t$ *of (at most) degree* t, *where* $0 \leq t \leq n - 1$, *such that* $F_i = g^{f(x_i)}$ *for all* $i = 1, \ldots, n$.

In other words, an algorithm $\mathcal{A}$ *has advantage* ϵ *in solving PDL in* $\mathbb{G}$ *if*

$$\Pr[\mathcal{A}(x_1, \ldots, x_n, g, g^{f(x_1)}, \ldots, g^{f(x_n)}) = f(X)] \geq \epsilon$$

where $f(X) \in \mathbb{Z}_q[X]_t$ *is (at most) a degree-*t *polynomial with* $0 \leq t \leq n-1$, *and the probability is over the random choice of generator* $g \in \mathbb{G}^*$ *and the distinct choice of* $x_1, \ldots, x_n$ *in* $\mathbb{Z}_q$.

Baghery [3] also presented a Non-Interactive Zero-Knowledge (NIZK) Proof-of-Knowledge (PoK) scheme π_{PDL}, that allows a prover to prove knowledge of a witness for R_{PDL} relation. The verifiability property of $\mathbf{\Pi_S}$ PVSS scheme [3,9] is proven under the PDL assumption.

2.3 Coding Theory and Dual Codes

We define a $[n, t+1, d]$ code RS to be a linear error-correcting code over $\mathbb{Z}_q$ of length n, dimension $t+1$, and minimum distance d. Its dual code $\mathsf{RS}^\intercal$ is the vector space that consists of all vectors $\mathbf{v}^\intercal \in \mathbb{Z}_q^n$ such that $\langle \mathbf{c}, \mathbf{v}^\intercal \rangle = 0$ for all $\mathbf{c}$ in RS. The dual code $\mathsf{RS}^\intercal$ of an $[n, t+1, d]$ code RS is an $[n, n-t-1, d^\intercal]$ code (for some $d^\intercal$). In this work, we will use the following basic linear algebra fact.

Lemma 1 ([8]). *If* $\mathbf{c}' \in \mathbb{Z}_q^n \setminus \mathsf{RS}$, *and* $\mathbf{v}^\intercal$ *is chosen uniformly at random in* $\mathsf{RS}^\intercal$, *then the probability that* $\langle \mathbf{c}', \mathbf{v}^\intercal \rangle = 0$ *is exactly* $1/q$.

The proof is provided in the full version of paper [4].

Moreover, in this work, we will always assume $n < q$, and we will use Reed-Solomon codes RS of the following form:

$$\mathsf{RS} = \{(f(1), f(2), \ldots, f(n)) : f(X) \in \mathbb{Z}_q[X], \deg(f(X)) \leq t\},$$

where $f(X)$ ranges over all polynomials in $\mathbb{Z}_q[X]$ of degree at most t. This is an $[n, t+1, n-t]$ code. Its dual $\mathsf{RS}^\intercal$ is an $[n, n-t-1, t+2]$ code, which can be defined as follows:

$$\mathsf{RS}^\intercal = \{(d_1 p(1), d_2 p(2), \ldots, d_n p(n)) : p(X) \in \mathbb{Z}_q[X], \deg(p(X)) \leq n-t\},$$

where the coefficients d_i are given by $d_i = \prod_{\substack{1 \leq j \leq n \\ j \neq i}} \frac{1}{i-j}$.

3 Pre-constructed Publicly Verifiable Secret Sharing

The definition of PVSS requires that given a secret f_0 and public keys $\mathsf{pk}_1, \ldots, \mathsf{pk}_n$ for a set of n parties $P_1, \ldots, P_n$, a dealer D proceeds as follows. First, the dealer creates shares $\{f_i\}_{i=1}^n$, and then encrypts each f_i under the corresponding pk_i, obtaining ciphertexts c_i for $i = 1, \ldots, n$. Finally, it publishes $\{c_i\}_{i=1}^n$ along with a proof π_{PVSS}, proving that the encrypted shares are well-formed. For instance, in the case of PVSS based on (n, t)-Shamir secret sharing, the proof guarantees that the encrypted shares are valid shares generated by the Shamir scheme. Specifically, any $t+1$ of n decrypted shares can be used to reconstruct the secret f_0, while any t decrypted shares reveal no information about the secret. As can be seen, the dealer in a PVSS scheme does not need to publish a commitment to (or an encryption of) the secret f_0. This is why in practical PVSS schemes [3,8,9,11], the dealer does not publish a commitment to f_0. Consequently, in current cryptographic protocols that use practical PVSS schemes [3,8,9,11] as a subroutine, if the main secret f_0 is needed, either at least $t+1$ shareholders collaborate to reconstruct it, or the dealer has to publish at least $O(t)$ field elements, and each party has to do $O(n)$ computation to compute f_0. For instance, in the SCRAPE randomness generation protocol [8], the dealer commits to all n shares $\{f_i\}_{i=1}^n$ separately and later opens them to verify and reconstruct f_0. This adds $O(n\lambda)$ bits communication and $O(n)$ computation cost to this final protocol, where λ is the security parameter and n is the number of parties. In the case of ALBATROSS [9], an improved version of SCRAPE, the dealer opens the secret polynomial itself, which again adds $O(t\lambda)$ bits communication and $O(n)$ computation costs to the final protocol, where $t \approx n/2$ is the threshold parameter. Given the revealed polynomial, a verifier needs to evaluate a degree-t polynomial n times and recompute n exponentiations to check if the commitments are valid.

Above all, as shown in [23, Sections 5 and 6], some applications of PVSS schemes, such as universally verifiable e-voting and threshold binding ElGamal, require the commitment (i.e., $C_0 = g^{f_0}$) or encryption of the main secret f_0 to be published by the dealer. Obviously, this feature exceeds the requirements of a standard PVSS scheme and is absent in [3,8,9,11]. The only exception is the less efficient PVSS scheme proposed by Schoenmakers [23] and its paring-based variant [20]. In Schoenmakers' scheme, the dealer publishes $C_0 = g^{f_0}$ in the proof π_{PVSS}, as a commitment to the first coefficient of the underlying secret polynomial. One may note that is occurred due to the following reasons. First, in Shamir secret sharing, the secret is typically embedded in $f(0) = f_0$. Consequently, in the Feldman VSS where the dealer publishes commitments to the coefficient of the secret polynomial, $C_0 = g^{f(0)} = g^{f_0}$ serves as the commitment to the first coefficient. However, if the secret would be embedded differently in Shamir secret sharing, for instance by setting $f(-1) = f_0$, Feldman VSS would still work, but the commitment to the main secret, $g^{f(-1)}$, would not be published. One might argue that given $g^{f(i)}$ for $i = 1, \ldots, n$, it is possible to publicly compute $g^{f(j)}$ at an arbitrary point j, such as the index of main secret, using Lagrange interpolation in the exponent. However, this would require $O(n)$ exponentiations. More importantly, in packed Shamir secret sharing and packed PVSS schemes [9], where the l secrets $f_0, f_{-1}, \ldots, f_{-(l-1)}$ are embedded to different points, e.g., $f(0), f(-1), \ldots, f(-(l-1)))$, the secret is not solely $f(0)$. Thus, commitments to the secrets would not necessarily be published in a standard PVSS scheme.

In applications where the dealer needs to publish the encryption of $f_0 = f(0)$ under a specific public key pk_0, such as threshold binding ElGamal [23, Section 6.1], in addition to proof π_{PVSS}, the dealer publishes $y_{f_0} = \mathsf{pk}_0^{f_0}$ along with a DLEQ proof π_{DLEQ} (using Fig. 1) to show that $y_{f_0} = \mathsf{pk}_0^{f_0} \wedge C_0 = g^{f_0}$. This again adds extra communication and computation costs to the final protocol.

To address the concerns outlined above and develop more efficient, versatile, and broadly applicable PVSS schemes, we introduce Pre-Constructed PVSS (PPVSS) and present practical constructions. We start by defining the syntax for PPVSS schemes, adapting it from the standard PVSS syntax with some extensions. Next, we propose a general strategy to efficiently convert a Shamir-based PVSS scheme into a PPVSS protocol.

3.1 Definitions

Next, we introduce our definition for PPVSS schemes, which can be viewed as a natural extension of the standard PVSS definitions adapted from [3,8,9,23].

Definition 7. *A Pre-constructed PVSS (PPVSS) protocol consists of four algorithms of* ($\mathsf{Initial}$, Share, Verify, $\mathsf{Reconstruct}$) *as follows:*

1. $\mathsf{Initial}(1^\lambda) \rightarrow (\{\mathsf{pk}_i, \mathsf{sk}_i\}_{i=1}^n, h_0 \text{ or } (\mathsf{pk}_0, \mathsf{sk}_0))$: *Given* 1^λ, *in this phase, each party* $\{P_i\}_{i=1}^n$ *registers public key* pk_i *and withholds the corresponding secret key* sk_i. *The parties and dealer also agree on a commitment key* h_0 *or a specific public key* pk_0 *with the secret key* sk_0, *which will be used in the sharing phase while committing to or encrypting the main secret.*
2. $\mathsf{Share}(n, t, f_0, \{\mathsf{pk}_i\}_{i=1}^n, h_0 \text{ or } \mathsf{pk}_0) \rightarrow (\{y_i\}_{i=0}^n, \pi_{PPVSS})$: *Given secret* f_0, *it first secret shares* f_0 *and obtains the shares* $\{f_i\}_{i=1}^n$. *Next, it encrypts the share* f_i *under* pk_i *and obtains ciphertexts* $\{y_i\}_{i=1}^n$. *It also commits to (resp. encrypts)* f_0 *using* h_0 *(resp.* pk_0*) and obtains* y_0. *Then, it generates a publicly verifiable NIZK proof* π_{PPVSS} *that* y_0 *is indeed commitment to (or encryption of) main secret* f_0 *under* h_0 *(resp.* pk_0*), and* $\{y_i\}_{i=1}^n$ *are encryptions of a valid sharing of* f_0. *Finally, returns* $(y_0, y_1, \ldots, y_n, \pi_{PPVSS})$.
3. $\mathsf{Verify}(n, t, \{\mathsf{pk}_i, y_i\}_{i=0}^n, \pi_{PPVSS}) \rightarrow$ `true/false`: *In this phase, anyone (not necessarily a participant in the protocol) can verify non-interactively the values* $\{y_i\}_{i=0}^n$ *using* $(\{\mathsf{pk}_i\}_{i=0}^n, \pi_{PPVSS})$, *and output either* `true/false`.
4. $\mathsf{Reconstruct}$: *This phase can be done in two ways:*
   (a) *(Optimistic)* $\mathsf{Reconstruct}^{\mathsf{opt}}((h_0, y_0, f_0, r_0) \text{ or } (\mathsf{pk}_0, y_0, \mathsf{sk}_0)) \rightarrow \{f_0, \mathsf{false}\}$:
      - *Given the commitment key* h_0, *the commitment* y_0 *and the opening values* (f_0, r_0), *a verifier checks if* (f_0, r_0) *are valid opening for* y_0. *If so, the verifier returns* f_0; *otherwise it returns* `false`.
      - *Given the public key* pk_0, *the ciphertext* y_0 *and the secret key* sk_0, *the algorithm decrypts* y_0 *and returns* f_0;
   (b) *(Pessimistic)* $\mathsf{Reconstruct}^{pes}(\{y_i, \mathsf{sk}_i\}_{i \in Q, |Q|=t+1}) \rightarrow \{f_0, \mathsf{false}\}$: *Given any* $t+1$ *of the encrypted shares and secret keys, e.g.,* $\{y_i, \mathsf{sk}_i\}_{i=1}^{t+1}$, *it returns either the main secret* f_0, *or* `false`. *This can be done in two phases: decryption of the shares and share pooling. In the first step, every party* $P_i \in Q$ *decrypts the share* f_i *from the ciphertext* y_i *by using its secret key* sk_i, *and publishes* f_i *together with a NIZK proof* π_i^{Dec} *that this value is indeed a correct decryption of* y_i. *In the share pooling phase, a verifier* V *(not necessarily from the participants) first checks whether the proofs* $\{\pi_i^{Dec}\}_{i=1}^{t+1}$ *are correct. If the check passes for less than* t *parties in* Q *then* V *returns* false; *otherwise* V *applies a reconstruction procedure to the set of valid shares, i.e.,* $\{f_i\}_{i=1}^{t+1}$, *and calculates and returns* f_0.

Similar to a PVSS scheme [8,23], a PPVSS scheme needs to satisfy the following security guarantees.

- **Correctness**: If the dealer and parties follow the protocol, then the Verify algorithm will return true and the Reconstruct by both approaches will return f_0. More formally, for any integers $n > 1$ and $t < n$ a PPVSS is called correct, if for $(\{\mathsf{pk}_i, \mathsf{sk}_i\}_{i=1}^n, h_0 \text{ or } (\mathsf{pk}_0, \mathsf{sk}_0)) \leftarrow \mathsf{Initial}(1^\lambda)$, we have:

$$\Pr\left[\begin{array}{l}(\{y_i\}_{i=0}^n, \pi_{PPVSS}) \leftarrow \mathsf{Share}(n, t, f_0, \{\mathsf{pk}_i\}_{i=1}^n, h_0 \text{ or } \mathsf{pk}_0) : \\ \mathtt{true} \leftarrow \mathsf{Verify}(n, t, \{\mathsf{pk}_i, y_i\}_{i=0}^n, \pi_{PPVSS})\end{array}\right] = 1,$$

$$\Pr\left[\begin{array}{l}(\{y_i\}_{i=0}^n, \pi_{PPVSS}) \leftarrow \mathsf{Share}(n, t, f_0, \{\mathsf{pk}_i\}_{i=1}^n, h_0 \text{ or } \mathsf{pk}_0), \\ f_0' \leftarrow \mathsf{Reconstruct}^{opt}((h_0, y_0, f_0, r_0) \text{ or } (\mathsf{pk}_0, y_0, \mathsf{sk}_0)) \quad \vee \\ f_0' \leftarrow \mathsf{Reconstruct}^{pes}(\{y_i, \mathsf{sk}_i\}_{i\in Q, |Q|=t+1}) : f_0' = f_0\end{array}\right] = 1\,.$$

- **Verifiability**: If Verify algorithm returns true, then with high probability the values $\{y_i\}_{i=1}^n$ are encryptions of a valid sharing of some secret, and y_0 is a commitment (or a ciphertext under pk_0) to the same secret. Furthermore if the check in the (pessimistic) $\mathsf{Reconstruct}^{pes}$ phase passes then the communicated values f_i are indeed the shares of the secret distributed by the dealer. Alternatively, if the check in the (optimistic) $\mathsf{Reconstruct}^{opt}$ phase passes then the input value f_0 is the main secret, shared in the sharing phase. More formally, given λ, for any integers $n \geq 2t + 1$ and $t \geq 0$, a PVSS is called verifiable if for any PPT adversaries $\mathcal{A}$, we have:

$$\Pr\left[\begin{array}{l}(\{\mathsf{pk}_i, \mathsf{sk}_i\}_{i=1}^n, h_0 \text{ or } (\mathsf{pk}_0, \mathsf{sk}_0)) \leftarrow \mathsf{Initial}(1^\lambda), \\ (\{y_i\}_{i=0}^n, \pi_{PPVSS}) \leftarrow \mathcal{A}(n, t, \{\mathsf{pk}_i\}_{i=1}^n, h_0 \text{ or } \mathsf{pk}_0), \\ \mathtt{true} \leftarrow \mathsf{Verify}(n, t, \{\mathsf{pk}_i, y_i\}_{i=0}^n, \pi_{PPVSS}) : \\ \exists s, \forall Q \in [n], s \leftarrow \mathsf{Reconstruct}^{pes}(\{y_i, \mathsf{sk}_i\}_{i\in Q, |Q|\geq t+1}), \\ \vee \;\; s \leftarrow \mathsf{Reconstruct}^{opt}((h_0, y_0, s, r_0) \text{ or } (\mathsf{pk}_0, y_0, \mathsf{sk}_0))\end{array}\right] \geq 1 - \mathsf{negl}(\lambda)\,,$$

  where Q is the set of honest parties.
- **IND1-Secrecy (Indistinguishability of Secrets)**: Prior to the reconstruction phase, the public information together with the secret keys sk_i of any set of at most t parties, excluding sk_0, gives no information about the secret f_0. This is formalized by the following indistinguishability game adapted from [8,20]. We say that for any integers $n > 1$ and $t < n$, the PVSS scheme satisfies *IND1-Secrecy* if for any polynomial-time adversary $\mathcal{A}$ corrupting at most t parties, excluding the owner of sk_0, $\mathcal{A}$ has negligible advantage in the following game played against a challenger.
  1. The challenger runs $\mathsf{Initial}(1^\lambda)$ of the PPVSS and obtains $(\{\mathsf{pk}_i, \mathsf{sk}_i\}_{i=1}^n, h_0$ or $(\mathsf{pk}_0, \mathsf{sk}_0))$ and sends all public information along with the secret information of all corrupted parties to the $\mathcal{A}$.
  2. The challenger chooses secrets s_0 and s_1 at random in the space of secrets. Furthermore, it chooses $b \in \{0, 1\}$ uniformly at random and runs $\mathsf{Share}(n, t, s_0, \{\mathsf{pk}_i\}_{i=1}^n, h_0 \text{ or } \mathsf{pk}_0)$ algorithm of the PPVSS scheme with s_0 as the secret and obtains $(\{y_i\}_{i=0}^n, \pi_{PPVSS})$. It then sends $\mathcal{A}$ all public information generated in that phase, together with s_b.

3. $\mathcal{A}$ outputs a guess $b' \in \{0, 1\}$.

The advantage of $\mathcal{A}$ is defined as $\left|\Pr[b = b'] - \frac{1}{2}\right|$.

3.2 Building a PPVSS from a Shamir-Based PVSS

From the definition of PVSS schemes presented in Definition 7, we observe that a PPVSS extends the functionality of PVSS schemes by committing to the main secret and providing a unique and efficient reconstruction approach. These features make a PPVSS scheme more useful and versatile than standard PVSS schemes. Over the past decade, a wide range of practical PVSS schemes have been proposed, achieving significant performance [3,8–10,18,19,21].

In this section, we introduce a general strategy that enables the efficient transformation of a Shamir-based PVSS scheme into an alternative PPVSS scheme with minimal computational and communication overhead. This strategy provides a generic and efficient approach to constructing a PPVSS scheme from a Shamir-based PVSS scheme. Our key observation is that in (n, t)-Shamir-based secret sharing protocols, both the main secret f_0 and the individual shares $\{f_i\}_{i=1}^n$ are distinct evaluations of a unique degree-t polynomial $f(x)$. In a publicly verifiable secret-sharing scheme, given individual public keys $\{\mathsf{pk}_i\}_{i=1}^n$, the dealer proves, in a publicly verifiable manner, that each individual share f_i encrypted under public key pk_i is an evaluation of a unique degree-t polynomial $f(x)$ at point i. Building on this, we observe that in a PVSS scheme with public keys $\{\mathsf{pk}_i\}_{i=1}^n$, if a dealer can convince a public verifier that $y_i = \mathsf{Enc}(f(i), \mathsf{pk}_i)$ for $i = 1, \ldots, n$, then the dealer can be slightly modified to prove the same statement for $i = 0, 1, \ldots, n$ as well. Here, pk_0 can represent the public key of a specific party in the target application, or it can be a public key whose secret key is unknown to any party. It is worth mentioning that any public key encryption scheme can act as a computationally hiding and perfectly binding commitment scheme if the committer (or encryptor) does not know the secret key. Thus, pk_0 can be set either as a specific party's public key in the target application or as the commitment key in a commitment scheme.

Applying this subtle modification to the Share algorithm of the underlying PVSS scheme yields a modified Share' algorithm for a new PPVSS scheme, which returns $n+1$ ciphertexts (or n ciphertexts and 1 commitment) along with a proof π_{PPVSS} to verify the correctness of the new sharing phase. Consequently, a verifier in the resulting PPVSS scheme would run the verification algorithm of the underlying PVSS scheme using $n+1$ ciphertexts and $n+1$ public keys (or n public keys and one commitment key). We demonstrate that this subtle modification has minimal impact on the efficiency of the underlying PVSS scheme while significantly enhancing its functionality. Furthermore, it enables a new approach to secret reconstruction in the resulting PPVSS scheme, which, in practice, can be considerably more efficient than current methods.

In Fig. 2, we present a general construction for building a PPVSS scheme $\Lambda' = (\mathsf{Initial}', \mathsf{Share}', \mathsf{Verify}', \mathsf{Reconstruct}')$ using a Shamir-based PVSS scheme $\Lambda = (\mathsf{Initial}, \mathsf{Share}, \mathsf{Verify}, \mathsf{Reconstruct})$.

Initial′: In addition to running the Initial algorithm of the underlying PVSS scheme, parties agree on a commitment key pk_0, or a public key pk_0 with its associated secret key sk_0 which is only known to a specific party.

Share′: Given (n, t), a secret f_0, $\{\mathsf{pk}_i\}_{i=1}^n$, and the commitment or public key pk_0, the dealer runs the Share algorithm of the underlying PVSS scheme for $i = 0, 1, \dots, n$ and obtains π_{PPVSS}. Specifically, the dealer proceeds as follows:

1. Samples a uniformly random polynomial $f(x)$ of degree t with $f(0) = f_0$ and coefficients in $\mathbb{Z}_q$. Then, for $i = 0, 1, \dots, n$, sets $f_i = f(i)$.
2. Using $\{\mathsf{pk}_i, i, f_i\}_{i=0}^n$, computes the encrypted shares $\{y_i\}_{i=0}^n$, where y_0 is the encryption/commitment of f_0 under pk_0.
3. Runs the proof generation procedure of the underlying PVSS scheme with inputs $(\{\mathsf{pk}_i, y_i\}_{i=0}^n, f(x))$ and obtains the proof π_{PPVSS}.
4. Finally, broadcasts $(y_0, y_1, \dots, y_n, \pi_{PPVSS})$.

Verify′: Given (n, t), $\{\mathsf{pk}_i, y_i\}_{i=0}^n$, and π_{PPVSS}, a verifier runs the Verify algorithm of Λ for $i = 0, 1, \dots, n$ and outputs either `true` or `false`.

Reconstruct′: This phase can proceed in one of two approaches:

1. **Approach 1 (Optimistic Case with Commitment):** The dealer publishes the opening information for y_0, such as f_0 (and any associated randomness r_0 if needed). Then, given pk_0 and y_0, parties verify the validity of the revealed value f_0 (and associated randomness r_0 if needed) and return either f_0 (if the opening was valid) or false.
2. **Approach 2 (Pessimistic Case):** Given any $t+1$ of the encrypted shares and secret keys, e.g., $\{y_i, \mathsf{sk}_i\}_{i=1}^{t+1}$, parties run the Reconstruct algorithm of the underlying PVSS scheme and return either f_0 or false.

Fig. 2. A general construction for building a Shamir-based PPVSS scheme $\Lambda' = (\mathsf{Initial}', \mathsf{Share}', \mathsf{Verify}', \mathsf{Reconstruct}')$ from a Shamir-based PVSS scheme Λ.

Efficiency of Resulting PPVSS Scheme. The efficiency of the new protocol Λ' closely aligns with that of the original protocol Λ, with only a marginal increase. Specifically, the efficiency of the new algorithms is approximately $1/n$ times more than the original ones, implying that running the algorithms of the PPVSS scheme Λ' is comparable to executing the original algorithms in the PVSS scheme for $n + 1$ parties instead of n parties. The new PPVSS scheme Λ' achieves enhanced functionality and efficiency with minimal cost.

We will discuss the security of resulting PPVSS scheme, later in the context of particular instantiations and the proposed protocols.

4 On Practical PPVSS Schemes

The strength of the scheme proposed in Fig. 2 lies in its generality and efficiency, as it only requires a secure PVSS scheme Λ. Over the past decades, various PVSS schemes with different trade-offs have been proposed [3,8,9,11,18,20,23]. We compare the efficiency of well-known PVSS schemes in App. ??.

In this section, we instantiate the general construction from Fig. 2 using two efficient PVSS schemes [3,8] in the RO and plain models and construct two novel and practical PPVSS schemes. The proposed PPVSS schemes exhibit various trade-offs in terms of efficiency and security and the second construction uses bilinear pairing groups. We first highlight two less efficient PVSS schemes from the literature that can act as a PPVSS scheme, which in the dealer also publishes commitments to the (pre-constructed) secret.

4.1 Schoenmakers' PVSS Scheme Is a PPVSS Scheme as Well

Among current constructions for PVSS schemes, one notable protocol was introduced by Schoenmakers [23]. We refer to the full version of paper [4] for an overview of his construction. His proposed PVSS scheme is constructed in the RO model and is distinguished by its versatility, being applicable in many protocols. Specifically, this PVSS scheme can be used for random beacons, universally verifiable e-voting, binding ElGamal, revocable cash, and many other applications [23]. This versatility is primarily because, in Schoenmakers' construction, as part of the proof, the dealer uses Feldman VSS and publishes commitments to the coefficients of the secret polynomial $f(x)$, which includes a commitment to the first coefficient. The commitment to the first coefficient can also be considered a commitment to the main secret. This additional property is precisely what a type of PPVSS schemes needs to guarantee, compared to standard PVSS schemes. In [20], Heidarvand and Villar proposed a pairing-based variant of Schoenmakers' PVSS scheme, which removes the need for a random oracle and similarly publishes a commitment to the main secret. Thus, Schoenmakers' scheme [23] and its pairing-based variant proposed in [20] can also be considered as (special) PPVSS schemes, where in both cases, the dealer publishes a commitment to the pre-constructed secret as well. Despite their versatility, Schoenmakers' PPVSS scheme [23] and its pairing-based variant [20] are significantly less efficient compared to more recent PVSS schemes. Notably, their verification costs are dominated by $O(n^2)$ exponentiations.

Since the introduction of Schoenmakers' (P)PVSS [23], and its pairing-based variant [20], several follow-up and more efficient PVSS schemes have been developed [3,8,9,11,18], reducing the verification complexity to $O(n)$. Although all the recent PVSS schemes are considerably more efficient compared to the PPVSS schemes from [20,23], they all are limited in terms of applicability and are mostly used in a restricted number of applications (e.g., distributed randomness generation). Consequently, many protocols based on (P)PVSS, such as universally verifiable e-voting and threshold binding ElGamal [23], still need to rely on Schoenmakers' construction [23] or its pairing-based variant [20], which both are too slow, rendering them impractical for large-scale applications. In PPVSS schemes build with our proposed construction, with minimal computational overhead, the dealer can publish either or both the encryption and/or commitment of the main secret f_0, providing greater flexibility.

4.2 A Practical PPVSS Scheme in the Random Oracle Model

In this section, we instantiate the general construction from Fig. 2 using the RO-based PVSS scheme proposed by Baghery [3], so-called Π_S, which can also be considered as a formally proven and non-packed version of the PVSS scheme initially proposed by Cascudo and David [9]. The resulting PPVSS scheme $\Lambda_{RO} = (\mathsf{Initial}', \mathsf{Share}', \mathsf{Verify}', \mathsf{Reconstruct}')$ is summarized in Fig. 3. The key differences between the original scheme and the resulting PPVSS scheme are highlighted in gray color. The resulting RO-based PPVSS scheme can be seen as the first alternative to the RO-based (P)PVSS scheme proposed by Schoenmakers [23], offering greater flexibility and more efficient verification, requiring $O(n)$ exponentiations instead of $O(n^2)$. This improvement allows us to revisit all the applications discussed in [23], and enhance their performance.

Theorem 1 (RO-Based PPVSS). *Under the Polynomial Discrete Logarithm (PDL) and Decisional Diffie-Hellman (DDH) assumptions, the PPVSS scheme (outlined in Fig. 3), is secure against an static adversary in the random oracle model. That is, (i) the protocol satisfies Correctness, (ii) it satisfies Verifiability under PDL assumption, and both the reconstruction algorithms described in* $\mathsf{Reconstruct}'$ *phase result in the secret* g^{f_0} *distributed by the dealer (for any qualified set of shareholders in case of approach 2), (iii) it satisfies IND1-Secrecy under DDH assumption, and any non-qualified set of shareholders is unable to distinguish between the shares of two secrets.*

Proof. **Correctness.** If the dealer and parties follow the protocol honestly, the verification and reconstruction processes yield the expected results. At the end of initialization phase, parties register public keys ($\{\mathsf{pk}_i := g^{s_i}\}_{i=1}^n, \mathsf{pk}_0$ or (pk_0, s_0)) and store the associated secret keys $\{s_i\}_{i=1}^n$ (or $\{s_i\}_{i=0}^n$) for the reconstruction phase. Given (n, t), the secret f_0, public keys $\{\mathsf{pk}_i\}_{i=1}^n$, and the commitment or public key pk_0, the dealer proceeds as follows: samples a polynomial $f(x)$ of degree t such that $f(0) = f_0$ and generates the encrypted shares $\{y_i = \mathsf{pk}_i^{f(i)}\}_{i=0}^n$, where y_0 is the encryption or commitment of f_0 under pk_0. Then, it samples $r(x)$ of degree t and sets $c_i = \mathsf{pk}_i^{r(i)}$ for $i = 0, 1, \ldots, n$. Next, it computes the challenge value $d = \mathcal{H}(y_0, y_1, \ldots, y_n, c_0, c_1, \ldots, c_n)$ and $z(x) = r(x) + df(x)$. Finally, it broadcasts $\pi_{PPVSS} := (d, z(x))$ and $y_0, y_1, \ldots, y_n$. By substituting these values in the verification equation, we observe that

$$d == \mathcal{H}(y_0, y_1, \ldots, y_n, \frac{\mathsf{pk}_0^{z(0)}}{y_0^d}, \frac{\mathsf{pk}_1^{z(1)}}{y_1^d}, \ldots, \frac{\mathsf{pk}_n^{z(n)}}{y_n^d})$$

$$= \mathcal{H}(y_0, y_1, \ldots, y_n, \frac{\mathsf{pk}_0^{r(0)+df(0)}}{\mathsf{pk}_0^{df(0)}}, \frac{\mathsf{pk}_1^{r(1)+df(1)}}{\mathsf{pk}_1^{df(1)}}, \ldots, \frac{\mathsf{pk}_n^{r(n)+df(n)}}{\mathsf{pk}_n^{df(n)}})$$

$$= \mathcal{H}(y_0, y_1, \ldots, y_n, \mathsf{pk}_0^{r(0)}, \mathsf{pk}_1^{r(1)}, \ldots, \mathsf{pk}_n^{r(n)}) = \mathcal{H}(y_0, y_1, \ldots, y_n, c_0, c_1, \ldots, c_n).$$

During the optimistic reconstruction phase, given $(g, \mathsf{pk}_0, y_0, f_0)$, clearly $y_0 = \mathsf{pk}_0^{f_0}$ and the algorithm will always return f_0. For the pessimistic case, given any

Initial′: As in the Initial phase of the original PVSS scheme [3,9], given the generator g for $\mathbb{G}$, for $i = 1, \ldots, n$, each party P_i register their public key $\mathsf{pk}_i = g^{s_i}$, and store the secret key s_i. The parties also agree on $\mathsf{pk}_0 \neq g$ as the commitment key, or a target public key. In case of former, pk_0 is sampled randomly from $\mathbb{G}$, and in case of later, it is registered by the target person P_0 as $\mathsf{pk}_0 = g^{s_0}$, where $s_0 \in \mathbb{Z}_q$ is the secret key of the target person.

Share′: Given the parameters (n, t), a secret f_0, the public keys $\{\mathsf{pk}_1, \ldots, \mathsf{pk}_n\}$, and the commitment or public key pk_0, the dealer acts as follows:

1. Samples a uniformly random polynomial $f(x)$ of degree t with $f(0) = f_0$ and coefficients in $\mathbb{Z}_q$. Then, for $i = 0, 1, \ldots, n$ sets $f_i = f(i)$.
2. Sets the encrypted shares $y_0 = \mathsf{pk}_0^{f_0}, y_1 = \mathsf{pk}_1^{f_1}, \ldots, y_n = \mathsf{pk}_n^{f_n}$. Note that, depending on the target application, in practice, the secret key of pk_0 might be unknown, or it can be known for a specific party.
3. Based on the proof scheme π_{PDL} (presented in [3]), samples a new random degree-t polynomial $r(x)$ with coefficients in $\mathbb{Z}_q$ and sets $c_i = \mathsf{pk}_i^{r(i)}$ for $i = 0, 1, \ldots, n$.
4. Given the random oracle $\mathcal{H}$, compute $d = \mathcal{H}(y_0, y_1, \ldots, y_n, c_0, c_1, \ldots, c_n)$ and $z(x) = r(x) + df(x)$.
5. Finally, broadcasts $(y_0, y_1, \ldots, y_n, \pi_{PPVSS} := (d, z(x))$.

Verify′: Given (n, t), $(\mathsf{pk}_0, \mathsf{pk}_1, \ldots, \mathsf{pk}_n, y_0, y_1, \ldots, y_n)$, and $\pi_{PPVSS} = (d, z(x))$, a verifier first checks if $z(x)$ is a degree-t polynomial. If so, given the random oracle $\mathcal{H}$, it checks the following equation and outputs `true/false`

$$d == \mathcal{H}(y_0, y_1, \ldots, y_n, \frac{\mathsf{pk}_0^{z(0)}}{y_0^d}, \frac{\mathsf{pk}_1^{z(1)}}{y_1^d}, \ldots, \frac{\mathsf{pk}_n^{z(n)}}{y_n^d}).$$

Reconstruct′: This phase can proceed in one of two approaches:

1. Approach 1 (Optimistic Case): The dealer publishes f_0. Then, given (g, pk_0, y_0), a verifier (not necessarily from the parties) checks if $y_0 == \mathsf{pk}_0^{f_0}$ and returns either g^{f_0} (if the check passes) or false.
2. Approach 2 (Pessimistic Case): Parties run the Reconstruct algorithm of Π_S PVSS scheme and return either g^{f_0} or false. To this end,
   (a) They first use their secret key s_i, and obtain their share $F_i := g^{f_i}$ from y_i by computing $F_i = y_i^{1/s_i}$. Then, they publish F_i plus a NIZK proof that the value F_i is a correct decryption of y_i. To this end, the party P_i needs to prove knowledge of an s_i such that, $(\mathsf{pk}_i = g^{s_i}) \wedge (y_i = F_i^{s_i})$, which can be done by the NIZK proof scheme for the DLEQ relation (given in Fig. 1).
   (b) Then, given any $t+1$ valid values of F_i, w.l.o.g. for $i = 1, \ldots, t+1$, the secret $g^{f_0} = g^{f(0)}$, can be obtained by Lagrange interpolation,

$$\prod_{i=1}^{t+1} F_i^{\lambda_i} = \prod_{i=1}^{t+1} (g^{f_i})^{\lambda_i} = g^{\sum_{i=1}^{t+1} f_i \lambda_i} = g^{f(0)} = g^{f_0},$$

where $\lambda_i = \prod_{j \neq i} \frac{j}{j-i}$ is a Lagrange coefficients.

Fig. 3. Λ_{RO}: an efficient RO-based PPVSS scheme based on the PVSS scheme Π_S.

$t+1$ shares and their secret keys, e.g., $\{y_i, s_i\}_{i \in Q, |Q|=t+1}$, the parties run the Reconstruct algorithm of the original PVSS scheme and this also always yields f_0 if the shares will be generated honestly.

Verifiability. For the verifiability, we show that if Verify algorithm returns true, then the values $\{y_i\}_{i=1}^n$ are encryptions of a valid sharing of some secret, and y_0 is a commitment (or a ciphertext under pk_0) to the same secret. Furthermore if the check in the (pessimistic) Reconstruct^{pes} phase passes then the communicated values f_i are indeed the shares of the secret distributed by the dealer and the reconstruction with any $t+1$ of valid shares will reach to the same secret g^{f_0}. Alternatively, if the check in the (optimistic) Reconstruct^{opt} phase passes then the output value g^{f_0} is the main secret, shared in the sharing phase. This is achieved by showing that the NIZK argument deployed in the new PPVSS scheme satisfies special soundness under PDL problem for the relation $y_i = \mathsf{pk}_i^{f(i)}$ for $i = 0, 1, 2, \ldots, n$, where $f(x)$ is a (at most) degree-t witness polynomial. In other words, akin to the case of original PVSS scheme [3], we show that given two acceptable transcripts of the (interactive) protocol, any $t+1$ honest shareholders can use theirs secret keys and extract a unique (at most) degree-t polynomial from the dealer, which is a solution for the PDL problem. This implies that both the reconstitution approaches will result in a unique secret g^{f_0}. Let, $(c_i, d, z(x))$ and $(c_i, d', z'(x))$ be two acceptable transcripts of the (interactive) protocol, for $i = 0, 1, \ldots, n$. From the verification equation, we know that

$$\mathsf{pk}_i^{z(i)} = c_i(y_i)^d \quad , \quad \mathsf{pk}_i^{z'(i)} = c_i(y_i)^{d'} \quad \text{for } i = 0, 1, , \ldots, n \; .$$

Note that, as pointed in [3], the verification equation can be written in the above form as well. This implies that,

$$\mathsf{pk}_i^{z(i)-z'(i)} = y_i^{d-d'} \Rightarrow y_i = \mathsf{pk}_i^{\frac{z(i)-z'(i)}{d-d'}} \qquad \text{for } i = 0, 1, \ldots, n \; . \tag{2}$$

Then, if all $n \geq 2t+1$ of the checks in the verification pass successfully, given the (pessimistic) reconstruction protocol detailed in Fig. 3, any set of $t+1$ honest parties can decrypt $\{y_i\}_{i \in Q, |Q|=t+1, i \neq 0}$, as $F_i := y_i^{1/s_i}$, and rewrite the last equation as below,

$$g^{z(i)-z'(i)} = F_i^{d-d'} \Rightarrow F_i = g^{\frac{z(i)-z'(i)}{d-d'}} \qquad \text{for } i \in Q, \; |Q| = t+1, i \neq 0.$$

Note that at this stage parties need to give NIZK proof for DLEQ relation for their correct decryption, therefore malicious parties will be aborted. Now, since $z(x)$ is a degree-t polynomial, and since from $f_i := \frac{z(i)-z'(i)}{d-d'}$ for $i \in Q, |Q| = t+1, i \neq 0$, we obtain $t+1$ *distinct* evaluations of a (witness) degree-t polynomial $\frac{z(x)-z'(x)}{d-d'}$, therefore an extractor can use $\{f_i\}_{i \in Q, |Q|=t+1, i \neq 0}$ and reconstruct (extract) a *unique* (at most) degree-t polynomial $f(x)$, which is a solution for the PDL problem. This implies that, in the secret reconstruction with pessimistic approach, any set of $t+1$ honest parties, can use their individual (decrypted) shares $F_i := y_i^{1/s_i}$, employ Lagrange interpolation (as in Fig. 3), and evaluate a unique degree-t polynomial $f(x)$ in the *exponent* at any point. By evaluating $g^{f(x)}$ at point 0, they can obtain a unique secret value $g^{f(0)}$.

Note that in the case of $i = 0$, from Eq. (2), we can write

$$\mathsf{pk}_0^{z(0)-z'(0)} = y_0^{d-d'} \Rightarrow y_0 = \mathsf{pk}_0^{\frac{z(0)-z'(0)}{d-d'}}$$

which is a discrete logarithm solution. This implies that $\frac{z(0)-z'(0)}{d-d'}$ is the constant term of the same (up to) degree-t witness polynomial $f(x)$, extracted using the pessimistic reconstruction approach. Consequently, we conclude $y_0 = \mathsf{pk}_0^{f(0)} = \mathsf{pk}_0^{f_0}$. Thus, in secret reconstruction using the optimistic approach, given the opening information f_0, anyone can verify its validity and compute the unique secret g^{f_0}. In the scenario where pk_0 is the public key of a specific party, given the associated secret key s_0, one can compute the unique secret $F_0 := g^{f_0}$ by calculating y_0^{1/s_0}.

IND1-Secrecy. We show that, if there exists an adversary $\mathcal{A}$ which can break the IND1-secrecy property of the PPVSS scheme from Fig. 3, then there exists an adversary $\mathcal{B}$ which can use $\mathcal{A}$ as a subroutine to break the Decisional Diffie-Hellman (DDH) assumption with the same advantage.

Without loss of generality, we assume $\mathcal{A}$ corrupts the $t-1$ first parties (excluding the owner of s_0). Let $(h, h^\alpha, h^\beta, h^\gamma)$ be an instance of the DDH problem. We assume the values of α or β are nonzero. Now $\mathcal{B}$, using $\mathcal{A}$, can simulate an IND1 game as follows:

1. The challenger sets $g = h^\alpha$ and runs the initial phase of the protocol. For $t \le i \le n$ and $i = 0$, $\mathcal{B}$ selects uniformly random values $u_i \leftarrow \mathbb{Z}_q$ (implicitly defining $s_i = u_i/\alpha$) and sends the values $\mathsf{pk}_i = h^{u_i}$ to $\mathcal{A}$.
2. For $1 \le i \le t-1$, $\mathcal{A}$ chooses uniformly random values $s_i \leftarrow \mathbb{Z}_q$ and sets $\mathsf{pk}_i = g^{s_i}$ and sends this to the challenger.
3. For $1 \le i \le t-1$, the challenger chooses uniformly random values $f_i \leftarrow \mathbb{Z}_q$ and sets $v_i = h^{f_i}$ and $y_i = \mathsf{pk}_i^{f_i}$.
For $t \le i \le n$, it generates the values $v_i = h^{p(i)}$, where $p(x)$ is the unique polynomial of degree at most t determined by $p(0) = \beta$ and $p(i) = f_i$ for $i = 1, \ldots, t-1$. Note that $\mathcal{B}$ does not know β, but it does know $h^\beta = h^{p(0)}$ and $h^{f_i} = h^{p(i)}$ for $1 \le i \le t-1$, so it can use Lagrange interpolation in the exponent to compute the adequate v_i. It also creates the values $y_i = v_i^{u_i}$ for $t \le i \le n$ and $y_0 = (h^\beta)^{u_0}$. From all the computed values $\{\mathsf{pk}_i, y_i\}_{i=0}^n$, and given the challenge value of the interactive proof scheme, the simulator can sample a random degree-t polynomial $z'(x)$ and set $c_i' := \mathsf{pk}_i^{z'(i)}/y_i^d$ for $i = 0, 1, \ldots, n$. Finally, it sends all this information together with the value h^γ (which plays the role of s_b in the IND1 game) to $\mathcal{A}$.
4. $\mathcal{A}$ makes a guess b'. If $b' = 0$, $\mathcal{B}$ guesses that $\gamma = \alpha \cdot \beta$. If $b' = 1$, $\mathcal{B}$ guesses that γ is a random element in $\mathbb{Z}_p$.

The information that $\mathcal{A}$ receives in step 3 is distributed exactly like a sharing of the value $g^\beta = h^{\alpha \cdot \beta}$ with the PPVSS. Consequently, $\gamma = \alpha \cdot \beta$ if and only if the value h^γ sent to $\mathcal{A}$ is the secret shared by the PPVSS. It is now easy to see that the guessing advantage of $\mathcal{B}$ is the same as the advantage of $\mathcal{A}$. □

4.3 An Efficient PPVSS Scheme in the Plain Model

The PPVSS scheme proposed in Sect. 4.2 is built in the random oracle model. In this section, we present an efficient PPVSS scheme based on pairings in the plain model. To this end, we instantiate the general construction from Fig. 2 using the pairing-based PVSS scheme proposed by Cascudo and David [8], that relies on Decisional Bilinear Square (DBS) assumption [20]. Similarly, the resulting pairing-based PPVSS scheme can be seen as the first alternative to the paring-based PPVSS scheme proposed by Heidarvand and Villar [20], offering greater flexibility and more efficient verification, requiring $O(n)$ exponentiations and $O(n)$ pairings instead of $O(nt)$ exponentiations and $O(n)$ pairings.

As in the underlying PVSS scheme, in the new PPVSS scheme, the dealer initially uses pairings to prove the equality of the encrypted and committed shares, i.e., $\{y_i, c_i\}_{i=0}^n$. Subsequently, the verifier employs the dual-code trick to check that the committed shares $\{c_i\}_{i=0}^n$ are valid and properly formed. It is important to note that the equality proof provided by the dealer ensures that the correctness of the committed shares $\{c_i\}_{i=0}^n$ implies that the encrypted shares $\{y_i\}_{i=0}^n$ are also correct and well-formed.

Let $(q, \mathbb{G}, \mathbb{G}_T, e)$ be a description of a bilinear group and (g, h) be two independently chosen generators of $\mathbb{G}$. Let RS be the linear error correcting code equivalent to the (n, t)-threshold Shamir secret sharing scheme and $\mathsf{RS}^\intercal$ be its dual code. The resulting PPVSS scheme $\Lambda_{Plain} = (\mathsf{Initial}', \mathsf{Share}', \mathsf{Verify}', \mathsf{Reconstruct}')$ is summarized in Fig. 4. As in Λ_{RO}, the key differences between the original scheme [20] and the new PPVSS scheme are highlighted.

As in the original and prior PVSS schemes in the plain model [8,20], we present our PPVSS schemes over a symmetric bilinear group, also known as Type-I bilinear groups. However, as in original PVSS case, we note that our proposed PPVSS scheme can be adapted to asymmetric bilinear groups, where pairing-friendly curves enable more efficient pairing algorithms.

Security. The algorithms of new PPVSS scheme are similar to the underlying PVSS scheme [8], while the optimistic reconstruction is specific for the new PPVSS scheme. We have made adjustments in the security proof of underlying PVSS scheme to adapt for our protocol under the Decisional Bilinear Square (DBS) assumption. This proof leverages pairing-based verification, ensuring that any maliciously constructed encrypted shares $y_0, y_1, \ldots, y_n$ will pass verification with probability no higher than $1/q$, while $c_0, c_1, \ldots, c_n$ reveal no information about the secret $e(h, h)^{f_0}$ under the DBS assumption.

Theorem 2. *Under the DBS assumption, the PPVSS scheme Λ_{Plain} outlined in Fig. 4 satisfies IND1-secrecy against a static PPT adversary in the plain model.*

Proof. We show that, if an adversary $\mathcal{A}$ can break the IND1-secrecy property of PPVSS scheme Λ_{Plain}, then we can build another adversary $\mathcal{B}$ that can exploit $\mathcal{A}$ to break the Decisional Bilinear Square (DBS) assumption with equivalent advantage. Without loss of generality, we assume $\mathcal{A}$ corrupts the t first parties (excluding the owner of s_0).

Assume an instance $(g, g^\alpha, g^\beta, T)$ is given, where $\mathcal{B}$ must determine whether $T = e(g^\alpha, g^\alpha)^\beta$ or $T = e(g^\alpha, g^\alpha)^\gamma$ for a random $\gamma \leftarrow \mathbb{Z}_q$. Obviously if $\alpha = 0$ or $\beta = 0$ then the problem is trivial, so we assume these values are nonzero. Now $\mathcal{B}$, using $\mathcal{A}$ in an IND1 game as follows:

1. The challenger sets $h = g^\alpha$ and runs the Setup phase of PPVSS in plain model. For $t < i \leq n$ and $i = 0$, A_{DBS} selects uniformly random values $u_i \leftarrow \mathbb{Z}_q$ (these can be thought of implicitly defining s_i as $s_i = u_i/\alpha$) and sends the values $pk_i = g^{u_i}$ to $\mathcal{A}$.

Initial′: Let $(q, \mathbb{G}, \mathbb{G}_T, e)$ be a description of a bilinear group and (g, h) be two independently chosen generators of $\mathbb{G}$. As in the **Initial** phase of the original PVSS scheme [8], given the generator h, for $i = 1, \ldots, n$, each party P_i register their public key $\mathsf{pk}_i = h^{s_i}$, and store the secret key s_i. The parties also agree on $\mathsf{pk}_0 \neq h$ as the commitment key, or a target public key. In case of former, pk_0 is sampled randomly from $\mathbb{G}$, and in case of later, it is registered by the target person P_0 as $\mathsf{pk}_0 = h^{s_0}$, where $s_0 \in \mathbb{Z}_q$ is the secret key of P_0.

Share′: Given the parameters (n, t), a secret f_0, the public keys $\{\mathsf{pk}_1, \ldots, \mathsf{pk}_n\}$, and the commitment or public key pk_0, the dealer defines the secret $S = e(h, h)^{f_0}$ and acts as follows:

1. Samples a uniformly random polynomial $f(x)$ of degree t with $f(0) = f_0$ and coefficients in $\mathbb{Z}_q$. Then, for $i = 0, 1, \ldots, n$ sets $f_i = f(i)$.
2. Sets the encrypted shares $y_0 = \mathsf{pk}_0^{f_0}, y_1 = \mathsf{pk}_1^{f_1}, \ldots, y_n = \mathsf{pk}_n^{f_n}$. Note that, depending on the target application, in practice, the secret key of pk_0 might be unknown, or it can be known for a specific party.
3. Sets the commitments $c_i = g^{f_i}$ for $i = 0, 1, \ldots, n$.
4. Finally, broadcasts $\pi_{PPVSS} := (c_0, c_1, \ldots, c_n)$ and $(y_0, y_1, \ldots, y_n)$.

Verify′: Given (n, t), $(\mathsf{pk}_0, \mathsf{pk}_1, \ldots, \mathsf{pk}_n, y_0, y_1, \ldots, y_n)$, and $\pi_{PPVSS} = (c_0, c_1, \ldots, c_n)$, a verifier first checks if $e(y_i, g) = e(\mathsf{pk}_i, c_i)$, for $i = 0, 1, \ldots, n$. If so, it samples a random codeword $v^{\mathsf{T}} = (v_0^{\mathsf{T}}, v_1^{\mathsf{T}}, \ldots, v_n^{\mathsf{T}})$ of the dual code RS^{T} corresponding to RS, the instance of Shamir's (n, t)-threshold secret sharing used by dealer, and checks if:

$$c_0^{v_0^{\mathsf{T}}} \prod_{i=1}^{n} c_i^{v_i^{\mathsf{T}}} == 1$$

and outputs either `true`/`false`.

Reconstruct′: This phase can proceed in one of two approaches:

1. Approach 1 (Optimistic Case): The dealer publishes f_0. Then, given (h, pk_0, y_0), a verifier (not necessarily from the parties) checks if $y_0 == \mathsf{pk}_0^{f_0}$ and returns either $S = e(h^{f_0}, h)$ or false.
2. Approach 2 (Pessimistic Case): Parties run the **Reconstruct** algorithm of the original PVSS scheme [8] and return either $S = e(h^{f_0}, h)$ or false. To this end,
   (a) Parties in a qualified set Q first use their secret key s_i, and obtain their share $F_i := h^{f_i}$ from y_i by computing $F_i = y_i^{1/s_i}$. Then, they publish F_i. Note that here the NIZK proof for the correctness of decryption is empty.
   (b) Given $\{\mathsf{pk}_i, c_i, F_i\}_{i \in Q}$, a verifier checks if $e(\mathsf{pk}_i, F_i) = e(y_i, h)$ for every $P_i \in Q$.
   (c) If the check succeeds, they reconstruct $h^{f_0} = h^{f(0)}$ by Lagrange interpolation as,
   $$\prod_{P_i \in Q} F_i^{\lambda_i} = \prod_{P_i \in Q} (h^{f_i})^{\lambda_i} = h^{\sum_{P_i \in Q} f_i \lambda_i} = h^{f(0)} = h^{f_0},$$
   where $\lambda_i = \prod_{j \neq i} \frac{j}{j-i}$ is a Lagrange coefficients.
   (d) They return $S = e(h^{f_0}, h)$ or false if fewer than $t + 1$ valid shares were collected.

Fig. 4. Λ_{Plain}: an efficient PPVSS scheme in the plain model.

2. For $1 \leq i \leq t$, $\mathcal{A}$ chooses uniformly random values $s_i \leftarrow \mathbb{Z}_q$ and sets $\mathsf{pk}_i = h^{s_i}$ and sends this to the challenger.
3. For $1 \leq i \leq t$, the challenger chooses uniformly random values $f_i \leftarrow \mathbb{Z}_q$ and sets $c_i = g^{f_i}$ and $y_i = \mathsf{pk}_i^{f_i}$.
4. For $t < i \leq n$ and $i = 0$, the challenger generates the values $c_i = g^{f(i)}$ where $f(X)$ is a unique (at most) degree-t polynomial, determined by $f(0) = e(h, h)^{\beta} = e(g^{\alpha}, g^{\alpha})^{\beta}$ and $f(i) = f_i$ for $i = 1, \ldots, t$. The challenger now sends T (which plays the role of s_b in the IND1 game) to $\mathcal{A}$.
5. At the end of sharing phase, the value T is sent as part of the game response. If $\mathcal{A}$'s guess $b' = 0$, then $\mathcal{B}$ guesses that $T = e(g^{\alpha}, g^{\alpha})^{\beta}$; if $b' = 1$, it guesses $T = e(g^{\alpha}, g^{\alpha})^{\gamma}$. This ensures that $\mathcal{B}$'s advantage mirrors that of $\mathcal{A}$.

This completes the proof. □

Theorem 3. *If the dealer does not construct values* (c_i, y_i) *of the right form in the sharing phase (i.e. either* $\log_g c_i \neq \log_{\mathsf{pk}_i} y_i$ *for some* i*, or* $\log_g c_i = \log_{\mathsf{pk}_i} y_i = f_i$ *for all* $0 \leq i \leq n$ *but the values* $\{f_i\}_{i=1}^n$ *do not constitute a valid sharing of* $f_0 \in \mathbb{Z}_q$ *with the* (n,t)*-threshold Shamir secret sharing scheme), then this is detected in the verification phase with probability at least* $1 - 1/q$.

Proof. For all $i = 0, \ldots, n$ the relation of $\log_g c_i = \log_{\mathsf{pk}_i} y_i$ is verified by checking that $e(y_i, g) = e(\mathsf{pk}_i, c_i)$. Note that if $a = \log_g c_i \neq \log_{\mathsf{pk}_i} y_i = b$ for some i, then $e(y_i, g) = e(\mathsf{pk}_i, g)^b \neq e(\mathsf{pk}_i, g)^a = e(\mathsf{pk}_i, c_i)$ and the check fails with probability 1. Now with probability ϵ, for every $0 \leq i \leq n$, there exists f_i with $c_i = g^{f_i}$ and $y_i = \mathsf{pk}_i^{f_i}$. Now the values f_i are a valid sharing of f_0 with the (n,t)-threshold Shamir secret sharing scheme if and only if the vector $\vec{F} = (f_0, f_1, \ldots, f_n) \in \mathsf{RS}$, where RS is the liner error correcting code equivalent to the (n,t)-threshold Shamir secret sharing. Suppose that $\vec{F} := (f_0, f_1, \ldots, f_n) \notin \mathsf{RS}$. Let, $\mathsf{RS}^\intercal$ denotes the dual code of RS. Then, since the codeword $\vec{V}^\intercal := (v_0^\intercal, v_1^\intercal, \ldots, v_n^\intercal) \in \mathsf{RS}^\intercal$ is sampled uniformly at random, then $\langle \vec{F}, \vec{V}^\intercal \rangle \neq 0$ except with probability $1/q$, where $\langle \vec{F}, \vec{V}^\intercal \rangle$ denotes the inner product of two vectors $\vec{F}$ and $\vec{V}^\intercal$ as $\langle \vec{F}, \vec{V}^\intercal \rangle = \sum_{i=0}^n f_i \cdot v_i^\intercal$. But then, from the verification equation, we will have

$$\prod_{i=0}^n c_i^{v_i^\intercal} = \prod_{i=0}^n g^{f_i \cdot v_i^\intercal} = g^{\langle \vec{F}, \vec{V}^\intercal \rangle} \neq 1.$$

Hence if the values $\{f_i\}_{i=1}^n$ are not a valid Shamir sharing of f_0, then the check fails with probability $1 - 1/q$. This completes the proof. □

Theorem 4. *In the reconstruction phase of new PPVSS scheme, if the dealer or parties communicate invalid values, this is detected by the verifier. Namely, i) if a party in* Q *communicates an erroneous decryption share* y_i *in the pessimistic reconstruction phase, this is detected by the verifier with probability* 1. *i) if a dealer publishes an invalid* f_0 *in the optimistic reconstruction phase, then this is catched with probability* 1.

Proof. For the pessimistic case we observe that, if $y_i = h^a$ with $a \neq f_i$ then $e(pk_i, y_i) = e(pk_i, h)^a \neq e(pk_i, h)^{s_i} = e(f_i, h)$. For the optimistic case, we note that given $(h, \mathsf{pk}_0, y_0, f_0)$, a verifier checks if $y_0 == \mathsf{pk}_0^{f_0}$, which can be seen as a perfectly binding commitment scheme and the check fails with probability 1 if $y_0 \neq \mathsf{pk}_0^{f_0}$. □

In App. ??, we discuss the homomorphic property of new PPVSS schemes.

4.4 Empirical Performance of Λ_{RO} PPVSS Scheme and Comparison

We conducted a detailed analysis of the concrete efficiency of the proposed PPVSS schemes and compared them with relevant constructions from the literature. A summary of the results is presented in Table 1.

In addition, we evaluated the practical performance of the new RO-based PPVSS scheme through a prototype implementation in Rust and compared its performance with the (P)PVSS scheme proposed by Schoenmakers [23][1]. From the results in Table 1, we observe that the reconstruction phases of both new PPVSS schemes are as efficient as those of comparable schemes. Therefore, we focus primarily on the performance of the sharing and verification phases, as well as the communication size. Our experiments are done using the Ristretto Group under `Curve25519` and the hash function `Blake3` for the random oracle. The tests were run on MacBook Pro with an M4 Pro CPU with 24GB RAM. Both sharing and verification were limited to 8 threads to utilize the 8 performance cores available. All numbers are averaged over 100 iterations. The implementation results for several parameter sets are summarized in Table 2.

Table 2. Implementation results of Λ_{RO} PPVSS scheme and comparison with Schoenmakers' scheme [23]. n: Number of parties, t: Threshold value, $|\mathbb{Z}_q| = |\mathbb{G}| = 256$ bits.

(n, t)	Metrics	Schoenmakers [23]	Λ_{RO} PPVSS (Fig. 3)
(256, 127)	Sharing	4.87 ms	2.47 ms
	Verification	123.58 ms	2.10 ms
	Dealer's Broadcast	20 KB	12 KB
(512, 255)	Sharing	10.51 ms	6.21 ms
	Verification	482.70 ms	4.97 ms
	Dealer's Broadcast	40 KB	24 KB
(1024, 511)	Sharing	24.73 ms	17.96 ms
	Verification	1.91 s	13.68 ms
	Dealer's Broadcast	80 KB	48 KB

The implementation results also confirm that the new PPVSS protocol improves upon Schoenmakers' scheme [23] in all aspects and offers significantly faster verification. For $(n, t) = (512, 255)$, the new scheme achieves verification times that is approximately $97\times$ faster in comparison to the Schoenmakers' scheme, and this gap increases for the large values of n.

5 A Practical Universally Verifiable E-Voting Protocol

In [23, Sections 5 and 6], Schoenmakers proposed a variety of applications based on his (P)PVSS scheme, including a universally verifiable e-voting protocol, threshold software key escrow, and threshold binding ElGamal encryption. Our analysis shows that these applications are specifically suited for PPVSS schemes

[1] Our source code for the implementations is publicly available at https://github.com/KULeuven-cosic/ppvss-evoting.

and crucially rely on the dealer's ability to commit to the main secret or encrypt it under a specific public key–features that are absent in standard, more efficient PVSS schemes [3,8,9,11]. Our proposed PPVSS schemes, presented in Sect. 4, directly address these limitations.

In the full version of paper [4], we revisit the threshold software key escrow and threshold binding ElGamal encryption applications proposed by Schoenmakers [23] and present a more efficient variant of each. The threshold binding ElGamal encryption application relies on the dealer encrypting the main secret under a specific public key, a property readily achievable with our proposed PPVSS schemes. The threshold software key escrow application relies on the dealer publishing a commitment to the main secret.

As another important application of PPVSS schemes, in this section, we use our proposed RO-based PPVSS scheme (from Fig. 3) to revisit Schoenmakers' universally verifiable e-voting protocol and improve its overall performance. Notably, the new e-voting protocol requires $O(mn)$ exponentiations, rather than $O(mn^2)$, in the verification phase, where n and m denote the number of talliers and voters, respectively. This improvement makes our proposal considerably more efficient in practice, particularly for elections with large values of n. We begin by briefly outlining Schoenmakers' original e-voting protocol [23, Section 5] before presenting our revised variant.

5.1 Schoenmakers' Universally Verifiable E-Voting Protocol

Schoenmakers' proposed e-voting protocol follows the model for universally verifiable elections introduced by Benaloh et al. [7]. This model assumes the availability of a public bulletin board where all participants can post messages. The players in the scheme consist of a set of tallying authorities (talliers) $A_1, \ldots, A_n$, a set of voters $V_1, \ldots, V_m$ and a set of passive observers. These two sets need not be disjoint. As an instance, in small-scale elections like board-room elections, each player may be both a voter and a tallier. Schoenmakers' protocol leverages his proposed (P)PVSS scheme to achieve public verification while maintaining voter privacy. It consists of three main phases. In the first phase, voters use the (P)PVSS scheme to cast their encrypted ballots on the public bulletin board. Since voter anonymity is not a requirement in this scheme, double voting can be easily prevented by checking the votes and verifying the validity of ballots before accepting them. In the second phase, the bulletin board verifies the ballots and obtain the list of valid votes $\{V_i\}_{j=1}^{m}$. After a successful verification phase, in the third phase, the talliers use their private keys to collectively compute the final tally, by accumulating all valid ballots and decrypting the accumulated ballot. Figure 5 summarizes the procedure of Schoenmakers' e-voting protocol.

5.2 Schoenmakers' E-Voting Protocol Revisited

Leveraging the proposed RO-based PPVSS scheme from Fig. 3, next we revisit Schoenmakers' e-voting protocol and present a more efficient version. Given the

Initialization Phase: In this phase, the initialization of the PPVSS scheme has been completed, and each tallier A_i has sampled a secret key $x_i \in \mathbb{Z}_q$ and registered public key $\mathsf{pk}_i = G^{x_i}$. They also agree on pk_0 as the commitment key.

Ballot Casting Phase: Given the public keys of tallies, to casts a vote $v \in \{0, 1\}$, a voter acts as below:

1. Samples a random secret value $s \in \mathbb{Z}_q$.
2. Using the public keys of talliers $\{\mathsf{pk}_i\}_{i=0}^n$ and the secret value s, runs the distribution protocol for his PVSS (or our PPVSS) scheme and obtains the encrypted shares and the associated proof π_{PVSS} (or π_{PPVSS}).
3. Computes the value $U = G^{s+v}$ and using the protocol given in Sec. 2.1 constructs a well-formedness proof π_U, showing that indeed $v \in \{0, 1\}$, without revealing any information on v. The proof π_U refers to the value of $C_0 = h^s$ (or $y_0 = \mathsf{pk}_0^s$) which is published as part of π_{PVSS} (or π_{PPVSS}) in the (P)PVSS (or PPVSS) distribution protocol, and shows that:

$$\log_G U = \log_h C_0 \vee \log_G U = 1 + \log_h C_0 \text{ (or } \log_G U = \log_{\mathsf{pk}_0} y_0 \vee \log_G U = 1 + \log_{\mathsf{pk}_0} y_0 \text{)}.$$

The ballot for voter V consists of the output of the (P)PVSS (or PPVSS) distribution protocol (which consists of encryption of shares and the proof π_{PVSS} (or π_{PPVSS})), the value U (which can be seen as an encryption of the vote), and proof π_U (which proves the well-formedness of U).

Ballot Verification Phase: Once voters submitted their ballots, the ballots are checked by the bulletin board. Note that both proofs π_{PVSS} (or π_{PPVSS}) and π_U are publicly verifiable and can be checked by anyone.

Tallying Phase: Suppose voters $\{V_j\}_{j=1}^m$, have all cast valid ballots. The tallying protocol consists of the following step:

1. Talliers first accumulate all the respective encrypted shares, under the same public keys, by computing the values $Y_i^\star$, where the index j ranges over all voters:
$$Y_i^\star = \prod_{j=1}^m Y_{ij} = y_i^{\sum_{j=1}^m p_j(i)}.$$
2. Next, each tallier A_i applies the reconstruction protocol of Schoenmakers' (P)PVSS (or our PPVSS) scheme to the value $Y_i^\star$, which will produce $S^\star = G^{\sum_{j=1}^m p_j(0)} = G^{\sum_{j=1}^m s_j}$, due to the homomorphic property of the (P)PVSS (or PPVSS) scheme.
3. Using $\{U_j\}_{j=1}^m$, talliers compute $U^\star = \prod_{j=1}^m U_j = G^{\sum_{j=1}^m s_j + v_j}$. Then, using $S^\star$ and $U^\star$ they compute $V^\star = \frac{U^\star}{S^\star} = G^{\sum_{j=1}^m v_j}$. Given $V^\star$, the tally $V = \sum_{j=1}^m v_j$, $0 \leq V \leq m$, can be computed efficiently.

Fig. 5. A universally verifiable e-voting protocol based on Schoenmakers' (P)PVSS [23] and our proposed PPVSS. The highlighted texts are particular for the new variant.

new PPVSS scheme, the revision is straightforward. Essentially, in Schoenmakers' e-voting protocol (summarized in Fig. 5) we replace his (P)PVSS scheme with our proposed PPVSS scheme and adapt the rest of the protocol accordingly. With this replacement, using our PPVSS scheme, each voter will publish $y_0 = \mathsf{pk}_0^s$ as the commitment to their random secret s, which will serve the role of C_0 in Schoenmakers' voting protocol. Figure 5 presents the resulting e-voting protocol and highlights its key difference with the original scheme.

5.3 Efficiency Comparisons and Benchmarks

Efficiency of Schoenmakers' E-voting Protocol. The efficiency of Schoenmakers' e-voting protocol can be summarized as follows. In the first phase, each voter acts as the dealer in Schoenmakers' (P)PVSS scheme and distributes a random secret s. This requires each voter (i.e., the dealer) to compute $4.5n$ exponentiations and n evaluations of a degree-t polynomial. Using C_0 and U, each voter also runs the proof scheme from Sect. 2.1 and generates a proof π_U. This proof consists of $(4|\mathbb{G}|, 4|\mathbb{Z}_q|)$ elements and requires an additional 6 exponentiations in the group. In the second phase, the verifier needs to run the verifier of both Schoenmakers' (P)PVSS protocol and the NIZK proof scheme from Sect. 2.1 to check the validity of all ballots submitted by $\{V_j\}_{j=1}^m$. The computational cost of this step is approximately $m(nt + 4.5n)$ exponentiations, where m and n are the number of voters and talliers, respectively, and $t = \lfloor \frac{n-1}{2} \rfloor$ is the threshold value. In the third phase, each tallier A_i needs to compute $Y_i^\star$, run the reconstruction of Schoenmakers' (P)PVSS scheme, check the openings of other talliers and compute the final tally by calculating the discrete logarithm of $V^\star = G^{\sum_{j=1}^m}$. The total cost for this step is approximately $5t$ exponentiations and $n + t$ multiplications in the underplaying group.

Efficiency of New E-voting Protocol. In the first phase of new e-voting protocol, each voter compute $2n$ exponentiations and $2n$ evaluations of a degree-t polynomial. Using y_0 and U, each voter also runs the proof scheme from Sect. 2.1 and generates a proof π_U, which consists of $(4|\mathbb{G}|, 4|\mathbb{Z}_q|)$ elements and requires an additional 6 exponentiations in the group. In the second phase, the verifier needs to verify both proofs π_{PPVSS} and π_U to check the validity of all ballots submitted by $\{V_j\}_{j=1}^m$. The computational cost of this step is approximately

Table 3. Implementation results of the universally verifiable e-voting protocols proposed in [23] and Sect. 5 for different types and sizes of elections. n: Number of talliers, t: Threshold value (number of malicious talliers), m: Number of voters, $|\mathbb{Z}_q| = |\mathbb{G}| = 256$ bits, s: seconds, ms: milliseconds, B: Byte, K: Kilo, M: Million.

Election, (n, t, m)	Metrics	Schoenmakers [23]	Our Scheme (Fig. 5)
Election 1	Ballot Casting Time	4.65 ms	2.63 ms
(board-room)	Voter's Communication	20.28 KB	12.28 KB
(256, 127, 256)	Verification of One Ballot	121.15 ms	2.30 ms
	Tallying Time	11.18 ms	11.18 ms
Election 2	Ballot Casting Time	9.92 ms	6.43 ms
(board-room)	Voter's Communication	40.28 KB	24.28 KB
(512, 255, 512)	Verification of One Ballot	481.19 ms	5.33 ms
	Tallying Time	27.91 ms	27.91 ms
Election 3, 4, 5	Ballot Casting Time	0.56 ms	0.42 ms
(large-scale)	Voter's Communication	1648 B	1104 B
$(17, 8, m)$	Verification of One Ballot	1.24 ms	0.41 ms
$m = 50$K	Tallying Time	1.31 s	1.31 s
$m = 100$K	Tallying Time	2.61 s	2.61 s
$m = 1$M	Tallying Time	25.70 s	25.70 s

$2nm$ exponentiations and nm degree-t polynomial evaluations, where n and m are the number of talliers and voters, respectively. The tallying phase (i.e., the third phase) is identical for both protocols, therefore have the same efficiency.

Empirical Performance of E-voting Protocols. In addition, we assessed the practical performance of both e-voting protocols by implementing them in Rust and comparing their performance. As in case of PPVSS schemes, our experiments are done using the Ristretto Group under `Curve25519` and the hash function `Blake3` for the random oracle. The tests were run on MacBook Pro with an M4 Pro CPU with 24GB RAM. All three phases, ballot casting, ballot verification, and tallying were limited to 8 threads to utilize the 8 performance cores available. All numbers are averaged over 100 iterations. We have summarized our implementation results for various parameter sets in Table 3.

Upon comparing the implementation outcomes, it becomes apparent that the new e-voting protocol outperforms Schoenmakers' scheme in all metrics. Notably, it yields a remarkable acceleration in the verification phase, particularly for large value of n, making it practical for even large-scale board-room elections. As an instance, the new scheme achieves verification times that are approximately $52\times$ and $90\times$ faster in comparison to the Schoenmakers' scheme for each voter with the parameter pairs (n, t) equal to $(256, 127)$ and $(512, 255)$. In large-scale elections, we observe that for $(n, t, m) = (17, 8, 100K)$, ballot casting takes just 0.42 milliseconds, each voter needs to broadcast 1104 bytes of data, each ballot can be verified in 0.26 ms, and vote tallying is completed in 2.62 s.

6 Conclusion

In this paper, we introduced Pre-constructed PVSS (PPVSS), an extension of standard PVSS schemes that offers improved flexibility and efficiency by requiring the dealer to publish a commitment (or an encryption) to the main secret. This new design, combined with a novel secret reconstruction approach, directly addresses the limitations of existing PVSS schemes in applications that require the dealer's commitment to the secret itself, such as e-voting, threshold key escrow, and other transparency-focused protocols [23].

A major contribution of our work is a general strategy for transforming Shamir-based PVSS schemes into PPVSS schemes, applicable across a wide range of PVSS schemes. This flexibility enables PPVSS schemes to support a broader array of applications, including areas such as distributed key generation and randomness generation protocols. Our constructions include both RO-based and plain-model PPVSS schemes, both of which are built on state-of-the-art PVSS protocols [3,8,9]. Through theoretical analysis and practical evaluation, we showed that these PPVSS schemes not only match the security properties of PVSS but also improves upon current alternative protocols in terms of efficiency and flexibility. The RO-based scheme, in particular, enables the revision of universally verifiable e-voting protocol from [23], that improves its overall performance and significantly reduces the computational complexity of ballot verification, especially in settings with a high number of talliers.

While our focus has been on PVSS schemes where the secret is g^{f_0} and parties can only reconstruct g^{f_0} in the reconstruction phase, we believe our general strategy can readily apply to other PVSS schemes where the secret is shared directly as f_0, e.g., [10,19]. In addition, we revisited only a select few applications of PPVSS schemes, emphasizing their adaptability and potential for improved efficiency. Given the inherent flexibility of PPVSS, we anticipate that these schemes could find even wider applicability in cryptographic protocols. This opens new avenues for future research to explore additional applications where PPVSS can offer advantages over traditional PVSS schemes.

We primarily examined PPVSS schemes based on the Discrete Logarithm (DL) assumption. However, constructing PPVSS schemes based on alternative assumptions, such as lattice-based cryptography, presents an interesting direction for further study, potentially broadening the scope of applications and enhancing security against quantum adversaries.

Our work used one positive feature of PPVSS schemes–publishing an encryption or commitment of the main secret under a specific public key–across three revisited applications. We also introduced a new reconstruction approach that may improve efficiency in PVSS-based protocols by supporting constant communication and verification costs under an optimistic reconstruction method. This approach leverages the assumption that in some applications, each participant acts as a dealer at least once, and a majority of participants are honest. In such cases, this optimistic reconstruction approach can streamline the reconstruction phase and reduce overall computational overhead.

In summary, our work provides a flexible, efficient PPVSS framework that expands the practical capabilities of secret sharing schemes, setting the stage for future advancements in publicly verifiable threshold protocols and their applications in secure and decentralized systems.

Acknowledgments. This work was supported by the Flemish Government through the Cybersecurity Research Program with grant number VOEWICS02.

References

1. Atapoor, S., Baghery, K., Cozzo, D., Pedersen, R.: VSS from distributed ZK proofs and applications. In: Guo, J., Steinfeld, R. (eds.) Advances in Cryptology - ASIACRYPT 2023 - 29th International Conference on the Theory and Application of Cryptology and Information Security, Guangzhou, China, 4–8 December 2023, Proceedings, Lecture Notes in Computer Science. Springer, Heidelberg (2023). https://doi.org/10.1007/978-981-99-8721-4_13
2. Backes, M., Kate, A., Patra, A.: Computational verifiable secret sharing revisited. In: Lee, D.H., Wang, X. (eds.) ASIACRYPT 2011. LNCS, vol. 7073, pp. 590–609. Springer, Heidelberg (2011). https://doi.org/10.1007/978-3-642-25385-0_32
3. Baghery, K.: A unified framework for computational verifiable secret sharing. In: Jager, T., Pan, J. (eds.) Public-Key Cryptography - PKC 2025 - 28th IACR International Conference on Practice and Theory of Public-Key Cryptography, Roros, Norway, 12–15 May 2025, Proceedings. LNCS. Springer, Heidelberg (2025). https://doi.org/10.1007/978-3-031-91829-2_4

4. Baghery, K., Knapen, N., Nicolas, G., Rahimi, M.: Pre-constructed publicly verifiable secret sharing and applications. Cryptology ePrint Archive, Paper 2025/576 (2025)
5. Ben-Or, M., Goldwasser, S., Wigderson, A.: Completeness theorems for non-cryptographic fault-tolerant distributed computation (extended abstract). In: 20th Annual ACM Symposium on Theory of Computing, Chicago, IL, USA, 2–4 May 1988, pp. 1–10. ACM Press (1988)
6. Benaloh, J.C.: Secret sharing homomorphisms: keeping shares of a secret secret (extended abstract). In: Odlyzko, A.M. (ed.) CRYPTO 1986. LNCS, vol. 263, pp. 251–260. Springer, Heidelberg (1987). https://doi.org/10.1007/3-540-47721-7_19
7. Benaloh, J.C., Yung, M.: Distributing the power of a government to enhance the privacy of voters (extended abstract). In: Halpern, J.Y. (ed.) 5th ACM Symposium Annual on Principles of Distributed Computing, Calgary, Alberta, Canada, 11–13 August 1986, pp. 52–62. Association for Computing Machinery (1986)
8. Cascudo, I., David, B.: SCRAPE: scalable randomness attested by public entities. In: Gollmann, D., Miyaji, A., Kikuchi, H. (eds.) ACNS 2017. LNCS, vol. 10355, pp. 537–556. Springer, Cham (2017). https://doi.org/10.1007/978-3-319-61204-1_27
9. Cascudo, I., David, B.: ALBATROSS: publicly AttestabLe BATched randomness based on secret sharing. In: Moriai, S., Wang, H. (eds.) ASIACRYPT 2020. LNCS, vol. 12493, pp. 311–341. Springer, Cham (2020). https://doi.org/10.1007/978-3-030-64840-4_11
10. Cascudo, I., David, B.: Publicly verifiable secret sharing over class groups and applications to DKG and YOSO. In: Joye, M., Leander, G. (eds.) Advances in Cryptology – EUROCRYPT 2024, Part V, vol. 14655 of Lecture Notes in Computer Science, Zurich, Switzerland, 26–30 May 2024, pp. 216–248. Springer, Cham (2024). https://doi.org/10.1007/978-3-031-58740-5_8
11. Cascudo, I., David, B., Garms, L., Konring, A.: YOLO YOSO: fast and simple encryption and secret sharing in the YOSO model. In: Agrawal, A., Lin, D. (eds.) Advances in Cryptology – ASIACRYPT 2022, Part I, vol. 13791 of Lecture Notes in Computer Science, Taipei, Taiwan, 5–9December 2022, pp. 651–680. Springer, Cham (2022). https://doi.org/10.1007/978-3-031-22963-3_22
12. Chaum, D., Pedersen, T.P.: Wallet databases with observers. In: Brickell, E.F. (ed.) CRYPTO 1992. LNCS, vol. 740, pp. 89–105. Springer, Heidelberg (1993). https://doi.org/10.1007/3-540-48071-4_7
13. Chor, B., Goldwasser, S., Micali, S., Awerbuch, B.: Verifiable secret sharing and achieving simultaneity in the presence of faults (extended abstract). In: 26th Annual Symposium on Foundations of Computer Science, Portland, Oregon, 21–23October 1985, pp. 383–395. IEEE Computer Society Press (1985)
14. Cramer, R., Damgård, I., Schoenmakers, B.: Proofs of partial knowledge and simplified design of witness hiding protocols. In: Desmedt, Y.G. (ed.) CRYPTO 1994. LNCS, vol. 839, pp. 174–187. Springer, Heidelberg (1994). https://doi.org/10.1007/3-540-48658-5_19
15. Feldman, F.A.: Fast spectral tests for measuring nonrandomness and the DES. In: Pomerance, C. (ed.) CRYPTO 1987. LNCS, vol. 293, pp. 243–254. Springer, Heidelberg (1988). https://doi.org/10.1007/3-540-48184-2_22
16. Feldman, P.: A practical scheme for non-interactive verifiable secret sharing. In: 28th Annual Symposium on Foundations of Computer Science, Los Angeles, CA, USA, 12–14 October 1987, pp. 427–437. IEEE Computer Society Press (1987)
17. Fiat, A., Shamir, A.: How to prove yourself: practical solutions to identification and signature problems. In: Odlyzko, A.M. (ed.) CRYPTO 1986. LNCS, vol. 263, pp. 186–194. Springer, Heidelberg (1987). https://doi.org/10.1007/3-540-47721-7_12

18. Gentry, C., Halevi, S., Lyubashevsky, V.: Practical non-interactive publicly verifiable secret sharing with thousands of parties. In: Dunkelman, O., Dziembowski, S. (eds.) Advances in Cryptology – EUROCRYPT 2022, Part I, vol. 13275 of Lecture Notes in Computer Science, Trondheim, Norway, 30 May–3 June 2022. Springer, Cham (2022). https://doi.org/10.1007/978-3-031-06944-4_16
19. Groth, J.: Non-interactive distributed key generation and key resharing. Cryptology ePrint Archive, Report 2021/339 (2021)
20. Heidarvand, S., Villar, J.L.: Public verifiability from pairings in secret sharing schemes. In: Avanzi, R.M., Keliher, L., Sica, F. (eds.) SAC 2008. LNCS, vol. 5381, pp. 294–308. Springer, Heidelberg (2009). https://doi.org/10.1007/978-3-642-04159-4_19
21. Kate, A., Mangipudi, E.V., Mukherjee, P., Saleem, H., Thyagarajan, S.A.K.: Non-interactive VSS using class groups and application to DKG. Cryptology ePrint Archive, Report 2023/451 (2023)
22. Pedersen, T.P.: Non-interactive and information-theoretic secure verifiable secret sharing. In: Feigenbaum, J. (ed.) CRYPTO 1991. LNCS, vol. 576, pp. 129–140. Springer, Heidelberg (1992). https://doi.org/10.1007/3-540-46766-1_9
23. Schoenmakers, B.: A simple publicly verifiable secret sharing scheme and its application to electronic voting. In: Wiener, M. (ed.) CRYPTO 1999. LNCS, vol. 1666, pp. 148–164. Springer, Heidelberg (1999). https://doi.org/10.1007/3-540-48405-1_10
24. Shamir, A.: How to share a secret. Commun. Assoc. Comput. Mach. **22**(11), 612–613 (1979)
25. Stadler, M.: Publicly verifiable secret sharing. In: Maurer, U. (ed.) EUROCRYPT 1996. LNCS, vol. 1070, pp. 190–199. Springer, Heidelberg (1996). https://doi.org/10.1007/3-540-68339-9_17
26. Verheul, E.R., van Tilborg, H.: Binding ElGamal: a fraud-detectable alternative to key-escrow proposals. In: Fumy, W. (ed.) EUROCRYPT 1997. LNCS, vol. 1233, pp. 119–133. Springer, Heidelberg (1997). https://doi.org/10.1007/3-540-69053-0_10
27. Young, A., Yung, M.: Auto-recoverable auto-certifiable cryptosystems. In: Nyberg, K. (ed.) EUROCRYPT 1998. LNCS, vol. 1403, pp. 17–31. Springer, Heidelberg (1998). https://doi.org/10.1007/BFb0054114

Blockchains and Decentralized Systems

HCC: A Language-Independent Hardening Contract Compiler for Smart Contracts

Jens-Rene Giesen[1](✉), Sebastien Andreina[2], Michael Rodler[3], Ghassan Karame[4], and Lucas Davi[1]

[1] University of Duisburg-Essen, Essen, Germany
{jens-rene.giesen,lucas.davi}@uni-due.de
[2] NEC Laboratories Europe, Heidelberg, Germany
sebastien.andreina@neclab.eu
[3] Amazon Web Services, Düsseldorf, Germany
m@mrodler.eu
[4] Ruhr University Bochum, Bochum, Germany
ghassan@karame.org

Abstract. Developing secure smart contracts remains a challenging task. Existing approaches are either impractical or leave the burden to developers for fixing bugs. In this paper, we propose the first practical smart contract compiler, called HCC, which automatically inserts security hardening checks at the source-code level based on a novel and language-independent code property graph (CPG) notation. The high expressiveness of our developed CPG allows us to mitigate all of the most common smart contract vulnerabilities, namely reentrancy, integer bugs, suicidal smart contracts, improper use of tx.origin, untrusted delegate-calls, and unchecked low-level call bugs. Our large-scale evaluation on 10k real-world contracts and several sets of vulnerable contracts from related work demonstrates that HCC is highly practical, outperforms state-of-the-art contract hardening techniques, and effectively prevents all verified attack transactions without hampering functional correctness.

1 Introduction

Smart contracts are becoming increasingly supported by most modern blockchain platforms. When used within existing cryptocurrencies such as Ethereum, smart contracts often handle very large amounts of cryptocurrency. Unfortunately, the supporting software engineering tooling around smart contracts is still in its infancy. Important safety and security features prevalent in modern-day software engineering cycles are either not integrated or are not made sufficiently usable [42].

Several high-profile attacks on the Ethereum blockchain, such as the *TheDAO* attack, the *Parity Multisig Wallet* attack, and the more recent *Bacon Protocol* and *Orion Protocol* attacks [56,57] have fueled research to strengthen the security of smart contracts. While the bulk of the research on smart contract security is rooted in formal methods and verification [20,22,23,41], other

M. Fischlin and V. Moonsamy (Eds.): ACNS 2025, LNCS 15825, pp. 123–152, 2025.
https://doi.org/10.1007/978-3-031-95761-1_5

proposals approach smart contract security from a testing perspective and utilize symbolic execution [24,30] or fuzzing [36,59] to generate inputs and identify bugs and security vulnerabilities. However, as we will argue in Sect. 2.1, existing solutions are impractical for smart contract developers as they typically are hard to use and suffer from a high false positive and negative rate. Most importantly, the majority of existing approaches require heavy involvement from software developers for patching vulnerabilities and sorting out false alarms.

On the other hand, existing proposals targeting automated smart contract bytecode rewriting [37,63] are not able to handle complex attack patterns such as reentrancy. They are also incompatible with the upcoming eWASM bytecode format [12]. Further, security checks inserted into the bytecode of a smart contract are specific to one execution environment (e.g., the Ethereum virtual machine), which makes them hardly verifiable by most developers as they do not understand bytecode semantics. Similarly, contract repair tools operating as source-to-source compilers [25,29] either rely on developer-specified invariants, do not support many real-world contracts, or provide limited effectiveness.

Contributions. In this paper, we propose the first practical smart contract compiler, called HCC (hardening contract compiler), that automatically inserts security checks at the source-code level. HCC ensures full transparency for smart contract developers and is fully compatible with other source code related workflows. To do so, we develop a novel code-property graph (CPGs) [61] for smart contracts to detect a wide range of vulnerabilities (Sect. 3). Our design overcomes a set of unique challenges (Sect. 2.2), namely: (1) it supports inter-procedural and inter-contract analysis, (2) it accurately determines mitigation points (to avoid false positives), (3) it efficiently hardens against bugs without breaking legitimate behavior, and (4) it provides support for a highly dynamic smart contract ecosystem involving both permissioned and permissionless blockchains. Due to our CPG notation, HCC can be applied to any smart contract platform and programming language, which is especially important considering the high dynamics in this quite young application domain. For showcasing our work, our prototype implementation of HCC targets the Solidity language for Ethereum contracts (Sect. 4) which is by far the most popular smart contract language. In addition, we provide a detailed analysis of how HCC can be applied to Hyperledger Fabric (Sect. 6), one of the most popular enterprise blockchains. Note that Fabric drastically differs from Ethereum in terms of programming language and blockchain design, allowing us to demonstrate the high expressiveness of our CPG. We are not aware of any approach that is capable of supporting different blockchain platforms.

We demonstrate in detail HCC's effectiveness on all known patterns of reentrancy and integer bugs, while ensuring that it does not prevent legitimate reentrancy required for flash loans. These two bug classes are responsible for the most notorious and disastrous attacks observed in existing blockchains. In addition, HCC is capable of mitigating suicidal smart contracts, improper use of `tx.origin`, untrusted *delegatecall* and unchecked low-level call bugs.

We conducted an extensive evaluation (Sect. 5) based on a dataset of 10k Solidity smart contracts. Our dataset also includes vulnerable contracts based on the state-of-the-art datasets [38,50,64]. To comprehensively test for functional correctness, we apply a differential testing method on 31 629 actual blockchain transactions within these datasets. Moreover, we experimentally compare HCC with existing source-level contract repair tools [29]. Our experiments show that these do not support many real-world contracts and often fail to protect against real-world exploits (Sect. 5.3). Finally, to demonstrate the real-world impact of HCC, we evaluated it against the 25 top-valued Ethereum contracts with source code available as reported by etherscan.io. We harden these contracts with HCC and replay 49 265 transactions using a differential testing method. None of those transactions failed—demonstrating the high practical value of HCC. We also evaluate the runtime effects of the mitigations in Sect. 5.4.

We also integrated HCC with Hyperledger Fabric and our results show that HCC was able to fix all the vulnerabilities reported in the five ERC-20 token contracts from the Osiris [50] dataset. We open source HCC at https://github.com/uni-due-syssec/hcc.

2 Problem Statement and Related Work

2.1 Background & Related Work

Code Analysis Tooling. Basic syntax directed analysis usually relies on the abstract syntax tree (AST) and is effective at providing immediate feedback to the developer. However, it cannot precisely discover complex security vulnerabilities [61]. Various static analysis tools translate smart contract code into a custom Datalog-based intermediate representation (IR) [5,6,18,53]. While these approaches provide good analysis capabilities, they usually do not scale and often do not faithfully model the EVM's semantics [40]. Similarly, symbolic execution-based approaches for smart contracts [10,15,24,26,27,35,50,52,60] achieve high precision, but suffer from scalability issues in practice.

Further, existing code analysis tools require developers to choose between coverage and precision. Good coverage often entails many false alarms, bearing the risk that developers simply start to ignore them. A recent study shows that even experienced developers fail to correctly identify vulnerabilities in smart contracts using such tools [42]. On the other hand, tools with a low number of false alarms tend to miss vulnerabilities. Moreover, the majority of existing code analysis tools focus on reporting potential vulnerabilities, but do not provide any guidance on how to fix and harden the contract.

Contract Hardening. Several automated mitigation mechanisms have been proposed [8,14,25,29,38,51]. On-chain solutions [38,51] either require changes to the blockchain ecosystem or to smart contract deployment. Bytecode-level analysis [15,24,26,27,50] and hardening tools [14,37,63] suffer from imprecision due to the lack of high-level information (e.g., source types and control flow), which was a major source for false alarms in prior work [38]. As such, these approaches cannot easily cover bug classes that involve complex control-flows and data-flows such as reentrancy. Moreover, hardening on the bytecode level [14,37,63] does not allow developers to inspect the modified contract. In contrast, source-to-source compilation approaches [25,29,62] allow developers to inspect the introduced changes. For instance, Solythesis [25] inserts runtime checks into Solidity contracts. However, this requires manual specification of the invariants. Hence, incorrect or incomplete invariants (i.e., specification bugs) would lead to vulnerable smart contracts. SCRepair [62] and sGuard [29] both leverage symbolic analysis techniques, thereby suffering from the same scalability issues as code analysis tools discussed above. To tackle this shortcoming, sGuard [29] develops a custom symbolic analysis. However, as our analysis in Sect. 5.3 shows, sGuard does still not support many complex, real-world contracts and often does not prevent well-known exploits.

2.2 Challenges

Contrary to the majority of existing software, it is cumbersome to publish a timely update to a vulnerable smart contract. In fact, there are a number of challenges that emerge when developing effective and practical hardening compilers for smart contracts, namely:

Challenge 1: Dynamic Ecosystem. Smart contract ecosystems and programming languages are continuously evolving. There are a number of permissionless and permissioned blockchain platforms supporting various languages (e.g., Solidity, Go, Java, Rust). To avoid building a special-purpose compiler for each blockchain platform, our goal is to devise a general-purpose compiler that works independently of the platform specifics and languages. To date, there does not exist any approach that tackles this challenge.

Challenge 2: Developer-Friendliness & False Alarms. Existing approaches require developers to manually investigate each warning to sort out false alarms and fix true vulnerabilities. Hence, there is a pressing need for a novel approach to smart contract security that focuses on developer usability and eliminates the necessity for them to acquire domain-specific expertise, particularly in light of the ever-evolving ecosystem (c.f., Challenge 1). Moreover, it is imperative that any security solution implemented preserves the integrity of legitimate operations This calls for the development of security checks that are: (1) sufficiently generic to harden against all bug flavors of a specific bug pattern, and (2) at the same time not too strict to prevent legitimate executions.

Challenge 3: Inter-Procedural and Inter-Contract Analysis. Smart contracts suffer from various subtle errors in the program code, e.g., unexpected reentrant calls leading to inconsistent state updates. Detecting a wide range of complex smart contract bugs necessarily requires inter-procedural and inter-contract analysis. However, doing so for smart contracts is highly challenging since they can (1) create new smart contracts at runtime, (2) use different types of memory for runtime data and persistent state, (3) be invoked through different

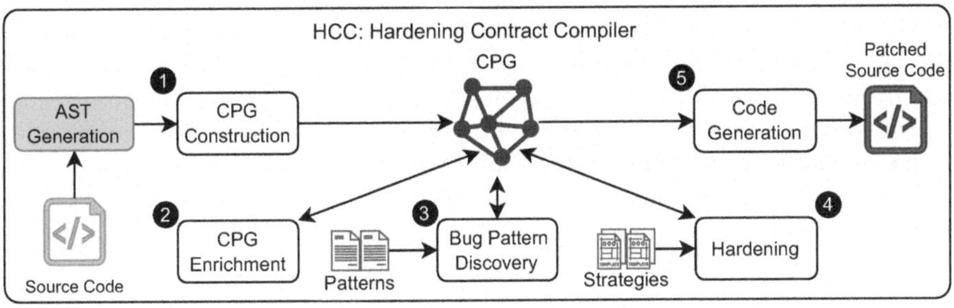

Fig. 1. Architecture of HCC.

entry functions, and (4) interact with other contracts, e.g., by invoking public functions of other contracts; highlighting the need for a novel graph schema that accurately models all the peculiarities of smart contracts.

Challenge 4: Determining Mitigation Points. Knowing where to insert security checks is a key requirement for hardening against attacks. This can be particularly challenging when the bug is, e.g., in a program loop. If the bug is in the loop header for the increment or decrement operation, there is a need to investigate the entire loop to validate whether and how the affected variable is processed inside the loop body in order to avoid missing potential vulnerabilities.

3 HCC: Hardening Contract Compiler

To solve the aforementioned challenges, we introduce HCC, a novel Hardening Contract Compiler that leverages code property graphs (CPGs), A CPG is a graph model of a program which consists of an AST (abstract syntax tree) enriched with information on control-flows and data-flows. Originally, CPGs have been proposed to detect memory safety bugs in the Linux kernel [61]. While memory safety bugs are not relevant for smart contracts—as the latter do not perform low-level memory operations—the superiority of CPGs in encoding the programs' control-flow and data-flow provides means to protect smart contracts independently of the programming language.

We generate the CPG by instrumenting the compilation process of smart contracts. Figure 1 shows the five phases of HCC's compilation process: (1) CPG construction (2) CPG enrichment, (3) bug pattern discovery, (4) hardening, and (5) code generation.

First, HCC transforms the compilers' generated AST into HCC's novel CPG representation. This step also includes determining the target compiler version to correctly generate matching code (Challenge 1). Second, the *enrichment* phase performs several analysis passes which are especially necessary to determine unresolvable function calls, i.e., calls to other contracts (Challenge 3). Third, HCC initiates a vulnerability scan based on CPG graph traversals. To do so, we generated generic CPG patterns to model diverse smart contract bugs

(Challenge 3 and 4). Fourth, we insert hardening patches—again based on generic templates—for insecure code. Fifth, HCC emits the hardened AST as source code and continues the ordinary compilation process.

As shown in Fig. 1, HCC does not remove vulnerabilities but rather adds hardening checks to prevent exploitation. The reasoning for this design decision is based on lessons learned from previous code analysis tools that way too often misjudged or missed contract vulnerabilities (see Sect. 2.1). In doing so, we follow a similar design to the mitigation techniques used in the Desktop world, i.e., control-flow integrity (CFI) assumes that program code will never be free of bugs. We note that, in contrast to traditional compiler-based hardening techniques like CFI [1], we apply our patches to the source code, which allows developers to review the checks.

Note that our modular design enables HCC to integrate existing detection and patching strategies, while requiring minimal integration efforts. For yet unknown bug types, additional enrichment steps can be easily included to perform the necessary analysis and CPG extension. Before we will explain each phase in detail, we introduce our notation.

Notation. The notation we use throughout this paper are listed in Table 1. For a given source code, let $\mathcal{S}$ denote the set of all statements. A statement $s \in \mathcal{S}$ represents a complete line of code (e.g., until the ";" or "{" symbols for languages such as Java and Solidity). Statements can contain one or multiple expressions $e \in \mathcal{E}$ that represent a valid unit of code, $\mathcal{E}$ defined as the set of all expressions. For example, the following assignment statement isEven $= (a\%2) == 0$; contains two binary expressions: the equality comparison as the first expression, itself nested with an arithmetic expression performing the modulo operation and four unary expressions: the two constants 0 and 2, and the two variables isEven and a. We use the $\overleftarrow{e}$ (resp. $\overrightarrow{e}$) notation to access the left (resp. right) element of a binary expression $e \in \mathcal{E}$. By e^r, we denote recursive accesses to all sub-expressions of e, like $\overleftarrow{e}$ and $\overrightarrow{e}$, until the expression cannot be resolved further. We denote the set of expressions in a given statement s as $\mathcal{E}_s$, and define the top level expression of a statement as $\widehat{e} \in \mathcal{E}_s$. We write $\mathcal{S}_{\rightarrow s}$ (resp. $\mathcal{S}_{s\rightarrow}$) to designate the former (resp. subsequent) statements of $s \in \mathcal{S}$ in the execution flow.

Since programming languages are based on functions, we define the subset $\mathcal{S}_f \subseteq \mathcal{S}$ for statements part of a given function f from the set of all defined functions $\mathcal{F}$. Functions are further defined through their arguments, $\mathcal{A}_f$, and their local variables, $\mathcal{L}_f$. We refer to the set of persistent variables (e.g., the database of the smart contract) by $\mathcal{P}$. Since access and updates of the persistent variables need to be strictly monitored to prevent attacks, we additionally define the set $\mathcal{U} = \{s \in \mathcal{S} : \exists p \in \mathcal{P} \mid s \text{ updates } p\}$, as the set of all statements s that *update* a persistent variable, and its filtered version $\mathcal{U}_p = \{s \in \mathcal{S} : s \text{ updates } p\}$, the set of statements $s \in \mathcal{U}$ that update a specific persistent variable $p \in \mathcal{P}$. Using the previous notation, we define a smart contract c from the set of all smart contracts $\mathcal{C}$ as the sets of persistent variables $c.\mathcal{P}$, and functions $c.\mathcal{F}$ declared in the contract c. Additionally, we define the helper notations: we write $r \rightarrow t$, $r \in \mathcal{E}$ to mean r refers to t, where t is any variable or function. We denote the set of binary operations, such as additions, by $\mathcal{E}^{BO}$ and the set of binary comparisons, such as equality, by $\mathcal{E}^{BC}$. The set of call expression $\mathcal{E}^{C}$ refers to expressions e referencing a function f, i.e., $e \in \mathcal{E}_s | e \rightarrow f$. Note that f can be either a defined ($f \in \mathcal{F}$) or undefined ($f \notin \mathcal{F}$) function. For $c \in \mathcal{E}^{C}$, $addr(c)$ refers to the callee contract of c. Finally, we denote by $\mathcal{V}_x$ the set of statements vulnerable to vulnerability type x.

❶ CPG Construction. In contrast to an AST, the CPG is a directed graph that consists of diverse types of nodes and directed edges. Nodes and edges are labeled and can have an arbitrary number of properties. In HCC, the AST is the prerequisite for generating the CPG. Common parser generators such as ANTLR [11] support many different programming languages, and enable the creation of compatible ASTs directly from source code for various source languages. HCC encodes the sets and elements from Table 1 in the CPG as nodes and edges. In the CPG, nodes are labeled according to their semantics, e.g., the node representing a function $f \in \mathcal{F}$ is referred to as `Function` and variables are denoted by the label `Variable`. Labeling every piece of data in the CPG effectively creates a schema that facilitates further processing and analysis. Since HCC's internal CPG representation preserves the general structure of the original AST, the CPG contains a node for every high-level syntactic element. This enables HCC to insert hardening patches by augmenting the AST.

Set	Members
$\mathcal{C}$	All contracts defined in the source code.
$\mathcal{P}$	Set of all persistent variables.
$c.\mathcal{P}$	Persistent variables declared in contract $c \in \mathcal{C}$.
$\mathcal{F}$	Set of all declared functions.
$\mathcal{A}_f$	Function arguments of $f \in \mathcal{F}$.
$\mathcal{L}_f$	Local variables declared in $f \in \mathcal{F}$.
$\mathcal{S}$	All statements in the source code.
$\mathcal{E}$	All expressions in the source code.
$\mathcal{V}_x$	All instances of vulnerability x.
	Subsets of $\mathcal{S}$
$\mathcal{S}_f$	Statements in function $f \in \mathcal{F}$.
$\mathcal{S}_{\rightarrow s}$	Set of statements former to s.
$\mathcal{S}_{s\rightarrow}$	Set of statements subsequent to s.
$\mathcal{U}$	Statements $s \in \mathcal{S}$ updating any $p \in \mathcal{P}$.
$\mathcal{U}_p$	Statements $s \in \mathcal{S}$ updating $p \in \mathcal{P}$.
	Subsets of $\mathcal{E}$
$\mathcal{E}_s$	Expressions in $s \in \mathcal{S}$, $\mathcal{E}_s \subseteq \mathcal{E}$.
$\mathcal{E}^{C}$	Set of function call expressions.
$\mathcal{E}^{BO}$	Set of binary operation expressions.
$\mathcal{E}^{BC}$	Set of binary comparison expressions.
	Further Notation
$a \rightarrow b$	Reference, $a \in \mathcal{E}$ refers to any b.
$addr(c)$	The callee contract for any $c \in \mathcal{E}^{C}$.
$\widehat{e}$	$e \in \mathcal{E}_s$: the top-level expression of statement s.
e^{r}	Recursively resolve all expressions of $e \in \mathcal{E}$.

Table 1. Definition of the notation for HCC.

During CPG construction, HCC resolves identifiers, e.g., function and variable names, and inserts edges between those identifiers and the variable or function they reference, thereby encoding $a \rightarrow b$. For instance, we insert an edge from a function call expression to the invoked function to encode inter-procedural control-flow information (c.f. Challenge 3). This connects function call sites with their underlying implementation to provide inter-procedural control-flow information, which is crucial to tackle Challenge 3. HCC encodes the control flow for $\forall s \in \mathcal{S}_f$ by creating nodes labeled *Statement*. Furthermore, HCC inserts an edge between f and the first statement control-flow-wise in f, $s_1 \in \mathcal{S}_f$, with the label *body*. The statements are ordered in $\mathcal{S}_f$, so $s_1, s_2 \in \mathcal{S}_f$ indicates that s_1 precedes s_2. HCC encodes this control-flow-wise order in the CPG through *leads* edges, i.e., it creates a *leads* edge from s_1 to s_2. This facilitates processing and analysis of the control-flow.

❷ **CPG Enrichment.** Typically, compilers convert the AST into a compiler-specific intermediate representation (IR) which encodes the program's control-flows and data-flows. While prior work similarly translate the AST into a custom IR [13,23,49], HCC performs control-flow and data-flow analysis directly in the CPG by enriching it with control and data-flow information. In contrast to IR-based approaches, the CPG allows us to maintain the AST ensuring the possibility for both code analysis and hardening. HCC determines unresolvable function calls and built-in API calls to obtain inter-procedural control-flow data (Challenge 3). It also performs intra-procedural data-flow analysis to detect accesses to variables. These analysis passes query the CPG and store the results inside the CPG for additional processing.

❸ **Bug Pattern Discovery.** The bug pattern discovery phase is a key phase in HCC. Here, we express bug patterns in the form of sub-graphs of the CPG. The presence of a bug pattern in the CPG indicates that the contract is susceptible to this bug type. In practice, HCC queries the CPG for bug patterns through graph traversals on the CPG. We refer to distinct matches of a bug pattern in the CPG as a bug instance $v \in \mathcal{V}x$. HCC adds a node to the CPG for each detected bug. Depending on the bug type, this node has unique properties and edges to other CPG nodes. The properties include statements affected by the bug and the mitigation point (Challenge 4). We developed our own static analysis passes that prioritize a low number of missed bugs rather than only patching truly vulnerable code. That said, similarly to control-flow integrity approaches [1], we aim at hardening the contract code at potentially exploitable points rather than relying on a complete removal of vulnerabilities, which is as of today an unreachable goal.

❹ **Hardening.** HCC generates hardening patches for the bug instances discovered in the previous phase. To do so, it utilizes hardening templates to construct CPG-level patches against vulnerabilities. The templates are closely related to vulnerability types. Hence, we define templates for all individual vulnerability patterns to cover all possible instances $v \in \mathcal{V}_x$. We designed HCC's automated analysis and hardening such that the potential for accidentally breaking legitimate contract functionality is very low (Challenge 2). In Sects. 4.2 to 4.3 we provide detailed descriptions of the hardening templates. To perform hardening, HCC queries the CPG for all bug instances and applies the corresponding hardening template. In doing so, HCC resolves and inserts missing expressions in the template. HCC augments the CPG by inserting nodes to the CPG as required by the template.

❺ **Code Generation.** HCC generates the hardened source code as its last step in the compilation workflow. HCC traverses the hardened CPG, i.e., the hardened AST sub-graph of the CPG, to generate the hardened source code, taking into account the target compiler version (Challenge 1). The rewritten source code is then ready for further review or verification, compilation, and deployment.

4 Application to Ethereum

In this section, we describe our implementation of HCC for Solidity smart contracts in Ethereum. Ethereum is the most popular smart contract platform, has been intensively investigated in research, and is currently being used by several startups [9,31,47]. Reentrancy vulnerabilities are the most exploited bugs in Ethereum and continue to frequently cause losses of millions of USD [4,55,56,58]. Reentrancy has been extensively investigated in previous research [29,36,38,64], allowing us to use these previous results as ground truth [37,38,50,64] in the evaluation of our prototype. As reentrancy features a quite complex attack pattern involving interaction between multiple contracts, it is a perfect target to demonstrate the power of our CPG-based approach.

Thanks to its generic CPG model, HCC is able to mitigate all the major vulnerabilities in Ethereum [19]. In Sect. 4.3, we describe how HCC covers suicidal smart contracts, improper use of `tx.origin` for access control, untrusted DelegateCall and unchecked low-level call bugs. For the interested reader, we provide implementation details and analysis queries in the extended version of this paper [17].

4.1 Creating CPGs from Solidity ASTs

HCC constructs the CPG by calling the Solidity compiler (solc) [48], parsing its JSON-based AST output, and loading the AST into the graph database. While the AST is loaded into our database, HCC assigns labels to AST nodes, and adds edges for data-flows and control-flows. That is, HCC generates labels and properties to the CPG that represent high-level concepts that are common in smart contracts (e.g., contract, data structure, and function definitions).

Consider the smart contract shown in Listing 1.1 which serves as an on-chain wallet and as a running example to illustrate every phase of HCC. Given sufficient balance, the *withdraw* function allows users to withdraw an amount from the contract. The *removeAccount* function conveniently allows users to withdraw all their funds. Without HCC's hardening (highlighted lines), the *withdraw* function suffers from a reentrancy vulnerability since the balance is updated (Line 15) after an external call (Line 13) which transfers the amount. Figure 2 depicts the CPG that HCC creates for the original vulnerable contract (prior to hardening). CPG nodes for *Contract*, *Function* and *StateVariable* are examples of high-level concepts that are common in Solidity smart contracts. As becomes evident, HCC utilizes labels to differentiate between the different concepts.

```
1  contract Vulnerable {
2    mapping (address => uint) balance;
3  +  mapping(address => bool) balance_lock;
4
5    ...
6
7    function withdraw(uint amount) public {
8  +  require(!balance_lock[msg.sender],
9  +  "[HCC] balance_lock[msg.sender] ...");
10
11     if (balance[msg.sender] >= amount) {
12 +     balance_lock[msg.sender] = true;
13       msg.sender.call.value(amount)("");
14 +     balance_lock[msg.sender] = false;
15       balance[msg.sender] -= amount;
16     }
17   }
18   function removeAccount() public {
19     withdraw(balance[msg.sender]);
20   }
21 }
```

Listing 1.1: Solidity contract vulnerable to a reentrancy attack. Here, the state update of the *balance* variable happens after the external call of the same function. HCC inserts the highlighted lines during its hardening phase.

While transforming the AST into the CPG, HCC already resolves references between identifiers and their entity, i.e., $(a \to b)$. Note that HCC recognizes different kinds of reference semantics: (1) data dependencies (green edges), (2) function call references (brown edges), and (3) *write state* semantics (red edges). As shown in Line 11, the condition of the *IfStatement* depends on the *balance* state variable, which is declared in Line 2. As a result, HCC inserts the green edge to connect the *IfStatement* and *StateVariable* nodes to represent this data dependency. Similarly, the function call to the *withdraw* function on Line 19 refers to the function definition on Line 7. This relationship is represented in Fig. 2 with the brown edge connecting the *FunctionCall* node from within the *removeAccount* function with the *Function* node.

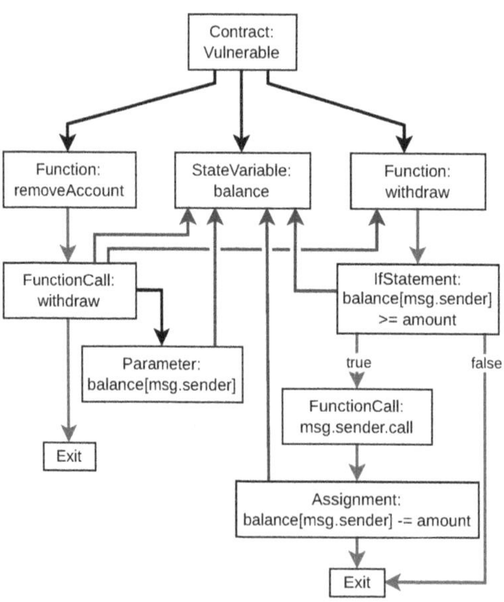

Fig. 2. The CPG HCC constructs for the code from Listing 1.1.

Lastly, to represent the assignment to the *balance* state variable on Line 15, HCC inserts the red edge between the *Assignment* node and the *StateVariable* node to encode the *write state* semantics. This encodes $b' \to b, b' \in \mathcal{E}, b \in c.\mathcal{P}$, which is subsequently used to construct the set $\mathcal{U}_p$.

However, there are cases where a reference to an entity exists in the AST *before* the entity is declared or defined. Whenever HCC cannot resolve a reference, the reference is stored in a temporary list of unresolved references. HCC attempts to resolve the references again as part of its CPG enrichment phase. Note that during CPG construction, HCC also inserts control-flow edges (blue edges) between the individual statements of a function to encode $\mathcal{S}_f$.

Control flow constructs such as *IfStatements* or loops are more involved and require special attention to prevent hampering the scalability of HCC's analyses, e.g., a naive model of control flow for loops would introduce cycles, i.e., $\mathcal{S}_{\rightarrow s} \cap \mathcal{S}_{s\rightarrow} \neq \emptyset,\ s \in \mathcal{S}$. Hence, for *if* statements, we connect the statement with two different types of edges matching the `then` branch (*true* label) and `else` branch (*false* label). Similarly, we introduce two different kinds of control-flow edges for loops: one that connects the loop header statement with the loop body (true case), and one that connects the last statement of the loop's body with the loop header.

Call Analysis. Especially for the case of reentrancy, it is crucial to know the location of external function calls. Hence, HCC iterates over all function call expressions $c \in \mathcal{E}^C$ in the CPG and explicitly labels each external call. External calls are function calls that either target another contract, or statements that utilize low-level functions that are associated with the *address* type of Solidity, i.e., $c \in \mathcal{E}^C \wedge addr(c) \neq \text{self} \wedge c \rightarrow f' \wedge f' \notin c.\mathcal{F}$. HCC assumes that control *may* change to any public function of the caller contract. To detect all cases of external calls (direct or indirect), HCC applies an analysis consisting of two stages. Consider again Listing 1.1 where Line 13 contains an external call. As ① in Fig. 3 shows, HCC adds in the first stage the external call label (*ext. call* label) to the corresponding call expression node in the CPG. In the second stage, HCC propagates information about external calls to higher abstraction levels to simplify the bug patterns and hardening strategies, i.e., HCC labels the statement nodes that contain an external call, as well as the *Function* nodes, whose statements contain external calls. In our example, HCC first assigns the *external call* label to the *FunctionCall* node at ②. Afterwards, it also labels the *Function* node representing the *withdraw* function (③).

After this analysis iteration, HCC can detect external function calls that it could not detect before. At first sight, the *FunctionCall* at Line 19 seems like an internal function call, because is calls the *withdraw* function that exists in the same smart contract. However, after the two stages, HCC knows that the *withdraw* function performs an external call, so internal function calls to the *withdraw* function perform the external call transitively. Fortunately, switching back and forth between the described analysis stages already covers this: upon executing the first analysis stage again, HCC now considers the *withdraw* function as *performing an external*. Hence, it labels the *FunctionCall* node within the *removeAccount* function as an external call at ④. During the second analysis stage of the call analysis, HCC propagates this information further, i.e., to the *Function* node of *removeAccount* (⑤).

Similar to external calls, HCC also identifies *delegate calls* and *constructor calls* to cover the full space of reentrancy attacks [38]. HCC identifies the former using the same approach as external calls, but assigns the label *delegate call* in addition to the label *external call*. For the latter, we analyze Solidity's *new* expressions to check whether the constructor performs an external call. As the *new* keyword is ambiguous in Solidity (e.g., could be used for new in-memory data types), we need to identify constructor calls that indeed create new contracts and label them as *external calls*.[1] Prior solutions for reentrancy detection treat constructor calls either as completely trusted or fully untrusted [38]. In contrast, HCC can precisely analyze whether a create-based reentrancy is possible since it analyzes the constructor code.

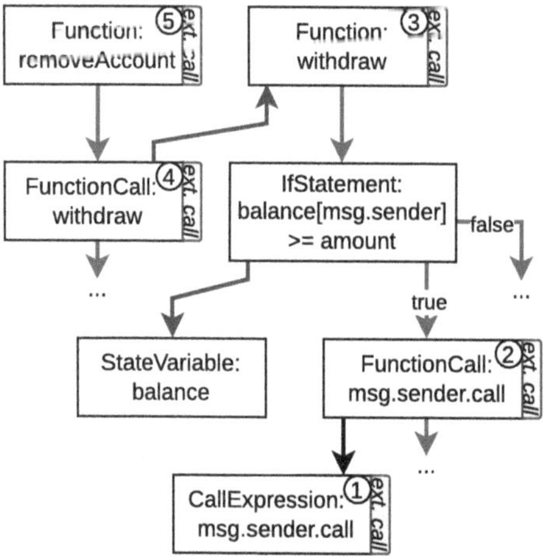

Fig. 3. Call Analysis during CPG enrichment for Listing 1.1.

Write State Analysis. To find statements that update state, HCC constructs the set $\mathcal{U}$ following a two-step approach similar to the call analysis. First, HCC collects all *state updates*–that is, statements that change either state variables or a local variable stored in storage. Consider Line 15 which updates the *balance* variable. HCC labels the *Assignment* node in the CPG as a *state update*, as well as the surrounding *withdraw* function. Further, HCC adds a new edge to the CPG (red edge in Fig. 2), which directly connects the state update statement with the target state variable, thereby encoding the insertion of $s \in \mathcal{S}$ into $\mathcal{U}$. Moreover, HCC adds s to the set of statements writing to a state variable, i.e., $s \in \mathcal{U}_p, p \in c.\mathcal{P}$. Second, HCC collects all statements containing internal function calls that update the contract's state and treats these function calls and their surrounding functions just like the original state update statements above. Further, HCC includes these function calls in the sets $\mathcal{U}$ and $\mathcal{U}_p$. We indicate this in Fig. 2 with the red edge connecting the *FunctionCall* node of the *removeAccount* function with the *StateVariable* node. Similar to the call analysis, HCC propagates the edges and labels until no new labels were added to the CPG.

4.2 Reentrancy Hardening

Reentrancy vulnerabilities enable attackers to reenter a smart contract when the internal state of a smart contract is inconsistent, i.e., when a public function in the victim contract performs an external call to another contract. Reentrancy bugs are challenging to detect, mostly due to concurrent accesses to state variables in all functions of the smart contract. Several classes of reentrancy attacks have been studied in the past [36,38]: (1) same-function reentrancy, in which an attacker maliciously reenters a publicly callable function of the

[1] Note that creating new contracts by means of the new expression requires the source code of the contract to be created. Hence, HCC's CPG already contains the contract to be created.

victim contract that operates on an inconsistent state (see Listing 1.1), (2) cross-function reentrancy, where the inconsistent internal state is only exploitable in a sequence of publicly callable functions operating on the same state, (3) delegate-based reentrancy, which is similar to a same-function reentrancy in which a *delegatecall* replaces either the external call or the state update, and (4) create-based reentrancy, that happens when the victim contract creates a new contract by calling its constructor before updating the internal state. To concisely describe HCC's reentrancy detection, we define $\mathcal{D} = \{c \in \mathcal{E}^C : c \rightarrow \text{delegatecall}\}$ as the set of low-level delegate calls.

HCC's detection of reentrancy patterns consists of two main steps. First, HCC queries the CPG for state updates $u \in \mathcal{U}$. In our example in Listing 1.1, a state update happens at Line 15, which corresponds to the *Assignment* node ① in Fig. 4. Second, HCC queries the CPG for an external call that precedes the state update. Note that we denote control-flow prior to hardening as dashed blue edges in Fig. 4. Starting at the *Assignment* node ① in Fig. 4, HCC follows the dashed blue control-flow edge ②, which in this case directly refers to the external call ③, i.e.:

$$\mathcal{V}_{Re} = \{e, u \in \mathcal{S}_f : \ u \in \mathcal{U} \cap \mathcal{S}_{e\rightarrow} \ \wedge \ \exists\, c \in \mathcal{E}^C \cap \mathcal{E}_s \ \wedge \ addr(c) \notin \{\text{self}\} \wedge \ c \rightarrow f' \ \wedge \ f' \notin \mathcal{F}\}$$

$\mathcal{V}_{Re}$ captures pairs of statements, where the first statement is a function call to an unimplemented function, and the second statement is a state update. At this point, HCC already detects the reentrancy vulnerability, as there is a path that leads from an external call to a state update. Hence, HCC inserts the red *Vulnerability* node ④ into the CPG for a same-function reentrancy vulnerability. As Fig. 4 shows, HCC connects the *Vulnerability* node with the *Assignment* node ① and the *FunctionCall* node ③. HCC uses the *Assignment* during the hardening phase to fully capture all parameters for the mutex locks. To detect cross-function reentrancy vulnerabilities $v = (e, u) \in \mathcal{V}_{Re}$, HCC also queries the CPG for *cross-functions* $\mathcal{F}_v^{\times}$, i.e., functions that operate on the state variable $p \in c.\mathcal{P}$:

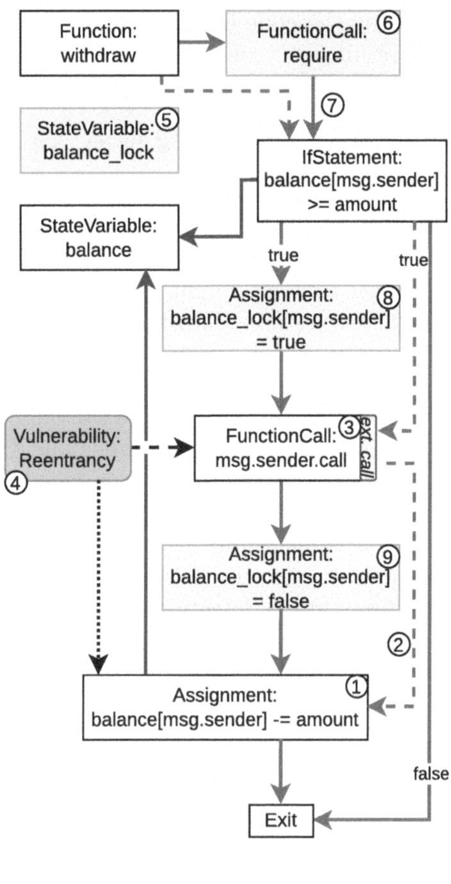

Fig. 4. Reentrancy Analysis and Hardening for Listing 1.1.

$$\mathcal{F}_v^{\times} = \{f \in \mathcal{F} : \ \exists s \in \mathcal{S}_f \cap \mathcal{U}_p : \ \exists p : \ u \rightarrow p\}$$

For a given $v \in \mathcal{V}_{Re}$, this query returns the set of functions that write to the same state as the vulnerable function containing the reentrancy. If *cross-functions* exist ($\mathcal{F}_v^\times \neq \varnothing$), HCC connects the *Vulnerability* node with the corresponding *Function* nodes $f \in \mathcal{F}_v^\times$.

This generic approach covers the same-function and cross-function variants of reentrancy patterns. Since the call analysis from the CPG enrichment phase also labels *delegate calls* and constructor calls as *external calls*, i.e., $\mathcal{D} \subseteq \mathcal{E}^C$, this approach also covers delegate-based reentrancy in which a delegate call is performed before a state update. However, there is a special case ($\mathcal{V}_{Rd}$) in which a *delegate call* is preceded by an *external call*. In Ethereum, *delegate calls* allow executing the code of the target contract within the calling contracts' context. As a result, HCC considers these cases as susceptible to reentrancy:

$$\mathcal{V}_{Rd} = \{e, d \in \mathcal{S}_f : \mathcal{D} \cap \mathcal{E}_d \neq \varnothing \wedge d \in \mathcal{S}_{e\rightarrow} \wedge \exists c \in \mathcal{E}^C \cap \mathcal{E}_e \wedge addr(c) \notin \{\text{self}\} \wedge c \rightarrow f' \wedge f' \notin \mathcal{F}\}$$

Similar to $\mathcal{V}_{Re}$, this query returns pairs of statements in order of control-flow with the first one being an external call, but the second statement must contain a delegate call. However, it is undecidable which state variable–if any–the target contract might write to, so HCC omits the query for $\mathcal{F}_v^\times$. HCC inserts a *Vulnerability* node into the CPG and connects it to the external call inserting a full contract lock for this case.

In HCC, the detection of create-based reentrancy ($\mathcal{V}_{Rn}$) works similar to $\mathcal{V}_{Re}$. However, instead of external calls, HCC queries for constructor calls which are followed by a state update. The CPG-based analysis allows HCC to also analyze the constructor that is being called, even though this constructor is part of another contract, thereby tackling Challenge 3. In this way, HCC only reports a vulnerability if the constructor contains an external call. For create-based reentrancy, HCC also conducts the cross-function analysis $\mathcal{F}_v^\times$. Formally, we express HCC's detection for create-based reentrancy as follows:

$$\mathcal{V}_{Rn} = \{n, u \in \mathcal{S}_f : u \in \mathcal{U} \cap \mathcal{S}_{n\rightarrow} \wedge \exists c \in \mathcal{E}^C \cap \mathcal{E}_n \wedge addr(c) \text{ is undef.} \wedge c \rightarrow f' \wedge \exists e \in \mathcal{S}_{f'} \wedge \exists c' \in \mathcal{E}^C \cap \mathcal{E}_e \wedge addr(c') \notin \{\text{self}'\} \wedge c' \rightarrow f' \wedge f' \notin \mathcal{F}\}$$

While this query is similar to $\mathcal{V}_{Re}$, it differs in that it does explicitly look for a function $f \in \mathcal{F}$, but with an undefined address. This is exactly the case for constructors, as there does not exist an address when the constructor is called. Notably, this pattern only includes sequences where the constructor contains an external call.

For every vulnerability $v \in \mathcal{V}_R = \{\mathcal{V}_{Re} \cup \mathcal{V}_{Rd} \cup \mathcal{V}_{Rn}\}$, HCC inserts a vulnerability node into the CPG and labels it according to the vulnerability type, e.g., *create-based reentrancy*. Finally, HCC inserts edges between the vulnerability node and the nodes returned from the detection queries. These edges show which role a node fulfills in the detected bug pattern and are later used by the hardening strategies.

HCC follows three steps to harden against reentrancy vulnerabilities $(c, u) = v \in \mathcal{V}_R$: (1) create a *lock* variable, (2) insert guard statements that check the locks in the vulnerable function and the *cross-functions*, and (3) wrap the external call in locking and unlocking statements. In our example, HCC first adds the *StateVariable* ⑤ node to the CPG in Fig. 4 (Line 3 in Listing 1.1), i.e., p' for $p : u \rightarrow p$. HCC considers indices of arrays and mappings, as well as member accesses when constructing *lock* variables. This avoids false alarms that are present in prior work [29,38], as those approaches lock the entire contract. We provide further details about the false alarms in the extended version of our paper [17]. The state variable in our example is a *mapping* of *address* to *uint*. HCC follows the same access pattern as the affected state variable, which means that the *lock* variable is a *mapping* from *address* to *bool*. This does not lock the entire contract and allows for cascading withdrawal.

Next, HCC constructs a guard statement g that checks whether p' is locked, and inserts it at the start of the vulnerable function $f \in \mathcal{F} : u \in \mathcal{S}_f$ so that $s_0 \in S_f = g$. In Fig. 4, the green *FunctionCall* node ⑥ represents g. HCC also adds a guard statement to the *cross-functions* as they operate on the same state variable, $g = s_0 \forall f \in \mathcal{F}_v^{\times}$. After node insertion, HCC adjusts the control-flow of the function to integrate the inserted code. The *Function* node in Fig. 4 has two outgoing control-flow edges. The dashed blue edge represents the control-flow before the hardening phase. After HCC adds code to the CPG, it redirects the control-flow, so that the solid blue edge and edge ⑦ represent the control-flow after hardening.

As the last step during hardening, HCC wraps the *external call* in *lock* (l) and *unlock* (l') statements, i.e., *Assignment* statements l ⑧ and l' ⑨ that set the lock to *true* and *false*, respectively. Similar to the guard statements, HCC adjusts the control-flow of the function so that the hardening code is executed: $l \in \mathcal{S}_{\rightarrow c} \wedge l' in \mathcal{S}_{c\rightarrow}$.

Flash loans. Flash loans are a popular mechanism in DeFi, enabling instant loans that do not need any collateral and whose durations span only a single blockchain transaction. Flash loans rely on legitimate reentrancy, as a borrower must be able to receive and repay the loan within the same transaction. Listing 1.2 shows a flash loan function: In Lines 4 and 5, the contract checks that it has enough funds to provide the loan to the borrower. At Line 6, the contract transfers the funds to the borrower before calling the borrowers' callback—that is, granting control over the execution to the borrower—in Line 8. Finally, the flash loan contract finishes execution after checking that it has at least the same balance as before the loan plus fees in Lines 10 and 11.

Similar to most other static analysis tools [5,6,18,53], HCC does not prevent this legitimate form of reentrancy. HCC detects that locking is not required, as the flash loan functionality does not require the loan provider to update state.

In case the flash loan contract requires additional DeFi features such as lending and bonding, which should not be executed in the same transaction [7, 21], HCC supports the inclusion of an additional configuration file that specifies sets of mutually exclusive functionalities that users are not allowed to be executed within a single transaction. HCC then automatically adds a locking mechanism (based on bitmaps) to prevent the unwanted behavior.

4.3 Covering Additional Vulnerabilities

```
function flashLoan(uint256 amount) external {
  IFlashBorrower r = msg.sender;

  uint256 before = t.balanceOf(address(this));
  require(before >= amount, "Not enough tokens");
  t.transfer(msg.sender, amount);

  require(r.onFlashLoan(...), "Callback failed");

  uint256 after = t.balanceOf(address(this));
  require(after >= before + fee, "Loan not repaid");
}
```

Listing 1.2: A minimal flash loan function.

Due to the high expressiveness of our CPG, HCC also hardens against other vulnerabilities than reentrancy, namely 1) suicidal smart contracts, 2) dangerous use of the global variable `tx.origin` for access control purposes, 3) performing low-level *delegatecalls* to untrusted addresses, and 4) unchecked low-level calls.

HCC also supports hardening against arithmetic bugs and truncation bugs. Starting with version 0.8, the Solidity compiler automatically inserts checks for arithmetic bugs. However, these checks are only available in the newest compiler versions, leaving legacy contracts at risk. Further, past exploits against ERC-20 token [37,50] have shown that these vulnerabilities can lead to severe losses. Due to incompatibilities between Solidity versions, automatically upgrading contracts to versions above 0.8 is out of scope. To remedy this, we also implemented integer bug hardening for HCC to support legacy contracts and describe it in detail in the extended version of our paper [17].

Suicidal Smart Contracts Hardening. The global *selfdestruct* function destroys the smart contract. That is, it prevents all further code execution on its address and transfers the balance to an address given as a function parameter. Suicidal smart contracts suffer from access control bugs that unintentionally allow any entity to call the *selfdestruct* function [43]. To prevent exploitation, HCC captures every call expression to the *selfdestruct* function. During CPG enrichment, it then queries the CPG for an owner check, i.e., any check comparing addresses to either *msg.sender* or the unsafe *tx.origin*, before the control-flow reaches the call. To better capture this, we define the set of ownership checks OC as follows:

$$OC = \{s \in \mathcal{S} : \exists e \in \mathcal{E}_s \cap \mathcal{E}^{BC} : \exists r \in (\overleftarrow{e} \cup \overrightarrow{e})^r \wedge (r \rightarrow \text{tx.origin} \vee r \rightarrow \text{msg.sender})\}$$

OC is the set of all comparison statements where *msg.sender* or the unsafe *tx.origin* is used. Such statements indicate that access control is defined based on the transaction issuer. HCC analyzes owner checks during CPG enrichment. Using this set, we detect the *selfdestruct* vulnerability as follows:

$$\mathcal{V}_{sd} = \{s \in \mathcal{S} : \exists c \in \mathcal{E}^C \cap \mathcal{E}_s \wedge c \rightarrow \text{selfdestruct} \wedge \nexists o : \{o \in OC \wedge o \in \mathcal{S}_{\rightarrow s}\}\}$$

$\mathcal{V}_{sd}$ first selects all statements containing a call to *selfdestruct*, and filters out statements preceded by an ownership check.

The contract in Listing 1.3 is suicidal because the *destroy* function lacks access control before the call to *selfdestruct* at Line 6. To detect this, HCC collects the statement at Line 6, and then queries the CPG for a preceding owner check. As HCC adds Lines 2, 3 and 5 during the hardening phase, HCC's query for the owner check returns an empty result, i.e., $OC = \varnothing$. Based on this, HCC deems the contract as vulnerable at Line 6.

To mitigate this type of vulnerability, HCC inserts checks comparing the *owner* of the smart contract with *msg.sender*. Here, HCC first queries the CPG for a state variable called *owner* which has an address type. If this variable does not exist, HCC will use the variable first declared in the contract with an address type. However, if none of the state variables have a suitable type (as in our example from Listing 1.3), HCC will declare an appropriate state variable (Line 2) and set its value to *msg.sender* in the constructor (Line 3) of the smart contract. Once HCC determines (or creates) the owner variable, HCC adds an assertion before the call to *selfdestruct* which compares this variable to *msg.sender* (Line 5).

Using `tx.origin` for Access Control. Smart contracts can access the account address that initiated the current transaction sequence through the global variable *tx.origin*, which is the bottom-most address in the call stack. Hence, the *tx.origin* variable should not be used for authorization or access control purposes to avoid impersonation attacks. Listing 1.4 depicts the source code of a smart contract that is susceptible to an impersonation attack (here, the check in Line 2 relies on `tx.origin` instead of `msg.sender`). A malicious contract, when being called by the owner of this contract, can then execute the *destroy* function granting authorization through *tx.origin* [46] and cause denial of service.

HCC detects this vulnerability by checking comparison expressions of addresses against the *tx.origin* global variable. Namely, HCC detects this vulnerability as follows:

$$\mathcal{V}_{to} = \{s \in \mathcal{S} : \exists e \in \mathcal{E}_s \cap \mathcal{E}^{BC} : \exists r \in (\overleftarrow{e} \cup \overrightarrow{e})^r | r \rightarrow \text{tx.origin}\}$$

$\mathcal{V}_{to}$ matches statements s containing a binary comparison $e \in \mathcal{E}^{BC}$, where one of the operands is *tx.origin*. In our example, this is the assert statement at Line 2 . HCC replaces the variable *tx.origin* in the comparison expression with

```
1 contract Suicidal {
2 +address owner;
3 +constructor(){owner=msg.sender;}
4  function destroy() public {
5 +  assert(msg.sender == owner);
6    selfdestruct(msg.sender);
7  }
8 }
```

Listing 1.3: A suicidal Ethereum smart contract written in Solidity. The highlighted lines show the patches inserted by HCC.

```
1 function destroy() public {
2  assert(+msg.sender-tx.origin==owner);
3  selfdestruct(owner);
4 }
```

Listing 1.4: This function is vulnerable to impersonation attacks. We highlight code inserted (green) and removed (red) by HCC.

the variable *msg.sender*, which is always the top-most caller address in the call stack.

Hardening Untrusted DelegateCalls. The low-level function *delegatecall* allows a smart contract to execute code portions deployed at another address within its own context. Since the callee code acts on the storage and balance of the caller contract, *delegatecall* into untrusted smart contracts may act maliciously [44]. Listing 1.5 shows an example of this vulnerability: Without the check inserted by HCC (Line 2), the DelegateCall in Line 3 executes code from an arbitrary contract. To detect this vulnerability, HCC queries the CPG for all *delegatecall* expressions existing in the CPG. Using the CPG's data-flow information, HCC queries for the origin of the target contract's address and only trusts addresses from a state variable $p \in c.\mathcal{P}$. It is impossible to infer the trustworthiness of an unknown call target statically. Indeed, we argue that this is an access control problem: attackers must be unable to *delegatecall* into malicious contracts, but privileged users are allowed to do so. For this reason, if the target address originates in a source other than a state variable (e.g., a function parameter or global variable) HCC also queries the CPG for an owner check in the same way as described for suicidal smart contracts. Using the set of delegate calls $\mathcal{D}$ (Sect. 4.2) and the set of ownership checks (Sect. 4.3), HCC detects this vulnerability as follows:

$$\mathcal{V}_{dc} = \{s \in \mathcal{S}_f : \exists d \in \mathcal{D} \cap \mathcal{E}_s \mid addr(d) \notin c.\mathcal{P} \wedge$$
$$addr(d) \in \{\mathcal{A}_f \cup \mathcal{L}_f \cup \{\text{msg.sender}\}\} \wedge \nexists o : \{o \in OC \wedge o \in \mathcal{S}_{s\rightarrow} \cup \mathcal{S}_{\rightarrow s}\}\}$$

This pattern matches all statements that contain a delegate call and filters out all those statements that are preceded or succeeded by an owner check.

To mitigate this vulnerability, HCC adds Line 2 to perform an owner check before the *delegatecall*.

Unchecked Low-Level Calls. Low-level calls to transfer Ether may result in the execution of another smart contract. Execution failure of the callee smart contract reverts the Ether transfer and state changes of the callee contract, while the caller resumes execution. The absence of exception handling can result in locked Ether or denial of service because the caller updates its state despite the transfer being reverted [45]. Consider Listing 1.6: the call at Line 4 may fail and

```
1 function call(address target) public {
2 +  assert(msg.sender == owner);
3    target.delegatecall(...);;
4 }
```

Listing 1.5: This function deliberately executes attacker-controlled code in its own context. We highlight the runtime checks inserted by HCC in green.

```
1 function withdraw(uint val) public {
2  require(balance[msg.sender] >= val);
3  balance[msg.sender] -= val;
4 +(bool ok, ) = msg.sender.call{...}();
5 +require(ok);
6 }
```

Listing 1.6: A function that might lead to state inconsistency. We highlight the runtime checks inserted by HCC in green.

msg.sender does not receive the funds. However, without the checks inserted by HCC (green highlights), the state update at Line 3 happens regardless of the calls' success. Even worse, this state inconsistency might lead to locked Ethers, i.e., funds that cannot be removed from the smart contract. HCC detects this vulnerability by collecting all low-level call expressions from the CPG that are top-level expressions in a statement. All of them indicate that the call is neither stored in a variable nor checked immediately:

$$\mathcal{V}_{ul} = \{s \in \mathcal{S} : \exists\, c \in \mathcal{E}^C \cap \mathcal{E}_s : \widehat{c} \wedge addr(c) \notin \{\text{self}\} \wedge \\ c \rightarrow \text{call} \vee c \rightarrow \text{delegatecall}\}$$

To mitigate the vulnerability, HCC wraps the low-level call in a *require* statement, only allowing resumption of the smart contract if the low-level call succeeds (Lines 4 and 5).

5 Evaluation

We evaluate the application of HCC to Solidity smart contracts based on functional correctness and effectiveness. The former is vital as to ensure that contracts still perform as expected. For the latter, we focus on reentrancy and integer bugs to compare HCC's effectiveness to previous work [37,38,50,64]. Lastly, we evaluate the runtime effects of HCC's hardenings for vulnerabilities described in Sect. 4.3 to 4.3.

Methodology. We utilize the same differential testing approach as in [37] based on a large set of important real-world contracts. To do so, we run a modified Ethereum node based on *geth* to compare execution traces of transactions using both the original and the hardened bytecode. To measure functional correctness, we ensure that both transaction traces contain the same state updates (i.e., storage writes), ether transfers, and external calls (i.e., any interaction with the blockchain state) in the same order. We re-execute transactions targeting the smart contract which were successful on the original unhardened contract code. This is due to the fact that (1) we cannot determine functional correctness of failing transactions, and (2) HCC aims at not changing the functional behavior, hence it does not affect the conditions that lead to the failure of transactions in the original contract. We evaluate HCC on contracts that fulfill the following criteria: (1) the source code of the contract is available (2) the contract is programmed in Solidity, (3) the source code is compatible to a *solc* version of 0.4.12 or above and (4) *solc* compiles the original source code without errors (and also without the *stack too deep* issue in the Solidity compiler when adding new local variables [54]).

5.1 Functional Correctness

We collected the top 25 high-value accounts with balances ranging from 20 000 to 7.2 million Ether in August 2022 that fulfill the above criteria. We first harden

```
function batchTransfer(address[] receivers,
                                          uint  value)
                 public whenNotPaused returns (bool) {
  uint256 cnt = receivers.length;
+ assert((uint256(cnt) == 0 ) ||
+    (uint256(cnt) * value / uint256(cnt) == value));
  uint256 amount = uint256(cnt) * value;
  require(cnt > 0  && cnt <= 20 );
  require(value > 0  && balance[msg.sender] >= amount);
  ...
```

Listing 1.7: The vulnerable function of the exploited BEC Token contract. Highlighted lines mark the runtime checks added by HCC.

the contracts against exploits that target reentrancy and integer bugs. Next, we apply differential testing to determine whether all tested transactions work as intended. We excluded deployment transactions as they cannot be replayed since contracts have already been deployed. Further, we measure the gas overhead induced by the hardening checks.

Table 2 shows the results of our functional evaluation. Replaying 49 265 transactions required one week execution and none of the transactions failed, i.e., HCC preserves functional correctness for all the top 25 Ethereum contracts. Notice the varying gas overhead across different contracts. This is because (1) even slight differences in compiler versions and parameters between the original smart contract and the hardened smart contract can lead to lower gas cost through compiler optimization, (2) the number of inserted runtime checks varies across contracts, (3) not all transactions trigger a runtime check. As some contracts in Table 2 have a negative value in the minimum gas overhead, we measured the effect of using different compiler versions for patched and unpatched contracts in a separate experiment. Our results show that the gas overhead deviates only minimally (between -0.24 % and +0.52 %) when measurements are done across different compiler versions—which also explains the negative values in Table 2. Indeed, using different versions of the compiler before and after hardening can result in lower gas costs.

We note that all contracts where HCC inserts reentrancy hardening, i.e., where the RE checks column is not zero in Table 2, are variants and extensions of multi-signature wallet contracts [16]. As such, they share large parts of their code, so that HCC inserts a similar number of reentrancy and integer bug runtime checks. We find the gas overhead for these contracts largely tolerable. For instance, contract $0 \times 2265 \ldots 1e41$, which exhibits the highest overhead, has a mean and maximum gas increase of 35 149 and 99 916. This is equivalent to a mean increase of 0.0012 Ether and a maximum increase of 0.0034 Ether (avg. of 34 GWei per gas). We point out that, in a non-reentrant transaction, it costs 10 000 gas to store/remove each lock flag (storage writes). With the introduction of transient storage operations (TSOs) [2], relying on transient storage could reduce the overhead of locking by 99% as it would require only 100 gas to store/remove the lock. However, since the majority of the contracts in our dataset predate TSO, we opted not to rely on TSOs.

Further, our results show that integer bug mitigation results in a very low overhead ranging from 0.14 % to 10.8 % with an average of 2.82 %. In comparison,

Table 2. Top-25 evaluated Ethereum contracts. RE/IO stand for inserted runtime checks for reentrancy hardening and integer overflow patching.

Contract	# Transactions		Gas Overhead (gas)						Checks		Compile
	Total	Success	mean	SD	mean (%)	min	max	median	RE	IO	Time (s)
`0x6ba3...c351`	4 789	4 789	17 503	20 978	15.88%	3	43 777	3	3	14	7.97
`0x2265...1e41`	60	60	35 149	19 144	32.75%	3	99 916	41 945	2	14	7.79
`0x3d92...7c18`	1 783	1 783	29 979	19 920	26.61%	3	43 937	43 103	2	14	7.50
`0x51fd...7ee2`	630	630	12 111	10 833	9.85%	−128	23 150	21 119	1	14	8.04
`0x74fe...4af7`	159	159	17 806	8 127	20.45%	−56	22 708	21 417	1	14	7.15
`0x3262...658a`	9	9	24 027	21 490	21.92%	3	43 937	42 975	2	14	7.55
`0xb8d2...84d0`	6 055	6 055	6 166	14 874	5.41%	0	94 698	3	2	14	7.82
`0x7da8...6cf9`	384	384	106	407	0.14%	−493	2 603	−63	0	10	6.79
`0xc61b...193c`	22	22	0	0	0.0%	0	0	0	0	0	3.93
`0x67b6...9c7a`	11 888	11 888	4 824	1 436	2.62%	0	9 537	4 494	0	4	12.53
`0xa646...0a2b`	160	160	7 183	24 829	10.8%	−488	114 680	276	0	14	6.89
`0x3d45...1cd1`	44	44	327	311	0.29%	0	994	175	0	14	6.87
`0x8dc2...9a20`	68	68	0	0	0.0%	0	0	0	0	0	3.92
`0x0000...05fa`	11 016	11 016	6 804	18 481	7.91%	0	475 580	4 751	0	8	5.66
`0x674b...bd3f`	39	39	174	22	0.18%	170	314	170	0	16	10.27
`0x2134...d469`	98	98	716	993	1.02%	−65	3 426	358	0	9	7.68
`0xc02a...6cc2`	9 861	9 861	285	205	0.88%	33	834	399	0	5	5.28
`0x23ea...062f`	1 448	1 448	699	1 518	1.6%	−27 745	788	788	0	1	5.17
`0xa646...0a2b`	160	160	7 183	24 829	10.80%	−488	114 680	276	0	14	6.89
`0xcafe...5f2c`	752	752	1 363	9 348	1.124%	−52 937	150 697	87	0	14	6.94
Total/**Average**	49 265	49 265	**9 718**		**9.90%**	**−4 737**	**62 312**	**9 113**	13	207	**7.13**

the gas overhead of reentrancy mitigation is typically higher due to the storage writes. Nonetheless, this overhead is largely tolerable.

5.2 Hardening Effectiveness

To evaluate the hardening effectiveness of HCC, we leverage existing datasets that contain smart contracts with known vulnerabilities [38,50,64] and harden the respective contracts with HCC. We evaluate the effectiveness of the two hardening mechanisms separately. Hence, we construct two distinct datasets, one for each vulnerability class, and apply the differential testing approach described above.

Integer Bug Hardening. We evaluate the effectiveness of integer bug hardening on five ERC-20 token contracts from the Osiris [50] dataset, which all have confirmed vulnerabilities that have been actively exploited [37]. We harden the five contracts against integer bugs with HCC and compile the hardened source code to bytecode using the standard Solidity compiler. We replay and re-execute a total of 31 216 transactions, of which 68 transactions are confirmed attacks. Table 3 shows that HCC effectively prevents all confirmed attack transactions—with a hardening effectiveness of 100 % for integer bugs. Moreover, HCC does not hamper the legitimate behavior of the studied contracts, i.e., all the benign transactions do not raise an alarm in HCC, and their traces' effects are the same as the original one. Overall, HCC introduces an average runtime gas overhead of 1.64 %.

We now describe in detail the token contract belonging to the BeautyChain (BEC) token to demonstrate how HCC hardens integer bugs. We select the BEC contract because it was actively exploited, resulting in a loss of 10^{58} BEC tokens [34]. While the BEC contract is compatible with the ERC-20 standard for token transfers, it also implements custom functionality, such as the ability to transfer an amount of tokens to multiple receivers in its *batchTransfer* function. Listing 1.7 shows the function that implements this behavior for the BEC token contract. Note that the highlighted lines (5 and 6) are added only after hardening through HCC. The *batchTransfer* function takes an array of addresses (*receivers*) and an integer as its input (*value*). All addresses in the receivers array will receive an amount of tokens equal to *value*. Interestingly, the developers were aware of integer bugs as they use the *sub* and *add* functions of the SafeMath library [32] in this function. However, the *batchTransfer* function is vulnerable to an integer overflow due to a missing check before the multiplication in line 7, demonstrating that using SafeMath does not ensure full hardening against integer overflows. Since both multiplication operands, i.e., the length of the array and *value*, are inputs to this publicly callable function, an attacker can construct an exploit transaction by providing selected values for the parameters that trigger the multiplication overflow in line 7. Consequently, the *amount* variable overflows to a very low value or even to zero, which bypasses the check in line 9. Due to the inserted overflow check in lines 5 and 6 of Listing 1.7, the multiplication overflow becomes unexploitable.

We further analyze the effectiveness of HCC's integer bug hardening by extending our dataset to all contracts of the original OSIRIS dataset [50]. 134 vulnerable contracts were deemed suitable for our experiment based on our criteria list described in Sect. 5. To accurately perform this experiment, we need to ensure that OSIRIS does not report integer vulnerabilities for vulnerable code that is protected by HCC's inserted hardening checks, because our implementation for integer vulnerabilities does not remove the vulnerability but rather inserts runtime checks that prevent exploitation. Hence, we carefully sort out OSIRIS alarms for non-exploitable vulnerabilities. Our evaluation results show that none of hardened contracts raised an alarm, which demonstrates the effectiveness of automated integer bug hardening with HCC.

Reentrancy Hardening. For this experiment, we selected 5 contracts from the Sereum dataset [38] meeting the following conditions: (a) source code is available, (b) the contract uses a HCC-compatible solidity version, and (c) we manually identified at least one true attack transaction, i.e., the contract is not a false positive. Additionally, we included all contracts susceptible to reentrancy from the Ever-Evolving Game [64] dataset. We hardened the contracts against reentrancy bugs with HCC and compile the hardened source code to bytecode using the standard Solidity compiler.

We replayed and re-executed 109 transactions, including 54 confirmed attack transactions. HCC's hardening introduces an average gas overhead of 11.95 %. Table 3 shows that HCC prevents *all* confirmed attack transactions, achieving 100 % patch effectiveness for reentrancy hardening, while all the benign transactions do not raise any alarm in HCC. In contrast to the EEG dataset, we discovered two new reentrant transactions (contract 0x85d2...ea0b and 0x516d...29a9). We analyzed the transactions and confirmed that those are indeed reentrant calls correctly prevented by HCC.

5.3 Practicality

We compared HCC coverage and effectiveness to the sGUARD [29] state-of-the-art source-to-source compiler to demonstrate the high practicality of HCC. To this end, we conducted a large-scale experiment on 10 000 contracts sampled from etherscan.io without any filtering using a timeout of one minute per contract and 64GB memory budget. Note that a timeout of one minute is sufficient even for complex real-world contracts, as the compilation times in Tables 2 and 3 show. HCC successfully processes 7 174 (71.74%), while sGUARD processes only 3 286 (32.86%).

One might think that a timeout of one minute is too short for symbolic execution-based approaches. Hence, we additionally compiled the 15 contracts containing known integer overflow and reentrancy vulnerabilities as well as the

Table 3. HCC effectiveness for ERC-20 tokens (upper part) and reentrancy (lower part).

Contract	Checks	# Transactions		Gas Overhead		Compile
		Total	Attacks	mean (%)	median (gas)	Time (s)
BEC	5	9 296	1	0.43%	103	4.04
HXG	8	1 284	10	4.37%	2 884	4.36
SCA	31	286	1	3.32%	1 590	5.20
SMT	14	9 816	1	4.36%	1 743	3.93
UET	14	10 534	55	3.41%	1 571	4.23
Total/**Average**	72	31 216	68	**3.16 %**	**1579**	**4.35**
`0x0eb...43e`	1	2	1	1.32%	551	4.54
`0x2c4...e9d`	5	1	1	-	-	5.48
`0x72f...82e`	3	2	1	0.17%	408	6.29
`0x85d...a0b`	5	26	26	-	-	5.80
`0x516...9a9`	5	8	8	-	-	5.90
`0xd4c...69e`	2	8	1	3.02%	642	6.48
`0x4a8...a38`	1	43	10	11.00%	27	6.85
`0xaae...0b8`	1	8	2	0.38%	424	5.01
`0xb4c...999`	1	7	3	47.46%	10 918	4.71
`0xb7c...4f7`	1	4	1	20.31%	942	4.21
Total/**Average**	25	109	54	**11.95 %**	**1987**	**5.52**

Top-25 contracts with sGUARD using a timeout of 12 hours per contract. Note that a timeout of 12 h for all 10 000 contracts is not possible as it would require months to complete the experiment. Even with this excessive timeout, only 17 of the 40 contracts are compiled by sGUARD, whereas HCC compiles 36 out of 40 contracts. In particular, sGUARD processes only 4 of the Top-25 contracts successfully, while HCC is able to successfully compile 20 contracts. In addition, sGUARD does not add any patch to any contract of our integer bug dataset, including the real-world ERC20 Token contracts that were actively exploited in 2018.

We also observed that existing approaches hamper legitimate transactions (false positive) when checking for reentrancy vulnerabilities.

For instance, sGUARD applies a locking mechanism similar to OpenZeppelin's *ReentrancyGuard* [33], i.e., it creates a single mutex-lock for the whole contract. As mentioned in Sect. 4.2, this locking strategy prevents legitimate access patterns, like withdrawals from different accounts within the same transaction, that cannot lead to state-inconsistency. In contrast, HCC's locking strategy is field- and offset-sensitive as it considers both, fields of data structures and indices to mappings without limits to nesting, thereby allowing these access patterns.

Vulnerability	Deployment Overhead	Execution Overhead
Suicidal	107.9%	42.0%
`tx.origin`	0.0%	0.0%
Untrusted *delegatecall*	14.6%	1.6%
Unchecked call	2.7%	0.2%
Average	31.3%	10.9%

Table 4. Gas overhead introduced byHCC's hardening patches.

5.4 Other Runtime Metrics

Similar to reentrancy and integer bug hardening, we also evaluate the gas overhead of HCC's other mitigations (Sect. 4.3 to 4.3) in a separate experiment. As there are very few real-world transactions that trigger these vulnerabilities and their functions, we perform this experiment based on the code samples in Listing 1.3 to 1.6.

As shown in Table 4, the execution and deployment overheads with HCC's hardening code of all contracts are negligible, except for the contract from Listing 1.3. This outlier is due to the fact that the additional runtime check doubles the code size of the function, as otherwise the *destroy* function would only consist of the function call to the *selfdestruct* function, which is very cheap in terms of gas costs. Similarly, the hardened version of Listing 1.3 introduces a larger code size and deployment overhead due the insertion of the constructor and the *owner* variable. Note that deployment overhead is negligible, as it is a one-time cost.

6 Application to Hyperledger Fabric

Hyperledger Fabric [3] is one of the most popular permissioned blockchain platforms, which supports Golang-based smart contracts. To apply HCC to Hyperledger Fabric, we apply the following adaptations. Since not all compilers generate an AST in a machine-readable format, and in order to reduce the differences in ASTs generated by language-specific compilers (such as the Golang compiler for Golang code), we make use of a generic parser generator such as ANTLR [11]. ANTLR can generate AST models for many existing programming languages, such as Golang. As ANLTR provides a uniform parsing behavior across all the supported languages, it ensures minimal modifications to the CPG enrichment phase, as we do not need to account for compiler-specific behavior for each new programming language.

The code generation phase requires minimal adaptation to emit valid code in the programming language considered, Golang in this case. Since the logical operators are usually similar across languages, we only need to change the error reporting mechanism. This requires changing the *assert* (*condition*) used in Solidity to the standard"if not condition, return error" of Golang as follows:

```
if(!condition) {
  return nil, errors.New("HCC: Illegal Operation") }
```

Lastly, we modify the CPG enrichment phase to match platform-specific APIs to their existing equivalent (of Ethereum or any other already-integrated platform). Indeed, different smart contract platforms each provide their own specific APIs on how to interact with other smart contracts and how to access the storage system. In the case of Fabric, this includes Fabric's storage access patterns (i.e., the *PutState* and *GetState* methods) and external call patterns (Fabric's *InvokeChaincode* method).

We note that, when incorporating Fabric support into HCC, only 101 lines of code were added, and 8 lines of code were modified (excluding the code associated with the AST generation step). These represent approximately 2.75%, of the overall 3953 lines of code.

Note that, while reentrancy attacks are specific to Ethereum, other types of attacks, such as integer overflows and underflows, are directly applicable to Fabric's smart contracts. This also means that the bug discovery and hardening phases for integer bugs (c.f., Sect. 4.3) can be reused without any modifications. Owing to Golang's type inference, it is not always easy to differentiate between signed and unsigned integers in the AST, as type information is not always available. For this reason, when HCC cannot ensure with certainty the type, it always assumes that the type is signed as it creates additional checks compared to the unsigned version, ensuring the effectiveness of the hardening regardless of whether the actual type (although part of the check may be superfluous if the type was unsigned).

Evaluation of HCC on Fabric. We evaluate our integration of HCC with Fabric using the five ERC-20 token contracts from the Osiris [50] dataset.

Contract	LOC Overhead	Execution Overhead	Execution Overhead (ns)
BEC	14%	2.8%	4
HXG	38%	30.2%	78
SCA	34%	29.8%	151
SMT	36%	28.2%	96
UET	33%	26.8%	52
Average	31%	23.5%	76.2

Table 5. Execution overhead introduced by HCC in Hyperledger Fabric.

To do so, we translate vulnerable functions from Solidity to Golang and then apply HCC on the resulting smart contract. We then measure the overhead introduced (in LOC and execution time) in each function by HCC. Table 5 shows our results; here each point is averaged over 1000 independent runs. Our results show that HCC introduces an average code overhead of 31%; this corresponds to adding the 3 lines required for each assert introduced by HCC. On the other hand, HCC introduces an average of 23.5% in terms of execution times (around 76 nanoseconds). Note that this overhead varies between BEC and the other considered contracts. This is mainly due to the fact that the BEC contract has only one patch which introduces little overhead. Recall that the Fabric framework requires a few seconds to process a transaction—as such, an overhead of hundreds of nanoseconds can be easily tolerated.

Beyond Hyperledger Fabric, we argue that the reliance on ANTLR ensures support for many smart contract based languages since ANTLR has grammars targeted at many popular programming languages, such as Java, C++, C#, Python. This means that HCC can support a wide variety of blockchain platform such as Hyperledger Sawtooth [39] and Neo [28], which use Python, Java, or C#, without incurring significant changes in the AST generation step.

7 Conclusion

While the popularity and adoption of blockchain technologies steadily increase, little attention is paid to developing secure contracts. HCC is the first practical language-independent approach that keeps the developer out of the loop, hardening smart contracts against a variety of attacks. It introduces a new and generic smart contract representation, namely a code-property graph, which allows modeling of diverse vulnerabilities in Ethereum and Hyperledger Fabric thereby addressing the high dynamics in this application domain. We demonstrate that HCC is applicable to complex and high-value state-of-the-art contracts in Ethereum preventing all known reentrancy and integer bugs.

Acknowledgements. This work has been partially funded by the Deutsche Forschungsgemeinschaft (DFG, German Research Foundation)—CROSSING (SFB 1119) 236615297 within project T1, EXC 2092 (CASA) 39078197—and the European Union ERC CONSEC under grant No. 101042266 and ECH2020 TeraFlow Project under grant agreement No. 101015857. The views and opinions expressed are those of the authors only and do not necessarily reflect those of the European Union or the

European Research Council Executive Agency. Neither the European Union nor the granting authority can be held responsible for them.

References

1. Abadi, M., et al.: Control-flow Integrity. In: Proceedings of the ACM Conference on Computer and Communications Security (2005). https://doi.org/10.1145/1102120.1102165.
2. Akhunov, A., Salem, M.: EIP-1153: Transient storage opcodes [DRAFT], June 2018. https://eips.ethereum.org/EIPS/eip-1153. Accessed 25 Mar 2022
3. Androulaki, E., et al.: Hyperledger fabric. In: Proceedings of the Thirteenth EuroSys Conference (2018). https://doi.org/10.1145/3190508.3190538
4. Benson, J.: Grim Finance Hacked for $30 Million in Fantom Tokens. en-US, December 2021. https://decrypt.co/88727/grim-finance-hacked-30-million-fantom-tokens. Accessed 25 Mar 2022
5. Bose, P., et al.: SAILFISH: Vetting Smart Contract State-Inconsistency Bugs in Seconds (2021). arXiv: 2104.08638
6. Brent, L., et al. Vandal: A Scalable Security Analysis Framework for Smart Contracts (2018). arXiv: 1809.03981
7. Callens, V., Meghji, Z., Gorzny, J.: Temporarily Restricting Solidity Smart Contract Interactions (2024). arXiv: 2405.09084 [cs.CR]
8. Chen, T., et al.: SODA: a generic online detection framework for smart contracts. In: Annual Network and Distributed System Security Symposium (NDSS) (2020)
9. ConsenSys. Blockchain Technology Solutions|Ethereum Solutions. en-us. May 2022. https://consensys.net/. Accessed 12 Mar 2022
10. ConsenSys. Mythril (2018). https://github.com/ConsenSys/mythril. Accessed 01 Mar 2021
11. ANTLR Developers. ANTLR (2014). https://www.antlr.org/. Accessed 01 Feb 2021
12. ewasm. Ethereum WebAssembly (ewasm) (2018). https://ewasm.readthedocs.io/. Accessed 01 Mar 2021
13. Feist, J., Greico, G., Groce, A.: Slither: a static analysis framework for smart contracts. In: 2019 IEEE/ACM 2nd International Workshop on Emerging Trends in Software Engineering for Blockchain (WETSEB) (2019)
14. Torres, C.F., Jonker, H., State, R.: Elysium: context-aware bytecode-level patching to automatically heal vulnerable smart contracts. In: Proceedings of the 25th International Symposium on Research in Attacks, Intrusions and Defenses. RAID 2022. Limassol, Cyprus: Association for Computing Machinery, pp. 115–128, October 2022
15. Frank, J., Aschermann, C., Holz, T.: ETHBMC: a bounded model checker for smart contracts. In: USENIX Security Symposium, USENIX Security 2020 (2020)
16. Stefan George. gnosis/MultiSigWallet (2019). https://github.com/gnosis/MultiSigWallet/blob/master/contracts/. Accessed 01 Apr 2021
17. Giesen, J.-R., et al.: HCC: A Language-Independent Hardening Contract Compiler for Smart Contracts (2024). https://doi.org/10.48550/ARXIV.2203.00364
18. Grech, N., et al.: Gigahorse: thorough, declarative decompilation of smart contracts. In: IEEE/ACM International Conference on Software Engineering (ICSE) (2019)

19. NCC Group. Decentralized Application Security Project (DASP) - Top 10 (2018). https://www.dasp.co/index.html. Accessed 17 Nov 2022
20. Hildenbrandt, E., et al.: KEVM: a complete formal semantics of the Ethereum virtual machine. In: IEEE Computer Security Foundations Symposium (CSF) (2018). https://doi.org/10.1109/CSF.2018.00022
21. SourceHat Labs Inc.: Peapods Finance Smart Contract Audit Report. en-us. January 2024. https://sourcehat.com/audits/PeapodsFinance/. Accessed 01 July 2024
22. Jiao, J., et al.: Semantic understanding of smart contracts: executable operational semantics of solidity. In: IEEE Symposium on Security and Privacy (2020). https://doi.org/10.1109/SP40000.2020.00066
23. Sukrit, K., et al.: ZEUS: analyzing safety of smart contracts. In: Proceedings Network and Distributed System Security Symposium. Internet Society (2018)
24. Krupp, J., Rossow, C.: teEther: gnawing at ethereum to automatically exploit smart contracts. In: USENIX Security Symposium (USENIX Security 2018) (2018)
25. Li, A., Choi, J.A., Long, F.: Securing smart contract with runtime validation. In: Proceedings of ACM SIGPLAN International Conference on Programming Language Design and Implementation (PLDI) (2020). https://doi.org/10.1145/3385412.3385982
26. Luu, L., et al.: Making smart contracts smarter. In: Proceedings of the 2016 ACM SIGSAC Conference on Computer and Communications Security (2016)
27. Mossberg, M., et al.: Manticore: a user-friendly symbolic execution framework for binaries and smart contracts. In: 34th IEEE/ACM International Conference on Automated Software Engineering (ASE) (2019). https://doi.org/10.1109/ASE.2019.00133
28. Neo-Project. Neo-Project (2016). https://neo.org/. Accessed 01 Apr 2021
29. Nguyen, T.D., Pham, L.H., Sun, J.: SGUARD: towards fixing vulnerable smart contracts automatically. In: 2021 IEEE Symposium on Security and Privacy (S&P), pp. 1215–1229 (2021). https://doi.org/10.1109/SP40001.2021.00057
30. Nikolić, I., et al.: Finding the greedy, prodigal, and suicidal contracts at scale. In: Proceedings of the Annual Computer Security Applications Conference (2018)
31. OpenSea. OpenSea, the largest NFT marketplace. OpenSea (2017). https://opensea.io/. Accessed 12 May 2022
32. OpenZeppelin. Digital currency Ethereum is cratering because of a $50 million hack (2017). https://github.com/OpenZeppelin/openzeppelin-contracts/blob/d6a45ef14e64e034cc14fce16b073d3b4e8a4f91/contracts/SafeMath.sol. Accessed 01 May 2022
33. OpenZeppelin: ReentrancyGuard (2018). https://docs.openzeppelin.com/contracts/3.x/api/utils#ReentrancyGuard. Accessed 01 May 2022
34. p0n1. A disastrous vulnerability found in smart contracts of BeautyChain (BEC) (2018). https://medium.com/secbit-media/a-disastrous-vulnerability-found-in-smart-contracts-of-beautychain-bec-dbf24ddbc30e. Accessed 01 May 2022
35. Permenev, A., et al.: Verx: safety verification of smart contracts. In: IEEE Symposium on Security and Privacy (S&P) (2020)
36. Rodler, M., et al.: EF/CF: high performance smart contract fuzzing for exploit generation. In: IEEE European Symposium on Security and Privacy (EuroS&P). IEEE (2023, to appear)
37. Rodler, M., et al.: EVMPatch: timely and automated patching of ethereum smart contracts. In: USENIX Security Symposium, USENIX Security 2021 (2021)

38. Rodler, M., et al.: Sereum: protecting existing smart contracts against re-entrancy attacks. In: Proceedings of the Network and Distributed System Security Symposium (NDSS) (2019)
39. Hyperledger Sawtooth. Hyperledger Sawtooth (2018). https://sawtooth.hyperledger.org/. Accessed 01 Apr 2021
40. Schneidewind, C., Scherer, M., Maffei, M.: the good, the bad and the ugly: pitfalls and best practices in automated sound static analysis of Ethereum smart contracts. In: Leveraging Applications of Formal Methods, Verification and Validation: Applications - International Symposium on Leveraging Applications of Formal Methods (ISoLA) (2020). https://doi.org/10.1007/978-3-030-61467-6_14
41. Schneidewind, C., et al.: eThor: practical and provably sound static analysis of Ethereum smart contracts. In: CCS 2020: ACM SIGSAC Conference on Computer and Communications Security (2020). https://doi.org/10.1145/3372297.3417250.
42. Sharma, T., et al.: Exploring security practices of smart contract developers, April 2022. arXiv:2204.11193 [cs]. Accessed 04 May 2022
43. SWC-106 - Unprotected SELFDESTRUCT Instruction. en. https://swcregistry.io/docs/SWC-106. Accessed 17 Nov 2022
44. SWC-112 - Delegatecall to Untrusted Callee. en. https://swcregistry.io/docs/SWC-112. Accessed 17 Nov 2022
45. SWC-113 - DoS with Failed Call. en. https://swcregistry.io/docs/SWC-113. Accessed 17 Nov 2022
46. SWC-115 - Authorization through tx.origin. en. https://swcregistry.io/docs/SWC-115. Accessed 17 Nov 2022
47. Polygon technology. Bring the World to Ethereum | Polygon. en-us. May 2022. https://polygon.technology/ . Accessed 12 May 2022
48. The Solidity Programming Language. Solidity Developers (2015). https://github.com/ethereum/solidity/
49. Tikhomirov, S., et al.: SmartCheck: static analysis of Ethereum smart contracts. In: IEEE/ACM International Workshop on Emerging Trends in Software Engineering for Blockchain (WETSEB@ICSE) (2018)
50. Torres, C.F., Schütte, J., et al.: Osiris: hunting for integer bugs in Ethereum smart contracts. In: 34th Annual Computer Security Applications Conference (ACSAC 2018) (2018)
51. Torres, C.F., et al.: ÆGIS: smart shielding of smart contracts. In: Proceedings of the ACM SIGSAC Conference on Computer and Communications Security, CCS 2019 (2019). https://doi.org/10.1145/3319535.3363263
52. Torres, C.F., et al.: ConFuzzius: a data dependency-aware hybrid fuzzer for smart contracts. In: IEEE European Symposium on Security and Privacy (EuroS&P) (2021). https://doi.org/10.1109/EuroSP51992.2021.00018
53. Tsankov, P., et al.: Securify: practical security analysis of smart contracts. In: Proceedings of the ACM SIGSAC Conference on Computer and Communications Security (2018)
54. Waas, M.: Stack Too Deep (2020). https://soliditydeveloper.com/stacktoodeep. Accessed May 2021
55. White, M.: Dolomite exchange exploited for $1.8 million. en-us. Mar 2024. https://www.web3isgoinggreat.com/?id=dolomite-exchange-hack. Accessed 29 Apr 2024
56. White, M.: "NFT mortgage lender" Bacon Protocol is hacked for $1 million. en-us, March 2022. https://web3isgoinggreat.com/?id=bacon-protocolhacked-for-1-million. Accessed 28 Apr 2024

57. White, M.: Orion Protocol suffers $2.9 million hack. en-us. February 2023. https://web3isgoinggreat.com/?blockchain=ethereum&id=orion-protocolsuffers-2-9-million-hack. Accessed 07 Feb 2023
58. Williams, C.: $8.2M Lost as Visor Finance Suffers Latest DeFi Hack. en-US, December 2021. https://cryptobriefing.com/8-2m-lost-visor-financesuffers-latest-defi-hack/. Accessed 25 Mar 2022
59. Wüstholz, V., Christakis, M.: Harvey: a greybox fuzzer for smart contracts. In: ESEC/FSE 2020: ACM Joint European Software Engineering Conference and Symposium on the Foundations of Software Engineering (2020). https://doi.org/10.1145/3368089.3417064
60. Xue, Y., et al.: Cross-contract static analysis for detecting practical reentrancy vulnerabilities in smart contracts. In: 2020 35th IEEE/ACM International Conference on Automated Software Engineering (ASE), pp. 1029–1040 (2020)
61. Yamaguchi, F., et al.: Modeling and discovering vulnerabilities with code property graphs. In: IEEE Symposium on Security and Privacy (2014). https://doi.org/10.1109/SP.2014.44
62. Yu, X.L., et al.: Smart contract repair. ACM Trans. Softw. Eng. Methodol. **29**(4), 1–32 (2020). https://doi.org/10.1145/3402450
63. Zhang, Y., et al.: SMARTSHIELD: automatic smart contract protection made easy. In: IEEE International Conference on Software Analysis, Evolution and Reengineering (2020). https://doi.org/10.1109/SANER48275.2020.9054825
64. Zhou, S., et al.: An ever-evolving game: evaluation of real-world attacks and defenses in Ethereum ecosystem. In: USENIX Security Symposium, USENIX Security 2020 (2020)

Double Auction Meets Blockchain: Consensus from Scored Bid-Assignment

Xiangyu Su[1(✉)], Xavier Défago[1], Mario Larangeira[1,2], Kazuyuki Mori[3], Takuya Oda[1,4], Yasumasa Tamura[1,5], and Keisuke Tanaka[1]

[1] Institute of Science Tokyo, 2-12-1 Ookayama, Meguro-ku, Tokyo, Japan
{su.x.4029,rebello.m.f72a}@m.isct.ac.jp, {defago,keisuke}@comp.isct.ac.jp
[2] Input Output, Global, Singapore, Singapore
mario.larangeira@iohk.io
[3] Mitsubishi Electric Corporation, 8-1-1 Tsukaguchi-honmachi, Amagasaki, Hyogo, Japan
Mori.Kazuyuki@ab.MitsubishiElectric.co.jp
[4] The University of Kitakyushu, 1-1 Hibikino Wakamatsu-ku, Kitakyushu, Fukuoka, Japan
t-oda@kitakyu-u.ac.jp
[5] Hokkaido University, Kita 14, Nishi 9, Kita-ku, Sapporo, Hokkaido, Japan
ytamura@ist.hokudai.ac.jp

Abstract. A double auction system, where buyers and sellers trade through bids, requires a transparent and immutable mechanism to record allocation results. This demand can be met with robust ledgers that ensure persistence and liveness, as exemplified by the Bitcoin blockchain (EuroCrypt '15). While existing blockchain-aided auction systems often rely on secure smart contracts or layer-2 techniques, this work proposes a more fundamental approach by constructing a provably secure blockchain protocol directly from the computation of bid allocations. The core component is an alternative proof-of-work (PoW) scheme based on a scored generalized multiple assignment problem (SGMAP), integrated into a tailored blockchain protocol. Unlike conventional PoW-based protocols, our leader selection is driven by block scores derived from the SGMAP scoring function, which is designed to be flexible enough to define the difficulty level and accommodate real-life requirements of the underlying double auction system. We prove persistence and a modified liveness property for our design, and present implementation results to validate its robustness and practicality.

Keywords: Double Auctions · Scored Generalized Multiple Assignment Problem · Alternative Proof-of-Work · Blockchain Consensus

This work was supported by the JST CREST under Grant JPMJCR2113, and the JSPS KAKENHI under Grant JP24H00071 and Grant JP21K11882.

M. Fischlin and V. Moonsamy (Eds.): ACNS 2025, LNCS 15825, pp. 153–183, 2025.
https://doi.org/10.1007/978-3-031-95761-1_6

1 Introduction

In a double auction system, multiple buyers and sellers issue (buy or sell) bids to buy or sell some products. Eligible bids are matched, *i.e.*, buy bids are allocated with sell bids, and vice versa, into trading agreements according to some predefined conditions, *e.g.*, the buy bid's price is higher than the sell bid's price. A necessary functionality in such a system is to securely record the trading history so users can perform accordingly. In a decentralized environment, a public ledger that ensures consensus is usually used for this purpose, preventing any single party from tampering with the data.

The problem of consensus, in which multiple participants are made to agree on common decisions, has been studied across five decades in the context of distributed systems [22,23]. Due to the popularity of Bitcoin and other cryptocurrencies, consensus and its embodiment as a blockchain protocol has gained a much broader interest, taking the form of a distributed robust ledger, ensuring consensus through the properties of persistence and liveness [16]. It is natural to consider blockchain as the public ledger in double auction systems. In fact, numerous studies have investigated blockchain-aided double auction systems (with some in the context of peer-to-peer energy trading) [7,12–14,19,24–26,28,33,35,36]. As we will show in the detailed literature review (Sect. 1.2), most of these works are built atop secure smart contracts and layer-2 techniques. However, the assumption of smart contracts being secure is unfalsifiable [27], let alone the genuinely higher transaction fee incurred by using smart contacts. In contrast, this work aims to build consensus on blockchain that directly utilizes mechanisms in double auctions, *e.g.*, bidding operations and the allocation of bids. Through this, our protocol can handle more general double auction models (as explained in Sect. 1.1) and can be proven secure without relying on smart contracts.

1.1 Our Approach and Contributions

The first step is to clarify our double auction model.

Our Double Auction Model. We consider a single-product[1] periodic double auction system, in which the underlying market is cleared periodically so that users can perform product and payment transmission accordingly in real life. Bids are issued to buy/sell the product with three attributes: type (*i.e.*, indicating to buy or to sell), unit-price, and quantity. Each bid is associated with a lifespan attribute, indicating whether it is time-wise available to be matched with other bids. Unlike conventional double auctions, *e.g.*, uniform price auction or k-double auction, we introduce a more flexible mechanism that enables many-to-many assignments between buy and sell bids. This model can find use cases in real-life applications like peer-to-peer energy trading.

[1] The multi-product case can be achieved by executing multiple instances of our protocol in parallel.

Concretely, a buy bid can be matched with multiple sell bids (and vice versa) if the following conditions hold:

1. The price in the buy bid is higher than the price in the sell bid;
2. The sum of the quantity in the multiple sell (buy) bids does not exceed the quantity of the buy (sell) bid;
3. All the bids are within their lifespan.

Based on 2 and 3, we define the *"residual"* (later Definition 5) that inherits the price and lifespan of the original bid while its quantity is the subtraction of the matched parts from the original quantity. Finally, a matched buy-sell bid pair is a trading agreement in which the buyer transfers the payment, and the seller delivers the product. Note that our double auction model can be extended to impose more constraints, *e.g.*, including a preference list for each bid so that it only buys from sellers (sells to buyers) in the list. However, this paper will focus on the three conditions mentioned above, which are the bare minimum requirements for our many-to-many double auction model. Our blockchain protocol will be general enough to cover extensions made to this model.

A Brief Description of Our Approach. To integrate double auctions into blockchain protocols, we first define a bid layer to the data structure to support bidding operations (*i.e.*, issuing buy/sell bids). Atop the bid layer, we refine transactions as matched buy-sell bid pairs, and blocks as the containers of bids and transactions, *i.e.*, each block keeps a list of buy/sell matched transactions. The allocation of buy and sell bids (*i.e.*, forming transactions) is formalized into a Scored Generalized Multiple Assignment Problem (SGMAP, which is a many-to-many match design in our auction model). We define a generic scoring function that evaluates assignment results.

Later, by directly associating the SGMAP with our refined blockchain data structure, *i.e.*, directly relating it to our auction model, and lifting the scoring function's domain to the space of blocks, we propose the core component of our blockchain protocol: an alternative proof-of-work (PoW) scheme, namely the proof-of-bid-assignment (PoBA) scheme. Similar to the mempool of transactions in conventional blockchain protocols, we introduce the concept of "bidpool" to cope with double auctions and in accordance with our proposed bid layer. Our PoBA starts with each user maintaining such a pool according to her view of the blockchain. At the beginning of each time slot[2], the user collects bids from the previous slot and updates her bidpool. By sampling the bidpool, the user generates a block with its corresponding score by solving the semanticized SGMAP. We require the user to include the input bid set in her block so that the block and score can be verified by all other users.

Note that we do not require *optimality*, *i.e.*, the best possible combination of buy/sell bids, in block generation. This is due to a unique feature of our protocol: we encourage competition among users so that the protocol will eventually put

[2] We divide time into discrete units call slots, details can be found in Sect. 2.

forth a chain of blocks with the highest overall score (*i.e.*, the highest-score rule). Concretely, for blockchain selection, we first consider a tree structure for each user's intermediate view of block candidates (from multiple users in each time slot). Hence, each branch (from root to leaf) on the tree is a valid blockchain. Then, with an accumulation function defined over the depth of each block on the branch, we extend the score of blocks to the score of branches. Thereby, users can select the highest-scored branch accordingly, *i.e.*, each branch has a score associated given by the score accumulation of its blocks.

Our security proof is quite involved. We first abstract away from concrete computations in the PoBA by directly sampling blocks with corresponding scores from the distribution determined by the generic scoring function. We model this approach under the universal sampler model [20] (with necessary modifications). Our modeling is similar to how hash computation is modeled (*i.e.*, by queries to a random oracle) in conventional hash-PoW-based blockchain protocols, *e.g.*, Bitcoin [16], and the way that we use the universal sampler is similar to [5]. To justify how suitable this modeling approach is, we provide theoretical insights in Sect. 5.1 and implement the PoBA scheme under various conditions, *i.e.*, using different initial bid distributions and solving strategies, in Sect. 6. Then, we prove *persistence* by analyzing the dynamics of honest users' views (*i.e.*, represented by their local trees of blocks) concerning scores (of blocks and branches) following the given (arbitrary) distribution. Moreover, we show *block-liveness*, a variant of the standard liveness property, yields directly from our protocol design. Note that the original liveness property indicates state changes in a protocol. Hence, the adaptation of liveness is necessary and reasonable because in our refined data structure, a single transaction (*i.e.*, a matched buy-sell bid pair) cannot change the state of the protocol as in UTXO-based blockchain protocols, *e.g.*, Bitcoin [16]. In contrast, our protocol changes its state when a block (containing the sets of bids and transactions) is inserted into all honest users' local trees. Thus, the security of our protocol is based on the persistence and block-liveness properties.

Our Contribution. It is threefold: (1) a blockchain data structure that supports bidding operations in double auction systems; (2) an alternative PoW scheme (*i.e.*, the PoBA) based on the problem of assigning buy and sell bids concerning a generic scoring function (*i.e.*, the SGMAP); (3) design a blockchain protocol for double auction systems based on the PoBA scheme and prove security for our novel consensus mechanism (*i.e.*, the score-based blockchain selection). Additionally, we implement the PoBA scheme and provide a full network simulation for our protocol. The link can be found in Sect. 6.

1.2 Related Works

Our literature review focuses on two aspects: (1) blockchain-aided double auction systems; (2) alternative PoW-based blockchain protocols.

Firstly, most works rely on blockchains enabled by smart contracts (SC) or layer-2 techniques [7,12,14,19,25,26,28,33,35,36], with some assuming a trusted execution environment (TEE) [13,24]. While most works focused on implementation and engineering, [28], built atop state channels, provided a (UC-based) security proof that requires stronger liveness than relying only on smart contracts. Our work is unique in that it focuses on the consensus layer of a blockchain-aided auction system, utilizing an alternative PoW scheme (our PoBA scheme) that integrates auction mechanisms, *i.e.*, the computation of bid allocations. We further propose a novel blockchain selection mechanism tailored to PoBA to achieve consensus. Our design is securely proven for key consensus properties (Table 1).

Table 1. Comparison with related works.

Works	Techniques	Focus of Analysis
[7,19,25,26,33,35,36]	SC & Secure blockchain	SC-based privacy and security
[13,24]	SC & TEE	Sealed-bids auction & TEE-based security
[12,14]	SC	Sealed-bids auction & SC programming
[28]	SC & State channel	Dispute resolution via SC (UC-based)
This work	Scored bid-assignment problem & The highest-score rule	Consensus: Persistence & Block-liveness

Secondly, we list several works that inspired our design. The aim here is not to make a direct comparison, but rather to trace the relevant research trends. In [16], the authors provided the first rigorous security proof for Hash-PoW-based blockchain protocols. Weighted variants of such protocols, that can optimize network throughput, were later proven secure in [17,21]. However, the computationally wasteful mining mechanism in the Hash-PoW highlighted the need for alternative tasks (*i.e.*, alternative PoW schemes) to secure blockchain protocols. Hence, secure protocols based on "useful work" were proposed [4,11] to leverage computing power for meaningful purposes. While our PoBA design is unique compared to existing works, it incorporates the concept of weight-based consensus from [21] into the generic scoring function and uses the allocation of bids as the useful work. While our consensus mechanism differs from the weight-based ones, we notice that our PoBA can be applied to [21]'s framework by lifting the score distribution via transformation functions [32].

1.3 Organization

The remainder is organized as follows. Section 2 defines the notations and the general model of protocol execution. The following sections present our main contributions: Sect. 3 introduces the tailored data structure and basic abstractions from our double auction model; Sect. 4 proposes our blockchain protocol by specifying an SGMAP-based PoBA scheme and the score-based blockchain selection mechanism; Sect. 5 models the PoBA scheme using a universal sampler and proves the security of our protocol; and finally, Sect. 6 implements the PoBA scheme under various conditions and validates our analysis approach.

2 Preliminaries

We use λ for the security parameter. For any integer $a \le b$, let $[a..b] \triangleq \{a, a+1, \ldots, b\}$. If $a \ge 0$, let $[a]_0 \triangleq \{0, \ldots, a\}$, and if $a \ge 1$, let $[a] \triangleq \{1, \ldots, a\}$. Given a set X, $x \xleftarrow{\$} X$ denotes that x is uniformly and randomly sampled from X, and $x \xleftarrow{\mathcal{D}} X$ denotes that x is randomly sampled from X following distribution $\mathcal{D}$. Given an algorithm Alg, $x \leftarrow \mathsf{Alg}$ denotes that x is assigned the output of the algorithm Alg on fresh randomness. The (key:value) term denotes a mapping from a key key to the value value. A collision-free hash function is denoted by $H : \{0,1\}^* \to \{0,1\}^\lambda$.

We further employ a digital signature scheme $\mathsf{SIG} \triangleq (\mathsf{KGen}, \mathsf{Sign}, \mathsf{Verify})$ that satisfies correctness and existential unforgeability under adaptive chosen message attack. The formal definition is given in Appendix A.1. In particular, we say a signature is valid if $\mathsf{SIG.Verify}$ outputs 1.

Protocol Execution Model. Based on the formalization methodology and model outlined in [16] (including its subsequent refinements, *e.g.*, [9,30], that operate under weaker assumptions closer to real-life environments), we specify general settings of our protocol as follows. The protocol adopts the standard Interactive Turing Machines (ITM) Model for its execution [6]. A protocol refers to algorithms for a set of nodes (users) to interact with each other. All corrupted nodes are considered to be controlled by an adversary $\mathcal{A}$ who can read inputs and set outputs for these nodes.

Time and Slots. Time is divided into discrete units called slots, indexed by an integer $t \ge 0$. Following [9], users are equipped with (approximately) synchronized clocks that indicate the current slot. The length of each slots is adjusted to be long enough so that any discrepancies between users' local time are insignificant. Here, we assume the existence of a (not necessarily fully) synchronized clock $\mathcal{T}$, secured by the signature scheme SIG with a key pair $(\mathsf{sk}_\mathcal{T}, \mathsf{pk}_\mathcal{T})$. It replies users' queries with $(\sigma_\mathcal{T}, t) \leftarrow \mathcal{T}(m)$ *s.t.* $(\sigma_\mathcal{T}, t) \leftarrow \mathsf{SIG.Sign}(\mathsf{sk}_\mathcal{T}, m, t)$, where m is the query message and t is the current slot index. This assumption can be instantiated using the *trusted* checkpoints approach proposed in [8], which was later extended to the *decentralized* setting in [1].

Synchrony. We adapt the δ-synchronous setting [6] to our slot-based execution model, where $\delta \in \mathbb{N}$ represents a known upper bound of the actual network delay, shared by all users. Suppose an honest user sends a message in slot t, the message is guaranteed to be received by all honest users in any slot $t' \ge t + \delta$. We assume the delayed diffuse functionality [9] (described in Appendix A.2).

Rushing Adversary. The rushing network adversary can: (1) receive honest user messages first; (2) decide for each recipient whether to inject additional messages; (3) decide the order of message delivery; (4) diffuse its (the adversary's) messages after seeing all honest messages. Further, we need a constraint on the adversary (formally in Assumption 1) to argue the security of our protocol.

Permissionless Setting. We adopt the permissionless model from [31]. Specifically, in each slot t, exactly $n_t \in \mathbb{N}$ users participate in the protocol, with a corruption fraction f_t (*i.e.*, $f_t \cdot n_t$ corrupted nodes). Upon joining, an honest user is informed by the protocol of the parameters (n_t, f_t, δ). We assume an honest majority, meaning the corruption fraction satisfies $f_t < 1/2$ for all $t \geq 0$.

Corruption Model. This paper focuses on the static corruption model, where honest users cannot be corrupted after spawned. However, as discussed in [18, 30], the static corruption can be relaxed to a constrained adaptive one (*i.e.*, a model permitting corruption only at the end of a slot) by employing key-evolving cryptographic primitives[3]. While [30] extended this approach to support a *fully* adaptive corruption model (*i.e.*, honest users can be corrupted at any point during protocol execution), further research is required to adapt their analysis to our specific protocol.

3 Our Formalization of Blockchain-Aided Auctions

This section starts our formalization by presenting the refined blockchain data structure and abstractions of our double auction model.

3.1 Refined Data Structure

We add a bid layer to support bidding operations, *i.e.*, the issuance of buy/sell bids. Recall our double auction model (in Sect. 1.1), a bid is issued at a generation slot and will expire at an expiration slot to either: (1) buy a quantity of the product at an initial unit-price (anything lower is acceptable); or (2) sell a quantity of the product at an initial unit-price (anything higher is acceptable). Hence, we define each bid to consist of four attributes: type (*i.e.*, buy or sell), unit-price, quantity, and lifespan (*i.e.*, represented by the generation and expiration slot indices). Additionally, we secure the integrity of bids with a hash function $H(\cdot)$ and a signature scheme $\mathsf{SIG}{=}(\mathsf{KGen}, \mathsf{Sign}, \mathsf{Verify})$ (from Sect. 2). Next, a trading agreement, usually called a transaction in the context of blockchain protocols, is redefined as a buy-sell bid pair with the corresponding matched unit-price and matched quantity. We further refine the block's definition to be the container of the sets of bids and transactions with necessary metadata, *e.g.*, the hash of the previous block and signatures.

The Definitions. Formally, we define them as follows.

Definition 1 (Bid). *A bid, issued by a user* u *with a key pair* $(\mathsf{sk_u}, \mathsf{pk_u})$ *from the signature scheme* SIG*, is defined as* $\mathsf{bid} \triangleq (\mathsf{bid_{raw}}, \mathsf{slotInfo}, \mathsf{aux_u})$*, and is associated with an identifier* $\mathsf{bidID}{=}H(\mathsf{bid})$*. The space of bids is denoted by* $\mathbb{BID}$.

[3] Proposed in [18] and explored in [30] under the term "erasure model", this approach allows honest parties to securely erase their secret internal state upon corruption.

- $\mathsf{bid}_{\mathsf{raw}} \triangleq (\mathsf{type}, p, q)$ *is the bid's raw content where:* $\mathsf{type} \in \{\mathsf{buy}, \mathsf{sell}\}$ *indicates the bid's type (i.e., being a buy/sell bid); and* $p, q > 0$ *denote the bid's unit-price and quantity, respectively;*
- $\mathsf{slotInfo} \triangleq (t_{\mathsf{Gen}}, t_{\mathsf{Exp}}, \mathsf{pk}_{\mathcal{T}}, \sigma_{\mathcal{T}})$ *is the bid's lifespan information where:* $t_{\mathsf{Gen}}, t_{\mathsf{Exp}}$ *denotes the bid's generation and expiration slot indices s.t.* $-1 \leq t_{\mathsf{Gen}} < t_{\mathsf{Exp}}$[4]*; and* $(\mathsf{pk}_{\mathcal{T}}, \sigma_{\mathcal{T}})$ *is the time server's public key and its signature on the bid's raw content and slot indices:* $\sigma_{\mathcal{T}} \leftarrow \mathsf{SIG.Sign}(\mathsf{sk}_{\mathcal{T}}, (\mathsf{bid}_{\mathsf{raw}}, t_{\mathsf{Gen}}, t_{\mathsf{Exp}}))$*;*
- $\mathsf{aux}_{\mathsf{u}} \triangleq (\mathsf{pk}_{\mathsf{u}}, \sigma_{\mathsf{u}})$ *is the user's public key and her signature on the bid's raw content and lifespan information:* $\sigma_{\mathsf{u}} \leftarrow \mathsf{SIG.Sign}(\mathsf{sk}_{\mathsf{u}}, (\mathsf{bid}_{\mathsf{raw}}, \mathsf{slotInfo}))$.

Definition 2 (Transaction). *A transaction is defined as* $\mathsf{tx} \triangleq (\mathsf{bidID}_1, \mathsf{bidID}_2, p_{\mathsf{tx}}, q_{\mathsf{tx}})$ *where:* $\mathsf{bidID}_1, \mathsf{bidID}_2$ *are the identifiers of two bids of different types (i.e., a buy bid and a sell bid); and* $p_{\mathsf{tx}}, q_{\mathsf{tx}} > 0$ *denote the matched unit-price and quantity. The space of transactions is denoted by* $\mathbb{TX}$.

Definition 3 (Block). *A block, generated by* u *with* $(\mathsf{sk}_{\mathsf{u}}, \mathsf{pk}_{\mathsf{u}})$ *from* SIG*, is defined as* $\mathsf{bk} \triangleq (\mathsf{bk}_{\mathsf{raw}}, \mathsf{slotInfo}, \mathsf{aux}_{\mathsf{u}})$ *and is associated with an identifier* $\mathsf{bkID} = H(\mathsf{bk})$*. The space of blocks is denoted by* $\mathbb{BK}$.

- $\mathsf{bk}_{\mathsf{raw}} \triangleq (\mathsf{prevHash}, \mathsf{BIDs}, \mathsf{TXs})$ *is the block's raw content where:* $\mathsf{prevHash}$ *is the identifier (i.e., hash) of the block's direct predecessor;* BIDs *denotes a set of bids where each element is in the mapping form* $(\mathsf{bidID}{:}\mathsf{bid}) \in \mathsf{BIDs}$*; and* TXs *denotes a set of transactions where* $\mathsf{tx} \in \mathsf{TXs}$*;*
- $\mathsf{slotInfo} \triangleq (t_{\mathsf{Gen}}, \mathsf{pk}_{\mathcal{T}}, \sigma_{\mathcal{T}})$ *is the block's generation information where:* $t_{\mathsf{Gen}} \geq 0$ *denotes the block's generation slot index; and* $(\mathsf{pk}_{\mathcal{T}}, \sigma_{\mathcal{T}})$ *is the time server's public key and its signature on the block's raw content and slot index:* $\sigma_{\mathcal{T}} \leftarrow \mathsf{SIG.Sign}(\mathsf{sk}_{\mathcal{T}}, (\mathsf{bk}_{\mathsf{raw}}, t_{\mathsf{Gen}}))$*;*
- $\mathsf{aux}_{\mathsf{u}} \triangleq (\mathsf{pk}_{\mathsf{u}}, \sigma_{\mathsf{u}})$ *is the user's public key and her signature on the block's raw content and generation information:* $\sigma_{\mathsf{u}} \leftarrow \mathsf{SIG.Sign}(\mathsf{sk}_{\mathsf{u}}, (\mathsf{bk}_{\mathsf{raw}}, \mathsf{slotInfo}))$.

For completeness, we recall the definition of a blockchain: a linked list of blocks, on which the first block is called the genesis block, denoted by bk^G, containing initial users' public keys. Later, we will consider a tree structure (to be explained in Sect. 4.3) to analyze users' local views. In order to distinguish an arbitrary blockchain from the highest-scored one, we use the term "branch" to describe the former and "chain" for the latter.

Definition 4 (Chain). *Let* $||$ *denote block concatenation. That is, for any* $i \geq 0$*, if* $\mathsf{bk}^{i-1} || \mathsf{bk}^i$ *(let* $\mathsf{bk}^{-1} = \mathsf{bk}^G$*), the* $\mathsf{prevHash}$ *entry of* bk^i *equals to* bk^{i-1}*'s identifier* $\mathsf{bkID}^{i-1} = H(\mathsf{bk}^{i-1})$*. Then, a blockchain for* $t \geq 0$ *is defined as the concatenation of blocks:* $\mathsf{chain}^t \triangleq \mathsf{bk}^G || \mathsf{bk}^0 || \cdots || \mathsf{bk}^t$ *where* bk^G *is the genesis block. Moreover, for any* $\tau \in [t]_0$*, we use* $\mathsf{chain}^{t\lceil \tau}$ *to denote the blockchain without* τ*-rightmost blocks, i.e.,* $\mathsf{chain}^{t\lceil \tau} \triangleq \mathsf{bk}^G || \mathsf{bk}^0 || \cdots || \mathsf{bk}^{t-\tau}$.

[4] In particular, we call a bid initial if $t_{\mathsf{Gen}} = -1$, indicating that the bid was issued before the first block was generated. Moreover, we require $t_{\mathsf{Gen}} < t_{\mathsf{Exp}}$ because the bid allocation has at least one slot delay by our protocol design (see Sect. 4.2).

Concrete Configurations and Their Rationale. Here, we further specify several configurations concerning our double auction model.

Firstly, the bid's definition is extensible by including more attributes, *e.g.*, the preference list mentioned before (in Sect. 1.1). We can even integrate a reputation system by letting each bid include a signed (by some trusted authorities) reputation score of its issuer, and then design our generic scoring function (to be explained in the following sections) to take the reputation score into consideration. However, the current Definition 1 is sufficient for our protocol design, and hence, the following of this work will proceed under this definition.

Bids, and hence their identifiers, are designed to be unique, unlike transactions, which do not require uniqueness. That is, there can be multiple transactions with the same $(\mathsf{bidID}_1, \mathsf{bidID}_2, p_{\mathsf{tx}}, q_{\mathsf{tx}})$. However, we consider that, in any block, a $(\mathsf{bidID}_1, \mathsf{bidID}_2, p_{\mathsf{tx}})$ tuple appears only once in transactions. This is because if multiple transactions share the same $(\mathsf{bidID}_1, \mathsf{bidID}_2, p_{\mathsf{tx}})$, their q_{tx} can be aggregated, allowing them to be unified into a single transaction.

Moreover, recall that our double auction model aims to enable many-to-many assignments between buy and sell bids. To facilitate this, we introduce the concept of residuals, which represents the remaining quantity of a bid after it has been partially matched with bids of the opposite type. The formal definition is given in the form of a mapping *w.r.t.* a bid and a transaction involving that bid. For simplicity, we inherently assume that all bids and transactions are "valid": the three conditions outlined in our double auction model hold, and signatures and identifiers are correctly computed.

Definition 5 (Residual Bids). *Let* $(\mathsf{bidID}{:}\mathsf{bid})$ *be the mapping form of a bid where* $\mathsf{bid}{=}(\mathsf{bid}_{\mathsf{raw}}, \mathsf{slotInfo}, \mathsf{aux}_{\mathsf{u}})$ *and* $\mathsf{bid}_{\mathsf{raw}}{=}(\mathsf{type}, p, q)$. *Given a transaction* $\mathsf{tx}{=}(\mathsf{bidID}, \cdot, p_{\mathsf{tx}}, q_{\mathsf{tx}})$ *that involves the given bid, we denote the residual bid of* bidID *w.r.t.* tx *with* $(\mathsf{bidID}{:}\mathsf{rbid})$ *s.t.: if* $q{>}q_{\mathsf{tx}}$, $\mathsf{rbid}{\overset{\Delta}{=}}(\mathsf{rbid}_{\mathsf{raw}}, \mathsf{slotInfo}, \mathsf{aux}_{\mathsf{u}})$ *where* $\mathsf{rbid}_{\mathsf{raw}}$ $=(\mathsf{type}, p, q' = q{-}q_{\mathsf{tx}})$*; otherwise (i.e.,* $q{=}q_{\mathsf{tx}}$*),* $\mathsf{rbid}{\overset{\Delta}{=}}\perp$.

We note that tx in the definition should be valid *w.r.t.* bid, *i.e.*, to have $q{\geq}q_{\mathsf{tx}}$. Moreover, when $q{=}q_{\mathsf{tx}}$, we consider the bid is fully matched, *i.e.*, $\mathsf{rbid} = \perp$.

Given another transaction $\mathsf{tx}'{=}(\mathsf{bidID}, \mathsf{bidID}'', p'_{\mathsf{tx}}, q'_{\mathsf{tx}})$, we can extract the residual of $(\mathsf{bidID}{:}\mathsf{rbid})$ by further subtracting q'_{tx} from q', *i.e.*, the new residual bid is defined as $(\mathsf{bidID}{:}\mathsf{rbid}')$: if $q'{>}q'_{\mathsf{tx}}$, $\mathsf{rbid}'_{\mathsf{raw}}{\overset{\Delta}{=}}(\mathsf{type}, p, q'{-}q'_{\mathsf{tx}})$; otherwise, $\mathsf{rbid}'{\overset{\Delta}{=}}\perp$. This process can be repeated recursively until the residual quantity reaches 0 or the bid expires. The recursive nature of residual bids (while preserving their identifiers) allows us to save block space by only storing original ("non-residual") bids in the bid sets, *i.e.*, $\mathsf{bidID} = H(\mathsf{bid})$ for any $(\mathsf{bidID}{:}\mathsf{bid}) \in \mathsf{BIDs}$. Users can ambiguously extract the latest quantity of any bid concerning its identifier with the given blockchain. Note that the equation for identifiers above does not hold for residual bids as their quantities have changed.

Concretely, for a blockchain $\mathsf{chain}^t{=}\mathsf{bk}^G||\mathsf{bk}^0||\dots||\mathsf{bk}^t$ with $t{\geq}0$, let BIDs^i and TXs^i be the bid set and transaction set in each block bk^i for all $i \in [t]_0$, respectively. Note that each $(\mathsf{bidID}{:}\mathsf{bid})$ should exist only once in a bid set on chain^t by our configuration, we denote the set of transactions involving bidID with $T^t_{\mathsf{bidID}} \triangleq \{\mathsf{tx}|\mathsf{tx}{=}(\mathsf{bidID}, \cdot, p_{\mathsf{tx}}, q_{\mathsf{tx}}) \in \bigcup_{i\in[t]_0} \mathsf{TXs}^i\}$[5] for each (bidID:bid) $\in \bigcup_{i\in[t]_0} \mathsf{BIDs}^i$. Then, let q be the quantity of bid, the latest quantity of the residual bid associated with bidID, denoted by q', can be derived by the equation (as before, only meaningful when $q' > 0$)

$$q' = q - \sum_{\mathsf{tx} \in T^t_{\mathsf{bidID}}} q_{\mathsf{tx}}. \tag{1}$$

One concern with this configuration (*i.e.*, storing only original bids in blocks) is that block verification may become less efficient because the latest residual of each bid is not explicitly recorded. However, we argue that users can track residuals locally on a block-by-block basis, for example, by updating T_{bidID} with transactions from $\mathsf{TXs}^{t+1} \in \mathsf{bk}^{t+1}$ that involve bidID.

3.2 Abstraction of Bid Assignment

Now, we abstract the process of allocating bids in our double auction model, then present a scored variant of the generalized multiple assignment problem (SGMAP, which is many-to-many) [29]. Precisely, we consider two sets $B{=}\{b_i \triangleq (\mathsf{B}, p_i, q_i)\}_{i\in[m]}$ and $S{=}\{s_i \triangleq (\mathsf{S}, p_j, q_j)\}_{j\in[n]}$ (where $m, n{\geq}1$) as the problem's input. Here, each element (*i.e.*, $b{\in}B$ and $s{\in}S$) consists of a flag that indicates in which set the element is in (*i.e.*, B for set B and S for set S, ensuring the two sets are disjoint); and two value attributes *s.t.* $p, q{>}0$. The corresponding space of the sets are denoted by $\mathbb{B}{=}\{B|\forall p, q{>}0\}$ and $\mathbb{S}{=}\{S|\forall p, q{>}0\}$.

Then, a match between $b_i{\in}B$ and $s_j{\in}S$ concerning value attributes can be represented by their indices as (i, j, p_{ij}, q_{ij}) where p_{ij}, q_{ij} denote the assigned values. By considering the attributes in terms of our double auction model (*i.e.*, B for buying, S for selling, p for price, and q for quantity), we directly yield a requirement: $q_{ij}{\geq}0$, in which $q_{ij}{=}0$ indicates there is *no* match between b_i and s_j. Next, we can impose the first two constraints[6] from the model. Recall that a buy bid can be matched to a sell bid if: (1) the buy bid's price is higher than the sell bid's price[7]; (2) the residual quantity of both bids is no less than 0 after being matched together. We formally write these constraints as follows:

$$q_{ij} \geq 0 \land p_{ij} \in [p_j, p_i] \text{ if } q_{ij} \neq 0; \qquad \sum_{j=0}^{n-1} q_{ij} \leq q_i \land \sum_{i=0}^{m-1} q_{ij} \leq q_j. \tag{2}$$

Finally, we define the scoring function that evaluates assignment results. Let the set of assignment results for the input sets (B, S) be denoted as $A_{B,S}{=}$

[5] We omit writing "or $\mathsf{tx}{=}(\cdot, \mathsf{bidID}, p_{\mathsf{tx}}, q_{\mathsf{tx}})$" in T^t_{bidID} because the two bid identifiers in a transaction are symmetric, and bidID can only exist in one position.

[6] The third one involves lifespan, which will be discussed later concerning the correctness of our PoBA scheme.

[7] In practice, it is convenient to consider a deterministic pricing strategy as in the k-double auction model, *i.e.*, given $k{\in}[0, 1]$, set $p_{ij}{=}k{\cdot}p_j{+}(1{-}k){\cdot}p_i$.

$\{(i, j, p_{ij}, q_{ij}) | \forall (i, j) \in [m] \times [n] \wedge (p_{ij}, q_{ij})$ satisfies conditions in Eq. 2$\}$. Then, the generic scoring function is defined over the space of assignment results as $s : \mathbb{A} \to \mathbb{R}$ where $\mathbb{A} = \{A_{B,S} | \forall (B, S) \in \mathbb{B} \times \mathbb{S}\}$.

The next formal definition yields directly from the early explanation.

Definition 6 (The SGMAP). *Given two sets* $B = \{(\mathsf{B}, p_i, q_i)\}_{i \in [m]}$ *and* $S = \{(\mathsf{S}, p_j, q_j)\}_{j \in [n]}$ *with* $m, n \geq 1$ *and any* $p, q > 0$. *The SGMAP is to find a set* $A_{B,S} = \{(i, j, p_{ij}, q_{ij})\}$ *that satisfies conditions in Eq. 2 and evaluate the set with the generic scoring function given above, i.e.,* $s(A_{B,S})$.

Note that it is easy to find a valid solution to the SGMAP as any random assignment set that satisfies conditions in Eq. 2 is sufficient. In contrast, the difficulty of finding an optimal solution depends on the scoring function. Proven in [29], the optimization problem is NP-complete even when the scoring function is just a linear combination of q_{ij} for $(i, j) \in [m] \times [n]$. We will review this in Sect. 5.1 and present experiments with concrete examples in Sect. 6.

4 Our Protocol

This section first semanticizes the SGMAP with our refined blockchain data structure to yield an alternative PoW scheme, namely proof-of-bid-assignment (PoBA). Then, by specifying the process of users preparing their input bid set (to the PoBA) and the selection of blockchain (after generating blocks from the PoBA), we build a blockchain protocol based on the PoBA scheme.

4.1 The PoBA Scheme

We first semanticize the definition of SGMAP (Definition 6) with the raw content of bids (Definition 1) and transactions (Definition 2).

Definition 7 (The SGMAP, Semanticized). *Let* $\mathsf{Bs} = \{(\mathsf{bidID{:}b}) | \mathsf{b} \in \{\mathsf{bid}, \mathsf{rbid}\}\}$ *be a set of (residual) bids where* bidID *is the identifier of the original bid corresponding to* b. *Extract the buy and sell bid subset:*

$$B = \{(\mathsf{bidID}_i{:}\mathsf{b}_i) | \mathsf{b}_{\mathsf{raw},i} = (\mathsf{buy}, p_i, q_i)\}_{i \in [m]},$$
$$S = \{(\mathsf{bidID}_j{:}\mathsf{b}_j) | \mathsf{b}_{\mathsf{raw},j} = (\mathsf{sell}, p_j, q_j)\}_{j \in [n]},$$

s.t. $\mathsf{Bs} = B \cup S$ *and* $B \cap S = \emptyset$. *The SGMAP is to find a transaction set* $\mathsf{TXs} = \{(\mathsf{bidID}_i, \mathsf{bidID}_j, p_{ij}, q_{ij})\}$ *so that* p_{ij}, q_{ij} *satisfies conditions in Eq. 2. By abuse of notations, the score of the transaction set is* $s(\mathsf{TXs})$ *(i.e.,* $s : \mathbb{TX}^* \to \mathbb{R}$*).*

Next, we want users to generate blocks by solving the semanticized SGMAP in our PoBA. Hereby, we lift the range of the generic scoring function from transaction sets to blocks by considering a transforming function $T{:}\mathbb{R} \times \{0,1\}^* \to \mathbb{R}$. Concretely, the score of a given block that embeds a transaction set, *i.e.*, $\mathsf{TXs} \in \mathsf{bk}$, is denoted by $s_{bk}(\mathsf{bk}) = T(s(\mathsf{TXs}), \mathsf{bk} \backslash \mathsf{TXs})$ (*i.e.*, $s_{bk}{:}\mathbb{BK} \to \mathbb{R}$) where $\mathsf{bk} \backslash \mathsf{TXs} \stackrel{\Delta}{=} (\mathsf{prevHash}, \mathsf{BIDs}, \mathsf{slotInfo}, \mathsf{aux_u})$ is the other content in the block (by Definition 3).

Finally, the PoBA scheme $\mathsf{PoBA} \stackrel{\Delta}{=} (\mathsf{Solve}, \mathsf{Verify})$ is specified as follows.

Construction 1 (The PoBA). *Let $H:\{0,1\}^*\rightarrow\{0,1\}^\lambda$ be a collision-free hash function, and let $s_{bk}:\mathbb{BK}\rightarrow\mathbb{R}$ be a generic scoring function that evaluates blocks. For any user* u, *denote her blockchain at the beginning of slot $t+1\geq 0$ with* $\mathsf{chain}^t = \mathsf{bk}^G||\cdots||\mathsf{bk}^t$ ($\mathsf{chain}^{-1}\triangleq\mathsf{bk}^G$). *She performs* Solve *and* Verify *s.t.:*

- Solve(chain^t, Bs) *takes as input the blockchain and a set of bids*[8]. *It outputs an extended blockchain* $\mathsf{chain}^t||\mathsf{bk_u}$ *where* $\mathsf{bk_u}=((H(\mathsf{bk}^t),\mathsf{BIDs},\mathsf{TXs}),(t+1,\mathsf{pk}_\mathcal{T},\sigma_\mathcal{T}),(\mathsf{pk_u},\sigma_\mathsf{u}))$ *s.t.:*
  - *For any* (bidID:b)$\in$Bs, *if* $H(\mathsf{b})=\mathsf{bidID}\wedge(\mathsf{bidID{:}b})\notin\bigcup_{i\in[t]_0}\mathsf{BIDs}^i$, *the bid set* BIDs $\in\mathsf{bk_u}$ *contains* (bidID:b);
  - TXs *is a valid solution to the semanticized SGMAP regarding* Bs;
  - *Signatures* $(\sigma_\mathcal{T},\sigma_\mathsf{u})$ *are generated according to Definition 3.*
- Verify(chain'^{t+1}) *takes as input a blockchain. Parse* $\mathsf{chain}'^{t+1}=\mathsf{chain}'^t||\mathsf{bk_{u'}}$[9], *i.e.,* $\mathsf{bk_{u'}}$ *is generated by* u'. *Parse* $\mathsf{bk_{u'}}=((\mathsf{prevHash},\mathsf{BIDs},\mathsf{TXs}),(t_\mathsf{Gen},\mathsf{pk}_\mathcal{T},\sigma_\mathcal{T}),(\mathsf{pk_{u'}},\sigma_\mathsf{u'}))$. *It outputs* $(1,s_{bk}(\mathsf{bk_{u'}}))$ *if the following conditions hold (i.e., the input blockchain is valid); Otherwise, it outputs* $(0,\perp)$.
  1. *The blockchain being extended is valid:* $(1,\cdot)\leftarrow$Verify(chain'^t). *In particular, we extend this verification to the genesis block, i.e.,* Verify(chain^{-1}) $=1$;
  2. *Parse* $\mathsf{chain}'^t=\mathsf{bk}^G||\cdots||\mathsf{bk}'^t$, *we have* $\mathsf{prevHash}=H(\mathsf{bk}'^t)$;
  3. *The bid set satisfies, for each* (bidID:bid)$\in$BIDs, *that: (1)* $H(\mathsf{bid})=\mathsf{bidID}$; *(2)* $(\mathsf{bidID{:}bid})\notin\bigcup_{i\in[t]_0}\mathsf{BIDs}'^i$; *(3)* bid*'s lifespan* $(t_\mathsf{Gen},t_\mathsf{Exp})$ *satisfies* $t_\mathsf{Gen}\leq t<t_\mathsf{Exp}$[10]; *(4) the signatures* $(\sigma_\mathcal{T},\sigma_{\mathsf{u}'',\mathsf{bid}})$ *in* bid *are valid;*
  4. *The transaction set satisfies, for each* $(\mathsf{bidID}_1,\mathsf{bidID}_2,p_\mathsf{tx},q_\mathsf{tx})\in\mathsf{TXs}$, *that: (1)* $\mathsf{bidID}_1,\mathsf{bidID}_2\in\bigcup_{i\in[t]_0}\mathsf{BIDs}'^i\cup\mathsf{BIDs}$ *where* $\mathsf{BIDs}'^i\in\mathsf{bk}'^i\in\mathsf{chain}'^t$; *(2) Extract all transactions from* $\mathsf{chain}'^t||\mathsf{bk_{u'}}$ *for* $\mathsf{bidID}_1,\mathsf{bidID}_2$:

$$T^{t+1}_{\mathsf{bidID}_1}=\{\mathsf{tx}|\mathsf{tx}=(\mathsf{bidID}_1,\cdot,p_\mathsf{tx},q_\mathsf{tx})\in\bigcup_{i\in[t]_0}\mathsf{TXs}'^i\cup\mathsf{TXs}\},$$

$$T^{t+1}_{\mathsf{bidID}_2}=\{\mathsf{tx}|\mathsf{tx}=(\cdot,\mathsf{bidID}_2,p_\mathsf{tx},q_\mathsf{tx})\in\bigcup_{i\in[t]_0}\mathsf{TXs}'^i\cup\mathsf{TXs}\}.$$

The conditions given by Eq. 2 hold for both bidID_j, $j\in\{1,2\}$, *i.e.,*

$$p_\mathsf{tx}\in[p_2,p_1]\wedge\forall j\in\{1,2\},\sum_{\{\mathsf{tx}\in T^{t+1}_{\mathsf{bidID}_j}\}}q_\mathsf{tx}\leq q_j,$$

where (p_j,q_j) *is the price and quantity of* $(\mathsf{bidID}_j{:}\mathsf{bid}_j)\in\bigcup_{i\in[t]_0}\mathsf{BIDs}'^i\cup\mathsf{BIDs}$. *Note that* bid_1 *is for buying and* bid_2 *is for selling, hence,* $p_2\leq p_1$.
  5. *The generation slot* $\mathsf{bk_{u'}}.t_\mathsf{Gen}=t+1$, *and the signatures* $(\sigma_\mathcal{T},\sigma_\mathsf{u'})$ *are valid.*

[8] Bs is the user's local input to solve the semanticized SGMAP, which may contain residual bids given by chain^t. Intuitively, the bid set BIDs in the newly generated block should contain non-residual bids from Bs that are not included in chain^t.

[9] u' and u may not share the same view of the blockchain, *i.e.*, $\mathsf{chain}'^t\neq\mathsf{chain}^t$.

[10] We require valid blocks of slot $t+1$ only contain bids issued up to the end of slot t to prevent on-the-fly bid issuance for artificially boosting block scores.

We say the PoBA is correct, if $\mathsf{Verify}(\mathsf{chain}^t||\mathsf{bk_u})=(1, s_{bk}(\mathsf{bk_u}))$ for any *valid* Bs and $(\mathsf{chain}^t||\mathsf{bk_u})\leftarrow\mathsf{Solve}(\mathsf{chain}^t, \mathsf{Bs})$. The preparation of the input bid set Bs and its validity will be clarified below. On a high level, and consistent with our configurations (Sect. 3.1), each user can extract residual bids locally and maintain a pool of bids (referred to as the "bidpool" Pool) based on their view of the blockchain. However, to address practical constraints, such as limited block sizes, we introduce an inherent parameter $\mathsf{N}\in\mathbb{N}$ that imposes an upper bound on the size of $\mathsf{Bs} \subseteq \mathsf{Pool}$, *i.e.*, $|\mathsf{Bs}| \leq \mathsf{N}$.

4.2 Bidpool Update and Validation

A bidpool is analogous to the mempool in conventional blockchain protocols, with the difference that a bidpool stores bids instead of transactions. A user's bidpool is maintained by two aspects: (1) the user's view of the blockchain, *i.e.*, extracting the latest residual bids and removing them from the bidpool if their residual quantity reaches 0; (2) the non-residual bids issued in previous slots but not included in the user's bidpool.

Concretely, for each user, at the beginning of slot $t{+}1{\geq}0$, denote her bidpool and her blockchain of slot t with Pool^t and chain^t ($\mathsf{Pool}^{-1}{=}\emptyset$ and $\mathsf{chain}^{-1}{=}\mathsf{bk}^G$), respectively. Moreover, we write the set that consists of bids in the second aspect.

$$B^t \triangleq \{(\mathsf{bidID{:}bid})|H(\mathsf{bid}){=}\mathsf{bidID} \wedge \mathsf{bid}.t_{\mathsf{Gen}}{\leq}t{<}\mathsf{bid}.t_{\mathsf{Exp}} \wedge (\mathsf{bidID{:}bid}){\notin}\mathsf{Pool}^t\} \quad (3)$$

Here, following the requirement in block verification (Verify in Construction 1), the set B^t only collects bids with $t_{\mathsf{Gen}}{\leq}t$. For $t{=}{-}1$, we denote $B^{-1}\triangleq\{(\mathsf{bidID{:}bid})| \mathsf{bid}.t_{\mathsf{Gen}}{=}-1\}$, *i.e.*, consisting of initial bids (Definition 1).

Then, the update algorithm $\mathsf{UpdatePool}(\mathsf{Pool}^t, \mathsf{chain}^t, B)$ outputs the bidpool of slot $t{+}1$, *i.e.*, Pool^{t+1}. We specify $\mathsf{UpdatePool}$ in Algorithm 1. Finally, we say Pool^{t+1} is valid *w.r.t.* chain^t if there are no duplicates or conflicts, as formally defined in Definition 8. Therefore, given chain^t, any subset $\mathsf{Bs}^{t+1} \subseteq \mathsf{Pool}^{t+1}$ is considered a valid input set for the PoBA scheme in slot $t{+}1$.

Definition 8 (Validity of Bidpools). *Let* Pool^{t+1} *be a user's bidpool in slot* $t{+}1{\geq}0$, *and let* $\mathsf{chain}^t{=}\mathsf{bk}^G||\ldots||\mathsf{bk}^t$ *be the valid blockchain in her view at the beginning of slot* $t{+}1$ *(by Construction 1).* Pool^{t+1} *is valid w.r.t.* chain^t *if the following conditions hold for any* $(\mathsf{bidID{:}b}){\in}\mathsf{Pool}^{t+1}$*:*

- $\mathsf{b}.p, \mathsf{b}.q{>}0$, *and* $\mathsf{b}.t_{\mathsf{Gen}}{\leq}t{<}\mathsf{b}.t_{\mathsf{Exp}}$*;*
- *If* $\exists(\mathsf{bidID{:}bid}) \in \mathsf{chain}^t$, b *is identical to* bid *except with* $\mathsf{b}.q$ *is computed by Eq. 1 concerning* $\mathsf{bid}.q$[11]*;*
- *Otherwise, i.e.,* b *is non-residual,* $H(\mathsf{b}){=}\mathsf{bidID}$ *and* $(\mathsf{b}.\sigma_{\mathcal{T}}, \mathsf{b}.\sigma_{\mathsf{u}})$ *are valid.*

It is straightforward to see that, given any valid Pool^t (*w.r.t.* any chain^{t-1}), a valid chain^t, and B^t as defined by Eq. 3, the Pool^{t+1} obtained from $\mathsf{UpdatePool}$ is valid *w.r.t.* chain^t. This holds even when chain^t deviates from chain^{t-1} (*i.e.*, $\mathsf{chain}^{t\lceil 1}{\neq}\mathsf{chain}^{t-1}$) due to unsettled blockchain selection.

[11] $\mathsf{b}.q{=}\mathsf{bid}.q$ when the transaction set involving bidID (*i.e.*, T^t_{bidID}) on chain^t is empty.

Algorithm 1: In any $t+1 \geq 0$, UpdatePool is parameterized by a bidpool Pool^t, a blockchain chain^t, and a set of bids B^t given by Eq. 3.

// Parse $\mathsf{chain}^t = \mathsf{bk}^G || \mathsf{bk}^0 || \ldots || \mathsf{bk}^t$.
// For any $i \in [t]_0$, recall $\mathsf{bk}^i_{\mathsf{raw}} = (H(\mathsf{bk}^{i-1}), \mathsf{BIDs}^i, \mathsf{TXs}^i)$.
function $\mathsf{UpdatePool}(\mathsf{Pool}^t, \mathsf{chain}^t, B^t)$;
if $t = -1$ **then**
    Return $\mathsf{Pool}^0 = B^{-1}$;
    // Pool^{-1} is empty, and no bids in chain^{-1}.
else
    Set $\mathsf{Pool}^{t+1} = \mathsf{Pool}^t \cup B^t$;
    // $\mathsf{Pool}^t \cap B^t = \emptyset$ by definition.
    for $(\mathsf{bidID{:}bid}) \in \bigcup_{i \in [t]_0} \mathsf{BIDs}^i$ **do**
        if $(\mathsf{bidID{:}bid}) \notin \mathsf{Pool}^{t+1}$ **then**
            Add $(\mathsf{bidID{:}bid})$ to Pool^{t+1} ;
            // chain^t may contain previously unnoticed bids.
        end
    end
    // Note that Pool^{t+1} inherits residual bids from Pool^t.
    // To distinguish, denote with $\mathsf{b} \in \{\mathsf{bid}, \mathsf{rbid}\}$.
    for $(\mathsf{bidID{:}b}) \in \mathsf{Pool}^{t+1}$ **do**
        if $\mathsf{b}.t_{\mathsf{Exp}} < t+1$ **then**
            Remove $(\mathsf{bidID{:}b})$ from Pool^{t+1} ;
        end
        Let $T^t_{\mathsf{bidID}} = \{\mathsf{tx} | \mathsf{tx} = (\mathsf{bidID}, \cdot, p_{\mathsf{tx}}, q_{\mathsf{tx}}) \in \bigcup_{i \in [t]_0} \mathsf{TXs}^i\}$;
        // The case of $\mathsf{tx} = (\cdot, \mathsf{bidID}, p_{\mathsf{tx}}, q_{\mathsf{tx}})$ follows identically.
        Compute $q' = \mathsf{b}.q - \sum_{\mathsf{tx} \in T^t_{\mathsf{bidID}}} q_{\mathsf{tx}}$;
        if $q' > 0$ **then**
            Set $\mathsf{b}' = \mathsf{b}$, except with $\mathsf{b}'.q = q'$;
        else
            Remove $(\mathsf{bidID{:}b})$ from Pool^t;
        end
    end
    Return Pool^{t+1}
end

4.3 Score-Based Blockchain Selection

Alongside correctness, the difficulty level is another crucial property for alternative PoW schemes, *i.e.*, users must contribute enough computing power to generate valid blocks. Otherwise, they may generate massive amounts of blocks in a short time period so that the network fails to finalize on a chain of blocks. In contrast, as in Sect. 3.2, finding a valid SGMAP solution (hence, a PoBA block) does not require intensive computing power, *i.e.*, no difficulty.

We tackle this difference by proposing a novel blockchain selection mechanism that encourages users to compete using their blocks (*w.r.t.* scores). One potential challenge arises when the overall bidpool size is insufficient, *i.e.*, there are not enough input bids to even reach the desired optimization difficulty of the SGMAP. To mitigate this, we suggest issuing "dummy" bids in a publicly verifiable manner, *e.g.*, using verifiable random functions over outputs from a publicly available randomness beacon. This approach may also facilitate the dynamic adjustment of the PoBA difficulty.

Concretely, since each user may generate and diffuse multiple valid blocks in each slot, we utilize a directed tree (precisely, forest due to potentially missing blocks) to store blocks locally. Our score-based selection requires *honest* users to extend their block-tree with newly received blocks and select the highest-scored branch on the tree as their blockchain, *i.e.*, the highest-score rule. Hereby, we further extend the score of blocks to branches to support this mechanism.

Starting with definitions, we first consider a master-tree at the end of slot $t \geq 0$, denoted by mtree^t, that contains all valid blocks generated (*not* diffused) by users up to slot t. It is a directed tree with the genesis block bk^G as the root. Its vertices correspond to blocks, and edges correspond to the hash link between blocks. As in graph theory: (1) vertex height is defined as the number of edges from the vertex to the root; (2) tree height is defined as the number of edges in the longest path from a leaf vertex to the root. Hence, mtree^t is of height $t+1$, and blocks are generated in the same slot if vertices in mtree^t are of the same height. Because we assume a rushing adversary controlling block diffusion (while constrained by the bound δ as detailed in Sect. 2), honest users may only see a part of the master-tree. Hence, a user's view, denoted by $\mathsf{tree}_{\mathsf{u}}^t$, is a sub-tree of the master tree.

Definition 9 (Master-Tree and User-Tree). *Let bk^G be the genesis block. For any $\ell \geq 0$ and all $i \in [n]$ where $n \geq 1$ is the number of users participating the protocol in slot $t \in [\ell]_0$, let $BK_i^t = \{\mathsf{bk}_i^t\}$ denote the set of valid blocks generated by user u_i. Then, $BK^t = \bigcup_{i \in [n]} BK_i^t$ denotes the set of all valid blocks generated in slot t by all users. The master-tree of slot ℓ is defined as $\mathsf{mtree}^\ell = (V, E)$ where $V = \bigcup_{t \in [-1..\ell]} BK^t$ and $E = \bigcup_{t \in [\ell]_0} \{(\mathsf{bk}^{t-1}, \mathsf{bk}^t) | \mathsf{bk}^t.\mathsf{prevHash} = H(\mathsf{bk}^{t-1})\}$ with $\mathsf{bk}^{-1} = \mathsf{bk}^G$ being the only element in BK^{-1}. A user-tree of u, denoted by $\mathsf{tree}_{\mathsf{u}}^\ell = (V_{\mathsf{u}}, E_{\mathsf{u}})$, satisfies $\mathsf{tree}_{\mathsf{u}}^\ell \subseteq \mathsf{mtree}^\ell$.*

Next, we define branches *w.r.t.* a given block-tree (master or user), which is a chain of blocks (Definition 4).

Definition 10 (Branch on Tree). *Let $G^\ell = (V^\ell, E^\ell)$ be a block-tree (master or user) of slot $\ell \geq 0$. A branch is defined as $\mathsf{branch}^t = \mathsf{bk}^G || \mathsf{bk}_{i_1}^0 || \ldots || \mathsf{bk}_{i_t}^t$ $(t \leq \ell)$ s.t. $\mathsf{branch}^t \subseteq G^\ell$ and the vertex represents $\mathsf{bk}_{i_t}^t$ on G^ℓ is a leaf vertex.*

We later distinguish the notations of branch and chain by using branch^t for an arbitrary branch on a given block-tree, and chain^ℓ for the highest-scored branch. Next, we define the score of branches by introducing an accumulating function $acc: \mathbb{N} \to \mathbb{R}$ *s.t.* it takes as input the height of vertices on the given branch.

Definition 11 (Score of Branches and Highest-Score Rule). *Let $\mathsf{branch}^t \subseteq G^\ell$ be a branch as in Definition 10 where $\ell \geq 0$ and $t \in [\ell]_0$. Parse it* *with* $\mathsf{branch}^t{=}\mathsf{bk}^G||\mathsf{bk}^0_{i_1}||\ldots||\mathsf{bk}^t_{i_t}$. *The score of* branch^t *is defined as follows:*

$$S_{\mathsf{branch}^t}=\sum_{j=0}^{t} acc(t)\cdot s_{bk}(\mathsf{bk}^j). \tag{4}$$

Therefore, our highest-score rule requires honest users with $\mathsf{tree}^\ell_\mathsf{u}$ *to adopt the blockchain that satisfies* $\mathsf{chain}^\ell \triangleq \arg\max_{\mathsf{branch}^t\subseteq\mathsf{tree}^\ell_\mathsf{u}} S_{\mathsf{branch}^t}$.

It is important to note that block or branch scores may not be strictly ordered for certain scoring functions, *e.g.*, the concrete example we provided for implementation in Sect. 6. However, it is convenient to consider the hash value of blocks or branches as a tiebreaker, *e.g.*, with the lower one being preferred.

4.4 Protocol Description

The execution starts at time 0 slot index $t{=}0$, and the genesis block bk^G, containing public keys of initial users, is known to all users.

Considering our periodic auction model, each user u start their slot $t{+}1{\geq}0$ following the instruction of the global clock $\mathcal{T}$. Denote the view of u on her bidpool and user-tree at the end of slot t with $\mathsf{Pool}^t_{\mathsf{u}'}$ and $\mathsf{tree}^t_{\mathsf{u}'}$, respectively (where $\mathsf{Pool}^{-1}_{\mathsf{u}'}{=}\emptyset$ and $\mathsf{tree}^{-1}_{\mathsf{u}'}{=}\{\mathsf{bk}^G\}$). Note that due to our permissionless setting, u may not participate in slot t. Hence, we use u' as the subscript to emphasize that u may obtain her bidpool and user-tree from another user. Moreover, we require $\mathsf{PoBA.Verify}(\mathsf{branch}){=}(1,\cdot)$ for any $\mathsf{branch}{\subseteq}\mathsf{tree}^t_{\mathsf{u}'}$, hence, the user can select her blockchain $\mathsf{chain}^t_{\mathsf{u}'}$ following the highest-score rule (Definition 11). Denote u's view on the non-residual bid set with B^t_u (by Eq. 3).

The user first updates her bidpool by executing $\mathsf{Pool}^{t+1}_\mathsf{u}{\leftarrow}\mathsf{UpdatePool}(\mathsf{Pool}^t_{\mathsf{u}'}, \mathsf{chain}^t_{\mathsf{u}'}, B^t_\mathsf{u})$. She can then run $\mathsf{PoBA.Solve}$ on several $\mathsf{Bs}{\subseteq}\mathsf{Pool}^{t+1}_\mathsf{u}$ instances, with the inherent upper bound parameter *s.t.* $|\mathsf{Bs}|{\leq}\mathsf{N}$, to obtain multiple block candidates. Let $BK^{t+1}_\mathsf{u}{\triangleq}\{\mathsf{bk}^{t+1}_{\mathsf{u},j}\}_{j\in[\mathsf{ite}]}$ be the set of candidates where $\mathsf{chain}^t_{\mathsf{u}'}||\mathsf{bk}^{t+1}_{\mathsf{u},j}\leftarrow \mathsf{PoBA.Solve}(\mathsf{chain}^t_{\mathsf{u}'}, \mathsf{Bs}_j)$, and $\mathsf{ite}{\in}\mathbb{N}$ is the maximum number of $\mathsf{PoBA.Solve}$ iterations. Note that ite is bounded by the computing power of the user and the length of each slot. If the user is honest, she only diffuses the highest-scored candidate $\mathsf{bk}^{*t+1}_\mathsf{u}{\triangleq}\arg\max_{\mathsf{bk}^{t+1}_{\mathsf{u},j}\in BK^{t+1}_\mathsf{u}} s_{bk}(\mathsf{bk}^{t+1}_{\mathsf{u},j})$ with the corresponding blockchain $\mathsf{chain}^{t+1}_\mathsf{u}{\triangleq}\mathsf{chain}^{t-1}_{\mathsf{u}'}||\mathsf{bk}^{*t+1}_\mathsf{u}$.

Additionally, each user helps propagate other user's blockchains. A significant concern is the potential strain on network bandwidth. However, it is crucial for our security analysis (as in Lemma 1) that users propagate, at a minimum, their locally highest-scored blockchain in each slot. To reduce network traffic, we propose that during each slot, users propagate a received blockchain only if it surpasses their current highest-scored blockchain. Additionally, users should avoid retransmitting identical information to prevent redundancy.

Finally, the update process of tree-view is specified with $\mathsf{UpdateTree}$ (Algorithm 2). At the end of slot $t{+}1$, u is responsible for reporting her confirmed blockchain $\mathsf{chain}_{\mathsf{u}}^{t+1\lceil\tau} \subseteq \mathsf{tree}_{\mathsf{u}}^{t+1}$, to the protocol *w.r.t.* a parameter τ (to be estimated in Sect. 5.2). The description of our protocol can be found in Appendix B, and discussions concerning the incentive model in Appendix C.

Algorithm 2: In any slot $t+1 \geq 0$, UpdateTree is parameterized by a user-tree tree^{t+1} and a blockchain candidate $\mathsf{chain}^{t'}$.

---

function $\mathsf{UpdateTree}(\mathsf{tree}^{t+1}, \mathsf{chain}^{t'})$;
Parse $\mathsf{tree}^{t+1} = \{V, E\}$;
`// Verify the input blockchain candidate.`
Run $(b, \cdot) \leftarrow \mathsf{PoBA.Verify}(\mathsf{chain}^{t'})$;
if $b = 0$ **then**
    Return tree^{t+1}
else
    `// ` $\mathsf{chain}^{t'}$ `is valid with` $t' = t+1$.
    `// Parse` $\mathsf{chain}^{t'} = \mathsf{chain}^{t+1} = \mathsf{bk}^{G} || \mathsf{bk}^{0} || \ldots || \mathsf{bk}^{t} || \mathsf{bk}^{t+1}$.
    for $i \in [t]_0$ **do**
        `// Find the first block not in tree.`
        if $\mathsf{bk}^{i-1} \in \mathsf{tree}^{t+1}$ *and* $\mathsf{bk}^{i} \notin \mathsf{tree}^{t+1}$ **then**
            Set $V' = V \cup \{\mathsf{bk}^{j}\}_{j \in [i..t+1]}$;
            Set $E' = E \cup \{(\mathsf{bk}^{j}, \mathsf{bk}^{j+1})\}_{j \in [i-1..t]}$;
            Return $\mathsf{tree}^{t+1} = (V', E')$
        end
    end
end

---

5 Security Analysis

The first step of our analysis is to model the computation in the PoBA scheme. We follow the approach similar to [5] under the universal sampler model [20].

5.1 Modeling the PoBA

Recall that PoW can be modeled by queries to the random oracle [16]. Extending this methodology, we model the computation of the PoBA as queries to a modified universal sampler [5,20], which is an "advanced" random oracle that can sample from any given distribution. This approach abstracts away from concrete algorithms and focus on the distribution of block scores instead. This modeling choice is justified by the following observations: (1) for an appropriately chosen scoring function, *e.g.*, the linear combination of assigned quantities, the optimization version of the SGMAP is proven to be NP-complete [29]; (2) users need to sample an N-size bid set as the input to the PoBA from their bidpools in which stochasticity arises due to the uncertainty in problem inputs [10]. We will validate this approach with a concrete scoring function in Sect. 6.

Now, we show the definition of the modified universal sampler [5] and detail the interaction between users and the universal sampler.

Definition 12 (The Modified Universal Sampler [5]). *A universal sampler consists of algorithms* $\mathsf{US} \triangleq (\mathsf{Setup}, \mathsf{Sample})$ *that are performed as follows.*

- $\mathsf{Setup}(1^\lambda)$ *takes the security parameter* λ *and outputs sampler parameters* U*;*
- $\mathsf{Sample}(U, \mathsf{d}, \beta)$ *takes the parameters* U*, the program description* d *with a random seed for the program to generate samples. It outputs induced samples* p_{d}.

We specify the program description above with $\mathsf{d} \triangleq (\mathsf{PoBA.Solve}, s_{bk})$. In any slot $t+1 \geq 0$, a user u queries the universal sampler with $\beta \triangleq (\mathsf{Pool}_\mathsf{u}^{t+1}, \mathsf{chain}_\mathsf{u}^t; r_\mathsf{u}^{t+1})$ (*i.e.*, we write the randomness explicitly). Following the conventional modeling of computational power [16,21], we assume that, in each slot, each user can make up to $q>0$ queries to the universal sampler. This assumption derives from the limited length of slots in the *protocol*, where each user can perform $\mathsf{ite} \leq q$ executions of PoBA.Solve per slot. The total number of queries in a slot is bounded above by $Q \in \mathbb{N}$, which includes less than f fraction from the adversary, *i.e.*, $Q_\mathcal{A} < f \cdot Q$. We further clarify that the network or the adversary cannot delay queries, given that it is local oracle access.

Then, we require the universal sampler to have the single property of randomly sampling a block candidate bk *s.t.* its score $s_{bk}(\mathsf{bk})$ follows the distribution $\mathcal{D}$ determined by the scoring function $s_{bk}(\cdot)$. Denote the score space with $\mathbb{S} \triangleq s_{bk}(\mathbb{BK})$, we have $s_{bk}(\mathsf{bk}) \xleftarrow{\mathcal{D}} \mathbb{S}$. Moreover, the probability density function and the distribution function of $\mathcal{D}$ are denoted by $f(\cdot)$ and $F(\cdot)$ that satisfy $F(x) = \Pr[X \leq x] = \int_{\mathsf{smin}}^{x} f(t)dt$.

A Universal Sampler that Models PoBA.Solve

In any slot $t+1 \geq 0$, run $U \leftarrow \mathsf{US.Setup}(1^\lambda)$. Let $\mathbb{L}_\mathsf{u}^{t+1} = \{(\cdot,\cdot,\cdot,\cdot,\cdot)\}$ be the list kept by the universal sampler for user u, and let U^{t+1} denote the set of all users. We define $U \triangleq \bigcup_{\mathsf{u} \in \mathsf{U}^{t+1}} \mathbb{L}_\mathsf{u}^{t+1}$. The total size of lists is upper bounded by $Q \in \mathbb{N}$: $|U| \leq Q$.

On a query $(\mathsf{Pool}_\mathsf{u}^{t+1}, \mathsf{chain}_\mathsf{u}^t, r_\mathsf{u}^{t+1})$ **from** u**:**

- If: there exists a tuple $(\mathsf{Pool}_\mathsf{u}^{t+1}, \mathsf{chain}_\mathsf{u}^t, r_\mathsf{u}^{t+1}, \mathsf{bk}_\mathsf{u}^{t+1}, s_{bk}(\mathsf{bk}_\mathsf{u}^{t+1})) \in \mathbb{L}_\mathsf{u}^{t+1}$, then, return $(\mathsf{bk}_\mathsf{u}^{t+1}, s_{bk}(\mathsf{bk}_\mathsf{u}^{t+1}))$;
- Else if: $|\mathbb{L}_\mathsf{u}^{t+1}| > q$ when u is honest or $|U| > Q$, then return $\perp$;
- Else: return $(\mathsf{bk}_\mathsf{u}^{t+1}, s_{bk}(\mathsf{bk}_\mathsf{u}^{t+1})) \leftarrow \mathsf{US.Sample}(U, (\mathsf{PoBA.Solve}, s_{bk}), (\mathsf{Pool}_\mathsf{u}^{t+1}, \mathsf{chain}_\mathsf{u}^t, r_\mathsf{u}^{t+1}))$ *s.t.* $s_{bk}(\mathsf{bk}_\mathsf{u}^{t+1}) \xleftarrow{\mathcal{D}} \mathbb{S}$, and add $(\mathsf{Pool}_\mathsf{u}^{t+1}, \mathsf{chain}_\mathsf{u}^t, r_\mathsf{u}^t, \mathsf{bk}_\mathsf{u}^{t+1}, s_{bk}(\mathsf{bk}_\mathsf{u}^{t+1}))$ to $\mathbb{L}_\mathsf{u}^{t+1}$.

5.2 Persistence and Block-Liveness

Persistence and liveness [16] are the core properties of our protocol. For persistence, we adopt a refined version from [11]. Whereas for liveness, it is derived from two basic properties called chain growth and chain quality [16]. We observe (1) chain growth follows from our slot-based execution setting (Sect. 2); and (2) our score-based design eliminates the need of chain quality. That is, the chain quality requires the fraction of adversarial blocks in a time interval to be on par with the fraction of adversarial users. Otherwise, adversaries can exclude typical transactions in their blocks, so the protocol cannot achieve liveness. However, in our case, with a well-designed scoring function (concerning the underlying double auction system), adversaries cannot gain advantages from such an attack as it lowers the block score. Hence, the possibility of the adversarial blocks being selected is lowered. Based on these observations, we define a "block-liveness" property for our protocol instead of the conventional transaction liveness.

Definition 13 (Persistence and Block-Liveness). *Formally, we define:*

- *Persistence: For any two honest users with blockchains* $\mathsf{chain}_1^{t_1}, \mathsf{chain}_2^{t_2}$ *at slot* $t_1, t_2 \geq 0$*, respectively. Without loss of generality, let* $t_1 \leq t_2$*. Persistence with parameter* $\tau \in \mathbb{N}$ *indicates that* $\mathsf{chain}_1^{t_1}$*, is a prefix of* $\mathsf{chain}_2^{t_2}$ *after removing the rightmost* τ *blocks, i.e.,* $\mathsf{chain}_i^{t_1\lceil\tau} \subseteq \mathsf{chain}_2^{t_2}$*;*
- *Block-liveness: For any honest user with* chain^t *in slot* $t \geq 0$*, block-liveness states that for any* $i \in [t]_0$*,* chain^i *is extended by exact one block.*

In an honest user's local block-tree, the persistence is proven by: (1) the highest-scored branch of each slot will eventually be known to all honest users; (2) the selected branches of different slots have a long enough common prefix. If a block or branch is known to all honest users, it is disclosed. The δ-bounded network guarantees that honestly generated blocks are always disclosed after δ slots. The adversary is empowered to learn all generated blocks, thereby knowing the master-tree in any given slot. However, we require the adversary to always send the highest-scored blockchain of each slot to at least one honest user. This assumption is made to rule out the possibility of a selfish mining attack, which is particularly challenging to analyze due to its game-theoretic nature [2].

Assumption 1. Let $\mathcal{A}$ be the rushing adversary who holds the master-tree mtree^t of slot $t \geq 0$. For any $i \in [t]_0$, if $\mathsf{chain}^i = \arg\max_{\mathsf{branch}^i \subseteq \mathsf{mtree}^i} S_{\mathsf{branch}^i}$, at least one honest user receives chain^i by the end of slot i.

Thereby, we have the following Lemma 1 (proof is in Appendix D).

Lemma 1. *Given a* δ*-synchronous network, for any slot* $t \geq 0$*, if* $\mathsf{chain}^t \subseteq \mathsf{mtree}^t$ *is the highest-scored branch in* t*,* chain^t *will be disclosed for any* $\ell \geq t+\delta+1$*.*

The knowledge of the highest-scored branches of each slot is not enough to prove persistence. Even in the master-tree in which everything is known, given two conjunctive slots, the highest-scored branches may be different from each other, *e.g.*, a high-but-not-highest-scored branch gets extended by an extremely high-scored block so that the new branch is selected in the next slot. This situation causes the blockchain to be unstable and prevents honest users from agreeing on the same blockchain. There are two types of persistence violations: (1) the newly selected branch does not extend previously selected ones so that consensus can get reset (Fig. 1a); (2) the change of branch selection frequently happens so that consensus cannot be settled (Fig. 1b).

(a) A chain get **substituted** after selected for multiple slots.

(b) Chains **swing** among branches over conjunctive slots.

Fig. 1. Persistence Violations: Substitution and Swing. The circle denotes the blocks on the branches, and the double circle denotes the branch being selected as the highest-scored one.

The first case, we analyze the probability of existing any branch that deviates the selected chain for $\tau{\geq}1$ slots getting selected in slot $t{+}1$. We denote the chain selected in slot t with $\mathsf{chain}^t{=}\mathsf{chain}^{t\lceil\tau}||\mathsf{bk}_\mathsf{c}^{t-\tau+1}||\ldots||\mathsf{bk}_\mathsf{c}^t$, and *w.l.o.g.*, let $\mathsf{branch}^t{=}\mathsf{chain}^{t\lceil\tau}||\mathsf{bk}_\mathsf{b}^{t-\tau+1}||\ldots||\mathsf{bk}_\mathsf{b}^t$ be a branch *s.t.* $\mathsf{bk}_\mathsf{c}^i{\neq}\mathsf{bk}_\mathsf{b}^i$ for all $i{\in}[t{-}\tau{+}1..t]$. The violation indicates that there exists a block $\mathsf{bk}_\mathsf{b}^{t+1}$ that extends branch^t *s.t.* $S_{\mathsf{branch}^t||\mathsf{bk}_\mathsf{b}^{t+1}}{>}\max_{\mathsf{bk}_\mathsf{c}^{t+1}} S_{\mathsf{chain}^t||\mathsf{bk}_\mathsf{c}^{t+1}}$ where $\mathsf{bk}_\mathsf{c}^{t+1}$ denotes the block candidates extending chain^t. We conclude with Lemma 2 (proof in Appendix E).

Lemma 2. *Let $\mathcal{D}$ be the score distribution determined by $s_{bk}(\cdot)$. Let mtree^{t+1} be the master-tree of any slot $t{+}1{\geq}\tau{\geq}1$. Assuming at least one honest user, there exists an accumulating function $acc(\cdot)$ (Definition 11) s.t. the violation case mentioned above occurs with probability less than $\mathsf{O}(c^{-\tau})$ where $c{>}1$ is a constant value given by $acc(\cdot)$.*

The second violation occurs when the adversary finds the highest-scored *block* in multiple conjunctive slots as honest users stick to the highest-scored branch.

Lemma 3. *Given $\mathcal{D}$ and mtree^{t+1} the same as Lemma 2. Assuming the fraction of adversarial computing power is $f{<}1$ (i.e., $Q_{\mathcal{A}}{<}f{\cdot}Q$), chain swinging occurs during $\tau{\geq}1$ conjunctive slots with probability $\mathsf{O}(f^\tau)$.*

To prove this lemma, we remark that for any distribution, the probability of the adversary finding the highest-scored block is upper bounded by its computing power fraction f. Finally, by Lemma 1 and by applying the Markov chain approach to Lemma 2, 3, we have the theorem for persistence.

Theorem 1 (Persistence). *Let $c{>}1$ be the constant value given by $acc(\cdot)$ and $f{<}1$ be the fraction of adversarial computing power, the protocol parameterized by $\tau{\geq}\delta+1$ satisfies persistence with probability $1-\mathsf{O}(c^{-\tau+\delta}+f^{\tau-\delta})$.*

For completeness, we show Theorem 2. The proof is straightforward. Assume the one honest user is unaware of any other blocks. She can trivially extend her block-tree by generating blocks locally and selecting the blockchain accordingly.

Theorem 2 (Block-liveness). *Assuming at least one honest user, the protocol satisfies block-liveness unconditionally.*

6 Implementation

The implementation is for the PoBA scheme using a concrete scoring function: $s_{bk}(\mathsf{bk}) = \sum_{i,j} p_{ij} \cdot q_{ij}$ where $(\mathsf{bidID}_i, \mathsf{bidID}_j, p_{ij}, q_{ij}) \in \mathsf{TXs}$ is the transaction set embedded bk. The code for PoBA and a functional network simulation for our PoBA-based blockchain protocol can be found in the anonymous repository[12].

Setup. Our implementation begins with an SGMAP under the given scoring function, using a bid set of size N=5. We deliberately selected a small N to shorten the solving time, as our primary focus is on validating the output distribution rather than the runtime. To solve this sub-problem, we utilized the SLSQP solver from Python's SciPy package [34]. Next, we prepared two bid sets under different distributions: (1) Bids with uniformly distributed $p \in (0, 1]$ and $q \in [1..10]$; (2) Bids with (normally distributed) $p \sim \mathcal{N}(0.5, 0.01)$ and $q \sim \mathcal{N}(5.5, 4)$, which are further clipped (and rounded) to range $(0, 1]$ (for p) and $[1..10]$ (for q), respectively. Both sets are much larger than N to simulate the bidpool.

For the optimization process, we utilize two stochastic algorithms in conjunction with the SLSQP solver: simulated annealing (SA) and stochastic local search (SLS). In each iteration, these algorithms explore possible solutions by moving elements in and out of the current sub-problem. To demonstrate the solving process, our simulations run with a maximum of 100 iterations for each algorithm. For large-scale experiments focusing on the score distribution, each algorithm is set to 20 iterations to simulate the limited computing power and shorten the solving time. We conduct the following two series of experiments: (1) Optimization process visualization: Each algorithm (SA and SLS) is run once on the uniformly distributed bids to visualize the score during 100 iterations; and (2) Score distribution analysis: Each algorithm is run 5000 times on both uniform and normal bid distributions, with each run limited to 20 iterations.

Visualization and Analysis. The following figures visualize the score history during 100 iterations using SA (Fig. 2a) and SLS (Fig. 2b). Both results show noticeable fluctuations in block scores throughout the iterations, highlighting the stochastic nature of finding the optimal PoBA solution *w.r.t.* the given scoring function. Consequently, by requiring users in the PoBA scheme to adhere to a generic enough stochastic solving algorithm, it becomes unlikely that any single user will consistently dominate the block generation.

[12] https://anonymous.4open.science/r/poba-chain.

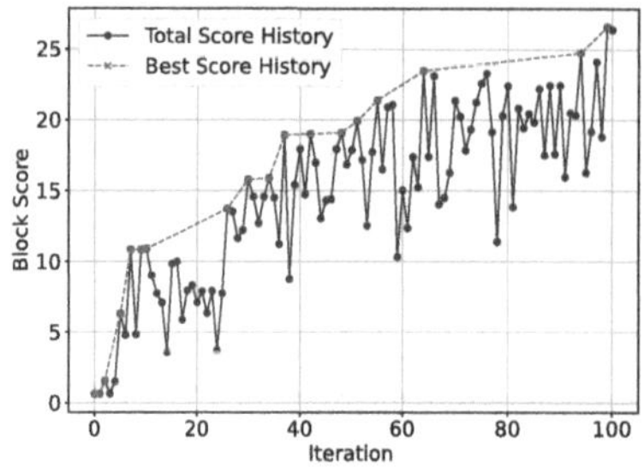

(a) Score history with the SA.

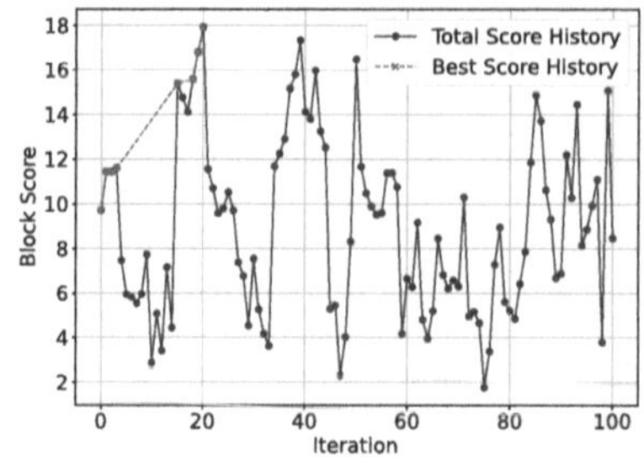

(b) Score history with the SLS.

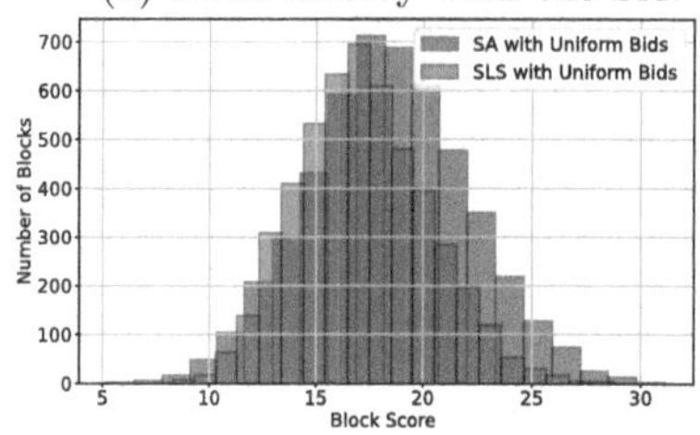

(c) Uniform bids using SA and SLS.

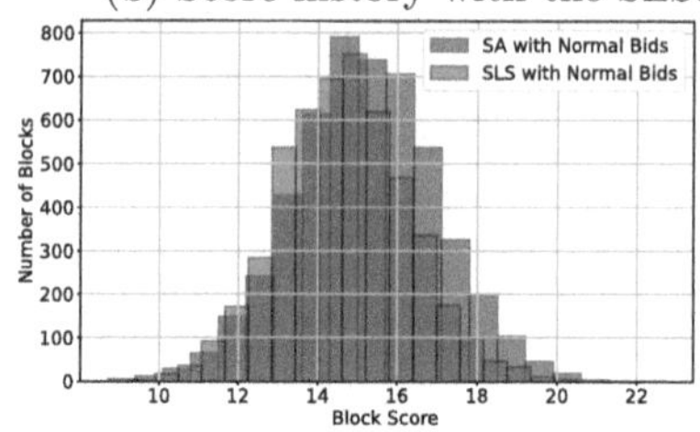

(d) Normal bids using SA and SLS.

Fig. 2. Optimization process visualization and score distribution analysis.

Next, we illustrate the results of the score distribution in Fig. 2c and Fig. 2d, comparing different algorithms (SA and SLS) applied to uniformly and normally sampled bids. We consider that our bid set simulates a user's bidpool, which should exhibit some consistency across the network. Although slight shifts are observed in the results, the overall distribution of the best scores remains stable. This stability arises from two key factors: (1) the scores naturally align with the distribution defined by the scoring function; and (2) the resulting distribution is influenced by the generalized extreme value (GEV) distribution (according to the extreme value theory) as each trial involves multiple iterations in our experiments. The stability in our results suggests that, given an input bid distribution, a generic stochastic solving algorithm prevents any user from gaining a significant advantage in finding higher-scored blocks, as the scores are consistently shaped by both the scoring function and the GEV distribution.

The implementation results suggest that we can reliably focus on the score distribution without overly concerned with specific settings, thereby validating our use of the universal sampler model for the generic scoring function.

7 Final Remarks

We proposed a novel blockchain consensus protocol that can be applied to double auction systems, hence having practical applications, *i.e.*, peer-to-peer energy trading. Our construction is somewhat similar to PoW, *i.e.*, relying on computational power. However, it was repurposed for a more useful work, *i.e.*, allocating buy and sell bids. Concretely, we introduced a Scored Generalized Multiple Assignment Problem, SGMAP, and semanticized the problem with our thoroughly redesigned (to accommodate bidding and bid allocation) blockchain data structure. The resulting scheme is proof-of-bid-assignment (PoBA), the core component of our proposed score-based blockchain protocol. Finally, we presented significantly involved security analysis and experimental results to substantiate the security. Concretely, we analyzed honest users' local chain dynamics under our score-based blockchain selection rule to prove persistence; and showed liveness concerning a variant that focuses on block dynamics instead of transactions.

A Auxiliary Definitions

This section provides supplementary definitions and descriptions.

A.1 Digital Signatures Scheme

The algorithms in a signature scheme $\mathsf{SIG}{=}(\mathsf{KGen}, \mathsf{Sign}, \mathsf{Verify})$ works as follows.

- $\mathsf{KGen}(1^\lambda)$ takes as input λ and outputs a key pair $(\mathsf{sk}, \mathsf{pk})$;
- $\mathsf{Sign}(\mathsf{sk}, m)$ takes as input the secret key sk and a message m. It outputs a signature σ on m under sk;
- $\mathsf{Verify}(\mathsf{pk}, m, \sigma)$ takes as input the public key pk, the message m and the signature σ. It outputs 1 if the signature is valid and 0 otherwise.

The correctness and the existential unforgeability under adaptive chosen message attacks (EUF-CMA) are defined as follows.

Definition 14 (Correctness). *A signature scheme satisfies correctness, if for any* $\lambda > 0$ *and* $(\mathsf{sk}, \mathsf{pk}) \leftarrow \mathsf{KGen}(1^\lambda)$*:* $\Pr[\mathsf{Verify}(\mathsf{pk}, m, \mathsf{Sign}(\mathsf{sk}, m)) = 1] = 1$.

Definition 15 (EUF-CMA). *A signature scheme satisfies EUF-CMA, if for any adversary that has access to a signing oracle $\mathcal{O}_{\mathsf{Sign}}(\mathsf{sk}, \cdot)$ with queries $m \in \mathsf{Q}$, the following probability is negligible of λ for any $\lambda > 0$ and $(\mathsf{sk}, \mathsf{pk}) \leftarrow \mathsf{KGen}(1^\lambda)$:*

$$\Pr\left[(m^*, \sigma^*) \leftarrow \mathcal{A}^{\mathcal{O}_{\mathsf{Sign}}}(\mathsf{pk}) | m^* \notin \mathsf{Q} \wedge \mathsf{Verify}(m^*, \sigma^*, \mathsf{pk}) = 1\right].$$

A.2 The Diffuse Functionality

Based on [9,16], we describe the delayed diffuse functionality tailored to our protocol setting (recall Sect. 2). The functionality is parameterized by $\delta \in \mathbb{N}$ and denoted by $\mathsf{DDiffuse}_\delta$. It keeps rounds, executing one round per slot. $\mathsf{DDiffuse}_\delta$ interacts with the environment $\mathcal{Z}$, users in slot $t \geq 0$, *i.e.*, u_i for all $i \in [n_t]$, and an adversary $\mathcal{A}$. It works as follows in each round:

- $\mathsf{DDiffuse}_\delta$ maintains a $\mathsf{RECEIVE}(i)$ string defined for each user u_i. A user u_i, if activated, is allowed to fetch the contents of her personal $\mathsf{RECEIVE}(i)$ string at any time. Moreover, users can instruct the functionality to diffuse a potentially empty message m. Activated users are allowed to diffuse once in a round;
- When the adversary is activated, it is allowed to: (1) Read all $\mathsf{RECEIVE}(\cdot)$; (2) Read all diffuse requests and deliver messages to their corresponding $\mathsf{RECEIVE}(\cdot)$ in any order it prefers; (3) For any message m obtained from a diffuse request and any user u_i, $\mathcal{A}$ can move m into a special string $\mathsf{DELAYED}(i)$ instead of $\mathsf{RECEIVE}(i)$;
- At the end of each round, $\mathsf{DDiffuse}_\delta$ ensures that any message to u_i that was either (1) diffused in this round and not put to $\mathsf{DELAYED}(i)$; or (2) removed from the string $\mathsf{DELAYED}(i)$ in this round and delivered to $\mathsf{RECEIVE}(i)$. Moreover, if any message currently present in $\mathsf{DELAYED}(i)$ was originally diffused at least δ slots ago, then $\mathsf{DDiffuse}_\delta$ removes it from $\mathsf{DELAYED}(i)$ and appends it to $\mathsf{RECEIVE}(i)$;
- Upon receiving a create instruction from $\mathcal{Z}$ with a user-tree tree, $\mathsf{DDiffuse}_\delta$ spawns a new user with tree as her local tree and informs her with (n_t, f_t, δ).

B Formal Protocol Description

The PoBA-Based Blockchain Protocol $\Pi^{n,\delta,k,\tau,s_{bk}(\cdot),acc(\cdot)}_{\mathcal{T},\mathsf{PoBA},\mathsf{UpdatePool},\mathsf{UpdateTree}}$

In each slot $t{+}1{\geq}0$ given by the global clock $\mathcal{T}$, the protocol Π is executed by n users (with honest majority). We assume δ is the known network delay and $k{\in}[0,1]$ is a constant that determines the auction price. Given a generic scoring function $s_{bk}(\cdot)$, an accumulating parameter function $acc(\cdot)$, the PoBA scheme PoBA, and the algorithms (UpdatePool, UpdateTree), instructions for an honest user u with an tuple output from slot t, *i.e.*, $(\mathsf{Pool}^t_{\mathsf{u}'}, \mathsf{tree}^t_{\mathsf{u}'}, B^t_{\mathsf{u}})$, are as follows.

- **Select local blockchain:** $\mathsf{chain}^t \stackrel{\Delta}{=} \arg\max_{\mathsf{branch}^t \subseteq \mathsf{tree}^t_{\mathsf{u}'}} S_{\mathsf{branch}^t}$;
- **Update bidpool:** Run $\mathsf{Pool}^{t+1}_{\mathsf{u}} \leftarrow \mathsf{UpdatePool}(\mathsf{Pool}^t_{\mathsf{u}'}, \mathsf{branch}^t, B^t_{\mathsf{u}})$ for each $\mathsf{branch}^t \subseteq \mathsf{tree}^t_{\mathsf{u}'}$ *s.t.* $\mathsf{Pool}^{t+1}_{\mathsf{u}}$ is valid *w.r.t.* chain^t;
- **Generate block candidates:** $\mathsf{chain}^t || \mathsf{bk}^{t+1}_{\mathsf{u},j} \leftarrow \mathsf{PoBA.Solve}(\mathsf{chain}^t, \mathsf{Bs}_j)$ where $\mathsf{Bs}_j {\subseteq} \mathsf{Pool}^{t+1}_{\mathsf{u}}$ and $|\mathsf{Bs}_j| {\leq} \mathsf{N}$ *s.t.* $BK^{t+1}_{\mathsf{u}} \stackrel{\Delta}{=} \{\mathsf{bk}^{t+1}_{\mathsf{u},j}\}_{j \in [\mathsf{ite}]}$;
- **Diffuse the best candidate:** Let the best block candidate $\mathsf{bk}^{*t+1}_{\mathsf{u}} \stackrel{\Delta}{=} \arg\max_{\mathsf{bk}^{t+1}_{\mathsf{u},j} \in BK^{t+1}_{\mathsf{u}}} s_{bk}(\mathsf{bk}^{t+1}_{\mathsf{u},j})$ and diffuse $\mathsf{chain}^{*t+1}_{\mathsf{u}} \stackrel{\Delta}{=} \mathsf{chain}^t || \mathsf{bk}^{*t+1}_{\mathsf{u}}$;
- **Update user-tree:** $\mathsf{tree}^{t+1}_{\mathsf{u}} \leftarrow \mathsf{tree}^t_{\mathsf{u}'}$, and for each valid chain'^{t+1} received in slot $t{+}1$, $\mathsf{tree}^{t+1}_{\mathsf{u}} \leftarrow \mathsf{UpdateTree}(\mathsf{tree}^{t+1}_{\mathsf{u}}, \mathsf{chain}'^{t+1})$;
- **Collect new bids:** Collect valid bids to $B^{t+1} \stackrel{\Delta}{=} \{(\mathsf{bidID{:}bid}) | H(\mathsf{bid}) = \mathsf{bidID} \wedge \mathsf{bid}.t_{\mathsf{Gen}} \leq t{+}1 < \mathsf{bid}.t_{\mathsf{Exp}} \wedge (\mathsf{bidID{:}bid}) \notin \mathsf{Pool}^{t+1}_{\mathsf{u}}\}$;
- **Report confirmed ledger:** When queried by the protocol Π, select $\mathsf{chain}^{t+1}_{\mathsf{u}} \stackrel{\Delta}{=} \arg\max_{\mathsf{branch}^{t+1} \subseteq \mathsf{tree}^{t+1}_{\mathsf{u}}} S_{\mathsf{branch}^{t+1}}$ and output $\mathsf{chain}^{t+1\lceil\tau}_{\mathsf{u}}$.

C Discussion: Incentive Model and Rational Analysis

Our security analysis (Sect. 5) is based on *assumptions* of the fraction of adversarial users and their behaviors. Note that this work does *not* analyze the reasons behind these assumptions based on users' rationality as in [2,3,15]. Instead, we present an intuition of the hardness of our rational analysis here.

Like conventional blockchain protocols, there are two layers of incentive: inherent (*e.g.*, transaction fee) and explicit (*e.g.*, block reward). The inherent incentive in our case derives from where users can tweak transactions to benefit themselves, *e.g.*, assigning higher buy prices for their sell bids or lower sell prices for their sell bids. However, prioritizing their own bids in the solving algorithm will potentially sacrifice the block scores. Hence, their blocks may fail to be selected in the confirmed blockchain. The trade-off between this inherent reward and the scarification of block scores requires a case-by-case analysis with respect to concrete scoring functions.

It is even more complicated to consider explicit incentives. A well-chosen scoring function and our highest-score rule will impose the selected blockchain to benefit the underlying double auction system. Hence, as long as the rushing adversary cannot disturb consensus (proven with respect to persistence and liveness), we regard our protocol as secure. However, in practice, the computation in the PoBA can be unfair so that some users may dominate the block generation. Explicit incentives, like block rewards, will intensify this unfairness.

Moreover, as pointed out by [15], the reason of honest users following protocol instruction is also a crucial aspect for rational analysis, which, unfortunately, is unclear for our protocol[13]. Recall that we inherently assume that users in the PoBA will compete with each other for higher-scored blocks. An instant deficiency caused by replacing honest users with rational agencies is that rational agencies will generate blocks embedding random (but valid) transaction sets to save computing power. Then, even under our highest-score rule, the selected blockchain is far from meaningful for the underlying double auction system.

Therefore, we deliberately leave the design of the incentive model and rational analysis as future work.

D Proof of Lemma 1

We prove Lemma 1 as follows.

Proof. Consider the rightmost block on $\mathsf{chain}^t = \mathsf{bk}^G || \ldots || \mathsf{bk}^t$. If bk^t is generated by an honest user, it will be disclosed after δ slots by the network setting. Otherwise, by Assumption 1, at least one honest user receives bk^t in slot t. Because chain^t is the highest-scored branch in mtree^t, and the user's block-tree is a sub-graph of mtree^t, the user will also adopt chain^t as her highest-scored branch of slot t. Then, she (honest) will generate a block atop it in slot $t+1$. Therefore, for any $\ell \geq t + \delta + 1$, chain^t is disclosed. □

E Proof of Lemma 2

We prove Lemma 2 as follows.

Proof of Lemma 2). For $\tau=1$, let $\mathsf{branch}_{\mathsf{c}}^{t+1} = \mathsf{chain}^{t-1} || \mathsf{bk}_{\mathsf{c}}^{t} || \mathsf{bk}_{\mathsf{c}}^{t+1}$ and $\mathsf{branch}_{\mathsf{b}}^{*t+1} = \mathsf{chain}^{t-1} || \mathsf{bk}_{\mathsf{b}}^{*t} || \mathsf{bk}_{\mathsf{b}}^{*t+1}$ be two branches in slot $t+1$ where chain^{t-1}, $\mathsf{chain}^{t-1} || \mathsf{bk}_{\mathsf{c}}^{t}$ are the selected blockchains in slot $t-1$ and t. If a particular $\mathsf{branch}_{\mathsf{b}}^{*t+1}$ substitutes $\mathsf{branch}_{\mathsf{c}}^{t+1}$ (*i.e.*, $\mathsf{branch}_{\mathsf{b}}^{*t+1}$ gets selected), we write the probability with $\Pr[\tau=1, \mathsf{branch}_{\mathsf{b}}^{*t+1}]$ as follows (the subscript of the scoring function is omitted).

$$\Pr[\tau=1, \mathsf{branch}_{\mathsf{b}}^{*t+1}] = \Pr[s(\mathsf{bk}_{\mathsf{c}}^{t}) - s(\mathsf{bk}_{\mathsf{b}}^{*t}) \geq 0, \quad c_{0,1} \cdot (s(\mathsf{bk}_{\mathsf{c}}^{t}) - s(\mathsf{bk}_{\mathsf{b}}^{*t})) + (s(\mathsf{bk}_{\mathsf{c}}^{t+1}) - s(\mathsf{bk}_{\mathsf{b}}^{*t+1})) \leq 0] \tag{5}$$

[13] The solution may not be as simple as granting block rewards.

Here, we consider a constant value given by the accumulating function, *i.e.*, $c_{0,1}=\frac{acc(t)}{acc(t+1)}$. Denote random variables that represents the scores of the tuple $(\mathsf{bk}_\mathsf{c}^t, \mathsf{bk}_\mathsf{b}^{*t}, \mathsf{bk}_\mathsf{c}^{t+1}, \mathsf{bk}_\mathsf{b}^{*t+1})$ with $(X_\mathsf{c}^t, X_\mathsf{b}^t, X_\mathsf{c}^{t+1}, X_\mathsf{b}^{t+1})$. Then, write the subtraction of scores with $Y^t{=}X_\mathsf{c}^t - X_\mathsf{b}^t$ and $Y^{t+1}{=}X_\mathsf{c}^{t+1} - X_\mathsf{b}^{t+1}$. Following the universal sampler model, $(X_\mathsf{c}^t, X_\mathsf{b}^t, X_\mathsf{c}^{t+1}, X_\mathsf{b}^{t+1})$ are independent and follow the same distribution $\mathcal{D}_X{=}\mathcal{D}$ on $[\mathsf{smin}, \mathsf{smax}]$. Hence, Y^t and Y^{t+1} are independent, and distributed identically and *symmetrically* on $[\mathsf{smin}{-}\mathsf{smax}, \mathsf{smax}{-}\mathsf{smin}]$. We denote the distribution of Y^t and Y^{t+1} with $\mathcal{D}_Y$, and let $f_Y(\cdot)$ and $F_Y(\cdot)$ be the probability density function and the distribution function of $\mathcal{D}_Y$. Therefore, the probability $\Pr[\tau{=}1, \mathsf{branch}_\mathsf{b}]$ can be rewritten in the form of random variables

$$\Pr[(Y^t{\ge}0){\wedge}c_{0,1}{\cdot}Y^t + Y^{t+1}{\le}0)]. \tag{6}$$

Consider the event: $\{Y^t{=}y{\wedge}Y^{t+1}{\le}{-}c_{0,1}y\}$ for all $y{\in}[0, \mathsf{smax}{-}\mathsf{smin}]$. For simplicity, we rewrite $r{=}\mathsf{smax}{-}\mathsf{smin}$. By Y^t being independent of Y^{t+1}, we have Eq. 6$=\int_0^r \int_{-r}^{-c_{0,1}y} f_Y(y)f_Y(x)\mathrm{d}x\mathrm{d}y$. Then, we can estimate the upper bound with a trick that scales up $f_Y(\cdot)$ with two coefficients $c_1, c_2 > 0$,

$$f_Y(y)\begin{cases} \le c_1{\cdot}e^{-c_2\cdot y^2}, & \text{if } y \in [-r, r]; \\ =0, & \text{otherwise.} \end{cases} \tag{7}$$

Note that $f_Y(y)$ is a probability density function, hence, it satisfies $\int_{-r}^r f_Y(y)$ $\mathrm{d}y{=}1$. Then, for c_1, c_2, we have the estimation: $\int_{-\infty}^{\infty} c_1{\cdot}e^{-c_2\cdot y^2}\mathrm{d}y{\ge}1$, which is $c_1^2/c_2{\ge}\pi^{-1}$. The manipulation of inequality gives us that:

$$\text{Eq. 6}{\le}\int_0^\infty \int_{-\infty}^{-c_{0,1}y} e^{-y^2}{\cdot}e^{-x^2}\mathrm{d}x\mathrm{d}y{=}\frac{{c_1}^2}{2c_2}\cdot\tan^{-1}\left(\frac{1}{c_{0,1}}\right){\le}\frac{{c_1}^2}{2c_2{\cdot}c_{0,1}}.$$

That is, $\Pr[\tau{=}1, \mathsf{branch}_\mathsf{b}^{*t+1}]{\le}{c_1}^2/(2c_2{\cdot}c_{0,1})$ for any $c_1, c_2{\ge}0, c_1^2/c_2{\ge}\pi^{-1}$ where $c_{0,1}{=}\frac{acc(t)}{acc(t+1)}$.

Next, the probability for any $\mathsf{branch}_\mathsf{b}^{t+1}$, denoted by $\Pr[\tau{=}1]$, should consider a joint event, *i.e.*, let q be the number of possible $\mathsf{branch}_\mathsf{b}^{t+1}$. Recall that Q is the upper bound of the total number of queries in each slot. Hence, $q{\le}Q$. Finally, for $\tau{=}1$, we have $\Pr[\tau{=}1]{\le}1-\left(1-\frac{c_1^2}{2c_2\cdot c_{0,1}}\right)^Q$.

The case of $\tau > 1$ follows the same methodology of $\tau{=}1$. Consider a branch that satisfies $\mathsf{branch}_\mathsf{b}^t \cap \mathsf{chain}^t = \mathsf{chain}^{t\lceil\tau}$. Denote the distinct blocks on $\mathsf{branch}_\mathsf{b}^t$ with bk_b^i for $i{\in}[t{-}\tau{+}1..t]$, and the blocks on chain^t with bk_c^i for $i{\in}[t{-}\tau{+}1..t]$. For the new blocks generated in slot $t{+}1$, denote them with $\mathsf{bk}_\mathsf{b}^{t+1}$ for $\mathsf{branch}_\mathsf{b}$ and $\mathsf{bk}_\mathsf{c}^{t+1}$ for $\mathsf{branch}_\mathsf{c}$ (*i.e.*, $\mathsf{chain}^t||\mathsf{bk}_\mathsf{c}^{t+1}$ is no longer the highest-scored branch, hence restated as $\mathsf{branch}_\mathsf{c}^{t+1}$). By rewriting Eq. 6, the probability of $\mathsf{branch}_\mathsf{c}^{t+1}$ substituted by a particular $\mathsf{branch}_\mathsf{b}^{*t+1}$, denoted by $\Pr[\tau{>}1, \mathsf{branch}_\mathsf{b}^{*t+1}]$, is:

$$\Pr\left[\left(\bigwedge_{i\in[t-\tau+1..t]}\left(\sum_{j=t-\tau+1}^{i}\frac{acc(j)}{acc(i)}{\cdot}Y^j{\ge}0\right)\right)\wedge\left(\sum_{i=t-\tau+1}^{t+1}\frac{acc(i)}{acc(t+1)}{\cdot}Y^i{\le}0\right)\right]. \tag{8}$$

Here, $Y^i = X_{\mathsf{c}}^i - X_{\mathsf{b}}^i$ for all $i \in [t-\tau+1..t]$ are independent and distributed identically with $\mathcal{D}_Y$ on $[\mathsf{smin}-\mathsf{smax}, \mathsf{smax}-\mathsf{smin}]$. Note that we normalize the coefficient of the last Y in the sum with $\frac{acc(j)}{acc(i)}$ (when $j{=}i$) and $\frac{acc(i)}{acc(t+1)}$ (when $i{=}t{+}1$). For simplicity, we rewrite $\frac{acc(j)}{acc(i)}$ with $c(j,i)$, hence $c(i,i){=}1$, and we have ($r_1{=}0$):

$$\begin{aligned}
\text{Eq. 8} &= \int_{r_1}^{r} \cdots \int_{r_\tau}^{r} \Pi_{i=t-\tau+1}^{t} \Pr[Y^i{=}y_i] \cdot \Pr\left[Y^{t+1} \le - \sum_{i=t-\tau+1}^{t} c(i,t{+}1) \cdot y_i\right] \mathrm{d}y_i^\tau \\
&= \int_{r_1}^{r} \cdots \int_{r_\tau}^{r} \Pi_{i=t-\tau+1}^{t} f_Y(y_i) \cdot F_Y\left(- \sum_{i=t-\tau+1}^{t} c(i,t{+}1) \cdot y_i\right) \mathrm{d}y_i^\tau \\
&= \int_{r_1}^{r} \cdots \int_{r_\tau}^{r} \int_{-r}^{-\sum_{i=t-\tau+1}^{t} c(i,t+1)\cdot y_i} \Pi_{i=t-\tau+1}^{t} f_Y(y_i) \cdot f_Y(x) \mathrm{d}x \mathrm{d}y_i^\tau. \qquad (9)
\end{aligned}$$

We denote the lower bound of random variable $Y^{t-\tau+i}$ for any $i \in [1..\tau]$ as r_i. Hence $r_i = -\sum_{j=t-\tau+1}^{i} c(j,i) \cdot y_j$. Here, we use a small trick to scale Eq. 9. Note that r_i is not necessarily larger than 0. We scale $y_{t-\tau+i}$ down to $-r$ for all $i \in [1..\tau]$. Then, the upper bound of Y^{t+1} is $Y^{t+1} \le \widetilde{r_{\tau+1}} \overset{\Delta}{=} -c(t-\tau+1, t{+}1) y_{t-\tau+1} + r \cdot \sum_{j=2}^{\tau} c(t-\tau+j, t{+}1)$. By $\int_{-r}^{r} f_Y(y_{t-\tau+i}) \mathrm{d}y_{t-\tau+i} \le 1$ for any $i \in [1..\tau]$, we have:

$$\text{Eq. 9} \le \int_0^r \int_{-r}^{\widetilde{r_{\tau+1}}} f_Y(y_{t-\tau+1}) f_Y(x) \mathrm{d}x \mathrm{d}y_{t-\tau+1}. \qquad (10)$$

Finally, utilizing the same trick for $f_Y(\cdot)$ as in Eq. 7, we have:

$$\text{Eq. 10} \le= \frac{{c_1}^2}{c_2} \cdot \tan^{-1}\left(\frac{1}{c(t-\tau+1, t{+}1) - \sum_{j=2}^{\tau} c(t-\tau+j, t{+}1)}\right)$$

In order to obtain a similar result as the case of $\tau = 1$, *i.e.*, $\Pr[\tau{>}1, \mathsf{branch}_{\mathsf{b}}^{*t+1}] \le \frac{{c_1}^2}{c_2 \cdot c(t-\tau+1, t+1)}$, we need to further scale the sum formula to a higher-order infinitesimal of $c(t-\tau+1, t{+}1)$, which can be achieved when setting $acc(t){=}c^t$ and $c > 2$. In this situation, for any $c_1, c_2 {\ge} 0$ and $c_1^2/c_2 \ge \pi^{-1}$, the probability for any $\mathsf{branch}_{\mathsf{b}}^{t+1}$ concerning our universal sampler model is:

$$\Pr[\tau > 1] \le 1 - \left(1 - \frac{c_1^2}{c_2 \cdot c(t{-}\tau{+}1, t{+}1)}\right)^Q$$

Combining the discussion above, we consider a constant value $c > \max\{2, \frac{c_1^2}{c_2}\}$ for $acc(t){=}c^t$. Then, $\Pr[\tau{\ge}1] {\le} 1 - \left(1 - \frac{c_1^2}{c_2 \cdot c^{-\tau}}\right)^Q$ is of the same order as $Q \cdot c^{-\tau}$. Since we only use the upper bound of total queries to the universal sampler instead of honest queries, our conclusion holds even there is at least one honest user. Finally, we conclude the first violation case occurs with probability $\mathsf{O}(c^{-\tau})$. □

References

1. Badertscher, C., Gazi, P., Kiayias, A., Russell, A., Zikas, V.: Ouroboros chronos: permissionless clock synchronization via proof-of-stake. Cryptology ePrint Archive, Report 2019/838 (2019). https://eprint.iacr.org/2019/838
2. Badertscher, C., Garay, J., Maurer, U., Tschudi, D., Zikas, V.: But why does it work? a rational protocol design treatment of bitcoin. In: Nielsen, J.B., Rijmen, V. (eds.) EUROCRYPT 2018. LNCS, vol. 10821, pp. 34–65. Springer, Cham (2018). https://doi.org/10.1007/978-3-319-78375-8_2
3. Badertscher, C., Lu, Y., Zikas, V.: A rational protocol treatment of 51% attacks. In: Malkin, T., Peikert, C. (eds.) CRYPTO 2021. LNCS, vol. 12827, pp. 3–32. Springer, Cham (2021). https://doi.org/10.1007/978-3-030-84252-9_1
4. Ball, M., Rosen, A., Sabin, M., Vasudevan, P.N.: Proofs of work from worst-case assumptions. In: Shacham, H., Boldyreva, A. (eds.) CRYPTO 2018. LNCS, vol. 10991, pp. 789–819. Springer, Cham (2018). https://doi.org/10.1007/978-3-319-96884-1_26
5. Blocki, J., Zhou, H.-S.: Designing proof of human-work puzzles for cryptocurrency and beyond. In: Hirt, M., Smith, A. (eds.) TCC 2016. LNCS, vol. 9986, pp. 517–546. Springer, Heidelberg (2016). https://doi.org/10.1007/978-3-662-53644-5_20
6. Canetti, R.: Universally composable security: a new paradigm for cryptographic protocols. In: 42nd FOCS, pp. 136–145. IEEE Computer Society Press (2001). https://doi.org/10.1109/SFCS.2001.959888
7. Constantinides, T., Cartlidge, J.: Block auction: a general blockchain protocol for privacy-preserving and verifiable periodic double auctions. In: Xiang, Y., Wang, Z., Wang, H., Niemi, V. (eds.) 2021 IEEE Blockchain 2021, Melbourne, Australia, 6–8 December 2021, pp. 513–520. IEEE (2021). https://doi.org/10.1109/BLOCKCHAIN53845.2021.00078
8. Daian, P., Pass, R., Shi, E.: Snow White: robustly reconfigurable consensus and applications to provably secure proof of stake. In: Goldberg, I., Moore, T. (eds.) FC 2019. LNCS, vol. 11598, pp. 23–41. Springer, Cham (2019). https://doi.org/10.1007/978-3-030-32101-7_2
9. David, B., Gaži, P., Kiayias, A., Russell, A.: Ouroboros praos: an adaptively-secure, semi-synchronous proof-of-stake blockchain. In: Nielsen, J.B., Rijmen, V. (eds.) EUROCRYPT 2018. LNCS, vol. 10821, pp. 66–98. Springer, Cham (2018). https://doi.org/10.1007/978-3-319-78375-8_3
10. Dyer, M.E., Frieze, A.M.: Probabilistic analysis of the generalised assignment problem. Math. Program. **55**, 169–181 (1992). https://doi.org/10.1007/BF01581197
11. Fitzi, M., Kiayias, A., Panagiotakos, G., Russell, A.: Ofelimos: combinatorial optimization via proof-of-useful-work - a provably secure blockchain protocol. In: Dodis, Y., Shrimpton, T. (eds.) CRYPTO 2022, Part II. LNCS, vol. 13508, pp. 339–369. Springer, Heidelberg (2022). https://doi.org/10.1007/978-3-031-15979-4_12
12. Galal, H.S., Youssef, A.M.: Verifiable sealed-bid auction on the ethereum blockchain. In: Zohar, A., Eyal, I., Teague, V., Clark, J., Bracciali, A., Pintore, F., Sala, M. (eds.) FC Workshop. LNCS, vol. 10958, pp. 265–278. Springer, Heidelberg (2018). https://doi.org/10.1007/978-3-662-58820-8_18
13. Galal, H.S., Youssef, A.M.: Trustee: full privacy preserving vickrey auction on top of ethereum. In: Bracciali, A., Clark, J., Pintore, F., Rønne, P.B., Sala, M. (eds.) FC 2019. LNCS, vol. 11599, pp. 190–207. Springer, Cham (2020). https://doi.org/10.1007/978-3-030-43725-1_14

14. Galal, H.S., Youssef, A.M.: Publicly verifiable and secrecy preserving periodic auctions. In: Bernhard, M., et al. (eds.) FC 2021. LNCS, vol. 12676, pp. 348–363. Springer, Heidelberg (2021). https://doi.org/10.1007/978-3-662-63958-0_29
15. Garay, J.A., Katz, J., Maurer, U., Tackmann, B., Zikas, V.: Rational protocol design: cryptography against incentive-driven adversaries. In: 54th FOCS, pp. 648–657. IEEE Computer Society Press (2013). https://doi.org/10.1109/FOCS.2013.75
16. Garay, J., Kiayias, A., Leonardos, N.: The bitcoin backbone protocol: analysis and applications. In: Oswald, E., Fischlin, M. (eds.) EUROCRYPT 2015. LNCS, vol. 9057, pp. 281–310. Springer, Heidelberg (2015). https://doi.org/10.1007/978-3-662-46803-6_10
17. Garay, J.A., Kiayias, A., Leonardos, N., Panagiotakos, G.: Bootstrapping the blockchain, with applications to consensus and fast PKI setup. In: Abdalla, M., Dahab, R. (eds.) PKC 2018. LNCS, vol. 10770, pp. 465–495. Springer, Cham (2018). https://doi.org/10.1007/978-3-319-76581-5_16
18. Gilad, Y., Hemo, R., Micali, S., Vlachos, G., Zeldovich, N.: Algorand: scaling byzantine agreements for cryptocurrencies. Cryptology ePrint Archive, Report 2017/454 (2017). https://eprint.iacr.org/2017/454
19. Górski, T., Bednarski, J.: Modeling of smart contracts in blockchain solution for renewable energy grid. In: Moreno-Díaz, R., Pichler, F., Quesada-Arencibia, A. (eds.) EUROCAST 2019. LNCS, vol. 12013, pp. 507–514. Springer, Cham (2020). https://doi.org/10.1007/978-3-030-45093-9_61
20. Hofheinz, D., Jager, T., Khurana, D., Sahai, A., Waters, B., Zhandry, M.: How to generate and use universal samplers. In: Cheon, J.H., Takagi, T. (eds.) ASIACRYPT 2016. LNCS, vol. 10032, pp. 715–744. Springer, Heidelberg (2016). https://doi.org/10.1007/978-3-662-53890-6_24
21. Kamp, S.H., Magri, B., Matt, C., Nielsen, J.B., Thomsen, S.E., Tschudi, D.: Weight-based nakamoto-style blockchains. In: Longa, P., Ràfols, C. (eds.) LATINCRYPT 2021. LNCS, vol. 12912, pp. 299–319. Springer, Cham (2021). https://doi.org/10.1007/978-3-030-88238-9_15
22. Lamport, L.: Time, clocks, and the ordering of events in a distributed system. Commun. ACM **21**(7), 558–565 (1978). https://doi.org/10.1145/359545.359563
23. Lamport, L., Shostak, R.E., Pease, M.C.: The byzantine generals problem. ACM Trans. Program. Lang. Syst. **4**(3), 382–401 (1982). https://doi.org/10.1145/357172.357176
24. Liu, B., Yang, Y., Wang, R., Hong, Y.: Poster: Privacy preserving divisible double auction with A hybridized tee-blockchain system. In: 41st IEEE ICDCS 2021, Washington DC, USA, 7–10 July 2021, pp. 1144–1145. IEEE (2021). https://doi.org/10.1109/ICDCS51616.2021.00128
25. Liu, L., Du, M., Ma, X.: Blockchain-based fair and secure electronic double auction protocol. IEEE Intell. Syst. **35**(3), 31–40 (2020). https://doi.org/10.1109/MIS.2020.2977896
26. Ma, X., Xu, D., Wolter, K.: Blockchain-enabled feedback-based combinatorial double auction for cloud markets. Future Gener. Comput. Syst. **127**, 225–239 (2022). https://doi.org/10.1016/J.FUTURE.2021.09.009
27. Naor, M.: On cryptographic assumptions and challenges. In: Boneh, D. (ed.) CRYPTO 2003. LNCS, vol. 2729, pp. 96–109. Springer, Heidelberg (2003). https://doi.org/10.1007/978-3-540-45146-4_6
28. Nguyen, T.D.T., Thai, M.T.: A blockchain-based iterative double auction protocol using multiparty state channels. CoRR (2020). https://arxiv.org/abs/2007.08595

29. Park, J.S., Lim, B.H., Lee, Y.: A lagrangian dual-based branch-and-bound algorithm for the generalized multi-assignment problem. Manag. Sci. **44**(12), 271–275 (1998)
30. Pass, R., Seeman, L., Shelat, A.: Analysis of the blockchain protocol in asynchronous networks. In: Coron, J.-S., Nielsen, J.B. (eds.) EUROCRYPT 2017. LNCS, vol. 10211, pp. 643–673. Springer, Cham (2017). https://doi.org/10.1007/978-3-319-56614-6_22
31. Pass, R., Shi, E.: Thunderella: blockchains with optimistic instant confirmation. In: Nielsen, J.B., Rijmen, V. (eds.) EUROCRYPT 2018. LNCS, vol. 10821, pp. 3–33. Springer, Cham (2018). https://doi.org/10.1007/978-3-319-78375-8_1
32. Roussas, G.: An introduction to probability and statistical inference, pp. 207–243. Elsevier, Academic Press (2015). https://doi.org/10.1016/B978-0-12-800114-1.00006-8
33. Thakur, S., Breslin, J.G., Malik, S.: Privacy-preserving energy trade using double auction in blockchain offline channels. In: Prieto, J., Martínez, F.L.B., Ferretti, S., Guardeño, D.A., Nevado-Batalla, P.T. (eds.) 4th IEEE BLOCKCHAIN 2022, L'Aquila, Italy, 13-15 July 2022. Lecture Notes in Networks and Systems, vol. 595, pp. 289–302. Springer, Heidelberg (2022). https://doi.org/10.1007/978-3-031-21229-1_27
34. Virtanen, P., et al.: SciPy 1.0: fundamental algorithms for scientific computing in python. Nat. Methods **17**(3), 261–272 (2020). https://doi.org/10.1038/s41592-019-0686-2
35. Wongsamerchue, T., Leelasantitham, A.: An electronic double auction of prepaid electricity trading using blockchain technology. J. Mobile Multimedia **18**(6), 1829–1850 (2022). https://doi.org/10.13052/JMM1550-4646.18616
36. Zhang, S., Miao, P., Wang, B., Dong, B.: A privacy protection scheme of microgrid direct electricity transaction based on consortium blockchain and continuous double auction. IEEE Access **7**, 151746–151753 (2019). https://doi.org/10.1109/ACCESS.2019.2946794

SoK: Measuring Blockchain Decentralization

Christina Ovezik[1(✉)], Dimitris Karakostas[1], Mary Milad[1], Daniel W. Woods[1], and Aggelos Kiayias[1,2]

[1] University of Edinburgh, Edinburgh, UK
{c.ovezik,dkarakos,mmilad,dwoods2,akiayias}@ed.ac.uk
[2] IOG, Edinburgh, UK

Abstract. In the context of blockchain systems, the importance of decentralization is undermined by the lack of a widely accepted methodology to measure it. To address this gap, we set out a systematization effort targeting the decentralization measurement workflow. To facilitate our systematization, we put forth a framework that categorizes all measurement techniques used in previous work based on the resource they target, the methods they use to extract resource allocation, and the functions they apply to produce the final measurements. We complement this framework with an empirical analysis designed to evaluate whether the various pre-processing steps and metrics used in prior work capture the same underlying concept of decentralization. Our analysis brings about a number of novel insights and observations. First, the seemingly innocuous choices performed during data extraction, such as the size of estimation windows or the application of thresholds on the resource distribution, have important repercussions when calculating the level of decentralization. Second, exploratory factor analysis suggests that in Proof-of-Work (PoW) blockchains, participation on the consensus layer is not correlated with decentralization, but rather captures a distinct signal, unlike in Proof-of-Stake (PoS) systems, where the different metrics align under a single factor. These findings challenge a long-held assumption within the blockchain community that higher participation drives higher decentralization. Finally, we combine the results of our empirical analysis with first-principles reasoning to derive practical recommendations for researchers that set out to measure blockchain decentralization, and we further systematize the existing literature in line with these recommendations.

1 Introduction

The security, reliability, fairness, and even legal status of blockchain systems is determined in part by their level of decentralization. In practice, decentralization concerns how critical resources, such as tokens or mining power, are distributed across participants [50]. A system is considered centralized if a small number of parties—or, in the extreme case, a single party—controls a large share of the resources that secure the blockchain protocol. Prospective users or developers

M. Fischlin and V. Moonsamy (Eds.): ACNS 2025, LNCS 15825, pp. 184–214, 2025.
https://doi.org/10.1007/978-3-031-95761-1_7

of blockchain systems may want to monitor centralization in block production, as it increases the risk of attacks, like double spending or censorship. Similarly, centralization of token ownership can increase the potential for market manipulation. Regulators also evaluate decentralization levels to treat blockchain-based assets and classify them as securities or commodities [16,19,60]. Thus, decentralization metrics can be used by a wide range of participants across the blockchain ecosystem, to make quantitative assessments and comparisons of blockchain systems across different layers and over time.

Despite the fundamental importance of decentralization in blockchain systems, there is no widely accepted method for how to measure it in the blockchain and distributed systems literature.[1] This gap in the literature motivated us to systematize the process of measuring blockchain decentralization. Specifically, we put forward a framework for standardizing decentralization measurements, which involves addressing three critical questions: (1) What is the resource of interest, whose allocation one should measure? (2) How can its distribution be extracted from the available information? (3) Which functions should be applied to the distribution to produce the final decentralization measurement?

Regarding question (1), the existing literature focuses predominantly on the distribution of protocol participating resources (e.g., hashing power or stake) or the distribution of tokens to different participants.

In terms of question (2), there is a wide variety of approaches that demand careful systematization. One key issue is that the distribution of resources may not lend itself immediately to extraction. For instance, the amount of resources, such as computational power, held by consensus participants cannot be observed directly. Instead, block production is typically used as a proxy for it, but this approach requires caution—for instance, inferring hashing power from the number of produced blocks involves fixing an estimation window, the choice of which can significantly influence the outcome of the analysis. Other considerations include how to attribute blocks or tokens to entities and whether to prune the data set of token holders to approximate the most useful segment of the token ownership distribution, given the pseudonymity of addresses.

Finally, regarding question (3), a plethora of functions have been put to the test in the literature. Given the overlapping nature of many of these functions, the interesting part from a systematization perspective is to identify what exactly they measure and to what extent their estimation truly captures decentralization.

Contributions. Our first contribution is the development of a framework that describes the core workflow of blockchain decentralization measurements. This includes: (1) choice of resource; (2) data pre-processing, and in particular choices on (2a) clustering, (2b) resource estimation, (2c) population estimation, (2d)

[1] An illustratory example can be found in the proceedings of the SEC vs. Ripple case, where the SEC argued that the XRP token was centralized and hence a security, while Ripple argued the opposite. Ultimately, the lack of a widely accepted methodology for assessing decentralization led to Ripple being exonerated from most accusations [1]. (NB: this ruling is currently under appeal by the SEC).

measurement frequency, and (2e) inclusion thresholds; and (3) choice of decentralization metric. This enables us to describe a decentralization measurement pipeline that we implement to analyze existing systems and metrics.[2]

We then systematize the blockchain decentralization literature using the above framework, to showcase how prior work has approached the various steps of the measurement workflow. We observe that the literature lacks a unified methodology for addressing these concerns, with studies making a wide variety of choices, frequently without complete justification.

Using our measurement framework we conduct an empirical analysis using data from five live blockchain systems, demonstrating that different methodological choices taken in the literature have a significant impact on decentralization estimates. In particular, our analysis reveals that the results can be manipulated via arbitrary decisions on how to pre-process data, such as removing wallets with balance below a certain threshold, or aggregating block data over an arbitrary time period.

We review decentralization metrics from prior work and perform exploratory factor analysis to uncover the underlying constructs they capture. A key finding is that participation, namely the number of entities that actively command resources, and decentralization, namely how such entities share these resources, do not always align, with distinct factors emerging to represent the two in some cases. This challenges the common assumption that high participation inherently leads to high decentralization in blockchain systems.

Combining the results of our analysis with reasoning from first principles, we derive a range of recommendations for researchers who set out to measure decentralization in blockchain systems.

Scope. Our framework applies to fungible resources distributed across entities that participate in a blockchain system. The canonical applications are tokens distributed across users, and computational power or stake distributed across block producers. The framework can also extend to layer-2 blockchains or DeFi applications, such as those involving on-chain governance tokens. However, it is not suitable for blockchain layers involving non-fungible resources, such as the network layer, where the graph structure must be incorporated into any analysis of decentralization. We further note that our pragmatic approach differs from prior systematizations that have focused on conceptualizing decentralization [50,72].

Roadmap. The remainder of this paper is organized as follows. Section 2 describes a framework that identifies the decisions required to measure blockchain decentralization. Section 3 systematizes the existing literature, classifying prior work based on our framework. Section 4 presents our own empirical analysis that highlights how arbitrary decisions can manipulate estimates of decentralization. Section 5 combines the findings from the analysis with reasoning from

[2] The Edinburgh Decentralization Index (EDI) implements our proposed measurement pipeline to create an online dashboard that tracks and compares the decentralization of live blockchain systems: https://informatics.ed.ac.uk/blockchain/edi.

first principles to derive recommendations for future measurements, with the overarching goal of providing standardized, architecture agnostic estimates of decentralization at the consensus and tokenomics layers, and describes the existing literature vis-à-vis those recommendations. Finally, Sect. 6 offers a summary of our findings and proposes directions for future research.

2 Systematization Framework

Our first contribution is a systematization of the decisions researchers must make when measuring decentralization in blockchain systems. These decisions are: (1) determining which data to collect (layer/resource); (2) pre-processing collected data, which involves choices about (2a) clustering, (2b) resource estimation windows, (2c) population estimation, (2d) measurement frequency, and (2e) inclusion thresholds; and (3) choosing which metrics to use to derive insights about decentralization.

Some of these questions are straightforward and have been addressed in prior work, while others are more nuanced and are frequently overlooked during the measurement process. In the following paragraphs, we will discuss each step in detail and explain why all are critical for a robust decentralization analysis.

2.1 Blockchain Layers and Resources

Ideally, a decentralization measurement process would take a blockchain system as input and output a value that describes its overall degree of decentralization. However, blockchains are multilayered systems and some layers may exhibit higher decentralization than others.

This means that any decentralization analysis begins, explicitly or implicitly, by choosing which layer to focus on.[3]

A number of recent research works have been dedicated to identifying the different layers of blockchain systems relevant to decentralization [50,57,72]. The four layers that are common across all of them are: consensus, tokenomics,[4] network, and governance.

The consensus layer captures direct participation in the protocol, which happens through the creation of blocks that extend the ledger. This layer carries direct security implications—for example, if an entity controls the majority of block production, it can launch a "51% attack" and double-spend coins [3].

The tokenomics layer focuses on the distribution of wealth within a system. This layer is strongly tied to the utility of the system and is also particularly important from a policymaking perspective, with critical decisions depending on the structure of token ownership. For instance, a recent U.S. bill proposes

[3] Developing a unified index to represent the decentralization of all layers has been posed as an open question in the literature [50], yet there is no known methodology to date that achieves this.

[4] There is no consistent name for this layer in the literature. We adopt the term "tokenomics" from [50], but it has also been referred to as "wealth" [72] or "incentives" [57].

classifying a blockchain asset as a security if there exists a single entity that controls more than 20% of its total token supply [29].

The network layer concerns the peer-to-peer protocol underpinning the blockchain, focusing on aspects like node distribution and connectivity. Decentralization on this layer is vital for ensuring that information can propagate effectively and without being censored.

The governance layer encompasses all decision-making activity that is relevant to a blockchain, which can take place off-chain, e.g., through forums or traditional corporate structures, or on-chain, using mechanisms that assign voting rights to tokens.

Out of these layers, consensus and tokenomics have received by far the most attention in the relevant literature, with numerous studies attempting to measure the decentralization of block production or wealth in popular blockchains. In contrast, there are only a handful of studies that address the decentralization of the network layer [21,24,28]. Governance of layer-1 blockchains has also received very little attention in decentralization studies [4,31], though recently some studies have explored the governance decentralization of DeFi projects [7,30,65]. Notably, in systems that employ on-chain governance, voting rights are represented by tokens, hence the methodology described for the tokenomics layer can be applied to measure decentralization on the governance layer, too, including that of DeFi applications. Nonetheless, given the limited research on these layers, we consider it premature to systematize the decentralization measurement process for network and governance. Instead, we focus our systematization efforts on the consensus and tokenomics layers from now on.

A further benefit of focusing on consensus and tokenomics is that these layers are consistent across systems, as all blockchains generate blocks and issue tokens. Moreover, consensus and tokenomics data can be obtained directly or inferred from the blockchain itself, allowing for transparent data processing and analysis.

To assess the decentralization of a given layer, one must first identify the layer's key resource and determine how it is distributed among participating entities [50]. This process is straightforward in some cases—for example, the tokenomics layer can be assessed by examining the distribution of the system's native token. In some layers, however, the "ideal" resource is not directly observable, thus necessitating the use of a "proxy" resource. This is true for the consensus layer, where the goal is to measure how the *power* to create blocks is distributed, yet only the outcomes of the block creation process can be observed.

2.2 Data Pre-processing

The process of turning arbitrary, possibly complex and semantically related, data into an element of the domain of a decentralization metric function introduces various interesting pre-processing choices. In particular, these steps include clustering addresses controlled by the same entity, estimating distributions that are not directly observable, potentially pruning these distributions, and capturing snapshots of them at different points in time. In the following, we explore the steps required to transform raw ledger data into distributions that can form the input of the metric functions.

Clustering of Blocks and Addresses. Clustering is the process of linking all resources associated with a single real-world entity. It is a crucial step in a decentralization analysis, as unclustered data can yield misleading decentralization estimates. At the consensus layer, the goal is to attribute all blocks to the real-world entity that created them, such as a mining pool. At the tokenomics layer, clustering involves grouping seemingly unlinked addresses under the entity that controls them.

Notably, this step hinges on defining what constitutes an "entity", which can be a contestable subject in itself. For instance, in the consensus layer, a mining pool could be treated as a single entity or as a collection of individual miners, each regarded as a separate entity. In the tokenomics layer, similar considerations arise when dealing with custodial wallets, shared accounts, or corporations that have multiple subsidiaries. In line with prior work on characterizing entities in blockchain ecosystems, we consider all organizations, such as exchanges or mining pools, to be distinct entities [32].

In UTxO-based ledgers, such as Bitcoin, clustering is particularly important, as the system's design inherently drives users to have multiple addresses. Over the years, various heuristics have been proposed to cluster these addresses based on the transaction graph. One such heuristic takes advantage of transactions that consume the assets of multiple addresses [54]. Intuitively, the ability to spend assets from multiple addresses suggests a direct link between these addresses, e.g., that one wallet controls all of them. This heuristic is the oldest and most widely applied [26,32,46,54,56]. Another heuristic involves identifying a transaction's "change" address and linking it to the input addresses [2]. For the case of Cardano, an additional heuristic has been developed, which leverages its on-chain delegation mechanism and groups together addresses that share the same "stake key", since this key can be used to withdraw rewards [11].

In account-based blockchains, like Ethereum, addresses are typically reused, making clustering less critical compared to UTxO-based systems. Nonetheless, clustering can still be useful for identifying entities that control multiple addresses. Among the proposed heuristics for these blockchains, the most effective involves clustering addresses that receive funds from the same exchange-generated deposit address [67].

Finally, a crowd-sourced method for enhancing the clustered information is "tagging". In this case, researchers use public information from blockchain explorers, social media, or other sources to attribute addresses to their owners. The effectiveness of tagging is difficult to assess, since the information is often manually gathered or provided by proprietary means. Alternatively, self-tagging allows parties to voluntarily disclose ownership of resources. Although this is rare on the tokenomics layer, it is prevalent on the consensus layer, where mining pools often announce a block's production by including their name within it, effectively advertising their operation.

Resource Estimation Window. In some cases, the distribution of resources can be directly observed from the ledger. For example, the token balance of each address is publicly available and updated in real time. In other cases, like the consensus layer of Proof-of-Work (PoW) blockchains, this is not as straightforward. The resource of interest there is the computational (or mining) power of each block producer. Since this power cannot be observed directly, it must be estimated, typically using produced blocks as a proxy. Specifically, when looking at a window of n blocks, an entity that creates x of the observed blocks is assumed to control a fraction $\frac{x}{n}$ of the total mining power. A critical consideration here is the trade-off between statistical confidence and time-specificity. A larger sample size increases statistical confidence but may overlook temporal changes. On the other hand, using only few blocks, e.g., produced within a single day, provides high time-specificity but lacks statistical power to draw reliable conclusions [47].

For Proof-of-Stake (PoS) blockhains, similar considerations arise. Although the stake distribution can be observed from the blockchain, not all PoS protocols use this exact distribution in their consensus process. For example, some systems employ a periodic sub-selection of parties to run the consensus protocol, which only reflects a small part of the stake distribution.[5] Since the resource of interest in consensus is protocol-participating power, extracting this from the stake distribution would need to take into account protocol-specific details, such as how each protocol implements the sub-selection mechanism. To avoid complexities specific to each system and remain agnostic to PoS architectures, researchers may instead apply the same approach as for PoW systems, using block production to estimate the consensus power distribution.

Population Estimation. A related but distinct challenge is estimating the total population of active participants at a given time. Since mining is a probabilistic process, miners may fail to produce *any* blocks during specific time periods, even if they contribute computational power. If the population of active participants is not estimated separately, unsuccessful miners will be excluded, skewing metrics that rely on the full distribution.

A simple method is to use a broader observation window than the resource estimation window, considering an entity active if it produces at least one block within this larger timeframe. In general, increasing the size of the population estimation window will better capture unsuccessful miners, but risks capturing entities who are no longer active. Another approach is to track the oldest and most recent blocks produced by each miner and assume they were active during the intervening period. A more sophisticated method could involve statistical inference through the analysis of block production patterns. Ideally, the population estimation method should include all entities contributing computational power during the resource estimation window, while excluding past or future participants that were not active during this period.

Measurement Frequency. Another choice to make during a decentralization analysis is how often to sample the data. Analyzing a snapshot of the system

[5] An example of this is Cosmos, where only the top X validators (currently X = 180) are selected to participate in consensus, while all the rest are considered inactive [39].

requires only a single data point, so it is easier to measure. However, conducting a longitudinal analysis can capture trends over time or assess how specific events impact the system's decentralization levels. In such historical analyses, collecting enough measurement points is crucial to provide a granular view of how the system evolved over time. If the measurement frequency is too low, important shifts or fluctuations in decentralization could be missed.

Notably, the measurement frequency is distinct from the resource and population estimation windows. While estimation windows impact how resources or participants are distributed within a timeframe, measurement frequency determines how often those windows are sampled.

Inclusion Thresholds. Finally, researchers must decide whether to analyze the entire distribution or restrict it by applying inclusion criteria. This is particularly relevant for the tokenomics layer, where token distribution typically exhibits a long tail, with thousands or millions of addresses controlling tiny amounts of assets, e.g., "dust" wallets [53]. Therefore, it may be reasonable to consider some of these addresses inactive and exclude them from the analysis, to avoid skewing metrics that are sensitive to the tail of the distribution. Importantly, while other pre-processing steps can be performed in parallel, inclusion criteria should always be applied after clustering and resource/population estimation.

2.3 Decentralization Metrics

A decentralization metric is a function $M : \mathbb{R}^* \to \mathbb{R}$, where the domain is a distribution of fungible resources across a number of parties and the output is a real number. Various metrics have been used over the years to measure the decentralization of blockchain systems, either crafted for them, or borrowed from fields like economics and information theory. Here, we focus on the metrics that have been used at least twice in the blockchain decentralization literature.

Shannon Entropy. Shannon entropy, also known as information entropy, measures the average degree of "unpredictability" inherent to the outcomes of a random variable [61]. Formally, it is defined as: $\mathrm{H}(X) := -\sum_{x \in \mathcal{X}} p(x) \log p(x)$, where X is a discrete random variable that takes values in $\mathcal{X}$ and $p(x)$ is the probability of an outcome $x \in \mathcal{X}$. Higher entropy corresponds to greater uncertainty (i.e., smaller probabilities for each possible value), while lower entropy reflects more predictable outcomes.

For instance, in the context of blockchains, if the random variable represents block creators and the block distribution is treated as a probability distribution over possible outcomes, entropy reveals how difficult it is to predict who creates blocks. Intuitively, higher entropy values indicate greater decentralization [69]. To take an extreme example, in a highly centralized setting where all blocks are produced by a single entity, entropy would be 0, as there is no uncertainty regarding who may create some block.

Gini Coefficient. The Gini coefficient is a widely used measure of inequality, typically applied in economics to quantify income or wealth disparities [6,23].

To define Gini, we consider two curves. First, the Lorenz curve, which plots the proportion of the total assets (y-axis) that are cumulatively controlled by the bottom x of entities. Second, the line of equality, i.e., the line at 45 degrees starting at (0, 0). The Gini coefficient is the ratio of the area between the Lorenz curve and the line of equality over the total area under the line of equality: $G = \frac{A-B}{A}$, where $A = \frac{n\sum_{i=1}^{n} x_i}{2}$ and $B = \sum_{i=1}^{n} ix_i$.

A Gini value of 0 represents perfect equality, whereas 1 indicates complete centralization of assets to a single entity. Notably, the Gini coefficient takes into account the entire distribution, including zero values. For example, the Gini of $X = \{3, 2, 1\}$ differs significantly from that of $Y = \{3, 2, 1, 0\}$ (0.22 vs 0.42). Therefore, to obtain accurate Gini values, it is essential to capture a complete view of resource distribution among parties, e.g., including block producers who attempted to produce blocks within a given time period but failed. A closely related metric to Gini is the Theil index, which intends to capture the lack of diversity, or the redundancy, in a population [14]. While the Theil index has been discussed in the blockchain decentralization literature [48], it has never been measured empirically.

Nakamoto Coefficient. The Nakamoto coefficient (NC) represents the minimum number of parties that collectively control a majority of resources [64]. This metric was introduced in the context of blockchains and is commonly used in blockchain analysis, particularly when examining block production data. In a distribution with n entities in which entity i controls fraction s_i of the total resources, the Nakamoto coefficient is defined as: NC $= min\{k \in [1, ..., n] : \sum_{i=1}^{k} s_i > 0.5\}$. Notably, some research works, e.g., [43], use ≥ 0.51 instead of > 0.5 in their definition of the Nakamoto coefficient. We attribute this to the misnomer of the "51% attack", which may lead people to believe that 51% of resources are needed to compromise the security of a ledger, when in fact a majority ($> 50\%$) suffices [41].

The NC can be particularly useful when analyzing decentralization, as it identifies the minimum number of parties that need to collude, in order to gain a majority of the resources under question. This quantity is highly relevant when arguing about a distributed ledger's security, which often relies on the assumption that a majority of power is honest, e.g., in the case of Bitcoin (PoW) [20] or Ouroboros (PoS) [36].

τ-decentralization Index. An intuitive generalization of the Nakamoto coefficient is the number of entities that collectively control more than any τ fraction of the total resources. Formally, this is defined as $min\{k \in [1, ..., n] : \sum_{i=1}^{k} s_i > \tau\}$, where n is the total number of entities in the system and s_i is the share of resources controlled by entity i. Different values of τ may be interesting to explore, depending on the context. For instance, the liveness threshold of systems like Algorand [22] or Ethereum PoS [8,9] is 33%, instead of 50% so exploring this value of τ can be particularly useful there.

Notably, this metric has been used in the literature before, but without a consistent name. For instance, Nadler *et al.* use the term "top $n\%$" for it and calculate it for the top 99% [49]. Additionally, τ is similar to the N_ϵ "centralization level", which states that N parties control $1 - \epsilon$ of all resources, introduced by Chu *et al.* [13].

Concentration Ratios. Concentration ratios have long been employed in economics to assess the degree of market concentration within an industry. For a given number n, the concentration ratio CR_n represents the combined market share of the n largest firms in an industry. The most commonly used concentration ratios in economic analysis are CR_3, CR_4, and CR_5 [62]. Formally, the n-concentration ratio of a market is defined as: $CR_n = \sum_{i=1}^{n} s_i$, where s_i is the market share of the ith largest entity.

In blockchain studies, concentration ratios have been applied several times to analyze decentralization, though they are commonly called "mining power ratios" [21]. We adopt the more neutral term "concentration ratios", as it aligns with the historical usage of the metric and allows for broader application to any resource, such as the distribution of wealth in the system, rather than solely to mining power.

Herfindahl–Hirschman Index (HHI). The Herfindahl–Hirschman index is a market concentration metric, measuring the size of entities w.r.t. the industry in which they operate [33]. The HHI is computed as the sum of the squares of each entity's percentage of market control: HHI $= \sum_{i=1}^{n}(s_i)^2$, where s_i is the market share of entity i and n is the number of all entities. The HHI ranges from 0 to 10,000, with 0 indicating the existence of many small entities and 10,000 indicating a monopoly.

Interestingly, because the HHI has been used by antitrust authorities, there exist guidelines to interpret its results. For instance, US agencies classify markets in three types, based on the HHI: i) unconcentrated markets: HHI below 1,500; ii) moderately concentrated markets: HHI between 1,500 and 2,500; iii) highly concentrated markets: HHI above 2,500 [34]. Similar guidelines could be developed for evaluating blockchain decentralization.

Number of Parties. Finally, a crude method that has been used to estimate decentralization is to count the number of entities controlling any amount of the resource of interest. This approach provides a straightforward quantitative assessment, as a higher number of active participants generally indicates a more decentralized system, though, notably, it does not account for power disparities between participants.

3 Literature Systematization

Using the framework of Sect. 2, we now review prior work and evaluate how it addresses the questions outlined above. Table 1 summarizes this classification, organized in chronological order of publication.

To compile the articles included in Table 1, we performed a systematic search using three databases: Google Scholar, Semantic Scholar, and DBLP. We used the keywords "measuring blockchain decentralization" and selected among the results the studies that conducted empirical decentralization measurements. As discussed in the previous section, our systematization focuses on layers with fungible resources, so we exclude articles on the network layer. Using this initial sample, we applied a backward and forward reference search (snowballing) to identify additional relevant studies and applied the same selection criteria to them.

Importantly, Table 1 includes only measurement studies, that is, works that analyze data from real-world blockchain systems to derive insights about their decentralization. Our work is also informed by complementary literature, such as systematizations of blockchain decentralization dimensions [50,57,72], game-theoretic treatments of decentralization [5], simulation-based analyses [52], or studies that propose (de)centralization indices without conducting direct measurements [13]. However, these contributions are orthogonal to our systematization and were therefore excluded from the table.

In cases where certain decisions were not explicitly discussed in some paper, we made reasonable assumptions to complete the table. Specifically, since none of the studies discussed population estimation as a distinct decision, we assumed it aligned with the resource estimation window. Also, if clustering was not explicitly mentioned, we assumed that no clustering was employed.

Table 1 reveals that there is no standardized approach in the literature for performing the steps identified in our framework, undermining one's ability to compare results across studies. In the following paragraphs, we elaborate on how each step of the framework has been addressed in prior research.

Layers and Resources. A number of studies measure decentralization on the consensus [10,21,25,40,43–45,48,69] and tokenomics [10,12,31,37,38,49,56,58, 69] layers. For the consensus layer, most works measure the distribution of produced blocks, with the exception of two studies [70,71] that instead analyze the distribution of rewards among block producers. For the tokenomics layer, all studies used the system's native token as the resource of interest.

Clustering. Notably, the bulk of reviewed studies did not use any clustering techniques to link resources controlled by a single entity [24,30,31,38,40,43–45,48,66,69–71]. This omission likely results in an overestimation of decentralization in their findings. Among the studies that did apply clustering, some relied on blockchain explorers for resource attribution through tagging [7,21,25,55,68], whereas others used primary heuristics [10,25,49,55], such as multi-input transactions.

Resource Estimation Window. The two broad approaches for the resource estimation window are time-based windows and block-based windows. Most commonly a time-based window is employed, with most studies opting for windows like one day [43,45,68,70], one week [10,21,25,43,45,69,71], or one month [24,40,43–45,66]. A single study also used longer windows, including three

Table 1. Measurement approaches in blockchain decentralization literature, ordered chronologically. The metrics are: Shannon Entropy (SE), Gini coefficient (G), Nakamoto coefficient (NC), Herfindahl-Hirschman index (HHI), concentration ratios (CR), τ-decentralization index (T), and number of parties (#P).

Ref	Resource	Clustering	Resource estimation window	Population estimation	Measurement frequency	Inclusion threshold	Metrics
[21]	Blocks	Tagging	1 week			Top 20	$CR_{1,3,4}$
[66]	Blocks	-	1 month			-	CR_3
[69]	Blocks	-	1 week		Once	-	SE
	Tokens	-	N/A		Once	Top 10,000	SE
[55]	Blocks	Tagging, Multi-input	2,016 Blocks			-	G, NC
[24]	Blocks	-	1,3 Months1 year All-time		Once	-	SE, G, NC, #P
[68]	Blocks	Tagging	1 Day			-	NC,$CR_{3,5}$
[40]	Blocks	-	1 month		Once	Top 10, 20, 30	SE, NC, $CR_{1,2,4}$, $T_{0.33}$
[49]	Tokens	Other heuristics	N/A		1 month	Top 500	G, NC, $CR_{5,10,50,100,500}$, $T_{0.99}$, #P
[30]	Tokens	-	N/A		Once	> tx fees	G, NC
[43]	Blocks	-	1 Day1 week1 month		1, 0.5 Day 1, 0.5 week 1, 0.5 month	-	SE, G, NC
[71]	Rewards	-	1 week			-	NC, $CR_{3,5}$
[38]	Tokens	-	N/A		Unclear	Top 30, 50, 100	SE, G, NC
[31]	Tokens	-	N/A		Once	Top 1,000	SE, G
[7]	Tokens	Tagging	N/A		6 Months	> tx fees	SE, G
[44]	Blocks	-	1 month			Top 10, 20, -	SE, #P
[48]	Blocks	-	20 Blocks		1 Block	-	G
[10]	Blocks	Multi-input	1 week			-	NC
	Tokens	Multi-input, Other heuristics	N/A		1 week	-	G
[25]	Blocks	Tagging, Other heuristics	1 week		1 Day	-	G, NC, HHI, $T_{0.33}$
[45]	Blocks	-	1 Day1 week1 month			-	SE, G, NC
[70]	Rewards	-	1 Day			-	SE, G, NC, HHI

months, one year, and even the entire history of the ledger [24]. Regarding block-based windows, one study aligned the number of blocks with Bitcoin's difficulty adjustment period [55], while another used a window of 20 blocks [48].

Population Estimation. An interesting finding is that estimating the population of block producers was never identified as a distinct choice in the literature. Therefore, we assume that the population was inferred from the resource estimation window, which is why the two columns are merged in all entries of Table 1.

As a reminder, the estimation windows are only relevant for the consensus layer, where the power distribution is not directly available. In contrast, the wealth distribution in the tokenomics layer can be directly observed from the blockchain, hence these considerations do not apply (marked as N/A).

Measurement Frequency. In longitudinal studies, the measurement frequency was often conflated with the resource estimation window. For instance, some authors used a single term, such as "granularity", to refer to both concepts. Notably, Lin *et al.* [43] were the first to propose the use of sliding windows, effectively decoupling the estimation window from the measurement frequency (though they still used the term "granularity" for both of them). This approach was also followed by Grandjean *et al.* [25], who employed a "7-day rolling window", from which we infer that the measurements were conducted daily, even though not explicitly stated. On the other hand, several studies analyzed only a single snapshot of the system [24,30,31,40,69].

Inclusion Threshold. Approximately half of the reviewed studies employed inclusion thresholds on the distribution under consideration. In the consensus layer, some works quantified decentralization among the top 10–30 block producers [21,40,44], while the rest did not apply any threshold. In tokenomics, inclusion criteria were more prevalent. Some researchers focused exclusively on the top-X wealthiest entities, with X ranging from 30 to 10,000 [31,38,49,69]. Others focused on entities that control a minimum amount of tokens, most often above the fees required to issue a transaction [7,30]. Nonetheless, the selection of these thresholds is often arbitrary and lacks clear justification.

Decentralization Metrics. Several metrics have been employed in the literature to measure blockchain decentralization on the consensus and tokenomics layers. Starting from concentration ratios [21,40,49,66,68]—or "mining power ratios" as often referred to in this literature—various metrics were gradually incorporated into the blockchain decentralization toolkit. Overall, the Gini coefficient [7,10,24,25,30,31,38,43,45,48,49,55,70] and the Nakamoto coefficient [10,24,25,30,38,40,43,45,49,70,71] were most frequently used across the reviewed literature. Notably, there are studies that measure the Nakamoto coefficient without explicitly naming it [55,68], and the same goes for those that measure its generalization, the τ-decentralization index [25,40,49]. Shannon entropy has also been used extensively over the years [7,24,31,38,40,43–45,69,70], while the Herfindahl–Hirschman index has been included in more recent works [25,70]. In some cases, simply counting the number of participants (block producers or token holders) was also used as a measure of decentralization [24,44,49]. Notably, no metric was consistently applied across all studies, making it difficult to draw meaningful comparisons among their results.

4 Empirical Analysis

We now analyze the impact of the methodological decisions outlined above using data from live blockchain systems. We collected historical data from five ledgers: Bitcoin, Cardano, Ethereum, Litecoin, and Tezos. Notably, Ethereum transitioned from Proof-of-Work to Proof-of-Stake on September 2022 [35], so we treat it as two different systems, Ethereum PoW and Ethereum PoS. Our selection is diverse in terms of Sybil resilience mechanisms[6] and balance models[7]. By analyzing these varied design architectures, we increase confidence that our conclusions generalize, especially when results are consistent across systems.

In the following paragraphs, we discuss our approach for each step of the process, and present the results of our analysis. The pipeline of our methodology can be seen in Fig. 1.

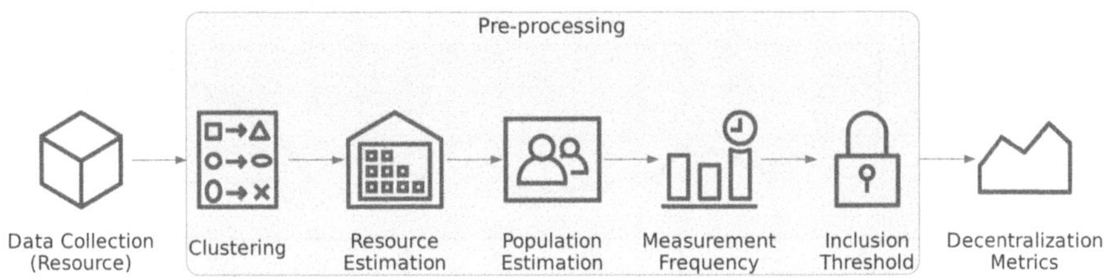

Fig. 1. Decentralization measurement pipeline.

Data Collection (Resource). In line with most prior work, we used blocks as the resource for estimating power distributions on the consensus layer. For the tokenomics layer, we use the system's native token as the resource, an approach consistently adopted in the relevant literature. As discussed in Sect. 2, we do not analyze the governance layer due to lack of sufficient measurement studies on layer-1 blockchains.

We collected historical data for both layers from Big Query's public datasets [18] and, in some cases, from our own full nodes. Due to space constraints, we refer to Appendix A.1 for more information on the collection process and a description of the relevant data.

Clustering. For both layers, we collected attribution data to determine how resources are distributed among real-world entities rather than addresses. This includes tags associated with known pools, addresses controlled by known entities (e.g., exchanges), and information on legal links between organizations, such

[6] Bitcoin, Ethereum Pow, and Litecoin are Proof-of-Work. Cardano, Ethereum PoS, and Tezos are Proof-of-Stake.

[7] Bitcoin, Cardano, and Litecoin use UTxOs. Ethereum and Tezos are account-based.

as acquisitions of mining pools.[8] We use blockchain explorers[9] and community projects [15] to collect off-chain data. For Bitcoin, we also implemented the multi-input heuristic [54], using the transaction graph retrieved from a full node, and for Cardano, we grouped addresses that shared the same stake key [11].

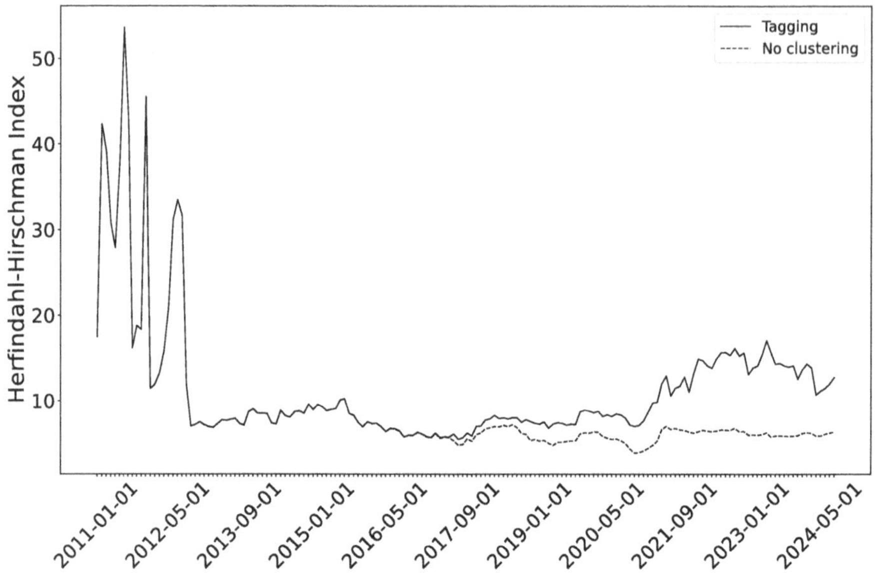

Fig. 2. Bitcoin tokenomics HHI values with and without clustering (tagging).

We conduct an analysis to assess the effectiveness of tagging, as this has not been thoroughly addressed in the literature. Figure 2 illustrates the HHI results for Bitcoin on the tokenomics layer, comparing the outcomes of tagging as a clustering method (solid lines) with the baseline of unclustered data (dashed lines). From 2016 onward, the two lines begin to diverge, indicating that tagging successfully grouped enough addresses to influence the results.[10] As expected, clustering increases centralization under the HHI, since it aggregates the same resources into fewer entities.[11]

Resource Estimation Window. Prior research on estimation windows for the consensus layer suggests that short windows, including the 1-day window used occasionally in the literature, do not provide enough statistical confidence to reliably estimate metrics like the Nakamoto Coefficient, especially for low

[8] For example, the mining pool BTC.COM was acquired BIT Mining [42], so after the point of the acquisition, blocks created by BTC.COM are attributed to BIT Mining.
[9] Such explorers are Etherscan, BitInfoCharts, and blockchain.com.
[10] Recall that higher HHI signifies greater centralization.
[11] Notably, this would not necessarily be true under the Gini Coefficient.

Table 2. Spearman correlations of Bitcoin's Gini values on tokenomics data, calculated with different inclusion thresholds.

	Top 100	Top 500	Top 1000	Top 10000	Top 50%	> tx fees	All
Top 100	1.00	0.17	−0.17	0.30	0.14	0.16	0.16
Top 500	0.17	1.00	0.82	0.34	−0.49	−0.71	−0.20
Top 1000	−0.17	0.82	1.00	0.24	−0.78	−0.93	−0.93
Top 10000	0.30	0.34	0.24	1.00	−0.54	−0.29	−0.76
Top 50%	0.14	−0.49	−0.78	−0.54	1.00	0.88	0.88
> tx fees	0.16	−0.71	−0.93	−0.29	0.88	1.00	1.00
	0.16	−0.20	−0.93	−0.76	0.88	1.00	1.00

throughput ledgers like Bitcoin [47]. In contrast, windows of 7 or more days were shown to provide statistical confidence in the results. Therefore, we adopted a 7-day window for aggregating blocks and estimating the distribution of block production power.

Population Estimation. We opted for the simple method of using an additional observation window for estimating the population of block producers at a given point in time. We evaluated the effects of different window sizes, to determine how the population estimation window can impact decentralization estimates. Figure 3 shows the results of the Gini coefficient on monthly Bitcoin data, using different window sizes for estimating the population of block producers. For the 'All' line, the population includes all entities that created at least one block between 2018–2024. This estimate includes miners who were inactive during certain periods. In contrast, the '0' line only accounts for the entities that produced blocks in each specific month. This estimate ignores active participants that were unsuccessful in producing blocks during the resource estimation window. The remaining lines estimate the population at each time period by looking X windows backwards and X windows forwards, for $X \in \{1, 12\}$. The significant discrepancy between the different lines shows that the population window is an important criterion when estimating decentralization. In our analysis, we use the entire history for population estimation, leaving a thorough evaluation of the optimal choice to future work.

Measurement Frequency. In a longitudinal study, the measurement frequency, together with the size of the study window, determines the number of data points for analysis. Although measurement frequency is a distinct choice, it should be selected in conjunction with estimation windows, as it determines whether the data contains overlapping or non-overlapping windows. For example, if the estimation window is seven days, weekly sampling produces non-overlapping windows, whereas daily sampling results in overlapping windows.

Overlapping windows are appropriate for descriptive statistics. However, when conducting inferential statistics, overlapping windows inflate the number

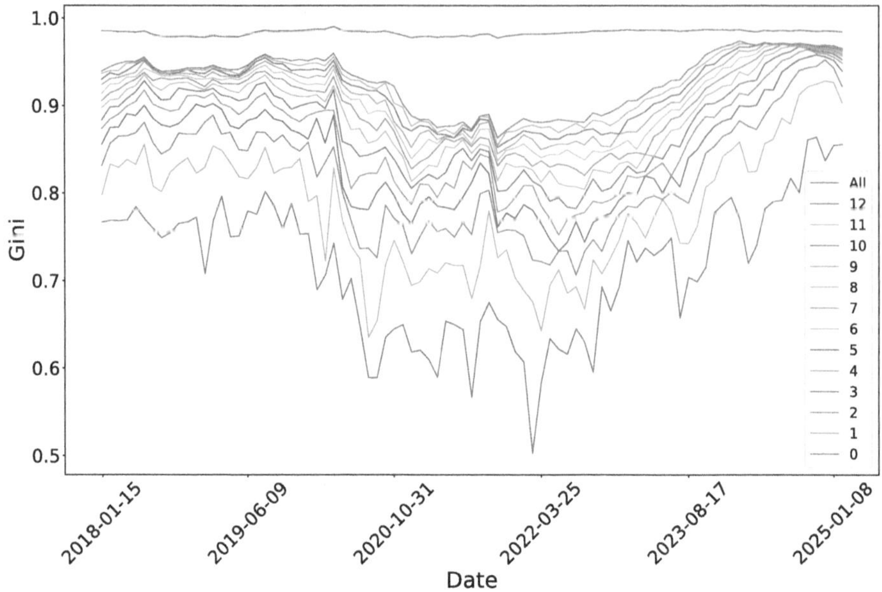

Fig. 3. Bitcoin consensus Gini values with different population estimation windows. 'All' assumes that an entity who mined once is active for the entire study window, 0 means that only miners that produced blocks within the given window are counted, whereas a number between 1 and 12 indicates the number of windows before and after the measurement window that are also used to estimate the population.

of data points without meaningfully increasing the number of observations, since the same underlying data is repeatedly counted. As our analysis involves such statistics (see metrics paragraph below), we opted for non-overlapping windows. Specifically, we sample consensus data weekly and tokenomics data monthly.

Inclusion Thresholds. We also explored the role of thresholds, given they were widely used in prior work, particularly for the tokenomics layer. The motivation behind using thresholds is to provide clearer insights, by removing low-resource entities, such as unusable "dust" wallets. However, it is unclear whether the results of decentralization analyses are robust to different threshold choices.

We tested all types of thresholds found the literature, i.e., accounting only for the top X wealthiest entities (with X ranging from 100 to 10,000), entities that control enough tokens to issue transactions, or all entities. We also included an additional type of threshold that considers only the top X% wealthiest entities—specifically we looked at the top 50%. Table 2 presents the Spearman correlations between the Gini values for Bitcoin, calculated on tokenomics data using the various inclusion thresholds.

Our analysis suggests that thresholds focused on the top X entities show little correlation with one another. This means that the arbitrary decision of which

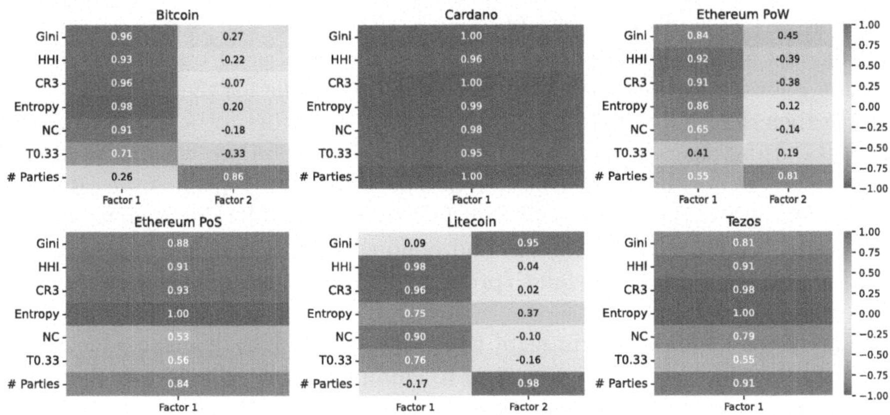

Fig. 4. Factor analysis results for decentralization metrics on the consensus layer.

threshold to choose (Top 100 vs 500 vs 1000) meaningfully changes estimates of decentralization trends, potentially enabling manipulation of the results by selectively adjusting the threshold. In contrast, the remaining thresholds (top 50%, more than the transaction fees, and all entities) show high correlation, suggesting that they provide more robust and reliable results. Note, this does not mean that these three thresholds result in the same values in absolute terms, but rather that they capture the same trends. In the rest of our experiments, we continue by using the entire distributions, without applying any thresholds.

Decentralization Metrics. Our objective in this part of the analysis is to examine the relationships between the various metrics used in the literature and to determine whether they capture a common underlying notion of decentralization. To achieve this, we employ exploratory factor analysis (EFA) [17], a statistical tool that has been widely used across different disciplines, including in studies of government decentralization [59].

In EFA, the observed variables—in this case the metrics—are analyzed to infer latent variables, or factors, that capture the data in a more succinct manner. If all metrics perfectly captured the same underlying notion of decentralization, the analysis would reveal a single factor. Conversely, if the metrics reflect different constructs, the analysis would produce multiple factors. In such cases, we expect metrics representing similar aspects to group together by loading onto the same factor. We also analyze correlations between metrics to confirm the results in a more intuitive way.

As EFA is sensitive to outliers [17], we first identify and treat outliers, defined as values that are greater than 3 standard deviations away from the mean. For treatment, we attempted several popular transformations and observed their effect on the data, in line with prior work [17]. We then used the Kaiser-Meyer-Olkin (KMO) test to determine whether our data was adequate for factor analysis [63]. All three versions of our data (untouched, outliers removed, and outliers transformed) were deemed suitable across all ledgers. The Box-Cox transformation was found to most uniformly reduce the number of outliers while still passing relevant adequacy tests, so we adopted that one for the analysis.

We then determine the appropriate number of factors to be extracted from the data, using eigenvalues according to the Kaiser criterion, which states that eigenvalues greater than 1 are considered to be significant [17]. Then, we calculate the loadings using the number of latent factors suggested by the eigenvalues. We also tested a number of orthogonal and oblique rotations to best capture these factors, but opted for the default (promax) because it made little difference to the results.

The factor loadings inform us of which latent variables describe which metrics, and therefore, which metrics tend to clump together. The higher the absolute value of a loading, the bigger the influence that the factor has on the metric. If two metrics load onto the same factor, but with different signs (positive/negative), it means that they capture the same concept, but in different directions.

Figure 4 illustrates the results of the factor analysis on the consensus layer, with the metrics calculated using 7-day resource estimation windows, all-time population estimation window, 7-day frequency, clustering (tagging) and no thresholds. We observe that for three of the ledgers (Cardano, Ethereum PoS and Tezos) all metrics load onto a single factor, suggesting they capture the same underlying concept of decentralization. However, the other three (Bitcoin, Ethereum PoW and Litecoin) all exhibit two factors, with the number of parties consistently loading strongly onto the second factor, suggesting that it captures a different signal compared to the other metrics. The pairwise Spearman correlations between the metrics also revealed that the number of participants in these blockchains is either uncorrelated or even inversely correlated with other decentralization metrics.

The same analysis was conducted for tokenomics, with the metrics calculated using monthly frequency, clustering (tagging) and no thresholds. However, the results were more nuanced on this layer, with no consistent narrative emerging across the different systems.[12]

5 Discussion and Recommendations

This section discusses our systematization and measurement results, with a focus on offering forward-looking recommendations. These recommendations are derived through reasoning from first principles and, where applicable, by interpreting the findings of our empirical analysis. Table 3 summarizes our suggestions for which options to choose and which to avoid when addressing the various dimensions of the decentralization measurement process. Additionally, the table connects our recommendations to the reviewed literature, offering an overview of the proportion of studies that adopted each choice.

[12] The EFA results for the tokenomics layer, as well as the correlation tables for both consensus and tokenomics can be found in the extended version of this paper [51].

Resource. The choice of resource is straightforward in tokenomics, as there is general agreement that tokens serve as the primary resource for this layer. In contrast, the consensus layer offers two approaches that have been used in the literature. In line with most prior work, we propose using blocks as the resource there, as they better reflect participation in the consensus process. The alternative method, which relies on block rewards, is less robust due to variations in reward structures across different systems, and even within a single system over time.

Clustering. Figure 2 demonstrated that tagging had a significant influence on Bitcoin's HHI estimates since 2016. The lack of difference before then is likely because the information sources did not tag legacy blocks. Based on this observation, we conclude that future studies can reasonably rely on tagging, particularly when analyzing established blockchains with sufficient public attribution data. In addition, implementing heuristics tailored to the architecture of a blockchain system—such as the multi-input heuristic for UTXO-based ledgers—can further enhance the clustering results, as demonstrated in the literature for Bitcoin [26,46], Ethereum [67] and Cardano [11].

Resource Estimation Window. As discussed earlier, prior work has already addressed the question of choosing an appropriate window size for estimating resource distribution in blockchains. In line with [47], we recommend using a window of at least 7 days when estimating block distributions, especially for low throughput ledgers like Bitcoin. Additionally, we caution researchers against using windows smaller than 150 blocks, as it has been demonstrated that Bitcoin failed the relevant hypothesis test in over half of the cases when aggregating over a daily window, which roughly corresponds to this block count [47].

Population Estimation. Figure 3 reveals how influential the size of the observation window can be when estimating the population at a given time period. The population window must strike a balance between capturing the unsuccessful but active participants, while also excluding those inactive during the relevant time period. We recommend choosing a window that is larger than the resource estimation window but smaller than the total observation period. A rule of thumb could be to look at one window backward and one window forward for each resource window. Further research is needed to determine whether more sophisticated methods, such as statistical inference, could provide more accurate population estimates compared to this heuristic.

Measurement Frequency. The data in a longitudinal analysis should be sampled frequently enough to capture temporal changes. For example, sampling the data only once a year might overlook significant trends that occurred throughout the year. We recommend experimenting with various sampling intervals to

Table 3. Summary of our recommendations for various steps of the decentralization measurement workflow, along with the adoption rates for each recommended or discouraged choice based on the relevant articles listed in Table 1. Note that the denominators in the adoption rates vary, as some decisions are only applicable to specific contexts (e.g., the consensus layer) and therefore only pertain to studies addressing those cases.

Workflow step	Recommended		Discouraged	
	Decision	Adoption	Decision	Adoption
Resource	Blocks (consensus) Tokens (tokenomics)	13/15 7/7	Rewards (consensus)	2/15
Clustering	Tagging Heuristics	5/20 5/20	No clustering	14/20
Resource estimation window (REW)	$\geq$ 7 days	12/15	< 150 blocks	5/15
Population estimation window (PEW)	REW < PEW < study window	0/15	PEW < REW	0/15
Inclusion threshold	None (consensus) > tx fees (tokenomics)	12/15 2/7	Top X	7/20
Decentralization metrics	NC, HHI (consensus)	9/15	# Parties	3/20

ensure the chosen frequency does not obscure significant change between measurements. We advise against using overlapping windows—i.e., sampling more frequently than the resource estimation window—when performing inferential statistics, as this can inflate the number of data points without adding observations.

Inclusion Threshold. At the consensus layer, an entity that produces a block is, by definition, active. Consequently, applying thresholds there would inevitably exclude active participants, leading to skewed decentralization estimates. For this reason, we advise against the use of thresholds in the consensus layer.

In contrast, thresholds may be justified in the tokenomics layer, as inactive addresses can still hold tokens. However, Table 2 demonstrated that the different top-X thresholds used in the literature yield decentralization estimates that are not correlated with each other. This indicates that arbitrary threshold choices can significantly impact results, potentially enabling manipulation by selectively adjusting the threshold. Interestingly, other types of thresholds showed stronger correlations with one another and with estimates derived from the entire distribution, suggesting that they provide more robust and reliable results. We consider the transaction fee threshold to be a reasonable choice, as it effectively excludes entities with no economic power in the system, while ensuring that the broader distribution remains representative.

Metrics. The results of the factor analysis on the consensus layer (Fig. 4) suggest that the blockchains we examined are divided into two categories. In the first category, all metrics load onto a single factor, whereas in the second two factors emerge, with the number of parties consistently loading onto the second factor, separate from most other metrics. Upon closer inspection, we observe that the first group comprises only PoS blockchains (Cardano, Ethereum PoS and Tezos), while the second only PoW ones (Bitcoin, Ethereum PoW and Litecoin). This allows us to speculate that this architectural choice has an impact on how effectively a blockchain system can translate participation into decentralization.

In particular, in PoW systems, decentralization and participation emerge as distinct factors, suggesting that increasing participation is not sufficient to achieve greater decentralization. This may be due to economies of scale, where larger mining operations benefit from lower costs and more efficient hardware, thereby consolidating control over block production. At any rate, it appears that merely counting the number of participants is not representative of decentralization, so we advise against using it in decentralization analyses of these systems.

In contrast, for PoS blockchains, all metrics cluster onto a single factor, which we interpret as decentralization itself, as the metrics were selected to capture this concept. The fact that the number of parties is clustered together with the other metrics here indicates that PoS blockchains are more effective at aligning decentralization with participation than their PoW counterparts.

Having identified that many of the metrics used in prior work capture the same underlying signal, the next goal is to decide on the most useful ones. This can only be done by reasoning from first principles, as there is no ground truth with which to validate metrics. We proceed by discussing each metric in turn.

Entropy and Gini are both tail-sensitive metrics that take the entire distribution into consideration. The main strengths of entropy are its simple mathematical definition and long scientific heritage. However, it has weaknesses when it is applied to quantifying blockchain decentralization. Most fundamentally, a blockchain for which one actor holds more than 50% of the resources can have an arbitrarily high entropy value if the number of participants is sufficiently high. Hence, relying on entropy to measure decentralization could create a false sense of security. Another problem lies in interpreting values as there is no clear rationale, unlike some other metrics.

Gini was designed to quantify how fairly resources, be it wealth or income, are distributed across society. This allows for comparisons between centralization of tokens, a form of wealth, and centralization of wealth in society, which can help with interpreting values. Gini also has an intuitive graphical explanation. However, it is highly sensitive to the tail of the distribution, which can pose challenges in blockchain measurements if the clustering of addresses is not entirely successful. Inaccurate clustering may lead to skewed Gini values, potentially misrepresenting the level of decentralization.

In contrast, the Nakamoto coefficient, τ-decentralization index and concentrations ratio are all tail-insensitive metrics that only account for the head of a distribution. The Nakamoto Coefficient and τ are better in that they capture information about how many parties need to coordinate to subvert the system, when the τ threshold is set with specific attacks in mind. While $\tau = 0.5$, aka the Nakamoto Coefficient, can warn about the potential for 51% attacks, it is not designed to warn about similar attacks in systems with security thresholds lower than 50%, such as Algorand [22] or Ethereum PoS [8,9], which require two thirds of consensus participants to be honest. We suggest using the Nakamoto coefficient when measuring consensus decentralization of systems that require an honest majority, and $\tau = 0.33$ for systems that require $\frac{2}{3}$ of honest participants.

Finally, HHI includes a contribution from the tail of the distribution, but discounts it via a quadratic term. Originally designed to quantify market concentration, the HHI is easily adaptable to the block production market of blockchains. Its values are also easier to interpret thanks to established guidelines [34].

6 Conclusion

We developed a framework that distills the decentralization measurement process into three distinct steps: (i) determining which data to collect (layer/resource), (ii) extracting the distribution of resources, and (iii) choosing which decentralization metrics to use. Notably, step (ii) requires a number of impactful choices to be made in the form of pre-processing, which involve (a) clustering, (b) resource estimation, (c) population estimation, (d) measurement frequency, and (e) inclusion thresholds. We reviewed existing literature and classified it based on our framework. Our investigation revealed that prior work lacks a systematic way for choosing which metrics to use and which pre-processing steps to follow—instead, most such choices were made in an arbitrary manner.

To make the landscape of various choices easier to navigate, we conducted an empirical analysis using data from five different blockchains on the consensus and tokenomics layers, and we combined the results of the analysis with first-principles reasoning to derive recommendations for future researchers. Our findings advise against some of the approaches that have been employed in the literature, such as examining only the top X wealthiest entities when measuring decentralization on the tokenomics layer. We also showed that the choice of population estimation window, which has not received any attention in prior work, can significantly impact decentralization estimates when using metrics that take the entire population into account, such as the Gini coefficient.

A large part of our analysis was dedicated to exploring the relationship between the different metrics that have been proposed for measuring decentralization, and using factor analysis to determine whether they capture the same latent constructs. An interesting finding that stemmed from this analysis is that in Proof-of-Work blockchains participation on the consensus layer is not correlated with decentralization, but rather captures a distinct signal. This suggests that, perhaps contrary to popular belief, higher levels of participation are not always associated with greater decentralization. This insight has significant implications for the design and governance of blockchain systems, as developers and stakeholders should consider mechanisms that not only encourage broad participation but also ensure that power among participants is widely distributed.

Future Work. Our work motivates various avenues for further research. While we are confident in our recommendations at the consensus layer, tokenomics presents additional challenges. Clustering there is more difficult because participants do not disclose token ownership, unlike mining pools that typically advertise which blocks they produce. It is also hard to know whether an address is abandoned forever or simply storing tokens long-term. Additionally, identifying the optimal mechanism for population estimation is a challenging, albeit necessary, step. The community should prioritize research that addresses these problems.

A natural future direction would be to apply our methodology to additional layers of blockchain systems, e.g., Governance or Network, and explore whether there exists a stronger relationship between participation and decentralization there. Improving decentralization measurement for other layers of blockchain systems, such as network or governance, will involve solving two core problems. First, researchers need to address inconsistent and missing data when relying on off-chain data sources. Second, fungible resources must be identified for these layers, or methods must be developed to appropriately weigh non-fungible resources according to their influence. We recommend that researchers conduct primary research in this area before attempting premature systematization.

Moreover, the community adopting standardized measures of decentralization could unlock exciting research opportunities. For example, event studies could analyze how decentralization dynamics shift in response to governance decisions, regulatory changes, or market shocks. This line of research could help identify which specific mechanisms or components (e.g., more sophisticated reward sharing schemes or proposer-builder separation methods) are successful in translating participation into decentralization in the context of a blockchain system, which is particularly relevant given the inconsistencies observed in PoW blockchains.

Table 4. Observation period and number of blocks captured for each ledger on the consensus layer.

Ledger	Observation period	#Blocks
Bitcoin	Jan 2018 - Oct 2024	361,762
Cardano	Jan 2018 - Dec 2023	6,858,920
Ethereum PoW	Jan 2018 - Sep 2022	10,709,818
Ethereum PoS	Sep 2022 - Oct 2024	5,331,582
Litecoin	Jan 2018 - Sep 2024	1,423,055
Tezos	Jun 2018 - Dec 2022	2,926,050

Table 5. Observation period for each ledger on the tokenomics layer.

Ledger	Observation period
Bitcoin	Jan 2011 - Aug 2024
Cardano	Jan 2018 - Dec 2024
Ethereum PoW	Jan 2016 - Sep 2022
Ethereum PoS	Sep 2022 - Aug 2023
Litecoin	Jan 2013 - Aug 2024
Tezos	Jan 2019 - Aug 2024

A Appendix

A.1 Data Description and Sources

For the consensus layer, we collect data about the blocks that were produced in each ledger. Specifically, for each block in the canonical chain, we obtain its number, timestamp, address(es) that received rewards for it and any ledger-specific fields that can potentially be used to identify its creator (for example, in Bitcoin this can be an encoded "tag" of a mining pool). For tokenomics, we collect data about each address that holds a non-zero amount of the system's native token and its corresponding "balance". Note that in account-based systems, such as Ethereum, the balance of an address can be retrieved directly from the ledger, while in UTXO-based systems, such as Bitcoin, the balance is derived from all the inputs and outputs of the transactions that an address has been involved in. Both block and balance information, as described above, can be obtained directly from the blockchain. We collect these on-chain data from Google Big Query's public datasets [18].

The data we collected for each ledger spans at least 5 years, with monthly observations. A special case is Ethereum, where we have (almost) 5 years of data for Ethereum PoW, but only one year of data for Ethereum PoS, starting from when the "merge" took place in 2022. Tables 4 and 5 provide details on the time period that was used for the different blockchains for each layer, as well as some additional information, such as the number of blocks captured in the data.

A.2 Attribution of Blocks

In the consensus layer, we needed to attribute each block to the entity that created it. To perform this analysis, we made the following assumptions.

First, we assume that self-reported block creation information is accurate. For example, in the case of Bitcoin, when a block $\mathcal{B}$'s coinbase parameter contains a tag which is known to be used by a mining pool $\mathcal{P}$, we assume that $\mathcal{B}$ was created by $\mathcal{P}$. This assumption is in line with other research works, e.g., [21], and we consider it realistic for a number of reasons. First, a pool is incentivized to claim ownership of its blocks, in order to attract more users. Large pools produce blocks often, thus offering a more stable income to their participants compared to small pools. Given that parties with small hashing power join pools in order to observe steadier and more frequent rewards, it is safe to assume that pools aim at maximizing the number of blocks which they claim to have produced. Second, a creator that wants to hide its identity has no incentive to attribute its block to a third party. In particular, a party that wants to hide its participating power can simply leave the coinbase parameter empty. Nonetheless, if this assumption is violated, i.e., if a party "fakes" the creation of a block by a mining pool, our analysis would present fake positives, by inflating the power of that particular pool.

Our second assumption is that the address which receives the block's rewards is controlled by the party that creates it. This holds in most cases, when the block is created in a straightforward manner by a single user or by a traditional mining pool.[13] However, there exist more complex settings, where the address that collects the rewards is collectively controlled by a set of parties, each operating (partially) on its own. Such example is Ethereum's smart contract-based pools like Lido[14] and Rocketpool.[15] These pools utilize a smart contract, which gives to its members access to funds that enable them to participate in consensus. Each member runs its own node and, when chosen, creates blocks unilaterally. However, the block's rewards are collected by the smart contract's address and distributed to the members based on their funds' contributions. We treat cases of quasi-centralized pools as fully centralized, but future work could explore the nuances behind these designs and enhance our results.

To assign blocks to entities, we first consider the coinbase parameter, where applicable. If a block contains a tag of a known pool, then we assume that the block has been created by that pool. In Cardano, every block is attributed to a known pool, since it includes the pool's ticker, which is registred on chain. When such identification occurs, all addresses that receive fees from the block are also attributed to the entity, i.e., we assume that the same entity controls them.

If a block's coinbase parameter does not contain a known tag, then we look into its coinbase transaction. Specifically, we identify if an address that receives fees from the block is controlled by a known entity, as identified in the previous step, or if an address has previously received fees from a block with a known tag. In addition, addresses of known entities are often publicly available. A special case is Tezos, where blocks do not include a field similar to the coinbase parameter. However, the addresses and public keys of the block creators are public, because they are used for the stake delegation mechanism.[16] Therefore, in line with previous research [55], we combine various fields and information sources to map addresses to real-world identities. Finally, if none of the previous steps

[13] In such pools, the address is controlled by the pool's operator, which is the party that also constructs the block that the members use for mining.

[14] https://lido.fi.

[15] https://rocketpool.net.

[16] A community project with this information is tzkt.io.

is successful in attributing a block to a known entity, then we attribute it to the set of addresses that receive fees from it.

Notably, in the consensus layer, while the resource is the same across all blockchains, the entities associated with that resource can vary. In most blockchains, the roles of proposing, validating and building blocks, as well as receiving fees for the transactions included in these blocks, are consolidated under a single entity, such as a mining or stake pool. However, this is not the case in Ethereum PoS, as the introduction of Proposer-Builder Separation (PBS) has significantly altered the landscape of block production [27]. Under PBS, the task of proposing blocks is separated from the task of building them—validators propose blocks, but specialized block builders assemble the blocks and collect transaction fees. This distinction is critical because block builders, not proposers, have the capacity to selectively include or censor transactions. Even though validators are the ones to eventually approve a block, a malicious block builder could censor a transaction without being noticed by lightweight validators, who do not keep a full copy of the mempool and validate the builder's actions (akin to mining pool leaders and members). We therefore choose to focus on block builders rather than proposers (validators) when evaluating the consensus layer of Ethereum PoS.

References

1. Securities and Exchange Commission v. Ripple Labs Inc. U.S. District Court for the Southern District of New York (2020). Case No. 1:20-cv-10832, filed Dec. 22, 2020, terminated Aug. 7 2024
2. Androulaki, E., Karame, G.O., Roeschlin, M., Scherer, T., Capkun, S.: Evaluating user privacy in bitcoin. In: Sadeghi, A.-R. (ed.) FC 2013. LNCS, vol. 7859, pp. 34–51. Springer, Heidelberg (2013). https://doi.org/10.1007/978-3-642-39884-1_4
3. Aponte-Novoa, F.A., Orozco, A., Villanueva-Polanco, R., Wightman, P.: The 51% attack on blockchains: a mining behavior study. IEEE Access **9**, 140549–140564 (2021)
4. Azouvi, S., Maller, M., Meiklejohn, S.: Egalitarian society or benevolent dictatorship: the state of cryptocurrency governance. In: Financial Cryptography and Data Security: FC 2018 International Workshops, BITCOIN, VOTING, and WTSC, Nieuwpoort, Curaçao, 2 March 2018, Revised Selected Papers 22, pp. 127–143. Springer (2019)
5. Bahrani, M., Garimidi, P., Roughgarden, T.: Centralization in block building and proposer-builder separation. In: Financial Cryptography and Data Security 2024: Twenty-Eighth International Conference (2024)
6. Bank, W.: Gini index. https://data.worldbank.org/indicator/SI.POV.GINI
7. Barbereau, T., Smethurst, R., Papageorgiou, O., Rieger, A., Fridgen, G.: Defi, not so decentralized: the measured distribution of voting rights (2022)
8. Buterin, V., et al.: Combining ghost and casper. arXiv preprint arXiv:2003.03052 (2020)
9. Buterin, V., Reijsbergen, D., Leonardos, S., Piliouras, G.: Incentives in ethereum's hybrid casper protocol. Int. J. Netw. Manage **30**(5), e2098 (2020)

10. Campajola, C., Cristodaro, R., Collibus, F.M.D., Yan, T., Vallarano, N., Tessone, C.J.: The evolution of centralisation on cryptocurrency platforms. arXiv preprint arXiv:2206.05081 (2023)
11. Chegenizadeh, M., Niya, S.R., Tessone, C.J.: Heuristic-based address clustering in cardano blockchain. In: Proceedings of the 1st ChainScience Conference in Boston, MA, USA (2023)
12. Cheng, L., Zhu, F., Liu, H., Miao, C.: On decentralization of bitcoin: an asset perspective. arXiv preprint arXiv:2105.07646 (2021)
13. Chu, S., Wang, S.: The curses of blockchain decentralization (2018)
14. Conceição, P., Ferreira, P.: The young person's guide to the theil index: suggesting intuitive interpretations and exploring analytical applications (2000)
15. Known bitcoin pools (2025). https://github.com/bitcoin-data/mining-pools. Accessed 13 Jan 2025
16. Council of the European Union: Proposal for a regulation of the European parliament and of the council on markets in crypto-assets, and amending directive (EU) 2019/1937 (MICA) (2022). https://data.consilium.europa.eu/doc/document/ST-13198-2022-INIT/en/pdf
17. Fabrigar, L.R., Wegener, D.T.: Exploratory Factor Analysis. Oxford University Press (2011)
18. Fernandes, S., Bernardino, J.: What is bigquery? In: Proceedings of the 19th International Database Engineering & Applications Symposium, pp. 202–203 (2015)
19. Financial Stability Board: Decentralised financial technologies: Report on financial stability, regulatory and governance implications (2019). https://www.fsb.org/wp-content/uploads/P060619.pdf
20. Garay, J., Kiayias, A., Leonardos, N.: The bitcoin backbone protocol: analysis and applications. In: Oswald, E., Fischlin, M. (eds.) EUROCRYPT 2015. LNCS, vol. 9057, pp. 281–310. Springer, Heidelberg (2015). https://doi.org/10.1007/978-3-662-46803-6_10
21. Gencer, A.E., Basu, S., Eyal, I., van Renesse, R., Sirer, E.G.: Decentralization in bitcoin and ethereum networks (2018)
22. Gilad, Y., Hemo, R., Micali, S., Vlachos, G., Zeldovich, N.: Algorand: scaling byzantine agreements for cryptocurrencies. In: Proceedings of the 26th Symposium on Operating Systems Principles, pp. 51–68 (2017)
23. Gini, C.: Measurement of inequality of incomes. Econ. J. **31**(121), 124–125 (1921)
24. Gochhayat, S.P., Shetty, S., Mukkamala, R., Foytik, P., Kamhoua, G.A., Njilla, L.: Measuring decentrality in blockchain based systems. IEEE Access **8**, 178372–178390 (2020)
25. Grandjean, D., Heimbach, L., Wattenhofer, R.: Ethereum proof-of-stake consensus layer: participation and decentralization. arXiv preprint arXiv:2306.10777 (2023)
26. Harrigan, M., Fretter, C.: The unreasonable effectiveness of address clustering. In: 2016 International IEEE Conferences on Ubiquitous Intelligence & Computing, Advanced and Trusted Computing, Scalable Computing and Communications, Cloud and Big Data Computing, Internet of People, and Smart World Congress (UIC/ATC/ScalCom/CBDCom/IoP/SmartWorld), Toulouse, France, 18–21 July 2016, pp. 368–373. IEEE Computer Society (2016). https://doi.org/10.1109/UIC-ATC-SCALCOM-CBDCOM-IOP-SMARTWORLD.2016.0071. https://doi.org/10.1109/UIC-ATC-ScalCom-CBDCom-IoP-SmartWorld.2016.0071
27. Heimbach, L., Kiffer, L., Ferreira Torres, C., Wattenhofer, R.: Ethereum's proposer-builder separation: promises and realities. In: Proceedings of the 2023 ACM on Internet Measurement Conference, pp. 406–420 (2023)

28. Howell, A., Saber, T., Bendechache, M.: Measuring node decentralisation in blockchain peer to peer networks. Blockchain Res. Appl. **4**(1), 100109 (2023)
29. H.R.4763 - 118th Congress (2023-2024): Financial innovation and technology for the 21st century act, h.r.4763 (2024). https://www.congress.gov/bill/118th-congress/house-bill/4763
30. Jensen, J.R., von Wachter, V., Ross, O.: How decentralized is the governance of blockchain-based finance: empirical evidence from four governance token distributions (2021)
31. Jia, Y., Xu, C., Wu, Z., Feng, Z., Chen, Y., Yang, S.: Measuring decentralization in emerging public blockchains. In: 2022 International Wireless Communications and Mobile Computing (IWCMC), pp. 137–141 (2022). https://doi.org/10.1109/IWCMC55113.2022.9825341
32. Jourdan, M., Blandin, S., Wynter, L., Deshpande, P.: Characterizing entities in the bitcoin blockchain. In: Tong, H., Li, Z.J., Zhu, F., Yu, J. (eds.) 2018 IEEE International Conference on Data Mining Workshops, ICDM Workshops, Singapore, Singapore, 17–20 November 2018, pp. 55–62. IEEE (2018). https://doi.org/10.1109/ICDMW.2018.00016
33. U.S. Department of Justice: Herfindahl-hirschman index. https://www.justice.gov/atr/herfindahl-hirschman-index
34. U.S. Department of Justice: Horizontal merger guidelines (08/19/2010) (2010). https://www.justice.gov/atr/horizontal-merger-guidelines-08192010
35. Kapengut, E., Mizrach, B.: An event study of the ethereum transition to proof-of-stake. Commodities **2**(2), 96–110 (2023)
36. Kiayias, A., Russell, A., David, B., Oliynykov, R.: Ouroboros: a provably secure proof-of-stake blockchain protocol. In: Katz, J., Shacham, H. (eds.) CRYPTO 2017. LNCS, vol. 10401, pp. 357–388. Springer, Cham (2017). https://doi.org/10.1007/978-3-319-63688-7_12
37. Kondor, D., Pósfai, M., Csabai, I., Vattay, G.: Do the rich get richer? An empirical analysis of the bitcoin transaction network. PLoS ONE **9**(2), e86197 (2014)
38. Kusmierz, B., Overko, R.: How centralized is decentralized? Comparison of wealth distribution in coins and tokens. In: 2022 IEEE International Conference on Omni-layer Intelligent Systems (COINS), pp. 1–6. IEEE (2022)
39. Kwon, J., Buchman, E.: Cosmos whitepaper. A Netw. Distrib. Ledgers **27**, 1–32 (2019)
40. Li, C., Palanisamy, B.: Comparison of decentralization in DPoS and PoW blockchains (2021)
41. Li, X., Jiang, P., Chen, T., Luo, X., Wen, Q.: A survey on the security of blockchain systems. Futur. Gener. Comput. Syst. **107**, 841–853 (2020)
42. BIT Mining Limited: BIT mining limited announces first closing of btc.com businesses acquisition (2021). https://ir.btcm.group/news/pressDetail/316
43. Lin, Q., Li, C., Zhao, X., Chen, X.: Measuring decentralization in bitcoin and ethereum using multiple metrics and granularities. In: 2021 IEEE 37th International Conference on Data Engineering Workshops (ICDEW), pp. 80–87. IEEE (2021)
44. Liu, J., Zheng, W., Lu, D., Wu, J., Zheng, Z.: Understanding the decentralization of DPoS: perspectives from data-driven analysis on EOSIO (2022)
45. Liu, J., Liu, L., Li, Z., Li, C.: Demonitor: monitoring decentralization in blockchains using bigquery. In: 2023 IEEE International Conference on Blockchain and Cryptocurrency (ICBC), pp. 1–2. IEEE (2023)
46. Meiklejohn, S., et al.: A fistful of bitcoins: characterizing payments among men with no names. Commun. ACM **59**(4), 86–93 (2016). https://doi.org/10.1145/2896384

47. Milad, M., Ovezik, C., Karakostas, D., Woods, D.W.: Statistical confidence in mining power estimates for pow blockchains. In: Companion Proceedings of the ACM on Web Conference 2024, pp. 1752–1760 (2024)
48. Mueller-Bloch, C., Andersen, J., Spasovski, J., Hahn, J.: Understanding decentralization of decision-making power in proof-of-stake blockchains—an agent-based simulation approach. Eur. J. Inf. Syst. (2022). https://doi.org/10.1080/0960085X.2022.2125840
49. Nadler, M., Schär, F.: Decentralized finance, centralized ownership? An iterative mapping process to measure protocol token distribution (2020)
50. Ovezik, C., Karakostas, D., Kiayias, A.: SoK: a stratified approach to blockchain decentralization. In: Financial Cryptography and Data Security 2024: Twenty-Eighth International Conference. Springer (2024)
51. Ovezik, C., Karakostas, D., Milad, M., Kiayias, A., Woods, D.W.: Sok: measuring blockchain decentralization. arXiv preprint arXiv:2501.18279 (2025)
52. Ovezik, C., Kiayias, A.: Decentralization analysis of pooling behavior in cardano proof of stake. In: Proceedings of the Third ACM International Conference on AI in Finance, pp. 18–26 (2022)
53. Pérez-Solà, C., Delgado-Segura, S., Navarro-Arribas, G., Herrera-Joancomartí, J.: Another coin bites the dust: an analysis of dust in utxo-based cryptocurrencies. Roy. Soc. Open Sci. **6**(1), 180817 (2019)
54. Reid, F., Harrigan, M.: An analysis of anonymity in the bitcoin system. In: PASSAT/SocialCom 2011, Privacy, Security, Risk and Trust (PASSAT), 2011 IEEE Third International Conference on and 2011 IEEE Third International Conference on Social Computing (SocialCom), Boston, MA, USA, 9–11 October 2011, pp. 1318–1326. IEEE Computer Society (2011). https://doi.org/10.1109/PASSAT/SOCIALCOM.2011.79
55. Romiti, M., Judmayer, A., Zamyatin, A., Haslhofer, B.: A deep dive into bitcoin mining pools: an empirical analysis of mining shares. arXiv preprint arXiv:1905.05999 (2019)
56. Ron, D., Shamir, A.: Quantitative analysis of the full bitcoin transaction graph. In: Sadeghi, A.-R. (ed.) FC 2013. LNCS, vol. 7859, pp. 6–24. Springer, Heidelberg (2013). https://doi.org/10.1007/978-3-642-39884-1_2
57. Sai, A.R., Buckley, J., Fitzgerald, B., Gear, A.L.: Taxonomy of centralization in public blockchain systems: a systematic literature review (2020)
58. Sai, A.R., Buckley, J., Le Gear, A.: Characterizing wealth inequality in cryptocurrencies. Front. Blockchain **4**, 730122 (2021)
59. Schneider, A.: Decentralization: conceptualization and measurement. Stud. Comp. Int. Dev. **38**, 32–56 (2003)
60. U.S. Securities and Exchange Commission: Framework for "investment contract" analysis of digital assets. US Securities and Exchange Commission **3** (2019)
61. Shannon, C.E.: A mathematical theory of communication. Bell Syst. Tech. J. **27**(3), 379–423 (1948)
62. Shepherd, W.G.: Concentration ratios, pp. 2029–2031. Palgrave Macmillan UK, London (2018). https://doi.org/10.1057/978-1-349-95189-5_520
63. Shrestha, N.: Factor analysis as a tool for survey analysis. Am. J. Appl. Math. Stat. **9**, 4–11 (2021). https://doi.org/10.12691/ajams-9-1-2
64. Srinivasan, B.S., Lee, L.: Quantifying decentralization (2017). https://news.earn.com/quantifying-decentralization-e39db233c28e
65. Sun, X., Stasinakis, C., Sermpinis, G.: Decentralization illusion in decentralized finance: evidence from tokenized voting in MakerDAO polls (2023)

66. Valdivia, L.J., Del-Valle-Soto, C., Rodriguez, J., Alcaraz, M.: Decentralization: the failed promise of cryptocurrencies. IT Prof. **21**(2), 33–40 (2019)
67. Victor, F.: Address clustering heuristics for ethereum. In: Financial Cryptography and Data Security: 24th International Conference, FC 2020, Kota Kinabalu, Malaysia, 10–14 February 2020 Revised Selected Papers 24, pp. 617–633. Springer (2020)
68. Wang, C., Chu, X., Qin, Y.: Measurement and analysis of the bitcoin networks: a view from mining pools. In: 2020 6th International Conference on Big Data Computing and Communications (BIGCOM), pp. 180–188. IEEE (2020)
69. Wu, K., Peng, B., Xie, H., Huang, Z.: An information entropy method to quantify the degrees of decentralization for blockchain systems. In: 2019 IEEE 9th International Conference on Electronics Information and Emergency Communication (ICEIEC), pp. 1–6. IEEE (2019)
70. Yan, T., Li, S., Kraner, B., Zhang, L., Tessone, C.J.: Analyzing reward dynamics and decentralization in ethereum 2.0: an advanced data engineering workflow and comprehensive datasets for proof-of-stake incentives. arXiv preprint arXiv:2402.11170 (2024)
71. Zeng, L., et al.: Characterizing ethereum's mining power decentralization at a deeper level. In: IEEE INFOCOM 2021-IEEE Conference on Computer Communications, pp. 1–10. IEEE (2021)
72. Zhang, L., Ma, X., Liu, Y.: SoK: blockchain decentralization (2023)

Automated Selfish Mining Analysis for DAG-Based PoW Consensus Protocols

Patrik Keller(✉)

University of Innsbruck, Innsbruck, Austria
patrik.keller@student.uibk.ac.at

Abstract. Selfish mining is strategic rule-breaking to maximize rewards in proof-of-work protocols [4]. Markov Decision Processes (MDPs) are the preferred tool for finding optimal strategies in Bitcoin [7,16] and similar linear chain protocols [22]. Protocols increasingly adopt DAG-based chain structures [19], for which MDP analysis is more involved [3]. To date, researchers have tailored specific MDPs for each protocol [3, 7,8,12,16,22]. Protocol design suffers long feedback loops, as each protocol change implies manual work on the MDP. To overcome this, we propose a generic attack model that covers a wide range of protocols, including Ethereum Proof-of-Work, GhostDAG [17], and Parallel Proof-of-Work [11]. Our approach is modular: we specify each protocol as a concise program, and our tooling then derives and solves the selfish mining MDP automatically.

Keywords: Proof-of-Work · Consensus · Incentives · Attack Search

1 Introduction

In the context of proof-of-work cryptocurrencies, "selfish mining" entails the deliberate deviation from the protocol to maximize personal rewards, e.g., by temporarily withholding blocks. The first selfish mining strategy was proposed by Eyal and Sirer in 2014 against Bitcoin [4]. Soon after, other researchers started to employ Markov Decision Processes (MDPs) to identify and evaluate optimal behavior [7,16]. Using these strategies, attackers controlling more than a third of the system's hash rate can reap excessive rewards. Depending on the communication assumptions, the threshold is even lower.

In 2019, Zhang and Preneel [22] comprehensively mapped and analyzed various defense mechanisms. Their findings indicate that all designs for improving incentive compatibility compromise at least one of the other security properties. Many recent protocol attempt to close this gap by adopting a directed acyclic graph (DAG) structure [1,11,12,15,17]. But MDP-modeling requires enumerating all feasible states, and doing this for arbitrary DAGs is not tractable. Hence, the DAG-based protocols have, so far, escaped MDP-based selfish mining analysis.

Fortunately, recent research has provided new options for analysing complex protocols. Probabilistic Termination [3] enables the *exact* solution of selfish mining MDPs with a tenfold efficiency improvement. When this approach meets its

M. Fischlin and V. Moonsamy (Eds.): ACNS 2025, LNCS 15825, pp. 215–243, 2025.
https://doi.org/10.1007/978-3-031-95761-1_8

limits, one can turn to *approximating* reinforcement learning techniques [2,8,12], which can handle arbitrarily large state spaces, including infinite ones [18].

The remaining bottleneck arises from tailoring the MDPs. So far, this involved a lot of manual work, basically starting from scratch for each protocol [3,7,8,12,16,22]. To overcome this, we propose a generic attack model that covers a wide range of DAG protocols. We specify each protocol as a concise program. Our tooling then generates the selfish mining MDP automatically.

We demonstrate our tooling by specifying and analyzing multiple protocols. Bitcoin allows to validate our approach against existing results. Ethereum Proof-of-Work and its Byzantium update serve as examples for (mostly) linear-chain protocols that carefully introduce DAG structure to adjust the reward scheme and chain preference rule. GhostDAG [17] and Parallel Proof-of-Work [11] represent the newer class of DAG-protocols that, so far, has been considered out of reach for MDP-based analysis. Notable results are that the optimal selfish mining policies against Ethereum, Byzantium, and GhostDAG involve creating more than one fork, and that relatively weak miners can benefit from selfish mining in GhostDAG. The most resilient protocol is Parallel Proof-of-Work.

We proceed as follows: Sect. 2 provides relevant background information on MDPs; Sect. 3 enumerates our assumptions and sketches the approach; Sect. 4 explains how we specify protocols; Sect. 5 documents how we search optimal selfish mining policies in automatically derived MDPs; Sect. 6 introduces two optimizations reducing the size of the state space; Sect. 7 documents all experiments and presents the results; Sect. 8 discusses our work and concludes.

2 Markov Decision Processes (MDP)

Finding incentive attacks against proof-of-work consensus protocols involves sequential decision-making, where an attacker must make a series of choices over time. The outcomes of these decisions are non-deterministic due to the inherently stochastic nature of mining. We use Markov Decision Processes (MDP) to model the problem and find the most profitable behavior.

An MDP is a probabilistic state machine. The *agent*, observes the current state of the system and chooses an *action*. The MDP defines probabilistic state transitions, specifying the probability distribution for the next state based on the current state and the chosen action. In our case, the agent models the attackers. The defenders are not agents, they react passively to the actions of the attacker.

A sequence of state transitions, starting from the (probabilistic) initial state until the process ends, is called an *episode*. Each state transition may have an effect, such as assigning a reward. The agent's goal is to maximize a function of the effects (objective function), in our case, expected mining rewards per time.

The strategy an agent uses to decide which action to take in each state is called a *policy*. Solving an MDP is about finding a policy that maximizes the objective function. For us, the optimal policy is the worst-case attack.

A good, textbook-sized introduction to the topic is provided by Sutton and Barto [18]. The book offers a formal mathematical description of MDPs and covers solving algorithms from first principles. These methods can be broadly categorized as follows:

Linear programming: The Bellman equations provide an optimality condition for the policy. This induces a linear programming problem which can be solved exactly.

Dynamic programming: Algorithms such as value iteration and policy iteration use the Bellman equations to define an iterative optimization step. Repeatedly applying this step converges to the optimal policy. When problem sizes become too large for linear programming, these methods offer practical solutions without losing much accuracy.

Approximate methods: Modern reinforcement learning (RL) techniques, such as Q-learning or policy gradient methods, train a simplified surrogate model by observing the probabilistic state machine. The resulting policies may not be optimal in the original MDP, but these methods are highly versatile: they are applicable when exact solutions are infeasible and effective even when the underlying MDP is unknown or changes over time.

Dynamic programming has been successfully applied to Bitcoin [3,7,16] and Ethereum Proof-of-Work [3]. Approximating methods have been applied to more complex protocols [8] or objective functions [2].

All these have in common that the researchers manually craft one MDP per problem and protocol. Our goal is to derive MDPs automatically from the protocol specification. We will use dynamic programming to provide optimal baseline results for small problem instances. Applying RL to solve bigger problem instances approximately is an option for future work.

3 Protocol-Generic Attack Space

We propose a protocol-generic state and action space (attack space) that is tractable for MDP-based analysis while still covering a useful range of attacks.

Assumptions. We achieve tractability by exploiting the following assumptions.

A1. Participants (miners) exchange blocks via reliable broadcast, and this is the only form of communication.

A2. Blocks reference other blocks by their content, inducing a directed acyclic graph (BlockDAG) with a single root block (genesis).

A3. Appending a new block to the DAG requires a proof-of-work. There is only one type of proof-of-work and the solving time is exponentially distributed.

A4. The broadcast primitive delivers the blocks in topological order, i.e., a block is delivered only after all its parents have been delivered.

A5. Honest behavior follows deterministically from the structure of the BlockDAG and the order in which the individual blocks were delivered.

A6. We focus on consensus protocols: in ideal conditions, excluding attacks and communication delays, all miners agree on an ordering of (a subset of) the blocks which we call *linear history*.
A7. We model all dishonest participants as a single agent, the *attacker*.
A8. The attacker may withhold and ignore blocks but otherwise behaves honestly.
A9. We analyse selfish mining in the equilibrium state where the difficulty adjustment algorithm (DAA) has fully adjusted to the available hash rate and the attacker's policy.

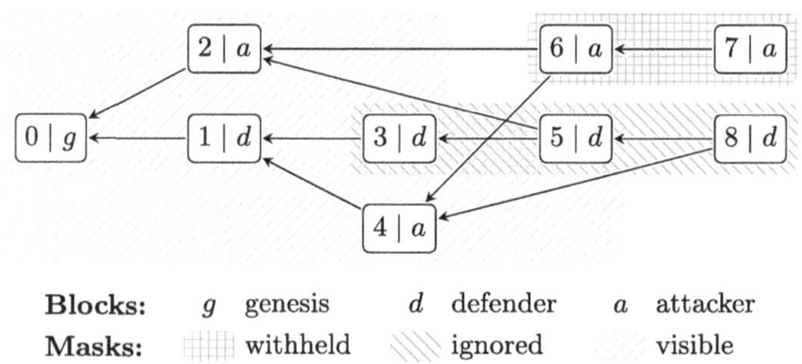

Fig. 1. Example state. Vertices are blocks and arrows indicate parents. The available actions are `Release(6)`, `Consider(3)`, and `Continue`. Block 8 was just mined; it will become visible during the next `Continue` action.

State Space. The assumptions A1–A3 and A7–A9 allow us to track the relevant state in a few variables:

1. An adjacency list, describing the structure of the BlockDAG.
2. A vector describing which blocks where mined by whom.
3. An ignorance mask, describing which blocks are ignored by the attacker.
4. A withholding mask, describing which blocks are withheld by the attacker.
5. A visibility mask, describing which blocks have been delivered to the defender.
6. Protocol-specific local states of the defender and the attacker.

We do not consider the full cross product of these variables, as most combinations are invalid. Due to topological delivery (A4), a block can become visible only after all parents are visible. Similarly, a block must remain ignored while any parent is ignored. Naturally, the attacker can only withhold their own blocks. As the blocks are delivered to the defender in topological order anyways, we apply the topological constraints to the withholding mask as well. Additionally, the protocol-specific local states follow deterministically from the stepwise modification of the other variables (A5).

Figure 1 shows an example state. We visualize the BlockDAG and the three masks for ignoring, withholding, and visibility. We omit the miners' local states.

Figure 7 in Appendix B shows another example with our attack space instantiated for the Bitcoin protocol.

Action Space. The original selfish mining MDP for Bitcoin uses only four actions (see Appendix B). We here use an (a-priori) unbounded number of actions and group them as follows.

Consider(b) to stop ignoring block b.
Release(b) to stop withholding block b.
Continue to wait until the next block is mined.

Induced by the topological restrictions of the state space, only of subset of actions is available at a time.

Bounding the State and Action Spaces. Exact MDP solving techniques work only if the number of states is finite. This is clearly not the case, as the BlockDAG grows continuously. We address this by truncating parts of the BlockDAG that are irrelevant for future protocol execution: stale blocks and the prefix of the linear history that all miners already agree upon (common history). Moreover, we define a limit on the number of blocks in the BlockDAG. In states that meet this limit, we force the attacker to behave honestly taking away the options to withhold and ignore blocks. By the consensus assumption A6, the miners will agree on a linear history. The common history will be truncated and the policy loops back to a smaller state. This bounds the number of actions as well.

Discussion of the Assumptions. Most of the Assumptions A3–A9 are uncontroversial and backed by related work. We here give special attention to the last three and defer the rest of our arguments to Appendix A.

Assumption A7 restricts our model to a single attacking agent. This is conservative, as it allows dishonest participants to collude and coordinate their attack. This assumption is common practice since defenders typically cannot rule out collusion among the attackers [6]. To address scenarios where attackers do not collude, our model can be expanded for multiple agents. We think the main challenge here lies in defining a suitable scenario. In the most obvious case where all participants act rationally, security collapses entirely [5].

In Assumption A8, we force the attacker to base their attack on ignoring and withholding blocks alone. We not think this is overly restrictive:

First, as we lay out in Appendix B, our attack space fully covers selfish mining against Bitcoin. We confirm this numerically in Sect. 7.2.

Second, we deem it necessary from a practical point of view. It allows us to derive the structure of the BlockDAG from honest behavior. The alternative approach, starting from arbitrary blocks, checking them against the protocol's block validity rule, and then enumerating all valid choices, is not tractable.

Third, using local information alone, withholding is indistinguishable from benign network delays. In the absence of network delays and withholding, local knowledge is global knowledge and consensus is easily solved. We think, dealing with withholding is the key aspect of proof-of-work consensus.

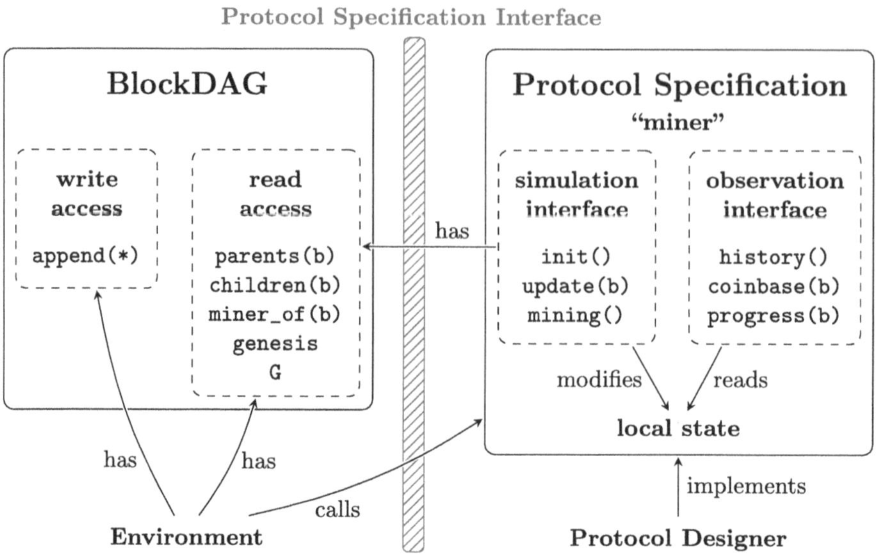

Fig. 2. The protocol designer specifies the protocol according to the protocol specification interface (Sect. 4.1). Our tooling (the environment) derives an MDP and searches the optimal policy for selfish mining (Sect. 5).

Assumption A9 encapsulates the details of difficulty adjustment. The DAA observes timestamps in the linear history and, in response, adjusts the difficulty of the proof-of-work puzzle. The goal is to maintain a (roughly) constant growth rate for the linear history, even though the available hash rate changes over time. This creates a feedback loop from the result of consensus (linear history, time) to the communication primitive (rate-limited by proof-of-work).

Expectedly, the attacker's actions affect the difficulty in the long term. In fact, selfish mining in Bitcoin becomes profitable (expected reward per time) only after the DAA has adjusted to the policy.

We are aware that the DAA can be gamed, e.g., by faking time stamps [20] or tactically leaving and re-joining the system [14,21]. Following related work [3, 4,16], we keep our model tractable by assuming the DAA is in a stable state.

4 Specification of Protocols

Our analysis framework is generic with respect to the protocol. We here explain how the protocols are specified. The other sections assume the protocol specification as an input.

The *protocol designer* specifies the protocol by implementing the mining software in a constrained programming *environment* which provides essential functionality like proof-of-work, reliable broadcast, and the BlockDAG. The *protocol implementation interface* is depicted in Fig. 2.

4.1 Protocol Specification Interface

The protocol designer specifies the miner's behavior as Python functions, which the environment calls during execution. We chose Python over pseudocode as this avoids ambiguity, enables automated testing and formatting, and closes the gap between the paper and the analytical code: the listings in this paper are the actual protocol implementations we feed into the automated analysis.

4.1.1 BlockDAG

The specification can access the BlockDAG as follows.

`parents(b)`, `children(b)` return the parents and children of block `b`.
`miner_of(b)` returns the miner of block `b` and `me` identifies the miner themselves.
`genesis` is the unique root block and `G` is the set of all blocks.
`height(b)` returns the distance of block `b` to `genesis`.

Later, we use additional DAG-related terminology:

- The *past* and *future* refer to the transitive closures of the parent and children relationships. The past of block B includes the parents of B as well as the parents of any other block in the past of B. The future is defined respectively for the children relationship.
- We say block A confirms block B to imply that B is in the past of A.

Recall from Sect. 3, that we restrict the visibility of blocks for the defender and let the attacker ignore blocks. This happens in a topological manner: `parents(b)` always returns all parents, `children(b)` and `G` might be subsets.

Also note that this interface does not allow direct modifications of the BlockDAG—only the environment can append new blocks.

4.1.2 Simulation Interface

The protocol designer implements three functions: `init`, `update`, and `mining`, which together model the miner's behavior. These functions can persist state across calls by setting attributes on the `state` object. Attribute names can be chosen freely, but we assume the values are hashable.

`init()` initializes the miner's local `state`. The environment calls this at the beginning of the protocol execution. The function has no return value.

`update(b)` updates the miner's local `state` with respect to a new block `b`. The environment calls this function to deliver blocks right after they become visible or stop being ignored. The function has no return value.

`mining()` returns the parents of the next block to be mined. This specifies how the miner *intends to* extend the BlockDAG. The actual extension is left to the environment and happens only if the miner was successful at proof-of-work.

Reflecting our assumptions in Sect. 3, the protocol designer assumes that new blocks are automatically and reliably dissipated to all miners (A1. Delivery happens in a topological order (A4).

Listing 1. Specification of the Bitcoin Protocol

```
1  def init():
2      state.head = genesis
3
4  def mining():
5      return {state.head}
6
7  def update(block):
8      if height(block) > height(state.head):
9          state.head = block
10
11 def history():
12     def history_of(block):
13         if block == genesis:
14             return [genesis]
15         else:
16             return history_of(parents(block).pop()) + [block]
17
18     return history_of(state.head)
19
20 def progress(block):
21     return 1
22
23 def coinbase(block):
24     return [(miner_of(block), 1)]
```

4.1.3 Example (Bitcoin)

In Bitcoin, the miner extends the longest chain of blocks, one block at a time. The `init()` function initializes `state.head = genesis`. The `update(b)` function checks whether the new block `b` has a longer history than `state.head`, and if so, updates `state.head = b`. The `mining()` function returns `state.head` as the single parent for the new block. We specify this in Listing 1, Lines 1–9.

4.1.4 Observation Interface

The protocol designer implements three functions: `history`, `coinbase`, and `progress`, which inform the analyst about the miner's state. These functions can read but not modify the `state` object.

`history()` returns a list of blocks, the miner's opinion on the linear history.

`coinbase(b)` defines the rewards allocated by block b. It returns a list of tuples `(r, v)`, where `r` denotes the recipient and `v` the size of the reward.

`progress(b)` defines the feedback for difficulty adjustment. It returns a non-negative number defining the progress of block b. We assume the linear history grows at a constant rate, denoted in (expected) progress per time (A9).

4.1.5 Example (Bitcoin, Cont'd)

In Bitcoin, the linear history is the longest chain of blocks. For each block `b` in the linear history, `coinbase(b)` assigns a unit reward to the miner of `b`. Similarly, there is one unit of progress per block. We specify this in Listing 1, Lines 11–24. Note, `set.pop()` removes and returns an arbitrary element of `set`. This is deterministic because the set is singleton.

4.2 Overview of the Specified Protocols

Besides Bitcoin, we have specify Ethereum Proof-of-Work, its Byzantium update, GhostDAG [17], and Parallel Proof-of-Work [11]. We here provide short descriptions for each, shortly highlighting the core design ideas, and defer the full listings to Appendix C.

4.2.1 Ethereum

can be seen as an extension to Bitcoin. Like in Bitcoin, miners append their blocks to the longest chain, the history is the longest chain, and each block on the longest chain contributes one unit of progress for difficulty adjustment. New is that miners reference blocks off the longest chain as uncles and that these uncles get a full block reward. This compensates the miner's of blocks that would have missed their reward in Bitcoin.

Ethereum sets a time horizon h, expressed in numbers of blocks added to the longest chain, before which uncles have to be merged into the main chain. Otherwise, they become orphans like in Bitcoin. The Ethereum cryptocurrency was deployed with $h = 7$, we set $h = 3$ throughout the paper.

We provide the full specification in Listing 2 in Appendix C.

4.2.2 Byzantium

was deployed as an upgrade to the Ethereum cryptocurrency. The overall chain structure stays intact, with the sole exception that a block can reference at most two uncles. Besides that, Byzantium modifies the consensus rule, progress, and rewards. Miners now extend the *heaviest* chain, where uncles add the same weight as regular blocks. Similarly, uncles add the same progress as regular blocks. Uncle rewards are now discounted based on the distance to the block merging them into the chain, while the merging block gets a small bonus reward for each uncle. Like Ethereum, Byzantium was deployed with horizon $h = 7$. We set horizon $h = 3$ throughout the paper. The full specification is available in Listing 3 in Appendix C.

4.2.3 GhostDAG

breaks with the notion of a longest or heaviest chain—miners just confirm all unconfirmed blocks. The total order is established after the fact, for all blocks in the DAG. GhostDAG comes with an heuristic for detecting longer phases of uncooperative behavior (private mining). Blocks contributed by the (honest) majority are colored blue, the others red. In the linear history, blue blocks take precedence over red blocks. Blue blocks allocate one unit of reward to their miner, blue blocks none. Similarly, blue blocks contribute one unit of progress to the chain, red blocks none. Note that the publication [17] does not specify rewards and progress—we fill these gaps.

The heuristic for coloring blocks can be tuned through a natural number parameter k. Higher k allows for more parallelism in the DAG without punishing the minority miners. The extreme setting $k = 0$ roughly resembles Bitcoin. We set $k = 3$ throughout the paper. The full specification is available in Listings 4 and 5 in Appendix C.

4.2.4 Parallel Proof-of-Work

uses two categories of blocks: votes and summaries. Appending the next summary requires referencing k votes confirming the parent summary. The summaries form a linear chain and this chain constitutes the linear history. As long as there are not enough votes for the next summary, miners append votes confirming the longest chain. In case of ties, miners vote for the chain with the most votes already. All blocks, both votes and summaries, assign a unit reward to their miner and contribute a unit progress to the difficulty adjustment.

Like in GhostDAG, higher k allows for more parallelism. The minimal setting $k = 1$ roughly resembles Bitcoin. We set $k = 3$ throughout the paper.

In the original proposal [11] summaries are not mined. Instead there is a form of leader election: only the miner of the smallest vote (by hash) may append the next summary. Later, the author has proposed a simplification [9] that works without public key cryptography. Here, the summaries are mined like votes and this proof-of-work is the only form of authorization. This is what we specify and analyse in this paper. The full specification is available in Listing 6 in Appendix C.

5 Automated Attack Search

We now integrate the protocol-generic attack space from Sect. 3 with the protocol specification in Sect. 4. We will derive and solve MDPs that allow us to study the protocol's susceptibility to selfish mining, in a fully automated way.

Recall from Sect. 2 that an MDP is a probabilistic state machine, where the inputs are called actions and the outputs are effects. On each step of execution, the attacker observes the state and chooses the next action. The attacker's objective is a function of the effects, in our case, maximizing rewards per time.

Assuming the protocol specification is given as input, the automated analysis pipeline is as follows. We first define the transition function, which takes the current state and the chosen action as input and returns a discrete probability distribution for the next state (Sect. 5.1). After bounding the state space (Sect. 5.2) and defining the transitions' effects (Sect. 5.3), we derive an explicit tabular MDP (Sect. 5.4). Lastly, we define the objective function (Sect. 5.5) and find the optimal policy (Sect. 5.6).

5.1 State Transition Function

Recall from Sect. 3, that we model two miners, attacker and defender. The attacker ignores and withholds blocks using three types of actions `Consider(b)`, `Release(b)`, and `Continue`. We describe the associated state transitions as a function that modifies the current state in response to the chosen action.

If the attacker chooses to `Consider(b)`, we remove block `b` from the set of ignored blocks and deliver it by calling the attacker's `update` function with argument `b`. This transition is deterministic. The action is only possible, if `b` is currently ignored and none of the parents of `b` are ignored.

`Release(b)` removes block `b` from the set of withheld blocks. This is only possible, if `b` is currently withheld and none of the parents of `b` are withheld. The transition is deterministic. Note, the defender does not learn about `b` yet because communication is delayed.

`Continue` advances time until the next block is mined. This action is always available. It induces one out of four probabilistic transitions, depending on whether the attacker communicates quickly (probability γ) and who mines the next block (probability α for the attacker).

During the `Continue` action, the defender learns about all blocks that are neither withheld nor yet visible. Depending on the attacker's luck regarding message reordering, we modify the order of delivery. With probability γ, we deliver the attacker's blocks before the defender's blocks. Otherwise, with probability $1-\gamma$, we deliver the defender's blocks first. We deliver the blocks by calling the defender's `update` function. This always happens in topological order (A4).

After communication, we append a new block. With probability α, we call the attacker's `mining` function and mark the new block withheld and ignored. Otherwise, with probability $1-\alpha$, we call the defender's `mining` function and mark the new block ignored. Note, even if the defender mines the new block, it only becomes visible during the next round of communication. This enables us to model all honest system participants as a single miner.

As we lay out in Appendix B, our communication assumptions align with the traditional selfish mining model against Bitcoin [16]. Similarly, the traditional actions, *Wait*, *Adopt*, *Match*, and *Override*, can be reproduced with a combination of our actions, `Consider(b)`, `Release(b)`, and `Continue`.

5.2 State Space Cutoff

The state transition function induces an infinite number of states: the BlockDAG grows monotonically, one block per `Continue` action. Blocks are not removed and, throughout an episode, no state is visited twice.

Exact MDP solving techniques assume a finite number of states. We thus impose a limit on the size of the BlockDAG (number of blocks). In states that meet this limit, we force *honest behavior*. We make sure that all remaining policies loop within the restricted state space, by *removing stale blocks* and *truncating the common history*. The details are as follows.

Honest Behavior. We define the honest policy as follows:

1. If any block b is withheld, then `Release(b)`.
2. If any block b is ignored, then `Consider(b)`.
3. Else, `Continue`.

In states where the BlockDAG meets the size limit, we enforce this policy by taking away all other actions. The attacker becomes honest and, by Assumption A6, the miners will agree on the linear history.

Truncating the Common History. After applying the state transition function (Sect. 5.1), we identify irrelevant parts of the BlockDAG and remove them. Our heuristic is as follows:

1. Obtain the linear histories of both miners, attacker and defender.
2. Find the longest common prefix of the linear histories (common history).
3. Find the last block `b` in the common history such that none of the blocks in `past(b)` have any children outside of $\{$`b`$\} \cup$ `past(b)`.
4. Remove all blocks in `past(b)` from the BlockDAG.

Point 3 preserves the semantics of the BlockDAG: block `b` becomes the new genesis (A2) and none of the remaining blocks lose any of their parents.

Some protocols leave behind unconfirmed (stale) blocks, e.g., orphans in Bitcoin. Stale blocks violate the condition in Point 3 and effectively prevent common history truncation. We hence remove them in advance.

Removing Stale Blocks. We identify and remove state blocks as follows:

1. Mark all blocks that are invisible to either miner, `Honest` or `Attacker`.
2. Mark all blocks that either miner would reference next (`mining` function).
3. Mark all blocks that are in the past of any block marked before.
4. Remove all *unmarked* blocks from the BlockDAG.

Point 1 is a safeguard against removing blocks not relevant now but in the future.

5.3 Effects: Reward and Progress

Each state transition has two effects: reward and progress. We measure these on the common history, just before truncating it. We iterate the blocks on the common history, apply the `coinbase` and `progress` functions to each, and accumulate the results. The transition's reward is the accumulated reward assigned to the attacker. The transition's progress is the accumulated progress.

5.4 State Exploration

After state space truncation, the state transition function spans a finite attack space. We now explore all reachable states, noting the available actions, and tabulating the probabilistic state transitions together with their effects. This operation yields an *explicit* (or tabular) MDP suitable for policy search.

Importantly, we evaluate the (expensive) state transition function once for each input. Our attack search uses the cached results. Also note, that we can update the model parameters, α and γ, in the explicit MDP without re-evaluating the state transition function, because only five distinct probabilities are involved.

5.5 Objective Function: Reward per Progress

Selfish mining is about maximizing the expected reward per time, after the DAA has adjusted to the attack. As discussed in Sect. 3, the DAA creates a complex feedback loop between the miners' clocks, the overall hash rate, and the attacker's behavior. Assumption A9 allows us break this loop: the DAA is in a stable state already and the expected progress per time fixed. We hence can treat *reward per progress* as a proxy for reward per time.

Note that Bitcoin, GhostDAG, and Parallel, assign exactly one unit of reward per unit of progress. For these protocols, reward per progress equals relative reward, the objective function used in the traditional models [3,16].

We use reward per progress to capture the differences to Ethereum and Byzantium. In Ethereum, uncles are assigned full rewards but they do not count for progress. Byzantium discounts uncle rewards, partially reallocating some of the discount to the merging block, while all blocks induce the same amount of progress. For both protocols, relative reward does not capture all details.

5.6 Probabilistic Termination Optimization

Exact MDP solving algorithms expect that the objective is a linear function of the transition effects [3,16]. Our objective function, reward per progress, is not linear. However, as the same is true for relative reward, we can simply turn to the established solving techniques for the Bitcoin MDP [3,16].

We use probabilistic termination optimization (PTO) [3]. In short, the trick is to transform the (source) MDP, where all policies loop, into an MDP where all episodes terminate. In the terminating MDP, the expected progress per episode (horizon) is sufficiently independent from the policy. The authors prove that, as the horizon grows to infinity, any reward-maximizing policy in the terminating MDP also maximizes the reward per progress in the source MDP.

We derive terminating MDPs with horizon 100. Then we apply a standard dynamic programming algorithm, value iteration, to obtain an 10^{-4}-optimal policy. We then apply this policy to the *source* MDP and find its steady state using linear equations. After calculating the expected reward *and* progress at the steady state, we obtain the expected reward *per* progress by dividing those numbers. This is what we report in Sect. 7.

6 State Space Optimizations

We propose two optimizations to reduce the size of the state space: canonizing the BlockDAG and forcing the attacker to consider their own blocks.

Canonization. We use adjacency lists to track the evolution of the BlockDAG over time. The blocks are enumerated in the order in which they were mined (compare Fig. 1). However, for proof-of-work consensus protocols, the exact mining order does not matter. In fact, the true mining order is unknown to the participants; they rely on consensus to establish an order in the first place.

So, our default BlockDAG implementation is bound to create redundant states. E.g., the blocks in Fig. 1 can be relabelled in 69 ways without breaking the topological constraints (parents have lower ids than their children) and there are 35 options for the blocks in Fig. 7 in Appendix B.

We optionally merge these states during state exploration (Sect. 5.4) by relabelling the blocks canonically: We first derive a vertex coloring from the relevant block properties (who mined it and whether it is visible/ignored/withheld). We then find a canonical and color-preserving vertex labeling using appropriate third-party software, Nauty [13]. The protocol designer may provide assistive input for canonization by implementing a function that colors blocks depending on the miner's local state.

Note that the GhostDAG protocol assumes a deterministic topological ordering of blocks. We specify this using Python's builtin `hash` function (Lines 13 and 18 of Listing 4 in Appendix C). Canonization does not preserve these hashes (blocks are integers) and thus is an invalid operation for GhostDAG.

Force Consider. The traditional selfish mining model against Bitcoin [16] allows at most two distinct chains (one fork). In our attack model, the attacker can create many forks, by temporally ignoring their own blocks.

We optionally adopt the traditional behavior and force the attacker to consider their own blocks. This happens during the same transition in which the new block has been mined (as opposed to enforcing a consider action after the transition).

7 Results

We now apply the automatic analysis pipeline (Sect. 5) to the specified protocols (Sect. 4.2). We first focus on the size of the state space (Sect. 7.1). Then we validate our modeling choices (Sect. 3 and 5) against established models for Bitcoin (Sect. 7.2). This is followed by a comparison of the protocols to determine which is the least susceptible to selfish mining (Sect. 7.3). Lastly, we evaluate whether and how our state space optimizations (Sect. 6) affect the results on selfish mining (Section 7.4).

Reference Models. Throughout this section, we compare our generic model to the traditional models specific to Bitcoin [3, 16]. We obtain the reported numbers from implementing the state transition functions and effects as described in the respective papers (comp. Sect. 5.1 and 5.3). The remaining parts of the analysis are the same across models: we restrict the state space based on the number of blocks (Sect. 5.2), build a tabular MDP (Sect. 5.4), and optimize the policy for selfish mining (Sects. 5.5 and 5.6).

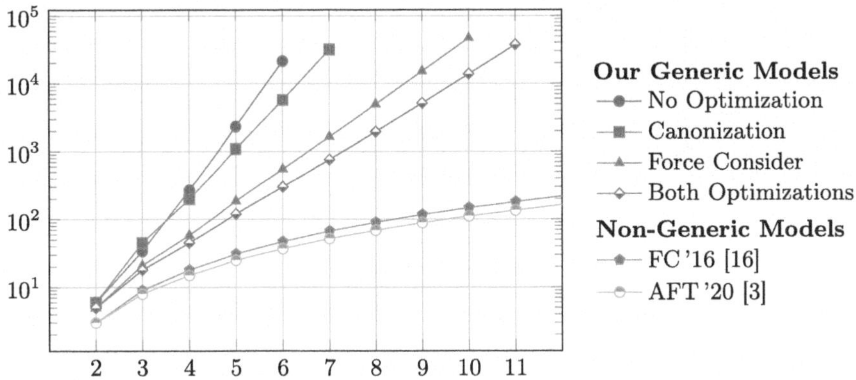

Fig. 3. Number of states of the Bitcoin MDP (y-axis) as a function of the BlockDAG's size limit (x-axis, number of blocks). We compare our model with optimizations turned on and off and add the traditional non-generic models [3,16] as a reference.

7.1 Size of the State Space

Recall from Sect. 5.2, that we limit the number of blocks in the BlockDAG to bound the number of states in the MDP. We expect the state size to grow as we increase the BlockDAG size limit. We now evaluate how fast.

We do this, by applying the analysis pipeline to the specified protocols, skipping the attack search itself. Instead we observe the number of states in the resulting MDP. We start with a BlockDAG size limit of 2 and increase it one-by-one, until the state size exceeds 100 000 states. This upper limit ensures that we can reproduce all results, including the following sections, within five hours on our consumer grade laptop ($\approx \$1\,000$).

Figure 3 visualizes the growth of the state space for Bitcoin, with state space optimizations turned on and off (Sect. 6). The optimizations are effective: when applying them both, we exceed the state size limit after 11 instead of 6 blocks. As a reference, we compare our generic model to the traditional models specific to Bitcoin [3,16]. Expectedly, the specific models have much smaller state sizes. Note that the plot is truncated on the right: the traditional models exceed the state size limit after 239 and 283 blocks respectively.

Table 1 expands this analysis for the other protocols, excluding the invalid optimization, canonization on GhostDAG. We report the maximum number of blocks explored ($s_{\max}$) before exceeding the state size limit of 100 000 states, and the number of states (n_6) when limiting the BlockDAG size to 6 blocks. For reference, we could explore the traditional model [16] up to $s_{\max} = 239$ before reaching 100 000 states, and it has $n_6 = 47$ states when limiting the BlockDAG to 6 blocks. For the second reference model [3], $s_{\max} = 283$ and $n_6 = 37$.

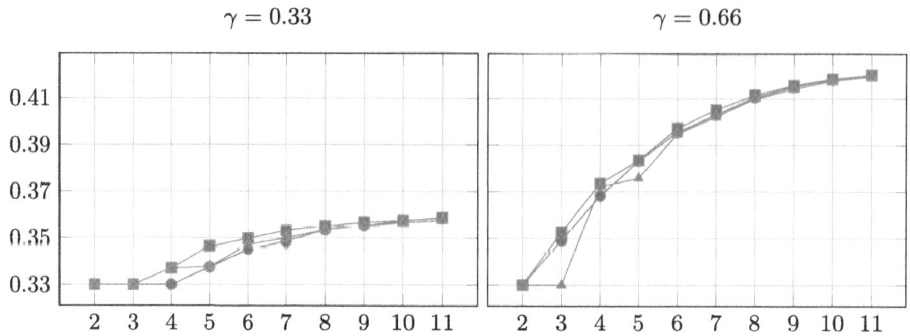

Fig. 4. Reward per progress of the optimal selfish mining policy against Bitcoin (y-axis) as a function of the BlockDAG size limit (x-axis, number of blocks). We compare our model (—●—) to the non-generic models presented at FC '16 [16] (—■—) and AFT '20 [3] (—▲—). We set the attacker's relative hash rate $\alpha = 0.33$ and communication advantage $\gamma \in \{0.33, 0.66\}$ (left/right). On our model, we enable BlockDAG canonization and force the attacker to consider their own blocks. Line $y = 0.33$ represents honest behavior.

7.2 Validation Against Traditional Models for Bitcoin

We now validate our protocol-generic model against existing models specific to Bitcoin [3,16]. We take 30 MDPs from Fig. 3: our model with both optimizations turned on, the two reference models, and BlockDAG size limits ranging from 2 to 11 blocks. We then apply the remaining analysis, policy optimization and evaluation (Sect. 5.6), with model parameters $\alpha = 0.33$ and $\gamma \in \{0.33, 0.66\}$. Figure 4 reports the results, denoted in (expected) reward per progress.

We make three observations: First, reward per progress grows monotonically for increasing BlockDAG size limit, independent of the model. This indicates that the BlockDAG size limit restricts the attacker. In a real setting, there is no

Table 1. State size scaling for all protocols and state space optimizations.

	No Opt.		Canonization		Force Consider		Both Opt.	
Protocol	s_{max}	n_6	s_{max}	n_6	s_{max}	n_6	s_{max}	n_6
Bitcoin	6	21327	7	5724	10	549	11	300
Ethereum	6	32961	7	10293	9	1179	10	596
Byzantium	6	33016	7	9879	9	1109	10	572
GhostDAG	6	46966			8	1527		
Parallel	7	9122	8	1654	8	2050	12	462

We grow the BlockDAG size limit (number of blocks), until the resulting model exceeds 100 000 states. We here report the maximum BlockDAG size limit (s_{max}) before reaching this limit, as well as the number of states (n_6) at a fixed size limit of 6 blocks. We omit the results for the invalid optimization, canonization on GhostDAG.

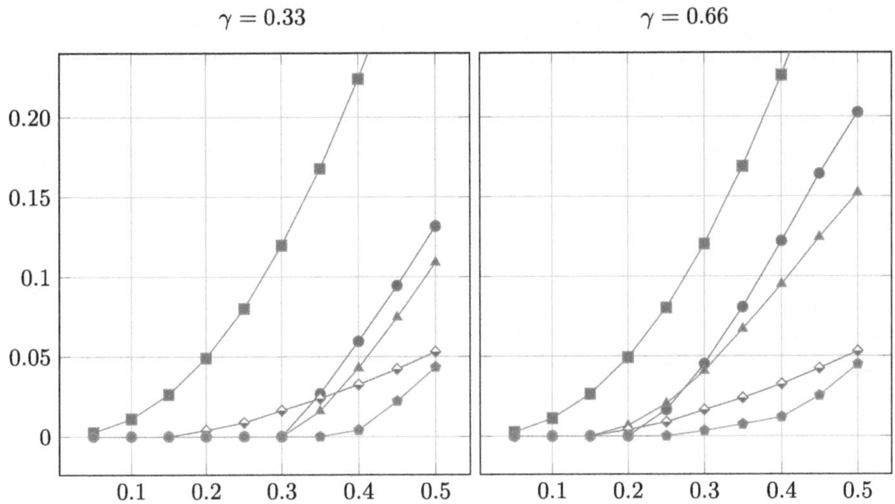

Fig. 5. Surplus of the optimal policy (y-axis, reward per progress minus α) as a function of the attacker's relative hash rate α (x-axis). We compare the protocols Bitcoin (—●—), Ethereum (—■—), Byzantium (—▲—), GhostDAG (—◇—), and Parallel Proof-of-Work (—⬟—). All results are obtained from our generic attack model with optimizations turned off. We set communication advantage $\gamma \in \{0.33, 0.66\}$ (left/right) and limit the BlockDAG to at most 6 blocks. Line $y = 0$ represents honest behavior.

BlockDAG size limit and the attacker's reward per progress could be even higher. Second, using the FC '16 model [16] as baseline, the error of our generic model is comparably sized to the error of the AFT '20 model [3]. Third, the effect of increasing the BlockDAG size limit by one, e.g. from 10 to 11, dominates the remaining differences between the models. All three models appear to converge on the same result.

7.3 Comparison of Protocols

We now evaluate selfish mining across all specified protocols: Bitcoin, Ethereum, Byzantium, GhostDAG, and Parallel Proof-of-Work. We take the 5 MDPs from Table 1, where the BlockDAG is limited to 6 blocks (n_6 column) and both optimizations are turned off. We then apply policy optimization and evaluation (Sect. 5.6), with model parameters $\alpha \in \{0.05, 0.1, \ldots, 0.45, 0.5\}$ and $\gamma \in \{0.33, 0.66\}$. Figure 5 reports the results, denoted in (expected) reward per progress minus α. This represents the *surplus* of selfish mining as compared to honest behavior. Note that we truncate the $\alpha = 0.5$ result for Ethereum, to give more detail to the other protocols. The truncated result can be read from Fig. 6 of the next experiment.

This comparison creates important insights for protocol design. First, the first Ethereum protocol is clearly off the table. Second, the fixes deployed with the Byzantium upgrade are effective. Compared to Bitcoin, Byzantium is less

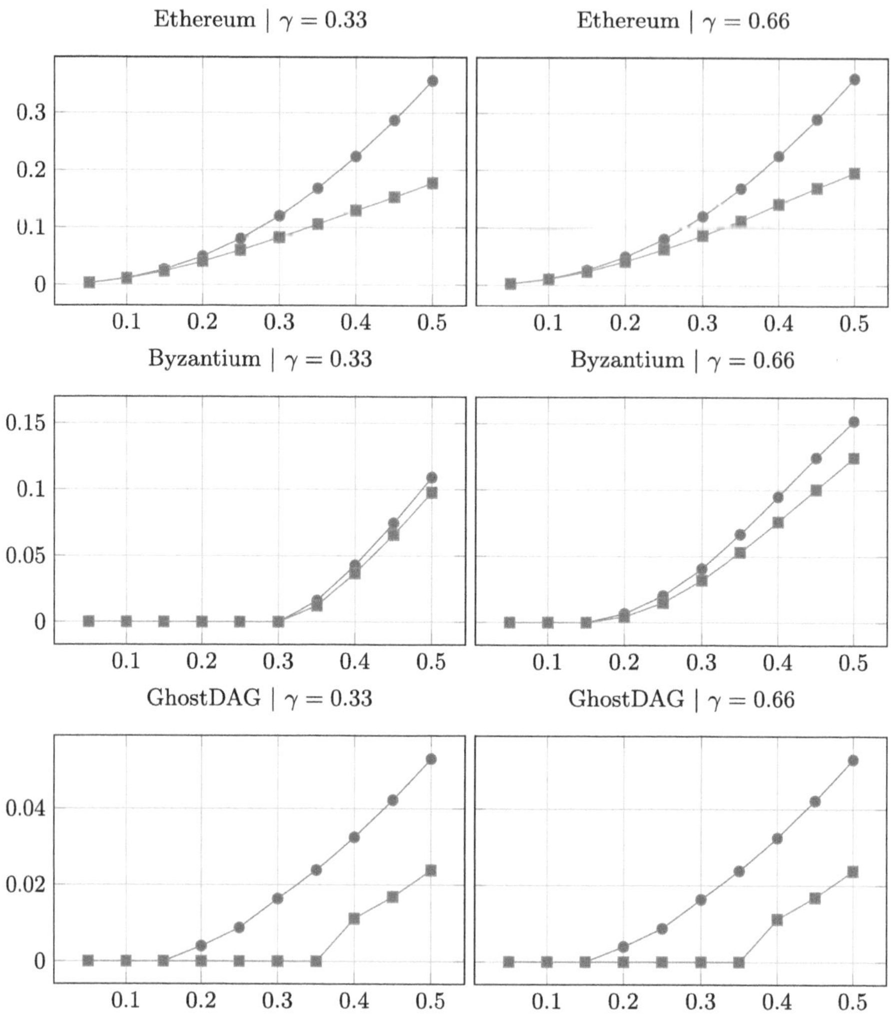

Fig. 6. Surplus of the optimal policy (y-axis, reward per progress minus α) as a function of the attacker's relative hash rate α (x-axis). We compare our generic model **with** (—●—) and **without** (—■—) **forcing the attacker to consider their own blocks**. We report the results for Ethereum (top), its Byzantium upgrade (middle), and GhostDAG (bottom); the other protocols, Bitcoin and Parallel Proof-of-Work, are not sensitive to this optimization. Note the different scales on the y-axis and see Fig. 5 for comparing results across protocols. We set communication advantage $\gamma \in \{0.33, 0.66\}$ (left/right) and limit the BlockDAG to at most 6 blocks. Line $y = 0$ represents honest behavior.

susceptible to selfish mining for most combinations of α and γ, and the difference is relatively small if not. Third, GhostDAG seems to be incentive incompatible for relatively weak attackers (low α) although it clearly outperforms Bitcoin and Byzantium for strong attackers. Forth, Parallel Proof-of-Work seems to hit a sweet spot, showing the lowest reward per progress for all parameter combinations.

This warrants further research. We are particularly interested in how GhostDAG's and Parallel's k-parameters affect the results and to which extent the results are skewed by our low BlockDAG size limit. We here set $k = 3$, while the designers of both protocols propose much higher values.

7.4 State Space Optimizations

We have presented two attack space optimizations in Sect. 6: canonization of the BlockDAG and forcing the attacker to consider their own blocks. We now check whether these optimizations affect the reward per progress after policy optimization. We take the 18 MDPs of Table 1, where the BlockDAG is limited to 6 blocks (all four n_6 columns). We then apply policy optimization and evaluation (Sect. 5.6), with model parameters $\alpha \in \{0.05, 0.1, \ldots, 0.45, 0.5\}$ and $\gamma \in \{0.33, 0.66\}$.

We do not observe substantial differences with the *Canonization* optimization turned on or off. Some protocols, however, are sensitive to the *Force Consider* optimization: Ethereum, Byzantium, and GhostDAG. Figure 6 shows the differences for these protocols with *Force Consider* turned on and off. As before, we report the (expected) reward per progress minus α, which represents the *surplus* of selfish mining as compared to honest behavior.

We observe that *Force Consider* reduces the surplus. This suggest that the optimal selfish mining strategy against Ethereum, Byzantium, and GhostDAG involves ignoring own blocks, at least temporally. We also conclude that the *Force Consider* optimization has to be applied with care.

8 Discussion and Conclusion

Our implementation is optimized for correctness and ease of presentation. The results reproduce on a \$ 1 000 laptop in a few hours. This comes at the cost of restricting the problem size (at most 100 000 states) and the size of the BlockDAG (6–11 blocks depending on model and protocol). This restricts the applicability of our tooling. E.g., the configuration of Parallel Proof-of-Work proposed by its authors [11] requests $k = 51$ parallel votes before growing the linear history by a single block. Restricting the size of the BlockDAG to anything below k is futile, and hence the proposed configuration escapes our treatment.

This raises the question, how far the problem size can be scaled after optimizing the implementation and reaching for more capable hardware. But considering the exponential growth in Fig. 3, we think algorithmic advances are inevitable. Modern reinforcement learning algorithms, e.g. DQN or PPO, should be an option, as they have been applied to similar problems before [2,12]. In principle, such techniques allow for unbounded state spaces, potentially opening a path to removing the BlockDAG size limit altogether. Beware though, that this comes at the cost of optimality. Our approach provides optimal policies and can serve as a baseline for evaluating approximate results in the future.

This brings us to other avenues for future research. We here measure two effects of the attacker's policy, reward and progress on the common chain (Sect. 5.3), and analyse a single objective function, reward per progress (Sect. 5.5), modeling the long term incentives after the DAA has adjusted to the policy. We deem it worthwhile to observe more effects, e.g., number of blocks mined and number of blocks rewritten on the defender's chain, to enable other relevant objective functions, e.g., for modelling consistency, liveness, and short term incentives.

We also see low hanging fruits to extend the range of protocols supported. E.g., some protocols use a "two-for-one trick" where the proof-of-work puzzle can have multiple possible solutions [1,15]. This can be modeled by coloring the blocks probabilistically, just when they are appended to the BlockDAG. The same mechanism would allow to (approximately) model hash-based precedence rules [12,17] which, we think, can be gamed. Turning to precedence rules, the random-tie breaking proposed by the inventors of selfish mining themselves [4], to reduce the negative effects of high communication advantages γ on Bitcoin, should be an interesting case study as well. Specifying this would require probabilistic state `update` functions—simple as long as the number of outcomes is finite.

Conclusion. We have presented a framework for finding optimal selfish mining attacks against a wide range of proof-of-work consensus protocols. Our work reproduces established results for well studied protocols, Bitcoin and Ethereum, and also covers protocols that have not been analyzed before (GhostDAG) or only with approximate policy optimization techniques (Parallel Proof-of-Work). A key feature of our approach is its modularity: the protocol designer specifies the protocol as a concise Python program, the subsequent analysis, including generating the selfish mining MDP and optimizing the policy, follows automatically. This modularity, combined with the release of all our tooling [10], enables rapid iteration during protocol design.

Acknowledgements. This work is inspired by a previous collaboration with George Bissias [12]. I would like to thank Rainer Böhme, George Bissias, Michael Fröwis, and the anonymous reviewers for their valuable feedback on earlier versions of this article.

A Discussion of the Remaining Assumptions

Our work is based on the nine Assumptions A3–A9, introduced in Sect. 3. We have discussed the three most important ones, A7–A9, in Sect. 3 already, and now cover the rest.

To A1: We assume reliable (or P2P or Bracha) broadcast, as it is largely orthogonal to consensus. Modelling consensus on top of reliable broadcast is common practice [6].

To A1 **and** A2**:** All messages are blocks and these must be organized as a DAG. This deliberately restricts our scope. In particular, we avoid modelling individual transactions and out-of-band communication.

To A2**:** We assume a connected DAG with single root block. Otherwise we would have to consider permanent splits and could not truncate the common chain.

To A3**:** We assume that all blocks require the same proof-of-work. This is a deliberate restriction to keep the state space tractable. Some interesting protocols use more than one puzzle, e.g., Fruitchains [15] and Colordag [1]. Modelling this is possible by randomly coloring the blocks. This however, would add another exponential factor to the state size (all possible colorings).

To A4**:** We assume all blocks are delivered in topological order. Typically protocols set an inductive block validity rule: a block with an invalid parent is invalid itself. Hence miners verify the blocks in topological order. Mining to confirm unverified blocks is risky. Other protocol designs are certainly viable, but we deliberately ignore them.

To A5**:** We assume deterministic behavior for a given BlockDAG and fixed order of delivery. This bounds the number of possible protocol-dependent local states: at most one per random transition explored. We need this, to explore the state space by traversing all possible state-action-transition paths.

To A6**:** We assume the protocol is a consensus protocol in the first place. This enables to bound the state space, by enforcing honest behavior and truncating the common chain.

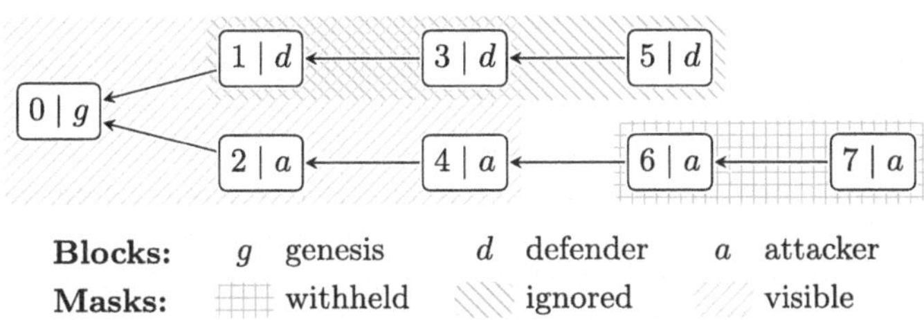

Fig. 7. Example state for the Bitcoin protocol. Vertices are blocks and arrows indicate parents. The available actions are `Consider(1)`, `Release(6)`, and `Continue`. Block 5 was just mined; it will become visible during the next `Continue` action. To emulate the traditional *Match* action, the attacker would `Release(6)` and then `Continue`. To emulate the *Override* action, the attacker would `Release(6)`, `Release(7)`, and then `Continue`.

B Traditional Selfish Mining Model for Bitcoin

We now present the traditional selfish mining model against Bitcoin [16]. Like our attack model (Sect. 3), it features two miners: the attacker and the defender. The defender extends the longest chain, breaking ties in order first seen. The attacker can fork the chain, mine blocks in private, and selectively release withheld blocks. The model is limited to one fork and there are at most two chains: the attacker mines the private chain and the defender mines the public chain. Figure 7 shows an example state in *our* generic model, reusing the notation of Fig. 1.

The traditional model has four actions: *Adopt*, *Match*, *Override*, and *Wait*. The *Adopt* action discards the private chain. The attacker will start a new fork from the most recent public block. With *Match*, the attacker releases just enough blocks to induce a block race between the public and the (released subset of the) private chain. With probability γ the block race is resolved in favor of the attacker, that is, the defender discards the public chain and continues mining on the (released subset of the) private chain. Otherwise, the defender continues mining the public chain. The *Override* action is similar to *Match*, but the attacker releases one additional block. This *forces* the defender to discard the public chain with probability one. Lastly, the *Wait* action lets the attacker continue mining on the private chain without doing anything. *All actions* induce one block being mined: with probability α the private chain grows by one, otherwise the public chain grows by one.

Note how γ models the communication advantage of the attacker. Honest Bitcoin miners resolve ties in favor of the block first received. High γ implies that the attacker can, in reaction to an honest node mining and sending block H, deliver his own block A to the remaining defenders before they learn about block H. These defenders will then discard the public chain in favor of the private chain. The second parameter, α, models the attacker's relative hash rate.

A key feature of this selfish mining model is its simple state space when implemented as MDP: two non-negative integers describe the lengths of the private and public chain and a ternary variable tracks the feasibility of *Match*. In the example in Fig. 7, there are 3 blocks on the public chain, 4 blocks on the private chain, and the *Match* action is feasible. The remaining information, e.g., block ids and the masks, is redundant.

The downside of such highly optimized MDPs is that they have to be tailored for each protocol individually. Our approach is to expand the state space such that it covers a wide range of protocols in one go. We do this, keeping the differences as small as possible: we do not introduce conflicting assumptions, use the same parameters (α and γ), and generalize the actions in a protocol-independent way.

C Protocol Specifications

This appendix provides the full protocol specifications that have been omitted in Sect. 4.2. Listing 2 specifies Ethereum Proof-of-Work. Listing 3 specifies Ethereum's Byzantium upgrade. Listing 4 specifies GhostDAG, with some helper functions deferred to Listing 5. Listing 6 specifies Parallel Proof-of-Work.

Listing 2. Specification of the Ethereum Protocol

```
h: int = 3

def init():
    state.head = genesis

def mining():
    return {state.head} | available_uncles()

def available_uncles():
    hist = history_of(state.head)
    allowed_parents = set(hist[-h - 1 : -2])
    uncles = set()
    leaves = {b for b in G if len(children(b)) == 0}
    for b in leaves:
        p, _ = parent_and_uncles(b)
        if p in allowed_parents:
            uncles.add(b)
    return uncles

def update(block):
    if height(block) > height(state.head):
        state.head = block

def history_of(block):
    if block == genesis:
        return [genesis]
    else:
        parent, _ = parent_and_uncles(block)
        return history_of(parent) + [block]

def parent_and_uncles(block):
    ranked = sorted(parents(block), key=lambda p: -height(p))
    if len(ranked) > 0:
        return ranked[0], set(ranked[1:])
    else:
        return None, set()

def history():
    return history_of(state.head)

def progress(block):
    return 1

def coinbase(block):
    _, uncles = parent_and_uncles(block)
    return [(miner_of(b), 1) for b in {block} | uncles]
```

Listing 3. Specification of the Byzantium Protocol

```
def mining():
    uncles = available_uncles()
    # choose at most 2 uncles, own blocks first
    ranked = sorted(uncles, key=lambda u: miner_of(u) != me)
    return {state.head} | set(ranked[0:2])

def update(block):
    prg_new = sum(progress(b) for b in history_of(block))
    prg_old = sum(progress(b) for b in history_of(state.head))
    if prg_new > prg_old:
        state.head = block

def progress(block):
    _, uncles = parent_and_uncles(block)
    return 1 + len(uncles)

def coinbase(block):
    _, uncles = parent_and_uncles(block)
    lst = [(miner_of(block), 1 + 0.3125 * len(uncles))]
    h = height(block)
    max_d = h + 1
    for u in uncles:
        d = h - height(u)
        lst.append((miner_of(u), (max_d - d) / max_d))
    return lst
```

The remaining functionality is inherited from Ethereum as specified in Listing 2.

Listing 4. Specification of the GhostDAG Protocol

```
k: int = 3

def mining():
    return tips(G)

def history_of(G):  # eprint.iacr.org/2018/104.pdf ; Alg. 1
    if len(G) == 1:
        return ({genesis}, [genesis])

    blue, hist = dict(), dict()
    for b in tips(G):
        blue[b], hist[b] = history_of(past(G, b))
    b_max = sorted(tips(G), key=lambda b: (-len(blue[b]), hash(b)))[0]
    blue = blue[b_max] | {b_max}
    hist = hist[b_max] + [b_max]

    ac = anticone(G, b_max)
    for b in sorted(ac, key=lambda b: (height(b), hash(b))):
        if is_k_cluster(G, blue | {b}):
            blue = blue | {b}
            hist = hist + [b]  # only blue blocks get a reward

    return (blue, hist)

def is_k_cluster(G, S):
    return all(len(anticone(G, b) & S) <= k for b in S)

def history():
    _blue, history = history_of(G)
    return history

# init() and fn update() do nothing
# progress() and coinbase() are like in Bitcoin
```

Listing 5. Specification of the GhostDAG Protocol (Utility Functions)

```
# protocol helper functions

def tips(subgraph):
    return {b for b in subgraph if len(children(b) & subgraph) == 0}

def past_or_future(relation, subgraph, block):
    acc = set()
    stack = set(relation(block)) & subgraph
    while len(stack) > 0:
        b = stack.pop()
        if b not in acc:
            acc.add(b)
            for p in set(relation(b)) & subgraph:
                stack.add(p)
    return acc

def past(subgraph, block):
    return past_or_future(parents, subgraph, block)

def future(subgraph, block):
    return past_or_future(children, subgraph, block)

def anticone(subgraph, block):
    return (
        subgraph
        - {block}
        - past(subgraph, block)
        - future(subgraph, block)
    )

# remaining protocol specification functions

def init():
    pass

def update(block):
    pass

def progress(block):
    return 1

def coinbase(block):
    return [(miner_of(block), 1)]
```

Listing 6. Specification of the Parallel Proof-of-Work Protocol

```
k: int = 3

def init():
    state.head = genesis

def mining():
    votes = children(state.head)
    if len(votes) >= k:
        # choose k votes, own votes first
        ranked = sorted(votes, key=lambda v: miner_of(v) != me)
        return set(ranked[0:k])
    return {state.head}

def update(block):
    if is_vote(block):
        block = parents(block).pop()
    if height(block) > height(state.head):
        state.head = block
    elif height(block) == height(state.head):
        if len(children(block)) > len(children(state.head)):
            state.head = block

def is_vote(block):
    return len(parents(block)) == 1

def history_of(block):
    if block == genesis:
        return [genesis]
    elif is_vote(block):
        return history_of(parents(block).pop())
    else:
        return history_of(parents(block).pop()) + [block]

def history():
    return history_of(state.head)

def progress(block):
    return k + 1

def coinbase(block):
    return [(miner_of(b), 1) for b in {block} | parents(block)]
```

References

1. Abraham, I., Dolev, D., Eyal, I., Halpern, J.Y.: Colordag: An incentive-compatible blockchain. In: 37th International Symposium on Distributed Computing, DISC 2023, 10–12 October 2023, L'Aquila, Italy. LIPIcs, vol. 281, pp. 1:1–1:22. Schloss Dagstuhl - Leibniz-Zentrum für Informatik (2023)
2. Bar-Zur, R., Abu-Hanna, A., Eyal, I., Tamar, A.: WeRLman: To tackle whale (transactions), go deep (RL). Cryptology ePrint 2022/175, IACR (2022)
3. Bar-Zur, R., Eyal, I., Tamar, A.: Efficient MDP analysis for selfish-mining in blockchains. In: Conference on Advances in Financial Technologies, pp. 113–131. ACM (2020)
4. Eyal, I., Sirer, E.G.: Majority is not enough: Bitcoin mining is vulnerable. In: Christin, N., Safavi-Naini, R. (eds.) FC 2014. LNCS, vol. 8437, pp. 436–454. Springer, Heidelberg (2014). https://doi.org/10.1007/978-3-662-45472-5_28
5. Ford, B., Böhme, R.: Rationality is self-defeating in permissionless systems. arXiv:1910.08820 (2019)
6. Garay, J., Kiayias, A.: SoK: a consensus taxonomy in the blockchain era. In: Jarecki, S. (ed.) CT-RSA 2020. LNCS, vol. 12006, pp. 284–318. Springer, Cham (2020). https://doi.org/10.1007/978-3-030-40186-3_13
7. Gervais, A., Karame, G.O., Wüst, K., Glykantzis, V., Ritzdorf, H., Capkun, S.: On the security and performance of proof of work blockchains. In: Conference on Computer and Communications Security, pp. 3–16. ACM (2016)
8. Hou, C., et al.: SquirRL: automating attack analysis on blockchain incentive mechanisms with deep reinforcement learning. In: Network and Distributed Systems Security Symposium. Internet Society (2021)
9. Keller, P.: Parallel proof-of-work with DAG-style voting and targeted reward discounting. arXiv:2312.03111v1 (2023)
10. Keller, P.: Protocol specifications, automated attack search, and reproducible experiments for this paper (2025). https://github.com/pkel/cpr/tree/3ef74c0055eb745da437adce7736b677f816fafd
11. Keller, P., Böhme, R.: Parallel proof-of-work with concrete bounds. In: Conference on Advances in Financial Technologies. ACM (2022)
12. Keller, P., Glickenhaus, B., Bissias, G., Gregory, G.: Tailstorm: A secure and fair blockchain for cash transactions. In: Conference on Advances in Financial Technologies. ACM (2023)
13. McKay, B.D., Piperno, A.: Practical graph isomorphism, II. J. Symb. Comput. **60**, 94–112 (2014)
14. Negy, K.A., Rizun, P.R., Sirer, E.G.: Selfish mining re-examined. In: Bonneau, J., Heninger, N. (eds.) FC 2020. LNCS, vol. 12059, pp. 61–78. Springer, Cham (2020). https://doi.org/10.1007/978-3-030-51280-4_5
15. Pass, R., Shi, E.: FruitChains: A fair blockchain. In: Symposium on Principles of Distributed Computing, pp. 315–324. ACM (2017)
16. Sapirshtein, A., Sompolinsky, Y., Zohar, A.: Optimal selfish mining strategies in Bitcoin. In: Financial Cryptography and Data Security. LNCS, vol. 9603, pp. 515–532. Springer (2016)
17. Sompolinsky, Y., Wyborski, S., Zohar, A.: Phantom Ghostdag: A scalable generalization of Nakamoto consensus. In: Conference on Advances in Financial Technologies, pp. 57–70. ACM (2021)
18. Sutton, R.S., Barto, A.G.: Reinforcement Learning: An Introduction, 2nd edn. Bradford Books (2018)

19. Wang, Q., Yu, J., Chen, S., Xiang, Y.: SoK: DAG-based blockchain systems. ACM Comput. Surv. **55**(12), 261:1–261:38 (2023)
20. Yaish, A., Stern, G., Zohar, A.: Uncle maker: (Time)stamping out the competition in ethereum. In: Proceedings of the 2023 ACM SIGSAC Conference on Computer and Communications Security, CCS 2023, Copenhagen, Denmark, 26–30 November 2023, pp. 135–149. ACM (2023)
21. Yaish, A., Tochner, S., Zohar, A.: Blockchain stretching & squeezing: Manipulating time for your best interest. In: Proceedings of the 23rd ACM Conference on Economics and Computation, EC 2022, pp. 65–88. ACM (2022)
22. Zhang, R., Preneel, B.: Lay down the common metrics: Evaluating proof-of-work consensus protocols' security. In: Symposium on Security and Privacy, pp. 1190–1207. IEEE (2019)

Sassafras: Efficient Batch Single Leader Election

Jeffrey Burdges[1], Elizabeth Crites[1(✉)], Handan Kılınç Alper[2], Alistair Stewart[1], and Sergey Vasilyev[1]

[1] Web3Foundation, Zug, Switzerland
{jeffrey,elizabeth,alistair,sergey}@web3.foundation
[2] =nil; Foundation, Limassol, Cyprus
handankilinc1@gmail.com

Abstract. In a single secret leader election (SSLE), a set of participants elect exactly one leader, who remains anonymous until they announce themselves by providing a proof. SSLE protocols are used in proof-of-stake blockchains to elect the leader who publishes the next block. Anonymity of the leader is an important security property, as the leader makes for an attractive target and may be subject to denial-of-service (DOS) attacks.

In this work, we propose a novel single leader election protocol, called *Sassafras*. We depart from the common approach of shuffling for constructing SSLE and instead employ a ring verifiable random function, which hides the identity of the leader within a ring of participants. Moreover, Sassafras is designed for *batch* leader elections, in which a single leader is selected for several elections at once. This allows the rate of leader election to match the rate of block production, an often-sought property not met by most SSLE protocols in the literature. We characterize single leader election with batching in the form of an ideal functionality in the Universal Composability (UC) framework and prove that Sassafras realizes this functionality. Sassafras is secure against an adaptive adversary, while achieving a slightly relaxed notion of anonymity for leaders. Sassafras features exceptionally low communication and computational complexity, outperforming other SSLE protocols by an order of magnitude or more.

1 Introduction

Leader election is an essential component of distributed systems, in particular in blockchain protocols to assign block producers. In the Byzantine setting, secrecy of the leaders is crucial for preventing denial-of-service (DOS) attacks. Most blockchain protocols [9,20,21,24,25,28] deploy secret *probabilistic* leader election (PLE), which elects leaders in expectation with respect to their power. Despite its efficiency, PLE has drawbacks due to its probabilistic nature: the election might result in multiple or no leaders, and the additional runoff procedure for selecting a leader increases the time needed to extend the blockchain. Moreover, PLE has been shown to achieve weaker blockchain security than *single* secret leader election (SSLE) [3], in which a exactly one leader is elected (see Sect. 1.1).

M. Fischlin and V. Moonsamy (Eds.): ACNS 2025, LNCS 15825, pp. 244–273, 2025.
https://doi.org/10.1007/978-3-031-95761-1_9

In this work, we present Sassafras, a *batch* single leader election protocol, in which a single leader is selected for several elections at once, and analyze its application as a replacement for PLE in existing blockchain protocols following the longest chain rule [9,20,21,24,25,28]. The batch capability of Sassafras enables scalable deployment as a leader election protocol for blockchain, as the rate of leader election aligns with the rate of block production. Moreover, Sassafras features exceptionally low communication and computational complexity. This is achieved by relaxing the secrecy achieved by some leaders, while maintaining enough anonymity to ensure security when deployed on a blockchain.

Overview of Sassafras. At a high level, Sassafras operates as follows. Parties first obtain a random number from a randomness beacon, and use it to generate n_t pseudorandom numbers (the number of tickets). The parties then determine which numbers qualify as winning, and anonymously publish, verify, and agree on these winners. The numbers are sorted to determine the order of the secret leaders, with the position of a number indicating its leader's rank.

The core challenge in Sassafras is generating verifiable random numbers while maintaining anonymity. While a standard verifiable random function (VRF) [29] could be used, the verification algorithm requires the public key of the generating party, which reveals their identity. To avoid this, Sassafras employs a *ring* verifiable random function [10], which ensures that the pseudorandom output is unique and verifiable, as in a VRF, but without revealing from which party in a set of public keys $\mathcal{PK}$ it was generated. In more detail, parties in Sassafras run the ring VRF evaluation algorithm n_t[1] times with inputs $r||i$ for $1 \leq i \leq n_t$ after obtaining r from the randomness beacon. They check if the evaluation outputs y_i fall below a fixed threshold – these are the winning outputs. To prove y_i has been generated correctly without revealing their identity, a party signs $r||i$, resulting in a signature σ_i that can be verified by anyone with $\mathcal{PK}$, but without identifying the signer. The winning tickets and their signatures are then published.

At this point, parties need a method of publishing the winning outputs and their signatures anonymously. If they publish them in clear, then their anonymity is immediately broken, even if σ_i can be verified without their keys, because an adversary could observe the network traffic and learn the source of any message. Thus, Sassafras requires an extra anonymity layer. The goal is to have a randomly selected party, which we call a repeater, receive a party's ticket y_i, σ_i. This is accomplished as follows. First, the party hides y_i, σ_i and the repeater's identity by encrypting y_i, σ_i using a shared symmetric key with the repeater. Then, they multicast the encryption to all parties.[2] In the end, the repeater capable

[1] We show how to choose the parameter n_t in Proposition 1. Specifically, as we discuss in Sect. 5, n_t should be at least 6 for $\ell = 2^{13}$ elections, under the assumption that the fraction of corrupt parties α is less than ≈ 0.3 with 2^{14} parties.

[2] Formally, Sassafras is secure in the $\mathcal{F}^s_{\mathsf{com}}$-hybrid model (Theorem 1), where $\mathcal{F}^s_{\mathsf{com}}$ is a secure diffusion functionality, which hides the message and the receiver. Here, we describe Sassafras with a simple and efficient instantiation using symmetric encryption. By "multicast the encryption to all parties," we mean via a standard diffusion functionality $\mathcal{F}_{\mathsf{com}}$. Details are given in Sect. 3.1.

of decrypting the ticket publishes y_i, σ_i on behalf of the sender party.[3] If the repeater is malicious, the anonymity of the sender is compromised. Otherwise, anonymity is preserved because the owner of y_i is known by the honest repeater only, and other parties are unable to decrypt the ciphertext. In the end, the output of the Sassafras protocol consists of the y_i-values with their signatures released by all repeaters. The sorted y_i-values determine the order of the leaders.

Let us now provide intuition for why the anonymity guarantees of Sassafras, despite the potential leakage of some leaders' identities, are sufficient to ensure the security of a blockchain deploying Sassafras. Suppose there are $\alpha = 1/3$ corrupt parties and 2/3 honest parties. For each election, one of these parties is randomly selected as the repeater. With probability $(2/3)(2/3) = 4/9$, both the ticket holder and the repeater will be honest. Thus, the identity of the honest leader is protected. With probability $(2/3)(1/3) = 2/9$, the ticket holder will be honest, but the repeater will be adversarial. In this case, the repeater learns the identity of the ticket holder and can attack her when she is due to be the next leader. (We later refer to this to as a "weakly corrupted" slot.) The ticket holder may be attacked by an adversary and unable to produce blocks; these slots do not contribute to the total number of blocks for reasoning about chain safety. For each slot, the probability that the adversary produces a block is at most 1/3, and the probability that an honest party produces a block is at least 4/9. In expectation, there will be more honest blocks appended to the current longest chain than adversarial blocks. From there, following an adaptation of the security proof for PLE-based proof-of-stake blockchains [4,9,21,30], which intuitively works by arguing that, by Chernoff bounds, for any long enough sequence of slots, there will be more honest blocks than adversarial ones, then we can find a k such that all public chains will include the same blocks that are more than k slots old. Thus, we see that even if an adversary can corrupt up to 1/3 of parties, the longest chain rule is not violated. A formal analysis is given in Sect. 4.2.

Our Contributions. The contributions of this work are as follows:

- We propose a novel batch SLE protocol, Sassafras, in which a single leader is selected for several elections at once. Sassafras is secure against adaptive corruption, while achieving a slightly relaxed notion of anonymity for leaders.
- To capture formally the properties of batch SLE, we define an ideal functionality $\mathcal{F}_{\mathsf{bsle}}$, which offers modularity and flexibility for batch SLE in the Universal Somposability (UC) framework. In particular, $\mathcal{F}_{\mathsf{bsle}}$ may be instantiated so that it is tailored to different unpredictability levels for leaders, ranging from perfect unpredictability of the leader to partial or no unpredictability, depending on the requirements of the real-world protocol. We prove that Sassafras realizes $\mathcal{F}_{\mathsf{bsle}}$ in the presence of an adaptive adversary.

[3] All repeaters publish all tickets at once (see Sect. 4).

Table 1. Single secret leader election (SSLE) protocols. n is the total number of participants, α is the fraction of corrupt parties, and $(1-\alpha)$ is the fraction of honest parties. Batch Election refers to running ℓ elections at once, and values are given per election. Comm. and Comp. are communication and computational complexity, respectively. Public is the fraction of leaders in a batch election that are leaked, and the unpredictability level of a leader (Definition 4) is the reciprocal, e.g., $\frac{1}{\alpha\sqrt{n}}$. For Sassafras, this is calculated in Proposition 1. SM is the Standard Model and UC is the Universal Composability model. ✗ means the protocol is insecure under our threat model, as described below; ✓ means it is secure in our model. The security model for WHISK [22] is marked '–' because no formal security analysis is provided. Other terms are defined below.

Protocol		Comm.	Comp.	Security			Primitives
		On-chain	On-chain	Public	Anon. Set	Model	
Single Election	IO-based [7]	$O(1)$	$O(1)$	–	$(1-\alpha)n$	SM, static, ✓	IO
	TFHE-based [7]	$O(\alpha n)$	$O(\alpha n)$	–	$(1-\alpha)n$	SM, static, ✓	LWE, TFHE
	Shuffle-1 [7]	$O(\sqrt{n})$	$O(\sqrt{n})$	–	$(1-\alpha)\sqrt{n}$	static, ✗	DH-based Shuffle
	Shuffle-2 [17]	$O(n)$	$O(n)$	–	$(1-\alpha)n$	UC, static, ✓	DH-based Shuffle
	Shuffle-3 [17]	$O(n)$	$O(n)$	–	$(1-\alpha)n$	UC, adaptive, ✓	DH-based Shuffle
	PEKS-based [18]	$O(\alpha n)$	$O(\log^2 n)$	–	$(1-\alpha)n$	UC, static, ✓	Functional Encryption
Batch Election	WHISK [22]	$O(\sqrt{n})$	$O(\sqrt{n})$	$-1.25\frac{\ln(1-\alpha)}{\sqrt{n}}n$	$(1-\alpha)\sqrt{n}$	– , ✗	DH-based Shuffle
	Sassafras	$\mathbf{O(1)}$	$\mathbf{O(1)}$	$(1-\alpha)\alpha n$	$\frac{(1-\alpha)n}{2}$	**UC, adaptive**	**Ring VRF**

– We show how Sassafras can be deployed on a blockchain to elect block producers. In particular, we show how PLE can be replaced with Sassafras, maintaining chain safety and scalability and achieving faster block finality. To the best of our knowledge, Sassafras is the most efficient SLE protocol both in terms of computational and communicational overhead to date. We provide a concrete efficiency analysis in Table 2 and Sect. 5.

1.1 Related Work

Single Secret Leader Election (SSLE): Most SSLE protocols [7,17,22] rely on (repeated) shuffling a commitment list, which incurs high overhead due to complex shuffle proofs [5] and makes them impractical for on-chain use. Boneh et al. [7] suggest shuffling smaller sublists to reduce overhead, but this also reduces the unpredictability of the leader (discussed further below). Another issue in some SSLE protocols [7,17] is the lack of an efficient design for *sequential* leader election, which is crucial in blockchain protocols for sequential block producing. Shuffle-based SSLE requires first shuffling the list, then finalizing it on-chain, and only afterward obtaining randomness from a beacon. Since these steps must be executed in sequence, a leader involved in shuffling could influence the process if they were to gain knowledge of the randomness too early. Existing randomness beacons [16,21,28,31] are too slow for the required sequentiality. For example, Drand [23] produces fresh randomness only every 30 s, but some blockchains produce a block every couple of seconds [9], or even multiple blocks per second [2, 6]. WHISK [22], a shuffle-based approach to SSLE following [7] and proposed for Ethereum[4], solves this issue by performing *batch* leader elections through a single randomness, as does Sassafras. Other approaches to SSLE, including functional encryption [18], indistinguishability obfuscation (IO), and threshold fully homomorphic encryption (TFHE) [7], are impractical due to the heavy cryptographic operations required.

We provide a comparison of SSLE protocols in Table 1, categorizing single ($\ell = 1$) and batch ($1 \leq \ell < n$) single leader election protocols. Communication complexity refers to the message sizes added to blockchain blocks for ℓ elections, while computational complexity covers the verifications within each block. Larger message sizes and complex verification algorithms slow down blockchain scalability by increasing propagation time. Thus, we focus on the verification cost and message overhead from the election mechanism. Table 1 shows the practicality of batch elections, as single-election protocols must run ℓ times to achieve the same result.

Table 2. The performance of existing SSLE protocols on a blockchain (See Sect. 5).

Protocol	Comm. On-chain	Comp. On-chain
Shuffle-1 [7]	123.7 MB	40.9 ms
Shuffle-2 [17]	4831.84 MB	5241.9 ms
Shuffle-3 [17]	17718.31 MB	11793.6 ms
PEKS-based [18]	301.47 MB	16.9 ms
WHISK [22]	90.44 MB	20 ms
Sassafras	7.64 MB ✓	7.81 ms ✓

Unpredictability of Batch SLEs: We now give a detailed comparison of the unpredictability levels achieved by WHISK and Sassafras under the assumption that the adversary can corrupt up to 1/3 of parties. These can be a combination of corrupted and weakly corrupted parties, captured by $\alpha + \alpha_w \leq 1/3$, where α_w is the maximum fraction of weak corruptions (e.g., DOS-type attacks). (See Sect. 4.2 for more details.) WHISK, like Sassafras, permits a fraction of leaders to be exposed, as seen in Table 1 (under "Public"). Out of one million validators on Ethereum, the proposed number of validators to run the WHISK protocol is $n = 2^{14} = 16384$. Now consider when $\alpha = \alpha_w = 1/6$, so that $\alpha n = (1/6)(16384) = 2730$ parties can be corrupted, and 2730 parties can be weakly corrupted. Sassafras results in $(1-\alpha)\alpha n = (1-1/6)(1/6)(16384) = 2276$ leaked leaders, but the anonymity set is of size $(1-\alpha)n/2 = 6826$, so the leaders remaining achieve good privacy, and, as discussed in the introduction, the leaked leaders still allow consensus to succeed. In contrast, WHISK only leaks $\frac{-1.25\ln(1-\alpha)}{\sqrt{n}}n = 29$ leaders, but the anonymity set is only of size $(1-\alpha)\sqrt{n} = 107$

[4] Ethereum currently deploys public leader election, where all leaders are known. They also assume $\alpha < 1/3$, as does every chain using traditional Byzantine Agreement that is asynchronously safe (e.g., Cosmos, Aptos, Sui, which also currently deploy public leader election). Thus, Sassafras makes an attractive option for deployment in most proof-of-stake blockchains.

for the remaining honest leaders. That is, all honest leaders in the set of 16384 parties can be easily targeted for weak corruption. Indeed, it is in the adversary's interest to simply weakly corrupt all $1/3n = 5460$ parties in its "corruption budget." Thus, WHISK is insecure under our threat model, as is the single election protocol of [7]. The main purpose of deploying SSLE protocols in blockchains is to mitigate against DOS attacks, which our model accounts for strongly, and Sassafras achieves by design.

Moreover, WHISK targets efficiency over other SSLE protocols by performing $\ell < n$ batch elections with $O(\sqrt{n})$ communication and computational complexity. Sassafras's efficiency surpasses that of WHISK by performing an arbitrary number (not restricted to $\ell < n$) of batch elections with $O(1)$ communication and computational complexity. A detailed efficiency comparison with WHISK can be found in Table 2 and Sect. 5.

Proof-of-Stake Protocols: As mentioned in the introduction, existing proof-of-stake (PoS) protocols that elect secret leaders are based on probabilistic leader election (PLE) [19–21,28,30], in which multiple leaders may be elected for a slot, or no leaders at all. The additional runoff procedure for selecting a leader increases the time needed to extend the blockchain. Concretely, Azouvi and Cappelleti show that the block finality time for a PoS protocol is decreased by 25% when SSLE is used versus PLE. Even more important, for an adversary who controls at most 1/3 of the parties, SSLE provides higher security than PLE against private attacks, a damaging attack where an adversary can create a private chain that overtakes the honest chain, breaking the security of a longest chain protocol. Specifically, they show that the common prefix parameter (how many blocks back all longest chains have the same prefix) against private attacks in a synchronous network with a perfect (i.e., unbiased) randomness beacon is decreased by roughly 25% against a malicious stake ratio α of 1/3 or 1/4. The same parameter decreases **70%** with an imperfect randomness beacon. While PLE-based PoS protocols provide security with more adversarial power (up to 1/2), they are significantly slower (25%) to finalize the blocks, while Sassafras provides security with less adversarial power (up to 1/3) but finalizes the blocks significantly faster.

2 Preliminaries

2.1 State Machine Replication (SMR)

Sassafras uses an SMR protocol to agree on a linearizable log[5]. In particular, this ensures that all parties reach consensus on the array of leaders. In SMR (Algorithm 1), each party maintains a replica of a deterministic state machine that updates an ordered set LOG using the algorithm Transition, which processes messages from the network. Time is divided into sequential slots [9,20,21,28], and SMR accesses a clock $\mathcal{F}_{\mathsf{clock}}$ [1,4,13,26] that increments slots monotonically. Parties update LOG whenever the slot changes. A command $cmd \in \mathsf{LOG}$ is considered final once marked as such by the algorithm Transition.

[5] Linearizability means orderability of logs.

Algorithm 1 STATEMACHINE

$\mathsf{LOG} = \emptyset$, $\mathsf{input} = \emptyset$, $\mathsf{Bucket} = \emptyset$
$\mathsf{sl} \leftarrow \mathcal{F}_{\mathsf{clock}}$ // learns the current slot sl from $\mathcal{F}_{\mathsf{clock}}$
run PROCESS1 **and** PROCESS1 in parallel

PROCESS1
while true **do**
  $\mathsf{sl}_c \leftarrow \mathcal{F}_{\mathsf{clock}}$
  if $\mathsf{sl}_c \geq \mathsf{sl}$ **then**
    $cmds \leftarrow \mathsf{Bucket}$
    clean Bucket
    $\mathsf{sl} = \mathsf{sl}_c + 1$
    input.APPEND($cmds||\mathsf{sl}_c$)
    LOG = TRANSITION(LOG, input)

PROCESS2
while true **do**
  fetch messages from the network (Figure 2)
  receive *cmds* from the network
  add *cmds* to Bucket

Definition 1 (Persistence). *Persistence guarantees that if cmd* $\in$ LOG *is final in an honest state machine, then it is going to be final in other state machines.*

Definition 2 (Liveness). *Liveness guarantees that cmd sent by an honest party becomes final in* Δ_{live}*-slots.*

2.2 Universal Composability (UC) Framework

The security of Sassafras is proven in the Universal Composability (UC) framework [12]. More background on UC security is provided in the full version [11]. A protocol π operates in *the hybrid world* when it runs in the real world but interacts with ideal functionalities.

Definition 3. *(UC-security of* π *[12]) Let* π *be a protocol executed in the real-world protocol and in the ideal world with the functionality* $\mathcal{F}$*. We say that* π *in the real world realizes* $\mathcal{F}$ *if for all probabilistic polynomial-time (PPT) adversaries* $\mathcal{A}$ *in the real world, there exists a PPT simulator* Sim *such that for any environment* $\mathcal{Z}$*, the ensembles of the output of* $\mathcal{Z}$ *are indistinguishable, i.e.,* $\{\mathsf{EXEC}(\lambda, z)_{\pi,\mathcal{A},\mathcal{Z}}\}_{z\in\{0,1\}^*} \approx \{\mathsf{EXEC}(\lambda, z)_{\mathcal{F},\mathsf{Sim},\mathcal{Z}}\}_{z\in\{0,1\}^*}$*. We call the real-world protocol UC secure if it realizes* $\mathcal{F}$*.*

3 Batch Single Leader Election

We formally define batch single leader election, which outputs single leaders for at least $\ell_{\min}$ elections. We define a functionality $\mathcal{F}_{\mathsf{bsle}}$ (Fig. 1), which models batch SLE in the ideal world with a dynamic set of parties $\mathcal{P}$. Thus, it supports changes in the set of parties during its execution. The environment $\mathcal{Z}$ creates parties and controls the adversary Sim according to the UC framework (Sect. 2.2). Each party $\mathsf{P}_i \in \mathcal{P}$ is assigned power pw_i, with the power distribution $\mathcal{D}[\mathsf{P}_i] = \frac{\mathsf{pw}_i}{\sum_{\mathsf{P}_j\in\mathcal{P}} \mathsf{pw}_j} = \rho_i$, representing the likelihood of P_i becoming a leader. Sim can adaptively corrupt up to an α-fraction of the total power, i.e., $\sum_{\mathsf{P}_i\in\mathcal{P}_\mathcal{A}} \mathcal{D}[\mathsf{P}_i] < \alpha$, where $\mathcal{P}_\mathcal{A}$ is the set of corrupted parties and $\beta = 1 - \alpha$.

An intuitive $\mathcal{F}_{\mathsf{bsle}}$ would randomly select one leader for each of the ℓ-elections and notify *only* the leader, ensuring fairness, unpredictability, robustness, and uniqueness (defined below). However, in real-world *batch* SLE, the leaders of ℓ-elections are not independent, unlike in single SLE, where elections are run separately ℓ times. This interdependence complicates efficient protocol design while preserving leader unpredictability. Therefore, we define $\mathcal{F}_{\mathsf{bsle}}$ to be adaptable to various leader unpredictability levels. It is modular, either resembling the intuitive $\mathcal{F}_{\mathsf{bsle}}$, with perfect unpredictability of leaders, or allowing more flexible designs for efficiency where anonymity of honest leaders is not perfect. We capture this by introducing an algorithm GETCLUE, whose specification depends on the desired unpredictability level of the batch SLE protocol.

$\mathcal{F}_{\mathsf{bsle}}$ is defined over parameters $\texttt{max-elect}, \ell_{\min}, n_t \in \mathbb{N}$, $c \in (0,1]$, $\gamma \in [0,1]$ and a PPT algorithm GETCLUE, which receives as an input an array and outputs a same-sized array including elements from clue domain $\mathcal{C}$. Each batch election is identified with $\mathsf{eid} = (e, \mathcal{P}, \mathcal{D})$. Leads stores leaders of elections where the set of parties $\mathcal{P}$ joining the batch election specified by Sim. $\mathcal{F}_{\mathsf{bsle}}$ keeps the information about each batch election in DB.
[Register.] Upon receiving a message ($\mathit{register}$, sid, P) from P, $\mathcal{F}_{\mathsf{bsle}}$ adds to the set of honest parties $\mathcal{P}_H$ and sends ($\mathit{registered}$, sid, P) to Sim.
[Batch Election.] Upon receiving a message (elect, sid, eid) from Sim, if $\mathsf{DB}[\mathsf{eid}]$ is defined, proceed to the the distribution phase below. Otherwise, set an empty list candidate election $\mathcal{C}$, let $\mathsf{counter} = 1$, and set $\mathsf{isDecided} = \mathsf{false}$. **Do the following until** $\mathsf{isDecided} = \mathsf{true}$:

- Run ELECT(eid) $\rightarrow$ Leads below:

```
ELECT(eid):
for P_i ∈ 𝒫 do
    τ_i ← cρ_i / ρ_max
    ℒ_i ← ∅
    for k ∈ [1, n_t] do
        ω_k ←$ [0, 1)
        if ω_k < τ_i: add P_i to ℒ_i then
return Leads ← SHUFFLE(∪_{i=1}^{n} ℒ_i)
```

- Obtain $\texttt{Clue} \leftarrow$ GETCLUE(Leads)*.
- Send ($\mathit{candidate}$, sid, eid, Leads_m, $\mathcal{I}_m$) to Sim. Here, $\mathcal{I}_m$ the list of elections that have a malicious leader and $\mathsf{Leads}_m[i] = \mathsf{Leads}[i]$ for all $i \in \mathcal{I}_m$.
- Add (Leak, $\texttt{Clue}$, Leads) to $\mathcal{C}$ and (eid, $\mathsf{counter}$, $\{k : \mathsf{Leads}[k] = \mathsf{P}_i\}$) to $\texttt{history}[\mathsf{P}_i]$ for all $\mathsf{P}_i \in \mathcal{P}_H$. Set $\mathsf{DB}[\mathsf{eid}] = (\texttt{Clue}, \mathsf{Leads})$.
  - **If** $\mathcal{F}_{\mathsf{bsle}}$ receives ($\mathit{re\text{-}elect}$, sid, eid) from Sim and $\mathsf{counter} < \texttt{max-elect}$, increment counter.
  - **Else if** $\mathcal{F}_{\mathsf{bsle}}$ receives (set, sid, eid, $\mathcal{P}$, c) from Sim where $c \leq \mathsf{counter}$, $\mathsf{DB}[\mathsf{eid}] = \mathcal{C}[c]$ and set $\mathsf{isDecided} = \mathsf{true}$.
  - **Else:** Set $\mathsf{isDecided} = \mathsf{true}$
- When $\mathsf{isDecided} = \mathsf{true}$, start the distribution phase.

[Distribution.] Get $\texttt{Clue}, \mathsf{Leads}$ from $\mathsf{DB}[\mathsf{eid}]$. Populate the array Leak of size $|\mathsf{Leads}|$ as follows: for each $\mathsf{Leak}[i]$ where $\mathsf{Leak}[i] \in \mathcal{P}_H$, get $b \leftarrow_\gamma \{0,1\}$ and if $b = 1$, let $\mathsf{Leak}[i] = \mathsf{Leads}[i]$. In the end, send ($\mathit{result}$, sid, eid, Leak, $\texttt{Clue}$, Leads_m, $\mathcal{I}_m$) to Sim. Then receive (abort, sid, eid, $\mathcal{L}_{\mathsf{abort}}$) from Sim, where $\mathcal{L}_{\mathsf{abort}} \subseteq \mathcal{I}_m$. If $|\mathsf{Leads}| - |\mathcal{L}_{\mathsf{abort}}| < \ell_{\min}$, abort. Otherwise, for all $k \in \mathcal{L}_{\mathsf{abort}}$, remove $\mathsf{Leads}[k]$ from Leads. Send (result, sid, eid, $\{k : \mathsf{Leads}[k] = \mathsf{P}_i\}$) to each $\mathsf{P}_i \in \mathcal{P}_H$.
[Reveal.] Upon receiving a message (reveal, sid, eid, P_i, k) from P_i, obtain Leads from $\mathsf{DB}[\mathsf{eid}]$. If $\mathsf{Leads}[k] = \mathsf{P}_i$ and the batch phase of eid is done, send (reveal, sid, eid, $\mathcal{P}$, P_i, k) to all $\mathsf{P} \in \mathcal{P}$.
[Corrupt.] Upon receiving a message ($\mathit{corrupt}$, sid, P_i), move P_i from $\mathcal{P}_H$ to $\mathcal{P}_A$. Send ($\mathit{corrupted}$, sid, $\texttt{history}[\mathsf{P}_i]$) to Sim.

Fig. 1. $\mathcal{F}_{\mathsf{bsle}}$ running ELECT.

[Batch Election in $\mathcal{F}_{\mathsf{bsle}}$]: $\mathcal{F}_{\mathsf{bsle}}$ receives a request of a batch election $\mathsf{eid} = (e, \mathcal{P}, \mathcal{D})$ from Sim. Here, eid is an identification of the election, where e is an identifier and $\mathcal{P}$ is the set of parties with power distribution $\mathcal{D}$. We remark that $\mathcal{P}$ can be specified by Sim arbitrarily. Thus, it can adapt to dynamically changing parties for each election. Recall that $\mathcal{P}$ and $\mathcal{D}$ must satisfy the assumption that $\sum_{\mathsf{P}_i \in \mathcal{P}_\mathcal{A}} \mathcal{D}[\mathsf{P}_i] < \alpha$ during the batch election.[6] After the request, $\mathcal{F}_{\mathsf{bsle}}$ runs $\textsc{Elect}(\mathsf{eid})$, which is an algorithm that randomly selects a leader with respect to their power for each election and returns the leaders list $\mathtt{Leads}$. $\textsc{Elect}$ is defined with fixed parameters $n_t \in \mathbb{N}$, the number of tickets, and $c \in (0, 1]$, used to determine the threshold for winning tickets. In $\textsc{Elect}$ in Fig. 1, each party P_i has a threshold value $\tau_i = c\frac{\mathcal{D}[\mathsf{P}_i]}{\rho_{\max}}$, where $\rho_{\max} = \max\{\mathcal{D}[\mathsf{P}]\}_{\mathsf{P} \in \mathcal{P}}$. We note that τ_i is proportional to the power of a party P_i, which is $\rho_i = \mathcal{D}[\mathsf{P}_i]$, and if $\mathcal{D}$ is an equal power distribution, then $\tau_i = c$ for all P_i.

$\textsc{Elect}$ selects n_t random elements in $[0, 1)$ for each party P_i and checks if they are less than the threshold c. If it is the case, P_i is added to a list $\mathcal{L}_i$ (see Lines 4-6 of $\textsc{GetClue}$). We note that c can be interpreted as a leader cutoff parameter, as it directly controls the expected number of random elements passing their respective thresholds across all parties. A smaller c increases the difficulty of selection, thereby reducing the number of potential leaders, while a larger c increases the selection probability. However, c does not affect the distribution of leaders in $\mathtt{Leads}$, as the probability that $\mathtt{Leads}[i] = \mathsf{P}_j$ is:

$$\Pr[\mathtt{Leads}[i] = \mathsf{P}_j] = \frac{\tau_j}{\sum_{\mathsf{P}_k \in \mathcal{P}} \tau_k} = \frac{\mathcal{D}[\mathsf{P}_j]}{\sum_{\mathsf{P}_k \in \mathcal{P}} \mathcal{D}[\mathsf{P}_k]} = \mathcal{D}[\mathsf{P}_j],$$

where $\mathcal{D}[\mathsf{P}_k] = \frac{\mathsf{pw}_k}{\sum_{\mathsf{P}_\ell \in \mathcal{P}} \mathsf{pw}_\ell}$. This shows that the leader selection process respects the distribution $\mathcal{D}$, ensuring fairness across all parties.

After running $\textsc{Elect}$, $\mathcal{F}_{\mathsf{bsle}}$ runs the algorithm $\textsc{GetClue}$, which outputs a list $\mathtt{Clue}$ in order of leadership where $|\mathtt{Clue}| = |\mathtt{Leads}|$. $\mathtt{Clue}$ stores some clues about the honest leaders, i.e., if $\mathtt{Leads}[k] \in \mathcal{P}_H$, $\mathtt{Clue}[k]$ is some clue in the clue domain $\mathcal{C}$. Otherwise, $\mathtt{Clue}[k] = \bot$. As an example, $\mathtt{Clue}[k]$ can be the number of times that an honest leader of the election k is a leader within ℓ-elections or a subset of honest parties that includes $\mathtt{Leads}[k]$.

After running $\textsc{Elect}$, $\mathcal{F}_{\mathsf{bsle}}$ gives the list of elections $\mathcal{I}_m$ with malicious leaders and their malicious leaders $\mathtt{Leads}_m$, where $\mathtt{Leads}_m[i] = \mathtt{Leads}[i]$ for all $i \in \mathcal{I}_m$ and for all malicious leaders in $\mathtt{Leads}$. If Sim disagrees with the result, $\mathcal{F}_{\mathsf{bsle}}$ reruns $\textsc{Elect}$, repeating the process until Sim agrees, or after at most $\mathtt{max\text{-}elect}$ attempts. After the agreement, $\mathcal{F}_{\mathsf{bsle}}$ initiates distribution of the result.

We remark that even though the parameter c does not have any effect on the fair leader election, it is included because it plays plays a crucial role in controlling the anonymity of leaders in Sassafras (see Lemma 2). Therefore, it might give the impression that the functionality is tailored specifically to Sassafras. However, having c in $\mathcal{F}_{\mathsf{bsle}}$ does not affect the generality of $\mathcal{F}_{\mathsf{bsle}}$, as it can be always set to 1, effectively disabling its influence.

[6] While $\mathcal{F}_{\mathsf{bsle}}$ could enforce this assumption directly, we choose to simplify the design by limiting Sim to respect this constraint.

[Distribution:] In the distribution phase, $\mathcal{F}_{\mathsf{bsle}}$ generates the array $\mathtt{Leak}$ by letting $\mathtt{Leak}[i] = \mathtt{Leads}[i]$ with probability γ, which is a fixed parameter of $\mathcal{F}_{\mathsf{bsle}}$. Note that if $\gamma = 0$, no honest leaders are revealed to Sim with the array $\mathtt{Leak}$. $\mathcal{F}_{\mathsf{bsle}}$ then gives $\mathtt{Leak}$, $\mathtt{Clue}$, and the list $\mathtt{Leads}_m, \mathcal{I}_m$ to Sim. Sim then sends a set $\mathcal{L}_{\mathsf{abort}} \subset \mathcal{I}_m$, indicating which malicious leaders are aborted. If $|\mathtt{Leads}| - |\mathcal{L}_{\mathsf{abort}}| < \ell_{\min}$, $\mathcal{F}_{\mathsf{bsle}}$ aborts. Otherwise, it removes the leaders in $\mathcal{L}_{\mathsf{abort}}$ and updates the leadership array to size $\ell - |\mathcal{L}_{\mathsf{abort}}|$. Finally, it informs the honest parties of their leadership roles.

We remark that $\mathtt{Clue}$ and $\mathtt{Leak}$ serve different purposes here: $\mathtt{Leak}$ reveals leaders of some elections, while $\mathtt{Clue}$ gives extra information about who the leader could be, i.e., $\Pr[\mathtt{Leads}[i] = \mathsf{P}_j | \mathtt{Clue}[i]] < \Pr[\mathtt{Leads}[i] = \mathsf{P}_j | \mathtt{Leak}[i] = \mathsf{P}_j] = 1$.

[Reveal:] If P reveals its leadership for the ith election, it informs $\mathcal{F}_{\mathsf{bsle}}$. $\mathcal{F}_{\mathsf{bsle}}$ sends a message to other parties saying P is the leader of i if $\mathtt{Leads}[i] = \mathsf{P}$.

[Corrupt:] When Sim corrupts P_i, $\mathcal{F}_{\mathsf{bsle}}$ adds it to a list of corrupted parties and gives information related to P_i in all previous batch elections that P_i joined.

We now describe the security properties that $\mathcal{F}_{\mathsf{bsle}}$ satisfies with respect to the algorithm GetClue.

Fairness: The leaders list $\mathtt{Leads}$ output by Elect ensures $\Pr[\mathtt{Leads}[i] = \mathsf{P}_j] = \mathcal{D}[\mathsf{P}_j]$ for all $\mathsf{P}_j \in \mathcal{P}$, meaning the probability of being selected as a leader is proportional to the weight in $\mathcal{D}$. During the distribution phase, the Sim can abort malicious leaders, altering $\Pr[\mathtt{Leads}[i] = \mathsf{P}_j]$ for adversarial parties. However, this does not reduce the likelihood of honest parties being selected, as only malicious leaders are removed, leaving honest leaders unaffected. Additionally, the relative proportion of honest leaders in $\mathtt{Leads}$ increases, preserving fairness for honest parties. Thus, $\mathcal{F}_{\mathsf{bsle}}$ maintains fairness across elections, even under adversarial interference.

Robustness: $\ell_{\min}$-robustness means that $\mathcal{F}_{\mathsf{bsle}}$ does not abort, i.e., $|\mathtt{Leads}| - |\mathcal{L}_{\mathsf{abort}}| < \ell_{\min}$. Intuitively, the parameters n_t and c should be selected in such a way that, even if all malicious leaders abort their leadership during the distribution phase, $\mathcal{F}_{\mathsf{bsle}}$ does not abort. Therefore, we have the following Lemma to ensure robustness with the right parameter selections for $\mathcal{F}_{\mathsf{bsle}}$:

Lemma 1. *$\mathcal{F}_{\mathsf{bsle}}$ is $\ell_{\min}$-robust except with the probability* $\exp(-\frac{(r-1)^2}{2r}\ell_{\min})$, *where* $r = \frac{cn_t\beta}{\rho_{\max}\ell_{\min}} > 1$ *and* $\beta = 1 - \alpha$.

The proof is given in the full version [11]. We note that malicious leaders may abort their leadership after the distribution phase, as their behavior cannot be controlled. However, such aborts do not affect the leadership of honest leaders. In contrast, aborts during the distribution phase can impact honest leaders, as $\mathcal{F}_{\mathsf{bsle}}$ aborts if it cannot ensure at least $\ell_{\min}$ leaders. Consequently, the robustness of $\mathcal{F}_{\mathsf{bsle}}$ is directly tied to ensuring sufficient honest leaders during the distribution phase.

Uniqueness: Since ELECT assigns a *single* leader for each election, $\mathcal{F}_{\mathsf{bsle}}$ satisfies uniqueness.

Unpredictability: This property quantifies the probability that an adversary can correctly guess the honest leader of an election [7], given its view. Defining unpredictability in batch elections is more complex than in single leader elections due to the interdependence between elections. For instance, in WHISK [22], when leaders reveal their leadership, the set of possible leaders for subsequent elections becomes smaller, increasing the simulator's chance of guessing the correct leader. A similar situation arises in Sassafras, where revealed or leaked leaderships influence the unpredictability of other elections.

In $\mathcal{F}_{\mathsf{bsle}}$, elections corresponding to honest parties in the `Leak` array do not provide unpredictability, as their leadership is explicitly exposed. The unpredictability of non-leaked honest leaders depends on the `Clue` and `Leak` arrays, as well as the set of honest leaders revealed during the reveal phase. To address these dependencies, we formally define the unpredictability of a leader with respect to the information provided by GETCLUE in $\mathcal{F}_{\mathsf{bsle}}$ below.

Definition 4 (θ-Unpredictability). *Let $\mathcal{F}_{\mathsf{bsle}}$ run a* ***specified*** GETCLUE *algorithm, and let* `Leads` *be an output of the* ELECT *run in $\mathcal{F}_{\mathsf{bsle}}$. $\mathcal{F}_{\mathsf{bsle}}$ satisfies θ-unpredictability if for all elections s such that s has not been revealed in the reveal phase of $\mathcal{F}_{\mathsf{bsle}}$ and s is not leaked by* `Leak`*, the probability of correctly guessing the honest leader* `Leads`$[s]$ *for all simulators* Sim *is bounded by Θ. Specifically, for all honest parties* P, $\Pr\left[\texttt{Leads}[s] = \mathsf{P} \,\middle|\, \texttt{R}, \texttt{Clue}, \texttt{Leak}, \texttt{Leads}[s] \notin \mathcal{P}_{\mathcal{A}}\right] \leq \Theta$, *where* `R` *is an array that records which parties have revealed their leadership and* `Clue` *is the output of* GETCLUE(`Leads`).

This definition ensures that the adversary's ability to guess the honest leader of an election is strictly bounded, even given the adversary's view consisting of `R`, `Clue`, and `Leak`.

Modularity of $\mathcal{F}_{\mathsf{bsle}}$: $\mathcal{F}_{\mathsf{bsle}}$ defines a batch SLE protocol with fairness, robustness, uniqueness and θ-unpredictability properties. The level of unpredictability θ achieved by $\mathcal{F}_{\mathsf{bsle}}$ strongly depends on the design of the abstract algorithm GETCLUE, which determines how `Clue` is generated. If the anonymity of an honest party is not a concern, GETCLUE can be designed such that $\theta = 1$, fully revealing leader information. In general, to meet the anonymity requirements of a batch SLE protocol, GETCLUE must be carefully defined to provide the maximum allowable information as quantified by the parameter θ.

Assume that $\mathcal{F}_{\mathsf{bsle}}$ is instantiated with a particular γ parameter and a **specific** GETCLUE algorithm, achieving θ-unpredictability with $\theta = \theta'$ under the given γ and GETCLUE. Its parameters $\ell_{\min}, \texttt{max-elect}, n_t, c$ are selected in accordance with Lemma 1. In this setting, any protocol π that securely realizes $\mathcal{F}_{\mathsf{bsle}}$ using the specified GETCLUE and parameters in the UC framework (Definition 3) inherits the fairness, robustness, uniqueness, and θ-unpredictability properties of $\mathcal{F}_{\mathsf{bsle}}$, where $\theta = \theta'$.

An instantiation of $\mathcal{F}_{\mathsf{bsle}}$ achieves perfect unpredictability, where $\theta = \rho_{\max}$, by setting $\gamma = 0$ (ensuring no leakage of honest leaders) and defining GETCLUE to output an empty array. In Sect. 4.1, we provide another instantiation of $\mathcal{F}_{\mathsf{bsle}}$ by specifying both $\gamma = \alpha$ and GETCLUE, and we demonstrate that the Sassafras protocol securely realizes this specific instance of $\mathcal{F}_{\mathsf{bsle}}$ with $\theta = \frac{\rho_{\max}}{\beta(1-\chi)}$ where $1 \geq \chi > c$.

3.1 Communication Model

We now describe the communication models $\mathcal{F}_{\mathsf{com}}$ and $\mathcal{F}^{s}_{\mathsf{com}}$ (Fig. 2) for parties running the batch SLE protocol. $\mathcal{F}_{\mathsf{com}}$ captures the diffusion functionality [4,21,26] with a bounded delay Δ, ensuring messages reach all parties within this limit. We alternatively introduce $\mathcal{F}^{s}_{\mathsf{com}}$, which is an extension of $\mathcal{F}_{\mathsf{com}}$ with a 'secure diffusion' option. With this, a sender can hide the message and the receiver, and only the size of the message is revealed.

$\mathcal{F}_{\mathsf{com}}$ creates an inbox $\mathcal{I}_i$ and a queue $\mathcal{Q}^{\Delta}_i$ for each party $\mathsf{P}_i \in \mathcal{P}$. $\mathcal{I}_i$ consists of tuples of sender and message, and $\mathcal{Q}^{\Delta}_i$ consists of tuples of sender, message and delay of the message.

Diffuse. Upon receiving a message (*diffuse*, sid, m) from a party P_S, set $D = 0$ and add (P_S, m, D) to $\mathcal{Q}^{\Delta}_i$ of all $\mathsf{P}_i \in \mathcal{P}$. Send (P_S, m) to Sim.

[**Secure Diffuse.**] Upon receiving a message (*secure_diffuse*, sid, m, P_j) from a party P_S, set $D = 0$, add (P_S, m, D) to $\mathcal{Q}^{\Delta}_j$, and add $(\mathsf{P}_S, \phi_i \leftarrow\!\!\$ \{0,1\}^{|m|}, D)$ to $\mathcal{Q}^{\Delta}_i$ for all $\mathsf{P}_i \in \mathcal{P} \setminus \{\mathsf{P}_j\}$. Finally, send $(\mathsf{P}_S, \mathsf{P}_i, |m|)$ to Sim.

Fetch. Upon receiving (*fetch*, sid) from P_i, for all (P_S, m_j, D_j) in $\mathcal{Q}^{\Delta}_i$, increment D_j. If $D_j = \Delta$, add (P_S, m_j) to $\mathcal{I}_i$, and remove (P_S, m_j, D_j) from $\mathcal{Q}^{\Delta}_i$. Send (*delayed*, sid, $\mathcal{Q}^{\Delta}_i$) to Sim. Receive (*send*, sid, $\mathcal{M} \subseteq \mathcal{Q}^{\Delta}_i$) from Sim. Add (P_S, m_j) to $\mathcal{I}_i$ for each $(\mathsf{P}_S, m_j, D_j) \in \mathcal{M}$, and remove (P_S, m_j, D_j) from $\mathcal{Q}^{\Delta}_i$. Send (*deliver*, sid, $\mathcal{I}_i$) to P_i and empty $\mathcal{I}_i$.

Fig. 2. $\mathcal{F}_{\mathsf{com}}$ without secure diffusion (the framed text) and $\mathcal{F}^{s}_{\mathsf{com}}$ with secure diffusion.

Realizing Secure Diffusion: Given $\mathcal{F}_{\mathsf{com}}$, we can instantiate $\mathcal{F}^{s}_{\mathsf{com}}$ with Diffie-Hellman (DH) key exchange and semantically secure encryption [15]. Each party runs DH key exchange with others and obtain shared keys, each of which is the hash of the DH key, i.e., hash of g^{ab} where a and b are DH private keys.[7] When sending a secret message to P, a party encrypts it with their shared key and sends it via $\mathcal{F}_{\mathsf{com}}$. All parties receive the encrypted message but only P can decrypt it, while others see random data. This setup [15] ensures message secrecy and receiver anonymity under the session-key security of the key exchange [14] and semantic security of the encryption scheme.

While this approach is secure, note that in the blockchain setting this means that every party that enters the system must ask every other party to engage

[7] For example, a key derivation hash function (KDF) is commonly used, which includes a salt to strengthen the key and make it usable for encryption.

in a key exchange with them. This has the disadvantages that each party needs to store a secret key for every other party and that parties need to know each others' network identities for key setup. Now consider the following optimization. For each message, the sender generates an ephemeral key pair $(\mathsf{esk}, \mathsf{epk})$, where $\mathsf{epk} = g^{\mathsf{esk}}$, and the encrypted message is $(\mathsf{epk}, \mathsf{H}(\mathsf{pk}_\mathsf{P}^{\mathsf{esk}}) \oplus m)$, where pk_P is the receiver's public key, m is the ticket, and H is a random oracle whose output is the same fixed length as m. This has receiver anonymity, as under the computational Diffie-Hellman assumption in the random oracle model, the message is indistinguishable from a random group element and random string without knowledge of the receiver's secret key. The sender only needs to know the receiver's public key and not its network identity, and the receiver does not need to know anything. Using ephemeral keys has the advantage that arbitrarily many messages can be sent to the same receiver with the same key and that the one-time pad can be used as the symmetric encryption scheme.

4 Sassafras

We now introduce our single leader election protocol, Sassafras. Sassafras is described in the hybrid world where the following ideal functionalities exist: a randomness beacon functionality $\mathcal{F}_{\mathsf{rand}}$ (Fig. 3), a ring VRF functionality $\mathcal{F}_{\mathsf{rvrf}}$ [10] (Fig. 4) and a secure diffusion communication channel functionality $\mathcal{F}^{s}_{\mathsf{com}}$ (Fig. 2). The Sassafras protocol does not use a functionality, but a State Machine Replication (SMR) protocol with properties defined in Sect. 2.1.

A ring VRF is a VRF that additionally allows the user to sign the VRF input and any extra message (e.g., auxiliary data) with a ring of public keys including their own, similar to ring signatures. The ring signature certifies that the VRF output has been generated with respect to one of the public keys in the ring.

To make the description of the protocol simpler and more compact, we avoid back and forth calls to the ring VRF functionality, and instead use the algorithms of a scheme that realizes $\mathcal{F}_{\mathsf{rvrf}}$ [10]. We note that this choice has clearly no effect on the security and correctness of the final scheme, as we show in Appendix C.

Ring Verifiable Random Function [10]**:** A ring verifiable random function consists of the following polynomial-time algorithms:

- $\mathsf{rVRF.Gen}(pp) \rightarrow (\mathsf{sk}, \mathsf{pk})$ takes as input public parameters pp and outputs a secret key and public key.
- $\mathsf{rVRF.Eval}(\mathsf{sk}_i, m) \rightarrow y$ takes as input a secret key sk_i and a message $m \in \{0,1\}^*$ and outputs a ring VRF evaluation y.
- $\mathsf{rVRF.CommitRing}(\mathcal{PK}, \mathsf{pk}_i) \rightarrow (\mathsf{comring}, \mathsf{opring}_i)$ takes as input a ring of public keys $\mathcal{PK} = \{\mathsf{pk}_1, \mathsf{pk}_2, \ldots, \mathsf{pk}_n\}$ and a $\mathsf{pk}_i \in \mathcal{PK}$ and outputs a deterministic commitment $\mathsf{comring}$ to $\mathcal{PK}$ and opening opring_i.
- $\mathsf{rVRF.OpenRing}(\mathsf{comring}, \mathsf{opring}_i) \rightarrow \mathsf{pk}_i$ takes as input a commitment $\mathsf{comring}$ and opening opring and outputs a public key pk_i.
- $\mathsf{rVRF.Sign}(\mathsf{sk}_i, \mathsf{comring}, \mathsf{opring}_i, m, \mathsf{aux}) \rightarrow \sigma$ takes as input a secret key, commitment and opening, message, and auxiliary data $\mathsf{aux} \in \{0,1\}^*$ (e.g., the context in which m is used) and outputs a signature σ on (m, aux).

- $\mathsf{rVRF.Verify}(\mathsf{comring}, m, \mathsf{aux}, \sigma) \rightarrow (b, y)$ takes as input a commitment, message, auxiliary data, and a purported signature and outputs a bit $b \in \{0, 1\}$ and a value y. $b = 1$ indicates acceptance and $b = 0$ indicates rejection.

$\mathsf{rVRF.CommitRing}$ and $\mathsf{rVRF.OpenRing}$ are optional algorithms, which are useful for succinct verification of large rings (else let $\mathsf{comring} = \mathcal{PK}$ and $\mathsf{opring}_i = \mathsf{pk}_i$). For example, $\mathsf{comring}$ could be a Merkle root of the keys in $\mathcal{PK}$, and opring the Merkle path of pk_i.

The security properties of a ring VRF, formally defined in $\mathcal{F}_{\mathsf{rvrf}}$ (Appendix B), are (1) correctness, (2) randomness: y is random and independent from the input and the key, (3) anonymity: y and σ do not leak any information about the public key of its signer except that the public key is in the ring, (4) unforgeability: an adversary should not be able to forge a ring VRF signature, and (5) uniqueness: there is only one valid y per key-input pair.

Finally, observe that the output of $\mathsf{rVRF.Eval}$ is independent of any specific ring. Consequently, the verification of two signatures for a given input using different rings results in the same evaluation value. This property allows a leader to disclose their identity as needed. For instance, suppose $y \leftarrow \mathsf{rVRF.Eval}(\mathsf{sk}_i, m)$ is verified via a ring VRF signature σ with a ring containing pk_i. Later, if the corresponding party wishes to affirm that y was generated using their key, they simply need to sign the same input with a ring containing only their key, i.e., $\mathcal{PK} = \{\mathsf{pk}_i\}$. This is precisely how leaders declare ownership of winning tickets in Sassafras.

Protocol Description: We now present the Sassafras protocol. Sassafras runs in the hybrid model $\mathcal{F}^s_{\mathsf{com}}, \mathcal{F}_{\mathsf{rand}}$ on top of State Machine Replication (SMR) (Sect. 2.1). Each party P_i generates a ring VRF key pair $(\mathsf{sk}, \mathsf{pk})$ by running $\mathsf{rVRF.Gen}(pp)$. All parties know the ring of public keys $\mathcal{PK} = \{\mathsf{pk}_i\}_{i=1}^n$, where n is the number of parties, and have equal power, i.e., $\mathcal{D}[\mathsf{P}] = \frac{1}{|\mathcal{P}|}$. Let $\mathsf{eid} = (e, \mathcal{P}, \mathcal{D})$, where e is an agreed identifier that makes $\mathsf{eid} = (e, \mathcal{P}, \mathcal{D})$ unique. Before the protocol begins, each party runs $\mathsf{rVRF.CommitRing}(\mathcal{PK}, \mathsf{pk}_i) \rightarrow (\mathsf{comring}, \mathsf{opring}_i)$. Sassafras then runs in six phases: *Randomness Generation, Preparation, Distribution, Submission, Sortition,* and *Revelation,* as follows.

1) Randomness Generation: Each P_i sends $(rand, \mathsf{sid}, \mathsf{eid})$ to $\mathcal{F}_{\mathsf{rand}}$ (Fig. 3) and receives randomness r_e . We employ this randomness beacon, wherein Sim can reset the randomness, because it is efficiently realizable on a blockchain [4,19,21].
2) Preparation: Parties prepare tickets using two parameters: $n_t \in \mathbb{N}$, the number of tickets, and a fixed parameter $c \in (0, 1]$ used to determine the threshold for winning tickets. Each P_i generates n_t ring VRF outputs $y_{ij} \leftarrow \mathsf{rVRF.Eval}(\mathsf{sk}_i, r_e||j||e)$ for $1 \leq j \leq n_t$ (i.e., $m = r_e||j||e$ in the ring VRF description above). An index j is marked as a winner if $y_{ij} < c$. For each winning $j \in [1, n_t]$ that P_i holds, it generates a ring VRF signature $\sigma_{ij} \leftarrow \mathsf{rVRF.Sign}(\mathsf{sk}_i, \mathsf{comring}, \mathsf{opring}_i, r_e||j||e, \bot)$[8], prepares a winning ticket (r_e, j, e, σ_{ij}), and adds the ticket to a list $\mathcal{L}_i$ of winning and non-winning tickets. For each $j \in [1, n_t]$ for which P_i is not the winner, P_i adds (r_e, Λ) to $\mathcal{L}_i$ anyway,

[8] aux does not serve any purpose in Sassafras, so is set to $\bot$.

Upon receiving $(rand, \mathsf{sid}, \mathsf{eid})$ from all honest parties in $\mathcal{P}$, if r_e is set, send $(rand, \mathsf{sid}, \mathsf{eid}, r_e)$ to all $\mathsf{P}_i \in \mathcal{P}$. Otherwise, sample r_e from $\{0,1\}^\lambda$ and send $(rand\_leak, \mathsf{sid}, \mathsf{eid}, r_e)$ to Sim. Then set counter $= 0$ and $\mathcal{C} = \emptyset$.

- Upon receiving the message $(rand\_reset, \mathsf{sid}, \mathsf{eid})$ from Sim, sample another randomness $r_e \leftarrow\!\!\$ \{0,1\}^\lambda$ if counter $<$ `max-reset`. Send the message $(rand\_leak, \mathsf{sid}, \mathsf{eid}, r_e)$ to Sim. Set the counter $=$ counter $+ 1$ and the candidate set $\mathcal{C} = \mathcal{C} \cup \{r_e\}$.
- Upon receiving the message $(rand\_set, \mathsf{sid}, \mathsf{eid}, r)$ from Sim, set $r_e = r$ if $r \in \mathcal{C}$.
- If no message is received from Sim or counter $=$ `max-reset`, move to the next step.

Send the message $(rand, \mathsf{sid}, \mathsf{eid}, r_e)$ to all $\mathsf{P}_i \in \mathcal{P}$.

Fig. 3. Functionality $\mathcal{F}_{\mathsf{rand}}$ for the randomness beacon.

in order to hide the number of winning tickets from the adversary. Here, Λ is an arbitrary message of size of (j, e, σ_{ij}).

Note that each party obtains exactly n_t ring VRF outputs from rVRF.Eval for inputs $r_e||j||e$, with $j \in [1, n_t]$, due to the *uniqueness* property of ring VRF, which prevents parties from increasing their chances of having more winning tickets.

3) Distribution: P_i selects a random party P_ℓ, called a *repeater*, for each ticket t (whether a winner or not) in $\mathcal{L}_i$. It then sends t to P_ℓ using $(secure\_diffuse, \mathsf{sid}, t, \mathsf{P}_\ell)$ via $\mathcal{F}^s_{\mathsf{com}}$, which hides the ticket's owner. (Recall that $\mathcal{F}^s_{\mathsf{com}}$ hides the message and the receiver with secure diffusion, which is necessary for unpredictability.)

When P_ℓ receives a ticket (r_e, j, e, σ_{ij}) from P_i, they verify it by checking that: (1) r_e is correct via $\mathcal{F}_{\mathsf{rand}}$, (2) $j \in [1, n_t]$, and (3) rVRF.Verify(comring, $r_e||j||e$, $\perp, \sigma_{ij})$ outputs $(1, y_{ij})$ with $y_{ij} < c$. If all checks pass, the ticket is considered valid (i.e., indeed a winning ticket).

4) Submission: For all ℓ, repeater P_ℓ sends all of the valid tickets it has received as a command to SMR (Algorithm 1) via $\mathcal{F}_{\mathsf{com}}$. The algorithm Transition(LOG, (r_e, j, e, σ_{ij})) of SMR verifies the ticket the same way the repeater does and, if it verifies, adds (r_e, j, e, σ_{ij}) to LOG. Note that all repeaters submit their tickets at the same time.

If a party sees that their repeater has not submitted their ticket(s) before the $\Delta_{\mathsf{subm}}{}^{th}$ slot (Sect. 2.1) after the randomness generation phase, they publish the tickets themselves, which reveals ownership. However, since a missing submission indicates that the repeater is malicious, the adversary gains no new information by this identity revelation. The submission phase ends Δ_{subm} slots after the randomness generation phase.

5) Sortition: After the submission phase, parties wait Δ_{live} (Sect. 2.1) slots to ensure all tickets are finalized by SMRs. They then sort the tickets by their y_{ij} values in descending order. The sorted list, `Tickets`, shows that $\texttt{Tickets}[u] = (r_e, j, e, \sigma_{ij})$ designates the signer of σ_{ij} as the leader of the uth election, with y_{ij} in u^{th} order. All parties can verify y_{ij} with rVRF.Verify(comring, $r_e||j||e, \perp, \sigma_{ij}) \rightarrow (1, y_{ij})$ without the ticket owner's key.

SMR ensures that all parties share the same, immutable leaders array. Due to the anonymity of ring VRF, parties do not know who generated the tickets,

except the repeaters. If a repeater is malicious, the anonymity of that ticket is compromised, but unpredictability is maintained for others (see Sect. 4.1).
6) Revelation: When P_i wants to announce their leadership of the kth election where $\texttt{Tickets}[k] = (r_e, j, e, \sigma_{ij})$, it outputs a signature $\bar{\sigma}_{ij}$ generated by $\mathsf{rVRF.Sign}(\mathsf{sk}_i, \{\mathsf{pk}_i\}, \mathsf{opring}_{\mathsf{self}}, r_e||j||e, \bot)$ where $(\{\mathsf{pk}_i\}, \mathsf{opring}_{\mathsf{self}}) \leftarrow \mathsf{CommitRing}(\{\mathsf{pk}_i\}, \mathsf{pk}_i))$. Here, the ring consists of *only* the signer's key. When a party to whom the leader wishes to show their leadership receives $\bar{\sigma}_{ij}$, it runs $\mathsf{rVRF.Verify}(\{\mathsf{pk}_i\}, r_e||j||e, \bot, \bar{\sigma}_{ij})$. If it outputs $(1, y_{ij})$, the party verifies the leader of the kth election is P_i.

Sassafras operates with equal powers like other protocols [7,17,18,22], but can be extended to non-equal powers by dividing a party's power into equal parts, generating a new key for each.

Intuition for Network-Layer Anonymity. Consider Sassafras with $\mathcal{F}^s_{\mathsf{com}}$ instantiated as in Sect. 3.1. Even for a strong adversary that has global view and can observe all the traffic between parties, traffic correlation for tickets sent to honest repeaters cannot be used to link leaders and their tickets. This is because: 1) tickets are encrypted via a shared key between leader and repeater, which makes the tickets sent to different receivers indistinguishable, 2) tickets sent by all leaders are of the same size, and 3) the repeaters send out all of the winning tickets they received at the same time, eliminating the possibility to correlation via timing signatures.

4.1 Security Analysis of Sassafras

We prove that Sassafras realizes the functionality $\mathcal{F}_{\mathsf{bsle}}$ running the algorithm GetClue (Algorithm 2) with parameter $\gamma = \alpha$ and the clue domain $\mathcal{C} = \{1, \ldots, n_t\}$. We first analyze the unpredictability of $\mathcal{F}_{\mathsf{bsle}}$ according to Definition 4 with this instantiation. We then show the UC security of Sassafras. GetClue

in our instantiation of $\mathcal{F}_{\mathsf{bsle}}$: The algorithm GetClue (Algorithm 2) starts by initializing a clue domain list $\mathcal{C}_i = \mathcal{C}$ for each party P_i. This domain represents the set of possible clue values available for that party. The algorithm then iterates over each leader $\texttt{Leads}[i]$ to assign a unique clue value. For the ith leader P_j, a clue k is sampled uniformly at random from the current clue domain $\mathcal{C}_j$ (Line 5). After sampling, the chosen clue k is removed from $\mathcal{C}_j$ (Line 6). This ensures that each clue value in $\mathcal{C}$ is used *exactly once* for each party, preventing reuse of the same clue for the same leader.

Let us denote clue sets of each party P_i by $\mathcal{C} \setminus \texttt{ClueLists}[\mathsf{P}_i]$ where $\texttt{ClueLists}[\mathsf{P}_i]$ is the remaining set at the return line of Algorithm 2. The clue set of a party in $\mathcal{F}_{\mathsf{bsle}}$ running Algorithm 2 corresponds to the winner index set of a party in Sassafras. In Sassafras, an index j is considered a winner index of a winning ticket if the random value generated by $\mathsf{rVRF.Eval}$ is less than the threshold c. This winning ticket then determines the leader of one of the elections k in Sassafras. In $\mathcal{F}_{\mathsf{bsle}}$ running GetClue (Algorithm 2), the process of obtaining the clue set works in reverse: first, a leader for an election is selected with probability $\frac{c\rho_i}{\rho_{\max}} = c$ by running Elect with the equal power distribution, and then a unique, non-repeated clue index is assigned to the leader uniformly at random. Despite the difference in process order, the distribution of the clue set of a party in $\mathcal{F}_{\mathsf{bsle}}$ is identical to the distribution of the winner index set of a party in Sassafras. We formally establish the equivalence of these distributions in the proof of Theorem 1. This mapping is crucial for proving the realization of $\mathcal{F}_{\mathsf{bsle}}$ using Algorithm 2.

Algorithm 2 GetClue(Leads)

```
set ClueLists of size |P|
for P_i ∈ P do
    ClueLists[P_i] ← C
for i ∈ {1, 2, ..., |Leads|} do
    k ←$ ClueLists[Leads[i]]
    remove k from ClueLists[Leads[i]]
    Clue[i] ← k
return Clue
```

Θ-Unpredictability: We show that unrevealed or non-leaked elections achieve a strong level of unpredictability, close to $\rho_{\max}$, even when `Clue` provides information about who is *not* the leader in other elections. For instance, if an honest party is the leader of the ith election, where $\texttt{Clue}[i] = k$, this implies that the same party cannot be the leader of another election j where $\texttt{Clue}[j] = k$, as the same clue value is not reused for the leadership of the same party.

Our result in Lemma 2 shows that smaller c makes `Clue` less useful for predicting leaders because the clue sets generated for each party vary significantly across parties. This variation arises because fewer attempts result in smaller and more distinct sets of indices for each party, reducing overlap and making it harder for the adversary to correlate clues across elections.

Lemma 2. *$\mathcal{F}_{\mathsf{bsle}}$ running* GetClue *in Algorithm 2 is Θ-unpredictable where* $\Theta = \frac{\rho_{\max}}{\beta(1-\chi)}$ *and* $1 \geq \chi > c$, *except with probability* $n_t \exp(-\beta\chi(\ln(\chi/c) - 1)/\rho_{\max})$.

Lemma 2 establishes that $\mathcal{F}_{\mathsf{bsle}}$ with GetClue from Algorithm 2 is θ-unpredictable, where $\theta = \frac{\rho_{\max}}{\beta(1-\chi)}$. This formally shows that a smaller c results in a smaller θ, bringing it closer to $\rho_{\max}$. Specifically, as c decreases, the lower bound of χ ($\chi > c$) also decreases, allowing χ to take smaller values. This increases $1 - \chi$ for those values, leading to an overall decrease in θ across certain ranges of χ. The proof of Lemma 2 is given in the full version [11]. We now state our main result.

Theorem 1. *Consider an instantiation of $\mathcal{F}_{\mathsf{bsle}}$ with Algorithm 2 where the parameter γ is set to α and parties have equal power. Sassafras realizes this instantiation $\mathcal{F}_{\mathsf{bsle}}$ in the $(\mathcal{F}_{\mathsf{rand}}, \mathcal{F}^{s}_{\mathsf{com}})$-hybrid model under the assumption that the underlying SMR has persistence and liveness with parameter Δ_{live} and the ring VRF scheme realizes $\mathcal{F}_{\mathsf{rvrf}}$ [10].*

We prove Theorem 1 in Appendix C. The intuition behind the proof is as follows: The output of ELECT run by $\mathcal{F}_{\mathsf{bsle}}$ and the leaders selected by Sassafras are in the same distribution, so Sim uses provided leaders $\mathtt{Leads}_m$ and $\mathtt{Clue}$ to output the same leaders in the real world. Similarly, since the distribution of clue sets of each party generated by GETCLUE in Algorithm 2 is the same as the winner index set of each party set in Sassafras, Sim uses $\mathtt{Clue}$ to simulate winner indices of Sassafras. Since we assume that the ring VRF scheme realizes $\mathcal{F}_{\mathsf{rvrf}}$, we replace the ring VRF scheme with $\mathcal{F}_{\mathsf{rvrf}}$ in Sassafras, which has a similar interface with the ring VRF definition given in Sect. 4 but via messages to $\mathcal{F}_{\mathsf{rvrf}}$. Then, we construct a simulator Sim, which simulates in the real world the honest parties of Sassafras, $\mathcal{F}_{\mathsf{rand}}, \mathcal{F}_{\mathsf{rvrf}}, \mathcal{F}^{s}_{\mathsf{com}}$, and simulates the adversary in $\mathcal{F}_{\mathsf{bsle}}$. When Sim receives a candidate election from $\mathcal{F}_{\mathsf{bsle}}$, Sim generates a randomness r_e as in $\mathcal{F}_{\mathsf{rand}}$ and leaks r_e to the adversary $\mathcal{A}$ in Sassafras. If $\mathcal{A}$ agrees on r_e, Sim sets the election in $\mathcal{F}_{\mathsf{bsle}}$. Otherwise, it asks $\mathcal{F}_{\mathsf{bsle}}$ to re-elect. After the election is set, Sim randomly picks ring VRF evaluation values less than c for $\mathcal{F}_{\mathsf{rvrf}}$ such that they correspond to the leaders in $\mathtt{Leads}_m$ and $\mathtt{Leak}$.

For the unknown honest leaders, Sim prepares tickets so that they can be verified via $\mathcal{F}_{\mathsf{rvrf}}$. Since the verification of a ticket does not require the ticket owner, Sim as $\mathcal{F}_{\mathsf{rvrf}}$ can simulate the verification even though it does not know the corresponding leaders in $\mathcal{F}_{\mathsf{bsle}}$, i.e., it just outputs verified when the signature of these tickets is given. For each leader in $\mathtt{Leak}$, Sim randomly selects a malicious repeater to leak the ticket in the real world. Each leader in $\mathtt{Leads}$, generated by ELECT (run by $\mathcal{F}_{\mathsf{bsle}}$), has an attempt index $k \in [1, n_t]$ stored in $\mathtt{Clue}$. This index corresponds to the winner index from Sassafras's preparation phase. Sim then maps the selected evaluation value for the ith leader as $(r||k||e)$ in $\mathcal{F}_{\mathsf{rvrf}}$, where $\mathtt{Clue}[i] = k$ and $\mathtt{Leak}[i] = \mathsf{P}$. If some malicious tickets are not in SMR after Δ_{live} slots, Sim deduces that $\mathcal{A}$ aborted the leaderships tied to those tickets and aborts them in $\mathcal{F}_{\mathsf{bsle}}$. Due to SMR's persistence, $\mathcal{A}$ cannot change the ticket order once finalized, ensuring the leader order remains the same in both worlds after Sim informs $\mathcal{F}_{\mathsf{bsle}}$ of the aborted leaderships.

During the simulation, Sim handles adaptive corruptions as follows. Once an honest party is corrupted, Sim treats it as malicious in subsequent steps. A challenge arises because the party was previously simulated without knowing its leaderships, verified via the $\mathcal{F}_{\mathsf{rvrf}}$ database. After corruption, Sim must provide the correct evaluation value when requested, but initially lacks knowledge of the ticket's association. Therefore, Sim corrupts the same party in $\mathcal{F}_{\mathsf{bsle}}$, retrieves all past leaderships from $\mathcal{F}_{\mathsf{bsle}}$, and updates its database to associate the tickets and their evaluation values with the corrupted party.

4.2 Sassafras with Blockchain and Blockchain with Sassafras

Sassafras and blockchain have a symbiotic relationship: Sassafras depends on the blockchain for liveness and persistence, while the blockchain relies on Sassafras to select leaders for block generation. This mutual dependence is essential for robustness in other SSLE protocols as well [7,17,18,22].

We build Sassafras on top of a secure blockchain protocol, such as [4,9,21,30], which runs in epochs $(e_1, e_2, \ldots)$. Each epoch has slots $(e_i = \{\mathsf{sl}_1, \ldots, \mathsf{sl}_{\texttt{eplen}}\})$, where each slot is assigned to a set of parties via a secret PLE before starting e_i. Parties in their assigned slots produce blocks according to the protocol.

We replace the election mechanism of the protocol with Sassafras, which we call $\mathfrak{B}$. The parameters n_t and c are set so that Sassafras realizes $\mathcal{F}_{\mathsf{bsle}}$ with $\ell_{\min} = \texttt{eplen}$ (see Proposition 1). Sassafras is first executed for e_1 using another SMR before $\mathfrak{B}$'s genesis block is released. During e_i, parties run $\mathfrak{B}$ based on the election results of e_{i-1} and execute Sassafras in parallel to elect leaders for e_{i+1}, using $\mathsf{eid} = (\mathcal{P}, \mathcal{D}, e_i)$. Parties run the preparation phase and give tickets to repeaters. Each repeater submits their ticket as a blockchain transaction during the submission phase, which ends $\Delta_{\mathsf{subm}} < \texttt{eplen}$ slots later. At the end of e_i, parties finalize tickets with $\mathfrak{B}$ and run the sortition phase to select the leaders for e_{i+1}. The first `eplen` tickets in `Tickets` determine the leaders in order.

Security Analysis: We assume the same corruption model as in batch SLE and introduce a new type of corruption for blockchains, called *weak corruption*, which covers denial-of-service (DOS) attacks and is often overlooked in blockchain analyses, despite their relevance. The adversary $\mathcal{A}$ can weakly corrupt up to α_w-fraction of honest block producers. A weakly corrupted party cannot send or receive blocks during the attack. Afterward, the party receives all missed messages, but there is no guarantee that messages sent during the corruption were delivered.

Persistence in $\mathfrak{B}$ is ensured if the probability of having a slot with honest leader(s) is greater than 1/2 [27]. In our adversarial model, weakly corrupted leaders cannot send blocks, acting outside the protocol. So we analyze the probability that a slot leader is weakly corrupted as well in $\mathfrak{B}$ with Sassafras, classifying all such slots as malicious. After this, we apply the same security analysis as the underlying blockchain protocol [4,9,21,30].

We first analyze the security of $\mathfrak{B}$ in an adversarial model we call the no-abort model, and from this, deduce that $\mathfrak{B}$ is a secure SMR. In this model, we assume $\mathcal{A}$ publishes all winning tickets of malicious parties during Sassafras's distribution phase. This restriction simplifies the analysis of slots, as without it, $\mathcal{A}$ could manipulate the probability of having an honest leader by withholding tickets. In the no-abort model, Sim is restricted to always send $(\mathit{abort}, \mathsf{sid}, \mathsf{DB}, \mathcal{L}_{\mathsf{abort}} = \emptyset)$ in $\mathcal{F}_{\mathsf{bsle}}$. We note that aborting slots does not help $\mathcal{A}$ compromise the security of $\mathfrak{B}$, as the election remains fair, as will be shown in the analysis.

Analysis of Slots: We distinguish a slot sl as a public, malicious, or weak slot. Assuming that Sassafras realizes $\mathcal{F}_{\mathsf{bsle}}$ with Algorithm 2, so non-leaked election results are θ-unpredictable (Lemma 2) and fair, i.e., the probability that a slot is assigned to an honest party is $1 - \alpha$, we obtain the following:
Public Slot: sl is a public slot if the repeater of the ticket assigned for sl is malicious. The probability of being a public slot is $p_{\mathsf{pSlot}} = (1-\alpha)\alpha = \alpha - \alpha^2$.
Malicious Slot: sl is malicious if its leader is malicious. The probability of being a malicious slot is $p_{\mathsf{mSlot}} = \alpha$.

Weak Slot: sl is weak if its honest leader is weakly corrupted. If sl is public, $\mathcal{A}$ can weakly corrupt the leader with probability 1. If sl is neither public nor malicious, $\mathcal{A}$ can weakly corrupt up to α_w-fraction of parties, succeeding if one of them is the leader. Since the leader of sl is θ-unpredictable, the probability of a weak slot is $p_{\mathsf{wSlot}} = p_{\mathsf{pSlot}} + \theta\alpha_w n(1 - p_{\mathsf{mSlot}} - p_{\mathsf{pSlot}})$, where $n = |\mathcal{P}|$.

Next, we analyze the security of $\mathfrak{B}$ under the assumption that $p_{\mathsf{hSlot}} = 1 - p_{\mathsf{wSlot}} - p_{\mathsf{mSlot}} > \frac{1}{2}$. We conclude that $\mathfrak{B}$ provides at least the same security properties as its PLE-based version, which is secure when the probability of a slot having honest leaders exceeds 1/2 [27]. While persistence analysis for SLE can be improved [3], this is beyond the scope of this paper.

Theorem 2. *Assuming $p_{\mathsf{hSlot}} > \frac{1}{2}$ and Sassafras executed before the genesis block realizes $\mathcal{F}_{\mathsf{bsle}}$ with Algorithm 2, $\mathfrak{B}$ has the liveness and persistence properties in* ***the no-abort model*** *with the epoch length $\texttt{eplen} \geq \Delta_{\mathsf{subm}} + \Delta_{live}$.*

Theorem 3. *$\mathfrak{B}$ is a secure SMR* ***iff*** *$\mathfrak{B}$ is a secure SMR in the no-abort model.*

The proofs are straightforward and are given in the full version [11]. Theorems 1 and 2 show that Sassafras is secure with high probability, provided the parameters satisfy various assumptions defined in the theorems. We need to show what combinations of parameters are possible by instantiating $\mathfrak{B}$. For this we need to be specific about the negligible probabilities involved. The proof of the following proposition is given in Appendix D.

Proposition 1. *Given a failure probability $\epsilon > 0$ and an unpredictability $\theta < \frac{\rho_{\max}}{\alpha}$, we can find $\texttt{eplen}, c, n_t$ such that with probability at least $1-\epsilon$, Sassafras is robust (Lemma 1) and θ-unpredictable (Lemma 2) and the security of $\mathfrak{B}$ holds. Furthermore, given $\rho_{\max} \leq \frac{1}{n'}$ for some n' and $\beta = \Theta(1)$, we can take $\theta = \frac{2\rho_{\max}}{\beta}$, $\epsilon = \exp(-\Theta(n'))$, $\Omega(\log n') \leq \texttt{eplen} \leq O(n')$, $c = \Theta(1)$ and $n_t = \Theta(1)$.*

5 Conclusion

In this work, we propose a security model for batch single leader election in the UC framework and construct an efficient instantiation, Sassafras, which we prove secure in this model. In addition, we show how Sassafras can be deployed on a blockchain to elect block producers.

Sassafras has superior asymptotic performance over other single leader election protocols, as demonstrated in Table 1. To validate this, we conducted benchmark tests (see Appendix A) using the same parameters as WHISK [22] with $n = 2^{14}$ and $\texttt{eplen} = 2^{13}$ slots, as shown in Table 2. Using Proposition 1, we set $n_t = 6$, $c = 0.18$, with $\alpha_w = 0.005$. This requires $\alpha < 0.29$ to maintain $p_{\mathsf{hSlot}} > 0.5$. In our analysis, we quantify the computational and communication overhead of the election protocol, focusing on the verification of election messages in a block and the additional data added to the blockchain when electing $\texttt{eplen}$ leaders.

The communication overhead for electing $\texttt{eplen}$ leaders in Sassafras is the size of all winning tickets. Assuming each block contains 2 winning tickets, the additional verification cost per block is for verifying two ring signatures[9]. Using the ring VRF construction from Sect. A of [10], each ring signature totals 432 bytes and takes about 3.9 ms to verify. The communication cost is $n \times n_t \times c$, representing the expected number of winning tickets, resulting in a 7.64 MB overhead for electing `eplen` leaders. With 2 tickets per block, the verification cost is 7.8 ms. Shuffle-based protocols, whether shuffling the entire party set [17] or a subset of size $\sqrt{n}$ [7,22], need inclusion of shuffle proofs [5] in a block for each election. We obtained the associated costs using the figures provided in Table 1 of [5], wherein verification of a shuffle proof requires $4n$ group operations, and the proof consists of $11\sqrt{n}$ group elements and $5n$ field elements. Notably, our communication cost results align with the analyses presented in [7,17]. PEKS-based SSLE [18], as shown in Table 2 of [18], requires 250 MB on-chain. While more efficient than shuffle-based solutions, this still exceeds Sassafras's overhead. The computational cost of PEKS-based SSLE involves verifying two Bulletproofs [8] for encryption and decryption, as noted in [18], which remains reasonable for blockchain applications. For WHISK, we refer to the benchmark analysis in [22]. WHISK boasts computational cost comparable to that of PEKS-based solutions; however, its communication cost remains relatively high, and an order of magnitude higher than that of Sassafras.

In summary, our analysis shows that Sassafras outperforms other protocols in both computational and communication costs on-chain. Thus, Sassafras is an attractive option for real-world deployment, enabling scalable blockchain protocols with faster finalization [3] than probabilistic leader election.

A Details of Our Benchmark Analysis

In our benchmark analysis for Sassafras, we use the ring VRF scheme rVRF from Sect. A of [10], instantiated with the Groth16-based proving system SpecialG, as described in Sect. 5.1 of the same work.[10] This construction operates over bilinear groups $\mathbb{G}_1$ and $\mathbb{G}_2$ from the BLS12-381 curve, and a separate group $\mathbb{G}'$[11] from Curve25519. In this setting, $\mathbb{G}_1$ elements are 48 bytes, $\mathbb{G}_2$ elements are 96 bytes, and $\mathbb{G}'$ elements are 32 bytes in size. The groups $\mathbb{G}_1$ and $\mathbb{G}_2$ are used in pairing operations.

We benchmarked this construction on our local machine with an AMD Ryzen 9 5950X 16-Core Processor, with the following average costs: Group multiplication in $\mathbb{G}_1$: 157.83×10^{-3} ms, group multiplication in $\mathbb{G}_2$: 507.62×10^{-3} ms, group multiplication in $\mathbb{G}'$: 79.9×10^{-3} ms, and pairing operation: 1.0386 ms.

In Sassafras, the main additional computational cost per block comes from verifying two ring VRF tickets. The cost is dominated by the rVRF.Verify algorithm, which includes (1) verification of a Chaum-Pedersen DLEQ proof (see PedVRF.Verify in Sect. 4 of [10]), requiring 3 multiplications in $\mathbb{G}_1$ and 2 in $\mathbb{G}'$

[9] The number of winning tickets per block is a design decision of the blockchain protocol and can vary.

[10] Ring VRF has also been implemented in [32].

[11] $\mathbb{G}'$ is the group for the preout element, which is part of the ring VRF signature.

and (2) verification of a $\mathsf{SpecialG}$ (Groth16) proof (see Sect. 5.2 of [10]), which involves 1 multiplication in $\mathbb{G}_1$ and 3 pairing operations. The resulting ring signature consists of: a Pedersen commitment (32 bytes), a Groth16 proof (192 bytes), a Chaum-Pedersen proof (176 bytes) and one group element (32 bytes) for a total size of **432 bytes**.

Each $\mathsf{rVRF.Verify}$ call takes approximately 3.9 ms. Given that the expected number of winning tickets is $n \times n_t \times c$, the total communication overhead for electing `eplen` leaders in a batch is around 7.64 MB on-chain. Assuming each block carries two ring VRF proofs, the ticket verification overhead per block is approximately 7.8 ms.

For the shuffle-based protocols [7,17], we use Curve25519 for our benchmark analysis. We rely on the implementation results presented in Sect. A of [5] to derive the computational and communication overhead shown in Table 2. Bayer and Groth [5] state that verifying a shuffle proof requires $4n$ group operations, and the proof consists of $11\sqrt{n}$ group elements and $5n$ field elements. Notably, our communication cost measurements align with the estimates reported in [17].

For WHISK [22], we use the analysis provided directly in the original work.

For the PEKS-based protocol [18], we use both the BLS12-381 curve and Curve25519. Communication overhead is derived from Table 2 in [18], while computational cost is estimated based on the verification of two Bulletproofs [8] used for encryption and decryption, as also discussed in [18].

B Ring Verifiable Random Function

Here, we give the ring VRF functionality $\mathcal{F}_{\mathsf{rvrf}}$ defined in [10]. We refer to [10] for a complete description of $\mathcal{F}_{\mathsf{rvrf}}$. Note that W below is implicitly part of the output σ of $\mathsf{rVRF.Sign}$ in Sect. 4.

C Proof of Security for Sassafras

Proof. (of Theorem 1.) Since the ring VRF scheme realizes $\mathcal{F}_{\mathsf{rvrf}}$, we can replace the ring VRF scheme with $\mathcal{F}_{\mathsf{rvrf}}$, i.e.,

- $\mathsf{rVRF.Eval}$: For honest parties, replaced by sending the message $(\mathit{sign}, \mathsf{sid}, \mathcal{PK}, \mathsf{pk}, \mathsf{aux}, m)$ and for malicious parties sending the message $(\mathit{eval}, \mathsf{sid}, \mathsf{pk}, W, m)$ to $\mathcal{F}_{\mathsf{rvrf}}$.
- $\mathsf{rVRF.Sign}$: For honest parties, replaced by sending the message $(\mathit{sign}, \mathsf{sid}, \mathcal{PK}, \mathsf{pk}, \mathsf{aux}, m)$ and for malicious parties replaced by picking a signature arbitrarily and sending the message $(\mathit{verify}, \mathsf{sid}, \mathcal{PK}, W, m, \mathsf{aux}, \sigma)$ to $\mathcal{F}_{\mathsf{rvrf}}$.
- $\mathsf{rVRF.Verify}$: For all parties, replaced by sending the message $(\mathit{verify}, \mathsf{sid}, \mathcal{PK}, W, m, \mathsf{aux}, \sigma)$ to $\mathcal{F}_{\mathsf{rvrf}}$.

So, we can construct a simulator Sim in the $(\mathcal{F}^{s}_{\mathsf{com}}, \mathcal{F}_{\mathsf{rand}}, \mathcal{F}_{\mathsf{rvrf}})$-hybrid model.

[Simulation of leader election:] Sim generates the ring VRF verification key pk_i as defined in $\mathcal{F}_{\mathsf{rvrf}}$ in the real world whenever $\mathcal{F}_{\mathsf{bsle}}$ sends a registration message for an honest party P_i. It sets $\mathsf{eid} = (e, \mathcal{P}, \mathcal{D})$ as agreed in the real protocol. Here $\mathcal{D}$ is set to the equal power distribution. Then it sends $(elect, \mathsf{sid}, \mathsf{eid})$ to $\mathcal{F}_{\mathsf{bsle}}$ and waits for the election result. If Sim receives $(result, \mathsf{sid}, \mathsf{eid}, \mathtt{Leak}, \mathtt{Clue}, \mathtt{Leads}_m, \mathcal{I}_m)$, it means that the election for e has already been executed. In this case, it moves directly

$\mathcal{F}_{\mathsf{rvrf}}$ runs a PPT algorithm Gen_{sign} during the execution and is parametrized with sets $\mathcal{S}_{eval}$ and $\mathcal{S}_W$ where $\mathcal{S}_{eval}$ and $\mathcal{S}_W$ are generated by a setup function $\mathsf{Setup}(\lambda)$.
[Key Generation.] Upon receiving a message $(keygen, \mathsf{sid})$ from P_i, send $(keygen, \mathsf{sid}, \mathsf{P}_i)$ to the simulator Sim. Upon receiving a message $(verificationkey, \mathsf{sid}, \mathsf{sk}, \mathsf{pk})$ from Sim, verify that sk or pk has not been recorded before for sid in $\mathtt{verification\_keys}$. If it is the case, store the value sk, pk in the table $\mathtt{verification\_keys}$ under P_i and return $(verificationkey, \mathsf{sid}, \mathsf{pk})$ to P_i.
[Honest Ring VRF Signature and Evaluation.] Upon receiving a message $(sign, \mathsf{sid}, \mathsf{ring}, \mathsf{pk}_i, \mathsf{aux}, m)$ from P_i, verify that $\mathsf{pk}_i \in \mathsf{ring}$ and that there exists a public key pk_i associated to P_i in $\mathtt{verification\_keys}$. If it is not the case, ignore the request. If there exists no W' such that $\mathtt{anonymous\_key\_map}[m, W'] = \mathsf{pk}_i$, let $W \leftarrow\$ \mathcal{S}_W$ and let $\mathsf{out} \leftarrow\$ \mathcal{S}_{eval}$. Set $\mathtt{anonymous\_key\_map}[m, W] = \mathsf{pk}_i$ and set $\mathsf{evaluations}[m, W] = \mathsf{out}$. In any case (other than ignoring the request), obtain W, out where $\mathtt{anonymous\_key\_map}[m, W] = \mathsf{pk}_i$, $\mathsf{evaluations}[m, W] = \mathsf{out}$, and $(\mathsf{sk}, \mathsf{pk})$ is in $\mathtt{verification\_keys}$. Then run $\mathsf{Gen}_{sign}(\mathsf{ring}, \mathsf{sk}, \mathsf{pk}, \mathsf{aux}, m) \to \sigma$. Let $\sigma = (\sigma, W)$ and record $[m, \mathsf{aux}, W, \mathsf{ring}, \sigma, 1]$. Return $(signature, \mathsf{sid}, \mathsf{ring}, W, \mathsf{aux}, m, \mathsf{out}, \sigma)$ to P_i.
[Malicious Ring VRF Evaluation.] Upon receiving a message $(eval, \mathsf{sid}, \mathsf{pk}_i, W, m)$ from Sim, if pk_i is recorded under an honest party's identity or if there exists $W' \neq W$ where $\mathtt{anonymous\_key\_map}[m, W'] = \mathsf{pk}_i$, ignore the request. Otherwise, record in the table $\mathtt{verification\_keys}$ the value $(\bot, \mathsf{pk}_i)$ under Sim if $(\cdot, \mathsf{pk}_i)$ is not in $\mathtt{verification\_keys}$. If $\mathtt{anonymous\_key\_map}[m, W]$ has not been defined before, set $\mathtt{anonymous\_key\_map}[m, W] = \mathsf{pk}_i$ and let $\mathsf{out} \leftarrow\$ \mathcal{S}_{eval}$ and set $\mathsf{evaluations}[m, W] = \mathsf{out}$. In any case (other than ignoring the request), obtain $\mathsf{out} = \mathsf{evaluations}[m, W]$ and return $(evaluated, \mathsf{sid}, m, \mathsf{pk}_i, W, \mathsf{out})$ to P_i.
[Corruption:] Upon receiving $(corrupt, \mathsf{sid}, \mathsf{P}_i)$ from Sim, remove (x_i, pk_i) from $\mathtt{verification\_keys}[\mathsf{P}_i]$ and store them in $\mathtt{verification\_keys}$ under Sim. Return $(corrupted, \mathsf{sid}, \mathsf{P}_i)$.
[Malicious Requests of Signatures.] Upon receiving a message $(signs, \mathsf{sid}, W, \mathsf{aux}, m)$ from Sim, obtain all existing valid signatures σ such that $[m, \mathsf{aux}, W, \cdot, \sigma, 1]$ is recorded and add them in a list $\mathcal{L}_\sigma$. Return $(signs, \mathsf{sid}, W, \mathsf{aux}, m, \mathcal{L}_\sigma)$ to Sim.
[Ring VRF Verification.] Upon receiving a message $(verify, \mathsf{sid}, \mathsf{ring}, W, \mathsf{aux}, m, \sigma)$ from a party, do the following:

- If there exists a record $[m, \mathsf{aux}, W, \mathsf{ring}, \sigma, b']$, set $b = b'$.
- Else if $\mathtt{anonymous\_key\_map}[m, W]$ is an honest verification key and there exists a record $[m, \mathsf{aux}, W, \mathsf{ring}, \sigma', 1]$ for any σ', then let $b = 1$ and record $[m, \mathsf{aux}, W, \mathsf{ring}, \sigma, 1]$.
- Else relay the message $(verify, \mathsf{sid}, \mathsf{ring}, W, \mathsf{aux}, m, \sigma)$ to Sim and receive back the message $(verified, \mathsf{sid}, \mathsf{ring}, W, \mathsf{aux}, m, \sigma, b_{\mathsf{Sim}}, \mathsf{pk}_{\mathsf{Sim}})$. Then check the following:
  1. If $\mathsf{pk}_{\mathsf{Sim}}$ is an honest verification key, set $b = 0$.
  2. Else if $W \notin \mathcal{W}[m, \mathsf{ring}]$ and $|\mathcal{W}[m, \mathsf{ring}]| \geq |\mathsf{ring}_{mal}|$ where ring_{mal} is a set of malicious keys in ring, set $b = 0$.
  3. Else if there exists $W' \neq W$ where $\mathtt{anonymous\_key\_map}[m, W'] = \mathsf{pk}_{\mathsf{Sim}}$, set $b = 0$.
  4. Else set $b = b_{\mathsf{Sim}}$.

In the end, record $[m, \mathsf{aux}, W, \mathsf{ring}, \sigma, 0]$ if it is not stored. If $b = 0$, let $\mathsf{out} = \bot$. Otherwise, do the following:

- If $W \notin \mathcal{W}[m, \mathsf{ring}]$, add W to $\mathcal{W}[m, \mathsf{ring}]$.
- If $\mathsf{evaluations}[m, W]$ is not defined, sample $y \leftarrow\$ \mathcal{S}_{eval}$. Then, set $\mathtt{anonymous\_key\_map}[m, W] = \mathsf{pk}_{\mathsf{Sim}}$ and $\mathsf{evaluations}[m, W] = \mathsf{out}$.
- Otherwise, set $\mathsf{out} = \mathsf{evaluations}[m, W]$.

Finally, output $(verified, \mathsf{sid}, \mathsf{ring}, W, \mathsf{aux}, m, \sigma, \mathsf{out}, b)$ to the party.
[Corruption:] Upon receiving $(corrupt, \mathsf{sid}, \mathsf{P}_i)$ from Sim, remove $(\mathsf{sk}_i, \mathsf{pk}_i)$ from $\mathtt{verification\_keys}[\mathsf{P}_i]$ and store them in $\mathtt{verification\_keys}$ under Sim. Return $(corrupted, \mathsf{sid}, \mathsf{P}_i)$.

Fig. 4. Functionality $\mathcal{F}_{\mathsf{rvrf}}$.

to Simulation of the preparation phase below. Otherwise, if $\mathcal{F}_{\mathsf{bsle}}$ sends $(\mathit{candidate\_election}, \mathsf{sid}, \mathsf{eid}, \mathtt{Leads}_m, \mathcal{I}_m)$ where $\mathsf{eid} = (e, \mathcal{P}, \mathcal{D})$, Sim registers each honest party P_i in $\mathcal{P}$ to $\mathcal{F}_{\mathsf{rvrf}}$ if P_i is not registered before.

[Simulation of the randomness phase:] Sim simulates $\mathcal{F}_{\mathsf{rand}}$ as described in Figure 3. Whenever Sim receives a message $(\mathit{rand\_reset}, \mathsf{sid}, \mathsf{eid}')$, it sends $(\mathit{re\text{-}elect}, \mathsf{sid}, \mathsf{eid})$ to $\mathcal{F}_{\mathsf{bsle}}$ and receives new election results $\mathtt{Leads}_m$ from $\mathcal{F}_{\mathsf{bsle}}$. When the adversary sends the message $(\mathit{rand\_set}, \mathsf{sid}, \mathsf{eid}', k_{set})$, Sim finalizes the randomness as r_e, which is the randomness generated when $\mathsf{counter} = k_{set}$ as $\mathcal{F}_{\mathsf{rand}}$ does. Then, Sim sends the message $(\mathit{set\_election}, \mathsf{sid}, k_{set}, \mathsf{eid})$ to $\mathcal{F}_{\mathsf{bsle}}$ to finalize the election in the ideal world. Then, it receives the message $(\mathit{initial\_election}, \mathsf{sid}, \mathsf{eid}, \mathtt{Leak}, \mathtt{Clue}, \mathtt{Leads}_m)$ from $\mathcal{F}_{\mathsf{bsle}}$.

Before Sim sends the message $(\mathit{rand\_leak}, \mathsf{sid}, \mathsf{eid}', r_e)$ to $\mathcal{A}$ while simulating $\mathcal{F}_{\mathsf{rand}}$, it sets up ring VRF outputs that are supposed to be generated by $\mathcal{F}_{\mathsf{rvrf}}$ with a given randomness of eid' for each party. This setup is executed by Sim in a way that in the real world, it gives a consistent result with $\mathtt{Leads}_m, \mathtt{Leak}$ as described below.

[Setting up random outputs of $\mathcal{F}_{\mathsf{rvrf}}$ before *rand_leak*:] Sim selects winner ring VRF outputs randomly such that $y_1 < y_2 < \ldots < y_\ell$ where $\ell_{\max} = nn_t$ and $y_i < c$ after $\mathcal{F}_{\mathsf{bsle}}$ sends $(\mathit{mal\_leaders}, \mathsf{sid}, \mathsf{eid}, \mathtt{Leads}_m)$. We note that Sim does not know $|\mathtt{Leads}|$, where $\mathtt{Leads}$ is the output $\textsc{Elect}$ in $\mathcal{F}_{\mathsf{bsle}}$. Therefore, it considers the maximum possible size, which is $\ell_{\max}$. It stores $y_1, y_2, \ldots, y_{\ell_{\max}}$ to a history list $\mathsf{Log}_r[\mathsf{eid}, \mathsf{counter}]$, where $\mathsf{counter}$ is the current counter of $\mathcal{F}_{\mathsf{rand}}$. This information will be useful when $\mathcal{A}$ corrupts an honest party during the simulation. Next, Sim executes the step that we call the Malicious rVRF evaluation preparation with the input r_e that it selected while simulating $\mathcal{F}_{\mathsf{rand}}$:

[Malicious rVRF evaluation preparation:] Given r_e and the list $\mathcal{I}_{\mathsf{P}_i}$ of elections that a malicious party P_i is selected as a leader, Sim creates a list $\mathsf{evaluations}_{\mathcal{A}}$ to later populate $\mathsf{evaluations}$ of $\mathcal{F}_{\mathsf{rvrf}}$. Then, Sim behaves as follows: Sim maps each election in $\mathcal{I}_{\mathsf{P}_i}$ to a random, unique index between $[1, n_t]$. We note that it is possible to map each election to a *unique* index because $|\mathcal{I}_{\mathsf{P}_i}| \leq n_t$, as can be seen in $\textsc{Elect}$. For each $k \in \mathcal{I}_{\mathsf{P}_i}$, Sim gets the mapped index j, and sets $\mathsf{evaluations}_{\mathcal{A}}[r_e||j||e, \mathsf{pk}_i] := y_k$. If there exists W such that $\mathtt{anonymous\_key\_map}[r_e||j||e, W] = \mathsf{pk}_i$, i.e., the input $r_e||j||e$ has been evaluated before generating r_e, then Sim outputs an abort message $\textsc{Abort-Collision}$ and ends the simulation.

[Simulating $\mathcal{F}_{\mathsf{rvrf}}$:] After receiving $(\mathit{more\_info}, \mathsf{sid}, \mathsf{eid}, \mathtt{Leak}, \mathtt{Clue}, \mathtt{Leads}_m)$ from $\mathcal{F}_{\mathsf{bsle}}$, $\mathcal{F}_{\mathsf{rvrf}}$ does the following for the leaked honest leaders. For each $k \leq \ell = |\mathtt{Leak}| \leq \ell_{\max}$ such that $\mathtt{Leak}[k] \neq \perp$, Sim gets $j \leftarrow \mathtt{Clue}[k]$, $\mathsf{P}_i \leftarrow \mathtt{Leak}[k]$, then selects randomly W from $\mathcal{S}_W$ as $\mathcal{F}_{\mathsf{rvrf}}$ does. Then, it sets $\mathtt{anonymous\_key\_map}[r_e||j||e, W] := \mathsf{pk}_i$ and $\mathsf{evaluations}[r_e||j||e, W] := y_k$, where y_k is obtained from $\mathsf{Log}_r[\mathsf{eid}, k_{set}]$. If $\mathsf{evaluations}[r_e||j||e, W]$ has been already defined with another value, Sim outputs a message $\textsc{Abort-Collision}$ and ends the simulation.

For each $k \leq \ell$ such that $\texttt{Leak}[k] = \bot$, Sim gets $j \leftarrow \texttt{Clue}[k]$, then samples $W \leftarrow_{\$} \mathcal{S}_W$, and runs $\mathsf{Gen}_{sign}(\mathcal{PK}, W, r_e||j||e)$, which outputs a signature which are indistinguishable from random. Then, it sets $\mathsf{evaluations}[r_e||j||e, W] := y_k$. It also stores W in $\texttt{W}[k]$ and σ in $\texttt{signature}[k]$. If $\mathsf{evaluations}[r_e||j||e, W]$ has been already defined with another value, Sim outputs an abort message ABORT-COLLISION and ends the simulation. Remark that Sim cannot set $\texttt{anonymous\_key\_map}[r_e||j||e, W]$ at this point because honest leader of kth election is not known yet. However, it is not an issue because $\mathcal{A}$ does have any interface in $\mathcal{F}_{\mathsf{rvrf}}$ to learn it for any honest party.

Sim simulates honest ring VRF signature as described in the functionality. Whenever $\mathcal{F}_{\mathsf{rvrf}}$ receives a message $(eval, \mathsf{sid}, \mathsf{pk}_i, W, m)$ from the adversary, it checks if $\mathsf{evaluations}_{\mathcal{A}}[m, \mathsf{pk}_i]$ is defined before. If it is defined, it sets $\mathsf{evaluations}[m, W] = \mathsf{evaluations}_{\mathcal{A}}[m, \mathsf{pk}_i]$. Otherwise, it behaves as defined $\mathcal{F}_{\mathsf{rvrf}}$. Thus $\mathcal{A}$ obtains the ring VRF values which leads malicious parties to be the leaders as in $\texttt{Leads}_m$.

For the rest of the queries for $\mathcal{F}_{\mathsf{rvrf}}$, Sim behaves as described in $\mathcal{F}_{\mathsf{rvrf}}$.

[Simulation of the preparation phase:] Sim simulates the leaked elections as follows: We denote the corresponding y-values of leaked elections of an honest party P_i by set $\mathcal{Y}_i = \{y_{i_1}, y_{i_2}, \ldots, y_{i_t}\}$ where $\texttt{Leak}[i_k] = \mathsf{P}_i$ and $i_k \in [1, \ell]$ for all $k \in [1, t]$. For each $\mathsf{P}_i \in \mathcal{P}_h$, Sim obtains σ_{i_k} and its anonymous key W_{i_k} by sending the message $(sign, \mathsf{sid}, \mathcal{PK}, \mathsf{pk}_i, r_e||j||e)$ to $\mathcal{F}_{\mathsf{rvrf}}$ where $j \leftarrow \texttt{Clue}[i_k]$. In the end, Sim constructs a list $\mathcal{L}_i$ for each honest party P_i such that $\mathcal{L}_i = \{(r_e, j, e, W_{i_k}, \sigma_{i_k})\}$ similar to the preparation phase of Sassafras. Remark that $\mathcal{L}_i$ includes only the leaked tickets differently than Sassafras but it is indistinguishable because $\mathcal{A}$ does not learn the non-leaked tickets at this phase.

Sim also prepares a list of tickets for the non-leaked slots. It creates a special list $\mathcal{L}^*$ which represents the union of subsets of $\mathcal{L}_i$ in Sassafras which includes tickets that are not sent to $\mathcal{A}$. For each election $k \leq \ell$ such that $\texttt{Leak}[k] = \bot$, it gets $W = \texttt{W}[k], \sigma = \texttt{signature}[k]$. In the end, it adds the ticket (r_e, j, e, W, σ) to $\mathcal{L}^*$ where $j = \texttt{Clue}[k]$.

[Simulation of the distribution phase:] Here, Sim only knows the owner of an honest party's y value if its election is leaked. However, it is not a problem because the honest leaders of non-leaked slots cannot be known by the adversary. Sim distributes the leaked elections among the malicious parties. In more detail, Sim does the following for each honest P_i: For each element in $\mathcal{L}_i$, it picks randomly a *malicious* party P_j and sends the element to P_j via $\mathcal{F}^s_{\mathsf{com}}$. Note that an honest party sends n_t messages in the distribution phase. In order to simulate this, Sim sends some random messages $n_t - |\mathcal{L}_i|$-times to each party as $\mathcal{F}_{\mathsf{com}}$.

[Simulation of the submission phase:] During the submission, Sim behaves exactly the same as an honest party in Sassafras. Sim submits the tickets together with their signatures and proofs on behalf of the honest party who receives them from a malicious party. For each anonymous ticket in $\mathcal{L}^*$, Sim picks randomly an honest party and submits the ticket on behalf of this honest party.

In the end of the sortition phase, if there exits an honest ticket which is not finalized, Sim outputs the message ABORT-MISSING and the simulation ends. Otherwise, Sim checks which malicious tickets are not in LOG of SMR in order to find aborted slots. If y_{sl} is not obtained from the verification of one of the malicious ring signatures in LOG and $\mathsf{Leads}_m[k] = \mathsf{P}_i \in \mathcal{P}_m$, Sim adds k to the aborted slot list $\mathcal{S}_{\mathsf{abort}}$. It sends $(aborted\_slots, \mathsf{sid}, \mathcal{S}_{\mathsf{abort}})$ to $\mathcal{F}_{\mathsf{bsle}}$. After Sim sends the aborted slots to $\mathcal{F}_{\mathsf{bsle}}$, if the sortition of tickets changes in LOG and is finalized, then Sim outputs ABORT-INCONSISTENCY and the simulation ends.

[**Simulation of revealing:**] When $\mathcal{F}_{\mathsf{bsle}}$ sends $(reveal, \mathsf{sid}, \mathsf{eid}, k, \mathsf{P}_i)$, Sim obtains r_e from $\mathcal{F}_{\mathsf{rand}}$ run for eid'. It sends $(sign, \mathsf{sid}, \{\mathsf{pk}_i\}, W, r_e||j||e)$ to $\mathcal{F}_{\mathsf{rvrf}}$ where $j \leftarrow \mathtt{Clue}[k]$ and $r_e||j||e$ is from the kth sorted ticket with randomness r_e. Then it obtains $\hat{\sigma}$ from $\mathcal{F}_{\mathsf{rvrf}}$. Then, it publishes it via $\mathcal{F}^s_{\mathsf{com}}$. If $\mathtt{anonymous\_key\_map}[r_e||j||e, W]$ has not defined in $\mathcal{F}_{\mathsf{rvrf}}$'s simulation due to the unknown leader of election k, Sim sets $\mathtt{anonymous\_key\_map}[r_e||j||e, W] = \mathsf{pk}_i$.

[**Simulation of Corruption:**] When Sim receives a message $(corrupted, \mathsf{sid}, \mathtt{history}[\mathsf{P}_i])$ from $\mathcal{F}_{\mathsf{bsle}}$, Sim should not reveal $\mathcal{A}$ that P_i has been simulated. The only place that P_i's behaviour has been simulated is the elections that Sim did not know the leaderships of P_i. Now, after the corruption, Sim learns all the leaderships of P_i in the past even for the candidate elections thanks to the data $\mathtt{history}[\mathsf{P}_i]$ provided by $\mathcal{F}_{\mathsf{bsle}}$. Therefore, Sim can set $\mathtt{anonymous\_key\_map}$ of P_i for the inputs related to the past batch elections and the candidate batch elections: $\mathtt{history}[\mathsf{P}_i]$ consists of the tuples $(\mathsf{eid}, \mathsf{counter}, \mathcal{I}_{\mathsf{P}_i} = \{j : \mathsf{Leads}[j] = \mathsf{P}_i\})$ i.e., the elections that P_i is selected as a leader in the election number $\mathsf{counter}$. For each batch election $\mathsf{eid} = (e, \mathcal{P}, \mathcal{D}) \in \mathtt{history}[\mathsf{P}_i]$, Sim obtains $\mathsf{Log}_r[\mathsf{eid}, \mathsf{counter}]$ that it stored during the setting up random outputs and $r = \mathcal{C}[\mathsf{counter}]$ from $\mathcal{F}_{\mathsf{rand}}$ run for eid. In the end, it executes the same steps in the malicious rVRF evaluation preparation with the randomness r and $\mathcal{I}_{\mathsf{P}_i}$ (See [Malicious rVRF evaluation preparation] above).

Claim. The view of $\mathcal{Z}$ in its interaction with Sim is indistinguishable from the view in its interaction with the real honest parties.

Proof. We first analyze the indistinguishability of simulation of functionalities. The simulations of $\mathcal{F}_{\mathsf{rand}}, \mathcal{F}^s_{\mathsf{com}}$ are the same. Sim only simulates differently $\mathcal{F}_{\mathsf{rvrf}}$ but the output of $\mathcal{F}_{\mathsf{rvrf}}$ stays the same. It differently outputs ABORT-COLLISION when a given input $(\mathcal{PK}, r_e||j||e)$ is assigned to a value in $\mathsf{evaluations}$ for a party P_i. Since r_e is learnt by the adversary after e is started and it is random, the probability that any input such as $(\mathcal{PK}, r_e||j||e)$ is queried to $\mathcal{F}_{\mathsf{rvrf}}$ before e starts is negligible. The simulation of honest parties are indistinguishable since Sim behaves as described in Sassafras. Other difference is in the sortition phase. If a y-value is missing in the in the end of the sortition phase, Sim outputs ABORT-MISSING. Since sortition period takes Δ_{live}-slots, all honest tickets are going to be final in Δ_{live}-slots. The other abort message that Sim outputs during the sortition phase is ABORT-INCONSISTENCY. Since all honest tickets are final in the end of Δ_{live}-slots, they are considered as final for all honest parties and cannot be changed.

Additionally, we need to show that the output of ELECT and the leaders selected by Sassafras are in the same distribution since during simulation the output of simulated Sassafras comes from ELECT. They are in the same distribution because both ELECT and Sassafras select leaders using the same weight distribution $\mathcal{D}[\mathsf{P}_i]$ and threshold parameter c. In ELECT, a leader is selected if a random value ω_k is less than the threshold $\tau_i = \frac{c \cdot \mathcal{D}[\mathsf{P}_i]}{\max\{\mathcal{D}[\mathsf{P}_j]\}} = c$, which mirrors Sassafras's condition where a leader's ticket is winner if $\mathsf{rVRF.Eval} < c$. Thus, the probability of P_i being selected as a leader is identical in both processes.

Lastly, we need to show that the distribution of clue sets of each party generated by GETCLUE in Algorithm 2 is the same as the winner index set of each party set. In Sassafras, for each party P_i, a random value y is generated by $\mathsf{rVRF.Eval}$. If $y < c$, an index $j \in \mathcal{C}$ is selected as a winner index uniformly at random. This process repeats across elections, resulting in the winner index set for P_i. In $\mathcal{F}_{\mathsf{bsle}}$, leaders are first selected with probability c, and then a clue $j \in \mathcal{C}$ is assigned uniformly at random from the available clues for the leader. Each assigned clue is removed to ensure uniqueness. Both processes involve: (1) selecting a party P_i with probability c, and (2) assigning a unique index $j \in \mathcal{C}$ uniformly at random for each selected leader. Thus, the probability of any index j being included in the clue set of P_i in $\mathcal{F}_{\mathsf{bsle}}$ is identical to the probability of j being included in the winner index set of P_i in Sassafras. This completes the proof of Theorem 1. □

D Parameter Selection for Deploying Sassafras

Proof. (of Proposition 1.) We first consider the first part. We need to set the parameter $\texttt{eplen}$ so that the blockchain security holds with probability at least $1 - \epsilon/3$. The probability that the blockchain security in an epoch holds given that the election succeeded and Sassafras was θ-unpredictable is at least $1 - \exp(O(\texttt{eplen}))$. So, we can set $\texttt{eplen} = \Omega(\log 1/\epsilon)$ and have this fail with probability at most $\epsilon/3$.

Next, we need the election to succeed except with probability at most $\epsilon/3$. By Lemma 1, we need $\exp(-\frac{(r-1)^2}{2r}\texttt{eplen}) \leq \epsilon/3$ where $r = \frac{cn_t\beta}{\rho_{\max}\texttt{eplen}}$ has $r > 1$. Since $\frac{(r-1)^2}{2r}$ has derivative $\frac{(r-1)r-(r-1)^2}{2r^2} = \frac{(r-1)(r+1)}{2r^2} = \frac{1}{2} - \frac{1}{2r^2}$ which is positive when $r > 1$, if we can find an $r' > 1$ with $\exp(-\frac{(r'-1)^2}{2r'}\texttt{eplen}) = \epsilon/3$, for $r \geq r'$, we have $\exp(-\frac{(r-1)^2}{2r}\texttt{eplen}) \leq \epsilon/3$. Rearranging the equation for r' gives $r'^2 + 1 - 2r'(1 + \frac{\ln(3/\epsilon)}{\texttt{eplen}}) = 0$. The only solution of this with $r' > 1$ is $r' = (1 + \frac{\ln(3/\epsilon)}{\texttt{eplen}}) + \sqrt{(1 + \frac{\ln(3/\epsilon)}{\texttt{eplen}})^2 - 1} = 1 + \frac{\ln(3/\epsilon)}{\texttt{eplen}} + \sqrt{(\frac{\ln(3/\epsilon)}{\texttt{eplen}})^2 + 2(\frac{\ln(3/\epsilon)}{\texttt{eplen}})}$. Later, we will take $n_t = \lceil \frac{r'\rho_{\max}\texttt{eplen}}{c\beta} \rceil$ which ensures that $r > r'$, but for this we need c. The proof of the following lemma is given in the full version [11].

Lemma 3. *If* $n_t = \lceil \frac{r' \rho_{\max} \mathtt{eplen}}{c\beta} \rceil$ *and*

$$c \leq \chi^{\frac{\beta\chi}{\beta\chi+\rho_{\max}}} \exp(-1 - \frac{\rho_{\max}(\ln(3r'\rho_{\max}\mathtt{eplen}/\beta\epsilon + 3/\epsilon) - 1)}{\beta\chi + \rho_{\max}})$$

then Sassafras is $\frac{\rho_{\max}}{\beta(1-\chi)}$*-unpredictable.*

We need to set $\chi = 1 - \frac{\rho_{\max}}{\beta\theta}$ to obtain θ-unpredictability. With parameters satisfying these, each property holds except with probability $\epsilon/3$. By a union bound, all three properties hold except with probability ϵ: that the election does not abort, that Sassafras is θ-unpredictable, and that the chain properties hold. This gives the first part of the proposition. Note that c and so n_t do not depend on ϵ in an ideal way. n_t has a term $(1/\epsilon)^{\rho_{\max}/\beta\chi}$. This means if $\rho_{\max}/\beta\chi$ is large then it takes poly$(1/\epsilon)$ VRF attempts by each party in each epoch to get a small error probability where poly is a polynomial. However, in the case of $\mathcal{D}$ being the uniform distribution over many parties, $\rho_{\max}$ is small. This is why we consider the case $\rho_{\max} \leq \frac{1}{n'}$ for a large n'. In the case where probabilities are not equal, we would suggest capping $\rho_{\max}$.

Consider choosing $\chi, \mathtt{eplen}, c, n_t$ as above for the case $\rho_{\max} = 1/n'$, $\theta = 2\rho_{\max}/\beta$, $\beta = \Theta(1)$ and $\epsilon = \exp(-Cn')$ for some constant C. Then $\chi = 1/2$ and $\mathtt{eplen} > \Omega(\log(Cn'))$. We could take $\mathtt{eplen} = \Theta(\log(n'))$, however we did not give an explicit constant for the lower bound on $\mathtt{eplen}$ and there are practical reasons for making epochs long, because we need to perform Sassafras in every epoch of $\mathfrak{B}$. Thus, we consider a looser upper bound of $O(n')$.

Next note that $r' = 1 + \ln(3/\epsilon)/\mathtt{eplen} + \sqrt{(\ln(3/\epsilon)/\mathtt{eplen})^2 + 2(\ln(3/\epsilon)/\mathtt{eplen})} = O(1)$ since $\ln(3/\epsilon)/\mathtt{eplen} = O(1)$. Now we need to take $c \leq \chi^{\frac{\beta\chi}{\beta\chi+\rho_{\max}}} \exp(-1 - \frac{\rho_{\max}(\ln(3r'\rho_{\max}\mathtt{eplen}/\beta\epsilon+3/\epsilon)-1)}{\beta\chi+\rho_{\max}})$. Here $\beta\chi = \Theta(1)$ and so $\beta\chi + \rho_{\max} = \Theta(1)$. The first term, $\chi^{\frac{\beta\chi}{\beta\chi+\rho_{\max}}}$, is $\Theta(1)$. We have $3r'\rho_{\max}\mathtt{eplen}/\beta\epsilon + 3/\epsilon = O(1/\epsilon) = O(\exp(Cn'))$ and so $(\ln(3r'\rho_{\max}\mathtt{eplen}/\beta\epsilon + 3/\epsilon) - 1) = O(Cn')$. We obtain that $c \leq \exp(-O(C))$ and so we can take $c = \Omega_C(1)$. Then $n_t = \lceil \frac{r'\rho_{\max}\mathtt{eplen}}{c\beta} \rceil = O_C(1)$. Any choice of $C > 0$ gives the final part of the proposition. □

References

1. Alper, H.K.: Network time with a consensus on clock. IACR Cryptol. ePrint Arch. (2019). https://eprint.iacr.org/2019/1348
2. Aptos: The aptos blockchain: Safe, scalable, and upgradeable web3 infrastructure (2022). https://aptosfoundation.org/whitepaper/aptos-whitepaper_en.pdf
3. Azouvi, S., Cappelletti, D.: Private attacks in longest chain proof-of-stake protocols with single secret leader elections. In: Baldimtsi, F., Roughgarden, T. (eds.) AFT 2021, Arlington, Virginia, USA, September 26 - 28, 202, pp. 170–182. ACM (2021). https://doi.org/10.1145/3479722.3480996
4. Badertscher, C., Gazi, P., Kiayias, A., Russell, A., Zikas, V.: Ouroboros genesis: Composable proof-of-stake blockchains with dynamic availability. In: Lie, D., Mannan, M., Backes, M., Wang, X. (eds.) CCS 2018, Toronto, ON, Canada, October 15-19, 2018, pp. 913–930. ACM (2018). https://doi.org/10.1145/3243734.3243848

5. Bayer, S., Groth, J.: Efficient zero-knowledge argument for correctness of a shuffle. In: Pointcheval, D., Johansson, T. (eds.) EUROCRYPT 2012, Cambridge, UK, April 15-19, 2012. LNCS, vol. 7237, pp. 263–280. Springer (2012). https://doi.org/10.1007/978-3-642-29011-4_17
6. Blackshear, S., et al.: Sui lutris: a blockchain combining broadcast and consensus. In: Luo, B., Liao, X., Xu, J., Kirda, E., Lie, D. (eds.) CCS 2024, Salt Lake City, UT, USA, October 14-18, 2024. pp. 2606–2620. ACM (2024). https://doi.org/10.1145/3658644.3670286
7. Boneh, D., Eskandarian, S., Hanzlik, L., Greco, N.: Single secret leader election. In: AFT 2020, New York, NY, USA, October 21-23, 2020, pp. 12–24. ACM (2020). https://doi.org/10.1145/3419614.3423258
8. Bünz, B., Bootle, J., Boneh, D., Poelstra, A., Wuille, P., Maxwell, G.: Bulletproofs: short proofs for confidential transactions and more. In: SP 2018, May 21-23, 2018, San Francisco, California, USA, pp. 315–334. IEEE Computer Society (2018). https://doi.org/10.1109/SP.2018.00020
9. Burdges, J., et al.: Overview of polkadot and its design considerations. CoRR **abs/2005.13456** (2020). https://arxiv.org/abs/2005.13456
10. Burdges, J., Ciobotaru, O., Alper, H.K., Stewart, A., Vasilyev, S.: Ring verifiable random functions and zero-knowledge continuations. IACR Cryptol. ePrint Arch. (2023). https://eprint.iacr.org/2023/002
11. . Burdges, J., Crites, E., Alper, H.K., Stewart, A., Vasilyev, S.: Sassafras: efficient batch single leader election. IACR Cryptol. ePrint Arch. (2023) https://eprint.iacr.org/2023/031
12. Canetti, R.: Universally composable security: A new paradigm for cryptographic protocols. In: FOCS 2001, October 14-17, 2001, Las Vegas, Nevada, USA, pp. 136–145. IEEE Computer Society (2001). https://doi.org/10.1109/SFCS.2001.959888
13. Canetti, R., Hogan, K., Malhotra, A., Varia, M.: A universally composable treatment of network time. In: CSF 2017, Santa Barbara, CA, USA, August 21-25, 2017, pp. 360–375. IEEE Computer Society (2017). https://doi.org/10.1109/CSF.2017.38
14. Canetti, R., Krawczyk, H.: Analysis of key-exchange protocols and their use for building secure channels. In: Pfitzmann, B. (ed.) EUROCRYPT 2001, Innsbruck, Austria, May 6-10, 2001. LNCS, vol. 2045, pp. 453–474. Springer (2001). https://doi.org/10.1007/3-540-44987-6_28
15. Canetti, R., Krawczyk, H.: Universally composable notions of key exchange and secure channels. In: Knudsen, L.R. (ed.) EUROCRYPT 2002, Amsterdam, The Netherlands, April 28 - May 2, 2002. LNCS, vol. 2332, pp. 337–351. Springer (2002). https://doi.org/10.1007/3-540-46035-7_22
16. Cascudo, I., David, B.: SCRAPE: scalable randomness attested by public entities. In: Gollmann, D., Miyaji, A., Kikuchi, H. (eds.) ACNS 2017, Kanazawa, Japan, July 10-12, 2017. LNCS, vol. 10355, pp. 537–556. Springer (2017). https://doi.org/10.1007/978-3-319-61204-1_27
17. Catalano, D., Fiore, D., Giunta, E.: Adaptively secure single secret leader election from DDH. In: Milani, A., Woelfel, P. (eds.) PODC '22, Salerno, Italy, July 25 - 29, 2022 pp. 430–439. ACM (2022). https://doi.org/10.1145/3519270.3538424
18. Catalano, D., Fiore, D., Giunta, E.: Efficient and universally composable single secret leader election from pairings. In: Boldyreva, A., Kolesnikov, V. (eds.) PKC 2023, Atlanta, GA, USA, May 7-10, 2023. LNCS, vol. 13940, pp. 471–499. Springer (2023). https://doi.org/10.1007/978-3-031-31368-4_17
19. Chen, J., Micali, S.: Algorand: a secure and efficient distributed ledger. Theor. Comput. Sci. **777**, 155–183 (2019). https://doi.org/10.1016/J.TCS.2019.02.001

20. Daian, P., Pass, R., Shi, E.: Snow white: Robustly reconfigurable consensus and applications to provably secure proof of stake. In: Goldberg, I., Moore, T. (eds.) FC 2019, Frigate Bay, St. Kitts and Nevis, February 18-22, 2019. LNCS, vol. 11598, pp. 23–41. Springer (2019). https://doi.org/10.1007/978-3-030-32101-7_2
21. David, B., Gazi, P., Kiayias, A., Russell, A.: Ouroboros praos: an adaptively-secure, semi-synchronous proof-of-stake blockchain. In: Nielsen, J.B., Rijmen, V. (eds.) EUROCRYPT 2018, Tel Aviv, Israel, April 29 - May 3, 2018. LNCS, vol. 10821, pp. 66–98. Springer (2018). https://doi.org/10.1007/978-3-319-78375-8_3
22. Drake, J., Feist, D., Herold, G., Khovratovich, D., Maller, M., Simkin, M.: Whisk: a practical shuffle-based SSLE protocol for ethereum (2022). https://hackmd.io/@asn-d6/HyD3Yjp2Y
23. drand: Drand - a distributed randomness beacon daemon (2017). https://github.com/drand/drand
24. Garay, J.A., Kiayias, A., Leonardos, N.: The bitcoin backbone protocol: Analysis and applications. In: Oswald, E., Fischlin, M. (eds.) EUROCRYPT 2015, Sofia, Bulgaria, April 26-30, 2015. LNCS, vol. 9057, pp. 281–310. Springer (2015). https://doi.org/10.1007/978-3-662-46803-6_10
25. Hanke, T., Movahedi, M., Williams, D.: DFINITY technology overview series, consensus system. CoRR **abs/1805.04548** (2018). http://arxiv.org/abs/1805.04548
26. Katz, J., Maurer, U., Tackmann, B., Zikas, V.: Universally composable synchronous computation. In: Sahai, A. (ed.) TCC 2013, Tokyo, Japan, March 3-6, 2013. LNCS, vol. 7785, pp. 477–498. Springer (2013). https://doi.org/10.1007/978-3-642-36594-2_27
27. Kiayias, A., Quader, S., Russell, A.: Consistency of proof-of-stake blockchains with concurrent honest slot leaders. In: ICDCS 2020, Singapore, November 29 - December 1, 2020 pp. 776–786. IEEE Computer Society (2020). https://doi.org/10.1109/ICDCS47774.2020.00065
28. Kiayias, A., Russell, A., David, B., Oliynykov, R.: Ouroboros: a provably secure proof-of-stake blockchain protocol. In: Katz, J., Shacham, H. (eds.) CRYPTO 2017, Santa Barbara, CA, USA, August 20-24, 2017. LNCS, vol. 10401, pp. 357–388. Springer (2017). https://doi.org/10.1007/978-3-319-63688-7_12
29. Micali, S., Rabin, M.O., Vadhan, S.P.: Verifiable random functions. In: FOCS 1999, October 17-18, 1999, New York, NY, USA, pp. 120–130. IEEE Computer Society (1999). https://doi.org/10.1109/SFFCS.1999.814584
30. Pass, R., Shi, E.: The sleepy model of consensus. In: Takagi, T., Peyrin, T. (eds.) ASIACRYPT 2017, Hong Kong, China, December 3-7, 2017. LNCS, vol. 10625, pp. 380–409. Springer (2017). https://doi.org/10.1007/978-3-319-70697-9_14
31. Syta, E., et al.: Scalable bias-resistant distributed randomness. In: SP 2017, San Jose, CA, USA, May 22-26, 2017, pp. 444–460. IEEE Computer Society (2017). https://doi.org/10.1109/SP.2017.45
32. Web3 Foundation: Ring vrf implementation (2022). https://github.com/davxy/ark-vrf

Multi-party Computation

Oblivious Suffix Sorting: A Multi-Party Computation Scheme for Secure and Efficient Suffix Sorting

Kota Isayama[1], Koki Jimbo[2(✉)], Naohiro Okamoto[3], Kunihiko Sadakane[3], and Kazunari Tozawa[3]

[1] SMBC Nikko Securities Inc., Chiyoda-ku, Tokyo 100-8325, Japan
[2] Tokyo University of Science, Noda-shi, Chiba 278-8510, Japan
kjimbo@rs.tus.ac.jp
[3] The University of Tokyo, Bunkyo-ku, Tokyo 113-8656, Japan

Abstract. Private string search is a technique that enables the search for specific patterns or substrings within a larger text while preserving the privacy of both the search query and the text. This is particularly important in scenarios where sensitive information needs to be processed without revealing the content to computation parties, such as in federated learning applications within bioinformatics. A key component of string search is *suffix sorting*, which provides essential index data structures such as suffix arrays (SA) and FM-indexes. Despite the existence of efficient suffix sorting methods in the classical model, there have been no efficient methods in secure computation models.

In this paper, we propose efficient and secure schemes based on multi-party computation (MPC) that construct suffix arrays and FM-indexes. To our knowledge, this is the first scheme that surpasses naive methods, reducing the communication complexity from $O(n^2)$ to $O(n \log^2 n)$ and the number of online communication rounds from $O(n)$ to $O(\log^2 n)$, where n is the string length. We also give secure schemes for private string search and computing string similarity measures.

Keywords: multi-party computation · string search · suffix sorting

1 Introduction

String search is an important and commonly used task in information retrieval that finds a given pattern by a user from a set of strings stored in a database. Typical applications of string search are Web search, natural language processing, and genome analyses. Among these, applications to bioinformatics is particularly significant. For instance, in DNA sequencing alignment, text-searching techniques are used to construct a mapping of short DNA fragments (reads) to a reference genome, aiming to find the optimal placement or alignment. This mapping is a critical part of the preprocessing step for detailed analyses. These analyses help understand the functions of specific DNA subsequences; they have

M. Fischlin and V. Moonsamy (Eds.): ACNS 2025, LNCS 15825, pp. 277–307, 2025.
https://doi.org/10.1007/978-3-031-95761-1_10

led to the discovery of single nucleotide polymorphisms (SNPs) and the identification of mutations. Nowadays string databases contain huge amount of data and therefore it is common to use indexes for searching string databases, which are data structures constructed from the strings. Using indexes we can perform string searches in poly-logarithmic time to the database size.

For searching for arbitrary patterns such as DNA sequences, suffix trees [34] have been proposed and commonly used. With the rapid growth of database size, two problems arose; index size and index construction time. For the index size problem, suffix arrays [28] (SA) have been proposed as a simplified alternative of the suffix trees. Furthermore, compressed versions of the suffix arrays such as compressed suffix arrays [16] and FM-index (also referred to as BWT) [13] and compressed suffix trees [31] were proposed. Since the size of a DNA sequence often exceeds billions of characters, it is necessary to use indexes with small data size [11,26]. For the index construction time problem, the most time consuming task for constructing these indexes is suffix sorting, which is to sort all the suffixes in a string lexicographically. A naive algorithm takes $O(n^2 \log n)$ time for sorting suffixes of a string of length n. Efficient algorithms have been proposed which run in $O(n \log n)$ time [24,28] time and $O(n)$ time [19]. Once the suffix array is constructed, other indexes can be constructed easily from it in $O(n)$ time. Therefore efficient suffix sorting is an important task in string search.

However, most of these successful results do not focus on data privacy. In practice, there is a considerable demand to prevent the leakage of highly sensitive information from collected data, *e.g.,* individual genomic information and hospital records [12]. A classical approach for preserving privacy is data sanitization: a process to hide confidential information in databases. String sanitization [6] is, given a string, to change substrings containing privacy information to other substrings. However this may lose important information because we modify data.

In this paper, we consider the problem of private string search where string data are encrypted. We consider a scenario where data holders encrypt their data and store these encrypted data on external servers, such as cloud servers. This scenario is referred to as the outsourcing scenario. This outsourcing approach is aimed at practicality and is employed in similar studies such as [27,29]. Consistent with these studies, entities submitting queries (*e.g.,* a research institution) need not be the same as the data owner (*e.g.,* a hospital). Moreover, the server holding the encrypted data performs computations according to queries without decrypting the data. Therefore, there are three main security requirements: data privacy (ensuring no information leakage from the server's data), query privacy (ensuring no leakage of query information), and output privacy (ensuring that only the query submitter knows the results of the query).

We investigate privacy-preserving approaches to building data structures for text indexing, such as suffix arrays and FM-indexes. We mainly focus on developing methods to securely performing suffix sorting. The aim is to achieve efficient and private data processing, such as text searching and constructing accessible indexes for multiple strings. We use multi-party computation (MPC), which is one of the promising solutions for analyzing sensitive data while maintaining data privacy. In recent years, various privacy-preserving applications leveraging MPC have emerged. However, there are still challenges in securely and efficiently computing large-scale applications, including private string search, at practical speeds.

1.1 Related Work and Our Goals

We review several studies on private pattern matching techniques, such as finding the longest prefix match (LPM), set-maximal match, and substring match. Note that all the work assume that some string index such as suffix array, suffix tree, or BWT is constructed securely.

Mahdi *et al.* [27] proposed a scheme to find substring and set-maximal matches from a database in an outsourcing scenario, assuming pre-computation by a trusted third party. Their scheme computes the set-maximal match in a privacy-preserving manner using an encrypted suffix tree [27]. The scheme uses a garbled circuit [36] and AES in counter mode as the cryptographic tools to encrypt a pre-computed suffix tree. Although the search time is feasible, there is some information leakage to computation servers.

Shimizu *et al.* have extensively studied the problem of privately computing LPM and set-maximal matches. Recent work [29] proposes highly efficient solutions for computing LPM, surpassing earlier studies such as [33] and [32]. These solutions utilize secret-shared recursive oblivious transfer or homomorphic encryption to refer to special look-up tables constructed from the pre-computed BWT, FM-index or other pre-computed data structures such as wavelet matrix [9]. This enables the client to calculate query intervals corresponding to encrypted genomic data stored the servers while preventing access pattern leakage to the look-up tables.

As mentioned above, these algorithms rely on the existence of pre-computed string indexes. For example, [29] assumes that data owners to pre-compute the BWT and other data structures prior to encryption. Specifically, pre-computation by data-owners lead to the following issues to the protocol:

- It reduces the level of security for multiple queries (as stated in the proof of theorem 2 of [29]).
- It is designed to address a specific scenario. The correlated randomness required for data encryption must be tailored to the query length, limiting the operation to text searches of a predetermined query length.

Solutions that involve the data owner re-encrypting the data for each query inadvertently compel the data owner's involvement in the computation process, which is impractical. On the other hand, storing correlated randomness for data encryption on the server in advance, based on the number or length of queries, introduces another set of challenges. This method imposes significant storage burdens on the server because it requires storage on the order of $O(N|q||A|)$ for data of length N, with an alphabet size of $|A|$ and a query length of $|q|$. In the scheme of [27], re-encryption can be done without data owner, but the trusted third party has to be assumed. In any case, it is impossible to conceal the tree traversal pattern indifferent to the number of queries.

To reduce the burden on servers, clients, and owners while preventing data privacy breaches, we believe that data structures such as suffix arrays and BWT should be directly computed from encrypted data, particularly in scenarios where data outsourcing is necessary. As mentioned above, suffix sorting is the key technique for constructing string indexes and all the work mentioned in this subsection relies on it. Therefore, the goal of this study is to develop methods for computing the suffix sorting of a given string in a privacy-preserving manner. We refer to these methods as oblivious suffix sorting throughout this paper. We demonstrate that our oblivious suffix sorting protocols satisfy the following security and efficiency requirements.

Security. We focus on the situation where all sensitive data are outsourced to external computation servers. These servers are supposed to participate in the computation and some of them are allowed to be corrupted. It is assumed that the data and the query holders (client) may be distinct entities or organizations. We aim to achieve oblivious suffix sorting using the techniques of secure multi-party computation (MPC). Let the function to be computed by all servers be denoted as f, the data stored on the servers as T, and the query string as q, where T and q are the input for f. Our security goal is to prevent information leakage between servers, except for the lengths of T and q. During this process, the query holder does not participate in the computation, except to provide pre-shared randomness. Further, the holder does not gain any information other than q and $f(T, q)$. To achieve this goal all T, q and $f(T, q)$ are encrypted.

Efficiency. In this category, our goal is to surpass efficiency in terms of online communication and rounds complexity asymptotically compared with that of the naive solution, that is, sorting suffixes according to a character using secure stable sort techniques such as [2]. The estimation of efficiency will be based on the recent results of the 2-server + client-aided model given that many basic secure computations, such as secure AND operations and secure permutations, are currently most efficiently performed under this model. This naive solution requires $\mathrm{O}(n)$ online rounds for a string of length n. This automatically imposes on users $\mathrm{O}(n^2 \log^2 n)$ online communication bits, even when employing the state-of-art radix sort protocol, which asymptotically requires $\mathrm{O}(n \log^2 n)$ bits [2]. This volume of data could become unmanageable, especially when dealing with big data. Moreover, we demonstrate that our oblivious suffix sort provides efficient storage costs for text search compared with [29].

1.2 Methods and Contributions

We propose two oblivious suffix sorting algorithms, which are based on the plain-text suffix sorting algorithm of Larsson and Sadakane [24] and the algorithm of

Kärkkäinen *et al.* [19]. The former is not optimal but possesses a fast worst case time complexity $O(n \log n)$ for text length n; the "doubling" technique is the key component for achieving such worst case complexities. This technique helps reduce the number of recursions by "doubling" the length of referred prefixes of suffixes for each recursion, rendering the total number of sorting operations less than that using the naive approaches. The latter is a highly efficient suffix sort algorithm and requires only $O(n)$ time complexity for text length n. The basic idea of this algorithm is separating suffixes into two parts, sorting them, and finally merging the results. This procedure helps reduce not only the number of recursions (requiring $O(\log n)$ recursions) but also the alphabet size and length of the string by two thirds in each recursion.

The two aforementioned algorithms can be implemented in the context of secure computation using general MPC primitives, specifically the arithmetic black box and secure permutation functionalities described in Sect. 2.2. By utilizing the security notion of Universal Composability introduced by [8], subroutines based on these functionalities can run in parallel, making our oblivious suffix sort protocols more efficient.

To the best of the authors' knowledge, the proposed oblivious suffix sorting algorithms are the first protocol to compute the suffix array of a given string leaking only the input length in the MPC framework using communication of quasi-linear number of bits. Concretely, the costs of the two oblivious suffix sorting algorithms require asymptotically $O(n \log^3 n)$ (for the Larsson based one in Sect. 3.1) and $O(n \log^2 n)$ (for the Kärkkäinen based one in Sect. 3.3) communication bits with $O(\log^2 n)$ online communication rounds (for both algorithms) for text length n (the communication and round complexity of our scheme are evaluated in detail in Appendix D).

The primary contribution of this study is the secure and efficient constructions of SA and BWT, which naturally enable the following applications.

Applications. The data structure known as the longest common prefix (LCP), when combined with the SA, supports as many operations as a suffix tree with comparable efficiency [1]. It is proven that the LCP can be easily calculated from the SA in a plaintext setting [20]. Although our method differs significantly from that presented in [20], we demonstrate that the LCP can be also efficiently calculated using the SA with extra information in a privacy-preserving setting.

Once SA and BWT (and LCP) are calculated, the pattern search can be performed efficiently in the MPC model using oblivious RAM (ORAM) based MPC schemes. For instance, techniques such as those proposed by [18,21] enable secure array access with low communication and round complexity, enabling efficient pattern searches [13,28] automatically. The communication, round and storage complexities associated with the secure pattern searches with our oblivious suffix sorting are asymptotically evaluated in Sect. 4.

We further show our oblivious suffix sort can be also used to create indexes for multiple encrypted strings in Appendix E. As with the case of a single string, our oblivious protocol does not require any of the string owners to participate in the computation, nor does it assume the existence of a third party who can decrypt the encrypted strings to create these indexes. By performing suffix sorting on a concatenated string of multiple encrypted strings, we can securely compute the SA and the BWT for the concatenated string. These indexes can be used not only for text searching but also to measure the similarity between two given strings. We demonstrate that our oblivious suffix sorting techniques enable the secret calculation of similarity measures called Burrows Wheeler Similarity Distributions (BWSD) introduced by Yang [35].

2 Preliminaries

2.1 Notations and Definitions

Notations for Strings. Let A be a set of symbols, and let any string be composed of symbols from A. Throughout this paper, we assume A is encoded as a subset R of a ring of integers modulo m, denoted by $\mathbb{Z}_m$ for some $m \in \mathbb{N}$, where $R \subseteq \mathbb{Z}_m$. Thus, a string T is represented as a sequence of integers, and the lexicographical order between symbols corresponds to the standard order relation of integers in $\mathbb{Z}_m$. For $x_i, x_j \in R$, x_i is lexicographically smaller than x_j if and only if $x_i < x_j$, and they are equal if $x_i = x_j$.

Let $T[i]$ denote the i-th symbol of T, and let $T[i, j]$ denote the substring of T from the i-th to the j-th position (inclusive). The i-th suffix of $T \in R^n$ is denoted as $T[i, n-1]$ for $i \in \{0, \ldots, n-1\}$.

To define the lexicographical order between suffixes $T[i, n-1]$ and $T[j, n-1]$, we append a unique symbol \$, referred to as the sentinel symbol, to the end of T, resulting in a string T' of length $n+1$ (i.e., $T'[n] = \$$). The symbol \$ is the smallest in lexicographical order and does not appear elsewhere in T. This ensures a well-defined order between any two suffixes. Specifically, $T[i, n-1]$ is smaller than $T[j, n-1]$ if and only if:

$$(T'[i] < T'[j]) \vee (T'[i] = T'[j] \wedge T'[i+1, n] < T'[j+1, n]),$$

where the first differing symbol determines the order, with the comparison extending to subsequent symbols if the current symbols are equal.

Unless otherwise specified, T' throughout this paper denotes a string $T \in R^n$ with the sentinel symbol \$ appended (we may assume A is encoded as $R \subseteq \mathbb{Z}_m$ where $0 \notin R$, and \$ is encoded as 0). In Sects. 3.3 and Appendix E, we need a few more extra sentinel symbols as we consider SA of a string generated by concatenating multiple strings.

Additional Operations for Strings. A few additional operations as described below are required throughout the paper. For a bit sequence $B \in \mathbb{Z}_2^n$ of length n and for $k \in \mathbb{Z}_2$:

- $\mathsf{rank}_k(B, i)$ computes the number of k in prefix $B[0, i-1]$.
- $\mathsf{select}_k(B, i)$ computes the smallest $j \in \{0, \ldots, n-1\}$ that satisfies $\mathsf{rank}_k(B, j) = i$. If j does not exist, it returns n.

- $\mathsf{pred}_k(B,i)$ computes the position $j \in \{0,\ldots,i-1\}$ satisfies $B[j] = k$ and $B[l] = \neg k$ for all $j < l < i$ if exists, 0 otherwise.
- $\mathsf{succ}_k(B,i)$ computes the position $j \in \{i+1,\ldots,n-1\}$ satisfies $B[j] = k$ and $B[l] = \neg k$ for all $i < l < j$ if exists, n otherwise.

For a set of suffixes of a given string T denoted as $S_T := \{T'[i,n] : i \in \{0,\ldots,n\}\}$, a string $t \in S_T$ and subset $S \subseteq S_T$, we define the rank operation in different way as follows.

- $\mathsf{rank}(S,t)$ count the number of strings $s \in S$ that satisfy $s < t$.

For two given strings $S \in \mathbb{Z}_k^n, T \in \mathbb{Z}_m^n$, we write $S \odot T$ for the sequence of element-wise tuples, *i.e.*, $(S \odot T)[i] = (S[i], T[i])$ for $i \in \{0,\ldots,n-1\}$.

Suffix Array and BWT. *The suffix array* (SA) of a string, proposed by Manber and Myers [28], stores the starting positions of lexicographically sorted suffixes. It serves as an alternative to suffix trees [34], supporting efficient string operations such as full-text search. While SA demands more computation time than suffix trees, it requires less storage.

The suffix array I of a string T' is defined as an array representing the starting positions of T''s suffixes in lexicographical order. The array I satisfies the following condition for all $i \in \{0,\ldots,n-1\}$:

$$T'[I[i],n] < T'[I[i+1],n],$$

where $I[0] = n$ and $T'[I[0],n] = \$$ is lexicographically the smallest suffix.

The Burrows–Wheeler Transform (BWT), introduced by Burrows and Wheeler [7], transforms a string into another string containing the same symbols, but with substrings that tend to consist of repeated symbols grouped together. This property facilitates data compression, making BWT a widely used preprocessing technique for block-sort compression. Additionally, BWT is essential for constructing the FM-index [13], enabling efficient text searching with low memory usage.

Specifically, the BWT transforms a string T' into an array BW, where the i-th entry stores the preceding character of the i-th smallest suffix in T'. The array BW is defined as:

$$BW[i] = \begin{cases} T'[I[i]-1] & \text{if } I[i] \neq 0 \\ \$ & \text{if } I[i] = 0 \end{cases}$$

for $i \in \{0,\ldots,n\}$. Clearly, BW can be computed easily with suffix array.

A few examples showing the SA and BWT are given in Fig. 4 of Appendix B.

LCP Array. *The longest common prefix* (LCP) *array* is a complementary data structure to SA that can make the time complexity of some operations nearly as efficient as using suffix trees.

For a given string T', let $lcp(T'[i,n], T'[j,n])$ denote the length of the LCP between $T'[i,n]$ and $T'[j,n]$. The *LCP array* of T', denoted by $LCP_{T'}$, stores the LCP values between all lexicographically consecutive suffixes of T' and is defined as follows for $i \in \{0,\ldots,n-1\}$:

$$LCP_{T'}[i] = lcp(T'[I[i],n], T'[I[i+1],n])$$

FM-Index and Text-Search Application. The *FM-index* [13] is a data structure used for efficient text search. It stores the results of the LF function, defined as:

$$LF[i] = C[k] + \mathsf{rank}_k(BW, i)$$

where $k = BW[i]$ and the array $C[k]$ stores the number of symbols in T lexicographically smaller than k, with $C[\$] = -1$. The FM-index does not need to store the entire LF array; instead, it only requires C and BW with the ability to calculate rank_k on BW.

For a query string P of length p, the following text search algorithm determines the interval $[l,r]$, representing the range of suffixes in the lexicographically sorted order that match P:

Step 1 Set $c = P[p-1]$, $l = C[c]+1$, and $r = C[c+1]$. Initialize the counter $k = 1$.
Step 2 Update $[l,r]$ by setting $c = P[p-1-k]$, $l = C[c] + \mathsf{rank}_c(BW, l-1) + 1$, and $r = C[c] + \mathsf{rank}_c(BW, r)$. Increment k by 1.
Step 3 If $k = p-1$, terminate and return $[l,r]$. Otherwise, repeat Step 2.

Since the search starts from the last symbol of P and proceeds backwards, this method is referred to as 'backward search.' Examples of text search using the FM-index are shown in Figs. 4 and 4 in Appendix B.

2.2 Security Model

All of our proposed protocols are built by combining MPC primitives that realize various functionalities. Specifically, we design these protocols within the arithmetic black-box (ABB) model [10] and analyze their security using the universally composable (UC) security framework [8]. The ABB model serves as an abstraction of secret-sharing-based MPC schemes, modeling the ability of computation servers to perform basic arithmetic operations while preserving privacy. We assume ideal functionalities $\mathcal{F}_{ABB}$ and $\mathcal{F}_{perm}$, which define the secure operations available, and consider the $(\mathcal{F}_{ABB}, \mathcal{F}_{perm})$-hybrid model, where ideal calls to $\mathcal{F}_{ABB}$ and $\mathcal{F}_{perm}$ are allowed. Hereafter, we denote an ideal call to functionality $\mathcal{F}$ as $Y \leftarrow \mathcal{F}(X)$, where X and Y represent the input to and output from $\mathcal{F}$, respectively.

Functionalities. We describe the ideal functionalities $\mathcal{F}_{ABB}$ and $\mathcal{F}_{perm}$. The arithmetic domain is set to $\mathbb{Z}_m$ for some $m \in \mathbb{N}$, and $[\![x]\!]$ denotes the encryption of $x \in \mathbb{Z}_m$ under the protocol's encryption scheme. If $x \in \mathbb{Z}_2$, we use $[\![x]\!]^B$ to emphasize the binary domain. Negation is denoted by $\neg$ for $x \in \mathbb{Z}_2$. The functionalities are as follows:

- $\mathsf{XOR}([\![x]\!]^B, [\![y]\!]^B)$: Compute $[\![z]\!]^B \in \mathbb{Z}_2$ satisfying $z = x \oplus y$.
- $\mathsf{NOT}([\![x]\!]^B)$: Compute $[\![\bar{x}]\!]^B \in \mathbb{Z}_2$ satisfying $\bar{x} = \neg x$.
- $\mathsf{AND}([\![x]\!]^B, [\![y]\!]^B)$: Compute $[\![z]\!]^B \in \mathbb{Z}_2$ satisfying $z = x \wedge y$.
- $\mathsf{OR}([\![x]\!]^B, [\![y]\!]^B)$: Compute $[\![z]\!]^B \in \mathbb{Z}_2$ satisfying $z = x \vee y$.
- $\mathsf{Add}([\![v]\!], [\![w]\!])$: Compute $[\![z]\!] \in \mathbb{Z}_m$ satisfying $z = v + w$.
- $\mathsf{Mult}([\![v]\!], [\![w]\!])$: Compute $[\![z]\!] \in \mathbb{Z}_m$ satisfying $z = vw$.
- $\mathsf{SMult}(a, [\![w]\!])$: Compute $[\![z]\!] \in \mathbb{Z}_m$ satisfying $z = aw$.
- $\mathsf{IfThen}([\![x]\!]^B, [\![v]\!])$: Compute $[\![z]\!] \in \mathbb{Z}_m$ satisfying $z = xv$.
- $\mathsf{B2A}([\![x]\!]^B)$: Convert encryption of $x \in \mathbb{Z}_2$ into encryption of $x \in \mathbb{Z}_m$.

Note that the operations XOR, NOT, Add, and SMult are considered to require zero communication and round complexity, as justified in [10]. These operations are performed locally by each party, and their results are denoted as $[\![x]\!]^B \oplus [\![y]\!]^B$, $\neg[\![x]\!]^B$, $[\![v]\!] + [\![w]\!]$, and $a[\![w]\!]$, respectively. We also assume the functionality $\mathcal{F}_{perm}$, which supports secure permutations and secure stable sorting. Let $\mathfrak{S}_n$ denote the symmetric group of degree n. For a permutation $\sigma \in \mathfrak{S}_n$ and a vector $\boldsymbol{v} \in \mathbb{Z}_m^n$, the operation $\boldsymbol{v} \cdot \sigma \in R^n$ is defined as follows for all $i \in \{0, \ldots, n-1\}$.

$$(\boldsymbol{v} \cdot \sigma)[i] = \boldsymbol{v}[\sigma(i)]$$

For example, for the vector $\boldsymbol{v} = (2, 8, 5, 6, 1)$, the permutation $\sigma = (4, 0, 3, 1, 2)$ acts as $\boldsymbol{v} \cdot \sigma = (1, 2, 6, 8, 5)$. The notation $[\![\boldsymbol{w}]\!]$ denotes the encryption of a vector $\boldsymbol{w} := (\boldsymbol{w}[0], \ldots, \boldsymbol{w}[n-1]) \in \mathbb{Z}_m^n$. The encryption of vector $\boldsymbol{w} \in \mathbb{Z}_m^n$ means each entry of $\boldsymbol{w}$ is encrypted and $[\![\boldsymbol{w}]\!]$ is described as:

$$[\![\boldsymbol{w}]\!] = ([\![\boldsymbol{w}[0]]\!], \ldots, [\![\boldsymbol{w}[n-1]]\!]).$$

- $\mathsf{AppPerm}([\![\boldsymbol{w}]\!], [\![\sigma]\!])$: Compute $[\![\boldsymbol{v}]\!] \in \mathbb{Z}_m^n$ satisfying $\boldsymbol{v} = \boldsymbol{w} \cdot \sigma$ where $\sigma \in \mathfrak{S}_n$ and $\boldsymbol{w} \in \mathbb{Z}_m^n$,
- $\mathsf{AppInvPerm}([\![\boldsymbol{w}]\!], [\![\sigma]\!])$: Compute $[\![\boldsymbol{v}]\!] \in \mathbb{Z}_m^n$ satisfying $\boldsymbol{v} = \boldsymbol{w} \cdot \sigma^{-1}$ where $\sigma \in \mathfrak{S}_n$ and $\boldsymbol{w} \in \mathbb{Z}_m^n$,
- $\mathsf{RadixSort}([\![\boldsymbol{w}]\!])$: Compute $[\![\sigma]\!] \in \mathfrak{S}_n$ where σ is the stable sorting of $\boldsymbol{w}$, *i.e.*, $\boldsymbol{w} \cdot \sigma^{-1}$ is an array wherein all elements are in ascending order.

For the encryption of a degree n permutation $\sigma \in \mathfrak{S}_n$, denoted by $[\![\sigma]\!]$, we represent σ as a vector in $\mathbb{Z}_n^n$ and $[\![\sigma]\!]$ as the encryption of this vector. Specifically, $[\![\sigma]\!]$ is written as: $[\![\sigma]\!] = ([\![\sigma[0]]\!], \ldots, [\![\sigma[n-1]]\!])$. Several MPC protocols are available for computing $\mathcal{F}_{perm}$, with the protocols in [2] offering highly efficient computation. When input for $\mathsf{RadixSort}$ is the encryption of a Boolean vector, we use the notation $\mathsf{CountSort}$ instead of $\mathsf{RadixSort}$ to emphasize that the round and communication complexities are different.

Note that by combining the operations in $\mathcal{F}_{perm}$, we can extend the functionality RadixSort to accept a sequence of tuples as input, as described in [2]. Given the input $[\![\boldsymbol{w}]\!] \odot [\![\boldsymbol{w'}]\!]$, the extended RadixSort returns the encryption of the permutation $\sigma \in \mathfrak{S}_n$ that sorts $(\boldsymbol{w}, \boldsymbol{w'})$ using $\boldsymbol{w}$ as the primary key and $\boldsymbol{w'}$ as the secondary key. For simplicity, we will write a call to RadixSort for input $[\![\boldsymbol{w}]\!] \odot [\![\boldsymbol{w'}]\!]$ as $\mathsf{RadixSort}([\![\boldsymbol{w}]\!] \odot [\![\boldsymbol{w'}]\!])$.

The advantage of considering $(\mathcal{F}_{ABB}, \mathcal{F}_{perm})$-hybrid model is its adaptability to improvements in MPC primitives. For instance, if the efficiency of MPC primitives is enhanced, our protocols can seamlessly integrate these improvements. Additionally, this model allows protocols to operate under various cryptographic schemes (*e.g.*, , additive or Shamir's secret sharing, garbled circuits), as long as the required functionalities are securely implemented. This flexibility enables the development of protocols without dependence on specific security models, such as the type of adversary (semi-honest or malicious), the number of servers, or the use of particular cryptographic tools.

Our implementation (Appendix A) and computational cost estimation (Appendix D) are based on protocols in the secret-sharing and 2PC + client-aided model. This model is adopted due to its demonstrated UC-security and efficiency compared to other models. However, the building-block protocols from [2] are designed for the semi-honest setting, which means the implementation in this paper is secure only against semi-honest adversaries. Extending the protocols to support a malicious setting or additional servers would require modifications to all sub-protocols, which is beyond the scope of this work.

Universal Composability. In [8], an MPC framework, referred to as the universally composable (UC) framework, was proposed. This framework is aimed at discussing the possibility of using protocols in parallel while maintaining security. The universal composable theorem proved in [8] states that for an $\mathcal{F}$-hybrid protocol ρ, where even concurrent ideal calls to $\mathcal{F}$ are permitted, a protocol $\rho^{\mathcal{F}\to\pi}$ constructed by replacing each ideal call to $\mathcal{F}$ of ρ with π which computes $\mathcal{F}$ is at least as secure as ρ if π UC-securely computes $\mathcal{F}$.

Outline of Security Proofs. We use the result of [23], which states that every protocol that is perfectly secure in a stand-alone model with a straight line black-box simulator is also secure in a concurrent general composition. Owing to this result, along with the fact that all our protocols are deterministic, our tasks can be divided into the following two subtasks [14]: to prove our protocols are secure in a stand-alone model with a straight line black-box simulator and to prove the correctness of these protocols. The former is obvious because all our protocols do not require operations such as re-shares and reconstructions of secret shared elements. Therefore, for all our proposed protocols in Sect. 3 and Appendix E, we may omit the privacy proofs and only focus on proving the correctness.

We use the following additional operations which are already proved to satisfy UC-security assuming functionalities $\mathcal{F}_{ABB}$ and $\mathcal{F}_{perm}$ in [3,4]. Thus, their use does not impose extra burdens on our security proofs.

- $\mathsf{Propagate}([\![\boldsymbol{w}]\!]^B, [\![\boldsymbol{z}]\!])$: Compute $[\![\boldsymbol{v}]\!]$ where $\boldsymbol{v} \in R^n$ satisfies $\boldsymbol{v}[i] = \boldsymbol{z}[\mathsf{pred}_1(\boldsymbol{w}, i+1)]$.
- $\mathsf{GroupSum}([\![\boldsymbol{w}]\!]^B, [\![\boldsymbol{z}]\!])$: Compute $[\![\boldsymbol{v}]\!]$ where $\boldsymbol{v} \in R^n$ satisfies $\boldsymbol{v}[i] = 0$ if $\boldsymbol{w}[i] = 0$, and $\boldsymbol{v}[i] = \sum_{j=i}^{\mathsf{succ}_1(\boldsymbol{w},i)-1} \boldsymbol{z}[j]$ otherwise.
- $\mathsf{Equality}([\![x]\!], [\![y]\!])$: Compute $[\![b]\!]^B$ where $b \in \mathbb{Z}_2$ satisfies $b = 1$ if $x = y$, $b = 0$ otherwise.

For example, given the input $\boldsymbol{w} = (1,0,0,1,1,1,0,0)$ and $\boldsymbol{z} = (2,3,9,8,3,7,5,2)$, Propagate returns $\boldsymbol{v} = (2,2,2,8,3,7,7,7)$ and GroupSum returns $\boldsymbol{v} = (14,0,0,8,3,14,0,0)$. For both Propagate and GroupSum, the second input $\boldsymbol{z}$ is partitioned by $\boldsymbol{w}$ into smaller groups, each starting with 1 in $\boldsymbol{w}$ and extending to the position before the next 1. Within each partitioned group, Propagate duplicates the group's initial value across all positions within the group, and GroupSum computes the sum of all values in the group and stores this sum at the group's starting position, with zeros in the subsequent positions of the group.

3 Oblivious Suffix Sorting

In this section, we present our MPC scheme for oblivious suffix sorting. We introduce two protocols based on Larsson and Sadakane's algorithm [24] and the DC3 algorithm [19] in Sects. 3.1 and 3.3, respectively. Each protocol is tailored to optimize either concrete or asymptotic costs and demonstrates superior performance compared to the naive method described below. Additionally, we propose a protocol for oblivious LCP array construction in Sect. 3.2. To save space, the secure computation protocols Π_{LS}, Π_{DC3}, and Π_{LCP}, which correspond to the oblivious suffix sorting and LCP array construction described above, are presented together below. We define the functionalities SuffixSort and LCP as follows:

- $\mathsf{SuffixSort}([\![T']\!])$: compute $[\![I]\!]$ where $I \in \mathfrak{S}_{n+1}$ is the SA of string T'.
- $\mathsf{LCP}([\![T']\!])$: compute $[\![\boldsymbol{w}]\!]$ where $\boldsymbol{w}$ is the LCP array of string T'.

Note that the BWT of T' can be derived from the SA I in a constant number of communication rounds. Specifically, the parties first update $[\![I[i]]\!]$ to $[\![I[i]]\!] := [\![I[i]]\!] - 1$ for all i, and then simply apply the updated $[\![I]\!]$ to T' by invoking $\mathsf{AppPerm}([\![T']\!], [\![I]\!])$ to obtain the BWT.

Naive Suffix Sort. The simplest method for suffix sorting is to compare the lexicographical order of suffixes by examining their characters from the end. Representing each suffix as $S_i := T'[i, n]$ $(i \in \{0, \ldots, n\})$, the naive solution proceeds as follows.

First, compare the second-to-last character of the longest suffix S_0 with the last character of S_1 (*i.e.*, sorting $T'[n-1, n]$) to order S_0 and S_1 lexicographically. Next, compare the third-to-last character of S_0, the second-to-last character of S_1, and the last character of S_2 (*i.e.*, sorting $T'[n-2, n]$) and rearrange them lexicographically. Repeating this process, all $S_0, \ldots, S_n$ are sorted by the $(n-1)$-st round. In a privacy-preserving manner, the character order in each

Protocol 1. Π_{LS}

Inputs. $[\![T']\!]$ where $T' \in R^{n+1}$.
Output. $[\![I]\!]$ where $I \in \mathfrak{S}_{n+1}$ is the SA of T'.

1. $[\![I']\!] \leftarrow \mathsf{RadixSort}([\![T']\!])$
2. $[\![w]\!] \leftarrow \mathsf{AppInvPerm}([\![T']\!], [\![I']\!])$
3. $[\![L]\!]^B \leftarrow \mathsf{Grouping}([\![w]\!])$
4. $h := 1$
5. While $h < n$ do:
   /* labeling step */
   (a) $[\![V^{(0)}]\!] \leftarrow \mathsf{Propagate}([\![L]\!]^B, id)$
   (b) $[\![V^{(1)}]\!] \leftarrow \mathsf{AppPerm}([\![V^{(0)}]\!], [\![I']\!])$
   (c) $[\![V^{(2)}[i]]\!] := [\![V^{(1)}[i+h \mod n+1]]\!]$ for all $i \in \{0, \ldots, n\}$
   /* sorting step */
   (d) $[\![V]\!] := [\![V^{(1)}]\!] \odot [\![V^{(2)}]\!]$
   (e) $[\![I']\!] \leftarrow \mathsf{RadixSort}([\![V]\!])$
   (f) $[\![w^{(2)}]\!] \leftarrow \mathsf{AppInvPerm}([\![V^{(2)}]\!], [\![I']\!])$
   /* grouping step */
   (g) $[\![L_1]\!]^B := [\![L]\!]^B$
   (h) $[\![L_2]\!]^B \leftarrow \mathsf{Grouping}([\![w^{(2)}]\!])$
   (i) $[\![L[i]]\!]^B \leftarrow \mathsf{OR}([\![L_1[i]]\!]^B, [\![L_2[i]]\!]^B)$ for $i \in \{0, \ldots, n\}$
   (j) $h := 2h$
6. $[\![I]\!] \leftarrow \mathsf{AppInvPerm}(\boldsymbol{id}, [\![I']\!])$

Protocol 2. Π_{LCP}

Inputs. $[\![T]\!]$, where $T \in R^n$.
Output. $[\![\boldsymbol{w}]\!]$, where $\boldsymbol{w}[i] = LCP_{T'}[i]$ for all $i \in \{0, \ldots, n-1\}$.

1. $([\![I]\!], \{[\![V_h^{(1)}]\!]\}_{0 \leq h < \lceil \log n \rceil}) \leftarrow \Pi_{LS}([\![T]\!])$
2. $h := \lceil \log n \rceil - 1$
3. $[\![w[i]]\!] := 0$ for $i \in \{0, \ldots, n-1\}$
4. While $h \geq 0$ do:
   (a) $[\![V]\!] \leftarrow \mathsf{AppInvPerm}([\![V_h^{(1)}]\!], [\![I]\!])$
   (b) $[\![I^{(a)}[i]]\!] := [\![I[i]]\!] + [\![w[i]]\!]$ for $i \in \{0, \ldots, n-1\}$
   (c) $[\![I^{(b)}[i]]\!] := [\![I[i+1]]\!] + [\![w[i]]\!]$ for $i \in \{0, \ldots, n-1\}$
   (d) $[\![V^{(a)}]\!] \leftarrow \mathsf{BatchAccess}([\![V]\!], [\![I^{(a)}]\!])$
   (e) $[\![V^{(b)}]\!] \leftarrow \mathsf{BatchAccess}([\![V]\!], [\![I^{(b)}]\!])$
   (f) $[\![\boldsymbol{c}[i]]\!]^B \leftarrow \mathsf{Equality}([\![V^{(a)}[i]]\!], [\![V^{(b)}[i]]\!])$ for $i \in \{0, \ldots, n-1\}$
   (g) $[\![\boldsymbol{d}[i]]\!] \leftarrow \mathsf{IfThen}([\![\boldsymbol{c}[i]]\!]^B, 2^h)$ for $i \in \{0, \ldots, n-1\}$
   (h) $[\![\boldsymbol{w}[i]]\!] := [\![\boldsymbol{w}[i]]\!] + [\![\boldsymbol{d}[i]]\!]$ for $i \in \{0, \ldots, n-1\}$
   (i) $h := h - 1$

round can be computed using RadixSort, and the rearrangement is performed with AppInvPerm.

The communication cost of RadixSort for an array of length n is approximately $n \log^2 n$ using the state-of-the-art algorithm [2]. Thus, the total communication cost is $\sum_{i=2}^{n} i(\log i)^2$, approximated as $n^2 \log^2 n$ (as RadixSort dominates each round).

3.1 Oblivious Suffix Sorting Protocol Based on Larsson-Sadakane

We first propose a protocol for oblivious suffix sorting based on Larsson and Sadakane's algorithm [24].

Larsson and Sadakane's algorithm is defined iteratively: in the h-th iteration, the goal is to permute the suffixes with respect to the first 2^h symbols. Let T' be a string of length $n+1$ whose final symbol is \$. We say a permutation $I \in \mathfrak{S}_{n+1}$ is in h-order if the suffixes in T' are sorted by applying I in the lexicographical order with respect to the first h symbols. The h-th iteration of the algorithm provides a permutation I in 2^h-order from a permutation in 2^{h-1}-order, so that after $\log n$ iterations we can obtain a permutation in n-order, that is, the suffix array of T'.

The main idea of our protocol is to use the grouped vector technique. Larsson and Sadakane's algorithm achieves efficiency by operating not directly on the suffixes, but on numeric labels assigned to suffixes that share the same prefix. Similarly, in our protocol, we securely assign the same numeric label to all the suffixes with the same first 2^{h-1} symbols during the h-th iteration, which is used as a key for sorting. To implement this, we use an encrypted bit vector as an intermediate data for grouping suffixes with the same prefix. We define the functionality Grouping for oblivious grouping below. Appendix C provides a protocol for realizing Grouping.

- Grouping($[\![V]\!]$) : Compute $[\![L]\!]$ where $L \in \mathbb{Z}_2^n$ satisfying $L[0] = 1$, and $L[i] = 1$ if and only if $V[i] \neq V[i-1]$.

We describe a protocol for SuffixSort in Protocol 1. The protocol takes $O(\log^2 n)$ online communication rounds and $O(n \log^3 n)$ online communication bits. We provide the performance estimation in Appendix D. The underlying algorithm is a data-oblivious variant of the algorithm of [24] and consists of three key steps: labeling, sorting, and grouping. The role of each step in the h-th iteration is as follows:

- Labeling step (Steps 5a–5c). The goal is to assign the same numeric label to suffixes whose first 2^h symbols are the same. Each suffix is labeled with a pair of values: $V^{(1)}$ distinguishes the first 2^{h-1} symbols, and $V^{(2)}$ distinguishes the next 2^{h-1} symbols. Once $V^{(1)}$ is computed using Propagate with the bit vector L for grouping, $V^{(2)}$ can be easily computed due to the nature of string suffixes.
- Sorting step (Steps 5e–5f). This step aims to sort the suffixes in ascending order based on the first 2^h symbols. We can obtain the permutation I in 2^h-order by sorting $V^{(1)}$ as the primary key and $V^{(2)}$ as the secondary key. Because we use radix sort, we first sort the suffixes using $V^{(2)}$ as the key, then sort them again using $V^{(1)}$ as the key.
- Grouping step (Steps 5g–5i). The goal here is to generate a bit vector L for grouping the suffixes according to the first 2^h symbols. Using the secondary key $\boldsymbol{w}^{(2)}$ of the sorted array, we call Grouping to compute the bit vector L_2, and then compute the element-wise OR of L_2 and L to obtain the group information over the first 2^h symbols.

Correctness of Protocol Π_{LS}. In Step (1)–(5a), $\boldsymbol{w}$ is the stable sorted sequence of T' from the definitions of RadixSort and AppInvPerm. The bit sequence L has length $n+1$, which suffices $L[0] = 1$, $L[i] = 1$ if and only if $\boldsymbol{w}[i] \neq \boldsymbol{w}[i-1]$ from Grouping, and by Propagate, the array $V^{(0)}$ satisfies the following for all $i \in \{1, \ldots, n\}$.

$$V^{(0)}[i] = \begin{cases} id[i] & \text{if } \boldsymbol{w}[i] \neq \boldsymbol{w}[i-1] \\ V^{(0)}[i-1] & \text{otherwise} \end{cases}$$

By the definitions of RadixSort and AppInvPerm, $\boldsymbol{w}$ is the stable sorted sequence of T'. The functionality Grouping gives the bit vector L of length $n+1$, where

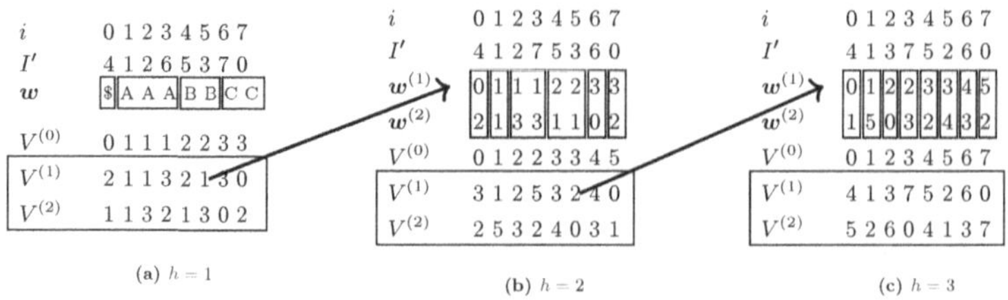

Fig. 1. Calculation Example of Π_{LS}

$L[0] = 1$ and $L[i] = 1$ if and only if $\boldsymbol{w}[i] \neq \boldsymbol{w}[i-1]$. Since $V^{(0)}$ is the output of $\mathsf{Propagate}([\![L]\!]^B, id)$, it holds that $V^{(0)}[i] < V^{(0)}[i+1]$ if and only if $\boldsymbol{w}[i] < \boldsymbol{w}[i+1]$. Using this, when $h = 1$ in Step (5), $T'[i] < T'[j]$ if and only if $V^{(1)}[i] < V^{(1)}[j]$ holds for any two distinct $i, j \in \{0, \ldots, n\}$. Therefore $T'[i, i+1] < T'[j, j+1]$ if and only if $(V^{(1)} \odot V^{(2)})[i] < (V^{(1)} \odot V^{(2)})[j]$ holds and I' calculated in (5e) is in the 2-order because $V^{(2)}$ is now an array in the i-th position wherein the order of a symbol following $T'[i]$ is stored.

If we assume that in the beginning of the k-th recursion ($h = 2^k$), $T'[i, i+h] < T'[j, j+h]$ if and only if $V^{(1)}[i] < V^{(1)}[j]$ holds, then clearly $T'[i, i+2h] < T'[j, j+2h]$ if and only if $(V^{(1)} \odot V^{(2)})[i] < (V^{(1)} \odot V^{(2)})[j]$ holds and I in (5e) is in the $2h$-order.

By induction, at the end of the $\lceil \log n \rceil - 1$-th recursion $T'[i, i+2^{\lceil \log n \rceil}] < T'[j, j+2^{\lceil \log n \rceil}]$ if and only if $(V^{(1)} \odot V^{(2)})[i] < (V^{(1)} \odot V^{(2)})[j]$ holds and I in (5e) is in the $2^{\lceil \log n \rceil}$-order. Now, clearly, $V^{(1)}[i]$ and $V^{(1)}[j]$ are distinct for any distinct $i, j \in \{n-2^k, \ldots, n\}$ at the end of any k-th recursion because $V^{(1)}[n] = 0$ holds for any k. Thus, at the end of the $\lceil \log n \rceil$-th recursion, there is an order-based relation between all two distinct elements of the array $V^{(1)} \odot V^{(2)}$. It can be said that I obtained in (6) is the SA of T'. □

Example. Fig. 1 illustrates the execution of Protocol 1 when the input string is "BAACBAC\$". The initial step performs sorting of the input string to obtain "\$AAABBCC", and then groups the same symbols, as shown in (a) of Fig. 1. In Labeling step of the h-th iteration, the parties assign a numeric label to each symbol in the sorted sequence by Propagate to obtain the label array $V^{(0)}$, and then compute the label array $V^{(1)}$ for the original sequence by invoking AppPerm and the label array $V^{(2)}$ by circularly shifting $V^{(1)}$ to the left by 2^{h-1} symbols. In Sorting step, the parties sort the numeric label $(V^{(1)}, V^{(2)})$ to obtain the sorted sequence $(\boldsymbol{w}^{(1)}, \boldsymbol{w}^{(2)})$ and the permutation I', as represented by an arrow in Fig. 1. In Grouping step, the parties call Grouping to generate the bit vector that partitions $\boldsymbol{w}^{(2)}$ into intervals according to the stored values, and compute the element-wise OR with the partition of $\boldsymbol{w}^{(1)}$, which corresponds to L already computed in the previous iteration. By repeating this procedure, the parties finally obtain $I = I'^{-1} = (7, 1, 5, 2, 0, 4, 6, 3)$, which corresponds to the SA of "BAACBAC\$".

3.2 Oblivious LCP Array Construction

We next propose a protocol for computing LCP arrays as an extension of Π_{LS}. Our data-oblivious algorithm is based on global accesses to group arrays constructed in Π_{LS}.

Base Algorithm. Let $\alpha^{(i)} = LCP_{T'}[i]$ for $i \in \{1, \ldots, n\}$. Let $k = \lceil \log n \rceil - 1$. We write $\alpha_j^{(i)}$ for the j-th bit (from the LSB) in the binary representation of $\alpha^{(i)}$. Note that $\alpha^{(i)} = \sum_{j=0}^{k} 2^j \alpha_j^{(i)}$. The value $\alpha^{(i)}$ can be computed as follows:

(a) Set $d = 0$ and $w_{-1}^{(i)} = 0$ for $i \in \{1, \ldots, n\}$.
(b) We check if the first 2^{k-d} characters of $T'[I[i] + w_{d-1}^{(i)}, n]$ and $T'[I[i+1] + w_{d-1}^{(i)}, n]$ match. If so, we set $\alpha_{k-d}^{(i)}$ to 1; otherwise, we set $\alpha_{k-d}^{(i)}$ to 0. Let $w_d^{(i)} = \sum_{j=k-d}^{k} 2^j \alpha_j^{(i)}$.
(c) We increment d by 1.
(d) If $d = k$, return $w_d^{(i)}$; otherwise, go back to Step (b).

We can easily verify that $w_k^{(i)} = LCP_{T'}[i]$ because the algorithm is simply the binary search based on the result of previous match $\alpha_{k-(d-1)}^{(i)}$ and $w_{d-1}^{(i)}$. As an example, consider calculating the length of the LCP for two strings "aabcabbcac· · ·" and "aabcabbabb· · ·", and assume that they are suffixes of some larger string, with $k = \lceil \log n \rceil - 1 = 3$. Initially, we examine the first $2^3 = 8$ characters of these strings to determine if they match. In this case, they do not match entirely, leading us to set $\alpha_3^{(i)} = 0$ and subsequently $w_0^{(i)} = 2^3 \alpha_3^{(i)} = 0$. In the next step, we check the first $2^2 = 4$ characters of each string, and we find that they match. Therefore, we update $\alpha_2^{(i)} = 1$ and calculate $w_1^{(i)} = 2^2 \alpha_2^{(i)} = 4$. Continuing in this manner, we confirm that the next $2^1 = 2$ characters also match, as do the subsequent $2^0 = 1$ character. We eventually obtain the value $w_3^{(i)} = 7$ which represents the length of LCP of these two strings.

To implement Step (b) within the setting of secure computation, it must have the capability to access any x symbols behind the starting position of all suffixes simultaneously. To satisfy this requirement, we propose a protocol $\Pi_{BatchAccess}$ for realizing the following functionality BatchAccess. The definition of $\Pi_{BatchAccess}$ is provided in Appendix C.

- BatchAccess($[\![\boldsymbol{v}]\!], [\![\boldsymbol{idx}]\!]$) : compute $\boldsymbol{w} \in R^n$ satisfying $\boldsymbol{w}[i] = \boldsymbol{v}[\boldsymbol{idx}[i]]$ for all $i \in \{0, \ldots, n-1\}$ where $\boldsymbol{v} \in R^n$ and $\boldsymbol{idx} \in \{0, \ldots, n-1\}^n$.

We describe a protocol for realizing LCP in protocol Π_{LCP}. The protocol uses all $V^{(1)}$ produced in each iteration of Π_{LS} to compute $\alpha_h^{(i)}$ for all $i \in \{1, \ldots, n\}$ and $h \in \{0, \ldots, \lceil \log n \rceil - 1\}$. We write $V_h^{(1)}$ for the 2^h-order group of T'. Although the protocol Π_{LS} is not designed to output each $V_h^{(1)}$, it can be easily modified to output them. We assume that Π_{LS} outputs all encrypted $V_h^{(1)}$.

Correctness of Protocol Π_{LCP}. Note that V is the array in which the 2^h-order of each suffix is indicated in corresponding position of T'. When $h = \lceil \log n \rceil$, $V^{(a)}[i]$ and $V^{(b)}[i]$ simply indicate the2^h-order of suffix $T'[I[i], n]$ and suffix $T'[I[i+1], n]$, respectively. Thus $\mathbf{c}[i] = 1$ at Step(4f) means that suffixes $T'[I[i], n]$ and $T'[I[i+1], n]$ have common prefix of length 2^h, and they do not when $\mathbf{c}[i] = 0$. Now, $\boldsymbol{w}[i]$ is $2^h \alpha^{(i)}_{\lceil \log n \rceil - 1}$ because $\mathbf{c}[i]$ and $\alpha^{(i)}_{\lceil \log n \rceil - 1}$ are clearly identical.

When $h = \lceil \log n \rceil - k$, suppose that $\boldsymbol{w}$ at Step(4h) satisfies the following

$$\boldsymbol{w}[i] = \sum_{j=1}^{k} 2^{\lceil \log n \rceil - j} \alpha^{(i)}_{\lceil \log n \rceil - j} \tag{1}$$

where $\alpha^{(i)}$ is the one defined at the top of Sect. 3.2. Then at $h = \lceil \log n \rceil - (k+1)$ iteration of the protocol, $V^{(a)}[i]$ indicates 2^h-order of suffix $T'[I[i + \boldsymbol{w}[i]], n]$ and $V^{(b)}[i]$ indicates that of $T'[I[i+1+\boldsymbol{w}[i]], n]$ according to definition of BatchAccess. If $V^{(a)}[i]$ and $V^{(b)}[i]$ are matched, then $\mathbf{c}[i] = 1$ at step(4f), and $\mathbf{c}[i] = 0$, otherwise. This indicates that $\mathbf{c}[i]$ is identical to $\alpha^{(i)}_{\lceil \log n \rceil - (k+1)}$, and thus, (1) is satisfied also in the $h = \lceil \log n \rceil - (k+1)$ case. By induction, $\boldsymbol{w}$ is identical to the LCP array of T. □

3.3 Oblivious Suffix Sorting Protocol Based on DC3

We next propose a protocol for oblivious suffix sorting that achieves low asymptotic complexity. The protocol is a privacy-preserving version of the difference cover modulo 3 (DC3) algorithm [19]. We assume that the alphabet set A is encoded to $R \subset \mathbb{Z}_m$ such that $0, 1, 2 \notin R$, which ensures three sentinel symbols smaller than any symbols in A. The input string T over A is supposed to be concatenated with these sentinel symbols at the tail of T in our oblivious DC3 algorithm. Let T' be a modified string of T with sentinel symbols appended as follows:

$$T'[i] = \begin{cases} T[i] & \text{if } 0 \leq i \leq n-1 \\ 2 & \text{if } i = n \\ 1 & \text{if } i = n+1 \text{ and } n+2 \leq 3(n'+1) \\ 0 & \text{if } i = n+2 \text{ and } n+3 = 3(n'+1) \\ 0 & \text{if } i \geq 3(n'+1) \end{cases}$$

The basic idea behind the DC3 algorithm is to divide the set of suffixes S_T of the input string T into three subsets $S^{(0)}$, $S^{(1)}$, and $S^{(2)}$ based on their starting positions. The subset $S^{(k)}$ is defined as $S^{(k)} := \{T'[i, 3n'+2] \mid i = k \pmod 3\}$, where $n' = \lfloor n/3 \rfloor$. Due to the properties of difference cover samples, it is sufficient to compute the sorting for only two of these three subsets to construct the suffix array of T.

We describe an asymptotically efficient protocol for suffix sorting in Protocol 3. The protocol takes $O(\log^2 n)$ online communication rounds and $O(n \log^2 n)$ online communication bits. Below is an outline of the protocol:

Protocol 3. Π_{DC3}

Inputs. $[\![T]\!]$, where $T \in R^n$.
Output. $[\![I]\!]$, where $I \in \mathfrak{S}_{n+1}$ is the SA of T.

1. $[\![T^{(j)}[i]]\!] := [\![T'[3i+j]]\!]$ for $i \in \{0,\dots,n'\}$, $j \in \{0,1,2,3,4\}$
   /* Reduction step */
2. $[\![R^{(1,2)}]\!] := ([\![T^{(1)}]\!] \odot [\![T^{(2)}]\!] \odot [\![T^{(3)}]\!]) \parallel ([\![T^{(2)}]\!] \odot [\![T^{(3)}]\!] \odot [\![T^{(4)}]\!])$
3. $[\![J]\!] \leftarrow \mathsf{RadixSort}([\![R^{(1,2)}]\!])$
4. For $(j,k) = (1,2),(2,3),(3,4)$ do:
   (a) $[\![U^{(j,k)}]\!] \leftarrow \mathsf{AppInvPerm}(([\![T^{(j)}]\!] \parallel [\![T^{(k)}]\!]), [\![J]\!])$
   (b) $[\![L^{(j)}]\!]^B \leftarrow \mathsf{Grouping}([\![U^{(j,k)}]\!])$
5. $[\![L[i]]\!]^B \leftarrow \mathsf{OR}([\![L^{(1)}[i]]\!]^B, \mathsf{OR}([\![L^{(2)}[i]]\!]^B, [\![L^{(3)}[i]]\!]^B))$ for $i \in \{0,\dots 2n'+1\}$
6. $[\![V]\!] \leftarrow \mathsf{Propagate}([\![L]\!]^B, \boldsymbol{id})$
7. $[\![T^{(1,2)}]\!] \leftarrow \mathsf{AppPerm}([\![V]\!], [\![J]\!])$
   /* Recursion */
8. $[\![I^{(1,2)}]\!] \leftarrow \mathsf{SuffixSort}([\![T^{(1,2)}]\!])$
   /* Merge step 1: sorting suffixes in $S^{(i)} \cup S^{(j)}$ */
9. $[\![\sigma^{(1,2)}]\!] \leftarrow \mathsf{AppInvPerm}(\boldsymbol{id}, [\![I^{(1,2)}]\!])$
10. $\pi^{(0,1)} := \boldsymbol{id}$
11. $\pi^{(0,2)} := (2n'+1, n'+1, n'+2, \dots, 2n'-1, 2n', 0, 1, \dots, n'-1, n')$
12. $[\![T^{(0,1)}]\!] := [\![T^{(0)}]\!] \parallel [\![T^{(1)}]\!]$
13. $[\![T^{(0,2)}]\!] := ([\![T^{(0)}]\!] \odot [\![T^{(1)}]\!]) \parallel ([\![T^{(2)}]\!] \odot [\![T^{(3)}]\!])$
14. For $(j,k) = (0,1),(0,2)$ do:
    (a) $[\![U^{(j,k)}]\!] \leftarrow \mathsf{AppPerm}([\![T^{(j,k)}]\!] \cdot \pi^{(j,k)}, [\![I^{(1,2)}]\!])$
    (b) $[\![\rho^{(j,k)}]\!] \leftarrow \mathsf{RadixSort}([\![U^{(j,k)}]\!])$
    (c) $[\![\sigma^{(j,k)}]\!] \leftarrow \mathsf{AppInvPerm}([\![\rho^{(j,k)}]\!], [\![I^{(1,2)}]\!]) \cdot \pi^{(j,k)^{-1}}$
    /* Merge step 2: sorting suffixes in $S^{(i)}$ */
15. For $(j,k) = (1,2),(0,1)$ do:
    (a) $[\![B^{(j,k)}]\!]^B \leftarrow \mathsf{AppInvPerm}((0^{n'+1} \parallel 1^{n'+1}), [\![\sigma^{(j,k)}]\!])$
    (b) $[\![C^{(j,k)}]\!] \leftarrow \mathsf{CountSort}([\![B^{(j,k)}]\!]^B)$
    (c) $[\![D^{(j,k)}]\!] \leftarrow \mathsf{AppPerm}([\![C^{(j,k)}]\!], [\![\sigma^{(j,k)}]\!])$
    /* Merge step 3: construction of inverse SA and SA */
16. $[\![\boldsymbol{p}^{(0)}[i]]\!] := [\![\sigma^{(0,1)}[i]]\!] + [\![\sigma^{(0,2)}[i]]\!] - [\![D^{(0,1)}[i]]\!]$ for $i \in \{0,\dots,n'\}$
17. $[\![\boldsymbol{p}^{(1)}[i]]\!] := [\![\sigma^{(0,1)}[i+n'+1]]\!] + [\![\sigma^{(1,2)}[i]]\!] - [\![D^{(1,2)}[i]]\!]$ for $i \in \{0,\dots,n'\}$
18. $[\![\boldsymbol{p}^{(2)}[i]]\!] := [\![\sigma^{(0,2)}[i+n'+1]]\!] + [\![\sigma^{(1,2)}[i+n'+1]]\!] - [\![D^{(1,2)}[i+n'+1]]\!] + (n'+1)$ for $i \in \{0,\dots,n'\}$
19. $[\![\sigma[3i+j]]\!] := [\![\boldsymbol{p}^{(j)}[i]]\!]$ for $i \in \{0,\dots,n'\}$, $j \in \{0,1,2\}$
20. $[\![I]\!] \leftarrow \mathsf{AppInvPerm}(\boldsymbol{id}, [\![\sigma]\!])$

- Reduction Step (Steps 2–7). This step generates a new string $T^{(1,2)}$ through numeric labeling. $T^{(1,2)}$ is a sequence with a length of two-thirds of T, where each symbol represents a label value assigned to a substring of length 3 starting at positions congruent to 1 (mod 3) or 2 (mod 3). The method of oblivious labeling is similar to Π_{LS}. By definition, the SA of $T^{(1,2)}$ corresponds to the sorting of suffixes in $S^{(1)} \cup S^{(2)}$.
- Recursion Step (Step 8). This step performs suffix sorting of $T^{(1,2)}$. It is well-defined because the input length reduces to two-thirds with each iteration. Remark that the parties must determine the exit condition for the recursion before the protocol begins. For example, by setting a threshold on the input

length of $T^{(1,2)}$ at Step 8, and switching to Π_{LS} when the length falls below this threshold, the correct calculation of $I^{(1,2)}$ can be ensured.

- Merge Step (Steps 9–20). This step securely computes the SA of T using the SA of $T^{(1,2)}$, in constant communication rounds. The property of difference cover samples allows us to determine the permutations $\sigma^{(0,1)}$, $\sigma^{(0,2)}$, $\sigma^{(0)}$, $\sigma^{(1)}$, and $\sigma^{(2)}$, which sort the suffixes in $S^{(0)} \cup S^{(1)}$, $S^{(0)} \cup S^{(2)}$, $S^{(0)}$, $S^{(1)}$, and $S^{(2)}$, respectively. Since these permutations store the rank of each suffix within its respective suffix set, we can derive the overall rank of each suffix across all suffixes as follows:

$$\mathsf{rank}(S_T, s) = \begin{cases} \mathsf{rank}(S^{(0)} \cup S^{(1)}, s) + \mathsf{rank}(S^{(0)} \cup S^{(2)}, s) - \mathsf{rank}(S^{(0)}, s) & \text{if } s \in S^{(0)} \\ \mathsf{rank}(S^{(1)} \cup S^{(2)}, s) + \mathsf{rank}(S^{(0)} \cup S^{(1)}, s) - \mathsf{rank}(S^{(1)}, s) & \text{if } s \in S^{(1)} \\ \mathsf{rank}(S^{(0)} \cup S^{(2)}, s) + \mathsf{rank}(S^{(1)} \cup S^{(2)}, s) - \mathsf{rank}(S^{(2)}, s) & \text{if } s \in S^{(2)} \end{cases} \quad (2)$$

The resulting rank values form the inverse suffix array of T, which can be inverted to obtain the SA of T.

Correctness of Protocol Π_{DC3}. For the same reason as in the protocol Π_{LS}, we can easily check that the reduction step correctly generate the new string $T^{(1,2)}$, where each label represents the order of the corresponding symbol in $R^{(1,2)}$.

In the merge step 1, since $I^{(1,2)}$ is the sorting of $R^{(1,2)}$, the permutation $\sigma^{(0,1)}$ indicates the sorting of $T^{(0,1)} \odot R^{(1,2)}$, which corresponds to the sorting of suffixes in $S^{(0)} \cup S^{(1)}$. Similarly, the permutation $\sigma^{(0,2)}$ is the sorting of $T^{(0,2)} \odot (R^{(1,2)} \cdot \pi^{(1,2)})$, which corresponds to the sorting of suffixes in $S^{(0)} \cup S^{(2)}$. The merge step 2 generates the arrays $D^{(0,1)}$ and $D^{(1,2)}$, which correspond to the results of radix sorting of $(0^{n'+1} \parallel 1^{n'+1}) \odot (S^{(0)} \cup S^{(1)})$ and $(0^{n'+1} \parallel 1^{n'+1}) \odot (S^{(1)} \cup S^{(2)})$, respectively. This means that the first and second half of $D^{(j,k)}$ correspond to $\{\mathsf{rank}(S^{(j)}, T'[3i+j, 3n'+2])\}_{0 \le i \le n'}$ and $\{\mathsf{rank}(S^{(k)}, T'[3i+k, 3n'+2]) + n' + 1\}_{0 \le i \le n'}$, respectively.

Because the equation (2) holds, the permutation σ indicates the inverse suffix array of T', and ApplInvPerm provides the inverse of σ, which is the SA of T'. □

Example. We present a computational example of Π_{DC3} when the input string T is "$CBBABBAB$". In preprocessing, the parties locally append sentinel symbols to T and obtain T' as "$CBBABBAB20\cdots$".

In reduction step, the parties first construct the sequence $R^{(1,2)}$ as $R^{(1,2)} :=$ ("BBA", "BBA", "$B20$", "BAB", "BAB", "200") . A call to RadixSort, followed by an oblivious permutation application, sorts $R^{(1,2)}$ in ascending order. By calling Grouping for each digit and computing the OR of the results, the parties obtain the bit vector that divides the sorted sequence of $R^{(1,2)}$ into intervals that store the same values, and by Propagate, all entries in each interval are labeled with a common value. Consequently, the parties obtain a new string $T^{(1,2)}$ of length 6 as $T^{(1,2)} := (3, 3, 1, 2, 2, 0)$.

In recursion step, the parties call SuffixSort with input $T^{(1,2)}$ to obtain the SA $I^{(1,2)}$ of $T^{(1,2)}$ as $I^{(1,2)} = (5, 2, 4, 3, 1, 0)$.

In merge step 1, the parties first construct $T^{(0,1)}$ and $T^{(0,2)}$, which correspond to the first symbols of the suffixes in $S^{(0)} \cup S^{(1)}$ and the first two symbols of the suffixes in $S^{(0)} \cup S^{(2)}$, respectively as $T^{(0,1)} = (\text{"}C\text{"}, \text{"}A\text{"}, \text{"}A\text{"}, \text{"}B\text{"}, \text{"}B\text{"}, \text{"}B\text{"})$ and $T^{(0,2)} = (\text{"}CB\text{"}, \text{"}AB\text{"}, \text{"}AB\text{"}, \text{"}BA\text{"}, \text{"}BA\text{"}, \text{"}20\text{"})$. Since $I^{(1,2)}$ is the sorting of suffixes in $S^{(1)} \cup S^{(2)}$, the parties can use it as a key to sort $T^{(0,1)}$ and $T^{(0,2)}$ according to their preceding substrings, resulting in $U^{(0,1)}$ and $U^{(0,2)}$ satisfying $U^{(0,1)} \odot (R^{(1,2)} \cdot I^{(1,2)}) = (\text{"}B200\text{"}, \text{"}AB20\text{"}, \text{"}BBAB\text{"}, \text{"}BBAB\text{"}, \text{"}ABBA\text{"}, \text{"}CBBA\text{"})$ and $U^{(0,2)} \odot (R^{(1,2)} \cdot I^{(1,2)}) = (\text{"}AB200\text{"}, \text{"}BAB20\text{"}, \text{"}ABBAB\text{"}, \text{"}CBBAB\text{"}, \text{"}BABBA\text{"}, \text{"}20BBA\text{"})$. By calling RadixSort to sort $U^{(0,1)}$ and $U^{(0,2)}$ according to their symbols, the parties can obtain the sorting of suffixes in $S^{(0)} \cup S^{(1)}$ and $S^{(0)} \cup S^{(2)}$, denoted by $\sigma^{(0,1)}$ and $\sigma^{(0,2)}$, respectively. In this example, the sorting results are $\sigma^{(0,1)} = (5, 1, 0, 4, 3, 2)$ and $\sigma^{(0,2)} = (5, 2, 1, 4, 3, 0)$.

The permutations $D^{(0,1)}$ and $D^{(1,2)}$ obtained in merge step 2 are $D^{(0,1)} = (2, 1, 0, 5, 4, 3)$ and $D^{(1,2)} = (2, 1, 0, 5, 4, 3)$. By definition, the first three entries of $D^{(i,j)}$ correspond to $\mathsf{rank}(S^{(i)}, s)$ for $s \in S^{(i)}$ and $i \in \{0, 1\}$. The last three entries of $D^{(i,j)}$ represent $\mathsf{rank}(S^{(j)}, s) + (n' + 1)$ for each $s \in S^{(j)}$ and $j \in \{1, 2\}$.

Now, the first three entries in $\sigma^{(i,j)}$ represent $\mathsf{rank}(S^{(i)} \cup S^{(j)}, s)$ for $s \in S^{(i)}$ and $i, j \in \{0, 1, 2\}$, while the last three entries correspond to $\mathsf{rank}(S^{(i)} \cup S^{(j)}, s)$ for $s \in S^{(j)}$ and $i, j \in \{0, 1, 2\}$. Therefore, the calculation of $\boldsymbol{p}^{(0)}$, $\boldsymbol{p}^{(1)}$, and $\boldsymbol{p}^{(2)}$ in merge step 3 corresponds to the calculation of the equation (2), which results in the parties obtaining I. These values are $\boldsymbol{p}^{(0)} = (8, 2, 1)$, $\boldsymbol{p}^{(1)} = (7, 6, 3)$, $\boldsymbol{p}^{(2)} = (5, 4, 0)$ and $I = (8, 6, 3, 7, 5, 2, 4, 1, 0)$.

4 Application: Pattern Matching

In the classical model, we can search for a pattern of length m in string T of length n in $O(m \log n)$ time using SA of it. If we use the LCP array, this can be improved to $O(m + \log n)$ time. Note that we have to convert the LCP array so that each entry stores the minimum LCP values in search ranges used for binary searches. This conversion uses only integer comparison and can be done easily in $O(\log n)$ rounds in classical model, and in $O(\log^2 n)$ rounds in our MPC model.

To perform pattern search in the MPC model, we can use oblivious RAM (ORAM) for efficient search. ORAMs can be classified into two: basic ORAM and Distributed ORAM (DORAM). An array A is stored in servers and a client asks to the servers to obtain an entry $A[i]$ of the array. For both ORAMs, the servers do not obtain any information about the values stored in the array and also the access patterns (index i of the array requested by the client). The difference is that in basic ORAMs, the client has i as plain text, whereas in DORAMs the client has only a share of i. Therefore DORAM is better for the outsourcing scenario.

For a basic ORAM, Holland *et al.* [17] proposed RankORAM, which supports access to an entry of RAM in one round. Its complexity is one communication round, amortized $4 \log n$ blocks of communication per access, and $O(n + \sqrt{n} \cdot B)$ bits of memory in a client, where n is the number of blocks in ORAM and B is the block size. Ichikawa [18] modified the RankORAM to work in a three-server

Table 1. Related studies on secure pattern matching. N and q stands for the length of the database string stored in servers and the length of the query string, respectively. H stands for the height of the suffix tree of the database string. Communication bits and randomness for ours depend on the implementation of DORAM; we use the values for a multi-server version of [21].

Protocol	Data Structure	Encryption	Leakage (per query)	Communication bits	Randomness (per query)
Ours	FM-index	ABB + Perm (2PC + 1)	None	$O(\|q\| \log^3 N)$	$O(\|q\| \log^2 N)$
Mahdi et al. [27]	Suffix Tree	AES, garbled circuits	Tree traversal pattern	$O(H)$	$O(H)$
Nakagawa et al. [29]	FM-index	2PC + 1, Secret Sharing	None	$O(\|q\| \log N)$	$N\|q\| \log N$

MPC model. Its complexity is $O(\log n)$ time in a client, $O(n)$ bits of memory in a client, and $O(1)$ blocks of communication. For a DORAM, Keller and Scholl [21] proposed a protocol to access an entry of RAM in $O(\log^2 n)$ rounds. We can store suffix arrays in an encrypted forms using these ORAMs, and perform efficient pattern searches.

The BWT of a string is also used in the FM-index [13], which is a space-efficient data structure for pattern search. The FM-index is regarded as a compressed version of the suffix array. Therefore we can support efficient pattern searches using the BWT. This search algorithm also runs in the MPC model by storing an encrypted BWT using ORAMs.

According to Table 1, both [27] and [29] enable highly efficient searches, yet, as discussed in Sect. 1.1, [27] differs from us in terms of security goals. [29] is also fast, but requires a significant amount of storage per query. Our method, while not as efficient as these, remains fast according to Appendix A.2 and has a lower storage cost.

Acknowledgments. This work was supported by JSPS, KAKENHI Grant Number JP21H05052, and JST, CREST Grant Number JPMJCR22M1, Japan. Kota Isayama participated in this research while affiliated with the University of Tokyo.

Disclosure of Interests. The authors have no competing interests to declare that are relevant to the content of this article.

A Experimental Results

We show preliminary results on constructing suffix arrays in the 2-server + client-aided MPC model. We used C language to implement the protocols and compiled with gcc version 12.2.0 and compiler options "-O3". Communication between parties are done using Unix TCP sockets. We simulated MPC in a computer; the two servers run on the same computer and therefore we do not consider latency for communication. This is enough for estimating running time for real applications because the amount of communication bits in a round is large and communication time is proportional to the amount of communication bits. The experiments are conducted on a PC (Dell Precision Tower 5810) with Intel Xeon CPU E5-1620 v4 @ 3.50GHz and 256 GB memory. Running times are real time measured by Unix "time" command. The input strings are random strings consisting of only `a` and `b` in an alphabet of size 256.

A.1 Suffix Sorting

We implemented three types of our suffix sorting protocols. Two of them are the DC3 protocol (Sect. 3.3) and the Larsson-Sadakane protocol (Sect. 3.1). The third one is a modified protocol of the Larsson-Sadakane protocol; we terminate the protocol when the number of groups is equal to the length of the input string. Note that this algorithm is not data oblivious because the parties can obtain the information of an upper bound of the LCP values, or equivalently the length of the longest repeated substrings in the input string. However this greatly reduces the running time of the Larsson-Sadakane protocol as shown in the experimental results below. These three protocols will be referred to as DC3, LS (full), and LS from now on. We used precomputed correlated randomness for multiplications [5] and AppPerm and AppInvPerm [2].

Figure 2 shows time for constructing suffix arrays by the three protocols. The X-axis and Y-axis show the lengths of input strings and time for constructing the suffix array of the input, respectively. Input lengths are from 2^{10} (1 K) to 2^{24} (16 M). The LS protocol is the fastest, though it leaks the information of an upper bound of the maximum LCP value. The DC3 protocol is slightly slower than the LS, and LS (full) is much slower than the others. This is because LS (full), LS, and DC3 has time complexity of $O(n \log^2 n)$, $O(n \log n \log h)$, and $O(n \log n)$, respectively, where h is the maximum LCP value. Note that the DC3 protocol is not linear time because we use a sorting protocol with $O(n \log n)$ running time. For random strings, the expected value of h is $O(\log n)$ [30] and therefore the expected time complexity of LS is $O(n \log n \log \log n)$.

We do not show a figure for the amount of communication bytes because it is almost proportional to running times. For a string of length 2^{20} (about one million), the amount of communication between two servers for DC3 protocol is 15,575,835,264 bytes for each server.

We also did experiments for plain text algorithms. We used the original implementations of the DC3 algorithm [19] and the Larsson-Sadakane algorithm (qsufsort.c) [24]. For a string of length 2^{20}, 100 times executions of DC3 and LS take 11.74 s and 14.98 s, respectively. Therefore our secure protocols take roughly 4,345 times and 1,530 times of the corresponding plain text algorithms, respectively. We need optimization of our protocols. The most time-consuming part of the protocols is integer sorting. We use radix sorting using 1-bit counting sort. The running time can be reduced using k-bit counting sort for $k > 1$, but the amount of communication bits increases.

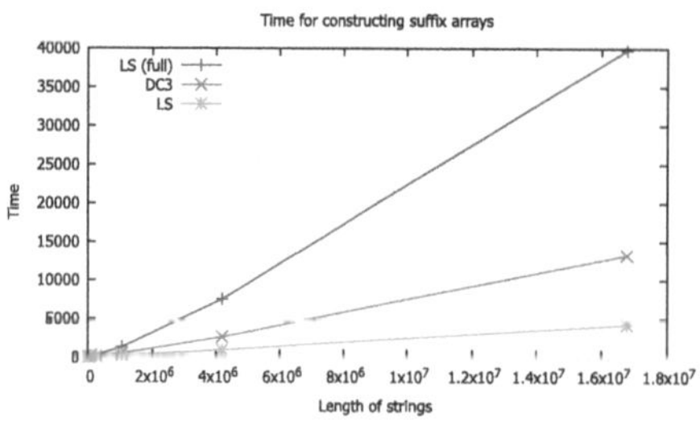

Fig. 2. Time for constructing suffix arrays.

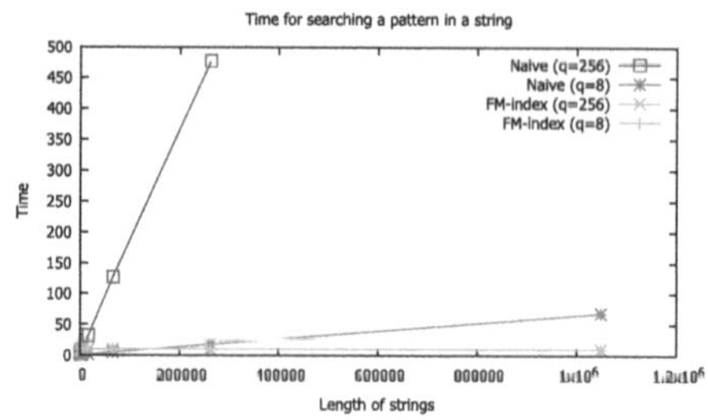

Fig. 3. Time for searching 100 patterns in a string.

A.2 Pattern Search

Next we show experimental results on searching a pattern P in a string T. We used two schemes; one is to use the FM-index and the other is a naive algorithm without using any index. For the algorithm using the FM-index, we first construct the FM-index of the string T and store it in the two servers using shares, then given a query string P, we search for it using the FM-index. The FM-index is stored using a basic ORAM based on a multi-server version of the RankORAM. Note that a client knows a query string and which entry of the FM-index is accessed. For the algorithm without using any index, we store the string T in the two servers using shares, and a query string P represented by shares is sent to the servers. The servers compute matches between the query string P and the substrings of T at every positions.

Figure 3 shows search time for patterns of length 8 in a string T of length 2^8 to 2^{20}. The X-axis show the length of T, and the Y-axis show the time for searching 100 random patterns in T. The alphabet size q is set to be 8 or 256. "Naive" shows the time for a naive matching algorithm without using any index, and "FM-index" shows the time using the FM-index data structure. As we expected, the search time by the naive algorithm without using any index is proportional to the string length because we have to read the whole string T, and that by our algorithm using the FM-index does not depend on the string length. Therefore our scheme is faster than a naive scheme for large databases.

B Examples of Suffix Arrays and BWT

We assume that the string to be processed is "tobeornottobe\$" where \$ is sentinel symbol described in Sect. 2.1. The SA stores the starting positions of lexicographically sorted suffixes in the original string. For example, the fourth smallest suffix "eornottobe\$" starts at position 3 in "tobeornottobe\$". The BWT of a string produces an array, BW, as shown in Fig. 4. The i-th element of BW stores the preceding symbol of the i-th smallest suffix. For instance, the preceding symbol of the fourth smallest suffix "eornottobe\$" is "b".

i	BW	SA	Suffix
0	e	13	$
1	o	11	be$
2	o	2	beornottobe$
3	b	12	e$
4	b	3	eornottobe$
5	r	6	nottobe$
6	t	10	obe$
7	t	1	obeornottobe$
8	e	4	ornottobe$
9	n	7	ottobe$
10	o	5	rnottobe$
11	t	9	tobe$
12	$	0	tobeornottobe$
13	o	8	ttobe$

i	LF	(a)	(b)	(c)
0	3	$ tobeornottob e	$ tobeornottob e	$ tobeornottob e
1	6	b e$tobeornott o	b e$tobeornott o	b e$tobeornott o
2	7	b eornottobe$t o	b eornottobe$t o	b eornottobe$t o
3	1	e $tobeornotto b	e $tobeornotto b	e $tobeornotto b
4	2	e ornottobe$to b	e ornottobe$to b	e ornottobe$to b
5	10	n ottobe$tobeo r	n ottobe$tobeo r	n ottobe$tobeo r
6	11	o be$tobeornot t	o be$tobeornot t	o be$tobeornot t
7	12	o beornottobe$ t	o beornottobe$ t	o beornottobe$ t
8	4	o rnottobe$tob e	o rnottobe$tob e	o rnottobe$tob e
9	5	o ttobe$tobeor n	o ttobe$tobeor n	o ttobe$tobeor n
10	8	r nottobe$tobe o	r nottobe$tobe o	r nottobe$tobe o
11	13	t obe$tobeorno t	t obe$tobeorno t	t obe$tobeorno t
12	0	t obeornottobe $	t obeornottobe $	t obeornottobe $
13	9	t tobe$tobeorn o	t tobe$tobeorn o	t tobe$tobeorn o

Fig. 4. Suffix Array and Burrows–Wheeler Transform for the String "tobeornottobe$", and Text Searching Algorithm Using FM-index

For the suffixes in Fig. 4, we assume the string is circular, with characters from the beginning of the original string appended to the end of each suffix, as illustrated in (a) of Fig. 4(a). The first symbols of all suffixes form the F-column (red), and the last symbols form the L-column (blue), which corresponds to the BW array in Fig. 4. The LF array in Fig. 4(a) indicates the position of each L-column symbol in the F-column. The FM-index stores the BW array and compact auxiliary arrays, enabling efficient calculation of the LF array with minimal memory usage (see Sect. 2.1).

The text search based on FM-index, often referred to as backward search, starts from the last symbol of the query string. We consider an example with a query string "tto" aiming to determine its lexicographical position among all suffixes of "tobeornottobe$". First, the interval in the F-column where the last query symbol "o" appears is determined as $[6, 9]$. Within this interval, the next query symbol "t" is checked in the L-column (the BW array), narrowing the interval to $[6, 7]$ ((**a**) of Fig. 4). Using the corresponding LF-interval, $[11, 12]$, the suffixes containing "to" as a prefix are identified ((**b**) of Fig. 4). Repeating the process, the next query symbol "t" in the L-column further narrows the interval to $[11, 11]$, and the corresponding LF-interval to $[13, 13]$. This confirms that "tto" is included in the 13th smallest suffix ((**c**) of Fig. 4).

C Building-Block Protocols

In this section, we define the protocols Grouping and BatchAccess, which serve as the building blocks for our oblivious suffix sorting scheme.

The protocol Π_{Grouping} implements the Grouping functionality and is used to securely compute Step (c) of Larsson and Sadakane's algorithm. As the oblivious equality tests in Step 2 can be performed in parallel, the protocol requires only a constant number of communication rounds. The correctness of Π_{Grouping} follows directly from the definition of Equality.

Protocol 4. Π_{Grouping}

Inputs. $[\![V]\!]$ where $V \in R^n$.
Output. $[\![L]\!]^B$, where $L \in \mathbb{Z}_2^n$, $L[0] = 1$, $L[i] = 1$ iff $V[i] \neq V[i-1]$.

1. $[\![L[0]]\!]^B := 1$
2. $[\![t[i]]\!]^B \leftarrow \mathsf{Equality}([\![V[i]]\!], [\![V[i-1]]\!])$ for $i \in \{1, n-1\}$
3. $[\![L[i]]\!]^B := \mathsf{NOT}([\![t[i]]\!]^B)$ for $i \in \{1, n-1\}$

Protocol 5. $\Pi_{BatchAccess}$

Inputs. $[\![\boldsymbol{v}]\!]$ and $[\![\boldsymbol{idx}]\!]$ where $\boldsymbol{v} \in R^n$ and $\boldsymbol{idx} \in \{0, \ldots, n-1\}^n$.

Output. $[\![\boldsymbol{w}]\!]$, where it satisfies $\boldsymbol{w}[i] = \boldsymbol{v}[\boldsymbol{idx}[i]]$ for all $i \in \{0, \ldots, n-1\}$.

/* Unary encoding */
1. $[\![I]\!] := 012\ldots(n-1) \,\|\, [\![\boldsymbol{idx}]\!]$
2. $B := 0^n \,\|\, 1^n$
3. $[\![\lambda]\!] \leftarrow \mathsf{RadixSort}([\![I]\!])$
4. $[\![L]\!]^B \leftarrow \mathsf{AppInvPerm}(B, [\![\lambda]\!])$
5. $[\![\sigma]\!] \leftarrow \mathsf{CountSort}([\![L]\!]^B)$
6. $[\![\lambda^{-1}]\!] \leftarrow \mathsf{AppInvPerm}(012\ldots 2n-1, [\![\lambda]\!])$
7. $[\![\pi]\!] \leftarrow \mathsf{AppInvPerm}([\![\lambda^{-1}]\!], [\![\sigma]\!])$
8. $[\![\rho[i]]\!] := [\![\pi[i+n]]\!] - n$ for all $i \in \{0, \ldots, n\}$
/* Concurrent reading */
9. $[\![X]\!] := [\![\boldsymbol{v}]\!] \,\|\, 0^n$
10. $[\![Y]\!] \leftarrow \mathsf{AppPerm}([\![X]\!], [\![\sigma]\!])$
11. $[\![\boldsymbol{q}]\!] \leftarrow \mathsf{Propagate}([\![\neg L]\!]^B, [\![Y]\!])$
12. $[\![\boldsymbol{r}]\!] \leftarrow \mathsf{AppInvPerm}([\![\boldsymbol{q}]\!], [\![\sigma]\!])$
13. $[\![\boldsymbol{p}[i]]\!] := [\![\boldsymbol{r}[i+n]]\!]$ for all $i \in \{0, \ldots, n-1\}$
14. $[\![\boldsymbol{w}]\!] \leftarrow \mathsf{AppInvPerm}([\![\boldsymbol{p}]\!], [\![\rho]\!])$

The protocol $\Pi_{BatchAccess}$ for realizing BatchAccess is similar to the oblivious reading protocol in [25]. All steps except Step 3 require only a constant rounds of communication rounds. The correctness proof is similar to that in [25].

D Performance Evaluation

In this section, we provide a performance evaluation of our proposed scheme. Note that our scheme is defined on top of the arithmetic black box model, so the concrete performance depends on the choice of the underlying MPC scheme. Here we consider secret-sharing-based semi-honest secure MPC schemes as instances of ABB in a *two-party computation setting.*

The two-party computation setting in this paper uses the GMW scheme [15] as the underlying system. This setting is the simplest case of dishonest majority settings, in which it is impossible to achieve MPC without a computational hardness assumption or a trusted third party. To isolate the problem, we consider the *offline/online paradigm*, which divides protocol execution into two phases. The offline phase is preprocessing to generate correlated randomness to be consumed in the online phase, which can run independently of the input values, using an additional security assumption mentioned above. The online phase, which runs after taking the input, only contains information-theoretically secure operations by consuming the correlated randomness. In this paper, we do not focus on any particular method to realize the offline phase, only considering the storage cost for correlated randomness.

Primitive Costs. Table 2 shows the communication and storage costs of the state-of-the-art two-party protocols for each primitive functionality. We assume here that $m = 2^\lambda$ and the size of each share is 1 for a secret boolean value, and λ for a secret value in $\mathbb{Z}_m$. The protocols realizing $\mathcal{F}_{perm}$ assumes that the input vector belongs to $\mathbb{Z}_m^n$. "Storage bits" indicates the size (in bits) of the correlated randomness that each party needs to store before performing the online phase of the protocol. "Rounds" and "Communication bits" are the number of *online* communication rounds and bits per party, respectively. Note that if the permutation input has already been used in another ApplnvPerm or AppPerm call, we can reduce complexity by reusing the intermediate data, as indicated by *. For simplicity, the table shows only the dominant terms for communication and storage bits.

Table 2. Communication and Storage Costs for Each Primitive in the Two-party Computation Setting.

Functionality	Rnds.	Communication bits	Storage bits	ref.
XOR	0	0	0	[15]
NOT	0	0	0	[15]
Add	0	0	0	[15]
SMult	0	0	0	[15]
AND	1	2	3	[5]
OR	1	2	3	[5]
Mult	1	2λ	3λ	[5]
B2A	1	1	$\lambda + 1$	[22]
IfThen	1	$\lambda + 1$	$2\lambda + 1$	[2]
AppPerm	3	$n(\lambda + 2\log n)$	$n(2\lambda + 4\log n)$	[2]
AppPerm*	1	$n\lambda$	$2n\lambda$	[2]
ApplnvPerm	2	$n(\lambda + 2\log n)$	$n(2\lambda + 4\log n)$	[2]
ApplnvPerm*	1	$n\lambda$	$2n\lambda$	[2]
RadixSort	$3\lceil \frac{\lambda}{2} \rceil$	$(5\lceil \frac{\lambda}{2} \rceil - 1)n\log n + 2n\lambda$	$(15\lceil \frac{\lambda}{2} \rceil - 6)n\log n + 2n\lambda$	[2]
CountSort	2	$n(1 + \log n)$	$n(1 + 3\log n)$	[2]
Propagate	5	$n(1 + 2\lambda + 3\log n)$	$n(1 + 4\lambda + 7\log n)$	[3]
GroupSum	5	$n(1 + 2\lambda + 3\log n)$	$n(1 + 4\lambda + 7\log n)$	[3]
Equality	2	$\lambda + \log \lambda$	$\lambda \log \lambda + 2\lambda$	[4]

Estimated Cost of Our Protocols. Table 3 shows the estimated communication and storage costs of our protocols. Evaluation is done by counting the number of calls to each primitive functionality. Round complexity estimation considers the case when parallelism is enabled. If the input values of primitive functionality calls are determined independently, these calls can be executed in parallel, reducing the number of communication rounds. On the other hand, when estimating communication bits and storage costs, we consider the total cost of all primitive functionality calls in the protocol. These estimated values are listed only for asymptotically dominant terms. Let $R = \mathbb{Z}_{2^\lambda}$. For simplicity, we set $\lambda = \log n$ for Protocols 1-2 and 5-6. We assume that $n_1 = n_2$ for Protocols 6. The cost of Protocol 2 does not include the cost of Protocol 1.

We describe an overview of the cost estimation for Protocol 3. We assume that the input length is $n \geq 4$. The costs required for each iteration with $n \geq 2^4$ and $\lambda = \log n$ are as follows:

$$(rnd.) = \frac{15}{2}\log n + 13$$

$$(comm.) = 10n\log^2 n + \left(\frac{169}{6} - 10C\right)n\log n + \left(\frac{61}{6} - 4C + 3\log\log n\right)n$$

$$(stor.) = 30n\log^2 n + \left(\frac{83}{3} - 30C + 3\log\log n\right)n\log n + \left(11 - \frac{5}{3}C\right)n$$

where $C = \log_2 \frac{2}{3}$. Note that the input length is reduced by a factor of two-thirds in each iteration. We set the threshold at $n = 2^4$, so the number of iterations k is approximately $\log_{\frac{3}{2}} n - 6 = -\frac{\log_2 n}{C} - 6$. The total costs can be obtained using the following equations:

$$\sum_{i=0}^{k}\left(\left(\frac{2}{3}\right)^i n\right)\log\left(\left(\frac{2}{3}\right)^i n\right) = 3n\log n + O(n)$$

$$\sum_{i=0}^{k}\left(\left(\frac{2}{3}\right)^i n\right)\log^2\left(\left(\frac{2}{3}\right)^i n\right) = 3n\log^2 n + 12Cn\log n + O(n)$$

Table 3. Communication and Storage Costs of Our Protocols in the Two-party Computation Setting.

#	Functionality	Rounds	Communication bits	Storage bits
1	LS	$3\log^2 n + \frac{17}{2}\log n + 1$	$n(5\log^3 n + \frac{21}{2}\log^2 n)$	$n(15\log^3 n + (2\log\log n + \frac{19}{2})\log^2 n)$
3	DC3	$6.4\log^2 n + 26.0\log n - 59.8$	$n(30\log^2 n + 45.2\log n)$	$n(99\log^2 n + 531.6\log n)$
2	LCP	$\frac{3}{2}\log^2 n + 17\log n + 2$	$n(10\log^3 n + 96\log^2 n)$	$n(30\log^3 n + (\log\log n + 183)\log^2 n)$
6	BDSW	$3\log^2 n + 11\log n - 9$	$n(5\log^3 n + \frac{49}{4}\log^2 n)$	$n(5\log^3 n + (2\log\log n + \frac{186}{4})\log^2 n)$
4	Grouping	2	$n(\lambda + \log\lambda)$	$n\lambda(\log\lambda + 1)$
5	BatchAccess	$\frac{3}{2}\log n + 14$	$n(5\log^2 n + 46\log n)$	$n(15\log^2 n + 87\log n)$

E Application: Global Similarity

In this section, we propose an oblivious suffix sort algorithm for a string formed by concatenating two distinct strings. Using the indexes from the suffix sort of the concatenated string, we show that the Burrows-Wheeler Similarity Distribution (BWSD) can be computed in a privacy-preserving manner. As noted in Sect. 1.2, this approach allows data owners to compute the indexes without decrypting their strings.

E.1 Oblivious Calculation of SA for Concatenated String of Two Distinct Strings

Let T_1 and T_2 be two strings of lengths n_1 and n_2, respectively. Define $n := n_1 + n_2$ and $n' := \max(n_1, n_2)$. To obtain new strings T_1' and T_2', append sentinel symbols $\$_1$ and $\$_2$ to T_1 and T_2, respectively, assuming $\$_1 < \$_2$.

The computation of the SA for the concatenated string, *i.e.*, a protocol that calculates the following functionality SuffixSortConcat is a central procedure for the similarity measure.

- $\mathsf{SuffixSortConcat}([\![T_1']\!], [\![T_2']\!])$: Compute $[\![\sigma]\!]$ where $\sigma \in S_{n+2}$ is the SA of concatenated string $T_1' \parallel T_2'$ and $|T_1'| = n_1 + 1$, $|T_2'| = n_2 + 1$ and $n = n_1 + n_2$.

The protocol $\Pi_{LS_{conc}}$ is for securely computing SA of the concatenated string, and it does not differ significantly from Π_{LS}. To save space, we describe only the parts that differ from Π_{LS} below:

- Step 1 computes $[\![\sigma]\!] \leftarrow \mathsf{RadixSort}([\![T_1']\!] \parallel [\![T_2']\!])$.
- The number of iterations in Step 5 becomes $max(n_1 + 1, n_2 + 1)$.
- Step 5 (c) computes the following:
  (c1) $[\![V^{(2)}[i]]\!] := [\![V^{(1)}[i + h \mod (n_1 + 1)]]\!]$ for $i \in \{0, \dots, n_1\}$
  (c2) $[\![V^{(2)}[i]]\!] := [\![V^{(1)}[n_1 + 1 + (i + h \mod (n_2 + 1))]]\!]$ for $i \in \{n_1 + 1, \dots, n + 1\}$

E.2 Oblivious Calculation of Burrows-Wheeler Similarity Distribution (BWSD)

The BWSD is a probability mass function designed to measure the similarity between two strings. Let the SA of the concatenated string $T_1'||T_2'$ be σ. Using σ, we define the following α:

$$\alpha[i] = \begin{cases} 0 & \text{if } \sigma[i] < n_1 + 1 \\ 1 & \text{if } \sigma[i] \geq n_1 + 1 \end{cases}$$

The array α indicates the origin of each suffix in the suffix-sorted $T_1'||T_2'$. For BWSD computation, we consider runs of consecutive 0s and 1s in α. Specifically, α can be expressed as $\alpha = 0^{k_1}1^{k_2}0^{k_3}\cdots 0^{k_{m-1}}1^{k_m}$ where $k_2, \dots, k_{m-1} \in \{1, \dots, n'\}$, $k_1, k_m \in \{0, \dots, n'\}$. Let t_{k_j} denote the total count of runs 0^{k_j} and 1^{k_j} in α, and let s be the total number of runs, $s = \sum_{k=1}^{n'} t_k$. The probability mass function $BWSD_{T_1', T_2'} : \{1, \dots, n'\} \to [0, 1]$ is simply defined by:

$$BWSD_{T_1', T_2'}(x) := \frac{t_x}{s}$$

Protocol 6. Π_{BDSW}

Inputs. $[\![T'_1]\!]$ and $[\![T'_2]\!]$ where $T'_1 \in R^{n_1+1}$ and $T'_2 \in R^{n_2+1}$.
Output. $([\![\boldsymbol{t}]\!], [\![s]\!])$ where $(\boldsymbol{t}, s) \in \mathbb{Z}_n^{n'} \times \mathbb{Z}_n$ is the pair that satisfies $\boldsymbol{t}[i] = t_i$ for all i and $s = \sum_{k=1}^{n'} \boldsymbol{t}[k]$.

1. $[\![\sigma]\!] \leftarrow \mathsf{SuffixSortConcat}([\![T'_1]\!], [\![T'_2]\!])$
2. $[\![\alpha]\!]^B \leftarrow \mathsf{AppPerm}((0^{n_1+1} \parallel 1^{n_2+1}), [\![\sigma]\!])$
3. $[\![\boldsymbol{f}[0]]\!]^B := 1$
4. $[\![\boldsymbol{f}[i]]\!]^B \leftarrow \mathsf{XOR}([\![\alpha[i]]\!]^B, [\![\alpha[i-1]]\!]^B)$ for $i \in \{1, \dots, n+1\}$
5. $[\![\boldsymbol{h}]\!] \leftarrow \mathsf{GroupSum}([\![f]\!]^B, 1^{n+2})$
6. $[\![\rho]\!] \leftarrow \mathsf{RadixSort}((012 \dots n') \parallel [\![h]\!])$
7. $[\![\boldsymbol{l}]\!] \leftarrow \mathsf{AppInvPerm}((012 \dots n') \parallel [\![h]\!]), [\![\rho]\!])$
8. $[\![L]\!]^B \leftarrow \mathsf{Grouping}([\![l]\!])$
9. $[\![\boldsymbol{b}]\!]^B \leftarrow \mathsf{AppInvPerm}((0^{n'+1} \parallel 1^{n+2})), [\![\rho]\!])$
10. $[\![\boldsymbol{b}[i]]\!] \leftarrow \mathsf{B2A}([\![\boldsymbol{b}[i]]\!]^B)$ for $i \in \{0, \dots, n+n'+2\}$
11. $[\![\boldsymbol{c}]\!] \leftarrow \mathsf{GroupSum}([\![L]\!]^B, [\![\boldsymbol{b}]\!])$
12. $[\![\boldsymbol{d}]\!] \leftarrow \mathsf{AppPerm}([\![\boldsymbol{c}]\!], [\![\rho]\!])$
13. $[\![\boldsymbol{f}[i]]\!] \leftarrow \mathsf{B2A}([\![\boldsymbol{f}[i]]\!]^B)$ for $i \in \{0, \dots, n+1\}$
14. $[\![s]\!] := \sum_{i=0}^{n+1} [\![\boldsymbol{f}[i]]\!]$
15. $[\![\boldsymbol{t}[i]]\!] = [\![\boldsymbol{d}[i]]\!]$ for $i \in \{1, \dots, n'\}$

Based on this function, the following two similarity measures are defined:

$$D_M(T'_1, T'_2) := \sum_{x=1}^{n'} x \frac{t_x}{s} - 1, \qquad D_E(T'_1, T'_2) := -\sum_{x=1}^{n'} (\frac{t_x}{s}) \log(\frac{t_x}{s})$$

The protocol Π_{BDSW} is for calculating $[\![\boldsymbol{t}]\!] \in \{0, \dots, n'\}^n$ and $[\![s]\!] \in \{0, \dots, n'\}$ that satisfy $\boldsymbol{t}[i] = t_i$ and s matches the definition above.

The Correctness of $\boldsymbol{\Pi_{BDSW}}$. The array $\boldsymbol{f}$ is constructed such that $\boldsymbol{f}[i] = 0$ if $\alpha[i] = \alpha[i-1]$, $\boldsymbol{f}[i] = 1$ otherwise. In other words, $\boldsymbol{f}$ records positions at which the first bit of each subsequence in α changes from 0 to 1. This can be interpreted as an array that records the starting positions of every run of α. Thus, the array $\boldsymbol{h}$ stores the length of every run at each position i, where $\boldsymbol{f}[i] = 1$ and $\boldsymbol{l}$ is the array that is stable sorted based on the length of runs after adding the index string $012 \dots n'$. This means that in $\boldsymbol{l}$, after each of the characters k that constituted the index string, the k is repeated as many times as the number of runs of length k that appear in α. By using $\mathsf{GroupSum}$ in Step (11), the number of runs of every length k is counted; therefore, $\boldsymbol{t}$ obtained at Step (15) is what we desire (number of 0s is excluded). Since each 1 in $\boldsymbol{f}$ indicates the starting position of a run, $\sum_{i=0}^{n+1} \boldsymbol{f}[i]$ is the total number of runs in α and s is the desired result. □

References

1. Abouelhoda, M.I., Kurtz, S., Ohlebusch, E.: Replacing suffix trees with enhanced suffix arrays. J. Disc. Algor. **2**(1), 53–86 (2004). https://doi.org/10.1016/S1570-8667(03)00065-0
2. Attrapadung, N., et al.: Oblivious linear group actions and applications. In: Vigna, G., Shi, E. (eds.) ACM CCS 2021, pp. 630–650. ACM Press (2021). https://doi.org/10.1145/3460120.3484584
3. Attrapadung, N., Morita, H., Ohara, K., Schuldt, J.C.N., Teruya, T., Tozawa, K.: Secure parallel computation on privately partitioned data and applications. In: Yin, H., Stavrou, A., Cremers, C., Shi, E. (eds.) ACM CCS 2022, pp. 151–164. ACM Press (2022). https://doi.org/10.1145/3548606.3560695
4. Attrapadung, N., Morita, H., Ohara, K., Schuldt, J.C.N., Tozawa, K.: Memory and round-efficient MPC primitives in the pre-processing model from unit vectorization. In: Suga, Y., Sakurai, K., Ding, X., Sako, K. (eds.) ASIACCS 22, pp. 858–872. ACM Press (2022). https://doi.org/10.1145/3488932.3517407
5. Beaver, D.: Efficient multiparty protocols using circuit randomization. In: Feigenbaum, J. (ed.) CRYPTO 1991. LNCS, vol. 576, pp. 420–432. Springer, Heidelberg (1992). https://doi.org/10.1007/3-540-46766-1_34
6. Bernardini, G., et al.: Hide and mine in strings: hardness, algorithms, and experiments. IEEE Trans. Knowl. Data Eng. **35**(6), 5948–5963 (2023). https://doi.org/10.1109/TKDE.2022.3158063
7. Burrows, M., Wheeler, D.J.: A block-sorting lossless data compression algorithm. SRS Res. Rep. **124** (1994)
8. Canetti, R.: Universally composable security: a new paradigm for cryptographic protocols. In: 42nd FOCS, pp. 136–145. IEEE Computer Society Press (2001). https://doi.org/10.1109/SFCS.2001.959888
9. Claude, F., Navarro, G.: The wavelet matrix. In: Calderón-Benavides, L., González-Caro, C., Chávez, E., Ziviani, N. (eds.) String Processing and Information Retrieval, pp. 167–179. Springer, Heidelberg (2012)
10. Damgård, I., Nielsen, J.B.: Universally composable efficient multiparty computation from threshold homomorphic encryption. In: Boneh, D. (ed.) CRYPTO 2003. LNCS, vol. 2729, pp. 247–264. Springer, Heidelberg (2003). https://doi.org/10.1007/978-3-540-45146-4_15
11. Durbin, R.: Efficient haplotype matching and storage using the positional burrows-wheeler transform (pbwt). Bioinformatics **30**(9), 1266–1272 (2014)
12. Erlich, Y., Narayanan, A.: Routes for breaching and protecting genetic privacy. Nat. Rev. Genet. **15**(6), 409–421 (2014). https://doi.org/10.1038/nrg3723
13. Ferragina, P., Manzini, G.: Indexing compressed text. J. ACM **52**(4), 552–581 (2005). https://doi.org/10.1145/1082036.1082039
14. Goldreich, O.: Foundations of Cryptography, vol. 2. Cambridge University Press, Cambridge (2004)
15. Goldreich, O., Micali, S., Wigderson, A.: How to play any mental game or a completeness theorem for protocols with honest majority. In: Aho, A. (ed.) 19th ACM STOC, pp. 218–229. ACM Press (1987). https://doi.org/10.1145/28395.28420
16. Grossi, R., Vitter, J.S.: Compressed suffix arrays and suffix trees with applications to text indexing and string matching. SIAM J. Comput. **35**(2), 378–407 (2005)
17. Holland, W., Ohrimenko, O., Wirth, A.: Single round-trip hierarchical oram via succinct indices (2022)

18. Ichikawa, A.: Round-efficient hierarchical multi-server oram. In: Symposium on Cryptography and Information Security (SCIS). The Institute of Electronics, Information and Communication Engineers (2023)
19. Kärkkäinen, J., Sanders, P., Burkhardt, S.: Linear work suffix array construction. J. ACM **53**(6), 918–936 (2006). https://doi.org/10.1145/1217856.1217858
20. Kasai, T., Lee, G., Arimura, H., Arikawa, S., Park, K.: Linear-time longest-common-prefix computation in suffix arrays and its applications. In: Amir, A. (ed.) CPM 2001. LNCS, vol. 2089, pp. 181–192. Springer, Heidelberg (2001). https://doi.org/10.1007/3-540-48194-X_17
21. Keller, M., Scholl, P.: Efficient, oblivious data structures for MPC. In: Sarkar, P., Iwata, T. (eds.) ASIACRYPT 2014. LNCS, vol. 8874, pp. 506–525. Springer, Heidelberg (2014). https://doi.org/10.1007/978-3-662-45608-8_27
22. Kikuchi, R., Ikarashi, D., Matsuda, T., Hamada, K., Chida, K.: Efficient bit-decomposition and modulus-conversion protocols with an honest majority. In: Susilo, W., Yang, G. (eds.) ACISP 2018. LNCS, vol. 10946, pp. 64–82. Springer, Cham (2018). https://doi.org/10.1007/978-3-319-93638-3_5
23. Kushilevitz, E., Lindell, Y., Rabin, T.: Information-theoretically secure protocols and security under composition. In: Kleinberg, J.M. (ed.) 38th ACM STOC, pp. 109–118. ACM Press (2006). https://doi.org/10.1145/1132516.1132532
24. Larsson, N.J., Sadakane, K.: Faster suffix sorting. Theor. Comput. Sci. **387**(3), 258–272 (2007). https://doi.org/10.1016/j.tcs.2007.07.017
25. Laud, P.: Parallel oblivious array access for secure multiparty computation and privacy-preserving minimum spanning trees. PoPETs **2015**(2), 188–205 (2015). https://doi.org/10.1515/popets-2015-0011
26. Li, H., Durbin, R.: Fast and accurate long-read alignment with burrows-wheeler transform. Bioinformatics **26**(5), 589–595 (2010). https://doi.org/10.1093/bioinformatics/btp698
27. Mahdi, M.S.R., Al Aziz, M.M., Mohammed, N., Jiang, X.: Privacy-preserving string search on encrypted genomic data using a generalized suffix tree. Inf. Med. Unlocked **23**, 100525 (2021). https://doi.org/10.1016/j.imu.2021.100525
28. Manber, U., Myers, G.: Suffix arrays: a new method for on-line string searches. SIAM J. Comput. **22**(5), 935–948 (1993). https://doi.org/10.1137/0222058
29. Nakagawa, Y., Ohata, S., Shimizu, K.: Efficient privacy-preserving variable-length substring match for genome sequence. Algor. Molec. Biol. **17**(1), 9 (2022). https://doi.org/10.1186/s13015-022-00211-1
30. Pittel, B.: Asymptotical growth of a class of random trees. Ann. Prob. **13**(2), 414–427 (1985)
31. Sadakane, K.: Compressed suffix trees with full functionality. Theory Comput. Syst. **41**(4), 589–607 (2007). https://doi.org/10.1007/S00224-006-1198-X
32. Shimizu, K., Nuida, K., Rätsch, G.: Efficient privacy-preserving string search and an application in genomics. Bioinformatics **32**(11), 1652–1661 (2016)
33. Sudo, H., Jimbo, M., Nuida, K., Shimizu, K.: Secure wavelet matrix: alphabet-friendly privacy-preserving string search for bioinformatics. IEEE/ACM Trans. Comput. Biol. Bioinf. **16**(5), 1675–1684 (2018)
34. Weiner, P.: Linear pattern matching algorithms. In: Proceedings of the 14th Annual Symposium on Switching and Automata Theory (Swat 1973), SWAT '73, pp. 1–11. IEEE Computer Society (1973). 10.1109/SWAT.1973.13

35. Yang, L., Zhang, X., Wang, T.: The burrows-wheeler similarity distribution between biological sequences based on burrows-wheeler transform. J. Theor. Biol. **262**(4), 742–749 (2010). https://doi.org/10.1016/j.jtbi.2009.10.033
36. Yao, A.C.: Protocols for secure computations. In: 23rd Annual Symposium on Foundations of Computer Science (FOCS 1982), pp. 160–164 (1982). https://doi.org/10.1109/SFCS.1982.38

Share&Shrink: Efficient and Delegatable MPC in One Broadcast then Asynchrony

Antoine Urban(✉) and Matthieu Rambaud

Télécom Paris and Institut polytechnique de Paris, Paris, France
{antoine.urban,matthieu.rambaud}@telecom-paris.fr

Abstract. We consider protocols for secure multi-party computation (MPC) under honest majority, i.e., for $n = 2t+1$ players of which t are corrupt, that achieve *guaranteed output delivery* (GOD), and operate in a single initial round of broadcast (BC), followed by steps of asynchronous peer-to-peer (P2P) messages. The power of closely related "hybrid networks" was studied in [Fitzi-Nielsen, Disc'09], [BHN, Podc'10] and [Patra-Ravi, IEEE Tr. Inf. Theory'18]. The interest of such protocols is that they go at the actual speed of the network, and security is preserved under arbitrary network conditions (past the initial BC).

We first consider a bare bulletin-board PKI setup, and leverage recent advances in multi-key homomorphic encryption [BJMS, Asiacrypt'20], to state the feasibility of honest majority MPC with GOD in a tight 1-BC-then-1 single step of asynchronous P2P messages.

We then consider efficiency. The only protocols adaptable to such a network model and setup are [BJMS, Asiacrypt'20], which does not scale well for many players, and [GLS, Crypto'15], which does not support input delegation from external resource-constrained owners (such as IoT devices or smartphones), limiting its practical use. Our main contribution is a generic design that enables MPC in 1BC-then-asynchronous P2P. It operates over ciphertexts encrypted under a (threshold) single-key encryption scheme, resulting in the smallest sizes expectable and efficient evaluation. It can be implemented from any homomorphic encryption scheme built from linear maps (e.g., GSW, CL, ...). Our main building block is the squishing of the verifiable input sharing ("Share"), in parallel with the distributed key generation (DKG) in the single BC, followed by threshold encryption ("Shrink") in one asynchronous step. Interestingly, it can be compiled into the first constant-round YOSO protocol in 1 BC.

Keywords: MPC · Verifiable Computation · Homomorphic Encryption · Yoso

1 Introduction

Byzantine broadcast (BC) and round-by-round synchronous communication are handy abstractions for designing simple multi-party computation protocols.

A. Urban—Supported by the Beyond5G project.
M. Rambaud—Supported by the French ANR Project ANR-21-CE39-0009-BARRACUDA.

M. Fischlin and V. Moonsamy (Eds.): ACNS 2025, LNCS 15825, pp. 308–338, 2025.
https://doi.org/10.1007/978-3-031-95761-1_11

However, in practice implementing a broadcast channel requires either multiple rounds of peer-to-peer communication [37,52,78] or special channels (such as blockchains), and is therefore costly and difficult in itself. This difficulty was pointed out in the comments of NIST's recent call for standardization of multiparty threshold-cryptography [1]. Moreover, implementing BC fails beyond $t < n/3$ corruptions if the network cannot deliver a number of consecutive synchronous rounds. An example is the protocol of [74] for the closely related primitive of consensus, without trusted distributed key generation (trusted DKG) setup, i.e., without distribution of correlated secrets to players by a trusted authority, which requires an expected 36 rounds. Thus significant effort is currently being put into minimizing the use of broadcast rounds in MPC [16,34,35,42,44,48,69]. We push further this line of work by asking for only one initial call to BC, i.e. a *broadcast-optimal* protocol as studied in [13,29,34,48], without any trusted DKG setup, followed by a fully asynchronous protocol. Beyond their security under network slowdowns, a further benefit of asynchronous protocols is that they go at the actual speed of the network, i.e., are *responsive* [30,69].

Since we aim at the (arguably gold standard) of guaranteed output delivery (GOD) under honest majority, this initial call to BC is necessary, as shown by an elementary split-brain attack [16]. Overall, two main approaches exist to design constant-round MPC protocols based on fully homomorphic encryption (FHE):

Threshold FHE-Based: A mainstream tool for round-efficient MPC is based on $(n,t)-$Threshold Fully Homomorphic Encryption schemes. The following generic approach or close variations [19], that may be called "DKG-then-Input-distribution" in two BC, consists of: (1) the distributed generation (DKG) of a common *threshold encryption key* ek, with private assignment of a *decryption key share* to each player, such that the scheme provides IND-CPA security against adversaries controlling up to t key shares. It is followed (2) by the broadcast of encrypted inputs under the common threshold encryption key. Then, players locally evaluate a circuit through an algorithm Eval on the encrypted inputs, that outputs a ciphertext. Finally, players (3) perform an asynchronous threshold decryption protocol using their key shares, so that any set of $t+1$ of them can recover the output.

Multikey-FHE-Based: Another popular tool to further reduce the number of rounds is to use a (n,n)-threshold Multikey-FHE scheme [25,55,56], for which no DKG is needed before the input distribution, effectively reducing the number of broadcast to just one: it starts (1) with the local generation of keys, directly followed by the broadcast of encrypted inputs under the different keys. Then, players proceed with the multikey evaluation of a circuit through an expensive algorithm MultikeyEval, before (2) performing a (n,n)-threshold decryption.

These two methods highlight a tradeoff: one allows efficient evaluation at the cost of one extra broadcast, while the other allows obtaining an MPC protocol in an optimal number of broadcasts with an expensive evaluation. In this work, our goal is to propose a new method that offers the best of both worlds:

A protocol with an efficient evaluation and only one initial broadcast.

Overall, our aim is to develop a new approach that eliminates the need for a DKG before the input distribution. To achieve this, we face two key challenges:

- ***Challenge 1: Delegation.*** We observe from the DKG-then-Input-distribution approach that calls to BC are used to provide players with *a common view on threshold-encrypted inputs.* In a breakthrough approach, Gordon et al. [38] proposed the first (n, t)-threshold multikey-FHE scheme enabling the construction of an MPC protocol with GOD requiring one single BC plus preliminary publication of input-independent material on a bulletin board PKI. However, it suffers from a practical issue. Indeed, as pointed out by [14], the most important property for deploying MPC in practice is the ability to *delegate* the costly computation to an untrusted cloud, in order to handle inputs coming from external resource-constrained input-owners (e.g. Iot devices, smartphones, ...) that, after the initial distribution of their inputs, do not take further part in the computation. Numerous techniques [11,26,41,65,68,72,79] have been proposed to achieve a secure and verifiable delegation of computation, scaling [2,6,17,18,65,71] to millions of inputs-owners. Unfortunately, the construction of [38] cannot enable delegation as explained in Sect. 6.1. Moreover, as it is based on GSW [47], sizes of ciphertexts are $d\times$ larger (where d is the lattice dimension, see Table 1) than those of the latest FHE schemes based on the ring-learning-with-errors (RLWE) assumption [61]. Unfortunately, the approach of [38] is not generic, and in particular, not portable to RLWE.
- ***Challenge 2: Efficient Evaluation.*** To remedy the latter issue, Badrinarayanan et al. [12] built an MPC protocol based on multikey-FHE using a more generic construction in 3 BC as presented in Sect. 6.2. However, this approach suffers from a major drawback: the sizes of their (multikey) ciphertexts are quadratic in the number $|\mathcal{Q}|$ of input-owners, and the same quadratic dependency applies to the multikey evaluation, making it impractical when scaling to a large number of input-owners as later demonstrated in Sect. 8. Part of this inefficiency is due to the use of the GSW-based multikey scheme from [66]. However, even using recent works [55,56] that reduced the overhead in homomorphic evaluation complexity to linear in $|\mathcal{Q}|$, the approach of [12] would still be $|\mathcal{Q}|\times$ less efficient than its counterparts based on single-key threshold FHE.

In this work, we then ask the following question:

Is there a generic method providing a common view on ciphertexts of inputs under a (threshold) single-key encryption (so of sizes independent of $|\mathcal{Q}|$), using no more than one broadcast, without a trusted DKG *setup?*

1.1 Results

Before we move to our main contribution, we first complete the theoretical picture of honest majority MPC with GOD from one initial round of broadcast.

Throughout this paper, we consider protocols with a bulletin board PKI setup (bPKI, see Sect. 2.4), which is synonymous with *"plain model with a broadcast before distributing inputs"*. This setup has been described as such in [12,38], while our bPKI syntax is used in [34,35] and [16][1].

A) Contribution 1: Feasibility of 1 BC+asynch P2P MPC with GOD under honest majority. We assume one initial access to a broadcast functionality BC, which guarantees output whatever the (non)behavior of the sender.

Theorem 1. *There exists an MPC protocol with GOD under honest majority, under the sole setup of a bulletin board PKI; which furthermore enjoys (i) termination in* 1BC*-then-*1 *step of asynchronous P2P messages; and (ii) allows inputs from external owners, i.e., which do not take part in the computation;*

The baseline is the protocol of [12], that, as stated, lacks properties (i) and (ii). In Sect. 7, we show how their three-round MPC protocol in the plain model can be modified to work in a single-BC model and support external input-owners.

Related Works. A series of recent works [34,35,48] have undertaken to fully characterize what MPC protocols with one initial broadcast round allow achieving across various setup settings, such as with or without a PKI or a Uniform Random String (URS). For instance, [34] studied the feasibility and impossibility of two-round MPC with different guarantees and broadcast patterns considering a model in which a PKI is available, and this was later extended in [35], assuming only a URS but no PKI or correlated randomness. In this work, we complete the picture by studying the case where a bulletin board PKI is available but no URS. The concurrent work of [48, Corollary 6.1] states the same result as Theorem 1. We detail in the full version of this work how our matching construction provides more guarantees and has a different complexity. Note that in our ePrint [76], there is an additional unpublished infeasibility result in the appendix.

B) Main Result: Share&Shrink. We answer positively the main question by proposing a new generic protocol in the bulletin-board PKI model, called Share&Shrink. Considering a set $\mathcal{Q}$ of input-owners wishing to delegate a computation on their inputs to a set of $n = 2t + 1$ players, our new protocol *simultaneously* addresses the main problems raised in Sect. 1: a) MPC with GOD in one Broadcast, b) Delegability, and c) Efficient Evaluation.

Overall, Share&Shrink performs *in parallel*: a DKG, and the distribution of inputs encrypted under a single threshold encryption key (thus of sizes independent of $|\mathcal{Q}|$). The broadcast BC is used **only once** in parallel by both players and input-owners. The second step is performed over asynchronous point-to-point channels. It leverages two main ingredients:

- First, any linear homomorphic encryption (ℓ-HE) scheme as defined in Definition 4. This includes close variations of some well-known schemes such as GSW [66] or BFV [39]. This linearity property allows us to express these schemes as a set of linear maps. In particular, encryption consists in the evaluation

[1] [16] assumes a trusted DKG setup, which is stronger than a bPKI.

of a linear map $\Lambda^{\mathsf{ek}}_{\mathsf{Enc}}$, parametrized by an encryption key ek, over the secret input.
- Second, (any) publicly verifiable secret sharing (PVSS) scheme [46,51], formalized as a functionality $\mathcal{F}_{\mathsf{LSS}}$ in Sect. 3.3. Recall that a PVSS sharing algorithm, on input a secret s, roughly consists in generating a (n,t)-linear secret sharing of s, encrypting each n shares with one of the n players keys, before returning the resulting vector of n ciphertexts. Interestingly, thanks to the linearity property of the sharing, one can compute linear combinations on the shared inputs.

Share & Shrink can be described as follows.

0. Setup. Each player non-interactively generates then publishes a public key in a bulletin board PKI, for any public-key encryption scheme (PKE). Players also retrieve a URS (see Sect. 2.4), as needed in most of the practical cases.
1. Share. Players run a DKG protocol in one broadcast round. The pattern is as in [43], possibly with the generation of a relinearization key as done in [77], if the ℓ-HE scheme is a RLWE-based scheme with fully homomorphic capabilities.
In parallel, input-owners broadcast PVSSs of their inputs and of encryption randomnesses.
2. Shrink. Each player obtains a common *threshold encryption key* ek and perform threshold encryptions of the shared inputs under ek, thereby "shrinking" them down to the sizes of ciphertexts encrypted under the (threshold) single-key ek. What makes threshold encryption work in *one step of peer-to-peer asynchronous messages*, is that it simply consists in the opening of a *linear map* $\Lambda^{\mathsf{ek}}_{\mathsf{Enc}}$, parametrized by ek, evaluated over the shared inputs (and the shared randomnesses), leveraging the functionality $\mathcal{F}_{\mathsf{LSS}}$ we introduced.

At the end, players obtain a common view on inputs encrypted under a single-key ek. They can proceed as in the DKG-then-Input-distribution method, i.e. with evaluation and later threshold decryption, which require no further broadcast.

In short, as shown in Table 1, Share&Shrink enables building a delegated MPC protocol with GOD in one broadcast with the following properties:

- ***Generic*** **(RLWE compatible)**, i.e. it is scheme-independent, and in particular can be built from RLWE-based schemes.
- ***Short ciphertexts size*** **(efficient Eval)**, i.e. the size of the ciphertexts undergoing homomorphic evaluation does not depend on the number of inputs-owners. This matters in practice as it is linked to computation complexity. Notably, the multikey ciphertexts used in previous works [12] have sizes that depend on $|\mathcal{Q}|$, leading to homomorphic operations complexity that also grows with $|\mathcal{Q}|$.

Theorem 2. (Share&Shrink). *For any linear homomorphic encryption scheme in the sense of Definition 4, and evaluation algorithm (or asynchronous* *protocol) over encrypted inputs in the sense of Sect. 5.1, there exists an MPC protocol under honest majority with GOD in the* bPKI *model, in 1* BC *followed by asynchronous P2P messages. It furthermore allows inputs from* external input-owners. *It operates on ciphertexts under a (threshold) single-key encryption, and in particular, their sizes are* independent *of the number* $|\mathcal{Q}|$ *of input-owners, and of* n. *Moreover, it can naturally be adapted to the YOSO model (see Sect. 9).*

Table 1. MPC for $n = 2t + 1$ players and $|\mathcal{Q}|$ input-owners, using FHE with lattice dimension d and modulus q, and assuming a URS and a bulletin-board PKI. The "Size" is the one of the ciphertexts which undergo homomorphic evaluation. "Delegability" means that input-owners can outsource the computation to a set of players. Protocols that must restart if a player aborts mid-process are not marked as GOD.

Protocol	1 BC + asynch P2P	GOD for $t < n/2$	Delegability	Size of ciphertexts
[54,63,64,67]	✗	✗	✓	$\|\mathscr{C}\|$
[25]	✓	✗	✗	$\|\mathcal{Q}\| \cdot \|\mathscr{C}\|$
[38]	✓	✓	✗	$\|\mathscr{C}\|$
[12] + Theorem 1	✓	✓	✓	$\|\mathcal{Q}\| \cdot \|\mathscr{C}\|$
Theorem 2	✓	✓	✓	$\|\mathscr{C}\|$

It has furthermore the *reusability* property of [12], i.e., messages from input-owners are independent of the circuit, allowing multiple circuits to be evaluated on a set of distributed inputs. [14] pointed out that not handling inputs from external lightweight owners, like mobile phones, is one of the main obstacles to the deployment of MPC. We thus believe that enabling delegation, and not having a complexity that grows with the number of input-owners, are significant advantages over previous works in 1BC then asynchrony [12,38].

1.2 More Related Works

Approach of [38]**:** Their protocol is detailed in Sect. 6.1 and based on a threshold multikey-FHE scheme. Unfortunately, as previously argued, their construction is not generic, i.e. cannot be built from any RLWE-based FHE scheme, and not delegable, i.e. cannot accommodate external input-owners.

Approach of [12]**.** Their protocol is described in Sect. 6.2 and leverages a multikey-FHE scheme. As previously argued in Sect. 1, its main drawback is that the multikey evaluation unavoidably introduces an overhead in $|\mathcal{Q}|$, even in $|\mathcal{Q}|^2$ in their construction that uses GSW, which makes it very expensive to use.

Approach of [7]**:** Another useful (non FHE-based) tool to locally evaluate a circuit on encrypted data is garbled circuits. Following Yao's seminal work [80], they have become a core concept for 2-party secure computation, enabling one player to "encrypt" a circuit while another privately evaluates it. For more than two players, it was extended by [15], and followed by numerous constant-round protocols [7–9,58,59]. However, garbled-circuit-based protocols face scalability issues as the circuit size grows linearly with the number of players, making the per-player communication cost depend on the circuit size $|C|$. In [7], this cost is $O(n^\tau|C| + n^{\tau+1}d)$, where $\tau > 2$ and d is the depth of C, increasing data processing and communication bandwidth requirements.

2 Model

General Notations. We denote $x \xleftarrow{\$} \mathscr{D}$ the sampling of x according to the distribution $\mathscr{D}$. Cardinality of a set X is denoted as $|X|$. For a finite set E, we denote the uniform distribution on E as $U(E)$. The set of positive integers $[1,\ldots,n]$ is denoted $[n]$. We denote vectors in bold, e.g., $\mathbf{v}$, and $\overrightarrow{\mathscr{D}}$ a vector of distributions. We denote by λ the security parameter throughout the paper.

We consider a positive integer d, denoted the *lattice dimension*; a monic polynomial f of degree d; $k < q$ positive integers denoted as plaintext and ciphertext moduli; and $R := \mathbb{Z}[X]/f(X)$. We denote $R_k = R/(k.R)$ and $R_q = R/(q.R)$ the residue rings of R modulo k and q. We denote $[.]_k$ the reduction of an integer modulo k into R_k. When applied to polynomials or vectors, these operations are performed coefficient-wise. All linear forms are succinctly specified as *formal linear combinations*, e.g., let $(\overline{x_i})_i$ denote *labels* of some variables $(x_i)_i$, then, $\sum_i \lambda_i\overline{x_i}$ denotes $\{(x_i)_i \rightarrow \sum_i \lambda_i x_i\}$.

2.1 Players, Input Owners and Corruptions

We consider $n = 2t + 1$ players $\mathscr{P} = (P_i)_{i\in[n]}$, which are probabilistic polynomial-time (PPT) machines, of public identities. We also consider PPT machines called *input-owners* $\mathcal{Q}$, and an *output-learner* $\mathcal{L}$, logically disjunct from players. Using the Universal Composability (UC) model [23] with static corruptions, we consider a PPT machine, denoted as the Environment Env. It fully controls an entity called the "dummy adversary" $\mathcal{A}$. At the start of the execution, $\mathcal{A}$ may corrupt up to t players of its choosing and any number of input-owners. They behave as instructed by $\mathcal{A}$. Without loss of generality, $\mathcal{A}$ corrupts exactly t players, indexed by $\mathcal{I} \subset [n]$. The remaining *honest* ones are indexed by $\mathcal{H} = [n] \setminus \mathcal{I}$. $\mathcal{A}$ notifies Env of every message received by corrupt players and from (simulated) functionalities. $\mathcal{A}$ can *rush*, i.e. all messaging functionalities (BC, bPKI, $\mathcal{F}_{\text{AT}}$) let $\mathcal{A}$ learn the messages sent by honest players before choosing those sent by corrupt ones.

2.2 Semi-malicious Corruptions

In our protocols and proofs, we will consider what we define as *Semi-Malicious Corruptions*, following [10, §A.2] [12,21,38]. Semi-maliciously corrupt players and input-owners continuously forward to $\mathcal{A}$ their outputs received from ideal functionalities, and act arbitrarily as instructed by $\mathcal{A}$. E.g., they can possibly not send some message although the protocol instructs them to. However, when a corrupt entity M inputs a message m to a messaging functionality $\mathcal{F}_{\text{AT}}$ or BC, then the sending of m must be compatible with the requirements of the protocol, with respect to: (i) all outputs of instances of $\overline{\mathcal{G}}_{\text{URS}}$, bPKI, BC, as defined in Sect. 2.4, and also $\mathcal{F}_{\mathsf{LSS}}$ as later introduced in Sect. 3.3, required for sending m, and (ii) an internal witness tape that M must have, of the form (x, r) with x an input and r of the same length as all random coins that an honest player would have been meant to have tossed upon sending m. M can however use conflicting (x, r) when sending different messages m, m'. Moreover, we also require that the semi-malicious adversary can only make BC^M to output v for some corrupt M only if: either v could have been input to BC^M by M itself according to the above rule, or, if $v = \perp$.

In summary, the adversary must have a witness tape containing: an input value of P, coins explaining the random choices of P, and the set of all broadcast values so far (possibly from other senders), including in our case the encryption keys, and, for each previous asynchronous step, a set of $t+1$ received messages. The latter requirement is new and specific to our asynchronous context. Recall that in [10], semi-malicious players simply had to explain their behavior based on previous broadcast messages. By contrast, in our model, nothing prevents them from arbitrarily picking the sets of $t+1$ messages. The observation which we make is that this new choosing power is useless, since our MPC protocol is made only of threshold openings of linear maps as teased in Sect. 1.1. Precisely, the choice of the $t+1$ messages *does not modify* the reconstructed value, from which semi-malicious players must build their next message.

2.3 Formalizing Eventual Delivery in UC

We now explain the high-level idea of the mechanism, denoted fetch -*and*-delay, used to formalize eventual delivery following [30,53]. Every ideal functionality $\mathcal{F}$, when it needs to eventually deliver (ssid, v) to some entity P, engages in the following interaction. It notifies $\mathcal{A}$ of the output id (ssid), and initializes a counter $D_{\mathsf{ssid}} \leftarrow 1$, which captures the delivery delay. Upon receiving (delay) from $\mathcal{A}$, it sets $D_{\mathsf{ssid}} \leftarrow D_{\mathsf{ssid}} + 1$. Upon receiving (fetch) from P, it sets $D_{\mathsf{ssid}} \leftarrow D_{\mathsf{ssid}} - 1$, as well as for all other counters related to pending outputs for P. In addition, we specify that it leaks (fetch) to $\mathcal{A}$[2]. It is left implicit that entities fetch as much as they can all. Since $\mathcal{A}$ is PPT, at some point, it gets exhausted from pressing the button delay. So, after sufficiently many fetches more, the counter drops down to 0. Then $\mathcal{F}$ can deliver (ssid, v) to P.

[2] This precision is not present in previous works [30,53,60], since that way, the adversary knows at any moment in time when an output will be delivered.

2.4 Ideal Functionalities

Broadcast with Eventual Termination (and Bulletin Board PKI). We formalize the ideal functionality BC of broadcast in the full version of this work. It is parametrized by a sender, and by a set of receivers. It has the following properties: (Termination) all honest receivers eventually output, and (Consistency) any two honest receivers output the same value. Finally, (Validity) if the sender is honest and inputs value m, all honest receivers output the same m.

From BC, we can describe the special case of a bulletin board PKI, denoted as bPKI. The difference with BC is that bPKI is accessible for players to submit their keys only before they receive inputs.

Remark 1. Notice that we *do not* impose any condition for the sending of some m on bPKI. Concretely, this is because the UC proof for implementing $\mathcal{F}_{\mathsf{LSS}}$, the main building block for our MPC protocol in Sect. 5.3, does not need extractable secret keys. The consequence is that our protocol can be instantiated with NIZKs with *non-necessary straight line* simulation extractability, so this allows more efficient NIZKs. Recent such examples are Bulleproofs and Spartan [36], of which the former are the ones used in [46] for our purpose.

(Asynchronous) Authenticated Message Transmitting: $\mathcal{F}_{\text{AT}}$***.*** We formalize in the full version the ideal functionality of asynchronous *public authenticated* message transmitting with eventual delivery delay. It is parametrized by a sender and a receiver, hence the terminology *authenticated.* It delivers every message sent within a finite delay D, although D can be adaptively increased by $\mathcal{A}$. It leaks the content of every message to $\mathcal{A}$, hence the terminology *public.*

Global Public Uniform Random String (URS): $\overline{\mathcal{G}}_{\text{URS}}$***.*** It samples uniformly at random a sequence of bits of pre-defined length κ, denoted URS, then outputs it to all players.

2.5 Ideal Functionality of MPC with Eventual Delivery: $\mathcal{F}_{\text{C}}$

The ideal functionality of MPC that we aim to UC implement, is formalized as $\mathcal{F}_{\text{C}}$ in Fig. 1. It returns to an output-learner $\mathcal{L}$ the evaluation of an arithmetic circuit $\mathrm{C} : (\mathscr{M} \cup \{\perp\})^n \rightarrow \mathscr{M}$ over inputs in $\mathscr{M}$. For simplicity: C has n input gates, one output gate, and $\mathcal{F}_{\text{C}}$ expects one single input from each owner.

The functionality works as follows. Upon receiving an input from any input-owner Q_i, it stores $(\mathsf{Q}_i, \overline{m_i})$[3] and leaks this to $\mathcal{A}$. Before delivering the output, $\mathcal{F}_{\text{C}}$ needs to wait for the inputs to be submitted. However, $\mathcal{A}$ may prevent corrupt owners from sending their inputs. To handle this, the functionality *i*) waits until it receives an input from every honest owner, *ii*) sets a timeout $T_{\mathcal{A}}$, and *iii*) sets to $\perp$ the inputs of the (corrupt) owners which did not give an input. Once the timeout expires, the output−available flag is permanently set to true and no more inputs can be submitted. Finally, the evaluation is eventually delivered after a finite delay chosen by $\mathcal{A}$ (guaranteed thanks to the fetch-and-delay mechanism explained in Sect. 2.3).

[3] Where $\overline{m_i}$ denotes the label of variable m_i.

$\mathcal{F}_{\mathsf{C}}$

Output format Initialize an empty vector $\mathbf{m} = \{\top\}^n$.

- Initialize output–available ← false.
- When all $m_i \neq \top$, $\forall i \in [n]$, set output–available = true. //it is now frozen

Formalizing timeout for inputs of corrupt players

- Initialize a counter $T_{\mathcal{A}} \leftarrow 1$ // the timeout.
- Upon receiving delay–inputs from $\mathcal{A}$, $T_{\mathcal{A}} \leftarrow T_{\mathcal{A}} + 1$.
- Upon receiving fetch from $\mathcal{L}$, $T_{\mathcal{A}} \leftarrow T_{\mathcal{A}} - 1$.
- When $T_{\mathcal{A}} = 0$ for the first time, freeze forever $T_{\mathcal{A}} = 0$. Then, for all $i \in \mathcal{I}$: if $m_i = \top$, then set $m_i \leftarrow \bot$.

Input (Only accessible while output–available = false) On input (input, $\widetilde{m_i} \in \mathscr{M}$) from any $\mathsf{Q}_i \in \mathcal{Q}$ for the first time, or possibly from $\mathcal{A}$ if Q_i is corrupt, set $m_i \leftarrow \widetilde{m_i}$, then store (input, $\mathcal{S}, m_i$), and *eventually-deliver* (stored, $\overline{m_i}$) to each player $P \in \mathscr{P}$. //eventually-delivers" consists of the fetch-and-delay mechanism explained in Section 2.3.

Formalizing eventual delivery

- Initialize a counter $D_R \leftarrow 0$ // the delivery delay.
- Upon receiving fetch from $\mathcal{L}$, $D_R \leftarrow D_R - 1$.
- When $D_R = 0$ for the first time, if no output was delivered yet to $\mathcal{L}$, wait until output–available = true, then deliver $y = \mathrm{C}(\mathbf{m})$ to $\mathcal{L}$.

Fig. 1. Functionality of secure circuit evaluation. Each input m_i is identified by a public label $\overline{m_i}$.

3 Cryptographic Ingredients

We now detail the main cryptographic ingredients needed for the remainder of the paper. After defining a Linear Homomorphic Encryption scheme in Sect. 3.1 and detailing an example in Sect. 3.2, we describe in Sect. 3.3, an ideal functionality for linear secret sharing, denoted $\mathcal{F}_{\mathsf{LSS}}$, and discuss its implementation.

Ring Learning with Errors. Let Ψ_q and $\mathscr{X}_q$ be distributions over R_q. The *decisional*-Ring Learning with Errors (RLWE) [61] assumption with parameter $(R_q, \mathscr{X}_q, \Psi_q)$ can be stated as follows: for a fixed secret sample $s \leftarrow \mathscr{X}_q$, then any polynomially long sequence of samples in R_q^2 of the form $(a_i, b_i = s \cdot a_i + e_i)_i$, where $a_i \leftarrow U(R_q)$, and $e_i \leftarrow \Psi_q$, is computationally indistinguishable from a uniform random sequence of elements of R_q^2.

Lemma 3 ***(Smudging lemma [10]).*** *For B_1, B_2 positive integers and $e_1 \in [-B_1, B_1]$ a fixed integer, sample e_2 uniformly at random in $[-B_2, B_2]$. Then the distribution of e_2 is statistically indistinguishable from that of $e_2 + e_1$ if $B_1/B_2 = \epsilon$, where $\epsilon = \epsilon(\lambda)$ is a negligible function.*

3.1 Toy Model of Linear Homomorphic Encryption Scheme

We observe that in many encryption schemes, key generation, encryption, and decryption are essentially *linear maps*. For simplicity's sake, we assume that all operations take place over $\mathbb{Z}/q\mathbb{Z}$-modules, where q is a known modulus[4]. A linear map between two $\mathbb{Z}/q\mathbb{Z}$-modules $g:(E,+)\to(F,*)$ satisfies $g(e_1+e_2)=g(e_1)*g(e_2)$ for $e_1,e_2\in E$, and, $g(a\cdot e)=a\cdot g(e)$ for all $a\in\mathbb{Z}/q\mathbb{Z}$. In such schemes, key generation is a linear function in a decryption key sk and some randomness, encryption is linear in a plaintext and some randomnesses, while decryption is, roughly, linear in sk. This linearity implies that there exists a public map which, given an offset (roughly: sk'), maps encryptions under sk into ciphertexts which have the same distribution as fresh encryptions under $\mathsf{sk}+\mathsf{sk}'$. This linearity also supports partial homomorphic operations, such as addition and/or multiplication, in some form. The following Definition 4 provides a wrapper for all such schemes, formalized using generic linear maps ($\Lambda_{\mathsf{EKeyGen}}$, Λ_{Enc} and Λ_{Dec}).

Definition 4 (Linear Homomorphic Encryption (ℓ-HE)**).** *A* ℓ-HE *scheme consists of a message space* $\mathscr{M}$*; spaces of decryption and encryption keys* $\mathscr{X}$, $\mathscr{E}k$*; randomness spaces* $\mathscr{B}_{Key}$ *and* $\overrightarrow{\mathscr{B}_{\mathsf{Enc}}}$*, both (subsets of) vector spaces over* $\mathbb{Z}/q\mathbb{Z}$ *modules; and a ciphertext space* $\mathscr{C}$*; along with the following PPT algorithms:*

- $\mathsf{Setup}(1^\lambda)$*: On input the security parameter* λ*, the setup algorithm outputs a set of public parameters* pp *and a uniform random string* a*.*
- $\mathsf{KeyGen}(\mathsf{pp},a)$*: On input some public parameters* pp*, and a URS* a*, the key generation algorithm samples a decryption key* $\mathsf{sk}\overset{\$}{\leftarrow}\mathscr{X}$ *and a key randomness* $\rho^{key}\overset{\$}{\leftarrow}\mathscr{B}_{Key}$*. When* $\mathscr{B}_{Key}$ *is not closed under addition, the randomness* ρ^{key} *is drawn small enough such that the sum of* n *such terms remains statistically within* $\mathscr{B}_{\mathrm{Key}}$*. In our multiparty setting, this ensures that a common key resulting from a sum of* n *keys remains valid, as illustrated in Eq. 1. The algorithm outputs an encryption key* $\mathsf{ek}\leftarrow\Lambda^{a}_{\mathsf{EKeyGen}}(\mathsf{sk},\rho^{key})\in\mathscr{E}k$[5]*, where* $\Lambda^{a}_{\mathsf{EKeyGen}}$ *is a public linear map with coefficients determined by the URS* a*.*
- $\mathsf{Enc}(\mathsf{pp},\mathsf{ek}\in\mathscr{E}k,m\in\mathscr{M})$*: On input public parameters* pp*, an encryption key* ek *and a plaintext* m*, the encryption algorithm samples a vector of randomnesses* $\boldsymbol{\rho}_{\mathsf{Enc}}\overset{\$}{\leftarrow}\overrightarrow{\mathscr{B}_{Enc}}$ *and outputs a ciphertext* $\mathsf{c}\leftarrow\Lambda^{\mathsf{ek}}_{\mathsf{Enc}}(m,\boldsymbol{\rho}_{\mathsf{Enc}})\in\mathscr{C}$*.*
- $\mathsf{Dec}(\mathsf{sk}\in\mathscr{X},\mathsf{c}\in\mathscr{C})$*: On input a ciphertext* c *and a decryption key* sk*, the decryption algorithm computes* $\mu\leftarrow\Lambda^{\mathsf{c}}_{\mathsf{Dec}}(\mathsf{sk})$*, and either outputs a plaintext* $m=\Omega_{\mathsf{Dec}}(\mu)$ *or* $\perp$*, where* Ω_{Dec} *denotes a non-linear decoding function.*

Examples. Definition 4 applies to various classical schemes such as BGN [20], exponentiated ElGamal [50,75], GSW [47] or CL [24], as discussed in the full version. Interestingly, this definition wraps schemes with varying homomorphic

[4] However, this formalization can be adapted to settings where q is unknown, such as in the CL case, where secret-sharing operates over $\mathbb{Z}$, as explained in [22].

[5] Sometimes with a *relinearization key* $\mathbf{rlk}\in\mathscr{R}lk$, which must also be linear in sk.

capabilities, from schemes supporting only homomorphic additions and scalar multiplications [24,50] to fully homomorphic schemes [47]. In particular, FHE schemes that satisfy Definition 4 are categorized as ℓ-FHE, with more details provided in Sect. 3.2.

MPC from **ℓ-HE.** Our main goal is to build a constant-round MPC protocol in 1 BC using efficient RLWE-based public-key FHE schemes. Modern schemes like BFV [39] or CKKS [27] require the generation of an extra "relinearization key" **rlk** for homomorphic evaluation of a circuit. To be compatible with our Share&Shrink protocol in 1 BC later described in Sect. 4, such FHE schemes must meet the ℓ-HE criteria outlined in Definition 4, i.e. to be built from linear maps, including for this relinearization key. Unfortunately, most RLWE-based schemes [54,64,67] do not satisfy this, as their **rlk** are quadratic in the decryption key sk. In Sect. 3.2, we consider the only known RLWE-based scheme that meets this requirement.

3.2 ℓ-BFV: A RLWE-Based ℓ-FHE Scheme with Linear Relinearization Key Generation

In [77], Urban and Rambaud introduced ℓ-BFV, a variant of the BFV FHE scheme, with a relinearization key generation that is linear in the decryption key, unlike the original [39].

Definition 5. *(ℓ-BFV [77]) ℓ-BFV is defined as a mere ℓ-HE scheme, augmented with an additional linear map, $\Lambda_{\mathsf{RlkGen}}$, for generating a relinearization key. ℓ-BFV takes two URSs as inputs: $\mathbf{a}$ and $\mathbf{d}_1$. Let $\mathscr{X}_q$, Ψ_q and $\mathscr{B}_{\mathsf{Enc},q}$ be distributions over R_q, with coefficients distributed according to a centered discrete Gaussian with standard deviation σ (resp σ_{Enc}) and truncated support over $[-B, B]$ (resp B_{Enc}) where σ and B are cryptosystem parameters. ℓ-BFV leverages the well-known gadget toolkit [25,47], including the following* gadget vector*: $\mathbf{g} \in R_q^l$, for some parameter $l \in \mathbb{N}$, and consists of the following PPT algorithms:*

- *ℓ-BFV.KeyGen(): Parse the URSs as $(\mathbf{a} \in R_q^l, \mathbf{d}_1 \in R_q^l)$, sample $e^{(\mathsf{pk})} \xleftarrow{\$} \Psi_q$ and $\mathsf{sk} \xleftarrow{\$} \mathscr{X}_q$, and set $a = \mathbf{a}[0]$. Define $\Lambda^a_{\mathsf{EKeyGen}} : (\mathsf{sk}, e^{(\mathsf{pk})}) \to (-a \cdot \mathsf{sk} + e^{(\mathsf{pk})}, a)$. Sample $r \leftarrow \mathscr{X}_q$, $\mathbf{e}_0^{(\mathbf{rlk})}, \mathbf{e}_2^{(\mathbf{rlk})} \leftarrow \Psi_q^l$, and define $\Lambda^{\mathbf{a},\mathbf{d}_1,\mathbf{g}}_{\mathsf{RlkGen}} : (\mathsf{sk}, r, \mathbf{e}_0^{(\mathbf{rlk})}, \mathbf{e}_2^{(\mathbf{rlk})}) \to (-\mathsf{sk} \cdot \mathbf{d}_1 + \mathbf{e}_0^{(\mathbf{rlk})} + r \cdot \mathbf{g}, \mathbf{d}_1, r \cdot \mathbf{a} + \mathbf{e}_2^{(\mathbf{rlk})} + \mathsf{sk} \cdot \mathbf{g})$
Output $\mathsf{ek} \leftarrow \Lambda^a_{\mathsf{EKeyGen}}(\mathsf{sk}, e^{(\mathsf{pk})}) = (-a \cdot \mathsf{sk} + e^{(\mathsf{pk})}, a) = (b, a)$, the relinearization key $\mathbf{rlk} \leftarrow \Lambda^{\mathbf{a},\mathbf{d}_1,\mathbf{g}}_{\mathsf{RlkGen}}(\mathsf{sk}, r, \mathbf{e}_0^{(\mathbf{rlk})}, \mathbf{e}_2^{(\mathbf{rlk})})$ and sk.*
- *ℓ-BFV.Enc$(\mathsf{ek} = (b, a), m \in R_k)$: Sample the $\overrightarrow{\text{encryption}}$ randomnesses $e_0^{(\mathsf{Enc})} \xleftarrow{\$} \mathscr{B}_{\mathsf{Enc},q}$, $e_1^{(\mathsf{Enc})} \xleftarrow{\$} \Psi_q$, and $u \xleftarrow{\$} \mathscr{X}_q$. Thus here: $\mathscr{B}_{Enc} = \mathscr{B}_{\mathsf{Enc},q} \times \Psi_q \times \mathscr{X}_q$. Define $\Lambda^{b,a}_{\mathsf{Enc}} : (\Delta m, u, e_0^{(\mathsf{Enc})}, e_1^{(\mathsf{Enc})}) \to (\Delta m + u \cdot b + e_0^{(\mathsf{Enc})}, u \cdot a + e_1^{(\mathsf{Enc})})$ with $\Delta = \lfloor q/k \rfloor$.
Output $\mathsf{c} \leftarrow \Lambda^{b,a}_{\mathsf{Enc}}(\Delta m, u, e_0^{(\mathsf{Enc})}, e_1^{(\mathsf{Enc})}) \in R_q^2$.*
- *ℓ-BFV.Dec(sk, c): Given a ciphertext $\mathsf{c} = (\mathsf{c}[0], \mathsf{c}[1]) \in R_q^2$, define $\Lambda^{\mathsf{c}}_{\mathsf{Dec}} : \mathsf{sk} \to \mathsf{c}[0] + \mathsf{c}[1] \cdot \mathsf{sk}$ and compute $\mu \leftarrow \Lambda^{\mathsf{c}}_{\mathsf{Dec}}(\mathsf{sk})$.
Output $m \leftarrow \left[\left\lfloor \frac{k}{q}(\mu) \right\rceil\right]_k := \Omega_{\mathsf{Dec}}(\mu) \in R_k$.*

ℓ-BFV is a fully homomorphic ℓ-FHE scheme that comes with a build-in Eval function for evaluating a circuit as later detailed in Sect. 5.1. It will server as our main example for our experiments in Sect. 8. Moreover, for later use in the security proof of our MPC protocol in Sect. 5.3, we recall in the full version of this paper the classical "IND-CPA under Joint Keys" Lemma [10], adapted in [77] for RLWE-based schemes such as ℓ-BFV.

3.3 Toy Functionality of LSS, and Instantiation in 1BC+1 Async P2P

The main ingredient in building a robust threshold scheme is a (n, t)-linear secret sharing scheme ((n, t)-LSS, formally defined in Def.9 in the full version), that divides a secret s into n shares, allowing only authorized subsets of $t+1$ of them to reconstruct the secret. Due to the linearity of the scheme, given shared secrets $m_1, \ldots, m_n$, some linear map Λ can be applied to compute the linear combination $\Lambda(\{m_i\}_i)$ on the shared inputs. The main technical challenge we face is that we consider in Sect. 8 an efficient ℓ-FHE scheme defined over polynomial rings, as introduced in Sect. 3.2. Unfortunately, Shamir's classic LSS scheme [73] is instantiated over a field $\mathbb{F}$, as it is based on polynomial interpolation and involves the computation of Lagrange coefficients, that require inverting elements of the form $\alpha_i - \alpha_j$, where α_i and α_j are public-points. Working over a field guarantees that all non-zero elements are units, hence that these coefficients exist. In the full version of this work, we recall known results [40, 77] for constructing a LSS scheme over rings. Following [77], we now abstract this linear secret sharing with linear combination capability through a functionality $\mathcal{F}_{\mathsf{LSS}}$ and provide an overview of its implementation from 1 BC in the bulletin-board PKI model. Note that our $\mathcal{F}_{\mathsf{LSS}}$ functionality is the first with eventual delivery (unlike [30]) *and* asynchronous opening (unlike [32]). Compared to the existing literature, this double constraint creates the new case to handle which we call 'Early Opening'. This deals with an honest player calling the output, i.e., sending its opening share, before the other players.

Functionality $\mathcal{F}_{\mathsf{LSS}}$. We specify in Fig. 2, an ideal functionality for secret sharing with linear combination capability and eventual delivery, denoted $\mathcal{F}_{\mathsf{LSS}}$. It is parametrized by i) a set $\mathscr{P}$ of n players, ii) a list $\mathscr{S}$ of entities of the senders, where each $\mathcal{S} \in \mathscr{S}$ has a list of inputs: $(x_{\mathcal{S},\alpha})_{\alpha \in X_S}$, identified by input labels $(\overline{x_{\mathcal{S},\alpha}})_{\alpha \in X_S}$. We denote $X_\mathcal{S}$ the list of indices α of inputs of sender $\mathcal{S}$. Finally iii), we consider an output-learner $\mathcal{L}$.

Setup. Before any sender starts interacting with $\mathcal{F}_{\mathsf{LSS}}$, it needs to wait until (Setup, P) is stored $\forall P \in \mathscr{P}$. However, the adversary $\mathcal{A}$ can choose to never instruct corrupt players to setup. To remedy this, we use the *fetch-and-delay* mechanism explained in Sect. 2.3 and introduce a timeout $T_\mathcal{A}$.

Input. Upon receiving (ready) from $\mathcal{F}_{\mathsf{LSS}}$, any $\mathcal{S} \in \mathscr{S}$ can then send its inputs $(x_{\mathcal{S},\alpha})_{\alpha \in X_S}$ of labels $(\overline{x_{\mathcal{S},\alpha}})_{\alpha \in X_S}$, after which $\mathcal{F}_{\mathsf{LSS}}$ notifies all the players. These values cannot be subsequently updated; $\mathcal{S}$ is committed to the submitted values.

$\mathcal{F}_{\mathsf{LSS}}$

Participants: A set $\mathscr{S}$ of senders, an output learner $\mathcal{L}$, and a set $\mathscr{P}$ of players.
Inputs (For each $S \in \mathscr{S}$): a list $(x_{S,\alpha})_{\alpha \in X_S}$, where each input $x_{S,\alpha}$ is identified by a unique predefined 'label' $\overline{x_{S,\alpha}}$.

Setup

- On input (Setup) from any $P \in \mathscr{P}$ for the first time, or possibly from $\mathcal{A}$ if P is corrupt: stores (Setup, P), and *eventually-delivers* (Setup, P) to each player $P \in \mathscr{P}$. //eventually-delivers" consists of the same fetch-and-delay mechanism as explained in Section 2.3.
- Initialize a counter $T_{\mathcal{A}} \leftarrow 1$ //Formalizing timing for setup of corrupt players
  - Upon receiving delay−Setup from $\mathcal{A}$, $T_{\mathcal{A}} \leftarrow T_{\mathcal{A}} + 1$.
  - Upon receiving fetch from any $P \in \mathscr{P}$, $T_{\mathcal{A}} \leftarrow T_{\mathcal{A}} - 1$.
  - When $T_{\mathcal{A}} = 0$ for the first time, freeze forever $T_{\mathcal{A}} = 0$. Then, send ready to every $\mathcal{S} \in \mathscr{S}$.

Input On input (input, $\overline{x_{S,\alpha}}, x_{S,\alpha} \in R_q$) from any $\mathcal{S} \in \mathscr{S}$ for the first time[a], or possibly from $\mathcal{A}$ if $\mathcal{S}$ is corrupt: first, if $x_{S,\alpha} = \perp$ then set it to 0, store (input, $\mathcal{S}, x_{S,\alpha}$), and *eventually-deliver* (stored, $\overline{x_{S,\alpha}}$)[b] to each player $P \in \mathscr{P}$.

$\mathcal{A}$ delaying eventual delivery

- Initialize $D \leftarrow 1$ // Delivery delay
- Upon receiving delay from $\mathcal{A}$, set $D \leftarrow D + 1$
- Upon receiving fetch from $\mathcal{L}$, $D \leftarrow D - 1$

Bookkeeping requests from honest players

- Initialize HOpeners $\leftarrow \{\}$[c]
- Upon receiving (LCOpen, ssid $= \Lambda$) from any *honest* player $P_i \in \mathscr{P}$, set HOpeners $\leftarrow$ HOpeners $\cup \{P_i\}$, set $D \leftarrow D - 1$ and leak (LCOpen, ssid $= \Lambda, P_i$) to $\mathcal{A}$.

LCOpen

- [Early Opening] If |HOpeners| ≥ 1 *and* if all $\overline{x_{S,\alpha}}$ appearing with nonzero coefficient in Λ are stored, then,
  1. if $\mathcal{L}$ is corrupt, leak $y := \Lambda((x_{S,\alpha})_{S,\alpha})$ to $\mathcal{A}$;
  2. if $\mathcal{L}$ is honest, upon receiving (open−order, Λ) from $\mathcal{A}$, if no output was delivered yet to $\mathcal{L}$, then send (ssid $= \Lambda, y := \Lambda((x_{S,\alpha})_{S,\alpha})$) to $\mathcal{L}$.
- [Collective Opening] If |HOpeners| $\geq t + 1$ *and* $D \leq 0$ *and* no output was delivered yet to $\mathcal{L}$, *and* if all $\overline{x_{S,\alpha}}$ appearing with nonzero coefficient in Λ are stored, then send (ssid $= \Lambda, y := \Lambda((x_{S,\alpha})_{S,\alpha})$ to $\mathcal{L}$.

[a]Once a sender $\mathcal{S}$ (or $\mathcal{A}$) send an input $x_{S,\alpha}$ with label $\overline{x_{S,\alpha}}$, the former cannot be subsequently updated.

[b]Appended with "$x_{S,\alpha} = \perp$" when this is the case.

[c]Recall that we consider in this description an unique Λ. If multiple are considered, then several sets HOpeners$_\Lambda$ must also be considered.

Fig. 2. Sharing with Linear Combination functionality for one single linear map Λ. sid omitted

Opening. Let $\mathsf{HOpeners}$ be a set of players, initially empty. Any player P_i can call LCOpen for some linear map Λ, and is then included in $\mathsf{HOpeners}$ (for some Λ). Upon receiving LCOpen for some linear map Λ from $t+1$ honest players, i.e. when $|\mathsf{HOpeners}| \geq t+1$, and if $\mathcal{F}_{\mathsf{LSS}}$ has stored all the inputs appearing with nonzero coefficient in Λ, then it eventually delivers its evaluation.

Implementation of $\mathcal{F}_{\mathsf{LSS}}$. Our goal is to build a protocol Π_{LSS} that implements $\mathcal{F}_{\mathsf{LSS}}$, i.e. that enables, after the unique round of broadcast, players to have a common view on a set of shared secrets. Subsequently, they can perform the threshold opening of the evaluation of *any* linear map over these shared secrets, using one step of all-to-all asynchronous peer-to-peer messages. Π_{LSS} is detailed in the full version. Overall it can be outlined as follows.

First, each player generates then registers its public key to bPKI. To send a secret s to $\mathcal{F}_{\mathsf{LSS}}$, i.e., to share it, the first step is to generate a (n,t)-linear secret sharing of s, yielding shares $\{s^{(i)}\}_{i\in[n]}$. Encrypt each share $s^{(i)}$ under P_i's public key. The resulting n-sized vector of ciphertexts is called a public verifiable secret sharing (PVSS). The term *verifiable* is used because when compiling to fully malicious security, NIZKs of knowledge of plaintexts and of a degree t polynomial are appended. For state-of-the-art implementations, see [46,51].

To open a linear map Λ over a set of shared secrets $(s_j)_j$: every P_i decrypts its encrypted shares $s_j^{(i)}$, then evaluates Λ on them. By linearity of the (n,t)-LSS scheme, the result is a partial opening share $z^{(i)}$ of $\Lambda((s_j)_j)$. Then, it sends $z^{(i)}$ to all via asynchronous P2P channels. Finally, from any $t+1$ partial opening shares, the desired linear combination $\Lambda((s_j)_j)$ is efficiently reconstructible.

We provide more details about the LSS instantiation over rings in the full version, and prove that Π_{LSS} does UC-implement $\mathcal{F}_{\mathsf{LSS}}$.

4 Share&Shrink: DKG & Encrypted Input Distribution in 1 BC + 1 Async. P2P

We follow the model and the formalism introduced in Sects. 2 and 3 and assume a linear homomorphic encryption scheme as in Definition 4, represented by a tuple of PPT algorithms ℓ-$\mathsf{HE} = (\mathsf{Setup}, \mathsf{KeyGen}, \mathsf{Enc}, \mathsf{Dec})$. Recall in particular that they are built from public fixed linear maps $\Lambda^{a}_{\mathsf{EKeyGen}}, \Lambda^{\mathsf{ek}}_{\mathsf{Enc}}, \Lambda^{\mathsf{c}}_{\mathsf{Dec}}$[6].

We now describe a protocol in the $\mathcal{F}_{\mathsf{LSS}}$-hybrid model, called Share&Shrink and formalized in Fig. 3, which performs a "DKG & Encrypted Input distribution" in 1 BC+asynch P2P. It allows players to obtain all-at-once: (i) a common threshold encryption key ek[7], (ii) a secret-shared decryption key sk; (formally: in $\mathcal{F}_{\mathsf{LSS}}$); and (iii) a common view on ℓ-HE ciphertexts of the inputs encrypted under ek. The challenge is that the input-owners have access to the broadcast to distribute their inputs *only before* the encryption key ek is known!

(0) **Setup:** Players receive some public parameters pp and a URS a.
In parallel, they Setup $\mathcal{F}_{\mathsf{LSS}}$ (concretely: publish PKE encryption keys).

[6] And possibly an extra $\Lambda_{\mathsf{RlkGen}}$ if the specific scheme requires a relinearization key.
[7] Possibly along with a common relinearization key $\mathbf{rlk}$, e.g. in the case of ℓ-BFV.

(1) **Broadcast:** Input-owners send (**Share**) their inputs m & encryption randomnesses $\boldsymbol{\rho}_{\mathsf{Enc}}$ to $\mathcal{F}_{\mathsf{LSS}}$ (concretely: broadcast PVSSs of them).
In parallel, based on public parameters pp and URS a, players generate additive contributions sk_i to the ℓ-HE decryption key, which they input to $\mathcal{F}_{\mathsf{LSS}}$; and ek_i to the threshold encryption key (using randomness ρ_i^{key}), which they broadcast (along with possibly extra material, e.g., a relinearization key for ℓ-BFV).
• **Local computation:** Then, each player locally computes the common threshold encryption key ek(See footnote 6), out of the contributions from the subset S of indices of non-aborting players. Precisely, $S \subset [n]$ are indices of those that broadcast correct material (including the PVSS, as captured by $\mathcal{F}_{\mathsf{LSS}}$). By linearity of the ℓ-HE scheme, this key is merely the sum of the contributions from S:

$$\mathsf{ek} = \Sigma_{i \in S} \Lambda^{a}_{\mathsf{EKeyGen}}(\mathsf{sk}_i, \rho_i^{\mathsf{key}}) = \Lambda^{a}_{\mathsf{EKeyGen}}(\Sigma_{i \in S}(\mathsf{sk}_i, \rho_i^{\mathsf{key}})) \quad (1)$$

(2) **Asynchronous step (Shrinking of the inputs):** Finally, players jointly compute threshold encryptions under ek of the shared inputs m_j. Con-

Share & Shrink protocol

Participants: n players $(P_i)_{i \in [n]}$, and $|\mathcal{Q}|$ input owners;
Inputs (for each input owner $\mathsf{Q}_j \in \mathcal{Q}$): plaintext m_j with label $\overline{m_j}$.

- (0) **Setup.** Each player P_i:
  - Sends (Setup) to $\mathcal{F}_{\mathsf{LSS}}$
  - Obtains some public parameters $\mathsf{pp} \leftarrow \ell\text{-HE.Setup}$, and a URS $a \leftarrow \overline{\mathcal{G}}_{\mathrm{URS}}$.
- (1) **Broadcast.**
  - Input and Randomness Distribution (I): Each $\mathsf{Q}_j \in \mathcal{Q}$:
    * Samples $\boldsymbol{\rho_j} \xleftarrow{\$} \overrightarrow{\mathscr{B}_{Enc}}$ and sends $(\mathsf{input}, \{\overline{m_j}, \overline{\boldsymbol{\rho_j}}\}, \{m_j, \boldsymbol{\rho_j}\})$ to $\mathcal{F}_{\mathsf{LSS}}$.
  - DKG (I): Each player P_i:
    * Computes $(\mathsf{sk}_i, \mathsf{ek}_i) \leftarrow \ell\text{-HE.KeyGen}(\mathsf{pp}, a)$. Sends $(\mathsf{input}, \overline{\mathsf{sk}_i}, \mathsf{sk}_i)$ to $\mathcal{F}_{\mathsf{LSS}}$ and broadcasts ek_i over BC^{P_i} //possibly along with $\mathbf{rlk}_i \in \mathscr{R}lk$.
- **Local computation.**
  - DKG (II): Upon the instances of BC of all players $(P_i)_{i \in [n]}$ having terminated, let S be the subset of indices of players that broadcast a ek_i and for which $\mathcal{F}_{\mathsf{LSS}}$ has acknowledged the receipt of an additive contribution to the decryption key. Each player P_i:
    * Computes $\mathsf{ek} = \Sigma_{i \in S} \mathsf{ek}_i$[a] and defines the (secret shared) decryption key as $\mathsf{sk} = \Sigma_{i \in S} \mathsf{sk}_i$ and its label as $\overline{\mathsf{sk}}$ //sk is accessible only through $\mathcal{F}_{\mathsf{LSS}}$
- (2) **Asynchronous step**
  - Input and Randomness Distribution (II): let S_{c} be the set of indices of input owners for which $\mathcal{F}_{\mathsf{LSS}}$ has acknowledged the receipt for all variables of Q_j's "input and randomness distribution" step. Each player P_i:
    * For each $j \in S_{\mathsf{c}}$, given labels $(\overline{m_j}, \overline{\boldsymbol{\rho_j}})$ and a key ek, sends $(\mathsf{LCOpen}, \Lambda^{\mathsf{ek}}_{\mathsf{Enc}}(\overline{m_j}, \overline{\boldsymbol{\rho_j}}))$ to $\mathcal{F}_{\mathsf{LSS}}$, and obtains a ciphertext c_j.

[a] And possibly a common relinearization key **rlk**.

Fig. 3. Share & Shrink Protocol

cretely, thanks to linearity of the ℓ-HE scheme, this can be done as threshold openings of the images of the m_j and of shared encryption randomnesses $\rho_{\mathsf{Enc},j}$ by the linear map $\Lambda^{\mathsf{ek}}_{\mathsf{Enc}}$, in one step of asynchronous P2P messages, as recalled in Sect. 3.3.

The outlined protocol differs fundamentally from related threshold-FHE works [54,63] which follow the pattern DKG-then-Input-distribution, since using Share& Shrink the Input Distribution is done without knowing a common key, which allows us *i*) to reduce the number of broadcast rounds to just one while guaranteeing output delivery, and *ii*) to keep short ciphertexts compared to [12].

5 MPC Protocol $\Pi^{\mathcal{F}_{\mathsf{LSS}}}_{\mathsf{MPC}}$

We now present our delegated MPC protocol that operates in one single initial BC followed by asynchronous P2P messages, leveraging a ℓ-HE scheme as defined in Definition 4 and our novel Share&Shrink protocol introduced in Sect. 4. First, we discuss the computation itself. Recall from Sect. 3.1 that Definition 4 wraps schemes with varying homomorphic capabilities, ranging from partially homomorphic, i.e. ℓ-HE schemes supporting only homomorphic additions and scalar multiplications, to somewhat homomorphic (supporting only a limited number of additions and multiplications), and finally to fully homomorphic. When using a scheme with the latter capabilities, specifically one that satisfies Definition 4, i.e. a ℓ-FHE scheme like ℓ-BFV (see Definition 5), players can locally evaluate any circuit on the encrypted inputs and produce an output ciphertext. While our primary focus is on evaluating circuits using FHE, we also consider other existing approaches for generating this output, using somewhat homomorphic ℓ-HE schemes following [28] or partially homomorphic ℓ-HE schemes following [16]. To formalize this, we introduce a generic evaluation protocol Eval in Sect. 5.1, to evaluate a circuit on ℓ-HE-encrypted ciphertexts in various ways. This protocol, possibly interactive over asynchronous channels, must be simulatable. We then review several known evaluation protocols that meet these criteria. Next in Sect. 5.2, we detail methods for threshold decryption, and finally describe our generic MPC protocol $\Pi^{\mathcal{F}_{\mathsf{LSS}}}_{\mathsf{MPC}}$ in the $\mathcal{F}_{\mathsf{LSS}}$-hybrid model in Sect. 5.3, which integrates these components.

5.1 (Asynchronous) Evaluation of a Circuit

Consider a linear homomorphic encryption scheme ℓ-HE (Definition 4), and players with input a set of ciphertexts $\{\mathsf{c}_j\}_{j\in[|\mathcal{Q}|]}$ of plaintexts $\{m_j\}_{j\in[|\mathcal{Q}|]}$ under a common threshold encryption key ek. We assume that there exists an asynchronous evaluation protocol Eval for any arithmetic circuit $\mathrm{C}\colon(\mathcal{M}\cup\{\perp\})^{|\mathcal{Q}|}\to\mathcal{M}$ with $|\mathcal{Q}|$ input gates, that outputs a ciphertext of the evaluation. Formally, we require that $\forall$ pp, $\mathbf{a}\leftarrow\ell\text{-HE.Setup}(1^\lambda)$, there exists a DKG in one BC that returns a threshold encryption key ek and, privately to the players, shares sk_i of the corresponding decryption key sk. Then for all $(m_j)_{j\in[|\mathcal{Q}|]}$, $\mathsf{c}_j\leftarrow\ell\text{-HE.Enc}(\mathsf{pp},\mathsf{ek},m_j)$

we require: ℓ-HE.Dec(sk, Eval(C, $c_1, \ldots, c_{|\mathcal{Q}|}$, ek[8])) = $C(m_1, \ldots, m_{|\mathcal{Q}|})$. We also require Eval to be simulatable. Such an Eval can be implemented in various ways, including:

- ℓ-FHE. When using a scheme with fully homomorphic capabilities as a particular kind of ℓ-HE scheme (as for ℓ-BFV, see Sect. 3.2), there exists a built-in non-interactive function Eval, simulatable from the knowledge of the threshold encryption key and of the relinearization key. Note that Eval introduces some noise when performing homomorphic operations. We refer to [77, Appendix C] for a complete noise analysis of the latter for ℓ-BFV. For correctness, the choice of practical cryptographic parameters, later discussed in Sect. 8, depends on the depth of the circuit being evaluated. For deeper circuits, one can use a *bootstrapping* algorithm that homomorphically brings back the size of the decryption noise of a ℓ-FHE ciphertext, roughly to that of a fresh ciphertext.
- [28]. Choudhury et al. proposed a protocol for circuit evaluation based on an efficient interactive multiparty bootstrapping protocol using pre-processed masks, for, in our case, a ℓ-HE scheme that supports a limited number of homomorphic operations. Players perform threshold decryptions of masked intermediary evaluations; and the simulator simulates the opening of a random value.
- [16]. From a common view of ℓ-HE encrypted inputs and decryption key shares assigned to each player, one can apply the asynchronous CDN-like [31] protocol of [16] to evaluate a circuit using a ℓ-HE scheme with only partial homomorphic properties, i.e. supporting only additions and scalar multiplications. Players open threshold decryptions of masked intermediary results. Since some masks can be inferred from each other by adversarially-chosen (but extractable) offsets, the simulator takes extra care.

5.2 Threshold Decryption

ℓ-HE decryption can be seen as a two steps process: (1) the interactive opening of a linear map $\Lambda^{\mathsf{c}}_{\mathsf{Dec}}$ applied to the (secret shared) decryption key sk, with public coefficients equal to the ciphertext c, (2) followed by local computation of a non-linear decoding function Ω_{Dec}. However, a direct adaptation from this decryption to the threshold setting is not straightforward when Ω_{Dec} is nontrivial. This is notably the case for the RLWE-based schemes, such as ℓ-BFV, that we now consider in the remainder of this section. Indeed, the output μ_{dec} of (1) allows recovering the plaintext, but also reveals a small *decryption noise* term that depends on the given ciphertext and the decryption key, as defined below:

Definition 6 (Decryption noise). *Let* $\mathsf{c} \in \mathscr{C}$, $m \in R_k$ *and* $\mathsf{sk} \in \mathscr{X}_q$. *We define the "decryption noise" as* $e^{(\mathsf{Dec})}(\mathsf{c}, \mathsf{sk}, m) := \Lambda^{\mathsf{c}}_{\mathsf{Dec}}(\mathsf{sk}) - \Delta.m$.

Asharov et al. [10] demonstrated that this noisy output of (1) reveals too much information about the decryption key. To prevent information leakage, [10] introduced the technique of adding additional noise to μ_{dec} before it can

[8] Possibly along an extra relinearization key.

be reconstructed. This "smudging" noise e_{sm} is, roughly, sampled uniformly in some large enough interval $[-B_{sm}, B_{sm}]$. Now consider an arithmetic circuit C, and denote B_{C} the upper-bound on the decryption noise of a ciphertext after evaluation of C, as defined below:

Definition 7 (Decryption noise after evaluation of a circuit: B_C). *For any layered arithmetic circuit C of multiplicative depth L, with input gates indexed by n, we consider the largest norm of the decryption noise $e^{(\mathsf{Dec})}(\mathsf{c}, \mathsf{sk}, y)$ of a ciphertext c, over the previous choices, and over the choices: of elements $(m_i \in R_k)_{i\in[n]}$, and of arbitrary fresh ℓ-BFV Encryptions of them $(\mathsf{c}_i)_{i\in[n]}$; denoting $\mathsf{c} := \mathsf{Eval}(C, (\mathsf{c}_i)_i, \mathbf{rlk}, \mathbf{b})$ and $y := C((m_i)_i)$.*

Recall that the multiplication of two ℓ-BFV ciphertexts involves two steps: the multiplication itself followed by a relinearization operation. Following [77], let us denote B_{fresh} the decryption noise of a newly encrypted ℓ-BFV ciphertext, and let B_{Add}, B_{Mult} and B_{Relin} be the upper bounds of the noise introduced by the addition, multiplication and relinearization operations, respectively. We can then estimate an upper bound on the decryption noise of the evaluated ciphertext as:

$$B_C \leq B_{\mathsf{fresh}} \cdot B_{\mathsf{Mult}}^L + B_{\mathsf{Add}} \cdot \frac{B_{\mathsf{Mult}}^L - 1}{B_{\mathsf{Mult}} - 1} + B_{\mathsf{Relin}} \cdot \frac{B_{\mathsf{Mult}}^{L-1} - 1}{B_{\mathsf{Mult}} - 1} \tag{2}$$

The choice of B_{sm} is crucial for both the security and correctness of our MPC protocol. This translates into the following two requirements:

1. First, the output of (1) $\mu_{\text{dec}} = \Lambda^{\mathsf{c}}_{\mathsf{Dec}}(\mathsf{sk})$ must be statistically close to the (scaled) plaintext circuit evaluation $\Delta \cdot y$. Then, some level of noise B_{sm} should exist so that adding a uniform noise $e_{\text{sm}} \in [-B_{sm}, B_{sm}]$ to both μ_{dec} and $\Delta \cdot y$, makes them indistinguishable, while leaving correct the result: $y = \Omega_{\mathsf{Dec}}(\mu_{\text{dec}} + e_{\text{sm}})$. Lemma 3 imposes a level of noise high enough so that $B_{\mathrm{C}}/B_{sm} \leqslant \text{negl}(\lambda)$.
2. Second, the correctness requirement imposes that B_{C} added with this smudging noise stays small, e.g. in the case of ℓ-BFV, we want that $B_{\mathrm{C}} + n \cdot B_{sm} \leq \Delta/2$.

Different methods exist for distributively opening μ_{dec} added with such noise:

- Most previous works [10,19,54] let each player P_i locally sample a smudging noise $e_{\text{sm},i} \xleftarrow{\$} [-B_{sm}, B_{sm}]$, multiply it by $n!^2$, then add it to its opening share of μ_{dec}, which it sends. The reason for multiplying by $n!^2$ is to clear-out the denominators of the Lagrange coefficients applied during reconstruction (see [4,19]) when Shamir LSS is used. This introduces an overhead of $n.n!^3$ on the ciphertext modulus q, and therefore, a $n\times$ blowup of the ciphertext size.
- To keep the ciphertext size small, an improved method [38,77] has been proposed, in which players do not anymore smudge their opening share of μ_{dec}, but open all at once the decryption μ_{dec} and a common shared noise e_{sm}, i.e., the linear map defined as:

$$\Lambda^{\mathsf{c}}_{\mathsf{Dec}+sm} : (\mathsf{sk}, e_{\text{sm}}) \to \Lambda^{\mathsf{c}}_{\mathsf{Dec}}(\mathsf{sk}) + e_{\text{sm}} \tag{3}$$

The distributed generation of the noise (one for every circuit to be evaluated) is simply by adding secret-shared contributions $e_{\text{sm},i}$ sampled in $[-B_{sm}, B_{sm}]$. As a result, the correctness constraint now imposes that the ciphertext expansion factor Δ has a dependency in n which is only linear, instead of cubic previously.

Protocol $\Pi_{\mathsf{MPC}}^{\mathcal{F}_{\mathsf{LSS}}}$

Participants: n players $\{P_i\}_{i\in[n]}$, and $|\mathcal{Q}|$ input-owners;
Inputs (for each $\mathsf{Q}_j \in \mathcal{Q}$): a plaintext m_j with label $\overline{m_j}$.

- **Share & Shrink.** Players and Input-Owners play the Share&Shrink protocol of Fig. 3 (with the added smudging noise sharing by players), in which each input-owner $\mathsf{Q}_j \in \mathcal{Q}$ has an input m_j.
  Denote $S_{\mathsf{c}} \subset [|\mathcal{Q}|]$ the indices of input-owners (resp. $S \subset [n]$ of players), for which no instance returned $\perp$.
  After Share&Shrink, players have a common view on i) a threshold encryption key ek^a, ii) a set of ciphertexts $\{\mathsf{c}_j\}_{j\in S_{\mathsf{c}}}$ encrypted under ek, iii) a shared decryption key sk in $\mathcal{F}_{\mathsf{LSS}}$, as well as, iv) a shared smudging noise e_{sm} in $\mathcal{F}_{\mathsf{LSS}}$.
- **Evaluation.** To evaluate a circuit C, each player runs $\mathsf{c} \leftarrow \mathsf{Eval}(\mathrm{C}, \{\mathsf{c}_j\}_{j\in S_{\mathsf{c}}}, \mathsf{ek}^a)$.
- **Threshold Decryption.** Players play the Threshold Decryption protocol of Section 5.2 with input the ciphertext c and the shared decryption key sk in $\mathcal{F}_{\mathsf{LSS}}$. They output the plaintext m obtained.

[a] Possibly along with a common relinearization key **rlk**.

Fig. 4. MPC protocol $\Pi_{\mathsf{MPC}}^{\mathcal{F}_{\mathsf{LSS}}}$

5.3 Protocol $\Pi_{\mathsf{MPC}}^{\mathcal{F}_{\mathsf{LSS}}}$ in ($\mathcal{F}_{\mathsf{LSS}}$, BC)-Hybrid Model, with External Resource $\overline{\mathcal{G}}_{\mathrm{URS}}$

Consider a ℓ-HE scheme satisfying Definition 4. Specifically, in this section we consider the RLWE-based ℓ-BFV scheme defined in Sect. 3.2 as an example (although other ℓ-HE schemes could have been used). We show in Fig. 4 how to build a delegated MPC protocol $\Pi_{\mathsf{MPC}}^{\mathcal{F}_{\mathsf{LSS}}}$ from the Share&Shrink protocol introduced in Sect. 4, an evaluation algorithm Eval as discussed in Sect. 5.1, and a threshold decryption protocol as detailed in Sect. 5.2.

***Sketch of UC Proof of Theorem* 2.** Following [23], a protocol *UC-implements* the ideal functionality $\mathcal{F}_{\mathrm{C}}$ if there exists a PPT *simulator* Sim, such that for every PPT *environment* Env, that controls a "dummy" adversary $\mathcal{A}$ *and* which may send inputs to honest participants *and* is forwarded their outputs in real-time, has negligible advantage in distinguishing between the following two executions:

- $\mathrm{REAL}_{\mathcal{A}}$: an actual execution of the MPC protocol $\Pi_{\mathsf{MPC}}^{\mathcal{F}_{\mathsf{LSS}}}$, with adversary $\mathcal{A}$ fully controlled by Env, and functionalities $\mathcal{F}_{\mathsf{LSS}}$, BC;

- IDEAL$_{\mathcal{F}_C,\mathsf{Sim}}$: an execution denoted as *ideal*, where Sim interacts with Env on behalf of $\mathcal{A}$. On the other side, Sim interacts with $\mathcal{F}_C$ on behalf of the corrupt participants, and also of $\mathcal{A}$. The honest dummy participants are connected to Env as in a real execution. But on the other side, they only interact with $\mathcal{F}_C$.

In detail, Sim initiates in its head, sets $\mathscr{P}$ of n players and $\mathcal{Q}$ of inputs-owners (delegating the computation), and may initially receive corruption requests from Env for arbitrarily many owners and up to t players, indexed by $\mathcal{I}$. It simulates functionalities $(\mathsf{BC}, \mathcal{F}_{\mathsf{LSS}})$ following a correct behavior, apart from the value returned by $\mathcal{F}_{\mathsf{LSS}}$ in the *Output Computation* step. In particular, recall that as BC and $\mathcal{F}_{\mathsf{LSS}}$ are securely implementable, they can be replaced in the following proof by their secure implementation without affecting the security of $\Pi_{\mathsf{MPC}}^{\mathcal{F}_{\mathsf{LSS}}}$ thanks to the composition theorem. Sim does the following:

- **Setup.** Simulates the setup of $\mathcal{F}_{\mathsf{LSS}}$ and retrieves the URS a from $\overline{\mathcal{G}}_{\text{URS}}$ and sends it to all on behalf of $\overline{\mathcal{G}}_{\text{URS}}$.
- **Distributed Key and Smudging Noise Generation:** Simulates a correct behavior of $\mathcal{F}_{\mathsf{LSS}}$. For every simulated honest player $(P_i)_{i\in\mathcal{H}}$:
  - ⋆ Samples $\mathsf{sk}_i \xleftarrow{\$} \mathscr{X}_q$, and sends it to $\mathcal{F}_{\mathsf{LSS}}$.
  - ⋆ Samples $e_{\text{sm},i} \xleftarrow{\$} [-B_{sm}, B_{sm}]$, and sends it to $\mathcal{F}_{\mathsf{LSS}}$.
  - ⋆ Samples $b_i \xleftarrow{\$} U(R_q)$, and sends $\mathsf{ek}_i = (b_i, a)$ over BC^{P_i}[9].
- **Input&Randomness Distribution:** Simulates correct behavior of $\mathcal{F}_{\mathsf{LSS}}$, and:
  - ⋆ $\forall$ simulated honest input-owners $\mathsf{Q}_j \in \mathcal{Q}$: sets $\widetilde{m_j} := 0$ and samples $\overrightarrow{\boldsymbol{\rho}_{\mathsf{Enc},j} \xleftarrow{\$} \mathscr{B}_{Enc}}$. Then sends $(\mathsf{input}, \{\overline{\widetilde{m_j}, \boldsymbol{\rho}_{\mathsf{Enc},j}}\}, \{\widetilde{m_j}, \boldsymbol{\rho}_{\mathsf{Enc},j}\})$ to $\mathcal{F}_{\mathsf{LSS}}$.
  - ⋆ $\forall$ simulated corrupt $\mathsf{Q}_j \in \mathcal{Q}$, upon receiving (c_j) from Env, uses sk to decrypt c_j into m_j and sets $\widetilde{m_j}{:=}0$ if $m_j{=}\bot$ or $\widetilde{m_j}{:=}m_j$ otherwise, and sends $(\mathsf{input}, \mathsf{Q}_j, m_j)$ to $\mathcal{F}_C$.

  As in the protocol, Sim sets $S_{\mathsf{c}} \subset [|\mathcal{Q}|]$ the indices of input-owners, resp. $S \subset [n]$ of the players, for which no instance returned $\bot$.
- **Threshold Encryption:** Simulates correct behaviors to compute key $\mathsf{ek}{:=}(\sum_{i\in S} b_i, a)$ (See footnote 8); to make $\mathcal{F}_{\mathsf{LSS}}$, $\forall j \in S_{\mathsf{c}}$, eventually output: $\left(\Lambda_{\mathsf{Enc}}^{\mathsf{ek}}(\widetilde{m}_j, \boldsymbol{\rho}_{\mathsf{Enc},j})\right)$.
- **Circuit Evaluation:** Simulates Eval as discussed in Sect. 5.1.
- **Output Computation:** Upon being leaked the evaluation y from $\mathcal{F}_C$, where by definition $y = \mathrm{C}(\{m_i\}_{i\in S_{\mathsf{c}}})$, then Sim simulates the following incorrect behavior:
  - ⋆ $\mathcal{F}_{\mathsf{LSS}}$ outputs $\left(\Lambda_{\mathsf{Dec}+sm}^{\mathsf{c}}, \Delta y + \Sigma_{j\in S} e_{\text{sm},j}\right)$ to $\mathcal{L}$. (See Eq. (3))

Recall that the view of Env consists of its interactions with $\mathcal{A}$/Sim, and of the outputs of the actual honest players. To show indistinguishability, we go through a series of hybrid games starting from the real execution. The first hybrid, $\mathsf{Hybrid}^{\mathcal{F}_{\mathsf{LSS}}}$, modifies the behavior of $\mathcal{F}_{\mathsf{LSS}}$ in the *Output Computation* step, to incorrectly return a simulated output $\mu^{\mathsf{Sim}} := \Delta.y + \Sigma_{j\in S} e_{\text{sm},j}$, where

[9] And possibly a relinearization key $\mathbf{rlk}_i$ depending on the chosen Eval.

$y := \mathsf{C}((m_j)_{j \in S_c})$ is the evaluation of the circuit on the actual inputs. Indistinguishability follows from the "smudging" Lemma 3. In the second hybrid, $\mathsf{Hybrid}^{\mathsf{key}}$, the additive contributions $(b_i)_{i \in \mathcal{H}}$ of honest players to the encryption key (See footnote 8) are replaced by a sample in $U(R_q)$. Then, in $\mathsf{Hybrid}^{\mathsf{Eval}}$, the *Evaluation* is simulated using techniques that depend on the Eval instantiation as discussed in Sect. 5.1. Finally, $\mathsf{Hybrid}^{\mathsf{0Share}}$ replaces the input of simulated honest input-owners by 0. By this point, honest players' decryption keys are no longer in use. Furthermore, since honest players sample their contributions ek_i to the common threshold encryption key independently, we can assume without loss of generality that corrupt contributions are generated after seeing the honest ones. We can thus apply the classical "IND-CPA under Joint Keys" Lemma [10], adapted in [77, §D] for RLWE-based schemes.

In conclusion, we arrived at a view produced by a machine that interacts only with Env and $\mathcal{F}_{\mathsf{C}}$. We discuss the adaptations needed to the broadcast-based compiler of [10, §E] to move from semi-malicious to malicious security in the full version.

6 Details on the Close Related Works

6.1 Details on the Approach of [38]

Let us recap their construction. Players first receive a uniform random string (denoted $\mathbf{B}$), and, (0) generate and submit GSW encryption keys in bPKI. To encrypt its input m_i, each player P_i (1) generates a ciphertext $\mathsf{c}_{i,i}$ of it under its own GSW encryption key and concatenates to it, encryptions of 0 under the $n-1$ keys of other players, all with the same encryption randomness (denoted $\mathbf{R}$). Such a vector of ciphertexts $\hat{\mathsf{c}}_i = (\mathsf{c}_{i,1}, \mathsf{c}_{i,2}, \ldots, \mathsf{c}_{i,n})$ is denoted as a *flexible ciphertext*, and is broadcast. *In parallel* (1), players complete the second step of a DKG, establishing a common threshold encryption key. Because a flexible ciphertext is generated using the same secret randomness for all the n GSW ciphertexts contained in it, players are able to Transform, locally and deterministically, a flexible ciphertext into a GSW ciphertext under the common threshold encryption key by linearity. Then, players locally evaluate the circuit, and finally (2) perform the threshold decryption, which can be done over asynchronous P2P channels, by our observation. Because the same encryption randomness is used, and given that t of these ciphertexts are encrypted under GSW encryption keys which were generated by the adversary $\mathcal{A}$, this a priori gives $\mathcal{A}$ an extra advantage to guess the plaintext of $\mathsf{c}_{i,i}$. For the security of GSW to hold, their encryption keys are thus scaled slightly larger ($m = \Omega((d+n)\log(q))$ vs $m = \Omega(d\log(q))$ in GSW), to apply the leftover-hash-lemma (LHL [38, lemma 1]).

Overall, this protocol has two main limitations:

1. ***It is not delegable*** The generation of the flexible ciphertext $\hat{\mathsf{c}}_i$ has, by construction the decryption key sk_i known by the corresponding player P_i (i.e. $\hat{\mathsf{c}}_i$ reveals the encrypted input m_i to the player P_i that owns the GSW decryption key sk_i). It is therefore impossible to accommodate external input-owners

without losing privacy, which prevents delegation and a fortiori lightweight input-owners.

2. ***It is not generic*** A second limitation of this technique is its reliance on the Leftover Hash Lemma (LHL) [49], making it unclear how to adapt the construction to other FHE schemes. Overall, adapting their approach to efficient RLWE-based cryptosystems faces significant challenges. Let us illustrate this issue by taking the ℓ-BFV scheme detailed in Sect. 3.2 as an example.
Suppose that the adversary is given one (or several) ℓ-BFV encryptions of 0 under semi-maliciously generated key(s) (a, b_i), i.e., $(u \cdot b_i + e_{0,i}^{(\mathsf{Enc})}, u \cdot a + e_{1,i}^{(\mathsf{Enc})})$, which would all be generated with the same secret randomness $u \leftarrow \mathscr{X}_q$. Then this may provide it with a distinguishing advantage when given a BFV encryption of some m under some honest key (a, b_j) which would re-use the same randomness u. A potential fix might involve modifying ℓ-BFV, e.g., defining $a := \mathbf{a}[0]$ as vectors with coordinates in R_q, and encryption randomness $\mathbf{u}$ equal to a random vector with entries in R_q. However, this fails because the LHL does not generally hold in such settings, as shown in [33, §1], due to a $1/d$ leakage of the secret randomness, making the outcome far from uniform. They also point that [62, Cor 7.5] showed that a weaker version of LHL, denoted "regularity", does apply in this setting, nonwithstanding the previous leakage issue, in the case where the distribution of secret randomness would be Discrete Gaussian with a sufficiently large parameter. Concretely, we would apply "regularity" to $\mathbf{A}.\mathbf{u}$, where $\mathbf{A}$ would be a matrix with n rows encoding all encryption keys. The problem is that for the applicability of "regularity", it is required that $\mathbf{A}$ be sampled uniformly, whereas in our setting we have t keys in $\mathbf{A}$ which are semi-maliciously generated, furthermore possibly depending on the other $t + 1$ honest keys. Thus, this situation could potentially leak substantial information on $\mathbf{u}$, and thus potentially enable to distinguish the outcome from random uniform, such as mentioned above [33, §1].

6.2 Details on the Approach of [12]

Let us recap their construction that leverages a multikey-FHE encryption scheme. Players (1) first run a distributed setup to generate public/secret key pairs and contributions to a uniform random string, that are then broadcast along with the public keys. Let $S_1 \subseteq [n]$ be the set of indices of players that sent a round-1 message. Players encrypt their inputs using a multikey-FHE scheme, then (2) broadcast the multikey ciphertexts along with PVSSs of their decryption keys. Let $S_2 \subseteq S_1$ be the set of indices of players that sent a round-2 message. Players then evaluate a circuit C on the encrypted inputs. From the secret-shared keys, it is described in [12] how honest players in round-3 can (3) *emulate* multikey-FHE reconstruction in one BC, as if it would have been performed by members of S_2 themselves, allowing the output to be recovered even with up to t corrupt players.

7 Proof of Theorem 1

Let us show how the 3-BC MPC protocol of [12] outlined in Sect. 6.2 can be cast in our model to (i) obtain termination in 1 BC-then-1 step of asynchronous P2P messages; and (ii) to allow inputs from external owners.

We first note that the first broadcast round is input-independent. Hence, we replace their round 1 by publication of public keys and URSs on bPKI. The modification to obtain (ii) is simply to allow any external input-owner to perform their round 2 broadcast, directed to the n players. In more detail, consider the subset $S_2 \subset [|\mathcal{Q}|]$ of owners which correctly shared their inputs and shares of multikey-FHE keys (in [12], S_2 is instead a subset of players). From these secret shared keys, it is described in [12] how honest players in round-3 can *emulate* multikey-FHE reconstruction, as if it would have been performed by members of S_2 themselves (their participation *as input-owners* is not needed anymore).

Finally, to obtain (i), we need to replace the broadcast in their third round with asynchronous P2P messages, such that the output after round 3 is unchanged: players still obtain the same common threshold decryption. We remark that their round 3 can be performed over asynchronous P2P channels, since the computation step performed by a player P at the end of round 3 is: *choose any* set $\mathcal{U}$ of $t+1$ valid decryption shares received in round-3 messages, then apply the local threshold decryption algorithm on them. So this step does not depend on whether all round-3 messages from honest players were received by P or not, but it may well be that t out-of-the $t+1$ valid decryption shares chosen by P, originate from corrupt players, without impacting decryption correctness.

8 Experimental Evaluation

We present a proof-of-concept implementation that shows that our approach leads to practical results. We instantiate Share&Shrink from the ℓ-BFV scheme presented in Sect. 3.2 and, for a fair comparison, we compare it to our Theorem 1 instantiated from an efficient multikey scheme [55] based on BFV, denoted MK-BFV. We consider inputs in R_k with $\log k = 16$, and parameters that achieve at least 128-bit of security level according to LWE-estimator [5]:

- For MK-BFV, we use the candidate parameter set described in [55, Table 2], recalled in Table 2, that supports circuits of depth 6.
- For Share&Shrink instantiated from ℓ-BFV, we use the same parameters as for MK-BFV in our specific single-key case.

Table 2. Experimental cryptographic parameters: Overview

$\log k$	$\log d$	$\log q$	l
16	14	438	8

We consider the following delegated setting:

- A number of input-owners ranging from 1 to 128, each owning inputs in R_k,
- A cluster of $n = 11$ or 50 players to perform the computation.

All experiments were performed on a MacBookPro with a 3.1 GHz Intel i5 processor, using Lattigo[10] as well as the implementation of MK-BFV done by [55][11].

8.1 Experiment#1: Mult Gate Computation

We first compare in Fig. 5a the running time of a Multiplication between two ciphertexts for different numbers of input-owners ranging from 1 to 64 (we can run MK-BFV with up to 64 input-owners, but RAM prevents scaling to 128).

Overall, this verifies that the running time is almost linear with the number of input-owners when using a multikey scheme, while Share&Shrink reduces this duration to a small constant, independent of $|\mathcal{Q}|$ as expected.

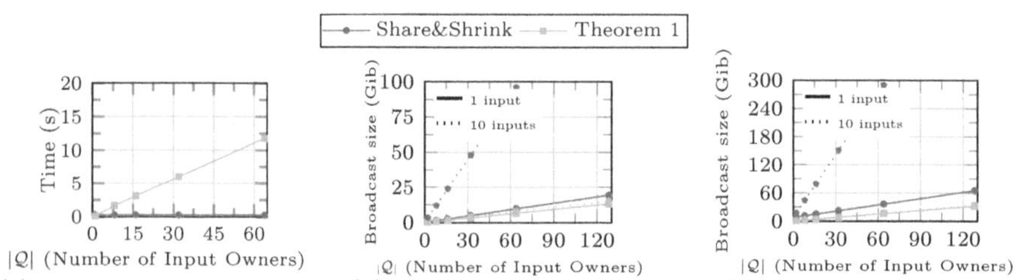

(a) Comparison of median Mult gate computation times of the Theorem 1 instantiated from the MK-BFV scheme [55] and Share&Shrink instantiated from ℓ-BFV.

(b) Comparison of the total broadcast size between the Theorem 1 instantiated from MK-BFV [55] and Share&Shrink for 1 and 10 inputs per owner, for $n = 11$.

(c) Comparison of the total broadcast size between the Theorem 1 instantiated from MK-BFV [55] and Share&Shrink for 1 and 10 inputs per owner, for $n = 50$.

Fig. 5. Experimental Results

8.2 Experiment #2: Broadcast Size

We compare in Fig. 5b the total broadcast size for $n = 11$ and a different number of input-owners ranging from 1 to 128 that each owns one or ten inputs in R_k, when using MK-BFV or Share&Shrink instantiated from ℓ-BFV. It comprises:

- An input-independent part that consists of the encryption and relinearization keys as well as a PVSS of some decryption key.

[10] https://github.com/tuneinsight/lattigo.
[11] https://github.com/SNUCP/MKHE-KKLSS/.

- An input-dependent part that consists either of MK-BFV ciphertexts or of PVSSs of inputs and randomnesses $e_0^{(\mathsf{Enc})}, e_1^{(\mathsf{Enc})}, u$ over R_q as required in Fig. 3.

Let us first provide some details about Fig. 5b. For the PVSS, we use the class-group-based public-key encryption scheme recently employed in [51], while omitting zero-knowledge proofs in our semi-malicious corruption model. For n players, the total bit-length of ciphertexts is $1752 \cdot (n+1)$ bits for a 256-bit plaintext, resulting in an asymptotic ciphertext expansion factor of 6.8. Following Sect. 3.2 and denoting $|\#\text{inputs}|$ the number of inputs per input-owner, the broadcast for Share&Shrink instantiated from ℓ-BFV is of size:

$$n \cdot |(3 \cdot l \cdot |R_q| + \mathsf{PVSS}(|R_q|))| + |\mathcal{Q}| \cdot |\#\text{inputs}| \cdot |\mathsf{PVSS}(3 \cdot |R_q| + |R_k|)|. \quad (4)$$

For Theorem 1 instantiated from MK-BFV, the broadcast is of size:

$$|\mathcal{Q}| \cdot (4 \cdot l \cdot |R_q| + \mathsf{PVSS}(|R_q|)) + |\mathcal{Q}| \cdot |\#\text{inputs}| \cdot 2|R_q|. \quad (5)$$

In Fig. 5b, we remark that for a small number of inputs per owner, Theorem 1 requires broadcasting a comparable amount of data than Share&Shrink. However, the greater the number of inputs per owner, the more the RHS of both Eqs. (4) and (5) dominates. Consequently, Share&Shrink requires a larger broadcast since a greater number of n-sized PVSSs are sent, which are larger than a MK-BFV ciphertext, whose size is $2|R_q|$.

Impact of the Number n of Players: For completeness, Fig. 5c illustrates the broadcast size for different numbers of input-owners when $n = 50$. In this case, for the PVSS, we use the LWE-based encryption scheme employed in [46]. For $n = 50$, this results in an amortized ciphertext expansion factor of 4.8. Overall, the results exhibit a similar dynamic to the $n = 11$ case shown in Fig. 5b.

In practice, we believe that it is reasonable to consider a small number n of powerful computation players and a very large number of resource-constrained input-owners sending few inputs.

9 YOSO MPC

A recent line of research [3,45,70] studies MPC with specialized computation models, that support a *dynamically* evolving set of players, i.e. where participants can join and leave the computation as desired, without interrupting the protocol. The rationale is that players may devote only a limited amount of time (and computational resources) to a computation that can last a long period. This computation model was captured by Gentry et al. [45] under the name **YOSO** (You Only Speak Once), where the computation is divided into a number of successive steps $d = 1, \ldots$. For each one of them, a committee $\mathcal{C}^{(d)}$ of *ephemeral players* carries out some local computation, each of them publishes a single message on a bulletin board, and then vanishes from the system. An attractive consequence of this model is the drastic reduction of the window for adaptive corruption of these players due to the unpredictable selection of committees of players for the computation. Unfortunately, this model inherently requires some form of consistent terminating broadcast (BC) at the end of each computation step, often modeled as a public ledger [45]. Roughly, this is needed for players to perform their computation on the same intermediary values.

It is not difficult to imagine building a YOSO MPC protocol from our Share&Shrink protocol in one single BC instantiated from an ℓ-FHE scheme presented in Sect. 5.3. Indeed, we have already dissociated the input-owners from the players, so the former can distribute their inputs in only one message without knowing the threshold encryption key. In order to fully move to the YOSO model, we can further dissociate the participants in the 3 rounds of the original protocol, by introducing the following committees:

- a key generation committee $\mathcal{C}^{(\mathsf{DKG})}$, whose members broadcast their contributions to the encryption key and PVSSs of their decryption keys;
- an input-owner committee $\mathcal{C}^{(\mathsf{owners})}$, whose members broadcast *in parallel* with $\mathcal{C}^{(\mathsf{DKG})}$, PVSSs of their inputs and encryption randomnesses;
- a shrinking committee $\mathcal{C}^{(\mathsf{Shrink})}$, which encrypts the distributed inputs under a common threshold encryption key, by sending opening shares for some linear form via asynchronous P2P channels to the next committee;
- and finally, a decryption committee $\mathcal{C}^{(\mathsf{Dec})}$, whose members locally perform the evaluation and the threshold decryption in one step of P2P messages.

We refer to [57] for further discussion about adaptions to be made to move to the YOSO setting.

Acknowledgments. We thank the reviewers of ACNS and Hieu Phan for their suggestions on a preliminary version of this work, which were all taken into account.

References

1. Compilation of public comments on multi-party threshold cryptography project (2023). https://csrc.nist.gov/files/pubs/ir/8214/c/ipd/docs/nistir-8214c-ipd-public-feedback.pdf
2. Delegated multi-key private matching for compute: Improving match rates and enabling adoption (2023). https://research.facebook.com/blog/2023/1/delegated-multi-key-private-matching-for-compute-improving-match-rates-and-enabling-adoption/
3. Acharya, A., Hazay, C., Kolesnikov, V., Prabhakaran, M.: SCALES: MPC with small clients and larger ephemeral servers. TCC (2022)
4. Agrawal, S., Boyen, X., Vaikuntanathan, V., Voulgaris, P., Wee, H.: Functional encryption for threshold functions (or fuzzy IBE) from lattices. In: PKC (2012)

5. Albrecht, M., et al.: Homomorphic Encryption Standard (2021)
6. Alon, B., Naor, M., Omri, E., Stemmer, U.: MPC for tech giants (GMPC): enabling gulliver and the lilliputians to cooperate amicably. In: CRYPTO (2024)
7. Ananth, P., Choudhuri, A.R., Goel, A., Jain, A.: Round-optimal secure multiparty computation with honest majority. In: CRYPTO (2018)
8. Ananth, P., Choudhuri, A.R., Goel, A., Jain, A.: Two round information-theoretic MPC with malicious security. In: EUROCRYPT (2019)
9. Ananth, P., Choudhuri, A.R., Goel, A., Jain, A.: Towards efficiency-preserving round compression in MPC. In: ASIACRYPT (2020)
10. Asharov, G., Jain, A., López-Alt, A., Tromer, E., Vaikuntanathan, V., Wichs, D.: Multiparty computation with low communication, computation and interaction via threshold FHE. In: EUROCRYPT (2012)
11. Babai, L., Fortnow, L., Levin, L.A., Szegedy, M.: Checking computations in polylogarithmic time. In: Proceedings of the Twenty-Third Annual ACM Symposium on Theory of Computing. STOC 1991 (1991)
12. Badrinarayanan, S., Jain, A., Manohar, N., Sahai, A.: Secure MPC: laziness leads to GOD. In: ASIACRYPT (2020)
13. Badrinarayanan, S., Miao, P., Mukherjee, P., Ravi, D.: On the round complexity of fully secure solitary MPC with honest majority. In: TCC (2023)
14. Barak, A., Hirt, M., Koskas, L., Lindell, Y.: An end-to-end system for large scale P2P MPC-as-a-service and low-bandwidth MPC for weak participants. In: CCS (2018)
15. Beaver, D., Micali, S., Rogaway, P.: The round complexity of secure protocols. In: Proceedings of the Twenty-Second Annual ACM Symposium on Theory of Computing, pp. 503–513 (1990)
16. Beerliová-Trubíniová, Z., Hirt, M., Nielsen, J.B.: Almost-asynchronous MPC with faulty minority. In: PODC 2010 (2010). We refer to eprint 2008/416
17. Bell, J.H., Bonawitz, K.A., Gascón, A., Lepoint, T., Raykova, M.: Secure single-server aggregation with (poly) logarithmic overhead. In: Proceedings of the 2020 ACM SIGSAC Conference on Computer and Communications Security (2020)
18. Bonawitz, K., et al.: Practical secure aggregation for privacy-preserving machine learning. In: CCS (2017)
19. Boneh, D., et al.: Threshold cryptosystems from threshold fully homomorphic encryption. In: CRYPTO (2018)
20. Boneh, D., Goh, E., Nissim, K.: Evaluating encryption schemes for pattern matching. In: EUROCRYPT 2005, pp. 40–62. Springer (2005)
21. Brakerski, Z., Halevi, S., Polychroniadou, A.: Four round secure computation without setup. In: TCC (2017)
22. Braun, L., Damgård, I., Orlandi, C.: Secure multiparty computation from threshold encryption based on class groups. In: CRYPTO (2023)
23. Canetti, R.: Universally composable security: a new paradigm for cryptographic protocols. In: FOCS (2001). We refer to eprint 2000/067 version 02/20/2020
24. Castagnos, G., Laguillaumie, F.: Linearly homomorphic encryption from DDH. In: CT RSA (2015)
25. Chen, H., Dai, W., Kim, M., Song, Y.: Efficient multi-key homomorphic encryption with packed ciphertexts with application to oblivious neural network inference. In: CCS (2019)
26. Chen, S., Cheon, J.H., Kim, D., Park, D.: Verifiable computing for approximate computation. Cryptology ePrint Archive (2019)
27. Cheon, J.H., Kim, A., Kim, M., Song, Y.: Homomorphic encryption for arithmetic of approximate numbers. In: ASIACRYPT (2017)

28. Choudhury, A., Loftus, J., Orsini, E., Patra, A., Smart, N.P.: Between a rock and a hard place: interpolating between MPC and FHE. In: ASIACRYPT (2013)
29. Cohen, R., Garay, J., Zikas, V.: Broadcast-optimal two-round MPC. In: EUROCRYPT (2020)
30. Coretti, S., Garay, J., Hirt, M., Zikas, V.: Constant-round asynchronous multi-party computation based on one-way functions. In: ASIACRYPT (2016)
31. Cramer, R., Damgård, I., Nielsen, J.B.: Multiparty computation from threshold homomorphic encryption. In: EUROCRYPT (2001)
32. Cramer, R., Damgård, I., Nielsen, J.: Secure Multiparty Computation and Secret Sharing. Cambridge University Press (2015)
33. Dachman-Soled, D., Gong, H., Kulkarni, M., Shahverdi, A.: Towards a ring analogue of the leftover hash lemma. J. Math. Cryptol. (2021)
34. Damgård, I., Magri, B., Ravi, D., Siniscalchi, L., Yakoubov, S.: Broadcast-optimal two round MPC with an honest majority. In: CRYPTO (2021)
35. Damgård, I., Ravi, D., Siniscalchi, L., Yakoubov, S.: Minimizing setup in broadcast-optimal two round MPC. In: EUROCRYPT (2023)
36. Dao, Q., Grubbs, P.: Spartan and bulletproofs are simulation-extractable (for free!). In: EUROCRYPT (2023)
37. Dolev, D., Reischuk, R.: Bounds on information exchange for byzantine agreement. J. ACM (JACM) **32**(1), 191–204 (1985)
38. Dov Gordon, S., Liu, F.H., Shi, E.: Constant-round MPC with fairness and guarantee of output delivery. In: CRYPTO (2015)
39. Fan, J., Vercauteren, F.: Somewhat practical fully homomorphic encryption. IACR ePrint (2012)
40. Fehr, S.: Span Programs over Rings and How to Share a Secret from a Module. Master's thesis, ETH Zurich (1998)
41. Fiore, D., Nitulescu, A., Pointcheval, D.: Boosting verifiable computation on encrypted data. In: Public-Key Cryptography–PKC (2020)
42. Fitzi, M., Nielsen, J.B.: On the number of synchronous rounds sufficient for authenticated byzantine agreement. In: DISC (2009)
43. Fouque, P.A., Stern, J.: One round threshold discrete-log key generation without private channels. In: PKC (2001)
44. Garay, J., Givens, C., Ostrovsky, R., Raykov, P.: Broadcast (and round) efficient verifiable secret sharing. In: ITC (2013)
45. Gentry, C., et al.: YOSO: you only speak once/secure MPC with stateless ephemeral roles. In: CRYPTO (2021)
46. Gentry, C., Halevi, S., Vadim, L.: Practical non-interactive publicly verifiable secret sharing with thousands of parties. In: EUROCRYPT (2022)
47. Gentry, C., Sahai, A., Waters, B.: Homomorphic encryption from learning with errors: conceptually-simpler, asymptotically-faster, attribute-based. In: CRYPTO (2013)
48. Goel, A., Jain, A., Prabhakaran, M., Raghunath, R.: On communication models and best-achievable security in two-round MPC. In: TCC (2021)
49. Impagliazzo, R., Levin, L.A., Luby, M.: Pseudo-random generation from one-way functions. In: Proceedings of the Twenty-First Annual ACM Symposium on Theory of Computing. STOC 1989 (1989)
50. ISO/IEC: ISO/IEC 18033-6:2019 it security techniques-encryption algorithms-part 6: Homomorphic encryption (2019). https://www.iso.org/obp/ui/#iso:std:iso-iec:18033:-6
51. Kate, A., Mangipudi, E.V., Mukherjee, P., Saleem, H., Thyagarajan, S.A.K.: Non-interactive VSS using class groups and application to DKG. In: CCS (2024)

52. Katz, J., Koo, C.Y.: On expected constant-round protocols for byzantine agreement. In: Annual International Cryptology Conference (2006)
53. Katz, J., Maurer, U., Tackmann, B., Zikas, V.: Universally composable synchronous computation. In: TCC (2011)
54. Kim, E., Jeong, J., Yoon, H., Kim, Y., Cho, J., Cheon, J.H.: How to securely collaborate on data: decentralized threshold he and secure key update. IEEE Access (2020)
55. Kim, T., Kwak, H., Lee, D., Seo, J., Song, Y.: Asymptotically faster multi-key homomorphic encryption from homomorphic gadget decomposition. In: CCS (2023)
56. Klemsa, J., Önen, M., Akin, Y.: A practical TFHE-based multi-key homomorphic encryption with linear complexity and low noise growth. In: ESORICS (2023)
57. Kolby, S., Ravi, D., Yakoubov, S.: Constant-round YOSO MPC without setup. Cryptology ePrint Archive, Paper 2022/187 (2022)
58. Lindell, Y., Pinkas, B., Smart, N.P., Yanai, A.: Efficient constant-round multi-party computation combining BMR and SPDZ. J. Cryptol. **32**, 1026–1069 (2019)
59. Lindell, Y., Smart, N.P., Soria-Vazquez, E.: More efficient constant-round multi-party computation from BMR and SHE. In: TCC (2016)
60. Liu-Zhang, C., Loss, J., Maurer, U., Moran, T., Tschudi, D.: MPC with synchronous security and asynchronous responsiveness. In: ASIACRYPT (2020)
61. Lyubashevsky, V., Peikert, C., Regev, O.: On ideal lattices and learning with errors over rings. J. ACM (2013)
62. Lyubashevsky, V., Peikert, C., Regev, O.: A toolkit for ring-LWE cryptography. In: EUROCRYPT (2013)
63. Mouchet, C., Bertrand, E., Hubaux, J.P.: An efficient threshold access-structure for RLWE-based multiparty homomorphic encryption. J. Cryptol. **36**(2), 10 (2023)
64. Mouchet, C., Troncoso-Pastoriza, J., Bossuat, J.P., Hubaux, J.P.: Multiparty homomorphic encryption from ring-learning-with-errors. PoPETS (2021)
65. Mouris, D., Masny, D., Trieu, N., Sengupta, S., Buddhavarapu, P., Case, B.: Delegated private matching for compute. Proc. Priv. Enhancing Technol. (2024)
66. Mukherjee, P., Wichs, D.: Two round multiparty computation via multi-key FHE. In: EUROCRYPT (2016)
67. Park, J.: Homomorphic encryption for multiple users with less communications. IEEE Access (2021)
68. Parno, B., Raykova, M., Vaikuntanathan, V.: How to delegate and verify in public: verifiable computation from attribute-based encryption. In: TCC (2012)
69. Patra, A., Ravi, D.: On the power of hybrid networks in multi-party computation. IEEE Trans. Inf. Theory (2018)
70. Rachuri, R., Scholl, P.: Le mans: dynamic and fluid MPC for dishonest majority. In: CRYPTO (2022)
71. Reyzin, L., Smith, A.D., Yakoubov, S.: Turning HATE into LOVE: compact homomorphic ad hoc threshold encryption for scalable MPC. In: CSCML (2021)
72. Schoenmakers, B., Veeningen, M., de Vreede, N.: Trinocchio: privacy-preserving outsourcing by distributed verifiable computation. In: ACNS (2016)
73. Shamir, A.: How to share a secret. Commun. ACM **22**(11), 612–613 (1979). https://doi.org/10.1145/359168.359176
74. Shrestha, N., Bhat, A., Kate, A., Nayak, K.: Synchronous distributed key generation without broadcasts. ePrint 2021/1635 (2021)
75. Tang, F., et al.: Solving small exponential ECDLP in EC-based additively homomorphic encryption and applications. IEEE Trans. Inf. Forensics Secur. **18**, 3517–3530 (2023)

76. Urban, A., Rambaud, M.: Share & shrink: (in-)feasibility of MPC from one broadcast-then-asynchrony, and delegated computation. Cryptology ePrint Archive, Paper 2022/378 (2022). https://eprint.iacr.org/2022/378
77. Urban, A., Rambaud, M.: Robust multiparty computation from threshold encryption based on RLWE. ISC (2024)
78. Wan, J., Momose, A., Ren, L., Shi, E., Xiang, Z.: On the amortized communication complexity of byzantine broadcast. In: Proceedings of the 2023 ACM Symposium on Principles of Distributed Computing, pp. 253–261 (2023)
79. Wu, W., Homsi, S., Zhang, Y.: Confidential and verifiable machine learning delegations on the cloud. Cryptology ePrint, Paper 2024/537 (2024)
80. Yao, A.C.: Protocols for secure computations. In: 23rd Annual Symposium on Foundations of Computer Science (SFCS 1982), pp. 160–164. IEEE (1982)

Delayed-Input Multi-party Computation

Michele Ciampi[1], Jure Sternad[2], and Yu Xia[1](✉)

[1] The University of Edinburgh, Edinburgh, UK
{michele.ciampi,yu.xia}@ed.ac.uk
[2] Aarhus University, Aarhus, Denmark
jsternad@cs.au.dk

Abstract. In this work, we consider the setting where the process of securely evaluating a multi-party functionality is divided into two phases: *offline* (or *preprocessing*) and *online*. The offline phase is independent of the parties' inputs, whereas the online phase does require the knowledge of the inputs. We consider the problem of minimizing the round of communication required in the online phase and propose a *round preserving* compiler that can turn a big class of multi-party computation (MPC) protocols into protocols in which only the last two rounds are input-dependent. Our compiler can be applied to a big class of MPC protocols, and in particular to all existing round-optimal MPC protocols. All our results assume no setup and are proven in the dishonest majority setting with black-box simulation. As part of our contribution, we propose a new definition we call *Multi-Party Computation with Adaptive-Input Selection*, which allows the distinguisher to craft the inputs the honest parties should use during the online phase, adaptively on the offline phase. This new definition is needed to argue that not only are the messages of the offline phase input-independent but also that security holds even in the stronger (and realistic) adversarial setting where the inputs may depend on some of the offline-phase protocol messages. We argue that this is the definition that any protocol should satisfy to be securely used while preprocessing part of the rounds. We are the first to study this definition in a setting where there is no setup, and the majority of the parties can be corrupted. Prior definitions have been presented in the Universal Composable framework, which is unfortunately not well suited for our setting (i.e., no setup and dishonest majority). As a corollary, we obtain the first four-round (which is optimal) MPC protocol, where the first two rounds can be preprocessed, and its security holds against adaptive-input selection.

Keywords: Secure multi-party computation · delayed-input · round-optimal · preprocessing

1 Introduction

Secure multiparty computation (MPC) [21,40] provides a solution to the problem of performing computation on private data by allowing a group of parties to jointly evaluate any function over their inputs in such a manner that

J. Sternad—The main part of the work was done when this author was a student at the University of Edinburgh.

M. Fischlin and V. Moonsamy (Eds.): ACNS 2025, LNCS 15825, pp. 339–368, 2025.
https://doi.org/10.1007/978-3-031-95761-1_12

no one learns anything beyond the output of the function. Since its conception, MPC has been extensively studied from different angles, in particular concerning: necessary *assumptions* [21,30,35], and *round complexity* [1,5,8,13,14,20,21,23,32,33,38,39]. Even in a setting where all but one party are corrupted, both of these topics are by now pretty well understood. In the plain model, where no setup is available, parties need at least four rounds of communication[1] to realize the coin-tossing functionality with black-box simulation [20,32]. A sequence of recent works showed that four rounds are also sufficient, relying on a variety of standard cryptographic assumptions [1,2,8,25]. In particular, in [12], the authors show a protocol that relies on the almost minimal assumption of malicious secure four-round Oblivious Transfer (OT), and recently, in [29] the authors show a protocol that relies on the underlying OT protocol in a black-box way (in this case the authors require the security of the OT protocol to hold against sub-exponential time adversaries). Another prolific line of research that aims to understand the concrete efficiency of MPC rather than focusing strictly on the round complexity is related to the area of secure computation with *preprocessing* [3–7,19,27,28,34,36,37]. In this, the MPC protocols are seen as composed of two phases: *offline* (or *preprocessing*) and *online*. In the offline phase, the parties do not know their inputs but exchange messages to generate some correlated randomness. In the online phase, the parties get access to their inputs and conclude the execution of the protocol by properly combining the inputs and the correlated randomness obtained during the offline phase. The idea behind this paradigm is to delegate most of the expensive operations to the offline phase (which can be run overnight or when there are no other critical activities that need computational resources). In this way, whenever the parties get access to their inputs, they can engage in the online phase and evaluate the output quickly.

In this work, we investigate whether it is possible to have the best of both worlds: a protocol that has optimal round complexity but where the majority of the messages can be exchanged during the offline phase and only a few messages (the last two) are exchanged during the online phase. We note that any generic ℓ-round MPC protocol must use the inputs of the parties at least in the $(\ell-1)$-th round[2]. Building on top of this fact, we consider the following natural question.

Is it possible to construct a round-optimal protocol for securely evaluating generic multiparty functionalities where all but the last two rounds of the protocol are preprocessed in the offline phase?

[1] Unless otherwise specified, the communication model we consider is simultaneous (i.e., all the parties can speak in the same round). In the multi-party setting, messages are sent over broadcast channels (one round corresponds to one message sent over broadcast).

[2] Assume by contradiction that this is not the case, then an adversary, upon receiving the last round of the protocol, can always locally compute the residual function with respect to multiple inputs.

A natural first step to answer this question is to look at existing round-optimal protocols and check in what round the inputs become needed. To the best of our knowledge, in the protocols proposed in [25,29], the parties *do need* their inputs already in the first two rounds. In [2,12] instead, only the last two rounds are input-dependent. Hence, it seems that the protocols of [2,12] already give a positive answer to the above question.

Unfortunately, this is not the case. These protocols are proven secure with respect to the standalone security definition of MPC. At a very high level, this notion guarantees that no adversary can distinguish real-world executions, where honest parties simply use their inputs and follow the protocol as prescribed, from an ideal-world execution, where honest parties are replaced with a simulator, which only has access to the output of the computation, and has no additional information on the honest parties' inputs. In this definition, it is crucial that the adversary engages exactly in one execution of the protocol, and moreover, the inputs the honest parties use are fixed at the beginning of the experiment (in both the real and the ideal world experiment). This, in particular, means that the distinguisher is not supposed to decide the inputs that the honest parties should use adaptively on, for example, the first two rounds of the protocol. The consequence of this is that even if a protocol is input-independent in the first two rounds, its security holds only if the honest parties' inputs are fixed before the protocol starts. This clearly defeats the entire purpose of the offline/online paradigm. It is indeed easy to design a protocol that is secure under the standard definition of MPC, but it becomes insecure if the distinguisher can decide the inputs adaptively on some of the protocol messages.

To see this more explicitly, consider a protocol Π, secure under the standard MPC security definition, and let us assume that the first two rounds of the protocol are input-independent. We now construct a new protocol Π', that works exactly as Π, but with the following modification. In the first round, each party samples and sends a random string. Upon receiving the input, each party compares the input with the random string, and if they are equal, then the party sends the input in the clear; otherwise, they simply follow the specification of Π. This protocol is secure under the standard MPC definition, due to the security offered by Π, and because the probability that the input of the party is equal to the random string is negligible. On the other hand, the protocol Π' is clearly not secure if the distinguisher is allowed to pick the input of the honest parties adaptively on the first round of the protocol.

This is, of course, an ad-hoc example, but it should be clear that one should not trust to execute a protocol in the offline/online setting, in which the inputs of the online phase are decided after the offline phase is concluded. Hence, it is natural to introduce a new definition that provides security in the very natural adversarial setting we are considering.

Our Contributions. Building on top of the above observation, we first devise a new security definition, which captures the ability of the distinguisher to pick the input adaptively on the first $\ell - R$ rounds of the protocol (assuming the protocol has ℓ rounds in total, with only the last R rounds requiring inputs from the parties, where $1 \leq R \leq \ell - 1$). We call this new security definition *MPC with Adaptive-Input Selection.* We provide our notion in four different flavours, extending the standard notions of security with *selective*, *selective identifiable*, *unanimous*, and *identifiable* aborts to our adaptive-input paradigm. We recall that the notion of security with unanimous abort guarantees that if an honest party gets the output, then all the honest parties get the output. The notion of identifiable abort is stronger as it guarantees that if honest parties do not get the output, then all the parties agree on the identity of a corrupted party. Another notion is selective identifiable abort, which means that every honest party can either get the output or identify a corrupted party (without having agreement among all honest parties). We also consider the less common selective variants of these notions, where no unanimity is guaranteed (i.e., some honest parties may abort and some others may not).

As our main contribution, we show how to turn a big class of MPC protocols that may require the inputs already to compute the first round into a new protocol that needs the inputs *only* in the last two rounds.

We require the input protocol to admit a simulator that can extract the inputs of the parties before the ℓ-th round and that after the extraction phase, it behaves in a straight-line (i.e., non-rewinding) manner. To the best of our knowledge, this is a property held by most MPC protocols that allow the evaluation of generic functionality. This, in particular, holds true for the protocols proposed in [2,12,25,29].

Moreover, the security of the output protocols satisfies our new definition of security with adaptive-input selection. Notably, our compiler is round-preserving. Hence, it can be applied to all the existing round-optimal protocols. Informally, we prove the following theorem.

Theorem(informal). Assuming the existence of an ℓ-round protocol Π that is secure with selective/selective-identifiable/identifiable/unanimous abort, there exists an ℓ-round protocol Π' where the first $\ell-2$ rounds are input independent. Moreover, Π' is secure with adaptive-input selection with selective/selective-identifiable/identifiable/unanimous abort.

All the results presented in this paper are with respect to black-box simulation, dishonest majority, static corruption, and in the plain model. Hence, we will not specify this in the remainder of the paper.

1.1 Technical Overview

We design a compiler that takes as input an ℓ-round MPC protocol Π and returns a new ℓ-round protocol $\hat{\Pi}$ where the first $\ell - 2$ rounds are independent of parties' inputs. Our compiler follows the paradigm proposed in [5], but it will require to significantly depart from [5] due to our requirement on the round complexity (we elaborate more on this later). Let f be the function that the parties wish to compute, and for simplicity, let us assume that each party has a one-bit input. The parties will execute Π (the non-delayed input protocol) to compute an n-bit-input functionality g.

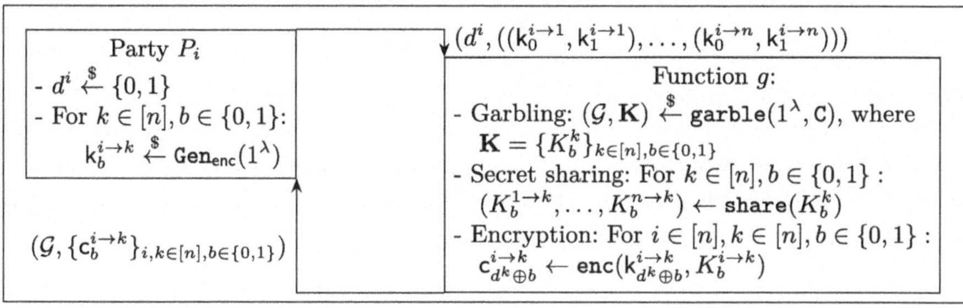

Fig. 1. $\mathtt{Gen}_{\mathsf{enc}}$ denotes the key generation algorithm of a symmetric key encryption scheme, and $\mathtt{enc}$ denotes its encryption algorithm. The garbling of the function f is done through the $\mathtt{garble}$ algorithm that takes as input the Boolean circuit $\mathtt{C}$ representing f and outputs the garbled circuit $\mathcal{G}$ along with the set of labels $\mathbf{K}$. A label $K_{x^k}^k$ is secret shared by running an n-out-of-n additive secret sharing algorithm $\mathtt{share}$ that takes as input the label and outputs n secret shares $K_{x^k}^{1\to k}, \ldots, K_{x^k}^{n\to k}$.

The functionality g computes a garbled circuit for the function f (the function the parties want to actually compute, and we denote the corresponding circuit as $\mathtt{C}$), performs an n-out-of-n secret sharing of each input label[3] and delivers the shares to the n parties as part of the output, together with the garbled circuit. More precisely, the shares are returned in a permuted order to hide which shares are related to the label for the bit b (with $b \in \{0,1\}$). The permutation is decided by the permutation bit d^i that each party P_i uses a part of the input to g.

Upon receiving the output of g, each party P_i broadcasts $z^i \leftarrow d^i \oplus x^i$ (where x^i corresponds to the input of P_i), and the share of the label related to its input. The bit z^i indicates which one, among the two shares related to the labels of the party P_i, each party P_j should broadcast in the next round. Once the selected shares have been broadcasted, each party can reconstruct exactly one label per input wire and evaluate the garbled circuit.

Unfortunately, there is a subtlety with the above approach. Indeed, the parties need to wait to receive the shares returned from the evaluation of g by the protocol Π (which requires ℓ rounds) and then exchange two additional rounds, one for sending the permutation bits and the other for sending the share-tag pairs. To make the compiler round-preserving, we need to depart significantly from prior BMR-like approaches considered in the literature so far and apply the following changes. The function g does not return the shares in the clear, but it returns an encryption of the shares. In more detail, for each $i \in [n]$, P_i receives encryptions of all the shares related to the input labels for 0 and 1 of all the parties. In addition, the party P_i receives a set of keys that allow it to decrypt all the ciphertexts containing the i-th share corresponding to its and all the other parties' labels.

[3] In the literature, the labels are sometimes called keys. We recall that each wire of a garbled circuit has a label/key corresponding to the input 0 and one corresponding to the input 1. In this case, the garbled circuit contains n wires, one per each party.

After the execution of g, each party possesses the encrypted shares of all the garbled circuit labels. To allow each party to decrypt the correct shares and to finally evaluate the garbled circuit, we let the parties broadcast $\overline{z}^i \leftarrow x^i \oplus d^i$. Similarly to what happened in the original protocol, in the last round, the parties send the keys corresponding to the permutation bits received in the previous round. This will enable the decryption of the labels and the evaluation of the garbled circuit.

At first glance, it looks like this modification did not help reduce the round complexity to ℓ. However, we observe that the encryption keys do not need to be decided by the functionality g and can instead be part of the input of g. Hence, the keys have been known to the parties since the beginning of the protocol, and upon receiving the permutation bit in the $(\ell - 1)$-th round, the parties can send the keys right away without needing to wait to receive the output of g. We refer the reader to Fig. 1 for a pictorial overview of the function g and how the input to the function is computed by each party and refer to Fig. 2 for a pictorial overview of the entire protocol.

We have overlooked yet another problem in the above discussion, which is related to the fact that parties may send incorrect keys, which may still reconstruct to labels that yield the garbled circuit evaluation to an incorrect (but different from $\perp$) output.[4] We solve this problem by letting g authenticate the labels. More details on this are provided in the technical section of the paper.

On the Need for a New Definition. As mentioned, the concept of MPC with pre-processing has been extensively studied. So, using the security definitions proposed in prior works would have been natural. To the best of our knowledge, most of these works are proven secure in the Universal Composable (UC) setting [9]. At a high level, in this setting, there is an adversary and an environment. The role of the environment (among others) is to decide when a protocol starts and what input the parties (both the honest and the corrupted parties) should use. As such, the UC framework captures very well the setting where the inputs of the honest parties are decided adaptively on the messages exchanged during the offline phase or on the messages of other protocols that are running concurrently. However, the UC framework and most of its relaxed versions [10] do not allow the simulator to rewind the environment. In particular, the simulator must be able to simulate in a straight-line fashion. Unfortunately, when no setup is available, and the majority of the parties are corrupted, it is impossible to construct such a straight-line simulator [11]. This is the reason why we could not adopt any of the existing definitions from the UC area, and we needed to modify the standard, standalone MPC security definition to capture the stronger adversarial setting we consider, which has been so far overlooked.

[4] Note that in the standard definition of the garbled circuit, nothing prevents an adversary from generating tampered labels that yield to an incorrect output (but different from $\perp$). This does not contradict the security of the garbled circuit, as the output obtained via this process may leak exactly the same (or less) information compared to the correct output.

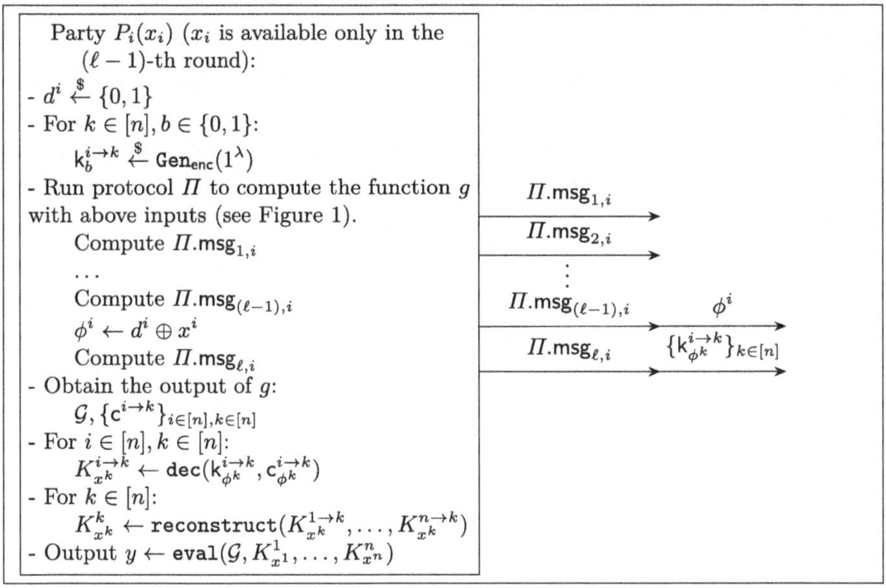

Fig. 2. $\mathsf{Gen}_{\mathsf{enc}}$ denotes the key generation algorithm of a symmetric key encryption scheme, and dec denotes its decryption algorithm. Each label $K_{x^k}^k$ is reconstructed by running the reconstruction algorithm $\mathtt{reconstruct}$ of the n-out-of-n secret sharing scheme. $\mathtt{eval}$ represents the evaluation algorithm of the garbling scheme that takes as input the garbled circuit $\mathcal{G}$ along with n garbled labels $K_{x^1}^1, \dots, K_{x^n}^n$ and outputs the evaluation of the circuit y. The protocol Π evaluates the function g on inputs d^i and $\{\mathsf{k}_b^{i\to k}\}_{k\in[n],b\in\{0,1\}}$ for each party P_i. We denote the message generated from the party P_i in the k-th of the protocol Π by $\Pi.\mathsf{msg}_{k,i}$. For simplicity, only the outgoing messages from the i-th party are shown. The protocol is symmetric, so all incoming messages are of the same form.

Overview of Multi-party Computation with Adaptive-Input Selection. In our new MPC definition, the real-world experiment is nearly the same as the one in the standard definition. The only difference is that after $\ell - R$ rounds, the adversary can decide the input of honest parties (denoted as x') in the experiment. The ideal world experiment is, instead, quite different. Instead of giving the simulator oracle access to the adversary $\mathcal{A}$, we provide oracle access to $\mathcal{P}(\mathcal{A})$, and call $\mathcal{P}$ a *proxy machine*.

$\mathcal{P}$ acts as a proxy between the adversary and the simulator with respect to all the protocol messages and never provides any information about the honest-parties inputs decided by the adversary. In more detail, we know that at some point, the adversary needs to decide what the inputs of honest parties x' are, and we do not want the simulator to know what x' is (as this would trivialize the definition). Whenever the adversary outputs x', $\mathcal{P}$ will send x' to the ideal functionality f without letting $\mathcal{S}$ know.

We also note that $\mathcal{S}$ might rewind, and $\mathcal{A}$ might change x' during rewinding. Therefore, we require $\mathcal{S}$ to signal that it has finished rewinding by sending a confirmation message ok to $\mathcal{P}$, and only at that point $\mathcal{P}$ will then send x' to the ideal functionality.

We show the ideal world experiment in the Fig. 3. The straight lines represent the flow of protocol messages between $\mathcal{S}$ and $\mathcal{A}$, while $\mathcal{P}$ acts as an intermediary, simply relaying these messages between the two entities. When $\mathcal{S}$ sends ok to $\mathcal{P}$ (indicated by dashed lines), $\mathcal{P}$ forwards x' to f (marked with dotted lines). Upon receiving x', f waits for $\mathcal{S}$ to obtain the inputs of corrupted parties, and then the ideal world experiment continues in the same way as the ideal world experiment of the standard MPC definition.

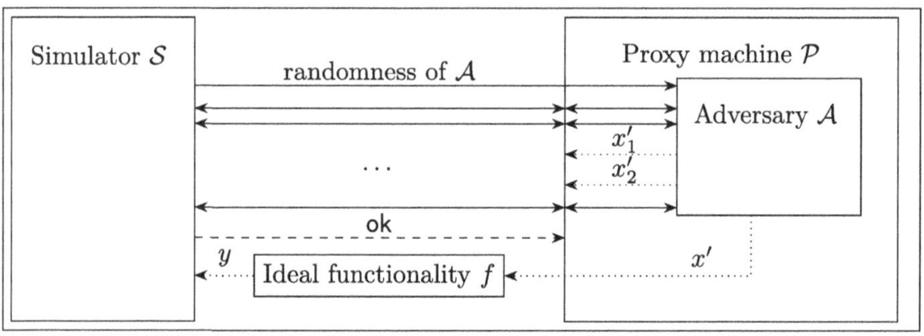

Fig. 3. The randomness that $\mathcal{A}$ should use and all messages from the simulator $\mathcal{S}$ to $\mathcal{P}$ are forwarded to $\mathcal{A}$. Similarly, all protocol messages of $\mathcal{A}$ are forwarded by $\mathcal{P}$ to $\mathcal{S}$ (denoted by straight lines), except the messages in which $\mathcal{A}$ attempts to send the input for honest parties x' (denoted by dotted lines). $\mathcal{P}$ blocks these messages unless it receives an ok command from $\mathcal{S}$. If ok is received, $\mathcal{P}$ forwards x' to the ideal functionality, which then waits for the inputs from the corrupted parties (likely extracted by $\mathcal{S}$) and returns the output y to $\mathcal{S}$.

Supported MPC Protocols. We mentioned that our compiler supports a big class of protocols. More formally, these protocols are all those that admit a simulator that 1) never generates the last-round message of the protocol before extracting the input of the corrupted parties and 2) after the simulator has queried the ideal functionality, it completes the simulation in a straight line (i.e., it does not perform any additional rewinding). We refer to these types of MPC protocol as a *Special-Extractable* protocol. We find it useful to assume that the non-delayed input protocol satisfies this property because the simulator we design will need to send simulated encryption keys in the last round of the protocol. Without knowing the corrupted parties' inputs, it is not clear how to generate these keys properly. This is why we require the first property. We require the second property to make sure that once the input is extracted, the simulator does not, for example, fully rewind the entire session. This would make our simulation more involved.

2 Preliminaries

We denote the *security parameter* with $\lambda \in \mathbb{N}$. We use "$\leftarrow$" as the assigning operator (e.g. if we assign the value of b to a, we write $a \leftarrow b$). For the randomized assignment, we use "$\xleftarrow{\$}$" where the randomness is not explicit. A randomized algorithm A is running in *probabilistic polynomial time* (PPT) if there exists a polynomial $\mathsf{poly}(\cdot)$ such that for every input x the running time of $A(x)$ is bounded by $\mathsf{poly}(|x|)$.

A function $f(\cdot)$ is *negligible in* λ, or just *negligible*, if for every positive polynomial $\mathsf{poly}(\cdot)$ and all sufficiently large λ it holds that $f(\lambda) < \frac{1}{\mathsf{poly}(\lambda)}$ [26]. In this paper, we use $\epsilon(\cdot)$ to denote a negligible function.

A *probability ensemble* $X = \{X(a,\lambda)\}_{a\in\{0,1\}^*,\lambda\in\mathbb{N}}$ is an infinite sequence of random variables indexed by a and $\lambda \in \mathbb{N}$. Two probability ensembles $X = \{X(a,\lambda)\}_{a\in\{0,1\}^*,\lambda\in\mathbb{N}}$ and $Y = \{Y(a,\lambda)\}_{a\in\{0,1\}^*,\lambda\in\mathbb{N}}$ are said to be *computationally indistinguishable*, denoted by $X \overset{c}{\equiv} Y$, if for every non-uniform polynomial-time algorithm $\mathcal{D}$ there exists a negligible function $\epsilon(\cdot)$ such that for every $a \in \{0,1\}^*$ and every $\lambda \in \mathbb{N}$, $\left|\Pr[\mathcal{D}(X(a,\lambda)) = 1] - \Pr[\mathcal{D}(Y(a,\lambda)) = 1]\right| \leq \epsilon(\lambda)$ [26].

2.1 Symmetric Encryption Scheme

Definition 1. *[22] A* symmetric encryption scheme *for the message space M is a tuple of three algorithms* $\mathtt{SE} = (\mathtt{Gen}_{\mathsf{enc}}, \mathtt{enc}, \mathtt{dec})$*:*

- $\mathtt{Gen}_{\mathsf{enc}}(1^\lambda)$*: Takes as input a unary representation of the security parameter λ, and outputs a key k.*
- $\mathtt{enc}(k,m)$*: Takes as input the symmetric key k and a message $m \in M$ to encrypt, and outputs a ciphertext c.*
- $\mathtt{dec}(k,c)$*: Takes as input the symmetric key k and a ciphertext c, and outputs a message or $\perp$ if decryption fails.*

A scheme $\mathtt{SE}$ *is* correct *if, for all $\lambda \in \mathbb{N}$, $k \xleftarrow{\$} \mathtt{Gen}_{\mathsf{enc}}(1^\lambda)$, $m \in M$, we have*

$$\Pr[\mathtt{dec}(k, \mathtt{enc}(k,m)) = m] = 1.$$

Definition 2. *[31] Let $\Pi = (\mathtt{Gen}_{\mathsf{enc}}, \mathtt{enc}, \mathtt{dec})$ be a symmetric encryption scheme with message space M. Let $\mathcal{A}$ be an adversary, which is formally just a (stateful) algorithm. We define an experiment $\mathtt{PrivK}^{\mathtt{eav}}_{\mathcal{A},\Pi}$ in the Fig. 2.1 as follows:*

Figure 2.1: The adversarial indistinguishability experiment $\mathtt{PrivK}^{\mathtt{eav}}_{\mathcal{A},\Pi}$.

1. *The adversary* $\mathcal{A}$ *outputs a pair of messages* $m_0, m_1 \in M$.
2. *A key* k *is generated using* $\mathtt{Gen}_{\mathsf{enc}}$, *and a uniform bit* $b \in \{0,1\}$ *is chosen. Ciphertext* $c \leftarrow \mathtt{enc}(k, m_b)$ *is computed and given to* $\mathcal{A}$. *We refer to* c *as the* challenge ciphertext.
3. $\mathcal{A}$ *outputs a bit* b'.
4. *The output of the experiment is defined to be* 1 *if* $b' = b$, *and* 0 *otherwise. We write* $\mathtt{PrivK}^{\mathtt{eav}}_{\mathcal{A},\Pi} = 1$ *if the experiment's output is* 1, *and say that* $\mathcal{A}$ succeeds.

Definition 3. *[31] Symmetric encryption scheme* $\Pi = (\mathtt{Gen}_{\mathsf{enc}}, \mathtt{enc}, \mathtt{dec})$ *with message space* M *is computationally indistinguishable if for every PPT* $\mathcal{A}$ *it holds that*

$$\Pr[\mathtt{PrivK}^{\mathtt{eav}}_{\mathcal{A},\Pi} = 1] = \frac{1}{2} + \epsilon(\lambda)$$

2.2 Message Authentication Code Scheme

Definition 4. *[31] A* message authentication code scheme *consists of three PPT algorithms* $\mathtt{MAC} = (\mathtt{Gen}_{\mathsf{mac}}, \mathtt{Mac}, \mathtt{Vrfy})$ *such that:*

1. *The* key-generation algorithm $\mathtt{Gen}_{\mathsf{mac}}$ *takes as input a unary representation of the security parameter* λ *and outputs a key* k *with* $|k| \geq \lambda$.
2. *The* tag-generation algorithm $\mathtt{Mac}$ *takes as input a key* k *and a message* $m \in \{0,1\}^*$, *and outputs a tag* t. *Since this algorithm may be randomized, we write this as* $t \xleftarrow{\$} \mathtt{Mac}_k(m)$.
3. *The* deterministic verification algorithm $\mathtt{Vrfy}$ *takes as input a key* k, *a message* m, *and a tag* t. *It outputs a bit* b, *with* $b = 1$ *meaning valid and* $b = 0$ *meaning invalid. We write this as* $b \leftarrow \mathtt{Vrfy}_k(m, t)$.

It is required that for every λ, *every key* k *output by* $\mathtt{Gen}_{\mathsf{mac}}(1^\lambda)$, *and every* $m \in \{0,1\}^*$, *it holds that* $\mathtt{Vrfy}_k(m, \mathtt{Mac}_k(m)) = 1$.

Definition 5. *[31]* $\Pi = (\mathtt{Gen}_{\mathsf{mac}}, \mathtt{Mac}, \mathtt{Vrfy})$ *is an computationally secure one-time* $\mathtt{MAC}$ *if for all PPT adversaries* $\mathcal{A}$ *it holds that:*

$$\Pr[\mathtt{Mac} - \mathtt{forge}^{\mathtt{1-time}}_{\mathcal{A},\Pi} = 1] \leq \epsilon(n)$$

in the $\mathtt{Mac} - \mathtt{forge}^{\mathtt{1-time}}_{\mathcal{A},\Pi}$ *experiment, as defined in Fig. 2.2:*

Figure 2.2: $\mathtt{Mac} - \mathtt{forge}^{\mathtt{1-time}}_{\mathcal{A},\Pi}$

1. *A key* k *is generated by running* $\mathtt{Gen}_{\mathsf{mac}}$.
2. *The adversary* $\mathcal{A}$ *outputs a message* m', *and* m' *is given to the challenger. Challenger returns a tag* $t' \xleftarrow{\$} \mathtt{Mac}_k(m')$.

3. $\mathcal{A}$ *outputs* (m, t).
4. *The output of the experiment is defined to be 1 if and only if (1)* $\mathtt{Vrfy}_k(m, t) = 1$ *and (2)* $m \neq m'$.

2.3 Garbling Scheme

Definition 6. *[18] A* garbling scheme *is a tuple of efficient algorithms* $\mathtt{GC} = (\mathtt{garble}, \mathtt{eval})$ *defined as follows.*

- $(\mathcal{G}, \boldsymbol{K}) \stackrel{\$}{\leftarrow} \mathtt{garble}(1^\lambda, \mathtt{C})$*: The algorithm* $\mathtt{garble}$ *takes as input a unary representation of the security parameter* λ *and a Boolean circuit* $\mathtt{C} : \{0,1\}^{\mathsf{L}} \to \{0,1\}^m$*, and outputs a garbled circuit* $\mathcal{G}$ *and* L *pairs of garbled labels* $\boldsymbol{K} = (K_0^1, K_1^1, \ldots, K_0^{\mathsf{L}}, K_1^{\mathsf{L}})$*. For simplicity, we assume that for every* $i \in [\mathsf{L}]$ *and* $b \in \{0,1\}$*, it holds that* $K_b^i \in \{0,1\}^\lambda$.
- $y \leftarrow \mathtt{eval}(\mathcal{G}, K_{\mathtt{sim}}^1, \ldots, K_{\mathtt{sim}}^{\mathsf{L}})$*: The algorithm* $\mathtt{eval}$ *takes as input the garbled circuit* $\mathcal{G}$ *and* L *garbled labels* $K_{\mathtt{sim}}^1, \ldots, K_{\mathtt{sim}}^{\mathsf{L}}$*, and outputs a value* $y \in \{0,1\}^m$.

We require the following properties of a garbling scheme:

- **Perfect Correctness.** We say $\mathtt{GC}$ satisfies *perfect correctness* if for any Boolean circuit $\mathtt{C} : \{0,1\}^{\mathsf{L}} \to \{0,1\}^m$ and $x = (x_1, \ldots, x_{\mathsf{L}})$ it holds that

$$\Pr[\mathtt{eval}(\mathcal{G}, \mathbf{K}[x]) = \mathtt{C}(x)] = 1,$$

  where $(\mathcal{G}, \mathbf{K}) \stackrel{\$}{\leftarrow} \mathtt{garble}(1^\lambda, \mathtt{C})$ with $\mathbf{K} = (K_0^1, K_1^1, \ldots, K_0^{\mathsf{L}}, K_1^{\mathsf{L}})$ and $\mathbf{K}[x] = (K_{x_1}^1, \ldots, K_{x_{\mathsf{L}}}^{\mathsf{L}})$.
- **Privacy.** We say that $\mathtt{GC}$ satisfies *privacy* if there exists a simulator $\mathtt{simGC}$ such that for every PPT adversary $\mathcal{A}$, it holds that

$$\Pr[\mathtt{GC}^{\mathtt{priv}} = 1] \leq \frac{1}{2} + \epsilon(\lambda),$$

  where $\mathtt{GC}^{\mathtt{priv}}$ experiment is defined in Fig. 2.3:

Figure 2.3: The garbling scheme privacy experiment $\mathtt{GC}^{\mathtt{priv}}$.

1. $\mathcal{A}$ constructs a circuit $\mathtt{C} : \{0,1\}^{\mathsf{L}} \to \{0,1\}^m$, outputs an input $x = (x_1, \ldots, x_{\mathsf{L}}) \in \{0,1\}^{\mathsf{L}}$ and sends them to the challenger.
2. Challenger chooses a random bit $b \in \{0,1\}$ and does the following:
   (a) if b = 0: $(\mathcal{G}, (K_0^1, K_1^1, \ldots, K_0^{\mathsf{L}}, K_1^{\mathsf{L}})) \stackrel{\$}{\leftarrow} \mathtt{garble}(1^\lambda, \mathtt{C})$. Set $K^i = K_{x_i}^i$ for $i \in [\mathsf{L}]$.
   (b) if b = 1: $(\mathcal{G}, K_{\mathtt{sim}}^1, \ldots, K_{\mathtt{sim}}^{\mathsf{L}}) \stackrel{\$}{\leftarrow} \mathtt{simGC}(1^\lambda, \mathtt{C}, \mathtt{C}(x))$. Set $K^i = K_{\mathtt{sim}}^i$ for $i \in [\mathsf{L}]$.
3. Challenger sends $\mathcal{G}, K^1, \ldots, K^{\mathsf{L}}$ to $\mathcal{A}$.
4. $\mathcal{A}$ outputs a bit b'.

5. $\mathcal{A}$ wins if $b = b'$, and we say that the experiment evaluates to 1 in this case.

2.4 Additive Secret Sharing Scheme

In our work, we will use *n-out-of-n secret sharing scheme*, which is also referred to as *additive secret sharing scheme*. We give the definition here:

Definition 7 (n-out-of-n secret sharing scheme). *A n-out-of-n secret sharing scheme is a pair of algorithms (*`share`*,* `reconstruct`*), such that:*

- `share` *is a randomized algorithm that on input a secret* m*, outputs a set of* n *shares* $(s_1, \ldots, s_n)$.
- `reconstruct` *is a deterministic algorithm that on input t shares* $(s_1, \ldots, s_n)$*, outputs the secret* m.

The scheme needs to satisfy the correctness *property if :* $\forall m$*, we have:*

$$\Pr_{\texttt{share}(m) \to (s_1,\ldots,s_n)} [\texttt{reconstruct}(s_1, \ldots, s_n) = m] = 1$$

In addition, the scheme satisfies perfect security *property if:* $\forall m, m'$, $\forall S \subseteq \{1, \ldots, n\}$*, where* $|S| < n$*, the following distributions are indistinguishable:*

$$\{(s_i : i \in S) \mid (s_1, \ldots, s_n) \leftarrow \texttt{share}(m)\}$$
$$\{(s'_i : i \in S) \mid (s'_1, \ldots, s'_n) \leftarrow \texttt{share}(m')\}$$

3 Secure Multiparty Computation (MPC)

We follow the real/ideal world simulation paradigm, and we adopt the security model of Cohen, Garay and Zikas [17].

Real-World. An n-party protocol $\Pi = (P_1, \ldots, P_n)$ is an n-tuple of probabilistic polynomial-time (PPT) interactive Turing machines (ITMs), where each party P_i is initialized with input $x_i \in \{0,1\}^*$ and random coins $r_i \in \{0,1\}^*$. We let $\mathcal{A}$ denote a special PPT ITM that represents the adversary and that is initialized with input that contains the identities of the corrupt parties, their respective private inputs and an auxiliary input.

The protocol is executed in rounds (i.e., the protocol is synchronous). Each round consists of a send phase and a receive phase, where parties can respectively send and receive messages. The communication in each round happens via a broadcast channel. During the execution of the protocol, the corrupt parties receive arbitrary instructions from the adversary $\mathcal{A}$, while the honest parties faithfully follow the instructions of the protocol. We consider the adversary $\mathcal{A}$ to be rushing, i.e., during every round, the adversary can see the messages the honest parties sent before producing messages for corrupt parties.

At the end of the protocol execution, the honest parties produce their outputs, and the adversary returns an arbitrary function of the corrupt parties' view. The view of a party during the execution consists of its input, random coins and the messages it sees during the execution.

Definition 8 (Real-world execution). *Let $\Pi = (P_1, \ldots, P_n)$ be an n-party protocol and let $\mathcal{J} \subseteq [n]$, of size at most t, denote the set of indices of the parties corrupted by $\mathcal{A}$. The joint execution of Π under $(\mathcal{A}, \mathcal{J})$ in the real world, on input vector $x = (x_1, \ldots, x_n)$, auxiliary input* aux *and the unary representation of the security parameter 1^λ, denoted $\mathtt{REAL}_{\Pi,\mathcal{J},\mathcal{A}(\mathsf{aux})}(x, 1^\lambda)$, is defined as the output vector of $P_1, \ldots, P_n$ and $\mathcal{A}(\mathsf{aux})$ resulting from the protocol interaction.*

Ideal-World. We describe ideal-world executions with selective abort (sa-abort), selective identifiable abort (si-abort) (recently introduced in [18]), unanimous abort (un-abort), identifiable abort (id-abort).

Definition 9 (Ideal Computation). *Consider* type $\in$ {sa-abort, un-abort, si-abort, id-abort}. *Let $f : (\{0,1\}^*)^n \to (\{0,1\}^*)^n$ be an n-party function and let $\mathcal{J} \subseteq [n]$, of size at most t, be the set of indices of the corrupt parties. Then, the joint ideal execution of f under $(\mathcal{S}, \mathcal{J})$ on input vector $x = (x_1, \ldots, x_n)$, auxiliary input* aux *to $\mathcal{S}$ and the unary representation of the security parameter 1^λ, denoted $\mathtt{IDEAL}^{\mathsf{type}}_{f,\mathcal{J},\mathcal{S}(\mathsf{aux})}(x, 1^\lambda)$, is defined as the output vector of $P_1, \ldots, P_n$ and $\mathcal{S}$ resulting from the following ideal process.*

1. Parties send inputs to trusted party*: An honest party P_i sends its input x_i to the trusted party for each $i \in [n]$. The simulator $\mathcal{S}$ may send to the trusted party arbitrary inputs for the corrupt parties. Let x'_i be the value actually sent as the input of party P_i.*
2. Trusted party speaks to simulator*: The trusted party computes $(y_1, \ldots, y_n) = f(x'_1, \ldots, x'_n)$. If there are no corrupt parties, proceed to step 4.. Otherwise the trusted party sends $\{y_i\}_{i \in \mathcal{J}}$ to $\mathcal{S}$.*
3. Simulator $\mathcal{S}$ responds to the trusted party as follows*:*
   (a) If type = sa-abort: *The simulator $\mathcal{S}$ can select a set of parties that will not get the output as $\mathcal{K} \subseteq [n] \setminus \mathcal{J}$. (Note that $\mathcal{K}$ can be empty, allowing all parties to obtain the output.) It sends* $(\mathtt{abort}, \mathcal{K})$ *to the trusted party.*
   (b) If type = un-abort: *The simulator can send* abort *to the trusted party. If it does, we take $\mathcal{K} = [n] \setminus \mathcal{J}$.*
   (c) If type = si-abort: *The simulator $\mathcal{S}$ can select a set of parties that will not get the output as $\mathcal{K} \subseteq [n] \setminus \mathcal{J}$. (Note that $\mathcal{K}$ can be empty, allowing all parties to obtain the output.) For each party j in $\mathcal{K}$, the simulator selects a corrupt party $i^*_j \in \mathcal{J}$ who will be blamed by party j. It sends* $(\mathtt{abort}, \mathcal{K}, \{j, i^*_j\}_{j \in \mathcal{K}})$ *to the trusted party.*
   (d) If type = id-abort: *If it chooses to abort, the simulator $\mathcal{S}$ can select a corrupt party $i^* \in \mathcal{J}$ who will be blamed, and send* $(\mathtt{abort}, i^*)$ *to the trusted party. If it does, we take $\mathcal{K} = [n] \setminus \mathcal{J}$.*
4. Trusted party answers parties*:*
   (a) *If the trusted party got* abort *from the simulator $\mathcal{S}$,*

i. *It sets the abort message* $\mathsf{abortmsg}$, *as follows:*
   - *if* $\mathsf{type} \in \{\mathsf{sa\text{-}abort}, \mathsf{un\text{-}abort}\}$, *we let* $\mathsf{abortmsg} = \perp$.
   - *if* $\mathsf{type} = \mathsf{si\text{-}abort}$, *we let* $\mathsf{abortmsg} = \{\mathsf{abortmsg}_j\}_{j\in\mathcal{K}} = (\perp, i_j^*)_{j\in\mathcal{K}}$.
   - *if* $\mathsf{type} = \mathsf{id\text{-}abort}$, *we let* $\mathsf{abortmsg} = (\perp, i^*)$.

ii. *The trusted party sends* y_j *to every party* P_j, $j \in [n] \setminus \mathcal{K}$.
If $\mathsf{type} = \mathsf{si\text{-}abort}$, *the trusted party then sends* $\mathsf{abortmsg}_j$ *to each party* P_j, $j \in \mathcal{K}$; *otherwise, the trusted party sends* $\mathsf{abortmsg}$ *to every party* P_j, $j \in \mathcal{K}$

(b) *Otherwise, it sends* y *to every* P_j, $j \in [n]$.

5. Outputs*: Honest parties always output the message received from the trusted party, while the corrupt parties output nothing. The simulator* $\mathcal{S}$ *outputs an arbitrary function of the initial inputs* $\{x_i\}_{i\in\mathcal{J}}$, *the messages received by the corrupt parties from the trusted party and its auxiliary input.*

Security Definitions. Now that we have described the ideal and the real-world experiment, we are ready to state the formal definition.

Definition 10. *Consider* $\mathsf{type} \in \{\mathsf{sa\text{-}abort}, \mathsf{un\text{-}abort}, \mathsf{si\text{-}abort}, \mathsf{id\text{-}abort}\}$. *Let* $f : (\{0,1\}^*)^n \to (\{0,1\}^*)^n$ *be an* n*-party function. A protocol* Π t*-securely computes the function* f *with* type *security if for every PPT real-world adversary* $\mathcal{A}$ *with auxiliary input* aux, *there exists a PPT simulator* $\mathcal{S}$ *such that for every* $\mathcal{J} \subseteq [n]$ *of size at most* t, *for all* $x \in (\{0,1\}^*)^n$, *for all* $\lambda \in \mathbb{N}$, *it holds that*

$$\mathtt{REAL}_{\Pi,\mathcal{J},\mathcal{A}(\mathsf{aux})}(x, 1^\lambda) \overset{c}{\equiv} \mathtt{IDEAL}^{\mathsf{type}}_{f,\mathcal{J},\mathcal{S}(\mathsf{aux})}(x, 1^\lambda).$$

3.1 Additional Notation

Let Π be an ℓ-round MPC protocol. Rather than viewing a protocol Π as an n-tuple of ITMs, it is convenient to view each ITM as a sequence of multiple algorithms: $\mathtt{frst\text{-}msg}_i$, to compute P_i's first messages to its peers; $\mathtt{nxt\text{-}msg}_i^k$, to compute P_i's k-th round messages for $(2 \le k \le \ell)$; and $\mathtt{output}_i$, to compute P_i's output. Thus, a protocol Π can be defined as $\{(\mathtt{frst\text{-}msg}_i, \mathtt{nxt\text{-}msg}_i^k, \mathtt{output}_i)\}_{i\in[n],k\in[\ell]\setminus\{1\}}$.

The syntax of the algorithms is as follows:

- $\mathtt{frst\text{-}msg}_i(x^i; r_i) \to \mathsf{msg}_{i,1}$ produces the first-round messages of party P_i to all parties.
- $\mathtt{nxt\text{-}msg}_i^k(x^i, \{\mathsf{msg}_{j,l}\}_{j\in[n],l\in\{1,\ldots,k-1\}}; r_i) \to \mathsf{msg}_{i,k}$ produces the k-th round messages of party P_i to all parties.
- $\mathtt{output}_i(x^i, \mathsf{msg}_{1,1}, \ldots, \mathsf{msg}_{n,1}, \ldots, \mathsf{msg}_{1,\ell}, \ldots, \mathsf{msg}_{n,\ell}; r_i) \to y_i$ produces the output returned to party P_i.

To not overburden the notation, we do not pass the random coin r as an explicit input of the cryptographic algorithms.

We have repeatedly mentioned that our compiler works for a big class of multi-party computation protocols (We denote this class of protocol as *Special-Extractable* MPC protocol, as per Definition 11). This property requires the

MPC simulator to be able to extract the inputs of the party before generating the last round of the protocol, and after the extraction, it behaves in a straight-line manner. All existing four-round protocols satisfy this property, and it is a property enjoyed by most of the MPC protocols.

Definition 11 (Special-Extractable MPC). *A secure multi-party protocol is Special-Extractable, if the simulator $\mathcal{S}$ (which exists by Definition 10) works in the following way. $\mathcal{S}$ queries the ideal-functionality (i.e., it returns the input of the corrupted parties) without ever sending the last protocol message to the adversary. Moreover, upon receiving the answer from the ideal functionality, $\mathcal{S}$ sends only one message to the adversary (on behalf of all the honest parties) and stops.*

4 Secure Computation with Adaptive-Input Selection

We now introduce the property of *delayed-inputness* for MPC protocols. To make it more general, for any ℓ-round MPC protocol, the inputs of parties are needed only in the last R rounds, where $1 \leq R \leq \ell - 1$.

Definition 12 (Delayed-input multi-party computation). *Let* $\Pi = \{(\texttt{frst-msg}_i, \texttt{nxt-msg}_i^k, \texttt{output}_i)\}_{i \in [n], k \in [l] \setminus \{1\}}$ *be an ℓ-round MPC protocol (satisfying Definition 10). Then, Π is* delayed-input *if the next-message functions* $\{(\texttt{frst-msg}_i, \texttt{nxt-msg}_i^k)\}_{i \in [n], k \in [\ell - R] \setminus \{1\}}$ *take as their first input a default value (e.g., 0^λ) in the place of the actual inputs of the parties. We note that* $1 \leq R \leq \ell - 1$.

The above definition just describes a syntactic property that the next-message function algorithms may satisfy. For delayed-input MPC protocols, we consider a security definition that allows the adversary to craft the inputs the honest parties should use in the real-world experiment adaptively on the first $\ell - R$ rounds. To capture this, we modify the standard definition of MPC (that we recall in Definition 10) as follows.

- The real-world experiment proceeds exactly like the real-world experiment of the standard MPC definition, with the difference that the adversary, upon generating the $(\ell - R)$-th round, also returns a special message $(\texttt{input}, x = \{x_i\}_{i \in \mathcal{I}})$, where $\mathcal{I}$ represents the indices of the honest parties. From that point on, the honest party P_i (for each $i \in \mathcal{I}$) will use the input x_i to evaluate the next message functions and complete the execution of the protocol.
- In the simulated experiment, we give the simulator black-box access to the adversary, but we prevent the simulator from getting the message $(\texttt{input}, x = \{x_i\}_{i \in \mathcal{I}})$ (clearly, a simulator having access to these messages would trivialize the security definition).
  To formalize this aspect, we give the simulator oracle access to a *proxy-machine* $\mathcal{P}(\cdot)$ and modify the ideal world experiment as follows. The proxy machine has black-box access to $\mathcal{A}$ (denoted with $\mathcal{P}(\mathcal{A})$) and acts as a proxy

between the adversary and the calling party (the simulator in our case) with respect to all the messages of the protocol Π. However, upon receiving the message $(\texttt{input}, x = \{x_i\}_{i\in\mathcal{I}})$ from $\mathcal{A}$, $\mathcal{P}(\mathcal{A})$ instructs the ideal functionality to use the inputs $\{x_i\}_{i\in\mathcal{I}}$ for the honest parties. The ideal functionality then waits for the simulator to receive the input of the corrupted parties, and upon receiving them, it returns the output to the simulator (that we recall, is the ideal world adversary). From that point on, the ideal world experiment behaves exactly like the ideal world experiment of the standard MPC definition. There is still another minor modification we need to do. The proxy delivers the inputs of the honest parties to the ideal functionality only after receiving an *ok* message from the simulator. This is needed as the simulator may want to rewind the adversary (rewinding the proxy machine), and this could cause $\mathcal{A}$ to send multiple `input` commands to the proxy machine. This, in turn, could make the proxy machine communicate to the ideal functionality some honest parties' inputs, which are not consistent with the inputs that appear in the final simulated thread. To avoid this, we let the simulator decide when is the right moment for $\mathcal{P}(\cdot)$ to send the inputs to the ideal functionality. Looking ahead, this *ok* command will be sent only after the simulator has decided that no more rewinds will be performed in the first $\ell - R + 1$ rounds.

We now propose a more formal definition of a real and ideal world and finally state the formal definition of adaptive-input selection secure MPC.

Real-World. Let $\{P_1, \dots, P_n\}$ be a set of n parties. Let $\mathcal{I}$ be the set of honest parties' indexes. In the real world, the adversary $\mathcal{A}$ engages in the execution of an ℓ-round delayed-input MPC protocol. The execution proceeds accordingly to the real world of the standard MPC definition (Definition 10), with the difference that in the $(\ell - R)$-th round, the adversary sends an additional message $(\texttt{input}, x = \{x_i\}_{i\in\mathcal{I}})$. For this point on, for each $i \in \mathcal{I}$, the party P_i uses the input x_i to complete the execution of the protocol against $\mathcal{A}$. We denote with $\mathtt{REAL}^{\mathsf{DI}}_{\Pi,\mathcal{J},\mathcal{A}(\mathsf{aux})}(1^\lambda)$ the output vector of $P_1, \dots, P_n$ and $\mathcal{A}(\mathsf{aux})$ resulting from the protocol interaction.

Ideal-world. The ideal world also follows the one described in the standard MPC definition (Definition 10), with the following difference. The ideal world is parametrized by a proxy machine $\mathcal{P}(\cdot)$. The proxy machine is initialized with an empty variable $\mathsf{HInputs}$, takes as input a PPT algorithm $\mathscr{A}$, and interacts with an additional algorithm called *caller* as follows.

- Upon receiving any message from the caller, forward this to $\mathscr{A}$.
- Upon receiving any message from $\mathscr{A}$, different from the command $(\texttt{input}, \cdot)$, forward this message to the caller.
- Upon receiving the message $(\texttt{input}, x)$ from $\mathscr{A}$, set $\mathsf{HInputs} \leftarrow x$.
- Upon receiving the message ok from the caller, parse $\mathsf{HInputs}$ as $\{x_i\}_{i\in\mathcal{I}}$, and send x_i to the ideal functionality on the behalf of the honest party P_i, for each $i \in \mathcal{I}$.

In summary, the honest parties' inputs are decided by $\mathcal{P}(\mathscr{A})$ (in particular, they are decided by $\mathscr{A}$). The inputs of the corrupted parties instead are decided by the ideal world adversary $\mathcal{S}$. When the ideal functionality receives the inputs from the honest and the corrupted parties, it acts exactly like the ideal world functionality described in Definition 10. We denote with $\mathtt{IDEAL}^{\mathsf{DI},\mathsf{type}}_{f,\mathcal{J},\mathcal{P}(\mathscr{A}),\mathcal{S}(\mathsf{aux})}(1^\lambda)$, the output vector of $P_1,\ldots,P_n$ and $\mathcal{S}$ resulting from the following ideal process.

We are now ready to state the formal definition of adaptive-input selection secure MPC.

Definition 13 (MPC with Adaptive-Input Selection). *Let $f : (\{0,1\}^*)^n \rightarrow (\{0,1\}^*)^n$ be an n-party function. A delayed-input protocol Π t-securely computes the function f with* type *security if for every PPT real-world adversary $\mathcal{A}$ with auxiliary input* aux*, there exists a PPT simulator $\mathcal{S}$ that has black-box access to $\mathcal{P}(\mathcal{A})$, such that for every $\mathcal{J} \subseteq [n]$ of size at most t, for all $\lambda \in \mathbb{N}$, it holds that*

$$\mathtt{REAL}^{\mathsf{DI}}_{\Pi,\mathcal{J},\mathcal{A}(\mathsf{aux})}(1^\lambda) \stackrel{c}{\equiv} \mathtt{IDEAL}^{\mathsf{DI},\mathsf{type}}_{f,\mathcal{J},\mathcal{P}(\mathcal{A}),\mathcal{S}(\mathsf{aux})}(1^\lambda).$$

We stress that the simulator does not directly query $\mathcal{A}$, but it has black-box access to $\mathcal{P}(\mathcal{A})$. This makes the definition non-trivial, preventing the simulator from obtaining the input that $\mathcal{A}$ would send via the command $(\mathtt{input}, x)$.

5 Our Compiler

In this section, we show how our compiler that turns an ℓ-round MPC protocol into an adaptive-input selection secure MPC protocol works. For simplicity, we describe our compiler for the case where $\ell = 4$ (which represents the minimal number of rounds) and $R = 2$, but extending the protocol to any ℓ and $R = 2$ is trivial. We also assume that each party has only one-bit input and argue that it is trivial to extend to inputs of arbitrary size by letting one party control multiple sub-parties of the one-input protocol. Before describing our compiler, we emphasize that our scheme works for a generic g. As such, we require the input of parties in the second last round ($R = 2$). We note that this is optimal, as for non-trivial functionality a protocol that requires the input only to compute the last round would trivially be susceptible to residual attacks. It is still an interesting open question describing a compiler that depending on the computed function, can adaptively decide whether $R = 1$ or $R = 2$, but we do not consider this *adaptive setting* in our paper.

Our construction makes use of the following tools:

- A four-round special-extractable malicious type secure MPC (Definition 10 and Definition 11) protocol $\Pi = \{(\mathtt{frst\text{-}msg}_i, \mathtt{nxt\text{-}msg}^k_i, \mathtt{output}_i)\}_{i\in[n],k\in\{2,3,4\}}$ against $t < n$ corruptions, which realizes the functionality g, formally specified in the Fig. 5.1 with $\mathsf{type} \in \{\mathsf{sa\text{-}abort}, \mathsf{si\text{-}abort}, \mathsf{un\text{-}abort}, \mathsf{id\text{-}abort}\}$. The j-th round message of the protocol Π sent by party P_i is denoted as $\mathsf{msg}_{j,i}$. The additional message introduced in the compiled protocol is denoted as $\widehat{\mathsf{msg}}_{j,i}$.

- A garbling scheme $\mathtt{GC} = (\mathtt{garble}, \mathtt{eval})$ (Definition 6).
- A symmetric encryption scheme $\mathtt{SE} = (\mathtt{Gen}_{\mathsf{enc}}, \mathtt{enc}, \mathtt{dec})$ (Definition 1), that is computationally indistinguishable as per Definition 3.
- A message authentication code scheme $\mathtt{MAC} = (\mathtt{Gen}_{\mathsf{mac}}, \mathtt{Mac}, \mathtt{Vrfy})$ (Definition 4) that is a one-time computationally-secure as per Definition 5.
- An additive secret sharing scheme $\mathtt{SS} = (\mathtt{share}, \mathtt{reconstruct})$ that satisfies Definition 7. Note that in Fig. 5.1 and Fig. 5.2, we directly use XOR operation $\bigoplus_{i \subset [n]}$ to achieve share and reconstruct.

We propose the formal description of the protocol in Fig. 5.2 and refer the reader to the introductory section for its informal description.

Figure 5.1: The functionality g

Input: Each party P_i for $i \in [n]$ provides the following input:

- $d^i \in \{0,1\}$
- $\mathsf{k}_{\mathsf{enc}}^{i \to k, b} \in \{0,1\}^\lambda$ for $k \in [n]$, $b \in \{0,1\}$

Output: Each party P_i for $i \in [n]$ gets the output $\mathcal{G}, \{\mathsf{c}^{i \to k}\}_{i \in [n], k \in [n]}, \{\mathsf{k}_{\mathsf{mac}}^{i \to k}\}_{i \in [n], k \in [n]}$.

1: $(\mathcal{G}, \mathbf{K}) \xleftarrow{\$} \mathtt{garble}(1^\lambda, C)$, where $\mathbf{K} = \{K_b^i\}_{i \in [n], b \in \{0,1\}}$ and C is the Boolean circuit for the function f
2: Sample uniformly random $K_b^{i \to k}$ for $i \in [n], k \in [n], b \in \{0,1\}$ such that $\bigoplus_{i \in [n]} K_b^{i \to k} = K_b^k$
3: **for** $i \in [n], k \in [n], b \in \{0,1\}$ **do**
4: Generate $\mathsf{k}_{\mathsf{mac}}^{i \to k, d^k \oplus b} \xleftarrow{\$} \mathtt{Gen}_{\mathsf{mac}}(1^\lambda)$
5: $\gamma_{d^k \oplus b}^{i \to k} \leftarrow \mathtt{Mac}_{\mathsf{k}_{\mathsf{mac}}^{i \to k, d^k \oplus b}}(K_b^{i \to k})$
6: $\mathsf{c}_{d^k \oplus b}^{i \to k} \leftarrow \mathtt{enc}(\mathsf{k}_{\mathsf{enc}}^{i \to k, d^k \oplus b}, (\gamma_{d^k \oplus b}^{i \to k} || K_b^{i \to k}))$
7: **end for**
8: **for** $i \in [n], k \in [n]$ **do**
9: $\mathsf{k}_{\mathsf{mac}}^{i \to k} \leftarrow (\mathsf{k}_{\mathsf{mac}}^{i \to k, 0}, \mathsf{k}_{\mathsf{mac}}^{i \to k, 1})$
10: $\mathsf{c}^{i \to k} \leftarrow (\mathsf{c}_0^{i \to k}, \mathsf{c}_1^{i \to k})$
11: **end for**

Figure 5.2: the protocol $\hat{\Pi}$ that computes f through four rounds of communication, where the first two rounds are independent of the parties' inputs

Private input: Each party P_i for $i \in [n]$ has private input $x^i \in \{0,1\}$.
Output: $y = f(x^1, \ldots, x^n)$ or $\bot$.

First round: Each party P_i does the following:

1. Sample uniformly random $d^i \xleftarrow{\$} \{0,1\}$ and $\{\mathsf{k}_{\mathsf{enc}}^{i \to k, b}\}_{k \in [n]} \xleftarrow{\$} \mathtt{Gen}_{\mathsf{enc}}(1^\lambda)$ for $b \in \{0,1\}$.
2. Set $x_g^i \leftarrow (d^i, \{\mathsf{k}_{\mathsf{enc}}^{i \to k, b}\}_{k \in [n], b \in \{0,1\}})$ and compute $\mathsf{msg}_{1,i} \leftarrow \mathtt{frst\text{-}msg}_i(x_g^i)$.

3. Send $\mathsf{msg}_{1,i}$ over broadcast channel.

Second Round: Each party P_i computes $\mathsf{msg}_{2,i} \leftarrow \mathtt{nxt\text{-}msg}_i^2(x_g^i, \tau_1)$ and sends it over broadcast channel, where τ_1 is the transcript of the protocol Π up to the first round.

Third Round: Each party P_i does the following:

1. Let τ_2 denote the transcript of the protocol Π up to second round.
2. Compute $\mathsf{msg}_{3,i} \leftarrow \mathtt{nxt\text{-}msg}_i^3(x_g^i, \tau_2)$.
3. Compute $\widehat{\mathsf{msg}}_{3,i} \leftarrow (\phi^i \leftarrow d^i \oplus x^i)$.
4. Send $(\mathsf{msg}_{3,i}, \widehat{\mathsf{msg}}_{3,i})$.

Fourth Round: Each party P_i does the following:

1. Upon receiving $\widehat{\mathsf{msg}}_{3,k}$ for $k \in [n] \setminus \{i\}$, compute $\widehat{\mathsf{msg}}_{4,i} \leftarrow (\{\mathsf{k}_{\mathsf{enc}}^{i\to k,\phi^k}\}_{k\in[n]})$.
2. Let τ_3 denote the transcript of the protocol Π up to third round.
3. Compute $\mathsf{msg}_{4,i} \leftarrow \mathtt{nxt\text{-}msg}_i^4(x_g^i, \tau_3)$.
4. Send $(\mathsf{msg}_{4,i}, \widehat{\mathsf{msg}}_{4,i})$.

Output Computation: Each party P_i does the following:

1. Let τ_4 denote the transcript of the protocol Π up to fourth round.
2. Compute the output of Π as $(\mathcal{G}, \{\mathsf{c}^{i\to k}\}_{i\in[n],k\in[n]}, \{\mathsf{k}_{\mathsf{mac}}^{i\to k}\}_{i\in[n],k\in[n]}) \leftarrow \mathtt{output}_i(x_g^i, \tau_4)$.
3. Obtain the shares of the labels, along with the tags by computing $(\gamma_{\phi^k}^{i\to k} || K_{x^k}^{i\to k}) \leftarrow \mathtt{dec}(\mathsf{k}_{\mathsf{enc}}^{i\to k,\phi^k}, \mathsf{c}_{\phi^k}^{i\to k})$ for $i \in [n], k \in [n]$.
4. Verify the correctness of the shares of the labels by checking that $\mathtt{Vrfy}_{\mathsf{k}_{\mathsf{mac}}^{i\to k,\phi^k}}(\gamma_{\phi^k}^{i\to k}, K_{x^k}^{i\to k}) = 1$ for $i \in [n], k \in [n]$. For each invalid pair $(\gamma_{\phi^j}^{k\to j}, K_{x^j}^{k\to j})$ output $(\mathtt{abort}, k)$.
5. Reconstruct the labels as $K_{x^k}^k = \bigoplus_{i\in[n]} K_{x^k}^{i\to k}$ for $k \in [n]$.
6. Output $y \leftarrow \mathtt{eval}(\mathcal{G}, K_{x^1}^1, \ldots, K_{x^n}^n)$.

5.1 The MPC Security Proof

We first provide an informal description of the proof and later discuss the proof in detail. The simulator $\mathcal{S}$ of the compiled protocol $\hat{\Pi}$ internally executes the simulator of input protocol Π, which we denote by $\mathcal{S}_\Pi$. To execute this simulator, we need to create a valid adversary for Π (i.e., an adversary that receives and sends only messages related to Π). We simulate such an adversary by means of an *augmented machine* $\mathcal{M}$. $\mathcal{M}$ internally runs the proxy machine $\mathcal{P}(\mathcal{A})$, and it filters out only the messages related to Π, forwarding these to $\mathcal{S}_\Pi$. Upon receiving a message from $\mathcal{S}_\Pi$, $\mathcal{M}$ enriches this message with all the other information that honest parties send in $\hat{\Pi}$ (this messages will be properly simulated as we will soon discuss), and forward everything to $\mathcal{P}(\mathcal{A})$. In summary, $\mathcal{P}(\mathcal{A})$ still receives messages of a format that is consistent with $\hat{\Pi}$, while $\mathcal{S}_\Pi$ believes that it is interacting with a valid adversary of Π (please see Fig. 5.3 to get a better idea of how this interaction works).

Given that $\mathcal{M}$ is a valid adversary for $\mathcal{S}_\Pi$, at some point $\mathcal{S}_\Pi$ extracts the input that the adversary is using to execute Π. Let us denote this input by x_g^j, where j denotes the input of the corrupted party (for simplicity, here we assume that there is only one corrupted party). Note that x_g^j encodes the random bit d^j

the adversary used to evaluate g. Our main simulator $\mathcal{S}$ can now infer the input of the adversary (the input for the functionality f) by computing $x^j \leftarrow \phi^j \oplus d^j$ (recall that ϕ^j is sent in the third round by the adversary). Having obtained x^j, $\mathcal{S}$ can query the ideal functionality f and simulate the garbled circuit (and the ciphertexts) accordingly. This simulated garbled circuit (and ciphertexts) will be used as input to $\mathcal{S}_\Pi$ ($\mathcal{S}$ is simulating the behaviour of g, which corresponds to the ideal functionality of $\mathcal{S}_\Pi$).

Theorem 1. *Assume Π is a four-round special-extractable malicious* type *secure multi-party computation protocol that adheres to Definition 10 and Definition 11, which realizes the functionality g, formally specified in the Fig. 5.1* (type $\in$ {sa-abort, si-abort, un-abort, id-abort}*). Let* GC *be a garbling scheme in line with Definition 6. Let* SE *be a symmetric encryption scheme (Definition 1) that is computationally indistinguishable as per Definition 3. Let* MAC *be a message authentication code scheme (Definition 4) that is a one-time computationally-secure as per Definition 5. Let* SS *be an additive secret sharing scheme satisfying Definition 7. Then the protocol $\hat{\Pi}$ (in Fig. 5.2) is malicious* type *delayed-input and adaptive-input selection secure.*

Proof. The core of our proof revolves around demonstrating that for every non-uniform PPT adversary $\mathcal{A}$ in the real world, a corresponding non-uniform probabilistic expected polynomial-time simulator $\mathcal{S}$ that has black-box access to $\mathcal{P}(\mathcal{A})$ exists in the ideal world:

$$\mathtt{REAL}^{\mathsf{DI}}_{\hat{\Pi},\mathcal{J},\mathcal{A}(\mathsf{aux})}(1^\lambda) \stackrel{c}{\equiv} \mathtt{IDEAL}^{\mathsf{DI,type}}_{f,\mathcal{J},\mathcal{P}(\mathcal{A}),\mathcal{S}(\mathsf{aux})}(1^\lambda).$$

As just mentioned, when the protocol Π is employed alongside $\hat{\Pi}$, there is a necessity for an intermediary or bridge between these protocols. We refer to this intermediary as the *augmented machine* $\mathcal{M}$[5]. This machine can simulate the majority of the simulator messages autonomously. For the few messages it cannot simulate, they are directly inputted into $\mathcal{M}$ by the simulator $\mathcal{S}$. A more profound reason for introducing the augmented machine $\mathcal{M}$ is to address potential rewinds that the simulator of Π might undertake. It is crucial to emphasize that whenever the inner protocol initiates a rewind of the augmented machine, these rewind messages will be forwarded to the proxy machine $\mathcal{P}(\mathcal{A})$, and correspondingly rewinds the adversary $\mathcal{A}$ and continues its execution. $\mathcal{M}$ operates two interfaces:

- **The left interface:** It acts as a proxy between $\mathcal{P}(\mathcal{A})$ and its external interface - the ideal-world simulator $\mathcal{S}_\Pi$ (which exists by the security assumption of the protocol Π) w.r.t. the messages of Π; or in the case of the hybrid experiment $\mathcal{H}_0$, its external interface is the execution of the protocol Π (simulated by $\mathcal{S}$).

[5] This is a standard technique used when proving the security of a protocol executed alongside another protocol. More examples of such techniques can be found in [15, 16, 24].

– **The right interface:** It interacts with the proxy machine $\mathcal{P}(\mathcal{A})$. $\mathcal{P}(\mathcal{A})$ will forward the messages to and from adversary $\mathcal{A}$ (the real-world adversary of the protocol $\hat{\Pi}$).

Figure 5.3: The simulator $\mathcal{S}$. For simplicity, we only consider one index i for the honest party and one index j for the corrupted party. We recall that ϕ^j is from $\widehat{\mathsf{msg}}_{3,j}$, and d^j is from x_g^j

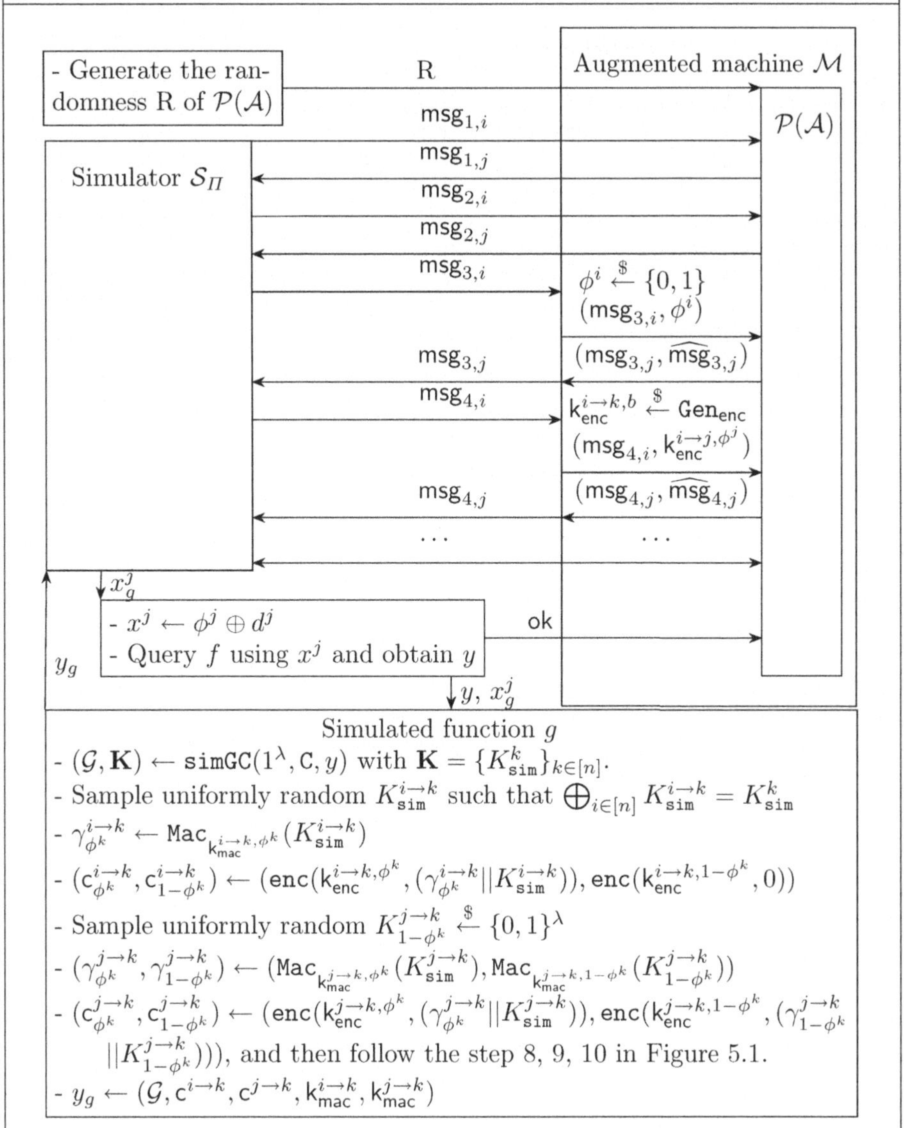

It is important to note that Π is secure under standard MPC definition, but $\mathcal{P}(\mathcal{A})$ needs to receive the command ok to decide the actual input of honest parties. We also need to describe how the simulator $\mathcal{S}$ generates this message. We specify the generation of ok in $\mathcal{S}$, and we let $\mathcal{M}$ forward this message to $\mathcal{P}(\mathcal{A})$ in the extraction phase.

While $\mathcal{M}$ interacts with the real-world adversary $\mathcal{A}$ for $\hat{\Pi}$ through $\mathcal{P}(\mathcal{A})$, it also acts as the adversary of the protocol Π for $\mathcal{S}_\Pi$. The details of $\mathcal{M}$ can be found in Fig. 5.4, and the simulator $\mathcal{S}$ is elaborated in Fig. 5.5.

Figure 5.4: The augmented machine $\mathcal{M}$

First round: Upon receiving the message $\mathsf{msg}_{1,i}$ (for $i \in \mathcal{I}$) in the left interface, forward $\mathsf{msg}_{1,i}$ to the right interface.
Upon receiving the message $\mathsf{msg}_{1,j}$ (for $j \in \mathcal{J}$) as the reply from the right interface, send the message $\mathsf{msg}_{1,j}$ to the left interface.
Second round: Upon receiving the message $\mathsf{msg}_{2,i}$ (for $i \in \mathcal{I}$) in the left interface, forward $\mathsf{msg}_{2,i}$ to the right interface.
Upon receiving the message $\mathsf{msg}_{2,j}$ (for $j \in \mathcal{J}$) as the reply from the right interface, send the message $\mathsf{msg}_{2,j}$ to the left interface.
Third round: Upon receiving the message $\mathsf{msg}_{3,i}$ (for $i \in \mathcal{I}$) in the left interface, compute uniformly random $\phi^i \xleftarrow{\$} \{0,1\}$, set $\widehat{\mathsf{msg}}_{3,i} \leftarrow (\phi^i)$ as in the protocol $\hat{\Pi}$, and output the messages $(\mathsf{msg}_{3,i}, \widehat{\mathsf{msg}}_{3,i})$ to the right interface.
Upon receiving the messages $\mathsf{msg}_{3,j}$ and $\widehat{\mathsf{msg}}_{3,j}$ (for $j \in \mathcal{J}$) from the right interface, send the message $\mathsf{msg}_{3,j}$ in the left interface.
Fourth round: Upon receiving the message $\mathsf{msg}_{4,i}$ (for $i \in \mathcal{I}$) in the left interface, compute $\mathsf{k}_{\mathsf{enc}}^{i\to k,b} \xleftarrow{\$} \mathsf{Gen}_{\mathsf{enc}}(1^\lambda)$ for $i \in \mathcal{I}, b \in \{0,1\}$, set $\widehat{\mathsf{msg}}_{4,i} \leftarrow (\{\mathsf{k}_{\mathsf{enc}}^{i\to k,\phi^k}\}_{k\in[n]})$ for $i \in \mathcal{I}$ as in the protocol $\hat{\Pi}$, and output the messages $(\mathsf{msg}_{4,i}, \widehat{\mathsf{msg}}_{4,i})$ to the right interface.
Upon receiving the messages $\mathsf{msg}_{4,j}$ and $\widehat{\mathsf{msg}}_{4,j}$ (for $j \in \mathcal{J}$) from the right interface, send the message $\mathsf{msg}_{4,j}$ in the left interface.
Extraction: Upon receiving the message ok in the left interface, forward it to the right interface.
Randomness passing: Upon receiving the randomness R of adversary $\mathcal{P}(\mathcal{A})$ in the left interface, forward it to the right interface.

Figure 5.5: The Simulator $\mathcal{S}$

$\mathcal{S}$ firstly runs $\mathcal{S}_\Pi$ against the adversary $\mathcal{M}$. According to Definition 13, this interaction is through the proxy machine $\mathcal{P}(\mathcal{A})$, where $\mathcal{P}(\mathcal{A})$ interacts with ideal functionality f and adversary $\mathcal{A}$ of protocol $\hat{\Pi}$. During this interaction, $\mathcal{S}_\Pi$ would be able to extract inputs from the corrupted parties. We assume the input from corrupted parties is $\{x_g^j\}_{j\in\mathcal{J}} = \{(d^j, \mathsf{k}_{\mathsf{enc}}^{j\to k,b})\}_{k\in[n],j\in\mathcal{J},b\in\{0,1\}}$. $\mathcal{S}_\Pi$ will extract the input and send it to $\mathcal{S}$. Then $\mathcal{S}$ proceeds to perform the following steps:

- Upon receiving $\{x_g^j\}_{j\in\mathcal{J}}$ issued by $\mathcal{S}_\Pi$, send ok to $\mathcal{M}$, and do the following:
  1. Retrieve ϕ^j from $\widehat{\mathsf{msg}}_{3,j}$ and set $x^j \leftarrow d^j \oplus \phi^j$ for $j \in \mathcal{J}$.

2. Query the ideal functionality f using x^j for $j \in \mathcal{J}$, and set $y \leftarrow f(x^1, \dots, x^n)$.
3. Generate $(\mathcal{G}, \mathbf{K}) \leftarrow \mathtt{simGC}(1^\lambda, \mathtt{C}, y)$, where $\mathbf{K} = \{K^1_{\mathtt{sim}}, \dots, K^n_{\mathtt{sim}}\}$.
4. Sample uniformly random $K^{i\to k}_{\mathtt{sim}}$ for $i \in [n], k \in [n]$ such that $\bigoplus_{i\in[n]} K^{i\to k}_{\mathtt{sim}} = K^k_{\mathtt{sim}}$
5. Sample $\mathsf{k}^{i\to k,\phi^k}_{\mathsf{mac}}, \mathsf{k}^{i\to k,1-\phi^k}_{\mathsf{mac}} \xleftarrow{\$} \mathtt{Gen}_{\mathsf{mac}}(1^\lambda)$ for $i \in [n], k \in [n]$
6. For each $i \in \mathcal{I}, k \in [n]$:
   (a) $\gamma^{i\to k}_{\phi^k} \leftarrow \mathtt{Mac}_{\mathsf{k}^{i\to k,\phi^k}_{\mathsf{mac}}}(K^{i\to k}_{\mathtt{sim}})$
   (b) $\mathsf{c}^{i\to k}_{\phi^k} \leftarrow \mathtt{enc}(\mathsf{k}^{i\to k,\phi^k}_{\mathsf{enc}}, (\gamma^{i\to k}_{\phi^k} || K^{i\to k}_{\mathtt{sim}}))$
   (c) $\mathsf{c}^{i\to k}_{1-\phi^k} \leftarrow \mathtt{enc}(\mathsf{k}^{i\to k,1-\phi^k}_{\mathsf{enc}}, 0)$
   (d) $\mathsf{k}^{i\to k}_{\mathsf{mac}} \leftarrow (\mathsf{k}^{i\to k,0}_{\mathsf{mac}}, \mathsf{k}^{i\to k,1}_{\mathsf{mac}})$
   (e) $\mathsf{c}^{i\to k} \leftarrow (\mathsf{c}^{i\to k}_0, \mathsf{c}^{i\to k}_1)$
7. For each $j \in \mathcal{J}, k \in [n]$:
   (a) Sample uniformly random $K^{j\to k}_{1-\phi^k} \xleftarrow{\$} \{0,1\}^\lambda$
   (b) $(\gamma^{j\to k}_{\phi^k}, \gamma^{j\to k}_{1-\phi^k}) \leftarrow (\mathtt{Mac}_{\mathsf{k}^{j\to k,\phi^k}_{\mathsf{mac}}}(K^{j\to k}_{\mathtt{sim}}), \mathtt{Mac}_{\mathsf{k}^{j\to k,1-\phi^k}_{\mathsf{mac}}}(K^{j\to k}_{1-\phi^k}))$
   (c) $(\mathsf{c}^{j\to k}_{\phi^k}, \mathsf{c}^{j\to k}_{1-\phi^k}) \leftarrow (\mathtt{enc}(\mathsf{k}^{j\to k,\phi^k}_{\mathsf{enc}}, (\gamma^{j\to k}_{\phi^k} || K^{j\to k}_{\mathtt{sim}})), \mathtt{enc}(\mathsf{k}^{j\to k,1-\phi^k}_{\mathsf{enc}}, (\gamma^{j\to k}_{1-\phi^k} || K^{j\to k}_{1-\phi^k})))$
   (d) $\mathsf{k}^{j\to k}_{\mathsf{mac}} \leftarrow (\mathsf{k}^{j\to k,0}_{\mathsf{mac}}, \mathsf{k}^{j\to k,1}_{\mathsf{mac}})$
   (e) $\mathsf{c}^{j\to k} \leftarrow (\mathsf{c}^{j\to k}_0, \mathsf{c}^{j\to k}_1)$
8. Send $\mathcal{G}, \{\mathsf{c}^{i\to k}\}_{i\in[n],k\in[n]}, \{\mathsf{k}^{i\to k}_{\mathsf{mac}}\}_{i\in[n],k\in[n]}$ to $\mathcal{S}_\Pi$.

– Continue running $\mathcal{S}_\Pi$ against the adversary $\mathcal{M}$, and outputs what $\mathcal{S}_\Pi$ outputs.

We now informally describe the following hybrid experiments and refer the reader to the Fig. 5.7 for the formal specification.

$\mathcal{H}_0$: Hybrid $\mathcal{H}_0$ is identical to the real world.

$\mathcal{H}_1$: Hybrid $\mathcal{H}_1$ is the same as hybrid $\mathcal{H}_0$ but the messages $\{\mathsf{msg}_{i,k}\}_{k\in[4]}$ are computed by the simulator $\mathcal{S}_\Pi$. The transition between $\mathcal{H}_0$ and $\mathcal{H}_1$ is justified by the malicious type security of Π - if an adversary could distinguish between the two hybrid experiments, it could break the security of the protocol Π.

$\mathcal{H}_2$: Hybrid $\mathcal{H}_2$ is the same as hybrid $\mathcal{H}_1$, but the ciphertexts $\mathsf{c}^{i\to j}_{1-\phi^j}$ that P_j does not decrypt at the output-computation phase (since it does not have the necessary keys) are encryption of 0. The transition between $\mathcal{H}_1$ and $\mathcal{H}_2$ is justified by the indistinguishability of the encryption scheme SE.

$\mathcal{H}_3$: Hybrid $\mathcal{H}_3$ is the same as hybrid $\mathcal{H}_2$, but the ciphertexts $\mathsf{c}^{j\to i}_{1-\phi^i}$ that P_j can decrypt but are not used at the output computation phase (since they do not correspond to P_i's input) are encryption of the uniformly random sampled bit strings that have the same length as the real garbled labels. The transition between $\mathcal{H}_2$ and $\mathcal{H}_3$ is justified by the perfect security of the additive secret sharing scheme SS - since the adversary can control at most $n-1$ parties, it can not collect enough shares to reconstruct the labels.

$\mathcal{H}_4$: Hybrid $\mathcal{H}_4$ is identical to the ideal world. In contrast to $\mathcal{H}_3$, the labels $\{K^k_{x^k}\}_{k\in[n]}$ are generated by $\mathcal{S}$ through the $\texttt{simGC}$ function. The transition between $\mathcal{H}_3$ and $\mathcal{H}_4$ is justified by the privacy of the garbling scheme $\texttt{GC}$.

In hybrids $\mathcal{H}_0, \mathcal{H}_1, \mathcal{H}_2, \mathcal{H}_3$, we use the augmented machine $\mathcal{M}_0(\cdot)$, and in hybrid $\mathcal{H}_4$, we use the augmented machine $\mathcal{M}_4(\cdot)$. The above augmented machines have the same left interface as $\mathcal{M}$ in Fig. 5.4. The right interface is against different adversaries according to different hybrid experiments. The description of the augmented machines is in Fig. 5.6.

Figure 5.6: The augmented machines $\mathcal{M}_0(\mathcal{A})$, $\mathcal{M}_4(\mathcal{A})$

First round: Upon receiving the message $\mathsf{msg}_{1,i}$ (for $i \in \mathcal{I}$) in the left interface, forward $\mathsf{msg}_{1,i}$ to $\mathcal{P}(\mathcal{A})$.
Upon receiving the message $\mathsf{msg}_{1,j}$ (for $j \in \mathcal{J}$) as the reply from $\mathcal{P}(\mathcal{A})$, send the message $\mathsf{msg}_{1,j}$ to the left interface.
Second round: Upon receiving the message $\mathsf{msg}_{2,i}$ (for $i \in \mathcal{I}$) in the left interface, forward $\mathsf{msg}_{2,i}$ to $\mathcal{P}(\mathcal{A})$.
Upon receiving the message $\mathsf{msg}_{2,j}$ (for $j \in \mathcal{J}$) as the reply from $\mathcal{P}(\mathcal{A})$, send the message $\mathsf{msg}_{2,j}$ to the left interface.
Third round: Upon receiving the message $\mathsf{msg}_{3,i}$ (for $i \in \mathcal{I}$) in the left interface, for $i \in \mathcal{I}$:

- Sample uniformly random $d^i \xleftarrow{\$} \{0,1\}$ and set $\phi^i \leftarrow d^i \oplus x^i$

- Sample uniformly random $\phi^i \xleftarrow{\$} \{0,1\}$

Then set $\widehat{\mathsf{msg}}_{3,i} \leftarrow (\phi^i)$ as in the protocol $\hat{\Pi}$, and output the messages $(\mathsf{msg}_{3,i}, \widehat{\mathsf{msg}}_{3,i})$ to $\mathcal{P}(\mathcal{A})$.
Upon receiving the messages $\mathsf{msg}_{3,j}$ and $\widehat{\mathsf{msg}}_{3,j}$ (for $j \in \mathcal{J}$) from $\mathcal{P}(\mathcal{A})$, send the message $\mathsf{msg}_{3,j}$ in the left interface.
Fourth round: Upon receiving the message $\mathsf{msg}_{4,i}$ (for $i \in \mathcal{I}$) in the left interface, compute $\mathsf{k}_{\mathsf{enc}}^{i\to k,b} \xleftarrow{\$} \mathsf{Gen}_{\mathsf{enc}}(1^\lambda)$ for $i \in \mathcal{I}, b \in \{0,1\}$, set $\widehat{\mathsf{msg}}_{4,i} \leftarrow (\{\mathsf{k}_{\mathsf{enc}}^{i\to k,\phi^k}\}_{k\in[n]})$ for $i \in \mathcal{I}$ as in the protocol $\hat{\Pi}$, and output the messages $(\mathsf{msg}_{4,i}, \widehat{\mathsf{msg}}_{4,i})$ to $\mathcal{P}(\mathcal{A})$.
Upon receiving the messages $\mathsf{msg}_{4,j}$ and $\widehat{\mathsf{msg}}_{4,j}$ (for $j \in \mathcal{J}$) from $\mathcal{P}(\mathcal{A})$, send the message $\mathsf{msg}_{4,j}$ in the left interface.
Extraction: Upon receiving the message ok in the left interface, forward it to $\mathcal{P}(\mathcal{A})$.
Randomness passing: Upon receiving the randomness R of adversary $\mathcal{P}(\mathcal{A})$ in the left interface, forward it to $\mathcal{P}(\mathcal{A})$.

We formally describe the hybrid experiments in Fig. 5.7. Before delving into the details, we provide brief instructions on how to interpret the figure. The primary guideline is to prioritize the most restrictive option for each step when multiple choices are available for a specific hybrid. For instance, in $\mathcal{H}_2$, we select the second option from the three available for step 2(c), as it is more constrained compared to the others. Additionally, we cannot choose the third option since it falls within a rectangle box, which exceeds the scope of $\mathcal{H}_2$. Consequently, $\mathcal{H}_2$ incorporates steps $1, 2.(a), 2.(b), 2.(d), 2.(e).i, 2.(e).ii$ from the rounded box, and $2.(c), 2.(e).iii$ from the dashed box. Thus, the points of divergence between $\mathcal{H}_2$ and $\mathcal{H}_1$ are steps $2.(c)$ and $2.(e).iii$. Similarly, we can discern the discrepancies between each hybrid experiment using this approach.

Figure 5.7: The hybrid experiments $\mathcal{H}_0, \mathcal{H}_1, \mathcal{H}_2, \mathcal{H}_3, \mathcal{H}_4$

$\mathcal{H}_0$, $\mathcal{H}_1$, $\mathcal{H}_2$, $\mathcal{H}_3$, $\mathcal{H}_4$

1. Run Π as honest party would against the adversary $\mathcal{M}_0(\mathcal{A})$.

1. Run $\mathcal{S}_\Pi$ against the adversary $\mathcal{M}_0(\mathcal{A})$, $\mathcal{M}_4(\mathcal{A})$
2. Upon receiving a set of queries $\{x_g^j\}_{j\in\mathcal{J}}$ issued by $\mathcal{S}_\Pi$, send ok to M and do the following:
   (a) Retrieve ϕ^j from $\widehat{\mathsf{msg}}_{3,j}$ and set $x^j \leftarrow d^j \oplus \phi^j$ (for $j \in \mathcal{J}$).
   (b) Compute $(\mathcal{G}, \mathbf{K}) \xleftarrow{\$} \mathtt{garble}(1^\lambda, \mathtt{C})$ where $\mathbf{K} = \{K_b^1, \ldots, K_b^n\}$, where $b \in \{0,1\}$.
   (c) Sample uniformly random $K_b^{i\to k} \xleftarrow{\$} \{0,1\}^\lambda$ for $b \in \{0,1\}, i \in [n], k \in [n]$ s.t. $\bigoplus_{i\in[n]} K_b^{i\to k} = K_b^k$

   (c) Sample uniformly random $K_{\phi^k}^{i\to k}$ for $i \in [n], k \in [n]$ such that $\bigoplus_{i\in[n]} K_{\phi^k}^{i\to k} = K_{\phi^k}^k$. Sample uniformly random $K_{1-\phi^k}^{i\to k}$ for $i \in [n], k \in [n]$ such that $\bigoplus_{i\in[n]} K_{1-\phi^k}^{i\to k} = K_{1-\phi^k}^k$. Set $K_{1-\phi^k}^{i\to k} \leftarrow 0$ for $i \in \mathcal{I}, k \in [n]$.

(c) Sample uniformly random $K_{\phi^k}^{i \to k}$ for $i \in [n], k \in [n]$ such that $\bigoplus_{i\in[n]} K_{\phi^k}^{i \to k} = K_{\phi^k}^{k}$. Sample uniformly random $K_{1-\phi^k}^{j \to k}$ for $j \in \mathcal{J}, k \in [n]$ without conditions. Set $K_{1-\phi^k}^{i \to k} \leftarrow 0$ for $i \in \mathcal{I}, k \in [n]$.

(b) Query the ideal functionality f using x^j for $j \in \mathcal{J}$, and set $y \leftarrow f(x^1, \ldots, x^n)$. Generate $(\mathcal{G}, \mathbf{K}) \leftarrow \mathtt{simGC}(1^\lambda, \mathtt{C}, y)$, where $\mathbf{K} = \{K_{\mathtt{sim}}^1, \ldots, K_{\mathtt{sim}}^n\}$.

(c) Sample uniformly random $K_{\mathtt{sim}}^{i \to k}$ for $i \in [n], k \in [n]$ s.t. $\bigoplus_{i\in[n]} K_{\mathtt{sim}}^{i \to k} = K_{\mathtt{sim}}^{k}$. Sample uniformly random $K_{1-\phi^k}^{j \to k}$ for $j \in \mathcal{J}, k \in [n]$ without conditions. Set $K_{1-\phi^k}^{i \to k} \leftarrow 0$ for $i \in \mathcal{I}, k \in [n]$.

(d) Sample $(\mathsf{k}_{\mathsf{mac}}^{i \to k, \phi^k}, \mathsf{k}_{\mathsf{mac}}^{i \to k, 1-\phi^k}) \xleftarrow{\$} \mathtt{Gen}_{\mathsf{mac}}(1^\lambda)$ for $i \in [n], k \in [n]$

(e) For each $i \in \mathcal{I}, k \in [n]$:

i. $(\gamma_{\phi^k}^{i \to k}, \gamma_{1-\phi^k}^{i \to k}) \leftarrow (\mathtt{Mac}_{\mathsf{k}_{\mathsf{mac}}^{i \to k, \phi^k}}(K_{x^k}^{i \to k}), \mathtt{Mac}_{\mathsf{k}_{\mathsf{mac}}^{i \to k, 1-\phi^k}}(K_{1-x^k}^{i \to k}))$

ii. $\mathsf{c}_{\phi^k}^{i \to k} \leftarrow \mathsf{enc}(\mathsf{k}_{\mathsf{enc}}^{i \to k, \phi^k}, (\gamma_{\phi^k}^{i \to k} || K_{x^k}^{i \to k}))$

iii. $\mathsf{c}_{1-\phi^k}^{i \to k} \leftarrow \mathsf{enc}(\mathsf{k}_{\mathsf{enc}}^{i \to k, 1-\phi^k}, (\gamma_{1-\phi^k}^{i \to k} || K_{1-x^k}^{i \to k}))$

i. $\gamma_{\phi^k}^{i \to k} \leftarrow \mathtt{Mac}_{\mathsf{k}_{\mathsf{mac}}^{i \to k, \phi^k}}(K_{\mathtt{sim}}^{i \to k})$

ii. $\mathsf{c}_{\phi^k}^{i \to k} \leftarrow \mathsf{enc}(\mathsf{k}_{\mathsf{enc}}^{i \to k, \phi^k}, (\gamma_{\phi^k}^{i \to k} || K_{\mathtt{sim}}^{i \to k}))$

iii. $\mathsf{c}_{1-\phi^k}^{i \to k} \leftarrow \mathsf{enc}(\mathsf{k}_{\mathsf{enc}}^{i \to k, 1-\phi^k}, 0)$

(f) For each $j \in \mathcal{J}, k \in [n]$:

i $(\gamma_{\phi^k}^{j \to k}, \gamma_{1-\phi^k}^{j \to k}) \leftarrow (\mathtt{Mac}_{\mathsf{k}_{\mathsf{mac}}^{j \to k, \phi^k}}(K_{x^k}^{j \to k}), \mathtt{Mac}_{\mathsf{k}_{\mathsf{mac}}^{j \to k, 1-\phi^k}}(K_{1-x^k}^{j \to k}))$

ii $(\mathsf{c}_{\phi^k}^{j \to k}, \mathsf{c}_{1-\phi^k}^{j \to k}) \leftarrow (\mathsf{enc}(\mathsf{k}_{\mathsf{enc}}^{j \to k, \phi^k}, (\gamma_{\phi^k}^{j \to k} || K_{\phi^k}^{j \to k})), \mathsf{enc}(\mathsf{k}_{\mathsf{enc}}^{j \to k, 1-\phi^k}, (\gamma_{1-\phi^k}^{j \to k} || K_{1-\phi^k}^{j \to k})))$

i. $(\gamma_{\phi^k}^{j \to k}, \gamma_{1-\phi^k}^{j \to k}) \leftarrow (\mathtt{Mac}_{\mathsf{k}_{\mathsf{mac}}^{j \to k, \phi^k}}(K_{\mathtt{sim}}^{j \to k}), \mathtt{Mac}_{\mathsf{k}_{\mathsf{mac}}^{j \to k, 1-\phi^k}}(K_{1-\phi^k}^{j \to k}))$

ii. $(\mathsf{c}_{\phi^k}^{j \to k}, \mathsf{c}_{1-\phi^k}^{j \to k}) \leftarrow (\mathsf{enc}(\mathsf{k}_{\mathsf{enc}}^{j \to k, \phi^k}, (\gamma_{\phi^k}^{j \to k} || K_{\mathtt{sim}}^{j \to k})), \mathsf{enc}(\mathsf{k}_{\mathsf{enc}}^{j \to k, 1-\phi^k}, (\gamma_{1-\phi^k}^{j \to k} || K_{1-\phi^k}^{j \to k})))$

(g) Set $\mathsf{k}_{\mathsf{mac}}^{i \to k} \leftarrow (\mathsf{k}_{\mathsf{mac}}^{i \to k, 0}, \mathsf{k}_{\mathsf{mac}}^{i \to k, 1})$, $\mathsf{c}^{i \to k} \leftarrow (\mathsf{c}^{i \to k, 0}, \mathsf{c}^{i \to k, 1})$ for $i \in [n], k \in [n]$

(h) Send $\mathcal{G}, \{\mathsf{c}^{i \to k}\}_{i\in[n],k\in[n]}, \{\mathsf{k}_{\mathsf{mac}}^{i \to k}\}_{i\in[n],k\in[n]}$ to $\mathcal{S}_\Pi$.

(i) Continue running $\mathcal{S}_\Pi$.

The formal proofs of the transitions between different hybrids are found in the full version of the paper.

Acknowledgments. We thank the reviewer of ACNS for suggesting making our new definitions more general, and overall improving the quality of our paper. We also acknowledge that this research is partially supported by the Input Output Research Hub (IORH) of the University of Edinburgh.

References

1. Ananth, P., Choudhuri, A.R., Jain, A.: A new approach to round-optimal secure multiparty computation. In: Katz, J., Shacham, H. (eds.) Advances in Cryptology – CRYPTO 2017, Part I. Lecture Notes in Computer Science, vol. 10401, pp. 468–499. Springer, Cham, Switzerland, Santa Barbara, CA, USA (Aug 20–24, 2017). https://doi.org/10.1007/978-3-319-63688-7_16
2. Badrinarayanan, S., Goyal, V., Jain, A., Kalai, Y.T., Khurana, D., Sahai, A.: Promise zero knowledge and its applications to round optimal MPC. In: Shacham, H., Boldyreva, A. (eds.) Advances in Cryptology – CRYPTO 2018, Part II. Lecture Notes in Computer Science, vol. 10992, pp. 459–487. Springer, Cham, Switzerland, Santa Barbara, CA, USA (Aug 19–23, 2018). https://doi.org/10.1007/978-3-319-96881-0_16
3. Beaver, D.: Precomputing oblivious transfer. In: Coppersmith, D. (ed.) Advances in Cryptology – CRYPTO'95. Lecture Notes in Computer Science, vol. 963, pp. 97–109. Springer Berlin Heidelberg, Germany, Santa Barbara, CA, USA (Aug 27–31, 1995). https://doi.org/10.1007/3-540-44750-4_8
4. Beaver, D.: Correlated pseudorandomness and the complexity of private computations. In: 28th Annual ACM Symposium on Theory of Computing. pp. 479–488. ACM Press, Philadephia, PA, USA (May 22–24, 1996). https://doi.org/10.1145/237814.237996
5. Beaver, D., Micali, S., Rogaway, P.: The round complexity of secure protocols (extended abstract). In: 22nd Annual ACM Symposium on Theory of Computing, pp. 503–513. ACM Press, Baltimore, MD, USA (May 14–16, 1990). https://doi.org/10.1145/100216.100287
6. Boyle, E., Gilboa, N., Ishai, Y.: Secure computation with preprocessing via function secret sharing. In: Hofheinz, D., Rosen, A. (eds.) TCC 2019: 17th Theory of Cryptography Conference, Part I. Lecture Notes in Computer Science, vol. 11891, pp. 341–371. Springer, Cham, Switzerland, Nuremberg, Germany (Dec 1–5, 2019). https://doi.org/10.1007/978-3-030-36030-6_14
7. Boyle, E., Gilboa, N., Ishai, Y., Nof, A.: Secure multiparty computation with sublinear preprocessing. In: Dunkelman, O., Dziembowski, S. (eds.) Advances in Cryptology – EUROCRYPT 2022, Part I. Lecture Notes in Computer Science, vol. 13275, pp. 427–457. Springer, Cham, Switzerland, Trondheim, Norway (May 30 – Jun 3, 2022). https://doi.org/10.1007/978-3-031-06944-4_15
8. Brakerski, Z., Halevi, S., Polychroniadou, A.: Four round secure computation without setup. In: Kalai, Y., Reyzin, L. (eds.) TCC 2017: 15th Theory of Cryptography Conference, Part I. Lecture Notes in Computer Science, vol. 10677, pp. 645–677. Springer, Cham, Switzerland, Baltimore, MD, USA (Nov 12–15, 2017). https://doi.org/10.1007/978-3-319-70500-2_22

9. Canetti, R.: Universally composable security: A new paradigm for cryptographic protocols. In: 42nd Annual Symposium on Foundations of Computer Science, pp. 136–145. IEEE Computer Society Press, Las Vegas, NV, USA (Oct 14–17, 2001). https://doi.org/10.1109/SFCS.2001.959888
10. Canetti, R., Cohen, A., Lindell, Y.: A simpler variant of universally composable security for standard multiparty computation. In: Gennaro, R., Robshaw, M.J.B. (eds.) Advances in Cryptology – CRYPTO 2015, Part II. Lecture Notes in Computer Science, vol. 9216, pp. 3–22. Springer Berlin Heidelberg, Germany, Santa Barbara, CA, USA (Aug 16–20, 2015). https://doi.org/10.1007/978-3-662-48000-7_1
11. Canetti, R., Kushilevitz, E., Lindell, Y.: On the limitations of universally composable two-party computation without set-up assumptions. In: Biham, E. (ed.) Advances in Cryptology – EUROCRYPT 2003. Lecture Notes in Computer Science, vol. 2656, pp. 68–86. Springer Berlin Heidelberg, Germany, Warsaw, Poland (May 4–8, 2003). https://doi.org/10.1007/3-540-39200-9_5
12. Choudhuri, A.R., Ciampi, M., Goyal, V., Jain, A., Ostrovsky, R.: Round optimal secure multiparty computation from minimal assumptions. In: Pass, R., Pietrzak, K. (eds.) TCC 2020: 18th Theory of Cryptography Conference, Part II. Lecture Notes in Computer Science, vol. 12551, pp. 291–319. Springer, Cham, Switzerland, Durham, NC, USA (Nov 16–19, 2020). https://doi.org/10.1007/978-3-030-64378-2_11
13. Ciampi, M., Ostrovsky, R., Siniscalchi, L., Visconti, I.: Delayed-input non-malleable zero knowledge and multi-party coin tossing in four rounds. In: Kalai, Y., Reyzin, L. (eds.) TCC 2017: 15th Theory of Cryptography Conference, Part I. Lecture Notes in Computer Science, vol. 10677, pp. 711–742. Springer, Cham, Switzerland, Baltimore, MD, USA (Nov 12–15, 2017). https://doi.org/10.1007/978-3-319-70500-2_24
14. Ciampi, M., Ostrovsky, R., Siniscalchi, L., Visconti, I.: Round-optimal secure two-party computation from trapdoor permutations. In: Kalai, Y., Reyzin, L. (eds.) TCC 2017: 15th Theory of Cryptography Conference, Part I. Lecture Notes in Computer Science, vol. 10677, pp. 678–710. Springer, Cham, Switzerland, Baltimore, MD, USA (Nov 12–15, 2017). https://doi.org/10.1007/978-3-319-70500-2_23
15. Ciampi, M., Ostrovsky, R., Siniscalchi, L., Waldner, H.: Round-optimal black-box multiparty computation from polynomial-time assumptions. Cryptology ePrint Archive, Paper 2023/1742 (2023). https://eprint.iacr.org/2023/1742, https://eprint.iacr.org/2023/1742
16. Ciampi, M., Ravi, D., Siniscalchi, L., Waldner, H.: Round-Optimal Multi-party Computation with Identifiable Abort, p. 335–364. Springer International Publishing (2022). https://doi.org/10.1007/978-3-031-06944-4_12, http://dx.doi.org/10.1007/978-3-031-06944-4_12
17. Cohen, R., Garay, J.A., Zikas, V.: Broadcast-optimal two-round MPC. In: Canteaut, A., Ishai, Y. (eds.) Advances in Cryptology – EUROCRYPT 2020, Part II. Lecture Notes in Computer Science, vol. 12106, pp. 828–858. Springer, Cham, Switzerland, Zagreb, Croatia (May 10–14, 2020). https://doi.org/10.1007/978-3-030-45724-2_28
18. Damgård, I., Ravi, D., Siniscalchi, L., Yakoubov, S.: Minimizing setup in broadcast-optimal two round MPC. In: Hazay, C., Stam, M. (eds.) Advances in Cryptology – EUROCRYPT 2023, Part II. Lecture Notes in Computer Science, vol. 14005, pp.

129–158. Springer, Cham, Switzerland, Lyon, France (Apr 23–27, 2023). https://doi.org/10.1007/978-3-031-30617-4_5

19. Dittmer, S., Ishai, Y., Lu, S., Ostrovsky, R.: Authenticated garbling from simple correlations. In: Dodis, Y., Shrimpton, T. (eds.) Advances in Cryptology – CRYPTO 2022, Part IV. Lecture Notes in Computer Science, vol. 13510, pp. 57–87. Springer, Cham, Switzerland, Santa Barbara, CA, USA (Aug 15–18, 2022). https://doi.org/10.1007/978-3-031-15985-5_3
20. Garg, S., Mukherjee, P., Pandey, O., Polychroniadou, A.: The exact round complexity of secure computation. In: Fischlin, M., Coron, J.S. (eds.) Advances in Cryptology – EUROCRYPT 2016, Part II. Lecture Notes in Computer Science, vol. 9666, pp. 448–476. Springer Berlin Heidelberg, Germany, Vienna, Austria (May 8–12, 2016). https://doi.org/10.1007/978-3-662-49896-5_16
21. Goldreich, O., Micali, S., Wigderson, A.: How to play any mental game or A completeness theorem for protocols with honest majority. In: Aho, A. (ed.) 19th Annual ACM Symposium on Theory of Computing, pp. 218–229. ACM Press, New York City, NY, USA (May 25–27, 1987). https://doi.org/10.1145/28395.28420
22. Goldwasser, S., Bellare, M.: Lecture notes on cryptography. Summer Course "Cryptography and Computer Security" at MIT (2008). http://www-cse.ucsd.edu/users/mihir/papers/gb.pdf
23. Goyal, V.: Constant round non-malleable protocols using one way functions. In: Fortnow, L., Vadhan, S.P. (eds.) 43rd Annual ACM Symposium on Theory of Computing, pp. 695–704. ACM Press, San Jose, CA, USA (Jun 6–8, 2011). https://doi.org/10.1145/1993636.1993729
24. Goyal, V., Jain, A., Ostrovsky, R., Richelson, S., Visconti, I.: Concurrent Zero Knowledge in the Bounded Player Model, pp. 60–79. Springer Berlin Heidelberg (2013). https://doi.org/10.1007/978-3-642-36594-2_4, http://dx.doi.org/10.1007/978-3-642-36594-2_4
25. Halevi, S., Hazay, C., Polychroniadou, A., Venkitasubramaniam, M.: Round-optimal secure multi-party computation. In: Shacham, H., Boldyreva, A. (eds.) Advances in Cryptology – CRYPTO 2018, Part II. Lecture Notes in Computer Science, vol. 10992, pp. 488–520. Springer, Cham, Switzerland, Santa Barbara, CA, USA (Aug 19–23, 2018). https://doi.org/10.1007/978-3-319-96881-0_17
26. Hazay, C., Lindell, Y.: Efficient Secure Two-Party Protocols. Springer Berlin Heidelberg (2010). https://doi.org/10.1007/978-3-642-14303-8
27. Hazay, C., Orsini, E., Scholl, P., Soria-Vazquez, E.: Concretely efficient large-scale MPC with active security (or, TinyKeys for TinyOT). In: Peyrin, T., Galbraith, S. (eds.) Advances in Cryptology – ASIACRYPT 2018, Part III. Lecture Notes in Computer Science, vol. 11274, pp. 86–117. Springer, Cham, Switzerland, Brisbane, Queensland, Australia (Dec 2–6, 2018). https://doi.org/10.1007/978-3-030-03332-3_4
28. Hazay, C., Scholl, P., Soria-Vazquez, E.: Low cost constant round MPC combining BMR and oblivious transfer. In: Takagi, T., Peyrin, T. (eds.) Advances in Cryptology – ASIACRYPT 2017, Part I. Lecture Notes in Computer Science, vol. 10624, pp. 598–628. Springer, Cham, Switzerland, Hong Kong, China (Dec 3–7, 2017). https://doi.org/10.1007/978-3-319-70694-8_21
29. Ishai, Y., Khurana, D., Sahai, A., Srinivasan, A.: Round-optimal black-box MPC in the plain model. In: Handschuh, H., Lysyanskaya, A. (eds.) Advances in Cryptology – CRYPTO 2023, Part I. Lecture Notes in Computer Science, vol. 14081, pp. 393–426. Springer, Cham, Switzerland, Santa Barbara, CA, USA (Aug 20–24, 2023). https://doi.org/10.1007/978-3-031-38557-5_13

30. Ishai, Y., Prabhakaran, M., Sahai, A.: Founding cryptography on oblivious transfer - efficiently. In: Wagner, D. (ed.) Advances in Cryptology – CRYPTO 2008. Lecture Notes in Computer Science, vol. 5157, pp. 572–591. Springer Berlin Heidelberg, Germany, Santa Barbara, CA, USA (Aug 17–21, 2008). https://doi.org/10.1007/978-3-540-85174-5_32
31. Katz, J., Lindell, Y.: Introduction to Modern Cryptography, Second Edition. Chapman & Hall/CRC Cryptography and Network Security Series, Taylor & Francis (2014). https://books.google.co.uk/books?id=OWZYBQAAQBAJ
32. Katz, J., Ostrovsky, R.: Round-optimal secure two-party computation. In: Advances in Cryptology - CRYPTO 2004, 24th Annual International CryptologyConference, Santa Barbara, California, USA, August 15-19, 2004, Proceedings. Lecture Notes in Computer Science, vol. 3152, pp. 335–354. Springer (2004). https://doi.org/10.1007/978-3-540-28628-8_21, https://iacr.org/archive/crypto2004/31520336/revised-Katz-Ostrovsky.pdf
33. Katz, J., Ostrovsky, R., Smith, A.: Round efficiency of multi-party computation with a dishonest majority. In: Biham, E. (ed.) Advances in Cryptology – EUROCRYPT 2003. Lecture Notes in Computer Science, vol. 2656, pp. 578–595. Springer Berlin Heidelberg, Germany, Warsaw, Poland (May 4–8, 2003). https://doi.org/10.1007/3-540-39200-9_36
34. Katz, J., Ranellucci, S., Rosulek, M., Wang, X.: Optimizing authenticated garbling for faster secure two-party computation. In: Shacham, H., Boldyreva, A. (eds.) Advances in Cryptology – CRYPTO 2018, Part III. Lecture Notes in Computer Science, vol. 10993, pp. 365–391. Springer, Cham, Switzerland, Santa Barbara, CA, USA (Aug 19–23, 2018). https://doi.org/10.1007/978-3-319-96878-0v13
35. Kilian, J.: Founding cryptography on oblivious transfer. In: 20th Annual ACM Symposium on Theory of Computing, pp. 20–31. ACM Press, Chicago, IL, USA (May 2–4, 1988). https://doi.org/10.1145/62212.62215
36. Nielsen, J.B., Nordholt, P.S., Orlandi, C., Burra, S.S.: A new approach to practical active-secure two-party computation. In: Safavi-Naini, R., Canetti, R. (eds.) Advances in Cryptology – CRYPTO 2012. Lecture Notes in Computer Science, vol. 7417, pp. 681–700. Springer Berlin Heidelberg, Germany, Santa Barbara, CA, USA (Aug 19–23, 2012). https://doi.org/10.1007/978-3-642-32009-5_40
37. Nielsen, J.B., Schneider, T., Trifiletti, R.: Constant round maliciously secure 2PC with function-independent preprocessing using LEGO. In: ISOC Network and Distributed System Security Symposium – NDSS 2017. The Internet Society, San Diego, CA, USA (Feb 26 – Mar 1, 2017). https://doi.org/10.14722/ndss.2017.23075
38. Pass, R.: Bounded-concurrent secure multi-party computation with a dishonest majority. In: Babai, L. (ed.) 36th Annual ACM Symposium on Theory of Computing, pp. 232–241. ACM Press, Chicago, IL, USA (Jun 13–16, 2004). https://doi.org/10.1145/1007352.1007393
39. Pass, R., Wee, H.: Constant-round non-malleable commitments from subexponential one-way functions. In: Gilbert, H. (ed.) Advances in Cryptology – EUROCRYPT 2010. Lecture Notes in Computer Science, vol. 6110, pp. 638–655. Springer Berlin Heidelberg, Germany, French Riviera (May 30 – Jun 3, 2010). https://doi.org/10.1007/978-3-642-13190-5_32
40. Yao, A.C.C.: How to generate and exchange secrets (extended abstract). In: 27th Annual Symposium on Foundations of Computer Science, pp. 162–167. IEEE Computer Society Press, Toronto, Ontario, Canada (Oct 27–29, 1986). https://doi.org/10.1109/SFCS.1986.25

Quantum-Safe Public Key Blinding from MPC-in-the-Head Signature Schemes

Sathvika Balumuri[1], Edward Eaton[1], and Philippe Lamontagne[1,2(✉)]

[1] National Research Council Canada, Ottawa, Canada
Philippe.Lamontagne2@cnrc-nrc.gc.ca
[2] Université de Montréal, Montreal, Canada

Abstract. Key blinding produces pseudonymous digital identities by rerandomizing public keys of a digital signature scheme. It provides privacy in decentralized networks. Current key blinding schemes are based on the discrete log assumption. Eaton, Stebila and Stracovsky (LATINCRYPT 2021) proposed the first post-quantum key blinding schemes from lattice assumptions. However, the large public keys and lack of QROM security means they are not ready to replace existing solutions. We present a general framework to build post-quantum signature schemes with key blinding based on the MPC-in-the-Head paradigm. This results in schemes that rely on well-studied symmetric cryptographic primitives and admit short public keys. We prove generic security results in the quantum random oracle model (QROM).

We instantiate our framework with the recent AES-based Helium signature scheme (Kales and Zaverucha, 2022) to obtain an efficient post-quantum key blinding scheme with small keys. Both Helium and the aforementioned lattice-based key blinding schemes were only proven secure in the ROM. This makes our results the first QROM proof of Helium and the first fully quantum-safe public key blinding scheme.

Keywords: Key Blinding · Anonymity · MPCitH · Quantum-Safe · QROM

1 Introduction

Decentralized services such as Tor's hidden services [24] or the GNU Name System [25] use a concept known as *public key blinding*[1] to provide privacy against the intermediate nodes that take part in the name resolution when a client attempts to connect to a service. This mechanism protects the anonymity of the server and circumvents censorship. In a digital signature scheme with public key blinding, the public key pk can be rerandomized using a seed τ into a blinded

[1] Not to be confused with blind signatures, which allows signing a message while being oblivious to its content.

M. Fischlin and V. Moonsamy (Eds.): ACNS 2025, LNCS 15825, pp. 369–397, 2025.
https://doi.org/10.1007/978-3-031-95761-1_13

key bpk, such that knowledge of τ and bpk does not allow one to compute pk; and such that only the secret key holder can produce valid signature for bpk.

Existing key blinding schemes are based on elliptic curve cryptography. Post-quantum schemes have been proposed [17] from lattice-based assumptions. The challenge in introducing new key blinding schemes is that their security does not directly reduce to the unforgeability of the underlying signature scheme and needs to be proven from scratch. In the case of post-quantum security, schemes that employ the random oracle methodology should be proven secure in the quantum random oracle model (QROM). Another challenge is that lattice-based post-quantum signatures schemes typically have large public keys, on the order of kilobytes for the Dilithium scheme selected for standardization by NIST. In the context of Tor's rendezvous spec, this is problematic since public keys represent identities that have to be handled manually by users.

Our work addresses all of these issues and more. We propose a general framework for constructing post-quantum key blinding schemes based on symmetric-key assumptions, with provably secure in the QROM and extremely short public keys.

1.1 Our Results

Our starting point is the idea of adding key blinding to the Picnic signature scheme which was sketched in [17]. We generalize it to any scheme where signatures consist of a message-dependent non-interactive zero-knowledge proof of knowledge (NIZKPoK) of the preimage of a one-way function constructed via Fiat-Shamir heuristic and the MPC-in-the-Head (MPCitH) paradigm[2]. We describe which properties those schemes and the underlying pseudorandom function must satisfy in order to yield an unforgeable and unlinkable key blinding scheme. The advantage of our modular approach is that signature with key blinding schemes can benefit from future improvements for signature schemes based on NIZKPoK[3]. Our proofs are in the quantum-accessible random oracle model (QROM) where the adversary may evaluate the random oracle on an arbitrary quantum superposition of inputs. Since previous works only proved security against classical random oracle queries, this makes our construction the first fully quantum-safe signature scheme with key blinding.

We use the Helium scheme of [21] to demonstrate our techniques. Helium offers several efficiency improvements over previous MPCitH-based schemes and it is an appealing candidate since it is solely based on well-studied symmetric primitives such as the AES block cipher and the SHAKE extendable output function and boasts small proof sizes for the AES circuit. We apply our framework to the Helium signature scheme to get a signature scheme with key blinding we call

[2] Although the MPCitH paradigm can be used to prove any NP statement, throughout this paper, we use the term to refer to proofs of statements about symmetric key primitives.

[3] For example, our techniques could apply to the recent VOLE-in-the-Head paradigm [1] which offers significant improvement in proof size over MPCitH.

blHelium. To prove that our scheme is secure in the QROM, we show that the proof system underlying Helium is a post-quantum proof of knowledge in the QROM. A direct corollary is that Helium is secure in the QROM, a question that was left open in [21].

The blinded public keys for our blHelium scheme are only 64 bytes for the version based on AES256, which makes it an ideal candidate for a post-quantum transition from ECDSA for the Tor and GNU networks and for other key blinding scheme that benefit from small keys.

We have implemented the AES128 version of our blHelium scheme as a fork of the Helium code. Even though this parameter choice is not post-quantum secure, it allows for a direct comparison with Helium to observe the overhead induced by key blinding. We observe that the blinded version is $2\times$ to $3\times$ slower and produces $2\times$ to $3\times$ larger signatures, which is to be expected based on the larger circuit size of the underlying one-way function.

1.2 Related Work

Public key blinding was first introduced as an anonymity protection feature of Tor's Rendezvous protocol [24]. Tor's key blinding scheme is based on discrete logarithm assumptions. Besides Tor, key blinding also has applications to the GNU Name System [25], private airdrop and rate-limited privacy pass [16]. Key blinding is just one of many public key rerandomization techniques. For an overview and comparison of signature schemes with key rerandomization, we refer the reader to [6].

The first post-quantum key blinding schemes were proposed in [17]. Their constructions are built from lattice-based post-quantum signature schemes and are only proven secure in the (classical) random oracle model. Their schemes also suffer from fairly long public keys (on the order of kilobytes). The general construction of key blinding for MPCitH schemes that we present was first sketched in the appendix of [17] for the Picnic signature scheme [7]. They briefly sketch a proof of unlinkability in the classical ROM, but provide no argument towards unforgeability.

Efforts have been made towards standardizing key blinding in an IETF technical specification draft [10]. The companion paper [16] provides security proofs for the scheme from the draft.

Multiparty computation in the head (MPCitH) is a technique for proving NP statements about arbitrary Boolean circuits introduced by [20]. This technique was refined by ZKBoo [18] and further improved in the paper that introduced Picnic [7], the first signature scheme built from the MPCitH framework to prove knowledge of a preimage of a one-way function. There have since been several improvements. Katz, Kolesnikov, and Wang [22] added a preprocessing phase to the MPC computation used in [7]. BBQ [8] is the first MPCitH signature scheme that instantiates the one-way function with the well studied AES block cipher. It mitigates the larger circuit size by avoiding private keys that lead to circuits which have the 0 byte as input to an s-box, allowing for an efficient computation of the nonlinear operation. Baum and Nof [3] introduces sacrificial multiplication triples (or beaver triples) to replace cut-and-choose checks, which leads to better soundness and less repetitions of the MPC protocol. The Banquet [2] signature scheme achieves 50% smaller signatures by running an MPC protocol that verifies the correctness of the circuit computation, instead of computing the result itself. Dobraunig, Kales, Rechberger, Schofnegger, and Zaverucha [11] offer additional improvements to AES-based MPCitH signature schemes and proposes a scheme based on the *Rain* cipher optimized for MPCitH. Helium [21] lifts multiple small fields $\mathbb{F}$ elements into a larger field $\mathbb{K}$, such that multiplying the $\mathbb{F}$ elements component-wise can be realised by a single operation on $\mathbb{K}$, a technique that was also used in Limbo [9].

2 Preliminaries

We let $\lambda \in \mathbb{N}$ be our security parameter throughout the paper. For two functions f, g let $f \circ g$ denote the function $x \mapsto f(g(x))$. Basic security notions of sets of functions are defined in Appendix A.1.

2.1 Digital Signature Schemes with Public Key Blinding

The definitions of this section are reproduced from previous work on signature schemes with key blinding [16,17].

Definition 1 (Digital Signature with Key Blinding). *A digital signature scheme with key blinding scheme is a tuple of algorithms:*

- $\mathsf{KGen}(1^\lambda)$*: returns a private key* sk *and an* identity *public key* pk
- $\mathsf{BlindPK}(\mathsf{pk}, \tau)$*: takes as input the identity public key* pk *and a blinding parameter* τ *and produces a* blinded public key bpk_τ.
- $\mathsf{Sign}(\mathsf{sk}, \tau, m)$*: produces a signature* σ *for* m *that is valid for the blinded key* bpk_τ.
- $\mathsf{Verify}(\mathsf{bpk}, m, \sigma)$*: returns* 1 *if* σ *is a valid signature of* m *for blinded key* bpk *and* 0 *otherwise.*

The scheme is (perfectly) correct if for $(\mathsf{sk}, \mathsf{pk}) \leftarrow \mathsf{KGen}(1^\lambda)$, *then for all* m *and* τ*:*

$$\mathsf{Verify}(\mathsf{BlindPK}(\mathsf{pk}, \tau), m, \mathsf{Sign}(\mathsf{sk}, \tau, m)) = 1 \ .$$

The unforgeability of signature schemes with key blinding is similar to that of regular unforgeability with the difference that we give the adversary control over which blinded key it targets for its forgery. The adversary is also allowed access to a signature oracle[4] for an arbitrary (polynomial) number of blinded keys.

[4] In [16], the adversary can request signatures with respect to the original (non-blinded) signature scheme. In the context of our framework, this is not possible since signatures for blinded keys are incompatible with the original scheme.

Definition 2 (Unforgeability – Chosen Message and Blinding Attack). *Let* (KGen, BlindPK, Sign, Verify) *be a key blinding signature scheme. The chosen message and blinding attack experiment* EUF-CMBA *is defined as the following game between a challenger and an adversary* $\mathcal{A}$*:*

- *The challenger samples* $(\mathsf{pk}, \mathsf{sk}) \leftarrow\!\!\$\, \mathsf{KGen}(1^\lambda)$ *and sends* pk *to* $\mathcal{A}$.
- $\mathcal{A}$ *can query a signing oracle* Sig *on message* m *and blinding parameter* τ *to receive* $\sigma = \mathsf{Sign}(m, \mathsf{sk}, \tau)$.
- $\mathcal{A}$ *sends its output* (m^*, σ^*, τ^*) *to the challenger who computes* $\mathsf{bpk}^* = \mathsf{BlindPK}(\mathsf{pk}, \tau^*)$ *and outputs 1 if* $\mathsf{Verify}(\mathsf{bpk}^*, m^*, \sigma^*) = 1$ *and if* (m^*, τ^*) *was not previously queried to the signing oracle. Otherwise it outputs 0.*

The advantage of an adversary $\mathcal{A}$ *for the* EUF-CMBA *game is defined as the probability* $\mathsf{Adv}_{\mathcal{A}}^{\text{EUF-CMBA}}$ *that the challenger outputs* 1.

The notion of privacy provided by key blinding is that of unlinkability. A scheme is unlinkable if an adversary cannot tell if two blinded keys originate from the same identity public key or from different keys. In the unlinkability experiment, we also allow the adversary to request new blinded keys at will and to request signatures of arbitrary messages with respect to the blinded keys.

Definition 3 (Unlinkability – Chosen Message and Blinding Attack). *Let* (KGen, BlindPK, Sign, Verify) *be a key blinding signature scheme. The* unlinkability under chosen message and blinding attack UL-CMBA *experiment is defined as the following game:*

- *The challenger samples* $(\mathsf{pk}_0, \mathsf{sk}_0) \leftarrow\!\!\$\, \mathsf{KGen}(1^\lambda)$.
- $\mathcal{A}$ *can query a blinding oracle* bl, *which on input* τ *returns* $\mathsf{bpk} \leftarrow \mathsf{BlindPK}(\mathsf{pk}_0, \tau)$.
- $\mathcal{A}$ *can query a signing oracle* Sig, *which on a message* m *and a blinding parameter* τ *returns* $\sigma = \mathsf{Sign}(m, \mathsf{sk}_0, \tau)$.
- $\mathcal{A}$ *sends a blinding parameter* τ^* *to the challenger. The challenger aborts the experiment if* τ^* *was previously queried to the blinding oracle.*
- *The challenger picks a new key pair* $(\mathsf{pk}_1, \mathsf{sk}_1) \leftarrow \mathsf{KGen}(1^\lambda)$, *samples a bit* $b \leftarrow\!\!\$\, \{0, 1\}$ *and sends* $\mathsf{bpk}_b^* \leftarrow \mathsf{BlindPK}(\mathsf{pk}_b, \tau^*)$ *to* $\mathcal{A}$.
- $\mathcal{A}$ *again has access to the blinding and signing oracle, but now the oracles use the key pair* $(\mathsf{sk}_b, \mathsf{pk}_b)$ *if* $\tau = \tau^*$ *and use the pair* $(\mathsf{sk}_0, \mathsf{pk}_0)$ *if* $\tau \neq \tau^*$.
- $\mathcal{A}$ *outputs a guess* b' *and wins if* $b' = b$.

The advantage of an adversary $\mathcal{A}$ *for the experiment is defined as the probability* $\mathsf{Adv}_{\mathcal{A}}^{\text{UL-CMBA}} = \left|\Pr[b = b'] - \frac{1}{2}\right|$.

2.2 Quantum Random Oracle Model

In the quantum random oracle model (QROM), the adversary has quantum oracle access to a unitary $\mathcal{O}^H : |c\rangle|x\rangle|y\rangle \mapsto |c\rangle|x\rangle|y \oplus c \cdot H(x)\rangle$ that computes a random function H in superposition. While the QROM does not permit observing and reprogramming random oracle queries as easily as in the classical ROM, there are now powerful tools for proving security in the QROM, which we present in the appendix (Sect. A.2).

2.3 Non-interactive Proof Systems in the QROM

Let $R \subseteq \mathcal{X} \times \mathcal{W}$ be a relation. A non-interactive proof system for R in the quantum random oracle model is a pair of oracle-aided algorithms $\Sigma = (\mathsf{P}^H, \mathsf{V}^H)$. The proof system is correct (or complete) if there is a negligible function $\kappa(\cdot)$ such that for every $(x, w) \in R$,

$$\Pr_H[\mathsf{V}^H(x, \pi) \mid \pi \leftarrow \mathsf{P}^H(x, w)] \geq 1 - \kappa(\lambda) \ . \tag{1}$$

Definition 4 (Post-Quantum Zero-Knowledge). *A non-interactive proof $\Sigma = (\mathsf{P}^H, \mathsf{V}^H)$ is post-quantum zero-knowledge (pqNIZK) if there is a simulator* Sim *and a function ε_{zk} such that for every QPT adversary $\tilde{\mathsf{V}}^H$ that makes at most q_H queries to H,*

$$\left|\Pr_H[\tilde{\mathsf{V}}^H(x, \pi) = 1 \mid \pi \leftarrow \mathsf{P}^H(x, w)] - \Pr_H[\tilde{\mathsf{V}}^{H_\Theta}(x, \pi) = 1 \mid (\pi, \Theta) \leftarrow \mathcal{S}^H(x)]\right| \leq \varepsilon_{\text{zk}}(\lambda, q_H) \tag{2}$$

where $\Theta = \{(x_1, y_1), \ldots, (x_t, y_t)\}$ is a list of assignments and H_Θ satisfies $H_\Theta(x_i) = y_i$ for every $(x_i, y_i) \in \Theta$ and is equal to H otherwise, and where $\varepsilon_{\text{zk}}(\lambda, q_H)$ is negligible in λ if q_H is polynomial in λ.

The soundness notion we will use is the definition of *online extractability* from [14]. We first present some notation. Let $\tilde{\mathsf{P}}$ be a dishonest prover that outputs an instance x, a proof π and some auxiliary (potentially quantum) information Z. Let $\mathsf{V}^H \leftrightarrow \tilde{\mathsf{P}}^H(1^\lambda)$ denote an execution of the proof, which we define as $(x, \pi, Z) \leftarrow \tilde{\mathsf{P}}^H(1^\lambda)$ followed by $v \leftarrow \mathsf{V}^H(x, \pi)$. The malicious prover may receive an additional input (e.g. a public key in the unforgeability game). For an interactive algorithm $\mathcal{E}$ (that we call the *online extractor*) which controls the interface to the random oracle, we let $\mathsf{V}^{\mathcal{E}} \leftrightarrow \tilde{\mathsf{P}}^{\mathcal{E}}(1^\lambda)$ denote the execution with the calls to H simulated by $\mathcal{E}$ and where $\mathcal{E}$ additionally outputs $w \in \mathcal{W}$. Let $[(x, \pi, v, Z)]_{\mathsf{V}^{\mathcal{O}} \leftrightarrow \tilde{\mathsf{P}}^{\mathcal{O}}(1^\lambda)}$ denote the distribution of the outputs of the execution with oracle $\mathcal{O} \in \{H, \mathcal{E}\}$ and let δ be the statistical distance.

Definition 5. *A non-interactive proof in the quantum random oracle model for a relation R is a* online extractable *against adaptive adversaries if there exists an online extractor $\mathcal{E}$, and functions ε_{sim} (the* simulation error*) and ε_{ex} (the* extraction error*), with the following properties. For any $\lambda \in \mathbb{N}$ and for any q-query dishonest prover $\tilde{\mathsf{P}}$,*

$$\delta([(x, \pi, v, Z)]_{\mathsf{V}^H \leftrightarrow \tilde{\mathsf{P}}^H(1^\lambda)}, [(x, \pi, v, Z)]_{\mathsf{V}^{\mathcal{E}} \leftrightarrow \tilde{\mathsf{P}}^{\mathcal{E}}(1^\lambda)}) \leq \varepsilon_{\text{sim}}(\lambda, q)$$

and

$$\Pr\big[v = 1 \wedge (x, w) \notin R : (x, \pi, v, Z, w) \leftarrow \mathsf{V}^{\mathcal{E}} \leftrightarrow \tilde{\mathsf{P}}^{\mathcal{E}}(1^\lambda)\big] \leq \varepsilon_{\text{ex}}(\lambda, q) \, .$$

Furthermore, the runtime of $\mathcal{E}$ is polynomial in $\lambda + q$, and $\varepsilon_{\text{sim}}(\lambda, q)$ and $\varepsilon_{\text{ex}}(\lambda, q)$ are negligible in λ whenever q is polynomial in λ.

Consider an execution of the proof system with honest verifier and a prover that has oracle access to the zero-knowledge simulator Sim. In this execution, verification is done with respect to the final state of the random oracle $\hat{H}$ has been reprogrammed at certain points from H by Sim. We let $(x, \pi, v, Z) \leftarrow V^{\hat{H}} \leftrightarrow \tilde{\mathsf{P}}^{H,\mathsf{Sim}}(1^\lambda)$ denote the outcome of this execution where $(x, \pi, Z) \leftarrow \tilde{\mathsf{P}}^{H,\mathsf{Sim}}$ and $v = \mathsf{V}^{\hat{H}(}x, \pi) \wedge x \notin Q_{\mathsf{Sim}}$ where Q_{Sim} is the list of queries made to the simulator.

Definition 6. *A non-interactive proof system in the QROM* $\Pi = (\mathsf{P}^H, \mathsf{V}^H)$ *is* conditionally simulation-sound with respect to a simulator Sim *if for all QPT provers* $\tilde{\mathsf{P}}^{H,\mathsf{Sim}}$ *with oracle access to* H *and* Sim*, there is a function* $\varepsilon_{\mathrm{ss}}$ *and an oracle algorithm* $\mathcal{B}^H$ *such that*

$$\delta\left([x, \pi, v, Z]_{V^{\hat{H}} \leftrightarrow \tilde{\mathsf{P}}^{H,\mathsf{Sim}}(1^\lambda)}, [x, \pi, v, Z]_{V^H \leftrightarrow \mathcal{B}^H(1^\lambda)}\right) \leq \varepsilon_{\mathrm{ss}}(\lambda, q_H, q_S, n) \quad (3)$$

where $\varepsilon_{\mathrm{ss}}(\lambda, q_H, q_S, n)$ *is negligible in* λ *whenever* q_H, q_S *and* n *are polynomial in* λ.

Definition 6 does not by itself imply any soundness notion. However, if a proof system is sound and satisfies Definition 6, then it is simulation-sound; similarly if it is (online) extractable, then it is simulation-sound (online) extractable.

On the Satisfiability of this Section's Definitions. The definitions from this section are somewhat strong, i.e. that extractability is online and simulation-sound. We have chosen to go with these stronger requirements because 1- they give tight bounds for reductions and 2- they are achievable using standard constructions. More precisely, the Fiat-Shamir transform applied to special-sound commit-and-open interactive proofs is online extractable [14,15]. Simulation-soundness and simulation-sound (extractability) of the Fiat-Shamir transform was shown by Unruh [27]; and it was observed in [12] that the argument also applies FS of multi-round proof systems.

3 Key Blinding for MPC-in-the-Head Signature Schemes

3.1 Blinding MPCitH Public Keys

Let $\mathcal{F} = \{f_k : \{0,1\}^\lambda \to \{0,1\}^\lambda\}_{k \in \{0,1\}^\lambda}$ be a family of pseudorandom functions. For $x \in \{0,1\}^\lambda$, we let $F_x : k \mapsto f_k(x)$. We consider signature schemes that are constructed as follows. Let $\Pi = (\mathsf{P}^H, \mathsf{V}^H)$ be a NIZKPoK for the relation $R = \{(y, k)) \mid y = F_x(k)\}$. It can be turned into a signature scheme as follows.

- Key generation: sample $x \in \{0,1\}^\lambda$ and $k \in \{0,1\}^\lambda$. Output $\mathsf{sk} := k$ and $\mathsf{pk} := (x, f_k(x))$.
- Signature: to sign a message m, use P on input $(\mathsf{pk}, \mathsf{sk})$ to produce a non-interactive zero-knowledge proof of knowledge of k such that $\mathsf{pk} = (x, f_k(x))$ that depends[5] on m.

[5] For example, if the proof system uses the Fiat-Shamir heuristic, m can be included in the random oracle queries that compute the verifier's challenge.

- Verification: run the verification protocol V on input pk.

For such protocols, we consider a generic blinding procedure which was first informally proposed in [17]. To blind a public key $\mathsf{pk} = (x, f_k(x))$ using a seed τ, one encrypts x a second time using a new key derived from pk and τ, for example using a cryptographic hash function G modelled as a random oracle. The new blinded public key is $\mathsf{bpk}_\tau = (x, f_{G(\tau,\mathsf{pk})}(\mathsf{pk}))$. Observe however that we want the same verification procedure for every blinded key (verification should depend only on the blinded public key and should not require knowledge of τ), so the value x cannot be itself encrypted. Moreover, unlinkability requires that we use the same input x for every public key, otherwise it becomes trivial to link blinded keys to the original key. Based on these observations, we conclude that each public key must use the same input x. It was shown in the full version of [7] that $k \mapsto f_k(x)$ is one-way for any input x if f_k is pseudorandom.

We now present our general framework for instantiating post-quantum digital signatures with key blinding from MPCitH. We assume for simplicity that the messages are of a fixed size $n(\lambda)$ determined by the security parameter.

Construction 1. Assume the following prerequisites:

- A security parameter $\lambda \in \mathbb{N}$
- A family of pseudorandom permutations $\mathcal{F} = \{f_k : \{0,1\}^{2\lambda} \rightarrow \{0,1\}^{2\lambda}\}_{k \in \{0,1\}^\lambda}$,
- A fixed input $\mathsf{inp} \in \{0,1\}^{2\lambda}$.
- $F : \{0,1\}^{2\lambda} \rightarrow \{0,1\}^{2\lambda}$ defined as $F(k, k') := f_{k'} \circ f_k(\mathsf{inp})$.
- Cryptographic hash functions $H, G : \{0,1\}^* \rightarrow \{0,1\}^\lambda$ (modelled as random oracles).
- A NIZKPoK $\Pi = (\mathsf{P}^H, \mathsf{V}^H)$ for the relation $R_F : \{0,1\}^{2\lambda \cdot n(\lambda)} \times \{0,1\}^{2\lambda}$ defined as $R_F = \{(y \| m, (k, k')) \mid y = F(k, k'), |m| = n(\lambda)\}$.

We define $\mathsf{blSig} = (\mathsf{KGen}, \mathsf{BlindPK}, \mathsf{Sign}, \mathsf{Verify})$ as the following signature scheme with key blinding:

- $\mathsf{KGen}(1^\lambda)$ returns $\mathsf{sk} \leftarrow\$ \{0,1\}^\lambda$ and $\mathsf{pk} = f_{\mathsf{sk}}(\mathsf{inp})$
- $\mathsf{BlindPK}(\mathsf{pk}, \tau)$ returns $\mathsf{bpk} = f_{G(\tau,\mathsf{pk})}(\mathsf{pk})$
- $\mathsf{Sign}(m, \mathsf{sk}, \tau)$ computes $\mathsf{pk} = f_{\mathsf{sk}}(\mathsf{inp})$ and $\mathsf{bpk} = \mathsf{BlindPK}(\mathsf{pk}, \tau)$ and returns $\mathsf{P}^H(\mathsf{bpk} \| m, \mathsf{sk}, G(\tau, \mathsf{pk}))$
- $\mathsf{Verify}(\mathsf{bpk}, m, \sigma)$ returns $\mathsf{V}^H(\mathsf{bpk} \| m, \sigma)$

In the remainder of this section, we show the security of our construction assuming certain properties of $\mathcal{F}$ and Π.

3.2 Security of (Blinded) Key Generation

Forging signatures for a scheme built from Construction 1 is at most as hard as finding preimages of F. The hardness of inverting F relies on the fact that if $\{f_k\}_k$ is a family of pseudorandom permutations, then for any x, $f_k(x)$ is one-way with respect to k, i.e. $\{F_x : k \mapsto f_k(x)\}_x$ is a one-way function family.

Lemma 1 ([7]). *Let* $\{f_k : \{0,1\}^\lambda \to \{0,1\}^\lambda\}_{k \in \{0,1\}^\lambda}$ *be a family of pseudorandom permutations, then* $F_x(k) := f_k(x)$ *is a one-way function for any* $x \in \{0,1\}^\lambda$.

The proof of Lemma 1 is found in the full version of [7]. It relies on the fact that the message space (or block size) of f is equal to its key space (or key size). Since the function F applies f twice with two different keys, the block size should be twice the key size.

Since F is actually built from the function family $\{f_{k'} \circ f_k\}_{(k,k')}$. It remains to show that this is a family of pseudorandom functions if f_k are pseudorandom.

Lemma 2. *If* $\{f_k\}_k$ *is a family of pseudorandom permutations, then* $\{f_{k'} \circ f_k\}_{(k,k')}$ *is also a family of pseudorandom permutations.*

Proof. Suppose there is a distinguisher $\mathcal{A}$ against the pseudorandomness game: it is given oracle access to either $f_{k'} \circ f_k$ for random k, k' or to a random function R, and tries to distinguish between both cases. We construct an adversary $\mathcal{B}$ against the pseudorandomness of f_k as follows: given an oracle $\mathcal{O}$ which is either f_k or a random function, sample a key k' and run $\mathcal{A}$ with oracle $f_{k'} \circ \mathcal{O}$.

Since $f_{k'}$ is a permutation, for a random R the function $f_{k'} \circ R$ is also random. Therefore, if $\mathcal{O} = f_k$, $\mathcal{A}$ has an oracle for $f_{k'} \circ f_k$ and if $\mathcal{O} = R$, $\mathcal{A}$ has an oracle for the random function $R' = f_{k'} \circ R$. We conclude that $\mathcal{B}$ distinguishes f_k from a random function with the same advantage as $\mathcal{A}$ distinguishes $f_{k'} \circ f_k$ from random. □

3.3 Unforgeability of Construction 1

We now want to show that forging valid signatures for blinded keys is at least as hard (asymptotically) as inverting the one-way function F. Recall that for breaking the unforgeability game, the adversary on input pk must produce τ^*, m^* and a valid proof of knowledge σ^* of (k, k') such that $\mathsf{BlindPK}(\mathsf{pk}, \tau^*) = F(k, k')$. The typical strategy of using the knowledge extractor of the NIZKPoK on σ^* does not directly work here. In particular the adversary could produce a proof for $(k, k') \neq (\mathsf{sk}, G(\tau^*, \mathsf{pk}))$, such that the knowledge extractor would not necessarily allow us recover the secret sk. Furthermore, the adversary has some control over the target blinded public key bpk for its forgery, however this control is limited to the choice τ which rerandomizes pk through the random oracle.

To precisely capture the problem the adversary needs to solve for forging signatures, we define the following NP relation.

Definition 7. *Let* $G : \{0,1\}^* \to \{0,1\}^\lambda$ *be a quantumly accessible random oracle, let* $\{f_k : \{0,1\}^{2\lambda} \to \{0,1\}^{2\lambda}\}_{k \in \{0,1\}^\lambda}$ *be a family of pseudorandom permutations and let* $\mathsf{inp} \in \{0,1\}^{2\lambda}$. *We define* $R_{G,f}$ *as the NP relation where the instances are of the form* $y \in \{0,1\}^{2\lambda}$ *and witnesses are tuples* (k, k', τ) *such that*

$$(y, (k, k', \tau)) \in R_{G,f} \iff f_{G(\tau,y)}(y) = f_{k'}(f_k(\mathsf{inp})) \ . \quad (4)$$

Using the fact that G is a random oracle, we can show that this relation is as hard as inverting F by reprogramming the oracle at a certain point. Let $\mathcal{A}^G$ be an adversary that on input y outputs a witness for $R_{G,f}$ after q queries to G with some probability p. We can invert F on a specific point z by sampling a key s, setting $y = f_s^{-1}(z)$, running $\mathcal{A}^G$ on input y, and reprogramming one of its oracle queries to output s. With probability p, $\mathcal{A}^G$ outputs (τ, k, k') such that $f_{G(\tau,y)}(y) = f_{k'}(f_k(\mathsf{inp}))$. With probability $\frac{1}{q}$, (τ, y) is the point that was programmed as $G(\tau, y) = s$, such that $z = f_s(y) = f_{k'}(f_k(\mathsf{inp}))$. Thus (k, k') is a preimage of z for F as required. We formalize this argument in the QROM using the measure-and-reprogram approach [12,13] with Lemma 3 whose proof is in Appendix B.

Lemma 3. *Let $\{f_k\}_{k\in\{0,1\}^\lambda}$ be a family of pseudorandom permutations. Let G be a quantum-accessible random oracle. If $F : (k, k') \mapsto f_{k'}(f_k(\mathsf{inp}))$ is a one-way function, then the relation $R_{G,f}$ is hard with advantage*

$$\mathsf{Adv}^{R_{G,f}}(\lambda) \leq (2q_G + 1)^2 \cdot \mathsf{Adv}_F^{\mathrm{OWF}}(\lambda) \tag{5}$$

where q_G is the number of queries to G.

Before going into the proof of unforgeability, we observe that unlike the unforgeability for regular digital signatures, in the EUF-CMBA game, the adversary can output a message m^* that was queried to the signature oracle, as long as τ^* differs. The proof thus requires bounding the probability of reusing a signature that was issued for m^* with a different τ. Only then can we move to standard techniques to bound the probability of producing a forgery. To this end, we make some assumptions about the functions f_k. We require that it is hard to find $\tau \neq \tau'$ such that $f_{G(\mathsf{pk},\tau)}(\mathsf{pk}) = f_{G(\mathsf{pk},\tau')}(\mathsf{pk})$. This is the case if we assume that G is collision resistant and that the f_k are key-collision-resistant[6] (Definition 11).

Theorem 1. *Let* blSig *be the signature scheme with key blinding form Construction 1. Assume that $\mathcal{F} = \{f_k\}_k$ is a family of key-collision-resistant pseudorandom permutations. Then* blSig *is* EUF-CMBA *in the QROM with advantage at most*

$$\begin{aligned}\mathsf{Adv}^{\mathrm{EUF\text{-}CMBA}}(\lambda) \leq \mathsf{Adv}^{R_{G,f}}(\lambda) &+ O(q_G^3 \cdot 2^{-\lambda}) + \mathsf{Adv}^{\mathrm{KCR}}(\lambda) \\ &+ q_s \cdot \varepsilon_{zk}(\lambda, q_H) + \varepsilon_{ss}(\lambda, q_H, q_S) \\ &+ \varepsilon_{sim}(\lambda, q_H) + \varepsilon_{ex}(\lambda, q_H) \ .\end{aligned}$$

where q_H, q_G and q_S are respectively the number of queries to H, G and Sig *made by the adversary; where $\varepsilon_{\mathrm{zk}}, \varepsilon_{\mathrm{sim}}, \varepsilon_{\mathrm{ss}}$ and $\varepsilon_{\mathrm{ex}}$ are defined in Sect. 2.3; and where* $\mathsf{Adv}^{\mathrm{KCR}}(\lambda)$ *is the advantage in the key-collision-resistance game (Definition 11).*

[6] Since keys are derived from the random function G, key-collision-resistance could potentially be replaced with a weaker assumption.

Proof. Let $\mathcal{A}^{G,H,\mathsf{Sig}}$ be an adversary against the EUF-CMBA experiment with Construction 1 that has access to a signature oracle Sig, to the QRO H for the proof system Π and to the QRO G used to blind public keys.

There are two scenarios for a forgery produced by $\mathcal{A}^{G,H,\mathsf{Sig}}$: either m^* was not queried to the signing oracle, or m^* was queried to Sig, but with a $\tau \neq \tau^*$. The first case requires the adversary to produce a new valid proof of knowledge and will be handled using standard techniques. The second case occurs if τ and τ^* lead to the same blinded public key. We handle the second and simpler case first.

The proof proceeds in a sequence of hybrid games, bounding the difference in the probability of winning between each hybrid. We start with the original EUF-CMBA game (Definition 2). Let WIN_i denote the event that the challenger outputs 1 in game i and let Q_{Sig} be the list of pairs (m, τ) queried to the signing oracle.

Game 0 (EUF-CMBA). $(\mathsf{pk}, \mathsf{sk}) \leftarrow \mathsf{KGen}(1^\lambda)$ and $(m^*, \sigma^*, \tau^*) \leftarrow \mathcal{A}^{G,H,\mathsf{Sig}}(\mathsf{pk})$

$$\text{WIN}_0 = \mathsf{Verify}(\mathsf{BlindPK}(\mathsf{pk}, \tau^*), m^*, \sigma^*) \wedge (m^*, \tau^*) \notin Q_{\mathsf{Sig}} \tag{6}$$

We modify this game by adding the condition that the challenger outputs 0 if there exist $\tau \neq \tau^*$ such that $(m^*, \tau) \in Q_{\mathsf{Sig}}$ and $G(\mathsf{pk}, \tau) = G(\mathsf{pk}, \tau^*)$
Game 1. $(\mathsf{pk}, \mathsf{sk}) \leftarrow \mathsf{KGen}(1^\lambda)$ and $(m^*, \sigma^*, \tau^*) \leftarrow \mathcal{A}^{G,H,\mathsf{Sig}}(\mathsf{pk})$

$$\text{WIN}_1 = \text{WIN}_0 \wedge \forall \tau \neq \tau^*, (m^*, \tau) \in Q_{\mathsf{Sig}} \implies G(\mathsf{pk}, \tau) \neq G(\mathsf{pk}, \tau^*) \tag{7}$$

Let COLL be the event $\exists \tau \neq \tau^* : (m^*, \tau) \in Q_{\mathsf{Sig}} \wedge G(\mathsf{pk}, \tau) = G(\mathsf{pk}, \tau^*)$. We have $\text{WIN}_1 = \text{WIN}_0 \wedge \neg\text{COLL}$. The difference between games 0 and 1 is thus

$$\begin{aligned} |\Pr[\text{WIN}_0] - \Pr[\text{WIN}_1]| &= |\Pr[\text{WIN}_0 \wedge \text{COLL}] + \Pr[\text{WIN}_0 \wedge \neg\text{COLL}] - \Pr[\text{WIN}_1]| \\ &\leq \Pr[\text{COLL}] \\ &\leq O(q_G^3 2^{-\lambda}) \end{aligned}$$

where the above bound comes from the bound on quantum collision finding (Lemma 6) for the quantum random oracle G.

Next, we get the challenger to abort whenever there is a τ in the list of queries that lead to the same blinded key as τ^*.
Game 2. $(\mathsf{pk}, \mathsf{sk}) \leftarrow \mathsf{KGen}(1^\lambda)$ and $(m^*, \sigma^*, \tau^*) \leftarrow \mathcal{A}^{G,H,\mathsf{Sig}}(\mathsf{pk})$

$$\text{WIN}_2 = \text{WIN}_1 \wedge \forall \tau \neq \tau^* : (m^*, \tau) \in Q_{\mathsf{Sig}} \implies f_{G(\mathsf{pk},\tau)}(\mathsf{pk}) \neq f_{G(\mathsf{pk},\tau^*)}(\mathsf{pk}) \tag{8}$$

We introduce the event KEYCOLL defined as $\exists \tau \neq \tau^* : (m^*, \tau) \in Q_{\mathsf{Sig}} \wedge f_{G(\mathsf{pk},\tau)}(\mathsf{pk}) = f_{G(\mathsf{pk},\tau^*)}(\mathsf{pk})$. Then, WIN_2 is the event $\text{WIN}_0 \wedge \neg\text{COLL} \wedge \neg\text{KEYCOLL}$ and

$$|\Pr[\text{WIN}_1] - \Pr[\text{WIN}_2]| \leq \Pr[\neg\text{COLL} \wedge \text{KEYCOLL}] \leq \mathsf{Adv}_{\mathcal{A}}^{\text{KCR}}(\lambda)$$

since, conditioned on $\neg$COLL, if event KEYCOLL occurs we can find a key collision by looking through the signature queries to find τ and τ^* such that $G(\mathsf{pk}, \tau) \neq G(\mathsf{pk}, \tau^*)$ is a key collision for f.

In the next game, the oracle $\mathsf{Sig}(m, \tau) = \mathsf{Sign}(m, \tau, \mathsf{sk})$ is replaced with the oracle $\mathsf{Sig}'(m, \tau) := \mathsf{Sim}(\mathsf{BlindPK}(\mathsf{pk}, \tau)\|m)$ where Sim is the zero-knowledge simulator of the NIZKPoK Π.

Game 3. $(\mathsf{pk}, \mathsf{sk}) \leftarrow \mathsf{KGen}(1^\lambda)$, $(m^*, \sigma^*, \tau^*) \leftarrow \mathcal{A}^{G,H,\mathsf{Sig}'}(\mathsf{pk})$, $\mathsf{Sig}'(m, \tau) := \mathsf{Sim}(\mathsf{BlindPK}(\mathsf{pk}, \tau)\|m)$

$$\text{WIN}_3 = \text{WIN}_2$$

Since the scheme is zero-knowledge (Definition 4) and by a union bound over the number of signature queries q_S, we have

$$|\Pr[\text{WIN}_3] - \Pr[\text{WIN}_2]| \leq q_S \cdot \varepsilon_{\mathsf{zk}}(\lambda, q_H) \tag{9}$$

Recall that in Game 3, the adversary can only win if

$$\forall \tau \neq \tau^*, (m^*, \tau) \in Q_{\mathsf{Sig}} \implies \mathsf{BlindPK}(\mathsf{pk}, \tau) \neq \mathsf{BlindPK}(\mathsf{pk}, \tau^*) \tag{10}$$

Furthermore, since the signature oracle Sig' now calls the zero-knowledge simulator, if we let $\mathsf{bpk}^* = \mathsf{BlindPK}(\mathsf{pk}, \tau^*)$, condition (10) implies that $\mathsf{bpk}^*\|m^* \notin Q_{\mathsf{Sim}}$ where Q_{Sim} is the list of queries to the zero-knowledge simulator. Thus, we can rewrite event WIN_3 as

$$\begin{aligned} \text{WIN}_3 &= \mathsf{Verify}(\mathsf{bpk}^*, m^*, \sigma^*) \wedge \mathsf{bpk}^*\|m^* \notin Q_{\mathsf{Sim}} \\ &= \mathsf{V}^{H_\theta}(\mathsf{bpk}^*\|m^*, \sigma^*) \wedge \mathsf{bpk}^*\|m^* \notin Q_{\mathsf{Sim}} \end{aligned}$$

where verification of the NIZKPoK is performed with respect to the reprogrammed oracle H_θ.

Given an efficient adversary $\mathcal{A}^{G,H,\mathsf{Sig}'}$ against Game 3, we construct an adversarial prover[7] $\mathcal{P}^{H,\mathsf{Sim}}$ against Π that takes input pk and runs $\mathcal{A}^{G,H,\mathsf{Sig}'}$:

- Whenever $\mathcal{A}^{G,H,\mathsf{Sig}'}$ makes a query to Sig' on input (m, τ), $\mathcal{P}^{H,\mathsf{Sim}}$ queries Sim on input $\mathsf{BlindPK}(\mathsf{pk}, \tau)\|m$.
- When $\mathcal{A}^{G,H,\mathsf{Sig}'}$ outputs (m^*, τ^*, σ^*), $\mathcal{P}^{H,\mathsf{Sim}}$ outputs the instance/proof pair $(x, \pi) = (\mathsf{BlindPK}(\mathsf{pk}, \tau^*)\|m^*, \sigma^*)$ along with auxiliary output $Z = \tau^*$.

To ensure that x has the correct form throughout the following games, we introduce the parameterized set $\mathcal{X}_{\mathsf{pk},\tau^*} := \{\mathsf{BlindPK}(\mathsf{pk}, \tau^*)\|m\}_{m \in \{0,1\}^{n(\lambda)}}$.

Game 4. $(\mathsf{pk}, \mathsf{sk}) \leftarrow \mathsf{KGen}(1^\lambda)$, $(x, \pi, \tau^*) \leftarrow \mathcal{P}^{H,\mathsf{Sim}}(\mathsf{pk})$,

$$\text{WIN}_4 = x \in \mathcal{X}_{\mathsf{pk},\tau^*} \wedge \mathsf{V}^{H_\theta}(x, \pi) \wedge x \notin Q_{\mathsf{Sim}}$$

We have that by definition of $\mathcal{P}^{H,\mathsf{Sim}}$,

$$\Pr[\text{WIN}_4] = \Pr[\text{WIN}_3] \ .$$

[7] $\mathcal{P}$ also has oracle access to G, but from this point on, we drop the superscript to lighten notation.

Let $\mathcal{B}^H$ be the malicious prover without access to Sim that emulates $\mathcal{P}^{H,\mathsf{Sim}}$ from Definition 6 (simulation-soundness). In the next game, we let (x, π, τ^*) be generated by $\mathcal{B}^H$ instead of $\mathcal{P}^{H,\mathsf{Sim}}$ and make verification with respect to the unprogrammed oracle H.

Game 5. $(\mathsf{pk}, \mathsf{sk}) \leftarrow \mathsf{KGen}(1^\lambda)$, $(x, \pi, \tau^*) \leftarrow \mathcal{B}^H(\mathsf{pk})$

$$\text{WIN}_5 = x \in \mathcal{X}_{\mathsf{pk},\tau^*} \wedge \mathsf{V}^H(x, \pi)$$

By Definition 6, we have

$$\Pr[\text{WIN}_5] = \Pr[\text{WIN}_4] \leq \varepsilon_{\text{ss}}(\lambda, q_H, q_S)$$

for ε_{ss} negligible in λ when q_H and q_S are polynomial in λ.

We now invoke the online knowledge extractor for $\mathcal{B}^H$ from Definition 5. In a first step, the random oracle is emulated by the extractor.

Game 6. $(\mathsf{pk}, \mathsf{sk}) \leftarrow \mathsf{KGen}(1^\lambda)$, $(x, \pi, (k, k'), \tau^*) \leftarrow \mathcal{B}^{\mathcal{E}}(\mathsf{pk})$

$$\text{WIN}_6 = x \in \mathcal{X}_{\mathsf{pk},\tau^*} \wedge \mathsf{V}^{\mathcal{E}}(x, \pi)$$

By Definition 5, we have

$$|\Pr[\text{WIN}_6] - \Pr[\text{WIN}_5]| \leq \varepsilon_{\text{sim}}(\lambda, q_H)$$

Next, we change the winning condition to also check that the witness produced by the knowledge extractor is a valid preimage for F.

Game 7. $(\mathsf{pk}, \mathsf{sk}) \leftarrow \mathsf{KGen}(1^\lambda)$, $(x, \pi, (k, k'), \tau^*) \leftarrow \mathcal{B}^{\mathcal{E}}(\mathsf{pk})$

$$\text{WIN}_7 = x \in \mathcal{X}_{\mathsf{pk},\tau^*} \wedge \mathsf{V}^{\mathcal{E}}(x, \pi) \wedge F(k, k') = \mathsf{BlindPK}(\mathsf{pk}, \tau^*)$$

Recall the relation $R_F = \{(x, (k, k')) \mid \exists m : x = y \| m \wedge y = F(k, k')\}$ which is proven by the NIZKPoK Π. The condition $x \in \mathcal{X}_{\mathsf{pk},\tau^*} \wedge F(k, k') = \mathsf{BlindPK}(\mathsf{pk}, \tau^*)$ implies that $(x, (k, k')) \in R_F$. By Definition 5, we thus have

$$|\Pr[\text{WIN}_7] - \Pr[\text{WIN}_6]| \leq \Pr[\mathsf{V}^{\mathcal{E}}(x, \pi) \wedge (x, (k, k')) \notin R_F] \leq \varepsilon_{\text{ex}}(\lambda, q_H)$$

We now define $\mathcal{M}$, an algorithm for the relation $R_{G,f}$ that, on input $y = \mathsf{pk}$, runs the online knowledge extractor on input pk to get k, k' and τ^*.

Game 7. $(\mathsf{pk}, \mathsf{sk}) \leftarrow \mathsf{KGen}(1^\lambda)$, $(k, k', \tau^*) \leftarrow \mathcal{M}(\mathsf{pk})$

$$\text{WIN}_8 = (\mathsf{pk}, (k, k', \tau^*)) \in R_{G,f}$$

We have

$$\Pr[\text{WIN}_8] \geq \Pr[\text{WIN}_7]$$

Since Game 0 is the EUF-CMBA game and Game 8 is finding a witness for the relation $R_{G,f}$, the statement follows by accounting for the errors across all games:

$$\begin{aligned}\Pr[\text{WIN}_0] \leq \Pr[\text{WIN}_8] &+ O(q_G^3 \cdot 2^{-\lambda}) + \mathsf{Adv}^{\text{KCR}}(\lambda) \\ &+ q_s \cdot \varepsilon_{\text{zk}}(\lambda, q_H) + \varepsilon_{\text{ss}}(\lambda, q_H, q_S) \\ &+ \varepsilon_{\text{sim}}(\lambda, q_H) + \varepsilon_{\text{ex}}(\lambda, q_H) \ .\end{aligned}$$

□

3.4 Unlinkability of Construction 1

We show unlinkability of Construction 1 in the QROM using a similar strategy as [17]. That is, we first use the zero-knowledge simulator to remove the signature oracle. Next, we remove the dependence on the identity public key pk of the blinded keys by first replacing $G(\tau, \mathsf{pk})$ with random values and then changing the blinding oracle so that it returns encryptions of independently generated public keys. This reduces the unlinkability game to the task of distinguishing many encryptions of the same plaintext from many encryptions of independent plaintexts. This corresponds to the notion of chosen plaintext indistinguishability security in a multi-user setting, defined in Sect. A.1.

Theorem 2. *Let* $\mathsf{blSig} = (\mathsf{KGen}, \mathsf{BlindPK}, \mathsf{Sign}, \mathsf{Verify})$ *be the blinded signature scheme of Construction 1 built from proof system* $\Pi = (\mathsf{P}^H, \mathsf{V}^H)$ *and he family of PRP* $\mathcal{F} = \{f_k\}_k$*. If* Π *is zero-knowledge (Definition 4) in the QROM and if* $\mathcal{F}$ *satisfies multi-user ciphertext indistinguishability (Definition 12) with advantage* $\mathsf{Adv}^{\text{MU-IND}}$ *then* blSig *is unlinkable under chosen message and blinding attack (Definition 3) in the QROM with advantage*

$$\mathsf{Adv}^{\text{UL-CMBA}}(\lambda) \leq \frac{1}{2} + \mathsf{Adv}^{\text{MU-IND}}(\lambda) + 2q_H\sqrt{\mathsf{Adv}^{\text{MU-IND}}(\lambda)} + q_S \cdot \varepsilon_{\text{zk}}(\lambda, q_H) \quad (11)$$

where q_G*,* q_H*,* q_S *and* q_B *are respectively the number of queries to the random oracles* G *and* H*, to the signing oracle and to the blinding oracle.*

Proof. We proceed by a game-hopping argument to reduce the unlinkability game to the multi-user indistinguishability of f_k. In each new game, we remove some part of the game that depends on the identity public key pk. We assume w.l.o.g. that the adversary never sends τ^* that was previously queried to the signature oracle since this would make the challenger abort. Let $\mathcal{A}_1^{G,H,\mathsf{bl},\mathsf{Sig}}$ and $\mathcal{A}_2^{G,H,\mathsf{bl},\mathsf{Sig}}$ denotes the two phases of the adversary (before and after the challenge blinded key).

Game 0 (UL-CMBA)

$$\begin{aligned}(\mathsf{sk}_i, \mathsf{pk}_i) &\leftarrow \mathsf{KGen}(1^\lambda), i \in \{0,1\}\\ \tau^* &\leftarrow \mathcal{A}_1^{G,H,\mathsf{bl},\mathsf{Sig}}(1^\lambda)\\ b &\leftarrow\$ \{0,1\}\\ \mathsf{bpk}^* &\leftarrow \mathsf{BlindPK}(\mathsf{pk}_b, \tau^*)\\ b' &\leftarrow \mathcal{A}_2^{G,H,\mathsf{bl},\mathsf{Sig}}(\mathsf{bpk}^*)\end{aligned}$$

$$\mathsf{bl}(\tau) := \begin{cases}\mathsf{BlindPK}(\mathsf{pk}_b, \tau) & \text{if } \tau = \tau^*\\ \mathsf{BlindPK}(\mathsf{pk}_0, \tau) & \text{if } \tau \neq \tau^*\end{cases}$$

$$\mathsf{Sig}(m, \tau) := \begin{cases}\mathsf{Sign}(m, \mathsf{sk}_b, \tau) & \text{if } \tau = \tau^*\\ \mathsf{Sign}(m, \mathsf{sk}_0, \tau) & \text{if } \tau \neq \tau^*\end{cases}$$

Game 0 is the UL-CMBA experiment.

$$\Pr[b' = b \mid \text{Game } 0] = \mathsf{Adv}_{\mathcal{A}}^{\text{UL-CMBA}}(\lambda) \quad (12)$$

By construction, the signature algorithm is

$$\mathsf{Sign}(m, \mathsf{sk}, \tau) = \mathsf{P}^H(\mathsf{BlindPK}(\mathsf{pk}, \tau) \| m, \mathsf{sk}, G(\tau, \mathsf{pk})).$$

In the next hybrid, we remove dependence of the signature algorithm on sk and $G(\tau, \mathsf{pk})$ by using the HVZK simulator for Π which depends only on the first argument.

Game 1

$$\begin{aligned}(\mathsf{sk}_i, \mathsf{pk}_i) &\leftarrow \mathsf{KGen}(1^\lambda), i \in \{0,1\} \\ \tau^* &\leftarrow \mathcal{A}_1^{G,H_\Theta,\mathsf{bl},\mathsf{Sig}}(1^\lambda) \\ b &\leftarrow\!\$\, \{0,1\} \\ \mathsf{bpk}^* &\leftarrow \mathsf{BlindPK}(\mathsf{pk}_b, \tau^*) \\ b' &\leftarrow \mathcal{A}_2^{G,H_\Theta,\mathsf{bl},\mathsf{Sig}}(\mathsf{bpk}^*)\end{aligned}$$

$$\mathsf{bl}(\tau) := \begin{cases}\mathsf{BlindPK}(\mathsf{pk}_b, \tau) & \text{if } \tau = \tau^* \\ \mathsf{BlindPK}(\mathsf{pk}_0, \tau) & \text{if } \tau \neq \tau^*\end{cases}$$

$$\mathsf{Sig}(m, \tau) := \begin{cases}\mathsf{Sim}(\mathsf{BlindPK}(\mathsf{pk}_b, \tau)\|m) & \text{if } \tau = \tau^* \\ \mathsf{Sim}(\mathsf{BlindPK}(\mathsf{pk}_0, \tau)\|m) & \text{if } \tau \neq \tau^*\end{cases}$$

Two changes are introduced in the above game: all calls to Sign are changed to corresponding calls to Sim, and the adversary's oracle H is replaced with a reprogrammed oracle H_Θ. By invoking the zero-knowledge property of Π (Definition 4) for the q_S simulated proofs, we have

$$|\Pr[b' = b \mid \text{Game 1}] - \Pr[b' = b \mid \text{Game 1}]| \leq q_S \cdot \varepsilon_{\text{zk}}(\lambda, q_H) \tag{13}$$

Next, we show how to remove dependence on pk from the symmetric key used to blind the public key. In game 2, whenever $\mathsf{BlindPK}$ is called, it returns $f_{k'}(\mathsf{pk})$ for a random $k' \in \{0,1\}^\lambda$ instead of $f_{G(\tau,\mathsf{pk})}(\mathsf{pk})$. We denote this as $f_\$(\mathsf{pk})$ below.

Game 2

$$\begin{aligned}(\mathsf{sk}_i, \mathsf{pk}_i) &\leftarrow \mathsf{KGen}(1^\lambda), i \in \{0,1\} \\ \tau^* &\leftarrow \mathcal{A}_1^{G,H_\Theta,\mathsf{bl},\mathsf{Sig}}(1^\lambda) \\ b &\leftarrow\!\$\, \{0,1\} \\ \mathsf{bpk}^* &\leftarrow f_\$(\mathsf{pk}_b) \\ b' &\leftarrow \mathcal{A}_2^{G,H_\Theta,\mathsf{bl},\mathsf{Sig}}(\mathsf{bpk}^*)\end{aligned}$$

$$\mathsf{bl}(\tau) := \begin{cases}f_\$(\mathsf{pk}_b) & \text{if } \tau = \tau^* \\ f_\$(\mathsf{pk}_0) & \text{if } \tau \neq \tau^*\end{cases}$$

$$\mathsf{Sig}(m, \tau) := \begin{cases}\mathsf{Sim}(f_\$(\mathsf{pk}_b)\|m) & \text{if } \tau = \tau^* \\ \mathsf{Sim}(f_\$(\mathsf{pk}_0)\|m) & \text{if } \tau \neq \tau^*\end{cases}$$

Since $\mathsf{BlindPK}$ is deterministic, we may assume without loss of generality that the adversary queries the bl oracle at most once per input τ to avoid the need for the oracles to record the keys.

Intuitively, the only way the adversary can detect this change in the behavior of the blinding oracle is if it has queried G on an input containing pk. We use the one-way to hiding technique of [26] (Lemma 5) to make this formal in the context of quantum access to G.

The one-way to hiding lemma allows us to relate the difference in winning probability between games 1 and 2 with the probability of extracting pk from the adversary's random oracle queries. To this end, define $\mathcal{E}^G$ to be an algorithm that simulates the interaction of $\mathcal{A}^{G,H_\Theta,\mathsf{bl},\mathsf{Sig}}$ with the challenger, and that picks one of the quantum queries of $\mathcal{A}$ to G at random, measures this query and outputs the result. Then, invoking Lemma 5 q_B times (once for each blinding query in which $G(\tau, \mathsf{pk})$ is replaced with a random value) implies that

$$|\Pr[b = b' \mid \text{Game 2}] - \Pr[b = b' \mid \text{Game 1}]| \leq 2q_B q_G \sqrt{\Pr[\mathsf{pk} \leftarrow \mathcal{E}^G]} \tag{14}$$

The probability that $\mathcal{E}$ outputs pk is at most the probability that an adversary recovers the plaintext pk from many encryptions of pk under f using different keys. It is trivially upper-bounded by

$$\Pr[\mathsf{pk} \leftarrow \mathcal{E}^G] \leq \mathsf{Adv}_{\mathcal{E}}^{\text{MU-IND}}(\lambda)$$

since one could turn its advantage into one for the MU-IND (Definition 12) game by sampling $\mathsf{pk}_0, \mathsf{pk}_1$, requesting ciphertexts $c_i = \mathsf{Enc}_{k_i}(\mathsf{pk}_b)$, sending $c_1, \ldots, c_n$ to the adversary which returns pk', and testing for $\mathsf{pk}' = \mathsf{pk}_0$.

We now change the blinding oracle again by replacing the real public key pk with a freshly sampled independent public key pk'. In game 3, when the adversary requests the blinding of the key with a seed τ, the challenger samples $k' \leftarrow\$ \{0,1\}^\lambda$ and $\mathsf{pk}' \leftarrow \mathsf{KGen}(1^\lambda)$ and returns $f_{k'}(\mathsf{pk}')$. We denote this as $f_\$(\$)$ in the game below (though pk is not necessarily uniformly distributed).

Game 3

$$\begin{aligned}(\mathsf{sk}_i, \mathsf{pk}_i) &\leftarrow \mathsf{KGen}(1^\lambda), i \in \{0,1\}\\ \tau^* &\leftarrow \mathcal{A}_1^{G, H_\ominus, \mathsf{bl}, \mathsf{Sig}}(1^\lambda)\\ b &\leftarrow\$ \{0,1\}\\ \mathsf{bpk}^* &\leftarrow f_\$(\$)\\ b' &\leftarrow \mathcal{A}_2^{G, H_\ominus, \mathsf{bl}, \mathsf{Sig}}(\mathsf{bpk}^*)\end{aligned} \qquad \begin{aligned}\mathsf{bl}(\tau) &:= f_\$(\$)\\ \mathsf{Sig}(m, \tau) &:= \mathsf{Sim}(f_\$(\$) \| m)\end{aligned}$$

We can relate the probability of success in this game with the multi-user indistinguishability of f_k. In game 3, the blinded keys that the adversary receives are encryptions of pk' under a secret key k' where both pk' and k' are unrelated to pk (and sk). If the adversary's behaviour changes in an observable way between games 2 and 3, then we can turn this into a distinguisher for the MU-IND property of f_k in the following way.

Let $\mathcal{D}$ be the following adversary against the MU-IND game:

- Let q_B be an upper-bound on the number of blinding queries made by $\mathcal{A}$. Sample $q_B + 1$ public keys $\mathsf{pk}_0, \ldots, \mathsf{pk}_n$ and query the MU-IND challenger on $(i, \mathsf{pk}_0, \mathsf{pk}_i)_{i \in [q_B]}$ to get the resulting ciphertexts $c_1, \ldots, c_{q_B}$ (which are either an encryption of pk_0 or pk_i with a key k_i).
- $\mathcal{D}$ now runs $\mathcal{A}$ by acting as the challenger in game 3 and by simulating its blinding oracle as follows: on $\mathcal{A}$'s ith query to bl, reply with c_i.
- Output whatever $\mathcal{A}$ outputs.

If $b = 0$ in the MU-IND game, then every c_i is an encryption of pk_0 and thus $\mathcal{A}$ is playing game 2. If $b = 1$, then each c_i is the encryption of a new public key pk_i, so $\mathcal{A}$ is playing game 3. By the MU-IND property of f_k, we have that

$$|\Pr[b = b' \mid \text{Game 3}] - \Pr[b = b' \mid \text{Game 2}]| \leq \mathsf{Adv}_{\mathcal{D}}^{\text{MU-IND}}(\lambda)$$

In game 3, bpk^* and the two oracles bl and Sig are independent of b. Therefore

$$\Pr[b = b' \mid \text{Game 3}] = \frac{1}{2}\ .$$

Summing up all the errors, we have

$$\mathsf{Adv}_{\mathcal{A}}^{\text{UL-CMBA}}(\lambda) \leq \frac{1}{2} + \mathsf{Adv}_{\mathcal{D}}^{\text{MU-IND}}(\lambda) + 2q_B q_H \sqrt{\mathsf{Adv}_{\mathcal{E}}^{\text{MU-IND}}(\lambda)} + q_S \cdot \varepsilon_{\mathsf{zk}}(\lambda, q_H) \ . \quad (15)$$

□

4 The blHelium Signature Scheme with Key Blinding

We now present our blHelium protocol, which follows Construction 1 instantiated with the AES block cipher and the Helium proof system [21]. We begin by giving a brief overview of the Helium signature scheme before describing the changes we make to equip it with key blinding, along with parameter choices. The detailed Helium proof system can be found in [21]. We prove its QROM security in Appendix C.

4.1 Overview of Helium

The scheme takes place over seven *phases*, representing the different message flows in the identification scheme prior to being converted to a signature scheme via the Fiat-Shamir transform (i.e., Phase 1 represents the first prover message, Phase 2 the first challenge, etc.). A high-level description of the proof system is as follows:

- **Committing to MPC Party Seeds.** Each MPC party's randomness is derived from a single seed which is committed to. The protocol runs through a distributed computation of AES, with each party holding a share of the secret key.
- **Checking of the MPC Computation.** Proving that the AES circuit was evaluated correctly means verifying correctness of the shares at each step of the MPC protocol. Every linear operation in the AES circuit can be evaluated locally. The non-linear S-box (a field inverse operation) is done efficiently by injecting shares of s and t such that $s \cdot t = 1$.
- **Challenging the Checking Protocol.** The injected shares of (s_i, t_i) must be checked for consistency. This is done efficiently by using polynomials S and T interpolated such that $S(i) = s_i$ and $T(i) = t_i$. The prover distributes shares of $P = S \cdot T$ to the parties. To verify correctness of the polynomials, a test $P(r) = S(r) \cdot T(r)$ is performed for a random r.

Verification consists of reconstructing the view of each MPC party whose seed was opened, testing for consistency. For a more thorough description of the protocol, we refer the reader to [21].

4.2 The blHelium Signature Scheme

At a high level, the blHelium signature scheme with key blinding follows Construction 1. We add a procedure to blind public keys and modify the signature and verification protocols of Helium to accommodate signing and verification according to blinded keys.

We describe a 128-bit version of blHelium to provide a direct comparison with Helium (which is implemented for 128-bit AES). However, this parameter set is not secure enough for most scenarios. We elaborate on this below before describing the 256-bit version, which is similar, but uses 256-bit AES and 4 blocks of 16 bytes instead of 2. The 128-bit blHelium consists of the following algorithms:

- KGen: The secret key sk is selected at random from the set of keys such that the circuits for $\text{AES}_{\mathsf{sk}}(\mathbf{0})$ and $\text{AES}_{\mathsf{sk}}(\mathbf{1})$ have no s-boxes which receives the 0 byte input[8]. The public key consists of $\mathsf{pk} = (\text{AES}_{\mathsf{sk}}(\mathbf{0}), \text{AES}_{\mathsf{sk}}(\mathbf{1}))$.
- BlindPK(pk, τ): computes $\mathsf{bk} \leftarrow G(\tau, \mathsf{pk}, t)$ and increments t until the circuits for $\text{AES}_{\mathsf{bk}}(\mathsf{pk}_0)$ and $\text{AES}_{\mathsf{bk}}(\mathsf{pk}_1)$ have no s-boxes which receives the 0 byte input. The blinded public key is $\mathsf{bpk} = (\text{AES}_{\mathsf{bk}}(\mathsf{pk}_0), \text{AES}_{\mathsf{bk}}(\mathsf{pk}_1))$.
- Sign(sk, τ, m): computes the blinding keys (bk, bpk) as in BlindPK and runs the Helium NIZKPoK to prove knowledge of sk and bk such that $\mathsf{bpk} = (\text{AES}_{\mathsf{bk}}(\text{AES}_{\mathsf{sk}}(\mathbf{0})), \text{AES}_{\mathsf{bk}}(\text{AES}_{\mathsf{sk}}(\mathbf{1})))$.
- Verify(bpk, m, σ): runs the verification protocol for the NIZKPoK.

4.3 blHelium Parameters and Performance

We consider two parameter sets for the blHelium scheme. The first uses the 128 bit AES block cipher as in Helium, but it suffers from some vulnerabilities. The 256 bits variants of AES offers a secure instantiation of blHelium.

128-bit blHelium. In the context of quantum adversaries 128-bit AES is not enough given that the Grover's unstructured search algorithm halves the security parameter asymptotically. More concretely, recent estimates of the resources required to break AES128 using Grover's algorithm have come up with a circuit depth in the order of 2^{80} [19].

However, even in the classical setting there are issues with instantiating Construction 1 with an 128-bit key cipher. An attacker only needs to find $\tau \neq \tau'$ that lead to the same blinded key to cheat the EUF-CMBA game. For Construction 1, this is at most as hard as finding a collision to a 128-bit hash function, which by the birthday bound is of complexity 2^{64} against classical attacks and even lower against quantum attacks. Note that strictly speaking this is a break of Definition 2, but the resulting forgery is valid for a message and blinded public key pair that was already produced by the signing oracle. All that the adversary has achieved is to find another blinding parameter which leads to the same blinded public key. Depending on the context, this might not be considered a security break, or it might be infeasible to carry out such an attack if, for example, the space of admissible τ is small.

We describe here our scheme based on 128-bit AES. We have implemented this version to provide a direct comparison with Helium (which is only available

[8] This step is necessary for the optimisation that computes the s-box as a field inverse.

for 128-bit AES). We encrypt two different plaintexts, first with sk, and then with bk. The choice of plaintext is arbitrary but must be fixed for all users – for simplicity we have chosen the all 0 and all 1 plaintext. This requires a total of two AES128 key schedules (which takes $2 \times 40 = 80$ s-boxes) and four AES128 encryptions (which takes $4 \times 160 = 640$ s-boxes) for a total of 720 s-boxes. Recall that s-box computation in the MPC protocol are checked using polynomial interpolation. Since the degree of each polynomial is limited by the field of size 128, we split these into 6 sets of polynomials $(S_i, T_i, P_i)_{i \in [6]}$, each being used to prove correctness of $720/6 = 120$ s-box computations. In contrast, Helium requires two sets of polynomials.

Helium and blHelium only use a subset of possible keys, since we restrict to AES circuits which have no substitution box that receives the 0 byte as input. Using the methodology of [8] which assumes the input to each s-box to be a uniformly random element of $\mathbb{F}_{2^8}$, we can estimate the fraction of keys for which the AES circuit has no 0-input s-box as $0.457 \approx (1 - \frac{1}{256})^{200}$. Therefore, the number of admissible keys is approximately 2^{127} (i.e. the key space is reduced roughly by half). Note also that for this reason, the BlindPK of blHelium presented in Sect. 4.2 differs slightly from Construction 1. It includes an additional parameter t that is incremented until $G(\tau, \mathsf{pk}, t)$ yields an admissible key.

We have implemented our 128-bit blHelium protocol as a fork of the Helium source code and have compared its per performance with Helium. Our focus in benchmarking is on signing and verification: key generation and blinding consist of only a handful AES operations and thus do not represent a significant burden. The sizes of signatures and the CPU time for signing and verification are reported in Fig. 1 and compared to Helium. We observe that signature and verification are 2× to 3× slower than Helium and signature size are 2× to 3× larger. This is to be expected from the fact that the circuit form our blHelium scheme evaluates 720 s-boxes instead of 200 for Helium (a factor of 3.6×).

	Helium+AES128			blHelium+AES128		
(N, M)	Sign	Verify	Size	Sign	Verify	Size
(17, 31)	8.169	7.605	17 580	16.816	14.086	52 424
(19, 30)	8.088	7.507	17 016	17.704	15.690	50 736
(31, 26)	8.342	7.810	14 760	20.095	17.569	43 984
(57, 22)	9.918	9.370	12 856	26.391	24.118	37 584
(107, 19)	12.513	12.448	11 420	38.459	35.607	32 776
(139, 18)	14.267	14.196	11 112	44.906	43.037	31 344
(185, 17)	17.881	17.900	10 500	55.109	52.827	29 608
(255, 16)	21.636	21.593	9 888	67.647	67.490	27 872
(371, 15)	28.132	28.698	9 516	90.303	88.953	26 376

Fig. 1. Benchmarking (signature sizes in bytes and signing and verification times in milliseconds) information for our implementation of blinded Helium and comparison with Helium for different parameters N and M representing the number of MPC parties and the number of repetitions, respectively. Timing is averaged over 100 iterations.

256-bit blHelium. The 256-bit version of blHelium is very similar to the 128-bit one, so we focus on the distinctions. It uses AES256, in which keys are composed of 32 bytes and the cipher operates on blocks of 16 bytes. Since we are encrypting twice for blinded public keys, the total key space is composed of 64 bytes. As explained in Sect. 3.2, we want the plaintext size to match the key size, therefore the AES256 version of blHelium uses 4 blocks of 16 bytes. This means the signature algorithm runs a total of 2 key schedules and 8 encryptions as part of the MPCitH computation. Encryption in AES256 consists of 14 rounds where each round performs an s-box on each of the 16 byte of the state for a total of 224 s-boxes per encryption circuit. Each key schedule consists of 56 s-boxes. Hence, a grand total of $2 \times 56 + 8 \times 224 = 1904$ s-boxes are involved in the circuit we need to run as part of the MPCitH proof. To prove knowledge of preimages for such a circuit using the Helium proof system, one would require $\lceil 1904/127 \rceil = 15$ polynomials to check the multiplication triples. To prevent division by 0, we can again use rejection sampling on the keys and estimate using the methods of [8] that roughly $\frac{1}{3}$ of keys are valid for the encryption circuit (that is, the circuit contains no 0-input s-box) for a loss of roughly 1.4 bits of security.

5 Conclusion and Open Questions

Our generic construction provides key blinding to any MPCitH signature schemes based on symmetric cryptography. They only rely on well-studied primitives and produce short public and blinded keys, which can be used as identifiers in anonymity networks. We have provided an implementation based on the Helium signature scheme that is ready to be experimented with.

A way to avoid introducing the relation $R_{G,f}$ in the proof of unforgeability would be to set the parameters such that key generation has a *lossy mode*, for example by having the block size larger than the key size. Would this lossy generator preserve the key-one-wayness of the encryption scheme? Is the tighter security reduction worth the increased overhead of running more encryption circuits?

We have not considered strong unforgeability for our construction, but we conjecture that it is implied by the concept of *computationally unique responses* for interactive proofs, which is known to imply strong unforgeability for Fiat-Shamir-based signatures [12,23,27].

Acknowledgments. We thank Thomas Bellebaum for spotting the attack against the EUF-CMBA game by finding collisions over τ which was not handled in a previous version of this paper. We also thank an anonymous reviewer for noticing an issue with the 128-bit parameters.

A Additional Preliminaries

A.1 Security Definitions for Symmetric Primitives

Definition 8 (One-Way Function). *A function $F : \mathcal{X} \to \mathcal{Y}$ is one-way (OWF) if for all QPT adversary $\mathcal{A}$,*

$$\Pr[F(x) = y \mid y \in_R \mathcal{Y}, x \leftarrow \mathcal{A}(y)] \leq \mathsf{negl}(\lambda) \ . \tag{16}$$

Definition 9 (Pseudorandom Function). *A family of function $\{f_k : \mathcal{X} \to \mathcal{Y}\}_{k\in\{0,1\}^\lambda}$ is a pseudorandom function family (PRF) if for all QPT oracle adversary $\mathcal{A}^{\mathcal{O}(\cdot)}$,*

$$\left|\Pr[\mathcal{A}^{f_k(\cdot)}(1^\lambda) = 1 \mid k \in_R \{0,1\}^\lambda] - \Pr[\mathcal{A}^{F(\cdot)}(1^\lambda) = 1]\right| \leq \mathsf{negl}(\lambda) \tag{17}$$

where F is a uniformly random function.

Definition 10 (Key-One-Way Function). *A family of function $\{f_k : \mathcal{X} \to \mathcal{Y}\}_{k\in\{0,1\}^\lambda}$ is key-one-way (KOW) if for all QPT adversary $\mathcal{A}$,*

$$\Pr[f_{k'}(x) = f_k(x) \mid k \in_R \{0,1\}^\lambda, x \in_R \mathcal{X}, k' \leftarrow \mathcal{A}(x, f_k(x))] \leq \mathsf{negl}(\lambda) \tag{18}$$

Definition 11 (Key Collision Resistant Function). *A family of function $\{f_k : \mathcal{X} \to \mathcal{Y}\}_{k\in\{0,1\}^\lambda}$ is key-collision-resistant (KCR) if for all QPT adversary $\mathcal{A}$,*

$$\Pr[f_{k'}(x) = f_k(x) \wedge k' \neq k \mid x \in_R \mathcal{X}, (k,k') \leftarrow \mathcal{A}(x)] \leq \mathsf{negl}(\lambda) \tag{19}$$

The following lemma establishes a relation between key-collision-resistance and key-one-wayness.

Lemma 4 ([5]). *Let $\mathcal{F} = \{f_k : \{0,1\}^n \to \{0,1\}^n\}_{k\in\{0,1\}^n}$ be a family of functions. Assuming there exist key collisions for $\mathcal{F}$ and that $\mathcal{F}$ is key-collision-resistant, then $\mathcal{F}$ is key-one-way.*

Definition 12. *Let $\{f_k : \mathcal{X} \to \mathcal{Y}\}_k$ be a family of permutations. The* multi-user indistinguishability *(MU-IND) experiment of parameter n is defined as follows:*

- *The challenger samples n keys $r_1, \ldots, r_n \leftarrow\$ \{0,1\}^\lambda$ and a bit $b \leftarrow\$ \{0,1\}$.*
- *The adversary may send queries of the form $(i, m_0, m_1) \in [n] \times \mathcal{X} \times \mathcal{X}$ to which the challenger responds to with $f_{r_i}(m_b)$.*
- *The adversary outputs a bit b'.*

The advantage of an adversary $\mathcal{A}$ in the MU-IND game is $\mathsf{Adv}_{\mathcal{A}}^{\text{MU-IND}}(\lambda) = \left|\Pr[b = b'] - \frac{1}{2}\right|$.

Multi-user security was studied in the context of public-key encryption in [4] where the authors found that it is implied by IND-CPA up to some loss in security. Their results also apply to the private-key setting, thus if we assume that AES, our chosen cipher for blHelium, satisfies chosen plaintext indistinguishability, then it is secure according to Definition 12.

A.2 Quantum Random Oracle Model

Theorem 3 (Measure-and-reprogram [12,13]**).** *Let $\mathcal{X}$ and $\mathcal{Y}$ be finite non-empty sets. There exists a black-box two-stage quantum algorithm $\mathcal{S}$ with the following property. Let $\mathcal{A}$ be an arbitrary oracle quantum algorithm that makes q queries to a uniformly random $H : \mathcal{X} \to \mathcal{Y}$ and that outputs some $x \in \mathcal{X}$ and a (possibly quantum) output z. Then, the two-stage algorithm $\mathcal{S}^{\mathcal{A}}$ outputs some $x \in \mathcal{X}$ in the first stage and, upon a random $\Theta \in \mathcal{Y}$ as input to the second stage, a (possibly quantum) output z, so that for any $x_\circ \in \mathcal{X}$ and any (possibly quantum) predicate V:*

$$\Pr_{\Theta}\big[x = x_\circ \wedge V(x, \Theta, z) : (x, z) \leftarrow \langle \mathcal{S}^{\mathcal{A}}, \Theta\rangle\big]$$
$$\geq \frac{1}{(2q+1)^2} \Pr_{H}\big[x = x_\circ \wedge V(x, H(x), z) : (x, z) \leftarrow \mathcal{A}^{H}\big] .$$

Furthermore, $\mathcal{S}$ runs in time polynomial in q, $\log|\mathcal{X}|$ and $\log|\mathcal{Y}|$.

Lemma 5 (One-Way to Hiding [26]**).** *Let $H : \mathcal{X} \to \mathcal{Y}$ be a quantumly accessible random oracle and let $\mathcal{A}^H$ be an adversary that makes at most q queries to H. Let $\mathcal{E}^H$ be an algorithm that picks $i \in [q]$ and $y \in \mathcal{Y}$ at random, runs $\mathcal{A}^H(x, y)$ until it's ith query, measures the input of the query in the computational basis and outputs the measurement outcome.*

$$\big|\Pr[1 \leftarrow \mathcal{A}^H(x, H(x))] - \Pr[1 \leftarrow \mathcal{A}^H(x, y)]\big| \leq 2q \cdot \sqrt{\Pr[x \leftarrow \mathcal{E}^H(x)]} \ . \quad (20)$$

Lemma 6 (Quantum Collision Finding [28]**).** *Let $H : \{0,1\}^* \to \{0,1\}^\lambda$ be a random oracle and let $\mathcal{A}^H$ be a QPT adversary that makes at most q queries to H. Then*

$$\Pr[H(x) = H(x') \wedge x \neq x' \mid (x, x') \leftarrow \mathcal{A}^H(1^\lambda)] \leq O(q^3 2^{-\lambda}) \quad (21)$$

B Additional Proofs

B.1 Proof of Lemma 3

We proceed as with the argument presented in Sect. 3.3, but use the measure-and-reprogram technique (Theorem 3) to insert s into a random oracle query. Let $\mathcal{A}^G$ be an adversary against $R_{G,f}$. Since Theorem 3 asks the adversary to output the point x which is reprogrammed, we define $\hat{\mathcal{A}}^G$ that on input y, runs $(\tau, k, k') \leftarrow \mathcal{A}^G(y)$ and outputs $x = (\tau, y)$ along with (τ, k, k'). Let $\mathcal{S}^{\hat{\mathcal{A}}}$ be the quantum algorithm from Theorem 3 for $\hat{\mathcal{A}}^G$. The reduction $\mathcal{R}$ for inverting F proceeds as follows:

1. On input $z \in \mathrm{Im}F$, sample s uniformly at random and set $y = f_s^{-1}(z)$.
2. Run the first stage of $\mathcal{S}^{\hat{\mathcal{A}}}$ on input y to get a point x.
3. Run the second stage of $\mathcal{S}^{\hat{\mathcal{A}}}$ with input s.
4. When $\mathcal{S}^{\hat{\mathcal{A}}}$ produces an output (x, τ, k, k'), output (k, k').

We now show that this reduction inverts F with probability polynomially related to the probability that $\mathcal{A}^G$ breaks relation $R_{G,f}$. Let $V_y(s,k,k')$ be the predicate that returns 1 if and only if $f_s(y) = f_{k'}(f_k(\mathsf{inp}))$ such that $(y,(\tau,k,k')) \in R_{G,f} \iff V_y(G(\tau,y),k,k') = 1$. Then by Theorem 3,

$$\begin{aligned}
&\Pr[z = f_{k'}(f_k(\mathsf{inp})) \mid (k,k') \leftarrow \mathcal{R}(z)] \\
&= \Pr[x = (\tau,y) \wedge f_s(y) = f_{k'}(f_k(\mathsf{inp})) \mid (x,\tau,k,k') \leftarrow \langle \mathcal{S}^{\hat{\mathcal{A}}}(y), s\rangle] \\
&= \Pr[x = (\tau,y) \wedge V_y(s,k,k') = 1 \mid (x,\tau,k,k') \leftarrow \langle \mathcal{S}^{\hat{\mathcal{A}}}(y), s\rangle] \\
&\geq \frac{1}{(2q_G+1)^2} \Pr[x = (\tau,y) \wedge V_y(G(x),k,k') = 1 \mid (x,\tau,k,k') \leftarrow \hat{\mathcal{A}}^G(y)]
\end{aligned}$$

where q_G is the number of queries to G made by $\hat{\mathcal{A}}^G$. Ignoring the inverse polynomial factor, the above probability corresponds to

$$\begin{aligned}
&\Pr[V_y(G(\tau,y),k,k') = 1 \mid (\tau,k,k') \leftarrow \mathcal{A}^G(y)] \\
&= \Pr[f_{G(\tau,y)}(y) = f_{k'}(f_k(\mathsf{inp})) \mid (\tau,k,k') \leftarrow \mathcal{A}^G(y)] \\
&= \Pr[(y,(\tau,k,k')) \in R_{G,f} \mid (\tau,k,k') \leftarrow \mathcal{A}^G(y)]
\end{aligned}$$

which is the advantage of $\mathcal{A}^G$ for finding a witness for relation $R_{G,f}$. □

C QROM Security of blHelium

In the following, we refer to the "Helium proof system" as the 7–message interactive proof from which the Helium signature scheme [21] is obtained through the Fiat-Shamir transform. The verifier checks the validity of the commitments, recreates the views of the MPC parties using the seeds, and verifies that they are consistent with the MPC protocol. We refer to [21] for the full details of the verifier.

C.1 Online Extractability

Our proof relies on online extractability in the QROM. The following Theorem is the online extractability with early extraction result (Corollary 4 in [15] with the simplified bound from Theorem 3).

Theorem 4 (Online Extractability with Early Extraction [15]**).** *Let $H : \{0,1\}^* \to \{0,1\}^n$ be a random function. There exists an extractable RO-simulator $\mathcal{S}$, with interfaces $\mathcal{S}.RO$ and $\mathcal{S}.E$, that satisfies the following properties. Let $\mathcal{A}$ be a two-round polynomial-time oracle adversary that outputs $t_1,\ldots,t_\ell$ in the first round and $x_1,\ldots,x_\ell \in \mathcal{X}$ and W after the second round, resulting in a transcript $[\boldsymbol{t},\boldsymbol{x},H(\boldsymbol{x}),W]_{\mathcal{A}^H}$. Let $[\boldsymbol{t},\boldsymbol{x},\boldsymbol{h},W]_{G^{\mathcal{A}}_{\mathcal{S}}}$ be the transcript where, when $\mathcal{A}$ outputs t_i, $\mathcal{S}.E$ is queried on t_i to obtain $\hat{x}_i \in \mathcal{X} \cup \{\perp\}$ and when*

$\mathcal{A}$ halts, $\mathcal{S}.RO$ is queried on $\mathcal{A}$'s outputs x_i to generate h_i. There are negligible functions δ_1 and δ_2 such that

$$\Pr_{G_{\mathcal{S}}^{\mathcal{A}}}[\exists i : x_i \neq \hat{x}_i \wedge h_i = t_i] \leq \delta_1 \tag{22}$$

and

$$\delta([\boldsymbol{t}, \boldsymbol{x}, H(\boldsymbol{x}), W]_{\mathcal{A}^H}, [\boldsymbol{t}, \boldsymbol{x}, \boldsymbol{h}, W]_{G_{\mathcal{S}}^{\mathcal{A}}}) \leq \delta_2 \tag{23}$$

for $\delta_1 + \delta_2 \leq 34\ell q/\sqrt{2^n} + 2365q^3/2^n$ where q is the number of oracle queries.

Note that [14] contains generic results about the online extractability of non-interactive proofs in the QROM. These results are framed in the context of three-message protocols. It is directly clear if they generalize to more rounds, so we present here a direct proof that Helium is online-extractable.

Theorem 5. *Assuming* commit *is a random oracle, then the* Helium *proof system instantiated with a post-quantum one-way function F is an online extractable proof system (Definition 5) for the relation $R_F = \{(x, w) : x = F(w)\}$ with extraction error ε_{ex} and simulation error ε_{sim} satisfying*

$$\varepsilon_{\text{sim}}(n, q) + \varepsilon_{\text{ex}}(n, q) \leq 34M \cdot N \cdot q/\sqrt{2^n} + 2365q^3/2^n + \max_{M_1, M_2, M_3} \left(\frac{2\,L-2}{|\mathbb{K}|}\right)^{M_1} \cdot \left(\frac{1}{2^8}\right)^{M_2} \cdot \left(\frac{1}{N}\right)^{M_3} \tag{24}$$

against quantum polynomial-time adversaries making q queries to commit *where n is the bit size of commitments and where $M_1 + M_2 + M_3 = M$ is the number of parallel repetitions.*

Proof. A quantum adversary $\mathcal{A}$ against Helium has quantum superposition access to the commitment oracle H_c = commit. We need to construct a knowledge extractor $\mathcal{E}$ whose success probability in producing a witness is related to $\mathcal{A}$'s probability of cheating the protocol. The extractor will simulate the random oracle H_c with the online extractable oracle $\mathcal{S}$ of [15] specified in Theorem 4. The extractor will run $\mathcal{A}$ by replacing H_c with the oracle interface $\mathcal{S}.RO$. After the prover's first message σ_1, $\mathcal{E}$ will use the extraction interface $\mathcal{S}.E$ on every commitment $\mathsf{com}_e^{(i)}$ for $e \in [M]$ and $i \in [N]$ to get either an oracle input $(\mathsf{salt}, e, i, \mathsf{seed}_e^{(i)})$ or a symbol $\perp$ which means that $\mathcal{A}$ did not query H_c on this input. Then, $\mathcal{E}$ proceeds in a similar fashion as the extractor of [21, Appendix A] in their proof of unforgeability of BN++ to compute the inputs and shares of the MPC parties.

In more details, when $\mathcal{A}$ produces its first message σ_1, $\mathcal{E}$ does the following:

- parse σ_1 as $(\mathsf{salt}, ((,_e^{(i)}, \mathsf{ct}_e^{(i)})_{i \in [N]}, \ldots),$
- for $i \in [N]$ and $e \in [M]$, use the $\mathcal{S}.E$ interface on input $,_e^{(i)}$ to get either $\hat{s}_e^{(i)}$ or $\perp$.
- For each $i \in [N]$ and $e \in [M]$ such that $\mathsf{seed}_e^{(i)}$ is successfully extracted, compute the input shares $\mathsf{sk}_e^{(i)}$ of party i for repetition e using the seed contained in $\hat{s}_e^{(i)}$.

– If there is an $e \in [M]$ for which $\mathsf{sk}_e = \sum_i \mathsf{sk}_e^{(i)}$ is a preimage for pk, output sk_e. Otherwise, output $\perp$.

We now show that the probability that $\mathcal{E}$ outputs a preimage sk is non-negligible if $\mathcal{A}$ produces a forgery with non-negligible probability.

We let $V(\boldsymbol{\sigma}, \boldsymbol{h})$ denote the probabilistic event that V accepts the transcript $(\boldsymbol{\sigma}, \boldsymbol{h})$. We denote by $\boldsymbol{s}_{h_3}$ the set of seeds announced when the challenge is $h_3 = (\bar{i}_e)_{e\in[M]}$, i.e. $\boldsymbol{s}_{h_3} = \{(\mathsf{salt}, e, i, \mathsf{seed}_e^{(i)}) \mid e \in [M], i \neq \bar{i}_e\}$. Similarly, let $\boldsymbol{y}_{h_3}$ denote the commitments to the revealed seeds; i.e. $\boldsymbol{y}_{h_3} = H_c(\boldsymbol{s}_{h_3})$.

We first bound the difference in probability between an execution with H_c and an execution with $\mathcal{S}.RO$.

$$
\begin{aligned}
\Pr[V(\boldsymbol{\sigma}, \boldsymbol{h})] &= \Pr[V(\boldsymbol{\sigma}, \boldsymbol{h}) \wedge H_c(\boldsymbol{s}_{h_3}) = \boldsymbol{y}_{h_3}] \\
&\leq \Pr[V(\boldsymbol{\sigma}, \boldsymbol{h}) \wedge \mathcal{S}.RO(\boldsymbol{s}_{h_3}) = \boldsymbol{y}_{h_3}] \\
&\quad + \Pr[H_c(\boldsymbol{s}_{h_3}) = \boldsymbol{y}_{h_3} \wedge H_c(\boldsymbol{s}_{h_3}) \neq \mathcal{S}.RO(\boldsymbol{s}_{h_3})] \\
&\leq \Pr[V(\boldsymbol{\sigma}, \boldsymbol{h}) \wedge \mathcal{S}.RO(\boldsymbol{s}_{h_3}) = \boldsymbol{y}_{h_3}] + \delta_1
\end{aligned}
$$

where δ_1 is the negl4igible error term of (22).

Next, we bound the probability that the values $\hat{s}_e^{(i)}$ obtained through the $\mathcal{S}.E$ interface differ from the committed values.

$$
\begin{aligned}
&\Pr[V(\boldsymbol{\sigma}, \boldsymbol{h}) \wedge \mathcal{S}.RO(\boldsymbol{s}_{h_3}) = \boldsymbol{y}_{h_3}] \\
&\leq \Pr[V(\boldsymbol{\sigma}, \boldsymbol{h}) \wedge \mathcal{S}.RO(\boldsymbol{s}_{h_3}) = \boldsymbol{y}_{h_3} \wedge \mathcal{S}.E(\boldsymbol{y}_{h_3}) = \boldsymbol{s}_{h_3}] \\
&\quad + \Pr[\mathcal{S}.RO(\boldsymbol{s}_{h_3}) = \boldsymbol{y}_{h_3} \wedge \mathcal{S}.E(\boldsymbol{y}_{h_3}) \neq \boldsymbol{s}_{h_3}] \\
&\leq \Pr[V(\boldsymbol{\sigma}, \boldsymbol{h}) \wedge \mathcal{S}.RO(\boldsymbol{s}_{h_3}) = \boldsymbol{y}_{h_3} \wedge \mathcal{S}.E(\boldsymbol{y}_{h_3}) = \boldsymbol{s}_{h_3}] + \delta_2 \\
&= \Pr[V(\boldsymbol{\sigma}, \boldsymbol{h}) \wedge \hat{\boldsymbol{s}}_{h_3} = \boldsymbol{s}_{h_3}] + \delta_2
\end{aligned}
$$

where $\hat{\boldsymbol{s}}_{h_3} = \mathcal{S}.E(\boldsymbol{y}_{h_3})$. We again take note of δ_2 and add it at the end.

The expression $\Pr[V(\boldsymbol{\sigma}, \boldsymbol{h}) \wedge \hat{\boldsymbol{s}}_{h_3} = \boldsymbol{s}_{h_3}]$ corresponds to the probability that V accepts when the committed seeds are the values $\hat{s}_e^{(i)}$ extracted by $\mathcal{E}$ through $\mathcal{S}.E$. Note that the prover sends $N \cdot M$ commitments $y_e^{(i)}$, so the values $\hat{s}_e^{(i)}$ are well defined for each $(i, e) \in [N] \times [M]$. We let $\mathsf{sk} \leftarrow \mathcal{E}$ denote the event that the seeds $\hat{s}_e^{(i)}$ allow $\mathcal{E}$ to compute the shares of the witness sk and $\perp \leftarrow \mathcal{E}$ its complement (when $\mathcal{E}$ outputs $\perp$). We have

$$
\begin{aligned}
&\Pr[V(\boldsymbol{\sigma}, \boldsymbol{h}) \wedge \hat{\boldsymbol{s}}_{h_3} = \boldsymbol{s}_{h_3}] \leq \\
&\quad \Pr[\mathsf{sk} \leftarrow \mathcal{E}] + \Pr[V(\boldsymbol{\sigma}, \boldsymbol{h}) \wedge \hat{\boldsymbol{s}}_{h_3} = \boldsymbol{s}_{h_3} \mid \perp \leftarrow \mathcal{E}] \ .
\end{aligned}
$$

We now look at this last probability that the verifier accepts when the extractor is unable to reconstruct a witness from the MPC shares.

Recall that the verifier recomputes the view of each party in the MPC protocol to the exception of the excluded party $\bar{i}$. Since $\hat{\boldsymbol{s}}_{h_3} = \boldsymbol{s}_{h_3}$, it computes those views using the extracted seeds $\hat{s}_e^{(i)}$. If $\mathcal{E}$ outputs $\perp$, then for every e it holds that the key $\hat{\mathsf{sk}}_e = \sum_i \hat{\mathsf{sk}}_e^{(i)}$ expanded from the seed $\hat{s}_e^{(i)}$ is not a valid preimage.

This means that at least one of the views computed by the verifier is inconsistent (i.e. that party cheated). In this case the verifier accepts if one of three things happen:

1. the prover injects invalid polynomials S, T and P (such that $S \cdot T \neq P$); or
2. the prover injects invalid multiplication triples; or
3. the view of the inconsistent party is not opened.

There are M parallel repetitions which must pass verification and the prover may try to cheat in a different round in each repetition. We analyze the probability of each event below. The probability that the prover cheats in all M repetitions corresponds to the *trivial* cheating probability in the proof of [15]. At this point, the rest of the analysis is entirely classical and is very similar to the proof of [21] and to other proofs of soundness for multi-round interactive proofs. We bound the probability that the verifier accepts when the MPC shares are computed using the extracted seeds $\hat{s}_e^{(i)}$, conditioned on the extraction failing.

Cheating the First Challenge. The first challenge h_1 is used to test the checking polynomials. In Helium, there are two checking polynomials P_1 and P_2 since there are not enough field elements in $\mathbb{F}_{2^8}$ to interpolate a single polynomial with the desired degree. For other one-way functions, there might be more polynomials, for example in blHelium, we use a total of 6 checking polynomials since we are effectively applying 4 AES circuits (see Sect. 4.3 for details). Let n_p denote the number of checking polynomials and C the total count of field inverse in the circuit such that the degree of each polynomial is $L = \lceil C/n_p \rceil$. By the Schwartz-Zippel Lemma, the probability that a random point R_e satisfies $S_e(R_e) \cdot T_e(R_e) - P_e(R_e) = 0$ is at most $\frac{2L-2}{|\mathbb{K}|}$ where $\mathbb{K}$ is the extension field of $\mathbb{F}_{2^8}$. The challenge h_1 is parsed as $(R_e)_{e \in [M]}$ where for each e, R_e is used to check that $S \cdot T = P$ by checking that $S(R_e) \cdot T(R_e) = P(R_e)$. If we let M_1 denote the number of parallel repetitions e for which the prover cheats in round 1, the probability that the adversary isn't caught is at most

$$\left(\frac{2L-2}{|\mathbb{K}|} \right)^{M_1} . \tag{25}$$

Cheating the Second Challenge. The second challenge h_2 is used to challenge the multiplication triples used to check $S_e(R_e) \cdot T_e(R_e) = P_e(R_e)$. The Helium protocol uses a dot-product checking protocol, which has soundness $1/|\mathbb{F}_{2^8}|$. If we let M_2 denote the number of repetitions where the adversary cheats in the second round, its probability of passing verification is at most

$$\left(\frac{1}{2^8} \right)^{M_2} .$$

Cheating the Third Challenge. The third challenge is used to challenge the views of the MPC protocol. If the prover did not cheat in any of the previous two rounds, then there is at least one party whose view is inconsistent with that of the others. The prover can cheat in this round if the inconsistent view is not challenged by the verifier. This occurs with probability $\frac{1}{N}$. There are $M_3 = M - M_1 - M_2$ repetitions where the adversary attempts to cheat in the last round. So the probability of success in this round is

$$\left(\frac{1}{N}\right)^{M_3} \tag{26}$$

To complete the proof, we add all the error terms and obtain the bound

$$\Pr[V(\boldsymbol{\sigma}, \boldsymbol{h}) = 1] \leq \Pr[\mathsf{sk} \leftarrow \mathcal{E}] + \delta_1 + \delta_2 + \max_{M_1, M_2, M_3} \left(\frac{2\,L-2}{|\mathbb{K}|}\right)^{M_1} \cdot \left(\frac{1}{|\mathbb{F}_{2^8}|}\right)^{M_2} \cdot \left(\frac{1}{N}\right)^{M_3}$$

where the bound $\delta_1 + \delta_2 \leq 34\ell q/\sqrt{2^n} + 2365q^3/2^n$ is given by Theorem 4. Since our extractor extracts $\ell = M \cdot N$ points, the Theorem statement follows. □

C.2 Simulation Soundness

The Helium signature scheme is obtained by applying the Fiat-Shamir transform on the Helium proof system. Simulation-soundness of the Fiat-Shamir transform in the QROM was first shown by Unruh [27, Theorems 22 and 24 of the full version]. More precisely, Unruh showed that if a 3-message public-coin proof system is sound (respectively extractable), then the non-interactive proof system obtained by applying the Fiat-Shamir transform is simulation-sound (respectively simulation-sound extractable). It was observed in [12] that Unruh's result extends to Fiat-Shamir applied to multi-round interactive proofs.

References

1. Baum, C., et al.: Publicly verifiable zero-knowledge and post-quantum signatures from VOLE-in-the-head. In: Handschuh, H., Lysyanskaya, A. (eds.) Advances in Cryptology – CRYPTO 2023, pp. 581–615. Springer, Cham (2023). https://doi.org/10.1007/978-3-031-38554-4_19
2. Baum, C., de Saint Guilhem, C.D., Kales, D., Orsini, E., Scholl, P., Zaverucha, G.: Banquet: short and fast signatures from AES. In: Garay, J.A. (ed.) Public-Key Cryptography – PKC 2021, pp. 266–297. LNCS. Springer, Cham (2021). https://doi.org/10.1007/978-3-030-75245-3_11
3. Baum, C., Nof, A.: Concretely-efficient zero-knowledge arguments for arithmetic circuits and their application to lattice-based cryptography. In: Kiayias, A., Kohlweiss, M., Wallden, P., Zikas, V. (eds.) PKC 2020. LNCS, vol. 12110, pp. 495–526. Springer, Cham (2020). https://doi.org/10.1007/978-3-030-45374-9_17
4. Bellare, M., Boldyreva, A., Micali, S.: Public-key encryption in a multi-user setting: security proofs and improvements. In: Preneel, B. (ed.) Advances in Cryptology—EUROCRYPT 2000, pp. 259–274. LNCS. Springer, Heidelberg (2000). https://doi.org/10.1007/3-540-45539-6_18
5. Buchmann, J., Dahmen, E., Ereth, S., Hülsing, A., Rückert, M.: On the security of the Winternitz one-time signature scheme. Int. J. Appl. Crypt. **3**(1), 84–96 (2013). https://doi.org/10.1504/IJACT.2013.053435

6. Celi, S., Griffy, S., Hanzlik, L., Perez-Kempner, O., Slamanig, D.: SoK: signatures with randomizable keys. In: Clark, J., Shi, E. (eds.) Financial Cryptography and Data Security, pp. 160–187. Springer, Cham (2025). https://doi.org/10.1007/978-3-031-78679-2_9
7. Chase, M., et al.: Post-quantum zero-knowledge and signatures from symmetric-key primitives. In: Proceedings of the 2017 ACM SIGSAC Conference on Computer and Communications Security, CCS 2017, pp. 1825–1842. Association for Computing Machinery, New York, NY, USA, October 2017. https://doi.org/10.1145/3133956.3133997
8. de Saint Guilhem, C.D., De Meyer, L., Orsini, E., Smart, N.P.: BBQ: using AES in picnic signatures. In: Paterson, K.G., Stebila, D. (eds.) Selected Areas in Cryptography – SAC 2019. LNCS, pp. 669–692. Springer, Cham (2020). https://doi.org/10.1007/978-3-030-38471-5_27
9. de Saint Guilhem, C.D., Orsini, E., Tanguy, T.: Limbo: efficient zero-knowledge MPCitH-based Arguments, CCS 2021, pp. 3022–3036. Association for Computing Machinery, New York, NY, USA, November 2021. https://doi.org/10.1145/3460120.3484595
10. Denis, F., Eaton, E., Lepoint, T., Wood, C.A.: Key blinding for signature schemes. Internet-Draft, Internet Engineering Task Force / Internet Engineering Task Force, July 2023. https://datatracker.ietf.org/doc/draft-irtf-cfrg-signature-key-blinding/04/
11. Dobraunig, C., Kales, D., Rechberger, C., Schofnegger, M., Zaverucha, G.: Shorter signatures based on tailor-made minimalist symmetric-key crypto. In: Proceedings of the 2022 ACM SIGSAC Conference on Computer and Communications Security, CCS 2022, pp. 843–857. Association for Computing Machinery, New York, NY, USA, November 2022. https://doi.org/10.1145/3548606.3559353
12. Don, J., Fehr, S., Majenz, C.: The measure-and-reprogram technique 2.0: multi-round fiat-shamir and more. In: Micciancio, D., Ristenpart, T. (eds.) CRYPTO 2020. LNCS, vol. 12172, pp. 602–631. Springer, Cham (2020). https://doi.org/10.1007/978-3-030-56877-1_21
13. Don, J., Fehr, S., Majenz, C., Schaffner, C.: Security of the Fiat-Shamir transformation in the quantum random-oracle model. In: Boldyreva, A., Micciancio, D. (eds.) Advances in Cryptology – CRYPTO 2019. LNCS, pp. 356–383. Springer, Cham (2019). https://doi.org/10.1007/978-3-030-26951-7_13
14. Don, J., Fehr, S., Majenz, C., Schaffner, C.: Efficient NIZKs and signatures from commit-and-open protocols in the QROM. In: Dodis, Y., Shrimpton, T. (eds.) Advances in Cryptology – CRYPTO 2022, pp. 729–757. Springer, Cham (2022). https://doi.org/10.1007/978-3-031-15979-4_25
15. Don, J., Fehr, S., Majenz, C., Schaffner, C.: Online-extractability in the quantum random-oracle model. In: Dunkelman, O., Dziembowski, S. (eds.) Advances in Cryptology – EUROCRYPT 2022. LNCS, pp. 677–706. Springer, Cham (2022). https://doi.org/10.1007/978-3-031-07082-2_24
16. Eaton, E., Lepoint, T., Wood, C.A.: Security analysis of signature schemes with key blinding (2023). https://eprint.iacr.org/2023/380
17. Eaton, E., Stebila, D., Stracovsky, R.: Post-quantum Key-blinding for authentication in anonymity networks. In: Longa, P., Ràfols, C. (eds.) LATINCRYPT 2021. LNCS, vol. 12912, pp. 67–87. Springer, Cham (2021). https://doi.org/10.1007/978-3-030-88238-9_4
18. Giacomelli, I., Madsen, J., Orlandi, C.: ZKBoo: faster zero-knowledge for Boolean circuits. In: SEC 2016, pp. 1069–1083. USENIX Association, USA, August 2016

19. Grassl, M., Langenberg, B., Roetteler, M., Steinwandt, R.: Applying Grover's algorithm to AES: quantum resource estimates. In: Takagi, T. (ed.) Post-Quantum Cryptography, pp. 29–43. Springer, Cham (2016). https://doi.org/10.1007/978-3-319-29360-8_3
20. Ishai, Y., Kushilevitz, E., Ostrovsky, R., Sahai, A.: Zero-knowledge from secure multiparty computation. In: Proceedings of the Thirty-Ninth Annual ACM Symposium on Theory of Computing, STOC 2007, pp. 21–30. Association for Computing Machinery, New York, NY, USA, June 2007. https://doi.org/10.1145/1250790.1250794
21. Kales, D., Zaverucha, G.: Efficient lifting for shorter zero-knowledge proofs and post-quantum signatures. Cryptology ePrint Archive, Paper 2022/588 (2022). https://eprint.iacr.org/2022/588
22. Katz, J., Kolesnikov, V., Wang, X.: Improved non-interactive zero knowledge with applications to post-quantum signatures. In: Proceedings of the 2018 ACM SIGSAC Conference on Computer and Communications Security, CCS 2018, pp. 525–537. Association for Computing Machinery, New York, NY, USA, October 2018. https://doi.org/10.1145/3243734.3243805
23. Kiltz, E., Lyubashevsky, V., Schaffner, C.: A concrete treatment of fiat-shamir signatures in the quantum random-oracle model. In: Nielsen, J.B., Rijmen, V. (eds.) EUROCRYPT 2018. LNCS, vol. 10822, pp. 552–586. Springer, Cham (2018). https://doi.org/10.1007/978-3-319-78372-7_18
24. Project Tor: Tor rendezvous specification version 3.0 (2020)
25. Schanzenbach, M., Grothoff, C., Fix, B.: The GNU name system. RFC 9498, November 2023. https://doi.org/10.17487/RFC9498
26. Unruh, D.: Revocable quantum timed-release encryption. J. ACM **62**(6), 49:1–49:76 (2015). https://doi.org/10.1145/2817206
27. Unruh, D.: Post-quantum security of Fiat-Shamir. In: Takagi, T., Peyrin, T. (eds.) ASIACRYPT 2017. LNCS, vol. 10624, pp. 65–95. Springer, Cham (2017). https://doi.org/10.1007/978-3-319-70694-8_3
28. Zhandry, M.: How to record quantum queries, and applications to quantum indifferentiability. In: Boldyreva, A., Micciancio, D. (eds.) CRYPTO 2019. LNCS, vol. 11693, pp. 239–268. Springer, Cham (2019). https://doi.org/10.1007/978-3-030-26951-7_9

Network Security

Opening Pandora's Packet: Expose IPv6 Implementations Vulnerabilities Using Differential Fuzzing

Enrico Bassetti[1](✉), Edoardo Di Paolo[2], Francesco Drago[3], Mauro Conti[3], and Angelo Spognardi[2]

[1] Delft University of Technology, Delft, The Netherlands
e.bassetti@tudelft.nl
[2] Sapienza University of Rome, Rome, Italy
{dipaolo,spognardi}@di.uniroma1.it
[3] University of Padua, Padua, Italy
francesco.drago.1@studenti.unipd.it, mauro.conti@unipd.it

Abstract. IPv6 is the next generation of the Internet Protocol that is being deployed around the world to replace IPv4. In the design of IPv6, extension headers allow the protocol to be flexible, enabling optional features, such as fragmentation or encryption. However, the complexity of this design often leads to vulnerabilities that can affect millions of hosts worldwide. In this paper, we propose a new methodology that exploits differential fuzzing to uncover and analyze vulnerabilities in IPv6 network stack implementations. We run a thorough set of experiments to validate the methodology on several operating systems, such as Windows, Linux, and FreeBSD, uncovering two firewall policies bypass and multiple fingerprinting possibilities. The results highlight the danger of vulnerabilities at this level of the network stack and underscore the importance of testing IPv6 as it becomes the core part of the Internet. Researchers and implementers can use our proposed methodology to look for security issues in other operating systems in a semi-automatic way.

Keywords: IPv6 · differential fuzzing · extension headers

1 Introduction

The Internet Protocol version 6 (IPv6) is the latest version of the Internet Protocol, which is currently being deployed worldwide alongside the current version 4. Although the adoption was slow at the beginning, it increased steadily during the last decade due to the IPv4 address shortage and the always-increasing number of hosts connected to the Internet, such as smartphones, servers, and Internet-of-Things appliances. Far from being only the successor of IPv4, IPv6 contains numerous changes and additions, including the "extension headers" feature designed to allow flexibility to extend the protocol while permitting a fixed-size IPv6 main header. Thanks to the fixed-size header, routers and middleboxes

M. Fischlin and V. Moonsamy (Eds.): ACNS 2025, LNCS 15825, pp. 401–423, 2025.
https://doi.org/10.1007/978-3-031-95761-1_14

can directly implement the parsing of the IPv6 main header in hardware, accelerating packet forwarding and filtering and increasing the performance of the network.

Unfortunately, even if IPv6 was designed based on the lesson learned from IPv4, the standard required several years to reach the current form, mainly due to issues found in the design of specific extensions, such as IP fragmentation. Operating systems developers have difficulties implementing and updating the network stack responsible for IPv6 to the latest specifications, especially when it comes to extension headers, as demonstrated by different works in the literature. Incomplete or faulty implementations open the door to a variety of vulnerabilities, such as firewall bypass and IDS/IPS evasion. Also, with the new paradigm of Software Defined Networking, different user-space implementations of network stacks are running in private and public networks and cloud environments, increasing the scope of potential attacks to millions of hosts worldwide. Thus, we need a more comprehensive approach to assess the correct handling of IPv6 packets with extension headers by operating systems and IP stacks.

Designing and implementing a testing suite that is both comprehensive and flexible (to accommodate new features) is a complex and long task. To overcome this problem, we propose a new methodology based on black box differential fuzzing. Our differential fuzzer works by comparing the output of multiple targets when they receive the same input. We use a differential fuzzer that generates special IPv6-crafted packets to trigger different behavior between operating systems. Although other works use differential fuzzing to uncover potential issues in specific code sections, to our knowledge, this is the first time that differential fuzzing is used for the IPv6 stack in an automatic setting to explore the network-level protocol security.

Contributions. The key contributions of this paper are as follows:

- We provide a novel technique to perform security testing of IPv6 extension headers implementations exploiting differential fuzzing.
- We validate our technique over widely used operating systems, such as Windows, macOS, Linux, Cisco IOS, and various BSDs. We describe and discuss the results obtained by the validation phase.
- We present some critical vulnerabilities we found in network stacks during the validation phase, such as bypass of firewall policies.
- We show that the same technique can be used to fingerprint operating systems based on different combinations of IPv6 extension headers and responses from the victim.
- We provide a prototype implementation and a dataset for further study.
- We also provide bits of advice for fuzzing and testing network stacks.

Availability. Our code and dataset are publicly available at https://github.com/netsecuritylab/ipv6-ext-headers-diff-fuzzer.

1.1 Observations and Goal

The strength of the IPv6 fixed-header design is the ability to add new headers to extend IPv6 beyond current capabilities by exploiting the Next Header field. However, the same design does not support enforcing a specific order of headers or whether they can be present multiple times. In fact, the IPv6 standard only "recommends" an order for headers [8], and it specifies that hosts must be able to cope with different orders and repetition of headers. The standard does not specify what to do in that case, except that the host is supposed to "attempt to process" those packets.

Our goal is to identify and uncover differences and vulnerabilities in IPv6 stack implementations in common operating systems. Differences may indicate that the standard is unclear or loose in those points; this may create vulnerabilities when proper conditions occur. When differences are found, it is important to study whether it is a legitimate implementation decision or not and if it represents a potential vulnerability. Also, highlighting differences between implementations, even when they are legitimate, allows the creation of fingerprinting tools and countermeasures or mitigations which are useful to researchers and defenders. The methodology we propose facilitates reaching this goal.

1.2 Research Questions

Motivated by the goal and the observations above on the way extension headers are designed in the standard, we formulate the following research questions:

- **RQ1** can we fingerprint the endpoint's operating system using IPv6 extension headers?
- **RQ2** can we use extension headers to trigger unexpected behavior (or crashes) in the remote endpoint?
- **RQ3** can we identify the presence of middleboxes using extension headers? Can we fingerprint them?
- **RQ4** can we use unexpected behavior/crashes to bypass middleboxes (such as firewall, IDS, IPS, etc.)?
- **RQ5** are operating system firewalls sufficient to protect/normalize extension headers in crafted packets?

The paper is organized as follows: Sect. 2 provides a brief background on IPv6 extension headers and differential fuzzing. Section 3 contains the approach we designed to tackle the problem. Section 4, 5, and 6 explains how we implemented and evaluated the methodology, describing and discussing the results. Section 7 present some mitigations, while Sect. 8 discuss the related works.

2 Background

This section introduces the structure and features of IPv6, focusing on extension headers (Sect. 2.1), and differential fuzzing, a technique used to identify discrepancies in the behavior of different system implementations (Sect. 2.2).

2.1 IPv6 and Extension Headers

The Internet Protocol version 6 (IPv6) is the latest version of the Internet Protocol designed to address the limitations of its predecessor, IP version 4. With the exponential growth of internet-connected devices, such as IoT devices, IPv4 address space has become insufficient, leading to address exhaustion. In contrast, IPv6 resolves this issue by utilizing a 128-bit address space, which supports approximately 2^{128} unique addresses. Given that the adoption of IPv6 has been steadily increasing in recent years[1], the study of the design and implementation of security measures for the new protocol is becoming increasingly important.

One of the distinguishing features of IPv6 is the design of a fixed-size header and a set of extension headers for additional features. Extension headers are additional headers that are stored between the main IPv6 header and the upper-layer header (if any). Figure 1 shows the main IPv6 header and two extension headers. They implement optional features, such as IP fragmentation, IPSec (authentication/encryption), Mobile IPv6, and others [18]. These headers are stored in a header chain: the *Next Header* field of the IPv6 main header is set to the type identifier for the first extension header. Subsequently, each extension header contains a *Next Header* field which indicates the next extension header type. The last IPv6 extension header contains the identifier for the upper layer protocol (e.g., TCP, UDP, ICMPv6). The preferred order and whether the extension headers can be repeated in the chain is specified in the RFC 8200 [8].

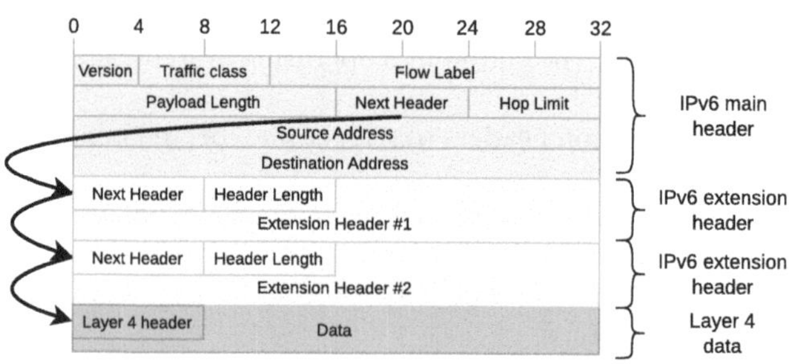

Fig. 1. IPv6 main header format with extension headers

Handling some IPv6 extension headers correctly has proven difficult due to the complexity of the overall IPv6 standard and too broad guidelines, as demonstrated by the different RFCs that defined and changed IPv6 since its initial release [7]. As shown in literature, not implementing the latest standard properly leaves operating systems vulnerable (Di Paolo et al. [9]). Motivated by this, we formulated the hypothesis that each operating system may have implemented the IPv6 extension header handling logic differently from the others.

[1] IPv6 adoption statistics by Google.

2.2 Differential Fuzzing

Fuzzing is a technique used to find vulnerabilities and bugs in software by providing invalid, unexpected, or random data inputs. It is widely used to uncover bugs and vulnerabilities in software implementations. Depending on the level of knowledge about the target system, fuzzing can be categorized into *black box*, when there is no knowledge about the internal implementation or structure of the target; *white box*, when the fuzzer has complete knowledge of the target; and *gray box*, when there is partial knowledge about the internals of the target.

Differential fuzzing is a specific fuzzing technique that focuses on uncovering discrepancies in the behavior of multiple implementations of a function, protocol, application, or system. Unlike traditional fuzzing, which tests a single system with randomly generated inputs to find vulnerabilities or bugs, differential fuzzing compares the outputs or states of different systems when subjected to the same inputs. Security researchers are approaching differential fuzzing to overcome the complexity of some protocols. For example, Bushart and Rossow used this technique to highlight vulnerabilities in common DNS resolvers [6].

3 Methodology

This section presents the methodology we designed, starting from an overview in Sect. 3.1, then describing the three stages of the analysis in Sect. 3.2, and concluding in Sect. 3.3 with the description of two scenarios where this methodology should be applied.

3.1 Methodology Overview

We propose a technique based on black box differential fuzzing to test IPv6 implementations on a large scale and verify whether we can exploit extension headers for different purposes than the one envisioned by the standard. The technique employs fuzzing from a remote machine by sending crafted packets to the target without instrumenting them, collecting and comparing all responses. We decided on a "remote" network stack fuzzing as network stacks are complex and stateful code, and we aim to uncover issues spanning the entire implementation (and not issues in, e.g., parsing functions). In these settings, fuzzing is a complex task, as it involves testing the code present in every layer traversed by the test packets—i.e., one cannot test the IPv6 main header parser without generating a lower layer frame. Additionally, network stacks usually live in the kernel space, which is notoriously difficult to instrument. The black box approach to fuzzing allows us to test the target without instrumenting the kernel, although the fuzzing performance may be suboptimal. A generalized schema of the idea is depicted in Fig. 2.

IPv6 is a complex protocol with several optional features that change how a packet is handled. For example, a Fragment Header requires the operating system to wait for other packets, reorder them, and decide what to do with overlapping fragments. Building a complete set of tests to cover all potential aspects of the protocol is unfeasible, and it will not scale with future extensions. For this reason, we can use differential fuzzing to compare the behavior and responses between different implementations. These differences may result from non-compliance or implementation bugs, or they might be two valid interpretations of the standard. In any case, they are worth investigating, as an attacker might exploit them, as we show later in this work.

One assumption of our design comes from the differential fuzzing itself, and it is that IPv6 network stacks are acting differently when it comes to errors in implementation. We assume that an error is not repeated identically across all operating systems. This may not happen, for example, with errors within the standard. For this reason, differences uncovered by this technique can be considered a lower-bound—when no interesting results are highlighted, further research must be done to uncover other potential problems and cases.

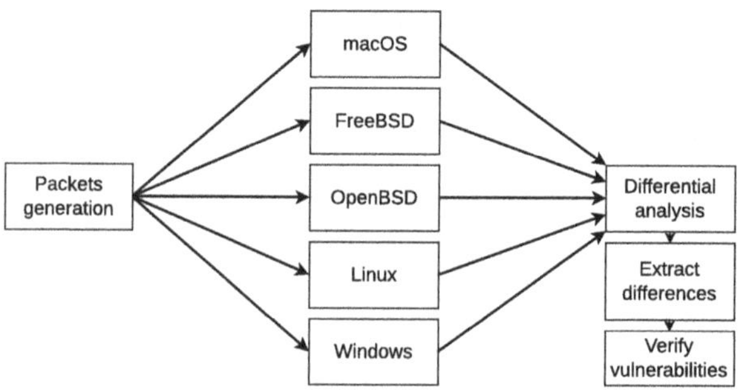

Fig. 2. Differential fuzzing over different operating systems. The fuzzer sends the same crafted packet to multiple operating systems and then compares the results.

3.2 Analysis Stages

We designed our test methodology in three stages: fuzzing, data analysis, and specific issue investigation.

Initial Fuzzing. We send crafted IPv6 packets to the target, storing the result in PCAP traces. The combination of packets includes: standard IPv6 packet with ICMPv6 Echo Request (for validation purposes), IPv6 packet with incorrect extension headers (indicated as Hop-by-Hop in the Next Header field while being ICMPv6, which is also different in size), IPv6 packet with no ICMPv6 header and no payload, and all permutations of the following extension headers: Hop-by-Hop, Routing, Fragment, Destination Option, Encapsulating Security Payload (ESP), Authentication Header (AH), an invalid extension header identifier, and the two identifiers marked as experimental in the standard. Additionally, every packet is sent multiple times with a different payload size, so the final packet size varies from 40 bytes for empty packets to 1500 bytes for packets with multiple extension headers and/or a larger payload. Finally, the test is executed once with a static source IP and a second time with a random source IP address for every single packet.

Data Analysis. After collecting all traces, we analyze them, comparing packets coming back from the victim for each test between operating systems. The comparison may also include packets coming from the attacker after going through the victim if the victim acts as a router (as in the scenario described in Sect. 3.3). Identical[2] packets can be ignored, as they describe identical behavior between stacks when handling them. The remaining packets describe those tests where IP stacks are different between O.S., and they are selected for an in-depth investigation to confirm whether the behavior is consistent even outside the fuzzing.

Issue Investigation. In this last phase, we analyze the behavior highlighted in the previous phase by developing and performing specific tests. The goals are: 1) confirm that the difference exists and that it is not created by the fuzzing noise, rate limits, or other mechanisms; 2) expand and understand the specific behavior to see whether it leads to a vulnerability (on the same hosts or when paired with other hosts).

3.3 Differential Fuzzing Scenarios

Since IP stacks may behave differently when a host forwards packets to other hosts, we included two scenarios in this testing methodology. The first is a simple scenario with two hosts directly connected in a network, as shown in Fig. 3. In this scenario, we use the name "attacker" for the host where the fuzzer is running and "victim" for the host under testing. A simple scenario with no router avoids the noise that might be generated by the router along the path (e.g., packet dropped or reordered) and also mimics an environment where an attacker is performing lateral movement between hosts in the same network.

In the second scenario, the traffic is going through a router, which is our current victim. The goal is to test the router itself to uncover differences between packet handling in different operating systems when forwarding a packet containing IPv6 extension headers. Some may affect the routing (such as the Hop-by-Hop header), while others should not. In this case, the "victim" becomes the router itself, while the destination endpoint is a host that the attacker controls (or at least from which they can get traffic traces). The scenario is depicted in Fig. 4.

[2] We expect some fields to change, which are not considered in our definition of "identical packet". One such field is the Hop Limit (previously known as TTL, Time To Live), which is decremented on each hop.

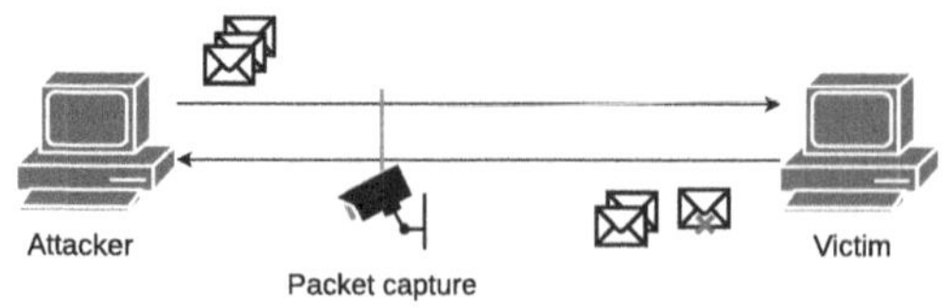

Fig. 3. Network diagram of the first scenario. The host named "attacker" performs the fuzzing, while the "victim" is the destination of the traffic. There are no middleboxes.

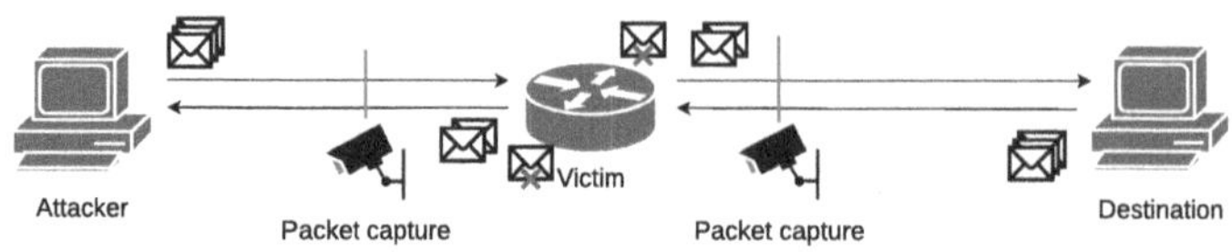

Fig. 4. Network diagram of our second setup, with one operating system acting as the attacker, connected to another operating system acting as a router. The router is also a victim of the tests and is used to access a third machine.

Some operating systems or network stacks cannot be used as routers. In these cases, the second scenario does not apply. Differences can still be highlighted using data obtained by fuzzing only in the first scenario.

4 Evaluation

In this section, we present the technologies and the tools we prepared to evaluate our approach, starting with a description of the fuzzer, the list of targets under evaluation, the motivation behind the list, and the environment where we conducted our experiments.

4.1 Targets

We evaluate our technique on widely used operating systems for workstations, servers, and smart devices. BSD operating systems, such as FreeBSD, NetBSD, and OpenBSD, have been included as they are often regarded to be more secure than other operating systems [19], and they are used as the basis for popular consumer and office appliances (e.g., Apple's AirPort Extreme and Time Capsules use NetBSD; pfSense, opnSense, and TrueNAS appliances use FreeBSD). Linux, Windows, and macOS have been included because of their popularity in workstations, routers, and servers, which makes them a tempting target for malicious actors. We also decided to include some mobile operating systems, such as Apple iOS and Android, to verify whether they inherit the same issues present in the operating systems from which they are derived. Finally, we included two popular router operating systems: Cisco IOS, which powers many enterprise-grade routers, and MikroTik RouterOS, a low-cost router targeting small offices and ISPs. Table 1 lists operating systems and versions we experimented with.

Table 1. Operating systems and versions we used to validate our testing methodology.

Operating systems	Kernel	Vagrant box
Linux Arch	6.7.9-arch1-1	20240315.221711
Linux Debian 12	6.1.0-18-amd64	20240319
Linux Ubuntu 23.04	5.15.0-91-generic	4.3.12
NetBSD	9.3 (GENERIC)	4.3.12
OpenBSD	6.9 GENERIC.MP#473	4.2.16
FreeBSD	13.1-RELEASE	4.2.16
FreeBSD	13.2-RELEASE	4.3.12
FreeBSD	14.0-RELEASE	4.3.12
Windows 10	10.0.19045	20240201.01
Windows 11	10.0.22621.1702	2202.0.2305
MacOS Sonoma 14.5	23.2.0	–
Android 11	4.14.180	–
Apple iOS	17.2.1	–
MikroTik RouterOS	6.49.13 (LTS)	6.49.13
MikroTik RouterOS	7.14.1 (stable)	7.14.1
Cisco IOS	15.2(4)M7	–

4.2 Environment

We followed the guidelines in the literature, such as those presented by Edwards et al. [10] on the methodology for repeatable networking experiments. Some operating systems we identified for our validation experiments run in a virtual machine (such as Linux and FreeBSD). We used Vagrant [20] to create and manage virtual machines, and a set of scripts to prepare the victim. Other operating systems are difficult to virtualize properly (such as Apple iOS, Cisco IOS, and Android). We decided to use physical devices for testing these systems. Table 1 enumerates all versions, for reproducibility.

4.3 Fuzzer

We implemented the fuzzing tool that generates the packets, as described earlier in Sect. 3. The tool uses the Python `scapy` library to create valid IPv6 packets and sends them with a delay to avoid overloading the victim. We extended `scapy` to support additional extension headers, including Encapsulating Security Payload (ESP), Authentication Header (AH), Experimental headers, and a custom-made extension header with an invalid identifier. The fuzzer generates all combinations for all headers, using default values for their fields. The fuzzing tool is also spoofing the source address for two main reasons: first, spoofing an address that is not in the local network speeds up the process as no Neighbor Discovery is necessary (provided that there is a route back to the attacker for replies); second, it avoids false positives and false negatives due to side effects that some packets may trigger in the system itself (e.g., incoming rate limiting per IP).

In order to make our experiments easy to reproduce, we also implemented a supervising code that prepares the environment, launches the victim's Vagrant box, starts `tcpdump` for the packet capture, performs the fuzzing using our tool, and exports the PCAPs traces. We started the packet capture and the fuzzing tool manually for physical machines.

4.4 Evaluation and Analysis

We performed all the experiments within both scenarios, storing different network traces: from one observation point (the victim) in the first scenario, and from two observation point in the second scenario (both sides of the victim router, to acquire the packet before and after it went into the router). We used the PCAP standard format to store the network traces to facilitate the analysis.

After the first phase, we analyzed the stored network traces using `scapy` to highlight differences, and then we investigated each case with Wireshark. In particular, we analyzed all packets coming back from the victim in the first scenario and all packets flowing across the router in the second scenario. In the former, we checked whether the reply was present, and if so, we looked for differences between replies across operating systems. In the latter, we checked whether every packet going inside the router (regardless of source and destination, request, or reply) was present when exiting the router at the expected interface and whether it was exactly the same as the one that entered the router. When testing with the firewall, we checked that the packet was not present when exiting the victim/router when it was supposed to be blocked.

When highlighting differences, we also considered ICMPv6 errors (and other packets in general). In particular, we consider a difference when two operating systems reply with different ICMPv6 errors or when one operating system is replying with an error, and the other is replying with the expected reply packet. Two packets are considered identical if they match byte-by-byte from the IPv6 header to the rest of the packet, except for the fields that are expected to change, such as the Hop Limit (formerly Time To Live). Also, Ethernet frames are not included in the comparison as they are outside the scope of this work.

While analyzing the data acquired after performing our experiment in the first scenario, we discovered that a combination of extension headers can trigger different responses depending on the target's operating system. Assuming that the target responds to some packets (e.g., ICMPv6 Echo Request, TCP SYN on an open port), we show that it is possible to identify its operating system, responding to **RQ1**. We discuss this vulnerability in detail in Sect. 5.2. We also noticed some interesting behavior on specific ICMPv6 Echo Request packets. Further investigations revealed a vulnerability in ICMPv6 packet handling, responding to **RQ2**. We discuss this vulnerability in detail in Sect. 5.3.

Then, we focused on the second scenario, where the victim is the router. By the standard, a router should forward IPv6 packets without processing extension headers, except for Hop-by-Hop and Routing extensions. So, we expect to find no alteration of packets or routing decisions based on extension headers. This assumption was confirmed by the data we obtained in this scenario, showing only negligible changes to packets in all but one case: FreeBSD mishandled packets with duplicated Fragment Header. This issue resulted in a severe vulnerability, leading to a bypass of firewall policies. We discuss this in detail in Sect. 5.1. This vulnerability partially responds to both **RQ3** and **RQ4**, demonstrating that we can use extension headers to trigger unexpected behaviors and fingerprint the operating system with these.

In total, we analyzed 28566 packets, highlighting 16181 different responses across all network stacks (including ICMPv6 diagnostic responses). Tests have been executed multiple times to avoid transient errors. We noticed no significant changes between different executions. By looking at the resulting network traces, we found that numerous differences derive from divergent implementations of valid IPv6 specifications. For example, the standard specifies that, in cases of unrecognized Next Header values, the node processing the packet *should*[3] discard the packet and send an ICMPv6 Parameter Problem back. As it is not required, some operating systems (e.g., Microsoft Windows) discard the packet silently.

5 Results and Discussion

In this section, we discuss the results by grouping them into three main parts: a critical vulnerability highlighted in FreeBSD due to a duplicated Fragment Header (Sect. 5.1), the fingerprint of a remote operating system due to the difference in handling extension headers (Sect. 5.2), and a vulnerability of some operating system when handling ICMPv6 Echo Request messages (Sect. 5.3).

5.1 Use IP Fragment Header to Bypass the pf Firewall

One of the features implemented by IPv6 extension headers is IP fragmentation. IPv6 implements fragmentation to handle packets larger than the smallest MTU for a given path [8]. However, differently from the previous version IPv4, the metadata related to the fragment (such as the offset in the original packet) are stored in an extension header. As described in this section, a special metadata settings in fragmented packets can be abused to launch different attacks, such as Denial-of-Service or firewall policy bypass.

Atomic Fragments. Atomic Fragments are a special type of fragments in IPv6. They are packets composed of only one fragment because the original packet does not need to be fragmented in the first place. Atomic Fragments have distinct characteristics: specifically, they have a fragment offset of 0, and

[3] "Should" keyword has a special meaning in RFCs. As described by RFC 2119 [5], it means that implementers can decide to ignore a part of the specification if they weigh and understand all the implications of that choice.

the more fragments flag is set to 0, indicating that they are the first fragment and there are no more fragments. The processing of these packets is discussed in RFC 6946 [11]. Figure 5 shows an example of an IPv6 packet with an Atomic Fragment header.

Gont et al. already describe how Atomic Fragments can be misused in two RFCs, one dated 2013, RFC 6946 [11] and a subsequent update in 2017, RFC 8021 [12]. They show that an attacker can create a Denial of Service by triggering the IP fragmentation (e.g., using an ICMPv6 Packet Too Big message) in a network that drops extension headers. While this is true also for non-atomic fragments, the previous version of the IPv6 standard required endpoints to generate Atomic Fragments when the declared MTU is lower than the IPv6 minimum MTU (1280). The current revised IPv6 standard RFC 8200 [8] revises this requirement and specifies that Atomic Fragments must not be generated in the presence of an ICMPv6 Packet Too Big with a low MTU. Operating systems still generate Atomic Fragments today. Firewalls, routers, and other network appliances are still expected to handle them for compatibility reasons.

Fig. 5. An example of an Atomic Fragment. An Atomic Fragment has both offset and M flag set to 0, indicating that this is the first and only fragment.

How to Handle Atomic Fragments. Handling these packets correctly, as described in RFC 6946 [11], is crucial for maintaining compatibility and security. Hosts such as firewalls and IDS/IPS should adhere to RFC 6946 when processing atomic fragments to avoid possible security threats. Foremost, a packet containing an atomic fragment must be considered in isolation from other packets/fragments; this means that there should be no interference with other packets. In fact, an atomic fragment should be reassembled only with its content. The "Unfragmentable Part" of the reassembled packet consists of all headers except the Fragment Header, where the offset and the more fragments flag are 0. The Next Header is set to the value found in the Next Header field of the Fragment Header.

FreeBSD Firewall Bypass Using Fragments. In the case of FreeBSD, the fuzzer triggered a peculiar behavior when two or more Atomic Fragment headers were present. The Fragment Header, as almost all extension headers, can appear at most once. However, nothing forbids attackers from creating IPv6 packets with multiple Fragment headers in the chain. An example of an IPv6 packet with multiple Fragment headers is shown in Fig. 6.

The FreeBSD firewall, `pf`, is responsible for reassembling the packet to match the ruleset. `pf` can also match fragments without reassembly, a technique used

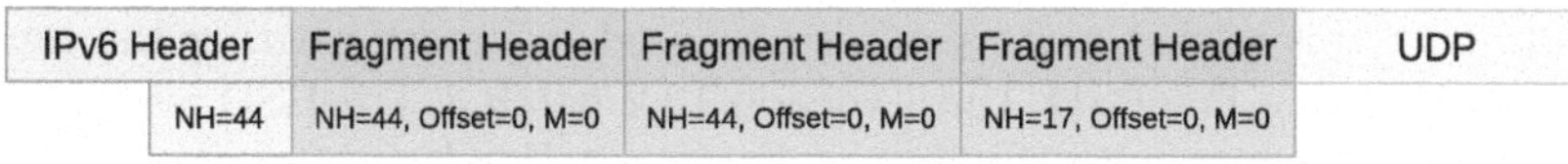

Fig. 6. IPv6 packet with three Atomic Fragment headers. The IPv6 specifications forbid duplication for almost all extension headers, including Fragment header.

when a basic stateless IP firewall/router is desired. However, it is common to have the reassembly option enabled in the "packet scrubbing" feature (many FreeBSD-based firewalls enable this by default, such as pfSense[4]) to allow the firewall to match packets at higher protocols, such as TCP, UDP, HTTP.

When FreeBSD receives a packet that contains the Fragment Header, it tries to reassemble it into the original packet, waiting for the next fragments. The reassembly phase starts immediately when the Fragment Header describes an Atomic Fragment. However, suppose the packet contains multiple Fragment Headers. In that case, FreeBSD is confused during the normalization phase: the packet skips the rest of the normalization function[5] and it assumes that the rest of the packet is the payload, including eventual per-fragment extension headers. Now, suppose no firewall rule blocks the packet at the IP level (e.g., rulesets that allow only specific protocols, ports, or combinations of IP and protocols, blocking all the rest). In that case, the packet is accepted as "unknown protocol" and forwarded to the destination, if the FreeBSD firewall is not the final recipient.

Additionally, removing the first Fragment Header results in a forwarded packet containing only one Fragment Header, which is completely legal. In fact, in one test, we experimented using FreeBSD as a firewall to protect a Linux machine. The Linux machine exposed a UDP service, which was blocked by the firewall policy in FreeBSD. We sent a UDP packet with two Fragment headers to the FreeBSD firewall, which, due to this vulnerability, skipped checking the rules, removed the first Fragment Header, and forwarded the packet to the Linux host. The Linux host accepted the packet. The Linux host would have rejected the packet if FreeBSD had not removed the duplicated Fragment Header. In other words, the firewall is not only vulnerable to this attack, but it is actually fixing the packet so that the victim accepts it.

We also tested the TCP protocol, and we were able to successfully connect to a service behind the firewall. The TCP SYN packet with a duplicated Fragment Header passes the firewall thanks to the vulnerability, and TCP SYN-ACK responses are allowed to go back by default, even if they have no Fragment Header at all. Additionally, FreeBSD creates an entry in the state table: subsequent packets do not need to have Fragment Headers after the SYN-ACK packet, as they match the existing state. However, a good ruleset for stateful firewalls should include blocking non-TCP SYN packets not associated with an existing connection in the state table, which partially mitigates this vulnerability for TCP.

[4] "Firewall & NAT", pfSense documentation.

[5] https://github.com/freebsd/freebsd-src/commit/76afcbb52492f9b3e72ee7d4c4ed0a54c25e1c48.

Note that this packet alone can also be used to detect whether the remote machine is running FreeBSD. Until version 13.2 patch 3, FreeBSD was the only one accepting packets with duplicated Fragment Header. After the release of versions 13.2p3 and 14, we noticed that FreeBSD is not responding at all, while other operating systems are still responding, as shown in Table 2.

Table 2. Multiple Atomic Fragment header handling by operating systems. Legend: ○ no replies, ◐ ICMPv6 Parameter Problem reply, ● ICMPv6 Echo reply (incorrect).

Operating System	No firewall	Firewall discarding packets
Linux (all tested versions)	◐	◐
NetBSD	○	○
OpenBSD	●	○
FreeBSD (until 13.2)	●	● +**Policy bypass**
FreeBSD 13.2+	●	○
Windows (all tested versions)	●	○
macOS	●	○
Android	◐	n/a
Apple iOS	●	n/a
RouterOS (all tested versions)	◐	◐
Cisco IOS	●	◐

5.2 Fingerprinting Using Extension Headers

Operating systems handle the presence of duplicated extension headers differently. As seen in Sect. 5.1, some network stacks do not completely adhere to the specifications, paving the way to various vulnerabilities. This subsection explores how we exploit the differences between network stacks to fingerprint the remote operating system, responding to **RQ1**.

Duplicated Extension Headers. After analyzing the result of the evaluation, we can select the minimum set of packets that allows us to reliably fingerprint the remote host. As shown in Table 3, this set contains three packets: first, one with a duplicated Fragment Header; then, a second packet with a duplicated Routing Header; finally, a third with a malformed extension header chain (e.g., Hop-by-Hop type in the Next Header while appending an ICMPv6 header).

By analyzing whether the remote host responds to these packets and what packet it sends back, we can determine the running kernel between Linux, NetBSD, OpenBSD, FreeBSD, Windows, macOS, and Cisco IOS. RouterOS and

Android use a modified version of the Linux kernel, indistinguishable in the data we obtained. In the case of FreeBSD, as expected, we can distinguish between systems running patched or non-patched kernel versions due to the vulnerability we presented earlier in Sect. 5.1.

Table 3. Responses to invalid extension headers combinations. ○ indicates no replies, ◐ indicates an ICMPv6 parameter problem, ● indicates an ICMPv6 Echo Reply.

Operating systems	2 x Fragment Header	2 x Routing Header	Malformed Header
Linux (all tested versions)	◐	●	○
NetBSD	○	○	○
OpenBSD	●	◐	○
FreeBSD (all tested versions)	●	●	○
Windows (all tested versions)	●	○	○
macOS	●	●	◐
Android	◐	●	○
Apple iOS	●	●	○
RouterOS (all tested versions)	◐	●	○
Cisco IOS	●	●	◐

IPsec-Related Extension Headers. We also noticed that different operating systems behave differently when presented with Encapsulating Security Payload (ESP) or the Authentication Header (AH) extension headers without being configured specifically for these. Fortunately, no operating system is passing packets to the upper layer (as there is no way for the operating system to verify the authentication or encryption in our setup). Figure 8 shows that Windows, NetBSD, and OpenBSD completely ignore these packets, while Linux and FreeBSD respond with an "ICMPv6 Parameter Problem".

Although we already have all the necessary data with the three packets described in the first paragraph Sect. 5.2, this further information may be used in specific conditions when a firewall is filtering some traffic while allowing IPSec traffic.

Extension Headers in ICMPv6 Errors. Network stacks send back ICMPv6 "Parameter Problem" packets to report to the source that they had problems parsing the incoming IPv6 packet header. It contains the original header, with indications on the specific error: *unknown Next Header field, unrecognized IPv6 option*, or *malformed header field.* In our testing, we purposefully triggered this behavior, and we discovered that different operating system behave differently when subjected to this traffic. In particular, Linux and macOS include the entire IPv6 header, including all extension headers, in the ICMPv6 Parameter Problem reply. Windows never replies to these probes. FreeBSD is peculiar in this case, as some ICMPv6 errors contain the header, and others do not. This indicates that the error is triggered during parsing and that the error is sent back with the current status of the parsing.

Figure 7 summarizes the differences. Although less precise, this can be used to fingerprint an host by sending a crafted packet with malformed header chain.

Operating systems	**Extension headers echoed back**
Linux (all versions)	●
NetBSD	●
OpenBSD	●
FreeBSD (all versions)	◐
Windows (all versions)	No response
macOS	●
Android	●
iOS	●
RouterOS (all versions)	●
Cisco IOS	●

Fig. 7. Extension headers in ICMPv6 Parameter Problem replies. Legend: ○ no extension headers, ◐ until the malformed one, ● all sent back.

Operating systems	**ESP**	**AH**
Linux (all versions)	◐	◐
NetBSD	○	○
OpenBSD	○	○
FreeBSD (all versions)	◐	◐
Windows (all versions)	○	○
macOS	○	○
Android	◐	◐
iOS	○	○
RouterOS (all versions)	◐	◐
Cisco IOS	○	○

Fig. 8. Responses using AH/ESP headers and no SPI in the victim. ○ indicates no responses, ◐ indicates an ICMPv6 parameter problem, ● indicates a complete reply.

5.3 ICMPv6 “zero” Vulnerability

Echo Requests. ICMPv6 is an essential component of IPv6, designed to facilitate error reporting and diagnostic functions [13]. As a successor to the ICMP used in IPv4, ICMPv6 provides mechanisms for reporting errors such as unreachable destinations or packet transmission issues, which are crucial for maintaining network stability and performance. Additionally, ICMPv6 supports important functionalities like Neighbor Discovery Protocol (NDP), which were previously delegated to different protocols (such as ARP) in IPv4.

ICMPv6 includes functionality to test the reachability of the endpoints. A host that wants to check whether a target is alive and reachable can send an ICMPv6 Echo Request. If the packet is delivered successfully (i.e., not blocked by a firewall or routing misconfiguration), the target host generates an ICMPv6 Echo Reply. Requests contain two fields (among others) that are used to match them with replies: identifier and sequence number. The identifier is supposed to

Table 4. Firewall mitigation effectiveness. Legend: ○ full mitigation, ◐ partial mitigation (replies to some packets), ● vulnerable to ICMPv6 "zero" (always replies).

Operating systems	"block-all" policy	"server" policy
Linux (all tested versions)	○	◐
NetBSD	○	○
OpenBSD	○	○
FreeBSD (until 13.1)	●	●
FreeBSD 13.2+	●	●
Windows (all tested versions)	●	●
macOS	◐	◐
RouterOS (all tested versions)	○	○

stay constant during a session of consecutive tests, while the sequence number is supposed to change (usually incremented by one in the sender) to match a specific request with the subsequent reply. These two values may start at zero.

ICMPv6 "zero" Echo Requests. Although our focus was on IPv6 extension headers, we also briefly tested our approach on ICMPv6 while developing the tool to respond to **RQ2**. In one iteration, we sent numerous Echo requests with both zero identifier and sequence numbers to targets with firewalls enabled and configured to block all non-essential traffic. We named these packets "ICMPv6 Zero Echo Requests". Note that these packets are legal by the standard [13].

Some operating systems are still replying to such packets despite being configured otherwise. In particular, Microsoft Windows is sending "Echo replies" back immediately, while FreeBSD starts replying only after ten packets on average. Other operating systems are discarding the Echo request correctly. An attacker interested in scanning and fingerprinting a remote host can use this technique to 1) discover whether the remote host is alive or not and 2) recognize whether it is running Windows, FreeBSD, or other operating systems.

We also experimented with diagnostic tools provided by the operating systems and Linux distributions, such as `ping`. By default, all tools use random identifiers. Linux and Windows utilities start from 1 when generating sequence numbers, while macOS, FreeBSD, NetBSD, and OpenBSD start from zero instead. This difference indicates what tool is generating Echo Requests.

5.4 Limitations

Black Box Fuzzing. We used black box fuzzing due to the complexity of instrumenting kernel code. Gray or white box approaches can better guide the fuzzing towards different code paths, thus potentially finding more vulnerabilities while using fewer resources. For this reason, the number of vulnerabilities we found is a lower bound.

Differential Fuzzing. Differential fuzzing uncovers differences in packet content and packet handling. This assumes that faulty implementations do not behave the same across all operating systems. For this reason, our approach is unable to highlight issues that are shared between all operating systems that are tested. This limitation can be partially mitigated by increasing the number of IPv6 stacks under testing, as this increases the chance that one stack implemented a specific combination differently from others.

Pre-shared Configuration. Some extension headers, such as the ESP and AH, are used together with a pre-shared configuration in the operating system. Having a valid "security association" requires the two endpoints to share some parameters beforehand. Given the context of our work, we limited our testing to cases without a "security association" between the two endpoints.

6 Extension Headers on the Internet

We collected a sample of one month of data from VSIX[6], an Internet Exchange Point (IXP) in Italy, to glimpse into the Internet traffic and see whether extension headers are being used. On average, the IXP is serving 55 Gb/s of total traffic. We sampled the traffic using a ratio of 1:4000, and we observed 60 thousands packets with Fragmentation header out of a total of 89 million packets (0.15%). No other extension header has been observed. We suppose that we see only Fragment headers because 1) extension headers implement features rarely needed, and 2) ISPs block packets with extension headers, as already shown by Hendriks et al. [14]. We confirmed the latter with a few local operators. Due to this, we decided not to perform tests on the Internet as the gathered data would be inaccurate. Nevertheless, even if these policies mitigate the vulnerabilities, these are still a threat in other networks, such as company and campus networks.

7 Mitigations

In this section, we present the same set of experiments done with built-in firewalls configured to block packets according to different policies. The aim is to study potential mitigations for the vulnerabilities presented in Sect. 5, and respond to **RQ5**. We define two possible sets of policies: "block-all" where every incoming IPv6 packet is blocked, except for the required one (e.g., NDP), and "server", that allows some services on TCP, UDP, and ICMPv6. The first policy is usually found on workstations, while the second is common on servers.

While testing "block-all", we have that some operating systems still respond to packets with extension headers when they are ICMPv6 "zero", whether the

[6] VSIX Internet Exchange Point. https://www.vsix.it/.

packet contains extension headers or not. This indicates that at least part of the ICMPv6 logic is bypassing the firewall. In evaluating "server", we have that some O.S. parse the extension headers before evaluating the policies and, if they see a malformed header, they send an ICMPv6 Parameter Problem.

Table 4 summarizes the results we found. Unlike others, macOS responds to the ICMPv6 parameter problem only once the firewall is enabled (no ICMPv6 Echo Replies), even if it is not vulnerable to the ICMPv6 "zero" attack, regardless of the policy. In general, due to blocked incoming packets, different packets are reduced to 2080, and they are related mostly to the ICMPv6 "zero" vulnerability.

When combined with the ICMPv6 "zero" Echo Request, we see that FreeBSD and Windows built-in firewalls are not blocking the packets generated by the fuzzer. As shown in the table, FreeBSD still responds to some combinations either with ICMPv6 Echo Replies or with ICMPv6 Parameter Problem, and Windows sends back ICMPv6 Echo Replies regardless of the firewall policy.

We suggest installing an external firewall in front of the vulnerable machine to block ICMPv6 Parameter Problems responses or, if possible, block incoming packets for protocols and extension headers not allowed in the first place.

8 Related Work

This section presents some works related to fuzzing and past research concerning IPv6 and extension headers in particular.

8.1 Network Fuzzing

Fuzzing is a widely used technique for identifying vulnerabilities, especially in complex algorithms such as parsers. Indeed, several studies have been proposed in the literature over the years. Perhaps the most famous one is "AFLNET" by Pham et al. [21], which combines mutation techniques with server state feedback. Rather than creating new packets, their approach involves replaying modified versions of previously captured packets. Hoque et al. [15] present a tool to find semantic bugs violating the temporal properties of network protocols. Becker et al. [4] describe a fuzzing framework for IPv6 based on machine learning exploiting reinforcement learning. The authors validated their proposal on IPv6 NDP. However, all these works focus only on testing one implementation for errors in execution, and they require instrumenting the kernel. The last one also does not consider using extension headers in the fuzzing process, even if it is focused on IPv6. Our approach does not require modifications to existing systems, allowing testing of proprietary, embedded, and hardware-implemented network stacks.

Differential fuzzing has been used for network protocols: Bushart and Rossow [6] found vulnerabilities in the DNS infrastructure through "ResolvFuzz", a differential fuzzer for DNS resolvers. Reen and Rossow [22] propose "DPIFuzz", a differential fuzzer for the QUIC protocol [16] that mutates QUIC streams based on feedback gathered by instrumenting the tools. However, network stacks live in kernel, which is difficult to instrument, if even possible. Additionally, proprietary and hardware-implemented network stacks cannot be instrumented if not designed for that. Our methodology does not have these limitations.

8.2 IPv6 Extension Headers

On IPv6, and specifically extension headers, several works are available in the literature. Hendriks et al. [14] present a measurement study on IPv6 extension headers traffic on the Internet. Atlasis and Rey in [1–3] discuss several IPv6 fragmentation attacks. They are able to perform a fingerprinting attack, IPS/IDS evasion, and firewall evasion, exploiting overlapping fragments and atomic fragments with other extension headers. Di Paolo et al. [9] propose a new model for testing compliance to RFCs on IPv6 fragmentation. A study by Lin et al. [17] introduces an adaptive model that leverages a set of rules derived from IDS/IPS rules to address threats related to the use of IPv6 extension headers. However, all these work target one single implementation with a defined set of tests, often designed around a single weakness of the IPv6 standard. These approaches are more effective for specific cases but can hardly be generalized to the IPv6 stack.

Despite the growth in IPv6 adoption, research on IPv6, specifically on extension headers, remains underdeveloped. To the best of our knowledge, our study is pioneering in this field as we introduce the first differential fuzzer targeting IPv6. This approach uncovers implementation differences and vulnerabilities that can arise because of a single faulty implementation and a combination of different operating systems in a network.

9 Conclusions

Our study provides a novel methodology for testing IPv6 implementations based on black box differential fuzzing. Our methodology is based on identifying differences in IPv6 implementation across different network stacks while subjected to specially crafted packets. The assumption, proven correct during the evaluation, is that different operating systems implement part of the IPv6 logic differently due to shortcomings and flexibility in the IPv6 RFC. To the best of our knowledge, we are the first to implement and validate such an approach on IPv6.

We found multiple vulnerabilities not reported in the past, spanning from operating system fingerprinting to a critical firewall bypass. Some of these vulnerabilities require the interaction between multiple components, such as the IPv6 extension header parsing logic and the on-board firewall, something never considered in other proposals, such as the one presented in the Related Works Sect. 8. In particular, we revealed that Atomic Fragments can be used to bypass firewall policies in the FreeBSD operating system. Additionally, we showed that it is possible to remotely fingerprint operating systems, exploiting IPv6 extension headers by comparing their different behaviors on specially crafted packets. We also revealed that some operating systems are vulnerable to an additional vulnerability that we named ICMPv6 "Zero" Echo. Moreover, we propose some possible mitigation for the vulnerability presented in this work.

While our approach is specifically tailored to IPv6 extension headers, it can also be adapted to other parts of the protocol, as demonstrated by the brief ICMPv6 experiment we presented in Sect. 5.3. In fact, our findings encourage more research on securing the entire IPv6, a critical part of the current Internet infrastructure. We are releasing the tool as open source to help the community secure their implementation and build over our work.

Future Works. Other parts of the IPv6 network stacks are still unexplored, such as the ICMPv6 packet handling. As seen in Sect. 5.3, even simple Echo Requests might expose incorrect network stacks and firewalls implementations and can lead to vulnerabilities. We are in the process of expanding our tools to include ICMPv6, as well as other core parts of IPv6, to illuminate other potential issues.

Responsible Disclosure. We responsibly disclosed the vulnerabilities to the FreeBSD Security Team and to Microsoft. The assigned CVE identifier are CVE-2023-4809 and CVE-2024-6640 for FreeBSD. Other non-critical issues have been reported using standard channels. The vulnerabilities have been patched since then.

Acknowledgments. We would like to thank VSIX (VSIX Internet Exchange Point https://www.vsix.it/) for enabling us to capture and analyze traffic at their IXP.

Disclosure of Interests. The authors have no competing interests to declare that are relevant to the content of this article.

A Appendix

A.1 Remarks on Network Testing and Network Bridges

During our evaluation, we noticed that some environments are interfering with IP packets, although this is unexpected to users. Initially, our environment was built over Proxmox[7], an open-source virtual machine hypervisor based on KVM and Debian Linux. Proxmox uses Linux bridges and OpenvSwitch bridges under the hood to connect virtual machines (via virtual NICs) and physical NICs.

Normally, Linux bridges are not supposed to interfere with IP packets, as they work at a lower level. However, a specific Linux bridge flag (`/proc/sys/net/bridge/bridge-nf-call-iptables`) forces all Ethernet frames in the bridge to pass by `netfilter` in the host/hypervisor Linux kernel for inspection. This is used to enforce policies at the link layer (e.g., it is used to block a virtual machine from spoofing addresses from neighbors, which is important in cloud environments that provide VMs to third parties). By forcing Ethernet frames into the `netfilter`, IP packets are validated and reassembled

[7] https://www.proxmox.com/en/.

by the Linux network stack, checked against the `netfilter` policies, and then fragmented again (if they were fragmented in the first place). The problem is, in this way, Linux is also blocking some crafted packets from reaching the victim, such as the one with multiple Fragment headers.

Researchers who rely on virtual machines and software solutions, in general, may want to check whether the underlying system is altering Ethernet frames and IP packets before doing experiments. We suggest planning for validation tests even for elements that are normally considered "passive" or "transparent". In the case of some hypervisors, such as Proxmox, these settings cannot be changed without extensive modifications: researcher may want to use `kvm` directly or with other hypervisors, such as `libvirt`/Vagrant, where the control on these flags are left to the user.

B Mitigating Extension Headers Vulnerabilities with Linux Netfilter

The Linux Netfilter framework supports intercepting packets before the reassembly by using the `NF_IP_PRI_CONNTRACK_DEFRAG` priority in the prerouting hook. In this phase, Netfilter can have rules matching the Next Header before the reassembly and parsing of extensions, allowing the creation of rules that can selectively block fingerprinting packets by matching unexpected Next Headers.

Note that the Linux Netfilter also supports "transparent" firewalls on Ethernet bridges. When the relevant option is enabled, packets are forced to enter the Linux Netfilter pipeline, effectively being subjected to the Linux validation and parsing code. Combining this with the priority in the prerouting hook, system operators can protect vulnerable systems using transparent firewalls to avoid changing the network layout. This can also be done transparently in a virtual environment where Linux is used as a host, such as in `kvm`-based hypervisors.

References

1. Atlasis, A.: Attacking IPv6 implementation using fragmentation. Blackhat Europe, pp. 14–16 (2012)
2. Atlasis, A.: Security impacts of abusing IPv6 extension headers. In: Black Hat Security Conference, pp. 1–10 (2012)
3. Atlasis, A., Rey, E.: Evasion of high-end IPS devices in the age of IPv6. Blackhat.com (2014)
4. Becker, S., Abdelnur, H.J., Engel, T., et al.: An autonomic testing framework for ipv6 configuration protocols. In: 4th International Conference on Autonomous Infrastructure, Management and Security, AIMS 2010. Springer (2010)
5. Bradner, S.O.: Key words for use in RFCs to Indicate Requirement Levels. RFC 2119 (1997). https://doi.org/10.17487/RFC2119. https://www.rfc-editor.org/info/rfc2119
6. Bushart, J., Rossow, C.: ResolFuzz: differential fuzzing of DNS resolvers. In: European Symposium on Research in Computer Security, pp. 62–80. Springer (2023)

7. Carpenter, B.E., Jiang, S.: Transmission and Processing of IPv6 Extension Headers. RFC 7045 (2013). https://doi.org/10.17487/RFC7045. https://www.rfc-editor.org/info/rfc7045
8. Deering, S., Hinden, R.: RFC 8200: Internet protocol, version 6 (IPv6) specification (2017)
9. Di Paolo, E., Bassetti, E., Spognardi, A.: A new model for testing IPv6 fragment handling. In: European Symposium on Research in Computer Security, pp. 277–294. Springer (2023)
10. Edwards, S., Liu, X., Riga, N.: Creating repeatable computer science and networking experiments on shared, public testbeds. ACM SIGOPS Oper. Syst. Rev. **49**(1), 90–99 (2015)
11. Gont, F.: Processing of IPv6 "Atomic" Fragments. RFC 6946 (2013). https://doi.org/10.17487/RFC6946. https://www.rfc-editor.org/info/rfc6946
12. Gont, F., Liu, W.S., Anderson, T.: Generation of IPv6 Atomic Fragments Considered Harmful. RFC 8021 (2017). https://doi.org/10.17487/RFC8021. https://www.rfc-editor.org/info/rfc8021
13. Gupta, M., Conta, A.: Internet Control Message Protocol (ICMPv6) for the Internet Protocol Version 6 (IPv6) Specification. RFC 4443 (2006). https://doi.org/10.17487/RFC4443. https://www.rfc-editor.org/info/rfc4443
14. Hendriks, L., Velan, P., Schmidt, R.d.O., de Boer, P.T., Pras, A.: Threats and surprises behind IPv6 extension headers. In: 2017 Network Traffic Measurement and Analysis Conference (TMA), pp. 1–9. IEEE (2017)
15. Hoque, E., Chowdhury, O., Chau, S.Y., Nita-Rotaru, C., Li, N.: Analyzing operational behavior of stateful protocol implementations for detecting semantic bugs. In: 2017 47th Annual IEEE/IFIP International Conference on Dependable Systems and Networks (DSN), pp. 627–638 (2017). https://doi.org/10.1109/DSN.2017.36
16. Langley, A., et al.: The QUIC transport protocol: design and internet-scale deployment (2017)
17. Lin, B., et al.: An adaptive detection model for IPv6 extension header threats based on deterministic decision automaton. Sci. Rep. **14**(1), 9534 (2024)
18. Loukola, M., Slytta, J.: New possibilities offered by IPv6. In: Proceedings 7th International Conference on Computer Communications and Networks (Cat. No. 98EX226), pp. 548–552. IEEE (1998)
19. Lucas, M.: Absolute OpenBSD, 2nd edn. Unix for the Practical Paranoid. No Starch Press (2013). https://books.google.nl/books?id=WAYvDwAAQBAJ
20. Palat, J.: Introducing vagrant. Linux J. **2012**(220), 2 (2012)
21. Pham, V.T., Böhme, M., Roychoudhury, A.: AFLNET: a greybox fuzzer for network protocols. In: 2020 IEEE 13th International Conference on Software Testing, Validation and Verification (ICST), pp. 460–465 (2020). https://doi.org/10.1109/ICST46399.2020.00062
22. Reen, G.S., Rossow, C.: DPIFuzz: a differential fuzzing framework to detect DPI elusion strategies for QUIC. In: Proceedings of the 36th Annual Computer Security Applications Conference, ACSAC 2020, pp. 332–344. Association for Computing Machinery, New York (2020). https://doi.org/10.1145/3427228.3427662

TAU: Trust via Asynchronous Updates for Satellite Network Resiliency

Quincy Bayer[1(✉)], Robert Esswein[1], Samuel Mergendahl[2], Jonathan Ruffley[3], Mai Abdelhakim[1], and Robert K. Cunningham[1]

[1] University of Pittsburgh, Pittsburgh, PA, USA
{quincy.bayer,robert.esswein,maia,robertkcunningham}@pitt.edu
[2] MIT Lincoln Laboratory, Lexington, MA, USA
samuel.mergendahl@ll.mit.edu
[3] Naval Nuclear Laboratory, West Mifflin, PA, USA
jonathan.ruffley@unnpp.gov

Abstract. Satellite networks are key enablers to many applications, including world-wide sensing and communications. Unlike their terrestrial counterparts, satellites are able to provide coverage in remote and hard-to-reach areas, including areas with regional conflicts. However, they are also susceptible to multiple security threats and potential failures. In addition to commonly used security techniques, it is essential to have algorithms that assess the trustworthiness of satellites as they operate, without limiting the satellites' abilities to perform their intended tasks. In this paper we focus on trust assessment methods that analyze the behavior of satellites to detect attacks and identify failed or compromised nodes in constellation networks. In this work, we (1) present a satellite threat model and enumerate possible attacks, (2) compare several existing trust assessment models when applied to low earth orbit satellite constellations, and (3) propose Trust via Asynchronous Updates (TAU), a novel trust algorithm model that is applicable to all modern satellite constellation networks. Model TAU uses finite state machines and asynchronous updates to track node behavior. Our custom simulator evaluates the performance of our algorithm in comparison to several previously proposed trust models. We consider two well-known attacks, the kinetic and black hole attacks, and show that the proposed Model TAU accurately identifies malicious satellites, with low false positive rate, in time comparable to previously proposed trust models while achieving lower computational complexity and communication overhead.

Keywords: Trust Assessment · Satellite Network · Network Security · Trust Algorithm · LEO Satellite · Decentralized Trust

1 Introduction

Due to dramatic reductions in launch costs [39], it has become feasible to deploy large constellations of satellites to low earth orbit (LEO) in order to cover the

M. Fischlin and V. Moonsamy (Eds.): ACNS 2025, LNCS 15825, pp. 424–452, 2025.
https://doi.org/10.1007/978-3-031-95761-1_15

earth with sensors and networks. Today's satellites provide important services such as navigation [19], observation [34], entertainment [6], and communication [10]. Compared to terrestrial systems, satellite networks can easily service remote locations serving more end users. Satellites are also fully contained, making them immune to failures of supporting systems, such as the power grid. With these advantages, customers are flocking to the industry, resulting in revenue projections exceeding six billion dollars [14]. However, increasing the number of satellites in a network increases the likelihood that one or more will fail [26]. This risk of failure is increased by the industry trend of industrializing the satellite production process. Many companies have begun using parts provided by third-party vendors opening up the satellites to supply chain vulnerabilities [29]. In addition, some satellite networks have offered communication and sensing that has been used in regional conflicts [47]. Because of their importance to political and commercial organizations, satellite networks have become attractive targets for cyber attackers [36].

Trust assessment or trust management algorithms can provide an effective method to mitigate against the growing cybersecurity concerns and failure conditions. These algorithms analyze network and operational behaviors of nodes in the network to identify abnormal or concerning behaviors. This information is then used to inform cooperative tasks, such as routing or distributed computation. These algorithms do not replace existing security techniques such as secure boot, security updates, or public-key encryption schemes but are intended to augment these features. There are several existing trust algorithms that have been proposed for various applications [1,2,20,27,38,43,49]. However, many of these algorithms were designed for terrestrial networks and are not tailored to satellite networks. Additionally, many existing methods have significant limitations such as circumventing node assessment, over-reliance on prior behaviors, and scalability limitations. These limitations will be explained and discussed in more detail in Sect. 4.

In this paper, we analyze several previously proposed trust algorithms for their applicability to LEO satellite constellations. To our knowledge, no such comparison has been done before, so this assessment is our first contribution. To do this we first create a uniform notation to describe how the different algorithms work. Next, we propose Trust via Asynchronous Updates (TAU): a novel decentralized trust assessment algorithm for identifying abnormally behaving nodes in distributed satellite communication networks. To evaluate the decentralized trust algorithms, we built a custom simulator and use it to assess the performance of each algorithm in the presence of attacks. We show that our decentralized trust algorithm is able to accurately identify malicious satellites, with a low false positive rate, in time comparable to previously proposed trust models. Additionally, Model TAU achieves this while having lower computational complexity and communication overhead than previous models.

This paper is structured as follows: Sect. 2 describes related work and background information such as our threat model. Section 3 describes decentralized trust algorithms and briefly explains the previously proposed algorithms that we will use as a comparison. Section 4 discusses several limitations that we have identified in various trust algorithms from literature. Section 5 describes our proposed Model TAU and how it addresses the limitations found in Sect. 4. Section 6 evaluates how our algorithm performs relative to the previously proposed algorithm. Finally, Sect. 7 summarizes the findings of this work.

2 Background

2.1 Related Work

In [16] and [24], the authors discuss ad hoc network security in the VANET and MANET domains specifically. Both of these works stress the importance of identifying nodes of the network that are behaving abnormally. Our work addresses these issues by advancing the research for identifying abnormal behavior in applications for satellite networks.

Prior work has examined attacks on satellite systems. An overview of possible attacks and mitigations, along with multiple descriptions of known attacks has been developed [13]. In addition, recent work has examined satellite vulnerabilities that stem from the fact that a large amount of information regarding the behavior of satellite networks must be made public in order to service consumers [17]. There has also been work on more advanced attacks such as the DoSat attack, a style of DDoS attack specially targeting satellite networks [28]. Our work builds off of this research by focusing on identifying abnormally behaving nodes in order to create more resilient satellite networks.

Several existing methods aim at securing an individual satellite system [15] such as secure boot [37] and access control [46]. Maintaining the security of an individual satellite is critical to maintaining the security of the network as a whole. However, these methods are not sufficient to ensure the resiliency of a satellite network as they may fail to detect attacks or failures in network operations. In this work, we choose to focus on detecting and locating abnormal behavior in a satellite constellation network after these methods have failed.

Trust assessment methods provide a promising way for detecting and identifying failed or compromised nodes in a network through monitoring and analyzing the behavior of nodes as the network operates. Trust assessment methods have been proposed in various fields such as inter-vehicle networks [38], ad hoc networks [43], fog IoT applications [49], and web services [9]. These methods are optimized for their respective domains. In this work, we will analyze various existing trust assessment approaches in the context of LEO satellite networks. We will point out the limitations of existing methods, especially if they are applied in a satellite network. Then we propose a novel trust assessment method, TAU, tailored to LEO constellation networks. We compare our proposed method with existing trust assessment techniques, including one designed for satellite networks [27].

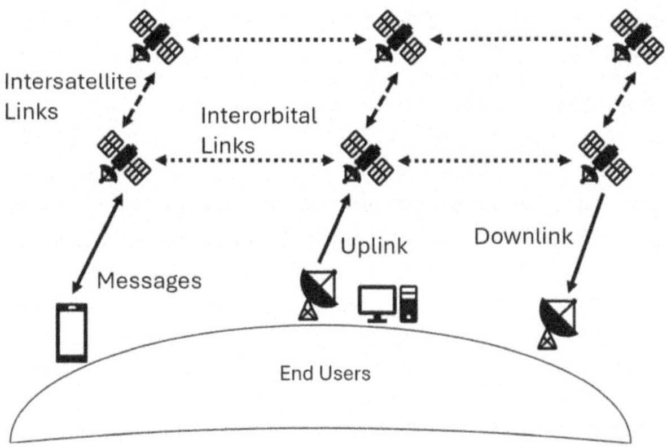

Fig. 1. An example of a LEO satellite network.

2.2 LEO Satellite Networks Are Still Relatively New

LEO satellite networks are positioned at altitudes less than 2000 km, which allows communication with terrestrial devices to have propagation delays of less than 10 milliseconds. In order to maintain their altitude, these satellites must maintain speeds of over 27,000 km per hour, causing them to orbit the Earth in around 90 min [32]. Because these LEO satellites change their position relative to the Earth during operation, long duration communication or long dwell sensing requires cooperation between multiple satellites [25].

Several of today's LEO satellite networks are connected in a mesh topology [3]. This allows satellites to send packets directly to adjacent satellites instead of repeated uplinking and downlinking. Inter-satellite communication is typically performed with laser transceivers [44]. These connections are both more efficient and more secure than radio frequency (RF).

In this work, we model a satellite network as a Walker-Delta constellation, an architecture popular with modern LEO satellite constellations, where multiple satellites follow the same path in an orbital plane [45]. In many such constellations, each satellite is connected to the two adjacent satellites within the same orbital plane and two corresponding satellites in each of the neighboring orbital planes [3,30]. See Fig. 1 for additional clarification of LEO satellite networks.

This approach is in contrast to older satellites, that were often in higher orbits and occasionally networked. Older satellite systems use a "bent pipe" approach where satellites simply relay all communications from one ground station or device to another with no inter-satellite communications [4].

2.3 Security Techniques Focus on a Satellite or a Link

Today's LEO satellites use many common security techniques, including secure boot [37], separation of privilege [31], and verification of software update integrity and authenticity [48]. Additionally, network links are protected by design:

transceivers establish point-to-point links that make it extremely difficult for neighboring devices to eavesdrop. Links are also often encrypted [35], which further prevents eavesdropping attempts.

Despite these security features, it has been shown that modern satellite networks are still at risk. At CYSAT 2023, the European Space Agency (ESA) and a cybersecurity team from Thales collaborated on a live demonstration where they hacked the ESA's OPS-SAT, an operational LEO satellite at the time [7]. They showed that even a satellite with modern cybersecurity features still had identifiable vulnerabilities that could be exploited. This demonstration was the result of the 2023 Hack-a-sat contest where several other groups reported finding additional vulnerabilities [31,46]. The results of this contest show that despite taking steps to improve their cybersecurity, individual satellites can still be compromised. Assuming that some satellites in the network remain uncompromised, they can use decentralized trust algorithms to enable intrusion detection in a scalable manner.

2.4 Threat and Attack Models

To simplify and focus this work, we examine the security of communication within the constellation.

We assume that a malicious attacker has physical access to the satellite or has remote access to the satellite network via a communications channel. Physical access can occur during satellite build, while the satellite is awaiting launch, or via anti-satellite systems while in orbit [5,23]. Physical access to the satellite enables uploading malicious software or physical damage to the system. We limit the attacker to compromising a few satellites. We believe that this is realistic, because a singleton satellite could be compromised by a worker with access during launch or by another satellite while in orbit as demonstrated by the annual Hack-a-sat competition [21]. This manual attack makes it difficult to scale. Constellations are often launched with multiple satellites that have identical design - we assume that it is possible for an attacker to inject malicious software into all satellites of a particular launch. In the OneWeb constellation, this typically ranges between 30–40 satellites which is about 5% of the final constellation [33]. We also assume that the entire network is not compromised. We assume that the regular process of testing and updating software will find and resolve issues between launches.

We assume that the entire network is known. This means that network administrators can generate certificates for all known network members and malicious entities cannot spread their malicious activities across multiple identities such as that of a Sybil attack [12].

We consider an attacker whose goal is to damage the efficacy of a satellite network by reducing the number of messages that are delivered to their destination satellite. To accomplish this, the attacker may force packets to be dropped by modifying the hardware and/or the software of multiple (but not all) satellites in a constellation network.

We consider two possible attacks, kinetic and black hole attacks. Kinetic attacks prevent satellite from operating correctly by physically attacking the system rather than using an electronic means. This could be physical destruction/damage [5] or a loss of functionality due to limitations of design decisions, such as battery depletion [41]. The black hole attack is a software attack that causes the malicious satellite to accept all packets, but then drop some or all of the packets that it receives [20]. By adjusting the ratio of packets it transmits, the affected node can retain other nodes' trust, thereby causing damage over a longer period of time.

3 Decentralized Trust Models

In an ideal case, a trusted third party would exist with complete knowledge of all satellite assessments by all satellites in the network. This entity would be capable of receiving input from all satellites simultaneously and would be able to make instantaneous decisions about which satellites are benign, which are compromised, and which require additional observation before a decision can be reached. In this ideal case, the trusted third entity would also be able to provide instantaneous feedback to inform any collaborative decision. Since information transfer to a global picture is not instantaneous, and there is no single repository of a network trust state, we use a decentralized algorithm where each satellite develops its own view and takes its own actions.

Decentralized trust algorithms use several types of trust assessments to achieve their objectives. Trust assessments based solely on interactions between each node and its neighbors are referred to as *direct trust*, which is usually updated after every such interaction. Some trust algorithms also collect assessments, or recommendations, created by other nodes regarding the node being analyzed. This is referred to as *indirect trust*. Because it involves communicating with other nodes, indirect trust is typically updated less frequently and is associated with a more complex computation than a direct trust assessment. Direct and indirect trust are combined to create *aggregate trust*, which is used to inform decisions involving other nodes.

We analyze four decentralized trust algorithms and describe their strengths, weaknesses, and varied applications. These algorithms highlight the breadth of approaches that have been used to perform decentralized trust assessments. We refer to the four algorithms from prior work that we analyze as Model A [2], Model G [20], Model L [27], and Model M [1]. This naming scheme is based on the first letter of the last name of the lead authors of each paper except for Model M which is the first letter of the name of the model used in the original paper. Each of these algorithms follow different approaches to trust assessment, and each has different strengths and weaknesses. See Table 1 for a summary of the notation and see Fig. 2 for an example of the node designation in a satellite network using the notation. For a comparison of the different aspects of the algorithms, see Table 2. The following sections will briefly describe each of the algorithms, using a standardized notation.

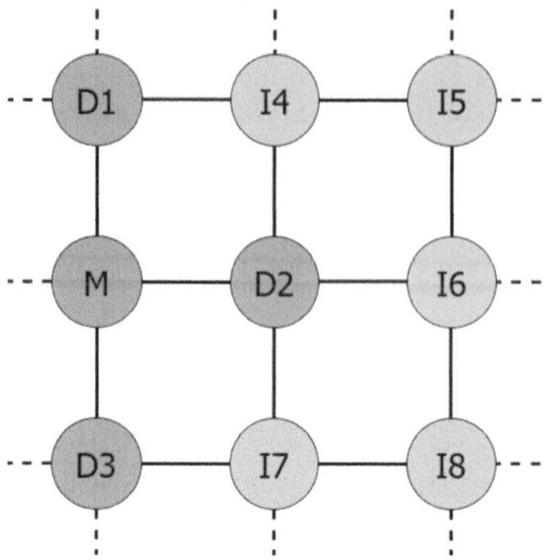

Fig. 2. Example network portion. The satellite represented by a green disc labeled M is evaluating the satellites around itself. It is evaluating the direct trust of satellites $D1$, $D2$, and $D3$ indicated by blue discs and it is evaluating the indirect trust of satellites $I4$, $I5$, $I6$, $I7$, and $I8$ indicated by yellow discs. In this network, k = 4 and n = 9. (Color figure online)

Table 1. Uniform notation used for trust algorithms

m	Node performing the analysis
a	Node being analyzed at a point in time
i	Other node in network. Exact definition varies
n	The number of nodes in the network
k	The number of directly reachable neighbors
$F_m(a)$	Packet count, m forwarded through a that arrived successfully
$L_m(a)$	Packet count, m forwarded through a that were lost
$D_m(a)$	Direct trust of a from the perspective of m
$I_m(a, i)$	Indirect trust of a from the perspective of i as stored at m
$A_m(a)$	Aggregate trust of a from the perspective of m
$W_m(a)$	Intermediate value used during trust computation of a from the perspective of m
$E_m(a)$	Entity trust of a from the perspective of m
$S_m(a)$	Number of successful connections with a from m
$U_m(a)$	Number of unsuccessful connections with a from m
$P_m(a)$	Positive event counter at m regarding a
$N_m(a)$	Negative event counter at m regarding a
$\Psi_m(a)$	Finite State Machine (FSM) state at m regarding a
$\Omega_{x,y}$	Threshold value under conditions x and y

Table 2. Properties of the algorithms evaluated in this work. The Communication column describes the number of bytes of packets generated for an indirect trust update. The Storage column describes the number of bytes necessary for maintaining the algorithm state at each satellite. The Direct and Indirect columns describe the computational complexity of the update functions when updating direct and indirect trust, respectively.

Model	Use Case	Comm.	Storage	Direct	Indirect
A [2]	IoT	0	$O(k)$	$O(1)$	-
G [20]	VANET	$O(n^3)$	$O(n^2)$	$O(1)$	$O(nk)$
L [27]	Satellite	$O(kn^2)$	$O(n^2)$	$O(1)$	$O(nk^2)$
M [1]	VANET	$O(n^3)$	$O(n^2)$	$O(1)$	$O(n)$
TAU	Satellite	$O(kn)$	$O(n^2)$	$O(1)$	$O(1)$

3.1 Model A

Model A is a trust and routing algorithm developed for Internet of Things (IoT) networks [2]. Model A only includes a direct trust component, which limits any node m to assessing the trustworthiness of the k directly connected satellites (i.e., direct neighbors).

Direct Trust via Interaction. To perform direct trust of a node's adjacent neighbors, node m counts the number of successful ($S_m(a)$) and unsuccessful ($U_m(a)$) connections between nodes m and a. Aggregate trust is equal to the direct trust ($A_m(a) = D_m(a) \in [0, 1]$) and is calculated as:

$$\textit{Model A: } D_m(a) = \frac{S_m(a) + 1}{S_m(a) + U_m(a) + 2}. \tag{1}$$

The analyzed node a is trusted by the main node m if $D_m(a)$ is above a threshold.

3.2 Model G

Model G is proposed for vehicular networks [20]. Model G uses fuzzy logic to combine several directly measured counting metrics along with indirect trust values to update a Q-learning table that is then used in a reinforcement learning model. Because this algorithm uses a reinforcement learning-based approach it can adapt to changes in its environment while accounting for learned prior node behavior.

Direct Trust via Fuzzy Logic. In Model G, there are three key features that are analyzed. Each neighbor node is measured for cooperativeness (the ratio of packets a node forwards relative to the average number of packets forwarded by neighbor nodes), honesty (the ratio of accurate packets sent by a node relative to the total number of packets it sent), and responsibility (the ratio of packets generated by a node relative to the average number of packets generated by neighbor nodes). These three ratios are combined using a fuzzy logic function to create a direct trust value ($D_m(a)$) for all neighbor nodes.

Indirect Trust via Q-Table. Model G stores a table of n trust values for each of the n nodes in the network which are all initialized to $I_m(a,i) = 0$. These values can grow without bound, and stabilize to different values depending on the size of the network with all trusted nodes having higher trust than all untrusted nodes. Whenever the measuring node m receives an indirect trust update message, the table values are updated using the following function:

$$\begin{aligned} \textit{Model G: } I_m(a,i) \leftarrow\ & \alpha \cdot [R + \gamma \cdot I_i(a,i)] \\ & + (1-\alpha) \cdot I_m(a,i). \end{aligned} \tag{2}$$

In this equation, α and γ are the learning and discount rates respectively. The authors used values of $\alpha = 0.7$ and $\gamma = 0.9$. R is the reward factor. It is equal to the direct trust $D_m(a)$ calculated at the main node m if it exists and 0 otherwise. The aggregate trust for each node is calculated as $A_m(a,m) = I_m(a,m) = \text{avg}_i I_m(a,i)$. For more details, refer to [20].

3.3 Model L

Model L is designed for satellite networks [27] and is based on Dempster-Shafer Theory [40]. It measures trust as a vector of three values corresponding to (Trustworthy, Untrustworthy, Questionable). By utilizing Dempster-Shafer Theory to combine data from multiple sources, this algorithm deals with subjective uncertainty in trust evaluation. However, its communication overhead and storage needs scale proportional to the number of satellites squared, limiting this approach to small networks (see Table 2).

Direct Trust via Trust Vector. Model L proposes a two-hop message probing scheme for measuring trust. Using this method, it counts the number of messages which are forwarded ($F_m(a)$) and lost ($L_m(a)$). This is used to create an interval direct trust vector calculated as:

$$\textit{Model L: } W_m(a) = \begin{pmatrix} v_t = \frac{F_m(a)}{F_m(a)+L_m(a)}, \\ v_u = \frac{L_m(a)}{F_m(a)+L_m(a)}, \\ v_q = 1 - v_t - v_u. \end{pmatrix} \tag{3}$$

The direct trust vector is initialized to $D_m(a) = (0,0,1)$ combined with the interval direct trust vector as a sliding average with learning rate α:

$$\textit{Model L: } D_m(a) \leftarrow (1-\alpha) \cdot D_m(a) + \alpha \cdot W_m(a). \tag{4}$$

Indirect Trust via Similarity Matrix. During each interval, a node will receive indirect trust vectors ($I_i(a, i)$) from each other node i in the network for each of its k neighbors. Using these vectors, node m constructs a k by k recommendation similarity matrix $R_m(a)$ using the Dempster-Shafer distance function to compare each pair of vectors. A full description of the distance function can be seen in [27]. The columns of the similarity matrix are summed and then normalized to create an array of discount factors. The trust vectors are each multiplied by their corresponding discount factor to get an array of indirect trust vectors ($I_m(a, i)$) which are then summed to create an overall indirect trust vector $I_m(a, m) = (v_t, v_u, v_q)$.

Aggregating Direct and Indirect Trust. To calculate the aggregate trust vector ($A_m(a, m) = (v_t, v_u, v_q)$), Model L takes the direct ($D_m(a, m)$) and indirect ($I_m(a, m)$) trust vectors and combines them using the Dempster-Shafer synthesis function. For details on this function and more information about the model as a whole, please refer to [27].

3.4 Model M

Model M is designed for vehicular ad-hoc networks [1]. This model uses two trust metrics to determine trust. The first metric, $E_m(a)$, is referred to as Entity Trust. This metric attempts to identify dishonest nodes within the pool of legitimate nodes by comparing a node's current behaviors with its past behaviors. The other metric, $A_m(a)$, is referred to as the data-centric trust metric. This metric is computed by aggregating the quality of prior messages with the indirect trust assessments of other nodes. Both metrics must be above given threshold values for a received message to be considered trusted.

Trust via Entity Verification. To perform entity verification, each node of the network stores an entity trust value $E_m(a)$. When node m receives a message from node a, the entity trust algorithm first determines if the message was received within a pre-defined range. The range is based on the size of the two antennas of the two devices. $E_m(a)$ is increased if the message was received within the range and decreased otherwise.

Trust via Data Verification. The data-centric trust metric counts the number of packets forwarded ($F_m(a)$) and lost ($L_m(a)$) by each of the main node's k neighbors. The model calculates a weighted ratio ($W_m(a)$) for each using the following equation:

$$\textit{Model M: } W_m(a) = \frac{\alpha \cdot \sum_{i=1}^{n} F_i(a)}{\alpha \cdot \sum_{i=1}^{n} F_i(a) + \beta \cdot \sum_{i=1}^{n} L_i(a)}, \tag{5}$$

where α and β are weights $0 < \alpha, \beta < 1$. This weighted ratio is intuitively different from the weighted ratio used in Model L. The weights α and β allow the developer to tune the severity of dropped messages relative to normal behavior. Since Model M updates trust after receiving a message, the weighted ratio is combined with a value $0 \leq M_{\text{Quality}} \leq 1$ that is indicative of the quality of the transmission. For our work, we assumed that the communication channels were lossless, so $M_{\text{Quality}} = 1$. The aggregate trust ($A_m(a)$) is calculated using:

$$\textit{Model M: } A_m(a) = \frac{1}{2} \frac{M_{\text{Quality}} \cdot W_m(a)}{M_{\text{Quality}} + W_m(a)}. \tag{6}$$

In addition to the metrics described here, Model M has two alternative trust assessment methods that are used based on conditions specific to vehicular ad hoc networks. For more details, please refer to [1].

4 Limitations of Prior Models

Limitations of prior trust assessment techniques can be divided into three main categories. First, node assessment can be circumvented allowing malicious nodes to avoid detection. Second, multiple models exhibit over-reliance on prior behavior, meaning that a node that behaves properly for a long time can use its past behavior to mask more recent malicious behavior. Finally, many algorithms require quadratic or higher amounts of resources with respect to the number of nodes, making the algorithm difficult to scale to the size of existing and planned satellite constellations.

4.1 Node Assessment can be Circumvented

There are several methods that can be used to directly assess the ability of a node to forward messages. The first method uses probe packets that return to the source node. Nodes can generate packets where the final destination is the same as the source and pass through one or multiple other nodes to "probe" the network. The assumption here is that if the packet returns to the source node, it knows that all other nodes on the route of the packet correctly forwarded the packet. However, a malicious node could mask its behavior because such probing packets are easily detectable. The malicious node only needs to compare the source and destination of a packet, and if they are the same, it knows that the packet is a probing packet. Then, the malicious node can route only probing packets, allowing it to drop any legitimate traffic without fear of detection.

The second method uses self reporting from a secure network interface. Secure hardware within an embedded system interface could be used to count the number of packets properly routed by embedded systems [42]. However, other work has demonstrated that specially crafted attacks on satellite hardware can inhibit these security measures, allowing a malicious node to fake its reliability [46]. It is unlikely that these issues will be fully resolved, so satellite trust algorithms must rely on metrics from other sources.

The third method uses acknowledgment packets (ACK) from reliable communication protocols such as TCP. When a node sends a packet to a particular destination, all nodes along the path are able to test if other nodes along the path are routing packets properly. If an ACK packet generated at the final destination returns along the same path, then all of these nodes are notified of all other nodes' proper operation. However, TCP does not guarantee that packets return to the source on the same route as was used to reach the destination. In this case, intermediate nodes might mark other nodes along the path as untrustworthy if the ACK packet is routed around those particular nodes. A source based routing algorithm (where the entire route is decided by the source node and stored in the packet) can account for this issue and is what we choose to use with the proposed Model TAU .

4.2 Over-Reliance on Prior Behaviors

Many trust algorithms have some feature to count the number of correct and incorrect behaviors that each node does, then use these metrics to determine the trust of the node. For relatively short time intervals, this works well, but it does not work with systems deployed for long periods of time. If a node behaves properly for a long time, suppose a year, before being attacked and taken over by a malicious entity, then that node might have millions or even billions of correct behaviors with only a few incorrect. When it suddenly switches to malicious behavior, it will take time proportional to how long the node behaved correctly before other nodes start to detect and react to the malicious node.

This concept can be seen in Fig. 3. In this figure, a benign and a malicious entity are depicted, with the malicious activity onset starting at two different times. In Fig. 3a, the malicious node acts maliciously from the start. In this graph, the trust value of the malicious entity remains below the trusted threshold, while the benign entity accumulates trust. In Fig. 3b, the malicious entity initially accumulates trust, so that when it later performs malicious actions, the entity remains in the trusted state longer. Although not shown, if the malicious behavior continues, the trust value will eventually go below the threshold.

4.3 Resource Use Limits Scalability

Most of the trust algorithms identified in literature rely on periodic updates from other nodes to maintain an accurate assessment of the network. The periodicity of the updates ensures that nodes know when to expect update packets and also works as a liveness test. In this context, a liveness test determines if another node is still operational. In this case, the lack of a signal indicates a problem with another node.

However, these periodic messages consume a large amount of bandwidth and result in large overhead, especially as the number of nodes increases. The overhead of different trust algorithms can be seen in Table 2. Multiple of the models rely on communication overhead which scales proportional to the number of satellites cubed, which will become a significant problem as the size of satellite networks continues to increase. It is noted that modern LEO constellations are

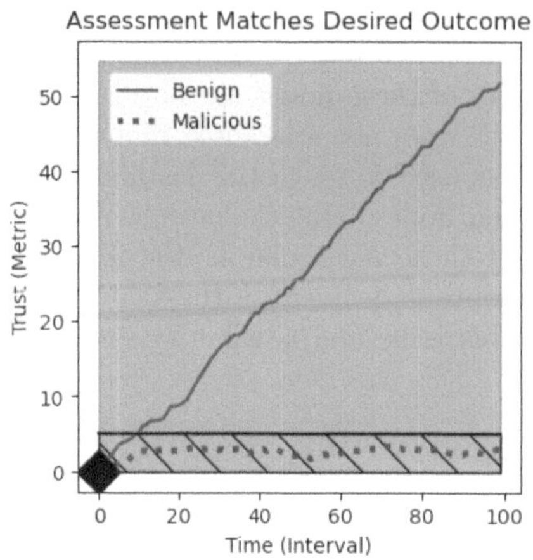

(a) Benign entity accumulates trust. Malicious entity attack occurs immediately after network initialization.

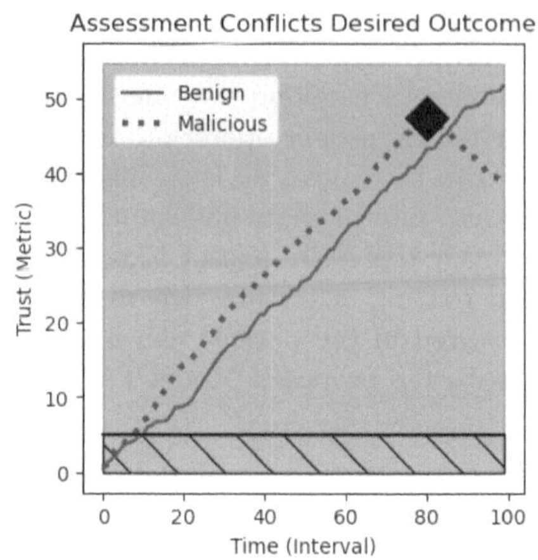

(b) Malicious entity attack is delayed until after it has exceeded the trust threshold.

Fig. 3. An illustration of different assessments based on the timing of the onset of malicious activity. The green region above the threshold with no hatch represents nodes above the "trusted" threshold, and the red hatched region below the threshold line represents nodes that are "untrusted" according to the trust metric. In both graphs, the blue solid line indicates the trust of the benign node and the purple dotted line indicates the trust of the malicious node. The black diamond shape indicates the time that the malicious node begins acting maliciously. (Color figure online)

continuing to grow in size as seen by Starlink, which has requested permission to add over 2000 additional satellites to the existing constellation [11].

5 The Proposed Model TAU

In this section, we present our proposed trust assessment algorithm for satellite networks, Model TAU . Model TAU is based on a finite state machine (FSM). Each satellite m maintains a 3-state FSM for each other satellite a in the network with the states being: Trusted (T), Questionable (Q), and Untrusted (U).

$$Model\ TAU : \Psi_m(a) \in \{T, Q, U\} \tag{7}$$

An FSM diagram with transition conditions can be seen in Fig. 4. State transitions occur after one or several asynchronous events e. Each event can increase the value of one of two counters $P_m(a)$ or $N_m(a)$. These counters track the positive and negative events associated with node a. The conditions for a transition are based on the current state of $\Psi_m(a)$ and the threshold values Ω.

The events that can trigger these transitions are direct trust measurements (the detection of forwarded and lost packets), indirect trust alerts, and direct

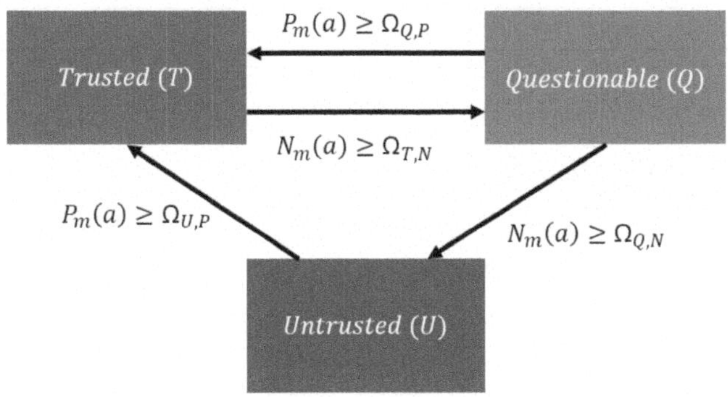

Fig. 4. The finite state machine used by the TAU trust algorithm. Transitions occur when one of the two counters ($P_m(a)$ or $N_m(a)$) exceeds the relevant threshold Ω. State transitions result in counters being reset.

intervention from a trusted authority, such as a ground station. These events can be designated either as positive or negative. Certain events are more reliable indicators of abnormal behavior than others, so we assign various weights e_w to each event e based on the type of event that has occurred and the current state of other nodes associated with the event. These weights are all positive integers with more important events having a larger effect on their respective counters.

Whenever a node a enters the Trusted state from the perspective of node m, m initializes $N_m(a) = 0$. This initialization occurs every time a node transitions to the Trusted state or after initialization. Whenever m experiences a negative event e, it increases the counter by the amount of the event weight:

$$Model\ TAU : N_m(a) \leftarrow N_m(a) + e_w. \tag{8}$$

Different events have different weights, so some events may cause the counter to increment more quickly than others. For example, if m receives a message from Trusted node i that says that node a is Untrusted, this event is weighted more heavily than node a dropping a single packet. Therefore the first event will increase $N_m(a)$ more than the second event. After $N_m(a)$ has reached a threshold of the Trusted state on the Negative counter denoted by $\Omega_{T,N}$, then $\Psi_m(a)$ will switch from Trusted to Questionable.

The Questionable state is for testing another satellite which is suspected of being malicious. Whenever a satellite enters the Questionable state from the perspective of m, m initializes the two counters ($P_m(a) = 0$ and $N_m(a) = 0$). Each counter has a separate threshold value designated as $\Omega_{Q,P}$ and $\Omega_{Q,N}$. Whenever a positive or negative event occurs, the event weight of that event will be added to the corresponding counter. Only one of the two counters will be affected by a particular event. This state is intended to be a temporary state, so whichever counter reaches its corresponding threshold first indicates the result of the test indicates which state $\Psi_m(a)$ should switch to. The logic for this state can be seen in Algorithm 1.

Algorithm 1: Questionable State Algorithm

Input: Event e with weight e_w, State $\Psi_m(a) \in \{T, Q, U\}$,
$0 \leq P_m(a) < \Omega_{Q,P}$, $0 \leq N_m(a) < \Omega_{Q,N}$,
Output: None
if e is Negative **then** $N_m(a) \leftarrow N_m(a) + e_w$
else $P_m(a) \leftarrow P_m(a) + e_w$
end if
if $N_m(a) \geq \Omega_{Q,N}$ **then** $\Psi_m(a) \leftarrow U$
end if
if $P_m(a) \geq \Omega_{Q,P}$ **then** $\Psi_m(a) \leftarrow T$
end if

The Questioning state serves as a transition between the Trusted and Untrusted states, resetting assessments built up over time. Consider a satellite which operates correctly 99% of the time. This satellite performs well, but will eventually generate enough negative events such that it drops into the Questionable state. However, during this test, the satellite will cause many more positive events than negative ones. This means that $P_m(a)$ will reach its corresponding threshold before $N_m(a)$ and move the satellite back to the Trusted state.

If a satellite a is in the Untrusted state, it means that the satellite entered the Questionable state and has continued to produce more negative events indicating abnormal behavior. This is likely indicative of an issue such as damage or corruption by a malicious entity. A satellite in this state can only move to a higher state after direct intervention from a trusted entity, such as an authenticated ground station. As satellites in LEO circle the Earth in only a few hours, they can reasonably expect to receive this direct intervention in a timely manner.

Figure 5 depicts how the FSM and counters change over time as a result of different observed activity. In this example, the node being analyzed starts in the Trusted state. Over time, the negative counter starts to grow until it reaches the threshold value. For this example, all of the thresholds are set to 6 to match the value used in our evaluation, i.e. $\Omega_{T,N} = \Omega_{Q,N} = \Omega_{Q,P} = 6$, but this is not a requirement of the algorithm. After $N_m(a)$ reaches the threshold, the counters are reset and $\Psi_m(a)$ changes from Trusted to Questionable. In the Questionable state, a produces more positive events than negative events, so $P_m(a)$ reaches its threshold value (6) faster. $\Psi_m(a)$ returns to the Trusted state and both of the counters are reset. a continues to cause negative events, so the state again changes to Questionable. However, this time the node causes more negative events which means that $N_m(a)$ reaches its threshold (6) first and finally causes the $\Psi_m(a)$ to transition to the Untrusted state.

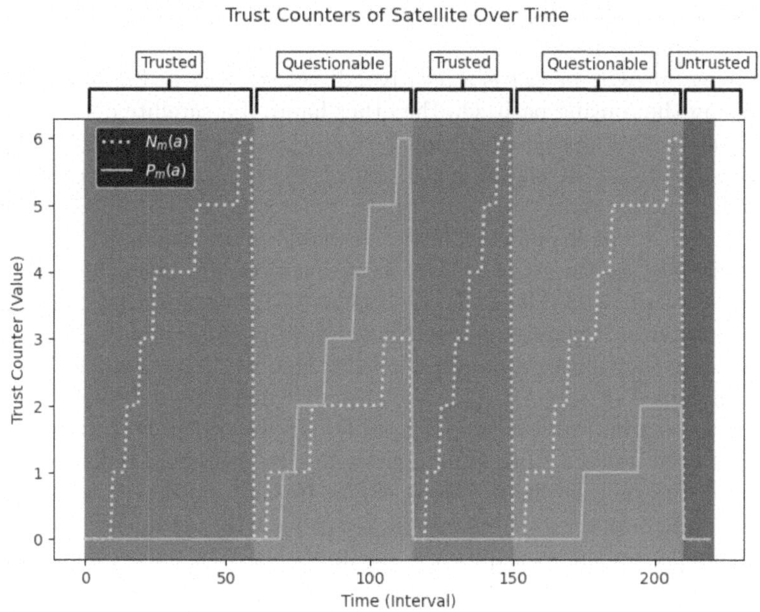

Fig. 5. An example runtime of the TAU model and the two counters as the behavior of a node being analyzed changes. The green, yellow and red regions correspond to $\Psi_m(a)$ being equal to Trusted, Questionable and Untrusted respectively as indicated by the labels above the figure. (Color figure online)

5.1 Direct Trust via Response Packets

While many prior trust algorithms use interactions and probing packets to perform direct trust assessment, we use an ACK packet system. ACK packets are generated whenever a packet arrives at its destination.

In the simplest case, the source and the destination are directly communicating. If an ACK packet is returned by the connected neighbor, this indicates a positive event. If no ACK is received within a preset time period, then this will be a negative event.

Next consider the case where the source and the destination nodes are not directly connected. In this case, the destination is still the only entity to create an ACK packet. The destination node can use source-based routing to ensure that the ACK packet travels along the same path that the original packet took to arrive to the source. Additionally, by having the destination node sign the ACK packet using a public key cryptography scheme, it can ensure that malicious intermediate nodes cannot generate the ACK packet instead.

When each intermediate node receives the ACK packet generated by the destination node, each intermediate node knows that none of the other nodes on the path have dropped the packet. Because this method uses a source-based routing algorithm, all nodes along the path know which intermediate nodes could potentially drop the packet.

Receiving an ACK packet is a positive, direct trust event for all of the nodes further along the routing path. On the other hand, if a satellite does not receive an ACK packet after a pre-defined time period (either because the original packet was dropped or the ACK packet was dropped) then this creates a negative event for all nodes further along the routing path, since it is not possible to determine where the packet was dropped from the available information. We assume that any message lacking an ACK packet must have a node behaving abnormally somewhere on its path. Packets that receive an ACK message exist on paths with only benign nodes. Benign nodes will have more positive events than negative events because they exist on more paths that result in a returned ACK packet.

Two examples of the ACK packet system can be seen in Fig. 6. In both examples, the original packet travels from node 1 to node 8 by passing through node 2 and then node 5. Node 8 then generates an ACK packet and sends it to node 5. In both examples, node 5 would count this as a positive event for node 8. In Fig. 6a, node 5 forwards the ACK packet to node 2, and node 2 forwards the packet to node 1. In this example, as a result of this ACK packet being properly forwarded, nodes 1 and 2 would count positive events for nodes 5 and 8, and node 1 would also count a positive event for node 2. In Fig. 6b, node 5 fails to forward the ACK packet. In this case, node 5 would still count a positive event for node 8, but nodes 1 and 2 would count negative events for nodes 5 and 8 instead.

There is an exception to the rule for applying negative events. If at least one node along the path of the message is known to be Untrusted ($\Psi_m(i) = U$), no negative events will be accumulated. We assume that all negative events will be caused by one of these nodes that are Untrusted and because the Untrusted state does not have a transition condition related to the negative event counter, there is no need to apply negative events to any node.

Consider again the example in Fig. 6. In Fig. 6b, node 5 failed to forward the ACK packet. If node 1 had come to the conclusion that node 5 was Untrusted, then it would not count the negative event for node 8 as node 5 is already Untrusted.

5.2 Indirect Trust via Asynchronous Updates

Models G, L, and M share indirect trust by sending their trust evaluation values for each node to all other nodes once in every set time interval. Low earth orbit satellite constellations do not have broadcast communications, so every time interval, all n satellites generate n messages with n values. This creates network communication overhead proportional to the number of satellites cubed, which can be problematic for larger constellations. To solve this issue we propose an asynchronous indirect trust update. We propose that whenever a counter goes over a threshold, triggering a change in state $\Psi_m(a)$, it announces this single piece of information to all other nodes in the network. Whether the state switched to a higher trust state or a lower trust state indicates whether this update is a

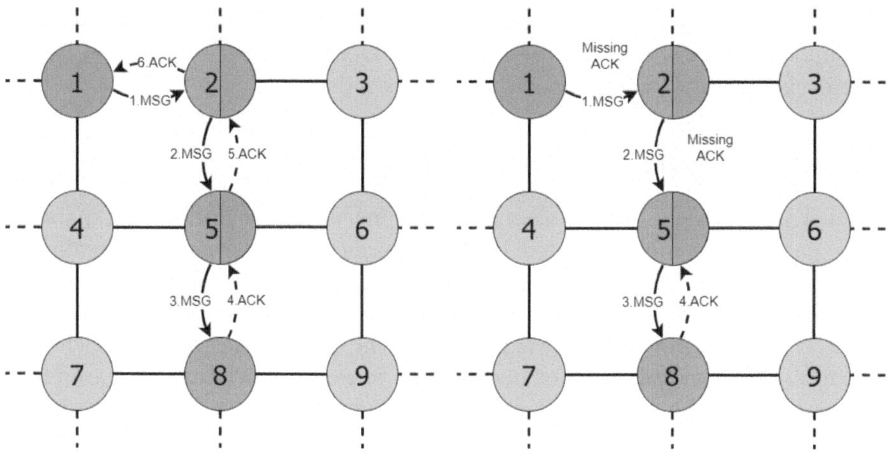

(a) (b)

Fig. 6. Two examples showing the flow of packet and ACK. The network shown is a subsection of the torus topology used by many modern satellite networks. In both examples, the packet travels from node 1 to node 8 via nodes 2 and 5. Nodes 1, 2, and 5 are all or partially green because they will evaluate the trust of other nodes as a result of this packet. Nodes 2, 5, and 8 are all or partially blue because they will have their trust evaluated by other nodes as a result of this packet. In Fig. 6a, all nodes forward the ACK packet appropriately. This results in nodes 1 and 2 counting positive events for nodes 5 and 8. In Fig. 6b, node 5 fails to forward the ACK packet, so nodes 1 and 2 never receive it. This results in nodes 1 and 2 counting negative events for nodes 5 and 8. Numbers attached to arrows indicate the order packets are sent.

positive or negative event for other nodes. When the network is performing normally, there are no significant changes in the trust values for any of the algorithms resulting in redundant communication. By limiting the indirect trust updates to only FSM transitions which occur infrequently, the communication overhead is significantly reduced.

Because the indirect trust updates are not occurring periodically, it is possible for attackers to drop this update packet without detection. For that reason, each satellite that receives an update sends it to all adjacent satellites unless that satellite has already transmitted the update. This results in routing around any malicious satellites that may maliciously drop the packet that would alert other nodes to its malicious behavior. Assuming that each satellite has $k = 4$ adjacent satellites, this asynchronous, indirect trust update corresponds to $k \cdot n = 4n$ overhead messages sent occasionally which is significantly less than the n^2 messages generated by Models G, L, and M.

There are two additional techniques we use to reduce communications overhead in the indirect update system. Only 1-hop neighbors of node a can report indirect trust updates about node a. The assumption is that 1-hop neighbors will have the most up to date information about a's behavior and additional nodes reporting updates will simply flood the network. Additionally, indirect trust updates from nodes that are themselves Questionable or Untrusted have a lower event weight as these reports are not as reliable.

5.3 Addressing the Limitations of Prior Models

Model TAU prevents node assessment circumvention by using ACK packets. These packets are not generated by the intermediate entities, so a malicious entity cannot fake them. This can be guaranteed by requiring the destination satellite to sign the ACK packet with a public key cryptography scheme. Also, the ACK packet provides knowledge about the node being analyzed whether the packet gets forwarded or not because the timeout, which indicates a missing ACK packet, can be used for trust algorithm purposes. This concept is similar to how a node can fail a liveness test if it does not generate a periodic update.

Additionally, Model TAU does not overly rely on prior node behaviors as all nodes start at the maximum level of trust. The FSM that Model TAU uses as a basis only has three states and the counters, which trigger transitions, are reset during every state transition. These state transitions are triggered by events rather than periodic time intervals which allows the model to remain reactive after long periods of time.

Finally, Model TAU scales well due to its asynchronous indirect trust update method. Traffic is only generated on state transitions, which should be infrequent events. On the other hand, periodic indirect trust updates that are used in existing work typically occur every few seconds, which consumes a significant amount of bandwidth.

6 Evaluation

To examine the different trust models, we developed a simulator for assessing the accuracy of the trust models' identification of malicious nodes in a satellite network. While designing our simulator, we assume each satellite has limited access to information about behavior across the network. Therefore, we implemented several features in the simulator to guarantee that each satellite operates with the information it would have received had the simulation occurred in a real satellite network. Each satellite has its own instance of the trust model. Each of these trust model instances stores only the information that would be stored at each satellite. Additionally, information is only shared between the different model instances as a result of an indirect trust update (whether it is synchronous or asynchronous).

6.1 Trust Algorithms are Compared in a Custom Simulator

Modern constellation systems range from a few tens to thousands of satellites [11, 22], and our simulator supports this. Older, but still relevant, LEO satellite constellations such as Globalstar and Iridium are relatively small with 48 and

66 satellites respectively [10,30]. For these tests, we chose an intermediate round number and used a 100 satellite network with 10 orbital planes of 10 satellites each. We intend to perform more scalability studies in future work.

The simulator is a discrete event simulator that updates indirect trust of the entire network once per time interval. Every interval, the network generates 100 packets and selects a source and destination node uniformly. For each experiment, we ran 20 independent iterations of the simulator for 20 intervals each. In each iteration, 10 nodes were selected uniformly from the network to be designated as malicious with behavior varying depending on the experiment. Each iteration uses a different set of malicious nodes.

6.2 Parameters of Model TAU Used By the Simulator

In examining the proposed Model TAU , we assumed that dropping and forwarding messages both have an event weight of 1. Indirect trust updates have event weights of 2, 1, and 0 when the reporting node is Trusted, Questionable, and Untrusted respectively. We chose to set the thresholds $\Omega_{T,N} = \Omega_{Q,N} = \Omega_{Q,P} = 6$. When considering how to set the thresholds, we considered the satellites that are far away from satellite a will be relying almost exclusively on indirect trust updates to make decisions. This means that the threshold cannot be larger than the number of satellites neighboring satellite a multiplied by the maximum indirect trust update event weight. Additionally, we wanted to account for the possibility that two adjacent satellites are both malicious, as the neighboring malicious satellite may not accurately report negative trust events about the satellite being analyzed. For that reason we set the thresholds equal to the number of 1-hop neighbors (k) minus 1 multiplied by the maximum indirect trust update event weight (2): (k-1)·max(weight) = (4-1)·2 = 6. These threshold and event weight values show comparable, and sometimes superior, results in terms of accuracy and efficiency. Even further optimization of these parameters is intended for future work.

6.3 Trust Algorithms are Evaluated with F-Scores

To examine the effectiveness of the various trust models, we consider a ground station view. At the end of each simulator interval, each node measures its current trust value for each neighbor relative to a threshold defined by the corresponding model. If there are more positive opinions regarding a node, that node is classified as Trusted. If there are more negative opinions about a node, that node is classified as Untrusted. If the opinions are equal in number, the node is classified as Questionable. This classification system allows us to analyze how effective the trust model is at identifying malicious nodes. We then compute the precision, recall, and F-score [18]. These metrics are calculated using the True Positives (TP), False Positives (FP) and False Negatives (FN) as follows:

$$\text{Precision} = \frac{\text{TP}}{\text{TP} + \text{FP}}, \text{Recall} = \frac{\text{TP}}{\text{TP} + \text{FN}}, \text{F-score} = 2\frac{\text{Precision} \cdot \text{Recall}}{\text{Precision} + \text{Recall}}.$$

TP is the number of malicious nodes classified as Untrusted, FP is the number of benign nodes classified as Untrusted, and FN is the number of malicious nodes classified as Questionable or Trusted. Note that the ideal scenario is that Precision, Recall, and F-score are all equal to 1.0 as this indicates that all abnormally behaving nodes have been identified and no benign nodes have been misclassified as Untrusted. In each experiment, we averaged the precision, recall, and F-score at each time interval across the different iterations for each of the trust models.

6.4 Experiment Overview

We conducted three experiments to assess performance. In each experiment, there were 10 malicious nodes in a network of 100 total nodes. The first and third experiments consider a kinetic attack and the second experiment considers a black hole attack. The first and second experiments assumed that the attack occurred immediately after network initialization, and the third experiment assumed that the attack was delayed until long after network initialization. We also performed a fourth experiment that used a delayed black hole attack, but the observations were similar to the results of the delayed kinetic attack experiment, so it was dropped for brevity.

Immediate Kinetic Attack Experiment. In our first experiment, we measured the performance of the trust algorithms assuming that the attack was introduced immediately after network initialization. In these results, the network was subjected to a ten node kinetic attack. The average precision, recall, and F-score at all intervals over all of the iterations can be seen in the first column of Fig. 7.

In this figure, we can see that all nodes, with the exception of those using Model G, quickly identified the malicious nodes as malicious, as indicated by having high recall. Additionally, Models A, L, and TAU had limited instances where Trusted nodes were misclassified as Untrusted which result in lower precision scores. Model G classified the entire network as Trusted, and was never able to identify the malicious nodes.

In this experiment, Model A achieves the highest F-score, and it achieves it faster than all the other models. Models L and TAU had slightly lower F-scores because their precision was slightly less than the best results. Model M did not perform as well in this experiment due to its high misclassification rate resulting in lower precision. Model G was not able to locate the malicious nodes in this experiment because of its low initial trust which resulted in low recall and F-score.

Immediate Black Hole Attack Experiment. In this experiment, the network experienced a black hole attack that randomly dropped 65% of all packets at ten nodes, starting immediately after network initialization. This matches the drop rate chosen by [27], although the results are not particularly sensitive to the

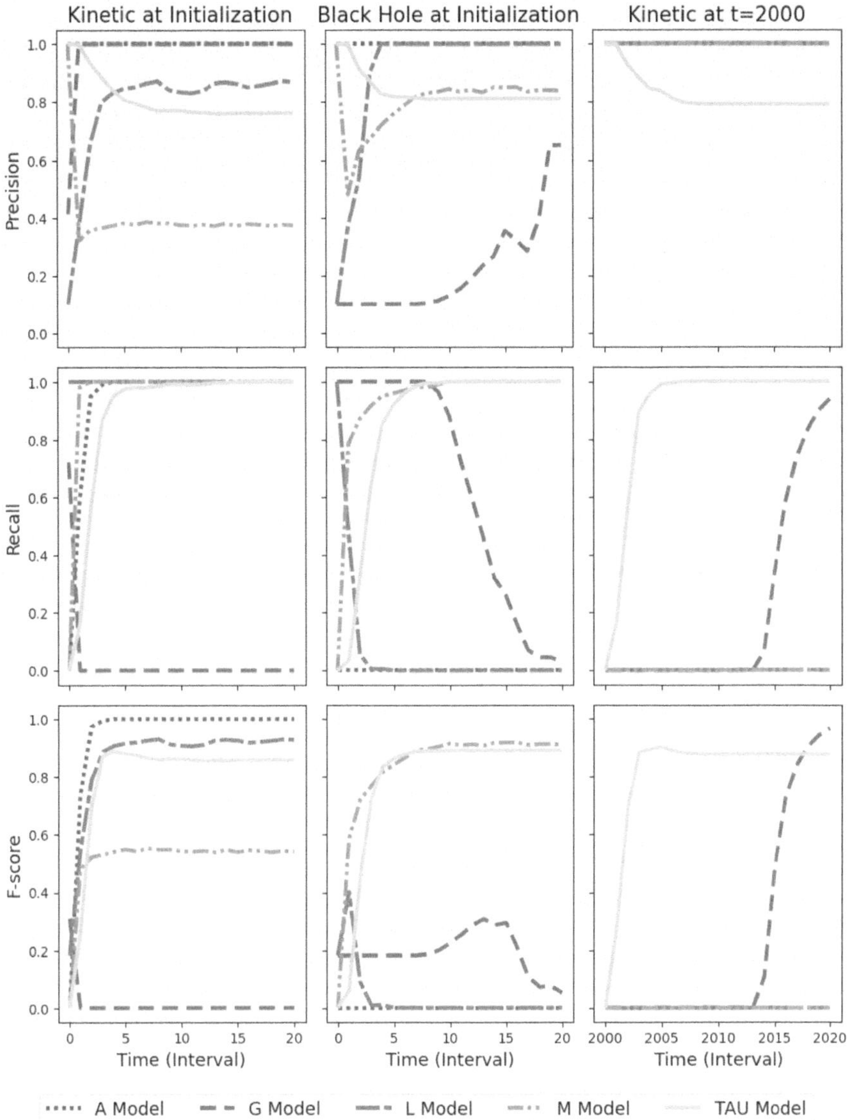

Fig. 7. Precision, recall, and F-score of all models under three conditions, as trust is gained or lost over time. Each experiment has ten malicious nodes. The first and third experiments experienced kinetic attacks. The second experiment experienced a black hole attack. The first and second experiments were performed under the assumption that the attack occurred immediately, at network initialization. The third experiment was performed under the assumption that the attack occurred 2000 intervals after network initialization. Model TAU accurately identifies malicious nodes as fast as, or faster than, other models, with significantly less overhead.

exact value selected. The average precision, recall, and F-score at all intervals over all of the iterations can be seen in the second column of Fig. 7.

In this experiment, Models A and L had almost no success in identifying the malicious nodes as demonstrated by low recall; however, these models maintained igh precision. Models M and TAU consistently identified the malicious nodes. These models tended to misclassify trustworthy nodes, especially when they were adjacent to multiple malicious satellites. This is why the stable precision values of the two models are below 1.0. While Model G initially classified the malicious nodes as Untrusted, it consistently abandoned these classifications as seen by the significant drop in recall starting at 10 intervals.

Models M and TAU achieved the best results in this experiment. Both were able to quickly identify the malicious nodes with limited misclassification. Model G suffers with its low initial trust value, and its performance under a black hole attack is similar to the immediate kinetic attack experiment. Model A suffers because it only confirms that the next node receives the packet. It does not attempt to determine the behavior of the other node after the transmission is complete, so it is not aware of the malicious behavior being performed.

Delayed Kinetic Attack Experiment. In this experiment, the network was subjected to the same kinetic attack as the first experiment but after many models reached stable values and 2000 intervals had occurred. The average precision, recall, and F-score at all intervals over all of the iterations can be seen in the third column of Fig. 7.

In this experiment, Models G and TAU were the only models able to identify the malicious nodes. All others had a recall of 0.0 at all intervals. Model G took significantly longer than Model TAU , but it was still able to locate the malicious nodes with no misclassifications. Model G performed much better in this experiment relative to the immediate kinetic attack experiment because it was able to build up trust for the trustworthy nodes before the attack was introduced. Model TAU was able to identify the malicious nodes just as quickly as in the previous experiment, but it still has a slight tendency to occasionally misclassify nodes adjacent to malicious nodes.

Models G and TAU were the superior models in this experiment, however there are some trade-offs. Model TAU had a much faster response time, but it has a tendency to misclassify nodes adjacent to malicious nodes when those nodes were adjacent to multiple malicious nodes. Model G had a much slower response time, but it consistently achieved 100% precision. The other three models performed significantly worse because of the over-reliance on prior behavior.

6.5 Scalability Results

In this section, we examine the complexity of the proposed TAU algorithm in terms of latency and memory requirements of the simulation, and compare it to existing trust algorithms. We focus on the synchronous trust update step because the latency caused by the other steps is negligible in comparison. All experiments were conducted on a Thinkbook 14 G2 ITL with a 11th Gen Intel(R) Core(TM) i5-1135G7 @ 2.40GHz. Additionally, we count the number of floats and integers that were maintained at each node, not including any intermediate values that are generated during the synchronous trust updates. For the three algorithms that use a synchronous trust update, we calculate the time it takes to complete the synchronous trust update as an average of all interval trust updates across all the experiments and iterations. The results can be seen in Table 3.

Both Models A and TAU do not use a synchronous trust update function, so they account for no computation time in the synchronous trust update step. Model M used several μs of computation, and Models L and G were four orders of magnitude higher than Model M. The experiments above show that the increased computation does not result in more accurate algorithms.

The final two columns of Table 3 show the floats and integers used by the different algorithms. Model A is extremely lightweight, so it used the lowest number of resources. Models G and L used a large number of floats which require more memory than integers. Models M and TAU mostly rely on integers rather than floats, but Model M uses floats to store the final trust results and it requires almost twice as many integers as the TAU model.

Table 3. Resources used by the different models. The Average Time column refers to the time it takes to complete a synchronous trust update. The Floats and Integers columns refer to the amount of memory that must be stored outside of the indirect trust update.

Model	Average Time	Floats	Integers
A	0.000 ms	1	8
G	8.130 ms	10403	300
L	5.468 ms	30603	0
M	0.093 ms	104	20000
TAU	0.000 ms	0	10200

6.6 Discussion

We presented an analysis of five models of trust that are commonly used in other domains. Model A is relatively simple compared to the other models, so it responds very quickly to kinetic attacks. In the immediate kinetic attack experiment, the Model A consistently reported the most accurate results in the shortest amount of time. However, Model A was unable to detect the black hole attacks due to the fact that it only relied on successful interactions rather than determining if the packet successfully arrived at its destination. Additionally Model A uses a continuous counter that doesn't reset for successful and unsuccessful interactions, so after a long period of time, Model A is not able to adapt and cannot account for the change in node behavior. This results in a very poor performance for the delayed kinetic attack experiment. **While Model A is lightweight and easy to implement, it has trouble identifying delayed or complex attacks.**

Model G is the only prior trust model that achieves some success in the delayed kinetic attack experiment, aided by its reinforcement learning approach. This model cannot handle attacks that occur at network initialization, because it needs time to build trust across the network. In the immediate kinetic attack, Model G initially misclassifies nodes as malicious due to the fact that it initially puts all nodes in a questionable state rather than in a trusted state. In the immediate black hole attack experiment, it often accredited dropped packets to other nodes resulting in very poor trust evaluation for the network as a whole. On the other hand, when Model G was given time to build up trust prior to introducing the attack model, it performed much better. In the delayed kinetic attack experiment, Model G was able to identify the malicious node after approximately 15 intervals as indicated by the spike in recall. **Model G is adaptable due to its reinforcement learning approach, but it has difficulty identifying attacks that occur immediately after initialization of the network.**

Model L is one of the best models for responding to the attack in the immediate kinetic attack experiment and one of the worst in the delayed kinetic attack experiment as indicated by the F-score. The poor performance in the delayed kinetic attack experiment occurs because Model L builds up too much trust and overrelies on prior node behavior. Additionally the fractional drop rate in the immediate black hole experiment allows the malicious nodes to avoid detection. **Model L was tailored for LEO satellite constellations, but limitations in the design make it difficult for the model to respond to more sophisticated attacks.**

Out of the three experiments, Model M performed best in the immediate black hole experiment. This model is able to correctly identify the malicious node with the least number of misclassifications relative to the other models. This is because Model M is optimized for identifying black hole attacks with only a partial drop rate. It performed poorly in the delayed kinetic attack experiment due to an over-reliance on prior behaviors. **Model M is optimized for identifying black hole attacks, but struggles because of the operational differences between satellite and VANET networks.**

The proposed Model TAU performed well on all three experiments as it was able to identify the malicious nodes in all cases, resulting in high recall. This model has a tendency to misclassify one of the nodes adjacent to a malicious node as untrusted due to a randomly high amount of traffic traveling through the adjacent node into the malicious node. This resulted in lower trust for that adjacent node as displayed by the drop in precision for all three experiments.

Future work includes extending the algorithm to include other sources of information including remote attestation and restarts in known-good states. We will also explore alternative methods for setting parameters, thresholds, and event weights.

Despite the superior performance of Model TAU using less overhead communication, it can be argued that algorithms that use synchronous communication are better as they have the added benefit of a liveness testr, the kinetic attack experiments show that Model TAU is able to quickly identify satellites that have stopped operating as a result of a kinetic attack. This demonstrates the model's ability to provide liveness tests without the use of a synchronous communication protocol.

In addition to the kinetic and black hole attacks addressed in this paper, we identified flooding and voting attacks as potential concerns for a satellite network [8,41]. Nodes that issue flooding attacks send extraneous messages to one or multiple neighbors, effectively using up all available bandwidth. Voting attacks occur when a satellite exploits a reputation system to alter how other nodes perceive the trust of nodes in the network. This can be achieved by slandering legitimate nodes or by advocating for malicious nodes. Successful voting attacks rely on the specifics of the trust algorithm they are opposing, making comparisons challenging, so we did not consider them in this work. Future work includes extending the algorithm to address both of these attacks.

7 Conclusion

In this work, we assessed multiple prior decentralized trust algorithms. Many earlier decentralized trust algorithms are optimized for their settings, which do not match today's satellite network configurations, and therefore hinder their ability to adapt to satellite-relevant attack scenarios. In response to this, we proposed a novel decentralized trust algorithm, TAU which is superior to the other existing trust models in its ability to detect kinetic and black hole attacks in satellite networks.

This new algorithm uses finite state machines to assess the trust of nodes in the network, giving this model higher computational efficiency relative to the existing models from prior works. Additionally, the proposed algorithm uses an asynchronous indirect trust update, driven by state transitions, which significantly reduces the communication overhead that occupies network traffic compared to the models from prior work. Model TAU was able to quickly and accurately identify abnormally behaving nodes that had been subjected to kinetic or black hole attacks. Despite having less computation complexity and a lower communication overhead, this model was able to outperform other algorithms in many different attack scenarios.

Acknowledgments. This research was supported by the NSF Center for Space, High-performance, and Resilient Computing (SHREC) industry and agency members and by the IUCRC Program of the National Science Foundation under Grant No. CNS-1738783. This work was funded in part by the Naval Nuclear Laboratory.

This material is based upon work supported under Air Force Contract No. FA8702-15-D-0001. Any opinions, findings, conclusions or recommendations expressed in this

Disclosure of Interests. The authors have no competing interests to declare that are relevant to the content of this article.

References

1. Ahmad, F., Kurugollu, F., Adnane, A., Hussain, R., Hussain, F.: Marine: man-in-the-middle attack resistant trust model in connected vehicles. IEEE Internet Things J. **7**(4), 3310–3322 (2020)
2. Ahmad, I., Yau, K.: A trust model for multi-hop 5G networks: a reinforcement learning approach. In: 2021 15th International Conference on Open Source Systems and Technologies (ICOSST), pp. 1–6 (2021)
3. Albulet, M.: Spacex non-geostationary satellite system: attachment a technical information to supplement schedules. US Federal Communications Commission, Washington, DC, USA, Rep. SAT-OA-20161115-00118 (2018)
4. Asato, M., Cagnon, R., Jocic, L.: A high-capacity, anti-jam ehf "bent-pipe" satellite/central-hub system architecture concept. In: Proceedings of MILCOM 1995, vol. 2, pp. 722–730 (1995). https://doi.org/10.1109/MILCOM.1995.483560
5. Barnes, J., Demirjian, K., Schmitt, E., Sanger, D.: Russia's advances on space-based nuclear weapon draw U.S. concerns. The New York Times, p. 8 (2024)
6. Blau, P.: Directv 15 – spacecraft & satellites. https://spaceflight101.com/spacecraft/directv-15/
7. Bonnet, M.: Thales seizes control of ESA demonstration satellite in first cyber-security exercise of its kind. Thales (2023). https://www.thalesgroup.com/en/worldwide/security/press_release/thales-seizes-control-esa-demonstration-satellite-first
8. Chen, X., Makki, K., Yen, K., Pissinou, N.: Sensor network security: a survey. IEEE Commun. Surv. Tutor. **11**(2), 52–73 (2009)
9. Conner, W., Iyengar, A., Mikalsen, T., Rouvellou, I., Nahrstedt, K.: A trust management framework for service-oriented environments. In: Association for Computing Machinery, WWW 2009, New York, NY, USA, pp. 891–900 (2009). https://doi.org/10.1145/1526709.1526829
10. Dietrich, F., Metzen, P., Monte, P.: The globalstar cellular satellite system. IEEE Trans. Antennas Propag. **46**(6), 935–942 (1998)
11. Dortch, M.: Request for orbital deployment and operating authority for the spacex gen2 ngso satellite system. US Federal Communications Commission, Washington, DC, USA, Rep. SAT-OA-20161115-00118 (2022)
12. Douceur, J.R.: The sybil attack. In: Druschel, P., Kaashoek, F., Rowstron, A. (eds.) Peer-to-Peer Systems, pp. 251–260. Springer, Heidelberg (2002)
13. Ear, E., Remy, J.L.C., Feffer, A., Xu, S.: Characterizing cyber attacks against space systems with missing data. In: 2023 IEEE Conference on Communications and Network Security (CNS), pp. 1–9 (2023)

14. Erwin, S.: Starlink soars: SpaceX's satellite internet surprises analysts with $6.6 billion revenue projection. Spacenews (2024)
15. Falco, G.: The vacuum of space cyber security. In: 2018 AIAA SPACE and Astronautics Forum and Exposition (2018). https://doi.org/10.2514/6.2018-5275
16. Ghori, M.R., Zamli, K.Z., Quosthoni, N., Hisyam, M., Montaser, M.: Vehicular adhoc network (vanet): review. In: 2018 IEEE International Conference on Innovative Research and Development (ICIRD), pp. 1–6 (2018)
17. Giuliari, G., Ciussani, T., Perrig, A., Singla, A.: ICARUS: attacking low earth orbit satellite networks. In: 2021 USENIX Annual Technical Conference (USENIX ATC 2021), pp. 317–331. USENIX Association (2021). https://www.usenix.org/conference/atc21/presentation/giuliari
18. Goutte, C., Gaussier, E.: A probabilistic interpretation of precision, recall and f-score, with implication for evaluation. In: Losada, D.E., Fernández-Luna, J.M. (eds.) Advances in Information Retrieval, pp. 345–359. Springer, Heidelberg (2005)
19. Green, C.G., Massatt, P., Rhodus, N.: The GPS 21 primary satellite constellation. Navigation **36**(1), 9–24 (1989)
20. Guleng, S., Wu, C., Chen, X., Wang, X., Yoshinaga, T., Ji, Y.: Decentralized trust evaluation in vehicular internet of things. IEEE Access **7**, 15980–15988 (2019)
21. Hack-a-sat. http://hackasat.com. Accessed 16 Nov 2024
22. Henri, Y.: The oneweb satellite system. In: Handbook of Small Satellites: Technology, Design, Manufacture, Applications, Economics and Regulation, pp. 1–10 (2020)
23. Kan, S.: China's anti-satellite weapon test. In: CRS Report for Congress. Congressional Research Service, Library of Congress (2007)
24. Khokhar, R.H., Ngadi, M., Mandala, S.: A review of current routing attacks in mobile ad hoc networks. Int. J. Comput. Sci. Secur. **2** (2008)
25. Kulu, E.: Satellite constellations-2021 industry survey and trends. In: Small Satellite Conference (2021)
26. LaBel, K.A., Gates, M.M., Barth, J.L., Johnston, A., Marshall, P.: Single event effect criticality analysis. NASA Headquarters/Code QW (1996)
27. Li, H., Shi, D., Zhou, R., Liao, D., Zhang, M., Zhou, Y.: Distributed trust evaluation mechanism of LEO satellites for 6G network. In: 2021 IEEE 23rd International Conference on High Performance Computing & Communications, pp. 819–824 (2021)
28. Lu, T., Ding, X., Shang, J., Zhao, P., Zhang, H.: DoSat: a DDoS attack on the vulnerable time-varying topology of LEO satellite networks. In: ACNS 2024: 22nd International Conference on Applied Cryptography and Network Security, pp. 265–282. Springer, Heidelberg (2024). https://doi.org/10.1007/978-3-031-54773-7_11
29. Machi, V.: 10 tech trends that will impact the satellite industry in 2024. Via Satellite (2023)
30. Maine, K., Devieux, C., Swan, P.: Overview of iridium satellite network. In: WESCON 1995, p. 483 (1995)
31. Maurice-Michel, D.: How I hacked an esa's experimental satellite. Deadf00d (2021). https://www.deadf00d.com/post/howto-hack-an-esa-experimental-satellite.html
32. May, A.: Low earth orbit: Definition, theory and facts. Space.com (2022)
33. McDowell, J.: Oneweb launch statistics (2024). https://planet4589.org
34. Neigh, C.: Satellites (2024). https://landsat.gsfc.nasa.gov/satellites/
35. Papoutsis, E., Howells, G., Hopkins, A., McDonald-Maier, K.: Key generation for secure inter-satellite communication. In: Second NASA/ESA Conference on Adaptive Hardware and Systems (AHS 2007), pp. 671–681 (2007). https://doi.org/10.1109/AHS.2007.67

36. Peled, R., Aizikovich, E., Habler, E., Elovici, Y., Shabtai, A.: Sok: evaluating the security of satellite systems. arXiv abs/2312.01330 (2023)
37. Rashmi, R., Karthikeyan, A.: Secure boot of embedded applications - a review. In: 2018 Second International Conference on Electronics, Communication and Aerospace Technology (ICECA), pp. 291–298 (2018). https://doi.org/10.1109/ICECA.2018.8474730
38. Rathore, H., Griffith, H.: Leveraging neuro-inspired reinforcement learning for secure reputation-based communication in connected vehicles. In: 2023 IEEE Conference on Communications and Network Security (CNS), pp. 1–6 (2023)
39. Roberts, T.G., Kaplan, S.: Space launch to low earth orbit: How much does it cost. Civil and Commercial Space Space Security (2020)
40. Shafer, G.: Dempster-shafer theory (1992, unpublished). http://www.glennshafer.com/assets/downloads/articles/article48.pdf
41. Shi, E., Perrig, A.: Designing secure sensor networks. IEEE Wirel. Commun. **11**(6), 38–43 (2004)
42. Shreejith, S., Fahmy, S.A.: Security aware network controllers for next generation automotive embedded systems. In: Proceedings of the 52nd Annual Design Automation Conference (2015)
43. Sun, Y.L., Han, Z., Yu, W., Liu, K.R.: A trust evaluation framework in distributed networks: vulnerability analysis and defense against attacks. In: Proceedings IEEE INFOCOM 2006. 25TH IEEE International Conference on Computer Communications, pp. 1–13 (2006)
44. Tesat-Spacecom: Laser products (2021). https://www.tesat.de/products#laser
45. Walker, J.G.: Satellite constellations. J. Br. Interplanet. Soc. **37**, 559 (1984)
46. Willbold, J., Schloegel, M., Vogele, M., Gerhardt, M., Holz, T., Abbasi, A.: Space odyssey: an experimental software security analysis of satellites. In: IEEE Symposium on Security and Privacy (2023)
47. Wood, G.: A suspicious pattern alarming the Ukranian military. The Atlantic (2024)
48. Yue, P., et al.: Low earth orbit satellite security and reliability: Issues, solutions, and the road ahead. IEEE Commun. Surv. Tutor. **25**(3), 1604–1652 (2023). https://doi.org/10.1109/COMST.2023.3296160
49. Zheng, X., Yang, S., Wang, X.: A reliable and decentralized trust management model for fog computing in industrial IoT. In: NOMS 2023-2023 IEEE/IFIP Network Operations and Management Symposium, pp. 1–6 (2023)

Cryptographic Primitives and Protocols

Spilling-Cascade: An Optimal PKE Combiner for KEM Hybridization

Céline Chevalier[1,2], Guirec Lebrun[1,3](✉), and Ange Martinelli[3]

[1] DIENS, École normale supérieure, CNRS, PSL University, Inria, Paris, France
guirec.lebrun@ens.fr
[2] CRED, Paris-Panthéon-Assas University, Paris, France
[3] ANSSI, Paris, France

Abstract. Hybrid Post-Quantum cryptography is a cautious approach that aims to guard against the threat posed by the quantum computer, through the simultaneous use of Post-Quantum (PQ) and classical (i.e. pre-quantum) cryptosystems, should the post-quantum schemes used prove insecure.

Regarding the hybridization of Key Encapsulation Mechanisms (KEMs), most recent studies focus on safely combining the symmetric keys output by a parallel execution of classical and Post-Quantum KEMs. While this architecture is straightforward, it appears to lack bandwidth optimization.

Hence, we propose a novel method for hybridizing several KEMs more effectively, by combining the underlying Public-Key Encryption schemes (PKEs) in an innovative variant of the cascade composition that we call "spilling-cascade", before turning the hybrid PKE into a KEM with a FO transformation. We prove that this architecture constitutes a robust combiner for encryption schemes up to IND-CPA security, which permits to eventually generate an IND-CCA-secure KEM.

In terms of performance, our spilling-cascade scheme has a better communication cost than the commonly used parallel combination, with a bandwidth gain of its ciphertext that ranges from 2.8% to 13% compared to the latter, depending on the number and the characteristics of the PKEs that are combined. Moreover, we prove that for given PKEs to hybridize, the ciphertext communication cost of the spilling-cascade is optimal.

Keywords: PKE combiner · KEM hybridization · Cascade · Post-Quantum Cryptography · Hybrid Key Exchange

1 Introduction

Faced to the looming threat posed by the quantum computer to the classical public-key cryptography, the American National Institute of Standards and

This work has been partially supported by the European Union - Next Generation EU through the "France Relance" program, and by the French government through the "France 2030" program, under the project RESQUE.

M. Fischlin and V. Moonsamy (Eds.): ACNS 2025, LNCS 15825, pp. 455–485, 2025.
https://doi.org/10.1007/978-3-031-95761-1_16

Technology (NIST) launched in 2017 a Post-Quantum Cryptography (PQC) competition aiming to select the best post-quantum Key Encapsulation Mechanism (KEM) and signature algorithms. KEMs, in particular, were chosen as basic bricks to ensure the public-key encryption functionality.

Informally, a KEM is a key transport mechanism between two users, a sender and a recipient, comprising key generation, encapsulation and decapsulation algorithms. During the encapsulation stage, the sender provides the KEM with a public key associated with the recipient and is given, as output, a symmetric key and a ciphertext. The decapsulation algorithm, fed by the recipient with their secret key and the exchanged ciphertext, outputs a symmetric key identical to the one given to the sender at the encapsulation (cf. Sect. 2.3 for a formal definition). In the PQ framework, many KEMs (e.g. [1,5,6,22,24,26]) – and in particular the lattice-based ones – are built by applying an operation named "Fujisaki-Okamoto (FO) transformation" [12,16,18] to an OW-CPA[1] or IND-CPA secure PKE, which turns the whole scheme into an IND-CCA KEM.

NIST's PQC competition reached a turning point in summer 2022, when a KEM (Crystals Kyber [26]) and several signature schemes were selected for standardization. One may thus be tempted to use Kyber from now on in order to avoid the "harvest now – decrypt later" attacks that may occur with a quantum computer. However, due to the lack of maturity of post-quantum cryptography as a field of research, especially when it comes to the parametrization of real-life implementations of PQ primitives, it appears much safer to hybridize KEMs by simultaneously using classical and PQ algorithms, in order to benefit from the best security of both worlds, yet at the cost of some overhead.

A natural KEM hybridization in the PQ framework is the "double" one, where a classical key exchange scheme is combined with a single PQ KEM. However, when it comes to sensitive data whose secrecy must be ensured for at least few decades (and which are, consequently, particularly vulnerable to the aforementioned "harvest now – decrypt later" attacks), some users may want to ensure that they do not rely on only one PQ cryptosystem that could be shown insecure in a couple of years, in which case the hybridization would have been totally useless. A n-hybridization ($n > 2$) with one classical algorithm and two or more PQ KEMs solves this problem, but it suffers from important computational and bandwidth overheads that should be limited as much as possible.

There are two different ways to carry out a KEM hybridization: either with a straightforward combination of the selected KEMs or by the combination of the PKEs comprised in these KEMs.

[1] One-Way Chosen-Plaintext Attacks. This encryption security model, which aims to prevent the full recovery of a plaintext by an adversary having access to an encryption oracle, is weaker than models relying on "semantic security", where the adversary tries to distinguish the ciphertexts associated to chosen plaintexts, with the help of an encryption oracle (IND-CPA) and potentially an adaptive decryption oracle (IND-CCA).

KEM Combination. The first method – the combination of KEMs seen as black-boxes – is the most common. Its classical architecture is the parallel composition (cf. Sect. 2.4) where all component KEMs are running in parallel and output their own symmetric key and related ciphertext. Then, a dedicated primitive named "key combiner" (a.k.a. "core function" in [13]) mixes the symmetric keys with the ciphertexts to produce a combined key.

Using KEMs as core components is a natural approach, since these primitives were precisely targeted by the NIST for standardization in its PQC competition. However, the parallel composition of KEMs appears not to be the most effective way to generate a hybrid KEM, for the following reasons:

- Regarding the computation cost, combining n KEMs that are built with a FO transformation means carrying out this FO transformation n times as well, whereas we would like to reduce this number to a single operation.
- More importantly, the bandwidth of a key exchange using such a hybrid KEM (n public-keys and n ciphertexts) is not optimized, and this issue is even more pronounced with PQ algorithms that already have an important communication cost.

PKE Combination. The other – less studied – method is the combination of the PKEs within the KEMs that we want to hybridize, in order to produce a hybrid PKE that a single FO transformation will turn into an IND-CCA KEM. The main idea here is to save the computation cost of $(n-1)$ FO transformations, since this one must be applied only once, on the hybrid PKE. Furthermore, as this (intermediate) hybrid PKE only gets to be OW-CPA or IND-CPA secure, the key combiner can afford to be simpler – and thus computationally more sober – than in the IND-CCA security model. Indeed, it was proved by [13] that merely XORing the keys of component IND-CPA KEMs was sufficient to ensure the same security for the hybrid algorithm[2].

To the best of our knowledge, the only study of a hybrid KEM based on a PKE combination is [19], which presents a generic construction where PKEs are run in parallel composition before the resulting hybrid PKE undergoes a single FO transformation. However, the gains of this construction, compared to a KEM combination, are purely computational and in particular, the bandwidth is left unaltered.

Outside the scope of public-key cryptography, the combination of secret-key encryption primitives has been far more studied, and notably the cascade composition (cf. Sect. 2.4). The early works of [10] and [21] focus on cascades of block ciphers; the former proves the security of the hybrid scheme against message-recovery attacks, whereas the latter shows that a cascade of ciphers is at least as secure as the first cipher but that the security of the construction cannot be ensured, in the corresponding security model, by the second cipher only.

[2] This result can be extended to the case of encryption schemes.

At a higher level, [15] proves that a cascade of encryption schemes yields IND-RCCA security[3] if at least one of its components achieves that security. In a similar study, [30] introduces the notion of "multi-encryption" and shows that the cascade scheme can reach IND-gCCA security (See footnote 3) in their slightly different multi-encryption security model.

Our Contributions and Outline of this Paper. We present in Sect. 3 of this paper a new way to combine encryption schemes, designed to keep the computational gains of the PKE parallel combination of [19] while offering a lighter bandwidth. This construction, that we call "spilling-cascade", is a mix between parallel and cascade combinations. We prove in Sect. 3.3 that our spilling-cascade scheme is an IND-CPA secure robust combiner for encryption schemes (in the sense of Definition 5), which is a sufficient condition to build an IND-CCA KEM from the hybrid PKE, *via* the appropriate FO transformation (cf. Sect. 2.3). We also study in Sect. 3.5 the functionalities offered by such an architecture, mainly the aforementioned KEM hybridization but also a lighter Authenticated Key Exchange (AKE) protocol that can be used, for instance, to implement the recent KEM-TLS proposal [27].

We then instantiate in Sect. 4 two types of spilling-cascade hybrid KEMs:

- a first one combining a classical encryption scheme (ElGamal) and a PQ PKE (Crystals Kyber);
- a second one, where another PQ PKE (either NTRU-HRSS [20], its variant npNTRU from [25] or BAT [11]) is added to the former double hybridization.

We also refer to some possible improvements that are further detailed in the full version, including one, named "Integrated Diffie-Hellman (IDH) KEM", in which the first classical PKE in the cascade chain is replaced by a Diffie-Hellman key agreement scheme.

Finally, we prove in Sect. 5 that the spilling-cascade architecture has an *optimal* ciphertext communication cost when it comes to PKE combination – under some conditions –, and we compare in practice the communication efficiencies of the instantiations from Sect. 4.

2 Preliminaries

In the whole paper, we include both symmetric and public-key cryptosystems under the generic term of "encryption scheme", our spilling-cascade combiner being proved secure for both primitives. However, for practical purpose, we use the notations of public-key cryptography in most instances and figures, as we use PKEs to build KEMs. This does not narrow the range of our study.

[3] IND-RCCA [4] and IND-gCCA [2] are relaxed versions of the IND-CCA security notion, designed to exclude trivial security failures in the IND-CCA model that come from "benign malleability".

2.1 Notations and Terminology

In all the document, sampling an element s from a space $\mathcal{S}$ with uniform distribution is represented by $s \leftarrow_{\$} \mathcal{S}$. The output of a probabilistic algorithm is represented by $\leftarrow$ and that of a deterministic algorithm is given by $:=$.

$[\cdot]$ denotes optional values or parameters. $\lfloor\ \rceil$ and $\lceil\ \rceil$ respectively denote the rounding and ceiling values of a decimal number.

Regarding bit-strings: $\cdot||\cdot$ is used for the concatenation operation. $|\cdot|$ represents the bit-length of a string; when applied on an arbitrary element, it denotes the bit-length of the string encoding that element. Moreover, we use the notation $a \sqsubseteq b$ to mean that the bit-string representing an arbitrary element a is included in the bit-string encoding another element b (and conversely for $a \sqsupseteq b$).

In the context of lattice-based cryptography, vectors are written in lower case bold characters, matrices in upper case characters and scalars in lower case roman characters.

2.2 Public-Key Encryption Scheme (PKE)

Definition 1 (Public-Key Encryption Scheme). *A probabilistic public-key encryption scheme, defined over finite message and ciphertext spaces $\mathcal{M}$ and $\mathcal{C}$, is a tuple of polynomial-time algorithms* (KeyGen, Enc, Dec) *such that:*

- **KeyGen** *takes as input the security parameter λ and probabilistically outputs a couple of public and private keys that lie in public and private key spaces $\mathcal{PK}$ and $\mathcal{SK}$:* $\boxed{(pk, sk) \leftarrow \text{KeyGen}(1^\lambda)}$.
- **Enc** *takes as input a public-key $pk \in \mathcal{PK}$ and a plaintext m. It maps the plaintext into the message space $\mathcal{M}$ – notably by adding a padding p if necessary – and probabilistically yields a ciphertext $c \in \mathcal{C}$. This algorithm becomes deterministic if its internal randomness r is considered as part of the parameters:* $\boxed{c \leftarrow \text{Enc}(pk, m) \quad \Leftrightarrow \quad c := \text{Enc}(pk, m; r)}$.
- **Dec** *takes as input a secret-key $sk \in \mathcal{SK}$ and a ciphertext $c \in \mathcal{C}$ and deterministically outputs a plaintext $m \in \mathcal{M}$:* $\boxed{m := \text{Dec}(sk, c)}$

Worst-Case Correctness. If the encryption scheme is *perfectly* correct, we have: $\forall m \in \mathcal{M}, \forall (pk, sk) \leftarrow \text{KeyGen}(1^\lambda),\ \text{Dec}(sk, \text{Enc}(pk, m) = m$.

However, many PKEs, especially in the post-quantum framework, do not have this property and it appears useful to statistically bound their correctness error. Specifically, the Fujisaki-Okamoto transformation (cf. below) considers that correctness error in its worst-case.

Definition 2 (Worst-Case Correctness (from [18])). *The worst-case correctness of a public-key encryption scheme* PKE, *with a message space $\mathcal{M}$ and a randomness space $\mathcal{R}$, is defined as:*

$$\delta^{wc} := \underset{(pk,sk)\leftarrow \text{KeyGen}(1^\lambda)}{\mathbb{E}} \left(\underset{m\in\mathcal{M}}{\text{Max}} \left\{ \underset{r\in\mathcal{R}}{\Pr} \left[\text{Dec}(sk, \text{Enc}(pk, m; r)) \neq m \right] \right\} \right) \quad (1)$$

γ-Spreadness. This property, issued from [12], lower-bounds the min-entropy of the ciphertexts output by an encryption scheme over its internal randomness, for every given message and key-pair from the message and keys spaces.

Definition 3 (γ-Spreadness of a PKE (from [12])). *A probabilistic public-key encryption scheme with message space $\mathcal{M}$, ciphertext space $\mathcal{C}$ and randomness space $\mathcal{R}$ is said to be γ-spread iff:*

$$\forall (pk, sk) \leftarrow \mathrm{KeyGen}(1^\lambda), \forall m \in \mathcal{M}, \quad \underset{c \in \mathcal{C}}{\mathrm{Max}} \left\{ \Pr_{r \in \mathcal{R}} [\mathrm{Enc}(pk, m; r) = c] \right\} \leq 2^{-\gamma} \tag{2}$$

IND-CPA Security. The security game corresponding to the IND-CPA security of public-key encryption schemes, with two experiments $\mathbf{Exp}^{\mathrm{IND-CPA-b}}$ ($b \in \{0, 1\}$), is detailed in Fig. 1. In this model, the advantage of any Probabilistic Polynomial-Time (PPT) adversary $\mathcal{A} = (\mathcal{A}_1, \mathcal{A}_2)$ (where $\mathcal{A}$ wins the security experiment $\mathbf{Exp}^{\mathrm{IND-CPA-b}}$ if its guessing bit $\hat{b}$ equals b) is:

$$\mathrm{adv}_{\mathcal{E}}^{\mathrm{IND-CPA}}(\mathcal{A}) = \left| \Pr[1 \leftarrow \mathcal{A}]_{\mathcal{E}}^{\mathrm{IND-CPA-1}} - \Pr[1 \leftarrow \mathcal{A}]_{\mathcal{E}}^{\mathrm{IND-CPA-0}} \right| \tag{3}$$

Experiment $\mathbf{Exp}_{\mathrm{PKE}}^{\mathrm{IND-CPA-b}}$

$(pk, sk) \leftarrow \mathrm{KeyGen}(1^\lambda)$
$(m^0, m^1, st) \leftarrow \mathcal{A}_1(pk)$
$c^* \leftarrow \mathrm{Enc}(pk, m^b)$
$\hat{b} \leftarrow \mathcal{A}_2(pk, c^*, m^0, m^1, st)$
return $\hat{b}$

Experiment $\mathbf{Exp}_{\mathrm{KEM}}^{\mathrm{IND-CCA-b}}$

$(pk, sk) \leftarrow \mathrm{KeyGen}(1^\lambda)$
$(k_0^*, c^*) \leftarrow \mathrm{Encaps}(pk)$
$k_1^* \leftarrow\$ \mathcal{K}$
$\hat{b} \leftarrow \mathcal{A}^{\mathcal{O}^{Decaps}}(pk, c^*, k_b^*)$
return $\hat{b}$

Decapsulation oracle $\mathcal{O}^{Decaps}(c \neq c^*)$

$k := Decaps(sk, c)$
return k

Fig. 1. IND-CPA security game for a public-key encryption scheme (left) and IND-CCA security game for a KEM (right).

2.3 Key Encapsulation Mechanism (KEM)

Definition 4 (Key Encapsulation Mechanism). *A KEM is a tuple of algorithms (KeyGen, Encaps, Decaps) defined as follows:*

- **KeyGen** *takes as input the security parameter λ and probabilistically outputs a couple of public and private keys:* $\boxed{(pk, sk) \leftarrow \mathrm{KeyGen}(1^\lambda)}$.
- **Encaps** *takes as input a public-key $pk \in \mathcal{PK}$ and probabilistically yields a symmetric key and an associated ciphertext c:* $\boxed{(k, c) \leftarrow \mathrm{Encaps}(pk)}$.

- **Decaps** *takes as input a secret-key* $sk \in \mathcal{SK}$ *and a ciphertext* $c \in \mathcal{C}$ *and deterministically outputs a symmetric key* k: $\boxed{k := \text{Decaps}(sk, c)}$ *or (for an explicit rejection) a symbol* $\perp$ *stating that the encapsulation is invalid.*

We say that the KEM is correct if:
$\forall (pk, sk) \leftarrow \text{KeyGen}(1^\lambda),\ \big(\text{Decaps}(sk, c), c\big) \leftarrow \text{Encaps}(pk).$

Security. The security generally expected for a KEM – and that was explicitly stated by the NIST for its PQC competition, is the IND-CCA(2) security. It relies on the indistinguishability of the output symmetric key, while the adversary has access to a decapsulation oracle (cf. Fig. 1 for the related security game).

FO Transformation. A common construction of an IND-CCA KEM in the (Quantum) Random Oracle Model ((Q)ROM) consists in applying, to an IND-CPA secure PKE, an operation called "Fujisaki-Okamoto (FO) transformation" [12,28]. [16] later proposes a modular approach of the original transformation, with several subroutines that must be selected according to the features of the underlying PKE. However, the security bounds given by [16] appear non-tight in the QROM. In this framework, [25], later improved by [18], uses the concept of "Disjoint Simulatability" (DS) to implement an alternate modular FO transformations with tighter security bounds in the QROM.

Composition. The FO transformation of [18] comprises two subroutines that transform any IND-CPA PKE into an IND-CCA scheme. In particular, the property of DS, that is naturally satisfied by many code-based and lattice-based PKEs, can be achieved by any PKE – through the "puncturing" (Punc) operation – at a negligible cost.

- "Punc" transformation: it turns any (probabilistic) IND-CPA secure PKE PKE_0 into another scheme PKE_1 with the Disjoint Simulatability (DS) property. To do so, this operation removes an arbitrary message $\hat{m}$ from the message space of the original scheme: $\boxed{\mathcal{M}_1 := \mathcal{M}_0 \backslash \{\hat{m}\}}$ and uses that message $\hat{m}$ to sample fake encryptions.
- $\text{FO}^{\not\perp}_{m[,c]} = \text{U}^{\not\perp}_{m[,c]} \circ T$ operation, with $\text{U}^{\not\perp}_{m[,c]}$ and T as defined in [16]:
  - T turns the IND-CPA secure and Disjoint Simulatable PKE PKE_1 into a deterministic OW-PCVA[4] scheme by deriving its internal randomness r from the input plaintext m instead of randomly drawing it: $\boxed{r := G(m[, pk])}$[5], with G a cryptographic hash function modeled as a

[4] The One-Way Plaintext-Checking and Validity Attacks (OW-PCVA) security notion is the OW-CPA security where the adversary has an additional access to both a Plaintext Checking Oracle (which states if a couple (plaintext, ciphertext) is related) and a Ciphertext Validity Oracle (asserting the validity of a proposed ciphertext).

[5] The inclusion in T operation of the recipient's public key, or part of it, corresponds to a multi-user variant [8] that is used, for instance, by ML-KEM.

quantum random oracle. In the decryption stage, the validity of the decrypted plaintext also generally needs to be checked *via* a re-encryption.
- $U^{\not\perp}_{m[,c]}$ derives the symmetric key from the random plaintext that was encapsulated (instead of straightly using this message as the key): $\boxed{k := H(m[,c])}$, with H a cryptographic hash function also modeled as a quantum random oracle.

In $FO^{\not\perp}_{m[,c]}$, any decapsulation error of the FO-built KEM is implicitly rejected, with a random key z that is output instead of the symmetric key.

Hence, the modular FO transformation from [18] can be summarized as follows – with straight and dashed arrows respectively denoting tight and non-tight reductions in the QROM:

$$\underset{\mathrm{PKE}_0}{\mathrm{IND\text{-}CPA}} \xrightarrow{\quad \mathrm{Punc} \quad} \underset{\mathrm{PKE}_1}{\mathrm{IND\text{-}CPA{+}DS}} \overset{\mathrm{U}^{\not\perp}_{m[,c]} \circ \mathrm{T}}{\dashrightarrow} \underset{\mathrm{KEM}}{\mathrm{IND\text{-}CCA}} \tag{4}$$

Security Bounds. Let us consider an IND-CPA secure PKE PKE_0, γ-spread and with a worst-case correctness δ^{wc} (cf. Sect. 2.2). According to Theorem 3.6 from [18], if we apply a FO transformation to that PKE, then for any adversary $\mathcal{A}$ against the IND-CCA security of the output KEM, there exist quantum adversaries $\mathcal{B}_1$ and $\mathcal{B}_2$ against the IND-CPA security of PKE_0, with running times similar to that of $\mathcal{A}$ and s.t.:

$$\begin{aligned} \mathrm{Adv}^{\mathrm{IND-CCA}}_{\mathrm{KEM}}(\mathcal{A}) \leq & (8 \cdot (3 \cdot q_G + 2 \cdot q_H + q_D + 6)^2 + 1) \cdot \delta^{wc} + \mathrm{Adv}^{\mathrm{IND-CPA}}_{\mathrm{PKE}_0}(\mathcal{B}_1) \\ & + 2 \cdot \sqrt{(q_G + q_H) \cdot \mathrm{Adv}^{\mathrm{IND-CPA}}_{\mathrm{PKE}_0}(\mathcal{B}_2) + \frac{4(q_G + q_H)^2}{|\mathcal{M}| - 1}} + 2^{-\gamma} \end{aligned} \tag{5}$$

q_D denotes the number of classical decapsulation queries of the adversary and q_G and q_H the number of queries to the random oracles G and H.

2.4 Combination of KEMs and Encryption Schemes

Robust Combiner. The combination of several primitives of the same type can be used to guaranty a certain property when some of the primitives that are combined – but we do not necessarily know which ones – fulfill themselves this property. The algorithm that mixes together these primitives is called a combiner, for which [15] has defined the notion of "robustness". We adapt hereunder this concept of robust combiner to the case of encryption schemes.

Definition 5 (Robust Combiner for Encryption Schemes). *Let s_{sec} be a predicate, associated with a security level SEC*[6]*, that takes as input an encryption scheme $\mathcal{E}$ and outputs 1 if $\mathcal{E}$ respects that security level, and 0 otherwise.*

[6] Such as OW-CPA, IND-CPA, IND-CCA...

A combiner for encryption schemes is an algorithm that takes as input n arbitrary encryption schemes $(\mathcal{E}_i)_{i \in [\![1,n]\!]}$ and that outputs a single encryption scheme $\mathcal{E}_{hy}$ – called hybrid. We say that this combiner is SEC robust if the output hybrid scheme yields SEC security, provided that at least one of its component schemes is itself SEC secure and regardless of any other assumptions about these component schemes:

$$\forall n \in \mathbb{N}^* \backslash \{1\}, \forall \mathcal{E}_{i \in [\![1,n]\!]}, \quad \sum\nolimits_{i=1}^{n} s_{sec}(\mathcal{E}_i) \geq 1 \Rightarrow \ s_{sec}(\mathcal{E}_{hy}) = 1 \tag{6}$$

We now present beneath the two main modes of combination of KEMs and encryption schemes: the parallel and cascade (sequential) compositions.

Parallel Composition. The common way to hybridize KEMs or encryption schemes is called the "parallel composition" (cf. [13] for KEM combination). This method consists in running in parallel each one of the n component primitives that we want to hybridize, in order to generate a combined public-key $pk := (pk_1, \ldots, pk_n)$, a combined ciphertext $c := (c_1, \ldots, c_n)$ and, in the case of KEMs, a combined key $k_c := \text{Comb}(k_1, \ldots, k_n, c)$, with Comb a key combiner.

Cascade Composition. The combination of n encryption schemes $(\mathcal{E}_i := (\text{KeyGen}_i, \text{Enc}_i, \text{Dec}_i))_{i \in [\![1,n]\!]}$ is called a cascade (a.k.a. sequential) composition if every ciphertext output by the first $n-1$ encryption schemes is given as input to the following encryption scheme:

$$\text{Enc}_{casc}((pk_1, \ldots, pk_n), m) := \text{Enc}_n(pk_n, \text{Enc}_{n-1}(pk_{n-1}, \ldots, \text{Enc}_1(pk_1, m))) \tag{7}$$

3 Spilling-Cascade Hybridization of Encryption Schemes

3.1 Description

Because the ciphertexts output by most post-quantum PKEs are much larger than their input plaintexts, it is not possible to combine these schemes in a regular cascade. We consequently conceive, for the purpose of PQ KEM hybridization, the spilling-cascade combination where only a part of the intermediate ciphertexts is encapsulated as in a regular cascade. The remaining part of these intermediate ciphertexts is joined to the last ciphertext c_n of the chain, in order to produce the global ciphertext of the hybrid scheme (cf. Fig. 2 & Fig. 3).

This architecture aims to keep most of the advantages brought by the regular cascade hybridization, compared to the more common parallel composition, when the regular cascade combination of encryption schemes appears impossible. It indeed performs a hybridization more effective than the parallel one in terms of bandwidth and can still be proved a robust combiner – in the sense of Definition 5 – under certain assumptions, as detailed beneath.

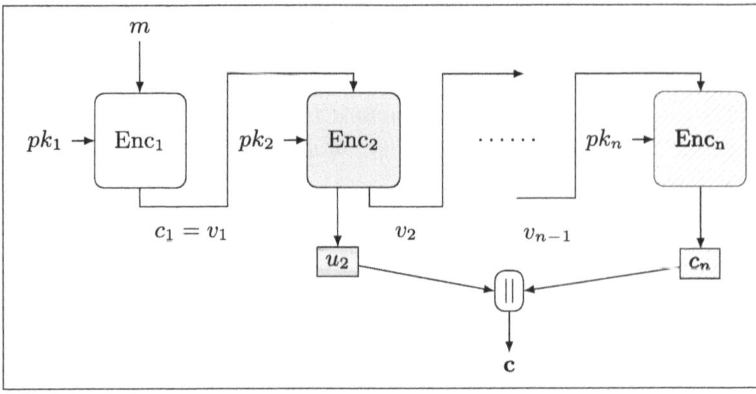

Fig. 2. Architecture of a $\{2\}$-spilling-cascade. In this instance, the encryption scheme $\mathcal{E}_2$ publicly displays a part u_2 of its ciphertext, whereas the other encryption schemes are combined in a regular (i.e. non spilling) cascade.

Definition 6 (Spilling-Cascade Combination of Encryption Schemes). *The combination of* n *encryption schemes* $(\mathcal{E}_i := (\mathrm{KeyGen}_i, \mathrm{Enc}_i, \mathrm{Dec}_i))_{i\in[\![1,n]\!]}$ *is called a* $\mathcal{S}$*-spilling-cascade composition if there exists a non-empty subset of the* $n-1$ *first indices,* $\mathcal{S} \subseteq \{1,\ldots,n-1\}$*, such that:*

1. *For every encryption scheme* $\mathcal{E}_j$*,* $j \in \mathcal{S}$*, in this subset – called a "spilling primitive" –, the generated ciphertext is of the form* $c_j = \{u_j, v_j\}$ *s.t.:*
   - u_j *is made public as part of the global ciphertext, along with the output* c_n *of the last scheme of the chain:* $\boxed{c_{sc} := \big((u_j)_{j\in\mathcal{S}}, c_n\big)}$*;*
   - v_j*, that has a bit-length corresponding to the input size of the following encryption algorithm* Enc_{j+1} $(|v_j| = |m_{j+1}|)$*, is given as input to that scheme:* $\boxed{c_{j+1} \leftarrow \mathrm{Enc}_{j+1}(pk_{j+1}, v_j)}$*.*
2. *Any encryption scheme* $\mathcal{E}_i$*,* $i \notin \mathcal{S}$*, outside the subset* $\mathcal{S}$ *is composed in regular cascade and thus feeds the next primitive* Enc_{i+1} *with its full ciphertext*[7] $c_i = v_i$ *s.t.* $|c_i| \leq |m_{i+1}|$ *:* $\boxed{c_{i+1} \leftarrow \mathrm{Enc}_{i+1}(pk_{i+1}, c_i)}$*.*

In this paper, we focus on a hybridization where all upstream primitives are spilling, that we call a fully spilling-cascade, as stated below.

Definition 7 (Fully Spilling-Cascade). *A fully spilling-cascade composition of* n *encryption schemes is a* $\{1,\ldots,n-1\}$*-spilling-cascade combination of these schemes, i.e. a spilling-cascade where* ***all*** *the* $n-1$ *first primitives* $(\mathcal{E}_i)_{i\in[\![1,n-1]\!]}$ *are spilling a part of their ciphertexts in the global ciphertext.*

[7] In the case where $|c_i| < |m_{i+1}|$, a padding p_i of size $|m_{i+1}| - |c_i|$ is added in order to map c_i to the message space $\mathcal{M}_{i+1}$ of the scheme $\mathcal{E}_{i+1}$, according to Definition 1 and as in the regular cascade construction of Sect. 2.4. This padding is determined by the specifications of the associated encryption scheme.

Spilling-cascade $\mathbf{Enc_{sc}}(pk, m, \mathcal{S})$

```
(pk_1, ..., pk_n) := Parse(pk)
c := ∅
v_0 := m
for i ∈ [[1, n − 1]] do :
   c_i ← Enc_i(pk_i, v_{i−1})
   if i ∈ S then :
      c_i := (u_i, v_i)
   else :
      c_i := v_i
   c := (c, u_i)
c_n ← Enc_n(pk_n, v_{n−1})
c := (c, c_n)
return c
```

Spilling-cascade $\mathbf{Dec_{sc}}(sk, c, \mathcal{S})$

```
(sk_1, ..., sk_n) := Parse(sk)
((u_i)_{i∈S}, c_n) := Parse(c)
v_{n−1} := Dec_n(sk_n, c_n)
for i ∈ [[n − 1, 1]] do :
   if i ∈ S then :
      c_i := (u_i, v_i)
   else :
      c_i := v_i
   v_{i−1} := Dec_i(sk_i, c_i)
m := v_0
return m
```

Fig. 3. Encryption and decryption algorithms of a $\mathcal{S}$-spilling-cascade encryption combiner. $\mathcal{S} \subseteq \{1, \ldots, n-1\}$ denotes the set of spilling primitives in the cascade chain. The key generation, identical to that of a parallel combination [19], is not detailed.

3.2 Partitioned-Ciphertext Encryption Schemes

The security offered by the spilling-cascade architecture is based on a property of encryption schemes, that we name "partitioned-ciphertext". It states that the ciphertexts yielded by such encryption schemes can be decomposed into two parts, c_r and c_m, such that c_r does not depend on the encrypted plaintext but rather (generally) on the randomness of the probabilistic encryption, whereas c_m comprises all the information related to the plaintext.

As it is proved hereunder, the security of a $\mathcal{S}$-spilling-cascade composition can be ensured if and only if the spilling primitives $(\mathcal{E}_j)_{j\in\mathcal{S}}$ of the chain have this partitioned-ciphertext property *and* if their c_m element is included in the encapsulated part v of their ciphertext: $\forall j \in \mathcal{S},\ c_{m_j} \sqsubseteq v_j$ (which, in turn, implies that $c_{r_j} \sqsupseteq u_j$).

Definition 8 (Partitioned-Ciphertext Encryption Scheme). *An encryption scheme $\mathcal{E} = (\mathrm{KeyGen}, \mathrm{Enc}, \mathrm{Dec})$ is said to have a "partitioned ciphertext" if any ciphertext c output by that scheme can be decomposed into two non-empty parts c_r and c_m[8] such that:*

1. *The bit-lengths of c_r and c_m are constant over the message space $\mathcal{M}$;*
2. *c_r does not depend on the plaintext m.*

More formally: $\forall pk \in \mathcal{PK},\ \forall r \in \mathcal{R},\ \forall (m, m') \in \mathcal{M}^2$, $(c_r, c_m) := \mathrm{Enc}(pk, m; r)$ and $(c'_r, c'_m) := \mathrm{Enc}(pk, m'; r)$ s.t.

1. $|c_r| = |c'_r|$ and $|c_m| = |c'_m|$

[8] As in Definition 6, the relative order of c_r and c_m in the ciphertext c is not determined in the general case.

2. $c_r = c'_r$.

A common instance of a partitioned-ciphertext classical encryption scheme is ElGamal, that yields a ciphertext of the form $c_{eg} := (c_r = g^r, c_m = m.X^r)$, with r a random coin and m the plaintext to encrypt.

Regarding PQ algorithms, the PKEs of three of the four KEMs that are most likely to be standardized in the future[9] have this partitioned-ciphertext property: BIKE, HQC and Kyber – which has a ciphertext $c_{ky} := (c_r = A^T.\mathbf{r} + \mathbf{e}_1, c_m = \mathbf{t}^T.\mathbf{r} + e_2 + \lfloor \frac{q}{2} \rceil .m)$, with $\mathbf{r}$ and m as for ElGamal.

We prove in Appendix A.1 the partitioned-ciphertext property of ElGamal and Kyber, that we precisely use in our instantiations of Sect. 4.

3.3 IND-CPA Security of Spilling-Cascade

Theorem 1. *The combination of n encryption schemes $(\mathcal{E}_i = (\text{KeyGen}_i, \text{Enc}_i, \text{Dec}_i))_{i \in [\![1,n]\!]}$ in a $\mathcal{S}$-spilling-cascade mode constitutes a robust IND-CPA secure combiner for encryption schemes, in the sense of Definition 5*[10]*, if and only if all spilling primitives are partitioned-ciphertext algorithms whose message-dependent part of the ciphertext (c_m) is encapsulated by the next encryption scheme in the chain: $\forall j \in \mathcal{S},\ c_{m_j} \sqsubseteq v_j$.*

Nota: Breaking the security of a spilling primitive – from the $n-1$ upstream schemes – in a spilling-cascade chain, due to a mathematical flaw or a sufficient computational power of the adversary, does not question at all the partitioned-ciphertext property of this encryption scheme. All information regarding the plaintext remains contained in the message-dependent part c_m of its ciphertext, which is encapsulated by the next encryption scheme in the spilling-cascade chain and thus never made public.

Proof Sketch. The conditions expected in Theorem 1 from any spilling primitive $\mathcal{E}_{s \in [\![1,n-1]\!]}$ in a spilling-cascade chain are the following:

- Condition 1: that spilling primitive $\mathcal{E}_s$ has a partitioned-ciphertext;
- Condition 2: the message-related part of its ciphertext is encapsulated by the following encryption scheme: $c_{m_s} \sqsubseteq v_s$.

Our proof consists of two statements, that correspond respectively to the "sufficient" and "necessary" conditions of the IND-CPA robustness of the spilling-cascade combiner:

[9] These promising algorithms are the current winner of round 3 of NIST's PQC competition (Crystals Kyber, standardized as "ML-KEM") as well as the remaining three candidates of the fourth round, studied as an alternative solution to Kyber (BIKE, ClassicMcEliece & HQC).

[10] In other terms, the hybrid scheme is IND-CPA secure if at least anyone of its component primitives is IND-CPA secure as well.

1. If, in a spilling-cascade combination of n encryption schemes, any spilling primitive respects both conditions 1 and 2, then that spilling-cascade is an IND-CPA robust combiner for encryption schemes.
2. Conversely, if the spilling-cascade is an IND-CPA robust combiner, then all spilling primitives from the spilling-cascade chain respect both conditions 1 and 2.

Proof of Statement 1. Let us consider n encryption schemes $(\mathcal{E}_i)_{i\in[\![1,n]\!]}$ such that all $n-1$ upstream primitives $(\mathcal{E}_i)_{i\in[\![1,n-1]\!]}$ either are non-spilling or respect both condition 1 and condition 2. We additionally consider that only a single encryption scheme in the chain, with index $j \in [\![1,n]\!]$, is IND-CPA secure.

For any encryption scheme that yields a ciphertext of the form $(u, v) \leftarrow \text{Enc}(pk, m)$ from a plaintext $m \in \mathcal{M}$, we note π_u and π_v the functions that respectively output u and v from that ciphertext: $u := \pi_u(\text{Enc}(pk, m))$ and $v := \pi_v(\text{Enc}(pk, m))$.

Without loss of generality, the ciphertext output by the spilling-cascade chain related to a plaintext $m \in \mathcal{M}$ can be written as:

$$\boxed{c_{sc} := \left((u_i)_{i\in[\![1,n-1]\!]}, c_n\right)} \tag{8}$$
$$\text{with } v_0 := m \quad \text{and} \quad \forall i \in [\![1,n]\!],\ c_i := (u_i, v_i) \leftarrow \text{Enc}_i(pk_i, v_{i-1}) \text{ s.t. } \forall i \notin \mathcal{S}, u_i = \emptyset.$$

Furthermore, we can express the ciphertext c_i of any encryption scheme located after the IND-CPA secure encryption scheme $\mathcal{E}_j$ in the spilling-cascade chain ($i > j$), in function of the encapsulated part v_j of that secure primitive:

$$\forall i \in [\![j+1,n]\!], c_i \leftarrow \text{Enc}_i(pk_i, \pi_v(\text{Enc}_{i-1}(pk_{i-1}, \ldots, \pi_v(\text{Enc}_{j+1}(pk_{j+1}, v_j))))) \tag{9}$$

Game 0. This is the experiment $\mathbf{Exp}_{spill-casc}^{\text{IND-CPA-0}}$ of the spilling-cascade security game (cf. Fig. 1). The ciphertext produced by the hybrid scheme from a plaintext m^0 is:

$$\begin{aligned} c_{sc} &:= \left((u_i^0)_1^{j-1}, u_j^0, (u_i^0)_{j+1}^{n-1}, c_n^0\right) \\ \text{with} : &\ \forall i \in [\![1, j-1]\!], c_i^0 := (u_i^0, v_i^0) \leftarrow \text{Enc}_i(pk_i, v_{i-1}^0) \quad \text{and} \quad v_0^0 := m^0 \\ &(u_j^0, v_j^0) \leftarrow \text{Enc}_j(pk_j, v_{j-1}^0) \\ &\forall i \in [\![j+1, n-1]\!], u_i^0 := \pi_u(\text{Enc}_i(pk_i, \ldots, \pi_v(\text{Enc}_{j+1}(pk_{j+1}, v_j^0)))) \\ &c_n^0 \leftarrow \text{Enc}_n(pk_n, \ldots, \pi_v(\text{Enc}_{j+1}(pk_{j+1}, v_j^0))) \end{aligned} \tag{10}$$

Game 1. We replace in this game the term v_{j-1}^0 by the encapsulated part $\tilde{v}_{j-1}$ of the encryption of a random message $\tilde{m}_{j-1}$ from the message space of $\mathcal{E}_{j-1}$: $\tilde{v}_{j-1} := \pi_v(\text{Enc}_{j-1}(pk_{j-1}, \tilde{m}_{j-1}))$, with $\tilde{m}_{j-1} \leftarrow\$ \mathcal{M}_{j-1}$.

Thus, we have (with the boxes representing the values changed compared to the previous game):

$$
\begin{aligned}
c_{sc} &:= \left((u_i^0)_1^{j-1}, \boxed{\tilde{u}_j}, \boxed{(\tilde{u}_i)_{j+1}^{n-1}}, \boxed{\tilde{c}_n} \right) \\
&\text{with} : \forall i \in [\![1, j-1]\!], c_i^0 := (u_i^0, v_i^0) \leftarrow \mathrm{Enc}_i(pk_i, v_{i-1}) \text{ and } v_0^0 := m^0 \\
&(\boxed{\tilde{u}_j}, \boxed{\tilde{v}_j}) \leftarrow \mathrm{Enc}_j(pk_j, \boxed{\tilde{v}_{j-1}}) \qquad (11) \\
&\forall i \in [\![j+1, n-1]\!], \boxed{\tilde{u}_i} := \pi_u(\mathrm{Enc}_i(pk_i, \ldots, \pi_v(Enc_{j+1}(pk_{j+1}, \boxed{\tilde{v}_j})))) \\
&\boxed{\tilde{c}_n} \leftarrow \mathrm{Enc}_n(pk_n, \ldots, \pi_v(\mathrm{Enc}_{j+1}(pk_{j+1}, \boxed{\tilde{v}_j})))
\end{aligned}
$$

The advantage of any attacker $\mathcal{A}$ to distinguish $(\tilde{u}_j, \tilde{v}_j)$ from (u_j^0, v_j^0), i.e. to distinguish Game 0 from Game 1, is bounded by the IND-CPA security of the scheme $\mathcal{E}_j$: $\epsilon_1 \leq adv_{\mathcal{E}_j}^{\mathrm{IND-CPA}}$.

Proof. From any adversary $\mathcal{A} = (\mathcal{A}_1, \mathcal{A}_2)$ trying to distinguish Games 0 and 1, we can build an adversary $\mathcal{B} = (\mathcal{B}_1, \mathcal{B}_2)$ against the CPA-indistinguishability of the encryption scheme $\mathcal{E}_j$, as described in Fig. 4:

- $\mathcal{B}_1$ gets as input the public-key of $\mathcal{E}_j$, generates all other public keys from the spilling-cascade chain and computes the hybrid ciphertext associated with a random message m^0 up to the $(j-1)$-th ciphertext c_{j-1}^0. The adversary also randomly draws a message $\tilde{m}_{j-1} \leftarrow_\$ \mathcal{M}_{j-1}$ and encrypts it under $\mathcal{E}_{j-1}$ to get $\tilde{c}_{j-1}$. $\mathcal{B}_1$ then outputs v_{j-1}^0 and $\tilde{v}_{j-1}$.
- $\mathcal{B}_2$ runs on the challenge $(c_j^*, v_{j-1}^0, \tilde{v}_{j-1})$. Its computes the ciphertexts of the encryption schemes $\mathcal{E}_{j+1}$ to $\mathcal{E}_n$, all issued from $v_j^* := \pi_v(c_j^*)$. The hybrid ciphertext generated this way is given to the adversary $\mathcal{A}_2$ that outputs a guessing bit $\hat{b}$ that is also output by $\mathcal{B}_2$.

Consequently, $\mathcal{A}$'s advantage is bounded as follows:
$\epsilon_1 = adv^{G0-G1}(\mathcal{A}) \leq adv_{\mathcal{E}_j}^{\mathrm{IND-CPA}}(\mathcal{B})$.

Adversary $\mathcal{B}_1(pk_j)$

- **for** $i \in [\![1, n]\!] \setminus \{j\}$:
  - $(pk_i, sk_i) \leftarrow \mathrm{KeyGen}_i(1^\lambda)$
- $v_0^0 := m^0 \leftarrow_\$ \mathcal{M}_1$
- **for** $i \in [\![1, j-1]\!]$:
  - $c_i^0 := (u_i^0, v_i^0) \leftarrow \mathrm{Enc}_i(pk_i, v_{i-1}^0)$
- $\tilde{m}_{j-1} \leftarrow_\$ \mathcal{M}_{j-1}$
- $\tilde{v}_{j-1} := \pi_v\left(\mathrm{Enc}_{j-1}(pk_{j-1}, \tilde{m}_{j-1})\right)$
- $st \leftarrow \mathcal{A}_1\left((c_i^0)_1^{j-1}, (pk_i)_1^n\right)$
- $st' := \left(st, (u_i^0)_1^{j-1}, (pk_i)_{i \in [\![1,n]\!] \setminus \{j\}}\right)$
- **return** $v_{j-1}^0, \tilde{v}_{j-1}, st'$

Adversary $\mathcal{B}_2(pk_j, c_j^*, v_{j-1}^0, \tilde{v}_{j-1}, st')$

- $(u_j^*, v_j^*) := \left(\pi_u(c_j^*), \pi_v(c_j^*)\right)$
- **for** $i \in [\![j+1, n]\!]$:
  - $c_i^* := (u_i^*, v_i^*) \leftarrow \mathrm{Enc}_i(pk_i, v_{i-1}^*)$
- $c^* := \left((u_i^0)_1^{j-1}, u_j^*, (u_i^*)_{j+1}^{n-1}, c_n^*\right)$
- $\hat{b} \leftarrow \mathcal{A}_2\left(pk_j, c^*, v_{j-1}^0, \tilde{v}_{j-1}, st'\right)$
- **return** $\hat{b}$

Fig. 4. Adversary $\mathcal{B} = (\mathcal{B}_1, \mathcal{B}_2)$ against the CPA-indistinguishability of the j-th encryption scheme $\mathcal{E}_j$ of a spilling-cascade, based on an adversary $\mathcal{A} = (\mathcal{A}_1, \mathcal{A}_2)$ against the indistinguishability of games G0 and G1.

Game 2. $\forall i \in [\![1, j-1]\!]$, we replace u_i^0 by u_i^1, which modifies the hybrid ciphertext as follows:

$$\begin{aligned} c_{sc} &:= \left(\boxed{(u_i^1)_1^{j-1}}, \tilde{u}_j, (\tilde{u}_i)_{j+1}^{n-1}, \tilde{c}_n\right) \\ \text{with}: &\forall i \in [\![1, j-1]\!], \boxed{u_i^1} := \pi_u(\text{Enc}_i(pk_i, \boxed{v_{i-1}^1})) \quad \text{and} \quad \boxed{v_0^1} := m^1 \end{aligned} \tag{12}$$

None of the u_i^0 and u_i^1 ($i \in [\![1, j-1]\!]$) are related in any way to the ciphertexts $\tilde{c}_k := (\tilde{u}_k, \tilde{v}_k) = \text{Enc}_k(pk_k, \tilde{v}_{k-1})$, $k \in [\![j, n]\!]$, since the latter *all* originate from the *random* element $\tilde{m}_{j-1}$ (through $\tilde{v}_{j-1}$).

Moreover, $\forall i \in [\![1, j-1]\!]$, u_i^0 and u_i^1 follow the exact same distribution independent of their associated plaintexts m_i^0 and m_i^1,

- either because of the "partitioned-ciphertext" property of the associated encryption scheme $\mathcal{E}_i$ and the fact that $c_{m_i} \sqsubseteq v_i$, which implies by definition that no information related to the plaintexts m_i^0 and m_i^1 is contained in u_i^0 and u_i^1,
- or because the scheme $\mathcal{E}_i$ is not spilling, and in that case $u_i^0 = u_i^1 = \varnothing$.

Consequently, the advantage of any attacker in distinguishing Game 2 from Game 1 is null: $\epsilon_2 = 0$.

Game 3. We replace in this game the term $\tilde{v}_{j-1}$ by v_{j-1}^1, which implies the following changes:

$$\begin{aligned} c_{sc} :=& \left((u_i^1)_1^{j-1}, \boxed{u_j^1}, \boxed{(u_i^1)_{j+1}^{n-1}}, \boxed{c_n^1}\right) \\ \text{with}: &(\boxed{u_j^1}, \boxed{v_j^1}) \leftarrow \text{Enc}_j(pk_j, \boxed{v_{j-1}^1}) \\ &\forall i \in [\![j+1, n-1]\!], \boxed{u_i^1} := \pi_u(\text{Enc}_i(pk_i, \ldots, \pi_v(\text{Enc}_{j+1}(pk_{j+1}, \boxed{v_j^1})))) \\ &\boxed{c_n^1} \leftarrow \text{Enc}_n(pk_n, \ldots, \pi_v(\text{Enc}_{j+1}(pk_{j+1}, \boxed{v_j^1}))) \end{aligned} \tag{13}$$

Similarly to the passage from Game 0 to Game 1, and using the same type of adversary than in Fig. 4, we can bound the advantage of any attacker trying to distinguish Game 3 from Game 2 by: $\epsilon_3 \leq adv_{\mathcal{E}_j}^{\text{IND-CPA}}$.

This game corresponds to the experiment $\mathbf{Exp}_{spill-casc}^{\text{IND-CPA}-1}$ of the spilling-cascade security game. Consequently, the security bound of the hybrid encryption scheme generated by a spilling-cascade combination of n primitives, with at least an IND-CPA secure component encryption scheme $\mathcal{E}_j$, is bounded by $adv_{\mathcal{E}_{sc}}^{\mathrm{IND-CPA}} \leq 2 \cdot adv_{\mathcal{E}_j}^{\mathrm{IND-CPA}}$, which completes the proof of statement 1.

Proof of Statement 2. Let us define the following logical proposals:

- **Robust**($\mathcal{SC}$): the spilling-cascade $\mathcal{SC}$ is an IND-CPA robust combiner;
- **IND-CPA**($\mathcal{E}$): the encryption scheme $\mathcal{E}$ is IND-CPA secure;
- **Cond1**($\mathcal{E}$): the encryption scheme $\mathcal{E}$ has a partitioned-ciphertext, therefore it respects the condition 1 expressed in the proof sketch of Sect. 3.3;
- **Cond2**($\mathcal{E}$): the encryption scheme $\mathcal{E}$ respects the condition 2 from that proof sketch by having the message-related part of its ciphertext encapsulated by the following encryption scheme: $c_{m_s} \sqsubseteq v_s$.

With $\mathcal{S}$ the spilling primitives in a spilling-cascade chain, statement 2 can be expressed as:

$$\mathbf{Robust}(\mathcal{SC}) \Rightarrow \forall \mathcal{E}_s \in \mathcal{S}, \mathbf{Cond1}(\mathcal{E}_s) \wedge \mathbf{Cond2}(\mathcal{E}_s) \tag{14}$$

$$\Leftrightarrow \quad \exists \mathcal{E}_s \in \mathcal{S} : \neg\mathbf{Cond1}(\mathcal{E}_s) \vee \neg\mathbf{Cond2}(\mathcal{E}_s) \Rightarrow \neg\mathbf{Robust}(\mathcal{SC}) \tag{15}$$

As per Definition 5, a combiner for encryption schemes is said to be IND-CPA robust if for every possible set $\mathcal{C}_n = (\mathcal{E}_i)_1^n$ of n component encryption schemes – and for all values of $n \geq 2$ –, the IND-CPA security of any one of these schemes implies that the output hybrid encryption scheme $\mathcal{E}_{hy}$ is itself IND-CPA secure:

$$\mathbf{Robust} \Leftrightarrow (\forall n \geq 2, \forall \mathcal{C}_n, \ \forall \mathcal{E}_j \in \mathcal{C}_n, \mathbf{IND\text{-}CPA}(\mathcal{E}_j) \Rightarrow \ \mathbf{IND\text{-}CPA}(\mathcal{E}_{hy})) \tag{16}$$

$$\Rightarrow \neg\mathbf{Robust} \Leftrightarrow (\exists n \geq 2, \exists \mathcal{C}_n, \ \exists \mathcal{E}_j \in \mathcal{C}_n : \mathbf{IND\text{-}CPA}(\mathcal{E}_j) \wedge \neg\mathbf{IND\text{-}CPA}(\mathcal{E}_{hy})) \tag{17}$$

Combining Eq. (15) and Eq. (17), statement 2 is rephrased as:

$$\exists \mathcal{E}_s \in \mathcal{S} : \neg\mathbf{Cond1}(\mathcal{E}_s) \vee \neg\mathbf{Cond2}(\mathcal{E}_s) \Rightarrow \exists n \geq 2, \exists \mathcal{C}_n = (\mathcal{E}_i)_i^n, \exists \mathcal{E}_j \in \mathcal{C}_n : \mathbf{IND\text{-}CPA}(\mathcal{E}_j) \wedge \neg\mathbf{IND\text{-}CPA}(\mathcal{E}_{hy}) \tag{18}$$

Therefore, to prove Eq. (18), we assume that its left-hand proposal is true and we need to find an instance of a set $\mathcal{C}_n$ of component encryption schemes, for a given number n of encryption schemes, that validates the right-hand proposal. We study separately the two cases $\exists \mathcal{E}_s \in \mathcal{S} : \neg\mathbf{Cond1}(\mathcal{E}_s)$ and $\exists \mathcal{E}_s \in \mathcal{S} : \neg\mathbf{Cond2}(\mathcal{E}_s)$.

Spilling Primitive with Non-Partitioned-Ciphertext (¬**Cond1***).* Let us consider a spilling-cascade combination of encryption schemes in which there is (at least) one spilling primitive with non-partitioned ciphertext. Then, one can always find at least one set of encryption schemes $\mathcal{C}_n$ in which one of the primitives is IND-CPA secure but not the output hybrid scheme.

For instance, we can set the number of component encryption schemes to $n = 2$, for simplicity's sake, and therefore combine together two schemes such that:

- The first scheme $\mathcal{E}_1$ is a spilling primitive wrapped around a (random) non-partitioned-ciphertext encryption scheme $\mathcal{E}'_1$, that only differs from the latter by adding, at the beginning of its ciphertext, the first bit b_{m_1} of its plaintext: $c_1 := (b_{m_1}, c'_1)$. Straightforwardly, such a scheme is also a non-partitioned-ciphertext scheme. We also choose that $\mathcal{E}_1$ includes that bit in the part of its ciphertext that is made public: $u_1 := (b_{m_1}, \bar{u}_1)$.
- The second scheme in the spilling-cascade chain is IND-CPA secure.

In such a case, any PPT adversary can win with probability 1 the security experiment on the CPA-indistinguishability of the spilling-cascade, by choosing two challenge plaintexts m^0 and m^1 starting respectively with 0 and 1, and by checking, in the challenge ciphertext $c^* := (u_1^*, c_2^*) = (b_{m_1}^*, \bar{u}_1^*, c_2^*)$ output by the spilling-cascade, to which plaintext corresponds the leaked bit $b_{m_1}^*$.

Spilling Primitive with $c_m \not\sqsubseteq v$ *(*$\neg$**Cond2***).* In this case, the spilling-cascade combiner comprises a partitioned-ciphertext spilling primitive that does not entirely encapsulate the message-related part c_m of its ciphertext into the following encryption scheme. In the most conservative hypothesis, it comes to leaking a single bit b_m from that c_m part into the part of the ciphertext that is made public: $b_m \sqsubseteq u$.

Once again, we can straightforwardly find an instance of two encryption schemes such that:

- The first scheme $\mathcal{E}_1$ is a spilling primitive based on a (random) partitioned-ciphertext encryption scheme $\mathcal{E}'_1$, with the first bit b_{m_1} of its plaintext added at the beginning of the *public* part u_1 of its ciphertext: $u_1 := (b_{m_1}, u'_1)$. $\mathcal{E}_1$ is obviously also partitioned-ciphertext, with $c_{r_1} = c'_{r_1}$ and $c_{m_1} = (c'_{m_1}, b_{m_1})$.
- The second scheme in the spilling-cascade chain is IND-CPA secure.

This setting also leaks, in the hybrid ciphertext c^*, the bit b_{m_1} that was spilled by the scheme $\mathcal{E}_1$. This leakage is sufficient for the adversary to win with probability 1 the IND-CPA security experiment of the spilling-cascade scheme, with the same method as in the previous case.

This proves Statement 2 and terminates the proof of Theorem 1.

3.4 Properties of the Hybrid PKE

As recalled in Eq. 6, the security bound of a FO transformation depends on the worst-case correctness δ^{wc} and the γ-spreadness of the underlying PKE. Therefore, it appears necessary to assess the value of these two properties for a hybrid PKE built from a spilling-cascade.

Lemma 1 (Hybrid Worst-Case Correctness and γ-Spreadness). *The combination in spilling-cascade of n encryption schemes $(\mathcal{E}_i = (\text{KeyGen}_i, \text{Enc}_i, \text{Dec}_i))_{i \in [\![1,n]\!]}$, each of which being γ_i-spread and with a worst-case correctness δ_i^{wc}, yields a γ_{sc}-spread hybrid PKE with a worst-case correctness δ_{sc}^{wc} s.t.:*

$$\gamma_{sc} \geq \gamma_n \qquad \text{and} \qquad \delta_{sc}^{wc} \leq \sum\nolimits_{i=1}^{n} \delta_i^{wc} \tag{19}$$

This lemma, whose proof is located in Appendix A.2, underlines that a FO transformation applied on a spilling-cascade-built hybrid encryption scheme has a security bound that is similar to the ones of the FO transformations carried out on the component schemes. Indeed, the γ-spreadness – that we want as high as possible – is lower-bounded by the one of the last scheme in the spilling-cascade chain, while the worst-case correctness – which should be minimized – only grows linearly with the number of component schemes.

3.5 Functionalities of a Spilling-Cascade

We present hereunder two functionalities brought by the spilling-cascade combination of encryption schemes.

KEM Hybridization. As mentioned in the introduction, the spilling-cascade architecture can be used for KEM hybridization, in order to maintain the security of the hybrid encapsulation scheme even in case of failure of some of its components. A (spilling-)cascade KEM hybridization is realized by combining the PKEs of the KEMs we want to associate in order to generate a hybrid PKE, which in turn is transformed into a hybrid KEM with a FO transformation.

Authenticated Key Exchange with Spilling-Cascade. The spilling-cascade combination may also be used in the context of an authenticated key exchange, where the parties are implicitly authenticated by additional KEMs instead of signatures. This approach, stated for instance by [3], appears particularly interesting in the framework of post-quantum authentication, as most current PQ signatures still suffer from a larger bandwidth than their KEM counterparts. This observation has led to KEM-TLS [27], a variant of TLS where signatures are replaced by a KEM-based implicit authentication. KEM-TLS however uses a classical parallel combination of its KEMs, and therefore could be improved with the use of our spilling-cascade.

Figure 5 compares a standard implicit Unilateral Authenticated Key Exchange (UAKE) with a similar protocol using a spilling-cascade combiner.

Here, the (spilling-)cascade architecture does no longer have to prevent the failure of some of the KEMs. It instead plays the role of a multi-key encryption scheme, for which several secret keys (the ephemeral one, used to refresh the randomness, as well as the recipient's static one, used as an authentication mean)

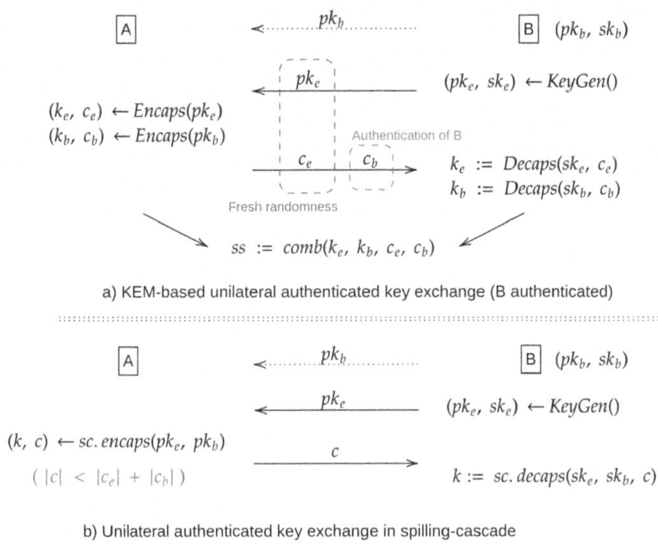

Fig. 5. KEM-based implicit UAKE, with authentication of party B. Figure *a* shows a standard authentication procedure, as proposed in [3]. Figure *b* details the variant with a spilling-cascade hybrid-KEM.

are needed to decrypt a ciphertext. In this paradigm, one can rely on the same algorithm for the whole spilling-cascade. As a consequence, the initial constraint of Theorem 1, stating that the upstream PKE must be partitioned ciphertext, may be relaxed (since this property is only needed, in the security proof of the spilling-cascade, when the first encryption scheme is broken and the second one remains secure).

4 Instantiations

We now detail the instantiation of two hybrid schemes that we consider as particularly relevant in real world applications. The communication costs associated with these instantiations are studied in Sect. 5.

4.1 Spilling-Cascade Double-Hybridization

The first hybrid KEM consists in a $\{1\}$-spilling-cascade combination of the classical ElGamal cryptosystem (on elliptic curves) and the PKE of the PQ KEM Crystals Kyber. As ElGamal has partitioned ciphertexts (cf. proof in Appendix A.1), according to Theorem 1, the resulting hybrid PKE has IND-CPA security and the related KEM, after a FO transformation, is IND-CCA secure.

4.2 Spilling-Cascade Triple-Hybridization

The second hybrid KEM combiner, adapted to highly sensitive data, comes from a triple hybridization in {1,2}-spilling-cascade composition, with one classical encryption scheme and two post-quantum PKEs (cf. Fig. 6). In this case, the choice of PQ algorithms is strongly constrained by the ciphertext length of the upstream PQ PKE and the input size of the downstream PQ PKE.

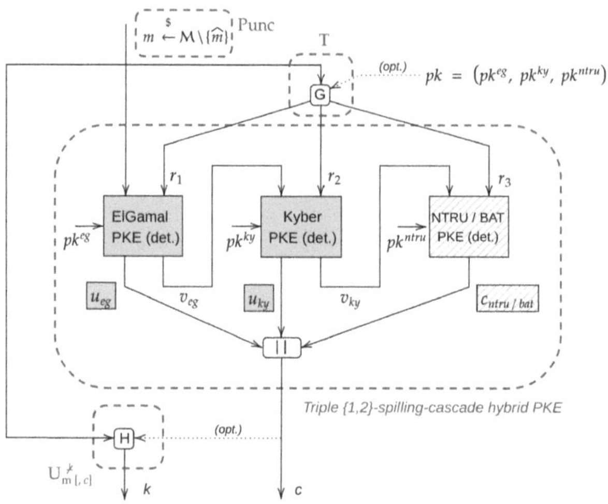

Fig. 6. Architecture of the triple hybridization in {1,2}-spilling-cascade ElGamal-Kyber-NTRU/BAT. The spilling PKEs, here both ElGamal and Kyber, are depicted in pink color. The dashed blue box represents the hybrid PKE and the dashed red boxes, the modular FO transformation. (Color figure online)

In our instantiation, the classical algorithm and the upstream PQ PKE are the same as in the double hybridization: ElGamal and Kyber. The security of the combiner is ensured by the fact that Kyber, which is a spilling primitive in the scheme along with ElGamal, is also a partitioned-ciphertext encryption scheme (cf. proof in Appendix A.1).

Regarding the downstream PQ algorithm, we consider two candidates both based on NTRU lattices: NTRU-HRSS [20] and the more recent algorithm BAT [11]. We also implement a variant of NTRU-HRSS proposed by [25], that we call npNTRU. This one is based on a tweak by [23] where the probabilistic NTRU-HRSS PKE is turned into a deterministic one by including the randomness r into the input of the PKE, along with the plaintext m (since it is possible to recover r as well in the decryption process). This tweak therefore increases the input size of this PKE, which is beneficial for the efficiency of the spilling-cascade..

The criteria considered for these choices were:

- The good performances of these algorithms, that make them realistic alternatives to Kyber in case this one would be broken.

- Their differences with Kyber in terms of mathematical foundations, so that a vulnerability on Kyber or even on the Module-Learning with Error problem would not necessarily compromise them.
- More importantly, the input lengths[11] of their PKEs, of 140 bytes for NTRU-HRSS, 160 bytes for BAT and 280 bytes for npNTRU, permit the encapsulation of the 128 byte-long c_m part of Kyber's ciphertext ($c_{m_{ky}} \sqsubseteq v_{ky}$), which is the necessary condition to implement a secure spilling-cascade combination of these KEMs.

Nota: NTRU-HRSS PKE takes as input a bit string that is encoded afterwards into a ternary polynomial. Because the original encoding algorithm does not permit to recover, in the decryption process, an arbitrary input given to the PKE (which is not a problem when NTRU is only used as a KEM), we had to slightly modify this encoding algorithm, as presented in the full version.

4.3 Enhanced Variations

We study two possible enhancements of our spilling-cascade KEM hybridization, that are detailed in the full version.

Integrated Diffie-Hellman (IDH) KEM. This is a spilling-cascade combination of one or several PQ PKEs with a Diffie-Hellman on Elliptic Curve (ECDH) key agreement scheme, in replacement of the classical encryption scheme. The idea here is to be more efficient in terms of bandwidth, given the fact that an ECDH key agreement scheme produces a ciphertext[12] lighter than a similar encryption algorithm (twice smaller, for instance, than its ElGamal counterpart).

Integration of the Public Keys. Another enhancement consists in the encapsulation in one another of the public keys of the PKEs to be hybridized, in order to gain once again some bandwidth. We provide here a method to encapsulate an ECDH or ElGamal public key in Kyber's one. This proposal is unfortunately not generically applicable to all classical or PQ algorithms, since it depends on the structure of the wrapping public key. However, the fact that Kyber and the ECDH schemes are the most commonly used key exchange primitives, respectively in the classical and Post-Quantum settings, mitigates this drawback.

5 Communication Cost

Even if the practical communication cost of the spilling-cascade's ciphertext relies on the characteristics of the encryption schemes used in the chain, we state it constitutes the *optimal* generic hybridization method of PKEs regarding the communication cost of the output ciphertext.

[11] For the parameters corresponding to the NIST security level 3.

[12] We model here the "ciphertext" of an ECDH key agreement scheme by the public DH element output by the sender. See the full version for additional details.

5.1 Communication Cost of the Spilling-Cascade

Definition 9 (Expansion Rate of an Encryption Scheme). *Let us consider an encryption scheme $\mathcal{E}$ that, for a given set of parameters depending on the security parameter λ, has a message space $\mathcal{M}$ with elements of bit-length $|m_\mathcal{E}|_\lambda$ and outputs ciphertexts of bit-length $|c_\mathcal{E}|_\lambda$. We define the expansion rate of $\mathcal{E}$ for the security parameter λ*[13] *as the ratio:*

$$\boxed{\tau_{\mathcal{E},\lambda} = \frac{|c_\mathcal{E}|_\lambda}{|m_\mathcal{E}|_\lambda}} \tag{20}$$

Spilling-Cascade Ciphertext Bandwidth. Let $(\mathcal{E}_i)_{i\in[\![1,n]\!]}$ be n encryption schemes with respective input size, output size and expansion rate $|m_i|$, $|c_i|$ and τ_i. Let us combine these schemes in spilling-cascade, with an arbitrary subset $\mathcal{S}$ of the $n-1$ first primitives spilling a part of their ciphertext. As in Definition 6, we note u_i the spilling (i.e. public) part of $\mathcal{E}_i$'s ciphertext and v_i the part of its ciphertext that is encapsulated by $\mathcal{E}_{i+1}$ (if the scheme is not spilling, then $u_i = \varnothing$ and $v_i = c_i$).

The spilling predicate s_i, associated with an encryption scheme $\mathcal{E}_i$ in the spilling-cascade chain, is defined as: $s_0 = 0$, $s_n = 1$ and $\forall i \in [\![1, n-1]\!], s_i = 1$ if $\mathcal{E}_i \in \mathcal{S}$ and 0 otherwise. The ciphertext size of the spilling-cascade combination of that schemes is:

$$|c_{sc}| = \sum_{i=1}^{n-1} \left(s_i\,|u_i|\right) + |c_n| = \sum_{i=1}^{n-1} s_i\left(|c_i| - |v_i|\right) + s_n\,|c_n| \tag{21}$$

For non-spilling schemes $\mathcal{E}_i \notin \mathcal{S}$, $s_i\,|u_i| = 0$. Moreover, according to Definition 6, spilling primitives $\mathcal{E}_j \in \mathcal{S}$ have an encapsulated ciphertext of the same bit-length as the elements of the message space of the following schemes: $|v_j| = |m_{j+1}|$. Consequently, $s_j(|c_j| - |v_j|) = s_j(\tau_j\,|m_j| - |m_{j+1}|)$ and:

$$\boxed{|c_{sc}| = \sum_{i=1}^{n} (s_i\tau_i - s_{i-1})\,|m_i|} \tag{22}$$

Nota: In comparison, the ciphertext bandwidth of the parallel combination of that same encryption schemes is: $|c_{par}| = \sum_{i=1}^{n} \tau_i\,|m_i|$.

5.2 Optimality of the Ciphertext Size

We define below the concept of encryption scheme with *bare ciphertext* that aims to exclude, in our Theorem 2, any cryptosystem where part of the ciphertext (padding or error correcting mechanism, for instance) is not required for

[13] The security parameter λ may be omitted when it is well-defined and remains unchanged in a given context, which is the case in this paper.

decryption. We also exclude from our analysis, through the concept of *efficiency*, combiners for encryption schemes that artificially decrease their bandwidth by truncating the ciphertext they output. In practice, to the best of our knowledge, all real-life cryptosystems have a bare ciphertext and all combiners for encryption schemes are efficient. Therefore, these two assumptions do not narrow the scope of Theorem 2.

Definition 10 (Encryption Scheme with Bare Ciphertext). *An encryption scheme $\mathcal{E}$ is said to have a bare ciphertext if any bit of the ciphertext c it outputs is necessary to successfully run its decryption algorithm* Dec.

Theorem 2 (Optimal Communication Cost). *For all sets $(\mathrm{PKE}_i)_{i=1}^{n}$ of n public-key cryptosystems with bare ciphertexts that are instantiable with a spilling-cascade, there exists no efficient, IND-CPA robust, combiner for PKEs that is compatible with these sets and that outputs a ciphertext smaller than that of the spilling-cascade, provided that one of the two following conditions applies:*

1. *This combination is fully-spilling: $\mathcal{S} = (\mathcal{E}_i)_{i=1}^{n-1}$ (cf. Definition 7);*
2. *Any non-spilling encryption scheme outputs ciphertexts of bit-length equal to the input size of the following primitive: $\forall \mathcal{E}_j \notin \mathcal{S}, |c_j| = |m_{j+1}|$.*

Nota: This theorem states the optimality of the spilling-cascade as a combination method generically applicable to all sets of PKEs respecting the security conditions from Theorem 1. On the contrary, we cannot exclude that there exists specific sets of PKEs that can be combined in a way that yields a ciphertext smaller than with the spilling-cascade. However, such combinations would lack the genericity that we require, and thus are not considered in Theorem 2.

Proof of Theorem 2. We proceed with a proof by contradiction. Let us assume that there exists an efficient IND-CPA robust combiner for PKEs $\mathscr{C}_{opt}$ (in the sense of Definition 5) that is compatible with any set of PKEs $(\mathrm{PKE}_i)_{i\in[\![1,n]\!]}$ instantiable with the spilling-cascade and that outputs a ciphertext smaller than that of the latter (cf. Eq. (22)). Let us assume moreover that one of the two conditions from Theorem 2 is respected: either all the $n-1$ first schemes are spilling, when combined in spilling-cascade, or the non-spilling schemes do not need paddings to fit in the message space of the following encryption schemes.

$$|c_{opt}| \;<\; |c_{sc}| \;=\; \sum\nolimits_{i=1}^{n} (s_i \tau_i - s_{i-1})\, |m_i| \;=\; \sum\nolimits_{i=1}^{n-1} s_i \left(|c_i| - |m_{i+1}|\right) + |c_n| \tag{23}$$

As a reminder, the spilling predicate s is defined as: $s_0 = 0$, $s_n = 1$ and $\forall i \in [\![1, n-1]\!], s_i = 1$ if $\mathcal{E}_i \in \mathcal{S}$ (spilling primitive) and 0 otherwise.

We now wonder whether the data comprised in $\mathscr{C}_{opt}$'s ciphertext is sufficient to recover the original plaintext m that was encrypted by $\mathscr{C}_{opt}$. Firstly, we prove below that the plaintext m encrypted by any IND-CPA robust combiner $\mathscr{C}$ can be recovered only if all its underlying decryption algorithms $(\mathrm{Dec}_i)_{i\in[\![1,n]\!]}$ are run successfully by the decryption algorithm $\mathrm{Dec}_{\mathscr{C}}$ of the hybrid scheme.

Proposition 1. *If a combiner $\mathscr{C}$ for PKEs is IND-CPA robust, in the sense of Definition 5, then its decryption algorithm* $\mathrm{Dec}_{\mathscr{C}}$ *runs the decryption algorithms* Dec_i *of* all *its component PKEs* $(\mathrm{PKE}_i)_{i\in[\![1,n]\!]}$.

Proof. We also prove this proposition by contradiction. Let us consider a combiner for PKEs $\mathscr{C}$ that is IND-CPA robust and that has a decryption algorithm $\mathrm{Dec}_{\mathscr{C}}$ that does not run the decryption algorithm of PKE_j – but it may use the $(\mathrm{KeyGen}_i)_{i\in[\![1,n]\!]}$ and $(\mathrm{Enc}_i)_{i\in[\![1,n]\!]}$ algorithms if needed, including those of the j-th scheme.

According to Definition 5, the hybrid PKE generated by the combiner must remain IND-CPA secure in the case where PKE_j is IND-CPA secure and all the other schemes are broken by the adversary. However, in such a case, the adversary appears able to break the IND-CPA security of the hybrid scheme, since the only IND-CPA secure component scheme PKE_j does not have its decryption algorithm Dec_j involved in the decryption process of the combiner. We note that the Enc_j algorithm – that is potentially run by $\mathrm{Dec}_{\mathscr{C}}$ – does not secure the hybrid scheme because it uses as input a public key, known by the adversary[14]. The hybrid PKE is therefore not IND-CPA secure, which contradicts the initial hypothesis and proves that an IND-CPA robust combiner must run all its component decryption algorithms.

Focus on the Decryption Process of $\mathscr{C}_{opt}$. The decryption algorithm of the combiner $\mathscr{C}_{opt}$ can run its component decryption algorithms either in parallel or sequentially. During that process, each algorithm Dec_i "consumes" a ciphertext of size $|c_i|$ from the hybrid ciphertext c_{opt} and outputs a plaintext m_i' of size $|m_i|$.

In the general case, this plaintext m_i' can be used as additional data to "feed" another decryption algorithm from the combiner; this is however possible only when the decryptions occur sequentially. Therefore, we consider in the rest of that proof the more conservative hypothesis of sequential decryptions within the combiner $\mathscr{C}_{opt}$, and without loss of generality, we consider a decryption order from Dec_n to Dec_1.

Consequently, after running the $n-1$ first decryption algorithms, we have consumed $\sum_{i=2}^{n}\big(|c_i|-|m_i|\big)$ data, which leaves available, for the last decryption algorithm Dec_1, data of size α s.t.:

$$\begin{aligned}
\alpha &= |c_{opt}| - \sum\nolimits_{i=2}^{n}\big(|c_i|-|m_i|\big)\\
&< |c_{sc}| - \sum\nolimits_{i=2}^{n}\big(|c_i|-|m_i|\big)\\
&< \sum\nolimits_{i=1}^{n-1} s_i\big(|c_i|-|m_{i+1}|\big) + |c_n| - \sum\nolimits_{i=2}^{n}\big(|c_i|-|m_i|\big)\\
&< s_1(|c_1|-|m_2|) + \sum\nolimits_{i=2}^{n-1}\underbrace{\big(s_i(|c_i|-|m_{i+1}|)+|m_i|-|c_i|\big)}_{\alpha_i} + |m_n| \qquad (24)
\end{aligned}$$

[14] This is a major difference with a combiner for secret-key cryptosystems, that can use the encryption algorithms of its component schemes even for the decryption process.

As any existing non-spilling scheme has a ciphertext size $|c_i| = |m_{i+1}|$ (due to condition 2 of Theorem 2), the associated $\alpha_i = |m_i| - |c_i| = |m_i| - |m_{i+1}|$ appears identical to the value of that term for spilling schemes. Therefore:

$$\alpha < s_1(|c_1| - |m_2|) + |m_2| < |c_1| \tag{25}$$

Because PKE_1 has a bare ciphertext – as stated as a prerequisite of Theorem 2 –, its decryption algorithm Dec_1 needs an input of size at least $|c_1|$. As shown in Eq. (25), the data available for Dec_1 is therefore too small to successfully retrieve the plaintext m_1 that was encrypted with Enc_1. Thus, as the combiner $\mathscr{C}_{opt}$ needs all its component decryption algorithms to work successfully in order to be IND-CPA robust, the failure of Dec_1 makes impossible to recover the original plaintext m and the combiner $\mathscr{C}$ turns out to be non-functional. This indicates that the ciphertext output by the spilling-cascade is the smallest possible for an efficient IND-CPA robust combiner for PKEs with bare ciphertexts, which terminates the proof of Theorem 2.

5.3 Practical Efficiency

In our instantiations of KEM hybridization (cf. Fig. 7), the best optimization brought by our spilling-cascade scheme exceeds 13%, in the case of the triple hybridization ElGamal_Kyber_npNTRU, with a reduction of 306 bytes in the output ciphertext.

	Hybridization	Parallel comb. |ct| (bytes)	Spill-casc. comb. |ct| (bytes)	Gain of spill-casc.
KEM hybridization	ElGamal_Kyber	1,152	1,120	2.8 %
	ElGamal_BAT	1,070	1,006	6.0 %
	ElGamal_Kyber_NTRU	2,290	2,121	7.4 %
	ElGamal_Kyber_BAT	2,158	1,966	8.9 %
	ElGamal_Kyber_npNTRU	2,290	1,984	13.4 %
Unilateral Authenticated Key Echange	Kyber_Kyber	2,176	2,144	1.5 %
	NTRU_NTRU	2,276	2,139	6.0 %
	BAT_BAT	2,012	1,852	8.0 %
	npNTRU_npNTRU	2,276	2,002	12.0 %

Fig. 7. Ciphertext communication costs of parallel and spilling-cascade combinations for different types of hybridizations and KEM-based authentications.

Even though its bandwidth improvement remains moderate, the spilling-cascade combination offers interesting perspectives for lighter constructions in the future, as its performances closely depend on the primitives involved, which may appear in the future more appropriate to such a combination. Furthermore, even a small decrease in the size of the data transmitted may avoid reaching the maximum transmission size of a packet in a network, and thus its fragmentation.

A Omitted Proofs

A.1 Proofs for Partitioned-Ciphertext Algorithms

We detail hereunder the proofs of the partitioned-ciphertext property of ElGamal and Kyber encryption schemes, used in the practical instantiations of Sect. 4.

Proposition 2. *ElGamal public-key encryption algorithm [9] is a partitioned-ciphertext encryption scheme.*

Proof. We recall that in a cyclic group G of order q, with a generator g, an ElGamal ciphertext corresponding to a plaintext $m \in \mathcal{M} = G$ if of the form: $\boxed{c_{eg} := (c_{r_{eg}} = g^r, c_m = m.X^r)}$, where $X := g^x$ is the recipient's public-key and $r \leftarrow_\$ \mathbb{Z}_q$ a secret random element drawn by the sender.

For a given set of parameters $\{G, q, g\}$, the sizes of the components $c_{r_{eg}}$ and $c_{m_{eg}}$ clearly remain constant for all messages $(m, m') \in \mathcal{M}^2$ (these messages are such that $|m| = |m'|$, since every plaintext is an element of the group G). Furthermore, $c_{r_{eg}}$ does not depend on the encrypted plaintext m but only on the randomness r, which completes the proof.

Proposition 3. *Crystals Kyber public-key encryption algorithm [3] is a partitioned-ciphertext encryption scheme.*

Proof. The ciphertext output by Kyber is of the form $\mathbf{c}_{kyber} := (\mathbf{u}, v)$, with

$$\boxed{\begin{aligned} c_{r_{ky}} &:= \mathbf{u} = \text{Compress}(A^T.\mathbf{r} + \mathbf{e}_1) \\ c_{m_{ky}} &:= v = \text{Compress}(\mathbf{t}^T.\mathbf{r} + e_2 + \left\lfloor \tfrac{q}{2} \right\rceil .m) \end{aligned}}$$

- The modulus $q = 3329$ is a fixed public parameter;
- $\mathbf{t}$ and $A = \text{Expand}(\rho)$ are issued from the recipient's public-key $\boxed{pk := \mathbf{t} \mid\mid \rho}$ (with $\rho \leftarrow_\$ \{0,1\}^{256}$);
- $\mathbf{e}_1$, e_2 and $\mathbf{r}$ are sampled from a secret seed $r \leftarrow_\$ \{0,1\}^{256}$.

As any semantically-secure encryption scheme, Kyber is "length-uniform" (cf. [15]), which implies that:
$\forall (pk, pk') \in \mathcal{PK}^2, \forall (m, m') \in \mathcal{M}^2, |m| = |m'| \Rightarrow |\text{Enc}(pk, m)| = |\text{Enc}(pk', m')|$. Furthermore, we also have a message space with elements of constant size (32 bytes). Consequently: $\exists \kappa \in \mathbb{N} : \forall m \in \mathcal{M}, |c_{r_{ky}}| + |c_{m_{ky}}| = \kappa$.

Furthermore, the element $c_{r_{ky}}$ does not depend on the plaintext m: it is a function of the recipient's public key (since the matrix A directly comes from the random seed $\rho \in pk$) and of the random seed r used to deterministically produce $\mathbf{r}$, $\mathbf{e}_1$ and e_2. It thus fulfills condition 2 of Definition 8 and implies that $|c_{r_{ky}}|$ is constant over $\mathcal{M}$. According to the previous paragraph, we can deduce that $|c_{m_{ky}}|$ is constant over $\mathcal{M}$ as well, which terminates the proof of the theorem.

A.2 Proof of Worst-Case Correctness and γ-Spreadness

The proof of Lemma 1 is realized in the framework of a double PKE combination. The general case of n combined schemes is straightforwardly deduced by induction.

Let us consider the hybrid PKE PKE_{sc} resulting from the combination in $\{1\}$-spilling-cascade of component PKEs PKE_1 and PKE_2 The hybrid key-pair yielded by the hybrid key generation algorithm is simply the tuple of key-pairs of the underlying PKEs: $(pk_{sc}, sk_{sc}) := ((pk_1, pk_2), (sk_1, sk_2))$.

Following the previous notations of this paper, we call u_1 the element of the ciphertext $c_1 := (u_1, v_1)$ output by Enc_1 that is part of the hybrid ciphertext, and v_1 the part of c_1 that is encapsulated by PKE_2 in the spilling-cascade chain. Furthermore, let π_u and π_v be the functions that output respectively u_1 and v_1 from the encryption of a plaintext $m_1 \in \mathcal{M}_1$: $u_1 := \pi_u(\text{Enc}_1(pk_1, m; r_1))$ and $v_1 := \pi_v(\text{Enc}_1(pk_1, m; r_1))$. The sets of all possible values u_1 and v_1 for a given plaintext m from the message space of PKE_1 are called $\mathcal{U}_1^m$ and $\mathcal{V}_1^m$:

$$\begin{cases} \mathcal{U}_1^m := \{u_1 := \pi_u(\text{Enc}_1(pk_1, m; r_1)), r_1 \in \mathcal{R}_1\}_{m \in \mathcal{M}_1} \\ \mathcal{V}_1^m := \{v_1 := \pi_v(\text{Enc}_1(pk_1, m; r_1)), r_1 \in \mathcal{R}_1\}_{m \in \mathcal{M}_1} \end{cases}$$

We proceed separately to the proofs of the two properties of γ-spreadness and worst-case correctness.

Proof of the γ-Spreadness. As PKE_2 is γ_2-spread, $\forall (pk_2, sk_2) \leftarrow \text{KeyGen}_2(1^\lambda)$, $\forall m_2 \in \mathcal{M}_2$, $\alpha_2^{m_2} = \underset{c_2 \in \mathcal{C}_2}{\text{Max}} \left\{ \Pr_{r_2} [\text{Enc}_2(pk_2, m_2; r_2) = c_2] \right\} \leq 2^{-\gamma_2}$.

Regarding the hybrid scheme:
$\forall m \in \mathcal{M}_{sc} = \mathcal{M}_1, \forall (pk_1, sk_1) \leftarrow \text{KeyGen}_1(1^\lambda), \forall (pk_2, sk_2) \leftarrow \text{KeyGen}_2(1^\lambda)$:

$$\alpha^m = \underset{c_{sc} \in \mathcal{C}_{sc}}{\text{Max}} \left\{ \Pr_{r_1, r_2} [\text{Enc}_{sc}((pk_1, pk_2), m; (r_1, r_2)) = c_{sc}] \right\} \tag{26}$$

$$\begin{aligned} &= \underset{u_1 \in \mathcal{U}_1^m, c_2 \in \mathcal{C}_2}{Max} \{ \Pr_{r_1} [\text{Enc}_1(pk_1, m_1; r_1) = (u_1, v_1)] \\ &\quad \times \Pr_{r_1, r_2} [\text{Enc}_2(pk_2, v_1; r_2) = c_2 \mid \text{Enc}_1(pk_1, m_1; r_1) = (u_1, v_1)] \} \end{aligned} \tag{27}$$

Let v_1^* be the element of $\mathcal{V}_1^m$ that maximizes the probability that its encryption by PKE_2 yields c_2: $\forall v_1 \in \mathcal{V}_1^m, v_1 \neq v_1^*$,

$$\begin{aligned} &\Pr_{r_1, r_2} [\text{Enc}_2(pk_2, v_1; r_2) = c_2 \mid \text{Enc}_1(pk_1, m_1; r_1) = (u_1, v_1)] \\ &\qquad \leq \Pr_{r_2} [\text{Enc}_2(pk_2, v_1^*; r_2) = c_2] \end{aligned} \tag{28}$$

As $\forall m \in \mathcal{M}_1$, $\mathcal{V}_1^m \subseteq \mathcal{M}_2$ and PKE_2 is γ_2-spread, we have:

$$\alpha^m \leq \underset{c_2 \in \mathcal{C}_2}{\text{Max}} \left\{ \Pr_{r_2} [\text{Enc}_2(pk_2, v_1^*; r_2) = c_2] \right\} = \alpha_2^{v_1^*} \tag{29}$$

$$\leq 2^{-\gamma_2} \tag{30}$$

This proves that if PKE_2 is γ_2-spread, the hybrid PKE is γ_{sc}-spread, with $\gamma_{sc} \geq \gamma_2$.

Proof of the Worst-Case Correctness. Let $\mathrm{Fail}(\mathrm{PKE}_i, (pk_i, sk_i), m_i; r_i)$ be the event of failure by PKE_i of the decryption of a ciphertext $c_i := \mathrm{Enc}_i(pk_i, m_i; r_i)$, with $m_i \in \mathcal{M}_i$, $r_i \in \mathcal{R}_i$ and $(pk_i, sk_i) \leftarrow \mathrm{KeyGen}_i(1^\lambda)$. We have:

$$\begin{aligned}\mathrm{Fail}_{sc} &= \mathrm{Fail}(\mathrm{PKE}_{sc}, (pk_{sc}, sk_{sc}), m \in \mathcal{M}_1, (r_1, r_2) \in \mathcal{R}_1 \times \mathcal{R}_2) &(31)\\ &\subseteq \mathrm{Fail}(\mathrm{PKE}_1, (pk_1, sk_1), m; r_1) \cup \mathrm{Fail}(\mathrm{PKE}_2, (pk_2, sk_2), v_1; r_2) &(32)\end{aligned}$$

Consequently, the probability of failure of the hybrid PKE is bounded as: $p_{sc} \leq p_1 + p_2$, with:

$$p_{sc} = \Pr_{r_1, r_2}\left[\mathrm{Dec}_{sc}(sk_{sc}, \mathrm{Enc}_{sc}(pk_{sc}, m; (r_1, r_2))) \neq m\right] \quad (33)$$

$$p_1 = \Pr_{r_1}\left[\mathrm{Dec}_1(sk_1, \mathrm{Enc}_1(pk_1, m; r_1)) \neq m\right] \quad (34)$$

$$p_2 = \Pr_{r_1, r_2}\left[\mathrm{Dec}_2(sk_2, \mathrm{Enc}_2(pk_2, v_1; r_2)) \neq v_1\right] \quad (35)$$

$$\begin{aligned}&= \sum\nolimits_{r_1} \Big(\Pr_{r_2}\left[\mathrm{Dec}_2(sk_2, \mathrm{Enc}_2(pk_2, v_1; r_2)) \neq v_1 \mid v_1 = \pi_v(\mathrm{Enc}_1(pk_1, m; r_1))\right]\\ &\qquad \times \Pr_{r_1}\left[v_1 = \pi_v(\mathrm{Enc}_1(pk_1, m; r_1))\right]\Big) \quad (36)\end{aligned}$$

Let us now consider the value $\tilde{v_1} \in \mathcal{V}_1^m$ that maximizes the probability of failure of the decryption algorithm Dec_2:

$$\begin{aligned}\forall v_1 \in \mathcal{V}_1^m, v_1 \neq \tilde{v_1}, &\Pr_{r_2}\left[\mathrm{Dec}_2(sk_2, \mathrm{Enc}_2\left(pk_2, v_1; r_2)\right) \neq v_1\right]\\ &\leq \Pr_{r_2}\left[\mathrm{Dec}_2(sk_2, \mathrm{Enc}_2(pk_2, \tilde{v_1}; r_2)) \neq \tilde{v_1}\right]\end{aligned} \quad (37)$$

We have:

$$\begin{aligned}p_2^{max} = \operatorname*{Max}_{m \in \mathcal{M}_1}\{p_2\} &\leq \operatorname*{\mathit{Max}}_{m \in \mathcal{M}_1}\Big\{\Pr_{r_2}\left[\mathrm{Dec}_2(sk_2, \mathrm{Enc}_2(pk_2, \tilde{v_1}; r_2)) \neq \tilde{v_1}\right]\\ &\qquad \times \sum\nolimits_{r_1} \Pr_{r_1}\left[v_1 = \pi_v(\mathrm{Enc}_1(pk_1, m; r_1))\right]\Big\} &(38)\\ &\leq \operatorname*{Max}_{m \in \mathcal{M}_1}\left\{\Pr_{r_2}\left[\mathrm{Dec}_2(sk_2, \mathrm{Enc}_2(pk_2, \tilde{v_1}; r_2)) \neq \tilde{v_1}\right]\right\} &(39)\end{aligned}$$

Since the set $\mathcal{V}_1^m$ is included in the message space of PKE_2 ($\mathcal{V}_1^m \subseteq \mathcal{M}_2$), we can bound the above inequality as follows:

$$p_2^{max} \leq \operatorname*{Max}_{m_2 \in \mathcal{M}_2}\left\{\Pr_{r_2}\left[\mathrm{Dec}_2(sk_2, \mathrm{Enc}_2(pk_2, m_2; r_2)) \neq m_2\right]\right\} \quad (40)$$

Finally, we have:

$$\delta_{sc}^{wc} = \mathop{\mathbb{E}}_{(pk_{sc},sk_{sc})}\left(\mathop{\text{Max}}_{m\in\mathcal{M}_1}\{p_{sc}\}\right) \le \mathop{\mathbb{E}}_{(pk_{sc},sk_{sc})}\left(\mathop{\text{Max}}_{m\in\mathcal{M}_1}\{p_1\} + \mathop{\text{Max}}_{m\in\mathcal{M}_1}\{p_2\}\right) \tag{41}$$

$$\le \mathop{\mathbb{E}}_{(pk_1,sk_1)}\left(\mathop{\text{Max}}_{m\in\mathcal{M}_1}\{p_1\}\right) + \mathop{\mathbb{E}}_{(pk_{sc},sk_{sc})}\left(\mathop{\text{Max}}_{m\in\mathcal{M}_1}\{p_2\} = p_2^{max}\right) \tag{42}$$

$$\le \mathop{\mathbb{E}}_{(pk_1,sk_1)}\left(\mathop{\text{Max}}_{m\in\mathcal{M}_1}\{p_1\}\right) + \mathop{\mathbb{E}}_{(pk_2,sk_2)}\left(\mathop{\text{Max}}_{m_2\in\mathcal{M}_2}\left\{\Pr_{r_2}[\text{Dec}_2(sk_2, \text{Enc}_2(pk_2, m_2; r_2)) \ne m_2]\right\}\right) \tag{43}$$

$$\delta_{sc}^{wc} \le \delta_1^{wc} + \delta_2^{wc} \tag{44}$$

References

1. Aguilar-Melchor, C., et al.: HQC. Technical report, National Institute of Standards and Technology (2022). https://csrc.nist.gov/Projects/post-quantum-cryptography/round-4-submissions
2. An, J.H., Dodis, Y., Rabin, T.: On the security of joint signature and encryption. In: Knudsen, L.R. (ed.) EUROCRYPT 2002. LNCS, vol. 2332, pp. 83–107. Springer, Heidelberg (2002). https://doi.org/10.1007/3-540-46035-7_6
3. Bos, J., et al.: CRYSTALS – Kyber: a CCA-secure module-lattice-based KEM. Cryptology ePrint Archive, Report 2017/634 (2017). https://eprint.iacr.org/2017/634
4. Canetti, R., Krawczyk, H., Nielsen, J.B.: Relaxing chosen-ciphertext security. In: Boneh, D. (ed.) CRYPTO 2003. LNCS, vol. 2729, pp. 565–582. Springer, Heidelberg (2003). https://doi.org/10.1007/978-3-540-45146-4_33
5. Chen, C., et al.: NTRU. Technical report, National Institute of Standards and Technology (2020). https://csrc.nist.gov/projects/post-quantum-cryptography/post-quantum-cryptography-standardization/round-3-submissions
6. D'Anvers, J.P., et al.: SABER. Technical report, National Institute of Standards and Technology (2020). https://csrc.nist.gov/projects/post-quantum-cryptography/post-quantum-cryptography-standardization/round-3-submissions
7. Dodis, Y., Katz, J.: Chosen-ciphertext security of multiple encryption. In: Kilian, J. (ed.) TCC 2005. LNCS, vol. 3378, pp. 188–209. Springer, Heidelberg (2005). https://doi.org/10.1007/978-3-540-30576-7_11
8. Duman, J., Hövelmanns, K., Kiltz, E., Lyubashevsky, V., Seiler, G.: Faster lattice-based KEMs via a generic Fujisaki-Okamoto transform using prefix hashing. In: Vigna, G., Shi, E. (eds.) ACM CCS 2021: 28th Conference on Computer and Communications Security, Virtual Event, Republic of Korea, pp. 2722–2737. ACM Press (2021). https://doi.org/10.1145/3460120.3484819
9. ElGamal, T.: A public-key cryptosystem and a signature scheme based on discrete logarithms. In: Blakley, G.R., Chaum, D. (eds.) Advances in Cryptology, pp. 10–18. Springer, Heidelberg (1985)

10. Even, S., Goldreich, O.: On the power of cascade ciphers. ACM Trans. Comput. Syst. **3**, 108–116 (1985)
11. Fouque, P.A., Kirchner, P., Pornin, T., Yu, Y.: BAT: small and fast KEM over NTRU lattices. IACR Trans. Cryptogr. Hardw. Embed. Syst. **2022**(2), 240–265 (2022). https://doi.org/10.46586/tches.v2022.i2.240-265
12. Fujisaki, E., Okamoto, T.: Secure integration of asymmetric and symmetric encryption schemes. In: Wiener, M. (ed.) CRYPTO 1999. LNCS, vol. 1666, pp. 537–554. Springer, Heidelberg (1999). https://doi.org/10.1007/3-540-48405-1_34
13. Giacon, F., Heuer, F., Poettering, B.: KEM combiners. In: Abdalla, M., Dahab, R. (eds.) PKC 2018. LNCS, vol. 10769, pp. 190–218. Springer, Cham (2018). https://doi.org/10.1007/978-3-319-76578-5_7
14. Goldreich, O., Lustig, Y., Naor, M.: On chosen ciphertext security of multiple encryptions. Cryptology ePrint Archive, Report 2002/089 (2002). https://eprint.iacr.org/2002/089
15. Herzberg, A.: Folklore, practice and theory of robust combiners. Cryptology ePrint Archive, Report 2002/135 (2002). https://eprint.iacr.org/2002/135
16. Hofheinz, D., Hövelmanns, K., Kiltz, E.: A modular analysis of the Fujisaki-Okamoto transformation. In: Kalai, Y., Reyzin, L. (eds.) TCC 2017. LNCS, vol. 10677, pp. 341–371. Springer, Cham (2017). https://doi.org/10.1007/978-3-319-70500-2_12
17. Hohenberger, S., Lewko, A., Waters, B.: Detecting dangerous queries: a new approach for chosen ciphertext security. In: Pointcheval, D., Johansson, T. (eds.) EUROCRYPT 2012. LNCS, vol. 7237, pp. 663–681. Springer, Heidelberg (2012). https://doi.org/10.1007/978-3-642-29011-4_39
18. Hövelmanns, K., Kiltz, E., Schäge, S., Unruh, D.: Generic authenticated key exchange in the quantum random oracle model. In: Kiayias, A., Kohlweiss, M., Wallden, P., Zikas, V. (eds.) PKC 2020. LNCS, vol. 12111, pp. 389–422. Springer, Cham (2020). https://doi.org/10.1007/978-3-030-45388-6_14
19. Huguenin-Dumittan, L., Vaudenay, S.: FO-like combiners and hybrid post-quantum cryptography. In: Conti, M., Stevens, M., Krenn, S. (eds.) CANS 2021. LNCS, vol. 13099, pp. 225–244. Springer, Cham (2021). https://doi.org/10.1007/978-3-030-92548-2_12
20. Hülsing, A., Rijneveld, J., Schanck, J., Schwabe, P.: High-speed key encapsulation from NTRU. In: Fischer, W., Homma, N. (eds.) CHES 2017. LNCS, vol. 10529, pp. 232–252. Springer, Cham (2017). https://doi.org/10.1007/978-3-319-66787-4_12
21. Maurer, U.M., Massey, J.L.: Cascade ciphers: the importance of being first. J. Cryptol. **6**, 55–61 (1993). https://doi.org/10.1007/BF02620231
22. Naehrig, M., et al.: FrodoKEM. Technical report, National Institute of Standards and Technology (2020). https://csrc.nist.gov/projects/post-quantum-cryptography/post-quantum-cryptography-standardization/round-3-submissions
23. Pipher, J.H.J., Silverman, J.H.: NTRU: a new high speed public-key cryptosystem. In: Draft from at CRYPTO 96 Rump Session (1996). http://web.securityinnovation.com/hubfs/files/ntru-orig.pdf
24. Pöppelmann, T., et al.: NewHope. Technical report, National Institute of Standards and Technology (2019). https://csrc.nist.gov/projects/post-quantum-cryptography/post-quantum-cryptography-standardization/round-2-submissions
25. Saito, T., Xagawa, K., Yamakawa, T.: Tightly-secure key-encapsulation mechanism in the quantum random oracle model. In: Nielsen, J.B., Rijmen, V. (eds.) EUROCRYPT 2018. LNCS, vol. 10822, pp. 520–551. Springer, Cham (2018). https://doi.org/10.1007/978-3-319-78372-7_17

26. Schwabe, P., et al.: CRYSTALS-KYBER. Technical report, National Institute of Standards and Technology (2022). https://csrc.nist.gov/Projects/post-quantum-cryptography/selected-algorithms-2022
27. Schwabe, P., Stebila, D., Wiggers, T.: Post-quantum TLS without handshake signatures. In: Ligatti, J., Ou, X., Katz, J., Vigna, G. (eds.) ACM CCS 2020: 27th Conference on Computer and Communications Security, Virtual Event, USA, pp. 1461–1480. ACM Press (2020). https://doi.org/10.1145/3372297.3423350
28. Targhi, E.E., Unruh, D.: Post-quantum security of the Fujisaki-Okamoto and OAEP transforms. In: Hirt, M., Smith, A. (eds.) TCC 2016. LNCS, vol. 9986, pp. 192–216. Springer, Heidelberg (2016). https://doi.org/10.1007/978-3-662-53644-5_8
29. Zhang, C., Cash, D., Wang, X., Yu, X., Chow, S.: Combiners for chosen-ciphertext security. In: Dinh, T.N., Thai, M.T. (eds.) Computing and Combinatorics, pp. 257–268. Springer, Cham (2016)
30. Zhang, R., Hanaoka, G., Shikata, J., Imai, H.: On the security of multiple encryption or CCA-security+CCA-security=CCA-security? In: Bao, F., Deng, R., Zhou, J. (eds.) PKC 2004. LNCS, vol. 2947, pp. 360–374. Springer, Heidelberg (2004). https://doi.org/10.1007/978-3-540-24632-9_26

Distributed Asynchronous Remote Key Generation

Mark Manulis and Hugo Nartz(✉)

PACY Lab @ RI CODE, Universität der Bundeswehr München, Munich, Germany
mark@manulis.eu, hugo.nartz@unibw.de

Abstract. Asynchronous Remote Key Generation (ARKG) is a primitive introduced by Frymann et al. at ACM CCS 2020. It enables a sender to generate a new public key pk' for a receiver ensuring only it can, at a later time, compute the corresponding private key sk'. These key pairs are indistinguishable from freshly generated ones and can be used in various public-key cryptosystems such as digital signatures and public-key encryption. ARKG has been explored for applications in WebAuthn credential backup and delegation, as well as for enhancing receiver privacy via stealth addresses.

In this paper, we introduce distributed ARKG (dARKG) aiming to provide similar security properties in a distributed setting. Here, a sender generates pk' for a group of n receivers and the corresponding sk' can only be computed by any sub-group of size $t \leq n$. This introduces threshold-based access protection for sk', enabling for instance a set of proxies to jointly access a WebAuthn account or claim blockchain funds.

We construct dARKG using one-round publicly verifiable asymmetric key agreement, called 1PVAKA, a new primitive formalized in this work. Unlike traditional distributed key generation protocols where users interact with one another, 1PVAKA is asynchronous and allows a third party to verify and generate a public key from users' outputs.

We discuss 1PVAKA and dARKG instantiations tailored for use with bilinear groups and demonstrate practicality with implementation and performance analysis for the BLS12-381 curve.

Keywords: Asynchronous Remote Key Generation · Distributed Key Generation · Unlinkability

1 Introduction

Background and Motivation. Asynchronous Remote Key Generation introduced by Frymann et al. [16] serves as a cryptographic encapsulation mechanism for generating asymmetric key pairs between a sender and a receiver. In ARKG, the sender utilizes a receiver's long-term public key pk to derive a fresh public key pk' along with credentials cred. These credentials enable the receiver to later derive the corresponding private key sk' from its own long-term secret key sk. The properties SK-security and PK-unlinkability ensure that only the intended

M. Fischlin and V. Moonsamy (Eds.): ACNS 2025, LNCS 15825, pp. 486–515, 2025.
https://doi.org/10.1007/978-3-031-95761-1_17

receiver can access sk' and that derived key pairs $(\mathsf{sk}', \mathsf{pk}')$ are indistinguishable from freshly generated ones. Consequently, derived keys can be utilized in various cryptographic applications such as digital signatures or public key encryption, provided they are structurally compatible.

The initial instantiation of ARKG aimed to produce Diffie-Hellman-like key pairs. Subsequent developments addressed other types of keys. The generalized construction outlined in [18] focuses on pairing-based cryptosystems while the one in [15], relying on split-KEMs [8], supports lattice-based cryptosystems like Dilithium [14] and Kyber [6]. Recent papers focus primarily on the original application of ARKG in the backup of WebAuthn credentials [2]. Wilson [27] leverages KEMs with key blinding properties derived from lattices to achieve a stronger form of SK-security. Brendel et al. [7] also constructed a post-quantum ARKG scheme based on KEMs and digital signatures, albeit under modified security definitions.

Applications of ARKG. Initially devised to address the backup of hardware authenticators like Yubikeys within the WebAuthn/FIDO2[1] framework, ARKG has found versatile applications. The primitive was used to enable delegation of WebAuthn accounts and the construction of a new class of proxy signatures with unlinkable warrants [17]. This allows an account holder to delegate access rights for multiple accounts to a proxy. The blinding property providing unlinkability in ARKG is also similar to the one used for public-key malleability in mercurial signatures which found application in anonymous credential delegation [13,23].

Beyond credentials delegation, the same techniques used in ARKG contribute to the realization of stealth addresses and signatures in blockchain transactions [15,18], enhancing receiver privacy while allowing fund claiming. In fact, the original scheme from [16] for DL-based key pairs uses techniques that power the stealth addresses on the Monero blockchain [29]. The recent post-quantum stealth signature scheme [24] also adopts similar algorithms for the generation of public and private keys.

Motivation for a Distributed Scheme. A derived public key pk' can be used immediately for application tasks, i.e., before the corresponding sk' is derived by the receiver. The reconstruction of sk' is not possible if the receiver is unavailable. Moreover, compromising the receiver's static private key sk (which is excluded in the ARKG security model) yields sk'.

From this perspective, the restriction to a sole receiver exhibits single points of failure and attacks which may negatively impact the aforementioned applications. For example, if a WebAuthn backup authenticator is compromised, the attacker will gain unconditional access to all accounts on which backup keys were registered. Similarly, in case of stealth addresses, the loss or compromise of a transaction receiver's static private key would prevent them from claiming the funds or allow the attacker to claim them instead.

[1] https://github.com/Yubico/libfido2.

We argue that a *distributed* ARKG (dARKG) functionality where the derived secret key sk' can only be reconstructed by a (threshold) set of receivers would help mitigate the aforementioned risks. The distributed setup may also enable additional use cases. Owners of WebAuthn or unlinkable blockchain accounts could delegate access to trusted parties to reconstruct the required ARKG private keys sk' when needed. This power of attorney situation might apply in cases ranging from unavailability due to travel to death of the owner. Additionaly, threshold-based reconstruction of sk' would enable delegation of such accounts with access control policies based on the number of users, which is of particular interest in enterprise scenarios.

1.1 Challenges and Design Rationale

The dARKG primitive must allow a *delegator* to use the long-term public keys of n *proxies* in order to derive a fresh public key pk' and associated credentials. At a later stage, a subset of proxies should be able to reconstruct the corresponding private key sk' (or shares of it) from their long-term keys and credentials. It is desirable for dARKG to be compatible with the already existing functionalities and security requirements [16] of ARKG. Of particular importance is also the need to preserve asynchrony during the generation of pk'.

A sensible approach to build the primitive is to use existing (Non-Interactive) Distributed Key Generation ((NI-)DKG) protocols, e.g. [20,21]. The public key resulting from such a scheme could be used as the input static public key for the original ARKG. Clearly, interactive DKG protocols are less suitable as they assume online presence of all players and hence stand in conflict with the asynchrony requirement. In contrast, NI-DKG, e.g. [20], players only broadcast one message to each other. While this provides asynchrony, in dARKG proxies may not even have any means to communicate with each other at the time the static public key is created. In fact, the dARKG applications previously mentioned assume that each proxy interacts only with the delegator and that these interactions are asynchronous. From this perspective, we need a somewhat different flavour of (NI-)DKG where the delegator, as a dedicated party, asynchronously receives messages from the proxies and computes the resulting static public key pk. Importantly, the delegator must also be able to validate payloads from the proxies to ensure robustness: if pk' was successfully derived, the later computation of sk' by t honest players must also succeed.

Key Agreement for dARKG. In our paper we thus first propose a new one-round publicly verifiable asymmetric key agreement, denoted 1PVAKA. Each user generates a share sh and a "dealing" d for a group of users identified using their long-term public keys $\mathsf{ek}_1, \dots, \mathsf{ek}_n$. A third party can verify individual dealings and aggregate them into a public static key pk and new dealings $\mathsf{f}_1, \dots, \mathsf{f}_l$ for the l qualified users. Qualified users can, using their long-term secret keys dk_i and those new dealings, reconstruct the corresponding static key sk.

With dARKG in mind, the main challenge in building 1PVAKA is for the third party (the delegator) to combine users' (proxies) outputs into a static public key, while ensuring future recoverability of the static private key. That is, misbehaviour of asynchronous users must be identifiable during a 1PVAKA key generation session before aggregating a public key pk for the group.

For that purpose, the following natural approach is insufficient. Suppose each participant encrypts its own ephemeral secret key using (multi-recipient) public-key encryption for each other participant and broadcasts these ciphertexts along with the corresponding ephemeral public key (forming dealing $(\mathsf{d}_i)_{i\in[n]}$). A third party then combines the ephemeral public keys into a static group key pk and uses the dealings as public information. In this configuration, a single malicious user could send incorrect ciphertexts (unrelated to the public key in their dealing) leading later to unrecoverability of the private key sk. This is unacceptable as the public key pk may be used for many cryptographic operations before sk is required. In our construction of 1PVAKA we therefore use Verifiable Encryption (VE) [9] to ensure public verifiability of ciphertexts encrypting ephemeral secret keys with respect to their counterpart public keys.

The asymmetric group key agreement presented in [28] does not support *public* verifiability as derived decryption keys are required to verify the derived group public key. Nevertheless, our 1PVAKA construction uses a similar technique related to the homomorphic structure of public/private keys. We also use additively homomorphic encryption (similarly to [20]) to compress the payload sent by the delegator to a proxy from $\mathcal{O}(n)$ to $\mathcal{O}(1)$ ciphertexts.

1.2 Our Contributions

In this work, we introduce a framework for dARKG, building upon the foundational principles of ARKG outlined in [16]. Essentially, the original scheme can be seen as a specialized instance within our distributed framework.

We establish the syntax of dARKG along with key security properties, adapting the original definitions of SK-security and PK-unlinkability to account for the challenges inherent to the distributed approach. In doing so, we enhance PK-unlinkability to a more robust form, as seen in [7,27]. Our overarching dARKG construction uses 1PVAKA alongside conventional building blocks such as threshold secret sharing, verifiable public key encryption and KEM.

We treat 1PVAKA as an independent primitive at the frontier between asymmetric group key agreement [28] and non-interactive DKG [20]. To produce generic transformations compatible with most asymmetric cryptosystems, we use the blinding Asymmetric Key Generation (AKG) abstraction from [18]. This extends the applicability of our dARKG scheme to diverse key pair types, including those suitable for pairing-based cryptosystems.

The security properties of both our general 1PVAKA and dARKG constructions are proven in the random oracle model. We present an instantiation of 1PVAKA using single-message multi-receiver VE for use with the BLS12-381 curve. This curve can be used for authentication in WebAuthn and major blockchains like Bitcoin and Ethereum, as well as for BLS-3 signatures increasingly employed in distributed scenarios. Finally, we provide a Jupyter notebook with detailed benchmarks for an implementation of our instantiation of

1PVAKA. The results are satisfying and highlight the communication costs vs. complexity costs trade-off we aimed for.

1.3 Outline of the Paper

We start in Sect. 2 by recalling selected building blocks used in our 1PVAKA and dARKG constructions, including asymmetric key generation and verifiable encryption. We introduce 1PVAKA in Sect. 3 along with definitions and a construction. Section 4 presents the framework, syntax, security definitions and our general construction for dARKG. In Sect. 5 we discuss an instantiations and experimental results.

2 Preliminaries

We define security of cryptographic primitives through experiments involving PPT adversaries $\mathcal{A}$ or $\mathcal{B}$. Notation $\mathcal{A}^{\mathcal{O}}$ specifies that $\mathcal{A}$ has access to oracle $\mathcal{O}$. Security parameters are denoted by λ and by $\mathsf{negl}(\lambda)$, we denote any function f such that $f(\lambda) = \lambda^{-\omega(1)}$. Unless otherwise noted, probabilities will be implicitly taken over the random coins of the underlying algorithms.

Let $n \in \mathbb{N}$, we write $[n]$ for the set $\{1, \ldots, n\}$. For $I \subset \mathbb{N}$, we denote by $[\mathsf{x}]_I$ the set $\{\mathsf{x}_i \mid i \in I\}$ when elements x_i are clearly defined from context. For integer an $n \in \mathbb{N}$, we abbreviate $[\mathsf{x}]_n := [\mathsf{x}]_{[n]}$.

2.1 Asymmetric Key Generation (AKG)

Introduced in [18], Asymmetric Key Generation (AKG) provides handles for manipulating generic asymmetric keys. We add to the AKG syntax the convenient key blinding algorithms defined in [27]. Let $(\mathbb{S}, +)$ and $(\mathbb{P}, \cdot)$ be abelian groups corresponding to a secret and a public key space. An AKG scheme for key spaces $\mathbb{S}$ and $\mathbb{P}$ is defined by the following three PPT algorithms:

$\mathsf{Setup}(1^\lambda) \rightarrow \mathsf{pp}$: The setup algorithm takes as input a security parameter λ in unary representation. It outputs corresponding public parameters pp.

$\mathsf{KGen}(\mathsf{pp}) \rightarrow (\mathsf{sk}, \mathsf{pk})$: The key generation algorithm takes as input public parameters pp. It outputs a private and public key pair $(\mathsf{sk}, \mathsf{pk}) \in \mathbb{S} \times \mathbb{P}$.

$\mathsf{Check}(\mathsf{pp}, \mathsf{sk}, \mathsf{pk}) \rightarrow b$: The check algorithm takes as input public parameters pp and a key pair $(\mathsf{sk}, \mathsf{pk})$. It outputs a bit b.

If the following two algorithms are available, the scheme is said to be *blinding*:

$\mathsf{BlindPK}(\mathsf{pk}, \tau) \rightarrow \mathsf{pk}_\tau$: The public key blinding algorithm takes a public key pk as input and randomness $\tau \in \{0,1\}^\lambda$. It outputs a blinded public key pk_τ.

$\mathsf{BlindSK}(\mathsf{sk}, \tau) \rightarrow \mathsf{sk}_\tau$: The secret key blinding algorithm takes a secret key sk as input and randomness $\tau \in \{0,1\}^\lambda$. It outputs a blinded secret key sk_τ.

Definition 1 (Correctness). *An AKG scheme is correct if it provides valid key pairs compatible under the group laws, i.e., for all $\lambda \in \mathbb{N}$, it holds that*

$$\Pr\left[\begin{array}{r} \mathsf{Check}(\mathsf{sk},\mathsf{pk}) \neq 1 \\ \vee\ \mathsf{Check}(\mathsf{sk}+\mathsf{sk}',\mathsf{pk}\cdot\mathsf{pk}') \neq 1 \end{array} : \begin{array}{r} \mathsf{pp} \leftarrow \mathsf{Setup}(1^\lambda) \\ (\mathsf{sk},\mathsf{pk}) \leftarrow \mathsf{KGen}(\mathsf{pp}) \\ (\mathsf{sk}',\mathsf{pk}') \leftarrow \mathsf{KGen}(\mathsf{pp}) \end{array}\right] = \mathsf{negl}(\lambda).$$

A blinding AKG is correct if additionally for all blinding factor $\tau \in \{0,1\}^\lambda$,

$$\Pr\left[\mathsf{Check}(\mathsf{sk}_\tau,\mathsf{pk}_\tau) \neq 1 : \begin{array}{r} \mathsf{pk}_\tau \leftarrow \mathsf{BlindPK}(\mathsf{pk},\tau) \\ \mathsf{sk}_\tau \leftarrow \mathsf{BlindPK}(\mathsf{sk},\tau) \end{array}\right] = \mathsf{negl}(\lambda).$$

Definition 2 (Security). *Let $\lambda \in \mathbb{N}$ and set $\mathsf{pp} \leftarrow \mathsf{Setup}(1^\lambda)$. We say that the key-secrecy property holds for an AKG scheme or that it is secure if for all PPT adversary $\mathcal{A}$, the following advantage is negligible in λ*

$$\mathsf{Adv}^{\mathsf{secrecy}}_{\mathsf{AKG},\mathcal{A}}(\lambda) := \Pr\left[\mathsf{Check}(\mathsf{sk}^\star,\mathsf{pk}) = 1 : \begin{array}{r} (\mathsf{sk},\mathsf{pk}) \leftarrow \mathsf{KGen}(\mathsf{pp}) \\ \mathsf{sk}^\star \leftarrow \mathcal{A}(\mathsf{pp},\mathsf{pk}) \end{array}\right].$$

A blinding AKG scheme is secure if additionally, blinded and fresh public keys are indistinguishable, i.e., the following advantage is negligible

$$\mathsf{Adv}^{\mathsf{blinding}}_{\mathsf{AKG},\mathcal{A}}(\lambda) := \Pr\left[b = b' : \begin{array}{r} (\mathsf{sk}_0,\mathsf{pk}_0),(\mathsf{sk}_\star,\mathsf{pk}_\star) \leftarrow \mathsf{KGen}(\mathsf{pp}) \\ \tau \leftarrow\!\$\ \{0,1\}^\lambda;\ \mathsf{pk}_1 \leftarrow \mathsf{BlindPK}(\mathsf{pk}_\star,\tau) \\ b \leftarrow\!\$\ \{0,1\};\ b' \leftarrow \mathcal{A}(\mathsf{pp},\mathsf{pk}_b) \end{array}\right].$$

2.2 Asynchronous Remote Key Generation

An Asynchronous Remote Key Generation (ARKG) scheme as defined in [16] is composed of five algorithms defined as follows:

$\mathsf{Setup}(1^\lambda) \rightarrow \mathsf{pp}$: The setup algorithm takes as input a security parameter 1^λ and outputs a description pp of the public parameters.

$\mathsf{KGen}(\mathsf{pp}) \rightarrow (\mathsf{sk},\mathsf{pk})$: The key generation algorithm takes as input public parameters pp. It outputs a private and public key pair $(\mathsf{sk},\mathsf{pk})$.

$\mathsf{DerivePK}(\mathsf{pp},\mathsf{pk},\mathsf{aux}) \rightarrow (\mathsf{pk}',\mathsf{cred})$: The public key derivation algorithm takes as input public parameters pp, a public key pk and auxiliary information aux. It returns a derived public key pk' and a credential cred.

$\mathsf{DeriveSK}(\mathsf{pp},\mathsf{sk},\mathsf{cred}) \rightarrow \mathsf{sk}'/\bot$: The secret key derivation algorithm takes as input public parameters pp, a secret key sk and credential cred. It returns a secret key sk' or $\bot$ on error.

$\mathsf{Check}(\mathsf{pp},\mathsf{sk}',\mathsf{pk}') \rightarrow b$: The check algorithm takes as input public parameters pp, a secret key sk' and a public key pk'. It returns a bit b.

$\mathsf{Exp}^{\mathsf{PKU}}_{\mathsf{ARKG},\mathcal{A}}(\lambda)$

$\mathsf{pp} \leftarrow \mathsf{Setup}$
$(\mathsf{pk}_0, \mathsf{sk}_0) \leftarrow \mathsf{KGen}(\mathsf{pp})$
$b \leftarrow\!\!\$\ \{0,1\}$
$b' \leftarrow \mathcal{A}^{\mathsf{O}^b_{\mathsf{pk}'}}(\mathsf{pp}, \mathsf{pk}_0)$
$\textbf{return } b \stackrel{?}{=} b'$

$\mathsf{Exp}^{\mathsf{KS}}_{\mathsf{ARKG},\mathcal{A}}(\lambda)$

$\mathsf{pp} \leftarrow \mathsf{Setup}$
$(\mathsf{sk}, \mathsf{pk}) \leftarrow \mathsf{KGen}(\mathsf{pp})$
$(\mathsf{sk}^\star, \mathsf{pk}^\star, \mathsf{cred}^\star) \leftarrow \mathcal{A}^{\mathsf{O}_{\mathsf{pk}'}, \boxed{\mathsf{O}_{\mathsf{sk}'}(\mathsf{sid}, \cdot)}}(\mathsf{pp}, \mathsf{pk})$
$\mathsf{sk}' \leftarrow \mathsf{DeriveSK}(\mathsf{pp}, \mathsf{sk}, \mathsf{cred}^\star)$
$\textbf{return } \mathsf{Check}(\mathsf{pp}, \mathsf{sk}^\star, \mathsf{pk}^\star) \stackrel{?}{=} 1$
$\quad \wedge\, \mathsf{Check}(\mathsf{pp}, \mathsf{sk}', \mathsf{pk}^\star) \stackrel{?}{=} 1$
$\quad \boxed{\wedge\, \mathsf{cred}^\star \notin \mathcal{L}_{\mathsf{sk}'}}$
$\quad \boxed{\wedge\, (\mathsf{pk}^\star, \mathsf{cred}^\star) \in \mathcal{L}_{\mathsf{pk}'}}$

Fig. 1. Security experiments for PK-unlinkability on the left and SK-secrecy on the right with strong (msKS, hsKS) and honest (hwKS, hsKS) variants.

Definition 3 (Correctness). *An* ARKG *scheme is correct if for all* $\lambda \in \mathbb{N}$

$$\Pr\left[\mathsf{Check}(\mathsf{pp}, \mathsf{sk}', \mathsf{pk}') = 1 \;:\; \begin{array}{r} \mathsf{pp} \leftarrow \mathsf{Setup}(1^\lambda);\; (\mathsf{sk}, \mathsf{pk}) \leftarrow \mathsf{KGen}(\mathsf{pp}) \\ (\mathsf{pk}', \mathsf{cred}) \leftarrow \mathsf{DerivePK}(\mathsf{pp}, \mathsf{pk}, \_) \\ \mathsf{sk}' \leftarrow \mathsf{DeriveSK}(\mathsf{pp}, \mathsf{sk}, \mathsf{cred}) \end{array}\right] = 1.$$

Definition 4 (Security). *The adversary has access to the following oracles in the security experiments:*

- $\mathsf{O}_{\mathsf{pk}'}(\mathsf{pk}, \mathsf{aux})$*: The public key derivation oracle is parameterized with a public key* pk *and takes optional input* aux*. It returns the output of* $\mathsf{DerivePK}(\mathsf{pp}, \mathsf{pk}, \mathsf{aux})$ *and stores* $(\mathsf{pk}', \mathsf{cred})$ *in list* $\mathcal{L}_{\mathsf{pk}'}$*.*
- $\mathsf{O}^b_{\mathsf{pk}'}(b, \mathsf{sk}_0, \mathsf{pk}_0)$*: This oracle is parameterized by a key pair* $(\mathsf{sk}_0, \mathsf{pk}_0)$ *and bit* b*. It returns* $(\mathsf{sk}', \mathsf{pk}')$ *derived using key pair* $(\mathsf{sk}_0, \mathsf{pk}_0)$ *when* $b = 0$ *or a freshly generated key pair if* $b = 1$*.*
- $\mathsf{O}_{\mathsf{sk}'}(\mathsf{sk}, \mathsf{cred})$*: The secret key derivation oracle is parameterized with a secret key* sk *and takes a credential* cred *as input. If* $(\cdot, \mathsf{cred}) \in \mathcal{L}_{\mathsf{pk}'}$ *exists, it returns the output of* $\mathsf{DeriveSK}(\mathsf{pp}, \mathsf{sk}, \mathsf{cred})$ *and adds* cred *to list* $\mathcal{L}_{\mathsf{sk}'}$*, otherwise* $\perp$*.*

An ARKG scheme provides PK-unlinkability if for all PPT adversary $\mathcal{A}$*, the following advantage is negligible in* λ

$$\mathsf{Adv}^{\mathsf{PKU}}_{\mathsf{ARKG},\mathcal{A}}(\lambda) = \left|\Pr\left[\mathsf{Exp}^{\mathsf{PKU}}_{\mathsf{ARKG},\mathcal{A}}(\lambda) = 1\right] - \frac{1}{2}\right|.$$

Similarly, it provides SK-secrecy if the following advantage is negligible in λ

$$\mathsf{Adv}^{\mathsf{KS}}_{\mathsf{ARKG},\mathcal{A}}(\lambda) = \Pr\left[\mathsf{Exp}^{\mathsf{KS}}_{\mathsf{ARKG},\mathcal{A}}(\lambda) = 1\right].$$

The PKU *and* KS *experiments are defined in Figure Fig. 1.*

2.3 Verifiable Encryption

We follow the non-interactive definitions in [9,19]. Let $\mathcal{R}$ be a binary relation, a Verifiable Encryption (VE) scheme for $\mathcal{R}$ is defined by the following algorithms:

$\mathsf{KGen}(1^\lambda) \rightarrow (\mathsf{dk}, \mathsf{ek})$: The key generation algorithm takes as input a security parameter 1^λ in unary form and outputs a key pair $(\mathsf{dk}, \mathsf{ek})$.

$\mathsf{Enc}(\mathsf{ek}, w) \rightarrow \mathsf{ct}$: The encryption algorithm takes as input a public key ek and a witness w. It outputs a ciphertext ct.

$\mathsf{Verify}(\mathsf{ct}, \mathsf{ek}, x) \rightarrow b$: The verification algorithm takes as input a ciphertext ct, a public key ek and a statement x. It returns a bit b.

$\mathsf{Dec}(\mathsf{dk}, \mathsf{ct}) \rightarrow w/\bot$: The decryption algorithm takes as input a decryption key dk and a ciphertext ct. It outputs a plaintext w or symbol $\bot$ on error.

Definition 5 (Correctness). *A VE scheme is correct if for all $\lambda \in \mathbb{N}$ and $(x, w) \in \mathcal{R}$, the following probability is negligible in λ*

$$\Pr\left[b \neq 1 \vee (x, w') \notin \mathcal{R} \; : \; \begin{array}{c}(\mathsf{dk}, \mathsf{ek}) \leftarrow \mathsf{KGen}(1^\lambda); \; \mathsf{ct} \leftarrow \mathsf{Enc}(\mathsf{ek}, w) \\ b \leftarrow \mathsf{Verify}(\mathsf{ct}, \mathsf{ek}, x); \; w' \leftarrow \mathsf{Dec}(\mathsf{dk}, \mathsf{ct})\end{array}\right].$$

Definition 6 (Security). *A VE scheme is valid if for all $\lambda \in \mathbb{N}$ and PPT adversary $\mathcal{A}$, the following advantage is negligible in λ*

$$\mathsf{Adv}^{\mathsf{validity}}_{\mathsf{VE},\mathcal{A}}(\lambda) := \Pr\left[\mathsf{Exp}^{\mathsf{validity}}_{\mathsf{VE},\mathcal{A}}(\lambda) = 1\right].$$

A VE scheme is Honest-Verifier Zero-Knowledge (HVZK) if for all $\lambda \in \mathbb{N}$, there exists a simulator Sim *such that for all PPT distinguisher $\mathcal{A}$ and $(x, w) \in \mathcal{R}$, the following advantage is negligible in λ*

$$\mathsf{Adv}^{\mathsf{hvzk}}_{\mathsf{VE},\mathcal{A}}(\lambda) := \left|\Pr\left[\mathsf{Exp}^{\mathsf{hvzk}}_{\mathsf{VE},\mathcal{A}}(\lambda) = 1\right] - \frac{1}{2}\right|.$$

The experiments $\mathsf{Exp}^{\mathsf{validity}}_{\mathsf{VE},\mathcal{A}}$ and $\mathsf{Exp}^{\mathsf{hvzk}}_{\mathsf{VE},\mathcal{A}}$ are defined in Figure Fig. 2.

3 A One-Round Key Agreement Scheme for dARKG

Distributed ARKG involves a communication model between the delegator and the many proxies. Assuming derived secret and public keys are uniquely bound to each another, an efficient non-interactive distributed ARKG scheme implies[2] the existence of an efficient multiparty non-interactive key-exchange scheme [5]. These schemes are notoriously difficult to construct, especially against adaptive adversaries [22,25]. We therefore focus on the next minimal constraint model allowing a single round between each proxy and the delegator but no communication between proxies.

[2] Assuming a threshold of $t = 1$, in ARKG suppose $\mathsf{DerivePK}$ now takes as input public keys $\mathsf{pk}_1, \ldots, \mathsf{pk}_n$ for a group of users and returns public values $(\mathsf{pk}', \mathsf{cred})$. Running $\mathsf{DeriveSK}(\mathsf{sk}_i, \mathsf{cred}) \rightarrow \mathsf{sk}'$ yields the unique secret key bound to pk' which is a secret value shared by all users of the group.

$\mathsf{Exp}^{\mathsf{validity}}_{\mathsf{VE},\mathcal{A}}(\lambda)$	$\mathsf{Exp}^{\mathsf{hvzk}}_{\mathsf{VE},\mathcal{A}}(\lambda)$
$(\mathsf{dk},\mathsf{ek}) \leftarrow \mathsf{KGen}(1^\lambda)$	$(\mathsf{dk},\mathsf{ek}) \leftarrow \mathsf{KGen}(1^\lambda)$
$(x,\mathsf{ct}) \leftarrow \mathcal{A}(\mathsf{dk},\mathsf{ek})$	$\mathsf{ct}_0 \leftarrow \mathsf{Enc}(\mathsf{ek}, w)$
$b \leftarrow \mathsf{Verify}(\mathsf{ct},\mathsf{ek},x)$	$\mathsf{ct}_1 \leftarrow \mathsf{Sim}(\mathsf{ek}, x)$
$w' \leftarrow \mathsf{Dec}(\mathsf{dk},\mathsf{ct})$	$b \leftarrow\$ \{0,1\}$
return $b == 1 \wedge (x, w') \notin \mathcal{R}$	$b' \leftarrow \mathcal{A}(\mathsf{ek}, x, \mathsf{ct}_b)$
	return $b == b'$

Fig. 2. Security experiments for Verifiable Encryption [9].

To accommodate this setup and simultaneously achieve modularity in our construction, we introduce a one-round publicly verifiable asymmetric key agreement scheme labeled 1PVAKA. Looking ahead to our dARKG construction, each proxy in a group selected by a delegator will asynchronously produce a 1PVAKA secret share and a dealing. The delegator will verify the dealings and compute a public key for the whole group.

Our definition of 1PVAKA is close in spirit to the ASGKA construction in [28] as well as Groth's NI-DKG scheme in [20]. It is, however, built generically upon an arbitrary AKG scheme, publicly verifiable and does not require re-sharing or thresholding mechanisms. The entity in charge of selecting the recovery threshold in our construction of dARKG will be the delegator, not the proxies.

3.1 Syntax and Security Definitions of 1PVAKA

Let Δ be an AKG scheme with key spaces $\mathbb{S}$ and $\mathbb{P}$. A one-round publicly verifiable asymmetric key agreement (1PVAKA) for Δ is defined by the following PPT algorithms:

$\mathsf{Setup}(1^\lambda, 1^m) \rightarrow \mathsf{pp}$: The setup algorithm takes as input a security parameter λ and a maximum group size m in unary representation. It outputs a description pp of the public parameters of the scheme.

$\mathsf{KGen}(\mathsf{pp}) \rightarrow (\mathsf{dk},\mathsf{ek})$: The key generation algorithm takes as input the public parameters pp. It outputs a long-term key pair $(\mathsf{dk},\mathsf{ek})$.

$\mathsf{Deal}([\mathsf{ek}]_n) \rightarrow (\mathsf{sh},\mathsf{d})$: The dealing algorithm takes as input n long-term public keys $[\mathsf{ek}]_n$. It outputs a secret share sh and a public dealing d.

$\mathsf{Verify}([\mathsf{ek}]_n, \mathsf{d}) \rightarrow b$: The verification algorithms takes as input public keys $[\mathsf{ek}]_n$ and a dealing d. It outputs a bit b.

$\mathsf{CombinePK}([\mathsf{d}]_l) \rightarrow (\mathsf{pk}, [\mathsf{f}]_l)$: The public key combination algorithm takes as input accepted dealings $[\mathsf{d}]_l$. It outputs a group AKG public key $\mathsf{pk} \in \mathbb{P}$ and new public dealings $[\mathsf{f}]_l$ or symbol $\perp$ on error.

$\mathsf{CombineSK}(\mathsf{dk},\mathsf{sh},\mathsf{f}) \rightarrow \mathsf{sk}$ or $\perp$: The secret key combination algorithm takes as input a decryption key dk, a secret share sh and dealing f. It outputs a group AKG secret key $\mathsf{sk} \in \mathbb{S}$ or symbol $\perp$ on error.

Definition 7 (Correctness). *A 1PVAKA scheme is correct if for all integers $\lambda, n, m \in \mathbb{N}$ with $n \leq m$, the following probability is negligible in λ*

$$\Pr\left[\bigwedge_{i\in[n]} \mathsf{Verify}([\mathsf{ek}]_n, \mathsf{d}_i) \neq 1 \;:\; \begin{array}{r} \mathsf{pp} \leftarrow \mathsf{Setup}(1^\lambda, 1^m) \\ (\mathsf{ek}_i, \mathsf{dk}_i) \leftarrow \mathsf{KGen}(\mathsf{pp}) \textbf{ for } i \in [n] \\ (\mathsf{sh}_i, \mathsf{d}_i) \leftarrow \mathsf{Deal}([\mathsf{ek}]_n) \textbf{ for } i \in [n] \end{array}\right].$$

If the sequence above succeeds, then for all $I \subset [n]$ and $i \in I$, the following probability should also be negligible in λ

$$\Pr\left[\Delta.\mathsf{Check}(\mathsf{sk}, \mathsf{pk}) \neq 1 \;:\; \begin{array}{r} (\mathsf{pk}, [\mathsf{f}]_I) \leftarrow \mathsf{CombinePK}([\mathsf{d}]_I) \\ \mathsf{sk} \leftarrow \mathsf{CombineSK}(\mathsf{dk}_i, \mathsf{sh}_i, \mathsf{f}_i) \end{array}\right].$$

We specify below the security concepts pertinent to 1PVAKA, starting with key secrecy. Any user is capable of retrieving the secret AKG group key sk from its share sh and its long-term secret key dk. Consequently, we permit exposure of either the share or the long-term secret key to adversaries but not both.

We accommodate for parallel executions of the scheme using session identifiers denoted sid stored in a set $\mathcal{S}$. A list $\mathcal{L}$ keeps track of session material in the form $\mathcal{L}[\mathsf{sid}] = ([\mathsf{ek}]_n, \mathsf{state})$: constant $[\mathsf{ek}]_n$ contains this session's long-term keys and list state contains the outputs $(\mathsf{sh}, \mathsf{d})$ of dealing queries. Two additional sets $\mathcal{E}$ and $\mathcal{K}$ respectively contain exposed session shares and exposed long-term keys.

Definition 8 (Key secrecy). *For a security parameter λ, integers s, k and a PPT adversary $\mathcal{A}$, we define the $\mathsf{Exp}^{(\mathsf{s,k})\text{-}\mathsf{secrecy}}_{\mathsf{1PVAKA},\mathcal{A}}(\lambda)$ security experiment as follows.*

1. ***Setup phase:*** *The challenger sets $\mathsf{pp} \leftarrow \mathsf{Setup}(1^\lambda, 1^m)$ and sends pp to $\mathcal{A}$.*
2. ***Query phase:*** *During the execution of the game, adversary $\mathcal{A}$ can adaptively make the following queries in arbitrary order. Only a single challenge query can be made, the others are polynomially limited. Invalid queries are ignored.*
   Key query: *The challenger generates a key pair $(\mathsf{dk}, \mathsf{ek}) \leftarrow \mathsf{KGen}(\mathsf{pp})$, stores dk and gives ek to $\mathcal{A}$.*
   Initialization query: *$\mathcal{A}$ submits a new session identifier $\mathsf{sid} \notin \mathcal{S}$ and public keys $[\mathsf{ek}]_n$ to the challenger. The query is ignored if a public key in $[\mathsf{ek}]_n$ was not generated during a key query. It registers the session $\mathcal{S} \leftarrow \mathcal{S} \cup \{\mathsf{sid}\}$ and defines $\mathcal{L}[\mathsf{sid}] := ([\mathsf{ek}]_n, \mathsf{state} := \varnothing)$.*
   Deal query: *$\mathcal{A}$ submits an ongoing session identifier $\mathsf{sid} \in \mathcal{S}$. The challenger fetches $([\mathsf{ek}]_n, \mathsf{state}) := \mathcal{L}[\mathsf{sid}]$. The query is ignored if $|\mathsf{state}| = n$. Otherwise the challenger computes $(\mathsf{sh}, \mathsf{d}) \leftarrow \mathsf{Deal}([\mathsf{ek}]_n)$, sends d to $\mathcal{A}$ and sets $\mathsf{state} \leftarrow \mathsf{state}||(\mathsf{sh}, \mathsf{d})$.*
   Expose share query: *$\mathcal{A}$ submits a session identifier sid and index i. The challenger fetches $(\mathsf{sh}, \mathsf{d}) \in \mathsf{state}[i]$ and sends sh to $\mathcal{A}$ or $\perp$ if no such element exists. It also sets $\mathcal{E} \leftarrow \mathcal{E} \cup \{(\mathsf{sid}, i)\}$.*
   Expose key query: *$\mathcal{A}$ submits a long-term public key ek. Otherwise, the challenger gives the corresponding decryption key ek to $\mathcal{A}$ if it exists and updates $\mathcal{K} \leftarrow \mathcal{K} \cup \{\mathsf{ek}\}$.*

Challenge query: *At some point during the game,* $\mathcal{A}$ *submits a session identifier* sid *and a challenge secret key* $\mathsf{sk}^\star$. *The challenger fetches* $([\mathsf{ek}]_n, \mathsf{state}) := \mathcal{L}[\mathsf{sid}]$ *with* $\mathsf{state} = (\mathsf{sh}_i, \mathsf{d}_i)_{i\in[n]}$ *and aborts if either*

- *more than* $n - s$ *elements* (sid, i) *belong to* $\mathcal{E}$
- *more than* k *public keys in* $[\mathsf{ek}]_n$ *belong to* $\mathcal{K}$
- *there exists* i *such that* $(\mathsf{sid}, i) \in \mathcal{E}$ *and* $\mathsf{ek}_i \in \mathcal{K}$.

The challenger computes $(\mathsf{pk}, [\mathsf{f}]_l) \leftarrow \mathsf{CombinePK}([\mathsf{d}]_l)$, *aborting on error.*

3. ***Output phase:*** *The challenger outputs the result of* $\Delta.\mathsf{Check}(\mathsf{sk}^\star, \mathsf{pk})$.

A 1PVAKA scheme satisfies (s, k)*-key-secrecy if for all security parameter* λ *and all PPT adversaries* $\mathcal{A}$, *the following advantage is negligible in* λ

$$\mathsf{Adv}^{\mathsf{(s,k)\text{-}secrecy}}_{\mathsf{1PVAKA},\mathcal{A}}(\lambda, m) := \Pr\left[\mathsf{Exp}^{\mathsf{(s,k)\text{-}secrecy}}_{\mathsf{1PVAKA},\mathcal{A}}(\lambda, m) = 1\right].$$

During the challenge query, the users are simulated by the game and thus considered honest. The first two abort conditions in the challenge query are parameterized by the minimal number of unexposed shares s and the maximal number of exposed long-term keys k. An adversary learning both the share and the long-term key of a user knows its full secret state and thus can reconstruct the secret key associated to pk. The last abort condition prevents this trivial attack.

The following definition of *robustness* states that an adversary controlling some parties cannot force an honest user to derive an incorrect secret key sk all the while producing valid dealings. Robustness is relevant in any situation where dealings are asynchronously computed by users and then collected, verified and processed by a third party. This notion is important as the combined public key pk may be used for an extended period of time before users retrieve their group secret key sk. It would not be acceptable for users to notice only at this later stage that sk has been poisoned and made unusable.

Definition 9 (Robustness). *A 1PVAKA scheme is robust if for all integers* λ, m *and all PPT adversary* $\mathcal{A}$, *the following advantage is negligible in* λ

$$\mathsf{Adv}^{\mathsf{robustness}}_{\mathsf{1PVAKA},\mathcal{A}}(\lambda, m) := \Pr\left[\,\mathsf{Exp}^{\mathsf{robustness}}_{\mathsf{1PVAKA},\mathcal{A}}(\lambda, m) = 1\right]$$

where experiment $\mathsf{Exp}^{\mathsf{robustness}}_{\mathsf{1PVAKA},\mathcal{A}}$ *is defined in Fig. 3.*

3.2 1PVAKA Construction from Verifiable Encryption

Let Δ be an AKG scheme with key spaces $\mathbb{S}$ and $\mathbb{P}$. Define binary relation $\mathcal{R}$ over $\mathbb{S} \times \mathbb{P}$ by $\mathsf{sk}\mathcal{R}\mathsf{pk}$ if and only if $\Delta.\mathsf{Check}(\mathsf{sk}, \mathsf{pk}) = 1$. Let Π be an m-times additively homomorphic verifiable encryption scheme for relation $\mathcal{R}$. That is to say, $\Pi.\mathsf{Enc}(\mathsf{ek}, \mathsf{sk}_1 + \cdots + \mathsf{sk}_m) = \mathsf{ct}_1 + \cdots + \mathsf{ct}_m$ where $\mathsf{ct}_k = \Pi.\mathsf{Enc}(\mathsf{ek}, \mathsf{sk}_k)$.

Definition 10 (Transformation from VE to 1PVAKA). *A generic construction of 1PVAKA using the above AKG and VE is described in Fig. 4.*

$\mathsf{Exp}^{\mathsf{robustness}}_{\mathsf{1PVAKA},\mathcal{A}}(\lambda, m)$

$\mathsf{pp} \leftarrow \mathsf{Setup}(1^\lambda, 1^m)$

$(\mathsf{dk}_1, \mathsf{ek}_1) \leftarrow \mathsf{KGen}(\mathsf{pp})$ // Register honest user

$(\mathsf{ek}_2, \ldots, \mathsf{ek}_n) \leftarrow \mathcal{A}(\mathsf{pp}, \mathsf{ek}_1)$

$(\mathsf{sh}_1, \mathsf{d}_1) \leftarrow \mathsf{Deal}([\mathsf{ek}]_n)$

$(\mathsf{d}_2, \ldots, \mathsf{d}_n) \leftarrow \mathcal{A}(\mathsf{d}_1)$ // Adaptively create dealings

$(\mathsf{pk}, [\mathsf{f}]_n) \leftarrow \mathsf{CombinePK}([\mathsf{d}]_n)$

$\mathsf{sk} \leftarrow \mathsf{CombineSK}(\mathsf{dk}_1, \mathsf{sh}_1, \mathsf{f}_1)$

return $(\neg \Delta.\mathsf{Check}(\mathsf{sk}, \mathsf{pk})) \wedge \bigwedge_{2 \leq k \leq n} \mathsf{Verify}([\mathsf{ek}]_n, \mathsf{d}_k)$

Fig. 3. Robustness security experiment for 1PVAKA. The adversary produces seemingly valid public dealings but the honest user gets an invalid secret key.

Correctness of the transformation follows from that of Δ and Π as well as the additively homomorphic property of Π.

Lemma 1 (Key secrecy of 1PVAKA). *Assuming Δ is secure and Π is HVZK, the 1PVAKA scheme defined above provides $(1,1)$-key secrecy. More precisely, for all λ, m and for every adversary $\mathcal{A}$ against the $\mathsf{Adv}^{(1,1)\text{-}\mathsf{secrecy}}_{\mathsf{1PVAKA},\mathcal{A}}$ experiment, there exists an adversary $\mathcal{B} = (\mathcal{B}_1, \mathcal{B}_2)$ such that*

$$\mathsf{Adv}^{(1,1)\text{-}\mathsf{secrecy}}_{\mathsf{1PVAKA},\mathcal{A}}(\lambda, m) \leq q\left(m\mathsf{Adv}^{\mathsf{hvzk}}_{\mathsf{VE},\mathcal{B}_1}(\lambda) + \mathsf{Adv}^{\mathsf{KS}}_{\mathsf{AKG},\mathcal{B}_2}(\lambda)\right)$$

where q is the number of sessions started in $\mathsf{Exp}^{(1,1)\text{-}\mathsf{secrecy}}_{\mathsf{1PVAKA},\mathcal{A}}$.

Proof. Let us start by explaining the choice of values for s and k. If more than 2 long-term keys are available to the adversary, this one can trivially compute the session secret key sk by deciphering two distinct dealings and win the game, so $k \in \{0, 1\}$. Up to $n - 1 \leq m - 1$ shares can be exposed to the adversary without reducing the hidden randomness of sk in $\mathsf{CombineSK}$. This is because the last share acts as a one-time-pad by addition: $\mathsf{sk} = \mathsf{sh}_1 + \cdots + \mathsf{sh}_l$.

Let us consider an attacker $\mathcal{A}$ for experiment $\mathsf{Exp}^{(\mathsf{s},\mathsf{k})\text{-}\mathsf{secrecy}}_{\mathsf{1PVAKA},\mathcal{A}}$. We build an attacker $\mathcal{B}_2$ for the $\mathsf{Exp}^{\mathsf{KS}}_{\mathsf{AKG},\mathcal{B}_2}$ experiment via game-hopping.

<u>$\mathsf{Game}_0(\lambda, m)$:</u> this game is defined exactly by $\mathsf{Exp}^{(\mathsf{s},\mathsf{k})\text{-}\mathsf{secrecy}}_{\mathsf{1PVAKA},\mathcal{A}}$, thus

$$\mathsf{Adv}^{(\mathsf{s},\mathsf{k})\text{-}\mathsf{secrecy}}_{\mathsf{1PVAKA},\mathcal{A}}(\lambda, m) = \Pr[\mathsf{Game}_0(\lambda, m) = 1].$$

<u>$\mathsf{Game}_1(\lambda, m)$:</u> this game is defined as $\mathsf{Game}_0(\lambda, m)$ with additional value samples at the start

$$\mathsf{sid}^\star \leftarrow_{\$} [q]; \;\; \mathsf{pk}^\star \leftarrow \mathbb{P}.$$

This session identifier is a guess by the reduction of the session that the adversary will choose to attack in the challenge query. The public key is sampled as

$\mathsf{Setup}(1^\lambda, 1^m)$

$\mathsf{pp}_\Delta \leftarrow \Delta.\mathsf{Setup}(1^\lambda)$

return $\mathsf{pp} := (\mathsf{pp}_\Delta, m)$

$\mathsf{KGen}(\mathsf{pp})$

return $(\mathsf{dk}, \mathsf{ek}) := \Pi.\mathsf{KGen}(1^\lambda)$

$\mathsf{Deal}([\mathsf{ek}]_n)$

$(\mathsf{sk}, \mathsf{pk}) \leftarrow \Delta.\mathsf{KGen}(\mathsf{pp}_\Delta)$

$[\mathsf{ct}]_n \leftarrow (\Pi.\mathsf{Enc}(\mathsf{ek}_i, \mathsf{sk}))_{i \in [n]}$

return $(\mathsf{sh} := \mathsf{sk}, \mathsf{d} := (\mathsf{pk}, [\mathsf{ct}]_n))$

$\mathsf{Verify}([\mathsf{ek}]_n, \mathsf{d} =: (\mathsf{pk}, [\mathsf{ct}]_n))$:

return $\bigwedge_{i \in [n]} \Pi.\mathsf{Verify}(\mathsf{ct}_i)$

$\mathsf{CombinePK}([\mathsf{d}]_l)$

parse $\mathsf{d}_i =: (\mathsf{pk}_i, [\mathsf{ct}_i]_l)$

$\mathsf{f}_j \leftarrow \sum_{i \neq j} (\mathsf{ct}_i)_j$ **for** $j \in [l]$

return $(\mathsf{pk} := \prod_{i \in [l]} \mathsf{pk}_i, [\mathsf{f}]_l)$

$\mathsf{CombineSK}(\mathsf{dk}, \mathsf{sh}, \mathsf{f})$:

$\mathsf{sk}' \leftarrow \Pi.\mathsf{Dec}(\mathsf{dk}, \mathsf{f})$

return $\mathsf{sk} := \mathsf{sh} + \mathsf{sk}'$

Fig. 4. Generic transformation from Verifiable Encryption to 1PVAKA.

challenge for the AKG key-secrecy experiment. The probability for the game to correctly guess sid is bound by $1/q$, thus

$$\Pr[\mathsf{Game}_0(\lambda, m) = 1] \leq q \Pr[\mathsf{Game}_1(\lambda, m) = 1].$$

$\underline{\mathsf{Game}_2(\lambda, m)}$: in this game, the oracle queries made by adversary $\mathcal{A}$ are answered honestly except for queries to $\mathsf{O}_{\mathsf{deal}}$ for the predicted session sid. In that session, no corruption by $\mathcal{A}$ will take place according to the conditions of success. It can thus be run entirely by the game with relevant shares being exposed to the adversary.

We assume that $n - s$ user shares are revealed and the reduction guesses the index of the $s \in \{1, 2\}$ non-revealed ones: i_0 (and i_1 if $s = 2$). This adds a factor of s/m to the reduction.

The deal queries are executed honestly for $k \in [n] \backslash \{i_0\}$ who receive shares sh_j and dealings d_j containing public keys pk_j. The game sets the following public key in the dealing of user i_0 to embed the challenge: $\mathsf{pk}_{i_0} := \mathsf{pk}^\star \cdot (\prod_{j \neq i} \mathsf{pk}_j)^{-1}$. In the previous expression we assume the dealing is ran with i_0 last, so $i_0 = n$. We can make this assumption without loss of generality as all players are honest.

During the oracle call to $\mathsf{O}_{\mathsf{deal}}$ for i_0, the game cannot run the verifiable encryption algorithm as it does not know the secret key $\mathsf{sk}^\star$ which acts as witness. However, according to the Honest Verifier Zero-Knowledge security assumption on Π, there exists a simulator Sim producing ciphertexts for input $\mathsf{pk}^\star$ indistinguishable from the real outputs of the encryption algorithm. Such ciphertexts ($n - 1 \leq m - 1$ of them) are used by the game to simulate the encryption of $\mathsf{sk}^\star$. The advantage of an adversary in distinguishing this particular execution from the real one is thus bound by that of an adversary $\mathcal{B}_1$ against the experiment $\mathsf{Exp}^{\mathsf{hvzk}}_{\mathsf{VE}, \mathcal{B}_1}$.

Finally, the adversary can expose the long-term key associated to either i_0 or i_1 if $k = 1$. With a minimum probability of 1/2, it will guess i_0 and will be able to test the aforementioned simulated ciphertexts and distinguish the two games. Summing up these results we obtain

$$|\Pr[\mathsf{Game}_1(\lambda, m) = 1] - \Pr[\mathsf{Game}_2(\lambda, m) = 1]| \leq \frac{2^k m}{s} \mathsf{Adv}^{\mathsf{hvzk}}_{\mathsf{VE},\mathcal{B}_1}(\lambda).$$

And $\frac{2^k m}{s} = m$ in both cases since $k = s - 1$ and $s \in \{1, 2\}$.

In this last game, the output public key of the challenge oracle is $\mathsf{pk}^\star$. As such, adversary $\mathcal{A}$ replies with a candidate secret key $\mathsf{sk}^\star$ for the AKG Key-Secrecy challenge public key. The advantage of an adversary in this game is thus bound by that of an adversary $\mathcal{B}_2$ against experiment $\mathsf{Exp}^{\mathsf{KS}}_{\mathsf{AKG},\mathcal{B}_2}$. Thus

$$\Pr[\mathsf{Game}_2(\lambda, m) = 1] \leq \mathsf{Adv}^{\mathsf{KS}}_{\mathsf{AKG},\mathcal{B}_2}(\lambda). \tag{1}$$

□

Lemma 2 (Robustness of 1PVAKA). *If the VE scheme Π is valid, then the 1PVAKA scheme obtained via our transformation is robust. More precisely, for all $\lambda, m \in \mathbb{N}$, there exists an adversary $\mathcal{B}$ against the $\mathsf{Exp}^{\mathsf{validity}}_{\mathsf{VE},\mathcal{B}}$ experiment such that*

$$\mathsf{Adv}^{\mathsf{robustness}}_{\mathsf{1PVAKA},\mathcal{A}}(\lambda, m) \leq m\mathsf{Adv}^{\mathsf{validity}}_{\mathsf{VE},\mathcal{B}}(\lambda).$$

Proof. Let us consider an attacker $\mathcal{A}$ against experiment $\mathsf{Exp}^{\mathsf{robustness}}_{\mathsf{1PVAKA},\mathcal{A}}$. We explicit an adversary $\mathcal{B}$ against the $\mathsf{Exp}^{\mathsf{validity}}_{\mathsf{VE},\mathcal{A}}$ experiment.

The challenger generates key pair $(\mathsf{ek}, \mathsf{dk})$ and sends it to $\mathcal{B}$. Set the challenge key pair as user $\mathcal{U}_1$'s long-term 1PVAKA key pair. Adversary $\mathcal{B}$ now starts using $\mathcal{A}$ against the $\mathsf{robustness}$ experiment. On line 4 of $\mathsf{Exp}^{\mathsf{robustness}}_{\mathsf{1PVAKA},\mathcal{A}}$, a share and a dealing are obtained for the first user by $(\mathsf{sh}_1, \mathsf{d}_1) \leftarrow \mathsf{Deal}(\mathsf{ek}_1, \ldots, \mathsf{ek}_n)$. In the $\mathsf{Exp}^{\mathsf{validity}}_{\mathsf{VE},\mathcal{A}}$ experiment against the challenger, we simulate $\mathcal{P}^*$ exactly as this first user, using $\mathcal{B}$ as intermediary.

Assuming $\mathcal{A}$ wins the $\mathsf{robustness}$ experiment, the first user has reconstructed a secret key sk which is not valid for public key pk. By the correctness of AKG, this means that for some k, one of the qualified ciphertexts $(\mathsf{ct}_{1,k})$ does not decrypt to the secret key corresponding to pk. Since $\mathsf{Verify}([\mathsf{ek}]_n, \mathsf{d}_k) = 1$ for all $k \in [n]$, adversary $\mathcal{B}$ won against the $\mathsf{validity}$ experiment by producing a ciphertext $\mathsf{ct}_{1,i}$ that decrypts to a statement which does not correspond to the public value provided to the verifier. □

4 Distributed Asynchronous Remote Key Generation

In this section we introduce the syntax and security properties of distributed ARKG (dARKG) as well as its generic construction from 1PVAKA. Throughout the entire section we consider the universe of proxies $\mathcal{U} = \{\mathcal{P}_i\}_{i \in [N]}$ as well as a single *delegator* $\mathcal{D}$ which may or may not be part of $\mathcal{U}$. Working with a unique delegator is not restrictive as they only execute algorithms on public inputs.

4.1 Syntax of dARKG

Let Δ be an AKG scheme with key spaces $\mathbb{S}$ and $\mathbb{P}$. A dARKG scheme for Δ is defined by the following PPT algorithms and protocol:

$\mathsf{Setup}(1^\lambda, 1^m) \rightarrow \mathsf{pp}$: The setup algorithm takes as input a security parameter λ as well as a maximum group size m in unary representation. It outputs a description pp of the public parameters available to the following algorithms.

$\mathsf{LTKGen}(\mathsf{pp}) \rightarrow (\mathsf{dk}, \mathsf{ek})$: The long-term key generation algorithm takes as input public parameters pp and outputs a long-term key pair $(\mathsf{dk}, \mathsf{ek})$.

$\mathsf{Deal}([\mathsf{ek}]_n) \rightarrow (\mathsf{sh}, \mathsf{d})$: The dealing algorithm ran by proxies takes as input a set of proxy public keys $[\mathsf{ek}]_n$. It outputs a share sh and a dealing d.

$\mathsf{Aggreg}([\mathsf{ek}]_n, [\mathsf{d}]_n) \rightarrow (\mathsf{qual}, \mathsf{pk}, [\mathsf{f}]_l)/\bot$: The aggregation algorithm ran by the delegator takes as input proxy public keys $[\mathsf{ek}]_n$ and dealings $[\mathsf{d}]_n$. It verifies dealings and outputs an AKG public key $\mathsf{pk} \in \mathbb{P}$, a set of qualified proxies $\mathsf{qual} \subset [n]$ of size $l \leq n$ and their new dealings $[\mathsf{f}]_l$ of $\bot$ on error.

$\mathsf{DerivePK}(\mathsf{pk}, [\mathsf{ek}]_l, [\mathsf{f}]_l, t, \mathsf{aux}) \rightarrow (\mathsf{pk}', [\mathsf{cred}]_l)$: The public key derivation algorithm ran by the delegator takes as input long term keys $[\mathsf{ek}]_l$, an AKG public key $\mathsf{pk} \in \mathbb{P}$, dealings $[\mathsf{f}]_l$, a threshold t and optional auxiliary information. It outputs a derived public key $\mathsf{pk}' \in \mathbb{P}$ and credentials $[\mathsf{cred}]_l$.

$\mathsf{DeriveSKSh}(\mathsf{dk}, \mathsf{sh}, \mathsf{cred}) \rightarrow \mathsf{sh}'/\bot$: The secret key share derivation algorithm takes as input a long-term decryption key dk, a share sh and credentials cred. It outputs a derived secret share sh' or $\bot$ on error.

$\mathsf{DeriveSK} \rightarrow \mathsf{sk}'$ or $\bot$: The secret key derivation protocol involves $t = |I|$ proxies of $\mathcal{U}$. Proxy $\mathcal{P}_i$'s secret input corresponds to a derived secret share sh'_i. It outputs a derived AKG secret key $\mathsf{sk}' \in \mathbb{S}$ or $\bot$ on failure.

In practice, proxies in $\mathcal{U}$ provide long-term public keys to the delegator $\mathcal{D}$ which selects some $([\mathsf{ek}]_n)$ at the start of a session. For a given session, proxies generate dealings for each others that the delegator verifies and aggregates. Public key pk is then bound to qualified proxies of $[\mathsf{ek}]_n$. Thereafter, the key pk' can be derived for that group along with credentials $[\mathsf{cred}]_l$. The threshold added during the public key derivation process produces recovery shares stored in the credentials. After the release of the credentials by the delegator, individual proxies can combine their respective credential, secret share and long-term key to derive new secret shares sh'. Finally, the latter can be used in a multiparty protocol to reconstruct the derived secret key sk' corresponding to pk'.

Technically, the derived shares sh' can be used directly, in a threshold signature protocol for instance. The reconstruction protocol is thus a simple matter of convenience to define correctness generically.

Definition 11 (Correctness). *Let λ, m, n, t be integers such that $t \leq n \leq m$ and let $I \subset [N]$ be a set of size n which we identify here with $[n]$ for convenience. Let $\mathsf{pp} \leftarrow \mathsf{Setup}(1^\lambda, 1^m)$. A dARKG scheme is correct if for all such selection of values, the execution sequence in Fig. 5 yields $\Delta.\mathsf{Check}(\mathsf{sk}', \mathsf{pk}') = 1$.*

$$\left.(\mathsf{dk}_i, \mathsf{ek}_i) \leftarrow \mathsf{LTKGen}(\mathsf{pp})\ \forall i \in [n]\right\} \quad (1)$$

$$\left.\begin{array}{l}(\mathsf{sh}_i, \mathsf{d}_i) \leftarrow \mathsf{Deal}([\mathsf{ek}]_n)\ \forall i \in [n] \\ \qquad\qquad \mathsf{Aggreg}([\mathsf{ek}]_n, [\mathsf{d}]_n) \rightarrow (\mathsf{qual}, \mathsf{pk}, [\mathsf{f}]_l)\end{array}\right\} \quad (2)$$

$$\left.\mathsf{DerivePK}(\mathsf{pk}, [\mathsf{ek}]_l, [\mathsf{f}]_l, t) \rightarrow (\mathsf{pk}', [\mathsf{cred}]_l)\right\} \quad (3)$$

$$\left.\begin{array}{l}\mathsf{sh}'_i \leftarrow \mathsf{DeriveSKSh}(\mathsf{dk}_i, \mathsf{sh}_i, \mathsf{cred}_i)\ \forall i \in \mathsf{qual} \\ \text{Sample a subset } J \subset \mathsf{qual} \text{ of size } t \text{ at random} \\ \mathsf{sk}' \leftarrow \mathsf{DeriveSK} \text{ protocol ran between proxies } \mathcal{P}_j \text{ for } j \in J\end{array}\right\} \quad (4)$$

Fig. 5. Correct execution flow of dARKG. Operations on the left are performed by the proxies, those on the right by the delegator. (1) Registration of long-term public keys. (2) Group key generation session for I. (3) Derivation of public key pk'. (4) Secret share generation and recovery of derived secret key sk'.

4.2 Security Properties of dARKG

In this section we adapt the security requirements for ARKG [16] to the distributed setting. The first, *PK-unlinkability*, requires that the scheme must output keys indistinguishable from freshly generated ones. The second, *SK-secrecy*, prevents unauthorized access to sk' and disturbance to the delegator's behaviour.

We assume that all proxies in $\mathcal{U}$ have generated long-term key pairs $(\mathsf{dk}_i, \mathsf{ek}_i)$, the public keys being available to the delegator. The security games execute algorithms Deal, Aggreg and $\mathsf{DerivePK}$ on behalf of the honest parties. This implies an honest but curious delegator and authenticated channels between proxies and delegator. Share exposure and proxy corruptions are handled through calls to oracles defined below.

Let us first define the oracles handling key generation and adversarial behaviour. We store exposed long-term keys in a set $\mathcal{K}$ and a set of session identifiers $\mathcal{S}$. Four lists $\mathcal{L}_{\mathsf{deal}}$, $\mathcal{L}_{\mathcal{C}}$, $\mathcal{L}_{\mathcal{E}}$, $\mathcal{L}_{\mathcal{E}'}$ indexed by session identifiers sid track sessions' dealing states, corrupted shares, exposed shares and exposed derived shares respectively. Finally, three lists $\mathcal{L}_{\mathsf{pk}}$, $\mathcal{L}_{\mathsf{pk}'}$ and $\mathcal{L}_{\mathsf{sk}'}$ track aggregated public keys, derived public keys and derived secret keys.

$\mathsf{O}_{\mathsf{Init}}([\mathsf{ek}]_n, \mathsf{sid})$: This initialization oracle takes as input long-term keys $[\mathsf{ek}]_n$ and a new session identifier $\mathsf{sid} \notin \mathcal{S}$. It sets $\mathcal{L}[\mathsf{sid}] := ([\mathsf{ek}]_n, \mathsf{state} := \varnothing)$.

$\mathsf{O}_{\mathsf{Deal}}([\mathsf{ek}]_n, \mathsf{sid}, \mathsf{out?})$: This oracle takes as input proxy public keys $[\mathsf{ek}]_n$, session identifier $\mathsf{sid} \in \mathcal{S}$ and an optional adversarial share-dealing pair out. It fetches $([\mathsf{ek}]_n, \mathsf{state}) := \mathcal{L}_{\mathsf{deal}}[\mathsf{sid}]$, aborting if $|\mathsf{state}| = n$. If $\mathsf{out} = \varnothing$, it honestly executes a dealing and sets $\mathsf{out} := (\mathsf{sh}, \mathsf{d}) \leftarrow \mathsf{Deal}(\mathsf{pp}, [\mathsf{ek}]_n)$. The oracle then updates the state $\mathsf{state} \leftarrow \mathsf{state}||\mathsf{out}$ and returns d to the adversary.

$\mathsf{O}_{\mathsf{LTKExpose}}(\mathsf{ek})$: This oracle takes as input a proxy public key ek. It adds ek to set $\mathcal{K}$ and returns the corresponding secret key dk.

$\mathsf{O}_{\mathsf{ShExpose}}(\mathsf{sid}, i)$: This oracle takes as input session identifier sid and index i. It fetches $(\mathsf{sh}, \mathsf{d}) := \mathsf{state}[i]$ with $([\mathsf{ek}]_n, \mathsf{state}) := \mathcal{L}_{\mathsf{deal}}[\mathsf{sid}]$, aborting if not found. The oracle updates $\mathcal{L}_{\mathcal{E}}[\mathsf{sid}] \leftarrow \mathcal{L}_{\mathcal{E}}[\mathsf{sid}] \cup \{i\}$ and returns sh.

$\mathsf{O}_{\mathsf{Sh'Expose}}(\mathsf{sid}, i, [\mathsf{cred}]_l)$: This oracle takes as input session identifier sid, index i and credentials $[\mathsf{cred}]_l$. It fetches $(\mathsf{qual}, \mathsf{pk}', [\mathsf{cred}']_l)$ in $\mathcal{L}_{\mathsf{pk}'}[\mathsf{sid}]$ (see $\mathsf{O}_{\mathsf{pk}'}$ below) and $([\mathsf{ek}]_n, L := \{(i, \mathsf{sh}_i, \mathsf{d}_i)\}_{i\in[n]}, n) := \mathcal{L}_{\mathsf{deal}}[\mathsf{sid}]$ aborting if not found. It executes $\mathsf{sh}' \leftarrow \mathsf{DeriveSKSh}(\mathsf{pp}, \mathsf{dk}_k, \mathsf{sh}_k, \mathsf{cred}'_k)$. The oracle updates $\mathcal{L}_{\mathcal{E}'}[\mathsf{sid}] \leftarrow \mathcal{L}_{\mathcal{E}'}[\mathsf{sid}] \cup \{(k, [\mathsf{cred}']_l)\}$ and returns sh' to the adversary.

$\mathsf{O}^{s,k}_{\mathsf{Check}}(\mathsf{sid})$: This oracle is parameterized by two integers s and k. It takes as input a session identifier sid and fetches $([\mathsf{ek}]_n, \mathsf{state}) := \mathcal{L}_{\mathsf{deal}}[\mathsf{sid}]$, aborting if not found. It computes and return a bit b given by

$$b \leftarrow (|\mathcal{L}_{\mathcal{E}}[\mathsf{sid}]| < n - s) \wedge (|\mathcal{K} \cap [\mathsf{ek}]_n| > k) \wedge (|\mathcal{L}_{\mathcal{E}}[\mathsf{sid}] \cap \mathcal{K}| > 0).$$

These conditions respectively correspond to a minimum of s non-exposed dealing shares, a maximum of k exposed long-term keys and no proxy having both its dealing share and long-term key exposed in session sid.

$\mathsf{O}_{\mathsf{Aggreg}}(\mathsf{sid})$: This oracle takes as input a session identifier sid. It aborts if $\mathcal{L}_{\mathsf{pk}}[\mathsf{sid}] \neq \varnothing$. The oracle fetches $([\mathsf{ek}]_n, \mathsf{state}) := \mathcal{L}_{\mathsf{deal}}[\mathsf{sid}]$, aborting if not found. We can assume w.l.o.g that $|\mathsf{state}| = n$, reducing $[\mathsf{ek}]_n$ if necessary. The oracle parses $(\mathsf{sh}_i, \mathsf{d}_i)_{i\in[n]} := \mathsf{state}$ and aggregates the dealings:

$$(\mathsf{qual}, \mathsf{pk}, [\mathsf{f}]_l) \leftarrow \mathsf{Aggreg}([\mathsf{ek}]_n, [\mathsf{d}]_n).$$

It updates $\mathcal{L}_{\mathsf{pk}}[\mathsf{sid}] := ([\mathsf{ek}]_n, \mathsf{qual}, \mathsf{pk}, [\mathsf{f}]_l)$ and sends these values to the adversary or aborts on error.

For the sake of brevity we set $\mathsf{O}_{1,2} := (\mathsf{O}_{\mathsf{Deal}}, \mathsf{O}_{\mathsf{LTKExpose}}, \mathsf{O}_{\mathsf{ShExpose}}, \mathsf{O}_{\mathsf{Aggreg}})$. This corresponds to adversarial handles for part one and two of a dARKG session as defined in Fig. 5. The following oracles extend those used in the security definitions of ARKG to the distributed setting.

$\mathsf{O}_{\mathsf{pk}'}(\mathsf{sid}, t)$: This oracle takes a session identifier $\mathsf{sid} \in \mathcal{S}$ and a threshold t as input. It fetches $([\mathsf{ek}]_n, \mathsf{qual}, \mathsf{pk}, [\mathsf{f}]_l) := \mathcal{L}_{\mathsf{pk}}[\mathsf{sid}]$ aborting if nonexistent. The oracle then derives a key $(\mathsf{pk}', [\mathsf{cred}]_l) \leftarrow \mathsf{DerivePK}(\mathsf{pk}, [\mathsf{ek}]_l, [\mathsf{f}]_l, t)$. It updates $\mathcal{L}_{\mathsf{pk}'}[\mathsf{sid}] \leftarrow \mathcal{L}_{\mathsf{pk}'}[\mathsf{sid}] \cup \{(\mathsf{qual}, \mathsf{pk}', [\mathsf{cred}]_l)\}$ and returns $(\mathsf{pk}', [\mathsf{cred}]_l)$.

$\mathsf{O}^b_{\mathsf{pk}'}(\mathsf{sid}, t)$: This challenge oracle parameterized by a bit b takes as input a session identifier and a threshold t. It executes $(\mathsf{pk}'_0, [\mathsf{cred}]_l) \leftarrow \mathsf{O}_{\mathsf{pk}'}(\mathsf{sid}, t)$, samples a fresh public key $\mathsf{pk}'_1 \leftarrow\$\ \mathbb{P}$ and returns $(\mathsf{pk}'_b, [\mathsf{cred}]_l)$.

$\mathsf{O}_{\mathsf{sk}'}(\mathsf{sid}, [\mathsf{cred}]_l)$: This oracle takes as input identifier sid as well as credentials. It executes $\mathsf{sh}_i \leftarrow \mathsf{O}_{\mathsf{Sh'Expose}}(\mathsf{sid}, i, [\mathsf{cred}']_l)$ for $i \in [l]$. The oracle updates $\mathcal{L}_{\mathsf{sk}'}[\mathsf{sid}] \leftarrow \mathcal{L}_{\mathsf{sk}'}[\mathsf{sid}] \cup \{[\mathsf{cred}]_l\}$ and returns $[\mathsf{sh}]_l$.

PK-unlinkability states that honestly derived public keys are indistinguishable from freshly sampled ones. Note that in our definition of oracle $\mathsf{O}_{\mathsf{pk}'}$, credentials for the requested session are returned along with a derived public key. This is stronger than the definition in [16,18] and more aligned with [7,27]. Note also that the original ARKG scheme in [16] satisfies this stronger property as its credentials can be similarly simulated.

$\mathsf{Exp}^{(s,k)\text{-}\mathsf{SK\text{-}secrecy}}_{\mathsf{dARKG},\mathcal{A}}(\lambda, m)$

$\mathsf{pp} \leftarrow \mathsf{Setup}(1^\lambda, 1^m)$

$(\mathsf{sid}, t) \leftarrow \mathcal{A}^{\mathsf{O}_{1,2}}(\mathsf{pp})$

if $\neg \mathsf{O}^{s,k}_{\mathsf{Check}}(\mathsf{sid}) \vee \mathcal{L}_{\mathsf{pk}}[\mathsf{sid}] = \varnothing$ **then return** 0

$\mathsf{O}_{3,4} := (\mathsf{O}_{\mathsf{pk}'}(\mathsf{sid}, t), \mathsf{O}_{\mathsf{Sh'Expose}}(\mathsf{sid}, \cdot, \cdot), \boxed{\mathsf{O}_{\mathsf{sk}'}(\mathsf{sid}, \cdot)})$

$(\mathsf{sk}^\star, \mathsf{pk}^\star, [\mathsf{cred}^\star]_l) \leftarrow \mathcal{A}^{\mathsf{O}_{3,4}}$

if $|\mathcal{L}_{\mathcal{E}'}[\mathsf{sid}]| > t$ **then return** 0

$\mathcal{V} \leftarrow\!\!\$$ subset of qual of size t

for $i \in \mathcal{V}$ **do** $\mathsf{sh}'_i \leftarrow \mathsf{DeriveSKSh}(\mathsf{dk}_i, \mathsf{sh}_i, \mathsf{cred}^\star_i)$

$\mathsf{sk}' \leftarrow \mathsf{DeriveSK}\langle [\mathsf{sh}]_t \rangle(\mathsf{pp})$

return $(\Delta.\mathsf{Check}(\mathsf{sk}^\star, \mathsf{pk}^\star) \stackrel{?}{=} 1) \wedge (\Delta.\mathsf{Check}(\mathsf{sk}', \mathsf{pk}^\star) \stackrel{?}{=} 1)$

$\boxed{\wedge [\mathsf{cred}^\star]_l \notin \mathcal{L}_{\mathsf{sk}'}[\mathsf{sid}]}$ $\boxed{\wedge (\mathsf{qual}, \mathsf{pk}^\star, [\mathsf{cred}^\star]_l) \in \mathcal{L}_{\mathsf{pk}'}[\mathsf{sid}]}$

$\mathsf{Exp}^{\mathsf{PKU}}_{\mathsf{dARKG},\mathcal{A}}(\lambda, m)$

$\mathsf{pp} \leftarrow \mathsf{Setup}(1^\lambda, 1^m)$

$\mathsf{sid} \leftarrow \mathcal{A}^{\mathsf{O}_{1,2}}(\mathsf{pp})$

$b \leftarrow\!\!\$ \{0, 1\}$

$b' \leftarrow \mathcal{A}^{\mathsf{O}^b_{\mathsf{pk}'}(\mathsf{sid}, \cdot)}$

return $(b \stackrel{?}{=} b')$

Fig. 6. SK-secrecy and PK-unlinkability experiments for dARKG with strong (msKS, hsKS) and honest variants (hwKS, hsKS).

Definition 12 (PK-unlinkability). *A dARKG scheme provides PK-unlinkability if for all* $\lambda, m \in \mathbb{N}$ *and any stateful PPT adversary* $\mathcal{A}$*, the following advantage is neglibile in* λ

$$\mathsf{Adv}^{\mathsf{PKU}}_{\mathsf{dARKG},\mathcal{A}}(\lambda, m) = \Pr\left[\mathsf{Exp}^{\mathsf{PKU}}_{\mathsf{dARKG},\mathcal{A}}(\lambda, m) = 1\right]$$

where the PKU *experiment is defined in Fig. 6.*

In the distributed model, SK-secrecy prevents an adversary from producing a key pair $(\mathsf{sk}^\star, \mathsf{pk}^\star)$ and credentials $[\mathsf{cred}^\star]_l$ for a challenge group key pk. Such an attacker deceives a group of proxies into deriving a common secret key sk' or shares for key $\mathsf{pk}^\star$ when it is already in possession of a secret key $\mathsf{sk}^\star$ for $\mathsf{pk}^\star$. Public key $\mathsf{pk}^\star$ and credentials $[\mathsf{cred}^\star]_l$ may or may not have been derived from pk. These scenarios yield four flavors of SK-secrecy as in [16]; namely, mwKS, hwKS, msKS and hsKS corresponding to malicious/honest and weak/strong variants.

Definition 13 (SK-secrecy). *Let* r *and* s *be two positive integers. A dARKG scheme provides* (s, k)*-SK-secrecy if for all* $\lambda, m \in \mathbb{N}$ *and any stateful PPT adversary* $\mathcal{A}$*, the following is negligible in* λ*:*

$$\mathsf{Adv}^{(s,k)\text{-}\mathsf{SK\text{-}secrecy}}_{\mathsf{dARKG},\mathcal{A}}(\lambda, m) = \Pr\left[\mathsf{Exp}^{(s,k)\text{-}\mathsf{SK\text{-}secrecy}}_{\mathsf{dARKG},\mathcal{A}}(\lambda, m) = 1\right]$$

where the $\mathsf{Exp}^{(s,k)\text{-}\mathsf{SK\text{-}secrecy}}_{\mathsf{dARKG},\mathcal{A}}$ *experiment is defined in Fig. 6.*

4.3 Generic Construction of dARKG using 1PVAKA

Let Δ be a blinding AKG with key spaces $\mathbb{S}$ and $\mathbb{P}$. We use a key-encapsulation mechanism $\Lambda = (\mathsf{KGen}, \mathsf{Encaps}, \mathsf{Decaps})$ with output key space X as defined in Appendix A.1. We work under the simplifying assumption that $\Lambda.\mathsf{KGen} = \Delta.\mathsf{KGen}$ which holds for ARKG instantiations presented in [15,16,18]. In the general case, if $\Lambda.\mathsf{KGen}$ outputs asymmetric keys for an AKG scheme with key spaces $\mathbb{S}'$ and $\mathbb{P}'$, one may use the combined blinding AKG with spaces $\mathbb{S} \times \mathbb{S}'$ and $\mathbb{P} \times \mathbb{P}'$. Another approach is to assume that the key pairs output by algorithms $\Delta.\mathsf{KGen}$ and $(\mathsf{DerivePK}, \mathsf{DeriveSK})$ need not be from the same distribution. This method is used in [27] and allows $\mathsf{DerivePK}$ to take as input two keys: one for Λ and one for Δ. While this approach is more flexible in the choice of KEM, it requires corresponding modifications to the syntax and security definitions.

The definitions of the following schemes are recalled in Appendix A. We use a message authentication code $\mathsf{MAC} = (\mathsf{Tag}, \mathsf{Verify})$ with key space K and a secret sharing scheme $\mathsf{TSS} = (\mathsf{Share}, \mathsf{Verify}, \mathsf{Recon})$. For threshold shares encryption we use a public-key encryption scheme $\Pi = (\mathsf{KGen}, \mathsf{Enc}, \mathsf{Dec})$. Lastly, we require a cryptographic hash function $\mathcal{H} : X \to \{0,1\}^\lambda$, a key derivation function $\mathsf{KDF} : X \to K$ and a 1PVAKA scheme for Δ denoted Γ.

Definition 14 (Generic construction for dARKG). *A generic construction of dARKG using the building blocks introduced above is described in Fig. 7.*

Correctness follows from that of the building blocks present in the construction.

Lemma 3 (SK-secrecy of dARKG). *Assume that the 1PVAKA scheme Γ provides (1,1)-key-secrecy, that* TSS *offers secrecy and that the VE scheme Π is HVZK. The dARKG scheme from Fig. 7 provides the* hwKS *flavour of SK-secrecy. More precisely, for every adversary $\mathcal{A}$ against the $\mathsf{Exp}^{(1,1)\text{-SK-secrecy}}_{\mathsf{dARKG},\mathcal{A}}$ experiment, there exist adversary $\mathcal{B} := (\mathcal{B}_1, \mathcal{B}_2, \mathcal{B}_3)$ such that*

$$\mathsf{Adv}^{(1,1)\text{-SK-secrecy}}_{\mathsf{dARKG},\mathcal{A}}(\lambda, m) \leq q_1 q_2 \Big(m^2 \mathsf{Adv}^{\mathsf{hvzk}}_{\mathsf{VE},\mathcal{B}_1}(\lambda) + \mathsf{Adv}^{\mathsf{privacy}}_{\mathsf{TSS},\mathcal{B}_2}(\lambda) + \mathsf{Adv}^{(1,1)\text{-secrecy}}_{\mathsf{1PVAKA},\mathcal{B}_3}(\lambda, m) \Big)$$

where q_1 and q_2 are the number of sessions started in $\mathsf{O}_{1,2}$ and $\mathsf{O}_{\mathsf{pk}'}$ respectively.

The term $m^2 \mathsf{Adv}^{\mathsf{hvzk}}_{\mathsf{VE},\mathcal{B}_1}(\lambda)$ above can be removed if one considers the weaker, original version of $\mathsf{O}_{\mathsf{pk}'}$ which does not return credentials. The above statement is in line with the recent work and definitions of [7].

Proof. Let us consider an attacker $\mathcal{A}$ for experiment KS of DARKG. We build an attacker $\mathcal{B}$ for the SK-security experiment of the 1PVAKA scheme using game-hopping.

<u>$\mathsf{Game}_0(\lambda, m)$:</u> this game is defined by the $\mathsf{Exp}^{(1,1)\text{-SK-secrecy}}_{\mathsf{dARKG},\mathcal{A}}(\lambda, m)$ experiment for the honest-weak variant, thus

$$\mathsf{Adv}^{(1,1)\text{-SK-secrecy}}_{\mathsf{dARKG},\mathcal{A}}(\lambda, m) = \Pr[\mathsf{Game}_0(\lambda, m) = 1].$$

```
Setup(1^λ, 1^m)
1 : pp_1 ← Δ.Setup(1^λ)
2 : pp_2 ← TSS.Setup(1^λ)
3 : pp_3 ← Γ.Setup(1^λ, 1^m)
4 : return pp := ((pp_i)_{i∈[3]}, H, KDF)

LTKGen(pp)
1 : (dk_Λ, ek_Λ) ← Λ.KGen(1^λ)
2 : (dk_Π, ek_Π) ← Π.KGen(1^λ)
3 : dk ← (dk_Λ, dk_Π)
4 : ek ← (ek_Λ, ek_Π)
5 : return (dk, ek)

Deal([ek]_n)
1 : return (sh, d) := Γ.Deal([ek]_n)

DerivePK(pk, [ek]_l, [f]_l, t, aux)
1 : (ct, K) ← Λ.Encaps(pk)
2 : τ, mk ← H(K), KDF(K)
3 : τ' ←$ S
4 : pk' ← Δ.BlindPK(pk, τ + τ')
5 : [s]_l ← TSS.Share(t, l, τ')
6 : [c]_l ← (Π.Enc(ek_{Π,i}, s_i))_{i∈[l]}
7 : [m]_l ← (ct, f_i, c_i, aux)_{i∈[l]}
8 : [μ]_l ← (MAC.Tag(mk, m_i))_{i∈[l]}
9 : [cred]_l ← (m_i, μ_i)_{i∈[l]}
10 : return (pk', [cred]_l)

Aggreg([ek]_n, [d]_n)
1 : qual ← ∅
2 : for i ∈ [n] do
3 :   if Γ.Verify([ek]_n, d_i) then
4 :     qual ← qual ∪ {i}
5 : (qual, pk, [f]_qual)
6 :   ← Γ.CombinePK([d]_qual)
7 : return (qual, pk, [f]_qual)

DeriveSKSh(dk, sh, cred)
1 : parse cred =: (m, μ)
2 : parse m =: (ct, f, c, aux)
3 : K ← Λ.Decaps(dk_Λ, ct)
4 : τ, mk ← H(K), KDF(K)
5 : if ¬MAC.Verify(mk, m, μ)
6 :   then return ⊥
7 : sk ← Δ.CombineSK(dk_Γ, sh, f)
8 : s ← Π.Dec(dk_Π, c)
9 : sh' ← (sk, s, τ)
10 : return sh'

DeriveSK⟨(P_i)_{i∈I}⟩
1 : Proxy P_i has input sh'_i = (sk, s_i, τ)
2 : τ' ← TSS.Recon([s]_I)
3 : sk' ← Δ.BlindSK(sk', τ + τ')
4 : return sk'
```

Fig. 7. Algorithms for our general dARKG construction.

$\underline{\mathsf{Game}_1(\lambda, m)}$: this game is defined as $\mathsf{Game}_0(\lambda, m)$ except that during oracle calls to $\mathsf{O}_{\mathsf{pk}'}$ inside $\mathsf{O}^b_{\mathsf{pk}'}$, in algorithm DerivePK, we change $\mathsf{pk}' \leftarrow \mathsf{BlindPK}(\mathsf{pk}, \tau + \tau')$ for $\mathsf{pk}' \leftarrow \mathsf{BlindPK}(\mathsf{pk}_0, \tau + \tau')$ for some $(\mathsf{sk}_0, \mathsf{pk}_0) \leftarrow \Delta.\mathsf{KGen}(\mathsf{pp})$. For consistency, whenever $\mathcal{A}$ queries $\mathsf{O}_{\mathsf{sk}'}$ with the same session identifier and credentials $[\mathsf{cred}]_l$ such that $[\mathsf{cred}]_l \in \mathcal{L}_{\mathsf{sk}'}[\mathsf{sid}]$, Line 9 of DeriveSKSh in $\mathsf{O}_{\mathsf{Sh'Expose}}$ is replaced with

$$\mathsf{sh}' \leftarrow (\mathsf{sk}_0, s, \tau).$$

Since $(\mathsf{sk}_0, \mathsf{pk}_0)$ is sampled from $\Delta.\mathsf{KGen}$, the blinding property makes output key pairs indistinguishable from freshly generated ones. The two games are thus indistinguishable and

$$\Pr[\mathsf{Game}_0(\lambda, m) = 1] = \Pr[\mathsf{Game}_1(\lambda, m) = 1].$$

$\underline{\mathsf{Game}_2(\lambda, m)}$: this game is defined as $\mathsf{Game}_1(\lambda, m)$ except that during oracle calls to $\mathsf{O}_{\mathsf{pk}'}$ inside $\mathsf{O}^b_{\mathsf{pk}'}$, in algorithm DerivePK we replace the ciphertexts on Line 6 with outputs from the HVZK simulator of the verifiable encryption scheme Π. The game is indistinguishable from $\mathsf{Game}_1(\lambda, m)$ under the HVZK assumption of Π and the assumption that TSS offers privacy. Indeed, since $t-1$ derived secret key shares have been exposed via oracle $\mathsf{O}_{\mathsf{Sh'Expose}}$, the information theoretic security of TSS implies that the adversary does not learn any information related to sk'. Since we simulate $tl \leq m^2$ ciphertexts in total, we therefore have

$$|\Pr[\mathsf{Game}_1(\lambda, m) = 1] - \Pr[\mathsf{Game}_2(\lambda, m) = 1]| \leq m^2 \mathsf{Adv}^{\mathsf{hvzk}}_{\mathsf{VE},\mathcal{B}_1}(\lambda) + \mathsf{Adv}^{\mathsf{privacy}}_{\mathsf{TSS},\mathcal{B}_2}(\lambda).$$

We now construct an adversary $\mathcal{B}$ against the $\mathsf{Exp}^{(1,1)\text{-secrecy}}_{\mathsf{1PVAKA},\mathcal{A}}$ experiment from an adversary $\mathcal{A}$ against $\mathsf{Game}_2(\lambda, m)$. $\mathcal{B}$ guesses a session identifier sid corresponding to the static key generation session that $\mathcal{A}$ will attack. It also guesses an oracle call to $\mathsf{O}_{\mathsf{pk}'}$ that $\mathcal{A}$ will use to create $\mathsf{pk}^\star$. This is possible as the adversary cannot forge $\mathsf{pk}^\star$ or $[\mathsf{cred}^\star]_l$ for the honest variant: see Line 12 of the SK-security game in Fig. 6).

According to the definition game $\mathsf{Game}_1(\lambda, m)$, adversary $\mathcal{B}$ can reply to this oracle call using the challenge query $(\mathsf{pk}, [\mathsf{f}]_l)$ from the challenger for the $\mathsf{Exp}^{(1,1)\text{-secrecy}}_{\mathsf{1PVAKA},\mathcal{A}}$ game. Indeed, both values can be set arbitrarily since pk is indistinguishable from a fresh key and $[\mathsf{f}]_l$ contains simulated ciphertexts, which is the only information that was previously bound to pk.

Adversary $\mathcal{A}$ then returns a secret public key pair $(\mathsf{sk}^\star, \mathsf{pk}^\star)$ among its outputs. Since this is the honest variant of the experiment, $\mathsf{pk}^\star$ has been legitimately created during session sid meaning $\mathsf{sk}^\star$ is a valid challenge answer for the $\mathsf{Exp}^{(1,1)\text{-secrecy}}_{\mathsf{1PVAKA},\mathcal{A}}$ experiment. By definition $\Delta.\mathsf{Check}(\mathsf{sk}^\star, \mathsf{pk}^\star) = \Delta.\mathsf{Check}(\mathsf{sk}^\star, \mathsf{pk})$ if $\mathcal{A}$ wins $\mathsf{Game}_2(\lambda, m)$. □

Lemma 4 (PK-unlinkability of dARKG). *Assume that Δ is blinding, Π is HVZK-secure and Λ is* ANO-CCA *secure. The dARKG scheme defined in Fig. 7 provides PK-unlinkability. More precisely, for every adversary against the* $\mathsf{Exp}^{\mathsf{PKU}}_{\mathsf{dARKG},\mathcal{A}}$ *experiment, there exists an adversary $\mathcal{B} := (\mathcal{B}_1, \mathcal{B}_2)$ such that*

$$\mathsf{Adv}^{\mathsf{PKU}}_{\mathsf{dARKG},\mathcal{A}}(\lambda, m) \leq q_1 q_2 \left(\mathsf{Adv}^{\mathsf{ANO\text{-}CCA}}_{\mathsf{KEM},\mathcal{B}_1}(\lambda) + m^2 \mathsf{Adv}^{\mathsf{hvzk}}_{\mathsf{VE},\mathcal{B}_2}(\lambda)\right)$$

where q_1 and q_2 are the number of sessions in $\mathsf{O}_{1,2}$ and calls to $\mathsf{O}_{\mathsf{pk}'}$.

Proof. The proof follows the one of PK-unlinkability of the original scheme in [16].

$\underline{\mathsf{Game}_0(\lambda, m)}$: this game is defined exactly as the $\mathsf{Exp}^{\mathsf{PKU}}_{\mathsf{dARKG},\mathcal{A}}$ experiment and thus

$$\mathsf{Adv}^{\mathsf{PKU}}_{\mathsf{dARKG},\mathcal{A}}(\lambda, m) = \Pr[\mathsf{Game}_0(\lambda, m) = 1].$$

$\underline{\mathsf{H}^1_i(\lambda, m)}$: recursively define a series of hybrid games by $\mathsf{H}^1_0(\lambda, m) = \mathsf{Game}_0(\lambda)$ and $\mathsf{H}^1_i(\lambda, m) = \mathsf{H}^1_{i-1}(\lambda, m)$ with the exception that during the i-th call to $\mathsf{O}^b_{\mathsf{pk}'}$:

- computation of the public key $\mathsf{pk}^\star$ in DerivePK executed in the internal call to $\mathsf{O}_{\mathsf{pk}'}(\mathsf{sid}, \cdot)$ is replaced by $\Delta.\mathsf{BlindPK}(\mathsf{pk}_{\mathsf{rand}}, \tau)$,
- computation of the derived secret share sh' executed in the internal call to $\mathsf{O}_{\mathsf{Sh'Expose}}(\mathsf{sid}, \cdot, \cdot)$ is replaced by $(\mathsf{sk}_{\mathsf{rand}}, s, \tau)$

where $(\mathsf{sk}_{\mathsf{rand}}, \mathsf{pk}_{\mathsf{rand}}) \leftarrow \Delta.\mathsf{KGen}(\mathsf{pp})$ is a fresh key pair. This simulation is perfect owing to the blinding property of Δ. Thus we have

$$\Pr[\mathsf{Game}_0(\lambda, m) = 1] = \Pr[\mathsf{H}^1_q(\lambda, m) = 1].$$

$\underline{\mathsf{H}^2_i(\lambda, m)}$: recursively define another series of hybrid games by $\mathsf{H}^2_0(\lambda, m) = \mathsf{H}^1_q(\lambda, m)$ and $\mathsf{H}^2_i(\lambda, m) = \mathsf{H}^2_{i-1}(\lambda, m)$ where instead of computing (ct, K) as an encapsulation of pk, the oracle uses a fresh key $(\mathsf{sk}_{\mathsf{rand}}, \mathsf{pk}_{\mathsf{rand}}) \leftarrow \Lambda.\mathsf{KGen}(\mathsf{pp})$. Since Λ is ANO-CCA, the simulation is perfect under the ANO-CCA assumption: the credentials in $\mathsf{H}^2_i(\lambda, m)$ are indistinguishable from those in $\mathsf{H}^1_i(\lambda, m)$. Thus,

$$|\Pr[\mathsf{H}^1_{q_2}(\lambda, m) = 1] - \Pr[\mathsf{H}^2_{q_2}(\lambda, m) = 1]| \leq q_2 \mathsf{Adv}^{\mathsf{ANO\text{-}CCA}}_{\mathsf{KEM},\mathcal{A}}.$$

$\underline{\mathsf{H}^3_i(\lambda, m)}$: these games are defined via $\mathsf{H}^3_0(\lambda, m) = \hat{\mathcal{H}}^2_q(\lambda, m)$ and $\mathsf{H}^3_i(\lambda, m) = \mathsf{H}^3_{i-1}(\lambda, m)$ except in the i-th oracle call to $\mathsf{O}^b_{\mathsf{pk}'}$, the ciphertexts created using Π in DerivePK are simulated using the HVZK property of Π. The capability of an adversary to distinguish the two games is bound by $\mathsf{Adv}^{\mathsf{hvzk}}_{\mathsf{VE},\mathcal{B}_3}(\lambda)$, thus

$$|\Pr[\mathsf{H}^2_{q_2}(\lambda, m) = 1] - \Pr[\mathsf{H}^3_{q_2}(\lambda, m) = 1]| \leq m q_2 \mathsf{Adv}^{\mathsf{hvzk}}_{\mathsf{VE},\mathcal{B}_3}(\lambda).$$

$\underline{\mathsf{H}^4_i(\lambda, m)}$: start this game series as $\mathsf{H}^4_0(\lambda, m) = \mathsf{H}^3_{q_2}(\lambda, m)$. The output of oracle $\mathsf{O}^b_{\mathsf{pk}'}$ contains a public key pk' and credentials $[\mathsf{cred}]_l$. Those values are generated in DerivePK: public key $\mathsf{pk}^\star$ is now indistinguishable from a freshly generated one by game $\mathsf{H}^1_q(\lambda, m)$ and cred was generated using a new encapsulation key $\mathsf{pk}_{\mathsf{rand}}$. The dealings for session sid are generated honestly which means the ciphertexts in $[\mathsf{m}]_l$ can all be simulated. This leads to the definition of $\mathsf{H}^4_i(\lambda, m)$ similarly to $\mathsf{H}^3_i(\lambda, m)$ and since $nm \leq m^2$ ciphertexts have been simulated per call:

$$|\Pr[\mathsf{H}^3_{q_2}(\lambda, m) = 1] - \Pr[\mathsf{H}^4_{q_2}(\lambda, m) = 1]| \leq m^2 q_2 \mathsf{Adv}^{\mathsf{hvzk}}_{\mathsf{VE},\mathcal{B}_3}(\lambda).$$

$\underline{\mathsf{Game}_1(\lambda, m)}$: define this game as $\mathsf{H}^4_{q_2}(\lambda, m)$. $[\mathsf{cred}]_l$ is now indistinguishable from credentials generated via a fresh session. The outputs of $\mathsf{O}_{\mathsf{pk}'}$ in $\mathsf{Game}_1(\lambda, m)$ are thus indistinguishable from freshly generated values and we have

$$\Pr[\mathsf{Game}_1(\lambda, m) = 1] \leq 1/2$$

Finally, the reduction must guess the session identifier sid which is output by the adversary during the first phase. This adds a factor q_1 to the advantage. □

5 Instantiation and Performance

We show how to instantiate 1PVAKA using additive ElGamal encryption and randomness re-use as in [4]. A proxy generates its contribution to the group key generation as a sample $(s, g_1^s) \leftarrow \Delta.\mathsf{KGen}(\mathsf{pp})$ and encrypts s for the other proxies. The public key is appended to the ciphertext along with additional verification information to form the dealing d. In the following, we describe a simple DDH-based Verifiable Encryption scheme (Fig. 8) that can be used with our results of Sect. 3 to produce a 1PVAKA instance. We also implemented a version using the pairing-friendly curve BLS12-381 and benchmarked the results. Both settings should have similar running time, since the main bottleneck is the computation of discrete logarithms using BSGS [26].

Let Δ be an AKG scheme with key spaces $\mathbb{S} = \mathbb{Z}_q$ and $\mathbb{P} = \mathbb{G} = \langle g \rangle$ a cyclic group of size q. We assume that the DDH assumption holds for the group $\mathbb{G}$. We also assume that for elements $x \in \mathbb{Z}_q$ up to a bound B, the discrete logarithm of g^x is computable efficiently. The integer $L := q/\log(B)$ then denotes the number of digits required to encrypt an element of $\mathbb{Z}_q$.

We consider the non-interactive Chaum-Pedersen proof system [12] in $\mathbb{G}$ denoted here by $(\mathcal{P}, \mathcal{V})$ to prove equality of discrete logarithms across distinct basis. Formally, it consists of two algorithms: a prover $\mathcal{P}$ and a verifier $\mathcal{V}$ such that for elements $g, h, G, H, w \in \mathbb{G}^4 \times \mathbb{Z}_q$ and $\pi \leftarrow \mathcal{P}(g, h, G, H, w)$, we have

$$\mathcal{V}(g, h, G, H, \pi) \Leftrightarrow w = \mathsf{dlog}_g(G) = \mathsf{dlog}_h(H).$$

We introduce a Verifiable Encryption scheme for Δ based on this system in Fig. 8. The scheme consists of L parallel ElGamal encryptions and makes use of their homomorphic properties.

The scheme is valid in the sense of Definition 6 as if Verify returns 1, by definition

$$\mathsf{dlog}_g(S) = \sum_k B^k(\mathsf{dlog}_g(c_k) - \mathsf{dk}r_k).$$

This equation implies that it is indeed the digits of $\mathsf{dlog}_g(S)$ that are encrypted within the ciphertexts. Ciphertext ct thus encrypts the discrete logarithm of S.

The Chaum-Pedersen proof system and its generalized version are HVZK according to [12, Proposition 3.3] and [11, Theorem 5], respectively. One can thus simulate a proof for arbitrary ciphertexts and statement $S \in \mathbb{G}$.

To build a 1PVAKA protocol from the above Verifiable Encryption scheme we use our transformation from Fig. 4. A dealing thus consists in sampling a random AKG key $(\mathsf{sk}, \mathsf{pk})$ and verifiably encrypting sk under the long-term key ek_i of each proxy in $[\mathsf{ek}]_n$. In the case of ElGamal ciphertext, an additional optimization is directly available. It consists in re-using the randomness $(r_k)_k$ under the different keys. This is possible as the messages encrypted, the digits of sk, are the same across all ciphertexts.

Encryption in the exponent is necessary for the public verifiability of our ciphertexts. This requires decomposing cleartexts s in base B as $s =: \sum_{0 \le k \le L} s_k B^k$ and encrypting each digit s_k separately to ensure that a search

$\mathsf{KGen}(\mathsf{pp})$

$\mathsf{dk} := x \leftarrow\!\!\$\ \mathbb{Z}_q^*$
$\mathsf{ek} := g^x$
return $(\mathsf{dk}, \mathsf{ek})$

$\mathsf{Enc}(\mathsf{ek}, s \in \mathbb{Z}_q^*)$

Write $s =: \sum_k s_k B^k$
for $0 \leq k \leq L$ **do**
    $r_k \leftarrow\!\!\$\ \mathbb{Z}_q^*$
    $c_k \leftarrow ek^{r_k} g^{s_k}$
$\mathsf{ct}_0, \mathsf{ct}_1 \leftarrow (g^{r_k})_k, (c_k)_k$
$R \leftarrow g^{\sum_k r_k B^k}$
$C \leftarrow \prod_k c_k^{B^k}$
$w \leftarrow \sum_k r_k B^k$
$\pi \leftarrow \mathcal{P}(g, \mathsf{ek}, g^{-s}C, R, w)$
return $\mathsf{ct} := (\mathsf{ct}_0, \mathsf{ct}_1 || \pi)$

$\mathsf{Verify}(\mathsf{ct}, \mathsf{ek}, S)$

$\mathsf{ct} =: ((R_k)_k, (c_k)_k || \pi)$
$R \leftarrow \prod_k R_k^{B_k}$
$C \leftarrow \prod_k c_k^{B^k}$
$b \leftarrow \mathcal{V}(g, \mathsf{ek}, S^{-1}C, R, \pi)$
return b

$\mathsf{Dec}(\mathsf{dk}, \mathsf{ct})$

$\mathsf{ct} =: ((R_k)_k, (c_k)_k || \pi)$
for $0 \leq k \leq L$ **do**
    $s_k \leftarrow R_k^{-dk} c_k$
return $s := \sum_k s_k B^k$

Fig. 8. Verifiable Encryption scheme based on ElGamal in the exponent and the Chaum-Pedersen system. We omit the range $[0, L]$ of k in the indices for clarity. Cleartexts are written in base B and L is the number of ciphertexts required to encrypt an element in base B.

of the cleartext space is possible via BSGS or Pollard's Rho algorithm. Assuming searching interval $[0, mB]$ for the discrete logarithm of a given element $g_1^{s_k}$ is efficient, we can actually perform aggregation of ciphertexts up to m times. More formally, the dealings of the i-th proxy in $[\mathsf{ek}]_n$ contain ciphertexts for the other proxies in the form $(g^{r_k}, \mathsf{ek}_j^{r_k} g^{s_{i,k}})$ for $k \in [0, L]$ where $j \in [n]$. After verifying those ciphertexts, the delegator aggregates them using the additive property of the scheme into $(g^{nr_k}, \mathsf{ek}_j^{nr_k} g^{(s_{1,k}+\cdots+s_{n,k})})$ which serve as new dealings, here intended for the j-the proxy. Since $n \leq m$, a search for each exponent in the ciphertext reveals the k-th digit of the combined secret key sk as $s_k := \sum_i s_{i,k}$. The corresponding public key is combined by the delegator as $\mathsf{pk} := \prod_i g^{s_i}$. We stress that available VE schemes for discrete logarithms [9,10,19] either use encryption in the exponent or more complicated MPC/NIZK techniques.

To simplify notations, we implicitly assume that during algorithm Deal, a user encrypts its own secret share s under its own public key. This is of course unnecessary and simply an artifact of our syntax for Deal not taking a proxy identifier as input. In reality the delegator knows which proxy is associated with which dealing. As such, it can easily keep track of the structure of a dealing (for whom the i-th ciphertext is addressed) and preform verification and combination accordingly. Removing this unnecessary ciphertext from the dealing slightly improves efficiency and security: the scheme goes from $(1, 0)$-SK-secure to $(1, 1)$-SK-secure. Indeed, a long-term key exposure now allows for decryption of all the shares for a given session except the encrypting proxy's share.

Regarding the choice of B and the resulting complexity of the scheme. Let γ be the largest integer for which computing the discrete logarithm of g^a for $a \in [0, \ldots, 2^\gamma]$ is efficient. For the scheme to remain n-times additively homomorphic for $n \leq m$, the maximum value for B is $2^\gamma/n$. Parameter q is of size roughly 2λ, thus if L represents the number of digits required to represent a member of $\mathbb{Z}_q$, we need $2^{2\lambda} \leq (2^\gamma/n)^L$ and set $L(n) = \lceil 2\lambda/(\gamma \log(2) - \log(n)) \rceil$. Since L grows as $\mathcal{O}(\log(n)^{-1})$, n is essentially negligible next to γ. Encryption in the exponent thus allows for a compression factor of $\mathcal{O}(n)$ during the DerivePK algorithm for the cost of a few additional ciphertexts per dealing.

Table 1. Runtime benchmarks for selected combinations of n and γ for 1PVAKA. The second row indicates the number of group elements (L) in a ciphertext. Rows three to six report the average runtime of the algorithms as a mean over ten executions. We observe the trade-off between the size $\mathcal{O}(L)$ of the dealings and the runtime of CombineSK which computes L discrete logarithms.

(n, γ)	$(4, 20)$	$(4, 25)$	$(4, 30)$	$(8, 20)$	$(8, 25)$	$(8, 30)$
L (# of ciphertexts)	22	17	13	22	17	13
Deal (in s)	1.09	1.23	1.4	2.78	2.81	2.69
Verify (in s)	0.8	0.79	0.82	0.98	0.91	0.9
CombinePK (in s)	0.0	0.01	0.01	0.03	0.03	0.03
CombineSK (in s)	2.93	8.88	46.48	3.22	10.43	43.83

Table 1 summarizes our experimentally obtained benchmarks for 1PVAKA, which dominates the runtime of the dARKG scheme in Fig. 7. The Jupyter notebook used for our experiments is publicly available[3]. Measurements were performed on a Dell Latitude 7430 laptop clocked at 4.8GHz with 16GB of RAM. Our implementation is not optimized and the discrete-logarithm bottleneck can be mitigated at the cost of heavier communications. The results are promising and decryption of dealings in CombineSK could even be parallelized, decreasing the execution time by a factor of 2 to 16. Our strategy of additively aggregating ciphertexts during CombinePK also pays off, saving n more discrete-logarithm searches per ciphertext. We are hopeful that the same technique can be applied to (verifiable) "naturally" homomorphic encryption to bring dealings size to $\mathcal{O}(n)$ and the run time of CombineSK to $\mathcal{O}(1)$.

6 Conclusion

In this work we introduced dARKG, a distributed version of ARKG [16] in which originally one delegator could derive a public key pk' for a single proxy who could at a later time derive the corresponding private key sk'. Our dARKG

[3] https://gitlab.com/rv5MDg/jupyter-notebook-darkg.

functionality and security properties are designed to be close to the original while allowing reconstruction of sk' by a group of receivers in a threshold manner. Our general dARKG scheme adds distributed trust and fault-tolerance to the aforementioned applications of ARKG in WebAuthn and blockchain transactions but also enables further applications when t-out-of-n structure is viewed as an access policy.

Acknowledgement. We acknowledge funding for Project LIONS as part of dtec.bw, which is funded by the European Commission under NextGenerationEU.

A Additional Building Blocks

A.1 Key Encapsulation

Let $\mathcal{K}$ be an arbitrary key space. A Key Encapsulation Mechanism (KEM) scheme (for key space $\mathcal{K}$) is defined by the following three PPT algorithms:

$\mathsf{KGen}(1^\lambda) \to (\mathsf{dk}, \mathsf{ek})$: The key generation algorithm takes as input the unary representation of the security parameter λ. It outputs an encapsulation key ek and a decapsulation key dk.

$\mathsf{Encaps}(\mathsf{ek}) \to (K, \mathsf{ct})$: The encapsulation algorithm takes as input an encapsulation key ek. It outputs a key $K \in \mathcal{K}$ and a ciphertext ct.

$\mathsf{Decaps}(\mathsf{dk}, \mathsf{ct}) \to K$ or $\perp$: The deterministic decapsulation algorithm takes as input a decapsulation key dk and a ciphertext ct. It outputs a key $K \in \mathcal{K}$ or $\perp$ indicating that the ciphertext is invalid.

Definition 15 (Correctness). *A KEM is correct if for all $\lambda \in \mathbb{N}$,*

$$\Pr\left[\begin{array}{c}(\mathsf{dk}, \mathsf{ek}) \leftarrow \mathsf{KGen}(1^\lambda),\ (K, \mathsf{ct}) \leftarrow \mathsf{Encaps}(\mathsf{ek}),\\ K' \leftarrow \mathsf{Decaps}(\mathsf{dk}, \mathsf{ct}) : K \neq K'\end{array}\right] = \mathsf{negl}(\lambda)$$

where the probability is taken over the random coins of KGen *and* Encaps.

We recall the standard notion of anonymity under chosen ciphertext attacks ($\mathsf{ANO\text{-}CCA}$) for KEM.

Definition 16 ($\mathsf{ANO\text{-}CCA}$ Security). *A KEM is said to be* $\mathsf{ANO\text{-}CCA}$ *secure if for all λ and PPT adversary $\mathcal{A}$, it holds that*

$$\mathsf{Adv}^{\mathsf{ANO\text{-}CCA}}_{\mathsf{KEM},\mathcal{A}}(\lambda) := \left|\Pr\left[\mathsf{Exp}^{\mathsf{ANO\text{-}CCA}}_{\mathsf{KEM},\mathcal{A}}(\lambda) = 1\right] - \frac{1}{2}\right| = \mathsf{negl}(\lambda).$$

where experiment $\mathsf{Exp}^{\mathsf{ANO\text{-}CCA}}_{\mathsf{KEM},\mathcal{A}}$ is defined in Figure Fig. 9 and the probability is taken over the random coins of the algorithms.

Experiment $\mathsf{Exp}^{\mathsf{ANO\text{-}CCA}}_{\mathsf{KEM},\mathcal{A}}(\lambda)$:	Oracle $\mathcal{O}_{\mathsf{Decaps}}(b, \mathsf{ct}^\star)$:
$(\mathsf{dk}_b, \mathsf{ek}_b) \leftarrow \mathsf{KGen}(1^\lambda)\ b \in \{0,1\}$	**if** $\mathsf{ct}^\star \stackrel{?}{=} \mathsf{ct}$
$b \leftarrow\!\!\$\ \{0,1\}$	**then return** $\perp$
$(K, \mathsf{ct}) \leftarrow \mathsf{Encaps}(\mathsf{ek}_b)$	**else**
$b' \leftarrow \mathcal{A}^{\mathcal{O}_{\mathsf{Decaps}}(\mathsf{dk},\cdot)}(\mathsf{ek}_0, \mathsf{ek}_1, K, \mathsf{ct})$	**return** $K := \mathsf{Decaps}(\mathsf{dk}_b, \mathsf{ct}^\star)$
return $b \stackrel{?}{=} b'$	

Fig. 9. ANO-CCA game for KEM.

A.2 Threshold Secret Sharing

Definition 17 ([1,3]). *A Threshold Secret Sharing scheme is a triple of algorithms* $\mathsf{TSS} := (\mathsf{Setup}, \mathsf{Share}, \mathsf{Recon})$ *defined as:*

- $\mathsf{Setup}(1^\lambda)$*: takes as input a security parameter* 1^λ *and outputs a description* pp *of the public parameters.*
- $\mathsf{Share}(\mathsf{pp}, n, t, S)$*: takes as input a public parameter, two integers* $t \leq n$ *and a secret* S*. It outputs* n *shares* $(s_i)_{i\in[n]}$*.*
- $\mathsf{Recon}(\mathsf{pp}, (s_i)_{i\in I})$*: takes as input a public parameter and* t *shares* $(s_i)_{i\in I}$ *with* $I \subseteq [n]$*. It either outputs a secret* S *or* $\perp$ *on error.*

A TSS scheme is correct if for all $\lambda \in \mathbb{N}$, $1 \leq t \leq n$, and $\mathsf{pp} \leftarrow \mathsf{Setup}(1^\lambda)$, for all secret S, and $I \subset \mathbb{N}$ with $|I| = t$, it holds that

$$\Pr\left[\ \mathsf{Recon}(\mathsf{pp}, (s_i)_{i\in I}) = S\right] = 1$$

for shares $(s_i)_{i\in[n]} \leftarrow \mathsf{Share}(\mathsf{pp}, n, t, S)$.
Security-wise, a TSS scheme offers *privacy* if the following advantage is negligible in λ

$$\mathsf{Adv}^{\mathsf{privacy}}_{\mathsf{TSS},\mathcal{A}(\lambda)} = \left|\Pr\left[\mathsf{Exp}^{\mathsf{privacy}}_{\mathsf{TSS},\mathcal{A}(\lambda)} = 1\right] - \frac{1}{2}\right| \leq \mathsf{negl}(\lambda)$$

where the $\mathsf{Exp}^{\mathsf{privacy}}_{\mathsf{TSS},\mathcal{A}(\lambda)}$ experiment is defined in Fig. 10.

A.3 Key Derivation Functions

Definition 18 (Key Derivation Function). *A key derivation function* $\mathsf{KDF} : K \times L \rightarrow K'$ *takes as input a key* k *and a label* l*. It outputs a new key* k' *not necessarily from the same key space as* k*.*

Security of KDF. A KDF is secure if the following advantage is negligible in λ for all PPT adversary $\mathcal{A}$

$$\mathsf{Adv}^{\mathsf{KDF}}_{\mathcal{A}}(\lambda) = \left|\Pr\left[\mathsf{Exp}^{\mathsf{IND}}_{\mathsf{KDF},\mathcal{A}}(\lambda) = 1\right] - \frac{1}{2}\right|,$$

where the indistinguishability IND experiment is defined in Fig. 10.

A.4 Message Authentication Code

Definition 19 (Message Authentication Code). *A Message Authentication Code (MAC) is a triple* $\mathsf{MAC} = (\mathsf{KGen}, \mathsf{Tag}, \mathsf{Verify})$. *Algorithm* $\mathsf{KGen}(1^\lambda)$ *takes as input a security parameter* 1^λ *and outputs a secret key* $mk \leftarrow\$ \{0,1\}^\lambda$, $\mathsf{Tag}(mk, m)$ *outputs a tag* μ *for a secret key* mk *and a message* m *and* $\mathsf{Verify}(mk, m, \mu)$ *outputs* 1 *if the tag* μ *is valid for* mk *and* m, *otherwise* 0.

A MAC scheme is said to be correct if and only if for every $\lambda \in \mathbb{N}, m \in \{0,1\}^*$,

$$(mk \leftarrow \mathsf{KGen}(1^\lambda);\ \mu \leftarrow \mathsf{Tag}(mk, m)) \Rightarrow \mathsf{Verify}(mk, m, \mu),$$

Security of MAC schemes. . Define oracle $\mathsf{O}_{\mathsf{Tag},mk}$ parameterized by a key mk and taking a message m as input. It returns the result of $\mathsf{Tag}(mk, m)$. A MAC is unforgeable if the following advantage is negligible in λ for all PPT adversary $\mathcal{A}$

$$\mathsf{Adv}^{\mathsf{UNF}}_{\mathsf{MAC},\mathcal{A}}(\lambda) = \Pr\left[\mathsf{Exp}^{\mathsf{UNF}}_{\mathsf{MAC},\mathcal{A}}(\lambda) = 1\right],$$

where the unforgeability UNF experiment is defined in Fig. 10.

$\mathsf{Exp}^{\mathsf{privacy}}_{\mathsf{TSS},\mathcal{A}(\lambda)}$	$\mathsf{Exp}^{\mathsf{IND}}_{\mathsf{KDF},\mathcal{A}}(\lambda)$	$\mathsf{Exp}^{\mathsf{UNF}}_{\mathsf{MAC},\mathcal{A}}(\lambda)$
$(t, n) \leftarrow \mathcal{A}(1^\lambda)$	$k \leftarrow\$ K$	$mk \leftarrow \mathsf{KGen}(1^\lambda)$
$\mathsf{pp} \leftarrow \mathsf{Setup}(1^\lambda, t, n)$	$l \leftarrow\$ L$	$(m^\star, \mu^\star) \leftarrow \mathcal{A}^{\mathsf{O}_{\mathsf{Tag},mk}}$
$m_0, m_1 \leftarrow\$ \{0,1\}^k$	$y_0 \leftarrow \mathsf{KDF}(k, l)$	**return** $m \neq m^\star$
$(s_i^0)_{i\in[n]} \leftarrow \mathsf{Share}(\mathsf{pp}, m_0)$	$y_1 \leftarrow\$ \{0,1\}^\lambda$	$\wedge\, \mathsf{Verify}(mk, m^\star, \mu^\star)$
$(s_i^1)_{i\in[n]} \leftarrow \mathsf{Share}(\mathsf{pp}, m_1)$	$b \leftarrow\$ \{0,1\}$	
$I \leftarrow\$ \{J \subset [n] \mid \#J < t\}$	$b' \rightarrow \mathcal{A}(y_b)$	
$b \leftarrow\$ \{0,1\}$	**return** $b' \stackrel{?}{=} b$	
$b' \leftarrow \mathcal{A}(\mathsf{pp}, m_0, m_1, (s_i^b)_{i\in I})$		
return $b \stackrel{?}{=} b'$		

Fig. 10. Security experiments for TSS, KDF and MAC.

References

1. Adams, D.Q., et al.: Lower bounds for leakage-resilient secret-sharing schemes against probing attacks. In: 2021 IEEE ISIT (2021)
2. Balfanz, D., et al.: Web authentication: an API for accessing public key credentials level 3. Technical report (2019). https://www.w3.org/TR/webauthn-3
3. Beimel, A.: Secret-sharing schemes: a survey. In: Chee, Y.M., et al. (eds.) IWCC 2011. LNCS, vol. 6639, pp. 11–46. Springer, Heidelberg (2011). https://doi.org/10.1007/978-3-642-20901-7_2

4. Bellare, M., Boldyreva, A., Staddon, J.: Randomness re-use in multi-recipient encryption schemeas. In: Desmedt, Y.G. (ed.) Public Key Cryptography – PKC 2003. Springer, Berlin Heidelberg (2002)
5. Boneh, D., Zhandry, M.: Multiparty key exchange, efficient traitor tracing, and more from indistinguishability obfuscation. Algorithmica **79**, 1233–1285 (2017)
6. Bos, J., et al.: CRYSTALS - Kyber: a CCA-secure module-lattice-based KEM. In: EuroS&P (2018)
7. Brendel, J., Clermont, S., Fischlin, M.: Post-quantum asynchronous remote key generation for fido2 account recovery. Cryptology ePrint Archive (2023). https://eprint.iacr.org/2023/1275
8. Brendel, J., Fischlin, M., Günther, F., Janson, C., Stebila, D.: Towards post-quantum security for signal's x3dh handshake. In: Selected Areas in Cryptography: 27th International Conference (2020). https://doi.org/10.1007/978-3-030-81652-0_16
9. Camenisch, J., Damgård, I.: Verifiable encryption, group encryption, and their applications to separable group signatures and signature sharing schemes. In: ASIACRYPT 2000 (2000). https://doi.org/10.1007/3-540-44448-3_25
10. Camenisch, J., Shoup, V.: Practical verifiable encryption and decryption of discrete logarithms. In: Boneh, D. (ed.) CRYPTO 2003. LNCS, vol. 2729, pp. 126–144. Springer, Heidelberg (2003). https://doi.org/10.1007/978-3-540-45146-4_8
11. Chase, M., Orrù, M., Perrin, T., Zaverucha, G.: Proofs of discrete logarithm equality across groups. Cryptology ePrint Archive, Paper 2022/1593 (2022). https://eprint.iacr.org/2022/1593
12. Chaum, D., Pedersen, T.P.: Wallet databases with observers. In: Brickell, E.F. (ed.) Advances in Cryptology – CRYPTO 1992. Springer, Berlin, Heidelberg (1993)
13. Crites, E.C., Lysyanskaya, A.: Delegatable anonymous credentials from mercurial signatures. In: Matsui, M. (ed.) CT-RSA 2019. LNCS, vol. 11405, pp. 535–555. Springer, Cham (2019). https://doi.org/10.1007/978-3-030-12612-4_27
14. Ducas, L., Lepoint, T., Lyubashevsky, V., Schwabe, P., Seiler, G., Stehlé, D.: Crystals–dilithium: Digital signatures from module lattices (2018). https://repository.ubn.ru.nl/bitstream/handle/2066/191703/191703.pdf
15. Frymann, N., Gardham, D., Manulis, M.: Asynchronous remote key generation for post-quantum cryptosystems from lattices. In: 2023 IEEE 8th European Symposium on Security and Privacy (EuroS&P), pp. 928–941. IEEE Computer Society (2023). https://doi.org/10.1109/EuroSP57164.2023.00059
16. Frymann, N., Gardham, D., Kiefer, F., Lundberg, E., Manulis, M., Nilsson, D.: Asynchronous remote key generation: an analysis of Yubico's proposal for W3C Webauthn. In: Proceedings of the 2020 ACM SIGSAC, pp. 939–954. Association for Computing Machinery (2020). https://doi.org/10.1145/3372297.3417292
17. Frymann, N., Gardham, D., Manulis, M.: Unlinkable delegation of Webauthn credentials. In: Atluri, V., Di Pietro, R., Jensen, C.D., Meng, W. (eds.) Computer Security - ESORICS 2022, vol. 13556, pp. 125–144. Springer Nature Switzerland, Cham (2022). https://doi.org/10.1007/978-3-031-17143-7_7
18. Frymann, N., Gardham, D., Manulis, M., Nartz, H.: Generalised asynchronous remote key generation for pairing-based cryptosystems. In: Tibouchi, M., Wang, X. (eds.) Applied Cryptography and Network Security. ACNS 2023. LNCS, vol. 13905, pp. 394–421. Springer, Cham (2023). https://doi.org/10.1007/978-3-031-33488-7_15
19. Gjøsteen, K., Haines, T., Müller, J., Rønne, P., Silde, T.: Verifiable decryption in the head. In: Nguyen, K., Yang, G., Guo, F., Susilo, W. (eds) Information

Security and Privacy. ACISP 2022. LNCS, vol. 13494, pp. 355–374. Springer, Cham (2022). https://doi.org/10.1007/978-3-031-22301-3_18
20. Groth, J.: Non-interactive distributed key generation and key resharing. Cryptology ePrint Archive, Paper 2021/339. https://eprint.iacr.org/2021/339
21. Komlo, C., Goldberg, I., Stebila, D.: A formal treatment of distributed key generation, and new constructions. Cryptology ePrint Archive, Paper 2023/292 (2023). https://eprint.iacr.org/2023/292
22. Koppula, V., Waters, B., Zhandry, M.: Adaptive multiparty NIKE. In: Kiltz, E., Vaikuntanathan, V. (eds.) Theory of Cryptography. TCC 2022. LNCS, vol. 13748, pp. 244–273. Springer, Cham (2022). https://doi.org/10.1007/978-3-031-22365-5_9
23. Mir, O., Bauer, B., Griffy, S., Lysyanskaya, A., Slamanig, D.: Aggregate signatures with versatile randomization and issuer-hiding multi-authority anonymous credentials. In: Proceedings of the 2023 ACM SIGSAC Conference on Computer and Communications Security, pp. 30–44. Association for Computing Machinery (2023). https://doi.org/10.1145/3576915.3623203
24. Pu, S., Thyagarajan, S.A., Döttling, N., Hanzlik, L.: Post quantum fuzzy stealth signatures and applications. In: Proceedings of the 2023 ACM SIGSAC Conference on Computer and Communications Security, pp. 371–385 (2023). https://doi.org/10.1145/3576915.3623148
25. Rao, V.: Adaptive multiparty non-interactive key exchange without setup in the standard model. Cryptology ePrint Archive, Paper 2014/910 (2014). https://eprint.iacr.org/2014/910
26. Shanks, D.: Class number, a theory of factorization, and genera, January 1971. https://doi.org/10.1090/pspum/020/0316385
27. Stebila, D., Wilson, S.: Quantum-safe account recovery for Webauthn. Cryptology ePrint Archive, Paper 2024/678 (2024). https://doi.org/10.1145/3634737.3661138
28. Wu, Q., Mu, Y., Susilo, W., Qin, B., Domingo-Ferrer, J.: Asymmetric group key agreement. In: Joux, A. (ed.) EUROCRYPT 2009. LNCS, vol. 5479, pp. 153–170. Springer, Heidelberg (2009). https://doi.org/10.1007/978-3-642-01001-9_9
29. Yu, G.: Blockchain stealth address schemes. Cryptology ePrint Archive, Paper 2020/548 (2020). https://eprint.iacr.org/2020/548

Anonymous Authenticated Key Exchange

José Ignacio Escribano Pablos[1], María Isabel González Vasco[2], Ángel Pérez del Pozo[3], and Claudio Soriente[4](✉)

[1] Guardedbox, Guadalajara, Spain
[2] Universidad Carlos III De Madrid, Madrid, Spain
[3] Universidad Rey Juan Carlos, Madrid, Spain
[4] NEC Laboratories Europe, Heidelberg, Germany
claudio.soriente@neclab.eu

Abstract. Authenticated Key Exchange (AKE) can be used in client-server applications for mutual authentication and key establishment. In scenarios where client authentication is neither feasible nor desirable, One-Sided AKE (OS-AKE) allows both parties to establish a key while only the server authenticates to the client. Thus, OS-AKE provides client anonymity with respect to the server, but does not allow the server to enforce any form of access control—that is, the server simply establishes a key with *any* client.

In this paper, we introduce *Anonymous* AKE (A-AKE) to strike a balance between classical client authentication of AKE and client anonymity of OS-AKE. In a nutshell A-AKE is an AKE protocol where (i) the server authenticates to the client, (ii) the server can enforce access control by deciding which clients are authorized to run the key-establishment protocol, (iii) a key is established between the server and the client only if the latter is one of the authorized clients as defined by the server, and (iv) the authorized client remains anonymous (within the set of all authorized clients) with respect to the server. We introduce a security model for A-AKE that extends popular AKE models and design a general framework for instantiating A-AKE protocols based on well-established cryptographic primitives. Finally, we instantiate several AKE protocols aiming at strong security guarantees in the classical and post-quantum settings. We implement a prototype of each instantiation and provide an experimental comparison of their performance.

Keywords: Authenticated key exchange · Anonymity · Post-quantum cryptography

1 Introduction

Authenticated Key Exchange (AKE) protocols allow two parties to mutually authenticate and establish a fresh shared cryptographic key [17,34]. Authentication is usually achieved by means of a shared secret (e.g., a password or a symmetric key) or certified public keys. In many practical client-server scenarios, mutual authentication is not desirable nor it is feasible. For example, in TLS key establishment, only the server may have a certified public key and no shared secret is available—most of the times, there has been no previous client-server

M. Fischlin and V. Moonsamy (Eds.): ACNS 2025, LNCS 15825, pp. 516–546, 2025.
https://doi.org/10.1007/978-3-031-95761-1_18

interaction. In such scenarios, One-sided AKE (OS-AKE) allows the two parties to establish a fresh cryptographic key while only the server proves its identity to the client [26]. Thus, OS-AKE allows clients to remain anonymous but does not provide the server with any means to enforce access control. That is, the server establishes a key with *any* client.

In this paper we initiate the study of *Anonymous* Authenticated Key Exchange (A-AKE) to strike a balance between classical client authentication of AKE and client anonymity of OS-AKE. We consider a scenario with a server and a set of registered clients, each with a public key certificate. We assume the server can, at any time, define a subset of the registered clients that are "authorized" to run the key exchange protocol. At each run, the server proves its identity to the client, while the client only proves to the server that it is one of the authorized clients, without revealing its identity. A-AKE finds application in client-server scenarios where the server wants to enforce access control whereas clients want to remain anonymous, e.g., whistle-blowing platforms and anonymous forums. Other scenarios that rely on a balance between authentication and anonymity, include VANETs [35] and IoT [51,58]. See Sect. 6 for a broader discussion.

We start by introducing a formal model for A-AKE that extends the classical AKE models of [4,17] to account for client anonymity and unlinkability. Our model provides strong security guarantees as both key secrecy and client anonymity/unlinkability of past sessions hold, even if long term keys are leaked. Next, we introduce a framework to build A-AKE protocols by means of well-established cryptographic primitives such as public-key encryption, digital signatures, and commitment schemes. Assuming these tools to be secure (in a rather standard sense), we prove that our generic construction achieves the targeted security and privacy guarantees.

Next, we use our framework to instantiate various versions of A-AKE. One version uses traditional discrete-logarithm based cryptographic primitives, while the others are built from so-called post-quantum primitives—which are believed to remain secure against quantum adversaries (see, for instance, [41]). Finally, we present a prototype of each instantiation and show the results of experiments designed to quantify their communication and computation overhead.

Related Work. AKE in the client-server setting has been extensively studied in the literature; most designs consider a scenario in which clients authenticate using either passwords [12,30] or public key certificates [33]. One-sided AKE (OS-AKE) allows anonymous clients to establish a secret key with an authenticated server [3,25,26,29]. As such, the server cannot enforce any access control on clients and simply establishes a key with any client. Anonymity with respect to external adversaries is considered in so-called *privacy-preserving* AKE (PPAKE) [24,46,52,59]. PPAKE is essentially an AKE protocol where the client's identity does not appear in (nor it can be inferred from) the protocol transcript, even if the adversary is active (i.e., may interact with the involved parties). PPAKE protocols, however, *do not* provide client anonymity with respect to the server. Table 1 compares A-AKE with relevant AKE protocols. We note that

Table 1. Comparison of Authenticated Key Exchange proposals. Column **PQ** shows whether there exists an implementation of the scheme relying only on post-quantum tools; column **Access Control** indicates whether the server can implement any access control policy on clients.

Protocol	Type	PQ	Client auth	Server auth	Client anonymity		Access Control
					external adv.	server	
NAXOS [17,34]	AKE	✗	PK-cert	PK-cert	✗	✗	✓
IKEv2 [33]	AKE	✗	PK-cert	PK-cert	✗	✗	✓
KEM-X3DH [28]	AKE	✓	PK-cert	PK-cert	✗	✗	✓
Zhao [59]	PPAKE	✗	PK-cert	PK-cert	✓	✗	✓
Schäge et al. [52]	PPAKE	✗	PK-cert	PK-cert	✓	✗	✓
Ramacher [46]	PPAKE	✗	PK-cert	PK-cert	✓	✗	✓
Ferreia et al. [24]	PPAKE	✗	shared-secret	shared-secret	✓	✗	✓
ntor [26]	OS-AKE	✗	None	PK-cert	✓	✓	✗
Ace [3]	OS-AKE	✗	None	PK-cert	✓	✓	✗
HybridOR [25]	OS-AKE	✓	None	PK-cert	✓	✓	✗
GC-Std [29]	OS-AKE	✓	None	PK-cert	✓	✓	✗
This Work	A-AKE	✓	PK-cert	PK-cert	✓	✓	✓

A-AKE is the only AKE protocol that keeps clients anonymous with respect to an internal adversary, while allowing the server to enforce access control on the set of clients.

On Anonymity in Anonymous Authentication Primitives. The anonymity definition we introduce (Sect. 2) requires that the set of authorized clients has at least two honest members. This requirement is common in other anonymous authentication primitives. For example, the anonymity definition of ring signatures [7,47] assumes that public keys of honest clients are well-formed and that the ring of the challenge signature contains at least two such public keys—whereas the remaining public keys are arbitrarily chosen by the adversary and may be not well-formed. Similarly, the definition of *full* anonymity of group signatures [5,10] assumes that `join` protocols are carried out correctly, that the adversary may see the whole join protocol transcript (including the secret key) for honest users, and that the challenge signature is computed with the signing key of one out of two honest group members. We note that knowing the public keys of the members of the anonymity set is essential to provide some sort of assurance to the client. For example, in a group signature scheme, the client should know the set of group members. Otherwise it may as well be the only group member and its signatures would lack any anonymity. One may hope to simply leak the size of the anonymity set rather than the identities of its members. For example, the server/group-manager may claim that the group has N members. Larger values of N would provide greater anonymity. However, it is not clear how a group member could verify such claim. The only option is for each group member to sign a statement where it claims to be a group member, so that other group members can verify. However, verifying such statements requires the public keys of the signers, so that the anonymity set is leaked. In practice, anonymity for a honest client can only be guaranteed if that client learns the public keys of other honest clients and checks that those public keys are part of its anonymity set. This can be realized by means of a PKI and our A-AKE protocols presented in Sect. 3 makes use of a PKI for this purpose.

Paper Roadmap. In Sect. 2 we introduce the proposed security model for A-AKE and describe the basic tools needed for our design. We detail our generic construction in Sect. 3, and present a formal security analysis of it in Sect. 4. Section 5 depicts the experimental results carried over several A-AKE prototypes, each constructed from a different set of basic tools. Experiments focused particularly on comparing different post-quantum primitives. Section 6 shows how to improve performance by using techniques from broadcast encryption; it also discusses alternative designs for authentication protocols that provide both anonymity and access control. We provide conclusions in Sect. 7.

2 Security Model

We build on classical security models for authenticated key-exchange [4,17], adapt them to the client-server setting, and add definitions for anonymity and unlinkability, including forward-secrecy and forward-anonymity. The latter ensures that transcripts of past key-exchanges do not leak the identity of the involved clients, even if the adversary learns the long term keys of all participants. A similar property was named *forward-privacy* in [46,59] and was tailored towards external adversaries; our definition of forward-anonymity also consider corruptions of client and server.

Participants. We consider a finite universe of *registered* clients $\mathcal{C} = \{C_1, \ldots, C_n\}$ and a server $S \notin \mathcal{C}$. At each execution, a set of clients $\mathcal{C}^{Auth} \subseteq \mathcal{C}$ are *authorized.* Each party $\mathcal{C} \cup \{S\}$ can take part in a polynomial number of (possibly concurrent) protocol executions. Each execution involves a client instance Π_i^j, with $i \in \{1, \ldots, n\}$ and $j \in \mathbb{N}$, and a server instance Π_S^w, with $w \in \mathbb{N}$. Each instance is associated with a set of variables:

- ltsk_i (resp. ltsk_S) contains all long term keys stored by client C_i (resp. the server S)
- pid_i^j (resp. pid_S^w) it is initialized with the servers identifier S; when execution ends, it additionally stores the indices of authorized clients
- sid_i^j (resp. sid_S^w) it is initialized with a null value; when execution ends, it stores a session identifier (if the execution is successful)
- sk_i^j (resp. sk_S^w)it is initialized with a null value; when execution ends, it stores an established session key (if the execution is successful)
- rev_i^j (resp. rev_S^w) stores a binary value, stating whether the session key corresponding to the instance has been revealed or not
- acc_i^j (resp. acc_S^w) stores a binary value, indicating whether the run is accepted as successful or not.

Adversarial Capabilities. We restrict to probabilistic polynomial time adversaries; whenever they are assumed to have access to quantum resources, we will make it explicit. Further, we will only consider adversaries that interact classically with any hash function (i.e., we restrict to the so-called *classical* random oracle model). The capabilities of an adversary $\mathcal{A}$ are made explicit through a number of *oracles* allowing $\mathcal{A}$ to interact with instances of any participant (client or server).

We will assume that index $i \in \{1, \ldots, n\} \cup \{S\}$, indicating that oracle queries can be made to client or server instances (except for the $\mathsf{Execute}$ oracle, where i is always a client index):

$\mathsf{Execute}(\Pi_i^j, \Pi_S^w)$. This oracle executes a complete protocol run among the specified unused instances (corresponding to client C_i and server S). The adversary obtains a transcript of all messages sent over the network. A query to the $\mathsf{Execute}$ oracle models passive eavesdropping.

$\mathsf{Send}(\Pi_i^j, M)$. This oracle sends message M to instance Π_i^j and returns the response generated by this instance. A query $\mathsf{Send}(\Pi_i^j, \mathsf{init})$ to an unused instance Π_i^j models a situation in which Π_i^j sends a first message in a protocol run (and the query returns this first message)

$\mathsf{Reveal}(\Pi_i^j)$. Yields the session key sk_i^j stored by the corresponding instance.

$\mathsf{Test}(\Pi_i^j)$. Provided that sk_i^j is defined, (i.e., $\mathsf{acc}_i^j = \mathsf{true}$ and $\mathsf{sk}_i^j \neq \mathsf{null}$), this oracle selects a bit b uniformly at random and returns the session key sk_i^j if $b = 1$ or a key of the same length chosen uniformly at random from the set of possible keys if $b = 0$. The adversary is allowed only one query to this oracle.

$\mathsf{Corrupt}(X)$. This oracle returns all long-term keys of party X, where X must be in $\mathcal{C} \cup \{S\}$.

Remark 1. Note that our model allows a single query to the Test oracle. There are security models for AKE which allow several queries to this oracle, all of them answered with the same choice of the bit b (see, for instance, [1]). However, as shown in [2], both models are equivalent with a loss factor equal to the total number of instances.

Correctness. We call an $\mathsf{A\text{-}AKE}$ protocol $\mathcal{P}$ *correct*, if in the presence of a passive adversary $\mathcal{A}$—i.e., $\mathcal{A}$ must not use the Send oracle—the following holds: for any client instance Π_i^j and server instance Π_S^w, if both $\mathsf{sid}_i^j = \mathsf{sid}_S^w$ and $\mathsf{acc}_i^j = \mathsf{acc}_S^w = \mathsf{true}$, we have $\mathsf{sk}_i^j = \mathsf{sk}_S^w \neq \mathsf{null}$ and $\mathsf{pid}_i^j = \mathsf{pid}_S^w$.

Key Secrecy. Modeling key secrecy requires ruling out trivial attacks (e.g., those where the adversary trivially learns the session key by revealing an instance involved in the attacked execution). The following definitions of partnering and freshness help us to rule out such attacks.

Definition 1 (Partnering). *A client instance Π_i^j is partnered with a server instance Π_S^w if*

- *C_i belongs to the authorized set linked to Π_S^w (i.e., $i \in \mathsf{pid}_S^w$).*

- *Both* acc_i^j *and* acc_S^w *are set to* true.
- *Their session identifiers are defined and coincide, i.e.,* $\mathsf{sid}_i^j = \mathsf{sid}_S^w$.

Additionally, we will assume that any instance is partnered with itself.

Definition 2 (Freshness). *A client instance* Π_i^j *is* fresh *if* $\mathsf{acc}_i^j = \mathsf{true}$ *and the adversary has not:*

- *queried* $\mathsf{Reveal}(\Pi_i^j)$ *nor* $\mathsf{Reveal}(\Pi_S^w)$, *with* Π_S^w *and* Π_i^j *being partnered,*
- *queried* $\mathsf{Corrupt}(C_i)$ *or* $\mathsf{Corrupt}(S)$ *and subsequently* Send *to some* $l \in \mathsf{pid}_i^j$, $(l \neq i)$.

Analogously, a server instance Π_S^w *is* fresh *if* $\mathsf{acc}_S^w = \mathsf{true}$ *and the adversary has not:*

- *queried* $\mathsf{Reveal}(\Pi_S^w)$ *nor* $\mathsf{Reveal}(\Pi_i^j)$, *with* Π_S^w *and* Π_i^j *being partnered,*
- *queried* $\mathsf{Corrupt}(C_i)$ *and subsequently* Send, *with* $i \in \mathsf{pid}_S^w$,
- *queried* $\mathsf{Corrupt}(S)$ *and subsequently* Send *to some* $j \in \mathsf{pid}_S^w$, $(j \neq S)$.

Now, the main goal of an external adversary attacking a key establishment protocol is to gain information on the key being established, which in particular would allow him to distinguish the actual key from a value selected uniformly at random from the key space. We denote by $\mathsf{Succ}(\lambda)$ the probability that the adversary, making a Test query to a fresh instance, guesses correctly the bit b of the Test oracle. In turn, the A-AKE-advantage of $\mathcal{A}$ is denoted by $\mathsf{Adv}_{\mathcal{A}}(\lambda)$ and defined as $\mathsf{Adv}_{\mathcal{A}}(\lambda) := |2 \cdot \mathsf{Succ}(\lambda) - 1|$.

Definition 3 (Key Secrecy). *An A-AKE protocol* $\mathcal{P}$ *provides* key secrecy, *if for every ppt adversary* $\mathcal{A}$ *who has access to* Execute, Send, Test, Corrupt *and* Reveal *oracles,* $\mathsf{Adv}_{\mathcal{A}}(\lambda) \leq \mathrm{negl}(\lambda)$ *holds for some negligible function* $\mathrm{negl}(\lambda)$, *where* λ *is the security parameter.*

Remark 2. Our definition of key secrecy implies forward secrecy, i.e., leakage of long term keys does not leak any information on previously established session keys. This is because a Corrupt query does not violate freshness as long as it is not followed by Send queries. Hence, the definition of key secrecy accounts for an adversary that corrupts a client and tests previous sessions where that client was involved.

Remark 3. Note that the freshness definition forbids Send to any authorized client or the server, in case Corrupt was queried earlier. Hence, active attacks that corrupt authorized clients are ruled out.

Remark 4. Similar to other AKE, our model rules out scenarios where a client that establishes a session key with the server, leaks the key to the adversary. This is because our definition of freshness rules out trivial wins of an adversary by forbidding Reveal on instances involved in the tested session. In practice, if the server learns that a client has leaked a session key, that client may be banned.

Banning misbehaving clients in AKE is easy since the server knows the identity of the client for each key-exchange. In A-AKE, however, this may not be possible, since the identity of the client is hidden from the server (see Sect. 6). Similarly, our model does not consider an uncorrupted client that helps the adversary to establish a session key with the server. We leave the definition of a stronger model that accommodates for such behavior as future work.

Definition 4 (Implicit Authentication). *An A-AKE protocol $\mathcal{P}$ provides* implicit authentication, *if whenever a client instance Π_i^j has accepted (i.e., acc_i^j is set to true) if there exists another instance Π_l^t partnered with it, then $l = S$. Furthermore, if a server instance Π_S^k accepts, and there is a partnered instance Π_l^t then $l \in \mathcal{C}^{Auth}$.*

Remark 5. Note that key secrecy as defined above implies implicit authentication: if a key is established, it must be shared by the partnered instances—i.e., the server and an authorized client—otherwise, key secrecy would be violated.

Anonymity and Unlinkability. We introduce now forward anonymity and forward unlinkability as natural extensions of the idea of forward security in the related contexts (see the recent survey [11] for a complete description of forward security notions). Informally, forward anonymity ensures that transcripts of past key-exchange protocols do not leak the identity of the involved clients, even if the adversary learns the long term keys of all participants. A similar property was named *forward privacy* in [46,59] and was tailored towards external adversaries whereas our definition of forward-anonymity also allows the adversary to corrupt the server and/or some clients (different from the targeted one).

(Forward) Anonymity. Consider the following experiment $\mathsf{Expt}_{\mathsf{Anon}}$ where a ppt adversary $\mathcal{A}$, equipped with Send, Corrupt, Execute and Reveal plays the following game with a challenger Ch :

- $\mathcal{A}$ calls $\mathsf{Corrupt}(S)$ getting the server's long term keys,
- $\mathcal{A}$ selects two different client indices i_0, i_1 and announces them to Ch,
- Ch chooses a bit b uniformly at random,
- Ch and $\mathcal{A}$ interact, where Ch follows the protocol specification acting as client C_{i_b} (and therefore using secret long term keys in ltsk_{i_b}) and $\mathcal{A}$ may call Send, Reveal, Execute and Corrupt at will; $\mathcal{A}$ is not allowed to generate a server instance Π_S^w such that $i_0 \in \mathsf{pid}_S^w$ and $i_1 \notin \mathsf{pid}_S^w$ or vice versa,
- $\mathcal{A}$ outputs a guess b^*.

Let $\mathsf{Succ}_{\mathsf{Anon}}(\lambda)$ be the probability that $b = b^*$, and, in turn, denote the corresponding advantage by $\mathsf{Adv}_{\mathsf{Anon},\mathcal{A}}(\lambda) := |2 \cdot \mathsf{Succ}_{\mathsf{Anon}}(\lambda) - 1|$.

Definition 5 ((Forward) Anonymity). *An A-AKE protocol $\mathcal{P}$ attains* anonymity, *if for every ppt adversary $\mathcal{A}$ who has access to* Execute, Send, Corrupt *and* Reveal *oracles, $\mathsf{Adv}_{\mathsf{Anon},\mathcal{A}}(\lambda) \leq \mathrm{negl}(\lambda)$ holds for some negligible function* $\mathrm{negl}(\lambda)$, *where λ is the security parameter.*

(Forward) Unlinkability. Consider the following experiment $\mathsf{Expt}_{\mathsf{Unlink}}$where a ppt adversary $\mathcal{A}$, equipped with Send, Corrupt, Execute and Reveal plays the following game with a challenger Ch :

- $\mathcal{A}$ calls Corrupt(S) getting the server's long term keys,
- $\mathcal{A}$ selects two different client indices i_0, i_1 and announces them to Ch,

  Phase 1: Ch chooses a bit b u.a.r. Ch and $\mathcal{A}$ interact , where Ch follows the protocol specification acting as client C_{i_b} (and therefore using secret long term keys in ltsk_{i_b}) and $\mathcal{A}$ may call Send, Reveal, Execute and Corrupt.

  Phase 2: Ch chooses a bit b' u.a.r. Ch and $\mathcal{A}$ interact (in a polynomial number of instances), where Ch follows the protocol specification acting as client $C_{i_{b'}}$ (and therefore using secret long term keys in $\mathsf{ltsk}_{i_{b'}}$) and $\mathcal{A}$ may call Send, Reveal, Execute and Corrupt.

  As above, $\mathcal{A}$ is not allowed to generate a server instance Π_S^w such that $i_0 \in \mathsf{pid}_S^w$ and $i_1 \notin \mathsf{pid}_S^w$ or vice versa.
- $\mathcal{A}$ outputs a guess bit b^* for the equality $b == b'$.

Let $\mathsf{Succ}_{\mathsf{Unlink}}(\lambda)$ be the probability that b^* is correct, and, in turn, denote the corresponding advantage by $\mathsf{Adv}_{\mathsf{Unlink},\mathcal{A}}(\lambda) := |2 \cdot \mathsf{Succ}_{\mathsf{Unlink}}(\lambda) - 1|$.

Definition 6 ((Forward) Unlinkability). *An A-AKE protocol $\mathcal{P}$ attains* unlinkability, *if for every ppt adversary $\mathcal{A}$ who has access to* Execute, Send, Corrupt *and* Reveal *oracles,* $\mathsf{Adv}_{\mathsf{Unlink},\mathcal{A}}(\lambda) \leq \mathrm{negl}(\lambda)$ *holds for some negligible function* $\mathrm{negl}(\lambda)$*, where λ is the security parameter.*

Note that forward security is captured in the above Definitions 5 and 6, as we let the adversary corrupt the server at the beginning of the security game and make Corrupt calls to any client at any moment of the game. In fact, we are modeling the situation where anonymity and unlinkability are preserved for clients even against a malicious server who has access to all clients' long term secret keys before protocol runs. We will show that the generic A-AKE protocol we present in Sect. 3 achieves both notions. This is possible in our design because a client's long term secret is only used to prove membership to the authorized set in a non-traceable way.

Remark 6. Note that Definition 6 implies Definition 5 because an adversary that wins the anonymity game with non-negligible advantage can be used in both phases of the unlinkability game to win it with a non-negligible advantage.

2.1 Tools

For a given parameter λ, we will consider two hash functions H and G fixed and publicly known, both ranging on $\{0,1\}^{p(\lambda)}$ for some polynomial p.

Public Key Encryption Scheme. A public key encryption scheme is a triplet of polynomial time algorithms (KeyGen, Enc, Dec) such that

- KeyGen a probabilistic key generation algorithm, which on input the security parameter 1^λ outputs a key pair $(\mathsf{sk}, \mathsf{pk})$ (both of length polynomial in λ)

- Enc is a probabilistic encryption algorithm, which on input a plaintext message m and a public key pk gives as output a ciphertext c. Both plaintext and ciphertext can be represented as bitstrings of polynomial size in λ.
- Dec is a deterministic decryption algorithm which takes a ciphertext c and a secret key sk as input and outputs either a plaintext m corresponding to c or an error message $\perp$.

A public key encryption scheme should satisfy a minimal correctness property, namely, for every message m and for every key pair $(\mathsf{sk}, \mathsf{pk})$ output by the key generation algorithm, the decryption algorithm, queried on input $c = \mathsf{Enc}(m, \mathsf{pk})$ and sk, should output m (with overwhelming probability). For simplicity, we will assume the encryption scheme to have no decryption errors.

The standard security notions used to formalize security for public key encryption schemes build around the notion of indistinguishability or semantic security (IND). In a nutshell, security states that a polynomial time adversary has only negligible advantage in the security parameter when trying to figure out which of two adversarially selected messages corresponds to a given challenge ciphertext. In the so-called IND-CPA setting, the adversary is only passive, while an IND-CCA adversary has some (limited) access to a decryption oracle. See [44] for the exact definitions of these security properties.

Signature Scheme. A signature scheme SIG is a triplet of polynomial time algorithms $(\mathsf{SIG.Gen},\ \mathsf{SIG.Sign},\ \mathsf{SIG.Vfy})$ such that

- $\mathsf{SIG.Gen}$ is a probabilistic key generation algorithm, which on input the security parameter 1^λ outputs a key pair sk, vk (both of length polynomial in λ)
- $\mathsf{SIG.Sign}$ is a probabilistic signing algorithm, which on input a message m and a secret key sk produces a signature σ. Both message and signature can be represented as a bitstring of polynomial size in λ
- $\mathsf{SIG.Vfy}$ is a deterministic verification algorithm which given a signature σ, a message m and a public key vk as input, produces a binary input indicating whether the signature is valid or not.

The standard security notion for signature schemes is *strong existential unforgeability with chosen message attacks*, sEUF-CMA. Given an adversary $\mathcal{A}$, we will denote by $\mathsf{Adv}_{\mathsf{SIG}}(\mathcal{A})$ the probability of success of $\mathcal{A}$ in producing an existential forgery. See [45] for related formal definitions.

Commitment Scheme. A commitment scheme COMM is a triplet of probabilistic polynomial time algorithms $(\mathsf{COMM.Gen},\ \mathsf{COMM.Comm},\ \mathsf{COMM.Vfy})$ such that:

- $\mathsf{COMM.Gen}$ is a probabilistic key generation algorithm, which on input the security parameter 1^λ outputs a public committing key ck (of polynomial length in λ)
- $\mathsf{COMM.Comm}$, the committing algorithm, is a probabilistic algorithm which on input a message m and a committing key ck produces a commitment *comm* and an opening value *open* (again, both represented as bitstrings of polynomial size in λ).

- COMM.Vfy is a deterministic algorithm which given a commitment *comm* and an opening value *open* produces a binary input indicating whether their consistent or not.

For simplicity, in the above definition we will assume that the committed message m is explicitly encoded in *open*. In particular, the protocol below assumes $m == open$ to avoid the definition of a "decode" operation that extracts the committed message from *open*.

Informally a commitment scheme COMM is binding if it is not possible for an adversary to efficiently compute two different opening values consistent with the same commitment *comm*. Also, loosely speaking COMM is said to be hiding if each *comm* is a secure (in the sense of IND-CCA) encryption of the committed message m. Both security properties may be defined in either an information-theoretical (unconditional) or computational sense. We will denote by $\mathsf{AdvCOMM}^{B}(\lambda)$ and $\mathsf{AdvCOMM}^{H}(\lambda)$ the advantages of an adversary when trying to violate binding and hiding (respectively). Abusing notation, $\mathsf{AdvCOMM}^{H,B}(\lambda)$, will denote the advantage of violating any of the two security notions. Indeed, both advantages should be negligible functions in the security parameter, for any (computationally) secure commitment scheme. For precise definitions, for instance, Definitions 20.1 and 20.2 from [53].

Pseudorandom Keyed Hash Function Family. A keyed hash function family is a function $H^* : \mathcal{X} \times \mathcal{K} \longrightarrow \mathcal{Y}$, where $\mathcal{X}$, $\mathcal{Y}$ and $\mathcal{K}$ are respectively the domain, the range and the key space of H^*. Given $k \in \mathcal{K}$ and $x \in \mathcal{X}$, we will use the notation $H^*_k(x)$ for $H^*(x, k)$. The function H^* is said to be pseudorandom if, for randomly chosen $k \in \mathcal{K}$, it is computationally hard for an adversary with oracle access to $H^*_k(\cdot)$ to distinguish its outputs from those of a random function with domain $\mathcal{X}$ and range $\mathcal{Y}$. See for instance [43] for precise definitions.

3 Anonymous Authenticated Key Exchange

In this section we present a framework to instantiate A-AKE with generic cryptographic primitives described in the previous section. Later on, we introduce several instantiations based on concrete primitives attaining different levels of security and performance.

3.1 Main Idea

Our generic A-AKE is executed by the server S and a client C_i from a set of registered clients $\mathcal{C} = \{C_1, \ldots, C_n\}$. At each run, S can select a set of authorized clients $\mathcal{C}^{Auth} \subseteq \mathcal{C}$ which may vary from one execution to another; a pair-wise key for S and C_i is established if and only if $C_i \in \mathcal{C}^{Auth}$.

In a nutshell, the idea behind our construction is as follows: the session key is computed as $\mathsf{sk} = H(n_S \| n_i)$, where H is a hash function and n_S and n_i are fresh random nonces chosen by S and C_i, respectively. Our protocol design does not protect the secrecy of n_S, so the entropy of the session key relies solely on n_i. The mechanism we propose to preserve client's anonymity works as follows. The server encrypts l times the nonce n_S, once for each authorized client in $\mathcal{C}^{Auth}$, using an IND-CPA public key encryption scheme. Each of these l encryptions is produced under the public encryption key of each of the authorized clients; in this way, if C_i is in the authorized set, it is able to retrieve n_S from one of the ciphertexts and compute the session key. If no further measures were taken, the server could easily break client's anonymity. In particular, S could encrypt different nonces for different clients and, later on, when the session key is used, learn the client's identity from the derived key. To overcome this problem, we enforce that the server encrypts the same nonce in each of the ciphertexts.

Round 0: Server

Choose $\mathcal{C}^{Auth} \subseteq \mathcal{C}$
$\rho_S \leftarrow_\$$
$(comm, open) := \mathsf{COMM.Comm}(\rho_S)$
$m_0 = (\mathcal{C}^{Auth}, comm)$
$\sigma_0 := \mathsf{SIG.Sign}(\mathsf{sk}_S; m_0)$
Send $M_0 = (m_0, \sigma_0)$

Round 1: Client i

Parse M_0 as (m_0, σ_0)
Parse m_0 as $(\mathcal{C}^{Auth}, comm)$
Assert $\mathsf{SIG.Vfy}(\mathsf{vk}_S; m_0; \sigma_0) == 1$
$n_i, \rho_i \leftarrow_\$$
$(comm_i, open_i) := \mathsf{COMM.Comm}(n_i)$
Send $M_1 = (comm_i, \rho_i)$

Round 2: Server

Parse M_1 as $(comm_i, \rho_i)$
$(\mathsf{sk}^*, \mathsf{pk}^*) := \mathsf{CCAPKE.Gen}(1^\lambda)$
$n_S \leftarrow_\$, \quad \mathbb{C} := \emptyset$
For $j \in \mathcal{C}^{Auth}$:
  $r_j := H^*_{\rho_S}(\rho_i, j)$
  $c_j := \mathsf{PKE.Enc}(pk_j; n_S; r_j)$
  $\mathbb{C} := \mathbb{C} \cup \{c_j\}$
$m_2 := (\mathcal{C}^{Auth}, \mathbb{C}, \mathsf{pk}^*, comm_i)$
$\sigma_2 := \mathsf{SIG.Sign}(\mathsf{sk}_S; m_2)$
Send $M_2 = (m_2, \sigma_2)$

Round 3: Client i

Parse M_2 as (m_2, σ_2)
Parse m_2 as $(\mathcal{C}^{Auth}, \mathbb{C}, \mathsf{pk}^*, comm^*)$
Assert $i \in \mathcal{C}^{Auth}$
Assert $comm^* == comm_i$
Assert $\mathsf{SIG.Vfy}(\mathsf{vk}_S; m_2; \sigma_2) == 1$
$n_S := \mathsf{PKE.Dec}(sk_i; c_i)$
If $n_S == \bot$ then
  $valid := FALSE$
  $n_S \leftarrow_\$$
Else
  $valid := TRUE$
$(comm_S, open_S) := \mathsf{COMM.Comm}(n_S)$
Send $M_3 = comm_S$

Round 4: Server

$\sigma_4 = \mathsf{SIG.Sign}(\mathsf{sk}_S; open)$
Send $M_4 = (open, \sigma_4)$

Round 5: Client i

Assert $valid$
Parse M_4 as $(open, \sigma_4)$
Assert $\mathsf{SIG.Vfy}(\mathsf{vk}_S; open; \sigma_4) == 1$
Assert $\mathsf{COMM.Vfy}(comm; open) == 1$
For $c_j \in \mathbb{C} \setminus \{c_i\}$:
  $r_j := H^*_{open}(\rho_i, j)$
  Assert $\mathsf{PKE.Enc}(pk_j; n_S; r_j) == c_j$
$\mathsf{acc}_i := 1$
$\mathsf{pid}_i := \mathsf{pid}_i \cup \mathcal{C}^{Auth}$
$\mathsf{sk}_i := H(n_S \| n_i)$
$\mathsf{sid}_i := G(\mathsf{sk}_i)$
$ctx_i := \mathsf{CCAPKE.Enc}(\mathsf{pk}^*; (open_i, open_S))$
Send ctx_i

Round 6: Server

$(open_i, open_S) \leftarrow \mathsf{CCAPKE.Dec}(\mathsf{sk}^*; ctx_i)$
Assert $open_S == n_S$
Assert $\mathsf{COMM.Vfy}(comm_i; open_i) == 1$
Assert $\mathsf{COMM.Vfy}(comm_S; open_S) == 1$
$\mathsf{acc}_S := 1$
$\mathsf{pid}_i := pid_i \cup \mathcal{C}^{Auth}$
$\mathsf{sk}_S := H(n_S \| n_i)$
$\mathsf{sid}_S := G(\mathsf{sk}_S)$

Fig. 1. A-AKEprotocol. Input for client i is sk_i; input for the server is $\mathsf{sk}_S, \mathcal{C}^{Auth}$. Public keys are fetched from the PKI. Function "Assert" checks if the predicate is TRUE; otherwise it sets the acc variable to 0 and aborts.

This is achieved by making the server send, in a subsequent message, the randomness used to encrypt the ciphertexts. Hence, the client can use that randomness to re-encrypt the nonce n_S—retrieved by decrypting one of the ciphertexts—under each of the public keys of the authorized clients and check for equality with each of the ciphertexts previously sent by the server. If any of these checks fails, the client aborts the protocol.

3.2 Description

We assume the availability of a *public key infrastructure* (PKI) to generate and distribute keys; alternatively, the server and each client can generate their key pairs and register the public parts with the PKI. We denote with $(\mathsf{sk}_S, \mathsf{vk}_S)$ the signing and verification key of the server. We denote with (sk_i, pk_i) the secret and public key of the i-th client. Further, the PKI runs $\mathsf{ck} \leftarrow \mathsf{COMM.Gen}()$, and makes ck public, along with all generated public keys $\mathsf{vk}_S, pk_1, \ldots, pk_n$. The PKI also picks a keyed hash function family as defined in [43] and makes it public. All messages sent by the server to the client are authenticated by means of digital signatures; messages sent by the client are not authenticated. We stress that the set of authorized clients $\mathcal{C}^{Auth}$ is dynamic and defined by the server in the initialization round of the key-agreement protocol. Figure 1 shows the pseudocode of the key-agreement protocol. Next, we provide a round by round overview of the protocol and explain our design choices.

Round 0: The server S chooses the set $\mathcal{C}^{Auth}$ of authorized clients and a random ρ_S. computes a commitment *comm* to ρ_S and sends both $\mathcal{C}^{Auth}$ and *comm* to the client.[1] Note that ρ_S is later used to define the key to the hash function H^*.

Round 1: The client C_i chooses nonces n_i (as its contribution to the session key) and ρ_i (its contribution to the input of hash function H^*); next, it builds a commitment $comm_i$ to n_i and sends it to S, together with ρ_i.

Round 2: The server S chooses a nonce n_S as its contribution to the session key. Hence, for every $j \in \mathcal{C}^{Auth}$, the server constructs a ciphertext c_j that encrypts n_S under the public encryption key pk_j of C_j. We draw the randomness r_j used to compute c_j by evaluating the keyed hash H^* on (ρ_i, j) using ρ_S as the key. In addition, the server generates a key pair $(\mathsf{sk}^*, \mathsf{pk}^*)$ for an IND-CCA PKE, that will be used later to establish a confidential communication channel from the client to the server. Finally S signs and sends to the client a message containing the ciphertexts $c_{i_1}, \ldots, c_{i_l}$, the public key pk^*, the set of authorized clients $\mathcal{C}^{Auth}$ and the commitment received from the client in Round 1.

Round 3: If $C_i \in \mathcal{C}^{Auth}$, it decrypts c_i to get nonce n_S, computes a commitment $comm_S$ to n_S and sends it to the server. If (despite being authorized) client C_i cannot obtain a valid decryption, it commits to a random value (and will subsequently abort in Round 5). Note that an authorized client will reply

[1] In practical deployments, we would expect the client to start the communication with an "start" message. We omit this message to improve readability.

with a commitment (instead of simply sending back the challenge n_S) in order to remain anonymous; otherwise the server could encrypt different nonces for different clients and tell the client identity from the nonce sent back by the client.

Round 4: The server opens its commitment to ρ_S.

Round 5: For each j, the client evaluates $H^*_{\rho_S}$ on the value (ρ_i, j) to recover the randomness r_j. Hence, the client re-encrypts n_S under pk_j and checks for equality with c_j received at Round 2. If any of the ciphertexts computed locally differs from the one received at Round 2, the client aborts: the server may have encrypted different nonces for different clients in an attempt to de-anonymize the client. Note that at this stage C_i also aborts if ciphertext c_i decrypted in Round 3 was not valid (in any case, the server will not be able to tell the difference). Otherwise the client sends the opening values of commitments $comm_i$ and $comm_S$ to the server, encrypted under pk^*. Encryption ensures that the nonce n_i is hidden from other parties, including the rest of authorized clients. Finally C_i sets the session key as $\mathsf{sk} = H(n_S \| n_i)$.

Round 6: The server retrieves n_S and n_i from the opening values and checks if n_S is equal to the nonce encrypted in Round 2. If this is the case, S computes the session key as $\mathsf{sk} = H(n_S \| n_i)$.

Remark 7. In the above description and in Fig. 1 we make explicit the randomness used to encrypt the nonce n_S. That is, we write $\mathsf{PKE.Enc}(\mathsf{pk}; m; r)$ to denote the encryption of message m under public key pk using randomness r. Thus, the resulting ciphertext can be seen as a deterministic function of those three inputs.

Remark 8. Note that the protocol overhead is dominated by the encryption/decryption and transmission of the l ciphertexts created by the server. In Sect. 6 we show how this overhead can be reduced by using broadcast encryption.

4 Security

We now state the theorems regarding the security of the A-AKE protocol of the previous section, the corresponding proofs can be found in the Appendix.

Theorem 1 (Key Secrecy). *Let* PKE *be an IND-CPA secure public key encryption scheme, H^* a pseudorandom keyed hash function,* CCAPKE *an IND-CCA secure public key encryption scheme,* SIG *a signature scheme attaining sEUF-CMA security and* COMM *a secure commitment scheme (all according to definitions in Sect. 2.1). Then, the protocol described in Fig. 1 is a* A-AKE *achieving key secrecy in the sense of Definition 3 in the random oracle model.*

Theorem 2 (Anonymity and Unlinkability). *Let* PKE *be an IND-CPA secure public key encryption scheme, H^* a pseudorandom keyed hash function,* CCAPKE *an IND-CCA secure public key encryption scheme,* SIG *a signature scheme attaining sEUF-CMA security and* COMM *a secure commitment scheme (all according to definitions in Sect. 2.1). Then, the protocol described in Fig. 1 is a* A-AKE *achieving both anonymity and unlinkability in the sense of Definitions 5 and 6.*

5 Implementation and Evaluation

In this section, we present several prototypes of the protocol presented in Fig. 1. Each prototype uses a different set of cryptographic primitives. In particular, we implemented one pre-quantum version of the A-AKE protocol and six post-quantum ones. All prototypes were written in Rust. Experiments were executed on a machine with an AMD EPYC^{TM} 7002P (Rome) 2.5 GHz processor with 256 GB of RAM.

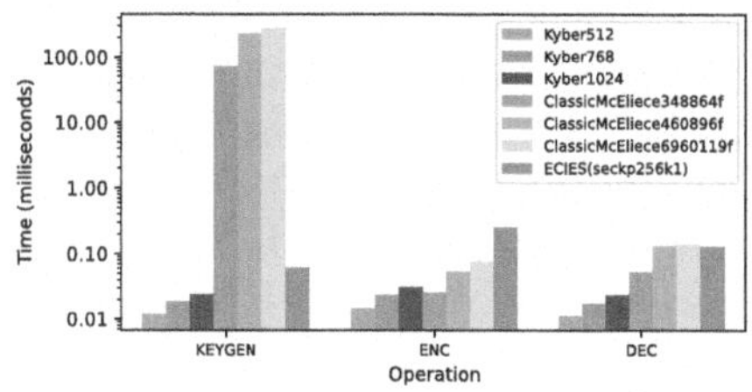

Fig. 2. Runtime comparison of key-generation, encryption and decryption for the encryption schemes we consider.

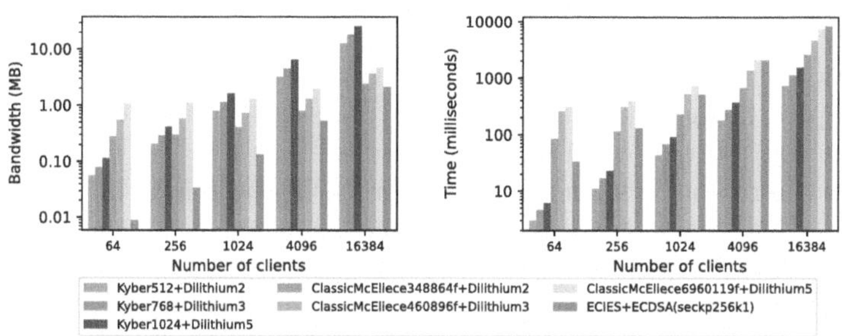

Fig. 3. Bandwidth (left) and runtime (right) comparison of the different prototypes as the number of authorized clients increases.

Common Tools. We have used the same symmetric tools for all implementations. Commitments were implemented by means of a hash function H, that is, $\mathsf{COMM.Comm}(m) = (H(m, r), r)$ is the commitment of message m for a random nonce r; H was set to SHA256 for the pre-quantum implementation and SHA3-256 for the post-quantum ones.

Pre-quantum Prototype. For encryption, we used ECIES (a hybrid encryption scheme in the so-called KEM-DEM paradigm) standardized in ANSI X9.63, IEEE 1363a, ISO/IEC 18033-2, and SECG SEC-1. For signatures, we used ECDSA (fixing the same parameter set for both primitives, `secp256k1` – see [18]). We selected the library 'ecies-rs' [23] for ECIES and 'k256' [50] for ECDSA. The former relies internally on the 'aes-gcm' [49] library to perform the symmetric operations of the hybrid scheme.

Post-quantum Prototypes. The post-quantum implementations use Kyber and Classic McEliece as KEMs and Dilithium as the signature scheme. Both Kyber and Dilithium are among the first schemes to be standardized by NIST [41], and Classic McEliece is following the NIST standardization process, standing out for providing small sized ciphertexts. We used the implementations available in LibOQS [42]. Among all available parameter sets for the KEMs, we selected Kyber512 and ClassicMcEliece348864f (level 1 as defined by NIST [40]), Kyber768 and ClassicMcEliece460896f (level 3), and Kyber1024 and ClassicMcEliece6960119f (level 5). We selected only a subset of all possible KEM+Signature combinations, attending to the security level of each primitive.[2] We derive a public key scheme by combining KEM and DEM, as in [20]. In our implementations, the DEM is provided by AES-GCM via the 'aes-gcm' [49] library.

5.1 Evaluation

We run a set of experiments to evaluate runtime and bandwidth requirements of our prototypes. When comparing the pre-quantum implementation (namely, ECIES+ECDSA) with the post-quantum ones, we refer to the post-quantum variants with the lowest level of security[3] so to have a fair comparison.

First, we measure (see Fig. 2) the time it takes to generate a key pair, encrypt, and decrypt a message for all of the encryption schemes we consider. We run each operation 100 times and report the average.

Kyber shows the best performance for each operation. In terms of key-generation, ECIES is 4 times worse than Kyber whereas Classic McEliece has the worst performance with 6000 times slow-down compared to Kyber. Further, Classic McEliece performs better than ECIES for encryption but decryption time is similar.

In the following experiments, we let l, the number of authorized clients, range from $2^6 = 64$ to $2^{14} = 16384$. For each setting, we run each experiment 100 times and report the average. In terms of bandwidth (Fig. 3, left), ECIES+ECDSA shows the best performance (0.0083 MB for $l = 64$, 0.13 MB for $l = 1024$, and 2.02 MB for $l = 16384$) but the gap with the variants based on Classic McEliece shrinks as the number of authorized clients increases. For example, the version that uses ClassicMcEliece348864f + Dilithium2 has a bandwidth requirement of 2.36 MB for $l = 16384$. The versions based on Kyber have lower bandwidth requirements than the ones based on Classic McEliece up to 512 authorized

[2] Namely, Kyber512+Dilithium2, ClassicMcEliece460896f+Dilithium2, Kyber768+Dilithium3, ClassicMcEliece460896f+Dilithium3, Kyber1024+Dilithium5, and ClassicMcEliece6960119f+Dilithium5.

[3] Kyber512+Dilithium2 or ClassicMcEliece460896f+Dilithium2.

clients. For larger numbers of authorized clients, the versions based on Kyber show the worse performance and requires around 10 MB for 16384 authorized clients. This is because the server sends one public key and l ciphertexts in Round 2. Classic McEliece has larger public keys but shorter ciphertexts compared to Kyber. Hence, for small values of l, the size of the Classic McEliece public key accounts for large fraction of the bytes sent by the server.

In terms of CPU time (Fig. 3, right), variants based on Kyber have the best performance (45 ms for $l = 1024$ or 750 ms for $l = 16384$). The variants based on Classic McEliece show the worse performance for small number of clients ($l \leq 1024$) whereas ECIES+ECDSA is the variant that performs the worse for larger values of l. The poor performance of variants based on Classic McEliece when l is small, is due to public key that the server must generate in Round 2.

Figure 4 breaks down the CPU time for each round of the protocol. Operations in Rounds 0, 1, 4, and 6 are independent of l and take at most 1 ms CPU time regardless of the cryptographic primitives used. Round 0 and round 4 exhibit roughly the same CPU time, dominated by signature generation. Round 1 is not shown in Fig. 4 since its CPU complexity is negligible and we wanted to keep the same y-axis for all rounds. During round 6, the server decrypts a ciphertext and verifies two commitments. The variants based on Kyber performs the best with less than 0.025 ms. This is because decryption in Kyber is faster than the same operation with Classic McEliece ciphertexts.

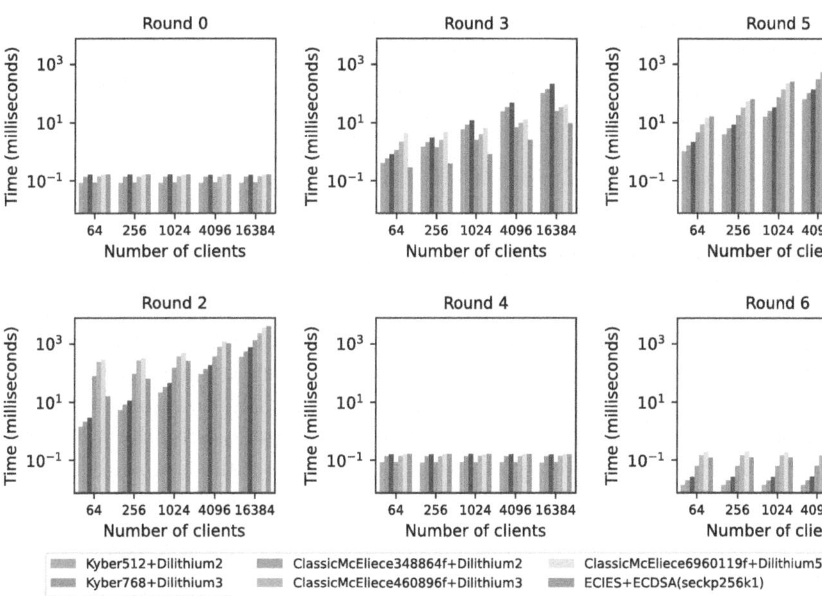

Fig. 4. Runtime of each round of the protocol in terms of the number of clients for each of the primitives we consider. Measurements for Round 1 are in the order of nanoseconds and are not visible.

Round 2 is the most involved one. In that round, Kyber-based variants show the best performance. Variants based on Classic McEliece perform worse than the ECIES+ECDSA one for small number of clients and this is due to the time it takes to generate a public key as described above. During Round 3, the client verifies the signature over the ciphertexts received in the previous round. This takes from a few ms for $l = 64$ to up to 200 ms for $l = 16384$. It is interesting to note the performance difference between Kyber+Dilithium and Classic McEliece+Dilithium even if they use the same signature scheme. This is because of the time it takes to process the signed message: the message is essentially a set of ciphertexts and Kyber ciphertexts have larger size compared to the ones of Classic McEliece. During Round 6, the server decrypts one ciphertext and verifies two commitments. Our results are line with the ones in Fig. 2: variants based on Kyber perform the best; performance of the ECIES-based variant is similar to the performance of the variants based on Classic McEliece.

Summary. We conclude that the choice of the primitives depends on the required security level, the number of authorized clients, and the available bandwidth. Notably, post-quantum security does not impact computational overhead; Kyber-based variants showed the best performance, even against the A-AKE variant based on less secure ECIES. This may be partially due to the maturity of the libraries we have used. The LibOQS library is a highly optimized one, due to the continuous focus on providing high-performance post-quantum primitives [42]. On the other side, post-quantum security has an impact on bandwidth as the number of bytes sent for PQ variants is 1.12 to 31 times worse than the bandwidth requirement of the A-AKE based on ECIES+ECDSA. We note, however, that the maximum bandwidth in our experiment was roughly 10 MBs (Kyber1024+Dilithium5) and that takes roughly 100 ms at 800 Mb/s speed.

6 Discussion

6.1 Protocol Variant Using Broadcast Encryption

Both the theoretical overhead evaluation of our protocol (Sect. 3) and the evaluation of the prototype (Sect. 5) show that the protocol bottleneck is the number of ciphertexts sent in Round 2. We now present an extension of the protocol from Sect. 3 which makes use of Broadcast Encryption (BE) to reduce the number of ciphertexts the server sends in Round 2 and, consequently, the number of ciphertexts a client needs to verify in Round 5. We first recall the so-called *Complete Subtree scheme* underlying this extension and then describe the proposed modifications to our protocol.

Symmetric Broadcast Encryption: Complete Subtree Scheme. Naor et al., introduce in [38] the so called *Subset-Cover framework*, which offers a unified treatment of several broadcast symmetric encryption schemes (e.g., [37,38]). This primitive allows a server to send an encrypted message to a group of clients, in such a way that only the members of certain subset of *authorized* clients are able to decrypt. Each time an encrypted message is broadcasted, the set of non-authorized or *revoked* clients may be chosen by the server. In a nutshell, the framework works as follows: the set of clients $\{C_1, \ldots, C_n\}$ is covered by a collection of subsets $\{S_j\}_{j \in J}$ and each of these subsets S_j is associated with a symmetric key k_j. In the setup phase each client C_i receives the key k_j for every subset S_j of the cover such that $C_i \in S_j$. Whenever the server S needs to broadcast a message for a set of authorized clients $\mathcal{C}^{Auth}$, a subcover $\{S_j\}_{j \in J'}$ (with $J' \subseteq J$) is determined in such a way that $\mathcal{C}^{Auth} = \cup_{j \in J'} S_j$. Then the plaintext is encrypted once for every key in $\{k_j\}_{j \in J'}$; in this way only clients in $\mathcal{C}^{Auth}$ are able to decrypt. One of the instantiations proposed in [38] is the *Complete Subtree (CS) scheme*. Here, clients $\{C_1, \ldots, C_n\}$ are assigned to leaves of a balanced binary tree. For each vertex v_j of this tree, consider the maximal subtree S_j rooted at that vertex. The cover $\{S_j\}_{j \in J}$ consists of all these subtrees. Naor et al. show that each client stores $log(n)$ keys and that any subset of clients may be covered with at most $r \cdot log(n/r)$ subtrees, where r is the number of non-authorized clients.

Modified Protocol Using the Complete Subtree Scheme. Once all n clients are registered, the PKI constructs the binary tree previously described, with one leaf per client. For each node v_j of the tree, the PKI runs $(sk_j, pk_j) \leftarrow \mathsf{PKE.Gen}(1^\lambda)$, makes public all the keys $\{pk_j\}_{j \in J}$ and securely transfers to each client the $log(n)$ secret keys corresponding to subtrees covering the client's leaf.

In a run of the A-AKE protocol (Fig. 1), during Round 2 the server computes a cover $\{S_j\}_{j \in J'}$ of the set of all authorized clients. Then, instead of sending the ciphertexts $c_{i_1}, \ldots, c_{i_l}$ for the original protocol, computes a ciphertext $c_j \leftarrow \mathsf{PKE.Enc}(pk_j, n_S; r_j)$ for each $j \in J'$. In Round 3, when a client needs to decrypt a ciphertext, it chooses one it is able to decrypt with one of its $log(n)$ secret keys. The rest of the protocol remains unchanged.

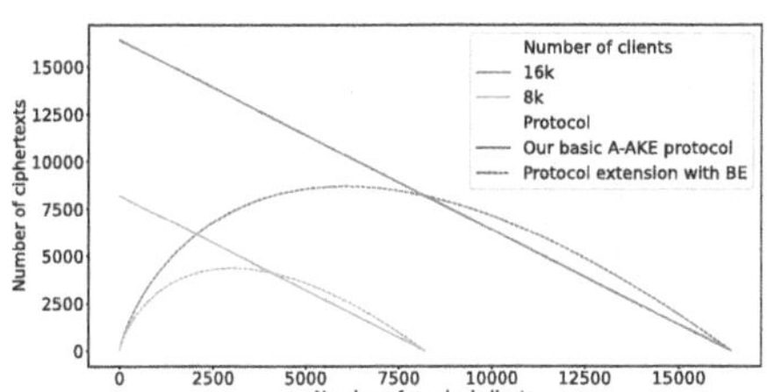

Fig. 5. Comparison between our basic A-AKE protocol and the BE extension.

Performance Improvement. Compared to the protocol of Fig. 1, the protocol just described reduces the number of ciphertexts (sent by the server in Round 2 and verified by the client in Round 5) from n to $r \cdot log(n/r)$, where r is the size of the set of non-authorized (revoked) clients, i.e., $r = |\mathcal{C} \setminus \mathcal{C}^{Auth}|$. At the same time, the number of keys held by each client increases from 1 to $log(n)$. Figure 5 shows the number of ciphertexts sent as a function of the number of revoked clients, both for our basic protocol of Fig. 1 and the BE extension described in this section. Results are shown for $n = 2^{13} \approx 8k$ and $n = 2^{14} \approx 16k$ clients. It can be seen that, for $r \leq n/2$ the BE extension performs better (in the sense of producing less ciphertexts) than the basic protocol, with big gains for small values of r. For example, for $n = 2^{14}$, and $r = 128$ the number of ciphertexts produced in the basic protocol is $c_B = 16256$ while the number of ciphertexts for the BE extension is $c_{BE} = 896$; for $r = 1024$ we have $c_B = 15360$ and $c_{BE} = 4096$, while for $r = 4096$, the number of ciphertexts is $c_B = 12288$ and $c_{BE} = 8192$. Note that, our BE extension allows to manage $n = 2^{14}$ clients in the worst case with roughly the same number of ciphertexts than the basic protocol needs for the worst case with half the clients, that is $n = 2^{13}$.

6.2 Alternative Constructions I

The basic idea of the protocol in Fig. 1 is to securely transfer a nonce from the server to the client while making sure that (i) only a client in the authorized set can recover the nonce, and that (ii) the same nonce is encrypted under all ciphertexts. Condition (i) guarantees client authentication, whereas condition (ii) ensures client anonymity. We could replace the encryption scheme of Fig. 1 used to send the server's nonce with any other encryption scheme that guarantees the above conditions. In the following we review some schemes that seem suitable for our problem and discuss advantages and shortcomings.

Public Key Encryption with Equality Test. One option is to send one ciphertext per client and use an encryption scheme that allows to check equality of messages under two ciphertexts.[4]

Such a scheme was proposed by Yang et al., [55] with the name of Public Key Encryption with Equality Testing (PKE-ET). In a nutshell, PKE-ET is defined as a tuple of algorithms (`keygen, enc, dec, test`) where the first three are the usual algorithms that define PKE and `test` is an algorithm that accepts two ciphertexts and outputs 1 if the two underlying plaintexts are equal. The scheme in [55] uses pairing for encryption, decryption, and equality testing. Further, the security definition of [55] only cover soundness for valid ciphertexts. That is one cannot produce two valid ciphertexts ctx, ctx', with different plaintexts, such that $\texttt{test}(ctx, ctx') = 1$. Nevertheless, no soundless guarantees are given if either ciphertext is not valid (i.e., not decryptable). In our settings, it means that a malicious server may be able to produce two ciphertexts ctx, ctx' such that only one decrypts correctly but $\texttt{test}(ctx, ctx') = 1$; hence the server can de-anonymize the client based on the fact that the client completes the protocol or aborts.

Plaintext-Checkable Encryption. Canard et al., [16], introduce the notion of Plaintext Checkable Encryption where a public `test` algorithm allows to test

[4] Note that such a scheme cannot satisfy the usual indistinguishability notion since the adversary can always test if the challenge ciphertext encrypts one of its chosen challenge messages. Nevertheless, ciphertexts in our scheme encrypt high-entropy nonces so that a weaker one-way security notion for the encryption scheme is sufficient.

if a putative message is encrypted under a ciphertext. Note that the security definitions of [16] include completeness and soundness, so that the above attack where one of the ciphertext is invalid is no longer viable. We could use PCE to encrypt the server's nonce under each of the client's keys. The client may decrypt the ciphertext encrypted under its key to obtain nonce n_S, and later use the `test` algorithm to check that (i) all ciphertexts are valid, and (ii) all ciphertexts encrypt the same message.

Verifiable Broadcast Encryption. Broadcast Encryption (BE) allows to reduce communication complexity due to the message sent by the server. *Verifiable* BE schemes are allow a party to tell if all potential recipients would decrypt the same message [22,27]. BEs that allow verifiability are the ones of Boneh, Gentry and Waters [9] and the one of Naor [39]. With verifiable BE we obtain a server's message of fixed size, at the cost of a public key that is linear in the number of clients. Further, the verifiable BE scheme of [9] uses bilinear maps and it is only secure against static adversaries.

6.3 Alternative Constructions II

Anonymous AKE protocols can be designed by combining an anonymous authentication scheme with a key-exchange (KE) protocol. In practice, client and server run a KE protocol (e.g., DHKE) and the client authenticates its messages by using an anonymous authentication scheme. In the following we review possible anonymous authentication schemes along with pros and cons when using them to build an A-AKE.

Group Signatures. In a Group Signature (GS) scheme [6], a group manager grants clients the ability to sign messages on behalf of the group, so that signatures are publicly verifiable but do not leak the identity of the signer. Group signatures are ill-suited for building anonymous AKE protocols because the group manager can reveal the identity of a signer. In practice, building an anonymous AKE by means of KE+GS requires a trusted third party as group manager.

Direct Anonymous Attestation. Direct Anonymous Attestation (DAA) [13] is a privacy-enhanced version of group signatures where anonymity cannot be revoked, not even by the group manager. Hence, one may build anonymous AKE protocols by means of KE+DAA where the server act as the DAA group manager (see, for instance, [54]). Available DAA protocols are based on pairings and designed for powerful clients (e.g., Intel workstations) [14]. Post-quantum DAA protocols have been proposed based on lattices [31], but they are still not practical as a signature takes hundreds of MBs. Boneh et al. [8], show how to build EPID—a variant of DAA—by using only symmetric-key primitives with signature sizes of a few MBs.

One subtle issue that arises when using DAA or EPID (as well as group signatures), is that clients have no guarantees on the size of the group (that is essentially their anonymity set). A malicious group manager could assign each client to a different group, thereby trivially breaking anonymity. A PKI and a public bulletin board would allow clients to verify that they all belong to the same group.

Ring Signatures. Ring Signatures (RS) are a sort of decentralized version of group signatures [7]. Ring signatures require no group manager, each user can sign (anonymously) on behalf of a "ring" of users, and the ring is arbitrarily chosen by the signer at signature time. Available ring signature schemes have signature size that is logarithmic in the size of the ring [36]. Post-quantum ring signature schemes have signatures that take few MBs [21]. Using ring signatures to build an anonymous AKE, requires a PKI for a client to fetch other client public keys to be included in its ring. A construction along these lines can be found in [19] for the group setting; i.e., there two users from a given group can establish a shared secret key without disclosing their identity to each other, just ensuring the membership to the prescribed group.

We also note that there are many (post-quantum) PKE but only few (post-quantum) ring signatures. Hence, our approach provides greater flexibility when choosing how to instantiate the scheme. Further, most post-quantum ring signatures leverage a NIZK that is taxing on the client. For example, the signature scheme in [32] requires 2.8 s to sign with a ring of 1024 members. If this scheme is combined with AKE, one should expect additional client time to process AKE-messages plus time required by the server. Our approach for the same number of clients takes <100 ms overall, when using Kyber+Dilithium.

6.4 Further Discussion

Applications. A-AKE strikes a balance between access control policies defined by the server and client anonymity. Application scenarios where A-AKE can be used include whistle-blowing platforms, anonymous online forums and IoT/VANETs applications. Regarding whistle-blowing platforms, previous work has shown that anonymity may affect credibility of reports [56,57]. A-AKE may allow only credible users (e.g., only company employees for whistle-blowing platforms set up to reveal wrongdoings within a company) to publish information, while published data remains anonymous. Similarly, previous work has shown that anonymous interactions on university forums improve participation (in terms of quantity, quality and length of posts) [15,48]. Hence, forum administrators may have an incentive in allowing user to remain anonymous while, at the same time, ensuring that only enrolled students may post content. In the context of IoT and VANETS, previous work has explored different mechanism for authorized-yet-anonymous reporting [35,58], including the use of anonymous credentials [51]. Similar authentication and anonymity guarantees may be provided by A-AKE.

Collusion with Authorized Clients. A-AKE cannot withstand non-authorized parties that collude with an authorized client. For example, in our protocol, a non-authorized party i may run the protocol with the server and ask an authorized client to decrypt one of the ciphertexts encrypting n_S—sent by the server during round 2. Knowledge of n_i (chosen during round 1) and of n_S

(received from a colluding authorized client) allows party i to a establish session key with the server. Our definition of freshness (see Definition 2) rules out such attacks by forbidding active adversaries (i.e., those that use the Send oracle) from corrupting authorized clients (see Remark 3).

Identifying Misbehaving Clients. A-AKE is vulnerable to attacks where an authorized client misbehaves by sharing the session key with another party (e.g., with another client that is not within the set of authorized clients).[5] We note that no key-establishment protocol is immune to a client that leaks the session key K.[6] Nevertheless, if the AKE server learns that K has been misused, it can identify the client engaged in the key-exchange protocol that output K. Due to the anonymity provisions of A-AKE, the server cannot identify the misbehaving client within the set of authorized clients. Mitigating this weakness requires "traitor tracing" solutions that, in turn, require a trusted third party that revokes anonymity of misbehaving clients. For example, client C_i may provide the server with a ciphertext c encrypting public key pk_i—under the public key of the tracing authority; the client should also prove that the ciphertext was honestly generated—i.e., it encrypts one of the authorized public keys—and prove knowledge of the secret key sk_i corresponding to pk_i. In case of misbehavior, the server can issue a request to the tracing authority that can decrypt c to identify the misbehaving client. We leave extensions to A-AKE to mitigate such issues as future work.

Complexity Comparison. We now briefly discuss the complexity of A-AKE—in terms of message flows—with that of some of the protocols included in Table 1.

AKE protocols, such as [28], take as little as two message flows and rely on key-encapsulation schemes and digital signatures. OS-AKE protocols like `ntor` [26] take two flows and use DH-like key exchange. State-of-the-art PPAKE protocols [46] use four flows and relies on rather standard cryptographic tools, such as, public key encryption, symmetric encryption and signature schemes.

A-AKE takes 7 flows and also uses standard cryptographic primitives (e.g., public key encryption—both IND-CPA and IND-CCA—a signature scheme and a commitment scheme).

All of these protocols assume a PKI to distribute certified public keys to all parties; OS-AKE uses the PKI only to certify the server's public key.

From the above discussion we conclude that privacy has an impact on the complexity of key-exchange protocols. For example, AKE protocols with no privacy are less complex that PPAKE protocols that provide privacy with respect to external parties. In turn, PPAKE protocols are less complex than A-AKE protocols that provide privacy with respect to external parties and the server.

---

[5] In our construction, the authorized client may as well leak n_i chosen during Round 1 and n_S obtained during round 3; knowledge of n_i and n_S allow any party to compute the session key.

[6] Unless the session key is computed and used in secure hardware like smart-cards.

7 Conclusions

Anonymous Authenticate Key Exchange (A-AKE) protocols strike a balance between client authentication of classical Authenticated Key Exchange protocols and client anonymity of One-Sided Authenticated Key Exchange protocols. A-AKE allows the server to freely decide which clients are authorized to establish a key with the server and, at the same time, keeps a client anonymous within the set of authorized clients. We have introduced a formal model for A-AKE that captures forward anonymity and unlinkability, apart from the classical key-secrecy property of key exchange protocols. We have also presented a general framework to build A-AKE by means of well established primitives. We have used our framework to instantiate A-AKE protocols in both pre-quantum and post-quantum settings. We have developed several prototypes and presented their performance by means of experiments.

Acknowledgments. This work has been partially funded by project CMAT-QREAL (reference 2024/00281/013) of the Spanish Agencia Estatal de Investigación and by NATO SPS project 5985. Further, this work has been partially been funded by the European Union (HORIZON-CL4-2022 P2CODE project No 101093069). The views and opinions expressed are those of the authors only and do not necessarily reflect those of the European Union or the European Research Council Executive Agency. Neither the European Union nor the granting authority can be held responsible for them.

A Appendix: Proofs

A.1 Proof for Theorem 1

The proof is set up in terms of several experiments or games, where a challenger interacts with the adversary confronting it with a counterfeit Test-challenge in the spirit of Definition 3.

In the sequel, we denote by qexe the number of $\mathsf{Execute}$ calls made by the adversary. Also, qsend will denote the number of Send queries. Similarly, qro_F will denote the number of queries $\mathcal{A}$ makes to a hash function $F \in \{H, G\}$.

We will denote by $\mathsf{Adv}_{\mathsf{SIG}}(\lambda)$ the advantage of an adversary aiming at violating the sEUF-CMA of SIG, by $\mathsf{Adv}_{\mathsf{PKE}}(\lambda)$ the advantage of an adversary aiming at violating the IND-CPA security of PKE and by $\mathsf{Adv}_{\mathsf{CCAPKE}}(\lambda)$ the advantage of an adversary aiming at violating the IND-CCA security of CCAPKE.

Similarly, $\mathsf{Adv}^{H}_{\mathsf{COMM}}(\lambda)$ will denote the advantage of an adversary violating the indistinguishability property of the commitment scheme COMM, while $\mathsf{Adv}^{B}_{\mathsf{COMM}}(\lambda)$ will denote his probability of violating the corresponding binding property.

Game 0. This first game corresponds to a real attack, in which all the parameters are chosen as in the actual scheme. By definition, $\mathsf{Adv}(\mathcal{A}, G_0) = \mathsf{Adv}(\mathcal{A})$.

Game 1.

In this game the hash functions H, G are simulated as Random Oracles; indeed, then the Random Oracle assumption implies that

$$\mathsf{Adv}(\mathcal{A}, G_1) = \mathsf{Adv}(\mathcal{A}, G_0)$$

Game 2.

This game will now abort with a gain for the adversary, if any of the messages the Client receives from Rounds 0, 2 or 4 (namely, M_0, M_2 or M_4) is not generated by the Server, yet accepted by the client. Clearly,

$$|\mathsf{Adv}(\mathcal{A}, G_2) - \mathsf{Adv}(\mathcal{A}, G_1)| \leq \mathsf{qsend} \cdot \mathsf{Adv}_{\mathsf{SIG}}(\lambda)$$

Game 3.

We change the simulation as follows: whenever the Client accepts a message in Round 2 (namely, M_2) replied from another session, it aborts with a win from the adversary. As M_2 contains a signature of M_1, a reply will only be accepted by the client if σ_2 is a valid signature for M_1, which happens with negligible probability (that of having a replayed a session handling the same commitment $comm_i$—even if it doesn't come from the same client's nonce n_i). Thus, either a certain client generated his nonce exactly as n_i or a different nonce n_i^* consistent with the commitment $comm_i$

$$|\mathsf{Adv}(\mathcal{A}, G_3) - \mathsf{Adv}(\mathcal{A}, G_2)| \leq negl(\lambda) + \mathsf{qsend} \cdot \mathsf{Adv}^B_{\mathsf{COMM}}(\lambda)$$

Game 4.

We change the simulation as follows: whenever the Client accepts a message in Round 4 (namely M_4) replied from another session (i.e., generated by the Server, but not fresh), we abort with a win for the adversary. Indeed, the checks in Round 5 step 3 will be successful if and only if for all $j \in \mathsf{pid}_S$ it holds $H^*_{\rho_S}(\rho_i, j) = H^*_{\bar{\rho}}(\bar{\rho}_i, j)$, where ρ_S is chosen by the Server in Round 2 of the tested instance, $\bar{\rho}$ is the nonce chosen by the server in the replayed session and $\bar{\rho}_i$ the corresponding input chosen by client i.

The probability of success in this Game for $\mathcal{A}$ differs only negligibly from the previous Game, as it is bounded by the probability of two evaluations of H^*,– under different keys and on different (known) inputs – to be equal. Due to the pseudorandomness property of H^* this probability is negligible in λ, as is the probability of two independent and uniformly chosen elements on the range of H^* to be equal. As a result,

$$|\mathsf{Adv}(\mathcal{A}, G_4) - \mathsf{Adv}(\mathcal{A}, G_3)| \leq negl(\lambda)$$

Game 5. This game will now abort with a gain for the adversary if M_3 in Round 3 is replied from another session and yet the Server accepts the session key in Round 6.

Now, in order to have $comm_S$ accepted in Round 6, the Server must have obtained a convincing M_5 containing a consistent $open_S$ value with the nonce

n_S selected by him in Round 2. Note the adversary may know the nonce $\overline{n_S}$ generated by the server in the replied session; however, due to the binding property of the commitment scheme, no opening value can be both consistent with n_S and $\bar{n_S}$ (so that the check in step 4 of Round 6 succeeds) unless these nonces are identical. As a result:

$$|\mathsf{Adv}(\mathcal{A}, G_5) - \mathsf{Adv}(\mathcal{A}, G_4)| \leq \mathsf{qsend} \cdot \mathsf{Adv}^{B}_{\mathsf{COMM}}(\lambda).$$

Gamo 6.

This game will now abort with a gain for the adversary, if the message sent in Round 3 is adversarially generated and yet the Server accepts the session key in Round 6.

Let $\mathcal{A}$ be an adversary succeeding in such task; the it must have either violated the binding property of COMM or have gained information about n_S from:

a) an actual message $M_3 = comm_S$ constructed by the client,
b) the ciphertexts $(c_{i_1}, \dots, c_{i_l})$.

Note that these are the only options; $\mathcal{A}$ cannot get a secret key from an authorized client l to decrypt c_l without violating freshness. First, a) is excluded by the hiding property of COMM. Second, to see why b) is also excluded, note that unless the adversary violates the pseudorandomness property of H^*, $(c_{i_1}, \dots, c_{i_l})$ are IND-CPA encryptions of the same value. Assuming this is so, if $\mathcal{A}$ gains information about n_S from them (i.e., if b) is the case), we may derive an adversary $\mathcal{B}$ from him, able to violate the IND-CPA security of the encryption scheme PKE.

Indeed, given any two messages m_0 and m_1, suppose c_b is an (IND-CPA) challenge ciphertext for an adversary $\mathcal{B}$. Now, $\mathcal{B}$ sets $c_1 := c_b$ and simulates the first two rounds of our Generic Protocol with one only client U_1, using m_0 as server's nonce n_S and interacting with $\mathcal{A}$, which goal is to produce a valid commitment to n_S. Then, if $\mathcal{A}$ does not succeed, $\mathcal{B}$ will assume the encrypted message was m_1, and thus output $b = 1$.

$$|\mathsf{Adv}(\mathcal{A}, G_6) - \mathsf{Adv}(\mathcal{A}, G_5)| \leq \mathsf{Adv}_{H^*,\mathrm{PRF}}(\lambda) + \mathsf{Adv}_{\mathsf{PKE}}(\lambda) + \mathsf{AdvCOMM}^{H,B}(\lambda)$$

where $\mathsf{Adv}_{H^*,\mathrm{PRF}}(\lambda)$ denotes the probability of violating the pseudorandomness property of H^*.

Game 7.

This game will now abort with a gain for the adversary, if the message sent in Round 5 is replayed from another session or adversarially generated and yet the Server accepts the session key in Round 6.

By the binding property of COMM, note that the message M_5 must be consistent with M_3, which can at this point only have been produced by the client (thus, from the correct n_S). We can argue as in the previous game that he cannot have information on n_S unless he has gained it from

a) the (honestly generated) $M_3 = comm_S$

b) the ciphertexts $(c_{i_1}, \ldots, c_{i_l})$.

Moreover, if he has no information on n_S then the probability that he can produce a ciphertext ctx_i^* passing the checks of Round 6 is bounded by the IND-CCA security of CCAPKE. Indeed, let $\mathcal{R}$ be the relation defined by the checks in Round 6; an adversary producing a message M_5 that passes all checks from Round 6 without holding any information on n_s would necessarily violate malleability w.r.t. ctx_i and, as a result,

$$|\mathsf{Adv}(\mathcal{A}, G_7) - \mathsf{Adv}(\mathcal{A}, G_6)| \leq \mathsf{Adv}_{\mathsf{PKE}}(\lambda) + \mathsf{AdvCOMM}^H(\lambda) + \mathsf{Adv}_{\mathsf{CCAPKE}}(\lambda)$$

Game 8. This game will now abort with a gain for the adversary, if M_1 is adversarially generated or replied from another session and yet the Server accepts the session key in Round 6. Note that this cannot happen: given that now all other interchanged messages are honestly generated by the corresponding parties, the actual $comm_i$ is included in M_2 and if this is not consistent with M_1 the client will reject the execution in Round 3.

Note that from this point on we can assume all messages come from legitimate parties and so the adversary can be considered passive.

Game 9. Now the simulation changes in that M_1 and M_5 are replaced by random values. Adv will only notice this change if the hiding property is violated or if he perceives inconsistency with M_5. As a result,

$$|\mathsf{Adv}(\mathcal{A}, G_9) - \mathsf{Adv}(\mathcal{A}, G_8)| \leq \mathsf{Adv}^H_{\mathsf{COMM}}(\lambda) + \mathsf{Adv}_{\mathsf{CCAPKE}}(\lambda)$$

Game 10.

Further, we change the simulation in that $\mathsf{sk}_i = \mathsf{sk}_S$ u.a.r., so clearly

$$|\mathsf{Adv}(\mathcal{A}, G_{10})| = negl(\lambda)$$

Also, it is easy to see that no information related to n_i is involved in the protocol transcript, thus, his only chance of distinguishing this game from the previous one is that he can distinguish truly random values from H outputs, which, by the random oracle assumption happens with negligible probability only. As a result, finally,

$$|\mathsf{Adv}(\mathcal{A}, G_{10}) - \mathsf{Adv}(\mathcal{A}, G_9)| \leq \mathsf{qro}_H \cdot negl(\lambda)$$

A.2 Proof for Theorem 2

Consider the anonymity game. The only way $\mathcal{A}$ may obtain non-negligible advantage in this game is using the Send oracle to send a message on behalf of the server in such a way that C_i continues with the protocol and C_j aborts (or vice versa). The reason for this fact is that the only piece of private information that could distinguish between the two clients are the secret decryption keys (sk_i and

sk_j respectively); and these secrets are only used for decryption of one ciphertext in Round 3. Subsequently, the obtained value n_S is re-encrypted under all public keys and the resulting ciphertexts are compared in Round 5 with the ciphertexts sent by the server in Round 2.

Now assume that, in the anonymity experiment, $\mathcal{A}$ is able to interact with the challenger in such a way that, if $sk_t = sk_i$ (that is, the challenger is playing as C_i), the session key is accepted by the challenger after Round 5. This is only possible if $\mathcal{A}$ has produced ciphertexts $\{c_\alpha\}_{\alpha=1}^{l}$ and a randomness r such that:

- If $r_\alpha = H_r^*(\rho_\alpha, \alpha)$ for each α
- and $n_S = \mathsf{PKE.Dec}(sk_i; c_i)$
- then $\mathsf{PKE.Enc}(pk_\alpha, n_S; r_\alpha) = c_\alpha$ for every α.

But we will show that if the challenger is playing as C_j (i.e. $sk_t = sk_j$) and faces the same messages, he will also accept after Round 5. Let $\overline{n_S} = \mathsf{PKE.Dec}(sk_j; c_j)$. As we have stated, $\mathsf{PKE.Enc}(pk_j, n_S; r_j) = c_j$. Therefore, because of the correctness of the PKE, we have that $\overline{n_S} = n_S$ and, consequently all the checks $\mathsf{PKE.Enc}(pk_\alpha, \overline{n_S}; r_\alpha) = c_\alpha$ will be successful and the challenger will also accept. From this we conclude that $\mathcal{A}$ has negligible advantage in the anonymity game.

Note that the proof for unlinkability is analogous to this anonymity proof, and therefore we omit it.

References

1. Abdalla, M., Bohli, J., Vasco, M.I.G., Steinwandt, R.: (password) authenticated key establishment: From 2-party to group. In: Theory of Cryptography Conference (TCC), pp. 499–514 (2007)
2. Abdalla, M., Fouque, P., Pointcheval, D.: Password-based authenticated key exchange in the three-party setting. In: Vaudenay, S. (ed.) Public Key Cryptography (PKC), pp. 65–84 (2005)
3. Backes, M., Kate, A., Mohammadi, E.: ACE: an efficient key-exchange protocol for onion routing. In: ACM Workshop on Privacy in the Electronic Society (WPES), pp. 55–64 (2012)
4. Bellare, M., Canetti, R., Krawczyk, H.: A modular approach to the design and analysis of authentication and key exchange protocols (extended abstract). In: ACM Symposium on the Theory of Computing, pp. 419–428 (1998)
5. Bellare, M., Micciancio, D., Warinschi, B.: Foundations of group signatures: formal definitions, simplified requirements, and a construction based on general assumptions. In: International Conference on the Theory and Applications of Cryptographic Techniques (EUROCRYPT), pp. 614–629 (2003)
6. Bellare, M., Shi, H., Zhang, C.: Foundations of group signatures: the case of dynamic groups. In: The Cryptographers' Track at the RSA Conference (CT-RSA), pp. 136–153 (2005)
7. Bender, A., Katz, J., Morselli, R.: Ring signatures: stronger definitions, and constructions without random oracles. In: Theory of Cryptography Conference (TCC), pp. 60–79 (2006)

8. Boneh, D., Eskandarian, S., Fisch, B.: Post-quantum EPID signatures from symmetric primitives. In: The Cryptographers' Track at the RSA Conference (CT-RSA), pp. 251–271 (2019)
9. Boneh, D., Gentry, C., Waters, B.: Collusion resistant broadcast encryption with short ciphertexts and private keys. In: International Cryptology Conference (CRYPTO), pp. 258–275 (2005)
10. Bootle, J., Cerulli, A., Chaidos, P., Ghadafi, E., Groth, J.: Foundations of fully dynamic group signatures. In: International Conference on Applied Cryptography and Network Security (ACNS), pp. 117–136 (2016)
11. Boyd, C., Gellert, K.: A modern view on forward security. Comput. J. **64**(4), 639–652 (2021)
12. Bradley, T., Jarecki, S., Xu, J.: Strong asymmetric PAKE based on trapdoor CKEM. In: International Cryptology Conference (CRYPTO), pp. 798–825 (2019)
13. Brickell, E.F., Camenisch, J., Chen, L.: Direct anonymous attestation. In: ACM Conference on Computer and Communications Security (CCS), pp. 132–145 (2004)
14. Brickell, E., Li, J.: Enhanced privacy ID: a direct anonymous attestation scheme with enhanced revocation capabilities. IEEE Trans. Dependable Secur. Comput. **9**(3), 345–360 (2012)
15. Brock, D., Ballweg, R., Wick, K., Byorth, K.: Online collaborative exercises: the implications of anonymous participation. J. Phys. Assist. Educ. **16**, 13–17 (2005)
16. Canard, S., Fuchsbauer, G., Gouget, A., Laguillaumie, F.: Plaintext-checkable encryption. In: The Cryptographers' Track at the RSA Conference (CT-RSA), pp. 332–348 (2012)
17. Canetti, R., Krawczyk, H.: Analysis of key-exchange protocols and their use for building secure channels. In: International Conference on the Theory and Application of Cryptographic Techniques (EUROCRYPT), pp. 453–474 (2001)
18. Certicom Research: Standards for efficient cryptography 2 (sec 2) (2010). https://www.secg.org/sec2-v2.pdf
19. Chow, S.S.M., Choo, K.R.: Strongly-secure identity-based key agreement and anonymous extension. In: Information Security Conference (ISC), pp. 203–220 (2007)
20. Cramer, R., Shoup, V.: Design and analysis of practical public-key encryption schemes secure against adaptive chosen ciphertext attack. SIAM J. Comput. **33**(1), 167–226 (2003)
21. Derler, D., Ramacher, S., Slamanig, D.: Post-quantum zero-knowledge proofs for accumulators with applications to ring signatures from symmetric-key primitives. In: International Conference on Post-Quantum Cryptography (PQCrypto), pp. 419–440 (2018)
22. Dowsley, R., Hanaoka, G., Imai, H., Nascimento, A.C.A.: Round-optimal deniable ring authentication in the presence of big brother. In: International Workshop on Information Security Applications (WISA), pp. 307–321 (2010)
23. ECIES Team: Elliptic curve integrated encryption scheme for secp256k1 in rust. https://github.com/ecies/rs
24. Ferreira, L.: Privacy-preserving authenticated key exchange for constrained devices. In: Applied Cryptography and Network Security (ACNS), vol. 13269, pp. 293–312 (2022)
25. Ghosh, S., Kate, A.: Post-quantum forward-secure onion routing - (future anonymity in today's budget). In: Applied Cryptography and Network Security (ACNS), pp. 263–286 (2015)
26. Goldberg, I., Stebila, D., Ustaoglu, B.: Anonymity and one-way authentication in key exchange protocols. Des. Codes Cryptogr. **67**(2), 245–269 (2013)

27. Hanaoka, G., Kurosawa, K.: Efficient chosen ciphertext secure public key encryption under the computational Diffie-Hellman assumption. In: International Conference on the Theory and Application of Cryptology and Information Security (ASIACRYPT), pp. 308–325 (2008)
28. Hashimoto, K., Katsumata, S., Kwiatkowski, K., Prest, T.: An efficient and generic construction for signal's handshake (X3DH): post-quantum, state leakage secure, and deniable. J. Cryptol. **35**(3), 17 (2022)
29. Ishibashi, R., Yoneyama, K.: Post-quantum anonymous one-sided authenticated key exchange without random oracles. In: Public-Key Cryptography (PKC), pp. 35–65 (2022)
30. Jarecki, S., Krawczyk, H., Xu, J.: OPAQUE: an asymmetric PAKE protocol secure against pre-computation attacks. In: International Conference on the Theory and Applications of Cryptographic Techniques (EUROCRYPT), pp. 456–486 (2018)
31. Kassem, N.E., Chen, L., Bansarkhani, R.E., El Kaafarani, A., Camenisch, J., Hough, P.: L-DAA: lattice-based direct anonymous attestation. Cryptology ePrint Archive, Paper 2018/401 (2018)
32. Katz, J., Kolesnikov, V., Wang, X.: Improved non-interactive zero knowledge with applications to post-quantum signatures. In: ACM Conference on Computer and Communications Security (CCS), pp. 525–537 (2018)
33. Kaufman, C., Hoffman, P., Nir, Y., Eronen, P., Kivinen, T.: Internet Key Exchange Protocol Version 2 (IKEv2) (2014). https://www.rfc-editor.org/rfc/rfc7296
34. LaMacchia, B.A., Lauter, K.E., Mityagin, A.: Stronger security of authenticated key exchange. In: Provable Security (ProvSec), pp. 1–16 (2007)
35. Li, H., Dán, G., Nahrstedt, K.: Lynx: Authenticated anonymous real-time reporting of electric vehicle information. In: 2015 IEEE International Conference on Smart Grid Communications (SmartGridComm), pp. 599–604 (2015)
36. Libert, B., Nguyen, K., Peters, T., Yung, M.: One-shot fiat-shamir-based NIZK arguments of composite residuosity and logarithmic-size ring signatures in the standard model. In: International Conference on the Theory and Applications of Cryptographic Techniques (EUROCRYPT), pp. 488–519 (2022)
37. Luby, M., Staddon, J.: Combinatorial bounds for broadcast encryption. In: Nyberg, K. (ed.) EUROCRYPT 1998. LNCS, vol. 1403, pp. 512–526. Springer, Heidelberg (1998). https://doi.org/10.1007/BFb0054150
38. Naor, D., Naor, M., Lotspiech, J.: Revocation and tracing schemes for stateless receivers. In: International Cryptology Conference (CRYPTO), pp. 41–62 (2001)
39. Naor, M., Pinkas, B.: Efficient trace and revoke schemes. In: Financial Cryptography (FC), pp. 1–20 (2000)
40. National Institute of Standards and Technology: Post-quantum cryptography PQC - security (evaluation criteria). https://csrc.nist.gov/projects/post-quantum-cryptography/post-quantum-cryptography-standardization/evaluation-criteria/security-(evaluation-criteria)
41. NIST: Post-Quantum Cryptography Standardization (2023). https://csrc.nist.gov/projects/post-quantum-cryptography/post-quantum-cryptography-standardization
42. Open Quantum Safe: Algorithms in liboqs. https://openquantumsafe.org/liboqs
43. Peng, C., Chen, R., Wang, Y., He, D., Huang, X.: Parameter-hiding order-revealing encryption without pairings. In: Tang, Q., Teague, V. (eds.) Public-Key Cryptography (PKC), pp. 227–256 (2024)
44. Pointcheval, D.: Provable Security for Public Key Schemes, pp. 133–190. Birkhäuser Basel, Basel (2005)

45. Pointcheval, D., Stern, J.: Security arguments for digital signatures and blind signatures. J. Cryptol. **13**(3), 361–396 (2000)
46. Ramacher, S., Slamanig, D., Weninger, A.: Privacy-preserving authenticated key exchange: stronger privacy and generic constructions. In: European Symposium on Research in Computer Security (ESORICS), pp. 676–696 (2021)
47. Rivest, R.L., Shamir, A., Tauman, Y.: How to leak a secret. In: Boyd, C. (ed.) ASIACRYPT 2001. LNCS, vol. 2248, pp. 552–565. Springer, Heidelberg (2001). https://doi.org/10.1007/3-540-45682-1_32
48. Roberts, L., Rajah-Kanagasabai, C.: "i'd be so much more comfortable posting anonymously": identified versus anonymous participation in student discussion boards. Aust. J. Educ. Technol. **29**, 612–625 (2013)
49. Rust Crypto: Pure rust implementation of the aes-gcm authenticated encryption with associated data (aead) cipher. https://docs.rs/aes-gcm
50. Rust Crypto: Secp256k1 (a.k.a. k-256) elliptic curve library written in pure rust with support for ecdsa. https://docs.rs/k256/latest/k256/
51. Sanchez, J., Bernabé, J.B., Skarmeta, A.F.: Integration of anonymous credential systems in IoT constrained environments. IEEE Access **6**, 4767–4778 (2018)
52. Schäge, S., Schwenk, J., Lauer, S.: Privacy-preserving authenticated key exchange and the case of ikev2. In: Public-Key Cryptography (PKC), pp. 567–596 (2020)
53. Smart, N.P.: Cryptography Made Simple. Information Security and Cryptography. Springer, Cham (2016)
54. Walker, J., Li, J.: Key exchange with anonymous authentication using DAA-SIGMA protocol. In: International Conference on Trusted Systems (INTRUST), pp. 108–127 (2010)
55. Yang, G., Tan, C.H., Huang, Q., Wong, D.S.: Probabilistic public key encryption with equality test. In: The Cryptographers' Track at the RSA Conference (CT-RSA), pp. 119–131 (2010)
56. Young, J., Courtney, J., Bennett, R., Ellis, T.S., Posey, C.: The impact of anonymous, two-way, computer-mediated communication on perceived whistleblower credibility. Inf. Technol. People **34**(3), 1119–1151 (2021)
57. Young, J., Farshadkhah, S.: Improving anonymous whistleblower credibility with self-sovereign identity. In: IFIP Dewald Roode Information Security Research Workshop, vol. 8, no. 11.13, pp. 1–25 (2021)
58. Zhang, Q., Wu, J., Zhong, H., He, D., Cui, J.: Efficient anonymous authentication based on physically unclonable function in industrial internet of things. IEEE Trans. Inf. Forensics Secur. **18**, 233–247 (2023)
59. Zhao, Y.: Identity-concealed authenticated encryption and key exchange. In: ACM Conference on Computer and Communications Security (CCS), pp. 1464–1479 (2016)

Key Recovery Attacks on Unpatched MEGA from Four Queries: Solving Approximate Divisor Problem with Help of Approximation of Squared Divisor

Naoki Shimoe(✉) and Noboru Kunihiro

University of Tsukuba, Ibaraki, Japan
s2420618@u.tsukuba.ac.jp, kunihiro@cs.tsukuba.ac.jp

Abstract. MEGA is a cloud storage platform that supports end-to-end encryption and aims to be designed to guarantee data confidentiality and integrity even against hostile servers. However, Backendal et al. (IEEE S&P 2023) and Heninger and Ryan (PKC2023) showed that a server can exploit the session ID exchange to recover the user's RSA private key with 512 and 6 login attempts, respectively. Furthermore, Albrecht et al. (Eurocrypt2023) constructed an ECB encryption oracle from MEGAdrop and reduced the number of required login attempts to two. The current version of MEGA is patched for these attacks.

We analyze the security of the session ID exchange in unpatched MEGA in more detail. To achieve this purpose, we evaluate the minimum number of login attempts required to recover the user's RSA private key without the ECB encryption oracle. Based on Heninger and Ryan's attack, we propose an attack that can recover the user's RSA private key with four login attempts without the ECB encryption oracle. To reduce the number of required login attempts, we introduce a problem of recovering an unknown divisor of a composite number given its approximation and an approximate of its square and propose an algorithm that solves this problem by refining its approximation.

Keywords: Cryptanalysis · Approximate divisor · MEGA · RSA

1 Introduction

MEGA is a large-scale cloud storage platform with approximately 300 million users as of June 2024 [11]. It is designed to protect its users' data and private keys from a malicious service provider. Therefore, its threat model assumes a powerful adversary who can manipulate its server. It must guarantee the confidentiality and integrity of its stored data and private keys even against such an adversary.

However, Backendal et al. [2] found five attacks that can violate the confidentiality and integrity of data on MEGA's servers under the above threat model. The RSA private key recovery attack is one of the five attacks. MEGA's RSA

M. Fischlin and V. Moonsamy (Eds.): ACNS 2025, LNCS 15825, pp. 547–571, 2025.
https://doi.org/10.1007/978-3-031-95761-1_19

private keys are encrypted using AES-ECB under the user's master key and stored on its server. Because of the malleability, the user cannot detect tampering and the attacker can freely overwrite it as long as the encoding format is not destroyed. In the attack, the adversary properly overwrites the user's RSA private key stored on the server. The adversary then sends the overwritten RSA private key to the client and uses it to collect information about the user's RSA private key from session IDs (SIDs) generated by the client. With information about the user's RSA private key collected from 512 login attempts by the client, the adversary can completely recover the user's RSA private key.

Heninger and Ryan [6] improved Backendal et al.'s RSA private key recovery attack and showed that the user's RSA private key can be recovered with six login attempts. Heninger and Ryan introduced a new problem called the Hidden Number Problem with Small Unknown Multipliers (HNP-SUM) and constructed an HNP-SUM from the SIDs for properly overwritten private keys. By solving this problem using a lattice-based method, the gap between AES plaintext blocks leaks. The adversary recovers partial information about the user's RSA private key from the gap.

Although MEGA patched its clients after receiving reports of these attacks, Albrecht et al. [1] showed that the user's RSA private keys can be recovered even against the patched MEGA with a large number of login attempts. To recover the user's RSA private key, we use an error code oracle and an ECB encryption oracle [1, section 2.2]. The ECB encryption oracle encrypts any 256 bit plaintext chosen by the adversary using AES-ECB under the user's master key and outputs the ciphertext. It is constructed from MEGAdrop. MEGAdrop allows us to upload a file F to a recipient's activated folder even if we don't have any MEGA account. The sender creates an obfuscated file encryption key k_F, encrypts k_F under the recipient's RSA public key and file F under k_F, and sends the encrypted key and file. The adversary exploits a vulnerability that allows the adversary to generate arbitrary obfuscated file encryption keys [2] and a mechanism in which the client replaces obfuscated file encryption keys encrypted under the client's RSA public key with ones encrypted using AES-ECB under the client's master key. Using the ECB encryption oracle, they reduced the number of login attempts required for the RSA private key recovery attack against unpatched MEGA to two.

1.1 Our Contribution

In this paper, we analyze in detail the security of unpatched MEGA's SID exchange protocol. We evaluate the minimum number of login attempts required to recover the user's RSA private key without the ECB encryption oracle. We propose a novel RSA private key recovery attack without the ECB encryption oracle by improving Heninger and Ryan's attack.

Contribution 1. We introduce a new subproblem to solve in our RSA key recovery attack. The adversary's goal is to recover q, which is an unknown divisor of a sufficiently large and known composite number N and is greater than or equal

Table 1. Comparison our work to the other works related to RSA key recovery attacks on unpatched MEGA

	login attempts	ECB encryption oracle
Backendal et al. [2]	512	-
Heninger and Ryan [6]	6	-
Albrecht et al. [1]	2	✓
Our paper	4	-

to N^{β}. Assume that the adversary is given the approximated values a_1, a_2 of q, q^2 and the bound N_1^{γ}, $N_2^{\gamma} \in \mathbb{N}$ of their errors. We express this setting as follow:

$$\begin{cases} q = a_1 + e_1 \ (|e_1| \leq N^{\gamma_1}) \\ q^2 = a_2 + e_2 \ ((|e_2| \leq N^{\gamma_2})) \end{cases}.$$

By combining the computation of an approximation of e_1 with Howgrave-Graham's lattice-based technique [8], we can recover q in polynomial time if

$$\max(\gamma_2, 2\gamma_1) < (1 + \beta)\beta.$$

This means that we can factorize an RSA modulus N, a product of two distinct primes p, q with the same bit-size, if both 1/4-fraction of the most significant bits of q and q^2 are leaked. We can recover q using our lattice-based method for the range of γ_1 and γ_2 where we cannot recover it using Howgrave-Gramam's [8] and Lu et al.'s [10, Section 3]. The problem we introduce can be viewed as a special version of the problem of solving simultaneous modular linear equations introduced by Lu et al. [10, Section 5]. However, unlike their method, our method does not require any assumptions about algebraic independence. This feature is important for our RSA key recovery attack on MEGA.

Contribution 2. By using the above technique, we reduce the number of required login attempts from six to four. As shown in Table 1, our proposed method requires the smallest number of login attempts among the RSA private key recovery attacks without the ECB encryption oracle. In our proposed attack, the adversary computes an approximation of the square of RSA prime q in addition to an approximation of q. Heninger and Ryan's attack only computes an approximation of q. Since the adversary in our proposed attack has the approximations of q and q^2, the adversary can employ our lattice-based method to recover q. Since our proposed attack exploits the same vulnerability as Heninger and Ryan's attack, it has no significant impact on the security of the current MEGA client. Although our attack depends on the implementation of MEGA and requires more login attempts than Albrecht et al.'s, its strategy may provide insight into a cryptanalysis of any other MEGA-like systems.

1.2 Roadmap

In Sect. 2, we recall the approximate divisor problem, its generalization and HNP-SUM, describe MEGA's RSA key and SID key exchange, and provide the brief explanation of Heninger and Ryan's attack on MEGA. In Sect. 3, we introduce our new method to recover an unknown divisor. In Sect. 4, we construct our new RSA key recovery attack on MEGA, analyze its success probability, and verify it through experiments. In Sect. 5, we conclude our discussion.

2 Preliminaries

2.1 Notation

Let $S[a : b]$ be byte a to b of the byte array S. Let $S[a : b]$ be the a-th byte of the byte array S. Let $||$ be the string concatenation operator. Let $\text{sgn}(*)$ be a function that returns -1, 0, or 1 when the real number $*$ is negative, 0, or positive, respectively. Let $U(a, b)$ be a discrete uniform distribution from integer a to integer b.

2.2 Approximate Divisor Problem and Its Generalization

Howgrave-Graham [8] showed the following theorem. The problem in this theorem is called the approximate divisor problem. This problem is solved by an algorithm based on Coppersmith's method [4].

Theorem 1 (Howgrave-Graham [8]). *Let N be a sufficiently large composite number. Let p be an unknown divisor of N and $p \geq N^\beta$ $(0 < \beta < 1)$. Let $a \in \mathbb{Z}$. Then, we can find $y \in \mathbb{Z}$ $(|y| \leq N^\gamma \in \mathbb{N},\ 0 \leq \gamma < \beta)$ satisfying*

$$a + y \equiv 0 \pmod{p}$$

in polynomial time, if

$$\gamma < \beta^2.$$

Lu et al. [10] generalized the approximate divisor problem so that the unknown factor can be a power of p and the modulus of the equation to be solved can be a power of p. They constructed an algorithm to solve the generalized approximate divisor problem described above and showed the following theorem.

Theorem 2 (Lu et al. [10]). *Let $v, w \in \mathbb{N}$. Let N be a sufficiently large composite number. Let p^v be an unknown divisor of N and $p \geq N^\beta$ $(0 < \beta < 1)$. Let $a \in \mathbb{Z}$. Then, we can find $y \in \mathbb{Z}$ $(|y| \leq N^\gamma \in \mathbb{N},\ 0 \leq \gamma < w\beta)$ satisfying*

$$a + y \equiv 0 \pmod{p^w},$$

in polynomial time, if

$$\gamma < vw\beta^2.$$

Lu et al. [10] also showed that Theorem 2 can be generalized to simultaneous modular equations assuming the following condition, which is often used in the multivariate setting of Coppersmith's method. We call the condition the algebraic independence condition.

Definition 1 (Algebraic Independence Condition). *The polynomials constructed from the output of the LLL algorithm are algebraically independent. The common roots of these polynomials can be found efficiently using the Gröbner basis technique.*

They showed the following theorem, which is a generalized version of Theorem 2 to simultaneous modular equations.

Theorem 3 (Lu et al. [10]). *Suppose we are given n non-zero integers $a_1, \dots, a_n$. Let $r, r_1, \dots, r_n \in \mathbb{N}$. Let N be a sufficiently large composite number with an unknown divisor p^r, and $p \geq N^\beta$ $(0 < \beta < 1)$. Under the algebraic independence condition of Definition 1, we can find all integer solutions $(y_1, \dots, y_n)$ that satisfy $|y_i| \leq N^{\gamma_i} \in \mathbb{N}$ $(0 \leq \gamma_i < r_i\beta,\ i = 1, \dots, n)$ and*

$$\begin{cases} a_1 + y_1 \equiv 0 \pmod{p^{r_1}} \\ \qquad\qquad\vdots \\ a_n + y_n \equiv 0 \pmod{p^{r_n}} \end{cases}$$

if

$$\sqrt[n]{\frac{\gamma_1 \cdots \gamma_n}{r r_1 \cdots r_n}} < \beta^{\frac{n+1}{n}} \text{ and } \beta \gg \frac{1}{\sqrt{\log N}}.$$

The run time of this algorithm is polynomial in $\log N$ *and exponential in* n.

2.3 Hidden Number Problem with Small Unknown Multipliers

Heninger and Ryan [6] introduced the following problem, which is a variant of Hidden Number Problem [3].

Definition 2 (Hidden Number Problem with Small Unknown Multipliers (HNP-SUM) [6]). *For $N, T, E \in \mathbb{N}$, $a_i \in \mathbb{Z}$ $(i = 1, \dots, n)$, there exist $x, t_i, e_i \in \mathbb{Z}$ such that*

$$\begin{cases} a_i \equiv t_i x + e_i \pmod{N} \\ |t_i| \leq T \\ |e_i| \leq E \end{cases}.$$

Let $G = \gcd(|t_1|, \dots, |t_n|)$. Given $N, T, E, a_i (i = 1, \dots, n)$, the goal is to find $(|t_1|, \dots, |t_n|)/G$.

Heninger and Ryan proposed a lattice-based heuristic algorithm to solve HNP-SUM. The following theorem holds for their proposed algorithm.

Theorem 4 (Heninger and Ryan[6]). *Let N, a_i, T, E, n generate an HNP-SUM instance shown in Definition 2. Let t_i be generated uniformly. Then, there exists a heuristic polynomial time algorithm that solves HNP-SUM when*

$$T^{(n+1)/(n-1)}E \lesssim N.$$

2.4 MEGA's RSA Private Key and SID Exchange Protocol

We explain MEGA's RSA private key and its encoding method, and then describe MEGA's SID exchange protocol.

We explain each element of the user's RSA private key $sk_{\mathsf{share}} = (q, p, d, u)$ and the RSA public key $pk_{\mathsf{share}} = (N, e)$. p and q are distinct 1024 bit prime numbers, and $N = pq$. The public exponent e varies depending on the type of client; if the client is a web client, $e = 257$, and if it is an SDK, $e = 17$. The private exponent d is $d = e^{-1} \bmod (p-1)(q-1)$. $u = q^{-1} \bmod p$ is a value used in efficient decryption using the Chinese Remainder Theorem [5].

We explain the encoding method of the user's RSA private key sk_{share}. Let $sk^{\mathsf{encoded}}_{\mathsf{share}}$ be the encoded RSA private key sk_{share}. sk_{share} is encoded in the following format.

$$sk^{\mathsf{encoded}}_{\mathsf{share}} \leftarrow \mathsf{len}(q) \,||\, q \,||\, \mathsf{len}(p) \,||\, p \,||\, \mathsf{len}(d) \,||\, d \,||\, \mathsf{len}(u) \,||\, u \,||\, P$$

Here P is padding, and $\mathsf{len}(*)$ is a function that encodes the bit length of the argument $*$ into a byte string of 2 bytes. p, q, d, u in $sk^{\mathsf{encoded}}_{\mathsf{share}}$ are byte strings. Since AES block is 16 byte and $sk^{\mathsf{encoded}}_{\mathsf{share}}$ is encrypted using AES-ECB, the padding P is set so that the byte length of $sk^{\mathsf{encoded}}_{\mathsf{share}}$ is a multiple of 16.

We explain the MEGA SID exchange protocol. The MEGA server randomly chooses a SID. The MEGA server creates a RSA plaintext M by padding the SID so that the MEGA client can retrieve it in the procedure as described below. The MEGA server encrypts M using the RSA public key pk_{share}. Let the resulting RSA ciphertext be C. The server sends the RSA ciphertext C and the user's RSA private key esk encrypted using AES-ECB to the client. We show the client-side process in Algorithm 1. The client decrypts and decodes the encrypted RSA private key esk to obtain sk_{share}. It then uses sk_{share} to decrypt the RSA ciphertext C. On lines 3–7 of Algorithm 1, the client performs the CRT-RSA decryption process [5] of the RSA ciphertext C. On lines 8–11 of Algorithm 1, a SID is generated from the decrypted result M'. The position at which the SID s is extracted from M' differs depending on the value of the 2nd byte of M'. When the server receives the SID s from the client, if $M[2] = \mathtt{0x00} \wedge M[3:44] = s$, or $M[2] \neq \mathtt{0x00} \wedge M[2:44] = s$, the SID exchange protocol is successful.

2.5 Heninger and Ryan's Attack on MEGA

We explain Heninger and Ryan's attack [6] on MEGA, which is the basis of our proposed method. They presented two types of RSA key recovery attacks: *small*

Algorithm 1. The client's procedure in MEGA's SID exchange protocol

Input: RSA ciphertext C, RSA secret key esk encrypted using AES-ECB under the user's master key k_M
Output: SID s

$sk_{\mathsf{share}}^{\mathsf{encoded}} \leftarrow \mathsf{AES\text{-}ECB.Dec}(k_M, esk)$
$(q, p, d, u) = sk_{\mathsf{share}} \leftarrow \mathsf{Decode}\left(sk_{\mathsf{share}}^{\mathsf{encoded}}\right)$
$d_p \leftarrow d \bmod p - 1$
$d_q \leftarrow d \bmod q - 1$
$M_p^{'} \leftarrow C^{d_p} \bmod p$
$M_q^{'} \leftarrow C^{d_q} \bmod q$
$M^{'} \leftarrow ((M_p^{'} - M_q^{'} \bmod p) \cdot u \mod p)q + M_q^{'}$
if $M^{'}[2] = \texttt{0x00}$ **then**
  $s \leftarrow M^{'}[3:45]$
else
  $s \leftarrow M^{'}[2:44]$
end if

attack and *fast attack*. Since we only use small attack in this paper, we do not introduce fast attack here.

We introduce some assumptions required for the attack. We assume that the byte length of u, d for the user's RSA private key sk_{share} is 128, 256, respectively. In this case, the byte length of $sk_{\mathsf{share}}^{\mathsf{encoded}}$ is 41×16. We also assume that $M^{'}[2] \neq$ 0x00 holds when the overwritten RSA private key is input to Algorithm 1. These assumptions hold with a high probability in the attack.

We explain the outline of the attack. According to the threat model, the adversary can control the MEGA server. The adversary recovers the user's RSA private key by the following steps.

1. Collect SIDs for the RSA ciphertext and the overwritten RSA private keys
2. Solve HNP-SUM constructed from the collected SIDs to recover the most significant 624 bits of q
3. Recover q from the most significant 624 bits of q

We explain the details of each step of the attack below.

Collecting SIDs for RSA Ciphertext and Overwritten RSA Private Keys. We introduce some notations useful to explain the attack, describe the items that an adversary sends in the SID exchange protocol, and then describe the corresponding client responses.

We represent the encoded RSA private key $sk_{\mathsf{share}}^{\mathsf{encoded}}$ and its AES-ECB ciphertext esk as 16-byte blocks. Since $sk_{\mathsf{share}}^{\mathsf{encoded}}$ consists of 41 blocks under the assumption, $sk_{\mathsf{share}}^{\mathsf{encoded}}$ is expressed as

$$sk_{\mathsf{share}}^{\mathsf{encoded}} = pt_1 || pt_2 || \cdots || pt_{41}$$

for 16-byte blocks $pt_1, \ldots, pt_{41}$. Let $ct_i = \textsf{AES-ECB.Enc}(k_M, pt_i)$, and the AES-ECB ciphertext esk of $sk_{\textsf{share}}^{\textsf{encoded}}$ is

$$esk = \textsf{AES-ECB.Enc}\left(k_M, sk_{\textsf{share}}^{\textsf{encoded}}\right) = ct_1||ct_2|| \cdots ||ct_{41}.$$

Here, we define the block-wise overwriting operation Overwrite. Let A be a byte string divided into blocks. Let a byte array $A^{'}$ obtained by overwriting the $i_1, \ldots, i_n$-th blocks of A with blocks $x_1, \ldots, x_n$, respectively. We denote this operation as $A^{'} \leftarrow \text{Overwrite}(A, (i_1, x_1), \ldots, (i_n, x_n))$.

We explain how to overwrite the encrypted RSA private key esk. The adversary changes only the value of u, which corresponds to the ciphertext blocks $ct_{33}, \ldots, ct_{41}$, while leaving the values of p, q, and d unchanged. To avoid failures in decoding and unpadding, the adversary overwrites esk without changing the ciphertext blocks ct_{33} and ct_{41} containing $\textsf{len}(u)$ and P, respectively. The adversary chooses $t \in \{0, 1, \ldots, 6\}$ and overwrites esk as shown below.

$$\begin{aligned}
esk_0^{'} &\leftarrow \text{Overwrite}(esk, (34, ct_{18}), (35, ct_{18}), \ldots, (40, ct_{18}))\\
esk_1^{'} &\leftarrow \text{Overwrite}(esk_0^{'}, (40 - t, ct_1))\\
esk_2^{'} &\leftarrow \text{Overwrite}(esk_0^{'}, (40 - t, ct_2))\\
&\vdots\\
esk_5^{'} &\leftarrow \text{Overwrite}(esk_0^{'}, (40 - t, ct_5))
\end{aligned}$$

The following holds for $i = 0, 1, 2, 3, 4, 5$.

$$\begin{cases} \text{Decode}(\textsf{AES-ECB.Dec}(k_M, esk_i^{'})) = (q, p, d, u_i^{'}) \\ u_i^{'} \neq u \end{cases}$$

pt_{18} is the most significant 11–26 bytes of d. The correct value of pt_{18} can be guessed with high probability in at most e brute force attempts. Therefore, we consider pt_{18} to be known. $pt_1, \ldots, pt_5$ are unknown blocks corresponding to the most significant 624 bits of q.

We explain items the adversary sends in the SID exchange and SIDs the client returns in response. The adversary randomly chooses plaintext M and calculates an RSA ciphertext $C = M^e \bmod N$. He uses the same ciphertext C throughout the attack. In each SID exchange, the adversary sends $(C, esk_i^{'})$ to the client. The client runs Algorithm 1 with $(C, esk_i^{'})$ as input, and the client returns the output $s_i^{'}$ of Algorithm 1. When inputting $(C, esk_i^{'})$ into Algorithm 1, we define $M^{'}$, calculated in line 7 of Algorithm 1, as $M_i^{'}$. By assumption, $s_i^{'} = M_i^{'}[2:44]$.

Constructing and Solving HNP-SUM to Recover the Most Significant Bits of q. We show that the adversary can obtain five equations for $\delta_j = pt_j - pt_{18}$ $(j = 1, 2, 3, 4, 5)$ and six SIDs $s_0^{'}, s_1^{'}, s_2^{'}, s_3^{'}, s_4^{'}, s_5^{'}$. Setting $M_p = M \bmod p$, $M_q = M \bmod q$, from lines 7 and 11 of Algorithm 1 we have

$$(M_p - M_q)u_i^{'}q + M_q \equiv M_i^{'}[1]2^{2040} + s_i^{'}2^{1696} + M_i^{'}[45:256] \pmod{N}. \quad (1)$$

Subtracting both sides of the Eq. (1) in case of $i = j$ ($j \in \{1, 2, 3, 4, 5\}$) from the Eq. (1) in case of $i = 0$, we have

$$\begin{aligned}(M_p - M_q)(u_j^{'} - u_0^{'})q \equiv &(M_j^{'}[1] - M_0^{'}[1])2^{2040} + (s_j^{'} - s_0^{'})2^{1696} \\ &+ M_j^{'}[45:256] - M_0^{'}[45:256] \pmod{N}.\end{aligned}$$

Let $a_j := (M_j^{'}[1] - M_0^{'}[1])2^{2040} + (s_j^{'} - s_0^{'})2^{1696}$ and $e_j := M_j^{'}[45:256] - M_0^{'}[45:256]$. Then,

$$(M_p - M_q)(u_j^{'} - u_0^{'})q \equiv a_j + e_j \pmod{N}.$$

Due to the way the user's RSA private key is overwritten, $u_j^{'} - u_0^{'} = 2^{128t+64}\delta_j$. Therefore, the above modular equation is

$$\delta_j 2^{128t+64}(M_p - M_q)q \equiv a_j + e_j \pmod{N}. \tag{2}$$

We show how to construct an HNP-SUM from (2), solve it to find δ_j, and recover the most significant 624 bits of q from δ_j. Let $x = 2^{128t+64}(M_p - M_q)q$, and from (2), the following equation holds.

$$\delta_j x \equiv a_j + e_j \pmod{N} \tag{3}$$

Integer x is unknown but doesn't depend on j. Integer a_j is recovered by brute-force guessing the value of $M_j^{'}[1] - M_0^{'}[1]$. Note that since there are at most 511 possible values for $M_j^{'}[1] - M_0^{'}[1]$, the number of times to exhaust all possible values is small. Integers δ_j and e_j are unknown, but we know that $|\delta_j| \leq 2^{128}$, $|e_j| \leq 2^{1696}$. Therefore, the adversary can create an instance of HNP-SUM

$$\begin{cases} \delta_j x \equiv a_j + e_j \pmod{N} \\ |\delta_j| \leq T := 2^{128} \\ |e_j| \leq E := 2^{1696} \end{cases} \quad (j = 1, \ldots, 5).$$

The above HNP-SUM can be solved from Theorem 4. In practice, the adversary solves HNP-SUM with 3 samples for computational efficiency. He or she solves HNP-SUM for each of $(\delta_1, \delta_2, \delta_3)$, $(\delta_1, \delta_2, \delta_4)$, and $(\delta_1, \delta_2, \delta_5)$. In the solution of HNP-SUM, the signs and greatest common divisor of its multipliers are lost. However, since δ_j is considered a random integer on $|\delta_j| \leq T$, the greatest common divisor is small with high probability. We can guess the correct signs and greatest common divisor with a small number of brute force attempts. When the correct δ_j is obtained, pt_j can be calculated from $pt_j = \delta_j + pt_{18}$. Therefore, the adversary can extract the most significant 624 bits of q from $pt_1||pt_2||pt_3||pt_4||pt_5$.

Recover q from the Most Significant Bits of q. The adversary completely recovers q from the most significant 624 bits of the found q. Let q_M be the most significant 624 bits of q, and q_L be the remaining bits of q. Then, the modular equation

$$q_M 2^{400} + y \equiv 0 \pmod{q} \ (|y| \leq 2^{400})$$

has a solution $y = q_L$. Since the solution can be calculated in polynomial time from Theorem 1, q is completely recovered. The other elements of the user's RSA private key can also be calculated from q, so the user's RSA private key is completely recovered.

3 Recovering an Unknown Divisor from its Approximation and an Approximation of its Square

We present a novel algorithm to recover an unknown divisor q of an integer N given an approximation of q and an approximation of its square q^2 simultaneously and show its success condition. To construct the algorithm, we adopt a strategy of refining the approximation of q by the approximation of q^2.

The success conditions when only given an approximation of q and when only given an approximation of q^2 are shown in Theorem 1 and 2, respectively.

Before proving a theorem for the algorithm to recover q, we present the following lemma for our refining strategy.

Lemma 1. *Let $q \in \mathbb{N}$ be unknown and greater than or equal to $L \in \mathbb{N}$. Let $a_1 \in \mathbb{N}$. Suppose that for a_1 there exists an unknown integer e_1 $(|e_1| \leq B_1)$ satisfying*

$$q = a_1 + e_1. \tag{4}$$

Let $a_2 \in \mathbb{N}$. Suppose that for a_2 there exists an unknown integer e_2 $(|e_2| \leq B_2)$ satisfying

$$q^2 = a_2 + e_2. \tag{5}$$

Then, we can calculate $a_1^{'}$ such that

$$q = a_1^{'} + e_1^{'} \quad \left(|e_1^{'}| \leq \left\lceil \frac{\max(B_1, 4B_2^2)}{L} \right\rceil\right)$$

in polynomial time.

Proof. First, we transform the given problem to make a condition $a_1 \geq L$ always hold. When $e_1 \leq 0$, the desired condition $a_1 \geq L$ always holds because $a_1 = q - e_1 \geq q \geq L$. Let $a_1 \leftarrow a_1 + B_1$ and $e_1 \leftarrow e_1 - B_1$. Then, the inequality

$e_1 \leq 0$ always holds. It is sufficient to calculate a' in polynomial time under the following conditions:

$$\begin{cases} q = a_1 + e_1 & (a_1 \geq L,\ |e_1| \leq 2B_1) \\ q^2 = a_2 + e_2 & (|e_2| \leq B_2) \end{cases}$$

We can complete this transformation only with one addition and one subtraction. Thus, it is done in polynomial time.

Next, we decompose e_1 into a known term and an unknown one. Substituting Eq. (4) into Eq. (5), we have

$$a_2 + e_2 = a_1^2 + 2a_1e_1 + e_1^2.$$

Transforming this equation, we have

$$e_1 = \frac{a_2 - a_1^2}{2a_1} + \frac{e_2 - e_1^2}{2a_1}. \tag{6}$$

Let $\alpha = \frac{a_2 - a_1^2}{2a_1}$, $\epsilon = \frac{e_2 - e_1^2}{2a_1}$. α is known while ϵ is unknown satisfying

$$\begin{aligned} |\epsilon| &= \frac{|e_2 - e_1^2|}{2a_1} \leq \frac{|e_2| + |-e_1^2|}{2a_1} \leq \frac{B_2 + 4B_1^2}{2a_1} < \frac{2\max(B_2, 4B_1^2)}{2a_1} \\ &= \frac{\max(B_2, 4B_1^2)}{a_1} \leq \frac{\max(B_2, 4B_1^2)}{L} \end{aligned}$$

Therefore, e_1 is expressed as the sum of the known term α and the unknown term ϵ.

Finally, we calculate a_1' from α and a_1. Substituting $e_1 = \alpha + \epsilon$ into the Eq. (4), we have

$$q = a_1 + \alpha + \epsilon.$$

Rounding α and ϵ, we have

$$q = a_1 + \lceil \alpha \rceil + \lfloor \epsilon \rceil.$$

We can set the upper bound of $|\lfloor \epsilon \rceil|$ to $\lceil \max(B_2, 4B_1^2)/L \rceil$. Let $a_1' = a_1 + \lceil \alpha \rceil$, and $e_1' = \lfloor \epsilon \rceil$. Then, the following holds.

$$a_1' + e_1' = q \quad \left(|e_1'| \leq \left\lceil \frac{\max(B_2, 4B_1^2)}{L} \right\rceil \right) \tag{7}$$

Since a_1 is known and α is calculated by subtracting, multiplying, and dividing known values once, a_1' can be calculated in polynomial time. □

Combining Lemma 1 and Theorem 1, we show the following theorem.

Theorem 5. *Let N be a sufficiently large composite number. Let q be an unknown divisor of N and $q \geq N^{\beta}$ $(0 < \beta < 1)$. Let $a_1 \in \mathbb{N}$. Suppose that for a_1 there exists an unknown integer e_1 $(|e_1| \leq N^{\gamma_1} \in \mathbb{N}, \gamma_1 < \beta)$ satisfying*

$$q = a_1 + e_1. \tag{8}$$

Let $a_2 \in \mathbb{N}$. Suppose that for a_2 there exists an unknown integer e_2 $(|e_2| \leq N^{\gamma_2} \in \mathbb{N}, \gamma_2 < 2\beta)$ satisfying

$$q^2 = a_2 + e_2. \tag{9}$$

Then, we can find q in polynomial time if

$$\max(\gamma_2, 2\gamma_1) < (1+\beta)\beta.$$

Proof. Since N is sufficiently large, $\log_N 4 = 2/\log_2 N$ is negligibly small. Thus, we always ignore $\log_N 4$ in this proof. Let $\varepsilon = \lceil N^{\max(\gamma_2, 2\gamma_1)-\beta} \rceil - N^{\max(\gamma_2, 2\gamma_1)-\beta}$. When $\max(\gamma_2, 2\gamma_1) > \beta$, $\log_N(1 + \varepsilon/N^{\max(\gamma_2, 2\gamma_1)-\beta}) < \log_N 2 = 1/\log_2 N$ is negligibly small. Thus, we ignore $\log_N(1+\varepsilon/N^{\max(\gamma_2, 2\gamma_1)-\beta})$ in this proof when $\max(\gamma_2, 2\gamma_1) > \beta$.

We construct an approximate divisor problem from the following equation derived from Lemma 1 and solve it.

$$q = a_1' + e_1' \quad \left(|e_1'| \leq \lceil N^{\max(\gamma_2, 2\gamma_1)-\beta} \rceil = N^{\max(\gamma_2, 2\gamma_1)-\beta}\left(1 + \frac{\varepsilon}{N^{\max(\gamma_2, 2\gamma_1)-\beta}}\right)\right)$$

We prove this theorem in the cases of $\max(\gamma_2, 2\gamma_1) \leq \beta$ and $\max(\gamma_2, 2\gamma_1) > \beta$ separately.

Case of $\max(\gamma_2, 2\gamma_1) \leq \beta$ Since $\lceil N^{\max(\gamma_2, 2\gamma_1)-\beta} \rceil \leq 1$, the possible candidates of q are $a_1' - 1, a_1', a_1' + 1$. We can recover q only by examining these three candidates.

Case of $\max(\gamma_2, 2\gamma_1) > \beta$ From the above equation, a modular equation

$$a_1' + y \equiv 0 \pmod{q} \quad \left(|y| \leq N^{\max(\gamma_2, 2\gamma_1)-\beta}\left(1 + \frac{\varepsilon}{N^{\max(\gamma_2, 2\gamma_1)-\beta}}\right)\right)$$

has a solution $y = e_1'$. From Theorem 1, we can solve the above approximate divisor problem in polynomial time if

$$\max(\gamma_2, 2\gamma_1) + \log_N\left(1 + \frac{\varepsilon}{N^{\max(\gamma_2, 2\gamma_1)-\beta}}\right) < (1+\beta)\beta.$$

Ignoring the negligible term $\log_N(1+\varepsilon/N^{\max(\gamma_2, 2\gamma_1)-\beta})$, the condition for solving the above approximate divisor problem in polynomial time is

$$\max(\gamma_2, 2\gamma_1) < (1+\beta)\beta. \tag{10}$$

Since we have e_1', we can calculate $q = a_1' + e_1'$. □

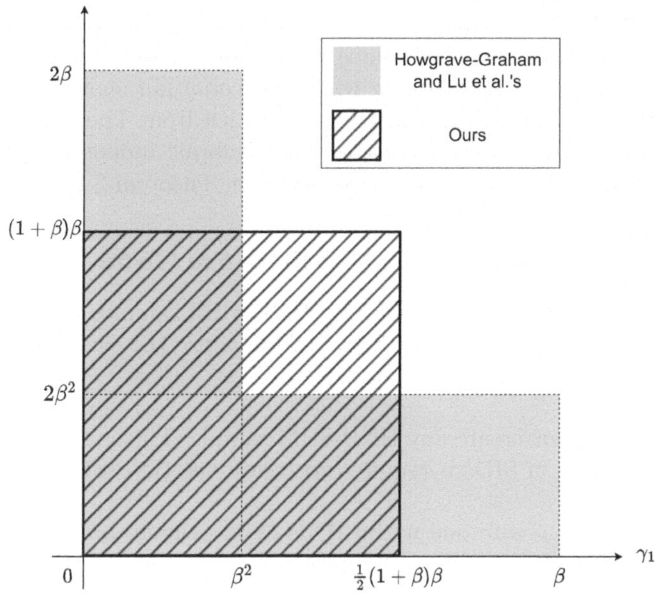

Fig. 1. Comparison of the conditions to recover q.

In the setting of Theorem 5, we compare the success condition of Theorem 5 with the success conditions of Theorem 1 and Theorem 2 ($v = 1, w = 2$). Figure 1 shows these conditions as the region of γ_1 and γ_2.

From Fig. 1, introducing our proposed method makes it possible to find q when

$$2\beta^2 < \gamma_2 < (1+\beta)\beta \text{ and } \beta^2 < \gamma_1 < \frac{1}{2}(1+\beta)\beta.$$

This is one of our main results. In the above range of γ_1 and γ_2, we cannot recover q by simply applying the algorithms of Theorem 1 and Theorem 2 to equations $q = a_1 + e_1$ and $q^2 = a_2 + e_2$, respectively. Our proposed method is effective when the leaked most significant bits of q and q^2 are small but well-balanced. In addition, it doesn't need the algebraic independence condition to hold while Theorem 3 does. We show in Sect. 4 that whether the algebraic independence condition holds is of practical importance.

4 Cryptanalyzing MEGA Without the ECB Encryption Oracle

We present a novel method to recover MEGA's RSA private key in four login attempts without the ECB encryption oracle. In our proposed method, the adversary obtains an approximation of q by solving HNP-SUM, similar to Heninger and Ryan's attack. By restricting the range of message M and parameter t, we calculate an approximation of q^2. Since we obtain the approximations of q and q^2 simultaneously, we can recover q when the condition shown in Theorem 5 holds. In theory, we also could construct an attack from Theorem 3. However, we verify through our experiments that the algebraic independence condition does not hold in this setting, and the attack from Theorem 3 fails.

4.1 HNP-SUM When Five or Less SIDs Are Given

We show what information is leaked from HNP-SUM samples when the number of login attempts is $b+1$ ($b \in \{0, \dots, 4\}$). We analyze the cases of $b = 0$, $b = 1$, $b = 2$, and $b = 3, 4$ separately.

Case $b = 0$ We cannot create any HNP-SUM sample. This is because, as shown in Sect. 2.5, one pair of SIDs is required to create one HNP-SUM sample.

Case $b = 1$ We can create one useful HNP-SUM sample, but we cannot solve HNP-SUM because the number of samples is small. There is also an HNP-SUM sample with the sign-inverted multiplier, but they do not contribute to solving the HNP-SUM according to Appendix A.

Case $b = 2$ We can obtain two useful HNP-SUM samples, but the number of useful HNP-SUM samples is too small to solve HNP-SUM. We can create a new HNP-SUM sample by combining the SID pair $(s_1^{'}, s_2^{'})$. However, it does not contribute to solving the HNP-SUM according to Appendix A because the multiplier of this HNP-SUM sample is $\delta_1 - \delta_2$. HNP-SUM samples with the sign-inverted multipliers also don't contribute. Therefore, the only useful HNP-SUM samples are those with multipliers δ_1, δ_2. Three or more HNP-SUM samples are required to solve HNP-SUM, so no information other than the HNP-SUM samples is leaked.

Case $b = 3, 4$ We obtain b HNP-SUM samples

$$\begin{cases} \delta_1 2^{128t+64}(M_p - M_q)q \equiv a_1 + e_1 \pmod{N} \\ \delta_2 2^{128t+64}(M_p - M_q)q \equiv a_2 + e_2 \pmod{N} \\ \quad\vdots \\ \delta_b 2^{128t+64}(M_p - M_q)q \equiv a_b + e_b \pmod{N} \end{cases}.$$

Since an HNP-SUM instance composed of these HNP-SUM samples is solved in Heninger and Ryan attack, $\delta_1, \delta_2, \dots, \delta_b$ can be recovered by solving HNP-SUM. Since pt_{18} is known, we can obtain $pt_1, pt_2, \dots, pt_b$, which contains the most significant $128b - 16$ bits of q.

To summarize the above discussion, when $b \leq 2$ we can only obtain HNP-SUM samples, while when $b = 3, 4$ we can obtain HNP-SUM samples, δ_i ($i = 1, 2, \dots, b$), and the most significant $128b - 16$ bit of p. Since we do not know how to recover the unknown values of HNP-SUM samples without solving HNP-SUM, we only analyze the cases of $b = 3, 4$.

We define the problem to be solved to recover the user's RSA private key. When the user logs in $b + 1$ times ($b \in \{3, 4\}$), the adversary tries to recover q from

$$\begin{cases} q = q_M 2^{1024-(128b-16)} + q_L \\ k_i(M_p - M_q)q \equiv a_i + e_i \pmod{N} \quad (i = 1, \ldots, b) \\ 0 < q_L < 2^{1024-(128b-16)} \\ 2^{128t+64} \leq k_i < 2^{128(t+1)+64} \\ |e_i| \leq E = 2^{1696} \end{cases}, \tag{11}$$

where $k_i \leftarrow |\delta_i| 2^{128t+64}$, $a_i \leftarrow (\mathrm{sgn}(\delta_i) \cdot a_i) \bmod N$, q_M, and N is given, and $t \in \{0, 1, \ldots, 6\}$ and M is chosen by the adversary.

4.2 Restricting the Range of Message

We analyze the leakage when the adversary chooses a message M in a more restricted range than in Heninger and Ryan's attack. Since the adversary controls the MEGA server, the adversary can choose an arbitrary message as a challenge for the SID exchange. In Heninger and Ryan's attack a message M is chosen randomly, while in our attack it is chosen so that

$$q < M < 2q.$$

Since the bit length of q is 1024 bit, when we set $M \leftarrow 2^{1024}$ for example, the above condition holds for M. When M is chosen in this way, $M_p = M - lp$ ($l \in \mathbb{Z}_{\geq 0}$), $M_q = M - q$. Then, the following holds.

$$k_i(M_p - M_q)q \equiv k_i(M - lp - M + q)q \equiv \delta_i 2^{128t+64} q^2 \pmod{N}$$

Therefore, when $q < M < 2q$, (11) is

$$\begin{cases} q = q_M 2^{1024-(128b-16)} + q_L \\ k_i q^2 \equiv a_i + e_i \pmod{N} \quad (i = 1, \ldots, b) \\ 0 < q_L < 2^{1024-(128b-16)} \\ 2^{128t+64} \leq k_i < 2^{128(t+1)+64} \\ |e_i| \leq E = 2^{1696} \end{cases}. \tag{12}$$

In our proposed attack, we assume that the adversary chooses a message M as shown above.

4.3 Finding the Quotients

We adjust the parameter t to find the quotient Q_i obtained by dividing $k_i q^2$ by N. Since we know k_i and the approximate value of q, we can calculate an approximate value of $k_i q^2$ from these values. We find Q_i by taking advantage of the fact that the quotient obtained by dividing the approximate value of $k_i q^2$ by N is close to Q_i.

We present the following proposition regarding the quotient obtained by dividing the product of a known number and an unknown number by a natural number.

Proposition 1. *Let p be expressed as $p = a + e$ using a known approximate value a and an unknown error value e $(0 < e \leq E < p)$. Let $N, k \in \mathbb{N}$. Let Q be the quotient obtained by dividing kp by N. Let $Q^{'}$ and $R^{'}$ be the quotient and remainder obtained by dividing ka by N, respectively. Let $Q^{''}$ be the quotient obtained by dividing $R^{'} + kE$ by N. Then,*

$$Q \in \{Q^{'} + l \mid l \in \mathbb{Z},\ 0 \leq l \leq Q^{''}\}.$$

In particular, when $kE < N$,

$$Q \in \{Q^{'}, Q^{'} + 1\}.$$

Proof. Multiplying both sides of $p = a + e$ by k, we have

$$kp = ka + ke.$$

Since $ka = Q^{'}N + R^{'}$, so

$$kp = Q^{'}N + R^{'} + ke.$$

Since $0 \leq R^{'} + ke < R^{'} + kE$, the quotient Q obtained by dividing kp by N is

$$Q \in \{Q^{'} + l \mid l \in \mathbb{Z},\ 0 \leq l \leq Q^{''}\}.$$

We consider the case of $kE < N$. Since $0 \leq R^{'} < N$, $0 \leq R^{'} + kE < 2N$. Therefore, the quotient $Q^{''}$ obtained by dividing $R^{'} + kE$ by N is either 0 or 1. From this, we can say that

$$Q \in \{Q^{'} + l \mid l \in \mathbb{Z},\ 0 \leq l \leq Q^{''}\} = \{Q^{'}, Q^{'} + 1\}. \qquad \square$$

We identify the range of t in which the number of candidates for the quotient Q_i is two. Using q_M and q_L, we express q^2 as

$$q^2 = q_M^2 2^{256(8-b)+32} + 2q_M q_L 2^{128(8-b)+16} + q_L^2.$$

If we set $e_{q^2} = 2q_M q_L 2^{128(8-b)+16} + q_L^2$, then

$$q^2 = q_M^2 2^{256(8-b)+32} + e_{q^2}.$$

Since $0 < q_L \leq 2^{128(8-b)+16}$ and $2^{128b+15} \leq q_M < 2^{128b+16}$,

$$\begin{aligned} 0 < e_{q^2} &< q_M 2^{256(8-b)+33} + 2^{256(8-b)+32} \\ &< q_M 2^{256(8-b)+34} \\ &< 2^{128(16-b)+50}. \end{aligned}$$

From Proposition 1, when $E_{q^2} := 2^{128(16-b)+50}$ and $k_i E_{q^2} < N$, there are two candidates for the quotient Q_i. Since $k_i < 2^{128(t+1)+64}$ and $2^{2047} < N$, the following inequation is sufficient to satisfy $k_i E_{q^2} < N$.

$$2^{128(t+1)+64} E_{q^2} < 2^{2047}$$

We identify the conditions under which this holds. Taking the logarithm to the base 2 on both of the sides and rearranging the equation, we have

$$t < b - 1 - \frac{115}{128}.$$

Since $b \in \{3, 4\}$ and $t \in \{0, 1, \ldots, 6\}$, the number of the candidates for the quotient Q_i is two when $t \leq b - 2$. Note that when $t > b - 2$, it is difficult to recover the quotient Q_i by brute force because there are more than 2^{64} candidates for it. Let us choose t from a set $\{0, \ldots, b - 2\}$.

If $t \leq b - 2$, the number of possible $(Q_1, \ldots, Q_b)$ is 8 when $b = 3$, and 16 when $b = 4$. Therefore, we can get the correct $(Q_1, \ldots, Q_b)$ by trying at most 16 candidates for $(Q_1, \ldots, Q_b)$. When $Q_1, \ldots, Q_b$ are guessed correctly, (12) is

$$\begin{cases} q = q_M 2^{1024-(128b-16)} + q_L \\ k_i q^2 = Q_i N + a_i + e_i \quad (i = 1, \ldots, b) \\ 0 < q_L < 2^{1024-(128b-16)} \\ 2^{128t+64} \leq k_i < 2^{128(t+1)+64} \\ |e_i| \leq E = 2^{1696} \end{cases}. \tag{13}$$

4.4 Calculating the Approximate Value of q^2

We transform

$$k_i q^2 = Q_i N + a_i + e_i \tag{14}$$

to make the left side q^2. Let $a_i^{'} = \lceil (Q_i N + a_i)/k_i \rceil$, and $e_i^{'} = \lfloor e_i/k_i \rfloor$. Dividing both sides of the Eq. (14), we have

$$q^2 = a_i^{'} + e_i^{'}.$$

Therefore, (13) becomes as follows.

$$\begin{cases} q = q_M 2^{1024-(128b-16)} + q_L \\ q^2 = a_i^{'} + e_i^{'} \quad (i = 1, \ldots, b) \\ 0 < q_L < 2^{1024-(128b-16)} \\ 2^{128t+64} \leq k_i < 2^{128(t+1)+64} \\ |e_i^{'}| \leq E^{'} = \lceil E/k_i \rceil \end{cases} \tag{15}$$

4.5 Recovering the User's RSA Private Key

From (15), the adversary has

$$\begin{cases} q = q_M 2^{1040-128b} + q_L \\ q^2 = a_i^{'} + e_i^{'} \quad (i = 1, \ldots, b) \\ 0 < q_L < 2^{1040-128b} \\ |e_i^{'}| \leq 2^{1632-128t} \end{cases}. \tag{16}$$

From Theorem 1 and Theorem 2, we cannot recover q using only the approximation to q or the approximation to q^2 shown above. Here, by applying Theorem 5, we aim to recover the user's RSA private key with fewer login attempts than the attack proposed by Heninger and Ryan that uses Theorem 1. We also present a variant of our proposed attack in which the phase of recovering q is replaced by the algorithm of Theorem 3.

For (16), we check the existence of pairs (b, t) for which the success condition shown in Theorem 5

$$\max(\gamma_2, 2\gamma_1) < (1 + \beta)\beta$$

holds, and those for which the success condition is shown in Theorem 3 (in $n = 2, r = 1, r_1 = 1, r_2 = 2$)

$$\sqrt{\gamma_1 \gamma_2 / 2} < \beta^{3/2}.$$

Since the pairs (b, t) are $(3, 0), (3, 1), (4, 0), (4, 1), (4, 2)$, we check whether the conditions hold for each (b, t).

Here, we introduce approximate values for the parameters $\beta, \gamma_1, \gamma_2$ in Theorem 5. Since N is 2047 or 2048 bit,

$$\beta \approx \log_N(q) = \frac{\log_2(q)}{\log_2(N)} \approx \frac{1024}{2048},$$

$$\gamma_1 = \log_N(2^{1040-128b}) = \frac{\log_2(2^{1040-128b})}{\log_2(N)} \approx \frac{1040 - 128b}{2048}$$

Since γ_2 depends on the value of k_i, we introduce the following values corresponding to the maximum and minimum values of γ_2.

- $\gamma_2^{\max} := \log_N(2^{1632-128t}) \approx (1632 - 128t)/2048$
- $\gamma_2^{\min} := \log_N(2^{1504-128t} - 1) \approx (1504 - 128t)/2048$

If the success conditions of Theorem 5 and Theorem 3 holds when $\gamma_2 = \gamma_2^{\max}$, then they hold for any γ_2. On the other hand, if the success conditions do not hold when $\gamma_2 = \gamma_2^{\min}$, then it does not hold regardless of the value of k_i. While β is always constant, γ_1, γ_2 depend on the values b, t the adversary set. We verify that the success conditions hold using the above approximate values.

Tables 2 and 3 shows whether the condition for finding q shown in Theorem 5 and Theorem 3 hold for each possible pair (b, t), respectively. As shown in Table 2, the success condition of Theorem 5 always holds when $(b, t) = (3, 1), (4, 1), (4, 2)$. It holds depending on the value of k_i when $(b, t) = (3, 0), (4, 0)$. Therefore, when $b = 3$, the number of login attempts required for the success of our proposed attack is the smallest, which is $4(= 3 + 1)$. Since Heninger and Ryan's attack requires six login attempts, our proposed attack can recover the user's RSA private key with two fewer login attempts than their attack. The success condition of Theorem 5 always holds when $(b, t) = (3, 1), (4, 1), (4, 2)$. Although Table 3 shows that the success condition of Theorem 3 always holds when $(b, t) = (3, 1), (4, 0), (4, 1), (4, 2)$, a variant of our proposed attack based on Theorem 3 may fail because of the algebraic independence condition. We check through our experiments whether this assumption holds.

Table 2. Whether the success condition of Theorem 5 is satisfied in the MEGA setting

b	t	β	γ_1	$\gamma_2^{\max}$	$\gamma_2^{\min}$	$\max(\gamma_2^{\max}, 2\gamma_1) < (1+\beta)\beta$	$\max(\gamma_2^{\min}, 2\gamma_1) < (1+\beta)\beta$
3	0	0.5	0.320	0.797	0.734		✓
3	1	0.5	0.320	0.734	0.672	✓	✓
4	0	0.5	0.258	0.797	0.734		✓
4	1	0.5	0.258	0.734	0.672	✓	✓
4	2	0.5	0.258	0.672	0.609	✓	✓

Table 3. Whether the success condition of Theorem 3 is satisfied in the MEGA setting

b	t	β	γ_1	$\gamma_2^{\max}$	$\gamma_2^{\min}$	$\sqrt{\gamma_1\gamma_2^{\max}/2} \leq \beta^{3/2}$	$\sqrt{\gamma_1\gamma_2^{\min}/2} \leq \beta^{3/2}$
3	0	0.5	0.320	0.797	0.734		✓
3	1	0.5	0.320	0.734	0.672	✓	✓
4	0	0.5	0.258	0.797	0.734	✓	✓
4	1	0.5	0.258	0.734	0.672	✓	✓
4	2	0.5	0.258	0.672	0.609	✓	✓

4.6 Success Probability of Our Attack

We show a success probability of our attack. Since our attack requires some assumptions introduced above, we examine the probabilities of these assumptions.

At first, we analyze the assumption about SIDs. The assumption is that $M_j'[2] \neq \texttt{0x00}$ for all SIDs s_j'. If this assumption does not hold, the attack will fail. Assuming that the decryption result M_j' follows a uniform distribution, the probability that $M_j'[2] \neq \texttt{0x00}$ is 255/256. Thus, the probability that the client returns the expected SIDs is $(255/256)^{b+1}$. For $b = 3, 4$, this probability is nearly equal to 0.98.

Next, we analyze the two assumptions about the RSA secret key. One is that its element u is 128 bytes, and the other is that its element d is 256 bytes. We calculate the lower bounds of $\Pr[u \geq 256^{127}]$ and $\Pr[d \geq 256^{255}]$ under a simple assumption that the values u and d follow discrete uniform distributions $U(1, p-1)$ and $U(1, (p-1)(q-1)-1)$, respectively. Under this assumption,

$$\begin{aligned}\Pr[u \geq 256^{127}] &= 1 - \Pr[u < 256^{127}] \\ &= 1 - \Pr[X < 256^{127} | X \sim U(1, p-1)] \\ &= 1 - \frac{256^{127} - 1}{p - 1} \\ &\geq 1 - \frac{256^{127}}{2^{1023}} \\ &= \frac{127}{128},\end{aligned}$$

and

$$\begin{aligned}\Pr[d \geq 256^{255}] &= 1 - \Pr[d < 256^{255}] \\ &= 1 - \Pr[X < 256^{255} | X \sim U(1, (p-1)(q-1)-1)] \\ &\approx 1 - \Pr[X < 256^{255} | X \sim U(0, N-1)] \\ &= 1 - \frac{256^{255}}{N} \\ &\geq 1 - \frac{256^{255}}{2^{2046}} \\ &= \frac{63}{64}.\end{aligned}$$

Thus, the probability that the RSA secret key satisfies the required assumptions is $\Pr[u \geq (256)^{127}] \cdot \Pr[d \geq (256)^{255}] \gtrsim (63/64) \cdot (127/128) \geq 0.97$.

Summarizing the above discussion, the success probability of our attack is approximately $0.98 \cdot 0.97 = 0.95$. However, even if our attack fails, we can simply retry it to make it successful, letting $k_i \leftarrow \delta_i 2^{128t+64-8h}$ $(h = 1, 2, \ldots)$ for all i. This attempt solves the problem of the incorrect value k_i when the assumptions about the RSA secret key do not hold. Taking this into account, the success probability is nearly equal to 0.98.

4.7 Experiment

We conduct two types of experiments[1]. One is an experiment on our proposed attack on MEGA, which is derived from our refining strategy. The other is an experiment on a variant of our proposed attack, which is derived from Lu et al.'s algorithm.

Setting of Our Experiments. We explain our experimental setting. The public exponent e is set to 257. We assume k_1, q_M and a_1 are given. Since these values are computed as shown in Heninger and Ryan's attack, we introduce this assumption to focus on validating our idea. The following cases are excluded from our experiments.

- The byte string of u is 127 bytes or less
- The byte string of d is 255 bytes or less
- $M_j^{'}[2] = \texttt{0x00}$.

We explain the implementation of our proposed attack from Theorem 5. We generate 100 RSA private keys randomly for $(b, t) = (3, 1), (4, 2)$ and apply our proposed attack to them. We also generate 100 RSA private keys randomly for $(b, t) = (5, 0)$ and apply Heninger and Ryan's attack to them. In our experiments, instead of using an actual MEGA client, we use an oracle that outputs k_1, a_1, and q_M based on the MEGA SID exchange protocol and RSA private key encoding format. We confirm whether q can be recovered using our proposed attack. We also measure the run time and lattice dimension used to recover q. The reason for measuring the lattice dimension is that the LLL algorithm dominates the run time in solving the approximate divisor problem, and the run time of the LLL algorithm is mainly affected by the dimension of the input lattice. Our experiments were implemented using Sage 9.8 and performed on a Mac OS Sonoma 14.4.1, Apple M1 CPU, and 16GB RAM.

We explain the implementation of the variant of our proposed attack. We randomly generate 10 RSA private keys for $(b, t) = (3, 1), (4, 0), (4, 1), (4, 2)$ and apply it to them. The case of $(b, t) = (3, 0)$ is excluded from our experiments because it is expected that the attack would take too long to be practical. Based on Howgrave-Graham's lemma [7], we choose the dimension of the lattice used in this attack so that two polynomials $h_1(x_1, x_2)$ and $h_2(x_1, x_2)$ derived from the output of the LLL algorithm have the desired roots. Instead of the running time, we measure the dimension of ring $\mathbb{Q}[x_1, x_2]$ modulo an ideal generated by polynomials $h_1(x_1, x_2), h_2(x_1, x_2)$. Since the algebraic independence condition does not hold when the dimension is non-zero, it is useful to verify the algebraic independence condition.

Exprimental Results. Table 4 shows the experimental results for our proposed attack ($b = 3, 4$) and Heninger and Ryan's one ($b = 5$).

[1] Our implementation is available at https://github.com/n-shimoe/mega_key_recovery_attack.

Table 4. The experimental results for the implementation of our proposed attack ($b = 3, 4$) and Heninger and Ryan's attack ($b = 5$)

b	t	$\bar{\gamma_1}$	$\bar{\gamma_2}$	lattice dim.	averaged time (s)	success rate
3	1	0.320	0.673	7	0.0123	100/100
4	2	0.258	0.611	4	0.00497	100/100
5	0	0.195	-	5	0.00439	100/100

Table 5. The experimental results for the implementation of the variant of our proposed attack

b	t	$\bar{\gamma_1}$	$\bar{\gamma_2}$	lattice dim.	ideal dim.
3	1	0.320	0.673	97 or 98	1
4	0	0.258	0.736	32	1
4	1	0.258	0.673	25	1
4	2	0.258	0.611	27	1

It shows that q is successfully recovered in all 100 trials. Thus, the effectiveness of our proposed method is verified under our introduced assumptions. It also shows that the average run time of our attack is at most three times longer than that of Heninger and Ryan's. Especially when $b = 4$, the average run time of our attack is almost as long as that of Heninger and Ryan's. Therefore, the adversary can run our attack without a significant loss in efficiency from Heninger and Ryan's attack.

Table 5 shows the experimental results for the variant of our proposed attack. It shows that the dimension of $\mathbb{Q}[x_1, x_2]$ modulo the ideal is 1 regardless of (b, t). Thus, the algebraic independence condition doesn't hold in this attack, and the algorithm of Theorem 3 is inappropriate in the MEGA setting.

5 Conclusion

Our RSA key recovery attack improves Heninger and Ryan's attack and can recover the user's RSA private key in unpatched MEGA with just four login attempts. Furthermore, unlike Albrecht et al.'s attack [1], our proposed attack does not require the ECB encryption oracle. Thus, our cryptanalysis makes the security of the SID exchange protocol clear. We show that key overwriting attacks can be improved by choosing messages or overwriting locations, and we provide insights for analysis of key overwriting attacks.

In a setting where approximations of q and q^2 are given simultaneously, we employ a strategy of refining the approximation of q. This enables us to recover q even under conditions where the algorithms of Theorem 1 and Theorem 2 cannot recover it. Moreover, we can avoid the algebraic independence condition using the strategy.

Acknowledgments. This work was supported by JST CREST Grant Number JPMJCR2113 and JSPS KAKENHI Grant Number JP23K21667.

A Why HNP-SUM with Three Samples Not Generated Randomly Cannot Be Solved

We define HNP-SUM with three samples for nonrandomly generated multipliers as

$$\begin{cases} t_1 x \equiv a_1 + e_1 \pmod{N} \\ t_2 x \equiv a_2 + e_2 \pmod{N} \\ t_3 x \equiv a_3 + e_3 \pmod{N} \\ c_3 t_3 = c_1 t_1 - c_2 t_2 \\ |t_i| \leq T \ \ (i = 1, 2, 3) \\ |e_i| \leq E \ \ (i = 1, 2, 3) \end{cases},$$

where the absolute value of $c_1, c_2, c_3 \in \mathbb{Z}$ is small and T is sufficiently large, and we show that this cannot be solved even if $ET^2 \lesssim N$ holds. We first show that HNP-SUM cannot be solved when $c_1 = 1, c_2 = 1, c_3 = 1$, and then generalize the result to small c_1, c_2, c_3.

We briefly explain the algorithm for solving HNP-SUM with 3 samples. In HNP-SUM algorithm, for the lattice $\mathcal{L}(B)$ generated by rows $\boldsymbol{b}_1, \boldsymbol{b}_2, \boldsymbol{b}_3$ and $\boldsymbol{b}_4$ of the matrix

$$B = \begin{pmatrix} E & 0 & 0 & a_1 \\ 0 & E & 0 & a_2 \\ 0 & 0 & E & a_3 \\ 0 & 0 & 0 & N \end{pmatrix},$$

we construct a sublattice $\mathcal{L}(B_{\mathsf{sub}})$ where:

$$\begin{aligned} \boldsymbol{v}_{i,j} &= t_j \boldsymbol{b}_i / \gcd(|t_i|, |t_j|) - t_i \boldsymbol{b}_j / \gcd(|t_i|, |t_j|) - k_{i,j} \boldsymbol{b}_4 \\ B_{\mathsf{sub}} &:= \{\boldsymbol{v}_{i,j} \mid i, j \in \{1, 2, 3\},\ i \neq j\} \end{aligned}$$

The rank of the sublattice $\mathcal{L}(B_{\mathsf{sub}})$ is 2. We assume that the first and second shortest vectors among the basis vectors of $\mathcal{L}(B)$ output by the LLL algorithm is the basis of $\mathcal{L}(B_{\mathsf{sub}})$. Then, we calculate the solution to HNP-SUM from the HNF of the basis matrix of $\mathcal{L}(B_{\mathsf{sub}})$ obtained by the LLL algorithm.

We show that the shortest vector among the basis vectors output by the LLL algorithm is not necessarily in the basis of $\mathcal{L}(B_{\mathsf{sub}})$ when $t_3 = t_1 - t_2$. Since $t_3 = t_1 - t_2$, the following holds

$$\begin{aligned} a_1 - a_2 - a_3 &\equiv (t_1 x - e_1) - (t_2 x - e_2) - (t_3 x - e_3) \\ &\equiv e_2 - e_1 + e_3 \pmod{N}. \end{aligned}$$

Thus, vector

$$\boldsymbol{v} := (E, -E, -E, e_2 - e_1 + e_3)$$

is on $\mathcal{L}(B)$. However, $\boldsymbol{v}$ is not on $\mathcal{L}(B_{\mathsf{sub}})$. Moreover, the upper bound of the norm $\|\boldsymbol{v}\|$ is $\sqrt{12}E$. Here, we introduce the following theorem about the LLL algorithm.

Theorem 6 (LLL [9]). *Let B_{LLL} be a full-rank ω-dimensional square matrix. Let $\mathcal{L}$ be a lattice generated by the row vectors of matrix B_{LLL}. The LLL algorithm outputs the basis $\boldsymbol{v}^*$ of $\mathcal{L}$ satisfying*

$$||\boldsymbol{v}^*|| \leq 2^{\frac{\omega-1}{4}} |\det B_{\mathsf{LLL}}|^{\frac{1}{\omega}}.$$

We prove that $\|\boldsymbol{v}\|$ is sufficiently smaller than $2^{3/4}(E^3N)^{1/4}$, and from Theorem 6 prove that $\boldsymbol{v}^* = \pm\boldsymbol{v}$ with high probability. Since $|e_i| \leq E$, $\|\boldsymbol{v}\| \leq \sqrt{12}E$. Since $ET^2 \lesssim N$ and T is sufficiently large,

$$\sqrt{12}E \leq 2^{3/4}ET^{1/2} \lesssim 2^{3/4}(E^3 N)^{1/4}.$$

Since $\sqrt{12}E$ is sufficiently smaller than $2^{3/4}ET^{1/2}$, $\sqrt{12}E$ is also sufficiently smaller than $2^{3/4}(E^3N)^{1/4}$. Therefore, $\|\boldsymbol{v}\|$ is sufficiently smaller than $2^{3/4}(E^3N)^{1/4}$, and $\boldsymbol{v}^* = \pm\boldsymbol{v}$ with high probability. From this, when $t_3 = t_1 - t_2$, there is a high probability that $\boldsymbol{v}^*$ is not a basis of $\mathcal{L}(B_{\mathsf{sub}})$, and HNP-SUM cannot be solved.

In the same way as above, when $c_3t_3 = c_1t_1 - c_2t_2$ for small $c_1, c_2, c_3 \in \mathbb{Z}$, vector

$$(E, -E, -E, c_2e_2 - c_1e_1 + c_3e_3) \in \mathcal{L}(B)$$

is the shortest basis vector output by the LLL algorithm with high probability. However, this vector is not on $\mathcal{L}(B_{\mathsf{sub}})$. Therefore, when $c_3t_3 = c_1t_1 - c_2t_2$ for small $c_1, c_2, c_3 \in \mathbb{Z}$, HNP-SUM cannot be solved. In particular, if an HNP-SUM sample has a sign-inverted multiplier of another one (for example, $c_1 = -1, c_2 = 0, c_3 = 1$), HNP-SUM cannot be solved.

References

1. Albrecht, M.R., Haller, M., Mareková, L., Paterson, K.G.: Caveat implementor! key recovery attacks on MEGA. In: Advances in Cryptology – EUROCRYPT 2023. LNCS, vol. 14008, pp. 190–218 (2023). https://doi.org/10.1007/978-3-031-30589-4
2. Backendal, M., Haller, M., Paterson, K.G.: MEGA: Malleable encryption goes awry. In: 2023 IEEE Symposium on Security and Privacy, pp. 146–163. IEEE (2023)
3. Boneh, D., Venkatesan, R.: Hardness of computing the most significant bits of secret keys in Diffie-Hellman and related schemes. In: Koblitz, N. (ed.) CRYPTO 1996. LNCS, vol. 1109, pp. 129–142. Springer, Heidelberg (1996). https://doi.org/10.1007/3-540-68697-5_11

4. Coppersmith, D.: Finding a small root of a univariate modular equation. In: Maurer, U. (ed.) EUROCRYPT 1996. LNCS, vol. 1070, pp. 155–165. Springer, Heidelberg (1996). https://doi.org/10.1007/3-540-68339-9_14
5. Garner, H.L.: The residue number system. In: Papers presented at the the 1959 western joint computer conference, IRE-AIEE-ACM 1959 (Western), pp. 146–153. ACM (1959)
6. Heninger, N., Ryan, K.: The hidden number problem with small unknown multipliers: Cryptanalyzing MEGA in six queries and other applications. In: Boldyreva, A., Kolesnikov, V. (eds.) Public-Key Cryptography – PKC 2023. LNCS, vol. 13940, pp. 147–176. Springer, Cham. (2023). https://doi.org/10.1007/978-3-031-31368-4_6
7. Howgrave-Graham, N.: Finding small roots of univariate modular equations revisited. In: Cryptography and Coding. In: Darnell, M. (eds.) LNCS, vol. 1355, pp. 131–142 (1997). https://doi.org/10.1007/BFb0024458
8. Howgrave-Graham, N.: Approximate integer common divisors. In: Silverman, J.H. (ed.) CaLC 2001. LNCS, vol. 2146, pp. 51–66. Springer, Heidelberg (2001). https://doi.org/10.1007/3-540-44670-2_6
9. Lenstra, A.K., Lenstra, H.W., Lovász, L.: Factoring polynomials with rational coefficients. Math. Ann. **261**, 515–534 (1982)
10. Lu, Y., Zhang, R., Peng, L., Lin, D.: Solving linear equations modulo unknown divisors: revisited. In: Iwata, T., Cheon, J.H. (eds.) ASIACRYPT 2015. LNCS, vol. 9452, pp. 189–213. Springer, Heidelberg (2015). https://doi.org/10.1007/978-3-662-48797-6_9
11. MEGA: About us - MEGA. https://mega.io/ja/about. Accessed 18 June 2024

Tighter Provable Security for TreeKEM

Karen Azari[1] and Andreas Ellison[2(✉)]

[1] University of Vienna, Faculty of Computer Science, Vienna, Austria
karen.azari@univie.ac.at
[2] ETH Zurich, Zurich, Switzerland
andreas.ellison@inf.ethz.ch

Abstract. The Messaging Layer Security (MLS) protocol, recently standardized in RFC 9420, aims to provide efficient asynchronous group key establishment with strong security guarantees. The main component of MLS, which is the source of its key efficiency and security properties, is a protocol called TreeKEM. Given that a major vision for the MLS protocol is for it to become the new standard for messaging applications like WhatsApp, Facebook Messenger, Signal, etc., it has the potential to be used by a huge number of users. Thus, it is important to better understand the security of MLS and hence also of TreeKEM. In previous work, TreeKEM was proven adaptively secure in the Random Oracle Model (ROM) with a polynomial loss in security by proving a result about the security of an arbitrary IND-CPA secure public-key encryption scheme in a public-key version of a security game called GSD. Unfortunately, the concrete security guarantees implied by this line of work are not sufficient for parameters used in practice.

In this work, we prove a tighter bound for the security of TreeKEM when DHIES is used for public-key encryption; DHIES is currently the only standardized scheme in MLS. Our bound implies meaningful security guarantees even for small practical parameters. We follow the above approach and first introduce a modified version of the public-key GSD game better suited for analyzing TreeKEM. We then provide a simple and detailed proof of security for DHIES in this game in the ROM and achieve a smaller security loss compared to the previous best result. Finally, we state the result on the security of TreeKEM implied by this bound and give an interpretation of the result with protocol parameters used in practice.

Keywords: Messaging Layer Security · TreeKEM · Secure Messaging · Group Key-Agreement · Adaptive Security · DHIES

1 Introduction

We all rely on messaging applications like WhatsApp, Facebook Messenger, Signal, etc. in our daily lives and take it for granted that our messages will be

K. Azari—Part of the work was done while the author was affiliated with ETH Zurich, Switzerland.

M. Fischlin and V. Moonsamy (Eds.): ACNS 2025, LNCS 15825, pp. 572–595, 2025.
https://doi.org/10.1007/978-3-031-95761-1_20

transmitted securely, for some definition of "secure". A common security feature expected from the protocol employed in a messaging application is end-to-end encryption, i.e. that only the end users of a messaging session can read the messages being sent and the service provider or any party with access to the communication channel learns nothing of their contents. The protocol should work in an asynchronous setting: we would like to send messages even when the recipient is offline, and we expect them to receive the message once they come online. For this, we must rely on a delivery service to store and deliver the messages. Of course, also this delivery service should learn nothing from the messages.

There are two more advanced security features expected from messaging protocols today, both related to security in case a user is compromised:

- forward secrecy (FS): the compromise should not reveal the contents of old messages
- post-compromise security (PCS): after the user recovers from the compromise, new messages are secure once again

As a user may well not know that they have been compromised, ensuring PCS requires regularly updating the key material used for encryption (in a way that the information leaked in a compromise *before* the update does not suffice to compute encryption keys used *after* the update). The more often the key material is updated, the stronger the level of PCS that is achieved. Thus, updating the key material should be an efficient operation.

For messaging between two users, the Double Ratchet protocol [16], the main component of the Signal Protocol, is a widely adopted solution used by major messaging applications such as Signal, WhatsApp, Facebook Messenger and more. It is well-studied and achieves all of the above security guarantees [9]. For messaging in a group of more than two users, a straightforward solution is to maintain 1:1 communication channels using the Double Ratchet protocol between every pair of users and send messages to the group by sending them to every member individually. This achieves very strong security guarantees but requires a number of encryption operations linear in the group size to send a message.

Another common solution is to use sender keys [5]: every user creates a symmetric key, their *sender key*, and distributes this sender key to every other user using 1:1 channels as before. A user sending a message then derives a symmetric encryption key for the message from their sender key, while continually updating their sender key (with each sent message) to provide FS. However, achieving PCS is costly: if a user is compromised, the sender keys of all users are leaked and recovering from the compromise requires each user to send a new sender key to every other user over the respective 1:1 channels, resulting in a number of operations linear in the group size per user and a quadratic number of operations in total. Moreover, dynamic group membership introduces additional complexity:

- adding a new member involves the new member sharing their sender key with all other group members

– removing a member requires distributing new sender keys in the group, just like recovering from a compromise

The Messaging Layer Security (MLS) protocol, recently standardized in [6], proposes a solution for group messaging with better efficiency and the same strong security guarantees as for the two-party case. Updating key material and adding or removing members can be achieved with a logarithmic number of operations (although the complexity may still degrade to linear in certain scenarios). At the core of MLS is a fairly recent primitive called a *continuous group key agreement* (CGKA) scheme [2] (this primitive was introduced only *after* the first draft of the MLS protocol). In essence, a CGKA scheme enables a group of users to agree on a *group key*, which they can then use to derive symmetric message encryption keys. This key must be indistinguishable from a random key for anyone outside the group eavesdropping on all communication. However, a CGKA scheme must also achieve FS and PCS, and support dynamic group membership. Hence, it must provide mechanisms for members to update their key material, add new users to the group and remove members from the group. Moreover, the scheme must work in the asynchronous setting with an untrusted service to deliver protocol messages.

The CGKA scheme used in the MLS protocol is called TreeKEM (initially proposed in [8]) and the majority of the literature on MLS is dedicated to analyzing TreeKEM or proposing better CGKA schemes. We refer the reader to [15, Section 1.3] for an in-depth overview of the literature. The TreeKEM protocol has undergone multiple changes since its inception. In this work, we refer to the version documented in RFC 9420. Given that the vision for the MLS protocol is for it to become the new standard for messaging protocols and that it has support from several large companies [10,11], it has the potential to be used by a huge number of users. Thus, understanding the security of MLS and hence also of TreeKEM is of great importance. This means having formal security guarantees about the security provided by TreeKEM (based on appropriate hardness assumptions).

1.1 The TreeKEM Protocol

Propose and Commit Syntax. As a CGKA scheme, TreeKEM must support operations for updating the key material of a group member, adding a new user and removing a member. The syntax for these operations has changed over time. In the current version of MLS, the protocol uses so-called *proposals* and *commits.* Whenever a user would like to have their key material updated, add a new user or remove a group member, they create a corresponding *update*, *add* or *remove proposal*, respectively, and share this proposal with the group. Any group member can then create a *commit* to apply a set of proposals, create a new group key and update their key material in the process. The commit object includes (encrypted) information such that every group member can update their view of the group and compute the new group key.

TreeKEM Dynamics. TreeKEM uses a full binary tree to model the group and every user is associated with a leaf in the tree (the remaining leaves may be left empty). Each user maintains a synchronized view of the tree, though different users will know more about different parts of the tree. The group key is derived from the root of the tree. Every node n in the tree has an associated key pair (pk_n, sk_n) output by Π.Gen where Π is a public-key encryption scheme. All public keys are known to all users. Let the *direct path* of a leaf be the path from the leaf's parent to the root. A leaf's *path to the root* refers to the same path but including the leaf as well. Every user at a leaf knows the secret key of their leaf and, in the usual case, the secret keys of all nodes on their direct path, though there can be exceptions to this rule. To illustrate the scheme and how commit operations are performed, we will consider a group with users $A, B, \ldots, G$ and H, as depicted in Fig. 1. In the following, we will use these labels for the users both to refer to the users themselves and to their nodes in the tree.

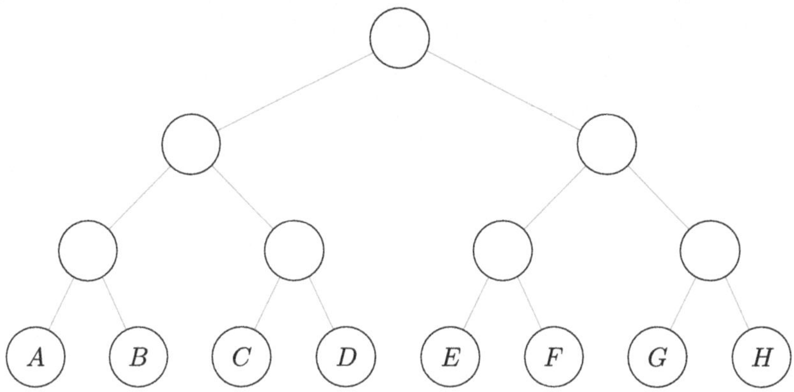

Fig. 1. Illustration of a group with users 8 users in the TreeKEM protocol.

Simple Commits. The idea behind this tree structure is that it allows for a user creating a commit with a new group key to share the new group key with the group using only a few encryptions, while still updating all the secrets the user knew in the tree in order to recover from a possible compromise (recall that in a CGKA scheme a commit also updates the committer's key material). To illustrate how a commit is performed and how the new group key is computed, say user A performs a commit. Let us consider commits without any proposals. TreeKEM specifies two hash functions $H_{\text{gen}}, H_{\text{dep}} \colon \{0,1\}^{\rho(\eta)} \to \{0,1\}^{\rho(\eta)}$ where $\rho(\eta)$ gives the number of random bits used by $\Pi.\text{Gen}(1^\eta)$. The depth of user A is $d = 3$. A will replace all the $d+1$ nodes on their path to the root with new nodes $A, p_1, \ldots, p_d$. (In practice A would just replace the information stored in the original nodes.) The key pairs for the new nodes are sampled as follows. For the leaf node A, user A simply samples a key pair by running $\Pi.\text{Gen}(1^\eta)$. For the remaining nodes, they first sample $s_1 \leftarrow \{0,1\}^{\rho(\eta)}$ and compute the key pair of the first parent p_1 as $\Pi.\mathsf{Gen}(1^\eta, H_{\text{gen}}(s_1))$. For $i \in \{2,\ldots,d\}$ they then compute $s_i := H_{\text{dep}}(s_{i-1})$ and set the key pair of p_i to be $\Pi.\mathsf{Gen}(1^\eta, H_{\text{gen}}(s_i))$. The new group key is $k := H_{\text{dep}}(s_d)$.

User A only needs to share (encryptions of) the seeds s_i for the other users to update their view of the tree and compute the new group key:

- To share the group key with user B, A computes the ciphertext $c_1 \leftarrow \Pi.\mathsf{Enc}_{pk_B}(s_1)$. B can then compute the seed s_1, then use that to compute the seeds $s_2,\ldots,s_d$, the key pairs of all new nodes on their path to the root and the group key k.
- To share the new group key with users C and D, A computes the ciphertext $c_2 \leftarrow \Pi.\mathsf{Enc}_{pk_X}(s_2)$, where X is the parent of the nodes C and D. Both C and D know the secret key sk_X of their parent and can decrypt c_2.
- To share the new group key with users E, F, G and H, A computes the ciphertext $c_3 \leftarrow \Pi.\mathsf{Enc}_{pk_Y}(s_3)$, where Y is the right child of the root node. Again, all users under Y know sk_Y and can thus decrypt c_3.

The commit c that A shares with all users includes the ciphertexts c_1, c_2 and c_3 and the public keys of all new nodes. Figure 2 illustrates the commit performed by A.

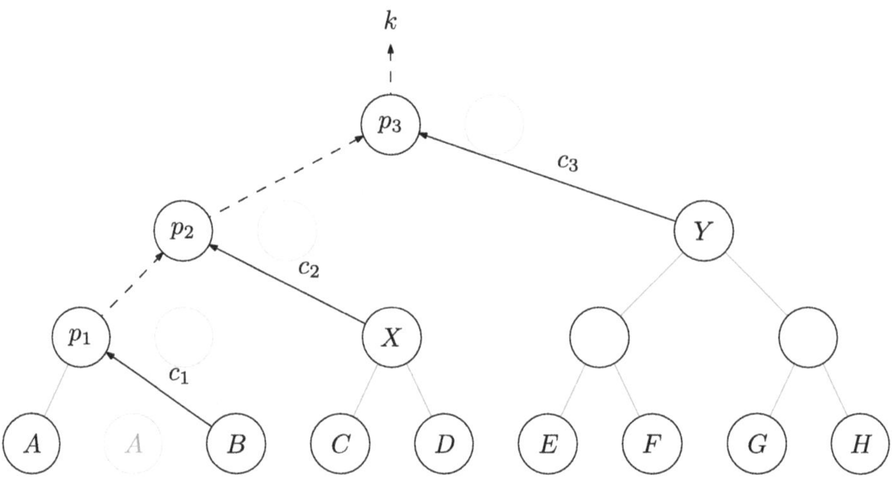

Fig. 2. The commit by user A described in the text. Dashed directed edges illustrate the fact that the target is related to the source via the hash function H_{dep}. The solid directed edges illustrate the fact that the seed of the target node is encrypted to the public key of the source node.

The nodes B, X and Y form the *copath* of A: the copath of a node v consists of the sibling of each node on v's path to the root, excluding the root itself. In the ideal case as above, a node performing a commit only has to compute one encryption for each node on its copath, i.e. logarithmically many encryptions in the total number of users.

The above concepts suffice to understand our main results. For a discussion of how proposals are incorporated into a commit, we refer the reader to Section C.1 of the appendix in the full version [4].

1.2 The GSD Game

The Generalized Selective Decryption (GSD) security game [14] was introduced precisely to analyze adaptive security for protocols based on a graph-like structure, as is the case with TreeKEM. It was initially defined for the private-key setting and later adapted to the public-key setting in [13].

In the GSD security game, given an encryption scheme a graph, the *GSD graph*, is constructed by the challenger where every node in the graph is associated with a symmetric key in the private-key setting, or a public/private key pair in the public-key setting. The adversary can then request encryptions of a node's (secret) key under the (public) key of another node. In the public-key setting, such an *encryption query* also reveals the latter node's public key. This creates an *encryption edge* in the graph, directed from the node whose (public) key was used for encryption to the node whose key was encrypted. The adversary can also corrupt any node, which reveals its (secret) key and allows the adversary to compute the (secret) key of any other node reachable from the corrupted node in the graph by performing decryptions along the path to the other node. At the end of the game the adversary chooses a node to be challenged on, the *challenge node*. A coin is then tossed and the adversary is given either the (secret) key of the challenge node or a uniformly random (secret) key and it must guess which scenario it is in. The possible choices for the challenge node must of course be restricted to nodes whose keys were not compromised through a corruption, meaning that the challenge node should never be reachable from a corrupted node in the graph. Further restrictions are also necessary which we do not go into here and refer the reader to Sect. 4.1. Figure 3 illustrates what an example GSD graph may look like.

The graph constructed in the public-key GSD game and the tree structure behind the TreeKEM protocol clearly resemble each other. Let Π the public-key encryption scheme in use, where $\Pi.\mathrm{Gen}(1^\eta)$ samples $\rho(\eta)$ random bits. We can make some small modifications to the public-key GSD game such that the operations performed in TreeKEM match the ones performed in this modified GSD game. Take the functions $H_{\mathrm{gen}}, H_{\mathrm{dep}}$ used in TreeKEM and first modify the game as follows:

- the key pair of a node v is generated by sampling a seed $s_v \in \{0,1\}^{\rho(\eta)}$ and computing $(pk_v, sk_v) = \Pi.\mathrm{Gen}(1^\eta, H_{\mathrm{gen}}(s_v))$
- encryption queries encrypt the seed of the target node instead of its secret key

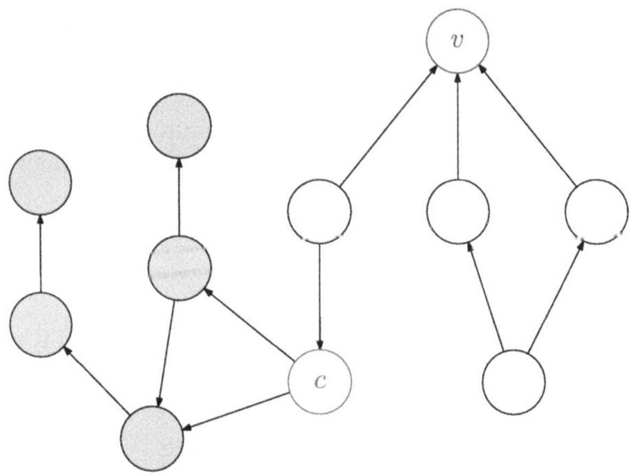

Fig. 3. An illustration of the GSD graph for an instance of the GSD game. The challenge node is v. The node c was corrupted, resulting in all nodes reachable from it being compromised, as marked with red color. (Color figure online)

Now the generation of key pairs and the encryptions computed in TreeKEM match what is done in this adapted GSD game. To model the fact that in TreeKEM the seed of a node may depend on the seed of another node through H_{dep} (as in the new direct path computed in a commit), we can introduce a new type of edge which we call a *seed dependency*: a seed dependency (u, v) implies that $s_v = H_{\text{dep}}(s_u)$.

1.3 Existing Security Proofs

The work in [13] made use of the relationship between the (public-key) GSD game and TreeKEM described in the previous section. They proved a polynomial bound for the adaptive security of the public-key GSD game in the Random Oracle Model (ROM) [7] for an arbitrary IND-CPA secure public-key encryption scheme. The core idea behind their proof is simple. Intuitively, the only way for an adversary to learn about the seed of an uncorrupted node for the first time is through the encryption edges into the node. The authors show that in the ROM, one can reduce security in the GSD game to the IND-CPA security of the public-key encryption scheme with a moderate security loss. They apply standard guessing arguments and a clever, albeit complicated, hybrid argument to achieve a security loss in $\mathcal{O}(N^2)$, where N is the number of nodes in the GSD graph. The N^2 loss stems from the fact that two nodes in the GSD graph need to be guessed correctly for the reduction to succeed.

This result implies a polynomial bound for the security of TreeKEM as a CGKA scheme as outlined in [13, Theorem 4] and subsequently proven in more detail in [3, Theorem 12], and was the first proof of adaptive security for TreeKEM. As far as we know, this is the tightest result on the security of TreeKEM in the literature.

1.4 Security Model

We prove adaptive CGKA security of TreeKEM for a single group and a single challenge query when the DHIES scheme is used. Additionally, our result easily extends to adversaries performing multiple challenge queries with the same security loss (irrespective of the number of challenges). Our security definition is very close to the definition provided in [3, Section 4.1.2], but gives the adversary less power. We provide a weaker definition in order to simplify the definition and proof. However, we are confident that the exact same result can be proven for the CGKA security definition in [3]. The additional power given to the adversary in [3] should only affect the set of commits that the adversary can ask to be challenged on in the CGKA security game (defined in [4, Section C.2]).

1.5 Contributions

Tighter GSD security for DHIES. In this work, we formally prove the adaptive security of a specific public-key encryption scheme, the DHIES scheme [1], in the adapted public-key GSD game described above, in the ROM. Focusing on the DHIES scheme allows us to achieve a tighter bound than the one in [13]. Each encryption of a seed s_v with DHIES is a tuple of the form $\langle g^x, c\rangle$ with $c \leftarrow \Pi_s.\mathrm{Enc}_k(s_v)$, where $k = H_{\mathrm{DH}}(g^{xy})$, g is a generator in the Diffie-Hellman group, Π_s is the private-key encryption scheme used in DHIES, H_{DH} is a hash function and y is the secret key of the source node of the encryption edge. By modelling H_{DH} as a random oracle, we know that in order for an adversary to learn anything from this encryption, intuitively, they must have either learned k by querying H_{DH} and then decrypting the ciphertext c, or they must have gleaned information from c without knowing the key k. We can reduce the first case to the hardness of the Diffie-Hellman problem with a security loss in $\mathcal{O}(N)$. To achieve a linear loss, we first guess the node v for which the Diffie-Hellman problem was solved on an outgoing encryption edge and exploit the self-reducibility property of the Diffie-Hellman problem in order to embed a single Diffie-Hellman challenge into all outgoing edges. The second case can be reduced to the security of the private-key encryption scheme with a security loss in $\mathcal{O}(\delta \cdot N)$ where δ is the maximum in-degree in the GSD graph. This follows from guessing the target node s_v and then applying a standard hybrid argument to the up to δ encryption edges ending in v.[1] In [4, Section B.4] we show that the security loss can be reduced to $\mathcal{O}(N)$ for a very specific set of schemes.

Besides providing a tighter bound, our proof has further significant advantages. Arguably, it is more intuitive and less complex than the ones in [3,13]. Furthermore, our approach can easily be adapted to prove the same security loss in a GSD game with multiple challenge queries. Both of these advantages stem from how we compute the challenge in our GSD definition. See Sect. 4.1 for details.

---

[1] The same hybrid argument does not work for directly reducing to the security of the public-key encryption scheme due to a technicality.

The Security of TreeKEM. Our final result for TreeKEM has a security loss in $\mathcal{O}(u \cdot (c \cdot \log(u) + p))$ reducing to EAV security[2] of the private-key encryption scheme and a loss in $\mathcal{O}(c \cdot \log(u) + p)$ reducing to the hardness of the Diffie-Hellman problem, where c is the number of commits, p the number of add or update proposals and u the number of users. As with GSD, our result holds irrespective of the number of challenge queries. The result in [13] implies a security loss of $\mathcal{O}((c \cdot \log(u) + p)^2)$ for a single challenge query, reducing to IND-CPA security of the public-key encryption scheme. This can be generalized to multiple challenges by a hybrid argument, involving an additional multiplicative loss in the number of challenges. When p is small such that $p \leq c \cdot \log(u)$, the losses simplify to $\mathcal{O}(c \cdot u \cdot \log(u))$ and $\mathcal{O}(c \cdot \log(u))$, respectively, as opposed to $\mathcal{O}((c \cdot \log(u))^2)$ in [13]. In this setting, our result guarantees 90 bits of security with 128-bit parameters and 210 bits with 256-bit parameters for large groups (under standard assumptions). When p is large, e.g. when many updates are applied in each commit, the losses simplify to $\mathcal{O}(c \cdot u^2)$ and $\mathcal{O}(c \cdot u)$ as opposed to $\mathcal{O}((c \cdot u)^2)$ in [13]. Our result guarantees 95 bits of security when a 128-bit Diffie-Hellman group is combined with 256-bit AES, while the result in [13] only guarantees 64 bits. Using 256-bit parameters gives a 209-bit security level.

1.6 Relation to MLS Security

The work in [3] provides a comprehensive security definition for group messaging protocols and reduces the security of MLS to the security of its underlying primitives, including the CGKA scheme. Since our proof can be adapted to go through with the CGKA definition used in this work, our result implies a tighter result for the security of MLS as a whole. However, the security proof of MLS in [3] has a very large (but polynomial) loss and even with our improved bound for TreeKEM we don't expect this to provide a meaningful level of security. Therefore, finding a tighter reduction for the MLS protocol as a whole is a crucial open problem on the path to proving meaningful security guarantees for the protocol.

2 Preliminaries

Our definitions were adapted from [12]. A summary of our notation, some simple lemmas, definitions for private-key and public-key encryption, IND-CPA security, EAV security, group-generation algorithms and the Decisional Diffie-Hellman (DDH) problem, and an explanation of the Random Oracle Model (ROM) can be found in [4, Section A].

2.1 DHIES

In the following definition we will refer to "key-derivation functions". This is only meant as a hint to the reader. We do not provide a definition here, as we will always model such a function as a random oracle.

[2] EAV security is implied by IND-CPA security. See [4, Section A.3] for details.

Definition 1 (DHIES[12, Construction 12.19]). *Let $\mathcal{G}$ a group-generation algorithm (for Diffie-Hellman groups). Let Π_s a private-key encryption scheme where* Π_s.Gen(1^η) *samples a key u.a.r. from $\{0,1\}^\eta$. Let $\mathcal{H}_{\mathrm{DH}} = \{H_{\mathrm{DH}}^{(\eta)} \mid \eta \in \mathbb{N}\}$ a family of key-derivation functions where $H_{\mathrm{DH}}^{(\eta)}\colon \{0,1\}^* \to \{0,1\}^\eta$. We write $H_{\mathrm{DH}} := H_{\mathrm{DH}}^{(\eta)}$ when η is clear from the context. Define the algorithms* Gen, Enc *and* Dec *as follows:*

- Gen*: on input 1^η run $\mathcal{G}(1^\eta)$ to obtain $(\mathbb{G}, q, g)$. Sample $x \leftarrow [q]$ and set $h_1 := g^x$. Set $pk := \langle \mathbb{G}, q, g, h_1 \rangle$ and $sk := \langle \mathbb{G}, q, g, x \rangle$, and output (pk, sk). The message space is the message space of Π_s.*
- Enc*: on input a public key $\langle \mathbb{G}, q, g, h_1 \rangle$ and a message m, sample $y \leftarrow [q]$, set $h_2 := g^y, k := H_{\mathrm{DH}}(h_1^y)$,[3] compute $c' \leftarrow \Pi_s.\mathrm{Enc}_k(m)$ and output the ciphertext $\langle h_2, c' \rangle$.*
- Dec*: on input a private key $\langle \mathbb{G}, q, g, x \rangle$ and a ciphertext $\langle h_2, c' \rangle$, compute $k := H(h_2^x)$ and output $\Pi_s.\mathrm{Dec}_k(c')$. If the ciphertext is not of the right form or* Π_s.Dec *outputs $\perp$, output $\perp$.*

The public-key encryption scheme $\Pi_{\mathrm{DH}} :=$ (Gen, Enc, Dec) *is called the Diffie-Hellman Integrated Encryption Scheme (DHIES).*

When using the DHIES scheme later on, we will set $pk := h$ and $sk := x$ in Gen *for simplicity. In practice $\mathbb{G}, q, g$ and H_{DH} will be known.*

Under the DDH assumption (i.e. the assumption that the DDH problem is hard relative to $\mathcal{G}$), using DHIES with an EAV secure private-key scheme gives an IND-CPA secure public-key encryption scheme in the ROM, as proven in [12, Theorem 12.12].

3 Our Concrete Result for TreeKEM

The following theorem describing the security of TreeKEM, stated informally here, is our main practical result. It bounds the advantage of any adversary creating c commits and p add or update proposals in a group with at most u users in distinguishing the group key of any uncompromised commit from a random bit string.

Theorem 1 (Informal). *If the DHIES scheme is used in TreeKEM, the private-key encryption scheme in DHIES is $(t, \varepsilon_{\mathrm{EAV}})$-EAV-secure and the DDH problem is $(t, \varepsilon_{\mathrm{DDH}})$-hard in the Diffie-Hellman group, then for all c, p, u, TreeKEM is $(\tilde{t}, \tilde{\varepsilon}, c, p, u)$-secure in the ROM with $\tilde{t} \approx t$ and*

$$\begin{aligned}\tilde{\varepsilon} &= 2 \cdot u \cdot (3 \cdot c \cdot \log(u) + p) \cdot \varepsilon_{\mathrm{EAV}} \\ &\quad + 2 \cdot (3 \cdot c \cdot \log(u) + p) \cdot \varepsilon_{\mathrm{DDH}} \\ &\quad + \mathrm{negl}\end{aligned}$$

[3] Where for $h \in \mathbb{G}$, $H_{\mathrm{DH}}(h)$ denotes the output of H_{DH} with the binary representation of h given as input.

where

- *c is the number of commits created*
- *p is the number of add or update proposals created*
- *u is the maximum number of users*
- *the term* negl = negl(η) *is negligible and much smaller than the other terms*

In [4, Section C] we restate the above theorem formally as Theorem 4. To this end, we also provide formal definitions for the syntax and security of propose and commit CGKA schemes and a high-level description of how to instantiate (the essence of) the TreeKEM protocol with our definitions.

Security Against Multiple Challenges. As noted in the introduction, although our security definitions only allow the adversary to make a single challenge query, it is straightforward to adapt our proof to show the same security loss with multiple challenge queries. See the note after [4, Theorem 4] for details.

3.1 Interpreting the Result

In the following, we will go through some concrete examples to see what level of security our proof guarantees for TreeKEM with different parameter choices. We will look at the `MLS_128_DHKEMX25519_AES128GCM_SHA256_Ed25519` cipher suite [6, Section 17.1] for 128-bit parameters, which uses Curve25519 as the Diffie-Hellman group and AES with a 128-bit key size for private-key encryption. We will assume that both Curve25519 and AES have a 128-bit security level and we will set $(t, \varepsilon_{\mathrm{EAV}}) = (t, \varepsilon_{\mathrm{DDH}}) = (2^{48}, 2^{-80})$.

For 256-bit parameters, we will look at the `MLS_256_DHKEMP521_AES256GCM_SHA512_P521` cipher suite, which uses curve P-521 and 256-bit AES. We will assume that P-521 and 256-bit AES have a 256-bit security level and set $(t, \varepsilon_{\mathrm{EAV}}) = (t, \varepsilon_{\mathrm{DDH}}) = (2^{128}, 2^{-128})$.

Large Groups with Hourly Commits and Frequent Updates. In this example we consider a large group of about 10'000 users, existing for 5 years and making one commit every hour. Then $u \leq 2^{14}$ and $c \leq 2^{16}$. We also assume that a significant fraction of the users will want to update with every commit. Then, assuming that add proposals are relatively rare, we can bound $p \leq c \cdot u = 2^{30}$. This implies $3 \cdot c \cdot \log(u) + p \leq 2^{31}$, dominated by p.

Then with 128-bit parameters we get

$$\tilde{\varepsilon} \leq 2^{46} \cdot \varepsilon_{\mathrm{EAV}} + 2^{32} \cdot \varepsilon_{\mathrm{DDH}} + \mathrm{negl} \leq \frac{1}{2^{33}}$$

with the $\varepsilon_{\mathrm{EAV}}$ term dominating the result. This only gives a security level of $\tilde{t}/\tilde{\varepsilon} \geq 2^{81}$. Since private-key encryption is relatively cheap, using 256-bit AES would have a small impact on the performance and would increase the security level to 95 bits (with the $\varepsilon_{\mathrm{DDH}}$ term now dominating).[4] Finally, using full 256-bit parameters yields 209 bits of security for TreeKEM.

[4] For this we set $(t, \varepsilon_{\mathrm{EAV}}) = (2^{48}, 2^{-208})$.

The previous best result in [13, Theorem 3] proved the bound

$$\tilde{\varepsilon} \leq 2 \cdot (3 \cdot c \cdot \log(u) + p)^2 \cdot \varepsilon + \text{negl}$$

where ε is the IND-CPA security of the underlying public-key encryption scheme. If we assume that DHIES has an x-bit security level as a public-key encryption scheme with x-bit parameters, the result implies 64 bits of security with 128-bit parameters (with no change when using 256-bit AES) and 192 bits with 256-bit parameters.

Few Updates. In this example we use the same number of users and commits, but assume that the number of proposals is small such that $p \leq c \cdot \log(u)$. In this case, we have $3 \cdot c \cdot \log(u) + p \leq 2^{22}$. Then our result guarantees 90 bits of security with 128-bit parameters, 104 bits with 256-bit AES and 218 bits with 256-bit parameters.

In contrast, the bound in [13] implies 82 bits with 128-bit parameters and 210 bits with 256-bit parameters.

Very Large Groups with One Commit Every Minute and Frequent Updates. In this example we consider more extreme values for c and u to highlight the gap between our result and the one in [13]. We assume a group of about 1 million users, existing for 50 years and making one commit every minute. Furthermore, we will again use $p \leq c \cdot u$. This means that $u \leq 2^{20}$, $c \leq 2^{25}$ and $3 \cdot c \cdot \log(u) + p \leq 2^{46}$.

These values imply 60 bits of security with 128-bit parameters, 80 bits with 256-bit AES and 188 bits with 256-bit parameters using our result. The result in [13] implies 34 bits of security with 128-bit parameters and 162 bits with 256-bit parameters.

4 Tighter GSD Security

In this section, we present the main theoretical result behind Theorem 1 in Theorem 2. To this end, we first define a modified version of the public-key GSD game from [13] and then proceed to prove Theorem 2 in detail.

4.1 Seeded GSD with Dependencies

The GSD game defined here is inspired by the definition of the public-key GSD game (Definition 7) and the proof of Theorem 3 in [13]. We have already motivated the differences in Sect. 1.2. We will call our adapted game *Seeded GSD with Dependencies* (SD-GSD). A very similar definition appears in [3], providing essentially the same abstraction over TreeKEM and also allowing for an adversary to provide the randomness used for encryption and key generation. However, our definition has one key difference: when asking to be challenged on a node with seed s, the adversary must distinguish $H_{\text{dep}}(s)$ from random as opposed to

s. This stays true to how the group key is computed in TreeKEM and provides two significant advantages:

- it allow us to significantly simplify our proof
- it enables one to easily prove the same bound when the adversary can make multiple challenge queries

On the other hand, the security implied by our definition is weaker (at least in the ROM), as it only guarantees that an adversary cannot compute the seed of the challenge node, whereas the other definitions guarantee that this seed cannot be distinguished from random.

Definition 2 (The SD-GSD Game). *Let* $\Pi = (\mathrm{Gen}, \mathrm{Enc}, \mathrm{Dec})$ *a public-key encryption scheme, where* $\mathrm{Gen}(1^\eta)$ *uses* $\rho(\eta)$ *random bits and* $\{0,1\}^{\rho(\eta)}$ *is a subset of the message space. Let* $\mathcal{H}_{\mathrm{gen}} = \{H_{\mathrm{gen}}^{(\eta)} \mid \eta \in \mathbb{N}\}, \mathcal{H}_{\mathrm{dep}} = \{H_{\mathrm{DH}}^{(\eta)} \mid \eta \in \mathbb{N}\}$ *families of functions with* $H_{\mathrm{gen}}^{(\eta)}, H_{\mathrm{dep}}^{(\eta)} \colon \{0,1\}^{\rho(\eta)} \to \{0,1\}^{\rho(\eta)}$*. We will write* $H_{\mathrm{gen}} := H_{\mathrm{gen}}^{(\eta)}, H_{\mathrm{dep}} := H_{\mathrm{dep}}^{(\eta)}$ *and* $\rho := \rho(\eta)$ *if* η *is clear from the context. Define the game* $\mathrm{Game}^{\text{SD-GSD}}_{(\Pi,\mathcal{H}_{\mathrm{gen}},\mathcal{H}_{\mathrm{dep}}),\eta}(\mathcal{A})$ *for an adversary* $\mathcal{A}$*:*

1. *The adversary* $\mathcal{A}$ *outputs* $n \in \mathbb{N}$ *and a list of dependencies* $D = \{(a_i, b_i)\}_{i=1}^m \subseteq [n]^2$*. For each* $v \in [n]$*:*
   (i) - ***Case*** $v = b_i$ ***for some*** i ***(***v ***is the target of some dependency):*** *set* $s_v = H_{\mathrm{dep}}(s_{a_i})$*.*
   - ***Otherwise:*** *sample* $s_v \leftarrow \{0,1\}^\rho$*.*

   We call s_v *the* seed *of the node* v *and a tuple* $(a, b) \in D$ *a* seed dependency.

   (ii) *Compute* $(pk_v, sk_v) = \mathrm{Gen}(1^\eta, H_{\mathrm{gen}}(s_v))$*.*

   Set $\mathcal{C} = E = \varnothing$*. We call the directed graph* $([n], E)$ *a* GSD graph *of* size n*.*
2. $\mathcal{A}$ *may adaptively make the following queries:*
   - $\mathrm{reveal}(v)$ *for* $v \in [n]$*:* $\mathcal{A}$ *is given* pk_v*.*
   - $\mathrm{encrypt}(u, v)$ *for* $u, v \in [n], u \neq v, (u, v) \notin E$*:* (u, v) *is added to* E *and* $\mathcal{A}$ *is given* $c \leftarrow \mathrm{Enc}_{pk_u}(s_v)$*.*
   - $\mathrm{corrupt}(v)$ *for* $v \in [n], v \notin \mathcal{C}$*:* $\mathcal{A}$ *is given* s_v *and* v *is added to* $\mathcal{C}$*. We call such a node* $v \in \mathcal{C}$ corrupted. *All nodes not reachable from any corrupted node in the graph* $([n], E \cup D)$ *are* safe *(while all other nodes are* unsafe*) and we call their seeds* hidden *(even if an unsafe node happens to have the same seed).*
3. $\mathcal{A}$ *outputs a node* $v \in [n]$*. We call* v *the* challenge node*.* $\mathcal{A}$ *bit* $b \leftarrow \{0,1\}$ *is sampled and* $\mathcal{A}$ *is given*

$$r = \begin{cases} H_{\mathrm{dep}}(s_v) & b = 0 \\ s & b = 1 \end{cases},$$

where $s \leftarrow \{0,1\}^\rho$*.*[5] $\mathcal{A}$ *may continue to do queries as before.*

[5] Note that (in general) r is not a hidden seed, as (with overwhelming probability) it is not the seed of any node.

4. *$\mathcal{A}$ outputs a bit b'. The output of the game is defined to be 1 if $b' = b$, and 0 otherwise.*

We require an adversary playing the above game to adhere to the following:

- *The challenge node is safe*
- *The challenge node is not the source of a seed dependency*[6]
- *Every node is the source and target of at most one seed dependency*[7]
- *The graph $([n], E \cup D)$ is acyclic and without self-loops*

It is interesting to note that previous definitions of the GSD game also included the following restrictions to the adversary:

- The challenge node always remains a sink in $([n], E)$
- reveal is never queried on the challenge node

Our proof in the ROM does not require these restrictions. If H_{dep} is modelled as a random oracle, then an encryption edge outgoing from the challenge node, or knowing its public key gives no advantage to $\mathcal{A}$, as by the assumption of H_{dep} being a random oracle the only way to learn information about $H_{\text{dep}}(s)$ is by querying s.

Definition 3 (SD-GSD Security). *Let $\Pi, \mathcal{H}_{\text{gen}}$ and $\mathcal{H}_{\text{dep}}$ as in Definition 2 above and let $t, \varepsilon, N, \delta$ functions in η. The triple $(\Pi, H_{\text{gen}}, H_{\text{dep}})$ is $(t, \varepsilon, N, \delta)$-*SD-GSD-secure *if for all η, for any adversary $\mathcal{A}$ constructing a GSD graph of size at most $N(\eta)$ and indegree at most $\delta(\eta)$ and running in time $t(\eta)$ we have*

$$\mathrm{Adv}^{\text{SD-GSD}}_{(\Pi,\mathcal{H}_{\text{gen}},\mathcal{H}_{\text{dep}}),\eta}(\mathcal{A}) := 2 \cdot \left(\Pr\left[\mathrm{Game}^{\text{SD-GSD}}_{(\Pi,\mathcal{H}_{\text{gen}},\mathcal{H}_{\text{dep}}),\eta}(\mathcal{A}) = 1\right] - \frac{1}{2} \right) \leq \varepsilon(\eta).$$

Since in this work we are interested in SD-GSD security for the case where H_{gen} and H_{dep} are modelled as random oracles and our focus is on the encryption scheme being used, we introduce the following definition for convenience.

Definition 4 (SD-GSD Security in the ROM). *A public-key encryption scheme Π is $(t, \varepsilon, N, \delta)$-*SD-GSD-secure in the ROM *if the triple $(\Pi, \mathcal{H}_{\text{gen}}, \mathcal{H}_{\text{dep}})$ is $(t, \varepsilon, N, \delta)$-SD-GSD-secure when H_{gen} and H_{dep} are modelled as random oracles. For security parameter η and an adversary $\mathcal{A}$, we write $\mathrm{Game}^{\text{SD-GSD}}_{\Pi,\eta}(\mathcal{A})$ to denote the game where H_{gen} and H_{dep} are modelled as random oracles and $\mathrm{Adv}^{\text{SD-GSD}}_{\Pi,\eta}(\mathcal{A})$ for $\mathcal{A}$'s advantage in this game.*

---

[6] Otherwise the adversary could learn the value of H_{dep} on the seed of the challenge node by creating a seed dependency with the challenge node as the source and corrupting the target node.

[7] If a node were the source node of multiple seed dependencies, then corrupting one target node would reveal the seeds of all target nodes. Additionally, the computation of seeds is not well-defined if a node is the target of multiple dependencies.

4.2 Proving SD-GSD Security for DHIES in the ROM

Theorem 2. *Let Π_{DH} denote the DHIES scheme instantiated with a group-generation algorithm $\mathcal{G}$ and a private-key encryption scheme Π_s. If Π_s is $(t, \varepsilon_{\text{EAV}})$-EAV-secure, the DDH problem is $(t, \varepsilon_{\text{DDH}})$-hard relative to $\mathcal{G}$ and the function H_{DH} in Π_{DH} is modelled as a random oracle, then for any δ, N with $\delta \leq N$, Π_{DH} is $(\tilde{t}, \tilde{\varepsilon}, N, \delta)$-SD-GSD-secure in the ROM with*[8]

$$\tilde{\varepsilon} = 2 \cdot \delta \cdot N \cdot \varepsilon_{\text{EAV}} + 2 \cdot N \cdot \varepsilon_{\text{DDH}} + \frac{2 \cdot m_{\text{DH}} \cdot N^2}{q} + \frac{m_s \cdot N}{2^{\rho-1}} + \frac{N^2}{2^{\rho-3}},$$

*where m_{s} is an upper bound on the number of queries made to either H_{gen} or H_{dep}, m_{DH} is an upper bound on the number of queries made to H_{DH}, q is a lower bound on the size of the group output by $\mathcal{G}$ and ρ is the number of random bits sampled by Π_{DH}.*Gen*, and with $\tilde{t} \approx t$.*[9]

In contrast, the result in [13] achieves a security loss in $\mathcal{O}(N^2)$ and reduces to the IND-CPA security of the public-key encryption scheme.

For ease of exposition, we will assume that $\mathcal{G}(1^\eta)$ is deterministic, as is the case in practice. We will therefore set $pk := h_1, sk := x$ in Π_{DH}.Gen, as $\mathbb{G}, q, g$ are implied by η. The results nevertheless hold also for the general case.

Intuition. Consider an arbitrary SD-GSD adversary $\mathcal{A}$. For an execution of $\text{Game}^{\text{SD-GSD}}_{\Pi_{\text{DH}},\eta}(\mathcal{A})$ we say "$\mathcal{A}$ *wins*" to denote the event $\text{Game}^{\text{SD-GSD}}_{\Pi_{\text{DH}},\eta}(\mathcal{A}) = 1$. For one argument, we will need to assume that all seeds sampled in the SD-GSD game are distinct, which happens with overwhelming probability. To this end, let C denote the event that there are two nodes with the same seed.

As usual with random oracles we proceed by a case distinction on whether they were queried on some interesting value. Accordingly, let Q_x denote the event that $\mathcal{A}$ queries H_x on a hidden seed for $x \in \{\text{gen}, \text{dep}\}$. Then we can write

$$\begin{aligned} \Pr\left[\mathcal{A} \text{ wins} \mid \overline{C}\right] &= \Pr\left[\mathcal{A} \text{ wins} \wedge Q_{\text{dep}} \mid \overline{C}\right] + \Pr\left[\mathcal{A} \text{ wins} \wedge \overline{Q_{\text{dep}}} \mid \overline{C}\right] \\ &\leq \Pr\left[\mathcal{A} \text{ wins} \wedge Q_{\text{dep}} \mid \overline{C}\right] + \Pr\left[\mathcal{A} \text{ wins} \mid \overline{C}, \overline{Q_{\text{dep}}}\right] \\ &\overset{(\dagger)}{=} \Pr\left[\mathcal{A} \text{ wins} \wedge Q_{\text{dep}} \mid \overline{C}\right] + \frac{1}{2} \\ &\leq \Pr\left[Q_{\text{s}} \mid \overline{C}\right] + \frac{1}{2} \\ &\overset{(\spadesuit)}{\leq} \Pr[Q_{\text{s}}] + \Pr[C] + \frac{1}{2}, \end{aligned} \tag{1}$$

where $Q_{\text{s}} := Q_{\text{gen}} \cup Q_{\text{dep}}$ (s for *seed*). Step (†) intuitively holds because without having queried H_{dep} for any hidden seed, in particular the seed s_v of the challenge

[8] Note that in the following equality we have omitted writing the argument η to the various functions and are implying that the equality holds for all η.

[9] We provide a more precise expression of the runtime in [4, Section B.1].

node v, $H_{\text{dep}}(s_v)$ is a uniformly random value from $\mathcal{A}$'s perspective. Therefore, it can do no better than guessing to distinguish $H_{\text{dep}}(s_v)$ from $s \leftarrow \{0,1\}^\rho$. Step (♠) follows from simple manipulations (see the proof for details).

The heart of the proof is to bound $\Pr[Q_s]$. When the adversary first triggers Q_s by querying the seed of some safe node w, it can only have learned the seed through encryptions $c_1 \leftarrow \Pi_{\text{DH}}.\text{Enc}_{pk_{u_1}}(s_w), \ldots, c_d \leftarrow \Pi_{\text{DH}}.\text{Enc}_{pk_{u_d}}(s_w)$ where $(u_1, w), \ldots, (u_d, w)$ are edges in the GSD graph (obtained through corresponding queries $\text{encrypt}(u_1, w), \ldots, \text{encrypt}(u_d, w)$). The only other potential source of information about s_w would be a seed dependency (p, w), but this tells $\mathcal{A}$ nothing: Since w is safe, p would also be safe and $H_{\text{dep}}(s_p)$ cannot have been queried due to the assumption that w was the first node to trigger Q_s. Without having queried $H_{\text{dep}}(s_p)$, by virtue of H_{dep} being a random oracle s_w has the same distribution as a seed without a dependency from $\mathcal{A}$'s perspective (uniformly random). See Fig. 4 for an illustration of node w in the GSD graph.

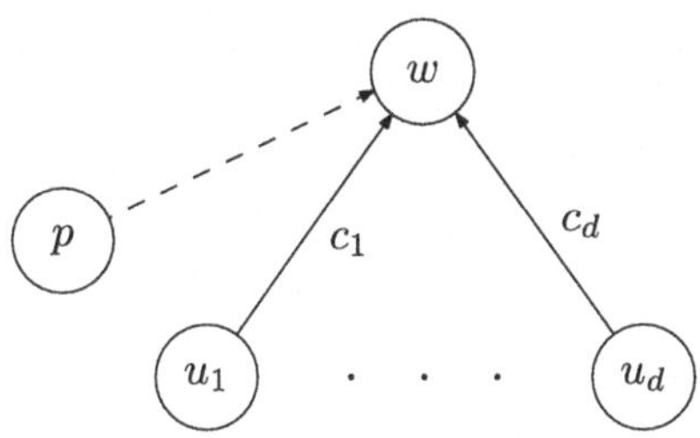

Fig. 4. Illustration of the GSD graph when Q_s is triggered at a node w. The dashed edge represents a seed dependency (p, w) and the remaining edges represent encryption queries $c_i \leftarrow \text{encrypt}(u_i, w)$.

The proof in [13] simply argued that this is not too likely if these encryptions were made with an IND-CPA secure scheme. In the context of the DHIES scheme we can say more about these encryptions and achieve a better reduction loss.

Let $(\mathbb{G}, q, g) = \mathcal{G}(1^\eta)$. Let $x_i = \log_g(pk_{u_i})$. Each encryption c_i is a tuple of the form $\langle g^{y_i}, \Pi_s.\text{Enc}_{k_i}(s_w)\rangle$ where $y_i \leftarrow [q]$ and $k_i = H_{\text{DH}}(g^{x_i \cdot y_i})$. Now we can again do a case distinction on whether H_{DH} was queried for (the encoding of) some group element $g^{x_j \cdot y_j}$ or not:

(i) If such a query was made, then $\mathcal{A}$ solved the Diffie-Hellman challenge (g^{x_j}, g^{y_j}). (Remember that we assumed that w is the first node for which Q_s is triggered and as before if w is safe, then so are the nodes u_i. Thus the adversary has not learned the exponent x_i through querying $H_{\text{gen}}(s_{u_i})$ for any i.)
(ii) If no such query was made, then from $\mathcal{A}$'s perspective all the k_i are independent, uniformly random keys and it still was able to learn s_w from the EAV secure encryptions $\Pi_s.\text{Enc}_{k_1}(s_w), \ldots, \Pi_s.\text{Enc}_{k_d}(s_w)$.

We can bound the probability of either of these events occurring using the hardness of the DDH problem relative to $\mathcal{G}$ and EAV security of Π_s, respectively.

To this end, we call a group element $h \in \mathbb{G}$ a *hidden Diffie-Hellman key* if $h = pk_u^{y_{u,v}}$, where (u, v) is an edge in the GSD graph, u is safe and $y_{u,v}$ is the exponent chosen in the DHIES encryption of s_v (i.e. $\mathcal{A}$ was given a ciphertext of the form $\langle g^{y_{u,v}}, \ldots \rangle$ when it queried encrypt(u, v)). Now analogously to above let Q_{DH} the event that $\mathcal{A}$ queries H_{DH} on a hidden Diffie-Hellman key, and let F_{DH} the event that $\mathcal{A}$ triggers Q_{DH} when Q_{s} has not (yet) been triggered. Then we can split the event Q_{s} into two cases as motivated above:

$$\Pr[Q_{\mathrm{s}}] = \Pr[Q_{\mathrm{s}} \wedge F_{\mathrm{DH}}] + \Pr\left[Q_{\mathrm{s}} \wedge \overline{F_{\mathrm{DH}}}\right].$$

We bound $\Pr[Q_{\mathrm{s}} \wedge F_{\mathrm{DH}}]$ and $\Pr\left[Q_{\mathrm{s}} \wedge \overline{F_{\mathrm{DH}}}\right]$ in Lemma 3 and Lemma 2, respectively.[10] Overall this gives us a bound on the advantage of $\mathcal{A}$ using (1).

Proof (of Theorem 2). Let δ, N functions in η (mapping to $\mathbb{N}$) with $\delta \leq N$. Let η arbitrary and let $\mathcal{A}$ an arbitrary SD-GSD adversary constructing a GSD graph of size at most $N(\eta)$ and indegree at most $\delta(\eta)$, making at most $m_{\mathrm{s}}(\eta)$ queries to H_{gen} or H_{dep} and at most $m_{\mathrm{DH}}(\eta)$ queries to H_{DH}, each of length at most $\gamma(\eta)$, and running in time $\tilde{t}(\eta)$. We will use the events defined above.

We have

$$\begin{aligned} \Pr[\mathcal{A} \text{ wins}] &= \Pr[\mathcal{A} \text{ wins} \wedge C] + \Pr\left[\mathcal{A} \text{ wins} \wedge \overline{C}\right] \\ &\leq \Pr[C] + \Pr\left[\mathcal{A} \text{ wins} \mid \overline{C}\right]. \end{aligned} \tag{2}$$

Let us first bound the probability of a seed collision. Let C_g the event that there is a collision among nodes that are not the source of a seed dependency. The seeds of these up to N nodes are sampled independently of each other u.a.r. from $\{0,1\}^\rho$, so by the birthday bound we have

$$\Pr[C_g] \leq \frac{N(N-1)}{2 \cdot 2^\rho}.$$

Now consider $\Pr\left[C \mid \overline{C_g}\right]$. The source seed of every seed dependency is distinct if $\overline{C_g}$. Therefore, given $\overline{C_g}$ every additional seed is sampled u.a.r. from $\{0,1\}^\rho$, with up to N seeds already being taken. Similar to proving the birthday bound, the probability that the i-th seed derived from a seed dependency collides with one of the already sampled seeds is at most $\frac{N+i}{2^\rho}$. Therefore,

$$\begin{aligned} \Pr\left[C \mid \overline{C_g}\right] &\leq \frac{N+0}{2^\rho} + \ldots + \frac{N+(N-1)}{2^\rho} \\ &= \frac{N^2}{2^\rho} + \frac{N(N-1)}{2 \cdot 2^\rho}. \end{aligned}$$

[10] To be precise, the event $Q_{\mathrm{s}} \wedge F_{\mathrm{DH}}$ is a superset of case (i) above. However, the argument applied in Lemma 3 gives the same bound for either event and this more general event has the advantage of being simpler.

Then

$$\begin{aligned}\Pr[C] &= \Pr[C \wedge C_g] + \Pr\left[C \wedge \overline{C_g}\right] \\ &\leq \Pr[C_g] + \Pr\left[C \mid \overline{C_g}\right] \\ &\leq \frac{N^2}{2^\rho} + \frac{N(N-1)}{2^\rho} \\ &\leq \frac{N^2}{2^{\rho-1}}.\end{aligned} \tag{3}$$

Next we justify step (†) in (1). Note that by the rules imposed on the adversary in the SD-GSD game, the challenge node v is safe and its seed is thus indeed hidden. If Q_{dep} does not hold, then $\mathcal{A}$ has not queried H_{dep} for s_v. Moreover, since v is the only node with seed s_v by $\overline{C}$, the SD-GSD challenger only ever queries H_{dep} for s_v when computing the challenge, so the challenger reveals no information about $H_{\text{dep}}(s_v)$ through its responses to other queries.[11] Thus, by virtue of H_{dep} being a random oracle, $H_{\text{dep}}(s_v)$ is a uniformly distributed value in $\{0,1\}^\rho$ from $\mathcal{A}$'s perspective. The value s follows the same distribution. Thus, $\mathcal{A}$ behaves the same when given either $r = s$ or $r = H_{\text{dep}}(s_v)$ and

$$\begin{aligned}\Pr\left[1 \leftarrow \mathcal{A} \mid \overline{C}, \overline{Q_{\text{dep}}}, b = 1\right] &= \Pr\left[1 \leftarrow \mathcal{A} \mid \overline{C}, \overline{Q_{\text{dep}}}, r = s\right] \\ &= \Pr\left[1 \leftarrow \mathcal{A} \mid \overline{C}, \overline{Q_{\text{dep}}}, r = H_{\text{dep}}(s_v)\right] \\ &= \Pr\left[1 \leftarrow \mathcal{A} \mid \overline{C}, \overline{Q_{\text{dep}}}, b = 0\right].\end{aligned} \tag{4}$$

Therefore

$$\begin{aligned}\Pr\left[\mathcal{A} \text{ wins} \mid \overline{C}, \overline{Q_{\text{dep}}}\right] = \;& \Pr\left[1 \leftarrow \mathcal{A} \mid \overline{C}, \overline{Q_{\text{dep}}}, b = 1\right] \cdot \frac{1}{2} \\ & + \Pr\left[0 \leftarrow \mathcal{A} \mid \overline{C}, \overline{Q_{\text{dep}}}, b = 0\right] \cdot \frac{1}{2} \\ \overset{(4)}{=} \;& \Pr\left[1 \leftarrow \mathcal{A} \mid \overline{C}, \overline{Q_{\text{dep}}}, b = 0\right] \cdot \frac{1}{2} \\ & + \Pr\left[0 \leftarrow \mathcal{A} \mid \overline{C}, \overline{Q_{\text{dep}}}, b = 0\right] \cdot \frac{1}{2} \\ = \;& \frac{1}{2}.\end{aligned}$$

Next, (♠) is easy to show

$$\Pr\left[Q_{\text{s}} \mid \overline{C}\right] \cdot (1 - \Pr[C]) = \Pr\left[Q_{\text{s}} \mid \overline{C}\right] \cdot \Pr\left[\overline{C}\right] = \Pr[Q_{\text{s}}] - \Pr[Q_{\text{s}} \wedge C]$$

$$\Longrightarrow$$

$$\Pr\left[Q_{\text{s}} \mid \overline{C}\right] \leq \Pr[Q_{\text{s}}] + \Pr[C].$$

[11] If collisions were possible, then another node u in the GSD graph could by chance have the same seed and the challenger could leak $H_{\text{dep}}(s_u) = H_{\text{dep}}(s_v)$, e.g. if u is the source of a seed dependency and the target node of the dependency is corrupted.

By Lemma 3 we have[12]

$$\Pr[Q_{\mathrm{s}} \wedge F_{\mathrm{DH}}] \leq N \cdot \varepsilon_{\mathrm{DDH}} + \frac{m_{\mathrm{DH}} \cdot N^2}{q}.$$

and by Lemma 2 we have

$$\Pr\left[Q_{\mathrm{s}} \wedge \overline{F_{\mathrm{DH}}}\right] \leq \delta \cdot N \cdot \varepsilon_{\mathrm{EAV}} + \frac{m_{\mathrm{s}} \cdot N}{2^{\rho}},$$

so we know that

$$\Pr[Q_{\mathrm{s}}] \leq N \cdot \varepsilon_{\mathrm{DDH}} + \delta \cdot N \cdot \varepsilon_{\mathrm{EAV}} + \frac{m_{\mathrm{DH}} \cdot N^2}{q} + \frac{m_{\mathrm{s}} \cdot N}{2^{\rho}}. \tag{5}$$

Then

$$\begin{aligned} \mathrm{Adv}_{\Pi,\eta}^{\text{SD-GSD}}(\mathcal{A}) &= 2 \cdot \left(\Pr[\mathcal{A} \text{ wins}] - \frac{1}{2}\right) \\ &\overset{(2),(1)}{\leq} 4 \cdot \Pr[C] + 2 \cdot \Pr[Q_{\mathrm{s}}] \\ &\overset{(3),(5)}{\leq} \tilde{\varepsilon}(\eta). \end{aligned}$$

Security Against Multiple Challenges. As noted already in the introduction, it is straightforward to prove the same result for an SD-GSD game with multiple challenge queries. In this SD-GSD game, the adversary would have access to an additional *challenge* oracle to perform a challenge on any node as in step 3 of the original game, with the bit b sampled once at the beginning of the game, and the seed s sampled fresh for every query. Of course, the adversary must ensure that the restrictions that apply to the challenge node in the original game apply to all challenge nodes in this new game.

To prove security in this multi-challenge SD-GSD game, the same case distinction can be performed as in (1) and, concerning step (†), it can be shown through a sequence of statistically indistinguishable hybrids that the adversary has no advantage if they did not trigger Q_{dep}.

Reducing to EAV Security. Recall case (ii) in the high-level discussion of Theorem 2: the adversary $\mathcal{A}$ was able to learn the seed s_w given the EAV secure encryptions $\Pi_s.\mathrm{Enc}_{k_1}(s_w), \ldots, \Pi_s.\mathrm{Enc}_{k_d}(s_w)$. We can see $\mathcal{A}$ as an adversary in a security game where $\mathcal{A}$ is given d EAV secure encryptions $c_1 \leftarrow \Pi_s.\mathrm{Enc}_{k_1}(m), \ldots, c_d \leftarrow \Pi_s.\mathrm{Enc}_{k_d}(m)$ of a message m with $k_i \leftarrow \Pi_s.\mathrm{Gen}(1^{\eta})$ and must compute m. If we can prove that beating such a game is hard, then we can bound the probability of $\mathcal{A}$ actually learning s_w in this way.

12 Note that we are again omitting the argument η from the functions on the right-hand side ($N, \varepsilon_{\mathrm{DDH}}$ and m_{DH} in this case).

This is exactly how we proceed in this section. Instead of asking the adversary to compute an encrypted message m, we turn to a more familiar decisional formulation as in the IND-CPA game (where the adversary may choose a pair m_0, m_1 and must distinguish whether the d ciphertexts encrypt m_0 or m_1). We call this security notion *EAV security under multiple (M) independent (I) encryptions of a single (S) pair of messages* (MIS-EAV).

Definition 5 (The MIS-EAV Game). *Let κ denote the security parameter and let Π a private-key encryption scheme. Define the game* $\text{Game}_{\Pi,\kappa}^{\text{MIS-EAV}}(\mathcal{A})$ *for an adversary $\mathcal{A}$:*

1. *The adversary $\mathcal{A}$ outputs $q \in \mathbb{N}$ and a pair of messages m_0, m_1 of the same length. We refer to q as the number of* queries *made by $\mathcal{A}$.*
2. *A bit $b \leftarrow \{0,1\}$ is sampled. For each $i \in [q]$, $\mathcal{A}$ is given an encryption $c_i \leftarrow \Pi.\text{Enc}_{k_i}(m_b)$ where $k_i \leftarrow \Pi.\text{Gen}(1^\kappa)$ is generated independently of the other keys.*
3. *$\mathcal{A}$ outputs a bit b'. The output of the game is defined to be 1 if $b' = b$, and 0 otherwise.*

Definition 6 (MIS-EAV Security). *A private-key encryption scheme Π is* (t, ε, q)-MIS-EAV-secure *if for all κ, for any adversary $\mathcal{A}$ making at most $q(\kappa)$ queries and running in time $t(\kappa)$ we have*

$$\text{Adv}_{\Pi,\kappa}^{\text{MIS-EAV}}(\mathcal{A}) := 2 \cdot \left(\Pr\left[\text{Game}_{\Pi,\kappa}^{\text{MIS-EAV}}(\mathcal{A}) = 1\right] - \frac{1}{2}\right) \leq \varepsilon(\kappa).$$

Similar to how IND-CPA security for a single encryption query implies IND-CPA security for q queries with a security loss of q by a standard hybrid argument, one can show that EAV security implies MIS-EAV security with the same loss. To see why, recall the hybrid argument for IND-CPA security (as discussed in e.g. [12, Theorem 12.6]): We define the sequence of hybrid games $G_0, \ldots, G_q$ where in the game G_i the first i encryption queries encrypt the second message and the remaining $q - i$ queries encrypt the first message. Then given an IND-CPA adversary $\mathcal{A}$ for multiple encryptions, an IND-CPA adversary $\mathcal{A}'$ is constructed to bound

$$|\Pr[\mathcal{A} \text{ outputs } 0 \text{ in game } G_{i-1}] - \Pr[\mathcal{A} \text{ outputs } 0 \text{ in game } G_i]|$$

for arbitrary i. The adversary $\mathcal{A}'$ simulates G_{i-1} or G_i to $\mathcal{A}$ depending on whether the ciphertext received from the (single-query) IND-CPA challenger, which gets passed on as the response to the i-th query, encrypts the first or the second message from the i-th pair of messages. $\mathcal{A}'$ then uses the encryption oracle to pass on the right encryptions to $\mathcal{A}$ for all other queries. Now notice that if we wanted to simulate to an MIS-EAV adversary we would not need access to an encryption oracle since for the MIS-EAV security game all the other encryptions can easily be generated by $\mathcal{A}'$ sampling the new keys itself.

The argument would of course also work without restricting the adversary to a single pair of messages. However, we make use of this restriction to provide a tighter reduction for a certain class of schemes in [4, Section B.4].

Lemma 1. *Let* Π *a private-key encryption scheme with finite message space. Let* $t_{\text{Gen}}, t_{\text{Enc}}$ *functions in* κ *that upper bound the runtime of* $\Pi.\text{Gen}$ *and* $\Pi.\text{Enc}$, *respectively. If* Π *is* (t, ε)*-EAV-secure, then for any function* q, Π *is* $(\tilde{t}, q \cdot \varepsilon, q)$*-MIS-EAV-secure with* $\tilde{t} = t - \mathcal{O}(q \cdot (t_{\text{Gen}} + t_{\text{Enc}}))$.

The details of the proof can be found in [4, Section B.2].

Lemma 2. *Recall the assumptions, variables and events from the statement and proof of Theorem 2. In particular, assume that* Π_s *is* $(t, \varepsilon_{\text{EAV}})$*-EAV-secure. Let* η *arbitrary and let* $\mathcal{A}$ *an SD-GSD adversary constructing a GSD graph of size at most* $N(\eta)$ *and indegree at most* $\delta(\eta)$*, making at most* $m_{\text{s}}(\eta)$ *queries to* H_{gen} *or* H_{dep} *and at most* $m_{\text{DH}}(\eta)$ *queries to* H_{DH}*, and running in time* $\tilde{t}(\eta)$*. Then*

$$\Pr\left[Q_{\text{s}} \wedge \overline{F_{\text{DH}}}\,\right] \leq \delta \cdot N \cdot \varepsilon_{\text{EAV}} + \frac{m_{\text{s}} \cdot N}{2^{\rho}}.$$

Intuition. By Lemma 1 we know that Π_s is MIS-EAV secure. Continuing the high-level argument before the proof of Theorem 2, consider the first moment that $\mathcal{A}$ triggers $Q_{\text{s}} \wedge \overline{F_{\text{DH}}}$ by querying the seed of some safe node w. As intended, it follows from the definition of the event F_{DH} that from $\mathcal{A}$'s perspective all DHIES ciphertexts it got from queries encrypt(u, w) for any u contain encryptions of s_w under independent, uniformly random keys using Π_s. Moreover, as already argued once, $\mathcal{A}$ has learned nothing from a potential seed dependency (p, w), so these encryptions are everything $\mathcal{A}$ had at its proposal to learn s_w.

We can use $\mathcal{A}$'s ability to compute the seed s_w of a safe node w from encryptions of s_w to construct an MIS-EAV adversary: We first guess a node w whose seed $\mathcal{A}$ may query first. Next, we give the MIS-EAV challenger s_w and some other independent seed s. We simulate the SD-GSD game to $\mathcal{A}$ and embed the encryptions from the MIS-EAV challenger when answering queries of the form encrypt(u, w) for any u. Now consider the behavior of $\mathcal{A}$ depending on which seed the challenger chooses to encrypt:

- If the challenger chooses to encrypt s_w, then $\mathcal{A}$ will trigger the event $Q_{\text{s}} \wedge \overline{F_{\text{DH}}}$ with the same probability as before. We can detect whether $Q_{\text{s}} \wedge \overline{F_{\text{DH}}}$ gets triggered since all seeds in the simulation are known. If $Q_{\text{s}} \wedge \overline{F_{\text{DH}}}$ occurs and we guessed w correctly, the event will be triggered at w and $\mathcal{A}$ will query s_w, telling us that the challenger encrypted s_w.
- If the challenger chooses to encrypt s, then $\mathcal{A}$ receives no information about s_w and has a negligible probability of querying it.

Thus, the advantage of the MIS-EAV adversary is about $\Pr\left[Q_{\text{s}} \wedge \overline{F_{\text{DH}}}\,\right]/N$, where the factor $1/N$ arises from guessing w, and using that Π_s is MIS-EAV secure we can bound this probability. Since we are only interested in checking whether the event was triggered for w, the adversary can abort when this is no longer possible (w is corrupted, some other hidden seed is queried, etc.). The details of the proof can be found in [4, Section B.2].

For a certain class of schemes, we can improve on Lemma 1 and achieve a tight reduction. This allows us to get rid of the factor δ in Lemma 2. However, we do not use this in our main result and refer the interested reader to [4, Section B.4].

Reducing to the DDH Problem

Lemma 3. *Recall the assumptions, variables and events from the statement and proof of Theorem 2. In particular, assume that the DDH problem is $(t, \varepsilon_{\text{DDH}})$-hard relative to $\mathcal{G}$. Let η arbitrary and let $\mathcal{A}$ an SD-GSD adversary constructing a GSD graph of size at most $N(\eta)$ and indegree at most $\delta(\eta)$, making at most $m_{\text{s}}(\eta)$ queries to H_{gen} or H_{dep} and at most $m_{\text{DH}}(\eta)$ queries to H_{DH}, and running in time $\tilde{t}(\eta)$. Then*

$$\Pr[Q_{\text{s}} \wedge F_{\text{DH}}] \leq N \cdot \varepsilon_{\text{DDH}} + \frac{m_{\text{DH}} \cdot N^2}{q}.$$

Intuition. We will bound the simpler event F_{DH}. This event tells us that there is some safe node a in the GSD graph with encryption edges to nodes $u_1, \ldots, u_d$, where the query encrypt(a, u_i) returned the ciphertext $\langle g^{y_i}, \Pi_s.\text{Enc}_{k_i}(s_{u_i})\rangle$ with $k_i = H_{\text{DH}}(g^{sk_a \cdot y_i})$, such that $g^{sk_a \cdot y_j}$ was the first hidden Diffie-Hellman key queried by $\mathcal{A}$ for some j. Moreover, at the time $g^{sk_a \cdot y_j}$ was queried, no hidden seed had yet been queried by $\mathcal{A}$, implying that $\mathcal{A}$ had not queried $H_{\text{gen}}(s_a)$ and thus had no information about sk_a besides pk_a (recall that $(pk_a, sk_a) = \Pi_{\text{DH}}.\text{Gen}(1^\eta, H_{\text{gen}}(s_a)))$.

It is interesting to note that our approach does not require that $\mathcal{A}$ has not queried H_{dep} for a hidden seed (i.e. that Q_{dep} was not triggered) as is implied by the event F_{DH}, because knowing $H_{\text{gen}}(s_a)$ is the only way to learn about sk_a. Regardless, we still want to have our definition of F_{DH} include this information, as the bound on $\Pr\left[Q_{\text{s}} \wedge \overline{F_{\text{DH}}}\,\right]$ in Lemma 2 relies on the fact that in the event of $Q_{\text{s}} \wedge \overline{F_{\text{DH}}}$ happening, Q_{DH} was not yet triggered when the event Q_{s} was triggered, i.e. when either the event Q_{gen} *or* the event Q_{dep} was triggered.

The intuition is clear that this means that $\mathcal{A}$ solved the Diffie-Hellman challenge (g^{sk_a}, g^{y_j}). What is not immediately clear is how to embed a *given* Diffie-Hellman challenge (g^x, g^y) from an instance of the DDH game and use $\mathcal{A}$ to tell whether the key k chosen by the challenger is the real key $g^{x \cdot y}$ or a uniformly random group element. An intuitive strategy would be to embed the challenge by setting $pk_a = g^x$ and $g^{y_j} = g^y$, which involves guessing u_j, and simply checking whether for any of the queries q_i to H_{DH} by $\mathcal{A}$, such that q_i encodes a group element in $\mathbb{G}$, it holds that $q_i = k$. Now:

- If $k = g^{x \cdot y}$, $\mathcal{A}$ triggers F_{DH} and we guessed a and u_j correctly, then indeed as described above $q_i = g^{sk_a \cdot y_j} = g^{x \cdot y} = k$ will hold for some i.
- If k is a random group element, then $\mathcal{A}$ has negligible probability of querying k, as no information about k is ever leaked to $\mathcal{A}$.

If we make sure not to change $\mathcal{A}$'s view of the game in the case $k = g^{x \cdot y}$ in this process, we can achieve an advantage of about $\Pr[F_{\text{DH}}]/N^2$, where one factor $1/N$ arises from guessing a and another from guessing u_j. Unfortunately, this would yield no improvement over the result from [13].

To avoid this issue, we can use the random self-reducibility of the DDH problem and avoid guessing u_j. Instead of embedding g^y into a single encryption edge, we embed it into all d encryption edges. To get a uniformly random exponent from y we set $y_j = y + r_j \mod q$ with $r_j \leftarrow [q]$. Given $g^{x \cdot y_j}$, we can easily compute $g^{x \cdot y}$:

$$g^{x \cdot y_j} = g^{x \cdot (y + r_j)} = g^{x \cdot y} \cdot g^{x \cdot r_j} \iff g^{x \cdot y} = g^{x \cdot y_j} \cdot \underbrace{((g^x)^{r_j})^{-1}}_{=: R_j}.$$

Now to determine whether k is the real Diffie-Hellman key, we check whether $q_i \cdot R_j = k$ for some i, j. This yields an advantage of about $\Pr[F_{\mathrm{DH}}]/N$ (and a slightly larger runtime). The details of the proof can be found in [4, Section B.5].

References

1. Abdalla, M., Bellare, M., Rogaway, P.: DHIES: an encryption scheme based on the Diffie-Hellman problem (1998). https://cseweb.ucsd.edu/~mihir/papers/dhies.pdf
2. Alwen, J., Coretti, S., Dodis, Y., Tselekounis, Y.: Security Analysis and improvements for the IETF MLS standard for group messaging. In: Micciancio, D., Ristenpart, T. (eds.) CRYPTO 2020. LNCS, vol. 12170, pp. 248–277. Springer, Cham (2020). https://doi.org/10.1007/978-3-030-56784-2_9
3. Alwen, J., Coretti, S., Dodis, Y., Tselekounis, Y.: Modular design of secure group messaging protocols and the security of MLS. In: Proceedings of the 2021 ACM SIGSAC Conference on Computer and Communications Security, pp. 1463–1483. CCS 2021, Association for Computing Machinery, New York, NY, USA (2021). https://doi.org/10.1145/3460120.3484820
4. Azari, K., Ellison, A.: Tighter provable security for TreeKEM. Cryptology ePrint Archive, Paper 2024/1878 (2024). https://eprint.iacr.org/2024/1878
5. Balbás, D., Collins, D., Gajland, P.: WhatsUpp with sender keys? Analysis, improvements and security proofs. In: Guo, J., Steinfeld, R. (eds.) Advances in Cryptology - ASIACRYPT 2023, pp. 307–341. Springer Nature Singapore, Singapore (2023). https://doi.org/10.1007/978-981-99-8733-7_10
6. Barnes, R., Beurdouche, B., Robert, R., Millican, J., Omara, E., Cohn-Gordon, K.: The messaging layer security (MLS) Protocol. RFC 9420 (2023). https://doi.org/10.17487/RFC9420, https://www.rfc-editor.org/info/rfc9420
7. Bellare, M., Rogaway, P.: Random oracles are practical: a paradigm for designing efficient protocols. In: Proceedings of the 1st ACM Conference on Computer and Communications Security, pp. 62–73. CCS 1993, Association for Computing Machinery, New York, NY, USA (1993). https://doi.org/10.1145/168588.168596
8. Bhargavan, K., Barnes, R., Rescorla, E.: TreeKEM: asynchronous decentralized key management for large dynamic groups a protocol proposal for messaging layer security (MLS). Research report, Inria Paris (2018). https://inria.hal.science/hal-02425247
9. Cohn-Gordon, K., Cremers, C., Dowling, B., Garratt, L., Stebila, D.: A formal security analysis of the signal messaging protocol. In: 2017 IEEE European Symposium on Security and Privacy (EuroS&P), pp. 451–466 (2017). https://doi.org/10.1109/EuroSP.2017.27
10. Hogben, G.: An important step towards secure and interoperable messaging (2023). https://security.googleblog.com/2023/07/an-important-step-towards-secure-and.html. Accessed 1 Nov 2023

11. IETF: Support for MLS (2023). https://www.ietf.org/blog/support-for-mls-2023/. Accessed 1 Nov 2023
12. Katz, J., Lindell, Y.: Introduction to Modern Cryptography, Third Edition. Chapman & Hall/CRC, 3rd edn. (2020)
13. Klein, K., et al.: Keep the dirt: tainted TreeKEM, adaptively and actively secure continuous group key agreement. In: 2021 IEEE Symposium on Security and Privacy (SP), pp. 268–284 (2021). https://doi.org/10.1109/SP40001.2021.00035
14. Panjwani, S.: Tackling adaptive corruptions in multicast encryption protocols. In: Vadhan, S.P. (ed.) TCC 2007. LNCS, vol. 4392, pp. 21–40. Springer, Heidelberg (2007). https://doi.org/10.1007/978-3-540-70936-7_2
15. Pascual Perez, G.: On the efficiency and security of secure group messaging. Ph.D. thesis, Institute of Science and Technology Austria (2024). https://doi.org/10.15479/at:ista:18088
16. Perrin, T., Marlinspike, M.: The double ratchet algorithm (2016). https://signal.org/docs/specifications/doubleratchet/. Accessed 5 Mar 2024

Author Index

M. Fischlin and V. Moonsamy (Eds.): ACNS 2025, LNCS 15825, pp. 597–599, 2025.
https://doi.org/10.1007/978-3-031-95761-1

The manufacturer's authorised representative in the EU is Springer Nature Customer Service Centre GmbH, Europaplatz 3, 69115 Heidelberg, Germany. If you have any concerns regarding our products, please contact ProductSafety@springernature.com

Printed and bound by CPI Group (UK) Ltd, Croydon, CR0 4YY
30/09/2026
02225560-0020